Leadership

Enhancing the Lessons of Experience   Seventh Edition

Richard L. Hughes
Robert C. Ginnett
Gordon J. Curphy

McGraw-Hill Irwin

ISBN   978-0-07-811265-2

MHID   0-07-811265-6

Vice president and editor-in-chief: *Brent Gordon*
Executive director of development: *Ann Torbert*
Managing development editor: *Laura Hurst Spell*
Development editor: *Jane Beck*
Vice president and director of marketing: *Robin J. Zwettler*
Marketing director: *Amee Mosley*
Associate marketing manager: *Jaime Halteman*
Vice president of editing, design, and production: *Sesha Bolisetty*
Project manager: *Dana M. Pauley*
Senior buyer: *Carol A. Bielski*
Design coordinator: *Joanne Mennemeier*
Senior media project manager: *Susan Lombardi*
Media project manager: *Suresh Babu, Hurix Systems Pvt. Ltd.*
Typeface: *10/12 Palatino*
Compositor: *Aptara®, Inc.*
Printer: *R. R. Donnelley*

Library of Congress Cataloging-in-Publication Data

Hughes, Richard L.
    Leadership : enhancing the lessons of experience / Richard L. Hughes, Robert C. Ginnett,
Gordon J. Curphy. — 7th ed.
        p. cm.
    Includes index.
    ISBN-13: 978-0-07-811265-2 (alk. paper)
    ISBN-10: 0-07-811265-6 (alk. paper)
    1. Leadership. I. Ginnett, Robert C. II. Curphy, Gordon J. III. Title.
HM1261.H84 2012
303.3′4—dc22
                                                                    2010052313

www.mhhe.com

About the Authors

Rich Hughes has served on the faculties of both the Center for Creative Leadership (CCL) and the U.S. Air Force Academy. CCL is an international organization devoted to behavioral science research and leadership education. He worked there with senior executives from all sectors in the areas of strategic leadership and organizational culture change. At the Air Force Academy he served for a decade as head of its Department of Behavioral Sciences and Leadership. He is a clinical psychologist and a graduate of the U.S. Air Force Academy. He has an MA from the University of Texas and a PhD from the University of Wyoming.

Robert Ginnett is an independent consultant specializing in the leadership of high-performance teams and organizations. He is the developer of the Team Leadership Model,© which provides the theoretical framework for many interventions in organizations where teamwork is critical. This model and its real-time application have made him an internationally recognized expert in his field. He has worked with hundreds of organizations including Novartis, Prudential, Fonterra, Mars, GlaxoSmithKlein, Boston Scientific, Daimler Benz, NASA, the Defense and Central Intelligence Agencies, the National Security Agency, United and Delta Airlines, Textron, and the United States Army, Navy, and Air Force. Prior to working independently, Robert was a senior fellow at the Center for Creative Leadership and a tenured professor at the U.S. Air Force Academy, where he also served as the director of leadership and counseling. Additionally, he served in numerous line and staff positions in the military, including leadership of an 875-man combat force in the Vietnam War. He spent over 10 years working as a researcher for the National Aeronautics and Space Administration, focusing his early work in aviation crew resource management, and later worked at the Kennedy Space Center in the post-*Challenger* period. Robert is an organizational psychologist whose education includes a master of business administration degree, a master of arts, a master of philosophy, and a PhD from Yale University.

Gordy Curphy is the president of C3, a human resource consulting firm that helps public and private sector clients achieve better results through people. Gordy has over 25 years of leadership and technical expertise in job analysis and competency modeling; hourly staffing systems; multirater feedback systems; performance management design and implementation; leadership development design, delivery, and evaluation; survey construction, administration, and analysis; assessment center methodology; executive coaching, training, and team building; succession planning; team and organizational effectiveness; and strategic and business planning.

Prior to forming his own consulting firm, Gordy spent 10 years as a vice president of institutional leadership at the Blandin Foundation and as a vice president and general manager at Personnel Decisions International. He is an industrial/organizational psychologist and a graduate of the U.S. Air Force Academy. He has an MA from the University of St. Mary's and a PhD in industrial/organizational psychology from the University of Minnesota.

Foreword

The first edition of this popular, widely used textbook was published in 1993, and the authors have continually upgraded it with each new edition including this one—the seventh. For this newest edition I've written *something* of a new foreword.

In a sense, no new foreword is needed; many principles of leadership are timeless. For example, their references to Shakespeare and Machiavelli need no updating. However, they have refreshed their examples and anecdotes, and they have kept up with the contemporary research and writing of leadership experts. Ironically, one of their most riveting new examples falls into the "Dark Side of Leadership" chapter, where they include the horrific example of Richard Fuld, the CEO who presided over the disintegration, destruction, and bankruptcy of Lehman Brothers, the fourth-largest investment bank in the world. Over a five-year period (when he was paid a total of $300,000,000), Fuld kept stretching the rubber band of increasingly risky investments while at the same time stretching another rubber band of tricky financial reporting until they both snapped simultaneously, bringing the world's financial system close to the brink of disaster. His actions cost the jobs of 25,000 employees and the loss of billions of dollars by investors. Yeoman work by other leaders avoided the brink but could not prevent a painful economic recession. This brutal example, in a perverse way, once again emphasizes the power of leadership.

Such examples keep this book fresh and relevant; but the earlier foreword, reprinted here, still captures the tone, spirit, and achievements of these authors' work:

Often the only difference between chaos and a smoothly functioning operation is leadership; this book is about that difference.

The authors are psychologists; therefore the book has a distinctly psychological tone. You, as a reader, are going to be asked to think about leadership the way psychologists do. There is much here about psychological tests and surveys, about studies done in psychological laboratories, and about psychological analyses of good (and poor) leadership. You will often run across common psychological concepts in these pages, such as personality, values, attitudes, perceptions, and self-esteem, plus some not-so-common "jargon-y" phrases like double-loop learning, expectancy theory, and perceived inequity. This is not the same kind of book that would be written by coaches, sales managers, economists, political scientists, or generals.

Be not dismayed. Because these authors are also teachers with a good eye and ear for what students find interesting, they write clearly and cleanly, and they have also included a host of entertaining, stimulating snapshots of leadership: cartoons, quotes, anecdotal Highlights, and personal glimpses from a wide range of intriguing people, each offered as an illustration of some scholarly point.

Also, because the authors are, or have been at one time or another, together or singly, not only psychologists and teachers but also children, students, Boy Scouts, parents, professors (at the U.S. Air Force Academy), Air Force officers, pilots, church members, athletes, administrators, insatiable readers, and convivial raconteurs, their stories and examples are drawn from a wide range of personal sources, and their anecdotes ring true.

As psychologists and scholars, they have reviewed here a wide range of psychological studies, other scientific inquiries, personal reflections of leaders, and philosophic writings on the topic of leadership. In distilling this material, they have drawn many practical conclusions useful for current and potential leaders. There are suggestions here for goal setting, for running meetings, for negotiating, for managing conflict within groups, and for handling your own personal stress, to mention just a few.

All leaders, no matter what their age and station, can find some useful tips here, ranging over subjects such as body language, keeping a journal, and how to relax under tension.

In several ways the authors have tried to help you, the reader, feel what it would be like "to be in charge." For example, they have posed quandaries such as the following: You are in a leadership position with a budget provided by an outside funding source. You believe strongly in, say, Topic A, and have taken a strong, visible public stance on that topic. The head of your funding source takes you aside and says, "We disagree with your stance on Topic A. Please tone down your public statements, or we will have to take another look at your budget for next year."

What would you do? Quit? Speak up and lose your budget? Tone down your public statements and feel dishonest? There's no easy answer, and it's not an unusual situation for a leader to be in. Sooner or later, all leaders have to confront just how much outside interference they will tolerate in order to be able to carry out programs they believe in.

The authors emphasize the value of experience in leadership development, a conclusion I thoroughly agree with. Virtually every leader who makes it to the top of whatever pyramid he or she happens to be climbing does so by building on earlier experiences. The successful leaders are those who learn from these earlier experiences, by reflecting on and analyzing them to help solve larger future challenges. In this vein, let me make a suggestion. Actually, let me assign you some homework. (I know, I know, this is a peculiar approach in a book foreword; but stay with me—I have a point.)

Your Assignment: To gain some useful leadership experience, persuade eight people to do some notable activity together for at least two hours that they would not otherwise do without your intervention. Your only restriction is that you cannot tell them why you are doing this.

It can be any eight people: friends, family, teammates, club members, neighbors, students, working colleagues. It can be any activity, except that it should be something more substantial than watching television, eating, going to a movie, or just sitting around talking. It could be a roller-skating party, an organized debate, a songfest, a long hike, a visit to a museum, or volunteer work such as picking up litter or visiting a nursing home. If you will take it upon yourself to make something happen in the world that would not have otherwise happened without you, you will be engaging in an act of leadership with all of its attendant barriers, burdens, and pleasures, and you will quickly learn the relevance of many of the topics that the authors discuss in this book. If you try the eight-person-two-hour experience first and read this book later, you will have a much better understanding of how complicated an act of leadership can be. You will learn about the difficulties of developing a vision ("Now that we are together, what are we going to do?"), of motivating others, of setting agendas and timetables, of securing resources, of the need for follow-through. You may even learn about "loneliness at the top." However, if you are successful, you will also experience the thrill that comes from successful leadership. One person *can* make a difference by enriching the lives of others, if only for a few hours. And for all of the frustrations and complexities of leadership, the tingling satisfaction that comes from success can become almost addictive. The capacity for making things happen can become its own motivation. With an early success, even if it is only with eight people for two hours, you may well be on your way to a leadership future.

The authors believe that leadership development involves reflecting on one's own experiences. Reading this book in the context of your own leadership experience can aid in that process. Their book is comprehensive, scholarly, stimulating, entertaining, and relevant for anyone who wishes to better understand the dynamics of leadership, and to improve her or his own personal performance.

David P. Campbell

Preface

Perhaps by the time they are fortunate enough to have completed six editions of a textbook, it is a bit natural for authors to believe something like, "Well, *now* we've got it just about right . . . there couldn't be too many changes for the next edition" (that is, *this* one). But as our experience consistently has been since the first edition, the helpful suggestions of users and reviewers always provide helpful grist for improvement. The changes made in this edition are far more extensive than we would have predicted a year ago, and we believe this edition is better because of them.

We have made a number of significant changes to this book's structure and format as well as the kind of normal updates you would expect (such as adding timely references, including new Highlights, and pruning dated stories). Let us briefly review here some of the major changes to this edition. Some of these can be characterized as a generalized effort to better integrate material covered in multiple chapters in previous editions into single chapters in this edition. For example, we have combined material from the first two chapters in all previous editions into the first chapter of this edition with an overall leaner and more consolidated treatment of the material. As another example, we have moved material about mentoring, coaching, and development planning from the chapter about leader behavior into the chapter about leader development while also eliminating material from earlier editions of the development chapter that over time had become somewhat out of date.

Another major change is the complete elimination of the chapter about assessing leadership. We struggled with this chapter through all previous editions in our efforts to adequately cover material that we believe important but that to many others is dry and perhaps not *that* important in an introductory course. We finally concluded that the cost of an entire chapter that either was *not* covered by many of our textbook users, or was found problematic by others who did, was simply not worth it. (Sneakily, we must admit that a little of that material might have found its way into other chapters.)

The chapter now called "Leadership, Ethics and Values" also includes many changes. There is an extended treatment of ethical leadership, and more explicit linkages are drawn among ethics, values, ethical leadership, authentic leadership, and servant leadership. In the spirit of consolidation and integration, some material about character development from other chapters in the previous edition is now included in this chapter instead. Finally, the "Leading across Cultures" section, which was in the "Leadership and Values" chapter of our sixth edition, is now part of "The Situation" chapter in this edition because it fits better there thematically.

Speaking about our chapter addressing the role of the situation in leadership, it also has undergone other significant changes. In general, these changes represent our effort to reorient the chapter more toward leadership issues than toward organizational behavior or management. Thus the chapter not only discusses the leadership challenges of leading globally but also explores the topic of organizational culture. The chapter also takes a new look at the role of leadership in dealing with increasing environmental change.

The final major change to this edition reorganizes the content covered in our sections about leadership skills into four chapters, each one now representing the final chapter in each of the book's four parts, and each chapter focusing on a distinctive aspect of a leader's challenges. There also are two new skills added: "Creating a Compelling Vision" and "Your First 90 Days as a Leader."

There are other changes to the seventh edition as well, though they are generally smaller in scope and less systematic than those just mentioned. For example, greater attention is now given to LMX theory in the "Contingency Theories" chapter; leading virtual teams gets more extended treatment in "Groups, Teams, and Their Leadership"; and new Highlights and Profiles in Leadership appear throughout the book.

As always, we are indebted to the superb editorial staff at McGraw-Hill/Irwin, including Jane Beck, our editorial coordinator, Laura Spell, the managing development editor, Dana Pauley, the project manager, and Jaime Halteman, our marketing manager. They all have been wise, supportive, helpful, and pleasant partners in this process, and it has been our good fortune to know and work with such a professional team. And as we noted at the beginning of this preface, we are also indebted to the individuals whose evaluations and constructive suggestions about the previous edition provided the foundation for many of our revisions. We are grateful for the scholarly and insightful comments from all of our reviewers:

John Anderson
Walsh College

Mark Arvisais
Towson University

David Lee Baker
Kent State University

Herbert Barber
Virginia Military Institute

Erich Baumgartner
Andrews University

Ellen Benowitz
Mercer County Community College

Kenneth Campbell
North Central College

Cheree Causey
University of Alabama–Tuscaloosa

Jeewon Cho
Montclair State University

Marie Gould
Peirce College

Donald Howard Horner
U.S. Naval Academy

Osmond Ingram Jr.
Dallas Baptist University

Karen Jacobs
LeTourneau University

Donna Rue Jenkins
National University

Lanny Karns
SUNY–Oswego

Stacey Kessler
Montclair State University

Paulette Laubsch
Fairleigh-Dickinson
University–Teaneck

Charles Changuk Lee
Chestnut Hill College

John Michael Lenti
University of South Carolina

Kristie Loescher
University of Texas–Austin

Lt. Col. Thomas Meriwether
Virginia Military Institute

Howard Rudd
College of Charleston

Cdr. Stephen Trainor
U.S. Naval Academy

Dennis Veit
University of Texas–Arlington

Deborah Wharff
University of North Carolina–
Pembroke

Eric Williams
University of Alabama–Tuscaloosa

Once again we dedicate this book to the leaders of the past from whom we have learned, the leaders of today whose behaviors and actions shape our ever-changing world, and the leaders of tomorrow who we hope will benefit from the lessons in this book as they face the challenges of change and globalization in an increasingly interconnected world.

Richard L. Hughes
Robert C. Ginnett
Gordon J. Curphy

Brief Contents

PART ONE:
Leadership Is a Process, Not a Position 1

Chapter 1: What Do We Mean by Leadership? 2

Chapter 2: Leader Development 43

Chapter 3: Skills for Developing Yourself as a Leader 88

PART TWO:
Focus on the Leader 117

Chapter 4: Power and Influence 118

Chapter 5: Leadership, Ethics and Values 150

Chapter 6: Leadership Attributes 188

Chapter 7: Leadership Behavior 242

Chapter 8: Skills for Building Personal Credibility and Influencing Others 277

PART THREE:
Focus on the Followers 317

Chapter 9: Motivation, Satisfaction, and Performance 331

Chapter 10: Groups, Teams, and Their Leadership 390

Chapter 11: Skills for Developing Others 436

PART FOUR:
Focus on the Situation 473

Chapter 12: The Situation 473

Chapter 13: Contingency Theories of Leadership 520

Chapter 14: Leadership and Change 556

Chapter 15: The Dark Side of Leadership 607

Chapter 16: Skills for Optimizing Leadership as Situations Change 657

Contents

Preface   viii

PART ONE
Leadership Is a Process, Not a Position   1

Chapter 1
What Do We Mean by Leadership?   2

Introduction   2
What Is Leadership?   3
  Leadership Is Both a Science and an Art   5
  Leadership Is Both Rational and Emotional   6
  Leadership and Management   8
Leadership Myths   11
  Myth: Good Leadership Is All Common Sense   11
  Myth: Leaders Are Born, Not Made   12
  Myth: The Only School You Learn Leadership from Is the School of Hard Knocks   13
The Interactional Framework for Analyzing Leadership   15
  The Leader   16
  The Followers   18
  The Situation   26
Illustrating the Interactional Framework: Women in Leadership Roles   27
There Is No Simple Recipe for Effective Leadership   34
Summary   35

Chapter 2
Leader Development   43

Introduction   43
The Action–Observation–Reflection Model   46
The Key Role of Perception in the Spiral of Experience   49
  Perception and Observation   49
  Perception and Reflection   51
  Perception and Action   52

Reflection and Leadership Development   54
  Single- and Double-Loop Learning   54
Making the Most of Your Leadership Experiences: Learning to Learn from Experience   57
  Leader Development in College   59
  Leader Development in Organizational Settings   61
  Action Learning   64
  Development Planning   66
  Coaching   69
  Mentoring   74
Building Your Own Leadership Self-Image   78
Summary   78

Chapter 3
Skills for Developing Yourself as a Leader   87

Your First 90 Days as a Leader   88
  Before You Start: Do Your Homework   88
  The First Day: You Get Only One Chance to Make a First Impression   89
  The First Two Weeks: Lay the Foundation   90
  The First Two Months: Strategy, Structure, and Staffing   92
  The Third Month: Communicate and Drive Change   93
Learning from Experience   94
  Creating Opportunities to Get Feedback   95
  Taking a 10 Percent Stretch   95
  Learning from Others   96
  Keeping a Journal   96
  Having a Developmental Plan   97
Building Technical Competence   98
  Determining How the Job Contributes to the Overall Mission   100
  Becoming an Expert in the Job   100
  Seeking Opportunities to Broaden Experiences   101

Building Effective Relationships with
Superiors   101
Understanding the Superior's World   102
Adapting to the Superior's Style   103
Building Effective Relationships with
Peers   104
Recognizing Common Interests and Goals   104
Understanding Peers' Tasks, Problems, and
Rewards   105
Practicing a Theory Y Attitude   105
Development Planning   106
Conducting a GAPS Analysis   107
Identifying and Prioritizing Development Needs:
Gaps of GAPS   109
Bridging the Gaps: Building a Development
Plan   110
Reflecting on Learning: Modifying Development
Plans   110
Transferring Learning to New Environments   112

PART TWO
Focus on the Leader   117

Chapter 4
Power and Influence   118

Introduction   118
Some Important Distinctions   118
Power and Leadership   121
Sources of Leader Power   122
A Taxonomy of Social Power   125
   Expert Power   125
   Referent Power   126
   Legitimate Power   128
   Reward Power   129
   Coercive Power   130
Concluding Thoughts about French and Raven's
Power Taxonomy   133
Leader Motives   134
Influence Tactics   137
Types of Influence Tactics   138
Influence Tactics and Power   139
A Concluding Thought about Influence
Tactics   142
Summary   142

Chapter 5
Leadership Ethics and Values   150

Introduction   150
Leadership and "Doing the Right
Things"   150
Values, Ethics, and Morals   152
Are There Generational Differences in
Values?   154
Moral and Ethical Reasoning and Action   157
Why Do Good People Do Bad Things?   166
Ethics and Values-Based Approaches to
Leadership   168
The Roles of Ethics and Values in
Organizational Leadership   172
Leading by Example: the Good, the Bad,
and the Ugly   174
Creating and Sustaining an Ethical
Climate   176
Summary   181

Chapter 6
Leadership Attributes   188

Introduction   188
Personality Traits and Leadership   189
What Is Personality?   189
The Five Factor or OCEAN Model of
Personality   192
Implications of the Five Factor or OCEAN
Model   196
Personality Types and Leadership   201
The Differences between Traits and Types   201
Psychological Preferences as a Personality
Typology   202
Implications of Preferences and Types   205
Intelligence and Leadership   208
What Is Intelligence?   208
The Triarchic Theory of Intelligence   210
Implications of the Triarchic Theory of
Intelligence   213
Intelligence and Stress: Cognitive Resources
Theory   218
Emotional Intelligence and Leadership   220
What Is Emotional Intelligence?   220

Can Emotional Intelligence Be Measured and Developed? 225
Implications of Emotional Intelligence 226
Summary 229

Chapter 7
Leadership Behavior 242

Introduction 242
Studies of Leadership Behavior 244
Why Study Leadership Behavior? 244
The Early Studies 246
The Leadership Grid 250
Competency Models 252
The Leadership Pipeline 255
Community Leadership 259
Assessing Leadership Behaviors: Multirater Feedback Instruments 262
Summary 268

Chapter 8
Skills for Building Personal Credibility and Influencing Others 277

Building Credibility 277
The Two Components of Credibility 278
Building Expertise 278
Building Trust 279
Expertise × Trust 281
Communication 283
Know What Your Purpose Is 285
Choose an Appropriate Context and Medium 285
Send Clear Signals 286
Actively Ensure That Others Understand the Message 287
Listening 288
Demonstrate Nonverbally That You Are Listening 289
Actively Interpret the Sender's Message 289
Attend to the Sender's Nonverbal Behavior 290
Avoid Becoming Defensive 290
Assertiveness 291
Use "I" Statements 293
Speak Up for What You Need 295

Learn to Say No 295
Monitor Your Inner Dialogue 295
Be Persistent 296
Conducting Meetings 296
Determine Whether It Is Necessary 297
List the Objectives 297
Stick to the Agenda 298
Provide Pertinent Materials in Advance 298
Make It Convenient 298
Encourage Participation 298
Keep a Record 299
Effective Stress Management 299
Monitor Your Own and Your Followers' Stress Levels 302
Identify What Is Causing the Stress 302
Practice a Healthy Lifestyle 303
Learn How to Relax 303
Develop Supportive Relationships 303
Keep Things in Perspective 304
The A-B-C Model 304
Problem Solving 306
Identifying Problems or Opportunities for Improvement 306
Analyzing the Causes 307
Developing Alternative Solutions 308
Selecting and Implementing the Best Solution 308
Assessing the Impact of the Solution 309
Improving Creativity 309
Seeing Things in New Ways 309
Using Power Constructively 311
Forming Diverse Problem-Solving Groups 311

PART THREE
Focus on the Followers 317

The Potter and Rosenbach Followership Model 320
The Curphy Followership Model 323

Chapter 9
Motivation, Satisfaction, and Performance 331

Introduction 331

Defining Motivation, Satisfaction, and
Performance   332
Understanding and Influencing Follower
Motivation   338
   Maslow's Hierarchy of Needs: How Does Context
   Affect Motivation?   340
   Achievement Orientation: How Does Personality
   Affect Motivation?   344
   Goal Setting: How Do Clear Performance Targets
   Affect Motivation?   346
   The Operant Approach: How Do Rewards and
   Punishment Affect Motivation?   351
   Empowerment: How Does Decision-Making
   Latitude Affect Motivation?   355
   Motivation Summary   360
Understanding and Influencing Follower
Satisfaction   362
   Global, Facet, and Life Satisfaction   364
   Three Theories of Job Satisfaction   369
   Affectivity: Is the Cup Half Empty or Half
   Full?   370
   Herzberg's Two-Factor Theory: Does Meaningful
   Work Make People Happy?   372
   Organizational Justice: Does Fairness
   Matter?   374
Summary   376

Chapter 10
Groups, Teams, and Their Leadership   390

Introduction   390
Individuals versus Groups versus
Teams   391
The Nature of Groups   393
   Group Size   394
   Developmental Stages of Groups   396
   Group Roles   396
   Group Norms   400
   Group Cohesion   402
Teams   406
   Effective Team Characteristics and Team
   Building   406
   Ginnett's Team Leadership Model   410
     Outputs   410

     Process   410
     Inputs   415
   Leadership Prescriptions of the Model   415
     Creation   415
     Dream   416
     Design   416
     Development   417
     Diagnosis and Leverage Points   418
   Concluding Thoughts about Ginnett's Team
   Leadership Model   422
Virtual Teams   424
Summary   428

Chapter 11
Skills for Developing Others   436

Setting Goals   436
   Goals Should Be Specific and Observable   437
   Goals Should Be Attainable but
   Challenging   437
   Goals Require Commitment   438
   Goals Require Feedback   439
Providing Constructive Feedback   439
   Make It Helpful   441
   Be Specific   442
   Be Descriptive   442
   Be Timely   443
   Be Flexible   443
   Give Positive as Well as Negative Feedback   444
   Avoid Blame or Embarrassment   444
Team Building for Work Teams   444
   Team-Building Interventions   445
   What Does a Team-Building Workshop
   Involve?   446
   Examples of Interventions   447
Building High-Performance Teams: The
Rocket Model   448
   Mission   450
   Talent   450
   Norms   451
   Buy-In   452
   Power   453
   Morale   453
   Results   454
   Implications of the Rocket Model   455

Delegating   457
  Why Delegating Is Important   457
    Delegation Frees Time for Other
    Activities   457
    Delegation Develops Followers   458
    Delegation Strengthens the
    Organization   458
  Common Reasons for Avoiding Delegation   458
    Delegation Takes Too Much Time   458
    Delegation Is Risky   458
    The Job Will Not Be Done as Well   459
    The Task Is a Desirable One   459
    Others Are Already Too Busy   459
  Principles of Effective Delegation   459
    Decide What to Delegate   459
    Decide Whom to Delegate To   460
    Make the Assignment Clear and Specific   460
    Assign an Objective, Not a Procedure   460
    Allow Autonomy, but Monitor
    Performance   461
    Give Credit, Not Blame   461
Coaching   462
  Forging a Partnership   463
  *Inspiring Commitment: Conducting a GAPS
  Analysis   464*
  *Growing Skills: Creating Development and
  Coaching Plans   465*
  *Promoting Persistence: Helping Followers Stick to
  Their Plans   466*
  *Transferring Skills: Creating a Learning
  Environment   467*
  Concluding Comments   468

PART FOUR
Focus on the Situation   473

Chapter 12
The Situation   475

Introduction   475
The Task   480
  *How Tasks Vary, and What That Means for
  Leadership   480*
  Problems and Challenges   482

The Organization   484
  From the Industrial Age to the Information Age   484
  The Formal Organization   486
  *The Informal Organization: Organizational
  Culture   489*
  A Theory of Organizational Culture   495
  *An Afterthought on Organizational Issues for
  Students and Young Leaders   498*
The Environment   498
  *Are Things Changing More Than They
  Used To?   499*
Leading across Societal Cultures   502
  What Is Societal Culture?   506
  The GLOBE Study   506
Implications for Leadership
Practitioners   511
Summary   512

Chapter 13
**Contingency Theories of
Leadership   520**

Introduction   520
Leader–Member Exchange (LMX)
Theory   521
  *Concluding Thoughts about the
  LMX Model   522*
The Normative Decision Model   523
  Levels of Participation   523
  Decision Quality and Acceptance   523
  The Decision Tree   525
  *Concluding Thoughts about the Normative
  Decision Model   528*
The Situational Leadership® Model   530
  Leader Behaviors   530
  Follower Readiness   532
  Prescriptions of the Model   532
  *Concluding Thoughts about the Situational
  Leadership® Model   533*
The Contingency Model   535
  The Least Preferred Coworker Scale   535
  Situational Favorability   537
  Prescriptions of the Model   538
  *Concluding Thoughts about the Contingency
  Model   540*

The Path–Goal Theory   542
Leader Behaviors   542
The Followers   543
The Situation   545
Prescriptions of the Theory   546
*Concluding Thoughts about the Path–Goal
Theory   547*
Summary   549

Chapter 14
Leadership and Change   556

Introduction   556
The Rational Approach to Organizational
Change   557
Dissatisfaction   560
Model   561
Process   564
Resistance   567
*Concluding Comments about the Rational
Approach to Organizational Change   570*
The Emotional Approach to Organizational
Change: Charismatic and Transformational
Leadership   573
Charismatic Leadership: A Historical Review   573
*What Are the Common Characteristics of
Charismatic and Transformational
Leadership?   580*
Leader Characteristics   581
Vision   581
Rhetorical Skills   582
Image and Trust Building   582
Personalized Leadership   583
Follower Characteristics   584
*Identification with the Leader and the
Vision   584*
*Heightened Emotional
Levels   585*
*Willing Subordination to the
Leader   585*
Feelings of Empowerment   585
Situational Characteristics   586
Crises   586
Social Networks   587
Other Situational Characteristics   587

Concluding Thoughts about the
Characteristics of Charismatic and
Transformational Leadership   587
Bass's Theory of Transformational and
Transactional Leadership   590
*Research Results of Transformational and
Transactional Leadership   592*
Summary   594

Chapter 15
The Dark Side of Leadership   607

Introduction   607
Bad Leadership   610
Managerial Incompetence   614
Managerial Derailment   620
The Six Root Causes of Managerial
Incompetence and Derailment   628
*Stuff Happens: Situational and Follower Factors in
Managerial Derailment   630*
*The Lack of Organizational Fit: Stranger in a
Strange Land   632*
*More Clues for the Clueless: Lack of Situational and
Self-Awareness   635*
*Lack of Intelligence, Subject Matter Expertise, and
Team-Building Know-How: Real
Genius   637*
Poor Followership: Fire Me, Please   640
*Dark-Side Personality Traits: Personality as a
Method of Birth Control   643*
Summary   648

Chapter 16
Skills for Optimizing Leadership as
Situations Change   657

Creating a Compelling Vision   657
Ideas: The Future Picture   658
*Expectations: Values and Performance
Standards   659*
*Emotional Energy: The Power and the
Passion   660*
Edge: Stories, Analogies, and Metaphors   661

Managing Conflict   662
  What Is Conflict?   662
  Is Conflict Always Bad?   663
  Conflict Resolution Strategies   664
Negotiation   668
  Prepare for the Negotiation   668
  Separate the People from the Problem   668
  Focus on Interests, Not Positions   668
Diagnosing Performance Problems
in Individuals, Groups, and
Organizations   669
  Expectations   670
  Capabilities   670
  Opportunities   671

  Motivation   671
  *Concluding Comments on the Diagnostic
  Model*   671
Team Building at the Top   671
  Executive Teams Are Different   672
  *Applying Individual Skills and
  Team Skills*   672
  Tripwire Lessons   673
Punishment   676
  Myths Surrounding the Use of Punishment   677
  Punishment, Satisfaction, and Performance   678
  Administering Punishment   682

Index   686

Leadership Is a Process, Not a Position

Part 1

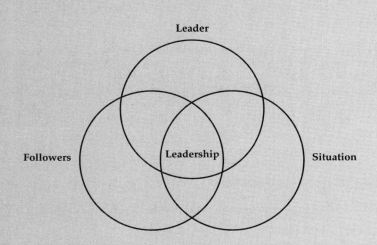

If any single idea is central to this book, it is that leadership is a process, not a position. The entire first part of this book explores that idea. One is not a leader—except perhaps in name only—merely because one holds a title or position. Leadership involves something happening as a result of the interaction between a leader and followers.

In Chapter 1 we define leadership and explore its relationship to concepts such as management and followership, and we also introduce the interactional framework. The interactional framework is based on the idea that leadership involves complex interactions between the leader, the followers, and the situations they are in. That framework provides the organizing principle for the rest of the book. Chapter 2 looks at how we can become better leaders by profiting more fully from our experiences, which is not to say that either the study or the practice of leadership is simple. Part 1 concludes with a chapter focusing on basic leadership skills. There also will be a corresponding skills chapter at the conclusion of each of the other three parts in this book.

Chapter 1

What Do We Mean by Leadership?

Introduction

In the spring of 1972, an airplane flew across the Andes mountains carrying its crew and 40 passengers. Most of the passengers were members of an amateur Uruguayan rugby team en route to a game in Chile. The plane never arrived. It crashed in snow-covered mountains, breaking into several pieces on impact. The main part of the fuselage slid like a toboggan down a steep valley, coming to rest in waist-deep snow. Although a number of people died immediately or within a day of the impact, the picture for the 28 survivors was not much better. The fuselage offered little protection from the extreme cold, food supplies were scant, and a number of passengers had serious injuries from the crash. Over the next few days, several surviving passengers became psychotic and several others died from their injuries. The passengers who were relatively uninjured set out to do what they could to improve their chances of survival.

Several worked on "weatherproofing" the wreckage; others found ways to get water; and those with medical training took care of the injured. Although shaken by the crash, the survivors initially were confident they would be found. These feelings gradually gave way to despair as search and rescue teams failed to find the wreckage. With the passing of several weeks and no sign of rescue in sight, the remaining passengers decided to mount expeditions to determine the best way to escape. The most physically fit were chosen to go on the expeditions because the thin mountain air and the deep snow made the trips difficult. The results of the trips were both frustrating and demoralizing: the expedition members determined they were in the middle of the Andes mountains, and walking out to find help was believed to be impossible. Just when the survivors thought nothing worse could possibly happen, an avalanche hit the wreckage and killed several more of them.

The remaining survivors concluded they would not be rescued, and their only hope was for someone to leave the wreckage and find help. Three of the fittest passengers were chosen for the final expedition, and everyone else's work was directed toward improving the expedition's chances of success. The three expedition members were given more food and were exempted from routine survival activities; the rest spent most of their energies securing supplies for the trip. Two months after the plane crash, the expedition members set out on their final attempt to find help. After hiking for 10 days through some of the most rugged terrain in the world, the expedition stumbled across a group of Chilean peasants tending cattle. One of the expedition members stated, "I come from a plane that fell in the mountains. I am Uruguayan . . ." Eventually 14 other survivors were rescued.

When the full account of their survival became known, it was not without controversy. It had required extreme and unsettling measures: the survivors had lived only by eating the flesh of their deceased comrades. Nonetheless, their story is one of the most moving survival dramas of all time, magnificently told by Piers Paul Read in *Alive*.[1] It is a story of tragedy and courage, and it is a story of leadership.

Perhaps a story of survival in the Andes is so far removed from everyday experience that it does not seem to hold any relevant lessons about leadership for you personally. But consider some of the basic issues the Andes survivors faced: tension between individual and group goals, dealing with the different needs and personalities of group members, and keeping hope alive in the face of adversity. These issues are not so different from those facing many groups we're a part of. We can also look at the Andes experience for examples of the emergence of informal leaders in groups. Before the flight, a boy named Parrado was awkward and shy, a "second-stringer" both athletically and socially. Nonetheless, this unlikely hero became the best loved and most respected among the survivors for his courage, optimism, fairness, and emotional support. Persuasiveness in group decision making also was an important part of leadership among the Andes survivors. During the difficult discussions preceding the agonizing decision to survive on the flesh of their deceased comrades, one of the rugby players made his reasoning clear: "I know that if my dead body could help you stay alive, then I would want you to use it. In fact, if I do die and you don't eat me, then I'll come back from wherever I am and give you a good kick in the ass."[2]

Lives of great men all remind us
We can make our lives sublime
And, departing, leave behind us
Footprints on the sands of time.
Henry Wadsworth Longfellow

What Is Leadership?

The Andes story and the experiences of many other leaders we'll introduce to you in a series of profiles sprinkled throughout the chapters provide numerous examples of leadership. But just what *is* leadership?

The halls of fame are open wide and they are always full. Some go in by the door called "push" and some by the door called "pull."

Stanley Baldwin, British prime minister in the 1930s

Remember the difference between a boss and a leader: a boss says, "Go!"—a leader says, "Let's go!"

E. M. Kelly

People who do research on leadership disagree more than you might think about what leadership really is. Most of this disagreement stems from the fact that **leadership** is a complex phenomenon involving the leader, the followers, and the situation. Some leadership researchers have focused on the personality, physical traits, or behaviors of the leader; others have studied the relationships between leaders and followers; still others have studied how aspects of the situation affect how leaders act. Some have extended the latter viewpoint so far as to suggest there is no such thing as leadership; they argue that organizational successes and failures often get falsely attributed to the leader, but the situation may have a much greater impact on how the organization functions than does any individual, including the leader.[3]

Perhaps the best way for you to begin to understand the complexities of leadership is to see some of the ways leadership has been defined. Leadership researchers have defined leadership in many different ways:

- The process by which an agent induces a subordinate to behave in a desired manner.[4]
- Directing and coordinating the work of group members.[5]
- An interpersonal relation in which others comply because they want to, not because they have to.[6]
- The process of influencing an organized group toward accomplishing its goals.[7]
- Actions that focus resources to create desirable opportunities.[8]
- Creating conditions for a team to be effective.[9]
- Getting results through others (the *ends* of leadership), and the ability to build cohesive, goal-oriented teams (the *means* of leadership). Good leaders are those who build teams to get results across a variety of situations.[10]
- A complex form of social problem solving.[11]

As you can see, definitions of leadership differ in many ways, and these differences have resulted in various researchers exploring disparate aspects of leadership. For example, if we were to apply these definitions to the Andes survival scenario described earlier, some researchers would focus on the behaviors Parrado used to keep up the morale of the survivors. Researchers who define leadership as influencing an organized group toward accomplishing its goals would examine how Parrado managed to convince the group to stage and support the final expedition. One's definition of leadership might also influence just *who* is considered an appropriate leader for study. Thus each group of researchers might focus on a different aspect of leadership, and each would tell a different story regarding the leader, the followers, and the situation.

Although having many leadership definitions may seem confusing, it is important to understand that there is no single correct definition. The various definitions can help us appreciate the multitude of factors that affect leadership, as well as different perspectives from which to view it. For example, in the first definition just listed, the word *subordinate* seems to confine leadership to downward influence in hierarchical relationships; it seems to exclude informal leadership. The second definition emphasizes the directing and controlling aspects of leadership, and thereby may deemphasize emotional aspects of leadership. The emphasis placed in the third definition on subordinates' "wanting to" comply with a leader's wishes seems to exclude any kind of coercion as a leadership tool. Further, it becomes problematic to identify ways in which a leader's actions are really leadership if subordinates voluntarily comply when a leader with considerable potential coercive power merely asks others to do something without explicitly threatening them. Similarly, a key reason behind using the phrase *desirable opportunities* in one of the definitions was precisely to distinguish between leadership and tyranny. And partly because there are many different definitions of leadership, there is also a wide range of individuals we consider leaders. In addition to stories about leaders and leadership we will sprinkle through this book, we will highlight several in each chapter in a series of Profiles in Leadership. The first of these is Profiles in Leadership 1.1, which highlights Peter Jackson.

All considered, we find that defining leadership as "the process of influencing an organized group toward accomplishing its goals" is fairly comprehensive and helpful. Several implications of this definition are worth further examination.

Leadership Is Both a Science and an Art

Saying leadership is both a science and an art emphasizes the subject of leadership as a field of scholarly inquiry, as well as certain aspects of the practice of leadership. The scope of the science of leadership is reflected in the number of studies—approximately 8,000—cited in an authoritative reference work, *Bass & Stogdill's Handbook of Leadership: Theory, Research, and Managerial Applications.*[12] However, being an expert on leadership research is neither necessary nor sufficient for being a good leader. Some managers may be effective leaders without ever having taken a course or training program in leadership, and some scholars in the field of leadership may be relatively poor leaders themselves.

However, knowing something about leadership research is relevant to leadership effectiveness. Scholarship may not be a prerequisite for leadership effectiveness, but understanding some of the major research findings can help individuals better analyze situations using a variety of perspectives. That, in turn, can tell leaders how to be more effective. Even so, because skills in analyzing and responding to situations vary greatly across leaders, leadership will always remain partly an art as

Any fool can keep a rule. God gave him a brain to know when to break the rule.
General Willard W. Scott

Peter Jackson

PROFILES IN LEADERSHIP 1.1

When Peter Jackson read *The Lord of the Rings* trilogy at the age of 18, he couldn't wait until it was made into a movie; 20 years later he made that movie himself. In 2004 *The Lord of the Rings: The Return of the King* took home 11 Academy Awards, winning the Oscar in every category for which it was nominated. This tied the record for the most Oscars ever earned by one motion picture. Such an achievement might seem unlikely for a producer/director whose film debut was titled *Bad Taste,* which it and subsequent works exemplified in spades. Peter Jackson made horror movies so grisly and revolting that his fans nicknamed him the "Sultan of Splatter." Nonetheless, his talent was evident to discerning eyes—at least among horror film aficionados. *Bad Taste* was hailed as a cult classic at the Cannes Film Festival, and horror fans tabbed Jackson as a talent to follow.

When screenwriter Costa Botes heard that *The Lord of the Rings* would be made into a live action film, he thought those responsible were crazy. Prevailing wisdom was that the fantastic and complex trilogy simply could not be believably translated onto the screen. But he also believed that "there was no other director on earth who could do it justice" (Botes, 2004). And do it justice he obviously did. What was it about the "Sultan of Splatter's" leadership that gave others such confidence in his ability to make one of the biggest and best movies of all time? What gave him the confidence to even try? And what made others want to share in his vision?

Peter Jackson's effectiveness as a leader has been due in large part to a unique combination of personal qualities and talents. One associate, for example, called him "one of the smartest people I know," as well as a maverick willing to buck the establishment. Jackson is also a tireless worker whose early successes were due in no small part to the combination of his ambition and dogged perseverance (Botes, 2004). His initial success was driven largely by his budding genius in making films on a low budget and with virtually no other staff. In reading others' comments who worked with him on the *LOTR* project, however, it's clear that his leadership continued to develop over the years. It was his ability to communicate a shared vision and inspire such extraordinary work from an incredibly large staff that made *LOTR* so spectacularly successful.

Source: Adapted from Costa Botes, *Made in New Zealand: The Cinema of Peter Jackson,* NZEDGE.com, May 2004.

---

well as a science. Highlight 1.1 provides further perspective on how the art and science of leadership are represented in somewhat distinctive research traditions.

Leadership Is Both Rational and Emotional

Leadership involves both the rational and emotional sides of human experience. Leadership includes actions and influences based on reason and logic as well as those based on inspiration and passion. We do not want to cultivate merely intellectualized leaders who respond with only logical predictability. Because people differ in their thoughts and feelings, hopes and dreams, needs and fears, goals and ambitions, and strengths and weaknesses, leadership situations can be complex. People are both rational and emotional, so leaders can use rational techniques and emotional appeals to influence followers, but they must also weigh the rational and emotional consequences of their actions.

A democracy cannot follow a leader unless he is dramatized. A man to be a hero must not content himself with heroic virtues and anonymous action. He must talk and explain as he acts—drama.

William Allen White, American writer and editor, Emporia Gazette

The Academic and Troubadour Traditions of Leadership Research

HIGHLIGHT 1.1

On a practical level, leadership is a topic that almost everyone is interested in at one time or another. People have a vested interest in who is running their government, schools, company, or church, and because of this interest thousands of books and articles have been written about the topic of leadership. Curphy and Hogan believe these works can be divided into two major camps. The **academic tradition** consists of articles that use data and statistical techniques to make inferences about effective leadership. Because the academic tradition is research based, for the most part these findings are written for other leadership researchers and are virtually uninterpretable to leadership *practitioners*. As such, leadership practitioners are often unfamiliar with the research findings of the academic tradition.

The second camp of leadership literature is the **troubadour tradition**. These books and articles often consist of nothing more than the opinions or score-settling reminiscences of former leaders. Books in the troubadour tradition, such as *Who Moved My Cheese?*, *What the CEO Wants You to Know*, *Winning*, and *Lead Like Jesus: Lessons from the Greatest Leadership Role Model of all Time*, are wildly popular, but it is difficult to separate fact from fiction or determine whether these opinions translate to other settings. People who are unfamiliar with the findings of the academic tradition and the limitations of the troubadour tradition find it difficult to differentiate research findings from opinion.

Perhaps the biggest challenge to improving the practice of leadership is to give practitioners timely, easily digestible, research-grounded advice on how to effectively lead others. The knowledge accumulated from 90 years of leadership research is of tremendous value, yet scientists have paid little attention to the ultimate consumers of their work—leaders and leaders-to-be. Leadership practitioners often want fast answers about how to be more effective or successful and understandably turn to popular books and articles that *appear* to provide timely answers to their practical concerns. Unfortunately, however, the claims in the popular literature are rarely based on sound research; they oversimplify the complexities of the leadership process; and many times they actually offer bad advice. Relatively little weight is given to well-researched leadership studies, primarily because the arcane requirements of publishing articles in scholarly journals make their content virtually unreadable (and certainly uninteresting) to actual leadership practitioners. One of the primary objectives of this book is to make the results of leadership research more usable for leaders and leaders-to-be.

Sources: G. J. Curphy, M. J. Benson, A. Baldrica, and R. T. Hogan, *Managerial Incompetence* (unpublished manuscript, 2007); G. J. Curphy, "*What We Really Know about Leadership (But Seem Unwilling to Implement)*" (presentation given to the Minnesota Professionals for Psychology and Applied Work, Minneapolis, MN, January 2004); R. T. Hogan, *Personality and the Fate of Organizations* (Mahwah, NJ: Lawrence Erlbaum Associates, 2007).

A full appreciation of leadership involves looking at both these sides of human nature. Good leadership is more than just calculation and planning, or following a checklist, even though rational analysis can enhance good leadership. Good leadership also involves touching others' feelings; emotions play an important role in leadership too. Just one example of this is the civil rights movement of the 1960s, which was based on emotions as well as on principles. Dr. Martin Luther King Jr. inspired many people to action; he touched people's hearts as well as their heads.

Aroused feelings, however, can be used either positively or negatively, constructively or destructively. Some leaders have been able to inspire others to deeds of great purpose and courage. On the other hand, as images of Adolf Hitler's mass rallies or present-day angry mobs attest, group frenzy can readily become group mindlessness. As another example, emotional appeals by the Reverend Jim Jones resulted in approximately 800 of his followers volitionally committing suicide.

The mere presence of a group (even without heightened emotional levels) can also cause people to act differently than when they are alone. For example, in airline cockpit crews, there are clear lines of authority from the captain down to the first officer (second in command) and so on. So strong are the norms surrounding the authority of the captain that some first officers will not take control of the airplane from the captain even in the event of impending disaster. Foushee[13] reported a study wherein airline captains in simulator training intentionally feigned incapacitation so the response of the rest of the crew could be observed. The feigned incapacitations occurred at a predetermined point during the plane's final approach in landing, and the simulation involved conditions of poor weather and visibility. Approximately 25 percent of the first officers in these simulated flights allowed the plane to crash. For some reason, the first officers did not take control even when it was clear the captain was allowing the aircraft to deviate from the parameters of a safe approach. This example demonstrates how group dynamics can influence the behavior of group members even when emotional levels are *not* high. (Believe it or not, airline crews are so well trained that this is *not* an emotional situation.) In sum, it should be apparent that leadership involves followers' feelings and nonrational behavior as well as rational behavior. Leaders need to consider *both* the rational and the emotional consequences of their actions.

Leadership and Management

In trying to answer "What is leadership?" it is natural to look at the relationship between leadership and management. To many, the word **management** suggests words like *efficiency, planning, paperwork, procedures, regulations, control,* and *consistency.* Leadership is often more associated with words like *risk taking, dynamic, creativity, change,* and *vision.* Some say leadership is fundamentally a value-choosing, and thus a value-laden, activity, whereas management is not. Leaders are thought to *do the right things,* whereas managers are thought to *do things right.*[14,15] Here are some other distinctions between managers and leaders:[16]

If you want some ham, you gotta go into the smokehouse.

Huey Long, governor of Louisiana, 1928–1932

- Managers administer; leaders innovate.
- Managers maintain; leaders develop.
- Managers control; leaders inspire.

- Managers have a short-term view; leaders, a long-term view.
- Managers ask how and when; leaders ask what and why.
- Managers imitate; leaders originate.
- Managers accept the status quo; leaders challenge it.

Zaleznik[17] goes so far as to say these differences reflect fundamentally different personality types: leaders and managers are basically different kinds of people. He says some people are managers *by nature*; other people are leaders *by nature.* One is not better than the other; they are just different. Their differences, in fact, can be useful because organizations typically need both functions performed well. For example, consider again the U.S. civil rights movement in the 1960s. Dr. Martin Luther King Jr. gave life and direction to the civil rights movement in America. He gave dignity and hope of freer participation in national life to people who before had little reason to expect it. He inspired the world with his vision and eloquence, and he changed the way we live together. America is a different nation today because of him. Was Dr. Martin Luther King Jr. a leader? Of course. Was he a manager? Somehow that does not seem to fit, and the civil rights movement might have failed if it had not been for the managerial talents of his supporting staff. Leadership and management complement each other, and both are vital to organizational success.

With regard to the issue of leadership versus management, the authors of this book take a middle-of-the-road position. We think of leadership and management as closely related but distinguishable functions. Our view of the relationship is depicted in Figure 1.1, which shows leadership and management as two overlapping functions. Although some functions performed by leaders and managers may be unique, there is also an area of overlap. In reading Highlight 1.2, do you see more good management in the response to the 1906 San Francisco earthquake, more good leadership, or both?

FIGURE 1.1
Leadership and Management Overlap

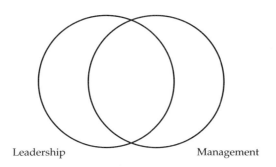

Leadership   Management

The Response of Leadership to a Natural Disaster

HIGHLIGHT 1.2

Much has been written about the inadequate response of local, state, and federal agencies to Hurricane Katrina. It may be instructive to compare the response of government agencies to a natural disaster on a different coast a century earlier: the San Francisco earthquake and fire of 1906.

While the precipitant disaster was the earthquake itself, much destruction resulted from the consequent fire, one disaster aggravating the impact of the other. Because of the earthquake, utility poles throughout the city fell, taking the high-tension wires they were carrying with them. Gas pipes broke; chimneys fell, dropping hot coals into thousands of gallons of gas spilled by broken fuel tanks; stoves and heaters in homes toppled over; and in moments fires erupted across the city. And because the earthquake's first tremors also broke water pipes throughout the city, fire hydrants everywhere suddenly went dry, making fighting the fires virtually impossible. In objective terms, the disaster is estimated to have killed as many as 3,000 people, rendered more than 200,000 homeless, and by some measures caused $195 billion in property loss as measured by today's dollars.

How did authorities respond to the crisis when there were far fewer agencies with presumed response plans to combat disasters, and when high-tech communication methods were unheard of? Consider these two examples:

- The ranking officer assigned to a U.S. Army post in San Francisco was away when the earthquake struck, so it was up to his deputy to help organize the army's and federal government's response. The deputy immediately cabled Washington, D.C., requesting tents, rations, and medicine. Secretary of War William Howard Taft, who would become the next U.S. president, responded by immediately dispatching 200,000 rations from Washington State. In a matter of days, every tent in the U.S. Army had been sent to San Francisco, and the longest hospital train in history was dispatched from Virginia.

- Perhaps the most impressive example of leadership initiative in the face of the 1906 disaster was that of the U.S. Post Office. It recovered its ability to function in short order without losing a single item that was being handled when the earthquake struck. And because the earthquake had effectively destroyed the city's telegraphic connection (telegrams inside the city were temporarily being delivered by the post office), a critical question arose: How could people struck by the disaster communicate with their families elsewhere? The city postmaster immediately announced that all citizens of San Francisco could use the post office to inform their families and loved ones of their condition and needs. He further stipulated that for outgoing private letters *it would not matter whether the envelopes bore stamps.* This was what was needed: Circumstances demanded that people be able to communicate with friends and family whether or not they could find or pay for stamps.

Perhaps this should remind us that modern leadership is not necessarily better leadership, and that leadership in government is not always bureaucratic and can be both humane and innovative.

Source: Adapted from S. Winchester, *A Crack in the Edge of the World: America and the Great California Earthquake of 1906* (New York: Harper Perennial, 2006).

The Romance of Leadership

HIGHLIGHT 1.3

This text is predicated on the idea that leaders can make a difference. Interestingly, though, while businesspeople generally agree, not all scholars do.

People in the business world attribute much of a company's success or failure to its leadership. One study counted the number of articles appearing in *The Wall Street Journal* that dealt with leadership and found nearly 10 percent of the articles about representative target companies addressed that company's leadership. Furthermore, there was a significant positive relationship between company performance and the number of articles about its leadership; the more a company's leadership was emphasized in *The Wall Street Journal,* the better the company was doing. This might mean the more a company takes leadership seriously (as reflected by the emphasis in *The Wall Street Journal*), the better it does.

However, the study authors were skeptical about the real utility of leadership as a concept.

They suggested leadership is merely a romanticized notion—an obsession people want and need to believe in. Belief in the potency of leadership may be a cultural myth that has utility primarily insofar as it affects how people create meaning about causal events in complex social systems. The behavior of leaders, the authors contend, does not account for much of the variance in an organization's performance. Nonetheless, people seem strongly committed to a basic faith that individual leaders shape organizational destiny for good or ill.

As you read this book and come to appreciate how many factors affect a group's success *besides* the talents of the individual leader, you might pay a price for that understanding. As you appreciate the *complexity* of leadership more, the *romance* of leadership might slightly diminish.

Source: J. R. Meindl, S. B. Ehrlich, and J. M. Dukerich, "The Romance of Leadership," *Administrative Science Quarterly* 30 (1985), pp. 78–102.

Leadership Myths

Few things pose a greater obstacle to leadership development than certain unsubstantiated and self-limiting beliefs about leadership. Therefore, before we begin examining leadership and leadership development in more detail, we will consider what they are not. We will examine several beliefs (we call them myths) that stand in the way of fully understanding and developing leadership.

Myth: Good Leadership Is All Common Sense

At face value, this myth says one needs only common sense to be a good leader. It also implies, however, that most if not all of the studies of leadership reported in scholarly journals and books only confirm what anyone with common sense already knows.

The problem, of course, is with the ambiguous term *common sense.* It implies a common body of practical knowledge about life that virtually any reasonable person with moderate experience has acquired. A simple experiment, however, may convince you that common sense may be less common than you think. Ask a few friends or acquaintances whether the old folk wisdom "Absence makes the heart grow fonder" is true or false. Most will say it is true. After that ask a different group whether the old folk wisdom "Out of sight, out of mind" is true or false. Most of that group will answer true as well, even though the two proverbs are contradictory.

A similar thing sometimes happens when people hear about the results of studies concerning human behavior. On hearing the results, people may say, "Who needed a study to learn that? I knew it all the time." However, several experiments[18,19] showed that events were much more surprising when subjects had to guess the outcome of an experiment than when subjects were told the outcome. What seems obvious after you know the results and what you (or anyone else) would have predicted beforehand are not the same thing. Hindsight is always 20/20.

The point might become clearer with a specific example; read the following paragraph:

> After World War II, the U.S. Army spent enormous sums of money on studies only to reach conclusions that, many believed, should have been apparent at the outset. One, for example, was that southern soldiers were better able to stand the climate in the hot South Sea islands than northern soldiers were.

This sounds reasonable, but there is a problem: the statement here is exactly contrary to the actual findings. Southerners were no better than northerners in adapting to tropical climates.[20] Common sense can often play tricks on us.

Put a little differently, one challenge of understanding leadership may be to know when common sense applies and when it does not. Do leaders need to act confidently? Of course. But they also need to be humble enough to recognize that others' views are useful, too. Do leaders need to persevere when times get tough? Yes. But they also need to recognize when times change and a new direction is called for. If leadership were nothing more than common sense, there should be few, if any, problems in the workplace. However, we venture to guess you have noticed more than a few problems between leaders and followers. Effective leadership must be something more than just common sense.

Myth: Leaders Are Born, Not Made

Some people believe being a leader is either in one's genes or not; others believe that life experiences mold the individual and that no one is born a leader. Which view is right? In a sense, both and neither. Both views are right in that innate factors as well as formative experiences influence many sorts of behavior, including leadership. Yet both views are wrong to the extent they imply leadership is *either* innate *or* acquired; what matters more is how these factors *interact*. It does not seem useful, we

If you miss seven balls out of ten, you're batting three hundred and that's good enough for the Hall of Fame. You can't score if you keep the bat on your shoulder.

Walter B. Wriston, chairman of Citicorp, 1970–1984

believe, to think of the world as composed of two mutually exclusive types of people, leaders and nonleaders. It is more useful to address how each person can make the most of leadership opportunities he or she faces.

It may be easier to see the pointlessness of asking whether leaders are born or made by looking at an alternative question of far less popular interest: Are *college professors* born or made? Conceptually the issues are the same, and here too the answer is that every college professor is both born *and* made. It seems clear enough that college professors are partly "born" because (among other factors) there is a genetic component to intelligence, and intelligence surely plays some part in becoming a college professor (well, at least a *minor* part!). But every college professor is also partly "made." One obvious way is that college professors must have advanced education in specialized fields; even with the right genes one could not become a college professor without certain requisite experiences. Becoming a college professor depends partly on what one is born with and partly on how that inheritance is shaped through experience. The same is true of leadership.

More specifically, research indicates that many cognitive abilities and personality traits are at least partly innate.[21] Thus natural talents or characteristics may offer certain advantages or disadvantages to a leader. Consider physical characteristics: A man's above-average height may increase others' tendency to think of him as a leader; it may also boost his own self-confidence. But it doesn't make him a leader. The same holds true for psychological characteristics that seem related to leadership. The stability of certain characteristics over long periods (for example, at school reunions people seem to have kept the same personalities we remember them as having years earlier) may reinforce the impression that our basic natures are fixed, but different environments nonetheless may nurture or suppress different leadership qualities.

Myth: The Only School You Learn Leadership from Is the School of Hard Knocks

Some people skeptically question whether leadership can develop through formal study, believing instead it can be acquired only through actual experience. It is a mistake, however, to think of formal study and learning from experience as mutually exclusive or antagonistic. In fact, they complement each other. Rather than ask whether leadership develops from formal study or from real-life experience, it is better to ask what kind of study will help students learn to discern critical lessons about leadership from their own experience. Approaching the issue in such a way recognizes the vital role of experience in leadership development, but it also admits that certain kinds of study and training can improve a person's ability to discern important lessons about leadership

Never reveal all of yourself to other people; hold back something in reserve so that people are never quite sure if they really know you.
Michael Korda, author, editor

Progress always involves risks. You can't steal second base and keep your foot on first.
Frederick B. Wilcox

from experience. It can, in other words, accelerate the process of learning from experience.

We argue that one advantage of formally studying leadership is that formal study provides students with a variety of ways of examining a particular leadership situation. By studying the different ways researchers have defined and examined leadership, students can use these definitions and theories to better understand what is going on in any leadership situation. For example, earlier in this chapter we used three different leadership definitions as a framework for describing or analyzing the situation facing Parrado and the survivors of the plane crash, and each definition focused on a different aspect of leadership. These frameworks can similarly be applied to better understand the experiences one has as both a leader and a follower. We think it is difficult for leaders, particularly novice leaders, to examine leadership situations from multiple perspectives; but we also believe developing this skill can help you become a better leader. Being able to analyze your experiences from multiple perspectives may be the greatest single contribution a formal course in leadership can give you. Maybe you can reflect on your own leadership over a cup of coffee in Starbucks as you read about the origins of that company in Profiles in Leadership 1.2.

Howard Schultz

PROFILES IN LEADERSHIP 1.2

Starbucks began in 1971 as a very different company than we know it as today. The difference is due in large part to the way its former CEO, Howard Schultz, reframed the kind of business Starbucks should be. Schultz joined Starbucks in 1981 to head its marketing and retail store operations. While on a trip to Italy in 1983, Schultz was amazed by the number and variety of espresso bars there—1,500 in the city of Turin alone. He concluded that the Starbucks stores in Seattle had missed the point: *Starbucks should be not just a store but an experience—a gathering place.*

Everything looks clearer in hindsight, of course, but the Starbucks owners resisted Schultz's vision; Starbucks was a retailer, they insisted, not a restaurant or bar. Schultz's strategic reframing of the Starbucks opportunity was ultimately vindicated when—after having departed Starbucks to pursue the same idea with another company—Schultz had the opportunity to purchase the whole Starbucks operation in Seattle, including its name.

Despite today's pervasiveness of Starbucks across the world, however, and the seeming obviousness of Schultz's exemplary leadership, the Starbucks story has not been one of completely consistent success. After Schultz retired as Starbucks CEO when it was a global megabrand, the company's performance suffered to the point Schultz complained that it was "losing its soul." He was asked to return as CEO in 2008, and it appears he has resurrected Starbucks by bringing new attention to the company's operating efficiency and by admitting, in effect, that some of his own earlier instinctive approach to company strategy and management may no longer be sufficient for the new global scale of Starbucks operation.

The Interactional Framework for Analyzing Leadership

Perhaps the first researcher to formally recognize the importance of the leader, follower, and situation in the leadership process was Fred Fiedler.[22] Fiedler used these three components to develop his contingency model of leadership, a theory of leadership that will be discussed in more detail in Chapter 13. Although we recognize Fiedler's contributions, we owe perhaps even more to Hollander's[23] transactional approach to leadership. We call our approach the **interactional framework.**

Several aspects of this derivative of Hollander's approach are worthy of additional comment. First, as shown in Figure 1.2, the framework depicts leadership as a function of three elements—the **leader,** the **followers,** and the **situation.** Second, a particular leadership scenario can be examined using each level of analysis separately. Although this is a useful way to understand the leadership process, we can understand the process even better if we also examine the **interactions** among the three elements, or lenses, represented by the overlapping areas in the figure. For example, we can better understand the leadership process if we not only look at the leaders and the followers but also examine how leaders and followers affect each other in the leadership process. Similarly, we can examine the leader and the situation separately, but we can gain even further understanding of the leadership process by looking at how the situation can constrain or facilitate a leader's actions and how the leader can change different aspects of the situation to be more effective. Thus a final important aspect of the framework is that leadership is the result of a complex set of interactions among the leader, the followers, and the situation. These complex interactions may be why broad generalizations about leadership are problematic: many factors influence the leadership process (see Highlight 1.3 on page 11).

FIGURE 1.2
An Interactional Framework for Analyzing Leadership

Source: Adapted from
E. P. Hollander, *Leadership Dynamics: A Practical Guide to Effective Relationships* (New York: Free Press, 1978).

An example of one such complex interaction between leaders and followers is evident in what have been called in-groups and out-groups. Sometimes there is a high degree of mutual influence and attraction between the leader and a few subordinates. These subordinates belong to the **in-group** and can be distinguished by their high degree of loyalty, commitment, and trust felt toward the leader. Other subordinates belong to the **out-group.** Leaders have considerably more influence with in-group followers than with out-group followers. However, this greater degree of influence has a price. If leaders rely primarily on their formal authority to influence their followers (especially if they punish them), then leaders risk losing the high levels of loyalty and commitment followers feel toward them.[24]

The Leader

This element examines primarily what the leader brings *as an individual* to the leadership equation. This can include unique personal history, interests, character traits, and motivation.

Source: *BIZZARO (NEW)* © Dan Pirari. King Features Syndicate.

Leaders are *not* all alike, but they tend to share many characteristics. Research has shown that leaders differ from their followers, and effective leaders differ from ineffective leaders, on various personality traits, cognitive abilities, skills, and values.[25-30] Another way personality can affect leadership is through temperament, by which we mean whether a leader is generally calm or is instead prone to emotional outbursts. Leaders who have calm dispositions and do not attack or belittle others for bringing bad news are more likely to get complete and timely information from subordinates than are bosses who have explosive tempers and a reputation for killing the messenger.

Another important aspect of the leader is how he or she achieved leader status. Leaders who are appointed by superiors may have less credibility with subordinates and get less loyalty from them than leaders who are elected or emerge by consensus from the ranks of followers. Often emergent or elected officials are better able to influence a group toward goal achievement because of the power conferred on them by their followers. However, both elected and emergent leaders need to be sensitive to their constituencies if they wish to remain in power.

More generally, a leader's experience or history in a particular organization is usually important to her or his effectiveness. For example, leaders promoted from within an organization, by virtue of being familiar with its culture and policies, may be ready to "hit the job running." In addition, leaders selected from within an organization are typically better known by others in the organization than are leaders selected from the outside. That is likely to affect, for better or worse, the latitude others in the organization are willing to give the leader; if the leader is widely respected for a history of accomplishment, she may be given more latitude than a newcomer whose track record is less well known. On the other hand, many people tend to give new leaders a fair chance to succeed, and newcomers to an organization often take time to learn the organization's informal rules, norms, and "ropes" before they make any radical or potentially controversial decisions.

A leader's legitimacy also may be affected by the extent to which followers participated in the leader's selection. When followers have had a say in the selection or election of a leader, they tend to have a heightened sense of psychological identification with her, but they also may have higher expectations and make more demands on her.[31] We also might wonder what kind of support a leader has from his own boss. If followers sense their boss has a lot of influence with the higher-ups, subordinates may be reluctant to take their complaints to higher levels. On the other hand, if the boss has little influence with higher-ups, subordinates may be more likely to make complaints to these levels.

The foregoing examples highlight the sorts of insights we can gain about leadership by focusing on the individual leader as a level of analysis. Even if we were to examine the individual leader completely, however, our understanding of the leadership process would be incomplete.

I must follow the people. Am I not their leader?
Benjamin Disraeli, 19th-century British prime minister

"I'll be blunt, coach. I'm having a problem with this 'take a lap' thing of yours . . ."

Source: © *Tribune Media Services, Inc. All Rights Reserved. Reprinted with permission.*

The crowd will follow a leader who marches twenty steps in advance; but if he is a thousand steps in front of them, they do not see and do not follow him.

Georg Brandes

The Followers

Followers are a critical part of the leadership equation, but their role has not always been appreciated, at least in empirical research (but read Highlight 1.4 to see how the role of followers has been recognized in literature). For a long time, in fact, "the common view of leadership was that leaders actively led and subordinates, later called followers, passively and obediently followed."[32] Over time, especially in the last cen-

The *First* Band of Brothers

HIGHLIGHT 1.4

Many of you probably have seen, or at least heard of, the award-winning series *Band of Brothers* that followed a company of the famous 101st Airborne division during World War II. You may not be aware that an earlier band of brothers was made famous by William Shakespeare in his play *Henry V*.

In one of the most famous speeches by any of Shakespeare's characters, the young Henry V tried to unify his followers when their daring expedition to conquer France was failing. French soldiers followed Henry's army along the rivers, daring them to cross over and engage the French in battle. Just before the battle of Agincourt, Henry's rousing words rallied his vastly outnumbered, weary, and tattered troops to victory. Few words of oratory have ever better bonded a leader with his followers than Henry's call for unity among "we few, we happy few, we band of brothers."

Hundreds of years later, Henry's speech is still a powerful illustration of a leader who emphasized the importance of his followers. Modern leadership concepts like vision, charisma, relationship orientation, and empowerment are readily evident in Henry's interactions with his followers. Here are the closing lines of Henry's famous speech:

> From this day to the ending of the world,
> But we in it shall be remembered—
> We few, we happy few, we band of brothers;
> For he today that sheds his blood with me
> Shall be my brother; be he ne'er so vile,
> This day shall gentle his condition;
> And gentlemen in England now-a-bed
> Shall think themselves accurs'd they were not here,
> And hold their manhoods cheap whiles any speaks
> That fought with us upon Saint Crispin's day.

Shakespeare's insights into the complexities of leadership should remind us that while modern research helps enlighten our understanding, it does not represent the only, and certainly not the most moving, perspective on leadership to which we should pay attention.

Source: N. Warner, "Screening Leadership through Shakespeare: Paradoxes of Leader–Follower Relations in *Henry V* on Film," *The Leadership Quarterly* 18 (2007), pp. 1–15.

All men have some weak points, and the more vigorous and brilliant a person may be, the more strongly these weak points stand out. It is highly desirable, even essential, therefore, for the more influential members of a general's staff not to be too much like the general.

Major General Hugo Baron von Freytag-Loringhoven, anti-Hitler conspirator

---

tury, social change shaped people's views of followers, and leadership theories gradually recognized the active and important role that followers play in the leadership process.[33] Today it seems natural to accept the important role followers play. Highlight 1.5 suggests some interesting interactions between leadership and followership in an arena familiar to you.

One aspect of our text's definition of leadership is particularly worth noting in this regard: Leadership is a social influence process shared among *all* members of a group. Leadership is not restricted to the influence exerted by someone in a particular position or role; followers are part of the leadership process, too. In recent years both practitioners and scholars have emphasized the relatedness of leadership and **followership.** As Burns[34] observed, the idea of "one-man leadership" is a contradiction in terms.

Obvious as this point may seem, it is also clear that early leadership researchers paid relatively little attention to the roles followers play in the

A Student's Perspective on Leadership and Followership

HIGHLIGHT 1.5

Krista Kleiner, a student at Claremont-McKenna College and active in its Kravis Leadership Institute, has offered these reflections on the importance for both students and college administrators of taking seriously the opportunities provided in the classroom for developing leadership and followership skills.

She notes that the admissions process to college (as well, we might add, as postcollege job searches) typically places significant emphasis on a person's leadership experience and abilities. Usually this is reflected in something like a list of "leadership positions held." Unfortunately, however, this system tends to overemphasize the mere acquisition of leadership titles and pays insufficient attention to the domain that is the most central and common element of student life: the classroom learning environment. Outstanding learning, she argues, is to a significant degree a collaborative experience between the formal leader (the teacher) and the informal followers (the students). The learning experience is directly enhanced by the degree to which effective participation by students contributes to their classroom groups, and this requires good leadership and good followership. The quality of one's contribution to the group could be

assessed via peer surveys, the results of which would be made available to the teacher. The surveys would assess dimensions of student contributions like these:

- Which students displayed particularly helpful leadership in work groups you participated in, and what did they do that was effective?
- Which students displayed particularly helpful followership in work groups you participated in that supported or balanced the leadership that emerged in the group or that was helpful to fellow group members?
- How have you contributed to the learning experience of your peers through your leadership–followership role in the classroom? How have you grown as a constructive leader and constructive follower through these experiences?

We hope these ideas challenge you to be a leader in your own student life and especially in this leadership course.

Source: K. Kleiner, "Rethinking Leadership and Followership: A Student's Perspective," in R. Riggio, I. Chaleff, and J. Lipman-Blumen (eds.), *The Art of Followership: How Great Followers Create Great Leaders and Organizations* (San Francisco: Jossey-Bass, 2008), pp. 89–93.

leadership process.[35,36] However, we know that the followers' expectations, personality traits, maturity levels, levels of competence, and motivation affect the leadership process too.[37-40]

The nature of followers' motivation to do their work is also important. Workers who share a leader's goals and values, and who feel intrinsically rewarded for performing a job well, might be more likely to work extra hours on a time-critical project than those whose motivation is solely monetary.

Even the number of followers reporting to a leader can have significant implications. For example, a store manager with three clerks working for him can spend more time with each of them (or on other things) than can a manager responsible for eight clerks and a separate delivery service; chairing a task force with 5 members is a different leadership activity than chairing a task force with 18 members. Still other relevant variables include followers' trust in the leader and their degree of confidence that he

Followership Styles

HIGHLIGHT 1.6

The concept of different styles of leadership is reasonably familiar, but the idea of different styles of followership is relatively new. The very word *follower* has a negative connotation to many, evoking ideas of people who behave like sheep and need to be told what to do. Robert Kelley, however, believes that followers, rather than representing the antithesis of leadership, are best viewed as collaborators with leaders in the work of organizations.

Kelley believes that different types of followers can be described in terms of two broad dimensions. One of them ranges from **independent, critical thinking** at one end to **dependent, uncritical thinking** on the other end. According to Kelley, the best followers think for themselves and offer constructive advice or even creative solutions. The worst followers need to be told what to do. Kelley's other dimension ranges from whether people are **active followers** or **passive followers** in the extent to which they are engaged in work. According to Kelley, the best followers are self-starters who take initiative for themselves, whereas the worst followers are passive, may even dodge responsibility, and need constant supervision.

Using these two dimensions, Kelley has suggested five basic styles of followership:

1. *Alienated followers* habitually point out all the negative aspects of the organization to others. While alienated followers may see themselves as mavericks who have a healthy skepticism of the organization, leaders often see them as cynical, negative, and adversarial.

2. *Conformist followers* are the "yes people" of organizations. While very active at doing the organization's work, they can be dangerous if their orders contradict societal standards of behavior or organizational policy. Often this style is the result of either the demanding and authoritarian style of the leader or the overly rigid structure of the organization.

3. *Pragmatist followers* are rarely committed to their group's work goals, but they have learned not to make waves. Because they do not like to stick out, pragmatists tend to be mediocre performers who can clog the arteries of many organizations. Because it can be difficult to discern just where they stand on issues, they present an ambiguous image with both positive and negative characteristics. In organizational settings, pragmatists may become experts in mastering the bureaucratic rules which can be used to protect them.

4. *Passive followers* display none of the characteristics of the exemplary follower (discussed next). They rely on the leader to do all the thinking. Furthermore, their work lacks enthusiasm. Lacking initiative and a sense of responsibility, passive followers require constant direction. Leaders may see them as lazy, incompetent, or even stupid. Sometimes, however, passive followers adopt this style to help them cope with a leader who expects followers to behave that way.

5. *Exemplary followers* present a consistent picture to both leaders and coworkers of being independent, innovative, and willing to stand up to superiors. They apply their talents for the benefit of the organization even when confronted with bureaucratic stumbling blocks or passive or pragmatist coworkers. Effective leaders appreciate the value of exemplary followers. When one of the authors was serving in a follower role in a staff position, he was introduced by his leader to a conference as "my favorite subordinate because he's a loyal 'No-Man.' "

Exemplary followers—high on both critical dimensions of followership—are essential to organizational success.

Leaders, therefore, would be well advised to select people who have these characteristics and, perhaps even more importantly, *create the conditions that encourage these behaviors.*

Source: Adapted from R. Kelley, *The Power of Followership* (New York: Doubleday Currency, 1992).

Paul Revere

PROFILES IN LEADERSHIP 1.3

A fabled story of American history is that of Paul Revere's ride through the countryside surrounding Boston, warning towns that the British were coming so local militia could be ready to meet them. As a result, when the British did march toward Lexington on the following day, they faced unexpectedly fierce resistance. At Concord the British were beaten by a ragtag group of locals, and so began the American Revolutionary War.

It has been taken for granted by generations of Americans that the success of Paul Revere's ride lay in his heroism *and* in the self-evident importance of the news itself. A little-known fact, however, is that Paul Revere was not the only rider that night. A fellow revolutionary by the name of William Dawes had the same mission: to ride simultaneously through a separate set of towns surrounding Boston to warn them that the British were coming. He did so, carrying the news through just as many towns as Revere did. But his ride was not successful; those local militia leaders weren't aroused and did not rise up to confront the British. If they had been, Dawes would be as famous today as Paul Revere.

Why was Revere's ride successful when Dawes's ride was not? Paul Revere started a word-of-mouth epidemic, and Dawes did not, *because of differing kinds of relationships the two men had with others.* It wasn't, after all, the nature of the news itself that proved ultimately important so much as the nature of the men who carried it. Paul Revere was a gregarious and social person—what Malcolm Gladwell calls a *connector.* Gladwell writes that Revere was "a fisherman and a hunter, a cardplayer and a theater-lover, a frequenter of pubs and a successful businessman. He was active in the local Masonic Lodge and was a member of several select social clubs." He was a man with a knack for always being at the center of things. So when he began his ride that night, it was Revere's nature to stop and share the news with anyone he saw on the road, and he would have known who the key players were in each town to notify.

Dawes was not by nature so gregarious as Revere, and he did not have Revere's extended social network. It's likely he *wouldn't* have known whom to share the news with in each town and whose doors to knock on. Dawes did notify some people, but not enough to create the kind of impact that Revere did. Another way of saying this is simply to note that the people Dawes notified didn't know *him* the way that Revere was known by those *he* notified.

It isn't just the information or the ideas you have as a leader that make a difference. It's also whom you know, and how many you know—and what they know about you.

Source: Adapted from Malcolm Gladwell, *The Tipping Point* (New York: Little, Brown and Company, 2002).

Never try to teach a pig to sing; it wastes your time and it annoys the pig.

**Paul Dickson,
baseball writer**

or she is interested in their well-being. Another aspect of followers' relations to a leader is described in Profiles in Leadership 1.3.

In the context of the interactional framework, the question "What is leadership?" cannot be separated from the question "What is followership?" There is no simple line dividing them; they merge. The relationship between leadership and followership can be represented by borrowing a concept from topographical mathematics: the Möbius strip. You are probably familiar with the curious properties of the Möbius strip: when a strip of paper is twisted and connected in the manner depicted in Figure 1.3, it has only one side. You can prove this to yourself by putting a pencil to any point on the strip and tracing continuously. Your pencil will cover the entire strip (that is, both "sides"), eventually returning to the point at which you started. To demonstrate the relevance of this curiosity to leadership, cut a strip of paper. On one side write *leadership,* and on the other side write *followership.* Then twist the strip and connect the two ends in the manner of the figure. You will have created a leadership/followership Möbius strip wherein the two concepts merge, just as leadership and followership can become indistinguishable in organizations.[41]

This does not mean leadership and followership are the same thing. When top-level executives were asked to list qualities they most look for

Source: © *Tribune Media Services, Inc. All Rights Reserved. Reprinted with permission.*

FIGURE 1.3
The Leadership/
Followership
Möbius Strip

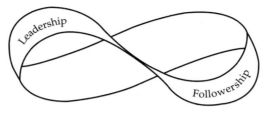

and admire in leaders and followers, the lists were similar but not identical.[42] Ideal leaders were characterized as honest, competent, forward-looking, and inspiring; ideal followers were described as honest, competent, independent, and cooperative. The differences could become critical in certain situations, as when a forward-looking and inspiring subordinate perceives a significant conflict between his own goals or ethics and those of his superiors. Such a situation could become a crisis for the individual and the organization, demanding a choice between leading and following.

As the complexity of the leadership process has become better understood, the importance placed on the leader–follower relationship itself has undergone dynamic change.[43,44] One reason for this is an increasing pressure on all kinds of organizations to function with reduced resources. Reduced resources and company downsizing have reduced the number of managers and increased their span of control, which in turn leaves followers to pick up many of the functions traditionally performed by leaders. Another reason is a trend toward greater power sharing and decentralized authority in organizations, which create greater interdependence among organizational subunits and increase the need for collaboration among them. Furthermore, the nature of problems faced by many organizations is becoming so complex and the changes are becoming so rapid that more and more people are required to solve them.

These trends suggest several different ways in which followers can take on new leadership roles and responsibilities in the future. For one thing, followers can become much more proactive in their stance toward organizational problems. When facing the discrepancy between the way things are in an organization and the way they could or should be, followers can play an active and constructive role collaborating with leaders in solving problems. In general, making organizations better is a task that needs to be "owned" by followers as well as by leaders. With these changing roles for followers, it should not be surprising to find that qualities of good followership are statistically correlated with qualities typically associated with good leadership. One recent study found positive correlations between the followership qualities of active engagement and independent thinking and the leadership qualities of dominance, sociability, achievement orientation, and steadiness.[45]

If you act like an ass,
don't get insulted if
people ride you.
Yiddish proverb

In addition to helping solve organizational problems, followers can contribute to the leadership process by becoming skilled at "influencing upward." Because followers are often at the levels where many organizational problems occur, they can give leaders relevant information so good solutions are implemented. Although it is true that some leaders need to become better listeners, it is also true that many followers need training in expressing ideas to superiors clearly and positively. Still another way followers can assume a greater share of the leadership challenge in the future is by staying flexible and open to opportunities. The future portends more change, not less, and followers who face change with positive anticipation and an openness to self-development will be particularly valued and rewarded.[46]

Thus, to an ever-increasing degree, leadership must be understood in terms of both leader variables and follower variables, as well as the interactions among them. But even that is not enough—we must also understand the particular situations in which leaders and followers find themselves.

Aung San Suu Kyi

PROFILES IN LEADERSHIP 1.4

In 1991 Aung San Suu Kyi already had spent two years under house arrest in Burma for "endangering the state." That same year she won the Nobel Peace Prize. Like Nelson Mandela, Suu Kyi is an international symbol of heroic and peaceful resistance to government oppression.

Until the age of 43, Suu Kyi led a relatively quiet existence in England as a professional working mother. Her life changed dramatically in 1988 when she returned to her native country of Burma to visit her sick mother. That visit occurred during a time of considerable political unrest in Burma. Riot police had recently shot to death hundreds of demonstrators in the capital city of Rangoon (the demonstrators had been protesting government repression). Over the next several months, police killed nearly 3,000 people who had been protesting government policies.

When hundreds of thousands of pro-democracy demonstrators staged a protest rally at a prominent pagoda in Rangoon, Suu Kyi spoke to the crowd. Overnight she became the leading voice for freedom and democracy in Burma. Today she is the most popular and influential leader in her country even though she's never held political office.

What prepared this woman, whose life was once relatively simple and contented, to risk her life by challenging an oppressive government? What made her such a magnet for popular support? Impressive as Aung San Suu Kyi is as a populist leader, it is impossible to understand her effectiveness purely in terms of her own personal characteristics. It is impossible to understand it independent of her followers—the people of Burma. Her rapid rise to prominence as the leading voice for democracy and freedom in Burma must be understood in terms of the living link she represented to the country's greatest modern hero—her father. He was something of a George Washington figure in that he founded the Burmese Army in 1941 and later made a successful transition from military leadership to political leadership. At the height of his influence, when he was the universal choice to be Burma's first president, he was assassinated. Suu Kyi was two years old. Stories about his life and principles indelibly shaped Suu Kyi's own life, but his life and memory also created a readiness among the Burmese people for Suu Kyi to take up her father's mantle of leadership.

The Situation

The situation is the third critical part of the leadership equation. Even if we knew all we could know about a given leader and a given set of followers, leadership often makes sense only in the context of how the leader and followers interact in a particular situation (see Profiles in Leadership 1.4 and 1.5).

Bill Gates's Head Start

PROFILES IN LEADERSHIP 1.5

Belief in an individual's potential to overcome great odds and achieve success through talent, strength, and perseverance is common in America, but usually there is more than meets the eye in such success stories. Malcolm Gladwell's best seller *Outliers* presents a fascinating exploration of how situational factors contribute to success in addition to the kinds of individual qualities we often assume are all-important. Have you ever thought, for example, that Bill Gates was able to create Microsoft because he's just brilliant and visionary?

Well, let's take for granted he *is* brilliant and visionary—there's plenty of evidence of that. The point here, however, is that's not always enough (and maybe it's *never* enough). Here are some of the things that placed Bill Gates, with all his intelligence and vision, at the right time in the right place:

- Gates was born to a wealthy family in Seattle that placed him in a private school for seventh grade. In 1968, his second year there, the school started a computer club—even before most *colleges* had computer clubs.

- In the 1960s virtually everyone who was learning about computers used computer cards, a tedious and mind-numbing process. The computer at Gates's school, however, was linked to a mainframe in downtown Seattle. Thus in 1968 Bill Gates was practicing computer programming via time-sharing as an eighth grader; few others in the world then had such opportunity, whatever their age.

- Even at a wealthy private school like the one Gates attended, however, funds ran out to cover the high costs of buying time on a mainframe computer. Fortunately, at about the same time, a group called the Computer Center Corporation was formed at the University of Washington to lease computer time. One of its founders, coincidentally a parent at Gates's own school, thought the school's computer club could get time on the computer in exchange for testing the company's new software programs. Gates then started a regular schedule of taking the bus after school to the company's offices, where he programmed long into the evening. During one seven-month period, Gates and his fellow computer club members averaged eight hours a day, seven days a week, of computer time.

- When Gates was a high school senior, another extraordinary opportunity presented itself. A major national company (TRW) needed programmers with specialized experience—exactly, as it turned out, the kind of experience the kids at Gates's school had been getting. Gates successfully lobbied his teachers to let him spend a spring doing this work in another part of the state for independent study credit.

- By the time Gates dropped out of Harvard after his sophomore year, he had accumulated more than *10,000 hours* of programming experience. It was, he's said, a better exposure to software development than anyone else at a young age could have had—and all because of a lucky series of events.

It appears that Gates's success is at least partly an example of the right person being in the right place at just the right time.

Source: Malcolm Gladwell, *Outliers: The Story of Success* (New York: Little, Brown and Company, 2008).

This view of leadership as a complex interaction among leader, fol-lower, and situational variables was not always taken for granted. To the contrary, most early research on leadership was based on the as-sumption that leadership is a general personal trait expressed independently of the situation in which the leadership is manifested. This view, commonly known as the **heroic theory,** has been largely discredited but for a long time represented the dominant way of conceptualizing leadership.[47]

In the 1950s and 1960s a different approach to conceptualizing leadership dominated research and scholarship. It involved the search for effective leader *behaviors* rather than the search for universal *traits* of leadership. That approach proved too narrow because it neglected important contextual, or situational, factors in which presumably effective or ineffective behaviors occur. Over time, the complexities of interactions among leader, follower, and situational variables increasingly have been the focus of leadership research.[48] (See Chapters 6, 7, and 13 for more detailed discussions of leader attributes, leader behaviors, and formal theories of leadership that examine complex interdependencies between leader, follower, and situational variables.) Adding the situation to the mix of variables that make up leadership is complicated. The situation may be the most ambiguous aspect of the leadership framework; it can refer to anything from the specific task a group is engaged in to broad situational contexts such as the remote predicament of the Andes survivors. One facet of the complexity of the situation's role in leadership is examined in Highlight 1.7.

Illustrating the Interactional Framework: Women in Leadership Roles

Not long ago if people were asked to name a leader they admired, most of the names on the resulting list could be characterized as "old white guys." Today the names on that same list would be considerably more heterogeneous. That change—which we certainly consider progress—represents a useful illustration of the power of using the interactional framework to understand the complexities of the leadership process.

A specific example is women in leadership roles, and in this section we'll examine the extent to which women have been taking on new leadership roles, whether there are differences in the effectiveness of men and women in leadership roles, and what explanations have been offered for differences between men and women in being selected for and succeeding in positions of leadership. This is an area of considerable academic research and popular polemics, as evident in many recent articles in the popular press that claim a distinct advantage for women in leadership roles.[49]

Decision Making in a Complex World

HIGHLIGHT 1.7

Decision making is a good example of how leaders need to behave differently in various situations. Until late in the 20th century, decision making in government and business was largely based on an implicit assumption that the world was orderly and predictable enough for virtually all decision making to involve a series of specifiable steps: assessing the facts of a situation, categorizing those facts, and then responding based on established practice. To put that more simply, decision making required managers to *sense, categorize,* and *respond.*

The Situation	The Leader's Job
Simple: predictable and orderly; right answers exist.	Ensure that proper processes are in place, follow best practices, and communicate in clear and direct ways.
Complex: flux, unpredictability, ambiguity, many competing ideas, lots of unknowns.	Create environments and experiments that allow patterns to emerge; increase levels of interaction and communication; use methods that generate new ideas and ways of thinking among everyone.

That process is actually still effective in simple contexts characterized by stability and clear cause-and-effect relationships that are readily apparent. Not all situations in the world, however, are so simple, and new approaches to decision making are needed for situations that have the elements of what we might call complex systems: large numbers of interacting elements, nonlinear interactions among those elements by which small changes can produce huge effects, and interdependence among the elements so that the whole is more than the sum of the parts. The challenges of dealing with the threat of terrorism are one example of the way complexity affects decision making, but it's impacting how we think about decision making in business as well as government. To describe this change succinctly, the decision-making process in complex contexts must change from sense, categorize, and respond to probe, sense, and respond.

In other words, making good decisions is about both *what* decisions one makes and understanding the role of the situation in affecting *how* one makes decisions.

Source: D.F. Snowden and M.E. Boone, "A Leader's Framework for Decision Making," *Harvard Business Review,* November 2007, pp. 69–76.

It is clear that women are taking on leadership roles in greater numbers than ever before. On the other hand, the actual percentage of women in leadership positions has stayed relatively stable. For example, a report released in 2010 by the U.S. Government Accountability Office indicated that women comprised an estimated 40 percent of managers in the U.S. workforce in 2007 compared with 39 percent in 2000.[50] And the percentage of women in top executive positions is considerably less encouraging. In a 2009 study by the nonprofit organization Catalyst, women made up only 13.5 percent of senior executive positions; almost 30 percent of companies in the Fortune 500 had no women in those top positions.[51]

Although these statistics are important and promising, problems still exist that constrain the opportunity for capable women to rise to the highest leadership roles in organizations (see Highlight 1.8). Many studies have considered this problem, a few of which we'll examine here. In a classic study of sex roles, Schein[52,53] demonstrated how bias in sex role stereotypes created problems for women moving up through managerial roles. Schein asked male and female middle managers to complete a survey in which they rated various items on a five-point scale in terms of how characteristic they were of men in general, women in general, or successful managers. Schein found a high correlation between the ways both male and female respondents perceived "males" and "managers," but no correlation between the ways the respondents perceived "females" and "managers." It was as though being a manager was defined by attributes thought of as masculine. Furthermore, it does not appear that the situation has changed much over the past two decades. In 1990 management students in the United States, Germany, and Great Britain, for example, still perceived successful middle managers in terms of characteristics more commonly ascribed to men than to women.[54] One area where views *do* seem to have changed over time involves women's perceptions of their own roles. In contrast to the earlier studies, women today see as much similarity between "female" and "manager" as between "male" and "manager."[55] To women, at least, being a woman and being a manager are not contradictory.

There have been many other studies of the role of women in management. In one of these, *Breaking the Glass Ceiling*,[56] researchers documented

Insights of a Woman Who Broke the Glass Ceiling

HIGHLIGHT 1. 8

Kim Campbell has distinguished herself in many ways. She was Canada's first female prime minister, and she now chairs the Council of Women World Leaders. In 2002 she was interviewed about the challenges and opportunities for women rising into senior leadership positions in organizations, and here are two brief excerpts of what she said:

You've held many positions that are traditionally filled by men. What's the greatest obstacle you've encountered?

There is a deeply rooted belief that women are not competent and can't lead. That's because there's an overlap in people's minds between the qualities that we associate with leadership and the qualities that we associate with masculinity—decisiveness, aggressiveness, competence. There is much less overlap between leadership qualities and those we associate with being feminine—an inclination toward consensus building, to be communal, expressive, nurturing. That's why for many people it was rather disturbing that I was prime minister. A woman wasn't supposed to be prime minister. I wasn't entitled to be there.

You've said that having women in leadership is more important now than ever. Why now?

We're living in a time when we see the frightening limitations of masculine cultures. Cultures that are totally masculine can give rise to fundamentalisms—they can be intolerant, narrow, violent, corrupt, antidemocratic. That's at a state level. At a corporate level, a macho culture made Enron possible.

Source: Excerpted from *Harvard Business Review,* 2002, pp. 20–21.

the lives and careers of 78 of the highest-level women in corporate America. A few years later the researchers followed up with a small sample of those women to discuss any changes that had taken place in their leadership paths. The researchers were struck by the fact that the women were much like the senior men they had worked with in other studies. Qualitatively, they had the same fears: They wanted the best for themselves and for their families. They wanted their companies to succeed. And not surprisingly, they still had a drive to succeed. In some cases (also true for the men) they were beginning to ask questions about life balance—was all the sacrifice and hard work worth it? Were 60-hour workweeks worth the cost to family and self?

More quantitatively, however, the researchers expected to find significant differences between the women who had broken the glass ceiling and the men who were already in leadership positions. After all, the popular literature and some social scientific literature had conditioned them to expect that there is a feminine versus a masculine style of leadership, the feminine style being an outgrowth of a consensus/team-oriented leadership approach. Women, in this view, are depicted as leaders who, when compared to men, are better listeners, more empathic, less analytical, more people oriented, and less aggressive in pursuit of goals.

In examining women in leadership positions, the researchers collected behavioral data, including ratings by both self and others, assessment center data, and their scores on the California Psychological Inventory. Contrary to the stereotypes and popular views, however, there were no statistically significant differences between men's and women's leadership styles. Women and men were equally analytical, people oriented, forceful, goal oriented, empathic, and skilled at listening. There were other differences between the men and women, however, beyond the question of leadership styles. The researchers did find (and these results must be interpreted cautiously because of the relatively small numbers involved) that women had significantly lower well-being scores, their commitment to the organizations they worked for was more guarded than that of their male counterparts, and the women were much more likely to be willing to take career risks associated with going to new or unfamiliar areas of the company where women had not been before.

Continued work with women in corporate leadership positions has both reinforced and clarified these findings. For example, the lower scores for women in general well-being may reflect the inadequacy of their support system for dealing with day-to-day issues of living. This is tied to the reality for many women that in addition to having roles in their companies they remain chief caretakers for their families. Further, there may be additional pressures of being visibly identified as proof that the organization has women at the top.

Other types of differences—particularly those around "people issues"—are still not evident. In fact, the hypothesis is that such supposed differences may hinder the opportunities for leadership development of women in the future. For example, turning around a business that is in trouble or starting a new business are two of the most exciting opportunities a developing leader has to test her leadership abilities. If we apply the "women are different" hypothesis, the type of leadership skills needed for successful completion of either of these assignments may leave women off the list of candidates. However, if we accept the hypothesis that women and men are more alike as leaders than they are different, women will be found in equal numbers on the candidate list.

Research on women leaders from medium-sized, nontraditional organizations has shown that successful leaders don't all come from the same mold. Such women tended to be successful by drawing on their shared experience as women, rather than by adhering to the "rules of conduct" by which men in larger and more traditional organizations have been successful.[57] Survey research by Judith Rosener identified several differences in how men and women described their leadership experiences. Men tended to describe themselves in somewhat transactional terms, viewing leadership as an exchange with subordinates for services rendered. They influenced others primarily through their organizational position and authority. The women, on the other hand, tended to describe themselves in transformational terms. They helped subordinates develop commitment to broader goals than their own self-interest, and they described their influence more in terms of personal characteristics like charisma and interpersonal skill than mere organizational position.

According to Rosener, such women leaders encouraged participation and shared power and information, but went far beyond what is commonly thought of as participative management. She called it **interactive leadership.** Their leadership self-descriptions reflected an approach based on enhancing others' self-worth and believing that the best performance results when people are excited about their work and feel good about themselves.

How did this interactive leadership style develop? Rosener concluded it was due to these women's socialization experiences and career paths. As we have indicated, the social role expected of women has emphasized that they be cooperative, supportive, understanding, gentle, and service-oriented. As they entered the business world, they still found themselves in roles emphasizing these same behaviors. They found themselves in staff, rather than line, positions, and in roles lacking formal authority over others so that they had to accomplish their work without reliance on formal power. What they had to do, in other words, was employ their socially acceptable behavioral repertoire to survive organizationally.

What came easily to women turned out to be a survival tactic. Although leaders often begin their careers doing what comes naturally and what fits within the constraints of the job, they also develop their skills and styles over time. The women's use of interactive leadership has its roots in

"That's what they all say, honey."

Source: © Tom Cheney, The New Yorker Collection, www.cartoonbank.com.

socialization, and the women interviewees believe that it benefits their organizations. Through the course of their careers, they have gained conviction that their style is effective. In fact, for some it was their own success that caused them to formulate their philosophies about what motivates people, how to make good decisions, and what it takes to maximize business performance.[37]

Rosener called for organizations to expand their definitions of effective leadership—to create a *wider* band of acceptable behavior so both men and women will be freer to lead in ways that take advantage of their true talents. The extent of the problem is suggested by data from a study looking at how CEOs, almost all male, and senior female executives explained the paucity of women in corporate leadership roles. Figure 1.4 compares the percentages of CEOs versus female executives who endorsed various possible explanations of the situation. It is clear that the CEOs attributed it primarily to inadequacies in the quantity and quality of experience of potential women

FIGURE 1.4
What Prevents Women from Advancing to Corporate Leadership?

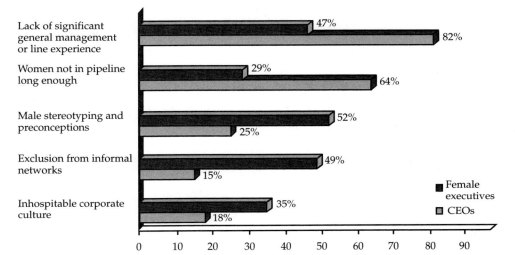

candidates for the top spots, whereas the females themselves attributed it to various forms of stereotyping and bias.

A more recent study sheds additional light on factors that affect the rise of women in leadership positions.[58] It identifies four general factors that explain the shift toward more women leaders.

The first of these is that *women themselves have changed*. That's evident in the ways women's aspirations and attitudes have become more similar to those of men over time. This is illustrated in findings about the career aspirations of female university students;[59] in women's self-reports of traits such as assertiveness, dominance, and masculinity;[60,61] and in the value that women place on characteristics of work such as freedom, challenge, leadership, prestige, and power.[62] The second factor is that *leadership roles have changed*, particularly with regard to a trend toward less stereotypically masculine characterizations of leadership. Third, *organizational practices have changed*. A large part of this can be attributed to legislation prohibiting gender-based discrimination at work, as well as changes in organizational norms that put a higher priority on results than on an "old boy" network. Finally, the *culture has changed*. This is evident, for example, in the symbolic message often intended by appointment of women to important leadership positions, one representing a departure from past practices and signaling commitment to progressive change.

Finally, in addition to the glass ceiling, another recently identified challenge for women is called the **glass cliff**. The glass cliff refers to the intriguing finding that female candidates for an executive position are *more* likely to be hired than equally qualified male candidates when an organization's performance is declining. At first that may seem like good news for women, but the picture is not quite so positive. When an organization's performance is declining, there is inherently an increased risk of failure. The increased likelihood of women being selected in those situations may actually reflect a greater willingness to put women in precarious positions;[63] it could also, of course, represent an increased willingness to take some chances when nothing else seems to be working.

There Is No Simple Recipe for Effective Leadership

Little things affect little minds.
Benjamin Disraeli, British prime minister, 1874–1880

To fill the gaps between leadership research and practice, this book will critically review major findings about the nature of leadership as well as provide practical advice for improving leadership. As our first step in that journey, the next chapter of the book will describe how leadership develops through experience. The remainder of the book uses the leader–follower–situation interaction model as a framework for organizing and discussing various theories and research findings related to leadership. In this study, it will become clear that while there is no simple recipe for effective leadership, there *are* many different paths to effective leadership.

As noted previously, it is important to understand how the three domains of leadership interact—how the leader, the followers, and the situation are all part of the leadership process. Understanding their interaction is necessary before you can draw valid conclusions from the leadership you observe around you. When you see a leader's behavior (even when it may appear obviously effective or ineffective to you), you should not automatically conclude something good or bad about the leader, or what is the right way or wrong way leaders should act. You need to think about the effectiveness of that behavior in *that* context with *those* followers.

As obvious as this advice sounds, we often ignore it. Too frequently we look at just the leader's behavior and conclude that he or she is a good leader or a bad leader apart from the context. For example, suppose you observe a leader soliciting advice from subordinates. Obviously it seems unreasonable to conclude that good leaders always ask for advice or that leaders who do not frequently ask for advice are not good leaders. The appropriateness of seeking input from subordinates depends on many factors, such as the nature of the problem or the subordinates' familiarity with the problem. Perhaps the subordinates have a lot more experience with this particular problem, and soliciting their input is the correct action to take in this situation.

Consider another example. Suppose you hear that a leader did not approve a subordinate's request to take time off to attend to family matters. Was this bad leadership because the leader did not appear to be taking care of her people? Was it good leadership because she did not let personal matters interfere with the mission? Again, you cannot make an intelligent decision about the leader's actions by looking at the behavior itself. You must always assess leadership in the context of the leader, the followers, and the situation.

The following statements about leaders, followers, and the situation make these points a bit more systematically:

- A leader may need to respond to various followers differently in the same situation.
- A leader may need to respond to the same follower differently in different situations.
- Followers may respond to various leaders quite differently.
- Followers may respond to each other differently with different leaders.
- Two leaders may have different perceptions of the same followers or situations.

All of these points lead to one conclusion: the right behavior in one situation is not necessarily the right behavior in another situation. It does *not* follow, however, that any behavior is appropriate in any situation. Although we may not be able to agree on the one best behavior in a given situation, we often can agree on some clearly inappropriate behaviors. Saying that the right behavior for a leader depends on the situation is not the same thing as saying it does not matter what the leader does. It merely recognizes the complexity among leaders, followers, and situations. This recognition is a helpful first step in drawing meaningful lessons about leadership from experience.

Summary

We have defined leadership as the process of influencing an organized group toward achieving its goals. The chapter also looked at the idea that leadership is both a science and an art. Because leadership is an immature science, researchers are still struggling to find out what the important questions in leadership are; we are far from finding conclusive answers to them. Even individuals with extensive knowledge of leadership research may be poor leaders. Knowing what to do is not the same as knowing when, where, and how to do it. The art of leadership concerns the skill of understanding leadership situations and influencing others to accomplish group goals. Formal leadership education may give individuals the skills to better understand leadership situations, and mentorships and experience may give individuals the skills to better influence others. Leaders must also weigh both rational and emotional considerations when attempting to influence others. Leadership sometimes can be accomplished through relatively rational, explicit, rule-based methods of assessing situations and determining actions.

Nevertheless, the emotional side of human nature must also be acknowledged. Leaders are often most effective when they affect people at both the emotional level and the rational level. The idea of leadership as a whole-person process can also be applied to the distinction often made between leaders and managers. Although leadership and management can be distinguished as separate functions, there is considerable overlap between them in practice.

Leadership is a process in which leaders and followers interact dynamically in a particular situation or environment. Leadership is a broader concept than that of leaders, and the study of leadership must involve more than just the study of leaders as individuals. The study of leadership must also include two other areas: the followers and the situation. In addition, the interactive nature of these three domains has become increasingly important in recent years and can help us to better understand the changing nature of leader–follower relationships and the increasing complexity of situations leaders and followers face. Because of this complexity, now, more than ever before, effective leadership cannot be boiled down to a simple recipe. It is still true, however, that good leadership makes a difference, and it can be enhanced through greater awareness of the important factors influencing the leadership process.

Key Terms

leadership, *4*
academic tradition, *7*
troubadour tradition, *7*
management, *8*
interactional framework, *15*
leader, *15*

followers, *15*
situation, *15*
interactions, *15*
in-group, *16*
out-group, *16*
followership, *19*
independent, critical thinking, *21*

dependent, uncritical thinking, *21*
active followers, *21*
passive followers, *21*
heroic theory, *27*
interactive leadership, *31*
glass cliff, *33*

Questions

1. We say leadership involves influencing organized groups toward goals. Do you see any disadvantages to restricting the definition to organized groups?

2. How would you define *leadership*?

3. Are some people the "leader type" and others not the "leader type"? If so, what in your judgment distinguishes them?

4. Identify several "commonsense" notions about leadership that, to you, are self-evident.

5. Does every successful leader have a valid theory of leadership?

6. Would you consider it a greater compliment for someone to call you a good manager or a good leader? Why? Do you believe you can be both?

7. Do you believe leadership can be studied scientifically? Why or why not?

8. To the extent that leadership is an art, what methods come to mind for improving one's "art of leadership"?

9. According to the interactional framework, effective leader behavior depends on many variables. It follows that there is no simple prescription for effective leader behavior. Does this mean effective leadership is merely a matter of opinion or subjective preference?

10. Generally leaders get most of the credit for a group's or an organization's success. Do you believe this is warranted or fair?

11. What are some other characteristics of leaders, followers, and situations you could add to those listed in Figure 1.2?

Activities

1. Describe the best leader you have personally known or a favorite leader from history, a novel, or a movie.

2. In this activity you will explore connotations of the words *leadership* and *management.* Divide yourselves into small groups and have each group brainstorm different word associations to the terms *leader* and *leadership* or *manager* and *management.* In addition, each group should discuss whether they would prefer to work for a manager or for a leader, and why. Then the whole group should discuss similarities and differences among the respective perceptions and feelings about the two concepts.

Minicase

Richard Branson Shoots for the Moon

The Virgin Group is the umbrella for a variety of business ventures ranging from air travel to entertainment. With close to 200 companies in over 30 countries, it is one of the largest companies in the world. At the head of this huge organization is Richard Branson. Branson founded Virgin over 30 years ago and has built the organization from a small student magazine to the multibillion-dollar enterprise it is today.

Branson is not your typical CEO. Branson's dyslexia made school a struggle and sabotaged his performance on standard IQ tests. His teachers and tests had no way of measuring his greatest strengths—his uncanny knack for uncovering lucrative business ideas and his ability to energize the ambitions of others so that they, like he, could rise to the level of their dreams.

Richard Branson's true talents began to show themselves in his late teens. While a student at Stowe School in England in 1968, Branson decided to start his own magazine, *Student.* Branson was inspired by the student activism on his campus in the 1960s and decided to try something different. *Student* differed from most college newspapers or magazines; it focused on the students and their interests. Branson sold advertising to major corporations to support his magazine. He included articles by ministers of Parliament, rock stars, intellectuals, and celebrities. *Student* grew to become a commercial success.

In 1970 Branson saw an opportunity for *Student* to offer records cheaply by running ads for mail-order delivery. The subscribers to *Student* flooded the magazine with so many orders that his spin-off discount music venture proved more lucrative than the magazine subscriptions. Branson recruited the staff of *Student* for his discount music business. He built a small recording studio and signed his first artist. Mike Oldfield recorded "Tubular Bells" at Virgin in 1973; the album sold 5 million copies, and Virgin Records and the Virgin brand name were born. Branson has gone on to start his own airline (Virgin Atlantic Airlines was launched in 1984), build hotels (Virgin Hotels started in 1988), get into the personal finance business (Virgin Direct Personal Finance Services was launched in 1995), and even enter the cola wars (Virgin Cola was introduced in 1994). And those are just a few highlights of the Virgin Group—all this while Branson has attempted to break world speed records for crossing the Atlantic Ocean by boat and by hot air balloon.

As you might guess, Branson's approach is nontraditional—he has no giant corporate office or staff and few if any board meetings. Instead he keeps each enterprise small and relies on his skills of empowering people's ideas to fuel success. When a flight attendant from Virgin Airlines approached him with her vision of a wedding business, Richard told her to go do it. He even put on a wedding dress himself to help launch the publicity. Virgin Brides was born. Branson relies heavily on the creativity of his staff; he is more a supporter of new ideas than a creator of them. He encourages searches for new business ideas everywhere he goes and even has a spot on the Virgin Web site called "Got a Big Idea?"

In December 1999 Richard Branson was awarded a knighthood in the Queen's Millennium New Year's Honours List for "services to entrepreneurship." What's next on Branson's list? He recently announced that Virgin was investing money in "trying to make sure that, in the not too distant future, people from around the world will be able to go into space." Not everyone is convinced that space tourism can become a fully fledged part of the travel industry, but with Branson behind the idea it just might fly.

1. Would you classify Richard Branson as a manager or a leader? What qualities distinguish him as one or the other?

2. As mentioned earlier in this chapter, followers are part of the leadership process. Describe the relationship between Branson and his followers.

3. Identify the myths of leadership development that Richard Branson's success helps to disprove.

Sources: http://www.johnshepler.com/articles/branson.html;
http://www.wma.com/richard_branson/summary/;
http://www.virgin.com/aboutvirgin/allaboutvirgin/thewholestory/;
http://www.virgin.com/aboutvirgin/allaboutvirgin/whosrichardbranson/;
http://www.qksrv.net/click-310374-35140;
http://www.guardian.co.uk/space/article/0,14493,1235926,00.html.

End Notes

1. P. P. Read, *Alive* (New York: J. B. Lippincott, 1974).
2. Ibid., p. 77.
3. J. R. Meindl and S. B. Ehrlich, "The Romance of Leadership and the Evaluation of Organizational Performance," *Academy of Management Journal* 30 (1987), pp. 90–109.
4. W. G. Bennis, "Leadership Theory and Administrative Behavior: The Problem of Authority," *Administrative Science Quarterly* 4 (1959), pp. 259–60.
5. F. Fiedler, *A Theory of Leadership Effectiveness* (New York: McGraw-Hill, 1967).
6. R. K. Merton, *Social Theory and Social Structure* (New York: Free Press, 1957).
7. C. F. Roach and O. Behling, "Functionalism: Basis for an Alternate Approach to the Study of Leadership," in *Leaders and Managers: International Perspectives on Managerial Behavior and Leadership*, eds. J. G. Hunt, D. M. Hosking, C. A. Schriesheim, and R. Stewar (Elmsford, NY: Pergamon, 1984).
8. D. P. Campbell, *Campbell Leadership Index Manual* (Minneapolis: National Computer Systems, 1991).
9. R. C. Ginnett, "Team Effectiveness Leadership Model: Identifying Leverage Points for Change," *Proceedings of the 1996 National Leadership Institute Conference* (College Park, MD: National Leadership Institute, 1996).
10. R. T. Hogan, G. J. Curphy, and J. Hogan, "What Do We Know about Personality: Leadership and Effectiveness?" *American Psychologist* 49 (1994), pp. 493–504.
11. M.D. Mumford, S. J. Zaccaro, F. D. Harding, T. O. Jacobs, and E. A. Fleishman, "Leadership Skills for a Changing World," *Leadership Quarterly* 11, no. 1 (2000), pp. 11–35.
12. B. M. Bass, *Bass and Stogdill's Handbook of Leadership*, 3rd ed. (New York: Free Press, 1990).
13. H. C. Foushee, "Dyads and Triads at 35,000 Feet: Factors Affecting Group Process and Aircrew Performance," *American Psychologist* 39 (1984), pp. 885–93.
14. W. G. Bennis and B. Nanus, *Leaders: The Strategies for Taking Charge* (New York: Harper & Row, 1985).
15. A. Zaleznik, "The Leadership Gap," *Washington Quarterly* 6, no. 1 (1983), pp. 32–39.
16. W. G. Bennis, *On Becoming a Leader* (Reading, MA: Addison-Wesley, 1989).
17. Zaleznik, "The Leadership Gap."

18. P. Slovic and B. Fischoff, "On the Psychology of Experimental Surprises," *Journal of Experimental Social Psychology* 22 (1977), pp. 544–51.

19. G. Wood, "The Knew-It-All-Along Effect," *Journal of Experimental Psychology: Human Perception and Performance* 4 (1979), pp. 345–53.

20. P. E. Lazarsfeld, "The American Soldier: An Expository Review," *Public Opinion Quarterly* 13 (1949), pp. 377–404.

21. For example, A. Tellegen, D. T. Lykken, T. J. Bouchard, K. J. Wilcox, N. L. Segal, and S. Rich, "Personality Similarity in Twins Reared Apart and Together," *Journal of Personality and Social Psychology* 54 (1988), pp. 1031–39.

22. Fiedler, *A Theory of Leadership Effectiveness.*

23. E. P. Hollander, *Leadership Dynamics: A Practical Guide to Effective Relationships* (New York: Free Press, 1978).

24. G. B. Graen and J. F. Cashman, "A Role-Making Model of Leadership in Formal Organizations: A Developmental Approach," in *Leadership Frontiers*, eds. J. G. Hunt and L. L. Larson (Kent, OH: Kent State University Press, 1975).

25. R. M. Stogdill, "Personal Factors Associated with Leadership: A Review of the Literature," *Journal of Psychology* 25 (1948), pp. 35–71.

26. R. M. Stogdill, *Handbook of Leadership* (New York: Free Press, 1974).

27. R. T. Hogan, G. J. Curphy, and J. Hogan, "What We Know about Personality: Leadership and Effectiveness," *American Psychologist* 49 (1994), pp. 493–504.

28. R. G. Lord, C. L. DeVader, and G. M. Allinger, "A Meta-Analysis of the Relationship between Personality Traits and Leadership Perceptions: An Application of Validity Generalization Procedures," *Journal of Applied Psychology* 71 (1986), pp. 402–10.

29. R. M. Kanter, *The Change Masters* (New York: Simon & Schuster, 1983).

30. E. D. Baltzell, *Puritan Boston and Quaker Philadelphia* (New York: Free Press, 1980).

31. E.P. Hollander and L.R. Offermann. Power and Leadership in Organizations." *American Psychologist* 45 (1990), pp. 179–89.

32. S. D. Baker, "Followership: The Theoretical Foundation of a Contemporary Construct," *Journal of Leadership & Organizational Studies* 14, no. 1 (2007), p. 51.

33. Baker, "Followership."

34. J. M. Burns, *Leadership* (New York: Harper & Row, 1978).

35. B. M. Bass, *Bass and Stogdill's Handbook of Leadership*, 3rd ed. (New York: Free Press, 1990).

36. Stogdill, *Handbook of Leadership.*

37. C. D. Sutton and R. W. Woodman, "Pygmalion Goes to Work: The Effects of Supervisor Expectations in the Retail Setting," *Journal of Applied Psychology* 74 (1989), pp. 943–50.

38. L. I. Moore, "The FMI: Dimensions of Follower Maturity," *Group and Organizational Studies* 1 (1976), pp. 203–22.

39. T. A. Scandura, G. B. Graen, and M. A. Novak, "When Managers Decide Not to Decide Autocratically: An Investigation of Leader-Member Exchange and Decision Influence," *Journal of Applied Psychology* 52 (1986), pp. 135–47.

40. C. A. Sales, E. Levanoni, and D. H. Saleh, "Satisfaction and Stress as a Function of Job Orientation, Style of Supervision, and the Nature of the Task," *Engineering Management International* 2 (1984), pp. 145–53.

41. Adapted from K. Macrorie, *Twenty Teachers* (Oxford: Oxford University Press, 1984).

42. J. M. Kouzes and B. Z. Posner, *The Leadership Challenge: How to Get Extraordinary Things Done in Organizations* (San Francisco: Jossey-Bass, 1987).

43. R. Lippitt, "The Changing Leader–Follower Relationships of the 1980s," *Journal of Applied Behavioral Science* 18 (1982), pp. 395–403.

44. P. Block, *Stewardship* (San Francisco: Berrett-Koehler, 1992).

45. G. F. Tanoff and C. B. Barlow, "Leadership and Followership: Same Animal, Different Spots?" *Consulting Psychology Journal: Practice and Research,* Summer 2002, pp. 157–65.

46. P. M. Senge. *The Fifth Discipline: The Art and Practice of the Learning Organization* (New York: Doubleday/Currency, 1990).

47. V. Vroom and A. G. Jago, "The Role of the Situation in Leadership," *American Psychologist* 62, no. 1 (2007), pp. 17–24.

48. Vroom and Jago, "The Role of the Situation in Leadership."

49. For example, M. Conlin, "The New Gender Gap: From Kindergarten to Grad School, Boys Are Becoming the Second Sex," *BusinessWeek,* May 26, 2003.

50. GAO, Women in Management: Female Managers' Representation, Characteristics, and Pay, GAO-10-1064T (Washington, D.C.: September 28, 2010).

51. http://catalyst.org/press-release/161/2009-catalyst-census-of-the-fortune-500-reveals-women-missing-from-critical-business-leadership. 10/05/2010.

52. V. Schein, "The Relationship between Sex Role Stereotypes and Requisite Management Characteristics," *Journal of Applied Psychology,* 57, 1973, pp. 95–100.

53. V. Schein, "Relationships between Sex Role Stereotypes and Requisite Management Characteristics among Female Managers, *Journal of Applied Psychology* 60, 1975, pp. 340–44.

54. V. Schein and R. Mueller, "Sex Role Stereotyping and Requisite Management Characteristics: A Cross Cultural Look, *Journal of Organizational Behavior* 13, 1992, pp. 439–447.

55. O. C. Brenner, J. Tomkiewicz, and V. E. Schein, "The Relationship between Sex Role Stereotypes and Requisite Management Characteristics Revisited," *Academy of Management Journal* 32 (1989), pp. 662–69.

56. A. M. Morrison, R. P. White, and E. Van Velsor, *Breaking the Glass Ceiling* (Reading, MA: Addison-Wesley, 1987).

57. J. B. Rosener, "Ways Women Lead," *Harvard Business Review* 68 (1990), pp. 119–25.

58. A. H. Eagly and L. L. Carli, "The Female Leadership Advantage: An Evaluation of the Evidence," *The Leadership Quarterly* 14 (2003), pp. 807–34.

59. A. W., Astin, S. A. Parrrott, W. S. Korn, and L. J. Sax, *The American Freshman: Thirty Year Trends* (Los Angeles: Higher Education Research Institute, University of California, 1997).

60. J. M. Twenge, "Changes in Masculine and Feminine Traits over Time: A Meta-analysis," *Sex Roles* 36 (1997), pp. 305–25.

61, J. M. Twenge, "Changes in Women's Assertiveness in Response to Status and Roles: A Cross-Temporal Meta-analysis, 1931–1993," *Journal of Personality and Social Psychology* 81, (2001), pp. 133–45.

62. A. M. Konrad, J. E. Ritchie, Jr., P. Lieb, and E. Corrigall, "Sex Differences and Similarities in Job Attribute Preferences: A Meta-analysis." *Psychological Bulletin* 126 (2000), pp. 593–641.

63. S. A. Haslam and Ryan, M. K., "The Road to the Glass Cliff: Differences in the Perceived Suitability of Men and Women for Leadership Positions in Succeeding and Failing Organizations," *The Leadership Quarterly* 19 (2008), pp. 530–46.

2

Leader Development

Introduction

In Chapter 1 we discussed the importance of using multiple perspectives to analyze various leadership situations. It's also true that there are multiple paths by which one's own leadership is developed. That's what this chapter is about: how to become a better leader. As an overview, we begin this chapter by presenting a general model that describes how we learn from experience. Next we describe how perceptions can affect a leader's interpretation of, and actions in response to, a particular leadership situation and why reflection is important to leadership development. The chapter also examines several specific mechanisms often used to help leaders become *better* leaders.

Perhaps a word here might be useful about titling this chapter *leader development*. We have done so deliberately to distinguish the phrase from *leadership development*. Although the two may seem synonymous to the reader, they have come to be treated by scholars and practitioners in the field as having distinct meanings. That wasn't always the case. Until a decade or so ago, scholars and practitioners, too, considered them essentially synonymous. Gradually, however, it became useful to use *leader development* when referring to methods intended to facilitate growth in an *individual's* perspectives or skills. For example, training designed to develop one's skill in giving feedback to another person would be considered leader development. Over the past decade, though, the term *leadership* has taken on a somewhat richer meaning transcending a focus on individual-level characteristics and skills even when the focus is on developing such qualities in *many* individuals. Paralleling a gradual shift in understanding that leadership is a process in which many people in an organization share in complex and interdependent ways (as we discussed in Chapter 1), the term *leadership development* has come to designate a focus on developing shared properties of whole groups or social systems such as the degree of trust among all the members of a team or department, or on enhancing the reward systems in an organization to better encourage collaborative behavior.[1] Although such things are frequently addressed throughout this text, the focus of this chapter will be on processes and methods designed to foster individual-level growth—hence the choice of chapter title.

And one more thing before we get into those substantive parts of the chapter: it might be useful to start with a fundamental question about the value of an academic course in leadership. Before the authors wrote this textbook, we and other colleagues taught an undergraduate course in leadership required of all cadets at the U.S. Air Force Academy. Undergraduate courses in leadership are fairly common now, but they weren't in the 1980s. For many decades the U.S. Air Force Academy and the U.S. Military Academy were among the few undergraduate schools offering such courses.

Because undergraduate leadership courses were somewhat uncommon then, the idea of an academic course in leadership was a novel idea to many faculty members from other departments. Some were openly skeptical that leadership was an appropriate course for an academic department to offer. It was a common experience for us to be asked, "Do you really think you can *teach* leadership?" Usually this was asked in a tone of voice that made it clear the questioner took it for granted that leadership couldn't be taught. Colleagues teaching leadership courses at other institutions have found themselves in similar situations.

Over time, we formulated our own response to this question, and it still reflects a core belief we continue to hold. Not coincidentally, that belief has been hinted at in the subtitle to every edition of our text: *Enhancing the Lessons of Experience*. Let us describe how that idea represents the answer to those skeptical questioners, and also how reflecting on their questions shaped these authors' thinking about one important objective of an academic course in leadership.

Just to be clear, we *don't* disagree completely with the premise of those skeptical questioners. We don't believe that merely taking a one-semester college course in leadership will make one a better leader. However, we believe strongly that it can lay a valuable foundation to becoming a better leader over time.

Here's our reasoning. If you accept that leadership can be learned (rather than just "being born" in a person), and if you also believe that the most powerful lessons about leadership come from one's own experience, then the matter boils down to the process of how we learn from experience. If one important factor in learning from experience pertains to how complex or multifaceted your conceptual lenses are for construing experience, then it's no big stretch to claim that becoming familiar with the complex variables that affect leadership gives you a greater variety of ways to make sense of the leadership situations you confront in your own life. In that way, completing a college course in leadership may not make you a better leader directly and immediately, but actively mastering the concepts in the course can nonetheless *accelerate the rate at which you learn from the natural experiences you have* during and subsequent to your course.

Leadership, like swimming, cannot be learned by reading about it.
**Henry Mintzberg,
scholar**

For efficiency, organizations that value developing their leaders usually create intentional pathways for doing so. In other words, leader development in most large organizations is not left to osmosis. There typically are structured and planned approaches to developing internal leaders or leaders-to-be. Formal training is the most common approach to developing leaders, even when research consistently shows that it's not the most effective method. It should not be surprising, then, that organizational members are often not satisfied with the opportunities generally provided within their organizations for developing as leaders. A recent study of more than 4,500 leaders from over 900 organizations found that only half were satisfied with their developmental opportunities.[2]

Findings like that do not prove that leader development opportunities are inherently inadequate or poorly designed. It must be remembered, for example, that developmental opportunities by their nature typically are not free despite whatever long-term advantages might accrue from them for both the individual and the organization. It would seem desirable, then, to ensure that developmental opportunities are provided based on our best understanding of leader development processes. Morgan McCall has summarized some of the key things we've learned about leader development over the last several decades in these seven general points:[3]

- To the extent that leadership is learned at all, it is learned from experience. In fact, about 70 percent of variance in a person's effectiveness in a leadership role is due to the results of her experience; only 30 percent is due to heredity.
- Certain experiences have greater developmental impact than others in shaping a person's effectiveness as a leader.
- What makes such experiences valuable are the challenges they present to the person.
- Different types of experience teach different leadership lessons.
- Some of the most useful experiences for learning leadership come in the jobs we're assigned to, and they can be designed to better enhance their developmental richness.
- Obstacles exist to getting all the developmental experiences we may desire, but we can still get many of them through our own diligence and with some organizational support.
- Learning to be a better leader is a lifelong pursuit with many twists and turns.

Leadership and learning are indispensable to each other.
John F. Kennedy

Of course we're not going to look at just these seven points! A fitting way to continue the chapter might be to look at Highlight 2.1, which identifies the most critical skills leaders will need in the years ahead. The feature offers several ideas for *what* leadership skills you might want to develop further. But knowing what you want to learn is only half the answer. It's also important to understand *how* to learn about leadership—and that's what we turn to next.

The Action–Observation–Reflection Model

Consider for a moment what a young person might learn from spending a year working in two very different environments: as a staff assistant in the U.S. Congress or as a carpenter on a house construction crew. Each activity offers a rich store of leadership lessons. Working in Congress, for example, would provide opportunities to observe political leaders both onstage in the public eye and backstage in more private moments. It would provide opportunities to see members of Congress interacting with different constituencies, to see them in political defeat and political victory, and to see a range of leadership styles. A young person could also learn a lot by working on a building crew as it turned plans and materials into the reality of a finished house: watching the coordination with subcontractors, watching skilled craftspeople train younger ones, watching the leader's reactions to problems and delays, watching the leader set standards and ensure quality work. At the same time, a person could work in either environment and *not* grow much if he or she were not disposed to. Making the most of experience is key to developing

What Skills Will Successful Leaders Need?

HIGHLIGHT 2.1

The Conference Board is a not-for-profit organization that conducts research, assesses trends, and makes forecasts about management to help businesses strengthen their performance and better serve society. In 2002 it identified critical skills leaders will need to be successful in the year 2010. The list, of course, is no longer a projection for the future; but the skills are still important ones:

- Cognitive ability—both raw "intellectual horsepower" and mental agility.
- Strategic thinking, especially with regard to global competition.
- Analytical ability, especially the ability to sort through diverse sources of information and see what's most important.
- The ability to make sound decisions in an environment of ambiguity and uncertainty.

- Personal and organizational communication skills.
- The ability to be influential and persuasive with different groups.
- The ability to manage in an environment of diversity—managing people from different cultures, genders, generations, and so on.
- The ability to delegate effectively.
- The ability to identify, attract, develop, and retain talented people.
- The ability to learn from experience.

Are your experiences in college developing these skills in you? Which of these skills might you want to develop further, and what experiences might best help you do so?

Source: *From A. Barrett and J. Beeson, "Developing Business Leaders for 2010," The Conference Board, 2002. Reprinted with permission of The Conference Board, www.conferenceboard.org.*

one's leadership ability. In other words, leadership development depends not just on the kinds of experiences one has but also on how one uses them to foster growth. A study of successful executives found that a key quality that characterized them was an "extraordinary tenacity in extracting something worthwhile from their experience and in seeking experiences rich in opportunities for growth."[4]

But how does one do that? Is someone really more likely to get the lessons of experience by looking for them? Why is it not enough just to be there? Experiential learning theorists, such as Kolb,[5] believe people learn more from their experiences when they spend time thinking about them. These ideas are extended to leadership in the **action–observation–reflection (A-O-R) model,** depicted in Figure 2.1, which shows that leadership development is enhanced when the experience involves three different processes: action, observation, and reflection. If a person acts but does not observe the consequences of her actions or reflect on their significance and meaning, then it makes little sense to say she has learned from an experience. Because some people neither observe the consequences of their actions nor reflect on how they could change their actions to become better leaders, leadership development through experience may be better understood as the growth resulting from repeated movements through all three phases rather than merely in terms of some objective dimension like time (such as how long one has been on the job). We believe the most productive way to develop as a leader is to travel along the **spiral of experience** depicted in Figure 2.1.

FIGURE 2.1
The Spiral of Experience

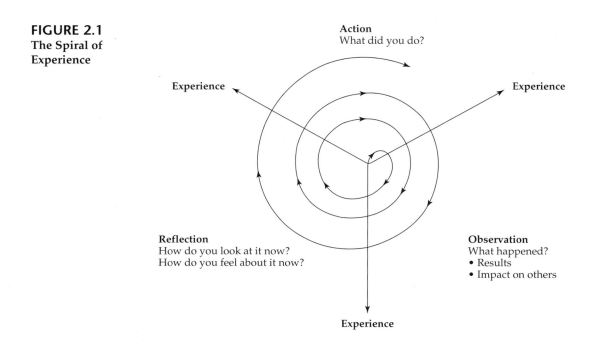

Action
What did you do?

Experience

Experience

Reflection
How do you look at it now?
How do you feel about it now?

Observation
What happened?
• Results
• Impact on others

Experience

Perhaps an example from Colin Powell's life will clarify how the spiral of experience pertains to leadership development. Powell held positions at the highest levels of U.S. military and civilian leadership as Chairman of the Joint Chiefs of Staff and U.S. Secretary of State, but in 1963 he was a 26-year-old officer who had just returned to the United States from a combat tour in Vietnam. His next assignment would be to attend a month-long advanced airborne Ranger course. Near the end of the course, he was to parachute with other troops from a helicopter. As the senior officer on the helicopter, Powell had responsibility for ensuring it went well. Early in the flight he shouted for everyone to make sure their static lines were secure—these are the cables that automatically pull the parachutes open when people jump. Nearing the jump site, he yelled for the men to check their hookups one more time. Here are his words describing what happened next:

> Then, like a fussy old woman, I started checking each line myself, pushing my way through the crowded bodies, running my hand along the cable and up to each man's chute. To my alarm, one hook belonging to a sergeant was loose. I shoved the dangling line in his face, and he gasped. . . . This man would have stepped out of the door of the helo and dropped like a rock.[6]

What did Powell learn from this experience?

> Moments of stress, confusion, and fatigue are exactly when mistakes happen. And when everyone else's mind is dulled or distracted the leader must be doubly vigilant. "Always check small things" was becoming another one of my rules.[7]

We shall not cease from exploration And the end of all our exploring Will be to arrive where we started And know the place for the first time.

T. S. Eliot

Let us examine this incident in light of the A-O-R model. *Action* refers to Powell's multiple calls for the parachutists to check their lines. We might speculate from his self-description ("like a fussy old woman") that Powell might have felt slightly uncomfortable with such repeated emphasis on checking the lines, even though he persisted in the behavior. Perhaps you, too, sometimes have acted in a certain manner (or were forced to by your parents) despite feeling a little embarrassed about it, and then, if it was successful, felt more comfortable the next time acting the same way. That seems to be what happened with Powell here. The *observation* phase refers to Powell's shocked realization of the potentially fatal accident that would have occurred had he *not* double-checked the static lines. And the *reflection* phase refers to the lesson Powell drew from the experience: "Always check the small things." Even though this was not a totally new insight, its importance was strongly reinforced by this experience. In a real sense Powell was "spiraling" through a lesson he'd learned from other experiences too, but embracing it even more this time, making it part of his style.

We also should note that Powell himself described his learning in a manner consistent with our interactional framework. He emphasized the situational importance of the leader's attention to detail, especially during moments of stress, confusion, and fatigue, when mistakes may be most likely to happen. Finally, it's worth noting that throughout Powell's autobiography he discusses many lessons he learned from experience. A key to his success was his ability to keep learning throughout his career.

The Key Role of Perception in the Spiral of Experience

Experience is not just a matter of what events happen to you; it also depends on how you perceive those events. Perception affects all three phases of the action–observation–reflection model and thus plays an important role in what anyone will extract from a leadership course or from any leadership situation. Human beings are not passive recorders of experiences that happen to them; rather, people actively shape and construct their experiences. To better understand how perception affects experience, we will examine its role in each part of the action–observation–reflection model. We will begin with the stage that seems to correspond most directly with perception—the observation phase.

Perception and Observation

Observation and perception both deal with attending to events around us. Both seem to take place spontaneously and effortlessly, so it is easy to regard them as passive processes. Our usual mental images of the perceptual process reflect this implicit view. For example, it is a common misconception that the eye operates essentially like the film in a continuously running camera. The fallacy of this passive view of perception is that it assumes we attend to all aspects of a situation equally. However, we do not see everything that happens in a particular leadership situation, nor do we hear everything. Instead we are selective in what we attend to and what we, in turn, perceive. One phenomenon that demonstrates this selectivity is called **perceptual set.** Perceptual sets can influence any of our senses, and they are the tendency or bias to perceive one thing and not another. Many factors can trigger a perceptual set, such as feelings, needs, prior experience, and expectations. Its role in distorting what we hear proved a costly lesson when a sympathetic airline pilot told his depressed copilot, "Cheer up!" The copilot thought the pilot had said, "Gear up," and raised the wheels while the plane was still on the ground.[8] Try your own ability to overcome perceptual set with the following exercise. Read through this narrative passage several times:

> **FINISHED FILES ARE THE RESULT OF YEARS OF SCIENTIFIC STUDY COMBINED WITH THE EXPERIENCE OF MANY YEARS.**

Make sure you have read it to yourself several times *before going any further.* Now go back to the text and count the number of times the letter *F* appears.

How many did you count? Three? Four? Five? Six? Most people do not get the correct answer (six) the first time. The most frequent count is three; perhaps that was how many you saw. If you did not find six, go back and try again. The most common error in this seemingly trivial task is overlooking the three times the word *of* appears. People easily overlook it because the word *of* has a *v* sound, not an *f* sound. Most people unconsciously make the task an auditory search task and listen for the sound of *F* rather than look for the shape of *F;* hence they find three *F*s rather than six. Listening for the sound constitutes a counterproductive perceptual set for this task, and having read the passage several times before counting the *F*s only exaggerates this tendency. Another reason people overlook the word *of* in this passage is that the first task was to *read* the passage several times. Because most of us are accomplished readers, we tend to ignore small words like *of*—they disappear from our perceptual set. Then, when we are asked to count the number of *F*s, we have already defined the passage as a reading task, so the word *of* is really not there for us to count. See Highlight 2.2 to learn about other factors that can affect our observational effectiveness.

It's not what we don't know that hurts, it's what we know that ain't so.

Will Rogers

There are strong parallels between this example of a perceptual set and the perceptual sets that come into play when we are enrolled in a leadership course or observe a leadership situation. For example, your instructor for this class may dress unstylishly, and you may be prejudiced in thinking that poor dressers generally do not make good leaders. Because of your biases, you may discount or not attend to some things your instructor has to say about leadership. This would be unfortunate because your instructor's taste in clothes has little to do with his or her ability to teach (which is, after all, a kind of leadership).

On Being Observant and Lucky and Learning from Experience

HIGHLIGHT 2.2

It's often said that some people have all the luck. Do you think that's true—are some people luckier than others? Richard Wiseman, a professor at the University of Hertfordshire, has written a book about just that question, and his findings are relevant to the role observation plays in our spiral of experience.

In one of his experiments, Wiseman placed advertisements in national newspapers asking for people to contact him who felt either consistently lucky or consistently unlucky. In one experiment, he gave both self-described lucky and unlucky people a newspaper to read and asked them to look it over and tell him how many photographs were inside.

Halfway through the paper he'd put a half-page message with two-inch lettering saying, "Tell the experimenter you have seen this and win $250."

The advertisement was staring everyone in the face, but the unlucky people tended to miss it whereas the lucky people tended to notice it. One reason may be related to the fact that Wiseman claims unlucky people are somewhat more anxious than lucky people, and that might disrupt their ability to notice things that are unexpected.

How observant are *you,* and might developing your own observation skills help you learn from experience more effectively?

Source: Adapted from Richard Wiseman, *The Luck Factor* (New York: Miramax Books, 2003).

A similar phenomenon takes place when one expects to find mostly negative things about another person (such as a problem employee). Such an expectation becomes a perceptual set to look for the negative and look past the positive things in the process. Stereotypes about gender, race, and the like represent powerful impediments to learning because they function as filters that distort one's observations. For example, if you do not believe women or minorities are as successful as white males in influencing others, you may be biased to identify or remember only instances where a woman or minority leader failed, and discount or forget instances where women or minority members succeeded as leaders. Unfortunately we all have similar biases, although we are usually unaware of them. Often we become aware of our perceptual sets only when we spend time reflecting about the content of a leadership training program or a particular leadership situation. Still another factor affecting the role observation plays in our ability to learn from experience is described in Highlight 2.2.

Perception and Reflection

Perceptual sets influence what we attend to and what we observe. In addition, perception also influences the next stage of the spiral of experience—reflection—because reflection is how we interpret our observations. Perception is inherently an interpretive, or a meaning-making, activity. One important aspect of this is a process called **attribution.**

Attributions are the explanations we develop for the behaviors or actions we attend to. For example, if you see Julie fail in an attempt to get others to form a study group, you are likely to attribute the cause of the failure to dispositional factors within Julie. In other words, you are likely to attribute the failure to form a study group to Julie's intelligence, personality, physical appearance, or some other factor even though factors beyond her control could have played a major part. This tendency to overestimate the dispositional causes of behavior and underestimate the environmental causes when others fail is called the **fundamental attribution error.**[9] People prefer to explain others' behavior on the basis of personal attributions even when obvious situational factors may fully account for the behavior.

On the other hand, if *you* attempted to get others to form a study group and failed, you would be more likely to blame factors in the situation for the failure (there was not enough time, or the others were not interested, or they would not be good to study with). This reflects a **self-serving bias**[10]—the tendency to make external attributions (blame the situation) for one's own failures yet make internal attributions (take credit) for one's successes. A third factor that affects the attribution process is called the **actor/observer difference.**[11] This refers to the fact that people who are observing an action are much more likely than the actor to make the fundamental attribution error. Consider, for example, a student who gets a bad score on an exam. The person sitting next to her (an observer) would

Common sense is the collection of prejudices acquired by age 18.
Albert Einstein

"Just don't make any personal appearances until after the election."

Source: Reprinted from *The Saturday Evening Post Magazine* © 1964. *The Saturday Evening Post Society.*

tend to attribute the bad score to *internal* characteristics (not very bright, weak in this subject) whereas the student herself would be more likely to attribute the bad score to *external* factors (the professor graded unfairly). Putting these factors together, each of us tends to see our own success as due to our intelligence, personality, or physical abilities, but others' success as more attributable to situational factors or to luck.

We note in concluding this section that reflection also involves higher functions like evaluation and judgment, not just perception and attribution. We will address these broader aspects of reflection, which are crucial to learning from experience, just ahead.

Perception and Action

We have seen how perception influences both the observation and reflection stages in the spiral of experience. It also affects the actions we take. For example, Mitchell and his associates[12-14] have examined how perceptions and biases affect supervisors' actions in response to poorly performing subordinates. In general, these researchers found that supervisors were biased toward making dispositional attributions about a subordinate's substandard performance and, as a result of these attributions, often recommended that punishment be used to remedy performance deficits.

Another perceptual variable that can affect our actions is the **self-fulfilling prophecy,** which occurs when our expectations or predictions play a causal role in bringing about the events we predict. It is not difficult to see how certain large-scale social phenomena may be affected this way. For example, economists' predictions of an economic downturn may, via the consequent decreased investor confidence, precipitate an economic crisis. But the self-fulfilling prophecy occurs at the interpersonal level, too. A person's expectations about another may influence how he acts toward her, and in reaction to his behavior she may act in a way that confirms his expectations.[15] An illustrative interaction sequence is shown in Figure 2.2.

Some of the best evidence to support the effects of self-fulfilling prophecies on leadership training was collected by Eden and Shani in the context of military boot camp.[16] They conducted a field experiment in which they told leadership instructors their students had unknown, regular, or high command potential. However, the students' actual command potential was never assessed, and unknown to the instructors, the students were actually randomly assigned to the unknown, regular, or high command potential conditions. Nevertheless, students in the high-potential condition had significantly better objective test scores and attitudes than the students in the unknown- or regular-potential conditions, even though instructors simultaneously taught all three types of students. Somehow the students picked up on their instructor's expectations and responded accordingly. Thus merely having expectations (positive or negative) about

FIGURE 2.2
The Role of Expectations in Social Interaction

Source: *From Edward E. Jones, "Interpreting Interpersonal Behavior: The Effects of Expectancies," Science 234, 3, October 1986, p. 43. Reprinted with permission from AAAS.*

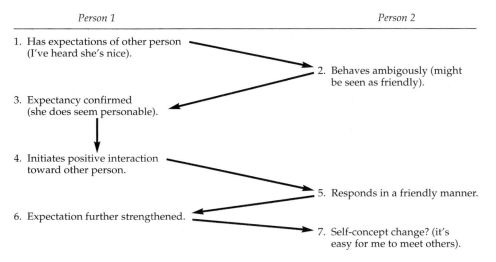

others can subtly influence our actions, and these actions can, in turn, affect the way others behave.

Reflection and Leadership Development

Perhaps the most important yet most neglected component of the action–observation–reflection model is reflection. Reflection is important because it can provide leaders with a variety of insights into how to frame problems differently, look at situations from multiple perspectives, or better understand subordinates. However, most managers spend relatively little time on this activity, even though the time spent reflecting about leadership can be fruitful. The importance of reflection in developing executive competence continues to be a major element of advancing scholarly thought and practice.[17]

Being ignorant is not so much a shame as being unwilling to learn.
Benjamin Franklin

One reason the reflection component is often neglected may be time pressure at work. Leaders are usually busy working in pressure-filled situations and often do not have time to ponder all the possible consequences of their actions or reflect on how they could have accomplished a particular action better. Sometimes it takes an out-of-the-ordinary experience to focus one's attention on developmental challenges (see Highlight 2.3). In addition, some leaders may not be aware of the value of reflection in leadership development. Intentional reflection might even prompt one to see potential benefits in experience not initially considered relevant to leadership in organizational settings (see Highlight 2.4).We hope this section will clarify the value of reflection and, in so doing, complement the emphasis, throughout the remainder of the book, on looking at leadership from different perspectives.

Single- and Double-Loop Learning

It is difficult for leaders to fundamentally change their leadership style without engaging in some kind of reflection. Along these lines, Argyris[18] described an intensive effort with a group of successful chief executive officers who became even better leaders through increased self-awareness. His model for conceptualizing this growth is applicable to any level of leader and is worth considering in more detail.

Argyris said that most people interact with others and the environment on the basis of a belief system geared to manipulate or control others, and to minimize one's own emotionality and the negative feelings elicited from others. This belief system also tends to create defensive interpersonal relationships and limits risk taking. People "programmed" with this view of life (as most of us are, according to Argyris) produce group and organizational dynamics characterized by avoidance of conflict, mistrust, conformity, intergroup rivalry, misperceptions of and miscommunications with others, ineffective problem solving, and poor decision making.

Leadership Development Dilemmas for Women

HIGHLIGHT 2.3

The Women's Leadership Program, offered by the Center for Creative Leadership (CCL), emphasizes receiving feedback, improving self-awareness, and setting leadership and life goals. Members of the CCL staff conducted a series of interviews with 60 executive women who had attended the program, and identified several salient issues these women were struggling with. Four particular themes stood out:

Wholeness and authenticity: These executive women desired to have whole and full lives. They felt job demands had forced their lives to become one-dimensional. Often they felt they had given up important parts of themselves: creativity, friendliness, musical talent, athletic performance, and so forth. Sometimes they felt their organizations required them to ignore or suppress some part of their true selves to succeed.

Clarity: After the program, many women developed great clarity about their own strengths, weaknesses, values, needs, priorities, and goals as leaders.

Connection: Many women expressed concerns that they did not have the degree of interpersonal connectedness with others they would have preferred. They expressed a desire for closer friendships and family ties. Many said they felt isolated in their organizations, with few confidants of either gender.

Control: One of the strongest themes identified in the interviews was the need to feel more in control. This need was manifested in a number of different ways, including the need to feel more comfortable exercising authority and a need to deal differently with organizational situations that made them feel helpless. Many women also expressed a desire to become more politically sophisticated.

To reflect on the overall findings of the study, it is encouraging that virtually all of these executive women believed they were continuing to grow both personally and professionally. The experiences of this group of executive women certainly support the view that development persists throughout life. Are any of these dilemmas issues for college students as well as executives? If so, do you believe they are any more problematic for female than for male students?

Source: Adapted from P. Ohlott, "Change and Leadership Development: The Experience of Executive Women," *Leadership in Action* 19, no. 5 (1999), pp. 8–12.

Most important for our purposes here, this belief system generates a certain kind of learning that Argyris called **single-loop learning.** Single-loop learning describes a kind of learning between the individual and the environment in which learners seek relatively little feedback that may significantly confront their fundamental ideas or actions. There is relatively little public testing of ideas against valid information. Consequently, an actor's belief system becomes self-sealing and self-fulfilling, and little time is spent reflecting about the beliefs. Argyris used the term *single-loop learning* because it operates somewhat like a thermostat: individuals learn only about subjects within the comfort zone of their belief systems. They might, for example, learn how well they are achieving a designated goal. They are far less likely, however, to question the validity of the goal or the values implicit in the situation, just as a thermostat does not question its

The Relevance of Women's Personal Experiences to Their Leadership Effectiveness

HIGHLIGHT 2.4

Record numbers of women are active in the managerial workforce. Not surprisingly, a widespread perception has arisen that the relationship between work and nonwork domains of women's lives is almost inherently one of conflict. Managerial women are described as constantly torn between the demands of their managerial and personal roles. Less attention has been paid to the question of possible benefits of combining employment and personal roles.

Psychologists have studied how the roles women play in their personal lives can affect their effectiveness at work. In telephone interviews with women managers, they asked this question (among others): *Are there any dimensions or aspects of your personal life that enhance your professional life?* Six themes characterized the women's responses:

- *Opportunities to enrich interpersonal skills* like motivating, respecting, and developing others—honed at home in raising children—are transferable to motivating, developing, and directing employees.

- *Psychological benefits* from overcoming obstacles, taking risks, and succeeding in personal arenas bolster esteem, self-confidence, energy, and courage.

- *Emotional support and advice* from friends and family who act as sounding boards and motivators allow one to vent feelings in a safe environment.

- *Handling multiple tasks* such as planning and juggling a busy family's schedules develops administrative skills such as prioritizing and planning.

- *Personal interests and background* provide skills and helpful perspectives for understanding and connecting with people at work.

- *Leadership opportunities* in volunteer, community organization, or family settings provide leadership lessons and increase comfort in authority roles.

Source: Adapted from: M. N. Ruderman, Patricia J. Ohlott, K. Panzer, and Sara N. King, "Benefits of Multiple Roles for Managerial Women," *Academy of Management Journal* 45, no. 2 (2002), pp. 369–86.

temperature setting. That kind of self-confrontation would involve double-loop learning.

Double-loop learning involves a willingness to confront one's own views and an invitation to others to do so, too. It springs from an appreciation that openness to information and power sharing with others can lead to better recognition and definition of problems, improved communication, and increased decision-making effectiveness. Mastering double-loop learning can be thought of as learning how to learn. With considerable collective work, including the difficult task of working through personal blind spots, Argyris's group of leaders did move to this stage. In other words, through reflection they learned how to change their leadership styles by questioning their assumptions about others, their roles in the organization, and their underlying assumptions about the importance of their own goals and those of the organization.

Making the Most of Your Leadership Experiences: Learning to Learn from Experience

This section builds on the ideas previously introduced in this chapter by giving leadership practitioners a few suggestions to enhance learning from experience. For decades, researchers have been studying the role of learning from experience as an important developmental behavior for people in executive positions. Although this research has contributed a great deal to *what* people need to learn to be successful (see Highlight 2.5 for a comparison of lessons men and women managers learn from experience), less is known about the process of learning or *how* we learn to be successful.

Bunker and Webb[19] asked successful executives to list adjectives describing how they felt while working through powerful learning events

What Do Men and Women Managers Learn from Experience?

HIGHLIGHT 2.5

For a quarter century or so, significant numbers of women have been represented in the management ranks of companies. During that period companies have promoted large pools of high-potential women, but relatively few of them have achieved truly top-level positions. Several factors probably account for this, but one possibility is that men and women learn differently from their work experiences. Researchers have studied how male and female executives describe the important lessons they've learned from their career experiences, and there are some interesting differences between the genders as well as significant overlap.

Most Frequent Lessons for Men and Women	For Men Only	For Women Only
Directing and motivating employees.	Technical/professional skills.	Personal limits and blind spots.
Self-confidence.	All about the business.	Taking charge of career.
Basic management values.	Coping with ambiguous situations.	Recognizing and seizing opportunities.
How to work with executives.	Shouldering full responsibility.	Coping with situations beyond your control.
Understanding other people's perspective.	Persevering through adversity.	Knowing what excites you.
Dealing with people over whom you have no authority.		
Handling political situations.		

Why would there be any learning differences between the genders? One hypothesis is that men and women managers tend to have different career patterns. For example, there is some evidence that women receive fewer truly challenging developmental opportunities. Do you believe there is any difference at your school between the opportunities provided to male and female students?

Source: Adapted from E. Van Velsor and M. W. Hughes, *Gender Differences in the Development of Managers: How Women Managers Learn from Experience* (Technical Report No. 145) (Greensboro, NC: Center for Creative Leadership, 1990).

and potent developmental experiences. Their typical responses were a combination of both positive and negative feelings:

Negatives	Positives
Pained	Challenged
Fearful	Successful
Frustrated	Proud
Stressed	Capable
Anxious	Growing
Overwhelmed	Exhilarated
Uncertain	Talented
Angry	Resourceful
Hurt	Learning

This pattern strongly supports the long-hypothesized notion of a meaningful link between stress and learning.[20] The learning events and developmental experiences that punctuate one's life are usually—perhaps always—stressful.[21-24]

Bunker and Webb note that executives try to be successful without experiencing stress. They are most comfortable when they can draw on a proven repertoire of operating skills to tackle a challenge they have conquered in the past. Combined with the organizational pressure to have "proven performers" in important positions, there is a tremendous initial pressure to "continue to do what we've always done." In stressful situations, this tendency may become even more powerful. What results is one of the great challenges of adult development: the times when people most need to break out of the mold created by past learning patterns are the times when they are most unwilling to do so. Being able to *go against the grain* of one's personal historical success requires an unwavering commitment to learning and a relentless willingness to let go of the fear of failure and the unknown.

To be successful, learning must continue throughout life, beyond the completion of one's formal education. The end of extrinsically applied education should be the start of an education that is motivated intrinsically. At that point the goal of studying is no longer to make the grade, earn a diploma, and find a good job. Rather, it is to understand what is happening around one, to develop a personally meaningful sense of what one's experience is about.[25]

This applies to the specific challenge of *becoming* and *remaining* an effective leader, too. People who lead in modern organizations need to be engaged in a never-ending learning process.[26] Ron Riggio of the Kravis Leadership Institute characterized this challenge well in observing that organizational leaders are practitioners of leadership at the same time they must continue to be students of leadership. "The practice of leadership,

Oprah Winfrey

PROFILES IN LEADERSHIP 2.1

In January 2007 doors opened for the first class of girls at the Oprah Winfrey Leadership Academy near Johannesburg, South Africa. The first admissions included about 150 seventh and eighth grade girls, with plans to expand to more than 400 girls in the seventh through twelfth grades by 2011. Winfrey's vision is that the academy will help develop the future women leaders of South Africa. This will be one more accomplishment for a woman who has her own television show, publishes two different magazines, was nominated for an Academy Award for acting in *The Color Purple,* made Dr. Phil famous, and whose recommendation can virtually guarantee a book's commercial success. She may be the most influential woman in the world.

No one would have predicted this from the poor and troubled family conditions she was born into. Her Grandmother Hattie Mae, however, who raised Oprah during her first six years, saw something special in her from the beginning. She taught Oprah to read before the age of 3, and at church Oprah was known as "the preacher" because of her

ability to recite Bible verses. As a teenager in school she was voted "most popular girl," and she placed second in a national competition for dramatic interpretation. At 18 she won the Miss Black Tennessee beauty pageant.

Even from an early age there were glimpses of the direction Oprah's life would take. As a child she played games "interviewing" everything from her corncob doll to crows on the fence, but her true start in broadcasting came at the age of 17 when she worked part-time at a local radio station while attending college. She became the youngest news anchor and the first black female news anchor at WLAC-TV in Nashville. In 1976 she moved to anchor the news in Baltimore, and in 1978 she became co-host of a local TV talk show. She moved to Chicago to host a talk show there, first airing in 1984; months later it was renamed *The Oprah Winfrey Show.* Its first national broadcast was in 1986, and the rest, as they say, is history. But Oprah is still making history—not only in virtually every facet of media but also in her philanthropic efforts to develop a generation of women leaders in South Africa.

Good flutists learn from experience; unfortunately, so do bad flutists.

Anonymous

I took a great deal o' pains with his education, sir; let him run the streets when he was very young, and shift for his-self. It's the only way to make a boy sharp, sir.

Charles Dickens,
Pickwick Papers

---

just like the practice of medicine, or law, or any other profession, is a continual learning process. The complexity of these professions means that one can always improve and learn how to do it better. The wise leader accepts this and goes through the sometimes painful process of personal leader development."[27]

Leader Development in College

Virtually everyone using this text is taking a college course in leadership for academic credit. But one academic course in leadership is only part of what at some schools is an entire curriculum of leadership studies. Riggio, Ciulla and Sorenson, representing three different institutions, have described the rise and key elements of leadership studies programs in liberal arts colleges, and note that there are now nearly 1,000 recognized leadership development programs in institutions of higher education.[28] Few, of them, though, are curriculum-based programs that offer academic credit in the form of, for example, an academic minor. As such programs continue to increase in number, several features should guide their design.

Steve Jobs

PROFILES IN LEADERSHIP 2.2

Steve Jobs is one of the most famous and successful business leaders in the world, even if also known as having a temperamental, aggressive, and demanding style with others. At the age of 20, with partner Steve Wozniak, he helped launch the personal computer revolution with Apple Computer and ultimately through its premier PC, the Macintosh. After leaving Apple, he founded another company, NeXT Computer, and in 1986 he bought a computer animation company called Pixar. The company's first film, *Toy Story,* made history by being the first entirely computer-animated feature film. Now back at Apple, Jobs has created even further revolutions in consumer technology products with the iPod, iPhone, and iPad.

In 2005 Jobs delivered the commencement address at Stanford. In that address he talked about one of the most difficult and yet most valuable experiences of his life: getting fired from Apple, the company that he had helped found. He and Wozniak started Apple, he said, in 1970 in his parents' garage. In 10 years it had grown into a $2 billion company. He could not believe it, amid that success, when he was fired by Apple's board of directors. "How can you get fired from a company you started? What had been the focus of my entire adult life was gone, and it was devastating." Yet now, reflecting on the opportunities that he was able to take advantage of because he left Apple, Jobs said to the graduating class, "I didn't see it then, but it turned out that getting fired from Apple was the best thing that ever could have happened to me."

STEVE JOBS ON LEADERSHIP

The only way to be truly satisfied is to do what you believe is great work. And the only way to do great work is to love what you do.

Be a yardstick of quality. Some people aren't used to an environment where excellence is expected.

Innovation distinguishes between a leader and a follower.

An educated man can experience more in a day than an uneducated man in a lifetime.

Seneca, Roman statesman, 1st century A.D.

All rising to a great place is by a winding stair.

Francis Bacon, philosopher

At liberal arts institutions, leadership studies programs should be multidisciplinary. As you will notice in this text, the field of leadership encompasses a broad range of disciplines including psychology, organizational behavior, history, education, management, and political science, to name just a few. Also, leadership studies need to be academically authorized courses of study (obvious as this may seem, one challenge to it was evident in the anecdote shared in the introduction to this chapter). Another important feature is that leadership programs need to deliberately cultivate values represented in the broader field, especially those that are particularly salient at each local institution. These values could include social responsibility and the expectation to become engaged in one's community; in such cases **service learning** is a common part of the programs. In other programs, global awareness is another guiding value. Finally, consistent with requirements across higher education, leadership studies programs should focus on expected developmental outcomes, with associated assessment and evaluation to determine program effectiveness.[29]

Some key curricular components of college-based leadership studies programs include coursework examining foundational theories and concepts in leadership (the kind this textbook is intended to support). In addition, coursework in ethics is vital to leadership studies. As just mentioned, service learning and other experiential learning opportunities should be provided and integrated with the classroom elements of the program. An understanding of group dynamics is critical to effective leadership, and its development requires student experiences interacting with others; leadership studies inherently require a social dimension of experience. Finally, as implied by the interdisciplinary nature of leadership studies, a variety of faculty from many different departments and disciplines should be involved in the program.[30]

Within leadership studies programs, various leader development methods may be used beyond service learning. Some courses or program elements might involve **individualized feedback** to students in the form of personality, intelligence, values, or interest test scores or leadership behavior ratings. **Case studies** describe leadership situations and are used as a vehicle for leadership discussions. **Role playing** is also a popular methodology. In role playing, participants are assigned parts to play (such as a supervisor and an unmotivated subordinate) in a job-related scenario. Role playing has the advantage of letting trainees actually practice relevant skills and thus has greater transferability to the workplace than do didactic lectures or abstract discussions about leadership. **Simulations** and **games** are other methods of leader development. These are relatively structured activities designed to mirror some of the challenges or decisions commonly faced in the work environment. A newer approach puts participants in relatively unfamiliar territory (such as outdoors rather than offices) and presents them physical, emotionally arousing, and often team-oriented challenges.

Leader Development in Organizational Settings

The title of this section does not imply that colleges and universities are not organizations; obviously they are. Nonetheless, college-based leadership studies differ in some significant ways from leader development programs one finds in the corporate sector or in the military. Most obvious, perhaps, is the fact that the essential purpose of college-based programs is to prepare students for their ultimate productive service as citizens, including in their own vocations. Our focus in this section is on methods of leader development provided in organizations not just for the individual's personal development but also (and maybe primarily) for the organization's benefit. Although all of the relatively short-term development methods just mentioned are used routinely in organizational programs, some of the most potent work-based leader development methods are longer-term in nature.

There are numerous leadership training programs aimed particularly toward leaders and supervisors in industry or public service. In many ways these have strong parallels to both the content and techniques used

What Do Children Believe about Leadership? "Wut Do Ldrs Do?"

HIGHLIGHT 2.6

A 5-year-old girl wrote and illustrated an unprompted "book" for her grandfather, a friend of the authors. We've included a few of the pages here. They convey what at least some young children believe are important qualities of leaders. You might ask yourself how valid this characterization is . . . and in what ways it is likely to be shaped by experiences between kindergarten and adulthood. The words are written entirely with a 5-year-old's phonetic spelling, so you'll need to be creative in interpreting the qualities!

If we were to apply our A-O-R model here, would you say this 5-year-old was learning from her experience?

Translation Frame A: What do leaders do?

Translation Frame B: They call 911 if someone gets hurt.

Translation Frame C: They get people excited to learn.

Translation Frame D: They be nice to people.

Translation Frame E: They help people.

in university-level courses on leadership. However, these programs tend to be more focused than a university course that typically lasts an entire semester. The content of industry programs also depends on the organizational level of the recipients; programs for first-level supervisors focus on developing supervisory skills such as training, monitoring, giving feedback, and conducting performance reviews with subordinates. Generally these programs use lectures, case studies, and role-playing exercises to improve leadership skills. The programs for midlevel managers often focus on improving interpersonal, oral communication, and written communication skills, as well as giving tips on time management, planning, and goal setting. These programs rely more heavily on individualized feedback, case studies, presentations, role playing, simulations, and **in-basket exercises** to help leaders develop. With in-basket exercises, participants are given a limited amount of time to prioritize and respond to a number of notes, letters, and phone messages from a fictitious manager's in-basket. This technique is particularly useful in assessing and improving a manager's planning and time management skills. In leaderless group discussions, facilitators and observers rate participants on the degree of persuasiveness, leadership, followership, or conflict each member manifests in a group that has no appointed leader. These ratings are used to give managers feedback about their interpersonal and oral communication skills.

In reviewing the general field of leadership development and training, Conger offered this assessment: "Leadership programs can work, and work well, if they use a multi tiered approach. Effective training depends on the combined use of four different teaching methods which I call personal growth, skill building, feedback, and conceptual awareness."[31] Some programs seek to stimulate leadership development by means of emotionally intense personal growth experiences such as river rafting, wilderness survival, and so forth. Leadership development through skill building involves structured activities focusing on the sorts of leadership skills featured in the final section of this book. Some approaches to leadership development emphasize individualized feedback about each person's strengths and weaknesses, typically based on standardized assessment methods. Feedback-based approaches can help identify "blind spots" an individual may be unaware of, as well as help prioritize which aspects of leadership development represent the highest priorities for development focus. Still other sorts of programs develop leadership by emphasizing its conceptual or intellectual components. An example of this approach would be an emphasis on theory and the use of case studies, common in many MBA programs. There are merits in each of these approaches, but Conger was on solid ground when he emphasized the value of combining elements of each.

In a related vein, others have emphasized that leader development in the 21st century must occur in more lifelike situations and contexts.[32]

Toward that end, they have advocated creating better practice fields for leadership development analogous to the practice fields whereon skills in competitive sports are honed, or practice sessions analogous to those in music training wherein those skills are sharpened. Increasingly leadership development is occurring in the context of work itself.[33]

Leadership programs for senior executives and CEOs tend to focus on strategic planning, developing and communicating a vision, public relations, and interpersonal skills. Many times the entire senior leadership of a company will go through a leadership program at the same time. One goal of such a group might be to learn how to develop a strategic plan for their organization. To improve public relations skills, some programs have CEOs undergo simulated, unannounced interviews with television reporters and receive feedback on how they could have done better.

In the following sections we discuss research surrounding four popular and increasingly common methods of leader development: action learning, development planning, coaching, and mentoring.

Action Learning

Perhaps the best way to appreciate the nature of **action learning** is to contrast it with more traditional **training programs**. The latter term refers to leadership development activities that typically involve personnel attending a class, often for several days or even a week. In such classes, many of the kinds of developmental activities already mentioned might be included such as exercises, instrument-based feedback, and various presentations on different aspects of leadership. The key point is that attendance at a training program inherently involves time away from immediate job responsibilities. And while the various exercises presumably address many common leadership issues such as communication, conflict, feedback, and planning, the inevitably artificial nature of such activities make transfer back to the actual work situation more difficult.

Action learning, on the other hand, is the use of actual work issues and challenges as the developmental activity itself. The basic philosophy of action learning is that for adults in particular, the best learning is *learning by doing*. Furthermore, action learning often is conducted in teams of work colleagues who are addressing actual company challenges; the members of action learning teams are placed into problem-solving roles and are expected to reach team decisions concerning the challenge or problem, and formally present their analysis and recommendations to others (often senior executives in their own company). Importantly, action learning also involves built-in opportunities for feedback and reflection for the participants about the perceived quality of their analysis and recommendations as well as, ideally, about aspects of their respective individual strengths and weaknesses as leaders working on the collaborative project together.

In the past 15 years or so, action learning has gone from being a relatively rare development vehicle to being found in many companies' internal

Innovative Approaches to Leader Development

HIGHLIGHT 2.7

Several well-established methods of leader development are highlighted in this chapter such as coaching and mentoring, but many innovative approaches are also worth noting. We've listed a few of them here, grouped into two broad categories: arts-based approaches and technology-based approaches.

ARTS-BASED APPROACHES

Some arts-based approaches may be described as "projective" because they involve some form of artistic creation or interpretation that allows participants to reveal inner thoughts and feelings (the name *projective* was originally associated with the Rorschach Inkblot test, a projective psychological test). For example, visual images (such as photographs or artwork) can provide a stimulus for a person to elaborate on in describing some leadership theme (the best team I've ever been on, what it feels like to work in this company, or the like). It's striking how rich and candid a person's reflections typically are when made in response to something tangible like an evocative image. Another projective technique would be to use simple building materials (like Legos) and instruct participants to create some depiction (perhaps of their organizational structure or strategy). Critical skills such as demonstrating empathy can be learned with dramatic and theatrical training (especially valuable for medical personnel). And films, which often have high emotional impact, can be used to facilitate rich discussions of various leadership issues.

TECHNOLOGY-BASED APPROACHES

Video games and virtual reality simulations also open new doors for leadership development because they share several distinctly advantageous characteristics for training and development. For one thing, they require speedy thought and action. Actions that might take weeks or longer to unfold in real life can be compressed into hours or minutes, and thus the pace of leadership can be heightened. These venues also encourage risk taking, and leadership roles in gaming or virtual reality contexts are often temporary, involving frequent swapping of roles. Even the U.S. Air Force has developed virtual reality simulations for leadership development in situations that are complex, ambiguous, and highly interdependent.

What kinds of experiences at your college might be untapped leadership laboratories?

Sources: S. S. Taylor and D. Ladkin, "Understanding Arts-Based Methods in Managerial Development," *Academy of Management Learning & Education* 8, no. 1 (2009), pp. 55–69;
B. Reeves, T. W. Malone, and T. O'Driscoll, "Leadership's Online Labs," *Harvard Business Review,* May 2008, pp. 59–66;
R. L. Hughes, and A. Stricker, "Outside-in and Inside-out Approaches to Transformation," in D. Neal, H. Friman, R. Doughty, and L. Wells (eds.), *Crosscutting Issues in International Transformation: Interactions and Innovations among People, Organizations, Processes, and Technology* (Washington, DC: Center for Technology and National Security Policy, National Defense University, 2009).

portfolios of leader development opportunities. Unfortunately, however, its demonstrated effectiveness for leader development, as distinguished from its use in generating fresh ideas for thorny company problems, has not kept pace with its increasing popularity and widespread use.

There are many reasons for this—not the least of which is that the links between a particular action learning project and its leadership challenges may be tenuous. Too often personnel are assigned to action learning teams assuming that they'll inevitably learn critical leadership lessons along the way; it usually doesn't happen so easily. If it were easy and automatic, we should expect more "leadership learning" from the experience of one's primary job and not need action learning at all. Furthermore, the very time-critical, high-visibility, and all-too-real elements that can make action learning problems so engaging and popular also often require a work pace that does not allow the kind of reflection we know is an important part of leader development. A final reason we'll mention here for why action learning projects may not achieve their desired leader development outcomes is because teams at work often fall prey to the same kinds of problems that you probably have experienced in team-based projects in your own academic coursework. It's one thing to *call* something a project requiring teamwork; it's quite another thing for the actual work on that project to truly *reflect* good teamwork. In poorly designed and supported action learning projects, the work might be dominated by one person or by just one perspective within the organization. Action learning holds great promise but has not yet delivered uniform results.[34]

Development Planning

How many times have you resolved to change a habit, only to discover two months later that you are still exhibiting the same behaviors? This is often the fate of well-intentioned New Year's resolutions. Most people do not even make such resolutions because the failure rate is so high. Given this track record, you might wonder if it is possible to change one's behavior, particularly if an existing pattern has been reinforced over time and is exhibited almost automatically. Fortunately, however, it *is* possible to change behavior, even long-standing habits. For example, many people permanently quit smoking or drinking without any type of formal program. Others may change after they gain insight into how their behavior affects others. Some will need support to maintain a behavioral change over time, whereas others seem destined to never change.[35,36,37]

Managers seem to fall into the same categories; some managers change once they gain insight, others change with social and organizational support, and others may not ever change. But do people just fall into one of these groups by accident? Is there any way to stack the odds in favor of driving behavioral change? Research provides several suggestions that leaders can take to accelerate the development of their own leadership skills, and we can use the development pipeline depicted in Figure 2.3 to categorize them.[38-43] They suggest five critical behavioral change questions, and leaders must provide positive answers to all five questions if they want to maximize the odds of enduring behavior change taking place.

Question 1: Do leaders know what behaviors need to change? Leaders are capable of exhibiting hundreds of different behaviors, but do they precisely know which behaviors they need to start, stop, or keep doing to build effective teams or achieve better results? The insight component of the development pipeline is concerned with giving leaders accurate feedback on their strengths and development needs, and 360-degree feedback

FIGURE 2.3
The PDI Development Pipeline®

Source: Copyright © 1991–2000, Personnel Decisions International Corporation. Reprinted with permission.

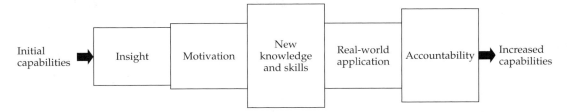

can provide useful information in this regard. Other sources of information about development needs can come from the results of an assessment center, a performance appraisal, or direct feedback from others.

Question 2: Is the leader motivated to change these behaviors? The next step in developing one's own leadership skills is working on development goals that matter. No leader has all of the knowledge and skills necessary to be successful; as a result most leaders have multiple development needs. Leaders need to determine which new skills will have the highest personal and organizational payoffs and build development plans that address these needs. The development plan should be focused on only one or two needs; plans addressing more than this tend to be overwhelming and unachievable. If leaders have more than two development needs, they should first work to acquire one or two skills before moving on to the next set of development needs.

Question 3: Do leaders have plans in place for changing targeted behaviors? Figure 2.3 indicates that acquiring new knowledge and skills is the next step in the development pipeline. For leaders, this means creating a written **development plan** that capitalizes on available books, seminars, college courses, e-learning modules, and so forth to acquire the knowledge underlying a particular development need (see Figure 2.4). For example, you can either learn how to delegate through the school of hard knocks or take a seminar to learn the best delegation skills. As we will see, knowledge alone is not enough to develop a new skill, but relevant books and courses can accelerate the learning process.[44] In addition, it is important not to underestimate the power of a written development plan. Leaders (and followers) who have a written plan seem more likely to keep development on their radar screens and take the actions necessary to acquire new skills.

Question 4: Do leaders have opportunities to practice new skills? Taking courses and reading books are good ways for leaders to acquire foundational knowledge, but new skills will be acquired only when they are practiced on the job. Just as surgeons can read about and watch a surgery but will perfect a surgical technique only through repeated practice, so too

The more you crash, the more you learn.

David B. Peterson, Personnel Decisions International

The only thing more painful than learning from experience is not learning from experience.

Archibald MacLeish, Librarian of Congress

FIGURE 2.4
Sample Individual Development Plan

Source: G. J. Curphy, *Personal Insights and Development Planning Training Manual* (North Oaks, MN: Curphy Consulting Corporation, 2007).

Individual Development Plan (IDP)

Name: Mark McMurray   **Supervisor: Steve Tolley**   **Planning Period: Apr-Dec 2008**

Development Goals	Action Plans – Developmental Activities & Resources (What, Who & How)	Time Line (Target Dates)	Criteria for Success (What will successful outcomes be?)
• Control reactions in stressful situations.	1. Set up a regular exercise routine (at least 5 times per week).	NLT 30 April 2008	Boss does not receive any reports of emotional outbursts from now until Dec 2008.
	2. Exercise at least 5 times per week for at least 45 minutes.	Review each week until end of year	
	3. Identify triggers and situations most likely to cause me to lose my temper.	NLT 30 April 2008	Higher manager ratings on end of year employee survey.
	4. Work with Steve Tolley to develop strategies to either avoid or cope with stressful situations.	Begin 30 April 2008	
• Develop more patience when dealing with others.	1. Identify those people or situations that cause me to lose patience.	NLT 15 May 2008	Be viewed as approachable and responsive by all staff – Manager, Peers, and Associates.
	2. Develop listening skills through consistent practice. Work with peers and direct reports to practice and demonstrate skills.	Begin 15 May 2008	Have a better understanding of key issues, role responsibilities, and resulting actions. As a result, achieve better results on the job.
	a) Wait my turn in conversation: work on not interrupting conversations.		
	b) Take notes in meetings to capture key messages and refer back to notes later.	Begin 15 May 2008	Higher manager ratings on end of year employee survey.
	c) Practice asking clarifying questions to probe issues and gain full understanding.		
	3. Engage in two-way dialogue on a consistent basis. End conversations with a clear understanding of the purpose, discussion points, and resulting action items.		
• Improve team building skills.	1. Work with key direct reports to develop a common set of assumptions, vision, and goals for the team.	30 May 2008	Team assumptions, vision, and goals submitted to Steve Tolley for approval.
	2. Work with Steve Tolley to review and upgrade team bench strength in light of team goals.	30 June 2008	Team consists of only A and B players as reviewed with Steve Tolley.
	3. Work with team to develop common meeting, communication, decision-making, and accountability norms.	30 July 2008	New norms written up, sent to all team members, and reviewed on a regular basis with the team.
	4. Work with Steve Tolley to develop strategies for motivating team members or acquiring the resources needed to achieve team goals.	30 July 2008	
	5. Review progress on team goals with team members and Steve Tolley.	Monthly	Team results.

will leaders acquire needed skills only if they practice them on the job. Therefore, good development plans use on-the-job experiences to hone needed leadership skills. Peterson maintains that most leadership positions offer ample opportunities to develop new skills, provided that leaders leverage all the experiences available to them. These on-the-job activities are so important to development that 70 to 80 percent of the action steps in a development plan should be job related.

Question 5: Are leaders held accountable for changing targeted behaviors? The last step in acquiring new skills is accountability, and there are several ways to make this happen with a development plan. One way to build in accountability is to have different people provide ongoing feedback on the action steps taken to develop a skill. For example, leaders could ask for feedback from a peer or direct report on their listening skills immediately after staff meetings. Another way to build accountability is to periodically review progress on development plans with the boss. This way the boss can look for opportunities to help the leader further practice developing skills and determine when it is time to add new development needs to the plan.

Development planning is more than a plan—it is really a process. Good development plans are constantly being revised as new skills are learned or new opportunities to develop skills become available. Leaders who take the time to write out and execute best-practice development plans usually report the most improvement in later 360-degree feedback ratings. Development planning provides a methodology for leaders to improve their behavior, and much of this development can occur as they go about their daily work activities.

Coaching

Development plans tend to be self-focused; leaders and followers use them as a road map for changing their own behaviors. When trying to change the behavior of followers, however, leaders can often do more than review followers' development plans or provide ongoing feedback. The next step in followers' development often involves coaching. Coaching is a key leadership skill that can help leaders improve the bench strength of the group, which in turn should help the group to accomplish its goals. Because of its role in development, coaching can also help to retain high-quality followers.[45,46] Because of these outcomes, coaching is a popular topic these days, but it is also frequently misunderstood.

Coaching is the "process of equipping people with the tools, knowledge, and opportunities they need to develop and become more successful."[47] In general, there are two types of coaching: informal and formal. **Informal coaching** takes place whenever a leader helps followers to change their behaviors. According to Peterson and Hicks, the best informal coaching generally consists of five steps[48] (see Table 2.1). In *forging a partnership*, leaders build a trusting relationship with their followers, identify followers' career goals and motivators, and learn how their followers view the organization and their situation.

The key question to be answered in this first step of coaching is "development for what?" Where do the followers want to go with their careers? Why do they want to go there? The answers to these questions help create

I really wanted to show people you can win all kinds of ways. I always coached the way I wanted to be coached. I know Lovie [Smith] has done the same thing. For guys to have success where it maybe goes against the grain, against the culture . . . I know I probably didn't get a couple of jobs in my career because people could not see my personality or the way I was going to do it . . . For your faith to be more important than your job, your family to be more important than your job . . . We all know that's the way it should be, but we're afraid to say that sometimes. Lovie's not afraid to say it and I'm not afraid to say it.

**Tony Dungy,
Super Bowl
winning coach,
Indianapolis Colts**

The best executive is one who has enough sense to pick good men to do what he wants done, and the self-restraint to keep from meddling while they do it.

**Theodore
Roosevelt, U.S.
president**

TABLE 2.1
The Five Steps of Informal Coaching

Source: D. B. Peterson and M. D. Hicks, *Leader as Coach: Strategies for Coaching and Developing Others* (Minneapolis, MN: Personnel Decisions International, 1996).

Forge a partnership: Coaching works only if there is a trusting relationship between the leader and his or her followers. In this step leaders also determine what drives their followers and where they want to go with their careers.

Inspire commitment: In this step leaders help followers determine which skills or behaviors will have the biggest payoff if developed. Usually this step involves reviewing the results of performance appraisals, 360-degree feedback, values, personality assessment reports, and so on.

Grow skills: Leaders work with followers to build development plans that capitalize on on-the-job experiences and create coaching plans to support their followers' development.

Promote persistence: Leaders meet periodically with followers to provide feedback, help followers keep development on their radar screens, and provide followers with new tasks or projects to develop needed skills.

Shape the environment: Leaders need to periodically review how they are role-modeling development and what they are doing to foster development in the workplace. Because most people want to be successful, doing this step well will help attract and retain followers to the work group.

a target or end goal as well as a personal payoff for development. Nevertheless, if a leader fails to build a relationship based on mutual trust with a follower, chances are the follower will not heed the leader's guidance and advice. Therefore, it is important that coaches also *determine the level of mutual trust,* and then improve the relationship if necessary before targeting development needs or providing feedback and advice. Too many inexperienced coaches either fail to build trust or take the relationship for granted, with the long-term result being little, if any, behavioral change, and a frustrated leader and follower.

Once career goals have been identified and a solid, trusting relationship has been built, leaders then need to *inspire commitment.* In this step, leaders work closely with followers to gather and analyze data to determine development needs. A leader and a follower may review appraisals of past performance, feedback from peers or former bosses, project reports, 360-degree feedback reports, and any organizational standards that pertain to the follower's career goals. By reviewing these data, the leader and the follower should be able to identify and prioritize those development needs most closely aligned with career goals.

The next step in the coaching process involves *growing skills.* Followers use their prioritized development needs to create development plans, and leaders in turn develop a **coaching plan** that spells out precisely what they will do to support the followers' development plans. Leaders and followers then review and discuss the development and coaching plans, make necessary adjustments, and execute the plans.

Just because a plan is developed does not mean it will be executed flawlessly. Learning often is a series of fits and starts, and sometimes followers either get distracted by operational requirements or get into developmental ruts. In the step called *promote persistence,* leaders help followers to manage the mundane, day-to-day aspects of development. Leaders can help followers refocus on their development by capitalizing on opportunities to give followers relevant, on-the-spot feedback. Once the new behavior has been practiced a number of times and becomes part of the follower's behavioral repertoire, leaders help followers *transfer the skills to new environments* by applying the skills in new settings and revising their development plans. In this step, leaders need to also ask themselves how they are role-modeling development and whether they are creating an environment that fosters individual development.

Tony Dungy

PROFILES IN LEADERSHIP 2.3

Now retired from coaching, Anthony Kevin "Tony" Dungy was the head coach of the Indianapolis Colts in 2007 when they won the Super Bowl. Dungy grew up in Michigan and played football for the University of Minnesota. Starting as a freshman at the quarterback position, Dungy set a number of school records for passing attempts, completions, passing yards, and passing touchdowns. Upon graduation Dungy played two years as a backup safety for the Pittsburgh Steelers (when they won the 1978 Super Bowl) and a year for the San Francisco 49ers. In his fourth NFL year Dungy was traded and subsequently cut from the New York Giants; he then took a job at the University of Minnesota as an assistant coach. He returned to the NFL as an assistant coach for the Pittsburgh Steelers. He worked for 13 years as a defensive backs coach and defensive coordinator for the Pittsburgh Steelers, Kansas City Chiefs, and Minnesota Vikings before taking over the head coaching position for the Tampa Bay Buccaneers in 1995. Under Dungy's leadership the Buccaneers went to the National Football League playoffs four times. But offensive woes during the playoffs caused the Buccaneer management to lose faith in Dungy, and they eventually let him go in 2001.

In early 2002 Dungy was hired as the head coach of the Indianapolis Colts, a team with a potent offense but poor defense. Dungy spent the next five years retooling the team's defense, and as a result his team had one of the best winning records in the NFL for those five years. Like his Tampa Bay team, the Colts were highly successful but regularly faltered in the playoffs until they beat the Chicago Bears 29–17 in Super Bowl XLI.

Dungy's coaching philosophy is quite different than other NFL head coaches. Rather than getting up early to review game films and leading practices by yelling and intimidation, Dungy believes good coaches are essentially teachers that do not belittle or scream at players. He also believes faith and family take priority over football, and he is active in such charitable programs as Big Brothers/Big Sisters, the Boys and Girls Club, and the Prison Ministry. Dungy's religious convictions are so strong that he once considered going into the prison ministry instead of coaching. Not only has Dungy been able to create a football dynasty in Indiana, he has also extended his reach in the NFL by having four of his assistant coaches move into head coaching positions with other NFL teams. As a matter of fact, Lovie Smith, the head coach of the Chicago Bears in Super Bowl XLI, was one of Dungy's former assistant coaches and subscribes to the same coaching philosophy.

Do you suspect that Dungy's and Smith's coaching philosophies are similar to those of most NFL coaches or different from them? If you think they're different, do you believe other coaches might try to emulate them based on their success?

Several points about informal coaching are worth additional comment. First, the five-step process identified by Peterson and Hicks can be used by leadership practitioners to diagnose why behavioral change is *not* occurring and what can be done about it. For example, followers may not be developing new skills because they do not trust their leader, the skills have not been clearly identified or are not important to them, or they do not have a plan to acquire these skills. Second, informal coaching can and does occur anywhere in the organization. Senior executives can use this model to develop their staffs, peers can use it to help each other, and so forth. Third, this process is just as effective for high-performing followers as it is for low-performing followers. Leadership practitioners have a tendency to forget to coach their solid or top followers, yet these individuals are often making the greatest contributions to team or organizational success. Moreover, research has shown that the top performers in a job often produce 20–50 percent more than the average performer, depending on the complexity of the job.[49] So if leaders would focus on moving their solid performers into the highest-performing ranks and making their top performers even better, chances are their teams might be substantially more effective than if they focused only on coaching those doing most poorly (see Figure 2.5).

Fourth, both "remote" coaching of people and coaching of individuals from other cultures can be particularly difficult.[50,51] It is more difficult for leaders to build trusting relationships with followers when they are physically separated by great distances. The same may be true with followers from other cultures—what may be important to, say, a Kenyan follower and how this person views the world may be very different from what his or her Dutch or Singaporean leader believes.

The kinds of behaviors that need to be developed can also vary considerably by culture. For example, one senior executive for a high-tech firm was coaching one of his Japanese direct reports on how to give better presentations to superiors. The follower's style was formal, stiff, and somewhat wooden, and the leader wanted the follower to add some humor and informality to his presentations. However, the follower said that by doing so he would lose the respect of his Japanese colleagues, so his commitment to this change was understandably low. What was agreed upon was that his style was effective in Japan but that it needed to change when he was giving presentations in the United States.

Informal coaching can help groups succeed as well as reduce turnover among employees, but what does it take to be a good informal coach? Research by Wenzel showed that the most effective informal coaches had a unique combination of leadership traits and skills. Leaders with higher levels of intelligence, dominance, and agreeableness were often more effective as coaches than those with lower scores. These leadership traits were the foundation for the relationship building, listening, assertiveness, and feedback skills associated with effective informal coaches. Good

FIGURE 2.5
What Were the Most Useful Factors in the Coaching You Received?

Source: "The Business Leader as Development Coach," *PDI Portfolio,* Winter 1996, p. 6.

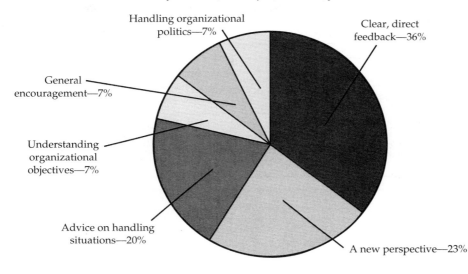

Handling organizational politics—7%

Clear, direct feedback—36%

General encouragement—7%

Understanding organizational objectives—7%

Advice on handling situations—20%

A new perspective—23%

informal coaches use these traits and skills to build trusting relationships with their followers, build best-practice coaching and development plans, and deliver tough and honest feedback when necessary.[52]

Most people are familiar with the idea of a personal fitness trainer—a person who helps design a fitness program tailored to a specific individual's needs and goals. **Formal coaching** programs provide a similar kind of service for executives and managers in leadership positions. Approximately 65 percent of the Global 1,000 companies use some form of formal coaching.[53] Formal coaching programs are individualized by their nature, but several common features deserve mention. There is a one-on-one relationship between the manager and the coach (that is, an internal or external consultant) that lasts from six months to more than a year. The process usually begins with the manager's completion of extensive tests of personality, intelligence, interests, and value; 360-degree feedback instruments; and interviews by the coach of other individuals in the manager's world of work. As the result of the assessment phase of this process, both the manager and the coach have a clear picture of development needs. The coach and the manager then meet regularly (roughly monthly) to review the results of the feedback instruments and work on building skills and practicing target behaviors. Role plays and videotape are used extensively during these sessions, and coaches provide immediate feedback to clients practicing new behaviors in realistic work situations. Another valuable outcome of coaching programs can involve clarification of

FIGURE 2.6
The Power of Coaching

Source: D. B. Peterson, *Individual Coaching Services: Coaching That Makes a Difference* (Minneapolis, MN: Personnel Decisions International, 1999).

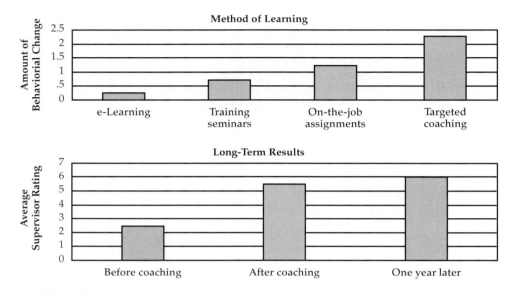

No man is so foolish but he may sometimes give another good counsel, and no man so wise that he may not easily err if he takes no other counsel than his own. He that is taught only by himself has a fool for a master.

Ben Jonson

Parents are the first leadership trainers in life.

Bruce Avolio, leadership researcher

managers' values, identification of discrepancies between their espoused values and their actual behaviors, and devising strategies to better align their behaviors with their values.

A formal coaching program can cost more than $100,000, and it is reasonable to ask if this money is well spent. A solid body of research shows that well-designed and well-executed coaching programs do in fact change behavior if, as Highlight 2.8 points out, certain conditions are met.[54,55,56,57] Figure 2.6 shows that coaching may be more effective at changing behavior than more traditional learning and training approaches. Moreover, the behavioral changes appear to be in place one year after the termination of a coaching program, indicating permanent behavioral change.[58] Such changes can be particularly important if the person making them—that is, the leader being coached—is highly placed or in a very responsible position. Most coaching candidates have hundreds, if not thousands, of subordinates, and usually oversee multimillion- or multibillion-dollar budgets. Thus the money spent on a coaching program can be relatively small in comparison to the budgets and resources the candidates control and as a result turn out to have a good return on investment.

Mentoring

In an organization, you also can gain valuable perspectives and insights through close association with an experienced person willing to take you

Some Critical Lessons Learned from Formal Coaching

HIGHLIGHT 2.8

1. **The person being coached must want to change.** It is difficult to get someone to change their behavior unless they want to change. Coaches need to ensure that coachees clearly understand the benefits of changing their behavior and the consequences if they do not change. Often it is much easier to get people to change when coaches link the new behaviors to coachees' values and career goals.

2. **Assessments are important.** Formal assessments involving personality, values, mental abilities, and multirater feedback are essential to understanding what behaviors coachees need to change, what is driving these needed changes, and how easy or difficult it will be to change targeted behaviors.

3. **Some behaviors cannot be changed.** Some behaviors are so ingrained or unethical that the best option may be termination. For example, one of the authors was asked to coach a married vice president who got two of his executive assistants pregnant in less than a year. Given that the coach was not an expert in birth control, the coach turned down the engagement.

4. **Practice is critical.** Good coaches not only discuss what needs to change, but also make coachees practice targeted behaviors. Often the initial practice takes place during coaching sessions, where the coach may play the role of another party and give the coachee feedback and suggestions for improvement. These practices are then extended to work, where the coachee must use these newly acquired behaviors in real-world situations.

5. **There is no substitute for accountability.** Superiors must be kept in the loop about coachees' progress and must hold them accountable for on-the-job changes. If coaches are working with potential derailment candidates, superiors must be willing to let coachees go if they do not make needed changes. Although fear and threats are not the best way to get people to change, some derailment candidates are in so much denial about their problems that it is only by fear of losing their high-status jobs that they are motivated to change.

As you read through this list of coaching "best practices," how might you distinguish good coaching from giving advice?

Sources: S. Berglas, "The Very Real Dangers of Executive Coaching," *Harvard Business Review,* June 2002, pp. 86–93; G. J. Curphy, "What Role Should I/O Psychologists Play in Executive Education?" in *Models of Executive Education,* R. T. Hogan (chair), presentation at the 17th Annual Society for Industrial and Organizational Psychology, Toronto, Canada, April 2002.

under her or his wing. Such an individual is often called a **mentor,** after the character in Greek mythology whom Odysseus trusted to run his household and see to his son's education when Odysseus went off to fight the Trojans. Now, 3,000 years later, Mentor's name is used to describe the process by which an older and more experienced person helps to socialize and encourage younger organizational colleagues.[59]

Mentoring is a personal relationship in which a more experienced mentor (usually someone two to four levels higher in an organization) acts as a guide, role model, and sponsor of a less experienced protégé. Mentors provide protégés with knowledge, advice, challenge, counsel, and support about career opportunities, organizational strategy and policy, office politics, and so forth. Although mentoring has a strong developmental component, it is not the same as coaching. One key difference is that mentoring may not target specific development needs. Protégés often meet with their mentors to get a different perspective on the organization or for advice on potential committee and task force assignments or promotion opportunities. Another difference is that this guidance is not coming from the protégé's immediate supervisor, but rather from someone several leadership levels higher in the organization. Protégés often do receive informal coaching from their bosses but may be more apt to seek career guidance and personal advice from their mentors. Another difference is that the mentor may not even be part of the organization. A mentor may have retired from the organization or may have been someone for whom the protégé worked a number of years earlier.

As in coaching, there are both formal and informal mentoring programs. *Informal mentoring* occurs when a protégé and mentor build a long-term relationship based on friendship, similar interests, and mutual respect. These relationships often begin with the protégé working in some part of the mentor's organization or on a high-visibility project for the mentor. *Formal mentoring* programs occur when the organization assigns a relatively inexperienced but high-potential leader to one of the top executives in the company. The protégé and mentor get together on a regular basis so the protégé can gain exposure and learn more about how decisions are made at the top of the organization. Often organizations implement formal mentoring programs to accelerate the development of female or minority protégés.[60,61,62]

Mentoring is quite prevalent in many organizations today. Researchers reported that 74 percent of the noncommissioned officers and officers in the U.S. Army had mentors and 67 percent of all U.S. Navy admirals had mentors sometime in their careers. Moreover, many admirals reported having an average of 3.5 mentors by the time they retired.[63,64,65] Other researchers have reported positive relationships between mentoring, personal learning, career satisfaction, pay, promotions, and retention.[66,67,68,69,70] But some of this research also found that formal mentoring programs were better than no mentoring programs but less effective than informal mentoring for protégé compensation and promotion.[71,72,73] The reason for these diminished results may be that most formal mentoring programs have a difficult time replicating the strong emotional bonds found in informal programs. In addition, most formal mentoring programs last only a year, whereas many informal mentoring relationships can last a lifetime (see Highlight 2.9).

Thomas examined the role mentoring played in the careers of minority leaders. He reported that minority leaders at the top of their organizations often had two key qualities. First, successful minority executives were concerned with getting the right experiences and developing the right foundation of leadership skills when they first joined the organization.

Overview of a Formal Mentoring Program

HIGHLIGHT 2.9

Menttium Corporation specializes in the development and delivery of formal mentoring programs for high-potential females. Most of the protégés have 6–20 years of professional experience, are often in midlevel management roles, and are matched with mentors from other organizations at the vice president level or higher. The Menttium 100 program is one year long and begins with a two-day kickoff conference. During this conference mentors and protégés meet each other, get an overview of the program, learn about important leadership and business topics, and network with other mentors and protégés. Over the course of the year mentors and protégés get together at least once a month, and protégés attend quarterly business education and networking events. The Ment-

tium 100 program seems to have a very positive impact on both mentors and protégés. For example:

- 75 percent of protégés said the program helped improve their leadership capabilities.

- 77 percent of protégés are more likely to stay with their parent companies.

- 80 percent of protégés believe their companies have benefited by their attending the program.

Although these results are promising, Menttium is currently engaged in a more rigorous, long-term study to assess the overall impact of its program on both mentors and protégés.

Source: Menttium, *Menttium 100: Cross-Company Mentoring for High Potential Women* (Minneapolis, MN: The Menttium Corporation, 2006).

Their focus was more on personal growth at each leadership level than with titles and rewards. Second, they had an extensive set of mentors and corporate sponsors who provided guidance and support over their careers. These mentors and sponsors helped the executives to develop the "three Cs" critical to advancement: confidence, competence, and credibility. Thomas also stated that the most successful white mentor–minority protégé relationships recognized that race was a potential barrier to advancement but were still able to bring up and work through touchy issues. Less successful white mentor–minority protégé relationships engaged in "protective hesitation," in which race or sensitive issues were avoided, ignored, or discounted.[74] Because of the benefits of informal mentoring, leadership practitioners should look for opportunities to build mentoring relationships with senior leaders whenever possible. However, it is important to realize that protégés cannot make these relationships happen by themselves. In many cases mentors seek out protégés, or mentors and protégés seek out each other to build relationships. But leaders and leaders-to-be can do a couple of things to improve the odds of finding a mentor. The first step is to do one's current job extremely well. Mentors are always looking for talent, and they are unlikely to take someone under their wing who appears unmotivated or incompetent. The second step is to look for opportunities to gain visibility and build social relationships with potential mentors. Working on a key task force, doing presentations for the executive committee, or signing up for community activities sponsored by a top executive are just a few pathways one could take to gain the attention of potential mentors.

Building Your Own Leadership Self-Image

This chapter has explored various aspects of how leadership develops, but we must acknowledge that not everyone *wants* to be a leader or believes he or she can be. John Gardner has argued that many of our best and brightest young people actually have been immunized against, and dissuaded from, seeking leadership opportunities and responsibilities.[75] Other young people, even if they want to be leaders, may not believe they have what it takes. Both groups, we believe, are selling themselves short.

For those who merely want to avoid the responsibilities of leadership, we encourage an openness of mind about leadership's importance and pervasiveness. We hope this book offers ways of thinking about leadership that make it at once more immediate, more relevant, and more interesting than it may have seemed before. For others, we encourage flexibility in self-image. Do not stay out of the leadership arena based on some self-defeating generalization such as "I am not the leader type." Experiment and take a few risks with different leadership roles. This will help you appreciate new facets of yourself as well as broaden your leadership self-image.

Summary

This chapter reviewed several major points regarding how leadership can be developed through both formal education and experience. One way to get more out of your leadership courses and experiences is through the application of the action–observation–reflection model. This model provides a framework for better understanding of leadership situations. In addition, being aware of the role perception plays in leadership development is important because it affects what you observe, how you interpret your observations, and what actions you take as a leader. Finally, remember that both education and experience can contribute to your development as a leader by enhancing your ability to reflect on and analyze leadership situations. Exposure to formal leadership education programs can help you develop multiple perspectives to analyze leadership situations, and the people you work with and the task itself can also provide you with insights on how to be a better leader. However, what you gain from any leadership program or experience is a function of what you make of it. Successful leaders are those who have "an extraordinary tenacity in extracting something worthwhile from their experience and in seeking experiences rich in opportunities for growth."[76] If you want to become a better leader, you must seek challenges and try to get all you can from any leadership situation or opportunity.

The chapter also examined several specific ways of changing behavior and developing leadership. For most people, behavior change efforts will be most successful if some formal system or process of behavioral change is put into place; these systems include development planning, informal and formal coaching programs, and mentorships. Development planning is the process of pinpointing development needs, creating development plans, implementing plans, and reflecting on and revising plans regularly. Good development plans focus on one or two development needs, capitalize upon on-the-job experiences, and specify sources of feedback. Organizations with formal development systems are likely to realize greater behavioral changes from more managers than organizations having no system or only an informal one.

Leaders can create development plans for themselves, and they can also help their followers with behavioral change through coaching or mentoring programs. Informal coaching programs often consist of a series of steps designed to create permanent behavioral changes in followers, and both leaders and followers play active roles in informal coaching programs. Formal coaching typically involves a formal assessment process and a series of one-on-one coaching sessions over a 6- to 12-month period. These sessions target specific development needs and capitalize on practice and feedback to acquire needed skills. Mentoring programs have many of the same objectives as coaching programs but take place between an individual (the protégé) and a leader several levels higher in the organization (the mentor).

Key Terms

action–observation–reflection model, *47*
spiral of experience, *47*
perceptual set, *49*
attribution, *51*
fundamental attribution error, *51*
self-serving bias, *51*
actor/observer difference, *51*
self-fulfilling prophecy, *53*

single-loop learning, *55*
double-loop learning, *56*
service learning, *60*
individualized feedback, *61*
case studies, *61*
role playing, *61*
simulations, *61*
games, *61*
in-basket exercises, *63*
action learning, *64*

training programs, *64*
development plan, *67*
development planning, *69*
coaching, *69*
informal coaching, *69*
coaching plan, *71*
formal coaching, *73*
mentor, *75*
mentoring, *75*

Questions

1. Not all effective leaders seem to be reflective by nature. How do you reconcile that with the concept of the spiral of experience and its role in leadership development?

2. Explain how you can use knowledge about each of the following to enrich the benefits of your own present leadership experiences:

    a. The action–observation–reflection model.

    b. The people you interact and work with.

    c. The activities you're involved in.

3. Using the role of teacher as a specific instance of leadership, discuss how a teacher's perceptual set, expectations of students, and attributions may affect student motivation and performance. Do you think some teachers could become more effective by becoming more aware of these processes? Would that be true for leaders in general?

4. If you were to design the perfect leadership development experience for yourself, how would you do so and what would it include? How would you know whether it was effective?

5. Do you think people have a need for growth and development?

6. One important aspect of learning from experience is observing the consequences of one's actions. Sometimes, however, the most significant consequences of a leader's actions do not occur for several years (for example, the ultimate impact of certain personnel decisions or a strategic decision to change a product line). Is there any way individuals can learn from the consequences of those actions in a way to modify their behavior? If consequences are so delayed, is there a danger they might draw the wrong lessons from their experiences?

7. What would a development plan for student leaders look like? How could you capitalize on school experiences as part of a development plan?

8. What would a leadership coaching or mentoring program for students look like? How could you tell whether the program worked?

Activities

1. Divide yourselves into groups, and in each group contrast what attributions you might make about the leadership style of two different individuals. All you know about them is the following:

	Person A	Person B
Favorite TV Show	*60 Minutes*	*Survivor*
Car	Ford Mustang	Volkswagen Beetle
Favorite Sport	American football	Mountain biking
Political Leaning	Conservative Republican	Liberal Democrat
Favorite Music	Country and western	New age

2. Read the development planning material in Chapter 11 of this book. Complete a GAPS analysis and create a development plan for yourself. Share your development plan with someone else in your class. Check with your partner in two to four weeks to review progress on your plans.

Minicase

Developing Leaders at UPS

UPS is the nation's fourth-largest employer with 357,000 employees worldwide and operations in more than 200 countries. UPS is consistently recognized as one of the "top companies to work for" and was recently recognized by *Fortune* as one of the 50 best companies for minorities. A major reason for UPS's success is the company's commitment to its employees. UPS understands the importance of providing both education and experience for its next generation of leaders—spending $300 million annually on education programs for employees and encouraging promotion from within. All employees are offered equal opportunities to build the skills and knowledge they need to succeed. A perfect example of this is Jovita Carranza.

Jovita Carranza joined UPS in 1976 as a part-time clerk in Los Angeles. Carranza demonstrated a strong work ethic and a commitment to UPS, and UPS rewarded her with opportunities—opportunities Carranza was not shy about taking advantage of. By 1985 Carranza was the workforce planning manager in metropolitan Los Angeles. By 1987 she was district human resources manager based in Central Texas. By 1990 she had accepted a move to district human resources manager in Illinois. She received her first operations assignment, as division manager for hub, package, and feeder operations, in Illinois in 1991. Two years later, she said yes to becoming district operations manager in Miami. In 1996 she accepted the same role in Wisconsin. By 1999 Carranza's progressive successes led UPS to promote her to president of the Americas Region. From there she moved into her current position as vice president of UPS Air Operations, based in Louisville, Kentucky.

The $1.1 billion air hub she currently oversees sprawls across the equivalent of more than 80 football fields. It can handle 304,000 packages an hour, its computers process nearly 1 million transactions per minute, and it serves as the lynchpin for the $33 billion business that has become the world's largest package delivery company.

Carranza attributes much of her success to her eagerness to take on new challenges: "The one error that people make early on in their careers is that they're very selective about opportunities so they avoid some, prefer others," she says. "I always accepted all opportunities that presented themselves because from each one you can learn something, and they serve as a platform for future endeavors."

It has also been important, she says, to surround herself with capable, skilled employees who are loyal to the company and committed to results. After nearly 30 years with UPS, Carranza says teamwork, interaction, and staff development are the achievements of which she is proudest: "Because that takes focus, determination, and sincerity to perpetuate the UPS culture and enhance it through people."

Carranza's corporate achievements, determination, drive, innovation, and leadership in business have earned her the distinction of being named *Hispanic Business Magazine*'s Woman of the Year. She credits her parents, both of Mexican descent, with teaching her "the importance of being committed, of working hard, and doing so with a positive outlook"—principles she says continue to guide her personal and professional life. These principles mirror those of the company whose corporate ladder she has climbed nonstop, an organization she says values diversity and encourages quality, integrity, commitment, fairness, loyalty, and social responsibility.

Among Carranza's words of wisdom: "Sit back and listen and observe," she says. "You learn more by not speaking. Intelligent people learn from their own experiences; with wisdom, you learn from other people's mistakes. I'm very methodical about that."

1. What are the major skills Jovita Carranza has demonstrated in her career at UPS that have made her a successful leader?

2. Consider the spiral of experience that Jovita Carranza has traveled. How has her experience affected her ability as a leader?

3. Take a look at the characteristics of successful leaders in Highlight 2.1. How many of these are demonstrated by Jovita Carranza?

Sources: http://www.ups.com; http://www.hispaniconline.com/vista/febhisp.htm; http://www.hispanicbusiness.com/news/newsbyid.asp?id=15535&page=3; http://www.socialfunds.com/csr/profile.cgi/1841.html.

End Notes

1. D.V. Day, "Leadership Development: A Review in Context," *Leadership Quarterly* 11, no. 4 (2000), pp. 581–613.

2. P. Bernthal and R. Wellins, "Trends in Leader Development and Succession," *Human Resource Planning* 29, no. 2 (2006), pp. 31–40.

3. M. McCall, "Recasting Leadership Development," *Industrial and Organizational Psychology* 3 (2010), pp. 3–19.

4. M. W. McCall Jr., M. M. Lombardo, and A. M. Morrison, *The Lessons of Experience: How Successful Executives Develop on the Job* (Lexington, MA: Lexington Books, 1988), p. 122.

5. D. Kolb, *Experiential Learning: Experience as the Source of Learning and Development* (Englewood Cliffs, NJ: Prentice-Hall, 1983).

6 C. Powell, with Joe Pirsico, *My American Journey* (New York: Random House, 1995), p. 109.

7. Ibid.

8. J. Reasonand K. Mycielska, *Absent-Minded? The Psychology of Mental Lapses and Everyday Errors* (Englewood Cliffs, NJ: Prentice Hall, 1982), p. 183.

9. L. Ross, "The Intuitive Psychologist and His Shortcomings: Distortions in the Attribution Process," in *Advances in Experimental Social Psychology*, vol. 10, ed. L. Berkowitz (New York: Academic Press, 1977), pp. 173–220.

10. D. T. Millerand M. Ross, "Self-Serving Biases in the Attribution of Causality: Fact or Fiction?" *Psychological Bulletin* 82 (1975), pp. 213–25.

11. E. E. Jones and R. E. Nisbett, "The Actor and the Observer: Divergent Perceptions of the Causes of Behavior," in *Attribution: Perceiving the Causes of Behavior*, eds. E. E. Jones, D. E. Kanouse, H. H. Kelley, R. E. Nisbett, S. Valins, and B. Weiner (Morristown, NJ: General Learning Press, 1972).

12. S. G. Green and T. R. Mitchell, "Attributional Processes of Leaders in Leader–Member Interactions," *Organizational Behavior and Human Performances* 23 (1979), pp. 429–58.

13. T. R. Mitchell, S. G. Green, and R. E. Wood, "An Attributional Model of Leadership and the Poor Performing Subordinate: Development and Validation," in *Research in Organizational Behavior*, eds. B. M. Staw and L. L. Cummings (Greenwich, CN: JAI, 1981), pp. 197–234.

14. T. R. Mitchelland R. E. Wood, "Supervisorsí Responses to Subordinate Poor Performance: A Test of an Attributional Model," *Organizational Behavior and Human Performance* 25 (1980), pp. 123–38.

15. E. E. Jones, "Interpreting Interpersonal Behavior: The Effects of Expectancies," *Science* 234, no. 3 (October 1986), pp. 41–46.

16. D. Eden and A. B. Shani, "Pygmalion Goes to Boot Camp: Expectancy, Leadership, and Trainee Performance," *Journal of Applied Psychology* 67 (1982), pp. 194–99.

17. K. D. Roglio and G. Light, "Executive MBA Programs: The Development of the Reflective Executive," *Academy of Management Learning & Education* 8, no. 2 (2009), pp. 156–73.

18. C. Argyris, *Increasing Leadership Effectiveness* (New York: John Wiley, 1976).

19. K. A. Bunkerand A. Webb, *Learning How to Learn from Experience: Impact of Stress and Coping*, Report No. 154 (Greensboro, NC: Center for Creative Leadership, 1992).

20. I. L. Janis, *Stress and Frustration* (New York: Harcourt Brace Jovanovich, 1971).

21. R. J. Grey and G. G. Gordon, "Risk-Taking Managers: Who Gets the Top Jobs?" *Management Review* 67 (1978), pp. 8–13.

22. D. C. Hambrick, "Environment, Strategy and Power within Top Management Teams," *Administrative Science Quarterly* 26 (1981), pp. 253–75.

23. G. Jennings, *The Mobile Manager* (New York: McGraw-Hill, 1971).

24. E. Schein, *Career Dynamics: Matching Individual and Organizational Needs* (Reading, MA: Addison-Wesley, 1978).

25. M. Csikszentmihalyi, *Flow: The Psychology of Optimal Experience* (New York: Harper & Row, 1990), p. 142.

26. R. T. Hogan and R. Warrenfelz, "Educating the Modern Manager," *Academy of Management Learning and Education* 2, no. 1 (2003), pp. 74–84.

27. R. E. Riggio, "Leadership Development: The Current State and Future Expectations," *Consulting Psychology Journal: Practice and Research* 60, no. 4 (2008), pp. 383–92.

28. R. E. Riggio, J. B. Ciulla, and G. J. Sorenson, "Leadership Education at the Undergraduate Level: A Liberal Arts Approach to Leadership Development," in S. E. Murphy and R. E. Riggio (eds.), *The Future of Leadership Development*, pp. 223–36 (Mahwah, NJ: Lawrence Erlbaum Associates).

29. Riggio, Ciulla, and Sorenson, "Leadership Education at the Undergraduate Level."

30. Riggio, Ciulla, and Sorenson, "Leadership Education at the Undergraduate Level."

31. J. Conger, "Can We Really Train Leadership?" *Strategy, Management, Competition,* Winter 1996, pp. 52–65.

32. M. Nevins and S. Stumpf, "21st-Century Leadership: Redefining Management Education," *Strategy, Management, Competition,* 3rd quarter 1999, pp. 41–51.

33. G. Hernez-Broomeand R. L. Hughes, "Leadership Development: Past, Present and Future," *Human Resource Planning* 27, no. 1 (2004), pp. 24–32.

34. J.A. Conger and G. Toegel. "Action Learning and Multirater Feedback: Pathways to Leadership Development?" in S.E. Murphy and R.E. Riggio (eds.), *The Future of Leadership Development*, pp. 107–125 (Mahwah, NJ: Lawrence Erlbaum Associates).

35. W. R. Miller, and S. Rollnick, *Motivational Interviewing: Preparing People to Change Addictive Behavior* (New York: Guilford Press, 1991).

36. J. Polivy and C. P. Herman, "If at First You Donít Succeed: False Hopes of Self-Change," *American Psychologist* 57, no. 9 (2002), pp. 677–89.

37. M. D. Peterson and M. D. Hicks, *Development FIRST: Strategies for Self-Development* (Minneapolis, MN: Personnel Decisions International, 1995).

38. J. F. Hazucha, S. A. Hezlett, and R. J. Schneider, "The Impact of 360-Degree Feedback on Management Skills Development," *Human Resource Management* 32 (1993), pp. 325–51.

39. C. D. McCauley, M. N. Ruderman, P. J. Ohlott, and J. E. Morrow, "Assessing the Developmental Components of Managerial Jobs," *Journal of Applied Psychology* 79, no. 4 (1994), pp. 544–60.

40. D. B. Peterson, and M. D. Hicks, *Leader as Coach: Strategies for Coaching and Developing Others* (Minneapolis, MN: Personnel Decisions International, 1996).

41. K. Behar, D. Arvidson, W. Omilusik, B. Ellsworth, and B. Morrow, *Developing Husky Oil Leaders: A Strategic Investment* (Calgary, Canada: Husky Energy, 2000).

42. D. B. Peterson, *The Science and Art of Self-Development.* Paper presented at the Arabian States Human Resource Management Society Annual Conference, Bahrain, October 2001.

43. G. J. Curphy, "Good Leadership is Hard to Find," *JobDig*, August 21–28, 2006, pp. 23–24.

44. W. Arthur, Jr., W. Bennett, Jr., P. S. Edens, and S. T. Bell. "Effectiveness of Training in Organizations: A Meta-analysis of Design and Evaluation Features." *Journal of Applied Psychology* 88 (2) (2003), pp. 234–45.

45. L. H. Wenzel, "Understanding Managerial Coaching: The Role of Manager Attributes and Skills in Effective Coaching." Unpublished doctoral dissertation, Colorado State University, 2000.

46. K. M. Wasylyshyn, B. Gronsky, and J. W. Hass, "Tigers, Stripes, and Behavior Change: Survey Results of a Commissioned Coaching Program," *Consulting Psychology Journal* 58, no. 2 (2006), pp. 65–81.

47. D.B. Peterson and M.D. Hicks. *Leader as Coach: Strategies for Coaching and Developing Others.* Minneapolis, MN: Personnel Decisions, International, 1996.

48. Ibid.

49. J. E. Hunter, F. L. Schmidt, and M. K. Judiesch, "Individual Differences in Output Variability as a Function of Job Complexity," *Journal of Applied Psychology* 74 (1990), pp. 28–42.

50. G. J. Curphy, *The Accelerated Coaching Program Training Manual* (North Oaks, MN: Curphy Consulting Corporation, 2003).

51. D. B. Peterson and M. D. Hicks, *Professional Coaching: State of the Art, State of the Practice* (Minneapolis, MN: Personnel Decisions International, 1998).

52. L. H. Wenzel, "Understanding Managerial Coaching: The Role of Manager Attributes and Skills in Effective Coaching." Unpublished doctoral dissertation, Colorado State University, 2000.

53. D. B. Peterson and M. D. Hicks, *Professional Coaching: State of the Art, State of the Practice* (Minneapolis, MN: Personnel Decisions International, 1998).

54. K. M. Wasylyshyn, B. Gronsky, and J. W. Hass, "Tigers, Stripes, and Behavior Change: Survey Results of a Commissioned Coaching Program," *Consulting Psychology Journal* 58, no. 2 (2006), pp. 65–81.

55. W.J.G. Evers, A. Brouwers, and W. Tomic. "A Quasi-Experimental Study on Management Coaching Effectiveness." *Consulting Psychology Journal* 58 no.3 (2006), pp. 174–182.

56. D.B. Peterson and J. Millier. "The Alchemy of Coaching: You're Good, Jennifer, But You Could Be Really Good." *Consulting Psychology Journal* 57 no.1 (2005), pp. 14–40.

57. S.V. Bowles and J.J. Picano. "Dimensions of Coaching Related to Productivity and Quality of Life." *Consulting Psychology Journal* 58 no.4 (2006), pp. 232–239.

58. Peterson, *Individual Coaching Services.*

59. J. A. Wilson and N. S. Elman, "Organizational Benefits of Mentoring," *Academy of Management Executive* 4 (1990), pp. 88–93.

60. Ragins, B. R., J. L. Cotton, and J. S. Miller. "Marginal Mentoring: The Effects of Types of Mentor, Quality of Relationship, and Program Design of Work and Career Attitudes." *Academy of Management Journal* 43, no. 6 (2000), pp. 1177–94.

61. Thomas, D. A. "The Truth about Mentoring Minorities: Race Matters." *Harvard Business Review,* April 2001, pp. 98–111.

62. Menttium. *Menttium 100: Cross-Company Mentoring for High Potential Women.* Minneapolis, MN: The Menttium Corporation, 2007.

63. A. G. Steinberg and D. M. Foley, "Mentoring in the Army: From Buzzword to Practice," *Military Psychology* 11, no. 4 (1999), pp. 365–80.

64. R. Lall, "Mentoring Experiences of Retired Navy Admirals," paper presented at Personnel Decisions International, Denver, CO, May 6, 1999.

65. S. C. De Janasz, S. E. Sullivan, and V. Whiting, "Mentor Networks and Career Success: Lessons for Turbulent Times," *Academy of Management Executive* 17, no. 3 (2003), pp. 78–88.

66. Menttium. *Menttium 100: Cross-Company Mentoring for High Potential Women.* Minneapolis, MN: The Menttium Corporation, 2007.

67. T.D. Allen, L. T. Eby, M. L. Poteet, E. Lentz, and L. Lima. "Career Benefits Associated with Mentoring for Protégés: A Meta-analysis." *Journal of Applied Psychology* 89 (1) (2004), pp. 127–36.

68. T.D. Allen, L. T. Eby, and E. Lentz. "The Relationship between Formal Mentoring Program Characteristics and Perceived Program Effectiveness." *Personnel Psychology* 59 (2006), pp. 125–53.

69. L.T. Eby and, M. Butts, A. Lockwood, and S. A. Simon. "Protégés' Negative Mentoring Experiences: Construct Development and Nomological Validation." *Personnel Psychology* 57 (2) (2004), pp. 411–48.

70. Abrahams, M. "Making Mentoring Pay." *Harvard Business Review*, June 2006, p. 21.

71. B.R. Ragins, J. L. Cotton, and J. S. Miller. "Marginal Mentoring: The Effects of Types of Mentor, Quality of Relationship, and Program Design of Work and Career Attitudes." *Academy of Management Journal* 43, no. 6 (2000), pp. 1177–94.

72. T.D Allen, L.T. Eby and E. Lentz. "Mentorship Behaviors and Mentorship Quality Associated with Formal Mentoring Programs: Closing the Gap between Research and Practice." *Journal of Applied Psychology* 91 (3) (2006), pp. 567–78.

73. T.D Allen, L.T. Eby and E. Lentz . "The Relationship between Formal Mentoring Program Characteristics and Perceived Program Effectiveness." *Personnel Psychology* 59 (2006), pp. 125–53.

74. D.A. Thomas. "The Truth about Mentoring Minorities: Race Matters." *Harvard Business Review,* April 2001, pp. 98–111.

75. J. W. Gardner, "The Antileadership Vaccine," essay in the Carnegie Corporation of New York annual report, 1965.

76. M. W. McCallJr., M. M. Lombardo, and A. M. Morrison, *The Lessons of Experience: How Successful Executives Develop on the Job* (Lexington, MA: Lexington Books, 1988).

Chapter 3

Skills for Developing Yourself as a Leader

One reason any person can improve his or her leadership effectiveness is that part of leadership involves skills, and skills can be practiced and developed. A further advantage of looking at leadership skills is that most people are less defensive about deficits in skills (which can be improved) than about suggested deficits in, say, personality. We will present a chapter about leadership skills following each of the four parts of the book, looking at skills that seem particularly relevant to various facets of our interactional framework. And because these skills chapters are quite different in purpose than the other chapters in the text, their format will be correspondingly different. Specifically, there will not be all the same closing sections found in the other chapters.

Not surprisingly, this first segment deals with some of the most fundamental, immediate, and yet in other ways most enduring challenges you will face as a leader. Key among these challenges is continuing to learn as a leader what you need to know now to be successful, and how to keep learning and developing throughout your life and career. The skills in this chapter will help in that effort. By the way, it might be useful to say more here about development planning, the last skill addressed in this chapter. Generally speaking, development planning would be considered an advanced leadership skill because it typically involves a leader developing her or his subordinates or followers. It's included with other skills in this introductory section so that you might think how to apply some of the ideas about development planning *to yourself*.

Here are the leadership skills we'll cover in this chapter:

- Your First 90 Days as a Leader
- Learning from Experience
- Building Technical Competence
- Building Effective Relationships with Superiors
- Building Effective Relationships with Peers
- Development Planning

Your First 90 Days as a Leader

People often find moving into a new leadership position to be a highly stressful work experience. Often these promotions involve relocations, working for new organizations and bosses, leading new teams, and being responsible for products or services that may be outside their immediate areas of expertise. Whether the move is from individual contributor to first-line supervisor or into senior executive positions, the stresses and strains of the first 90 days are both real and acute. Although the first three months give leaders unique opportunities to make smooth transitions, paint compelling pictures of the future, and drive organizational change, far too many new leaders stumble during this critical time period. This is unfortunate—these early activities often are instrumental to a leader's future success or failure. Many of these early mistakes are avoidable, and what follows is a roadmap for helping people make successful transitions into new leadership positions. It is important to note that the onboarding roadmap developed by Roellig and Curphy[1] is focused on external hires—those outside an organization who have been brought in to leadership positions. (See Figure 3.1.) Some of the steps in the onboarding roadmap can be ignored or need to be modified for individuals who have been promoted from within.

Before You Start: Do Your Homework

In all likelihood people wanting to move into a leadership role with another organization have already done a considerable amount of preparation for the interview process. Candidates should have read as much as

FIGURE 3.1
New Leader Onboarding Roadmap

Before You Start	The First Day	The First Two Weeks	The First Two Months	The Third Month
Prehire data gathering. Posthire activities.	Meet your boss. Meet your entire team.	Meet team members. Meet peers. Meet stars. Other meetings.	Obtain external perspectives. Strategy, structure, and staffing. Socialize decisions. Substantive issues. Get feedback.	Establish culture. Team off-site: Values. Strategy Ops rhythm. Improvement areas. Subteam analyses.

they can about the organization by reviewing its Web site, annual reports, press releases, and marketing literature. They should also use Facebook, LinkedIn, Plaxo, and other social networking sites to set up informational interviews with people inside the organization. These informational interviews will help candidates learn more about the organization's history and culture and provide additional insight about the vacant position. Sometime during the interview process candidates should also seek answers to the following five questions:

- Why is the organization looking for an outside hire for the position?
- What can make the function or team to be led more effective?
- What is currently working in the function or team to be led?
- What is currently not working in the function or team to be led?
- What about the function or team is keeping interviewers awake at night?

Once candidates have landed new positions, they should seek additional information about their new jobs as well as set up some of the activities that need to take place during their first two weeks at work. New hires should check with their bosses to see if they can get copies of the results or metrics pertaining to the group to be led, any presentations predecessors made about the group or department, budget information, contact information for their direct reports, and so forth. They should also ask their new bosses what they need to do to set up access cards and e-mail, office, and cell phone accounts, as being able to get into the facility and having functional computers and phones at the start. Prior to arrival, a new hire should also set up one-hour meetings with the boss and with the entire team on the first day and follow-up two- to three-hour one-on-one meetings with each team member during the first two weeks on the job.

The First Day: You Get Only One Chance to Make a First Impression

New leaders have two critical tasks the first day on the job: to meet their new boss and their new team. The first meeting should happen in the boss's office and be about an hour long. Here are some key topics to discuss in this meeting:

- Identifying the team's key objectives, metrics, and important projects.
- Understanding the boss's view of team strengths and weaknesses.
- Working through meeting schedules and communication styles. (How, when, and on what does the boss want to be kept informed?)
- Sharing plans for the day and the next several weeks.

New hires should end the discussion by arranging a follow-up meeting with their bosses to review progress and to ask whether weekly or monthly one-on-one meetings would be helpful.

New leaders should also meet with their entire teams the first day on the job. Depending on the size of the team, this meeting could be held in a small conference room or it could be in a large auditorium with Webcasts or conference calls to remote sites. It usually takes new leaders about an hour to share their backgrounds, the attributes and values they feel are important to success, expectations for themselves and employees, work habits and preferred ways of interacting, family and recreational activities, and what they plan on doing over the next few weeks. After sharing this information new leaders should ask team members whether they have any questions but should not expect many takers. Because team members do not know new leaders well, these initial meetings tend to have more one-way communication than interactive dialogue.

The First Two Weeks: Lay the Foundation

New leaders should spend the first two weeks meeting with many people both inside and outside the team. The key objectives for these meetings are to (1) learn as much as possible, (2) develop relationships, and (3) determine future allies. New leaders need to be particularly mindful about what they say or write in these meetings because they have no idea in whom they can confide. They also need to be aware of the fact that some of the people they are meeting with, for whatever reason, are not happy about their arrival and may not want them to succeed.

During the first two weeks new leaders will want to have one-on-one meetings with key team members. If the team has fewer than 15 people, new leaders should meet individually with everyone on the team; if the team is larger, new leaders should meet one-on-one with direct reports during the first two weeks and have small group or individual meetings with everyone else on the team sometime during the first 90 days. The one-on-one meetings usually last from two to three hours, and some of the critical questions to ask include these:

- *What is the team member working on?* New leaders should ask about major projects and where people are spending their time because this will help identify the critical issues facing the team.
- *What are the team member's objectives?* This is an important question that needs to be asked after the previous question. Often team members spend their time and energy working on projects that are completely unrelated to their work objectives, and new leaders need to understand what these gaps are and why they are occurring.
- *Who are the "stars" a level or two down in the organization?* This question may be omitted if new leaders are in charge of groups consisting of fewer than 15 people. But if groups are significantly larger, it is important for new leaders to know who their top performers are. In all likelihood direct reports will name many of the same people as stars, and

these high-performing individuals can play critical roles during the first 90 days of a new leader's tenure.

- *What are the people issues on the team?* This can be a difficult question to ask—new leaders don't want team members to think they are asking them to disparage others. However, it is important for new leaders to find out who is displaying inappropriate behavior or is difficult to work with. Once properly identified, new team leaders will need to address these people issues within the first 60 days in order to make clear who is in charge and to show what type of behavior will and will not be tolerated on the team.

- *What can the team do better?* Team members' answers to this question can help new leaders develop ideas for improving team performance. These answers also indicate whether team members are capable of thinking about, accepting, and driving change.

- *What advice do team members have for the new leader, and what can the new leader do to help team members?* New team leaders should close their meetings with these two questions and pay particular attention to what they can do to help their direct reports be successful. New leaders should avoid making any immediate promises but commit to closing the loop on those requests they will or will not fulfill sometime during the next two months.

Although new leaders should start building rapport during these one-on-one meetings, they should minimize their personal interactions with direct reports during their first two months on the job. Business lunches and team get-togethers are fine, but meeting with families and spouses during the first 60 days can make later structure and staffing decisions more difficult. New leaders need to make personnel decisions with team performance, not personal friendships, in mind.

During the first two weeks on the job new leaders should also schedule one-on-one meetings with all their peers. These meetings should last about an hour and take place in peers' offices; this will give new leaders opportunities to build rapport by observing office décor, diplomas, family pictures, awards, and so on. New leaders should discuss the following issues with peers:

- Their peers' objectives, challenges, team structure, and the like.
- Their perspectives on what the new leader's team does well and could do better.
- Their perspectives on the new leader's team members.
- How to best communicate with the boss.
- How issues get raised and decisions made on their boss's team.

New leaders should make it clear that they want and appreciate their peers' help. Scheduling regular meetings with their peers will build relationships and help new leaders stay ahead of potential conflicts or work issues. Unlike more personal meetings with direct reports, it is perfectly acceptable to socialize with peers and their families during the first 60 days. And because the boss will likely ask peers how the new leader is doing, meeting with peers on a regular basis becomes even more important.

If the team being led is fairly large, new leaders should also meet with their stars during the first two weeks on the job. Stars will be full of ideas for improving team performance, and these individuals are likely candidates for direct report positions should the new leader decide to change the structure of the team. If chosen for promotion, stars are likely to be loyal and well respected by others because they were widely recognized as being among the top performers on the team.

During the first two weeks new leaders should also try to meet with individuals who were once part of the team but have taken positions in other parts of the organization. These individuals can offer unique insights into the history of the team and team members, and this source of information should not be overlooked. The two other pieces of information new leaders should gather during the first two weeks are what the organization sees as the critical roles on the team and if there were any internal candidates for the team leader position. This information can be gathered from the boss, peers, former team members, the human resources representative, or the like. New leaders need this information to ensure they have the best talent filling key roles and to see if anyone on the team may be hoping they fail.

The First Two Months: Strategy, Structure, and Staffing

After their initial round of meetings with the boss, peers, and direct reports, new leaders need to spend the next six weeks gathering more information, determining the direction, and finalizing the appropriate structure and staffing for the team. Some of the tasks to be performed during this time include gathering benchmarking information from other organizations, meeting with key external customers and suppliers, and if appropriate, meeting with the former team leader. This additional information, when combined with the information gleaned from bosses, peers, direct reports, and stars, should help new team leaders determine the proper direction for their teams. This direction, or vision, may be more or less the same as what is already in place, or it may represent a significant change in direction. In either case, new leaders need to be able to articulate where the team has been and where it needs to go over the next one to three years, what it needs to accomplish, what changes will be needed to make this happen, and their expectations for team members. Depending on the new leader's vision, some of these changes may involve changing the team's structure and membership. In making these changes, new leaders need to remember that team strategy (vision and goals) should drive team structure, which in turn should drive team staffing decisions. Leaders who alter the strategy–structure–staffing sequence risk building dysfunctional, underperforming teams.

Although the first 90 days on the job provide a unique window for driving change, new leaders need to "socialize" their strategy, structure, and staffing ideas with their boss and peers before making any personnel decisions. Gathering input and working through potential disruptions with these two groups before moving ahead should improve buy-in and support for any change decisions. Once the proposed changes have been agreed to, new leaders need to have one-on-one meetings with all team members affected by any strategy, structure, and staffing decisions. During these meetings new leaders need to describe their vision and rationale for the changes and clarify roles and expectations for affected team members.

Although gathering additional information, developing the team's vision, and socializing key changes with affected parties take a considerable amount of time, new leaders must remember to stay focused on team performance. Team leaders may have less leeway to make needed changes if team performance drops precipitously during their first 60 days because dealing with day-to-day team issues will take up so much time that there will be little time left to drive change. Although it will be hard to obtain, new leaders should also seek feedback from others during their first two months with the organization. Possible sources for feedback include peers and recruiters. Recruiters have vested interests in seeing their placed candidates succeed and often tap their contacts within organizations to give new leaders feedback.

The Third Month: Communicate and Drive Change

At this point in a new leader's tenure he or she has developed a vision of the future and can articulate how the team will win; identified the what, why, and how of any needed changes; and defined a clear set of expectations for team members. The two major events for the third month are meeting with the entire team and meeting off-site with direct reports (if the team is large). The purpose of the first team meeting is for the new leader to share what he or she learned from whom during the information gathering process, his or her vision of the future, the new team structure and staffing model, his or her expectations for team members, and the rationale for any team changes. New leaders need to tie their changes to the attributes and values they shared during their first day on the job. Change is not about a new leader's PowerPoint presentation or the posters put up, but instead involves the tangible actions taken. And the actions team members pay the most attention to are the hiring, firing, promotion, restructuring, and staffing decisions made by new team leaders. One of the fastest ways to change the culture and norms of a team is to change the people in it.

If the group being led is large, the new leaders will want to have a separate second meeting with direct reports. This meeting may be from one to two days long and should be held off-site to minimize interruptions. The key issues to work through off-site include these:

- *Get agreement on the critical attributes and values of team members.* Although new leaders will have clear ideas about the values and attributes they are looking for in team members, they cannot be sure direct reports have fully bought into this set of attributes. New leaders should set aside time during the off-site meeting to finalize and clearly define the positive and negative behaviors for all the attributes and values they want to see in team members.
- *Create a team scorecard.* The new leader will paint a vision and some overall objectives for the future, but the direct report team needs to formulate a set of concrete, specific goals with timelines and benchmarks for measuring success.
- *Establish an operating rhythm.* Once the direction and goals have been clarified, the team will need to work on its meeting cadence and rules of engagement. The new leader and the direct report team need to determine how often they will meet, when they will meet, the purpose and content of the meetings, meeting roles and rules (sending substitutes to meetings, showing up to meetings on time, taking calls during meetings, and the like). This new meeting schedule should be published in a one-year calendar and sent to everyone in the group.
- *Establish task forces to work on key change initiatives.* In all likelihood a number of issues will need to be addressed by the team. Some of these issues can be discussed and resolved during the off-site meeting, whereas task forces might be a better venue for resolving other issues. The task forces should be staffed by stars, which will both improve the odds that good recommendations are made and allow the new leader to see the stars in action.

After finalizing team structure and staffing, creating a team scorecard, and establishing a new operating rhythm, new leaders should be well on the way to success. As stated at the beginning of this section, the first 90 days give new leaders a unique opportunity to put in place many of the components needed to drive long-term change in their teams. Thus they need to use this time wisely.

Learning from Experience

Leadership practitioners can enhance the learning value of their experiences by (1) creating opportunities to get feedback; (2) taking a 10 percent stretch; (3 learning from others; (4) keeping a journal of daily leadership events; and (5) having a developmental plan.

Creating Opportunities to Get Feedback

It may be difficult for leaders to get relevant feedback, particularly if they occupy powerful positions in an organization. Yet leaders often need feedback more than subordinates do. Leaders may not learn much from their leadership experiences if they get no feedback about how they are doing. Therefore, they may need to create opportunities to get feedback, especially from those working for them.

Leaders should not assume they have invited feedback merely by saying they have an open-door policy. A mistake some bosses make is presuming that others perceive them as open to discussing things just because they say they are open to such discussion. How truly open a door might be is in the eye of the beholder. In that sense, the key to constructive dialogue (that is, feedback) is not just expressing a policy but also being perceived as approachable and sincere in the offer.

Some of the most helpful information for developing your own leadership can come from asking for feedback from others about their perceptions of your behavior and its impact on your group's overall effectiveness. Leaders who take psychological tests and use periodic surveys or questionnaires will have greater access to feedback than leaders who fail to systematically solicit feedback from their followers. Unless leaders ask for feedback, they may not get it.

Taking a 10 Percent Stretch

Learning always involves stretching. Learning involves taking risks and reaching beyond one's comfort zone. This is true of a toddler's first unsteady steps, a student's first serious confrontation with divergent worlds of thought, and leadership development. The phrase *10 percent stretch* conveys the idea of voluntary but determined efforts to improve leadership skills. It is analogous to physical exercise, though in this context stretching implies extending one's behavior, not muscles, just a bit beyond the comfort zone. Examples could include making a point of conversing informally with everyone in the office at least once each day, seeking an opportunity to be chair of a committee, or being quieter than usual at meetings (or more assertive, as the case may be). There is much to be gained from a commitment to such ongoing "exercise" for personal and leadership development.

Several positive outcomes are associated with leaders who regularly practice the 10 percent stretch. First, their apprehension about doing something new or different gradually decreases. Second, leaders will broaden their repertoire of leadership skills. Third, because of this increased repertoire, their effectiveness will likely increase. And finally, leaders regularly taking a 10 percent stretch will model something valuable to others. Few things send a better message to others about the importance of their own development than the example of how sincerely a leader takes his or her own development.

One final aspect of the 10 percent stretch is worth mentioning. One reason the phrase is so appealing is that it sounds like a measurable yet manageable change. Many people will not offer serious objection to trying a 10 percent change in some behavior, whereas they might well be resistant (and unsuccessful) if they construe a developmental goal as requiring fundamental change in their personality or interpersonal style. Despite its nonthreatening connotation, though, an actual 10 percent change in behavior can make an enormous difference in effectiveness. In many kinds of endeavor the difference between average performers and exceptional performers is 10 percent. In baseball, for example, many players hit .275, but only the best hit over .300—a difference of about 10 percent.

Learning from Others

Leaders learn from others, first of all, by recognizing that they *can* learn from others and, importantly, from *any* others. That may seem self-evident, but in fact people often limit what and whom they pay attention to, and thus what they may learn from. For example, athletes may pay a lot of attention to how coaches handle leadership situations. However, they may fail to realize they could also learn a lot by watching the director of the school play and the band conductor. Leaders should not limit their learning by narrowly defining the sorts of people they pay attention to.

Similarly, leaders also can learn by asking questions and paying attention to everyday situations. An especially important time to ask questions is when leaders are new to a group or activity and have some responsibility for it. When possible, leaders should talk to the person who previously had the position to benefit from his or her insights, experience, and assessment of the situation. In addition, observant leaders can extract meaningful leadership lessons from everyday situations. Something as plain and ordinary as a high school car wash or the activities at a fast-food restaurant may offer an interesting leadership lesson. Leaders can learn a lot by actively observing how others react to and handle different challenges and situations, even common ones.

Keeping a Journal

Another way leaders can mine experiences for their richness and preserve their learning is by keeping a journal.[2] Journals are similar to diaries, but they are not just accounts of a day's events. A journal should include entries that address some aspect of leaders or leadership. Journal entries may include comments about insightful or interesting quotes, anecdotes, newspaper articles, or even humorous cartoons about leadership. They may also include reflections on personal events, such as interactions with bosses, coaches, teachers, students, employees, players, teammates, roommates, and so on. Such entries can emphasize a good (or bad) way somebody handled something, a problem in the making, the differences between people in their reactions to situations, or people in the news, a book, or a film. Leaders should also use their journals to "think on paper" about leadership readings from textbooks or formal leadership programs or to describe examples from their own experience of a concept presented in a reading.

There are at least three good reasons for keeping a journal. First, the process of writing increases the likelihood that leaders will be able to look at an event from a different perspective or feel differently about it. Putting an experience into words can be a step toward taking a more objective look at it. Second, leaders can (and should) reread earlier entries. Earlier entries provide an interesting and valuable autobiography of a leader's evolving thinking about leadership and about particular events in his or her life. Third, journal entries provide a repository of ideas that leaders may later want to use more formally for papers, pep talks, or speeches. As shown in Highlight 3.1, good journal entries give leaders a wealth of examples that they may use in speeches, presentations, and so on.

Having a Developmental Plan

Leadership development almost certainly occurs in ways and on paths that are not completely anticipated or controlled. That is no reason, how-

Sample Journal Entries

HIGHLIGHT 3.1

I went skiing this weekend and saw the perfect example of a leader adapting her leadership style to her followers and situation. While putting on my skis, I saw a ski instructor teaching little kids to ski. She did it using the game "red light, green light." The kids loved it and seemed to be doing very well. Later that same day, as I was going to the lodge for lunch, she was teaching adults, and she did more demonstrating than talking. But when she talked she was always sure to encourage them so they did not feel intimidated when some little kid whizzed by. She would say to the adults that it's easier for children, or that smaller skis are easier. She made the children laugh and learn, and made the adults less self-conscious to help them learn too. . . .

Today may not exactly be a topic on leadership, but I thought it would be interesting to discuss. I attended the football game this afternoon and could not help but notice our cheerleaders. I was just thinking of their name in general, and found them to be a good example (of leadership). Everyone gets rowdy at a football game, but without the direction of the cheerleaders there would be mayhem. They do a good job of getting the crowd organized and the adrenaline pumping (though of course the game is most important in that too!). It's just amazing to see them generate so much interest that all of the crowd gets into the cheering. We even chant their stupid-sounding cheers! You might not know any of them personally, but their enthusiasm invites you to try to be even louder than them. I must give the cheerleaders a round of applause. . . .

I've been thinking about how I used to view/understand leadership, trying to find out how my present attitudes were developed. It's hard to remember past freshman year, even harder to go past high school. Overall, I think my father has been the single most important influence on my leadership development—long before I even realized it. Dad is a strong "Type A" person. He drives himself hard and demands a great deal from everyone around him, especially his family and especially his only son and oldest child. He was always pushing me to study, practice whatever sport I was involved in at the time, get ahead of everybody else in every way possible.

ever, for leaders to avoid actively directing some aspects of their own development. A systematic plan outlining self-improvement goals and strategies will help leaders take advantage of opportunities they otherwise might overlook. This important skill is addressed in greater detail in the last part of this chapter.

A leader's first step in exercising control over his or her personal development is to identify some actual goals. But what if a leader is uncertain about what he or she needs to improve? As described earlier, leaders should systematically collect information from a number of different sources. One place a leader can get information about where to improve is through a review of current job performance, if that is applicable. Ideally, leaders will have had feedback sessions with their own superiors, which should help them identify areas of relative strength and weakness. Leaders should treat this feedback as a helpful perspective on their developmental needs. Leaders also should look at their interactions with peers as a source of ideas about what they might work on. Leaders should especially take notice if the same kind of problem comes up in their interactions with different individuals in separate situations. Leaders need to look at their own role in such instances as objectively as they can; there might be clues about what behavioral changes might facilitate better working relationships with others. Still another way to identify developmental objectives is to look ahead to what new skills are needed to function effectively at a higher level in the organization, or in a different role than the leader now has. Finally, leaders can use formal psychological tests and questionnaires to determine what their relative strengths and weaknesses as a leader may be.

On a concluding note, there is one activity leaders should put in their developmental plans whatever else might be included in them: a program of personal reading to broaden their perspectives on leadership. This reading can include the classics as well as contemporary fiction, biographies and autobiographies of successful leaders, essays about ethics and social responsibility, and assorted self-improvement books on various leadership and management issues. A vital part of leadership development is intellectual stimulation and reflection, and an active reading program is indispensable to that. Leaders might even want to join (or form) a discussion group that regularly meets to exchange ideas about a book everyone has read.

Building Technical Competence

Technical competence concerns the knowledge and repertoire of behaviors one can bring to bear to successfully complete a task. For example, a skilled surgeon possesses vast knowledge of human anatomy and surgical techniques and can perform an extensive set of highly practiced surgical procedures; a skilled volleyball player has a thorough understanding of the rules, tactics, and strategies of volleyball and can set, block, and serve effectively. Individuals usually acquire technical competence through formal education or training in specialized topics (such as law, medicine, accounting, welding, or carpentry), on-the-job training, or experience,[3] and many studies have documented the importance of technical competence to a person's success and effectiveness as both a leader and a follower. This section describes why technical competence is important to followers and leaders; it also provides ideas about how to increase readers' own technical competence.

There are many reasons why followers need to have a high level of technical competence. First, performance is often a function of technical competence.[4,5] Relatedly, research has shown that technical expertise plays a key role in supervisors' performance appraisal ratings of subordinates.[6,7] Second, followers with high levels of technical competence have a lot of expert power and at times can wield more influence in their groups than the leader does.[8,9] Third, individuals with high levels of technical competence may be more likely to be a member of a leader's in-group[10] and are more likely to be delegated tasks and asked to participate in decisions. Conversely, supervisors are more likely to use a close, directive leadership style when interacting with subordinates with poor technical skills.[11-14] Similarly, Blau[15] noted that organizations with relatively high numbers of technically competent members tended to have a flatter organizational structure; organizations with relatively fewer qualified members tended to be more centralized and autocratic. Thus, if followers wish to earn greater rewards, exert more influence in their groups, and have greater say in decisions, they should do all they can to enhance their technical competence.

There are also many reasons why it benefits leaders to have high levels of technical competence. First, technical competence has been found to be consistently related to managerial promotion rates. Managers having higher levels of technical competence were much more likely to rise to the top managerial levels at AT&T than managers with lower levels of technical competence.[16,17] Second, having a high level of technical competence is important because many leaders, particularly first-line supervisors, often spend considerable time training followers.[18] Perhaps nowhere is the importance of technical competence in training more readily apparent than in sports coaching; little is as frustrating as having a coach who knows less about the game than the team members. Third, leaders with high levels of technical competence seem to be able to reduce the level of role ambiguity and conflict in their groups,[19,20] and followers are generally more satisfied with leaders who have high rather than average levels of technical competence.[21,22] Finally, leaders who have a high level of technical competence may be able to stimulate followers to think about problems and issues in new ways, which in turn has been found to be strongly related to organizational climate ratings and followers' motivation to succeed.[23,24] Given these findings for both leaders and followers, we next discuss some practical advice for improving technical competence.

Determining How the Job Contributes to the Overall Mission

The first step in building technical competence is to determine how one's job contributes to the overall success of the organization. By taking this step, individuals can better determine what technical knowledge and which behaviors are most strongly related to job and organizational success. Next, people should evaluate their current level of technical skills by seeking verbal feedback from peers and superiors, reviewing past performance appraisal results, or reviewing objective performance data (such as test scores, team statistics, or the number of products rejected for poor quality). These actions will help individuals get a better handle on their own strengths and weaknesses, and in turn can help people be certain that any formal education or training program they pursue is best suited to meet their needs.

Becoming an Expert in the Job

Becoming an expert in one's primary field is often the springboard for further developmental opportunities. There are a number of ways in which individuals can become experts in their field, and these include enrolling in formal education and training programs, watching others, asking questions, and teaching others. Attending pertinent education and training courses is one way to acquire technical skills, and many companies often pay the tuition and fees associated with these courses. Another way to increase expertise in one's field is by being a keen observer of human behavior. Individuals can learn a lot by observing how others handle work coordination problems, achieve production goals, discipline team members, or help team members with poor skills develop. However, merely observing how others do things is not nearly as effective as observing and reflecting about how others do things. One method of reflection is trying to explain others' behaviors in terms of the concepts or theories described in this book. Observers should look for concepts that cast light on both variations and regularities in how others act and think about why a person might have acted a certain way. Additionally, observers can develop by trying to think of as many different criteria as possible for evaluating another person's actions.

It is also important to ask questions. Because everyone makes inferences regarding the motives, expectations, values, or rationale underlying another person's actions, it is vital to ask questions and seek information likely to verify the accuracy of one's inferences. By asking questions, observers can better understand why team practices are conducted in a particular way, what work procedures have been implemented in the past, or what really caused someone to quit a volunteer organization. Finally, perhaps nothing can help a person become a technical expert more than having to teach someone else about the equipment, procedures, strategies, problems, resources, and contacts associated with a job, club, sport, or activity. Teachers must thoroughly understand a job or position to effectively teach someone else. By seeking opportunities to teach others, individuals enhance their own technical expertise as well as that of others.

Seeking Opportunities to Broaden Experiences

Individuals can improve their technical competence by seeking opportunities to broaden their experiences. Just as a person should try to play a variety of positions to better appreciate the contributions of other team members, so should a person try to perform the tasks associated with the other positions in his or her work group to better appreciate how the work contributes to organizational success. Similarly, people should visit other parts of the organization to understand its whole operation. Moreover, by working on team projects, people get to interact with members of other work units and often can develop new skills. Additionally, volunteering to support school, political, or community activities is another way to increase one's organization and planning, public speaking, fund-raising, and public relations skills, all of which may be important aspects of technical competence for certain jobs.

Building Effective Relationships with Superiors

As defined here, superiors are individuals with relatively more power and authority than the other members of the group. Thus superiors could be teachers, band directors, coaches, team captains, heads of committees, or first-line supervisors. Needless to say, there are a number of advantages to having a good working relationship with superiors. First, superiors and followers sharing the same values, approaches, and attitudes will experience less conflict, provide higher levels of mutual support, and be more satisfied with superior–follower relationships than superiors and followers having poor working relationships.[25,26] Relatedly, individuals having good superior–follower relationships are often in the superior's in-group and thus are more likely to have a say in decisions, be delegated interesting tasks, and have the superior's support for career advancement.[27] Second, followers are often less satisfied with their supervisors and receive lower performance appraisal ratings when superior–follower relationships are poor.[28,29]

Although the advantages of having a good working relationship with superiors seem clear, one might mistakenly think that followers have little, if any, say in the quality of the relationship. In other words, followers might believe their relationships with superiors are a matter of luck: either the follower has a good superior or a bad one, or the superior just happens to like or dislike the follower, and there is little the follower can do about it. However, the quality of a working relationship is not determined solely by the superior, and effective subordinates do not limit themselves to a passive stance toward superiors. Effective subordinates have learned how to take active steps to strengthen the relationship and enhance the support they provide their superior and the organization.[30,31]

Wherever a person is positioned in an organization, an important aspect of that person's work is to help his superior be successful, just as an important part of the superior's work is to help followers be successful. This does not mean followers should become apple polishers, play politics, or distort information to make superiors look good. However, followers should think of their own and their superior's success as interdependent. Followers are players on their superior's team and should be evaluated on the basis of the team's success, not just their own. If the team succeeds, both the coach and the team members should benefit; if the team fails, the blame should fall on both the coach and the team members. Because team, club, or organizational outcomes depend to some extent on good superior–follower relationships, understanding how superiors view the world and adapting to superiors' styles are two things followers can do to increase the likelihood their actions will have positive results for themselves, their superiors, and their organizations.[32]

Understanding the Superior's World

Followers can do a number of things to better understand their superior's world. First, they should try to get a handle on their superior's personal and organizational objectives. Loyalty and support are a two-way street, and just as a superior can help subordinates attain their personal goals most readily by knowing what they are, so can subordinates support their superior if they understand the superior's goals and objectives. Knowing a superior's values, preferences, and personality can help followers understand why superiors act as they do and can show followers how they might strengthen relationships with superiors.

Second, followers need to realize that superiors are not supermen or superwomen; superiors do not have all the answers, and they have both strengths and weaknesses. Subordinates can make a great contribution to the overall success of a team by recognizing and complementing a superior's weaknesses and understanding his or her constraints and limitations. For example, a highly successful management consultant might spend over 200 days a year conducting executive development workshops, providing organizational feedback to clients, or giving speeches at various public events. This same consultant, however, might not be skilled in designing and making effective visual aids for presentations, or she might dislike having to make her own travel and accommodation arrangements. A follower could make both the consultant and the consulting firm more successful through his own good organization and planning, attention to detail, computer graphics skills, and understanding that the consultant is most effective when she has at least a one-day break between engagements.

A similar process can take place in other contexts, such as when subordinates help orient and educate a newly assigned superior whose expertise and prior experience may have been in a different field or activity.

In an even more general sense, subordinates can enhance superior–follower relationships by keeping superiors informed about various activities in the work group or new developments or opportunities in the field. Few superiors like surprises, and any news should come from the person with responsibility for a particular area—especially if the news is potentially bad or concerns unfavorable developments. Followers wishing to develop good superior–follower relationships should never put their superior in the embarrassing situation of having someone else know more about her terrain than she does (her own boss, for instance). As Kelley[33] maintained, the best followers think critically and play an active role in their organizations, which means followers should keep their superiors informed about critical information and pertinent opinions concerning organizational issues.

Adapting to the Superior's Style

Research has shown that some executives fail to get promoted (that is, are derailed) because they are unable or unwilling to adapt to superiors with leadership styles different from their own.[34] Followers need to keep in mind that it is their responsibility to adapt to their superior's style, not vice versa. For example, followers might prefer to interact with superiors face-to-face, but if their superior appreciates written memos, then written memos it should be. Similarly, a follower might be accustomed to informal interactions with superiors, but a new superior might prefer a more businesslike and formal style. Followers need to be flexible in adapting to their superiors' decision-making styles, problem-solving strategies, modes of communication, styles of interaction, and so on.

One way followers can better adapt to a superior's style is to clarify expectations about their role on the team, committee, or work group. Young workers often do not appreciate the difference between a job description and one's role in a job. A job description is a formalized statement of tasks and activities; a role describes the personal signature an incumbent gives to a job. For example, the job description of a high school athletic coach might specify such responsibilities as selecting and training a team or making decisions about lineups. Two different coaches, however, might accomplish those basic responsibilities in quite different ways. One might emphasize player development in the broadest sense, getting to know her players personally and using sports as a vehicle for their individual growth; another might see his role as simply to produce the most winning team possible. Therefore, just because followers know what their job is does not mean their role is clear.

Although some superiors take the initiative to explicitly spell out the roles they expect subordinates to play, most do not. Usually it is the subordinate's task to discern his or her role. One way followers can do this is to make a list of major responsibilities and use it to guide a discussion with the superior about different ways the tasks might be accomplished and the relative priorities of the tasks. Followers will also find it helpful to talk to others who have worked with a particular superior.

Finally, followers interested in developing effective relationships with superiors need to be honest and dependable. Whatever other qualities or talents a subordinate might have, a lack of integrity is a fatal flaw. No one—superior, peer, or subordinate—wants to work with someone who is untrustworthy. After integrity, superiors value dependability. Superiors value workers who have reliable work habits, accomplish assigned tasks at the right time in the right order, and do what they promise.[35]

Building Effective Relationships with Peers

The phrase *influence without authority*[36] captures a key element of the work life of increasing numbers of individuals. More and more people are finding that their jobs require them to influence others despite having no formal authority over them. No man is an island, it is said, and perhaps no worker in today's organizations can survive alone. Virtually everyone needs a co-worker's assistance or resources at one time or another. Along these lines, some researchers have maintained that a fundamental requirement of leadership effectiveness is the ability to build strong alliances with others, and groups of peers generally wield more influence (and can get more things done) than individuals working separately.[37] Similarly, investing the time and effort to develop effective relationships with peers not only has immediate dividends but also can have long-term benefits if a peer ends up in a position of power in the future. Many times leaders are selected from among the members of a group, committee, club, or team; and having previously spent time developing a friendly rather than an antagonistic relationship with other work group members, leaders will lay the groundwork for building effective relationships with superiors and becoming a member of superiors' in-groups. Given the benefits of strong relationships with peers, the following are a few ideas about how to establish and maintain good peer relationships.

Recognizing Common Interests and Goals

Although Chapters 4 through 8 describe a variety of ways people vary, one of the best ways to establish effective working relationships with peers is to acknowledge shared interests, values, goals, and expectations.[38] In order to acknowledge shared aspirations and interests, however, one must know what peers' goals, values, and interests actually are. Establishing informal communication links is one of the best ways to discover common interests and values. To do so, one needs to be open and honest in communicating one's own needs, values, and goals, as well as being willing to acknowledge others' needs, aspirations, and interests. Little can destroy a relationship with peers more quickly than a person who is overly willing to share his own problems and beliefs but unwilling to listen to others' ideas about the same issues. Moreover, although some people believe that participating in social gatherings, parties, committee meetings, lunches, company sport teams, or community activities can be a waste of time, peers with considerable referent power often see such activities as opportunities to establish and improve relationships with others. Thus an effective way to establish relationships with other members of a team, committee, or organization is to meet with them in contexts outside normal working relationships.

Understanding Peers' Tasks, Problems, and Rewards

Few things reinforce respect between co-workers better than understanding the nature of each other's work. Building a cooperative relationship with others depends, therefore, on knowing the sorts of tasks others perform in the organization. It also depends on understanding their problems and rewards. With the former, one of the best ways to establish strong relationships is by lending a hand whenever peers face personal or organizational problems. With the latter, it is especially important to remember that people tend to repeat behaviors that are rewarded and are less likely to repeat behaviors that go unrewarded. A person's counterproductive or negative behaviors may be due less to his personal characteristics ("He is just uncooperative") than to the way his rewards are structured. For example, a teacher may be less likely to share successful classroom exercises with others if teachers are awarded merit pay on the basis of classroom effectiveness. To secure cooperation from others, it helps to know which situational factors reinforce both positive and negative behaviors in others.[39] By better understanding the situation facing others, people can determine whether their own positive feedback (or lack thereof) is contributing to, or hindering the establishment of, effective relationships with peers. People should not underestimate the power of their own sincere encouragement, thanks, and compliments in positively influencing the behavior of their colleagues.

Practicing a Theory Y Attitude

Another way to build effective working relationships with peers is to view them from a Theory Y perspective (see Chapter 5 for more about Theory Y and a contrasting approach called Theory X). When a person assumes that others are competent, trustworthy, willing to cooperate if they can, and proud of their work, peers will view that person in the same light. Even if one practices a Theory Y attitude, however, it may still be difficult to get along with a few co-workers. In such cases it is easy to become preoccupied with the qualities one dislikes. This should be resisted as much as possible. A vicious cycle can develop in which people become enemies, putting more and more energy into criticizing each other or making the other person look bad than into doing constructive work on the task at hand. The costs of severely strained relationships can extend beyond the individuals involved. Cliques can develop among other co-workers, which can impair the larger group's effectiveness. The point here is not to overlook interpersonal problems, but rather to not let the problems get out of hand.

Practicing Theory Y does *not* mean looking at the world through rose-colored glasses, but it *does* mean recognizing someone else's strengths as well as weaknesses. Nevertheless, sometimes peers will be assigned to work on a task together when they don't get along with each other, and the advice "Practice a Theory Y attitude" may seem too idealistic. At such times it is important to decide whether to focus energy first on improving the relationship (before addressing the task) or to focus it solely on the task (essentially ignoring the problem in the relationship).

Cohen and Bradford[40] have suggested several guidelines for resolving this problem. It is best to work on the task if there is little animosity between the parties, if success can be achieved despite existing animosities, if group norms inhibit openness, if success on the task will improve the feelings between the parties, if the other person handles directness poorly, or if you handle directness poorly. Conversely, it is best to work on the relationship if there is great animosity between the parties, if negative feelings make task success unlikely, if group norms favor openness, if feelings between the parties are not likely to improve even with success on the task, if the other person handles directness well, *and* if you handle directness well.

Development Planning

Development planning is the systematic process of building knowledge and experience or changing behavior. Two people who have done a considerable amount of cutting-edge research in the development planning process are Peterson and Hicks.[41-43] These two researchers believe development planning consists of five interrelated phases. The first phase of development planning is identifying development needs. Here leaders identify career goals, assess their abilities in light of career goals, seek feedback about how their behaviors are affecting others, and review the organizational standards pertaining to their career goals. Once this information has been gathered, the second phase consists of analyzing these data to identify and prioritize development needs. The prioritized development needs in turn are used to create a focused and achievable development plan, the third phase of this process. The fourth phase in development planning is periodically reviewing the plan, reflecting on learning, and modifying or updating the plan as appropriate. As you

Change before you have to.

**Jack Welch,
former General
Electric CEO**

might expect, the action–observation–reflection (AOR) model, described in Chapter 2, is a key component during this phase of the development planning process. The last phase in development planning is transferring learning to new environments. Just because a leader can successfully delegate activities to a three-person team may not mean he will effectively delegate tasks or use his staff efficiently when he is leading 25 people. In that case the leader will need to build and expand on the delegation skills he learned when leading a smaller team. These five phases are well grounded in research—several studies have shown that approximately 75 percent of the leadership practitioners adopting these phases were successful in either changing their behaviors permanently or developing new skills. Because these five phases are so important to the development planning process, the remainder of this section will describe each phase in more detail.[44-46]

Conducting a GAPS Analysis

The first phase in the development planning process is to conduct a GAPS (goals, abilities, perceptions, standards) analysis. A GAPS analysis helps leadership practitioners to gather and categorize all pertinent development planning information. A sample GAPS analysis for an engineer working in a manufacturing company can be found in Figure 3.2. This individual wants to get promoted to a first-line supervisor position within the next year, and all of the information pertinent to this promotion can be found in her GAPS analysis. The specific steps for conducting a GAPS analysis are as follows:

- *Step 1: Goals.* The first step in a GAPS analysis is to clearly identify what you want to do or where you want to go with your career over the next year or so. This does not necessarily mean moving up or getting promoted to the next level. An alternative career objective might be to master one's current job—you may have just gotten promoted, and advancing to the next level is not important at the moment. Other career objectives might include taking on more responsibilities in your current position, taking a lateral assignment in another part of the company, taking an overseas assignment, or even cutting back on job responsibilities to gain more work–life balance. This last career objective may be appropriate for leaders who are starting a family or taking care of loved ones who are suffering from poor health. The two most important aspects of this step in the GAPS analysis are that leadership practitioners will have a lot more energy to work on development needs that are aligned with career goals, and in many cases advancing to the next level may not be a viable or particularly energizing career goal. This latter point may be especially true in organizations that have been recently downsized. Management positions often bear the brunt of downsizing initiatives, resulting in fewer available positions for those wishing to advance.

FIGURE 3.2
A Sample GAPS Analysis

Sources: D. B. Peterson and M. D. Hicks, *Leader as Coach* (Minneapolis, MN: Personnel Decisions International, 1996);
G. J. Curphy, *Career and Development Planning Workshop: Planning for Individual Development* (Minneapolis MN:
Personnel Decisions International, 1998).

Goals: Where do you want to go?	**Abilities:** What can you do now?
Step 1: Career objectives: Career strategies:	*Step 2:* What strengths do you have for your career objectives? *Step 3:* What development needs will you have to overcome?
Standards: What does your boss or the organization expect?	**Perceptions:** How do others see you?
Step 5: Expectations:	*Step 4:* 360-degree and performance review results, and feedback from others: • *Boss* • *Peers* • *Direct reports*

- *Step 2: Abilities.* People bring a number of strengths and development needs to their career goals. Over the years you may have developed specialized knowledge or a number of skills that have helped you succeed in your current and previous jobs. Similarly, you may also have received feedback over the years that there are certain skills you need to develop or behaviors you need to change. Good leaders know themselves—over the years they know which strengths they need to leverage and which skills they need to develop.

- *Step 3: Perceptions.* The perceptions component of the GAPS model concerns how your abilities, skills, and behaviors affect others. What are others saying about your various attributes? What are their reactions to both your strengths and your development needs? A great way of obtaining this information is by asking others for feedback or through performance reviews or 360-degree feedback instruments.
- *Step 4: Standards.* The last step in a GAPS analysis concerns the standards your boss or the organization has for your career objectives. For example, your boss may say you need to develop better public speaking, delegation, or coaching skills before you can get promoted. Similarly, the organization may have policies stating that people in certain overseas positions must be proficient in the country's native language, or it may have educational or experience requirements for various jobs.

When completing a GAPS analysis you may discover that you do not have all the information you need. If you do not, then you need to get it before you complete the next step of the development planning process. Only you can decide on your career objectives; but you can solicit advice from others on whether these objectives are realistic given your abilities, the perceptions of others, and organizational standards. You may find that your one-year objectives are unrealistic given your development needs, organizational standards, or job opportunities. In this case, you may need to either reassess your career goals or consider taking a number of smaller career steps that will ultimately help you achieve your career goal. If you are lacking information about the other quadrants, you can ask your boss or others whose opinions you value about your abilities, perceptions, or organizational standards. Getting as much up-to-date and pertinent information for your GAPS analysis will help ensure that your development plan is focusing on high-priority objectives.

Identifying and Prioritizing Development Needs: Gaps of GAPS

As shown in Figure 3.3, the goals and standards quadrants are future oriented; these quadrants ask where you want to go and what your boss or your organization expects of people in these positions. The abilities and perceptions quadrants are focused on the present: what strengths and development needs do you currently have, and how are these attributes affecting others? Given what you currently have and where you want to go, what are the gaps in your GAPS? In other words, after looking at all the information in your GAPS analysis, what are your biggest development needs, and how should these development needs be prioritized? You need to review the information from the GAPS model, look for underlying themes and patterns, and determine what behaviors, knowledge, experiences, or skills will be the most important to change or develop if you are to accomplish your career goals.

FIGURE 3.3
A Gaps-of-the-GAPS Analysis

Sources: D. B. Peterson and M. D. Hicks, *Leader as Coach* (Minneapolis, MN: Personnel Decisions International, 1996); G. J. Curphy, *The Leadership Development Process Manual* (Minneapolis, MN: Personnel Decisions International, 1998).

Where you want to go

Goals

Where you are now

Abilities

◄———— Gaps? ————►

Standards

Perceptions

Developmental Objectives
Current position: _____
_____
_____
_____
_____
_____
_____

Next proposed position: _____
_____
_____
_____
_____
_____

Bridging the Gaps: Building a Development Plan

A gaps-of-the-GAPS analysis helps leadership practitioners identify high-priority development needs, but it does not spell out what leaders need to do to meet these needs. A good development plan is like a road map: it clearly describes the final destination, lays out the steps or interim checkpoints, builds in regular feedback to keep people on track, identifies where additional resources are needed, and builds in reflection time so people can periodically review progress and determine whether an alternative route is needed. (See Figure 2.4 on page 68 for a sample development plan.) The specific steps for creating a high-impact development plan are as follows:

- *Step 1: career and development objectives.* Your career objective comes directly from the goals quadrant of the GAPS analysis; it is where you want to be or what you want to be doing in your career a year or so in the future. The development objective comes from your gaps-of-the-GAPS analysis; it should be a high-priority development need pertaining to your career objective. People should be working on no more than two to three development needs at any one time.

- *Step 2: criteria for success.* What would it look like if you developed a particular skill, acquired technical expertise, or changed the behavior outlined in your development objective? This can be a difficult step in development planning, particularly with "softer" skills such as listening, managing conflict, or building relationships with others.

- *Step 3: action steps.* The focus in the development plan should be on the specific, on-the-job action steps leadership practitioners will take to meet their development need. However, sometimes it is difficult for leaders to think of appropriate on-the-job action steps. Three excellent resources that provide on-the-job action steps for a variety of development needs are two books, *The Successful Manager's Handbook*,[47] and *For Your Improvement*,[48] and the development planning and coaching software *DevelopMentor*.[49] These three resources can be likened to restaurant menus in that they provide leadership practitioners with a wide variety of action steps to work on just about any development need.

- *Step 4: whom to involve and reassess dates.* This step in a development plan involves feedback—whom do you need to get it from, and how often do you need to get it? This step in the development plan is important because it helps keep you on track. Are your efforts being noticed? Do people see any improvement? Are there things you need to do differently? Do you need to refocus your efforts?

- *Step 5: stretch assignments.* When people reflect on when they have learned the most, they often talk about situations where they felt they were in over their heads. These situations stretched their knowledge and skills and often are seen as extremely beneficial to learning. If you know of a potential assignment, such as a task force, a project management team, or a rotational assignment, that would emphasize the knowledge and skills you need to develop and accelerate your learning, you should include it in your development plan.

- *Step 6: resources.* Often people find it useful to read a book, attend a course, or watch a recorded program to gain foundational knowledge about a particular development need. These methods generally describe the how-to steps for a particular skill or behavior.

- *Step 7: reflect with a partner.* In accordance with the action–observation–reflection model of Chapter 2, people should periodically review their learning and progress with a partner. The identity of the partner is not particularly important as long as you trust his or her opinion and the partner is familiar with your work situation and development plan.

Reflecting on Learning: Modifying Development Plans

Just as the development plan is a road map, this phase of development planning helps leaders to see whether the final destination is still the right one, if an alternative route might be better, and whether there is need for more resources or equipment. Reflecting on your learning with a partner is also a form of public commitment, and people who make public commitments are much more likely to fulfill them. All things considered, in most cases it is probably best to periodically review your progress with your boss. Your boss should not be left in the dark with respect to your development, and periodically reviewing progress with your boss will help ensure there are no surprises at your performance appraisal.

Transferring Learning to New Environments

The last phase in development planning concerns ongoing development. Your development plan should be a "live" document: it should be changed, modified, or updated as you learn from your experiences, receive feedback, acquire new skills, and meet targeted development needs. There are basically three ways to transfer learning to new environments. The first way is to constantly update your development plan. Another way to enhance your learning is to practice your newly acquired skills in a new environment. A final way to hone and refine your skills is to coach others in the development of your newly acquired skills. Moving from the student role to that of a master is an excellent way to reinforce your learning.

End Notes

1. M. Roellig and G. J. Curphy, *How to Hit the Ground Running: A Guide to Successful Executive On-Boarding* (Springfield, MA: Author, 2010).
2. M. Csikszentmihalyi, *Flow: The Psychology of Optimal Experience* (New York: Harper & Row, 1990).
3. G. Yukl, *Leadership in Organizations,* 2nd ed. (Englewood Cliffs, NJ: Prentice Hall, 1989).
4. G. J. Curphy, "Leadership Transitions and Succession Planning," in *Developing and Implementing Succession Planning Programs,* ed. J. Locke (chair). Symposium conducted at the 19th Annual Conference for the Society of Industrial and Organizational Psychology, Chicago, April 2004.
5. F. L. Schmidt and J. E. Hunter, "Development of a Causal Model of Job Performance," *Current Directions in Psychological Science* 1, no. 3 (1992), pp. 89–92.

6. W. C. Borman, L. A. White, E. D. Pulakos, and S. A. Oppler, "Models Evaluating the Effects of Rated Ability, Knowledge, Proficiency, Temperament, Awards, and Problem Behavior on Supervisor Ratings," *Journal of Applied Psychology* 76 (1991), pp. 863–72.

7. J. Hogan, "The View from Below," in *The Future of Leadership Selection*, ed. R. T. Hogan (chair). Symposium conducted at the 13th Biennial Psychology in the Department of Defense Conference, United States Air Force Academy, Colorado Springs, CO, 1992.

8. D. E. Bugental, "A Study of Attempted and Successful Social Influence in Small Groups as a Function of Goal-Relevant Skills," *Dissertation Abstracts* 25 (1964), p. 660.

9. G. F. Farris, "Colleagues' Roles and Innovation in Scientific Teams," Working Paper No. 552-71 (Cambridge, MA: Alfred P. Sloan School of Management, MIT, 1971).

10. D. Duchon, S. G. Green, and T. D. Taber, "Vertical Dyad Linkage: A Longitudinal Assessment of Antecedents, Measures, and Consequences," *Journal of Applied Psychology* 71 (1986), pp. 56–60.

11. H. D. Dewhirst, V. Metts, and R. T. Ladd, "Exploring the Delegation Decision: Managerial Responses to Multiple Contingencies," Paper presented at the Academy of Management Convention, New Orleans, LA, 1987.

12. C. R. Leana, "Power Relinquishment vs. Power Sharing: Theoretical Clarification and Empirical Comparison of Delegation and Participation," *Journal of Applied Psychology* 72 (1987), pp. 228–33.

13. A. Lowin and J. R. Craig, "The Influence of Level of Performance on Managerial Style: An Experimental Object-Lesson in the Ambiguity of Correlational Data," *Organizational Behavior and Human Performance* 3 (1968), pp. 68–106.

14. B. Rosen and T. H. Jerdee, "Influence of Subordinate Characteristics on Trust and Use of Participative Decision Strategies in a Management Simulation," *Journal of Applied Psychology* 59 (1977), pp. 9–14.

15. P. M. Blau, "The Hierarchy of Authority in Organizations," *American Journal of Sociology* 73 (1968), pp. 453–67.

16. A. Howard, "College Experiences and Managerial Performance," *Journal of Applied Psychology* 71 (1986), pp. 530–52.

17. A. Howard and D. W. Bray, "Predictors of Managerial Success over Long Periods of Time," in *Measures of Leadership*, ed. M. B. Clark and K. E. Clark (West Orange, NJ: Leadership Library of America, 1989).

18. K. N. Wexley and G. P. Latham, *Developing and Training Human Resources in Organizations* (Glenview, IL: Scott Foresman, 1981).

19. P. M. Podsakoff, W. D. Todor, and R. S. Schuler, "Leadership Expertise as a Moderator of the Effects of Instrumental and Supportive Leader Behaviors," *Journal of Management* 9 (1983), pp. 173–85.

20. T. G. Walker, "Leader Selection and Behavior in Small Political Groups," *Small Group Behavior* 7 (1976), pp. 363–68.

21. B. M. Bass, *Leadership and Performance beyond Expectations* (New York: Free Press, 1985).

22. D. D. Penner, D. M. Malone, T. M. Coughlin, and J. A. Herz, *Satisfaction with U.S. Army Leadership,* Leadership Monograph Series, no. 2 (U.S. Army War College, 1973).

23. B. J. Avolio and B. M. Bass, "Transformational Leadership, Charisma, and Beyond," in *Emerging Leadership Vista,* ed. J. G. Hunt, B. R. Baliga, and C. A. Schriesheim (Lexington, MA: D. C. Heath, 1988).

24. G. J. Curphy, "An Empirical Examination of Bass' 1985 Theory of Transformational and Transactional Leadership," PhD dissertation, University of Minnesota, 1991.

25. D. Duchon, S. G. Green, and T. D. Taber, "Vertical Dyad Linkage: A Longitudinal Assessment of Antecedents, Measures, and Consequences," *Journal of Applied Psychology* 71 (1986), pp. 56–60.

26. D. A. Porter, "Student Course Critiques: A Case Study in Total Quality in the Classroom," in *Proceedings of the 13th Biennial Psychology in Department of Defense Conference* (Colorado Springs, CO: U.S. Air Force Academy, 1992), pp. 26–30.

27. G. Yukl, *Leadership in Organizations,* 2nd ed. (Englewood Cliffs, NJ: Prentice Hall, 1989).

28. E. D. Pulakos and K. N. Wexley, "The Relationship among Perceptual Similarity, Sex, and Performance Ratings in Manager-Subordinate Dyads," *Academy of Management Journal* 26 (1983), pp. 129–39.

29. H. M. Weiss, "Subordinate Imitation of Supervisor Behavior: The Role of Modeling in Organizational Socialization," *Organizational Behavior and Human Performance* 19 (1977), pp. 89–105.

30. J. J. Gabarro, and J. P. Kotter, "Managing Your Boss," *Harvard Business Review* 58, no. 1 (1980), pp. 92–100.

31. R. E. Kelley, "In Praise of Followers," *Harvard Business Review* 66, no. 6 (1988), pp. 142–48.

32. Gabarro and Kotter, "Managing Your Boss."

33. Kelley, "In Praise of Followers."

34. M. W. McCall Jr. and M. M. Lombardo, "Off the Track: Why and How Successful Executives Get Derailed," Technical Report No. 21 (Greensboro, NC: Center for Creative Leadership, 1983).

35. J. M. Kouzes and B. Z. Posner, *The Leadership Challenge: How to Get Extraordinary Things Done in Organizations* (San Francisco: Jossey-Bass, 1987).

36. A. R. Cohen and D. L. Bradford, *Influence without Authority* (New York: John Wiley, 1990).

37. G. J. Curphy, A. Baldrica, M. Benson, and R. T. Hogan, *Managerial Incompetence,* unpublished manuscript, 2007.

38. A. R. Cohen and D. L. Bradford, *Influence without Authority* (New York: John Wiley, 1990).

39. Cohen and Bradford, *Influence without Authority.*

40. Cohen and Bradford, *Influence without Authority.*

41. D. B. Peterson and M. D. Hicks, *Professional Coaching: State of the Art, State of the Practice* (Minneapolis, MN: Personnel Decisions International, 1998).

42. D. B. Peterson and M. D. Hicks, "Coaching across Borders: It's Probably a Long Distance Call," *Development Matters,* no. 9 (1997), pp. 1–4.

43. D. B. Peterson and M. D. Hicks, *Leader as Coach: Strategies for Coaching and Developing Others* (Minneapolis, MN: Personnel Decisions International, 1996).

44. J. F. Hazucha, S. A. Hezlett, and R. J. Schneider, "The Impact of 360-Degree Feedback on Management Skills Development," *Human Resource Management* 32 (1993), pp. 325–51.

45. D. B. Peterson, "Skill Learning and Behavioral Change in an Individually Tailored Management Coaching and Training Program," unpublished doctoral dissertation, University of Minnesota, 1993.

46. S. A. Hezlett and B. A. Koonce, "Now That I've Been Assessed, What Do I Do? Facilitating Development after Individual Assessments," paper presented at the IPMA Assessment Council Conference on Public Personnel Assessment, New Orleans, LA, June 1995.

47. B. L. Davis, L. W. Hellervik, and J. L. Sheard, *The Successful Manager's Handbook*, 3rd ed. (Minneapolis, MN: Personnel Decisions International, 1989).

48. M. M. Lombardo and R. W. Eichinger, *For Your Improvement: A Development and Coaching Guide* (Minneapolis, MN: Lominger, 1996).

49. Personnel Decisions International, *DevelopMentor: Assessment, Development, and Coaching Software* (Minneapolis, MN: Personnel Decisions International, 1995).

Focus on
the Leader

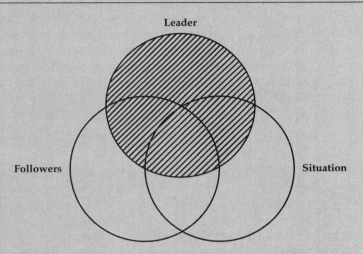

Part 2 focuses on the leader. The effectiveness of leadership, good or bad, is typically attributed to the leader much more than to the other elements of the framework. Sometimes the leader is the only element of leadership we even think of. One great leader's views were clear enough about the relative importance of leaders and followers:

> Men are nothing; it is the man who is everything. . . . It was not the Roman army that conquered Gaul, but Caesar; it was not the Carthaginian army that made Rome tremble in her gates, but Hannibal; it was not the Macedonian army that reached the Indus, but Alexander.
>
> **Napoleon**

Because the leader plays such an important role in the leadership process, the next four chapters of this book review research related to the characteristics of leaders and what makes leaders effective. Part 2 begins with a chapter about power and influence because those concepts provide the most fundamental way to understand the process of leadership. Chapter 5 looks at the closely related issues of leadership ethics and values. In Chapter 6 we consider what aspects of personality are related to leadership, and in Chapter 7 we examine how all these variables are manifested in effective or ineffective leader behavior.

Chapter 4

Power and Influence

Introduction

We begin Part 2 by examining the phenomenon of power. Some of history's earliest characterizations of leaders concerned their use of power. Shakespeare's plays were concerned with the acquisition and failing of power,[1] and Machiavelli's *The Prince* has been described as the "classic handbook on power politics."[2] Current scholars have also emphasized the need to conceptualize leadership as a power phenomenon.[3,4] Power may be the single most important concept in all the social sciences,[5] though scholars today disagree over precisely how to define power or influence. But it's not just scholars who have different ideas about power. The concept of power is so pervasive and complex that each of us probably thinks about it a little differently.

What comes to *your* mind when you think about power? Do you think of a person wielding enormous authority over others? Do you think of high office? Do you think of making others do things against their will? Is power ethically neutral, or is it inherently dangerous as Lord Acton said? ("Power corrupts, and absolute power corrupts absolutely.") Do you think a leader's real power is always obvious to others? What sorts of things might enhance or detract from a leader's power? What are the pros and cons of different ways of trying to influence people? These are the kinds of issues we will explore in this chapter.

Some Important Distinctions

Power has been defined as the capacity to produce effects on others[6] or the potential to influence others.[7] Although we usually think of power as belonging to the leader, it is actually a function of the leader, the followers, and the situation. Leaders have the potential to influence their followers' behaviors and attitudes. However, followers also can affect the leader's behavior and attitudes. Even the situation itself can affect a leader's capacity to influence followers (and vice versa). For example, leaders who can reward and punish followers may have a greater capacity to influence followers than leaders who cannot use rewards or punishments. Similarly, follower or situational characteristics may diminish a leader's potential to influence followers, such as when the latter belong to a strong, active union.

The fact that power is not merely a function of leaders is reflected in the continuing research on the use of power in organizations. Not only has there been ongoing research to examine the negotiation of power dynamics within and across organizations,[8] but also research examining power relationships between shareholders and governance boards[9] and power related to gender (a topic we will examine in more detail later in this chapter) in entrepreneurial relationships.[10]

Several other aspects of power also are worth noting. Gardner has made an important point about the exercise of power and its effects.[11] He stated that "power does not need to be exercised in order to have its effect—as any hold-up man can tell you."[12] Thus merely having the capacity to exert influence can often bring about intended effects, even though the leader may not take any action to influence his or her followers. For example, some months after the end of his term, Eisenhower was asked if leaving the White House had affected his golf game. "Yes," he replied, "a lot more people beat me now." Alternatively, power represents an inference or attribution made on the basis of an agent's observable acts of influence.[13] Power is never directly observed but rather attributed to others on the basis and frequency of influence tactics they use and on their outcomes.

Many people use the terms *power, influence,* and *influence tactics* synonymously,[14] but it is useful to distinguish among them. **Influence** can be defined as the change in a target agent's attitudes, values, beliefs, or behaviors as the result of influence tactics. **Influence tactics** refer to one person's actual behaviors designed to change another person's attitudes, beliefs, values, or behaviors. Although these concepts are typically examined from the leader's perspective (such as how a leader influences followers), we should remember that followers can also wield power and influence over leaders as well as over each other. Leadership practitioners can improve their effectiveness by reflecting on the types of power they and their followers have and the types of influence tactics that they may use or that may be used on them.

Whereas power is the *capacity* to cause change, influence is the degree of actual change in a target person's attitudes, values, beliefs, or behaviors. Influence can be measured by the behaviors or attitudes manifested by followers as the result of a leader's *influence tactics*. For example, a leader may ask a follower to accomplish a particular task, and whether or not the task is accomplished is partly a function of the leader's request. (The follower's ability and skill as well as access to the

The true leader must submerge himself in the fountain of the people.
V. I. Lenin

necessary equipment and resources are also important factors.) Such things as subordinates' satisfaction or motivation, group cohesiveness and climate, or unit performance measures can be used to assess the effectiveness of leaders' influence attempts. The degree to which leaders can change the level of satisfaction, motivation, or cohesiveness among followers is a function of the amount of power available to both leaders and followers. On one hand, leaders with relatively high amounts of power can cause fairly substantial changes in subordinates' attitudes and behaviors; for example, a new and respected leader who uses rewards and punishments judiciously may cause a dramatic change in followers' perceptions about organizational climate and the amount of time followers spend on work-related behaviors. On the other hand, the amount of power followers have in work situations can also vary dramatically, and in some situations particular followers may exert relatively more influence over the rest of the group than the leader does. For example, a follower with a high level of knowledge and experience may have more influence on the attitudes, opinions, and behaviors of the rest of the followers than a brand-new leader. Thus the amount of change in the attitudes or behaviors of the targets of influence is a function of the agent's capacity to exert influence and the targets' capacity to resist this influence.

Leaders and followers typically use a variety of tactics to influence each other's attitudes or behaviors (see Highlight 4.1 for a description of some nonverbal power cues common to humans). Influence tactics are the overt behaviors exhibited by one person to influence another. They range from emotional appeals, to the exchange of favors, to threats. The particular tactic used in a leadership situation is probably a function of the power possessed by both parties. Individuals with a relatively large amount of power may successfully employ a wider variety of influence tactics than individuals with little power. For example, a well-respected leader could make an emotional appeal, a rational appeal, a personal appeal, a legitimate request, or a threat to try to modify a follower's behavior. The follower in this situation may be able to use only ingratiation or personal appeals to change the leader's attitude or behavior.

At the same time, because the formal leader is not always the person who possesses the most power in a leadership situation, followers often can use a wider variety of influence tactics than the leader to modify the attitudes and behaviors of others. This would be the case if a new leader were brought into an organization in which one of his or her subordinates was extremely well liked and respected. In this situation, the subordinate may be able to make personal appeals, emotional appeals, or even threats to change the attitudes or behaviors of the leader, whereas the new leader may be limited to making only legitimate requests to change the attitudes and behaviors of the followers.

Gestures of Power and Dominance

HIGHLIGHT 4.1

We can often get clues about relative power just by paying attention to behaviors between two people. There are a number of nonverbal cues we might want to pay attention to. The phrase **pecking order** refers to the status differential between members of a group. It reminds us that many aspects of human social organization have roots, or at least parallels, in the behavior of other species. The animal kingdom presents diverse and fascinating examples of stylized behaviors by which one member of a species shows its relative dominance or submissiveness to another. There is adaptive significance to such behavioral mechanisms because they tend to minimize actual physical struggle and maintain a stable social order. For example, lower-ranking baboons step aside to let a higher-status male pass; they become nervous if he stares at them. The highest-status male can choose where he wants to sleep and whom he wants to mate with. Baboons "know their place." As with humans, rank has its privileges.

Our own stylized power rituals are usually so ingrained that we aren't conscious of them. Yet there is a "dance" of power relations among humans just as among other animals. The following are some of the ways power is expressed nonverbally in humans:

Staring: In American society, it is disrespectful for a person of lower status to stare at a superior, though superiors are not bound by a similar restriction. Children, for example, are taught not to stare at parents. And it's an interesting comment on the power relationship between sexes that women are more likely to avert their gaze from men than vice versa.

Pointing: Children are also taught that it's not nice to point. However, adults rarely correct each other for pointing because, more than mere etiquette, pointing seems to be a behavior that is acceptable for high-status figures or those attempting to assert dominance. An angry boss may point an index finger accusingly at an employee; few employees who wanted to keep their jobs would respond in kind. The same restrictions apply to frowning.

Touching: Invading another person's space by touching the person without invitation is acceptable when one is of superior status but not when one is of subordinate status. It's acceptable, for example, for bosses or teachers to put a hand on an employee's or a student's shoulder, respectively, but not vice versa. The disparity also applies to socioeconomic status; someone with higher socioeconomic status is more likely to touch a person of lower socioeconomic status than vice versa.

Interrupting: Virtually all of us have interrupted others, and we have all been interrupted ourselves. Again, however, the issue is who interrupted whom. Higher-power or status persons interrupt; lower-power or status persons are interrupted. A vast difference in the frequency of this behavior also exists between the sexes in American society. Men interrupt much more frequently than women do.

Source: D. A. Karp and W. C. Yoels, *Symbols, Selves, and Society* (New York: Lippincott, 1979).

Power and Leadership

And when we think we lead, we are most led.
Lord Byron

We began this chapter by noting how an understanding of power has long been seen as an integral part of leadership. Several perspectives and theories have been developed to explain the acquisition and exercise of power. In this section we will first examine various *sources* of power. Then we will look at how individuals vary in their personal *need* for power.

Sources of Leader Power

Where does a leader's power come from? Do leaders *have* it, or do followers *give* it to them? As we will see, the answer may be both . . . and more.

Something as seemingly trivial as the arrangement of furniture in an office can affect perceptions of another person's power. One vivid example comes from John Ehrlichman's book *Witness to Power.*[15] Ehrlichman described his first visit to J. Edgar Hoover's office at the Department of Justice. The legendary director of the FBI had long been one of the most powerful men in Washington, DC, and as Ehrlichman's impressions reveal, Hoover used every opportunity to reinforce that image. Ehrlichman was first led through double doors into a room replete with plaques, citations, trophies, medals, and certificates jamming every wall. He was then led through a second similarly decorated room into a third trophy room, and finally to a large but bare desk backed by several flags and still no J. Edgar Hoover. The guide opened a door behind the desk, and Ehrlichman went into a smaller office, which Hoover dominated from an impressive chair and desk that stood on a dais about six inches high. Erhlichman was instructed to take a seat on a lower couch, and Hoover peered down on Ehrlichman from his own loftier and intimidating place.

On a more mundane level, many people have experienced a time when they were called in to talk to a boss and left standing while the boss sat behind the desk. Probably few people in that situation misunderstand the power message there. In addition to the factors just described, other aspects of office arrangements also can affect a leader's or follower's power. One factor is the shape of the table used for meetings. Individuals sitting at the ends of rectangular tables often wield more power, whereas circular tables facilitate communication and minimize status differentials. However, specific seating arrangements even at circular tables can affect participants' interactions; often individuals belonging to the same cliques and coalitions will sit next to each other. By sitting next to each other, members of the same coalition may exert more power as a collective group than they would sitting apart from each other. Also, having a private or more open office may not only *reflect* but also *affect* power differentials between people. Individuals with private offices can dictate to a greater degree when they want to interact with others by opening or closing their doors or by giving instructions about interruptions. Individuals with more open offices have much less power to control access to them. By being aware of dynamics like these, leaders can somewhat influence others' perceptions of their power relationship.

Prominently displaying symbols like diplomas, awards, and titles also can increase one's power. This was shown in an experiment in a college setting where a guest lecturer to several different classes was introduced in a different way to each. To one group he was introduced as a student; to other groups he was introduced as a lecturer, senior lecturer, or professor, respectively. After the presentation, when he was no longer in the room, the class estimated his height. Interestingly, the same man was perceived by different groups as increasingly taller with each increase in academic status. The "professor" was remembered as being several inches taller than the "student."[16]

This finding demonstrates the generalized impact a seemingly minor matter like one's title can have on others. Another study points out more dramatically how dangerous it can be when followers are overly responsive to the *appearances* of title and authority. This study took place in a medical setting and arose from concern among medical staff that nurses were responding mechanically to doctors' orders. A researcher made telephone calls to nurses' stations in numerous different medical wards. In each, he identified himself as a hospital physician and directed the nurse answering the phone to administer a particular medication to a patient in that ward. Many nurses complied with the request despite the fact it was against hospital policy to transmit prescriptions by phone. Many did so despite never even having talked to the particular "physician" before the call—and despite the fact that the prescribed medication was dangerously excessive, not to mention unauthorized. In fact, 95 percent of the nurses complied with the request made by the most easily falsifiable symbol of authority, a bare title.[17] (See also Highlight 4.2.)

Even choice of clothing can affect one's power and influence. Uniforms and other specialized clothing have long been associated with authority and status, including their use by the military, police, hospital staffs, clergy, and so on. In one experiment, people walking along a city sidewalk were stopped by someone dressed either in regular clothes or in the uniform of a security guard and told this: "You see that guy over there by the meter? He's overparked but doesn't have any change. Give him a dime!" Whereas fewer than half complied when the requestor was dressed in regular clothes, over 90 percent did when he was in uniform.[18]

This same rationale is given for having personnel in certain occupations (such as airline crew members) wear uniforms. Besides identifying them to others, the uniforms increase the likelihood that in emergency situations their instructions will be followed. Similarly, even the presence of something as trivial as tattoos can affect the amount of power wielded in a group. One of the authors of this text had a friend named Del who was a manager in an international book publishing company. Del was a former merchant marine whose forearms were adorned with tattoos. Del would often take off his suit coat and roll up his sleeves when meetings were not going his way, and he often exerted considerably more influence by merely exposing his tattoos to the rest of the group.

A final situational factor that can affect one's potential to influence others is the presence or absence of a crisis. Leaders usually can exert more power during a crisis than during periods of relative calm. Perhaps this is because during a crisis leaders are willing to draw on bases of power they

He who has great power should use it lightly.

Seneca

The Milgram Studies

HIGHLIGHT 4.2

One intriguing way to understand power, influence, and influence tactics is to read a synopsis of Stanley Milgram's classic work on obedience and to think about how this work relates to the concepts and theories discussed in this chapter. Milgram's research explored how far people will go when directed by an authority figure to do something that might injure another person. More specifically, Milgram wanted to know what happens when the dictates of authority and the dictates of one's conscience seem incompatible.

The participants were men from the communities surrounding Yale University. They were led to believe they were helping in a study concerning the effect of punishment on learning; the study's legitimacy was enhanced by the study being conducted on the Yale campus. Two subjects at a time participated in the study—one as a teacher and the other as a learner. The roles apparently were assigned randomly. The teacher's task was to help the learner memorize a set of word pairs by providing electric shocks whenever the learner (who would be in an adjacent room) made a mistake.

A stern experimenter described procedures and showed participants the equipment for administering punishment. This "shock generator" looked ominous, with rows of switches, lights, and warnings labeled in 15-volt increments all the way to 450 volts. Various points along the array were marked with increasingly dire warnings such as *extreme intensity* and *danger: severe*. The switch at the highest level of shock was simply marked *XXX*. Every time the learner made a mistake, the teacher was ordered by the experimenter to administer the next higher level of electric shock.

In actuality, there was only one true subject in the experiment—the teacher. The learner was really a confederate of the experimenter. The supposed random assignment of participants to teacher and learner conditions had been rigged in advance. The real purpose of the experiment was to assess how much electric shock the teachers would administer to the learners in the face of the latter's increasingly adamant protestations to stop. This included numerous realistic cries of agony and complaints of a heart condition—all standardized, predetermined, tape-recorded messages delivered via the intercom from the learner's room to the teacher's room. If the subject (that is, the teacher) refused to deliver any further shocks, the experimenter prodded him with comments such as "The experiment requires that you go on" and "You have no other choice; you must go on."

Before Milgram conducted his experiment, he asked mental health professionals what proportion of the subjects would administer apparently dangerous levels of shock. The consensus was that only a negligible percentage would do so—perhaps 1 or 2 percent of the population. Milgram's actual results were dramatically inconsistent with what any experts had predicted. Fully 70 percent of the subjects carried through with their orders, albeit sometimes with great personal anguish, and delivered the maximum shock possible—450 volts!

Source: S. Milgram, "Behavioral Study of Obedience," *Journal of Abnormal and Social Psychology* 67 (1963), pp. 371–78.

normally forgo. For example, a leader who has developed close interpersonal relationships with followers generally uses her referent power to influence them. During crises or emergency situations, however, leaders may be more apt to draw on their legitimate and coercive bases of power to influence subordinates. That was precisely the finding in a study of bank managers' actions; the bank managers were more apt to use legitimate and coercive power during crises than during noncrisis situations.[19] This same phenomenon is observable in many dramatizations. In the television series *Star Trek, the Next Generation,* for example, Captain Picard normally uses his referent and expert power to influence subordinates. During emergencies, however, he will often rely on his legitimate and coercive power. Another factor may be that during crises followers are more willing to accept greater direction, control, and structure from leaders, whatever power base may be involved.

A Taxonomy of Social Power

French and Raven identified five sources, or bases, of power by which an individual can potentially influence others.[20] As shown in Figure 4.1, these five sources include one that is primarily a function of the leader; one that is a function of the relationship between leaders and followers; one that is primarily a function of the leader and the situation; one that is primarily a function of the situation; and finally, one that involves aspects of all three elements. Understanding these bases of power can give leadership practitioners greater insight about the predictable effects—positive or negative—of various sorts of influence attempts. Following is a more detailed discussion of French and Raven's five bases of social power.[21]

Expert Power

Expert power is the power of knowledge. Some people can influence others through their relative expertise in particular areas. A surgeon may wield considerable influence in a hospital because others depend on her knowledge, skill, and judgment, even though she may have no formal authority over them. A mechanic may be influential among his peers because he is widely recognized as the best in the city. A longtime employee may be influential because her corporate memory provides a useful historical perspective to newer personnel. Legislators who are experts in the

FIGURE 4.1
Sources of Leader Power in the Leader–Follower–Situation Framework

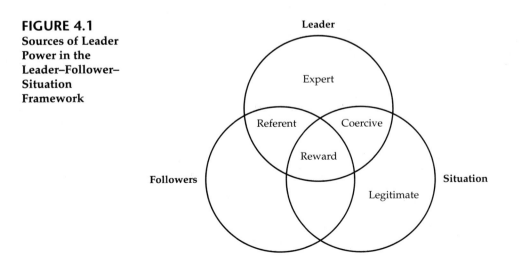

intricacies of parliamentary procedure, athletes who have played in championship games, and soldiers who have been in combat are valued for the lessons learned and the wisdom they can share with others.

Because expert power is a function of the amount of knowledge one possesses relative to the rest of the members of the group, it is possible for followers to have considerably more expert power than leaders in certain situations. For example, new leaders often know less about the jobs and tasks performed in a particular work unit than the followers do, and in this case the followers can potentially wield considerable influence when decisions are made regarding work procedures, new equipment, or the hiring of additional workers. Probably the best advice for leaders in this situation is to ask a lot of questions and perhaps seek additional training to help fill this knowledge gap. So long as different followers have considerably greater amounts of expert power, it will be difficult for a leader to influence the work unit on the basis of expert power alone.

Referent Power

One way to counteract the problems stemming from a lack of expertise is to build strong interpersonal ties with subordinates. **Referent power** refers to the potential influence one has due to the strength of the relationship between the leader and the followers. When people admire a leader and see her as a role model, we say she has referent power. For example, students may respond positively to advice or requests from teachers who are well liked and respected, while the same students might be unresponsive to less popular teachers. This relative degree of responsiveness is primarily a function of the strength of the relationship between the students and the different teachers. We knew one young lieutenant who had enormous referent power with the military security guards working for him due to his selfless concern for them, evident in such habits as bringing them hot chocolate and homemade cookies on their late-night shifts. The guards, sometimes taken for granted by other superiors, understood and valued the extra effort and sacrifice this young supervisor put forth for them. When Buddy Ryan was fired as head coach of the Philadelphia Eagles football team, many of the players expressed fierce loyalty to him. One said, "We'd do things for Buddy that we wouldn't do for another coach. I'd sell my body for Buddy."[22] That is referent power.

Another way to look at referent power is in terms of the role friendships play in making things happen. It is frequently said, for example, that many people get jobs based on whom they know, not what they know. This is true. But we think the best perspective on this issue was offered by David Campbell, who said, "It's not who you know that counts. It's what who you know *knows about you* that counts!" (personal communication).

Referent power often takes time to develop, but it can be lost quickly—just ask Tiger Woods. Furthermore, it can have a downside in that a desire to *maintain* referent power may limit a leader's actions in particular situations.

Power in an organization is the capacity generated by relationships.
Margaret A. Wheatley, futurist

For example, a leader who has developed a strong relationship with a follower may be reluctant to discipline the follower for poor work or chronic tardiness because such actions could disrupt the nature of the relationship between the leader and the follower. Thus referent power is a two-way street; the stronger the relationship, the more influence leaders and followers exert over each other. Moreover, just as it is possible for leaders to develop strong relationships with followers and, in turn, acquire more referent power, it is also possible for followers to develop strong relationships with

Michael Dell

PROFILES IN LEADERSHIP 4.1

The problem of having power you didn't know you had and might not even want.

It's hard to imagine anyone not recognizing the name Michael Dell. As founder of the computer company Dell, Inc., he created one of the most profitable computer companies in the world, with annual sales of up to $50 billion. Michael Dell has also become one of the wealthiest people in the world with a fourth-place listing on the *Forbes* rich Americans list in 2005 and an estimated worth of $18 billion. In July 2007 *USA Today* published its ranking of the 25 most influential business leaders in the last 25 years. Number 17 on this list was Michael Dell.

With just $1,000 in his pocket, Dell started PC's Limited in 1984. From his university dorm room Dell started building and selling personal computers from stock computer parts. In 1988 PC's Limited changed its name to Dell Computer Corporation and had an initial public offering (IPO) that valued the company at roughly $80 million. By 1992 Dell Computer Corporation was listed on the *Fortune* 500 list of the largest companies in the world, making Dell the youngest CEO ever to head a *Fortune* 500 company.

One of this book's authors worked with Michael Dell in the early 1990s (and wishes he had bought stock). He was chatting with Michael and describing the problems that can happen in large organizations when the leader has a lot of personal or referent power. Michael said, "Oh, I'm learning

about that. We've even got a name for that problem. We call them, 'Michael saids.'"

Here's an example of a "Michael said." One afternoon, Michael was walking around the plant and stopped to ask one of the assembly employees how things were going and what could be done to make things better. The assembler said that things were great but that occasionally there was some confusion with a particular electronic component (let's call it a resistor). Sometimes the resistors were red and sometimes they were green, and the red ones looked like another component. The assembler suggested that this problem could be eliminated if this particular resistor came only in green. Michael said that seemed like a reasonable solution and passed that information along to the people who bought resistors from the suppliers.

Six months later, Michael was having a meeting in his office when someone knocked on the door. It was a frazzled person who said he was terribly sorry to interrupt but there was a crisis down in manufacturing and production was about to stop. "Why?" asked Michael. The messenger said that the supplier of green resistors had a problem and the only resistors they could get were red and they couldn't use the red resistors. "Why not?" asked Michael. The messenger looked sheepishly at his feet and passed along the bad news. They couldn't use the red ones because "Michael said we could only use green resistors."

While referent and expert power may be good to use, as Dell and others have found out, there can be a potential downside of which you might not even be aware.

other followers and acquire more referent power. Followers with relatively more referent power than their peers are often the spokespersons for their work units and generally have more latitude to deviate from work unit norms. Followers with little referent power have little opportunity to deviate from group norms. For example, in an episode of the television show *The Simpsons,* Homer Simpson was fired for wearing a pink shirt to work (everybody else at the Springfield nuclear power plant had always worn white shirts). Homer was fired partly because he "was not popular enough to be different."

Legitimate Power

Legitimate power depends on a person's organizational role. It can be thought of as one's formal or official authority. Some people make things happen because they have the power or authority to do so. The boss assigns projects; the coach decides who plays; the colonel orders compliance with uniform standards; the teacher assigns homework and awards grades. Individuals with legitimate power exert influence through requests or demands deemed appropriate by virtue of their role and position. In other words, legitimate power means a leader has authority because she or he has been assigned a particular role in an organization. Note that the leader has this authority only while occupying that position and operating within the proper bounds of that role.

Legitimate authority and leadership are not the same thing. Holding a position and being a leader are not synonymous, despite the relatively common practice of calling position holders in bureaucracies the leaders. The head of an organization may be a true leader, but he or she also may not be. Effective leaders often intuitively realize they need more than legitimate power to be successful. Before he became president, Dwight Eisenhower commanded all Allied troops in Europe during World War II. In a meeting with his staff before the Normandy invasion, Eisenhower pulled a string across a table to make a point about leadership. He was demonstrating that just as you can pull a string, not push it, officers must lead soldiers and not push them from the rear.

It is also possible for followers to use their legitimate power to influence leaders. In these cases, followers can actively resist a leader's influence attempt by doing only work specifically prescribed in job descriptions, bureaucratic rules, or union policies. For example, many organizations have job descriptions that limit both the time spent at work and the types of tasks and activities performed. Similarly, bureaucratic rules and union policies can be invoked by followers to resist a leader's influence attempts. Often the leader will need to change the nature of his or her request or find another way to resolve the problem if these rules and policies are invoked by followers. If this is the case, the followers will have successfully used legitimate power to influence their leader.

Reward Power

Reward power involves the potential to influence others due to one's control over desired resources. This can include the power to give raises, bonuses, and promotions; to grant tenure; to select people for special assignments or desirable activities; to distribute desired resources like computers, offices, parking places, or travel money; to intercede positively on another's behalf; to recognize with awards and praise; and so on. Many corporations use rewards extensively to motivate employees. At McDonald's, for example, great status is accorded the All-American Hamburger Maker—the cook who makes the fastest, highest-quality hamburgers in the country. At individual fast-food restaurants, managers may reward salespeople who handle the most customers during rush periods. Tupperware holds rallies for its salespeople. Almost everyone wins something, ranging from pins and badges to lucrative prizes for top performers.[23] Schools pick teachers of the year, and professional athletes are rewarded by selection to all-star teams for their superior performance.

The potential to influence others through the ability to administer rewards is a joint function of the leader, the followers, and the situation. Leaders vary considerably in the types and frequency with which they give rewards, but the position they fill also helps determine the frequency and types of rewards administered. For example, employees of the month at Kentucky Fried Chicken are not given new cars; the managers of these franchises do not have the resources to offer such awards. Similarly, leaders in other organizations are limited to some extent in the types of awards they can administer and the frequency with which they can do so. Nevertheless, leaders can enhance their reward power by spending some time reflecting on the followers and the situation. Often a number of alternative or innovative rewards can be created, and these rewards, along with ample doses of praise, can help a leader overcome the constraints his or her position puts on reward power.

Although using reward power can be an effective way to change the attitudes and behaviors of others, in several situations it can be problematic. For example, the perception that a company's monetary bonus policy is handled equitably may be as important in motivating good work (or avoiding morale problems) as the amounts of the bonuses. Moreover, a superior may mistakenly assume that a particular reward is valued when it is not. This would be the case if a particular subordinate were publicly recognized for her good work when she actually disliked public recognition. Leadership practitioners can avoid the latter problem by developing good relationships with subordinates and administering rewards that they, not the leader, value. Another potential problem with reward power is that it may produce compliance but not other desirable outcomes like commitment.[24] In other words, subordinates may perform only at the level necessary to receive a reward and may not be willing to put forth the extra effort needed to make the

Unreviewable power is the most likely to self-indulge itself and the least likely to engage in dispassionate self-analysis.

Warren E. Burger, U.S. Supreme Court, Chief Justice, 1969–1986

organization better. An overemphasis on rewards as payoff for performance may also lead to resentment and feelings by workers of being manipulated, especially if it occurs in the context of relatively cold and distant superior–subordinate relationships. Extrinsic rewards like praise, compensation, promotion, privileges, and time off may not have the same effects on behavior as intrinsic rewards such as feelings of accomplishment, personal growth, and development. There is evidence that under some conditions extrinsic rewards can decrease intrinsic motivation toward a task and make the desired behavior less likely to persist when extrinsic rewards are not available.[25,26] Overemphasis on extrinsic rewards may instill an essentially contractual or economic relationship between superiors and subordinates, diluting important aspects of the relationship like mutual loyalty or shared commitment to higher ideals.[27] These cautions about reward power should not cloud its real usefulness and effectiveness. As noted previously, top organizations make extensive use of both tangible and symbolic rewards in motivating their workers. Furthermore, all leaders can use some of the most important rewards—sincere praise and thanks to others for their loyalty and work. The bottom line is that leaders can enhance their ability to influence others based on reward power if they determine what rewards are available, determine what rewards are valued by their subordinates, and establish clear policies for the equitable and consistent administration of rewards for good performance.

Finally, because reward power is partly determined by one's position in the organization, some people may believe followers have little, if any, reward power. This may not be the case. If followers control scarce resources, they may use the administration of these resources to get leaders to act as they want. Moreover, followers may reward their leader by putting out a high level of effort when they feel their leader is doing a good job, and they may put forth less effort when they feel their leader is doing a poor job. By modifying their level of effort, followers may in turn modify a leader's attitudes and behaviors. And when followers compliment their leader (such as for running a constructive meeting), it is no less an example of reward power than when a leader compliments a follower. Thus leadership practitioners should be aware that followers can also use reward power to influence leaders.

Coercive Power

You do not lead by hitting people over the head—that's assault, not leadership.

Dwight D. Eisenhower

Coercive power, the opposite of reward power, is the potential to influence others through the administration of negative sanctions or the removal of positive events. In other words, it is the ability to control others through the fear of punishment or the loss of valued outcomes. Like reward power, coercive power is partly a function of the leader, but the situation often limits or enhances the coercive actions a leader can take (see Highlight 4.3). Examples of coercive power include police giving tickets

Leadership Lessons from Abu Ghraib

HIGHLIGHT 4.3

Americans (and indeed people everywhere) were shocked by the pictures and reports emerging from the Abu Ghraib prison near Baghdad. What the U.S. military police guards did to the Iraqi prisoners was unconscionable. But we must look further up in the leadership hierarchy if we are to make sense of what happened and learn from it so we do not repeat these errors in the future. There are important leadership errors and lessons for us all.

A short review of the history of leadership might be helpful. If your grandparents happened to study leadership anytime from 1900 until about 1950, they would have read case studies of famous leaders. This "great man" theory of leadership hoped to unearth the traits that differentiated great leaders from lesser leaders. For the most part, this quest for the underlying innate leadership abilities stopped in the late 1940s when Ralph Stogdill published his findings that there was no clear set of traits responsible for great leaders.

From the 1950s to the 1980s, we decided that because leadership could not be comprehended by focusing solely on the leader, we should look at the relationship between the leader and the followers. As you will learn in Part 3 of this book, as the maturity and skills of the followers change, so should the behavior of the leader.

In the mid-1980s we started to consider the leadership implications of research done about 25 years earlier. We began to acknowledge that even if it were possible to know everything about a leader and everything about her or his followers, another variable powerfully affected leadership and performance: the situation (the focus of Part 4).

Two troubling studies clearly demonstrated this situational impact. The first, conducted by Stanley Milgram, was described in Highlight 4.2. The lesson learned was that reasonable, normal people, when put in a situation where authority told them to behave in a nefarious manner, for the most part did just that.

Ten years after Milgram's research, Phillip Zimbardo at Stanford University recruited students to serve as either "prisoners" or "guards" in a "prison" that was simulated in the basement of a campus building. Neither the guards nor the prisoners were given any instructions about how to behave. The experiment was to have lasted for approximately two weeks but was canceled after only six days because the "guards" were abusing their fellow student "prisoners" both physically and emotionally. It's not that the student guards were bad people; rather, they were put in a power situation that overcame their own beliefs and values. Fortunately an occasional noble hero rises to stand on higher moral ground. But as leaders, we cannot rely on that. For the masses, the situation is a powerful determinant of behavior. Incidentally, the Stanford Prison Experiment has its own Web site at www.prisonexp.org should you care to learn more about it.

Knowing what Milgram and Zimbardo demonstrated, it is at least possible to comprehend how someone like Pfc. Lynndie England, who according to her family would not even shoot a deer, could have become caught up in such barbarism. This is not to excuse her behavior but to help us understand it. And if we should not excuse the behavior of an undertrained soldier, we should be even less willing to excuse the leadership that put her and others in this situation without clear behavioral guidelines. After all, we've known about these studies for over 50 years!

Whether under the direction of authority as in the Milgram study, or under role assignments as in the Zimbardo study, the Abu Ghraib case showed a leadership vacuum that should not be tolerated.

And what about the business world? Leaders cannot claim they want and expect teamwork and collaboration from their subordinates if they place them in a situation that fosters competition and enmity. Neither can leaders claim that they want creativity from their subordinates if they have created a situation where the slightest deviation from rigid rules brings punishment. And perhaps most importantly, leaders can not expect egalitarian behaviors if people are put in highly differentiated power situations. People in organizations are smart. They are less likely to give you the behaviors you espouse in your speeches and more likely to give you the behavior demanded by the situation in which you place them. The leader's job is to create the conditions for the team to be successful, and the situation is one of the most important variables. What to consider in the situation will be discussed in more detail in Chapter 12.

for speeding, the army court-martialing AWOL soldiers, a teacher detaining disruptive students after school, employers firing lazy workers, and parents reprimanding children.[28] Even presidents resort to their coercive powers. Historian Arthur Schlesinger Jr., for example, described Lyndon Johnson as having a "devastating instinct for the weaknesses of others." Lyndon Johnson was familiar and comfortable with the use of coercion; he once told a White House staff member, "Just you remember this. There's

BEETLE BAILEY © King Features Syndicate.

only two kinds at the White House. There's elephants and there's ants. And I'm the only elephant."[29]

Coercive power, like reward power, can be used appropriately or inappropriately. It is carried to its extreme in repressive totalitarian societies. One of the most tragic instances of coercive power was the cult led by Jim Jones, which unbelievably self-exterminated in an incident known as the Jonestown massacre.[30] Virtually all of the 912 people who died there drank, at Jones's direction, from large vats of a flavored drink containing cyanide. The submissiveness and suicidal obedience of Jones's followers during the massacre were due largely to the long history of rule by fear that Jones had practiced. For example, teenagers caught holding hands were beaten, and adults judged slacking in their work were forced to box for hours in marathon public matches against as many as three or four bigger and stronger opponents. Jim Jones ruled by fear, and his followers became self-destructively compliant.

Perhaps the preceding example is so extreme that we can dismiss its relevance to our own lives and leadership activities. Yet abuses of power, especially abuses of coercive power, continue to make the news, whether we are seeing reports of U.S. military abuse in Iraq or Taliban abuse in Afghanistan. On the other hand, such examples provide a dramatic reminder that reliance on coercive power has inherent limitations and drawbacks. But this is not to say disciplinary sanctions are never necessary; sometimes they are. Informal coercion, as opposed to the threat of formal punishment, can also change the attitudes and behaviors of others. Informal coercion is usually expressed implicitly, and often nonverbally, rather than explicitly. It may be the pressure employees feel to donate to the boss's favorite charity, or it may be his or her glare when they bring up an unpopular idea. One of the most common forms of coercion is simply a superior's temperamental outbursts. The intimidation caused by a leader's poorly controlled anger is usually, in its long-term effects, a dysfunctional style of behavior for leaders.

It is also possible for followers to use coercive power to influence their leader's behavior. For example, a leader may be hesitant to take disciplinary action against a large, emotionally unstable follower. Followers can threaten leaders with physical assaults, industrial sabotage, or work slowdowns and strikes, and these threats can modify a leader's behavior. Followers are more likely to use coercive power to change their leader's behavior if they have a relatively high amount of referent power with their fellow co-workers. This may be particularly true for threats of work slowdowns or strikes.

Concluding Thoughts about French and Raven's Power Taxonomy

Can we reach any conclusions about what base of power is best for a leader to use? As you might have anticipated, we must say that's an unanswerable question without knowing more facts about a particular situation. For example, consider the single factor of whether a group is facing a crisis. This might affect the leader's exercise of power simply because leaders usually can exert more power during crises than during periods of relative calm. Furthermore, during crises followers may be more eager to receive direction and control from leaders.

Can we make any generalizations about using various sources of power? Actually, considerable research has examined French and Raven's ideas, and generally the findings indicate that leaders who rely primarily on referent and expert power have subordinates who are more motivated and satisfied, are absent less, and perform better.[31] However, Yukl[32] and Podsakoff and Schriesheim[33] have criticized these findings, and much of their criticism centers on the instrument used to assess a leader's bases of power. Hinkin and Schriesheim[34] developed an instrument that overcomes many of the criticisms, and future research should more clearly delineate the relationship between the five bases of power and various leadership effectiveness criteria.

Four generalizations about power and influence seem warranted. First, effective leaders typically take advantage of *all* their sources of power. Effective leaders understand the relative advantages and disadvantages of different sources of power, and they selectively emphasize one or another depending on their objectives in a given situation. Second, whereas leaders in well-functioning organizations have strong influence over their subordinates, *they are also open to being influenced by them.* High degrees of reciprocal influence between leaders and followers characterize the most effective organizations.[35] Third, leaders vary in the extent to which they share power with subordinates. Some leaders seem to view their power as a fixed resource that, when shared with others (like cutting a pie into pieces), reduces their own portion. They see power in zero-sum terms. Other leaders see power as an expandable pie. They see the possibility of increasing a subordinate's power without reducing their own. Needless to say, which view a leader subscribes to can have a major impact on the leader's support for power-sharing activities like delegation and participative management. A leader's support for power-sharing activities (or in today's popular language, *empowerment*) is also affected by the practice of holding leaders responsible for subordinates' decisions and actions as well as their own. It is, after all, the coach or manager who often gets fired when the team loses.[36,37] Fourth, effective leaders generally work to increase their various power bases (whether expert, referent, reward, or legitimate) or become more willing to use their coercive power.

Leader Motives

Thus far we have been looking at how different *sources* of power can affect others, but that's only one perspective. Another way of looking at the relationship between power and leadership involves focusing on the individual leader's personality. We will look most closely at the role personality plays in leadership in an upcoming chapter, but it will be nonetheless useful now to briefly examine how all people (including leaders) vary in their personal motivation to have or wield power.

People vary in their motivation to influence or control others. McClelland[38] called this the **need for power,** and individuals with a high need for power derive psychological satisfaction from influencing others. They seek positions where they can influence others, and they are often involved concurrently in influencing people in many different organizations or decision-making bodies. In such activities they readily offer ideas, suggestions, and opinions, and also seek information they can use in influencing others. They are often astute at building trusting relationships and assessing power networks, though they can also be quite outspoken and forceful. They value the tangible signs of their authority and status as well as the more intangible indications of others' deference to them. Two different ways of expressing the need for power have been identified: **personalized power** and **socialized power.** Individuals who have a high need for personalized power are relatively selfish, impulsive, uninhibited, and lacking in self-control. These individuals exercise power for their own needs, not for the good of the group or the organization. Socialized power, on the other hand, implies a more emotionally mature expression of the motive. Socialized power is exercised in the service of higher goals to others or organizations and often involves self-sacrifice toward those ends. It often involves an empowering, rather than an autocratic, style of management and leadership.

Although the need for power has been measured using questionnaires and more traditional personality inventories, McClelland and his associates have used the Thematic Apperception Test (TAT) to assess need for power. The TAT is a **projective personality test** consisting of pictures such as a woman staring out a window or a boy holding a violin. Subjects are asked to make up a story about each picture, and the stories are then interpreted in terms of the strengths of various needs imputed to the characters, one of which is the need for power. Because the pictures are somewhat ambiguous, the sorts of needs projected onto the characters are presumed to reflect needs (perhaps at an unconscious level) of the storyteller. Stories concerned with influencing or controlling others would receive high scores for the need for power.

The need for power is positively related to various leadership effectiveness criteria. For example, McClelland and Boyatzis[39] found the need for power to be positively related to success for nontechnical managers at AT&T, and Stahl[40] found that the need for power was positively related to managers' performance ratings and promotion rates. In addition, Fodor[41] reported that small groups of ROTC students were more likely to successfully solve a subarctic survival situation if their leader had a strong need for power. Although these findings appear promising, several cautions should be kept in mind. First, McClelland and Boyatzis[42] also reported that the need for power was unrelated to the success of technical managers at AT&T. Apparently the level of knowledge (that is, expert power) played a more important role in the success of the technical managers versus that of the nontechnical managers. Second, McClelland[43] concluded that although some need for power was necessary for leadership potential, successful leaders also have the ability to inhibit their manifestation of this need. Leaders who are relatively uninhibited in their need for power will act like dictators; such individuals use power impulsively, to manipulate or control others, or to achieve at another's expense. Leaders with a high need for power but low activity inhibition may be successful in the short term, but their followers, as well as the remainder of the organization, may pay high costs for this success. Some of these costs may include perceptions by fellow members of the organization that they are untrustworthy, uncooperative, overly competitive, and looking out primarily for themselves. Finally, some followers have a high need for power too. This can lead to tension between leader and follower when a follower with a high need for power is directed to do something.

Individuals vary in their motivation to manage, just as in their need for power. Miner[44] described the **motivation to manage** in terms of six composites:

- Maintaining good relationships with authority figures.
- Wanting to compete for recognition and advancement.
- Being active and assertive.
- Wanting to exercise influence over subordinates.
- Being visibly different from followers.
- Being willing to do routine administrative tasks.

Like McClelland, Miner also used a projective test to measure a person's motivation to manage. Miner's Sentence Completion Scale (MSCS) consists of a series of incomplete sentences dealing with the six components just described (such as "My relationship with my boss . . . "). Respondents are asked to complete the sentences, which are scored according to established criteria. The overall composite MSCS score (though not component scores) has consistently been found to predict leadership success in hierarchical or bureaucratic organizations.[45] Thus individuals who maintained respect for authority figures, wanted to be recognized, acted assertively, actively influenced subordinates, maintained "psychological distance" between themselves and their followers, and readily took on routine administrative tasks were more apt to be successful in bureaucratic organizations. However, Miner claimed that different qualities were needed in flatter, nonbureaucratic organizations, and his review of the MSCS[46] supports this view.

Findings concerning both the need for power and the motivation to manage have several implications for leadership practitioners. First, not all individuals like being leaders. One reason may be that some have a relatively low need for power or motivation to manage. Because these scores are relatively stable and fairly difficult to change, leaders who do not enjoy their role may want to seek positions where they have fewer supervisory responsibilities.

Second, a high need for power or motivation to manage does not guarantee leadership success. The situation can play a crucial role in determining whether the need for power or the motivation to manage is related to leadership success. For example, McClelland and Boyatzis[47] found the need for power to be related to leadership success for nontechnical managers only, and Miner[48] found that motivation to manage was related to leadership success only in hierarchical or bureaucratic organizations.

Third, to be successful in the long term, leaders may require both a high need for socialized power and a high level of activity inhibition. Leaders who impulsively exercise power merely to satisfy their own selfish needs will probably be ineffective in the long term. Finally, it is important to remember that followers, as well as leaders, differ in the need for power, activity inhibition, and motivation to manage. Certain followers may have stronger needs or motives in this area. Leaders may need to behave differently toward these followers than they might toward followers having a low need for power or motivation to manage.

Two recent studies offer a fitting conclusion to this section about power and the individual's motives and a transition to our next topic. Magee and Galinsky[49] not only have presented a comprehensive review of the nature of power in hierarchical settings but also have noted that the acquisition and application of power induce transformation of individual psychological process, with the result being manifested by actions to further increase power! This is not the first time this phenomenon has been observed (recall Lord Acton's words about power and corruption). That power actually transforms individual psychological processes as an underlying cause of this phenomenon is fascinating.

But just having power, by either situation or individual transformation, does not guarantee success. Treadway and colleagues[50] have presented research showing that while past work performance is a source of personal reputation and can increase an individual's power, this increase does not necessarily translate into influence over others. Many fail to achieve this increased influence due to their lack of political skills for influence, and the application of influence is our next topic.

Influence Tactics

Whereas power is the capacity or potential to influence others, influence tactics are the actual behaviors used by an agent to change the attitudes, opinions, or behaviors of a target person. Kipnis and his associates accomplished much of the early work on the types of influence tactics one person uses to influence another.[51] Various instruments have been developed to study influence tactics, but the Influence Behavior Questionnaire, or IBQ,[52] seems to be the most promising. Here is a detailed discussion of the different influence tactics assessed by the IBQ.

Types of Influence Tactics

The IBQ is designed to assess nine types of influence tactics, and its scales give us a convenient overview of various methods of influencing others. **Rational persuasion** occurs when an agent uses logical arguments or factual evidence to influence others. An example of rational persuasion would be when a politician's adviser explains how demographic changes in the politician's district make it important for the politician to spend relatively more time in the district seeing constituents than she has in the recent past. Agents make **inspirational appeals** when they make a request or proposal designed to arouse enthusiasm or emotions in targets. An example here might be a minister's impassioned plea to members of a congregation about the good works that could be accomplished if a proposed addition to the church were built. **Consultation** occurs when agents ask targets to participate in planning an activity. An example of consultation would be if a minister established a committee of church members to help plan the layout and use of a new church addition. In this case the consultative work might not only lead to a better building plan but also *strengthen member commitment* to the idea of a new addition. **Ingratiation** occurs when an agent attempts to get you in a good mood before making a request. A familiar example here would be a salesperson's good-natured or flattering banter with you before you make a decision about purchasing a product. Agents use **personal appeals** when they ask another to do a favor out of friendship. A sentence that opens with, "Bill, we've known each other a long time and I've never asked anything of you before" represents the beginning of a personal appeal, whereas influencing a target through the exchange of favors is labeled **exchange.** If two politicians agree to vote for each other's pet legislation despite minor misgivings about each other's bills, that is exchange. **Coalition tactics** differ from consultation in that they are used when agents seek the aid or support of others to influence the target. A dramatic example of coalition tactics occurs when several significant people in an alcoholic's life (such as spouse, children, employer, or neighbor) agree to confront the alcoholic in unison about the many dimensions of his or her problem. Threats or persistent reminders used to influence targets are known as **pressure tactics.** A judge who gives a convicted prisoner a suspended sentence but tells him to consider the suspension a "sword hanging over his head" if he breaks the law again is using pressure tactics. Finally, **legitimizing tactics** occur when agents make requests based on their position or authority. A principal may ask a teacher to be on the school's curriculum committee, and the

Don't threaten. I know it's done by some of our people, but I don't go for it. If people are running scared, they're not going to make the right decisions. They'll make decisions to please the boss rather than recommend what has to be done.

Charles Pilliod

teacher may accede to the request despite reservations because it is the principal's prerogative to appoint any teacher to that role. In practice, of course, actual tactics often combine these approaches. Rarely, for example, is an effective appeal purely inspirational without any rational elements.

Influence Tactics and Power

As alluded to throughout this chapter, a strong relationship exists between the relative power of agents and targets and the types of influence tactics used. Because leaders with high amounts of referent power have built close relationships with followers, they may be more able to use a wide variety of influence tactics to modify the attitudes and behaviors of their followers. For example, leaders with referent power could use inspirational appeals, consultations, ingratiation, personal appeals, exchanges, and even coalition tactics to increase the amount of time a particular follower spends doing work-related activities. Note, however, that leaders with high referent power generally do not use legitimizing or pressure tactics to influence followers because, by threatening followers, leaders risk some loss of referent power. Leaders who have only coercive or legitimate power may be able to use only coalition, legitimizing, or pressure tactics to influence followers.

Other factors also can affect the choice of influence tactics.[53] People typically use hard tactics (that is, legitimizing or pressure tactics) when an influencer has the upper hand, when they anticipate resistance, or when the other person's behavior violates important norms. People typically use soft tactics (such as ingratiation) when they are at a disadvantage, when they expect resistance, or when they will personally benefit if the attempt is successful. People tend to use rational tactics (the exchange and rational appeals) when parties are relatively equal in power, when resistance is not anticipated, and when the benefits are organizational as well as personal. Studies have shown that influence attempts based on factual, logical analyses are the most frequently reported method by which middle managers exert lateral influence[54] and upward influence.[55] Other important components of successful influence of one's superiors include thoroughly preparing beforehand, involving others for support (coalition tactics), and persisting through a combination of approaches.[56]

Findings about who uses different tactics, and when, provide interesting insights into the influence process. It is clear that one's influence tactic of choice depends on many factors, including intended outcomes and one's power relative to the target person. Although it may not be surprising that people select influence tactics as a function of their power relationship with another person, it is striking that this relationship holds true so universally across different social domains—for business executives, for parents and children, and for spouses. There is a strong tendency for people to resort to hard tactics whenever they have an advantage in clout if other tactics fail to get results.[57] As the bank robber Willie Sutton once

Gender Differences in Managing Upward: How Male and Female Managers Get Their Way

HIGHLIGHT 4.4

Both male and female managers in a *Fortune* 100 company were interviewed and completed surveys about how they influence upward—that is, how they influence their own bosses. The results generally supported the idea that female managers' influence attempts showed greater concern for others, whereas male managers' influence attempts showed greater concern for self. Female managers were more likely to act with the organization's broad interests in mind, consider how others felt about the influence attempt, involve others in planning, and focus on both the task and interpersonal aspects of the situation. Male managers, on the other hand, were more likely to act out of self-interest, show less consideration for how others might feel about the influence attempt, work alone in developing their strategy, and focus primarily on the task.

One of the most surprising findings of the study was that, contrary to prediction, female managers were less likely than male managers to compromise or negotiate during their influence attempts. The female managers were actually more likely to persist in trying to persuade their superiors, even to the point of open opposition. At first this may seem inconsistent with the idea that the female managers' influence style involved greater concern for their relatedness to others. However, it seems consistent with the higher value placed by the women managers on involvement. Perhaps female managers demonstrate more commitment to their issues, and greater self-confidence that they are doing the "right thing," precisely because they have already interacted more with others in the organization and know they have others' support.

While male and female managers emphasized different influence techniques, it is important to note that neither group overall was more effective than the other. Nonetheless, there may be significant implications of the various techniques for a manager's career advancement. At increasingly higher management levels in an organization, effectiveness may be defined primarily by its fit with the organization's own norms and values. Managers whose style most closely matches that of their superior may have an advantage in evaluations and promotion decisions. This may be a significant factor for women, given the highly skewed representation of males in the most senior executive ranks.

Source: K. E. Lauterbach and B. J. Weiner, "Dynamics of Upward Influence: How Male and Female Managers Get Their Way," *Leadership Quarterly 7*, no. 1 (1996), pp. 87–107.

> It is not power that corrupts, but fear. Fear of losing power corrupts those who wield it and fear of the scourge of power corrupts those who are subject to it.
>
> **Aung San Suu Kyi**

---

said, "You can get more with a kind word and a gun than you can get with just a kind word." This sentiment is apparently familiar to bank managers, too. The latter reported greater satisfaction in handling subordinates' poor performance when they were relatively more punishing.[58] Highlight 4.4 offers thoughts on how men and women managers sometimes use different influence techniques.

Although hard tactics can be effective, relying on them can change the way we see others. This was demonstrated in an experiment wherein leaders' perceptions and evaluations of subordinates were assessed after they exercised different sorts of authority over the subordinates.[59] Several hundred business students acted as managers of small work groups assembling model cars. Some of the students were told to act in an authoritarian manner, exercising complete control over the group's work; others

All forms of tampering with human beings, getting at them, shaping them against their will to your own pattern, all thought control and conditioning, is, therefore, a denial of that in men which makes them men and their values ultimate.

**A. A. Berle Jr.,
writer about
corporations**

were told to act as democratic leaders, letting group members participate fully in decisions about the work. As expected, authoritarian leaders used more hard tactics, whereas democratic leaders influenced subordinates more through rational methods. More interesting was the finding that subordinates were evaluated by the two types of leaders in dramatically different ways even though the subordinates of both types did equally good work. Authoritarian leaders judged their subordinates as less motivated, less skilled, and less suited for promotion. Apparently, bosses who use hard tactics to control others' behavior tend not to attribute any resultant good performance to the subordinates themselves. Ironically, the act of using hard tactics leads to negative attributions about others, which, in turn, tend to corroborate the use of hard tactics in the first place.

Finally, we should remember that using influence tactics can be thought of as a social skill. Choosing the right tactic may not always be enough to ensure good results; the behavior must be *skillfully executed*. We are not encouraging deviousness or a manipulative attitude toward others, merely recognizing the obvious fact that clumsy influence attempts often come across as phony and may be counterproductive. See Highlight 4.5 for some interesting ways influence skills are applied in the political arena.

To Be or Not to Be . . . a Porcupine

HIGHLIGHT 4.5

We have said that there are no simple recipes for leadership. This is evident in the various ways power and influence are exercised in the halls of the U.S. Congress. In *The Power Game*, author Hedrick Smith offers numerous examples of how Washington, DC, actually works. For example, interpersonal relationships play a key part in one's effectiveness; but there are many paths to interpersonal power and influence in government, as the following anecdotes point out.

Barney Frank, a Democratic congressman from Massachusetts, likens success in the House of Representatives to high school. Nobody in the House can give any other member an order, not even the speaker of the house. Neither can anyone be fired except by his or her own constituencies. That means, therefore, that those in Congress become influential by persuading people and having others respect but

not resent them. In that sense it's like high school. Sometimes, however, it may pay to be *unlikable,* at least in some situations. Former senator (and later secretary of state) Ed Muskie had a reputation for being a "porcupine"—for being difficult in the conference committees where final versions of legislation were hammered out. A former staff member said Muskie was the best porcupine of them all because nobody wanted to tangle with him. Muskie will "be gross. He'll smoke a god-awful cigar. He'll just be difficult, cantankerous." One reason Muskie was so successful as a legislator was precisely that he could be nearly impossible to deal with. People would rather ignore him and try to avoid fights or confrontations with his notorious temper. Muskie knew how to be a porcupine, and he used that behavior to advantage in authoring critical legislation.

Source: H. Smith, *The Power Game* (New York: Random House, 1988).

A Concluding Thought about Influence Tactics

In our discussion here, an implicit lesson for leaders is the value of being conscious of what influence tactics one uses and what effects are typically associated with each tactic. Knowledge of such effects can help a leader make better decisions about her or his manner of influencing others. It might also be helpful for leaders to think carefully about why they believe a particular influence tactic will be effective. Research indicates that some reasons for selecting among various possible influence tactics lead to successful outcomes more frequently than others. Specifically, thinking an act would improve an employee's self-esteem or morale was frequently associated with successful influence attempts. On the other hand, choosing an influence tactic because it followed company policy and choosing one because it was a way to put a subordinate in his place were frequently mentioned as reasons for unsuccessful influence attempts.[60] In a nutshell, these results suggest that leaders should pay attention not only to the actual influence tactics they use—to *how* they are influencing others—but also to *why* they believe such methods are called for. It is perhaps obvious that influence efforts intended to build others up more frequently lead to positive outcomes than influence efforts intended to put others down.

Summary	This chapter has defined *power* as the capacity or potential to exert influence, *influence tactics* as the behaviors used by one person to modify the attitudes and behaviors of another, and *influence* as the degree of change in a person's attitudes, values, or behaviors as the result of another's influence tactic. Because power, influence, and influence tactics play such important roles in the leadership process, this chapter provided ideas to help leaders improve their effectiveness. By reflecting on their different bases of power, leaders may better understand how they can affect followers and even expand their power. The five bases of power also offer clues to why subordinates can influence leaders and successfully resist leaders' influence attempts.

Leaders also may gain insight into why they may not enjoy certain aspects of their responsibilities by reflecting on their own need for power or motivation to manage; they may also better understand why some leaders exercise power selfishly by considering McClelland's concepts of personalized power and activity inhibition. Leaders can improve their effectiveness by finding ways to enhance their idiosyncratic credit and not permitting in-group and out-group rivalries to develop in the work unit.

Although power is an extremely important concept, having power is relatively meaningless unless a leader is willing to exercise it. The exercise of power occurs primarily through the influence tactics leaders and followers use to modify each other's attitudes and behaviors. The types of influence tactics used seem to depend on the amount of different types of power possessed, the degree of resistance expected, and the rationale behind the different influence tactics. Because influence tactics designed to build up others are generally more successful than those that tear others down, leadership practitioners should always consider why they are using a particular influence attempt before they actually use it. By carefully considering the rationale behind the tactic, leaders may be able to avoid using pressure and legitimizing tactics and find better ways to influence followers. Being able to use influence tactics that modify followers' attitudes and behaviors in the desired direction while they build up followers' self-esteem and self-confidence is a skill all leaders should strive to master.

Key Terms

power, *118*
influence, *119*
influence tactics, *119*
pecking order, *121*
expert power, *125*
referent power, *126*
legitimate power, *128*
reward power, *129*
coercive power, *130*
need for power, *135*

personalized
power, *135*
socialized power, *135*
projective personality
test, *135*
motivation to
manage, *136*
rational
persuasion, *138*

inspirational
appeals, *138*
consultation, *138*
ingratiation, *138*
personal appeals, *138*
exchange, *138*
coalition tactics, *138*
pressure tactics, *138*
legitimizing tactics, *138*

Questions

1. The following questions pertain to the Milgram studies (Highlight 4.2):
   a. What bases of power were available to the experimenter, and what bases of power were available to the subjects?
   b. Do you think subjects with a low need for power would act differently from subjects with a high need for power? What about subjects with differing levels of the motivation to manage?
   c. What situational factors contributed to the experimenter's power?
   d. What influence tactics did the experimenter use to change the behavior of the subjects, and how were these tactics related to the experimenter's power base?
   e. What actually was influenced? In other words, if influence is the change in another's attitudes, values, or behaviors as the result of an influence tactic, then what changes occurred in the subjects as the result of the experimenter's influence tactics?
   f. Many people have criticized the Milgram study on ethical grounds. Assuming that some socially useful information was gained from the studies, do you believe this experiment could or should be replicated today?

2. Some definitions of leadership exclude reliance on formal authority or coercion (that is, certain actions by a person in authority may work but should not be considered leadership). What are the pros and cons of such a view?

3. Does power, as Lord Acton suggested, tend to corrupt the power holder? If so, what are some of the ways it happens? Is it also possible subordinates are corrupted by a superior's power? How? Is it possible that superiors can be corrupted by a subordinate's power?

4. Some people say it dilutes a leader's authority if subordinates are allowed to give feedback to the leader concerning their perceptions of the leader's performance. Do you agree?

5. Is *leadership* just another word for *influence*? Can you think of some examples of influence that you would *not* consider leadership?

Activity

This activity will demonstrate how the five bases of power are manifest in behavior. Write the five bases of power on the board or put them on an overhead. Break students into five groups, and give each group a 3 × 5 card that lists one of the five bases of power. Give the group 10 minutes to plan and practice a 1-minute skit that will be presented to the rest of the class. The skit should demonstrate the base of power listed on the 3 × 5 card. After the skit is presented, the remaining groups should guess which base of power is being used in the skit. As an alternative, you might choose a project for out-of-class work. Another variation is to assign the groups the task of finding a 3- to 4-minute segment from a movie or video representing a base of power and bring that in to the class.

Minicase

The Prime Minister's Powerful Better Half

Ho Ching's power has been recognized by many. As chief executive officer of Temasek Holdings, she ranked number 18 on a list of Asia's most powerful businesspeople and number 24 on the *Forbes* list of the world's most powerful women. How did a shy, Stanford-educated electrical engineer end up with this kind of power? Ho was a government scholar who started off in civil service and ended up working for the Defense Ministry in Singapore. There she met and married Lee Hsien Loong, Singapore's current prime minister and the son of Lee Kwan Yew—one of modern Singapore's founding fathers. Ho's experience, education, and connections led to her appointment as chief executive of Temasek, where she oversees a portfolio worth over $50 billion and influences many of Singapore's leading companies.

Temasek Holdings was established in 1974 in an attempt by the Singapore government to drive industrialization. Through Temasek Holdings the Singapore government took stakes in a wide range of companies, including the city-state's best-known companies: Singapore Airlines, Singapore Telecommunications, DBS Bank, Neptune Orient Lines, and Keppel Corp. The company's Web site describes Temasek's "humble roots during a turbulent and uncertain time" and its commitment "to building a vibrant future [for Singapore] through successful enterprise." Ho's appointment to Temasek in May 2002 caused some controversy; as prime minister her husband has a supervisory role over the firm. Ho denies any conflict of interest:

> The issue of conflict does not arise because there are no vested interests. Our goal is to do what makes sense for Singapore, I don't always agree with him (Mr. Lee) and he doesn't always agree with me. We have a healthy debate on issues.

In her role as CEO, Ho is pushing for a more open policy and an aggressive drive into the Asian market. Under Ho's leadership Temasek has decided to publicly disclose its annual report with details of its performance—details that have formerly remained private and been known only to Temasek executives.

Ho is concentrating on broadening Temasek's focus beyond Singapore, most recently opening an office in India. At a recent conference of top Indian companies, Ho appealed to investors to look to India for opportunities for Asian growth:

> Since the Asian financial crisis in 1997, the word *Asia* had lost a bit of its sparkle. But that sparkle is beginning to return. In the 1960s and 1970s, the Asia economic miracle referred to East Asia, specifically Japan. The 1970s and 1980s saw the emergence of the four Asian Tigers of Korea, Taiwan, Hong Kong, and Singapore.

> Now is India's turn to stir, standing at an inflexion point, after 10 years of market liberalisation and corporate restructuring. Since 1997, Singapore's trade with India grew by 50 percent, or a respectable CAGR of about 7.5 percent. Confidence is brimming in India, and Indian companies began to reach out boldly to the world over the last five years.

> All these waves of development have shown that Asia, with a combined population of 3 billion, has been resilient. If Asia continues to work hard and work smart, honing her competitive strengths and leveraging on her complementary capabilities across borders, the outlook in the next decade or two looks very promising indeed.

1. We have described *power* as the capacity to cause change and *influence* as the degree of actual change in a target's behaviors. Ho Ching's power as a leader has been recognized by many, but would you describe Ho Ching as an influential leader? Why?

2. Based on the excerpt from Ho Ching's speech, what type of tactics does she use to influence the behavior of others?

3. Ho Ching has been named one of the most powerful leaders in Asia. What are her major sources of power?

Sources: http://www.fastcompany.com/online/13/womenofpr.html; http://www.forbes.com/finance/lists/11/2004/LIR.jhtml?passListId=11&passYear=2004& passListType=Person&uniqueId=OO5O&datatype=Person; http://www.businessweek.com/magazine/content/02_36/b3798161.htm; http://www.laksamana.net/vnews.cfm?ncat=31&news_id=5292; http://in.rediff.com/money/2004/apr/03spec.htm; http://www.theaustralian.news.com.au/ common/story_page/0%2C5744%2C10427548% 255E2703%2C00.html; http://in.news.yahoo.com/040812/137/2fgoc.html.

End Notes

1. N. Hill, "Self-Esteem: The Key to Effective Leadership," *Administrative Management* 40, no. 9 (1985), pp. 71–76.

2. D. Donno, "Introduction," in *The Prince and Selected Discourses: Machiavelli*, ed. and trans. D. Dunno (New York: Bantam, 1966).

3. J. W. Gardner, *On Leadership* (New York: Free Press, 1990); J. W. Gardener, *The Tasks of Leadership*, Leadership paper no. 2 (Washington, DC: Independent Sector, 1986).

4. T. R. Hinkin and C. A. Schriesheim, "Development and Application of New Scales to Measure the French and Raven (1959) Bases of Social Power," *Journal of Applied Psychology* 74 (1989), pp. 561–67.

5. J. M. Burns, *Leadership* (New York: Harper & Row, 1978).

6. R. J. House, "Power in Organizations: A Social Psychological Perspective," unpublished manuscript, University of Toronto, 1984.

7. B. M. Bass, *Bass and Stogdill's Handbook of Leadership*, 3rd ed. (New York: Free Press, 1990).

8. N. Levina and W. Orlikowski, "Understanding Shifting Power Relations within and across Organizations," *Academy of Management Journal* 52, no. 4 (2009), pp. 672–703.

9. J. Nelson, "Corporate Governance Practices, CEO Characteristics, and Firm Performance," *Journal of Corporate Finance*, 11 (2005), pp. 197–228.

10. D. E. Winkel and B. R. Ragins, "Navigating the Emotional Battlefield: Gender, Power, and Emotion in Entrepreneurial Relationships," *Academy of Management Proceedings* (2008), pp. 1–6.

11. Gardner, *On Leadership; Gardner, The Tasks of Leadership*.

12. Gardner, *On Leadership; Gardner, The Tasks of Leadership*.

13. C. A. Schriesheim and T. R. Hinkin, "Influence Tactics Used by Subordinates: A Theoretical and Empirical Analysis and Refinement of the Kipnis, Schmidt, and Wilkinson Subscales," *Journal of Applied Psychology* 75 (1990), pp. 246–57.

14. Bass, *Bass and Stogdill's Handbook of Leadership*.

15. J. Ehrlichman, *Witness to Power* (New York: Simon & Schuster, 1982).

16. P. R. Wilson, "The Perceptual Distortion of Height as a Function of Ascribed Academic Status," *Journal of Social Psychology* 74 (1968), pp. 97–102.

17. R. B. Cialdini, *Influence* (New York: William Morrow, 1984).

18. L. Bickman, "The Social Power of a Uniform," *Journal of Applied Social Psychology* (1974), pp. 47–61.

19. M. Mulder, R. D. de Jong, L. Koppelar, and J. Verhage, "Power, Situation, and Leaders' Effectiveness: An Organizational Study," *Journal of Applied Psychology* 71 (1986), pp. 566–70.

20. J. French and B. H. Raven, "The Bases of Social Power," in *Studies of Social Power*, ed. D. Cartwright (Ann Arbor, MI: Institute for Social Research, 1959).

21. French and Raven, "The Bases of Social Power."

22. Associated Press, January 9, 1991.

23. T. J. Peters and R. H. Waterman, *In Search of Excellence* (New York: Harper & Row, 1982).

24. G. Yukl, *Leadership in Organizations*, 2nd ed. (Englewood Cliffs, NJ: Prentice Hall, 1989).

25. E. L. Deci, "Effects of Contingent and Noncontingent Rewards and Controls on Intrinsic Motivation," *Organizational Behavior and Human Performance* 22 (1972), pp. 113–20.

26. E. M. Ryan, V. Mims, and R. Koestner, "Relation of Reward Contingency and Interpersonal Context to Intrinsic Motivation: A Review and Test Using Cognitive Evaluation Theory," *Journal of Personality and Social Psychology* 45 (1983), pp. 736–50.

27. M. M. Wakin, "Ethics of Leadership," in *Military Leadership*, ed. J. H. Buck and L. J. Korb (Beverly Hills, CA: Sage, 1981).

28. S. B. Klein, *Learning*, 2nd ed. (New York: McGraw-Hill, 1991).

29. F. Barnes, "Mistakes New Presidents Make," *Reader's Digest*, January 1989, p. 43.

30. F. Conway and J. Siegelman, *Snapping* (New York: Delta, 1979).

31. G. A. Yukl, *Leadership in Organizations*, 1st ed. (Englewood Cliffs, NJ: Prentice Hall, 1981).

32. Ibid.

33. P. M. Podsakoff and C. A. Schriesheim, "Field Studies of French and Raven's Bases of Power: Critique, Reanalysis, and Suggestions for Future Research," *Psychological Bulletin* 97 (1985), pp. 387–411.

34. T. R. Hinkin and C. A. Schriesheim, "Development and Application of New Scales to Measure the French and Raven (1959) Bases of Social Power," *Journal of Applied Psychology* 74 (1989), pp. 561–67.

35. G. Yukl, *Leadership in Organizations*, 2nd ed. (Englewood Cliffs, NJ: Prentice Hall, 1989).

36. E. P. Hollander and L. R. Offermann, "Power and Leadership in Organizations," *American Psychologist* 45 (1990), pp. 179–89.

37. J. Pfeffer, "The Ambiguity of Leadership," in *Leadership: Where Else Can We Go?* ed. M. W. McCall Jr. and M. M. Lombardo (Durham, NC: Duke University Press, 1977).

38. D. C. McClelland, *Power: The Inner Experience* (New York: Irvington, 1975).

39. D. C. McClelland and R. E. Boyatzis, "Leadership Motive Pattern and Long-Term Success in Management," *Journal of Applied Psychology* 67 (1982), pp. 737–43.

40. M. J. Stahl, "Achievement, Power, and Managerial Motivation: Selecting Managerial Talent with the Job Choice Exercise," *Personnel Psychology* 36 (1983), pp. 775–89.

41. E. Fodor, "Motive Pattern as an Influence on Leadership in Small Groups," paper presented at the meeting of the American Psychological Association, New York, August 1987.

42. D. C. McClelland and R. E. Boyatzis, "Leadership Motive Pattern and Long-Term Success in Management," *Journal of Applied Psychology* 67 (1982), pp. 737–43.

43. D. C. McClelland, *Human Motivation* (Glenview, IL: Scott Foresman, 1985).

44. J. B. Miner, "Student Attitudes toward Bureaucratic Role Prescriptions and the Prospects for Managerial Shortages," *Personnel Psychology* 27 (1974), pp. 605–13.

45. J. B. Miner, "Twenty Years of Research on Role Motivation Theory of Managerial Effectiveness," *Personnel Psychology* 31 (1978), pp. 739–60.

46. Miner, "Twenty Years of Research."

47. McClelland and Boyatzis, "Leadership Motive Pattern and Long-Term Success in Management."

48. Miner, "Twenty Years of Research."

49. J. C. Magee and A. D. Galinsky, "Social Hierarchy: The Self-Reinforcing Nature of Power and Status," *Academy of Management Annals* 2, no. 1 (2008), pp. 351–98.

50. D. C. Treadway, J. W. Breland, J. Cho, J. Yang, and A. B. Duke, "Performance Is Not Enough: Political Skill in the Longitudinal Performance–Power Relationship," *Academy of Management Proceedings* (2009), pp. 1–6.

51. D. Kipnis and S. M. Schmidt, *Profiles of Organizational Strategies* (San Diego, CA: University Associates, 1982).

52. G. A. Yukl, R. Lepsinger, and T. Lucia, "Preliminary Report on the Development and Validation of the Influence Behavior Questionnaire," in *Impact of Leadership,* ed. K. E. Clark, M. B. Clark, and D. P. Campbell (Greensboro, NC: Center for Creative Leadership, 1992).

53. D. Kipnis and S. M. Schmidt, "The Language of Persuasion," *Psychology Today* 19, no. 4 (1985), pp. 40–46.

54. B. Keys, T. Case, T. Miller, K. E. Curran, and C. Jones, "Lateral Influence Tactics in Organizations," *International Journal of Management* 4 (1987), pp. 425–37.

55. T. Case, L. Dosier, G. Murkison, and B. Keys, "How Managers Influence Superiors: A Study of Upward Influence Tactics," *Leadership and Organization Development Journal* 9, no. 4 (1988), pp. 4, 25–31.

56. Case et al., "How Managers Influence Superiors."

57. D. Kipnis and S. M. Schmidt, "The Language of Persuasion," *Psychology Today* 19, no. 4 (1985), pp. 40–46.

58. S. G. Green, G. T. Fairhurst, and B. K. Snavely, "Chains of Poor Performance and Supervisory Control," *Organizational Behavior and Human Decision Processes* 38 (1986), pp. 7–27.

59. D. Kipnis, "Technology, Power, and Control," *Research in the Sociology of Organizations* 3 (1984a), pp. 125–56.

60. L. Dosier, T. Case, and B. Keys, "How Managers Influence Subordinates: An Empirical Study of Downward Influence Tactics," *Leadership and Organization Development Journal* 9, no. 5 (1988), pp. 22–31.

Chapter 5

Leadership, Ethics, and Values

Introduction

In the previous chapter we examined many facets of power and its use in leadership. Leaders can use power for good or ill, and a leader's personal values and ethical code may be among the most important determinants of how that leader exercises the various sources of power available. That this aspect of leadership needs closer scrutiny seems evident enough in the face of the past decade's wave of scandals involving political, business, and even religious leaders who collectively rocked trust in both our leaders and our institutions. It should be sobering and worrisome that a serious presidential contender in one of our major parties not only had an ongoing extramarital affair during the campaign, which he lied about at the time (including his possible paternity of a child from that affair, later validated and admitted), but also managed to induce his own staff to cover it up. We might only wonder about what levels of honesty we could have expected from *that* White House had events unfolded differently. In the face of such depressing headlines about corrupt leadership, it is not surprising that scholarly and popular literature have turned greater attention to the question of ethical leadership.[1]

Leadership and "Doing the Right Things"

In Chapter 1 we referred to a distinction between leaders and managers that says leaders do the right things whereas managers do things right. But what are the "right things"? Are they the morally right things? The ethically right things? The right things for the company to be successful? And who says what the right things are?

Leaders face dilemmas that require choices between competing sets of values and priorities, and the best leaders recognize and face them with a commitment to doing what is right, not just what is expedient. Of course the phrase *doing what is right* sounds deceptively simple. Sometimes it takes great moral courage to do what is right, even when the right action seems clear. At other times, though, leaders face complex challenges that lack simple black-and-white answers. Whichever the case, leaders set a moral example to others that becomes the model for an entire group or organization, for good or bad. Leaders who themselves do not honor truth do not inspire it in others. Leaders concerned mostly with their own advancement do not inspire selflessness in others. Leaders should internalize a strong set of **ethics**—principles of right conduct or a system of moral values.

Leadership cannot just go along to get along . . . Leadership must meet the moral challenge of the day.

Jesse Jackson

Both Gardner[2] and Burns[3] have stressed the centrality and importance of the moral dimension of leadership. Gardner said leaders ultimately must be judged on the basis of a framework of values, not just in terms of their effectiveness. He put the question of a leader's relations with his or her followers or constituents on the moral plane, arguing (with the philosopher Immanuel Kant) that leaders should always treat others as ends in themselves, not as objects or mere means to the leader's ends (which does not necessarily imply that leaders need to be gentle in interpersonal demeanor or "democratic" in style). Burns took an even more extreme view regarding the moral dimension of leadership, maintaining that leaders who do not behave ethically do not demonstrate true leadership.

Whatever "true leadership" means, most people would agree that at a minimum it is characterized by a high degree of trust between leader and followers. Bennis and Goldsmith[4] described four qualities of leadership that engender trust: vision, empathy, consistency, and integrity. First, we tend to trust leaders who create a compelling *vision:* who pull people together on the basis of shared beliefs and a common sense of organizational purpose and belonging. Second, we tend to trust leaders who demonstrate *empathy* with us—who show they understand the world as we see and experience it. Third, we trust leaders who are *consistent.* This does not mean that we only trust leaders whose positions never change, but that changes are understood as a process of evolution in light of relevant new evidence. Fourth, we tend to trust leaders whose *integrity* is strong, who demonstrate their commitment to higher principles through their actions.

Another important factor affecting the degree of trust between leaders and followers involves fundamental assumptions people make about human nature. Several decades ago Douglas McGregor[5] explained different styles of managerial behavior on the basis of people's implicit attitudes about human nature, and his work remains quite influential today. McGregor identified two contrasting sets of assumptions people make about human nature, calling these **Theory X** and **Theory Y.**

In the simplest sense, Theory X reflects a more pessimistic view of others. Managers with this orientation rely heavily on coercive, external control methods to motivate workers, such as pay, disciplinary techniques, punishments, and threats. They assume people are not naturally industrious or motivated to work. Hence it is the manager's job to minimize the harmful effects of workers' natural laziness and irresponsibility by closely overseeing their work and creating external incentives to do well and disincentives to avoid slacking off. Theory Y, on the other hand, reflects a view that most people are intrinsically motivated by their work. Rather than needing to be coaxed or coerced to work productively, such people value a sense of achievement, personal growth, pride in contributing to their organization, and respect for a job well done. Peter Jackson, the director of the *Lord of the Rings* film trilogy, seems to exemplify a Theory Y view of human nature. When asked, "How do you stand up to executives?" Jackson answered, "Well, I just find that most people appreciate honesty. I find that if you try not to have any pretensions and you tell the truth, you talk to them and you treat them as collaborators, I find that studio people are usually very supportive."

There is nothing so fast as the speed of trust.
Stephen Covey

But are there practical advantages to holding a Theory X or Theory Y view? Evidently there are. There is evidence that success more frequently comes to leaders who share a positive view of human nature. Hall and Donnell[6] reported findings of five separate studies involving over 12,000 managers that explored the relationship between managerial achievement and attitudes toward subordinates. Overall, they found that managers who strongly subscribed to Theory X beliefs were far more likely to be in their lower-achieving group.

The dilemma, of course, is that for the most part both Theory X and Theory Y leaders would say they have the right beliefs and are doing the right things. This begs the question of what people generally mean by "right," which in turn raises an array of issues involving ethics, moral reasoning, values, and the influence they have on our behavior.

Values, Ethics, and Morals

Values are "constructs representing generalized behaviors or states of affairs that are considered by the individual to be important."[7] When Patrick Henry said, "Give me liberty, or give me death," he was expressing the value he placed on political freedom. The opportunity to constantly study and learn may be the fundamental value or "state of affairs" leading a person to pursue a career in academia. Someone who values personal integrity may be forced to resign from an unethical company. Values are learned through the socialization process, and they become internalized and for most people represent integral components of the self.[8] Thus values play a central role in one's overall psychological makeup and can affect behavior in a variety of situations. In work settings, values can affect decisions about joining an organization, organizational commitment, relationships with co-workers, and decisions about leaving an organization.[9] It is important for leaders to realize that

The Average Self-Rating on "Ethical Behavior" Is Way above Average

HIGHLIGHT 5.1

David Campbell is one of the world's most prolific researchers in the field of leadership. Among other things, he has authored numerous widely used surveys to assess various facets of leadership. The following story relates his efforts to develop an ethics scale for the Campbell Leadership Index (CLI).

In preliminary work on the CLI, it seemed obvious that ethics was central to the practice of good leadership and therefore should be one of the scales on the instrument (the CLI now includes 17 scales, including ambitious, enterprising, considerate, entertaining, organized, and productive). Consequently, in the early versions of the survey Campbell included adjectives such as *ethical, honest, trustworthy,* and *candid,* and negative adjectives such as *deceptive* and *scheming.* As with other CLI scales, this one was normed so that the average person would receive a score of 50 on the ethics

scale; obviously some would get higher scores and some lower scores.

During the CLI testing period, however, a major problem emerged: almost no one wanted to believe that he or she was merely average in ethical behavior, let alone below average. To soften the impact of such feedback, Campbell changed the name of the scale to "trustworthy" in the hope that this would retain the meaning but lessen the adverse reaction. But that change helped little. Eventually Campbell changed the name of the scale to "credible," which is more acceptable and also better captures the reasons why some executives may get low ratings on the scale despite self-perceptions of scrupulous honesty. The point, though, is not just the value of good PR, or what's in a name. Campbell's challenge in naming his scale underscores the difficulty of looking objectively at one's own behavior, and that, in turn, makes it difficult to look objectively at factors that affect ethical behavior.

individuals in the same work unit can have considerably different values, especially because we cannot see values directly. We can only make inferences about people's values based on their behavior.

Some of the major values that may be considered important by individuals in an organization are listed in Table 5.1. The instrumental values found in Table 5.1 refer to modes of behavior, and the terminal values refer to desired end states.[10] For example, some individuals value equality, freedom, and a comfortable life above all else; others may believe that family security and salvation are important goals. In terms of instrumental values, such individuals may think it is important always to act in an

TABLE 5.1
People Vary in the Relative Importance They Place on Values

Source: Adapted from M. Rokeach, *The Nature of Human Values* (New York: Free Press, 1973).

Terminal Values	Instrumental Values
An exciting life	Being courageous
A sense of accomplishment	Being helpful
Family security	Being honest
Inner harmony	Being imaginative
Social recognition	Being logical
Friendship	Being responsible

Glass, china, and repu-
tation are easily crack'd,
and never well mended.
  Benjamin Franklin

ambitious, capable, and honest manner, whereas others may think it is important only to be ambitious and capable. We should add that the instrumental and terminal values in Table 5.1 are only a few of those Rokeach has identified.

It's logical to wonder, of course, whether someone who values honesty is therefore a more honest person than one who may claim to value honesty less. To some extent that depends on what we know is an imperfect relationship between what people say and what people do, but it also makes salient certain subtle differences among seemingly similar terms.

Let's begin with ethics and morals—are they really the same thing? To some extent this depends on whom you ask. Technically speaking, ethics is a branch of philosophy dealing with principles of right conduct. Historically, ethics has focused on the *use of reason* to find appropriate principles or rules to govern conduct, whereas morality has dealt more with how various rules of conduct are applied in actual behavior. Admittedly, such a distinction between ethics and morality—between the head and the heart, as it were—may seem artificial to the average person. Even among philosophers who find it useful to distinguish ethics from morality, it is still important to admit that in a complex world "both must be used responsibly for us to be effective ethical actors."[11] In that pragmatic spirit, our approach here will be to minimize subtle philosophical distinctions and treat the terms *ethics* and *morals* (and ethical and moral reasoning) interchangeably.

What about values? Are values also essentially the same thing as ethics or morals? In answering that question, it's useful to remember that things that are valued are not necessarily those things that are valuable.[12] The question of what is ultimately valuable is at the heart of the discipline of ethics, which seeks general principles to guide all human conduct, even while recognizing that how people *do* act may be a different matter. You may find it useful to review some of the key distinctions in our own use of some of these words and phrases in Table 5.2

Are There Generational Differences in Values?

Various researchers have said that the pervasive influence of broad forces like major historical events and trends, technological changes, and economic conditions tends to create common value systems among people growing up at a particular time that distinguish them from people who grow up at different times.[13-15] They attribute much of the misunderstanding that may exist between older leaders and younger followers to the fact that their basic value systems were formulated during different social and cultural conditions, and these analyses offer a helpful perspective for understanding how differences in values can add tension to the interaction between some leaders and followers.

Zemke is another researcher who has looked at differences in values across generations and how those value differences affect their approaches

TABLE 5.2
Differentiating Key Terms

Ethics and Morals	Ethical and Moral Reasoning	Values
The "shoulds" and "oughts" of life.	Process used to make moral/ethical decisions.	Do not necessarily involve morals or ethics.
	Focus on "how" rather than "what" decision reached.	Often determined significantly by culture.
	Certain developmental theories posit that progressively higher stages of moral reasoning can be attained.	Beliefs in which individuals or groups have an emotional investment.

to work and leadership.[16] Following is his delineation of four generations of workers, each molded by distinctive experiences during critical developmental periods:

The Veterans (1922–1943): Veterans came of age during the Great Depression and World War II, and they represent a wealth of lore and wisdom. They've been a stabilizing force in organizations for decades, even if they are prone to digressions about "the good old days."

The Baby Boomers (1942–1960): These were the postwar babies who came of age during violent social protests, experimentation with new lifestyles, and pervasive questioning of establishment values. But they're graying now, and they don't like to think of themselves as "the problem" in the workplace even though they sometimes are. Boomers still have passion about bringing participation, spirit, heart, and humanity to the workplace and office. They're also concerned about creating a level playing field for all, but they hold far too many meetings for the typical Gen Xer.

The Gen Xers (1960–1980): Gen Xers grew up during the era of the Watergate scandal, the energy crisis, higher divorce rates, MTV, and corporate downsizing; many were latchkey kids. As a group they tend to be technologically savvy, independent, and skeptical of institutions and hierarchy. They are entrepreneurial and they embrace change. Having seen so many of their parents work long and loyally for one company only to lose their jobs to downsizing, Xers don't believe much in job security; to an Xer, job security comes from having the kinds of skills that make you attractive to an organization. Hence they tend to be more committed to their vocation than to any specific organization. In fact, the free-agency concept born in professional sports also applies to Xers, who are disposed to stay with an organization until a better offer comes along. Among the challenges they present at work is how to meet their need for feedback despite their dislike of close supervision. Xers also seek balance in their lives more than preceding generations; they work to live rather than live to work.

The Nexters (1980–): Also known as *millennials,* this is *your* generation, so any generalizations we make here are particularly risky! In general, however, Nexters share an optimism born, perhaps, from having been raised by parents devoted to the task of bringing their generation to adulthood; they are the children of soccer moms and Little League dads. They doubt the wisdom of traditional racial and sexual categorizing— perhaps not unexpected from a generation rich with opportunities like having Internet pen pals in Asia with whom they can interact any time of the day or night.

Some research has looked at how the values of Gen Xers impact the leadership process at work. One clear finding from this research involved the distinctively different view of authority held by Xers than previous generations. "While past generations might have at least acknowledged positional authority, this new generation has little respect for and less interest in leaders who are unable to demonstrate that they can personally produce. In other words, this generation doesn't define leading as sitting in meetings and making profound vision statements, but instead as eliminating obstacles and giving employees what they need to work well and comfortably."[17] Gen Xers expect managers to "earn their stripes" and not be rewarded with leadership responsibilities merely because of seniority. Often that attitude is interpreted as an indication of disrespect toward elders in general and bosses in particular. It may be more accurate, however, to characterize the attitude as one of skepticism rather than disrespect. Such skepticism could have arisen from the fact that Generation X grew up when there were relatively few heroes or leaders it could call its own. It also might have arisen from growing up in an environment of such pervasive marketing that anything smacking of "hype" is met with suspicion.[18] That skepticism is also evident in the fact that 53 percent of them believe that the soap opera *General Hospital* will be around longer than Medicare, and that a majority of them are more likely to believe in UFOs than that Social Security will last until their retirement.[19] Perhaps you can link some of these presumed characteristics of Gen Xers with some of the formative influences on their lives in Highlight 5.2.

Lest we overemphasize the significance of intergenerational differences, however, we should consider the results of a scientific sampling of over 1,000 people living in the United States that found *little* evidence of a generation gap in basic values. Indeed, the director of one of the largest polling organizations in the world called the results some of the most powerful he had seen in 30 years of public opinion research. They showed, he said, that even though young people have different tastes, they do *not* have a different set of values than their elders.[20] Considering the weight of

Question authority, but raise your hand first.

Bob Thaues

Main Events in the Lives of Gen Xers

HIGHLIGHT 5.2

A number of historical events over the past three and a half decades have had significant impacts on the lives and worldviews of today's emerging leaders.

GENERAL

1968 Martin Luther King Jr. assassinated

1969 U.S. lands on the moon

1973 Watergate scandal begins

1975 Vietnam war ends

1976 Energy crisis

1979 Iran hostage crisis

1981 Center for Disease Control's first published report on AIDS

1981 Reagan assassination attempt

1984 Ozone depletion detected

1984 Extensive corporate downsizing begins

1986 Space shuttle disaster

1986 Chernobyl disaster

1989 Berlin Wall falls

1990 Persian Gulf War

1991 USSR dissolves

2001 Terrorist attacks on World Trade Center

2003 Enron and other corporate scandals

2004 Southeast Asia tsunami kills over 200,000

2008 Election of first African-American president in U.S. history

TECHNOLOGICAL

1971 Intel's first chip developed

1972 First e-mail management program

1974 Videocassette recorder introduced on the consumer market

1975 Microsoft founded

1975 Personal computer introduced on the consumer market

1979 First commercial cellular telephone system

1980 CNN begins 24-hour broadcasting

1981 MTV launched

1991 World Wide Web launched

2001 Apple unveils the iPod

2006 You-Tube explodes on scene

2010 Facebook has 500,000,000 users

Source: Initially adapted from B. Baldwin and S. Trovas, *Leadership in Action* 21, no. 6 (January/February 2002), p. 17.

scholarly research on value differences across generations, it's been said that the idea of a generational gap in values may be more popular culture than good social science.[21]

Moral and Ethical Reasoning and Action

Until now our discussion has focused primarily on the content of people's values—that is, on *what* people claim to value. Equally important, however, is the question of *how one thinks about* value-laden issues, or what may be called ethical or moral dilemmas. Furthermore, the question of *how people actually act*, whatever their espoused values are, is a different matter still.

Moral reasoning refers to the process leaders use to make decisions about ethical and unethical behaviors. Moral reasoning does not refer to the morality of individuals per se, or their espoused values, but rather to the *manner by which they solve moral problems*. Values play a key role in the moral reasoning process because value differences among individuals often result in different judgments regarding ethical and unethical behavior. Kohlberg theorized that people progress through a series of developmental stages in their moral reasoning.[22] Each stage reflects a more cognitively complex way of analyzing moral situations than the preceding one, and the sequence of stages is fixed, or invariant. Moral reasoning is assessed using ethical dilemmas such as whether a man would be morally justified in stealing an overpriced drug to save his dying wife, and an individual's stage of moral reasoning is based on the *way the answer is explained* rather than the particular answer given. Two individuals, for example, may each argue that the husband was morally wrong to steal the drug—even in those extenuating circumstances—yet offer qualitatively different reasons for why the action was wrong. Similarly, two individuals may each argue the husband was morally justified in stealing the drug, yet offer different reasons for why it was justifiable. The focus is on the reasoning process rather than on the decision.

That distinction may be clearer if we look in greater detail at different ways of evaluating the husband's behavior. Table 5.3 outlines Kohlberg's six stages of moral development, as well as how a person at each stage might evaluate the husband's behavior. Note that the six stages themselves are organized into three higher-order levels: the **preconventional level,** in which a person's criteria for moral behavior are based primarily on *self-interest* such as avoiding punishment or being rewarded; the **conventional level,** in which the criteria for moral behavior are based primarily on *gaining others' approval* and *behaving conventionally;* and the **postconventional level,** in which the criteria are based on *universal, abstract principles* that may even transcend the laws of a particular society. Finally, to say moral development progresses in invariant stages does not imply that all individuals actually achieve the highest stages. Few adults do. How do you think, in that regard, a political leader at the conventional level may differ in behavior (such as in the "stands" he or she takes on issues) from one at the postconventional level?

You may find it interesting to reflect on the moral issues raised in Table 5.3. Obviously, different individuals may have disparate points of view on these ethical questions. But what actually moves an individual from one level to the next? In summarizing several decades of research on moral judgment, Rest highlighted fundamental, dramatic, and extensive changes that occur in young adulthood (the twenties and thirties) in how people define what is morally right or wrong.[23] Rest noted that formal education is strongly correlated with these, though no specific academic or personal experiences proved pivotal. Moral judgment is part of each person's general personal and social development, and individuals whose moral judgment develops most are those who "love to learn, seek new challenges, who enjoy intellectually stimulating environments, who are reflective, who make plans and set goals, who take risks, and who take responsibility for themselves in the larger social context of history and institutions, and who take responsibility for themselves

TABLE 5.3
Developmental
Levels and Stages of
Moral Reasoning

Source: Adapted from
L. Kohlberg, *The Psychology
of Moral Development: Essays
on Moral Development. Vol. 2.*
(San Francisco: Harper &
Row, 1984).

Descriptions of Stages	Examples of Moral Reasoning in Support of Stealing the Drug	Examples of Moral Reasoning against Stealing the Drug
Preconventional Level *Stage 1:* "Bad" behavior is that which is punished.	"If you let your wife die, you will get in trouble."	"If you steal the drug, you will get in trouble."
Stage 2: "Good" behavior is that which is concretely rewarded.	"If you do happen to get caught, you could give the drug back and not get much of a sentence."	"Even if you were caught and didn't get much of a sentence, your wife would probably die while you were in jail and it wouldn't do you much good."
Conventional Level *Stage 3:* "Good" behavior is that which is approved by others; "bad" behavior is that which is disapproved by others.	"If you don't steal the drug, you'll never be able to look anyone in the face again."	"Everyone would know you are a thief."
Stage 4: "Good" behavior conforms to standards set by social institutions; transgressions lead to feelings of guilt or dishonor.	If you have any sense of honor, you'd do your duty as a husband and steal the drug."	"If you stole the drug, however desperate you felt, you'd never be able to look at yourself in the mirror again."
Postconventional Level *Stage 5:* "Good" behavior conforms to community standards set through democratic participation; concern with maintaining self-respect and the respect of equals.	"If you don't steal the drug you'd lose your own respect and everyone else's too."	"We've all agreed to live by common rules, and any form of stealing breaks that bond."
Stage 6: "Good" behavior is a matter of individual conscience based on responsibly chosen commitments to ethical principles.	"If you didn't steal it, you might have satisfied the letter of the law, but you wouldn't have lived up to your own standards of conscience."	"Maybe others would have approved of your behavior, but stealing the drug would still have violated your own conscience and standards of honesty."

Gandhi

PROFILES IN LEADERSHIP 5.1

Gandhi was one of the great leaders in world history. No less an intellect than Albert Einstein wrote this about him: "Generations to come, it may be, will scarce believe that such a one as this ever in flesh and blood walked upon this earth." Viscount Louis Mountbatten, the last Viceroy of India, compared him to the Buddha and to Christ. As a young journalist, William L. Shirer chronicled Gandhi's rebellion against British colonialism in India and described his first meeting with Gandhi. In reading it here, think about what aspects of Gandhi's personality, behavior, vision, and values made him so charismatic a leader.

Gandhi was squatting on the floor in the corner of the verandah, spinning. He greeted me warmly, with a smile that lit up his face and made his lively eyes twinkle. The welcome was so disarming, his manner so friendly and radiant, that my nervousness evaporated before I could say a word. . . .

As our talk began I tried to take in not only what Gandhi was saying but how he looked. I had seen many photographs of him, but I was nevertheless somewhat surprised at his actual appearance. His face at first glance did not convey at all the stature of the man, his obvious greatness. It was not one you would have especially noticed in a crowd. It struck me as not ugly, as some had said—indeed it radiated a certain beauty—but it was not uncommon either. Age—he was 61—and fasting, and Indian sun and the strain of years in prison, of long, hard, nervous work, had obviously taken their toll, turned the nose down, widened it at the nostrils, sunk in his mouth just a little so that the lower lip protruded, and teeth were missing—I could see only two. His hair was closely cropped, giving an effect of baldness. His large ears spread out, rabbitlike. His gray eyes lit up and sharpened when they peered at you through his steel-rimmed spectacles and then they softened when he lapsed, as he frequently did, into a mood of almost puckish humor. I was almost taken aback by the gaiety in them. This was a man inwardly secure, who, despite the burdens he carried, the hardships he had endured, could chuckle at man's foibles, including his own.

He seemed terribly frail, all skin and bones, though I knew that this appearance was deceptive, for he kept to a frugal but carefully planned diet that kept him fit, and for exercise he walked four or five miles each morning at a pace so brisk, as I would learn later when he invited me to accompany him, that I, at 27 and in fair shape from skiing and hiking in the Alps below Vienna, could scarcely keep up. Over his skin and bones was a loosely wrapped dhoti, and in the chilliness of a north Indian winter he draped a coarsely spun white shawl over his bony shoulders. His skinny legs were bare, his feet in wooden sandals.

As he began to talk, his voice seemed high-pitched, but his words were spoken slowly and deliberately and with emphasis when he seemed intent on stressing a point, and gradually, as he warmed up, the tone lowered. His slightly accented English flowed rhythmically, like a poet's at times, and always, except for an occasional homespun cliché, it was concise, homely, forceful.

For so towering a figure, his humble manner at first almost disconcerted me. Most of the political greats I had brushed up against in Europe and at home had seemed intent on impressing you with the forcefulness of their personalities and the boldness of their minds, not being bashful at all in hiding their immense egos. But here was the most gentle and unassuming of men, speaking softly and kindly, without egotism, without the slightest pretense of trying to impress his rather awed listener.

How could so humble a man, I wondered, spinning away with his nimble fingers on a crude wheel as he talked, have begun almost single-handedly to rock the foundations of the British Empire, aroused a third of a billion people to rebellion against foreign rule, and taught them the technique of a new revolutionary method—nonviolent civil disobedience—against which Western guns and Eastern lathis were proving of not much worth? That was what I had come to India to find out.

Source: *Reprinted with the permission of Simon & Schuster, Inc. from GANDHI by William L. Shirer. Copyright © 1979 William L. Shirer.*

and their environs." At the same time, deliberate curricular attempts to affect moral judgment have been shown to be effective.

Interestingly, this does not necessarily mean that making moral or ethical judgments is an entirely rational process. While most people believe they behave ethically, there is considerable reason to believe that they are considerably more biased than they believe and that their actions fall short of their self-perceptions of ethical purity. Several unconscious biases affect our moral judgments, and paradoxically, the more strongly one believes that she is an ethical manager, the more one may fall victim to these biases.[24]

Research has identified four particular biases that can have a pervasive and corrosive effect on our moral decision making. One of these is **implicit prejudice.** Although most people purport to judge others by their merits, research shows that implicit prejudice often distorts their judgments. The insidious nature of implicit prejudice lies in the fact that one is by nature unconscious of it. When one is queried, for example, about whether one harbors prejudice against, say, Eskimos, one answers based on one's self-awareness of such attitudes. Some people are overtly racist or sexist, but offensive as such prejudice may be, it is at least something known to the person. In the case of implicit prejudice, however, people are unaware that their judgments about some group are systematically biased *without their awareness.*

This has been documented in a fascinating series of experimental studies designed to detect unconscious bias.[25] These studies require people to rapidly classify words or images as "good" or "bad." Using a keyboard, individuals make split-second classifications of words like "love," "joy," "pain," and "sorrow." At the same time, they sort images of faces that are black or white,

---

What are Critical Elements of Developing Ethical Leadership?

HIGHLIGHT 5.3

Howard Prince and his associates have developed an impressive and comprehensive proposal for ethical leadership development at the undergraduate level. Here is a summary of what they view as critical elements of such a program:

- Knowledge of leadership and ethics to provide a conceptual framework for understanding the practice of ethical leadership.
- Opportunities to practice leadership roles requiring collective action where the learner has some responsibility for outcomes that matter to others.
- Opportunities to study, observe, and interact with leaders, especially those who have demonstrated moral courage.

- Formal and informal assessment of the efforts of those learning to lead ethically.
- Feedback to the learner, and opportunities for the learner to reflect on that feedback.
- Strengthening the learner's personal ethics and core values.
- Inspiring students to think of themselves as leaders and to accept leadership roles and responsibilities, including students who had not previously thought of themselves as leaders.

Source: H. T. Prince, G .R. Tumlin, and S. L. Connaughton, "An Interdisciplinary Major in Ethical Leadership Studies: Rationale, Challenges, and Template for Building an Adaptable Program," *International Leadership Journal,* 2009, pp. 91–128.

young or old, fat or thin (depending on the type of bias being examined). The critical results indicating implicit prejudice involve subtle shifts in reaction time in associating a particular image (such as a black face) with "good" words. People who consciously believe they have no prejudice or negative feelings about particular groups, say black Americans or the elderly, are nonetheless systematically slower in associating "good" words with those faces than they are in associating white or young faces with them.

Another bias that affects moral decision making is **in-group favoritism.** Most of us can readily point to numerous favors and acts of kindness we've shown toward others, and we understandably regard such acts as indicators of our own generosity and kindly spirit. If the whole pattern of one's generous acts were examined, however, ranging from things like job recommendations to help on a project, there is typically a clear pattern to those whom we've helped: most of the time they're "like us." This may not seem surprising, but one needs to consider who's not being helped: people "not like us." In other words, when we may make an exception favoring an "on the bubble" job applicant who is "like us," and fail to make such an exception for an identical candidate who is "not like us," we have effectively discriminated against the latter.[26]

Overclaiming credit is yet another way we may fool ourselves about the moral virtue of our own decision making. In many kinds of ways we tend to overrate the quality of our own work and our contributions to the groups and teams we belong to.[27] This has been widely documented, but one of the most telling studies was a 2007 poll of 2,000 executives and middle managers conducted by *BusinessWeek* magazine. One question in that poll asked respondents, "Are you one of the top 10 percent performers in your company?" If people were objective in rating themselves, presumably 10 percent would have placed themselves in the top 10 percent. But that's not what the results showed. Overall, 90 percent of the respondents placed themselves in the top 10 percent of performers![28]

Finally, our ethical judgments are adversely impacted by **conflicts of interest.** Sometimes, of course, we may be conscious of a potential conflict of interest, as when you benefit from a recommendation to someone else (such as getting a sales commission for something that may not be in the consumer's best interest). Even then, though, we misjudge our own ability to discount the extent to which the conflict actually biases our perception of the situation in our own favor.[29]

Other research strikes even more fundamentally at the idea that progress in understanding ethical behavior and increasing its likelihood or prevalence can adequately be based on a purely rational or reasoning-based approach.[30] The nature of human information processing at the cognitive and neurological levels inherently involves nonconscious processes of association and judgment. In an earlier paragraph we introduced the term *implicit prejudice,* but the word *implicit* should not itself be deemed undesirable. Some of the most impressive—and distinctly human—aspects of our thinking are inherently tacit or implicit. For example, one line of study suggests that in making moral judgments people often follow something more like scripts than any formal and rational process of ethical reasoning. Behavioral scripts from one's religious tradition (such as the Good Samaritan story) may be subconsciously triggered and lead to ethical behavior without explicit moral reasoning.[31] Some go so far as to say that "moral reasoning is rarely the direct cause of ethical judgment."[32] While that kind of perspective initially may seem to represent a pessimistic outlook on the possibility of truly improving ethical conduct, the reality is not so gloomy. Advocates of this view recognize that constructive things can be done to enhance ethical decision making. They also propose that a more complete answer lies not only in enhancing ethical and moral reasoning but also in approaches that enhance people's awareness of their ways of construing or constructing moral dimensions of any situation.

So near is a falsehood to truth that a wise man would do well not to trust himself on the narrow edge.

Cicero

As noted earlier, just because we profess certain values or moral codes does not ensure we will act that way when confronted with situations that engage them. It should be no surprise that in general when people are confronted with situations they've never faced before, their behavior may be different than they might have predicted. Unexpected natural disasters or threatening engagements with ill-willed people easily come to mind as situations where our own behavior can surprise us. But it's also true that we don't always behave as ethically as we think we would in morally demanding situations.

Social psychologist Ryan Brown has studied how accurately people can forecast their own ethical behavior, and found that while their predictions were generally consistent with their personal values, their actual behavior often was not. The general design of these experiments placed individuals in situations where they could choose to behave rather selflessly or somewhat more selfishly. A typical situation required the individual to choose between one of two sets of anagrams to complete (ostensibly as part of a study having a different purpose): either a short set of anagrams that would take only about 10 minutes to complete, or a longer set that would take about 45 minutes to complete. Whichever set the subject did *not* select presumably would be given to another soon-to-arrive experimental subject. As it turned out, 65 percent of the participants acted selfishly, selecting the easier task for themselves. Maybe you're saying to yourself, "Well, of course . . . you'd be crazy not to choose the easier one for yourself if given the chance to get the same credit for it." Perhaps, but only 35 percent predicted that they would make a selfish choice. It seems that when we are asked to *forecast* our behavior, we take our actual personal values into account. But the results of these studies also make a persuasive case that our personal values represent how we think we ought to act rather than how we often actually do act.[33]

These results should give us some pause when, in the face of unethical behavior by others, we feel confident that we would have acted differently

What Would You Do?

HIGHLIGHT 5.4

Here are several situations in which values play a large part in determining your response. How would you act in each one, and by what principles or reasoning process do you reach each decision?

- Would you vote for a political candidate who was honest and competent and agreed with you on most issues if you also knew that person was alcoholic, sexually promiscuous, and twice divorced?

- Assume that as a teenager you smoked marijuana once or twice, but that was years ago. Would you answer truthfully on an employment questionnaire if it asked whether you had ever used marijuana?

- Your military unit has been ambushed by enemy soldiers and suffered heavy casualties. Several of your soldiers have been captured, but you also captured one of the enemy soldiers. Would you torture the captured enemy soldier if that were the only way of saving the lives of your own soldiers?

- Terrorists have captured a planeload of tourists and have threatened to kill them unless ransom demands are met. You believe that meeting the ransom demands is likely to lead to the safe release of those passengers, but also likely to inspire future terrorist acts. Would you meet the terrorists' demands (and probably save the hostages) or refuse to meet the terrorists' demands (and reduce the likelihood of future incidents)?

- If you were an elementary school principal, would you feel it was part of your school's responsibility to teach moral values, or only academic subject matter?

- Assume that you have been elected to your state's legislature and that you are about to cast the deciding vote in determining whether abortions will be legally available to women in your state. What would you do if your own strong personal convictions on this issue were contrary to the views of the majority of the people you represent?

Because responses to these various scenarios depend largely on one's values, it should be clear that in dealing with value-laden issues leaders must keep in mind that their own sentiments may not always prove a wise guide for action.

Source: Adapted from G. Stock, *The Book of Questions: Business, Politics, and Ethics* (New York: Workman Publishing, 1991).

---

facing the same situation. Such apparent overconfidence seems to be caused by the bias of idealizing our own behavior, and this bias, ironically, may leave us ill-prepared to make the most ethical choices when we actually confront ethically challenging situations. Being aware of this bias is a good first step in avoiding the same trap.[34]

It also helps to recognize that ethical decision making (and ethical leadership more generally) is not typically a matter of choosing the right action over the wrong one. A far more common and challenging situation involves choosing between two "rights," or what are often called **ethical dilemmas.** Rushworth Kidder has identified four ethical dilemmas that are so common to our experience that they serve as models or paradigms:[35]

- **Truth versus loyalty,** such as honestly answering a question when doing so could compromise a real or implied promise of confidentiality to others.

- **Individual versus community,** such as whether you should protect the confidentiality of someone's medical condition when the condition itself may pose threat to the larger community.

- **Short-term versus long-term,** such as how a parent chooses to balance spending time with children now as compared with investments in career that may provide greater benefits for the family in the long run.
- **Justice versus mercy,** such as deciding whether to excuse a person's misbehavior because of extenuating circumstances or a conviction that he or she has "learned a lesson."

Kidder offers three principles for resolving ethical dilemmas like these: ends-based thinking, rule-based thinking, and care-based thinking. **Ends-based thinking** is often characterized as "do what's best for the greatest number of people." It is also known as utilitarianism in philosophy, and it's premised on the idea that right and wrong are best determined by considering the consequences or results of an action. Critics of this view argue that it's almost impossible to foresee all the consequences of one's personal behavior, let alone the consequences of collective action like policy decisions affecting society more broadly. Even if outcomes could be known, however, there are other problems with this approach. For example, would this view ethically justify the deaths of dozens of infants in medical research if the result might save thousands of others?

Rule-based thinking is consistent with Kantian philosophy and can be colloquially characterized as "following the highest principle or duty." This is determined not by any projection of what the results of an act may be but rather by determining the kinds of standards everyone should uphold all the time, whatever the situation. In Kant's words, "I ought never to act except in such a way that I can also will that my maxim should become a universal law." Lofty as the principle may sound, though, it could paradoxically *minimize* the role that human judgment plays in ethical decision making by consigning all acts to a rigid and mindless commitment to rules absent consideration of the specific context of a decision ("If I let you do this, then I'd have to let *everyone* do it").

Care-based thinking describes what many think of as the Golden Rule of conduct common in some form to many of the world's religions: "Do what you want others to do to you." In essence, this approach applies the criterion of reversibility in determining the rightness of actions. We are asked to contemplate proposed behavior as if we were the *object* rather than the *agent*, and to consult our feelings as a guide in determining the best course.

It's important to emphasize that Kidder does not suggest that any one of these principles is always best. Rather, he proposes that it would be a wise practice when considering the rightness of an action to *invoke them all* and reach a decision only after applying each to the specific circumstances one is facing and weighing the collective analyses. In other words, one principle may provide wise guidance in one situation whereas a different one may seem most helpful in a different one. There can be such critical yet subtle differences across situations that all three principles should be tentatively applied before any final course of action is chosen.

Ask Yourself These Questions

HIGHLIGHT 5.5

An important foundation of behaving ethically at work is to become more self-conscious of one's own ethical standards and practices. The National Institute of Ethics uses the following questions in its self-evaluation to facilitate that kind of self-reflection:

- How do I decide ethical dilemmas?
- Do I have set ethical beliefs or standards?
- If so, do I live by these beliefs or standards?
- How often have I done something that I am ashamed of?
- How often have I done things that I am proud of?
- Do I admit my mistakes?
- What do I do to correct mistakes that I make?

- Do I often put the well-being of others ahead of mine?
- Do I follow the Golden Rule?
- Am I honest?
- Do people respect my integrity?
- What are the three best things that have ever happened to me?
- What is the most dishonest thing I have ever done?
- Did I ever rectify the situation?
- What is the most honest thing I have ever done?

All leaders should regularly ask themselves questions like these.

Source: *From N. Trautman, Integrity Leadership, Director, National Institute of Ethics, www.ethicsinstitute.com.*

Why Do Good People Do Bad Things?

An important aspect of ethical conduct involves the mental gymnastics by which people can dissociate their moral thinking from their actions. One's ability to reason about hypothetical moral issues, after all, does not ensure that one will *act* morally. Furthermore, one's moral actions may not always be consistent with one's espoused values. Bandura, in particular, has pointed out several ways people with firm moral principles nonetheless may behave badly without feeling guilt or remorse over their behavior. We should look at each of these.[36,37]

Moral justification involves reinterpreting otherwise immoral behavior in terms of a higher purpose. This is most dramatically revealed in the behavior of combatants in war. Moral reconstruction of killing is dramatically illustrated by the case of Sergeant York, one of the phenomenal fighters in the history of modern warfare. Because of his deep religious convictions, Sergeant York registered as a conscientious objector, but his numerous appeals were denied. At camp, his battalion commander quoted chapter and verse from the Bible to persuade him that under appropriate conditions it was Christian to fight and kill. A marathon mountainside prayer finally convinced him that he could serve both God and country by becoming a dedicated fighter.[38]

Another way to dissociate behavior from one's espoused moral principles is through **euphemistic labeling.** This involves using cosmetic words to defuse or disguise the offensiveness of otherwise morally repugnant or distasteful behavior. Terrorists, for example, may call themselves "freedom fighters," and firing someone may be referred to as "letting him or her go."**Advantageous comparison** lets one avoid self-contempt for one's behavior by comparing it to even more heinous behavior by others. ("If you think *we're* insensitive to subordinates' needs, you should see what it's like working for Acme.")

Through **displacement of responsibility** people may violate personal moral standards by attributing responsibility to others. Nazi concentration camp guards, for example, attempted to avoid moral responsibility for their behavior by claiming they were merely carrying out orders. A related mechanism is **diffusion of responsibility,** whereby reprehensible behavior becomes easier to engage in and live with if others are behaving the same way. When everyone is responsible, it seems, no one is responsible. This way of minimizing individual moral responsibility for collective action can be a negative effect of group decision making. Through **disregard** or **distortion of consequences,** people minimize the harm caused by their behavior. This can be a problem in bureaucracies when decision makers are relatively insulated by their position from directly observing the consequences of their decisions. **Dehumanization** is still another way of avoiding the moral consequences of one's behavior. It is easier to treat others badly when they are dehumanized, as evidenced in epithets like "gooks" or "Satan-worshippers." Finally, people sometimes try to justify immoral behavior by claiming it was caused by someone else's actions. This is known as **attribution of blame.**

How widespread are such methods of minimizing personal moral responsibility? When people behave badly, Bandura said, it is *not* typically because of a basic character flaw; rather, it is because they use methods like these to construe their behavior in a self-protective way.[39]

Darley suggested still another way people justify seemingly unethical conduct, and his observations illuminate certain common leadership practices. He said that ethical problems are almost inherent in systems designed to measure performance:[40]

> The more any quantitative performance measure is used to determine a group's or an individual's rewards and punishments, the more subject it will be to corruption pressures and the more apt it will be to distort and corrupt the action patterns and thoughts of the group or individual it is intended to monitor. . . . The criterial control system unleashes enormous human ingenuity. People will maximize the criteria set. However, they may do so in ways that are not anticipated by the criterion setters, in ways that destroy the validity of the criteria. The people "make their numbers" but the numbers no longer mean what you thought they did.[41]

Three general problems can arise when performance measurement systems are put in place. A person might cheat on the measurement system by exploiting its weaknesses either in hopes of advancement or through fear of falling behind. Even with the best will in the world, a person might act in a way that optimizes his or her performance measurements without realizing that this outcome was not what the system intended. Finally, a person may have the best interests of the system in mind and yet manipulate the performance measurement system to allow continuation of the actions that best fulfill his or her reading of the system goals. One major disadvantage of this particular approach is that it "takes underground" constructive dialogue about system goals or modifications in system measurements.

What, ethically, should one do when one is part of a performance measurement system? Darley suggested "that the time for the individual to raise the moral issue is when he or she feels the pressure to substitute accountability for morality, to act wrongly, because that is what the system requires. And that intervention might then be directed at the system, by honorably protesting its design."[42] For those who are governed by a performance measurement system, a constant moral vigilance is necessary—and it is needed most of all by those in leadership positions.

David Halberstam described another organization in which the "numbers game" had a corrupting effect.[43] In this case it was Ford Motor Company. In the eyes of those who worked in Ford plants around the country in the 1950s, Detroit "number crunchers" like Robert McNamara (later a secretary of defense during the Vietnam War) did not want to know the truth. McNamara and his people in Detroit kept making liberal agreements with the unions and at the same time setting higher and higher levels of production while always demanding increased quality. They talked about quality, but they did not give the plant managers the means for quality; what they really wanted was production. So the plant managers gave them what they wanted, numbers, while playing lip service to quality. Years later in Vietnam, some American officers, knowing McNamara's love of numbers, cleverly juggled the numbers and played games with body counts to make a stalemated war look more successful than it was. They did this not because they were dishonest but because they thought if Washington really wanted the truth it would have sought the truth in an honest way. In doing so they were the spiritual descendants of the Ford factory managers of the 1950s.

Beware of the man who had no regard for his own reputation, since it is not likely he should have any for yours.

George Shelley

Ethics and Values-Based Approaches to Leadership

Can you be a good leader without being a good person? Does it make any sense to say, for example, that Hitler was an effective leader even if he was an evil person? In that sense, while some might consider the phrase *ethical leadership* to be redundant, Avolio and his associates have defined ethical leadership as having two core components: the **moral person** and the **moral manager**.[44] The moral person is seen as a principled decision maker who cares about people and the broader society.[45] The actions of such people indicate they try to do the right things personally and professionally, and they can be characterized as honest, fair, and open. In addition, ethical leaders have clear ethical standards that they pursue in the face of pressure to do otherwise. More than being just moral people, ethical leaders are moral managers who "make ethics an explicit part of their leadership agenda by communicating an ethics and values message, by visibly and intentionally role modeling ethical behavior."[46] In recent years there has been a rekindling of interest in approaches to leadership that are inherently and explicitly based on the interdependence between effective leadership and certain value systems. This is in bold contrast to decades of tradition in the social sciences of being self-consciously "values-free" in pursuit of objectivity. Two prominent approaches in this movement are described in greater detail here.

Authentic leadership is grounded in the principle found in the familiar adage from Greek philosophy, "to thine own self be true." Authentic leaders exhibit a consistency between their values, their beliefs, and their actions.[47] The roots of authentic leadership are also in various expressions of the humanistic movement in psychology including Maslow's theory of self-actualization (see Chapter 9) and Carl Rogers's concept of the fully functioning person.[48] Central to both of these is the idea that individuals can develop modes of understanding and interacting with their social environments so as to become more truly independent of others' expectations of them (individual, group, and cultural) and guided more by the dictates of universal truths and imperatives. Such individuals manifest congruence between how they feel on the inside and how they act, between what they say and what they do. They have realistic self-perceptions, free from the blind spots and misperceptions of self that are common to most people. At the same time, they are accepting of themselves, their nature, and that of others too.

Authentic leaders have strong ethical convictions that guide their behavior not so much to avoid doing "wrong" things as to always try to do the "right" things, including treating others with respect and dignity. They know where they stand on fundamental values and key issues. Authentic leaders behave as they do because of personal conviction rather than to attain status, rewards, or other advantages. As Avolio puts it, authentic leaders both are self-aware and self-consciously align their actions with their inner values.[49] He points out that such authenticity is not just something you either "have or don't have." Authenticity as a leader is something that you must always be striving to enhance. It requires regularly identifying with your best self, checking in with your core values concerning your leadership agendas and operating practices, and verifying that your actions are aligned with the highest ethical and moral principles you hold. In this way, practicing authentic leadership becomes taking actions that serve high moral principles concerning relationships, social responsibilities, and performance standards.[50]

The most important thing in acting is honesty. Once you've learned to fake that, you're in.

Samuel Goldwyn, early film producer

One way to understand authentic leadership is to contrast it with what might be called *inauthentic* leadership. If you think of a leader who "plays a role," or puts on different acts with different audiences to manage their impressions, that is being inauthentic. For example, two detectives playing the roles of "good cop" and "bad cop" when interviewing a suspect are being inauthentic (you may believe that it makes sense for them to do so, but it's inauthentic nonetheless). A boss who exaggerates his anger at an employee's mistake to "teach a lesson" is being inauthentic. A leader who denies that her feelings were affected by critical feedback from her direct reports is being inauthentic.

The study of authentic leadership has gained momentum recently because of beliefs that (1) enhancing self-awareness can help people in organizations find more meaning and connection at work; (2) promoting transparency and openness in relationships—even between leader and followers—builds trust and commitment; and (3) fostering more inclusive structures and practices in organizations can help build more positive ethical climates.[51] In contrast to stereotypical notions of the stoic "hero leader" who shows no weakness and shares no feelings, authentic leaders are willing to be viewed as vulnerable by their followers—a vital component of building a trusting leader–follower relationship. Equally important to building trust is a leader's willingness to be transparent—in essence, to say what she means and mean what she says.[52]

Servant leadership has since 1970 described a quite different approach to leadership than that derived from a bureaucratic and mechanistic view of organizations wherein workers are thought of as mere cogs in a machine. In the latter, the leader's primary role may be understood as doing whatever it takes to ensure that things run smoothly, tasks are performed, and goals are met. This has commonly involved a hierarchical approach to leadership. From the contrasting perspective of servant leadership, the leader's role is literally to serve others.

The modern idea of servant leadership was developed and popularized by Robert Greenleaf after he read a short novel by Herman Hesse called *Journey to the East*.[53,54] This is the mythical story of a group of people on a spiritual quest. Accompanying the party is a servant by the name of Leo, whose nurturing character sustained the group on its journey until one day he disappeared. The group fell apart and abandoned its quest when it realized that it was helpless without its servant. Finally, after many years of continued searching, the story's narrator found the religious order that had sponsored the original quest. It turned out that Leo, whom the narrator had only known as a servant, was actually the order's revered leader. To Greenleaf, this story meant that true leadership emerges when one's primary motivation is to help others.

The idea of servant leadership, of course, has been around for thousands of years. It stems at least in part from the teachings of Jesus, who instructed his disciples that servanthood is the essence of worthy leadership (such as through the example of *him* washing *their* feet). Ten characteristics are often associated with servant leaders. As you'll see, most of them also seem in line with the idea of authentic leadership just described:[55]

- *Listening:* While all leaders need to communicate effectively, the focus is often on communicating *to* others; but servant leadership puts the emphasis on *listening* effectively to others.
- *Empathy:* Servant leaders need to understand others' feelings and perspectives.
- *Healing:* Servant leaders help foster each person's emotional and spiritual health and wholeness.
- *Awareness:* Servant leaders understand their own values, feelings, strengths, and weaknesses.
- *Persuasion:* Rather than relying on positional authority, servant leaders influence others through their persuasiveness.
- *Conceptualization:* Servant leaders need to integrate present realities and future possibilities.
- *Foresight:* Servant leaders need to have a well-developed sense of intuition about how the past, present, and future are connected.
- *Stewardship:* Servant leaders are stewards who hold an organization's resources in trust for the greater good.
- *Commitment to others' growth:* The ultimate test of a servant leader's work is whether those served develop toward being more responsible, caring, and competent individuals.
- *Building community:* Such individual growth and development is most likely to happen when one is part of a supportive community. Unfortunately numerous factors like geographic mobility and the general impersonalism of large organizations have eroded people's sense of community. Thus it is the servant leader's role to help create a sense of community among people.

Not surprisingly, the concept of servant leadership has detractors as well as adherents. The most common criticism is that although the idea of servant leadership has a certain popular appeal in what we might call its "soft" form (for example, leaders should be more concerned about others' well-being and development, should create a more developmental climate in their organizations, and should seek what's good for the whole organization rather than just their own advancement), when taken more literally and extremely the concept seems to suggest that serving others is an end in itself rather than a means to other organizational goals and purposes. That version strikes many as impractical even if laudable.

A recent scholarly review of the theory of servant leadership noted an almost irreconcilable conflict between the ideas of servant leadership and the inherent realities of organizational life: Servant leaders develop people, helping them to strive and flourish. Servant leaders want those they serve to become healthier, wiser, freer, and more autonomous. Servant leaders serve followers. But managers are hired to contribute to organizational goal attainment. These goals can be attained only by having subordinates (not followers) solving tasks that lead to productivity and effectiveness.[56]

A man who embodied some of the most central qualities of both authentic leadership and servant leadership is featured in Profiles in Leadership 5.1.

The Roles of Ethics and Values in Organizational Leadership

Subordinates cannot be left to speculate as to the values of the organization. Top leadership must give forth clear and explicit signals, lest any confusion or uncertainty exist over what is and is not permissible conduct. To do otherwise allows informal and potentially subversive "codes of conduct" to be transmitted with a wink and a nod, and encourages an inferior ethical system based on "going along to get along" or the notion that "everybody's doing it."

Richard Thornburgh, former U.S. attorney general

Just as individuals possess a set of personal values, so too do organizations have dominant values. Many times these values are featured prominently in the company's annual report, Web site, and posters. These values represent the principles by which employees are to get work done and treat other employees, customers, and vendors. Whether these stated values represent true operating principles or so much "spin" for potential investors will depend on the degree of alignment between the organization's stated values and the collective values of top leadership.[57,58] For example, many corporate value statements say little about making money, but this is the key organizational priority for most business leaders, and as such is a major factor in many company decisions. There is often a significant gap between a company's stated values and the way the company truly operates. Knowing the values of top leadership can sometimes tell you more about how an organization actually operates than will the organization's stated values. Two ancient and contrasting sets of values are described in Highlight 5.6.

In any organization, the top leadership's collective values play a significant role in determining the dominant values throughout the organization, just as an individual leader's values play a significant role in determining team climate. Related to the notion of culture and climate is employee "fit." Research has shown that employees with values similar to the organization or team are more satisfied and likely to stay; those with dissimilar values are more likely to leave.[59,60] Thus one reason why leaders fail is not due to a lack of competence but rather is due to a misalignment between personal and organizational values. Although the advantages of alignment between personal and organizational values may seem self-evident, leaders with *dissimilar* values may be exactly what some organizations need to drive change and become more effective.

Finally, values are often a key factor in both intrapersonal and interpersonal conflict. Many of the most difficult decisions made by leaders are choices between opposing values. A leader who valued both financial reward and helping others, for example, would probably struggle mightily when having to make a decision about cutting jobs to improve profitability.

Ancient Eastern Philosophies and the Boardroom

HIGHLIGHT 5.6

Thirty years ago a best-selling business book called *Theory Z* purported to help Western business leaders apply the art of Japanese management to their own circumstances. Since then other Eastern philosophies have also gained popularity among Western leaders, albeit often in simplified forms. One perspective that has become popular in the West is based on the Chinese philosopher Sun Tzu, whose classic work *The Art of War* was written 2,500 years ago. Another is the *Bhagavad Gita,* a sacred Indian text containing the wisdom of Lord Krishna, believed to have been written nearly as long ago. Different implications for leadership are derived from these classic writings, a few of which are noted here:

	The Art of War	*Bhagavad Gita*
On Material Incentives	People need extrinsic incentives to be motivated. Give your soldiers shares of the booty and conquered territory.	Never act for material rewards only. Focus instead on doing well, and good things will follow.
On Handling Followers	Rule with iron discipline. Maintain your authority over them, knowing that too much kindness toward your followers could make them useless.	Enlightened leaders are selfless and compassionate toward others. Followers who are treated as equals are more motivated to enthusiastically support their leader.
On the Ultimate Goal	Winning requires cleverness and sometimes even deception.	Success means satisfying multiple stakeholders.

It doesn't seem likely that these perspectives, which obviously have stood the test of time, could simply be either right or wrong. How do you reconcile their differences?

Source: Adapted from *BusinessWeek,* October 30, 2006.

A leader who highly valued financial reward and did *not* strongly value helping others (or vice versa) would have much less trouble making the same decision. Likewise, some leaders would have difficulties making decisions if friendships get in the way of making an impact, or when taking risks to gain visibility runs counter to maintaining comfortable levels of stability in a team or organization. Values also play a key role in conflict between groups. The differences between Bill O'Reilly and Al Franken, the Israelis and Palestinians, the Shiite and Sunni Muslims in Iraq, the Muslims and Hindus in Kashmir, and Christians and Muslims in Kosovo are all at least partly based on differences in values. Because values develop early and are difficult to change, it's usually extremely difficult to resolve conflicts between such groups.

In sum, it's vital for a leader to set a personal example of values-based leadership, and it is also important for leaders—especially senior ones—to make sure clear values guide *everyone's* behavior in the organization. That's likely to happen only if the leader sets an example of desired behavior. You might think of this as a necessary but not sufficient condition for principled behavior throughout the organization. If there is indifference or hypocrisy toward values at the highest levels, it is fairly unlikely that principled behavior will be considered important by others throughout the organization. Bill O'Brien, the former CEO of a major insurance company, likened an organization's poor ethical climate to a bad odor one gets used to:

> Organizations oriented to power, I realized, also have strong smells, and even if people are too inured to notice, that smell has implications. It affects performance, productivity, and innovation. The worst aspect of this environment is that it stunts the growth of personality and character of everyone who works there.[61]

Carried to an extreme, this can lead to the kinds of excesses all too frequently evident during the past decade:

> Who knew the swashbuckling economy of the 1990s had produced so many buccaneers? You could laugh about the CEOs in handcuffs and the stock analysts who turned out to be fishier than storefront palm readers, but after a while the laughs became hard. Martha Stewart was dented and scuffed [and subsequently convicted]. Tyco was looted by its own executives. Enron and WorldCom turned out to be the twin towers of false promises. They fell. Their stockholders and employees went down with them. So did a large measure of faith in big corporations.

> *Time Magazine*, January 2, 2003

Leading by Example: the Good, the Bad, and the Ugly

One of the most quoted principles of good leadership is "leadership by example." But what does it mean to exemplify ethical leadership and be an ethical role model? In one study, people from a range of organizations were interviewed about a person they knew who had been an ethical role model at work. Not all ethical role models exhibited exactly the same qualities, but four general categories of attitudes and behaviors seemed to characterize the group:[62]

- *Interpersonal behaviors*: They showed care, concern, and compassion for others. They were hardworking and helpful. They valued their relationships with others, working actively to maintain and sustain them. They tended to focus on the positive rather than the negative, and accepted others' failures.
- *Basic fairness*: A specific quality of their interpersonal behaviors was manifested in the fairness shown others. They were not only open to input

from others but actively sought it. They tended to offer explanations of decisions. They treated others respectfully, never condescendingly, even amid disagreements.

- *Ethical actions and self-expectations:* They held themselves to high ethical standards and behaved consistently in both their public and private lives. They accepted responsibility for and were open about their own ethical failings. They were perceived as honest, trustworthy, humble, and having high integrity.
- *Articulating ethical standards:* They articulated a consistent ethical vision and were uncompromising toward it and the high ethical standards it implied. They held others ethically accountable and put ethical standards above personal and short-term company interests.

Arguably the most important example for anyone is his or her boss, and it raises difficult and complex challenges when a boss is a *bad* ethical role model. This becomes a challenge far greater than merely the hypocrisy inherent in being told, "Do as I say, not as I do."

It should go without saying that those in responsible positions have a particular responsibility to uphold ethical standards—but what if they *don't?* What should you do when your own boss does not behave ethically?

One approach to addressing these challenges is to reject the notion that organizational leadership is synonymous with formal position or hierarchical power in the organization, and to embrace instead the idea that *all* organizational members have a role in organizational leadership, including responsibility for ethical leadership in the organization. The term **upward ethical leadership** has been used to refer to "leadership behavior enacted by individuals who take action to maintain ethical standards in the face of questionable moral behaviors by higher-ups."[63]

Nearly all men can stand adversity, but if you want to test a man's character, give him power.
Abraham Lincoln

However, there are almost always reasons that may constrain employee behavior in such situations, including fear of retribution by bosses. More generally, do employees feel they have a safe outlet for raising ethical concerns about misbehavior by superiors in the organization?

One variable that moderates an employee's likelihood of raising such concerns is the general quality of ethical climate in the organization. **Ethical climates** refer to those in which ethical standards and norms have been consistently, clearly, and pervasively communicated throughout the organization and embraced and enforced by organizational leaders in both word and example. **Unethical climates** are those in which questionable or outright unethical behavior exists with little action taken to correct such behavior, or (worse) where such misbehavior is even condoned.[64] It's likely that employees experience some degree of moral distress whenever a manager is perceived to behave unethically, but the distress is usually greater in unethical climates.

Even in ethical climates, however, some individuals may be more likely than others to address perceived ethical problems in an active and constructive manner. This inclination is likely to be enhanced among individuals who feel a sense of personal power. Employees tend to feel greater power, for example, if they believe they have attractive opportunities in the broader employment marketplace, if they're respected for their credibility and competence in the organization, and if others within the organization are somewhat dependent on them. Organizations can further enhance the likelihood that employees will address perceived ethical problems in an active and constructive manner by nurturing a culture that is not all "command and control," by fostering a sense of shared leadership more than hierarchy, and by valuing upward leadership.[65] In the end, though, the most powerful way organizations can enhance the likelihood that employees will address ethical problems in a constructive manner is by proactively creating an ethical climate throughout the organization, and that is not just a responsibility of informal ethical leaders throughout the organization but inescapably a responsibility of formal organizational leaders.

In fact, being in a formal leadership role imposes unique ethical responsibilities and challenges. Leaders more than followers (1) possess unique degrees of both legitimate and coercive power; (2) enjoy greater privileges; (3) have access to more information; (4) have greater authority and responsibility; (5) interact with a broader range of stakeholders who expect equitable treatment; and (6) must balance sometimes competing loyalties when making decisions.[66] With conditions like these, which sometimes also may represent seductive temptations to excuse one's own behavior, it is all the more important for leaders to take positive steps to create an ethical climate and hold themselves accountable to it.

> *It's important that people know what you stand for. It's equally important that they know what you won't stand for.*
>
> **Mary Waldrop**

Creating and Sustaining an Ethical Climate

So how do leaders do this? Several "fronts" of leadership action are needed to establish an ethical organizational climate:[67]

- *Formal ethics policies and procedures:* It's sometimes said that "you can't legislate morality," and the same may be said about legislating an ethical climate. Nonetheless, certain formal policies and procedures are probably necessary if not sufficient conditions for creating an ethical climate. These include formal statements of ethical standards and policies, along with reporting mechanisms, disciplinary procedures, and penalties for suspected ethical violations.

- *Core ideology:* A core ideology is basically an organization's heart and soul. It represents the organization's purpose, guiding principles, basic identity, and most important values. Starbucks is a good example. Starbucks' guiding principles include (1) respect and dignity for partners (employees); (2) embracing diversity; (3) applying the highest standards of excellence to the business; (4) developing "enthusiastically satisfied customers"; (5) contributing positively to local communities and to the environment more generally; and (6) maintaining profitability.[68]

- *Integrity:* The core ideology cannot be a mere set of boardroom plaques or other exhortations to behave well. The core ideology must be part of the fabric of every level and unit in the organization. Just as personal integrity describes an individual whose outward behavior and inward values are congruent and transparent, organizational integrity describes an organization whose pronouncements are congruent with its public and private actions at every level and in every office.

- *Structural reinforcement:* An organization's structure and systems can be designed to encourage higher ethical performance and discourage unethical performance. Performance evaluation systems that provide opportunities for anonymous feedback increase the likelihood that "dark side" behaviors would be reported, and thus discourage their enactment. Reward systems can promote honesty, fair treatment of customers, courtesy, and other desirable behaviors.

- *Process focus:* There also needs to be explicit concern with process, not just the achievement of tangible individual, team, and organizational goals. *How* those goals are achieved needs to be a focus of attention and emphasis too. When senior leaders set exceptionally high goals and show that they expect goals to be achieved whatever it takes, it's a recipe that may tempt and seemingly turn a blind eye to unethical behavior by employees.

Creating an ethical climate is not easy or just a matter of following a simple recipe. Conflicts over values can arise even when an organization has clearly published values that are embraced by everyone. That can happen when employees and leaders have divergent perceptions of whether the leader's behavior embodies important corporate values. At one company, for example, employees concluded that their CEO's behavior had betrayed the same corporate values that he had been instrumental in establishing. As they perceived the CEO's behavior deviating more and more from those values, employees gradually concluded that he had "sold out," and they became disillusioned with his leadership.

That disillusionment was a far cry from the initial perceptions employees had of their CEO. Consider the situation at Maverick when the CEO, John Bryant (both fictionalized names), started the company. Bryant located Maverick's offices in an unassuming warehouse district and gave each member of his small staff a festive company shirt with a logo on the back and his or her name stitched over the front pocket, like shirts mechanics wear. He provided a companywide profit-sharing plan, above-market salaries, and perks like free lunch on Friday, and he encouraged people to head home by six o'clock. He recruited employees whose varied races, backgrounds, and lifestyles broadcast Maverick's commitment to diversity, and on the weekends he let a minority youth organization use the company's offices. He spoke passionately to everyone about Maverick's people-oriented values and promoted them in company posters, client materials, and the employee handbook.

In short, Bryant did everything right. And by all accounts, Maverick in its early years was a great place to work—employees were motivated, loyal, hardworking, and enthusiastically committed to the company and the ideals Bryant promoted.[69]

Then the finger-pointing began. As the young company more than doubled in size during the 1990s, a remarkable shift occurred in how employees perceived the company and its leader. They came to see Bryant as a hypocrite, whose behavior violated everything he continued to proclaim the company stood for. As a consequence, employee commitment and creativity declined sharply.

What could account for such an unfortunate turnaround? That's not a simple question to answer, especially when the leader—Bryant himself—continued to see his own behavior in much more positive ways. Part of the answer to this enigma, it seems, involved a pivotal event in the company's history. In 1995 Bryant decided to double the size of the company's staff and operations. To him, this was a way to provide more professional growth and reward opportunities for staff. Employees, however, saw this as an act of greed on Bryant's part that would erode company values by disrupting the small, close-knit family the company had been. They also saw other decisions by him as similarly self-serving. When he decided to give long-term employees shares in the company as a reward for their hard work, for example, other employees perceived this as inconsistent with the company's commitment to equality. And while this was happening, no one let Bryant himself know that perceptions of him had taken a 180-degree turn.

In examining what happened at Maverick, it became clear that over time employees had *implicitly and unconsciously* shaped their understanding of the company's values to correspond more closely with their own. For example, employees came to believe that hierarchies of position and power were inconsistent with Maverick's values. In fact, no one had ever said anything like that. Thus Bryant's behavior *was* inconsistent with company values *as the employees had come to understand them,* even though it *wasn't* inconsistent with Bryant's understanding of the values on which he'd founded the company.

An important lesson for leaders in this story is hinted at in Bryant's own lack of awareness of the growing negative perceptions of his behavior. It's unlikely that subordinate members of an organization will offer unsolicited negative perceptions to leaders when they think the leaders have violated values. It's essential, then, for leaders themselves to invite discussion by regularly asking people what they're thinking and feeling. You don't want to be blindsided.

Another way to think about the essence of creating an ethical climate in organizations is to recognize that it is not simply the sum of the collective moralities of its members. Covey has developed and popularized an approach called **principle-centered leadership,**[70] which postulates a fundamental interdependence between the personal, the interpersonal, the managerial, and the organizational levels of leadership. The unique role of each level may be thought of like this:

> *Personal:* The first imperative is to be a trustworthy person, and that depends on both one's character *and* competence. Only if one is trustworthy can one have trusting relationships with others.
>
> *Interpersonal:* Relationships that lack trust are characterized by self-protective efforts to control and verify each other's behavior.
>
> *Managerial:* Only in the context of trusting relationships will a manager risk empowering others to make full use of their talents and energies. But even with an empowering style, leading a high-performing group depends on skills such as team building, delegation, communication, negotiation, and self-management.
>
> *Organizational:* An organization will be most creative and productive when its structure, systems (training, communication, reward, and so on), strategy, and vision are aligned and mutually supportive. Put differently, certain organizational alignments are more likely than others to nurture and reinforce ethical behavior.

Interestingly, the interdependence between these levels posited in principle-centered leadership is quite similar to recent conceptualizations of authentic leadership that also view it as a multilevel phenomenon. That is, authentic leadership can be thought of not only as a quality characterizing certain individual leaders but also as a quality of certain leader–follower dyads, groups or teams, and even organizations. Thus it makes just as much sense to talk about authentic organizations as it does to talk about authentic leaders.[71]

In concluding this chapter, we would be remiss not to explicitly address a question that has been implicit throughout it: *why* should a company go to the trouble of creating and sustaining an ethical climate?[72] One answer—perhaps a sufficient one—is because it's the right thing to do. Sometimes, however, it's too easy merely to assume that because something is the right thing to do there must be some costs or disadvantages associated with it. As is apparent from this chapter, it's not easy to create and sustain an ethical environment in an organization; it takes conviction, diligence, and commitment. In some ways, such continuing focus and effort can be thought of as a cost. However,

The Cult of Enron

HIGHLIGHT 5.7

Enron has come to represent the epitome of greed, ethical lapse, and spectacular failure in the business world. Its senior executives CEO Kenneth Lay and Jeffrey Skilling were blamed and prosecuted for the company's collapse and callous indifference to the welfare of its employees. But the problems at Enron ran deeper than just the shoddy ethics and illegal actions of a few people at the top. A large part of the problem was the Enron culture itself that people *throughout* the company perpetuated.

A root of the problem may be that Enron's culture had many characteristics of a cult. Cults are characterized as having these four qualities:

- Charismatic leadership.
- A compelling and totalistic vision.
- A conversion process.
- A common culture.

Here are some of the ways that Enron's corporate culture was like a cult. You can see how corporations as well as religious cults can encourage counterproductive conformity and penalize dissent.

CHARISMATIC LEADERSHIP

Enron's leaders created an aura of charisma around themselves through ever more dramatic forms of self-promotion. Skilling, for example, cultivated his image as the Enron version of Darth Vader, even referring to his traders as "Storm Troopers." The reputations of Skilling and other top executives at Enron were further reinforced by the ways in which they were lionized in respected business publications and by the opulent lifestyles they enjoyed.

COMPELLING AND TOTALISTIC VISION

Hyperbole was rampant at Enron, as in banners proclaiming its vision of being the "world's leading company." Such exalted self-images encourage members to feel a sense of privilege and destiny. Employees were bombarded with messages that they were the best and the brightest. Their commitment to organizational success had an almost evangelistic fervor, and workweeks of even 80 hours were considered normal.

CONVERSION AND INDOCTRINATION

From an employee's recruitment to Enron onward, communication was one-way: top-down. In the early stages this involved intense and emotionally draining rituals over several days wherein the recruit would hear powerful messages from the leaders. Group dynamics research has shown that such initiation rituals incline people to exaggerate the benefits of group membership in their minds. In Enron's case the purpose was to ingrain in employees a single-minded personal commitment to continued high rates of corporate growth.

COMMON CULTURE

Despite all the effort put into selecting new employees and imbuing them with a sense of privilege, a punitive internal culture was also nurtured through which all the psychic and material benefits of being in Enron could be withdrawn on a managerial whim. Enron was quick to fire any of these "best and brightest" who did not conform; they could be branded, almost overnight, as "losers" in others' eyes. This could happen for mere dissent with the corporate line as well as for failing to meet Enron's exceedingly high performance goals.

Source: D. Tourish and N. Vatcha, "Charismatic Leadership and Corporate Cultism at Enron: The Elimination of Dissent, the Promotion of Conformity, and Organizational Collapse," *Leadership* 1, no. 4 (2005), pp. 455–80.

Only mediocrities rise to the top in a system that won't tolerate wave making.

Lawrence J. Peter, author of *The Peter Principle*

I do believe in the spiritual nature of human beings. To some it's a strange or outdated idea, but I believe there is such a thing as a human spirit. There is a spiritual dimension to man which should be nurtured.

Aung San Suu Kyi

such focus and effort can pay dividends beyond an intrinsic sense of satisfaction.

Johnson has identified a number of tangible positive outcomes for an organization that creates an ethical climate. One of these is greater collaboration within the organization: an ethical climate produces greater trust within an organization, and trust is a key element underlying collaboration. Another positive outcome can be improved social standing and improved market share for the organization. Eighty-four percent of Americans said that if price and quality were similar, they would switch allegiance to companies associated with worthy causes. Over $2 trillion is now invested in mutual funds focusing on companies demonstrating commitment to the environment, ethics, and social responsibility.[73,74] There also is evidence that ethical companies often outperform their competitors.[75]

Similar tangible advantages were identified by Harvard professors John Kotter and James Heskett among companies that aligned espoused values with organizational practices. Such companies increased revenues by an average of 682 percent versus 166 percent for companies that didn't.[76] Paying attention to ethics and values *can* be good business.

Summary

This chapter has reviewed evidence regarding the relationships among ethics, values, and leadership. Ethics is a branch of philosophy that deals with right conduct. Values are constructs that represent general sets of behaviors or states of affairs that individuals consider important, and they are a central part of a leader's psychological makeup. Values affect leadership through a cultural context within which various attributes and behaviors are regarded differentially—positively or negatively.

It's not just the content of one's beliefs about right and wrong that matters, though. *How* one makes moral or ethical judgments, or the manner by which one solves moral problems, is also important and is referred to as moral reasoning. Some approaches to moral reasoning posit that it is developed by going through qualitative stages of successively more advanced moral reasoning.

Ethical action, of course, involves more than just the cognitive process of moral reasoning. That's why people's behavior does not always conform to how they predict they'll act, or with their espoused values. Furthermore, the thorniest ethical dilemmas people face tend not to involve choices between what is right or wrong but between two different "rights." In such cases it is useful to apply several different principles for resolving moral dilemmas.

Recently many approaches to leadership have explicitly addressed the interdependencies between effective leadership and particular value systems. The concepts of authentic leadership and servant leadership are among these. There also has been increased interest in recent years in the kinds of practices that can be instituted within organizations to enhance the likelihood that they will have ethical climates.

Key Terms

ethics, *151*
Theory X, *151*
Theory Y, *151*
values, *152*
moral reasoning, *157*
preconventional level, *158*
conventional level, *158*
postconventional level, *158*
implicit prejudice, *161*
in-group favoritism, *162*
overclaiming credit, *162*
conflicts of interest, *162*
ethical dilemmas, *164*
truth versus loyalty, *164*

individual versus community, *164*
short-term versus long-term, *165*
justice versus mercy, *165*
ends-based thinking, *165*
rule-based thinking, *165*
care-based thinking, *165*
moral justification, *166*
euphemistic labeling, *167*
advantageous comparison, *167*
displacement of responsibility, *167*

diffusion of responsibility, *167*
distortion of consequences, *167*
dehumanization, *167*
attribution of blame, *167*
moral person, *168*
moral manager, *168*
authentic leadership, *169*
servant leadership, *170*
upward ethical leadership, *175*
ethical climate, *175*
unethical climate, *175*
principle-centered leadership, *179*

Questions

1. Do you think it always must be "lonely at the top" (or that if it is not, you are doing something wrong)?

2. How do you believe one's basic philosophy of human nature affects one's approach to leadership?

3. Identify several values you think might be the basis of conflict or misunderstanding between leaders and followers.

4. Can a leader's public and private morality be distinguished? Should they be?

5. Can a bad person be a good leader?

6. Are there any leadership roles men and women should not have equal opportunity to compete for?

7. What is the relationship between an individual's responsibility for ethical behavior and the idea of organizational ethical climate? Does focus on the latter diminish the importance of the former or reduce the importance of individual accountability?

8. Could two different groups have quite different ethical climates if the same people were members of both?

Activities

1. Each person should select his or her own 10 most important values from the following list, and then rank-order those 10 from most important (1) to least important (10). Then have an open discussion about how a person's approach to leadership might be influenced by having different value priorities. The values are achievement, activity (keeping busy), advancement, adventure, aesthetics (appreciation of beauty), affiliation, affluence, authority, autonomy, balance, challenge, change/variety, collaboration, community, competence, competition, courage, creativity, economic security, enjoyment, fame, family, friendship, happiness, helping others, humor, influence, integrity, justice, knowledge, location, love, loyalty, order, personal development, physical fitness, recognition, reflection, responsibility, self-respect, spirituality, status, and wisdom.

2. Explore how the experiences of different generations might have influenced the development of their values. Divide into several groups and assign each group the task of selecting representative popular music from a specific era. One group, for example, might have the 1950s, another the Vietnam War era, and another the 1990s. Using representative music from that era, highlight what seem to be dominant concerns, values, or views of life during that period.

Minicase

Balancing Priorities at Clif Bar

Gary Erickson is a man of integrity. In the spring of 2000 Erickson had an offer of more than $100 million from a major food corporation for his company Clif Bar Inc. He had founded Clif Bar Inc. in 1990 after a long bike ride. Erickson, an avid cyclist, had finished the 175-mile ride longing for an alternative to the tasteless energy bars he had brought along. "I couldn't make the last one go down, and that's when I had an epiphany—make a product that actually tasted good." He looked at the list of ingredients on the package and decided he could do better. He called on his experience in his family's bakery, and after a year in the kitchen, the Clif Bar—named for Erickson's father—was launched in 1992. Within five years sales had skyrocketed to $20 million. He considered the $100 million offer on the table and what it meant for his company and decided against the deal. He realized that the vision he had for the company would be compromised once he lost control, so he walked away from the $100 million deal.

He has stuck to his vision and values ever since. His comm environmental and social issues are evident in everything he d environmental front, his company has a staff ecologist wh with reducing Clif Bar's ecological footprint on the plane

70 percent of the ingredients in Clif Bars are organic. A change in packaging has saved the company (and the planet) 90,000 pounds of shrink-wrap a year. And the company funds a Sioux wind farm to offset the carbon dioxide emissions from its factories. On the social side, Erickson launched a project called the 2,080 program (2,080 is the total number of hours a full-time employee works in one year). Through the 2,080 program employees are encouraged to do volunteer work on company time. Recently Erickson agreed to support (with salaries and travel expenses) employees who wanted to volunteer in Third World countries.

Erickson is also committed to his team. He thinks about things like, "What should our company be like for the people who come to work each day?" He sees work as a living situation and strives to make Clif Bar Inc.'s offices a fun place to be—there are plenty of bikes around; a gym and dance floor; personal trainers; massage and hair salon; a game room; an auditorium for meetings, movies, and music; dog days every day; and great parties.

As the company grows, however, maintaining such values may not be easy. Clif Bar already has 130 employees, and revenue has been rising by more than 30 percent a year since 1998, according to Erickson. "We're at a point where we have to find a way to maintain this open culture while we may be getting bigger," says Shelley Martin, director of operations. "It's a balancing act."

1. Without knowing Gary Erickson's age, where would you guess he falls in the four generations of workers as delineated by Zemke?
2. Consider the key work values in Table 5.1. Recalling that leaders are motivated to act consistently with their values, what values appear to be most important to Gary Erickson?
3. Clif Bar Inc. possesses a definite set of organizational values. If you visit the company Web site (www.clifbar.com), you will see evidence of these values: "Fight Global Warming" and "Register to Vote" are just as prominent as information about the product. Knowing some of the values of Gary Erickson, how closely aligned do you think the organizational values are to the way the company actually operates?

Sources: http://www.fortune.com/fortune/smallbusiness/managing/articles/0,15114,487527,00.html; http://www.clifbar.com; *The Costco Connection,* "Marathon Man," July 2004, p. 19.

End Notes

1. M. E. Brown and L. K. Trevino, "Ethical Leadership: A Review and Future Directions," *The Leadership Quarterly* 17 (2006), pp. 595–616.
2. J. W. Gardner, *On Leadership* (New York: Free Press, 1990).
3. J. M. Burns, *Leadership* (New York: Harper & Row, 1978).
4. W. Bennis and J. Goldsmith, *Learning to Lead* (Reading, MA: Perseus Books, 1997).
5. D. McGregor, *Leadership and Motivation* (Cambridge, MA: MIT Press, 1966).

6. J. Hall and S. M. Donnell, "Managerial Achievement: The Personal Side of Behavioral Theory," *Human Relations* 32 (1979), pp. 77–101.

7. L. V. Gordon, *Measurement of Interpersonal Values* (Chicago: Science Research Associates, 1975), p. 2.

8. W. L. Gardner, B. Avolio, F. Luthans, D. May, and F. Walumbwa, "'Can You See the Real Me?' A Self-Based Model of Authentic Leader and Follower Development," *Leadership Quarterly* 16 (2005), pp. 343–72.

9. R. E. Boyatzis and F. R. Skelly, "The Impact of Changing Values on Organizational Life," in *Organizational Behavior Readings*, 5th ed., ed. D. A. Kolb, I. M. Rubin, and J. Osland (Englewood Cliffs, NJ: Prentice Hall, 1991), pp. 1–16.

10. M. Rokeach, *The Nature of Human Values* (New York: Free Press, 1973).

11. C. A. Baird, *Everyday Ethics: Making Hard Choices in a Complex World* (Denver, CO: Tendril Press, 2005).

12. The Parr Center for Ethics, "What Is the Relationship between Values and Ethics?" University of North Carolina, http://parrcenter.unc.edu/ask/Ethics_Values.html, accessed November 18, 2009.

13. Boyatzis and Skelly, "The Impact of Changing Values on Organizational Life."

14. M. Maccoby, "Management: Leadership and the Work Ethic," *Modern Office Procedures* 28, no. 5 (1983), pp. 14, 16, 18.

15. M. Massey, *The People Puzzle: Understanding Yourself and Others* (Reston, VA: Reston, 1979).

16. R. Zemke, C. Raines, and B. Filipczak, *Generations at Work: Managing the Class of Veterans, Boomers, Xers, and Nexters in Your Workplace* (New York: AMA Publications, 2000).

17. J. J. Deal, K. Peterson, and H. Gailor-Loflin, *Emerging Leaders: An Annotated Bibliography* (Greensboro, NC: Center for Creative Leadership, 2001).

18. Deal, Peterson, and Gailor-Loflin, *Emerging Leaders:* An Annotated Bibliography.

19. E. Foley and A. LeFevre, *Understanding Generation X* (Zagnoli McEvoy Foley LLC, 2001), www.zmf.com.

20. E. C. Ladd, "Generation Gap? What Generation Gap?" *The New York Times*, December 9, 1994, p. A16.

21. F. Giancola, "The Generation Gap: More Myth Than Reality," *Human Resource Planning* 29, no. 4 (2006), pp. 32–37.

22. L. Kohlberg, *The Psychology of Moral Development: Essays on Moral Development*, Vol. 2 (San Francisco: Harper & Row, 1984).

23. J. Rest, "Research on Moral Judgment in College Students," in *Approaches to Moral Development: New Research and Emerging Themes*, ed. A. Garrod (New York: Teachers College Press, Columbia University, 1993), pp. 201–13.

24. M. R. Banaji, M. H. Bazerman, and D. Chugh, "How Ethical Are You?" *Harvard Business Review*, 2003, pp. 56–64.

25. A. G. Greenwald, D. E. McGhee, and J. L. K. Schwartz, "Measuring Individual Differences in Implicit Cognition: The Implicit Association Test," *Journal of Personality and Social Psychology* 74 (1998), pp. 1464–80.

26. Banaji, Bazerman, and Chugh, "How Ethical Are You?"

27. Ibid.

28. P. Coy, "Ten Years from Now," *BusinessWeek,* August 20 and 27, 2007, pp. 42–44.

29. Banaji, Bazerman, and Chugh, "How Ethical Are You?"

30. S. Sohenshein, "The Role of Construction, Intuition, and Justification in Responding to Ethical Issues at Work: The Sensemaking–Intuition Model," *Academy of Management Review* 32, no. 4, pp. 1022–1040.

31. Ibid.

32. J. Haidt, "The Emotional Dog and Its Rational Tail: A Social Intuitionist Approach to Moral Judgment," *Psychological Review* 108, pp. 814–34.

33. R. P. Brown and C. Barnes, *Thinking Hypothetically: A Value-Congruent Bias in Hypothetical Behavioral Forecasts,* in press.

34. R. T. Marcy, W. Gentry, and R. McKinnon, "Thinking Straight: New Strategies Are Needed for Ethical Leadership," *Leadership in Action,* 2008, pp. 3–7.

35. R. Kidder, *How Good People Make Tough Choices: Resolving the Dilemmas of Ethical Living* (New York: Harper Collins, 1995).

36. A. Bandura, *Social Foundations of Thought and Action* (Englewood Cliffs, NJ: Prentice Hall, 1986).

37. A. Bandura, "Mechanisms of Moral Disengagement," in *Origins of Terrorism: Psychologies, Ideologies, Theologies, States of Mind,* ed. W. Reich (Cambridge: Cambridge University Press., 1990), pp. 161–91.

38. Ibid., p. 164.

39. A. Bandura, "Self-Efficacy: Toward a Unifying Theory of Behavioral Change," *Psychological Review* 84 (1977), pp. 191–215.

40. J. Darley, "Inadvertent Moral Socialization in Military Simulations: Making Disasters Happen," keynote address at the Applied Behavioral Sciences Symposium, U.S. Air Force Academy, 1994.

41. Ibid.

42. Ibid.

43. D. Halberstam, *The Reckoning* (New York: Avon, 1986).

44. F. O. Walumbwa, B. Avolio, W. Gardner, T. Wernsing, and S. Peterson, "Authentic Leadership: Development of a Theory-Based Measure," *Journal of Management* 34, no. 1 (2008), pp. 89–126.

45. M. E. Brown and L. Trevino, "Ethical Leadership: A Review and Future Directions," *Leadership Quarterly* 17 (2006), pp. 595–616.

46. Ibid., p. 597.

47. F. O. Walumbwa, B. Avolio, W. Gardner, T. Wernsing, and S. Peterson, "Authentic Leadership: Development of a Theory-Based Measure," *Journal of Management* 34, no. 1 (2008), pp. 89–126.

48. C. Rogers, *On Becoming a Person: A Therapist's View of Psychotherapy* (London: Constable, 1961).

49. B. J. Avolio and T. S. Wernsing, "Practicing Authentic Leadership," in *Positive Psychology: Exploring the Best in People (Vol. 4: Exploring Human Flourishing),* ed. Shane Lopez (Santa Barbara: Praeger, 2008).

50. Ibid., p. 161.

51. B. J. Avolio and W. L. Gardner, "Authentic Leadership Development: Getting to the Root of Positive Forms of Leadership," *The Leadership Quarterly* 16 (2005), pp. 315–38.

52. B. J. Avolio and R. Reichard, "The Rise of Authentic Followership," in *The Art of Followership: How Great Followers Create Great Leaders and Organizations,* ed. R. E. Riggio, I. Chaleff, and J. Lipman-Bluman (San Francisco: Jossey-Bass, 2008), pp. 325–37.

53. L. Spears, "Practicing Servant-Leadership," *Leader to Leader* 34 (Fall 2004).

54. R. K. Greenleaf, *Servant Leadership* (New York: Paulist Press, 1977).

55. Spears, "Practicing Servant-Leadership."

56. J. A. Andersen, "When a Servant-Leader Comes Knocking . . ." *Leadership & Organization Development Journal* 30, no. 1 (2009), pp. 4–15.

57. R. T. Hogan, J. Hogan, and B. W. Roberts, "Personality Measurement and Employment Decisions: Questions and Answers," *American Psychologist* 51, no. 5 (1996), pp. 469–77.

58. R. T. Hogan and G. J. Curphy, "Leadership Matters: Values and Dysfunctional Dispositions," working paper, 2004.

59. Hogan, Hogan, and Roberts, "Personality Measurement and Employment Decisions."

60. Hogan and Curphy, "Leadership Matters."

61. B. O'Brien, "Designing an Organization's Governing Ideas," in *The Fifth Discipline Fieldbook,* ed. P. Senge et al. (New York: Doubleday, 1994), p. 306.

62. G. Weaver, L. Trevfino, and B. Agle, "Somebody I Look Up To: Ethical Role Models in Organizations," *Organizational Dynamics* 34, no. 4, pp. 313–30.

63. M. Uhl-Bien and M. Carsten, "Being Ethical When the Boss Is Not," *Organizational Dynamics* 36, no. 2 (2007), pp. 187–201.

64. Ibid.

65. Ibid.

66. C. E. Johnson, *Meeting the Ethical Challenges of Leadership: Casting Light or Shadow,* 2nd ed. (Thousand Oaks, CA: Sage, 2005).

67. C. E. Johnson, "Best Practices in Ethical Leadership, 2007," in *The Practice of Leadership: Developing the Next Generation of Leaders,* ed. J. Conger and R. Riggio (San Francisco: Jossey-Bass, 2006), pp. 150–71.

68. Ibid.

69. A. C. Edmondson and S. E. Cha, "When Company Values Backfire," *Harvard Business Review,* November 2002, pp. 18–19.

70. S. R. Covey, *Principle-Centered Leadership* (New York: Simon & Schuster, 1990).

71. F. J. Yammarino, S. D. Dionne, C. A. Schriesheim, and F. Dansereau, "Authentic Leadership and Positive Organizational Behavior: A Meso, Multi-Level Perspective," *The Leadership Quarterly* 19 (2008), pp. 693–707.

72. Johnson, "Best Practices in Ethical Leadership, 2007."

73. Ibid.

74. P. Kottler and N. Lee, *Corporate Social Responsibility: Doing the Most Good for Your Company and Your Cause* (New York: Wiley, 2005).

75. S. A. Waddock and S. B. Graves, "The Corporate Social Performance–Financial Performance Link," *Strategic Management Journal* 18 (1997), pp. 303–19.

76. J. P. Kotter and J. L. Heskett, *Corporate Culture & Performance* (New York: Free Press, 1992).

Chapter 6

Leadership Attributes

Introduction

In Chapter 1 leadership was defined as "the process of influencing an organized group toward accomplishing its goals." Given this definition, one question that leadership researchers have tried to answer over the past century is whether certain personal attributes or characteristics help or hinder the leadership process. In other words, does athletic ability, height, personality, intelligence, or creativity help a leader to build a team, get results, or influence a group? Put in the context of national U.S. presidential elections, are candidates who win the primaries and eventually go on to become president smarter, more creative, more ambitious, or more outgoing than their less successful counterparts? Do these leaders act in fundamentally different ways than their followers, and are these differences in behavior due to differences in their innate intelligence, certain personality traits, or creative ability? If so, could these same characteristics be used to differentiate successful from unsuccessful leaders, executives from first-line supervisors, or leaders from individual contributors? Questions like these led to what was perhaps the earliest theory of leadership, the **Great Man theory.**[1]

The roots of the Great Man theory can be traced back to the early 1900s, when many leadership researchers and the popular press maintained that leaders and followers were fundamentally different. This led to hundreds of research studies that looked at whether certain personality traits, physical attributes, intelligence, or personal values differentiated leaders from followers. Ralph Stogdill was the first leadership researcher to summarize the results of these studies, and he came to two major conclusions. First, leaders were not qualitatively different than followers; many followers were just as tall, smart, outgoing, and ambitious as the people who were leading them. Second, some characteristics, such as intelligence, initiative, stress tolerance, responsibility, friendliness, and dominance, were modestly related to leadership success. In other words, people who were smart, hardworking, conscientious, friendly, or willing to take charge were often more successful at building teams and influencing a group to accomplish its goals than people who were less smart, lazy, impulsive, grumpy, or not fond of giving orders.[2] Having "the right stuff" did not guarantee leadership success, but it improved the odds of successfully influencing a group toward the accomplishment of its goals.

Subsequent reviews involving hundreds of more sophisticated studies came to the same two conclusions.[3] Although these reviews provided ample evidence that people with the right stuff were more likely to be successful as leaders, many leadership researchers focused solely on the point that leaders were not fundamentally different than followers. However, given that most people in leadership positions also play follower roles (supervisors report to managers, managers report to directors, and so forth), this finding is hardly surprising. This erroneous interpretation of the findings, along with the rising popularity of behaviorism in the 1960s and 1970s, caused many leadership researchers to believe that personal characteristics could not be used to predict future leadership success and resulted in a shift in focus toward other leadership phenomena. Not until the publication of seminal articles published in the 1980s and 1990s did intelligence and personality regain popularity with leadership researchers.[4-6] Because of these articles and subsequent leadership research, we now know a lot about how intelligence and various personality traits help or hinder leaders in their efforts to build teams and get results.[7-10] This research also provided insight on the role that various situational and follower characteristics have in affecting how a leader's intelligence and personality play out in the workplace. The purpose of this chapter is to summarize what we currently know about personality, intelligence, and leadership. In other words, what does the research say about the leadership effectiveness of people who are smart, outgoing, innovative, and calm versus those who are dumb, shy, practical, and excitable? Do smarter people always make better leaders? Are there situations where tense and moody leaders are more effective than calm leaders? This chapter answers many common questions regarding the roles of personality, intelligence, creativity, and emotional intelligence in leadership effectiveness. As an overview, the chapter defines these four key attributes, reviews some key research findings for these attributes, and discusses the implications of this research for leadership practitioners.

Personality Traits and Leadership

What Is Personality?

Despite its common usage, Robert Hogan noted that the term **personality** is fairly ambiguous and has at least two quite different meanings.[6] One meaning refers to the impression a person makes on others. This view of personality emphasizes a person's *social reputation* and reflects not only a description but also an evaluation of the person in the eyes of others. From the standpoint of leadership, this view of personality addresses two distinct issues: "What kind of leader or person is this?" and "Is this somebody I would like to work for or be associated with?" In a practical sense, this view of personality comes into play whenever you describe the person you work for to a roommate or friend. For example, you might describe him or her as pushy, honest, outgoing, impulsive, decisive, friendly, and independent. Furthermore, whatever impression this leader made on you, chances are others would use many of the same terms of description. In that vein, many people would probably say that U.S. President Barack Obama is smart, self-confident, outgoing, articulate, ambitious, and level-headed.

The second meaning of personality emphasizes the underlying, unseen structures and processes inside a person that explain why we behave the way we do—why each person's behavior tends to be relatively *similar across different situations*, yet also *different from another person's behavior*. Over the years psychologists have developed many theories to explain how such unseen structures may cause individuals to act in their characteristic manner. For example, Sigmund Freud believed that the intrapsychic tensions among the id, ego, and superego caused one to behave in characteristic ways even if the real motives behind the behaviors were unknown to the person (that is, unconscious).[11] Although useful insights about personality have come from many different theories, most of the research addressing the relationship between personality and leadership success has been based on the **trait approach,** and that emphasis is most appropriate here.

Traits refer to recurring regularities or trends in a person's behavior, and the trait approach to personality maintains that people behave as they do because of the strengths of the traits they possess.[6] Although traits cannot be seen, they can be inferred from consistent patterns of behavior and reliably measured by personality inventories. For example, the personality trait of conscientiousness differentiates leaders who tend to be hardworking and rule abiding from those who tend to be lazy and are more prone to break rules. Leaders getting higher scores on the trait of conscientiousness on personality inventories would be more likely to come to work on time, do a thorough job in completing work assignments, and rarely leave work early. We would also infer that leaders getting lower scores on the trait of conscientiousness would be more likely to be late to appointments, make impulsive decisions, or fail to follow through with commitments and achieve results.

Personality traits are useful concepts for explaining why people act fairly consistently from one situation to the next. This cross-situational consistency in behavior may be thought of as analogous to the seasonal weather patterns in different cities.[12,13] We know that it is extremely cold and dry in Minneapolis in January and hot and humid in Hong Kong in August. Therefore, we can do a pretty good job of predicting what the weather will generally be like in Minneapolis in January, even though our predictions for any particular day will not be perfect. Although the average January temperature in Minneapolis hovers around 20°F, the temperature

There is an optical illusion about every person we ever meet. In truth, they are all creatures of a given temperament, which will appear in a given character, whose boundaries they will never pass: but we look at them, they seem alive, and we presume there is impulse in them. In the moment, it seems like an impulse; in the year, in the lifetime, it turns out to be a certain uniform tune, which the revolving barrel of the music box must play.

Ralph Waldo Emerson

Men acquire a particular quality by constantly acting a particular way. You become a just man by performing just actions, temperate by performing temperate actions, and brave by performing brave actions.

Aristotle

Angela Merkel

PROFILES IN LEADERSHIP 6.1

Angela Merkel is commonly acknowledged as one of the most powerful females in the world. Assuming office in November 2005, she is the first female to have been elected as chancellor of Germany and is the first person from the former German Democratic Republic to lead a unified Germany. She is also only the third female to serve on the G8 council and is currently the president of the European Union. At 53 she is also the youngest chancellor since World War II.

Merkel grew up in a rural community in Eastern Germany and showed an aptitude for math and science at an early age. A member of the communist youth movement in Eastern Germany, she went on to earn both undergraduate and doctoral degrees in physics, specializing in quantum chemistry. She spent much of the 1970s and 1980s in academic positions doing cutting-edge chemical research and publishing her work in such periodicals as *Molecular Physics* and *International Journal of Quantum Chemistry*. Chancellor Merkel did not get involved in politics until the fall of the Berlin Wall in 1989.

In the 1990s she was appointed to several ministerial positions in the Helmut Kohl government and was a young protégé of Chancellor Kohl's. A quick study, she learned the intricacies of national politics and international diplomacy under Kohl's mentorship and used this knowledge to run for and win national elections in Germany in 2005. Merkel currently leads a coalition of parties representing both the left and right wings of German politics. She is leading efforts to liberalize Germany's economy by allowing employers to increase the workweek from 35 to 40 hours and lay off employees during economic downturns. She also supports extending the life of Germany's nuclear power plants beyond 2020 and is opposed to Turkey becoming a full member of the European Union. Despite strong public outcry, Merkel supported the U.S. invasion of Iraq, has sent German soldiers to Afghanistan, endorsed global climate change legislation, and provided funds to support Greece, Portugal, and other European Union countries to prevent these countries from defaulting on their loans.

Given her background, what can you discern about Chancellor Merkel's public reputation, personality traits, values, and intelligence?

Sources: http://www.fullissue.com/index.php/angela-merkel-biography-1964-.html; http://www.imdb.com/name/nm1361767/bio; http://www.biography.com/articles/Angela-Merkel-9406424; http://www.economist.com/world/europe/displaystory.cfm?story_id=16116811.

ranges from $-30°F$ to $30°F$ on any single day in January. Similarly, knowing how two people differ on a particular personality trait can help us predict more accurately how they will tend to act in a variety of situations.

Just as various climate factors can affect the temperature on any single day, so can external factors affect a leader's behavior in any given situation. The trait approach maintains that a leader's behavior reflects an interaction between his or her personality traits and various situational factors (see, for example, Highlight 6.1). Traits play a particularly important role in determining how people behave in unfamiliar, ambiguous, or what we might call **weak situations.** On the other hand, situations that are governed by clearly specified rules, demands, or organizational policies—**strong situations**—often minimize the effects traits have on behavior.[14-18]

The strength of the relationship between personality traits and leadership effectiveness is often inversely related to the relative strength of the

Personality and the Presidency

HIGHLIGHT 6.1

Traits are unseen dispositions that can affect the way people act. Their existence can be inferred by a leader's consistent pattern of behaviors. For example, one way of examining a leader's standing on the trait of achievement orientation is to examine her or his achievements and accomplishments over a life span. Leaders with higher levels of achievement orientation tend to set high personal goals and are persistent in the pursuit of these goals. When considering the following leader's achievements and accomplishments, think about this person's standing on this personality trait, and try to guess who this person might be:

Age 23: lost a job.

Age 23: was defeated in a bid for state legislature.

Age 24: failed in a business venture.

Age 25: was elected to state legislature.

Age 26: sweetheart died.

Age 27: experienced several emotional problems.

Age 27: was defeated in a bid to be speaker of the house.

Age 34: was defeated for nomination to Congress.

Age 37: was elected to Congress.

Age 39: lost renomination to Congress.

Age 40: was defeated in a bid for land office.

Age 45: was defeated in a bid for U.S. Senate.

Age 47: was defeated for nomination to be vice president.

Age 49: was defeated in a second bid for U.S. Senate.

Age 51: was elected president of the United States.

The person was Abraham Lincoln.

situation; that is, personality traits are more closely related to leadership effectiveness in weak or ambiguous situations. Given the accelerated pace of change in most organizations today, it is likely that leaders will face even more unfamiliar and ambiguous situations in the future. Therefore, personality traits may play an increasingly important role in a leader's behavior. If organizations can accurately identify the personality traits of leadership and the individuals who possess them, they should be able to do a better job of promoting the right people into leadership positions. And if the right people are in leadership positions, the odds of achieving organizational success should be dramatically improved. The next section describes some research efforts to identify those personality traits that help leaders build teams and get results through others.

The Five Factor or OCEAN Model of Personality

Although personality traits provide a useful approach to describing distinctive, cross-situational behavioral patterns, one potential problem is the sheer number of traitlike terms available to describe another's stereotypical behaviors. As early as 1936 researchers identified over 18,000 trait-related adjectives in a standard English dictionary.[19] Despite this large number of adjectives, research has shown that most of the traitlike terms people use to describe others' behavioral patterns can be reliably categorized into five broad personality dimensions. Historically this five-dimension model was first identified as early as 1915 and independently verified in 1934, but over the years a number of researchers using diverse samples and assessment instruments have noted similar results.[5,20,21] Given the robustness of these findings, a compelling body of evidence appears to support these five dimensions of personality. These dimensions are referred to in personality literature as the **Five Factor Model (FFM) or OCEAN model of personality,** and most modern personality researchers endorse some version of this model.[5,22-28]

At its core, the Five Factor or OCEAN model of personality is a categorization scheme. Most, if not all, of the personality traits that you would use to describe someone else could be reliably categorized into one of the five OCEAN personality dimensions. A description of the model can be found in Table 6.1. The five major dimensions include openness to experience, conscientiousness, extraversion, agreeableness, and neuroticism. The first of these dimensions, **openness to experience,** is concerned with curiosity, innovative thinking, assimilating new information, and being open to new experiences. Leaders higher in openness to experience tend to be imaginative, broad-minded, and curious and are more strategic, big-picture thinkers; they seek new experiences through travel, the arts, movies, sports, reading, going to new restaurants, or learning about new cultures. Individuals lower in openness to experience tend to be more practical, tactical, and have narrower interests; they like doing things using tried-and-true ways rather than experimenting with new ways. Note that openness to experience is not the same thing as intelligence—smart people are not necessarily intellectually curious.

A key research question is whether people who are curious and big-picture thinkers are more effective leaders than those who are more pragmatic. Research has shown that openness to experience is an important component of leadership effectiveness and seems particularly important at higher organizational levels or for success in overseas assignments.[5,29-33] People with higher openness to experience scores take a more strategic

Why do people think artists are so special? It is just another job.
**Andy Warhol,
artist**

TABLE 6.1
The Five Factor or OCEAN Model of Personality

Factor	Behaviors/Items
Openness to experience	I like traveling to foreign countries. I enjoy going to school.
Conscientiousness	I enjoy putting together detailed plans. I rarely get into trouble.
Extraversion	I like having responsibility for others. I have a large group of friends.
Agreeableness	I am a sympathetic person. I get along well with others.
Neuroticism	I remain calm in pressure situations. I take personal criticism well.

approach to solving problems, and this can help CEOs and other senior leaders keep abreast of market trends, competitive threats, new products, and regulatory changes. And because people with higher openness to experience scores also like new and novel experiences, they often enjoy the challenges associated with living and leading in foreign countries. Nonetheless, there are many leadership positions where curiosity, innovation, and big-picture thinking are relatively unimportant. For example, production foremen on assembly lines, store managers at McDonald's, or platoon leaders for the U.S. Army do not need to be particularly strategic. These jobs put a premium on pragmatic decision-making rather than developing elegant solutions, so being higher in openness to experience in these roles can harm leadership effectiveness.

Conscientiousness concerns those behaviors related to people's approach to work. Leaders who are higher in conscientiousness tend to be planful, organized, and earnest, take commitments seriously, and rarely get into trouble. Those who are lower in conscientiousness tend to be more spontaneous, creative, impulsive, rule bending, and less concerned with following through with commitments. The characters Bart and Lisa Simpson from the television show *The Simpsons* provide a nice illustration of low and high conscientiousness trait scores. Lisa is organized, hardworking, and reliable and never gets into trouble; Bart is disorganized, mischievous, and lazy and rarely keeps promises. Research shows that individuals with higher conscientiousness scores are more likely to be effective leaders than those with lower scores.[5,25-33]

In many ways conscientiousness may be more concerned with management than leadership. That is because people with higher scores are planful, organized, and goal oriented and prefer structure; but they are also risk averse, uncreative, and somewhat boring and dislike change. Although the situation will determine how important these tendencies are for building teams and getting results, research has shown that conscientiousness is a good predictor of leadership potential. Along these lines, conscientiousness seems to be a particularly good predictor of leadership success in jobs that put a premium on following procedures, managing budgets, coordinating work schedules, monitoring projects, and paying attention to details. People having higher scores on conscientiousness would probably do well in the production foreman, store manager, and platoon leader jobs described earlier but may not be as effective if leading sales or consulting teams, college professors, or musicians.

Extraversion involves behaviors that are more likely to be exhibited in group settings and are generally concerned with getting ahead in life.[5,32] Such behavioral patterns often appear when someone is trying to influence or control others, and individuals higher in extraversion come across to others as outgoing, competitive, decisive, outspoken, opinionated, and self-confident. Individuals lower in extraversion generally prefer to work by themselves and have relatively little interest in influencing or competing with others. Because leaders' decisiveness, competitiveness, and self-confidence can affect their ability to successfully influence a group, build a team, and get results, it is not surprising that leaders often have higher extraversion scores than nonleaders.[5,27,28,32,34,35] You can see differences in people's standing on extraversion every time a group of people gets together. Some people in a group are going to be outgoing and will try to get the group to do certain things; others are more comfortable going along with rather than arguing over group activities.

This strong need to assume leadership positions in groups is often associated with taking risks, making decisions, and upward mobility. Many of the candidates on the television show *The Apprentice* have high extraversion scores. These candidates are willing to make decisions and vociferously argue why they shouldn't be fired when their projects go poorly. Those with lower extraversion scores often get "run over" by those with higher scores on their project teams. But as various episodes on this television show demonstrate, being the most decisive and domineering individual in a group does not guarantee project success. Many times those with the highest extraversion scores make poor decisions about their projects or fail to get the people on their projects to work together effectively. Although possessing too much extraversion can be problematic, in general people who are more decisive, self-confident, and outgoing seem to be more effective leaders, and thus extraversion is an important measure of leadership potential.

Another OCEAN personality dimension is **agreeableness,** which concerns how one gets along with, as opposed to gets ahead of, others.[5,30,32] Individuals high in agreeableness come across to others as charming, diplomatic, warm, empathetic, approachable, and optimistic; those lower in agreeableness are more apt to appear as insensitive, socially clueless, grumpy, cold, and pessimistic. Differences in agreeableness can easily be seen on the television show *American Idol.* Ellen DeGeneres has a high agreeableness score and never has a harsh word to say about any candidate, no matter how poorly he or she performs. Randy Jackson and Kara DioGuardi have moderate agreeableness scores and try to provide both positive and negative feedback to candidates. Simon Cowell has a very low agreeableness score and seemingly couldn't care less about how candidates feel about his feedback.

Although people with high agreeableness trait scores are well liked and tend to be better at building teams than those with lower scores, they can struggle with getting results through others. This is because persons with higher scores often have trouble making unpopular decisions or dealing with conflict and performance issues, which can negatively erode the effectiveness of their teams. Because of these difficulties, research has shown that agreeableness has had mixed results in predicting leadership effectiveness.[5,27,28,30,32]

Neuroticism is concerned with how people react to stress, change, failure, or personal criticism. Leaders lower in neuroticism tend to be thick-skinned,

Thermonuclear coaching sessions can be very effective techniques for getting the attention of pilots.
Anthony Burke,
F-16 pilot

A great leader's courage to fulfill his vision comes from passion, not position.
John Maxwell,
author

calm, and optimistic, tend not to take mistakes or failures personally, and hide their emotions; those higher in neuroticism are passionate, intense, thin-skinned, moody, and anxious and lose their tempers when stressed or criticized. Followers often mimic a leader's emotions or behaviors under periods of high stress, so leaders who are calm under pressure and thick-skinned can often help a group stay on task and work through difficult issues. Unfortunately the opposite is also true.

Differences in neuroticism can easily be observed in the judges on *American Idol.* Ellen DeGeneres has a high neuroticism score and readily shares her emotional reactions with candidates; Simon Cowell has a low neuroticism score and rarely displays any emotion on the show. Differences in emotional volatility certainly can affect a person's ability to build teams and get results, and research has shown that neuroticism is another good predictor of leadership potential.[5,27-35] Although lower neuroticism scores are generally associated with leadership effectiveness, people with low scores can struggle to rally the troops when extra effort is needed to achieve results or drive change. This is because these individuals are so flat emotionally that they have a hard time exhibiting any passion or enthusiasm. Charismatic leaders, on the other hand, often have higher neuroticism scores.[26]

Is that you, baby, or just a brilliant disguise?
Bruce Springsteen, musician

Implications of the Five Factor or OCEAN Model

The trait approach and the Five Factor or OCEAN model of personality give leadership researchers and practitioners several useful tools and insights. Personality traits help researchers and practitioners explain leaders' and followers' tendencies to act in consistent ways over time. They tell us why some leaders appear to be dominant versus deferent, outspoken versus quiet, planful versus spontaneous, warm versus cold, and so forth. Note that the behavioral manifestations of personality traits are often exhibited automatically and without much conscious thought. People high in extraversion, for example, will often maneuver to influence or lead whatever groups or teams they are a part of without even thinking about it. Although personality traits predispose us to act in certain ways, we can nonetheless learn to modify our behaviors through experience, feedback, and reflection.

As shown in Figure 6.1, personality traits are a key component of behavior and are relatively difficult to change. Moreover, because personality traits tend to be stable over the years and the behavioral manifestations of traits occur somewhat automatically, it is important for leaders and leaders-to-be to have insight into their personalities. For example, consider a leader who is relatively high in the trait of neuroticism and is deciding whether to accept a high-stress/high-visibility job. On the basis of his personality trait scores, we might predict that this leader could be especially sensitive to criticism and could be moody and prone to emotional outbursts. If the leader understood that he may have issues dealing with stress and criticism, he could choose not to take the position, modify the situation to reduce the level of stress, or learn techniques for

Level 5 Leadership

HIGHLIGHT 6.2

Over the past 20 years, some private corporations, such as Coca-Cola, General Electric, British Petroleum, IBM, and Walmart, have performed very well. People who invested $10,000 in these companies would have seen their investments increase four- to tenfold over this time. But some companies have outperformed even these high fliers. Jim Collins and his staff examined all the companies that appeared on the *Fortune* 500 list from 1965 to 1995 and found 11 companies that dramatically beat the others in returns. One critical component of this tremendous financial success was **Level 5 Leadership.** According to Collins, these companies had leaders with a unique combination of humility and will. As Collins says, Abraham Lincoln never let his ego get in the way of his dream of building a great, enduring nation. Similarly, these corporate leaders did not let their egos get in the way of building great companies. These leaders avoided the spotlight but focused on creating a company that delivered outstanding results. They also possessed an unbreakable resolve that channeled all their energy toward the success of their companies, as opposed to the pursuit of grand personal titles. All these leaders were calm in crises, were never boastful, took responsibility for failure, and were courteous and polite. These leaders set the tone for their respective organizations and spent a considerable amount of time surrounding themselves with the right people and building high-performing teams. As a result, these companies returned $471 for every dollar invested in 1965.

It is worth noting that Level 5 leaders act quite differently from stereotypical corporate executives. In the late 2000s senior executives would do all they could to get on television, and many of these leaders seemed more interested in personal aggrandizement than company success (consider Carly Fiorini, Ken Lewis, and Richard Fuld). Unfortunately it appears that many boards of directors have not paid attention to the key lessons of Collins's book—they continue to look for charismatic rather than Level 5 CEOs to run their organizations. Given the OCEAN model, how would Level 5 leaders score on the five personality factors?

Sources: J. Collins, *Good to Great* (New York: Harper Collins, 2001); R. Khurana, "The Curse of the Superstar CEO," *Harvard Business Review,* September 2002, pp. 60–67; J. A. Sonnenfeld and R. Khurana, "Fishing for CEOs in Your Own Backyard," *The Wall Street Journal,* July 30, 2002, p. B2; R. S. Peterson, D. B. Smith, P. V. Martorana, and P. D. Owens, "The Impact of Chief Executive Officer Personality on Top Management Team Dynamics: One Mechanism by Which Leadership Affects Organizational Performance," *Journal of Applied Psychology* 88, no. 5 (2003), pp. 795–808.

FIGURE 6.1
The Building Blocks of Skills

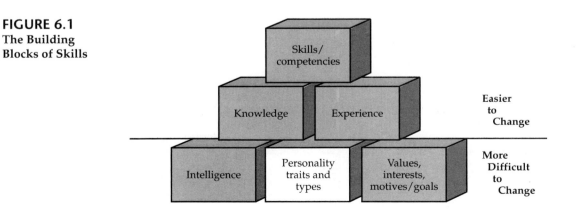

effectively dealing with these issues. A leader who lacked this self-insight would probably make poorer choices and have more difficulties coping with the demands of this position.[6]

The OCEAN model has proven useful in several other ways. Most personality researchers currently embrace some form of this model because it has provided a useful scheme for categorizing the findings of the personality–leadership performance research.[6,27-29,32] Because research has shown personality to be an effective measure of leadership potential, organizations now use the results of OCEAN personality assessments for hiring new leaders, for giving leaders developmental feedback about various personality traits, and as a key component in planning succession to promote leaders.[36]

One advantage of the OCEAN model is that it is a useful method for profiling leaders. An example of a school principal's results on an OCEAN personality assessment can be found in Figure 6.2. According to this profile, this leader will generally come across to others as self-confident, goal oriented, competitive, outgoing, liking to be the center of attention, but also distractible and a poor listener (high extraversion); optimistic, resilient, and calm under pressure (low neuroticism); reasonably warm and approachable (medium agreeableness); moderately planful, rule abiding, and earnest (medium conscientiousness); and a pragmatic, tactical thinker (low openness to experience). Other leaders will have different behavioral tendencies, and knowing this type of information *before* someone gets hired or promoted into a leadership position can help improve the odds of organizational success.

Another advantage of the OCEAN model is that it appears universally applicable across cultures.[6,29,33,37] People from Asian, Western European, Middle Eastern, Eastern European, and South American cultures seem to use the same five personality dimensions to categorize, profile, or describe others. Not only do people from different cultures describe others using the same five-factor framework—these dimensions all seem to predict job

FIGURE 6.2
Example OCEAN Profile

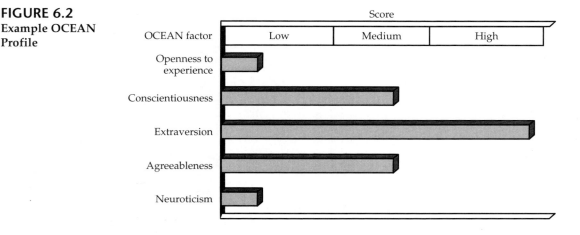

Personality and Life

HIGHLIGHT 6.3

Many organizations currently use personality testing as part of their process for hiring leaders or in leadership development programs. Despite their prevalence in both the private and public sector, there is still considerable controversy surrounding the use of personality testing in organizational settings. Some of the arguments against using personality testing are that (1) personality test scores are unrelated to job performance; (2) personality tests are biased or "unethical"; and (3) personality test results can be faked. These are important questions: if personality test scores are biased, are unrelated to job performance, and can be faked, there would be little reason to use them in work settings. However, a comprehensive review of personality research has recently revealed the following:

- Personality traits predict overall managerial effectiveness, promotion rates, and managerial level attainment.
- Personality traits predict leader emergence and effectiveness.
- Personality traits predict charismatic or transformational leadership.
- Personality traits predict expatriate performance.
- Personality traits predict goal setting, procrastination, creativity, and innovation.
- Personality traits predict overall job performance across virtually all job types.
- Personality traits predict absenteeism and other counterproductive work behaviors.
- Personality traits predict job and career satisfaction.
- Personality traits predict mortality rates, divorce, alcohol and drug use, health behaviors, and occupational attainment.

- Personality test scores predict teamwork and team performance.
- Personality test scores yield similar results for protected groups. In other words, males, females, African Americans, Hispanics, and Asian Americans generally score the same on personality tests.
- Personality tests results can be faked to some extent, but the degree to which test scores are faked depends on the test setting and administration. Faking, however, does not seem to affect the overall relationships between personality test results and work outcomes and can be detected and corrected.
- In all likelihood personality tests suffer less from adverse impact and faking than traditional selection techniques, such as résumés and job interviews.

These findings show that personality tests can help organizations hire leaders who have the potential to be effective and can help leaders hire followers who are more likely to be successful. The arguments against the use of personality testing simply do not stand up to the facts.

Sources: L. M. Hough and F. L. Oswald. "Personality Testing and Industrial–Organizational Psychology: Reflections, Progress, and Prospects," *Industrial and Organizational Psychology: Perspectives on Science and Practice* 1, no. 3 (2008), pp. 272–90; G. J. Curphy, *Hogan Assessment Systems Certification Workshop Training Manual* (Tulsa, OK: Hogan Assessment Systems, 2003); G. J. Curphy, "Comments on the State of Leadership Prediction," in *Predicting Leadership: The Good, the Bad, the Indifferent, and the Unnecessary*, in J. P. Campbell and M. J. Benson (chairs), symposium conducted at the 22nd Annual Conference for the Society of Industrial and Organizational Psychology, New York, April 2007.

and leadership performance across cultures. For example, in a comprehensive review of the research, Salgado reported that all five of the OCEAN dimensions predicted blue-collar, professional, and managerial performance in various European countries.[29] But the strength of the personality–job performance relationship depends on the particular job. Some jobs, such as sales, put a premium on interpersonal skills and goal orientation (extraversion and agreeableness), whereas manufacturing jobs put more of a premium on planning and abiding by safety and productivity rules (conscientiousness). Researchers often get much stronger personality–job performance relationships when the personality traits being measured have some degree of job relatedness.[6,27,28]

> *People believe what they want to believe and disregard the rest.*
>
> **Paul Simon and Art Garfunkel, musicians**

Robert "RT" Hogan

PROFILES IN LEADERSHIP 6.2

Robert Hogan has arguably been one of the most prominent and influential leadership researchers for the past 30 years. His papers and books are among the most widely cited in the behavioral sciences, and he is constantly asked to do keynote presentations to government, business, and academic audiences. His personality inventories are widely recognized as "best in class" and are used around the world to hire and develop everyone from truck drivers to CEOs. At this point well over 3 million individuals have taken one or more Hogan assessments, and the popularity of these instruments continues to grow.

Hogan grew up in east Los Angeles and was the first in his family to attend college. He attended UCLA and obtained an engineering degree on a Navy ROTC scholarship before spending the next seven years working on a destroyer in the U.S. Navy. It was in the navy that Hogan became interested in leadership and psychology; he read all he could about Freud, Jung, and other prominent psychologists while at sea. After leaving the navy Hogan became a parole officer for the Los Angeles police department. As a parole officer Hogan noticed that the process used to determine a juvenile's fate was completely at the whim of his or her parole officer and that there was no standardized system or process for keeping these individuals out of

trouble. Thinking there was a better way to do this, Hogan decided to attend UC Berkeley to obtain a PhD in personality psychology. While working on his graduate degree Hogan did personality testing on police officers and devised selection systems to combat unfair hiring and promotion practices. After graduation he spent some time as a professor at Johns Hopkins University before becoming a professor at the University of Tulsa. Hogan eventually became chair of the psychology department at the University of Tulsa while starting his own company, Hogan Assessment Systems.

A true entrepreneur, RT and his wife Joyce (who is also a well-known PhD psychologist) started Hogan Assessment Systems; the company now has 40 full-time employees and distributor partnerships around the globe. Hogan Assessment Systems has been a great way for RT and Joyce Hogan to mentor and develop graduate students and help junior faculty get published. They have also been able to leverage the data they have collected through their instruments to publish hundreds of articles and books about personality and leadership, many of which can be found in the most prestigious psychology journals. One of the authors of this textbook, Gordy Curphy, credits the Hogans with having a bigger impact on his thinking about leadership and success as a leadership consultant than anyone else he has worked with.

Personality Types and Leadership

The Differences between Traits and Types

Traits are not the only way to describe stereotypical behaviors. An alternative framework to describe the differences in people's day-to-day behavioral patterns is through **types,** or in terms of a **personality typology.** Superficially there may appear to be little difference between traits and types; even some of the same words are used to name them. Extraversion, for example, is the name of a factor in the OCEAN model, but another framework may talk about extraverted *types*. And these differences are more than skin-deep. We will emphasize only one aspect of these differences—the one we believe is most fundamental conceptually. Each personality factor in the OCEAN model (such as neuroticism) is conceptualized as a continuum along which people can vary, typically in a bell-curve distribution. A person may be relatively lower or higher on that trait, and the differences in behavioral patterns between any two people may be thought of as roughly proportional to how close or far apart they are on the scale. Types, on the other hand, are usually thought of as relatively *discrete categories*.

This distinction may be clearer with an example. Let us take the trait of dominance and compare it with a hypothetical construct we will call a "dominant type." Psychological typologies are often expressed in terms of polar opposites, so let us further suppose that our typology also refers to the bipolar opposite of dominant types, which we'll call submissive types. Importantly, people are considered to *be one or the other,* just as everyone is either male or female. If you are a dominant type, you are considered to be more like all the other dominant types than you are like any submissive type; if you are a submissive type, you are considered to be more like every submissive type than you are like any dominant type. In other words, typologies tend to put people into discrete psychological categories and emphasize the *similarities* among all people in the same category regardless of actual score (as long as it is in the "right" direction). Furthermore, typologies tend to emphasize *differences* between people of different types (such as between dominant and submissive types) regardless of actual score.

Figure 6.3 illustrates this point. The upper line refers to the continuum of the trait defined at one end by submissiveness and at the other end by dominance. The trait scores of four different individuals—Jim, John, Joe, and Jack—are indicated on the scale. You can infer from their relative positions on the scale that John is more like Joe than he is like either Jim or Jack. Now look at the lower line. This refers to the typology of submissive and dominant types. The theory behind personality types suggests that John is more like Jim than Joe, and Joe is more like Jack than John.

FIGURE 6.3
Traits and Types

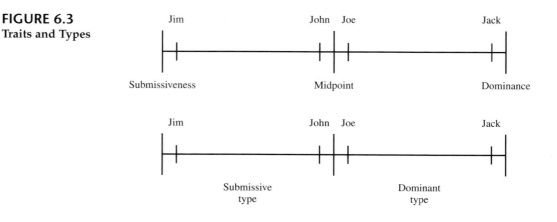

Psychological Preferences as a Personality Typology

One popular personality typology involves psychological preferences, or what we might call "mental habits." Like traits, our preferences play a role in the characteristic and unique ways we behave from day to day.

According to Jung,[38] preferences influence our choice of careers, ways of thinking, relationships, and work habits. Over 2 million people take the **Myers-Briggs Type Indicator (MBTI)** test every year,[39] which not only is the most popular measure of preferences but also makes it one of the most popular psychological tests. The MBTI is often used in college-level leadership and adult education courses, formal leadership training programs, and various team-building interventions. Moreover, numerous books and articles have been published about how the MBTI can be used to better understand oneself, co-workers, partners in intimate relationships, children, and educational and occupational choices. Because of the overall popularity of preferences and the MBTI, we believe it is worthwhile to review this framework and its most popular assessment instrument in some detail.

Somewhat paradoxically, one reason knowledge about our psychological preferences is important is precisely because it is so easy to forget about them. It is easy to forget how subjective and idiosyncratic preferences really are; we easily confuse our *preferences* with *the way things are or ought to be.* For example, those who value being organized may prefer *everyone* to be organized. They may get annoyed when working with others who are less organized than they are. In other words, it is easy to let preferences affect judgments about others (people "should" be organized, and therefore not being organized is a deficiency). Many people are unaware of the extent to which their preferences shape their perceptions of reality.

According to Myers and Myers,[40] there are four basic preference diménsions in which people can differ. These four dimensions include extraversion–introversion, sensing–intuition, thinking–feeling, and judging–perceiving. These four dimensions are bipolar, meaning that individuals generally prefer being either, say, extraverted or introverted. A more in-depth description of the day-to-day behavioral patterns of these four dimensions follows.

The **extraversion–introversion** dimension is fundamentally concerned with where people get their energy. Some leaders are naturally gregarious and outgoing. Their spontaneous sociability makes it easy for them to strike up conversations with anyone about almost anything. Not surprisingly, extraverts have a breadth of interests and a large circle of acquaintances. There are energized by being around others, but their tendency to "think out loud" and speak whatever is on their mind can sometimes get them into trouble. Other leaders are more comfortable being alone or with just a few others. Introverts can interact effectively with others, but they are fundamentally both more reserved and more deliberate than extraverts. Introverted leaders prefer to think things through and announce only final decisions, and followers may have a difficult time understanding the process such a leader used to reach his or her conclusions. Because introverts find being around others to be draining, they may come across as less approachable than extraverts. This preference dimension can be easily seen at parties and social settings. Extraverts work the crowd and are often the last to leave; introverts keep to themselves or talk to a small group of friends and leave early. Of course everyone needs to act in both introverted and extraverted ways at various times; however, some of us are more comfortable with one than the other.

The **sensing–intuition** dimension is concerned with how people look at data. Leader who prefer the sensing mode like facts and details; the focus of information gathering concerns the real, the actual, the literal, the specific, and the present. Hence sensing leaders tend to be practical, orderly, and down-to-earth decision makers. By contrast, leaders who rely on their intuition look for the big picture beyond particular facts and details; information is most meaningful for its pattern, trend, figurative meaning, and future possibilities. Intuitive leaders tend to be innovative and conceptual (though sometimes impractical) and are more comfortable with their hunches and inspirations. This preference dimension can often be seen in presentations. A sensing leader will use a relatively large number of slides to explain all the facts leading up to a practical decision. An intuitive leader will use a few slides to summarize key trends and describe the possible implications of these trends. Intuitive leaders sitting through a sensor's presentation might get bored with the details and think, "They just don't get it." Sensing leaders sitting through an intuitive's presentation will wonder, "Where are the data?" and ask questions about the assumptions and facts underlying the trends and conclusions.

Whereas the sensing–intuition dimension is concerned with how leaders and followers look at data, the **thinking–feeling** dimension is concerned with the considerations leaders prefer when making decisions. Thinking leaders like to analyze, criticize, and approach decisions impersonally and objectively. They use their heads to adopt a relatively detached stance toward decisions and pay more attention to operational, bottom-line considerations. Feeling leaders naturally empathize and appreciate, and they prefer to approach decisions personally and subjectively. They value humaneness and social harmony and use their hearts to weigh the impact of any decision on people. As an example, say a thinking leader was the head of a customer service support center, and his feeling follower just got a call that her child was sick at school and she needed to go pick her up. The leader's first thought might be "How will I be able to field customer calls during my follower's absence?" whereas the follower's first thought might be "I hope my child is okay." Similarly, the CEO of a large home improvement retail organization was a strong thinker, and one of his division presidents was a strong feeler. The CEO would look at monthly financial reports and make decisions that would improve shareholder value. The division president would look at these decisions and immediately think about how they would affect his 26,000 employees. Both the CEO and division president looked at the same reports; they just approached their decisions differently based on their preferences.

The **judging–perceiving** dimension describes the amount of information a leader needs before feeling comfortable making a decision. Judging leaders strive for closure; they like things settled and come across as decisive, methodical, and organized. Judgers get nervous *before* decisions get made and want to see only the minimal amount of information needed to make decisions. Although they make up their minds quickly, they may not have all the relevant facts and as a result can make poor decisions. Perceiving leaders like to keep their options open; they are curious, spontaneous, and flexible. Perceivers prefer to collect as much data as possible before making decisions and get nervous *after* they are made because they may not feel all the information was collected or analyzed correctly. Although perceivers are good at gathering and analyzing data, they sometimes are accused of suffering from "analysis paralysis." This personality preference can readily be seen in meetings. Judging leaders prefer to have an agenda, stick to it, and make as many decisions as possible in the meeting. Perceivers dislike agendas, do not mind going off on tangents, and may or may not make any decisions at meetings. They also have no problem revisiting decisions made in earlier meetings if new information comes to light. Judging followers can get frustrated working

I am the decider.
**George W. Bush,
U.S. president**

for perceiving leaders and vice versa over these meeting and decision-making issues.

As with personality traits, many leaders and followers exhibit the behaviors associated with their preference dimensions almost automatically, particularly in weak or stressful situations. However, it is important to note that people are not locked into exhibiting only those behaviors associated with their preferences. Leaders can and do exhibit behaviors associated with the opposite side of any preference dimension, but it takes personal insight and conscious energy and effort to do so. Moreover, the more extreme a preference score, the more likely the associated behaviors will be exhibited and the more effort it will take to exhibit nonpreference behaviors. One advantage of this framework is that the predominant preferences can be used to create 16 psychological types. For example, someone with high preferences for introversion, sensing, thinking, and judging would be categorized as an ISTJ type. A listing of the 16 types can be found in Table 6.2, and preference researchers believe that individuals within any particular type are more similar to each other than they are to individuals in any of the other 15 types.[39-41]

Implications of Preferences and Types

Preference advocates maintain that no one type is necessarily better than others in terms of leadership effectiveness, and that each type has unique strengths and potential weaknesses.[39-41] There is little published evidence to support this claim, but evidence shows that leaders are disproportionately distributed across a handful of types. As shown in Table 6.2, many more leaders are ISTJs, ESTJs, and ENTJs than other types. More research is needed concerning how preferences affect leadership, but it seems reasonable that awareness and appreciation of them can enhance any leader's effectiveness.

Although the MBTI is an extremely popular and potentially useful instrument, leadership practitioners need to be aware of its limitations and possible misuses. The four preference dimensions can provide useful insights about oneself and others, but the fundamental concept of type is problematic. First, types are not stable over time. Some research indicates that at least one letter in the four-letter type my change in half the people taking the test in as little as five weeks.[42] Data also show major development changes in distribution of types with age.[43] It is difficult to see how one should select individuals for teams or provide career guidance to others based on types if the types (or at least type scores) change, in some cases quickly. Furthermore, because the behavior of two people in the same type may vary as greatly as that of people of different types, the utility of typing systems remains uncertain.

But perhaps the most serious problem in using typologies concerns the way they are sometimes misused.[44] Unfortunately some people become so

TABLE 6.2   **The 16 Psychological Types**

Characteristics Frequently Associated with Each Myers-Briggs Type	
ISTJ (14%)[a] Serious, quiet, earn success by concentration and thoroughness. Practical, orderly, matter-of-fact, logical, realistic, and dependable. See to it that everything is well organized. Take responsibility. Make up their own minds as to what should be accomplished and work toward it steadily, regardless of protest or distractions.	**ISFJ** (2%) Quiet, friendly, responsible, and conscientious. Work devotedly to meet their obligations. Lend stability to any project or group. Thorough, painstaking, accurate. May need time to master technical subjects, as their interests are usually not technical. Patient with detail and routine. Loyal, considerate, concerned with how other people feel.
ISTP (2%) Cool onlookers—quiet, reserved, observing, and analyzing life with detached curiosity and unexpected flashes of original humor. Usually interested in impersonal principles, cause and effect, how and why mechanical things work. Exert themselves no more than they think necessary, because any waste of energy would be inefficient.	**ISFP** (1%) Retiring, quietly friendly, sensitive, kind, modest about their abilities. Shun disagreements, do not force their opinions or values on others, usually do not care to lead but are often loyal followers. Often relaxed about getting things done, because they enjoy the present moment and do not want to spoil it by undue haste or exertion.
ESTP (2%) Matter-of-fact, do not worry or hurry, enjoy whatever comes along. Tend to like mechanical things and sports, with friends on the side. May be a bit blunt or insensitive. Adaptable, tolerant, generally conservative in values. Dislike long explanations. Are best with real things that can be worked, handled, taken apart, or put together.	**ESFP** (1%) Outgoing, easygoing, accepting, friendly, enjoy everything and make things more fun for others by their enjoyment. Like sports and making things. Know what's going on and join in eagerly. Find remembering facts easier than mastering theories. Are best in situations that need sound common sense and practical ability with people as well as with things.
ESTJ (23%) Practical, realistic, matter-of-fact, with a natural head for business or mechanics. Not interested in subjects they see no use for, but can apply themselves when necessary. Like to organize and run activities. May make good administrators, especially if they remember to consider others' feelings and points of view.	**ESFJ** (2%) Warm-hearted, talkative, popular, conscientious, born cooperators, active committee members. Need harmony and may be good at creating it. Always doing something nice for someone. Work best with encouragement and praise. Little interest in abstract thinking or technical subjects. Main interest is in things that directly and visibly affect people's lives.
INFJ (1%) Succeed by perseverance, originality, and desire to do whatever is needed or wanted. Put their best efforts into their work. Quietly forceful, conscientious, concerned for others. Respected for their firm principles. Likely to be honored and followed for their clear convictions as to how best to serve the common good.	**INTJ** (9%) Usually have original minds and great drive for their own ideas and purposes. In fields that appeal to them, they have a fine power to organize a job and carry it through with or without help. Skeptical, critical, independent, determined, often stubborn. Must learn to yield less important points in order to win the most important.

INFP (1%)
Full of enthusiasms and loyalties, but seldom talk of these until they know you well. Care about learning, ideas, language, and independent projects of their own. Tend to undertake too much, then somehow get it done. Friendly, but often too absorbed in what they are doing to be sociable. Little concern with possessions or physical surroundings.

ENFP (2%)
Warmly enthusiastic, high-spirited, ingenious, imaginative. Able to do almost anything that interests them. Quick with a solution for any difficulty and ready to help anyone with a problem. Often rely on their ability to improvise instead of preparing in advance. Can usually find compelling reasons for whatever they want.

ENFJ (4%)
Responsive and responsible. Generally feel real concern for what others think or want, and try to handle things with due regard for other person's feelings. Can present a proposal or lead group discussion with ease and tact. Sociable, popular, sympathetic. Responsive to praise and criticism.

INTP (5%)
Quiet, reserved, impersonal. Enjoy especially theoretical or scientific subjects, logical to the point of hair splitting. Usually interested mainly in ideas, with little liking for parties or small talk. Tend to have sharply defined interests. Need careers where some strong interest can be used and useful.

ENTP (9%)
Quick, ingenious, good at many things. Stimulating company, alert, and outspoken. May argue for fun on either side of a question. Resourceful in solving new and challenging problems, but may neglect routine assignments. Apt to turn to one new interest after another. Skillful in finding logical reasons for what they want.

ENTJ (22%)
Hearty, frank, decisive, leaders in activities. Usually good in anything that requires reasoning and intelligent talk, such as public speaking. Are usually well-informed and enjoy adding to their fund of knowledge. May sometimes be more positive and confident than their experience in an area warrants.

*The percentage of managers falling into each of the 16 types.

Consulting Psychologists Press Inc. *Manual; A Guide to the Development and Use of Myers Briggs Type Indicator.* Palo Alto, CA: Author, 1993.

Perhaps no concept in the history of psychology has had or continues to have as great an impact on everyday life in the Western world as that of general intelligence.
**Sandra Scarr,
researcher**

enamored with simple systems for classifying human behavior that they begin to see *everything* through "type" glasses. Some people habitually categorize their friends, significant others, and co-workers into types. Knowledge of type should be a basis for appreciating the richness and diversity of behavior and the capabilities in others and ourselves. It is not meant to be a system of categorization that oversimplifies our own and others' behavior. Believing someone is a particular type can become a perceptual filter that keeps us from actually recognizing when that person is acting in a manner contrary to that type's characteristic style. Another misuse occurs when someone uses "knowledge" of type as an excuse or a rationalization for his own counterproductive behaviors ("I know I'm talking on and on and dominating the conversation, but after all, I'm an extravert"). In this case the misuse of type can become a self-fulfilling prophecy that may make it difficult for a leader to change a follower's behavior. The MBTI is a useful tool for enhancing awareness of oneself and others, but leaders need to understand that, like any tool, it can be misused.

Intelligence and Leadership

What Is Intelligence?

The first formal linkage between intelligence and leadership was established around 1115 BC in China, where the dynasties used standardized tests to determine which citizens would play key leadership roles in the institutions they had set up to run the country.[45] Using intelligence tests to identify potential leaders in the United States goes back to World War I, and

Anne Mulcahy

PROFILES IN LEADERSHIP 6.3

Anne Mulcahy became the first female CEO at Xerox in August 2001 and chairwoman in January 2002. In the late 1990s and early 2000s Xerox was rapidly losing market share, and its stock price was in a free fall. Over time Xerox had lost touch with its customers and the market and had not done a good job of reducing costs. Mulcahy logged 100,000 miles in her first year as CEO listening to employees and customers and then ordered a major restructuring that cut $1.7 billion in annual expenses, slashed 25,000 jobs, and shed $2.3 billion in noncore assets. Although these cuts were extremely painful, Mulcahy is widely credited with saving Xerox.

Anne Mulcahy had a very nontraditional path to the CEO role. She was the only girl in a family with four boys and was taught at an early age that she needed to compete equally with her siblings. This upbringing helped her to handle and listen to criticism, and these abilities in turn played a key role in her path to the top. She attended Marymount College before joining Xerox in 1976 as a field sales representative. Anne spent 15 years in sales before being named the vice president of Human Resources in 1992—a job she held for the next three years. She then spent a year as the vice president of Customer Operations Worldwide before being promoted to senior vice president and chief staff officer. A year later she became president of General Markets Operations, and from 2000 to 2001 she was the president and chief operating officer of Xerox. Her background in sales, human resources, customer service, and operations gave her a unique perspective on Xerox's customers, competitors, strategies, products, business models, and people, and she used this knowledge to formulate the company's turnaround and subsequent vision for growth.

Described as honest, straightforward, decisive, hardworking, disciplined, compassionate, and fiercely loyal to the Xerox brand, Mulcahy has consistently told the company "the good, the bad, and the ugly." Although many of her town hall meetings were quite contentious, she made a point of telling everyone the brutal facts surrounding Xerox. She also used these opportunities to convey a compelling vision of the company's future and what people needed to do to make her vision become reality. Employees appreciated Mulcahy's honesty, and her vision helped give them hope for the future. Her vision alone was not enough to turn around Xerox, however, and she quickly replaced direct reports who were not aligned with her vision or failed to deliver results. The company's financial performance and stock price steadily improved under Mulcahy's leadership, and in 2010 she retired from Xerox to spend more time with her family and on the other boards of directors she belonged to.

Given Anne Mulcahy's background, what do you think her personality traits are or personality type might be? How would you rate her analytic, practical, and creative intelligence?

Sources: http://www.referenceforbusiness.com/biography/M-R/Mulcahy-Anne-1952.html; http://news.xerox.com/pr/xerox/anne-m-mulcahy.aspx; http://investing.businessweek.com/businessweek/research/stocks/people/person.asp?personid=562620&ticker=XRX:US.

to a large extent this use of intelligence testing continues today. Over 100 years of very comprehensive and systematic research provides overwhelming evidence to support the notion that general intelligence plays a substantial role in human affairs.[46-54] Still, intelligence and intelligence testing are among the most controversial topics in the social sciences today. There is contentious debate over questions like how heredity and the environment affect intelligence, whether intelligence tests should be used in public schools, and whether ethnic groups differ in average intelligence test scores. For the most part, however, we will bypass such controversies here. Our focus will be on the relationship between intelligence and leadership.

We define **intelligence** as a person's all-around effectiveness in activities directed by thought.[46-55] What does this definition of intelligence have to do with leadership? Research has shown that more intelligent leaders are faster learners; make better assumptions, deductions, and inferences; are better at creating a compelling vision and developing strategies to make their vision a reality; can develop better solutions to problems; can see more of the primary and secondary implications of their decisions; and are quicker on their feet than leaders who are less intelligent.[46-64] To a large extent people get placed into leadership positions to solve problems, whether they are customer, financial, operational, interpersonal, performance, political, educational, or social in nature. Therefore, given the behaviors associated with higher intelligence, it is easy to see how a more intelligent leader will often be more successful than a less intelligent leader in influencing a group to accomplish its goals. Like personality traits, however, intelligence alone is not enough to guarantee leadership success. Plenty of smart people make poor leaders—just as few intelligent people are great leaders. Nevertheless, many leadership activities seem to involve some degree of decision-making and problem-solving ability, which means a leader's intelligence can affect the odds of leadership success in many situations.

As shown in Figure 6.4, intelligence is relatively difficult to change. Like personality, it is also an unseen quality and can be inferred only by observing behavior. Moreover, intelligence does not affect behavior equally across all situations. Some activities, such as following simple routines, put

Be willing to make decisions. That's the most important quality of a good leader.
George S. Patton, U.S. Army general

No psychologist has observed intelligence; many have observed intelligent behavior. This observation should be the starting point for any theory of intelligence.
I. Chien, researcher

FIGURE 6.4
The Building Blocks of Skills

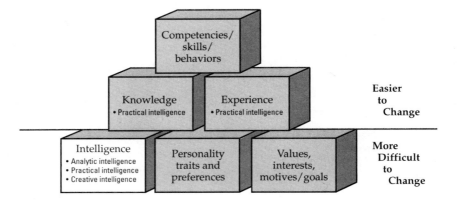

less of a premium on intelligence than others.[58,65] Finally, our definition of intelligence does not imply that intelligence is a fixed quantity. Although heredity plays a role, intelligence can be modified through education and experience.[46,51,57,65]

The Triarchic Theory of Intelligence

Intelligence and leadership effectiveness are related, but there is still an ongoing debate about the nature of intelligence. Many psychologists have tried to determine the structure of intelligence: is intelligence a unitary ability, or does it involve a collection of related mental abilities?[55,62,66,67] Other psychologists have said that the *process* by which people do complex mental work is much more important than determining the number of mental abilities.[50,51,68] One of the most comprehensive and compelling theories of intelligence developed and tested over the past 20 years is Sternberg's **triarchic theory of intelligence**.[50,51,56,57,68] It also offers some of the most significant implications for leadership. The triarchic theory focuses on what a leader *does* when solving complex mental problems, such as how information is combined and synthesized when solving problems, what assumptions and errors are made, and the like. According to this theory, there are three basic types of intelligence. **Analytic intelligence** is general problem-solving ability and can be assessed using standardized mental abilities tests. Analytic intelligence is important because leaders and followers who possess higher levels of this type of intelligence tend to be quick learners, do well in school, see connections between issues, and have the ability to make accurate deductions, assumptions, and inferences with relatively unfamiliar information.

There is still much, however, that analytic intelligence does not explain. Many people do well on standardized tests but not in life.[59,64,65,68] And some people do relatively poorly on standardized intelligence tests but develop ingenious solutions to practical problems. For example, Sternberg and his associates described a situation in which students in a school for the mentally retarded did very poorly on standardized tests yet consistently found ways to defeat the school's elaborate security system. In this situation the students possessed a relatively high level of **practical intelligence,** or "street smarts." People with street smarts know how to adapt to, shape, or select new situations to get their needs met better than people lacking street smarts (e.g., think of a stereotypical computer nerd and an inner-city kid both lost in downtown New York). In other words, practical intelligence involves knowing how things get done and how to do them. For leaders, practical intelligence is important because it involves knowing what to do and how to do it when confronted with a particular leadership situation, such as dealing with a poorly performing subordinate, resolving a problem with a customer, or getting a team to work better together.[64,68]

Because of its potential importance to leadership effectiveness, several other aspects of practical intelligence are worth noting. First, practical

The first method for estimating the intelligence of a ruler is to look at the men he has around him.
Niccolò Machiavelli, writer

Everyone is ignorant, only on different subjects.
Will Rogers, humorist

Why Athletes Can't Have Regular Jobs

HIGHLIGHT 6.4

The United States seems to put more emphasis on athleticism than intelligence, as least when it comes to the amounts of money allocated to athletic and academic scholarships. The following quotes illustrate the kind of returns the United States is getting from its athletic scholarships:

- Chicago Cubs outfielder Andre Dawson on being a role model: "I want all dem kids to do what I do, to look up to me. I want dem kids to copulate me."

- New Orleans Saints running back George Rogers when asked about the upcoming season: "I want to rush for 1,000 or 1,500 yards, whatever comes first."

- Torrin Polk, University of Houston receiver, on his coach: "He treats us like men. He lets us wear earrings."

- Senior basketball player at the University of Pittsburgh: "I am going to graduate on time, no matter now long it takes."

- Stu Grimson, Chicago Blackhawks wing, explaining why he keeps a color photograph of himself on his locker: "That's so when I forget how to spell my name, I can still find my clothes."

- Chuck Nevitt, North Carolina basketball player, explaining to his coach why he appeared nervous in practice: "My sister's expecting a baby, and I don't know if I am going to be an uncle or an aunt."

- Frank Layden, Utah Jazz President, on a former player: "I told him, 'Son, what is it with you? Is it ignorance or apathy?' He said, 'Coach, I don't know and I don't care.'"

- Football commentator and former player Joe Theisman: "Nobody in football should be called a genius. A genius is a guy like Norman Einstein."

- Shelby Metcalf, basketball coach at Texas A&M, recounting what he told a player who received four Fs and a D: "Son, looks to me like you're spending too much time on one subject."

- In the words of North Carolina State basketball player Charles Shackelford: "I can go to my left or right, I am amphibious."

Source: http://www.vegsource.com/talk/humor/messages/97.html.

intelligence is much more concerned with knowledge and experience than is analytic intelligence (see Figure 6.4). Leaders can build their practical intelligence by building their leadership knowledge and experience. Thus textbooks like this one can help you build your practical intelligence. Getting a variety of leadership experiences, and perhaps more important, reflecting on these experiences, will also help you build practical intelligence. But you should understand that it takes some time before you will become an "expert" at leadership—research shows that it takes 10 years to truly master any particular topic.[69]

Second, practical intelligence is *domain specific*. A leader who has a lot of knowledge and experience in leading a pharmaceutical research team may feel like a duck out of water when asked to lead a major fund-raising effort for a charitable institution. As another example, one of the authors worked with a highly successful retail company having over 100,000 employees. All the key leaders had over 20 years of retail operations and merchandising experience, but they also did poorly on standardized intelligence tests. The

Why Smart People Can't Learn

HIGHLIGHT 6.5

Being able to learn and adapt is a critical leadership skill, but it turns out that many professionals are not good at it. Leaders get paid to solve problems and are generally good at this, but many are lousy at determining what role *they* played in causing these problems. Leaders are good at **single-loop learning**—reviewing data and facts and identifying the underlying root causes from the information gathered—but are not good at **double-loop learning**—determining what they as leaders need to do differently to avoid problems in the future. The primary reason why many leaders are not good at double-loop learning is because most have not experienced real failure. Many people in positions of authority have enviable track records of success, so when things go badly they erroneously believe that it cannot be their fault because they have always been successful. Something else must be causing the group's substandard performance, such as underachieving followers, market conditions, difficult customers, government regulations, or cutthroat competitors. Thus many leaders react to failure by laying the blame on circumstances or other people. Although external factors can and do affect group performance, a leader's actions or inactions can also be a major cause of team failure. Before leaders point at external factors they need to ask how their actions contributed to the problem. Unfortunately it appears that the more formal education one has, the less likely it is that one will engage in double-loop learning. Intelligence alone will not help people extract the maximum value from their experiences—reflection also plays a key role in learning and adaptation.

Source: C. Argyris, "Teaching Smart People How to Learn," *Harvard Business Review*, May–June 1991, Reprint Number 91301.

We do know with certain knowledge that Osama bin Laden is either in Afghanistan, in some other country, or dead.

Donald Rumsfeld, former U.S. Secretary of Defense

company had successfully expanded in the United States (which capitalized on their practical intelligence), but their attempt to expand to foreign markets was an abysmal failure. This failure was due in part to the leaders' inability to learn, appreciate, or understand the intricacies of other cultures (analytic intelligence), their lack of knowledge and experience in foreign markets (practical intelligence), and in turn their development of inappropriate strategies for running the business in other countries (a combination of analytic and practical intelligence). Thus practical intelligence is extremely useful for leading in familiar situations, but analytic intelligence may play a more important role when leaders face new or novel situations.

Third, this example points out the importance of having both types of intelligence. Organizations today are looking for leaders and followers who have the necessary knowledge and skills to succeed (practical intelligence) and the ability to learn (analytic intelligence).[50,56,57,68,70] Fourth, high levels of practical intelligence may compensate for lower levels of analytic intelligence. Leaders with lower analytic abilities may still be able to solve complex work problems or make good decisions if they have plenty of job-relevant knowledge or experience. But leaders with more analytic intelligence, all things being equal, may develop their street smarts more quickly than leaders with less analytic intelligence. Analytic intelligence may play a lesser role once a domain of knowledge is mastered, but a more important role in encountering new situations.

The best way to have a good idea is to have a lot of ideas.
Dr. Linus Pauling, scientist

The third component of the triarchic theory of intelligence is **creative intelligence,** which is the ability to produce work that is both novel and useful.[50,51,57,68-73] Using *both* criteria (novel and useful) as components of creative intelligence helps to eliminate outlandish solutions to a potential problem by ensuring that adopted solutions can be realistically implemented or have some type of practical payoff. Several examples might help to clarify the novel and practical components of creative intelligence. The inventor of Velcro got his idea while picking countless thistles out of his socks; he realized that the same principle that produced his frustration might be translated into a useful fastener. The inventor of 3M's Post-it notes was frustrated because bookmarks in his church hymnal were continually sliding out of place, and he saw a solution in a low-tack adhesive discovered by a fellow 3M scientist. The scientists who designed the *Spirit* and *Opportunity* missions to Mars were given a budget that was considerably smaller than those of previous missions to Mars. Yet the scientists were challenged to develop two spacecraft that had more capabilities than the *Pathfinder* and the *Viking Lander.* Their efforts with *Spirit* and *Opportunity* were a resounding success, due in part to some of the novel solutions used both to land the spacecrafts (an inflatable balloon system) and to explore the surrounding area (both were mobile rovers).

Two interesting questions surrounding creativity concern the role of intelligence and the assessment of creative ability. Research shows that analytic intelligence correlates at about the .5 level with creative intelligence.[72] Thus the best research available indicates that analytic intelligence and creativity are related, but the relationship is imperfect. Some level of analytic intelligence seems necessary for creativity, but having a high level of analytic intelligence is no guarantee that a leader will be creative. And like practical intelligence, creativity seems to be specific to certain fields and subfields: Bill Gates cannot write music and Madonna cannot do math.[51,55,70,72-76]

Assessing creativity is no simple matter. Tests of creativity, or **divergent thinking,** differ from tests that assess **convergent thinking.** Tests of convergent thinking usually have a single best answer; good examples here are most intelligence and aptitude tests. Conversely, tests of creativity or divergent thinking have many possible answers.[77] Although Sternberg and his associates showed that it is possible to reliably judge the relative creativity of different responses, judging creativity is more difficult than scoring convergent tests.[70,72,78] For example, there are no set answers or standards for determining whether a movie, a marketing ad, or a new manufacturing process is truly creative. Another difficulty in assessing creativity is that it may wax and wane over time; many of the most creative people seem to have occasional dry spells or writer's block. This is different from analytic intelligence, where performance on mental abilities tests remains fairly constant over time.

The fastest way to succeed is to double the failure rate.
Thomas Watson Sr., IBM

Implications of the Triarchic Theory of Intelligence

Some 200 separate studies have examined the relationship between intelligence test scores and leadership effectiveness or emergence, and these

The Competent Hot Potato

HIGHLIGHT 6.6

What should leaders do when a follower is smart, competent, and creative (that is, has a high level of practical, analytic, and creative intelligence) but has difficulties getting along with other team members? Clearly creative followers with high levels of analytic intelligence and domain knowledge can help their teams make better decisions, but the cost of this knowledge is often strained relationships or high levels of turnover among teammates. Research shows that when given a choice, team members would prefer to work with a lovable but incompetent fool than an irritable but competent jerk. On one hand, team performance is likely to suffer if everyone on the team is happy but incompetent. On the other hand, performance is also likely to suffer when a toxic follower is part of a team. It appears that many managers resolve this dilemma by having competent jerks on their teams during the initial phases of projects—when ideas about project direction, possibilities, and solutions are being determined. Once these decisions are made, many managers then arrange to have the competent jerks leave their teams. The good news is that the team gets to capitalize on the competent jerks' expertise during the decision-making phase of the project but doesn't have to suffer their dysfunctional behavior during the execution phase. The

bad news is that a common way to get rid of competent jerks is to promote them. Many managers would rather see a toxic follower become a toxic leader rather than confront difficult performance issues. Subsequent bosses often repeat the "hot potato" process, helping toxic leaders move into roles with ever-increasing responsibilities.

Many times teammates share some of the blame with bosses for these questionable promotions. When teammates complain to their managers about competent jerks and the managers discuss these issues with the problematic individuals, competent jerks usually deny the allegations. And when competent jerks confront their teammates about these allegations, teammates are unwilling to share their complaints. With team members failing to provide feedback, leaders often are accused of harboring ill will toward the competent jerks. Oftentimes the only face-saving way out of this situation is to give a competent jerk a transfer to or promotion in another department.

Sources: J. Sandberg, "Sometimes Colleagues Are Just Too Bad to Not Get Promoted," *The Wall Street Journal,* August 17, 2005, p. A5; J. Casciaro and M. S. Lobo, "Competent Jerks, Lovable Fools, and the Formation of Social Networks," *Harvard Business Review,* June 2006, pp. 92–100.

You'll get hired for your intelligence, but fired for your personality.
Dianne Nilsen,
Account Executive

studies have been the topic of major reviews.[1,2,7,46-60,65,70] These reviews provide overwhelming support for the idea that leadership effectiveness or emergence is positively correlated with analytic intelligence. Nonetheless, the correlation between analytic intelligence and leadership success is not as strong as previously assumed. It now appears that personality is more predictive of leadership emergence and effectiveness than analytic intelligence.[5,26,27,28,32] Leadership situations that are relatively routine or unchanging, or that require specific in-depth product or process knowledge, may place more importance on personality and practical intelligence than analytic intelligence. Having a high level of analytic intelligence seems more important for solving ambiguous, complex problems, such as those encountered by executives at the top levels of an organization. Here leaders must be able to detect themes and patterns in seemingly unrelated information, make accurate assumptions about market conditions, or make wise

FIGURE 6.5
Average Intelligence Test Scores by Management Level

Source: N. Kuncel, "Personality and Cognitive Differences among Management Levels," unpublished manuscript (Minneapolis: Personnel Decisions International, 1996).

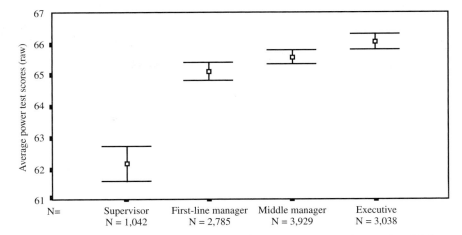

merger, acquisition, or divestiture decisions. Further evidence that higher levels of analytic intelligence are associated with top leaders can be found in Figure 6.5.

Although a high level of analytic intelligence is usually an asset to a leader, research also suggests that in some situations analytic intelligence may have a *curvilinear* relationship with leadership effectiveness.[1,79] When differences in analytic intelligence between leader and followers are too great, communication can be impaired; a leader's intelligence can become an impediment to being understood by subordinates. An alternative explanation for the curvilinear relationship between analytic intelligence and leadership effectiveness may have to do with how stress affects leader–subordinate interactions. Fiedler and his associates found that smart but inexperienced leaders were less effective in stressful situations than less intelligent, experienced leaders.[80-82] An example of this finding was clearly demonstrated in the movie *Platoon.* In one frantic scene an American platoon is ambushed by the Viet Cong. An inexperienced, college-educated lieutenant calls for artillery support from friendly units. He calls in the wrong coordinates, however, and as a result artillery shells are dropped on his own platoon's position rather than the enemy's position. The situation comes under control only after an experienced sergeant sizes up the situation and tells the artillery units to cease firing. This example points out the importance of *practical in-telligence* in stressful situations. Leaders revert to well-practiced behaviors under periods of high stress and change, and leaders with high levels of practical intelligence have a relatively broad set of coping and problem-solving behaviors to draw upon in these situations. Because of the levels of stress and change associated with many leadership positions today, systematically improving practical leadership skills through education and experience is important for leaders and leaders-to-be.

With respect to creative intelligence, perhaps the most important point leaders should remember is that their primary role is not so much to be

Silicon Valley doesn't have better ideas and isn't smarter than the rest of the world, but it has the edge in filtering ideas and executing them.

**Sergey Brin,
Google**

creative themselves as to *build an environment where others can be creative.* This is not to say that leaders should be uncreative, but rather that most innovations have roots in ideas developed by people closest to a problem or opportunity (that is, the workers). Leaders can boost the creativity throughout their groups or organizations in many ways, but particularly through selecting creative employees and providing opportunities for others to develop their creativity, and through broader interventions like making sure the motivation and incentives for others are conducive to creativity and providing at least some guidance or vision about what the creative product or output should look like.[84-95]

Leaders can do several things to improve the group and organizational factors affecting creativity. Leaders should be mindful of the effect various sorts of incentives or rewards can have on creativity; certain types of motivation to work are more conducive to creativity than others. Research has shown that people tend to generate more creative solutions when they are told to focus on their intrinsic motivation for doing so (the pleasure of solving the task itself) rather than focusing on extrinsic motivation (public recognition or pay).[83,96] When they need to foster creativity, leaders may find it more effective to select followers who truly enjoy working on the task at hand rather than relying on rewards to foster creativity.

Creativity can be hindered if people believe their ideas will be evaluated. Experiments by Amabile and Zhou showed that students who were told their projects were to be judged by experts produced less creative projects than students who were not told their projects would be judged.[97-98] A similar phenomenon can occur in groups. When a group knows its work must ultimately be evaluated, there is a pronounced tendency for members to be evaluative and judgmental too early in the solution-generating process. This tends to reduce the number of creative solutions generated, perhaps because of a generally shared belief in the value of critical thinking (and in some groups the norm seems to be the more criticism, the better) and of subjecting ideas to intense scrutiny and evaluation. When members of a group judge ideas as soon as they are offered, two dysfunctional things can happen. People in the group may censor themselves (not share all their ideas with the group) because even mild rejection or criticism has a significant dampening effect, or they may prematurely reject others' ideas through focus on an idea's flaws rather than its possibilities.[99] Given these findings, leaders may want to hold off on evaluating new ideas until they are all on the table, and should encourage their followers to do the same.

Finally, leaders who need to develop new products and services should try to minimize turnover in their teams and give them clear goals. Teams with unclear goals may successfully develop new or novel products, but these products may have low marketability or usefulness. An example illustrates this point. In the 1980s Texas Instruments (TI) decided to delve into the personal computer business. TI had a reputation for technical

TABLE 6.3
**Creativity Killers:
How to Squelch the
Creativity of Direct
Reports**

Sources: T. M. Amabile and
M. Khaire, "Creativity and
the Role of the Leader," *Harvard Business Review*, October
2008, pp. 100–10; T. M. Amabile and J. Zhou, in S. F. Dingfelder, "Creativity on the
Clock," *Monitor on Psychology*,
November 2003, pp. 56–58.

The following is a list of things leaders can do if they wish to stifle the creativity of their followers:

Take away all discretion and autonomy: People like to have some sense of control over their work. Micromanaging staff will help to either create yea-sayers or cause people to mentally disengage from work.

Create fragmented work schedules: People need large chunks of uninterrupted time to work on novel solutions. Repeated interruptions or scheduling "novel solution generation time" in 15-minute increments around other meetings will disrupt people's ability to be innovative.

Provide insufficient resources: People need proper data, equipment, and money to be creative. Cut these off, and watch creativity go down the tubes.

Focus on short-term goals: Asking a person to be creative at right this moment is like asking a comedian to be funny the first time you meet him. People can be creative and funny if given enough time, but focusing on only short-term outcomes will dampen creativity.

Create tight timelines and rigid processes: The tighter the deadlines and less flexible the processes, the more chance that innovation will be reduced.

Discourage collaboration and coordination: The best ideas often come from teams having members with different work experiences and functional backgrounds. By discouraging cross-functional collaboration, leaders can help guarantee that team members will offer up only tried and true solutions to problems.

Keep people happy: If you keep workers happy enough, they will have little motivation to change the status quo.

*Most artists have to
hack through a tangled
thicket of negativity,
logic, and procrastination on the way to creating anything. Peter
seems to be supernaturally free of any such
concerns. This is a guy
with a big wide conduit
running from the creative, imaginative part
of his brain, straight to
the place where most of
us keep our willpower.
That could be a recipe
for a monstrously selfish
ego. Again, Jackson's
ability to chase goals
doesn't come with that
type of baggage. He's
driven, and he's incredibly demanding, but he's
always focused on results, never on himself.*

**Costa Botes,
screenwriter**

excellence, and one of the best managers in the company was asked to head up the project. The manager did not have a clear sense of what customers wanted or what a personal computer should be able to do. This lack of clarity had some dramatic effects. As more and more engineers were added to the project, more innovative hardware ideas were added to the computer design. These additions caused the project to take much longer and cost a lot more than planned, but the TI personal computer ended up winning a number of major engineering awards. Unfortunately it was also a business disaster because the product failed to meet customer needs. Although Compaq computers arose from the ashes of TI's failure, the TI project serves as a good example of a concept called **creeping elegance.** Leaders without a clear vision of what a final project should look like may end up with something that fails to meet customer needs. Leaders need to provide enough room for creativity to flourish, but enough direction for effort to be focused.[87,90,91]

One industry that places a premium on creativity is the motion picture industry. Because creativity is so important to the commercial success of a

Innovation in Emerging Economies

HIGHLIGHT 6.7

For the past 100-plus years the West has been the center of innovation and creativity. Many modern conveniences we have become accustomed to were invented in the United States or Europe. But will the West remain the center of innovation? This is an important question: studies show that future job and economic growth will come from information- or knowledge-based work rather than manufacturing-based work. North America may lead the world in research spending, but globalization and information technology are helping other parts of the world to catch up. The emerging economies of Brazil, Russia, India, and China (BRIC) are graduating millions of scientists and engineers each year, and their

economies are becoming robust enough to generate strong domestic bases for new products.

Clever ideas can be found anywhere, and technology is helping to make these ideas into products. The expanding middle class of the BRIC countries is giving more people the income needed to purchase new products. With the number of scientists and engineers graduating from the BRIC countries and their rapidly expanding economies, it may only be a matter of time before the West is no longer the center of innovation. What do you think are the implications of these trends for leaders in the West or the BRIC countries?

Source: "Something New under the Sun," *The Economist*, October 13, 2007, pp. 3–4.

movie, it is relatively easy for a movie to succumb to creeping elegance. But how do movie directors successfully avoid creeping elegance when dealing with highly creative people having huge egos? Part of the answer may lie in the approach of two of Hollywood's most successful directors. Steven Spielberg and Ron Howard have said that before they shoot a scene they first have a clear picture of it in their own minds. If they don't have a clear picture, they sit down with the relevant parties and work it out. This shows the importance of having a clear vision when managing creativity.

Intelligence and Stress: Cognitive Resources Theory

In the preceding section we noted that intelligence may be a more important quality for leaders in some situations than others. You may be surprised to learn, however, that recent research actually suggests there are times when intelligence may be a disadvantage. A key variable affecting this paradoxical finding seems to be whether the leader is in a stressful situation. Recent research suggests that stress plays a key role in determining how a leader's intelligence affects his or her effectiveness. While it is not surprising that stress affects behavior in various ways, Fiedler and Garcia developed the **cognitive resources theory (CRT)** to explain the interesting relationships between leader intelligence and experience levels, and group performance in stressful versus nonstressful conditions.[100,101]

CRT consists of several key concepts, one of which is intelligence. Fiedler and Garcia defined intelligence as we have earlier—it is one's all-around effectiveness in activities directed by thought and is typically measured using standardized intelligence tests (in other words , analytic intelligence). Another key concept is experience, which represents the habitual behavior patterns, overlearned knowledge, and skills acquired for effectively dealing with task-related problems (that is, practical intelligence). Although experience is often gained under stressful and unpleasant conditions, experience also provides a "crash plan" to revert back to when under stress.[80-82,100,101] As Fiedler observed, people often act differently when stressed, and the crash plan describes this change in behavior patterns. For most CRT studies, experience has been defined as time in the job or organization. A third key concept in CRT is stress. Stress is often defined as the result of conflicts with superiors or the apprehension associated with performance evaluation.[82,101] This interpersonal stress is believed to be emotionally disturbing and can divert attention from problem-solving activities. In other words, people can get so concerned about how their performance is being evaluated that they may fail to perform at an optimal level. In sum, cognitive resources theory provides a conceptual scheme for explaining how leader behavior changes under stress to impact group performance.

Cognitive resources theory makes two major predictions with respect to intelligence, experience, stress, and group performance. First, because experienced leaders have a greater repertoire of behaviors to fall back on, leaders with greater experience but lower intelligence are hypothesized to have higher-performing groups under conditions of high stress. Experienced leaders have "been there before" and know better what to do and how to get it done when faced with high-stress situations. Leaders' experience levels can interfere with performance under low-stress conditions, however.

That leads to a second hypothesis. Because experience leads to habitual behavior patterns, leaders with high levels of experience tend to misapply old solutions to problems when creative solutions are called for. Experienced leaders rely too much on the tried and true when facing new problems, even under relatively low stress. Thus leaders with higher levels of intelligence but less experience are not constrained by previously acquired behavior patterns and should have higher-performing groups under low-stress conditions. In other words, experience is helpful when one is under stress but can hinder performance in the absence of stress.

These two major predictions of CRT can be readily seen in everyday life. For the most part, it is not the most intelligent but the most experienced members of sporting teams, marching bands, acting troupes, or volunteer organizations who are selected to be leaders. These leaders are often chosen because other members recognize their ability to perform well under the high levels of stress associated with sporting events and public performances. In addition, research with combat troops, firefighters, senior executives, and students has provided strong support for the two major tenets of CRT. [80-82,100,101]

Despite this initial empirical support, one problem with CRT concerns the apparent dichotomy between intelligence and experience. Fiedler and Garcia's initial investigations of CRT did not examine the possibility that leaders could be *both* intelligent and experienced. Subsequent research by Gibson showed not only that many leaders were both intelligent and experienced, but also that these leaders would fall back on their experience in stressful situations and use their intelligence to solve group problems in less stressful situations.[82]

Another issue with CRT concerns the leader's ability to tolerate stress. As Schonpflug and Zaccaro correctly pointed out, some leaders are better able than others to tolerate high levels of stress.[102,103] Some leaders have personalities characterized by low neuroticism scores, and they may do well in high-stress situations even when they lack experience because of their inherent ability to handle stress. Further research on this issue seems warranted.

In general, solid evidence appears to support the major tenets of CRT. Because of this research, CRT has several important implications for leaders. First, the best leaders may be smart *and* experienced. Although intelligence tests are good indicators of raw mental horsepower, it is just as important for leaders to broaden their leadership knowledge and experience if they want to succeed in high-stress situations. This latter point may be important today, when the additional stress of organizational downsizing may cause the performance of leaders to be scrutinized even more closely than in the past. In fact, this additional scrutiny may cause leaders who were previously successful to perform poorly.

Second, leaders may not be aware of the degree to which they are causing stress in their followers. If followers perceive that their performance is being closely watched, they are likely to revert to their crash plans in order to perform. If a situation calls for new and novel solutions to problems, however, such leader behavior may be counterproductive. A key point here is that leaders may be unaware of their impact on followers. For example, they may want to review their followers' work more closely in order to be helpful, but followers may not perceive it this way.

If you break it, you buy it.

Colin Powell, former U.S. secretary of state

Third, the level of stress inherent in the position needs to be understood before selecting leaders. Those filling high-stress leadership positions can either look for experienced leaders or reduce the stress in the situation so that more intelligent leaders can succeed. Another alternative could be to hire more intelligent leaders and put them through stress management training so the effects of stress are minimized.[81,82] It is also possible that experienced leaders may get bored if placed into low-stress positions.[7]

Emotional Intelligence and Leadership

What Is Emotional Intelligence?

So far we have discussed the role personality traits and types play in a leader's day-to-day behavioral patterns. We have also described

Intelligence and Judgment

HIGHLIGHT 6.8

Robert Hogan argues that the term "intelligent" applies mostly to decisions. Decisions that successfully solve problems or improve organizational performance are deemed "intelligent"; those that do not are usually described as "dumb." Decision making is critically important in business, politics, and warfare where money and people's lives are on the line. According to Hogan, an organization's success can be measured by the collective decisions it makes. Generally speaking, armies that win or companies that outperform their rivals make many more intelligent decisions than those that fail.

Good judgment occurs when leaders choose the right means to solve a problem and change course when information indicates to do so. Bad judgment occurs when people impose the wrong solution onto a problem and then stick with their solutions even when it is obviously not working. Many organizational failures boil down to top leaders picking the wrong solutions to solve problems or not adopting different solutions when presented with information showing that the initial approach is clearly failing. For example, the failure of General Motors had much to do with adopting and then sticking with a strategy of selling large trucks and SUVs in the face of climate change legislation, high gasoline prices, and an economic recession.

Given this definition of good versus bad judgment, how would you judge the Iraq war? After 9/11/2001 it was clear that the United States was at war, and its enemy was Al-Qaeda. The data linking Al-Qaeda to Iraq was sketchy, and the preponderance of evidence showed that Iraq did not have any weapons of mass destruction. There is no doubt that Saddam Hussein was an abusive dictator, but at the time many other abusive dictators posed bigger threats to the United States and world security than Saddam Hussein (consider Kim Jong-Il in North Korea). Al-Qaeda was well established in Afghanistan, but the United States instead opted to focus on Iraq. The war in Iraq has cost the United States 4,000 lives, 20,000 wounded soldiers, and a trillion dollars. Has this war reduced or eliminated the threat posed by Al-Qaeda? Was the decision to go to war with Iraq an exercise in good or poor judgment? How about the war in Afghanistan? What information would you need to answer these questions?

Source: R. T. Hogan, *Intelligence and Good Judgment*, unpublished manuscript (Tulsa, OK: Hogan Assessment Systems, 2009); P. Ingrassa, "How Detroit Drove into a Ditch," *The Wall Street Journal*, October 25–26, 2008, pp. W1–2.

the role analytic, practical, and creative intelligence play in solving problems and making decisions. And we have discussed how stress can affect a leader's ability to solve problems. An overwhelming body of evidence shows that these enduring patterns of behaviors and mental abilities have a big impact on leadership effectiveness, but we have not discussed the role emotions play in leadership success. To put it differently, do moods affect a person's ability to build teams and get results through others? Moods and emotions are constantly at play at work, yet most people are hesitant to discuss moods with anybody other than close friends. It also appears that moods can be contagious, in that the moods of leaders often affect followers in both positive and negative ways. And charismatic or transformational leaders use emotions as the catalyst for achieving better-than-expected results (see Chapter 14). Given the importance and prevalence of emotions in the workplace, there should be a wealth of research regarding mood and leadership effectiveness; but this is not the case. Researchers have begun to seriously examine the role of emotions in leadership only over the past 20 years.

The relationships between leaders' emotions and their effects on teams and outcomes became popularized by researcher Dan Goleman with the publication of the book *Emotional Intelligence.*[104] But what is emotional intelligence (EQ), and how is it the same as or different from personality traits or types or the three types of intelligence described in this chapter? Unfortunately there appear to be at least four major definitions of **emotional intelligence.** The term *emotional intelligence* can be attributed to two psychologists, Peter Salovey and John Mayer, who studied why some bright people fail to be successful. Salovey and Mayer discovered that many of them ran into trouble because of their lack of interpersonal sensitivity and skills, and defined emotional intelligence as a group of mental abilities that help people to recognize their own feelings and those of others.[105,106] Reuven Bar-On believed that emotional intelligence was another way of measuring human effectiveness and defined it as a set of 15 abilities necessary to cope with daily situations and get along in the world.[107] Rick Aberman defined emotional intelligence as the degree to which thoughts, feelings, and actions were aligned. According to Aberman, leaders are more effective and "in the zone" when their thoughts, feelings, and actions are perfectly aligned.[108,109] Daniel Goleman, a science writer for *The New York Times,* substantially broadened these definitions and summarized some of this work in his books *Emotional Intelligence* and *Working with Emotional Intelligence.*[104,110] Goleman argued that success in life is based more on one's self-motivation, persistence in the face of frustration, mood management, ability to adapt, and ability to empathize and get along with others than on one's analytic intelligence or IQ. Table 6.4 compares the Salovey and Mayer, Bar-On, and Goleman models of emotional intelligence.

Although these definitions can cause confusion for people interested in learning more about emotional intelligence, it appears that these four definitions of EQ can be broken down into two models: an ability model and a mixed model of emotional intelligence.[106,111] The ability model focuses on how emotions affect how leaders think, decide, plan, and act. This model defines emotional intelligence as four separate but related abilities, which include (1) the ability to accurately perceive one's own and others' emotions; (2) the ability to generate emotions to facilitate thought and action; (3) the ability to accurately understand the causes of emotions and the meanings they convey; and (4) the ability to regulate one's emotions. According to Caruso, Mayer, and Salovey, some

There is no single entity called EQ (emotional intelligence quotient) as people have defined it. One sympathetic interpretation of what journalists were saying is that there were a dozen unrelated things, which collectively might predict more than intelligence, things like warmth, optimism, and empathy. But there was nothing new about that. Instead, the story became this fabulous new variable that is going to outpredict intelligence. There is no rational basis for saying that.

John Mayer, EQ researcher

TABLE 6.4   **Ability and Mixed Models of Emotional Intelligence**

Sources: R. Bar-On, *Emotional Quotient Inventory* (North Tonawanda, NY: Multi-Health Systems, Inc., 2001); D. Goleman, *Working with Emotional Intelligence* (New York: Bantam Doubleday Dell, 1998); D. R. Caruso, J. D. Mayer, and P. Salovey, "Emotional Intelligence and Emotional Leadership," *in Multiple Intelligences and Leadership*, ed. R. E. Riggio, S. E. Murphy, and F. J. Pirozzolo (Mahwah, NJ: Lawrence Erlbaum Associates, 2002), pp. 55–74; online source: http://www.eiconsortium.org.

Ability Model	Mixed Models	
Mayer, Salovey, and Caruso	**Goleman et al.**	**Bar-On**
Perceiving emotions	Self-awareness	Intrapersonal
	Emotional awareness	Self-regard
	Accurate self-assessment	Emotional self-awareness
	Self-confidence	Assertiveness
		Independence
		Self-actualization
Managing emotions	Self-regulation	Adaptability
	Self-control	Reality testing
	Trustworthiness	Flexibility
	Conscientiousness	Problem solving
	Adaptability	
	Innovation	
Using emotions	Motivation	Stress management
	Achievement	Stress tolerance
	Commitment	Impulse control
	Initiative	
	Optimism	
Understanding emotions	Empathy	Interpersonal
	Understanding others	Empathy
	Developing others	Social responsibility
	Service orientation	Interpersonal relationship
	Diversity	
	Political awareness	General mood
		Optimism
	Social skills	Happiness
	Influence	
	Communication	
	Conflict management	
	Leadership	
	Change catalyst	
	Building bonds	
	Collaboration/cooperation	
	Team capabilities	

leaders might be good at perceiving emotions and leveraging them to get results through others, but have difficulties regulating their own emotions. Or they could be good at understanding the causes of emotions but not as good at perceiving others' emotions. The ability model

Scott Rudin

PROFILES IN LEADERSHIP 6.4

Few people know who Scott Rudin is, but many have seen his work. Rudin has been a Hollywood movie producer for over 20 years and has produced such movies as *The Addams Family, Sister Act, The Truman Show, A Civil Action, The Firm, Team America: World Police, Zoolander, The School of Rock, The Queen, Notes on a Scandal,* and many others. Rudin also has the reputation of being the most difficult boss to work for in Hollywood; it is estimated that he has fired over 250 assistants over the past five years. His caustic rants, shrieking threats, impulsive firings, and revolving door of assistants are legendary. For example, he allegedly once fired an assistant for bringing in the wrong breakfast muffin. Rudin describes his own leadership style as a cross between Attila the Hun and Miss Jean Brodie, and it is rumored that the role of Miranda Priestly in *The Devil Wears Prada* was loosely modeled after Rudin.

An extreme micromanager, Rudin is involved with every detail of the films he is producing. Because he is producing several films at any one time, it is not unusual for Rudin to make over 400 calls in a single day. Rudin's assistants start their days at 6:00 a.m. with a 30-page annotated list of phone calls that are to be set up that day. During the day assistants will also do anything from picking up dry cleaning to answering phones, scheduling appointments, arranging travel, buying birthday presents, dropping off kids, and so on—you name it, the assistant does it. So why do assistants put up with Rudin? The hours are long but the pay is good—most interns make $70,000–$150,000 per year. More importantly, aides who survive get a chance to rub shoulders with A-list talent and learn the ins and outs of the movie business. Plus the opportunities for advancement for those who survive are good—many of Rudin's aides have themselves become movie producers.

Given this background, what personality traits help Rudin to produce successful movies? How would Rudin stack up on the three types of intelligence? How would you rate Rudin's emotional intelligence?

Source: K. Kelly and M. Marr, "Boss-Zilla!" *The Wall Street Journal,* September 24–25, 2005, p. A1.

is not intended to be an all-encompassing model of leadership, but rather supplements the OCEAN and triarchic models of intelligence.[106,111] Just as leaders differ in neuroticism or practical intelligence, so do they differ in their ability to perceive and regulate emotions. The ability model of EQ is helpful because it allows researchers to determine if EQ is in fact a separate ability and whether it can predict leadership effectiveness apart from the OCEAN personality model and cognitive abilities.

The Goleman and Bar-On definitions of EQ fall into the mixed model category. These researchers believe emotional intelligence includes not only the abilities outlined in the previous paragraph but also a number of other attributes. As such, the mixed model provides a much broader, more comprehensive definition of emotional intelligence. A quick review of Table 6.4 shows that the attributes of emotional intelligence are qualities that most leaders should have, and Goleman, Boyatzis, and McKee maintain that leaders need more or less all of these attributes to be emotionally intelligent.[110,112,113] Moreover, the mixed model of emotional intelligence has been much more popular with human resource professionals and in the corporate world than the ability model. But does the mixed model really tell us anything different from what we already know? More specifically, is the mixed model different from the OCEAN personality model? Research shows that the mixed model assesses the same characteristics as the OCEAN model and is no more predictive of job performance and other important job outcomes than OCEAN personality assessments.[106,111,114-116] Goleman and Bar-On deserve credit for popularizing the notion that noncognitive abilities are important predictors of leadership success. But on the negative side, they also maintain that they have discovered something completely new and do not give enough credit to the 100 years of personality research that underlie many attributes in the mixed model.

Can Emotional Intelligence Be Measured and Developed?

The publication of *Emotional Intelligence* has encouraged an industry of books, training programs, and assessments related to measurement and development of emotional intelligence. Mayer, Salovey, and Caruso's Emotional Intelligence Test (MSCEIT) is a measure of the ability model of emotional intelligence; it asks subjects to recognize the emotions depicted in pictures, what moods might be helpful in certain social situations, and so forth.[106,117] Bar-On has self, self–other, youth, and organizational measures of emotional intelligence, such as the Bar-On Emotional Quotient—360 or EQi-S.[118]

The Emotional Competence Inventory (ECi) was developed by Goleman and consists of 10 questionnaires. These questionnaires are completed by the individual and nine others; the responses are aggregated and given to the participant in a feedback report. Because these researchers have defined emotional intelligence differently and use a different process to assess EQ, it is not surprising that these instruments often provide leaders with conflicting results.[119] Nevertheless, the U.S. Air Force Recruiting Service has used the EQ-i to screen potential recruiters and found that candidates scoring higher on the attributes of assertiveness, empathy, happiness, self-awareness, and problem solving were much less likely to turn over prematurely in the position and had a 90 percent chance of meeting their recruiting quotas.[119]

One issue that most EQ researchers agree on is that emotional intelligence can be developed. Goleman and Aberman have developed one- to five-day training programs to help leaders improve their emotional intelligence; Bar-On has developed 15 e-learning modules that are available at EQ University.com. One big adopter of EQ training has been the sales staff at American Express Financial Advisors (AEFA).

Leaders at AEFA discovered that the company had a well-respected set of investment and insurance products for customers, but many sales staff were struggling with how to respond to the emotions exhibited by clients during sales calls. Moreover, the best salespeople seem to be better able to "read" their clients' emotions and respond in a more empathetic manner. Since 1993 more than 5,500 sales staff and 850 sales managers at AEFA have attended a five-day training program to better recognize and respond to the emotions exhibited by clients. AEFA found that sales staff attending this program increased annual sales by an average of 18.1 percent, whereas those who did not attend training achieved only a 16.1 percent increase. However, this sample was small, and the comparison is somewhat unfair because the control group did not receive any kind of sales training in lieu of the EQ training.[119] Therefore, it is uncertain whether the EQ training content actually adds value over and above five days of sales training.

Implications of Emotional Intelligence

Aberman maintained that people can be extremely ineffective when their thoughts, feelings, and actions are misaligned—for example, arguing with someone on your cellular phone when driving on a highway.[108,109] It seems likely that leaders who are thinking or feeling one thing and actually doing something else are probably less effective in their ability to influence groups toward the accomplishment of their goals. The EQ literature should also be credited with popularizing the idea that noncognitive abilities, such as stress tolerance, assertiveness, and empathy, can play important roles in leadership success. Today many organizations are using *both* cognitive and noncognitive measures as part of the process of hiring or promoting leaders. Finally, the EQ literature has also helped to bring emotion back to the workplace. Human emotions are important aspects of one-on-one interactions and teamwork,[106,110,113,120-123] but too many leadership practitioners and researchers have chosen to ignore the role they play. When recognized and leveraged properly, emotions can be the motivational fuel that helps individuals and groups to accomplish their goals. When ignored or discounted, emotions can significantly impede a leader's ability to build teams or influence a group. As discussed in the personality section of this chapter, leaders who can empathize and get along with others are often more successful than those who cannot.

Some of the more recent research in emotional intelligence indicates that it moderates employees' reactions to job insecurity and their ability to cope with stress when threatened with job loss. Employees with lower EQ reported more negative emotional reactions and used less effective coping strategies when dealing with downsizing than those with higher

EQ.[124] Along these lines, other researchers report relationships between leaders' moods and followers' moods, job performance, job satisfaction, and creativity.[125] And Boyatzis, Stubbs, and Taylor accurately point out that most MBA programs focus more on cognitive abilities and developing financial skills than on those abilities needed to successfully build teams and get results through others.[126]

Given these results, is it possible to develop emotional intelligence? The answer to this question is yes, but the path taken to develop EQ would depend on whether the training program was based on an ability or mixed model of emotional intelligence. An ability-based EQ training program would focus on improving participants' ability to accurately perceive one's own and others' emotions, generate emotions to facilitate thought and action, accurately understand the causes of emotions and the meanings they convey, and regulate one's emotions. These programs make extensive use of videotapes, role plays, and other experiential exercises in order to help people better recognize, exhibit, and regulate emotion. Because the mixed model of EQ encompasses such a wide array of attributes, virtually any leadership development program could be considered an EQ training program.

Despite the positive contributions of emotional intelligence, the concept has several limitations. First, Goleman and his associates and Bar-On have not acknowledged the existence of personality, much less 100 years of personality–leadership effectiveness research. As shown in Table 6.5, Goleman's conceptualization of EQ looks similar to the OCEAN model found in Table 6.1. At least as conceptualized by these two authors, it is difficult to see how EQ is any different from personality. Second, if the EQ attributes are essentially personality traits, it is difficult to see how they will change as a result of a training intervention. Personality traits are difficult to change, and the likelihood of changing 20 to 40 years of day-to-day behavioral patterns as the result of some e-learning modules or a five-day training program seems highly suspect. As described in Chapter 1, people can change their behavior, but it takes considerable effort and coaching over the long term to make it happen. Finally, an important question to ask is whether EQ is really something new or simply a repackaging of old ideas and findings. If EQ is defined as an ability model, such as the one put forth by Mayer, Salovey, and Caruso, then emotional intelligence probably is a unique ability and worthy of additional research (see Figure 6.6). A leader's skills in accurately perceiving, regulating, and leveraging emotions seem vitally important in building cohesive, goal-oriented teams, and measures like the MSCEIT could be used in conjunction with OCEAN and cognitive abilities measures to hire and develop better leaders. But if EQ is defined as a mixed model, then it is hard to see that Goleman and his associates and Bar-On are really telling us anything new.

Ask yourself, what exactly is high potential? Then ask yourself, what is that potential for?
Rob Silzer, Baruch College, and Allen Church, Pepsico

TABLE 6.5
Comparison between the OCEAN Model and Goleman's Model of EQ

Goleman et al.	Likely OCEAN Correlates
Self-awareness	
Emotional awareness	Agreeableness
Accurate self-assessment	Neuroticism
Self-confidence	Extraversion
Self-regulation	
Self-control	Neuroticism, conscientiousness
Trustworthiness	Conscientiousness
Conscientiousness	Conscientiousness
Adaptability	Neuroticism, conscientiousness
Innovation	Openness to experience, conscientiousness
Motivation	
Achievement	Extraversion
Commitment	Extraversion
Initiative	Extraversion
Optimism	Neuroticism
Empathy	
Understanding others	Agreeableness
Developing others	Openness to experience
Service orientation	Agreeableness
Diversity	Agreeableness
Political awareness	Agreeableness
Social skills	
Influence	Extraversion, agreeableness
Communication	Extraversion
Conflict management	Agreeableness
Leadership	Extraversion
Change catalyst	Extraversion
Building bonds	Agreeableness
Collaboration/cooperation	Agreeableness
Team capabilities	Extraversion, agreeableness

FIGURE 6.6
Emotional Intelligence and the Building Blocks of Skills

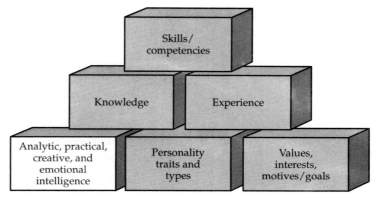

Assessing Leadership Potential

HIGHLIGHT 6.9

As the world of work shifts from manufacturing to information- or knowledge-based work, organizations are beginning to view talent as a strategic resource. Many manufacturing jobs in North America and Europe have shifted to Eastern Europe or Asia, and these jobs have been supplanted by those of software engineers, product designers, marketers, and salespeople at companies like Google, Apple, Microsoft, Intel, IBM, Oracle, and Facebook. Even traditional manufacturers, retailers, and consumer products companies such as GE, Dell, Best Buy, Target, Proctor & Gamble, and Pepsico are putting more emphasis on roles that design new products, brands, and marketing campaigns; manage supply chains; improve information transfer; or improve financial or operational results. And because of the growth potential of emerging markets and the shift in manufacturing, most large companies have sales, opérations, and suppliers located around the globe. Because it traditionally takes 20–30 years to develop an executive with marketing, sales, operations, finance, and international experience, one of the questions many organizations are asking is whether it is possible to shorten the executive development cycle. In other words, can organizations identify young leaders with the potential to be senior executives and then provide them with the experiences needed to make a successful transition to the C-suite? And can they significantly shorten the time to do this?

Because the companies with the best talent are likely to be the most successful, most *Fortune* 500 companies as well as the U.S. military have high-potential leadership programs. These programs identify people early in their professional careers and then put them into rotational programs that provide marketing, sales, human resource, finance, supply chain, and international experience. A key question for leaders-to-be is how to get identified as having high potential. Unfortunately there are as many answers to this question as there are companies with high-potential programs. High-potential talent identification programs range from FOBs (Friends of Bill, the CEO) to sophisticated talent assessments. The more sophisticated approaches typically use some combination of work values instruments, personality type and trait tests, mental abilities tests, EQ assessments, work simulations, and peer and boss feedback to identify candidates with "the right stuff." Many of the tools and techniques described in Chapters 5–7 make up these more sophisticated high-potential talent assessment batteries, so understanding these concepts should help leaders to gauge whether organizations take talent management seriously.

Source: R. Silzer and A. H. Church, "The Pearls and Perils of Identifying Potential," *Industrial and Organizational Psychology* 2 (2009), pp. 377–422.

Summary

This chapter has examined the relationships of personality, intelligence, and emotional intelligence with leadership emergence and effectiveness. In general, all these attributes can help a leader to influence a group toward the accomplishment of its goals, but by themselves they are no guarantee of leadership success. Often a situation will dictate which personality traits or types, components of intelligence, or emotional intelligence attributes will positively affect a leader's ability to build a team or get results through others.

Although the term *personality* has many different meanings, we use the term to describe one's typical or characteristic patterns of behavior. There are several different theories to describe why people act in characteristic ways, but the trait approach to personality has been the most thoroughly researched, and as such plays a key role in the chapter. The adoption of the OCEAN model of personality has helped to clarify the personality–leadership relationships, and researchers have noted that leadership success is positively correlated with the OCEAN personality dimensions of openness to experience, conscientiousness, extraversion, agreeableness, and neuroticism.

Personality types can also be used to categorize stereotypical behavioral patterns. The extraversion–introversion, sensing–intuition, thinking–feeling, and judging–perceiving personality dimensions can be combined to form 16 different types, and the majority of leaders can be found in 4 of these 16 types. Although the relationships between the 16 types and leadership effectiveness are not as strong as those with the OCEAN personality dimensions, the 16 personality types and associated dimensions give leaders valuable insights into human behavior.

A more recent theory for understanding intelligence divides it into three related components: analytic intelligence, practical intelligence, and creative intelligence. All three components are interrelated. Most research shows that leaders possess higher levels of analytic intelligence than the general population, and that more intelligent leaders often make better leaders. Analytic intelligence appears to confer two primary benefits upon leaders. First, leaders who are smarter seem to be better problem solvers. Second, and perhaps more important, smarter leaders seem to profit more from experience.

The roles of practical and creative intelligence in leadership are receiving increasing attention. Practical intelligence, or one's relevant job knowledge or experience, is proving to be extremely important for leaders. Leaders with higher levels of practical intelligence seem to be better at solving problems under stress. Moreover, practical intelligence seems to be the easiest of the three components to change. Creative intelligence involves developing new and useful products and processes, and creativity is extremely important to the success of many businesses today. It is important that leaders learn how to successfully stimulate and manage creativity, even more than being creative themselves.

In some ways emotional intelligence is a relatively new concept; it is generally concerned with accurately understanding and responding to one's own and others' emotions. Leaders who can better align their thoughts and feelings with their actions may be more effective than leaders who think and feel one way about something but then do something different about it. Although emotional intelligence has helped to point out the role emotions and noncognitive abilities play in leadership success, some of it seems to be nothing more than another label for personality. If this is the case, then emotional intelligence may be a leadership fad that will fade over time.

Key Terms

Great Man
theory, *188*
personality, *189*
trait approach, *190*
traits, *190*
weak situations, *191*
strong situations, *191*
Five Factor Model
(FFM) or OCEAN
model of
personality, *193*
openness to
experience, *193*
conscientiousness, *194*
extraversion, *194*
agreeableness, *195*
neuroticism, *195*

Level 5 Leadership, *197*
types, *201*
personality
typology, *201*
Myers-Briggs Type
Indicator (MBTI), *202*
extraversion–
introversion, *203*
sensing–intuition, *203*
thinking–feeling, *204*
judging–
perceiving, *204*
intelligence, *209*
triarchic theory of
intelligence, *210*
analytic
intelligence, *210*

practical
intelligence, *210*
single-loop
learning, *212*
double-loop
learning, *212*
creative
intelligence, *213*
divergent
thinking, *213*
convergent
thinking, *213*
creeping elegance, *217*
cognitive resources
theory (CRT), *218*
emotional
intelligence, *222*

Questions

1. What OCEAN personality traits or EQ components do you think would help professional sports players be more or less successful? Would successful coaches need the same or different personality traits and preferences? Would successful players and coaches need different traits for different sports?

2. How would you rank-order the importance of analytic intelligence, practical intelligence, creative intelligence, or emotional intelligence for politicians? Would this ranking be the same for college professors or store managers at a Walmart or 7-11 store?

3. Think of all the ineffective leaders you have ever worked or played for. What attributes did they have (or perhaps more importantly, lack) that caused them to be ineffective?

4. Individuals may well be attracted to, selected for, or successful in leadership roles early in their lives and careers based on their analytic intelligence. But what happens over time and with experience? Do you think *wisdom,* for example, is just another word for intelligence, or is it something else?

5. What role would downsizing play in an organization's overall level of practical intelligence?

6. We usually think of creativity as a characteristic of individuals, but might some organizations be more creative than others? What factors do you think might affect an organization's level of creativity?

7. Can better leaders more accurately perceive and leverage emotions? How could you determine if this was so?

1. Your instructor has access to a self-scored personality type assessment as well as an online OCEAN personality assessment. The online assessment takes about 10 minutes to complete and could be given as homework. Once the assessments are completed, you should review the feedback reports and discuss in class.

2. Your instructor can suspend a 30-foot rope approximately 2 feet off the ground. You and the rest of the class should get on one side of the rope. The rope represents an electrified fence, and your task is to get everyone successfully *over* the rope without touching it. You may not touch, lower, raise, or adjust the rope in any manner. You may not let any part of your skin or clothing touch the rope, nor can you drape anything over the rope to protect you from the "current." There are two rules you must follow to successfully navigate the rope. First, before starting to cross the rope, everyone in the group must form a line parallel to the rope and hold hands with the people on either side. These links with the other people in the group cannot be broken. Second, a quality error is committed if any group member touches the rope. If the group detects their own error, then only the person currently attempting to navigate the rope needs to start over. If the instructor catches the error but the group does not, then the instructor can have the entire group start over. This is analagous to catching a bad product before it is delivered to a customer instead of delivering defective products to customers. You will have about 25 minutes to plan and execute this exercise. After the exercise your group should discuss the role of personality traits as well as analytic, practical, creative, and emotional intelligence in the exercise.

Minicase

Lessons on Leadership from Ann Fudge

How do you rescue one of the largest advertising and media services firms in the world from a downward spiral? That is the question Martin Sorrell faced when his London-based WPP Group acquired Young & Rubicam in 2000. After many years on top, Y&R was starting to lose momentum—and clients. Kentucky Fried Chicken, United Airlines, and Burger King had all decided to take their advertising dollars elsewhere. Sorrell needed to stop the exodus, but how? Sorrell decided a fresh face was needed and started a search for a dynamic new CEO to revitalize Y&R. He found such a leader in Ann Fudge.

Ann Fudge was formerly president of Kraft Foods. At Kraft she had been responsible for the success of the $5 billion division that included well-known brands such as Maxwell House, Grape Nuts, Shredded Wheat, and General Foods International Coffees. Fudge's reputation as a charismatic leader who listens was a major issue for Sorrell when he went looking for a new CEO for

Y&R. Among the talents Fudge had to offer was an ability to interact effectively with all constituencies of a consumer business. Mattel Chairman and CEO Bob Eckert was Fudge's boss when he was president and CEO of Kraft. Of Fudge, Eckert says, "She is equally comfortable with consumers at the ballpark, factory workers on a production line, and executives in the boardroom. She could engage all three constituents in the same day and be comfortable. She is very comfortable with herself, and she's not pretending to be someone else. That's what makes her such an effective leader."

Fudge's commitment to her work and the people she works with is evident in the lessons she offers to other leaders:

1. Be yourself; do not feign behavior that you think will make you "successful."
2. Always remember it's the people, not you. A leader cannot be a leader if he/she has no followers. Be honest with people. Give them feedback. Put the right people in the right jobs. Surround yourself with the smartest people you can find—people who will offer differing perspectives and diversity of experience, age, gender, and race.
3. Touch your organization. It's easy to get stuck behind your desk. Fight the burden of paperwork and get out in the field. Don't be a remote leader. You cannot create a dynamic culture if people can't see, hear, and touch you. Let them know you as a person.
4. Steer the wheel with a strategic focus, yet maintain a wide peripheral vision. Know when to stop, speed up, slow down, brake quickly, swerve, or even gun it!

Fudge had a difficult decision to make when she was approached by Sorrell about the position at Y&R. She was in the midst of a two-year break—after 24 years working for corporate America, Fudge had decided to take some time for herself. She had left her position as president of Kraft Foods in 2001 based not on her dissatisfaction with her job, but on a desire to define herself by more than her career. "It was definitely not satisfaction, it was more about life," says Fudge about her sabbatical. During her two-year break she traveled, cycling around Sardinia and Corsica; she took up yoga; and she wrote a book called *The Artist's Way at Work*—a manual for improving creativity and innovation on the job.

Fudge took on the challenge and has not looked back. In her tenure at Y&R she has worked hard to get Y&R back on top. She has traveled the globe to visit Y&R employees. She frequently puts in 15-hour days pushing her strategy to focus on clients, encouraging teamwork, and improving creativity. A major undertaking for Fudge is to bring together the various business entities under the Y&R umbrella to better meet client needs. She's also trying to institute a Six Sigma method for creativity—looking for ways to increase productivity so employees have more time to be creative. Fudge's hard work is paying off. Y&R has recently added Microsoft and Toys R Us to its client list, and if Fudge has her way, the list will continue to grow until Y&R is back on top.

1. Where would Ann Fudge be placed in each of the Five Factor Model (FFM) categories?
2. Consider the components of creative intelligence from Table 6.3. Identify the key components that have affected Ann Fudge's success.
3. Ann Fudge decided to take a sabbatical to focus on her personal life. Based on her experience, what are the benefits of such a break? What might be some drawbacks?

Sources: Diane Brady, "Act Two: Ann Fudge's Two-Year Break from Work Changed Her Life. Will Those Lessons Help Her Fix Young & Rubicam?" *BusinessWeek,* March 29, 2004, p. 72; http://www.internet-marketing-brandin .com/News/african_american.htm; http://www.brandweek.com/brandweek/search/article_display.jsp?vnu_content_id1000506747; http://www.linkageinc.com/conferences/leadership/gild.

End Notes

1. R. M. Stogdill, *Handbook of Leadership* (New York: Free Press, 1974).
2. R. M. Stogdill, "Personal Factors Associated with Leadership: A Review of the Literature," *Journal of Psychology* 25 (1948), pp. 35–71.
3. R. D. Mann, "A Review of the Relationships between Personality and Performance in Small Groups," *Psychological Bulletin* 56 (1959), pp. 241–70.
4. R. G. Lord, C. L. DeVader, and G. M. Allinger, "A Meta-analysis of the Relationship between Personality Traits and Leadership Perceptions: An Application of Validity Generalization Procedures," *Journal of Applied Psychology* 71 (1986), pp. 402–10.
5. R. T. Hogan, G. J. Curphy, and J. Hogan, "What Do We Know about Personality: Leadership and Effectiveness?" *American Psychologist* 49 (1994), pp. 493–504.
6. R. T. Hogan, "Personality and Personality Measurement," in *Handbook of Industrial and Organizational Psychology,* Vol. 2, ed. M. D. Dunnette and L. M. Hough (Palo Alto, CA: Consulting Psychologists Press, 1991), pp. 873–919.
7. T. A. Judge, A. E. Colbert, and R. Ilies, "Intelligence and Leadership: A Quantitative Review and Test of Theoretical Propositions," *Journal of Applied Psychology* 89, no. 3 (2004), pp. 542–52.
8. T. A. Judge, J. E. Bono, R. Ilies, and M. W. Gerhardt, "Leadership and Personality: A Qualitative and Quantitative Review," *Journal of Applied Psychology* 87, no. 4 (2002), pp. 765–80.
9. S. J. Zaccaro, "Trait-Based Perspectives on Leadership," *American Psychologist* 62, no. 1 (2007), pp. 6–16.
10. R. T. Hogan, J. Hogan, and B. W. Roberts, "Personality Measurement and Employment Decisions: Questions and Answers," *American Psychologist* 51, no. 5 (1996), pp. 469–77.
11. S. Freud, *Group Psychology and the Analysis of the Ego,* trans. J. Strachey, 2nd ed. *The Standard Edition of the Complete Works of Psychological Works of Sigmund Freud, Vol. 2* (London: Hogarth Institute for Psycho-Analysis).

12. G. J. Curphy, *The Consequences of Managerial Incompetence*, presentation given at the 3rd Hogan Assessment Systems International Users Conference, Prague, Czech Republic, September 2004.

13. B. W. Roberts, "An Alternative Perspective on the Relation between Work and Psychological Functioning: The Reciprocal Model of Person–Environment Interaction," in *Personality and Organizational Behavior*, R. T. Hogan, Chair. Symposium presented at the 104th Annual Meeting of the American Psychological Association, Toronto, Canada, 1996.

14. G. J. Curphy, *Personality, Intelligence, and Leadership*, presentation given to the Pioneer Leadership Program at Denver University, Denver, CO, 1997.

15. G. J. Curphy, "Personality and Work: Some Food for Thought," in *Personality Applications in the Workplace: Thinking Outside the Dots*, R. T. Hogan (chair). Symposium presented at the 12th Annual Conference of the Society of Industrial and Organizational Psychology, St. Louis, MO, 1997.

16. G. J. Curphy, "New Directions in Personality," in *Personality and Organizational Behavior*. R. T. Hogan (chair). Symposium presented at the 104th Annual Meeting of the American Psychological Association, Toronto, Canada, 1996.

17. J. Hogan and B. Holland, "Using Theory to Evaluate Personality and Job-Performance Relations: A Socio-analytic Perspective," *Journal of Applied Psychology* 88, no. 1 (2003), pp. 100–12.

18. R. P. Tett and D. D. Burnett, "A Personality Trait-Based Interactionalist Model of Job Performance," *Journal of Applied Psychology* 88, no. 3 (2003), pp. 500–17.

19. G. W. Allport, and H. S. Odbert, "Trait-names: A Psycho-Lexical Study," *Psychological Monographs* 47 (1936), pp. 171–220.

20. J. J. Deary, "A (Latent) Big-Five Personality Model in 1915? A Reanalysis of Webb's Data," *Journal of Applied Psychology* 71, no. 5 (1996), pp. 992–1005.

21. L. L. Thurstone, "The Factors of the Mind," *Psychological Review* 41 (1934), pp. 1–32.

22. M. R. Barrick and M. K. Mount, "The Big Five Personality Dimensions and Job Performance: A Meta-analysis." *Personal Psychology* 44 (1991), pp. 1–26.

23. P. T. Costa Jr. and R. R. McCrae, "Domains and Facets: Hierarchical Personality Assessment Using the Revised NEO Personality Inventory," *Journal of Personality Assessment* 64 (1995), pp. 21–50.

24. M. R. Barrick, "Answers to Lingering Questions about Personality Research," paper presented at the 14th Annual Conference of the Society of Industrial and Organizational Psychology, Atlanta, GA, 1999.

25. C. J. Thoresen, J. C. Bradley, P. D. Bliese, and J. D. Thoresen, "The Big Five Personality Traits and Individual Job Growth Trajectories in Maintenance and Transitional Job Stages," *Journal of Applied Psychology* 89, no. 5 (2004), pp. 835–53.

26. J. E. Bono and T. A. Judge, "Personality and Transformational and Transactional Leadership," *Journal of Applied Psychology* 89, no. 5 (2004), pp. 901–10.

27. L. E. Hough and F. L. Oswald, "Personality Testing and Industrial-Organizational Psychology: Reflections, Progress, and Prospects," *Industrial and Organizational Psychology: Perspectives on Science and Practice* 1, no. 3 (2008), pp. 272–90.

28. D. S. Ones, S. Dilchert, C. Viswesvaran, and T. A. Judge, "In Support of Personality Assessment in Organizational Settings," *Personnel Psychology* 60, no. 4 (2007), pp. 995–1028.

29. J. F. Salgado, "Predicting Job Performance Using FFM and non-FFM Personality Measures," *Journal of Occupational and Organizational Psychology* 76, no. 3 (2003), pp. 323–46.

30. R. T. Hogan, "The Role of Big Five Personality Traits in Executive Selection," in *The Role of I/O Psychology in Executive Assessment and Development*, G. J. Curphy (chair). Paper presented at the 15th Annual Conference of the Society of Industrial and Organizational Psychology, New Orleans, LA, 2000.

31. G. J. Curphy and K. D. Osten, *Technical Manual for the Leadership Development Survey*, Technical Report No. 93–14 (Colorado Springs, CO: U.S. Air Force Academy, 1993).

32. R. T. Hogan, *Personality and the Fate of Organizations* (Mahwah, NJ: Lawrence Erlbaum, 2007).

33. F. Lievens, M. H. Harris, E. Van Keer, and C. Bisqueret, "Predicting Cross-Cultural Training Performance: The Validity of Personality, Cognitive Ability, and Dimensions Measures by an Assessment Center and a Behavior Description Interview," *Journal of Applied Psychology* 88, no. 3 (2003), pp. 476–89.

34. R. T. Hogan, J. Hogan, and R. Warrenfelz, *The Hogan Guide* (Tulsa, OK: Hogan Assessment Systems, 2008).

35. T. A. Judge and A. Erez, "Interaction and Intersection: The Constellation of Emotional Stability and Extraversion in Predicting Performance," *Personnel Psychology* 60 (2007), pp. 573–96.

36. G. J. Curphy, "Comments on the State of Leadership Prediction," in *Predicting Leadership: The Good, The Bad, the Indifferent, and the Unnecessary*, J. P. Campbell and M. J. Benson (chairs). Symposium conducted at the 22nd Annual Conference for the Society of Industrial and Organizational Psychology, New York, April 2007.

37. R. T. Hogan and J. Hogan, *The Leadership Potential Report* (Tulsa, OK: Hogan Assessment Systems, 2002).

38. C. G. Jung, *Psychological Types*, trans. R. F. C. Hall (Princeton, NJ: Princeton University Press, 1971).

39. N. L. Quenk, *In the Grip*, 2nd ed. (Mountain View, CA: CPP, Inc., 2000).

40. P. B. Myers and K. D. Myers, *The Myers-Briggs Type Indicator Step II (Form Q) Profile* (Palo Alto, CA: Consulting Psychologists Press, 2003).

41. N. L. Quenk and J. M. Kummerow, *The Myers-Briggs Type Indicator Step II (Form B) Profile* (Palo Alto, CA: Consulting Psychologists Press, 2001).

42. I. B. Myers and B. H. McCaulley, *Manual: A Guide to the Development and Use of the Myers-Briggs Type Indicator* (Palo Alto, CA: Consulting Psychologists Press, 1985).

43. W. H. Cummings, "Age Group Differences and Estimated Frequencies of the MBTI Types: Proposed Changes," *Proceedings of the Psychology in the Department of Defense Thirteenth Symposium* (Colorado Springs, CO: United States Air Force Academy, April 1992).

44. F. W. Gibson and G. J. Curphy, "The MBTI: Skewering a Sacred Cow," presentation given to the Colorado Organizational Development Network, Denver, CO, 1996.

45. P. H. Dubois, "A Test Dominated Society: China 1115 b.c.–1905," in *Testing Problems in Perspective*, ed. A. Anastasi. (American Council on Education, 1964).

46. R. D. Arvey et al., "Mainstream Science on Intelligence," *The Wall Street Journal*, December 13, 1994.

47. R. E. Riggio, "Multiple Intelligences and Leadership: An Overview," in *Multiple Intelligences and Leadership*, ed. R. E. Riggio, S. E. Murphy, and F. J. Pirozzolo (Mahwah, NJ: Lawrence Erlbaum Associates, 2002), pp. 1–7.

48. F. L. Schmidt and J. E. Hunter, "Development of a Causal Model of Job Performance," *Current Directions in Psychological Science* 1, no. 3 (1992), pp. 89–92.

49. S. Scarr, "Protecting General Intelligence: Constructs and Consequences for Interventions," in *Intelligence: Measurement, Theory, and Public Policy*, ed. R. L. Linn (Chicago: University of Illinois Press, 1989).

50. R. J. Sternberg, "The Concept of Intelligence: Its Role in Lifelong Learning and Success," *American Psychologist* 52, no. 10 (1997), pp. 1030–37.

51. R. J. Sternberg, "Creativity as a Decision," *American Psychologist*, May 2002, p. 376.

52. F. Schmidt, H. Le, I. Oh, and J. Schaffer, "General Mental Ability, Job Performance, and Red Herrings: Responses to Osterman, Hauser, and Schmitt," *The Academy of Management Perspectives* 21, no. 4 (2007), pp. 64–76.

53. T. A. Judge, R. Ilies, and N. Dimotakis, "Are Health and Happiness the Product of Wisdom? The Relationship of General Mental Ability to Education and Occupational Attainment, Health, and Well-Being," *Journal of Applied Psychology* 95, no. 3, pp. 454–68.

54. T. A. Judge, R. L. Klinger, and L. S. Simon, "Time Is on My Side: Time General Mental Ability, Human Capital, and Extrinsic Career Success," *Journal of Applied Psychology* 95, no. 1, pp. 92–107.

55. L. J. Cronbach, *Essentials of Psychological Testing*, 4th ed. (San Francisco: Harper & Row, 1984).

56. R. J. Sternberg, "WICS: A Model of Leadership in Organizations," *Academy of Management: Learning and Education* 2, no. 4 (2003a), pp. 386–401.

57. R. J. Sternberg, "A Model of Leadership: WICS," *American Psychologist* 62, no. 1 (2007), pp. 34–42.

58. J. F. Salgado, N. Anderson, S. Moscoso, C. Bertua, F. de Fruyt, and J. P. Rolland, "A Meta-analytic Study of General Mental Ability Validity for Different Occupations in the European Community," *Journal of Applied Psychology* 88, no. 6 (2003), pp. 1068–81.

59. J. Menkes, "Hiring for Smarts," *Harvard Business Review*, November 2005, pp. 100–11.

60. R. J. Herrnstein and C. Murray, *The Bell Curve: Intelligence and Class Structure in American Life* (New York: Free Press, 1994).

61. G. J. Curphy, "Concluding Remarks on Executive Assessment and Development," in *The Role of I/O Psychology in Executive Assessment and Development*, G. J. Curphy (chair). Symposium presented at the 15th Annual Conference of the Society for Industrial and Organizational Psychology, New Orleans, LA, 2000.

62. G. J. Curphy, "Early Leadership Talent Identification and Development," paper presented at the Conference for Executives of Saudi Aramco, Dhahran, Saudi Arabia, October 2001.

63. G. J. Curphy, "What Role Should I/O Psychologists Play in Executive Education?" in *Models of Executive Education*, R. T. Hogan (chair). Presentation given at the 17th Annual Society for Industrial and Organizational Psychology, Toronto, Canada, April 2002.

64. G. J. Curphy, "Leadership Transitions and Succession Planning," in *Developing and Implementing Succession Planning Programs*, J. Lock (chair). Symposium conducted at the 19th Annual Conference for the Society of Industrial and Organizational Psychology, Chicago, April 2004.

65. R. T. Hogan and J. Hogan, *The Hogan Business Reasoning Inventory* (Tulsa, OK: Hogan Assessment Systems, 2007).

66. B. Azar, "Searching for Intelligence Beyond G," *APA Monitor* 26, no. 1 (1995), p. 1.

67. H. Gardner, *Frames of Mind: The Theory of Multiple Intelligences* (New York: Basic Books, 1983).

68. R. J. Sternberg, *Beyond IQ: A Triarchic Theory of Human Intelligence* (New York: Cambridge University Press, 1985).

69. R. J. Sternberg, *Handbook of Creativity* (New York: Cambridge University Press, 1999).

70. R. J. Sternberg, "A Broad View of Intelligence: The Theory of Successful Intelligence," *Journal of Consulting Psychology* 55, no. 3 (2003b), pp. 139–54.

71. L. M. Kersting, "What Exactly Is Creativity?" *Monitor on Psychology*, November 2003, pp. 40–41.

72. R. J. Sternberg and T. I. Lubart, "Investing in Creativity," *American Psychologist* 52, no. 10 (1997), pp. 1046–50.

73. R. J. Sternberg, E. L. Grigorenko, and J. L. Singer, *Creativity: From Potential to Realization* (Washington DC: American Psychological Association Press, 2004).

74. J. C. Kaufman and J. Baer, "Hawking's Haiku, Madonna's Math: Why It Is Hard to Be Creative in Every Room," in *Creativity: From Potential to Realization*, ed. R. J. Sternberg, E. L. Grigorenko, and J. L. Singer (Washington DC: American Psychological Association Press, 2004).

75. T. Lubart and J. H. Guigard, "The Generality-Specificity of Creativity: A Multivariate Approach," in *Creativity: From Potential to Realization*, ed. R. J. Sternberg, E. L. Grigorenko, and J. L. Singer (Washington DC: American Psychological Association Press, 2004).

76. G. J. Feist., "The Evolved Fluid Specificity of Human Creative Talent," in *Creativity: From Potential to Realization*, ed. R. J. Sternberg, E. L. Grigorenko, and J. L. Singer (Washington DC: American Psychological Association Press, 2004).

77. J. P. Guilford, *The Nature of Human Intelligence* (New York: McGraw-Hill, 1967).

78. R. J. Sternberg, "What Is the Common Thread of Creativity? Its Dialectical Relationship to Intelligence and Wisdom," *American Psychologist* 56, no. 4 (2001), pp. 360–62.

79. E. E. Ghiselli, "Intelligence and Managerial Success," *Psychological Reports* 12 (1963), p. 89.

80. F. E. Fiedler, "The Effect and Meaning of Leadership Experience: A Review of Research and a Preliminary Model," in *Impact of Leadership*, ed. K. E. Clark, M. B. Clark, and D. P. Campbell (Greensboro, NC: Center for Creative Leadership, 1992).

81. F. E. Fiedler, "The Curious Role of Cognitive Resources in Leadership," in *Multiple Intelligences and Leadership,* ed. R. E. Riggio, S. E. Murphy, and F. J. Pirozzolo (Mahwah, NJ: Lawrence Erlbaum Associates, 2002), pp. 91–104.

82. F. W. Gibson, "A Taxonomy of Leader Abilities and Their Influence on Group Performance as a Function of Interpersonal Stress," in *Impact of Leadership,* ed. K. E. Clark, M. B. Clark, and D. P. Campbell (Greensboro, NC: Center for Creative Leadership, 1992).

83. M. A. Collins and T. M. Amabile, "Motivation and Creativity," in *Handbook of Creativity,* ed. R. J. Sterberg (New York: Cambridge University Press, 1999).

84. T. M. Amabile, E. A. Schatzel, G. B. Moneta, and S. J. Kramer, "Leader Behaviors and the Work Environment for Creativity: Perceived Leader Support," *The Leadership Quarterly* 15, no. 1 (2004), pp. 5–32.

85. R. Reiter-Palmon and R. Ilies, "Leadership and Creativity: Understanding Leadership from a Creative Problem Solving Perspective," *The Leadership Quarterly* 15, no. 1 (2004), pp. 55–77.

86. J. Zhou, "When the Presence of Creative Co-Workers Is Related to Creativity: Role of Supervisor Close Monitoring, Developmental Feedback, and Creative Personality," *Journal of Applied Psychology* 88, no. 3 (2003), pp. 413–22.

87. C. E. Shalley and L. L. Gilson, "What Leaders Need to Know: A Review of the Social and Contextual Factors That Can Foster or Hinder Creativity," *The Leadership Quarterly* 15, no. 1 (2004), pp. 33–53.

88. S. F. Dingfelder, "Creativity on the Clock," *Monitor on Psychology,* November 2003, p. 58.

89. M. Basadur, "Leading Others to Think Innovatively Together: Creative Leadership," *The Leadership Quarterly* 15, no. 1 (2004), pp. 103–21.

90. R. Florida and J. Goodnight, "Managing for Creativity," *Harvard Business Review,* July–August 2005, pp. 125–31.

91. R. Florida, R. Cushing, and G. Gates, "When Social Capital Stifles Innovation," *Harvard Business Review,* August 2002, p. 20.

92. M. D. Mumford, G. M. Scott, B. Gaddis, and J. M. Strange, "Leading Creative People: Orchestrating Expertise and Relationships," *The Leadership Quarterly* 13, no. 6 (2002), pp. 705–50.

93. R. J. Sternberg, "WICS: A Model of Leadership in Organizations," *Academy of Management: Learning and Education* 2, no. 4 (2003a), pp. 386–401.

94. X. Zhang and K. M. Bartol, "Linking Empowering Leadership and Employee Creativity: The Influence of Psychological Empowerment, Intrinsic Motivation, and Creative Process Engagement," *Academy of Management Journal* 53, no. 1 (2010), pp. 107–28.

95. T. M. Amabile and M. Khaire, "Creativity and the Role of the Leader," *Harvard Business Review,* October 2008, pp. 100–10.

96. T. M. Amabile, "Beyond Talent: John Irving and the Passionate Craft of Creativity," *American Psychologist* 56, no. 4 (2001), pp. 333–36.

97. T. M. Amabile, "The Motivation to Be Creative," in *Frontiers in Creativity: Beyond the Basics,* ed. S. Isaksen (Buffalo, NY: Bearly, 1987).

98. J. Zhou, "Feedback Valence, Feedback Style, Task Autonomy, and Achievement Orientation: Interactive Effects on Creative Performance," *Journal of Applied Psychology* 83, no. 2 (1998), pp. 261–76.

99. G. M. Prince, "Creative Meetings through Power Sharing," *Harvard Business Review* 50, no. 4 (1972), pp. 47–54.

100. F. E. Fiedler and J. E. Garcia, *New Approaches to Leadership: Cognitive Resources and Organizational Performance* (New York: John Wiley, 1987).

101. F. E. Fiedler, "Cognitive Resources and Leadership Performance," *Applied Psychology: An International Review* 44, no. 1 (1995), pp. 5–28.

102. W. Schonpflug, "The Noncharismatic Leader-Vulnerable," *Applied Psychology: An International Review* 44, no. 1 (1995), pp. 39–42.

103. S. J. Zaccaro, "Leader Resources and the Nature of Organizational Problems," *Applied Psychology: An International Review* 44, no. 1 (1995), pp. 32–36.

104. D. Goleman, *Emotional Intelligence* (New York: Bantam Doubleday Dell, 1995).

105. P. Salovey and J. D. Mayer, "Emotional Intelligence," *Imagination, Cognition, and Personality* 9 (1990), pp. 185–211.

106. J. D. Mayer, P. Salovey, and D. R. Caruso, "Emotional Intelligence: New Ability or Eclectic Traits?" *American Psychologist* 63, no. 6, pp. 503–17.

107. R. Bar-On, *The Emotional Quotient Inventory (EQ-i)* (Toronto, Canada: Multi-Health Systems, 1996).

108. R. Aberman, "Emotional Intelligence," paper presented at the Quarterly Meeting of the Minnesota Human Resource Planning Society, Minneapolis, MN, November 2000.

109. R. Aberman, "Emotional Intelligence and Work," presentation given to the Minnesota Professionals for Psychology Applied to Work, Minneapolis, MN, January, 2007.

110. D. Goleman, *Working with Emotional Intelligence* (New York: Bantam Doubleday Dell, 1998).

111. D. R. Caruso, J. D. Mayer, and P. Salovey, "Emotional Intelligence and Emotional Leadership," in *Multiple Intelligences and Leadership*, ed. R. E. Riggio, S. E. Murphy, and F. J. Pirozzolo (Mahwah, NJ: Lawrence Erlbaum Associates, 2002, pp. 55–74).

112. D. Goleman, R. Boyatzis, and A. McKee, "Primal Leadership: The Hidden Driver of Great Performance," *Harvard Business Review*, December 2001, pp. 42–53.

113. D. Goleman, R. Boyatzis, and A. McKee, *Primal Leadership: Realizing the Power of Emotional Intelligence* (Boston: Harvard Business School Press, 2002).

114. J. Antonakis, "On Why Emotional Intelligence Will Not Predict Leadership Effectiveness beyond IQ and the Big Five. An Extension and Rejoinder," *Organizational Analysis* 12, no. 2 (2004), pp. 171–82.

115. D. L. Van Rooy and C. Viswesvaran, "Emotinal Intelligence: A Meta-Analytic Investigation of Predictive Validity and Nomological Net," *Journal of Vocational Behavior* 65, pp. 71–95.

116. D. L. Joseph and D. A. Newman, "Emotional Intelligence: An Integrative Meta-Analysis and Cascading Model," *Journal of Applied Psychology* 95, no. 1, pp. 54–78.

117. J. D. Mayer, D. R. Caruso, and P. Salovey, " Selecting a Measure of Emotional Intelligence: The Case for Ability Testing," in *Handbook of Emotional Intelligence,* ed. R. Bar-On and J. D. A. Parker (New York: Jossey-Bass, 2000).

118. R. Bar-On, "The Bar-On Emotional Quotient Inventory (EQ-i): Rational, Description, and Summary of Psychometric Properties," in *Measuring Emotional Intelligence: Common Ground and Controversy,* ed. Glenn Geher (Hauppauge, NY: Nova Science Publishers, 2004), pp. 111–42.

119. T. Schwartz, "How Do You Feel?" *Fast Company,* June 2000, pp. 297–312.

120. V. U. Druskat, and S. B. Wolff, "Building the Emotional Intelligence of Groups," *Harvard Business Review,* March 2001, pp. 80–91.

121. T. Sy, S. Cote, and R. Saavedra, "The Contagious Leader: Impact of the Leader's Mood on the Mood of Group Members, Group Affective Tone, and Group Processes," *Journal of Applied Psychology* 90, no. 2 (2005), pp. 295–305.

122. C. Ting Fong, "The Effects of Emotional Ambivalence on Creativity," *Academy of Management Journal* 49, no. 5 (2006), pp. 1016–30.

123. T. Bradberry and J. Greaves, "Heartless Bosses?" *Harvard Business Review,* December 2005, p. 24.

124. P. J. Jordan, N. M. Ashkanasy, and C. E. J. Hartel, "Emotional Intelligence as a Moderator of Emotional and Behavioral Reactions to Job Security," *Academy of Management Review* 27, no. 3 (2002), pp. 361–72.

125. C. S. Wong, and K. S. Law, "The Effects of Leader and Follower Emotional Intelligence on Performance and Attitude: An Exploratory Study," *The Leadership Quarterly* 13, no. 3 (2002), pp. 243–74.

126. R. E. Boyatzis, E. C. Stubbs, and S. N. Taylor, "Learning Cognitive and Emotional Intelligence Competencies through Graduate Management Education," *Academy of Management Learning and Education* 1, no. 2 (2002), pp. 150–62.

Chapter 7

Leadership Behavior

Introduction

Researcher:	Are all the captains you fly with pretty much the same?
Aircrew Member:	Oh, no. Some guys are the greatest guys in the world to fly with. I mean they may not have the greatest hands in the world, but that doesn't matter. When you fly with them, you feel like you can work together to get the job done. You really want to do a good job for them. Some other captains are just the opposite . . . you just can't stand to work with them. That doesn't mean you'll do anything that's unsafe or dangerous, but you won't go out of your way to keep him or her out of trouble either. So you'll just sit back and do what you have to and just hope he or she screws up.
Researcher:	How can you tell which kind of captain you're working with?
Aircrew Member:	Oh, you can tell.
Researcher:	How?
Aircrew Member:	I don't know how you tell, but it doesn't take very long. Just a couple of minutes and you'll know.

Throughout this book we have been talking about different ways to assess leaders. But when all is said and done, how can we tell good leaders from bad ones? This is a critically important question: if we can specifically identify what leaders actually do that makes them effective, then we can hire or train people to exhibit these behaviors. One way to differentiate leaders is to look at what they do on a day-to-day basis. Some leaders do a good job of making decisions, providing direction, creating plans, giving regular feedback, getting their followers the resources they need to be successful, and building cohesive teams. Other leaders have difficulties making decisions, set vague or unclear goals, and ignore followers' requests

The truth of the matter is that you always know the right thing to do. The hard part is doing it.

Norman Schwartzkopf, U.S. Army

for equipment and subsequently cannot build teams. Although a leader's values, personality, and intelligence are important, variables like these have only an indirect relationship with leadership effectiveness. Their effect presumably comes from the impact they have on leader behavior, which appears to have a more direct relationship with a leader's ability to build teams and get results through others. One advantage of looking at leaders in terms of behavior instead of, say, personality is that behavior is often easier to measure; leadership behaviors can be observed, whereas personality traits, values, or intelligence must be inferred from behavior or measured with tests. Another advantage of looking at leader behavior is that many people are less defensive about—and feel in more control of—specific behaviors than they are about their personalities or intelligence.

Nonetheless, leaders with certain traits, values, or attitudes may find it easier to effectively perform some leadership behaviors than others. For example, leaders with higher agreeableness scores (as defined in Chapter 6) may find it relatively easy to show concern and support for followers but may also find it difficult to discipline followers. Likewise, leaders with a

Captains Thomas Musgrave and George Dalgarno

PROFILES IN LEADERSHIP 7.1

Three hundred miles south of New Zealand are the Auckland Islands. They are isolated and forbidding, and 150 years ago they brought almost certain death to ships that got too close. The howling sub-Antarctic winds drove ships onto the shallow reefs, and most sailors quickly drowned. Those who made it to shore died of exposure and starvation. The few who survived did so in dreadful conditions. In *Island of the Lost*, Joan Druett (2007) recounts the story of two parties who were shipwrecked in 1864 on opposite sides of the island; this is a story of leadership and teamwork.

The first, a party of five led by Captain Thomas Musgrave of England, behaved like Shackleton's crew stranded in the Weddell Sea. Encouraged by Musgrave, the men banded together in a common quest for survival. Over a period of 20 months, using material salvaged from their ship, they built a cabin, found food, rotated cooking duties, nursed one another, made tools, tanned seal hides for shoes, built a bellows and a furnace, made bolts and nails, and then built a boat that they used to sail to safety.

Meanwhile, 20 miles away, a Scottish ship led by Captain George Dalgarno went aground, and 19 men made it safely to shore. Dalgarno became depressed and went "mad," and the rest of the crew fell into despair, anarchy, and then cannibalism. A sailor named Robert Holding tried to encourage the others to act together to build shelter and find food, but other members of the crew threatened to kill and eat him. After three months, only three men were alive and subsequently rescued.

Although these events happened almost 150 years ago, the story has strong parallels to modern leadership. How did the leadership behaviors exhibited by Captains Musgrave and Dalgarno differ, and what impact did these behaviors have on their crews? Are there any parallels between these two captains and leaders in government, industry, or philanthropic organizations?

Sources: R. T. Hogan, *The Pragmatics of Leadership* (Tulsa, OK: Hogan Assessment Systems, 2007); G. J. Curphy and R. T. Hogan, *A Guide to Building High Performing Teams* (North Oaks, MN: Curphy Consulting Corporation, 2009); J. Druett, *Island of the Lost: Shipwrecked on the Edge of the World* (Chapel Hills, NC: Algonquin Books, 2007).

low affiliation value (Chapter 5) and who score low on the personality trait of extraversion (Chapter 6) will prefer working by themselves versus with others. Because behavior is under conscious control, we can always choose to change our behavior as leaders if we want to. However, the ease with which we exhibit or can change behavior will partly be a function of our values, personality, and intelligence.

Followers and the situation are the two other major factors to keep in mind when evaluating leadership behavior. As described in Chapter 6, strong situational norms can play pervasive roles in leaders' behavior. Similarly, follower and situational factors can help determine whether a particular leadership behavior is "bad" or "good." Say a leader gave a group of followers extremely detailed instructions on how to get a task accomplished. If the followers were new to the organization or had never done the task before, this level of detail would probably help the leader get better results through others. But if the followers were experienced, this same leader behavior would likely have detrimental effects. The same would be true if the company were in a financial crisis versus having a successful year.

This chapter begins with a discussion of why it is important to study leadership behavior. We then review some of the early research on leader behavior and discuss several ways to categorize different leadership behaviors. The next section describes a model of community leadership, and we conclude the chapter by summarizing what is currently known about a common leadership behavior assessment technique: the 360-degree, or multirater, feedback questionnaire.

Studies of Leadership Behavior

Why Study Leadership Behavior?

Thus far we have reviewed research on a number of key variables affecting leadership behavior, but we have not directly examined what leaders actually do to successfully build a team or get results through others. For example, what behaviors did Shane Aguero and Jerry Swope use to influence their platoon in Iraq (see Profiles in Leadership 7.2)? What did President Barack Obama specifically do to rescue the financial services and automotive industries, pass comprehensive health care legislation, more closely regulate banks, and deal with the oil spill in the Gulf of Mexico? What do Mark Zuckerberg, CEO of Facebook, and Eric Schmidt, the CEO of Google, do to keep their companies profitable? What exactly did James Cameron do to produce the movie *Avatar* or Craig Venter do to lead a laboratory that created the first artificial life? To answer questions like these, it is appropriate to turn our attention to leader behavior itself; if we could identify how successful leaders act compared with unsuccessful leaders, we could design leadership talent management systems allowing organizations to hire, develop, and promote the skills necessary for future success. Unfortunately, as we can see in the *Dilbert* comic strip, *The Office*

Lieutenant Shane Aguero and SFC Jerry Swope

PROFILES IN LEADERSHIP 7.2

Lt. Shane Aguero and SFC Jerry Swope were among the 21,000 soldiers from the First Calvary who were deployed to Iraq in early 2004. Their unit was responsible for patrolling the area known as Sadr City. The unit they were replacing had patrolled Sadr City for the past year and during that time reported only a single incident between the 2,500,000 Shiite residents and the U.S. Army. By all accounts the First Calvary was expecting to have similar relationships with the local population and believed its primary mission would be to provide local security and infrastructure improvement. But intelligence reports indicated that many of the Imams in Sadr City had started calling for the ouster of U.S. forces from Iraq; and in late March Paul Bremer, U.S. administrator of Iraq, closed down the local newspaper, *Al-Hawza,* because it was inciting violence. By early April intelligence reports indicated that "Sadr City was a volcano ready to explode."

Lt. Shane Aguero and the 17 members of Aguero's platoon, along with an Iraqi interpreter, were riding in four Humvees that were escorting three trucks collecting sewage from Sadr City on April 4. The drivers of the sewage trucks were getting more nervous as the day went on and at the end of the day quit their jobs—stating that they would be killed as collaborators if they remained. During the day the streets of Sadr City were busy with the normal bustle of a large city, but as the day came to a close the city streets became deserted. As Aguero's platoon was leaving Sadr City, they encountered a large crowd of people as well as a number of barriers that barred their travel on certain roads. They then came under gunfire. The gunfire started slowly at first, from one or two weapons of shooters who

were fairly spread out, but then quickly escalated into a full firefight involving hundreds of enemy soldiers. Aguero and his platoon were driving as fast as they could down the only street they could travel—a street that was lined with hundreds of members of the Mahdi Army and Sadr militia who were intent on killing everyone in the platoon.

Aguero ordered his platoon to park their four vehicles outside a three-story building and set up a defensive position on the roof. By this time one of his troops had been killed and one was wounded. SFC Jerry Swope remained in one of the Humvees to maintain radio contact with the Tactical Operations Center and coordinate a rescue. The building was rapidly surrounded by an overwhelming force of enemy soldiers who intimately knew the local terrain. Dozens of enemy shooters were closing in from all directions by taking five or six quick shots and then ducking to advance to better vantage points. Over the next four hours Aguero's platoon killed hundreds of Iraqis in repelling two massive frontal assaults (led by women and children acting as human shields), experienced eight casualties, and was dangerously close to "going black" (running out of ammunition). SFC Swope remained at the Humvee to coordinate the rescue efforts even though it had been hit by thousands of enemy rounds and its bulletproof glass had been shot out. It took three different rescue attempts to save Aguero's troops. The fighting was so intense that one of the rescue units experienced 47 casualties in an hour.

What behaviors did Lt. Aguero and SFC Swope exhibit that made them effective or ineffective leaders?

Source: M. Raddatz, *The Long Road Home* (New York: G. P. Putnam's Sons, 2007).

television series, and the explosive growth of management consulting firms, many people in positions of authority either do not know how to build teams or get results through others or do not realize how their behavior negatively affects the people who work for them.[1-10]

Before we describe the different ways to categorize what leaders do to build teams or influence a group, let's review what we know about

FIGURE 7.1
The Building Blocks of Skills

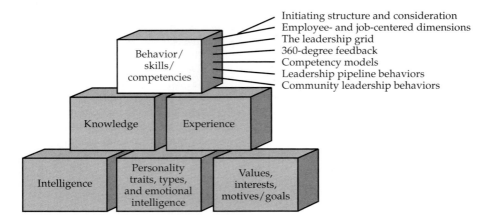

Initiating structure and consideration
Employee- and job-centered dimensions
The leadership grid
360-degree feedback
Competency models
Leadership pipeline behaviors
Community leadership behaviors

Behavior/skills/competencies

Knowledge | Experience

Intelligence | Personality traits, types, and emotional intelligence | Values, interests, motives/goals

leadership skills and behaviors. As shown in Figure 7.1, leadership behaviors (which include skills and competencies) are a function of intelligence, personality traits, emotional intelligence, values, attitudes, interests, knowledge, and experience. The factors in the bottom layer of blocks are relatively difficult to change, and they predispose a leader to act in distinctive ways. As described in Chapter 6, one's personality traits are pervasive and almost automatic, typically occurring without much conscious attention. The same could be said about how values, attitudes, and intelligence affect behaviors. Over time, however, leaders can learn and discern which behaviors are more appropriate and effective than others. It is always useful to remember the pivotal roles individual differences and situational variables can play in a leader's actions (see Profiles in Leadership 7.1 and 7.2).

The Early Studies

If you were asked to study and identify the behaviors that best differentiated effective from ineffective leaders, how would you do it? You could ask leaders what they do, follow the leaders around to see how they actually behave, or administer questionnaires to ask them and those they work with how often the leaders exhibited certain behaviors. These three approaches have been used extensively in past and present leadership research.

Much of the initial leader behavior research was conducted at Ohio State University and the University of Michigan. Collectively, the Ohio State University studies developed a series of questionnaires to measure different leader behaviors in work settings. These researchers began by collecting over 1,800 questionnaire items that described different types of leadership

We know what a person thinks not when he tells us what he thinks, but by his actions.

Isaac Bashevis Singer, writer

behaviors. These items were collapsed into 150 statements, and these statements were then used to develop a questionnaire called the **Leader Behavior Description Questionnaire (LBDQ)**.[11,12] To obtain information about a particular leader's behavior, subordinates were asked to rate the extent to which their leader performed behaviors like the following:

He lets subordinates know when they've done a good job.

He sets clear expectations about performance.

He shows concern for subordinates as individuals.

He makes subordinates feel at ease.

In analyzing the questionnaires from thousands of subordinates, the statistical pattern of responses to all the different items indicated that leaders could be described in terms of two independent dimensions of behavior called consideration and initiating structure.[13,14] **Consideration** refers to how friendly and supportive a leader is toward subordinates. Leaders high in consideration engage in many different behaviors that show supportiveness and concern, such as speaking up for subordinates' interests, caring about their personal situations, and showing appreciation for their work. **Initiating structure** refers to how much a leader emphasizes meeting work goals and accomplishing tasks. Leaders high in initiating structure engage in many different task-related behaviors, such as assigning deadlines, establishing performance standards, and monitoring performance levels.

The LBDQ was not the only leadership questionnaire developed by the Ohio State researchers. They also developed, for example, the Supervisory Descriptive Behavior Questionnaire (SBDQ), which measured the extent to which leaders in industrial settings exhibited consideration and initiating structure behaviors.[15] The Leadership Opinion Questionnaire (LOQ) asked leaders to indicate the extent to which they believed different consideration and initiating behaviors were important to leadership success.[16] The LBDQ-XII was developed to assess 10 other categories of leadership behaviors in addition to consideration and initiating structure.[17] Some of the additional leadership behaviors assessed by the LBDQ-XII included acting as a representative for the group, being able to tolerate uncertainty, emphasizing production, and reconciling conflicting organizational demands.

Rather than trying to describe the variety of behaviors leaders exhibit in work settings, the researchers at the University of Michigan sought to identify leader behaviors that contributed to effective group performance.[18] They concluded that four categories of leadership behaviors are related to effective group performance: leader support, interaction facilitation, goal emphasis, and work facilitation.[19]

Both goal emphasis and work facilitation are **job-centered dimensions** of behavior similar to the initiating structure behaviors described earlier.

Behaviors versus Skills

HIGHLIGHT 7.1

Leadership behaviors differ somewhat from leadership skills. A **leadership behavior** concerns a specific action, such as "setting specific performance goals for team members." A **leadership skill** consists of three components, which include a well-defined body of knowledge, a set of related behaviors, and clear criteria of competent performance. Perhaps leadership skills may be better understood by using a basketball analogy. People differ considerably in their basketball skills; good basketball players know when to pass and when to shoot and are adept at making layups, shots from the field, and free throws. Knowing when to pass and when to shoot is an example of the knowledge component, and layups and free throws are examples of the behavioral component of skills. In addition, shooting percentages can be used as one criterion for evaluating basketball skills. Leadership skills, such as delegating, can be seen much the same way. Good leaders know when and to whom a particular task should be delegated (knowledge); they effectively communicate their expectations concerning a delegated task (behavior); and they check to see whether the task was accomplished in a satisfactory manner (criteria). Thus a leadership skill is knowing when to act, acting in a manner appropriate to the situation, and acting in such a way that it helps the leader accomplish team goals.

Goal emphasis behaviors are concerned with motivating subordinates to accomplish the task at hand, and **work facilitation** behaviors are concerned with clarifying roles, acquiring and allocating resources, and reconciling organizational conflicts. Leader support and interaction facilitation are **employee-centered dimensions** of behavior similar to the consideration dimension of the various Ohio State questionnaires (see Table 7.1). **Leader support** includes behaviors where the leader shows concern for subordinates; **interaction facilitation** includes those behaviors where leaders act to smooth over and minimize conflicts among followers. Like the researchers at Ohio State, those at the University of Michigan also developed a questionnaire, the Survey of Organizations, to assess the degree to which leaders exhibit these four dimensions of leadership behaviors.[19]

Although the behaviors composing the task-oriented and people-oriented leadership dimensions were similar across the two research programs, there was a fundamental difference in assumptions underlying the work at the University of Michigan and that at Ohio State. Researchers at the University of Michigan considered job-centered and employee-centered behaviors to be at *opposite ends of a single continuum of leadership behavior.* Leaders could theoretically manifest either strong employee- *or* job-centered behaviors, but not both. On the other hand, researchers at Ohio State believed that consideration and initiating structure were *independent continuums.* Thus leaders could be high in both initiating structure and consideration, low in both dimensions, or high in one and low in the other.

TABLE 7.1
Early Leadership
Behavior
Dimensions

Ohio State Dimensions	University of Michigan Dimensions
Initiating structure	Goal emphasis and work facilitation
Consideration	Leader support and interaction facilitation

The key assumption underlying both research programs was that certain behaviors could be identified that are universally associated with a leader's ability to successfully influence a group toward the accomplishment of its goals. Here are the kinds of questions researchers were interested in:

- From the University of Michigan perspective, who tends to be more effective in helping a group to accomplish its goals—job- or employee-centered leaders?

- From the Ohio State perspective, are leaders who exhibit high levels of *both* task- and people-oriented behaviors more effective than those who exhibit *only* task or people behaviors?

- What role do situational factors play in leadership effectiveness? Are employee-centered leadership behaviors more important in nonprofit organizations or downsizing situations, whereas job-centered behaviors are more important in manufacturing organizations or start-up situations?

The answers to these questions have several practical implications. If leaders need to exhibit only job- or employee-centered behaviors, selection and training systems need to focus on only these behaviors. But if situational factors play a role, researchers need to identify which variables are the most important and train leaders in how to modify their behavior accordingly. As you might suspect, the answer to all these questions is "It depends." In general, researchers have reported that leaders exhibiting a high level of consideration or employee-centered behaviors have more satisfied subordinates. Leaders who set clear goals, explain what followers are to do and how to get tasks accomplished, and monitor results (that is, initiating structure or job-centered) often have higher-performing work units if the group faces relatively ambiguous or ill-defined tasks.[20-22] At the same time, however, leaders whose behavior is highly autocratic (an aspect of initiating structure) are more likely to have relatively dissatisfied subordinates.[20] Findings like these suggest that *no universal set of leader behaviors is always associated with leadership success.* Often the degree to which leaders need to exhibit task- or people-oriented behaviors depends on the situation, and this finding prompted the research underlying the contingency theories of leadership described in Chapter 13. If you review these theories, you will see strong links to the job- and employee-centered behaviors identified 50 years ago.

The Leadership Grid

The Ohio State and University of Michigan studies were good first steps in describing what leaders actually do. Other researchers have extended these findings into more user-friendly formats or developed different schemes for categorizing leadership behaviors. Like the earlier research, these alternative conceptualizations are generally concerned with identifying key leadership behaviors, determining whether these behaviors have positive relationships with leadership success, and helping people develop behaviors related to leadership success. One popular conceptualization of leadership is really an extension of the findings reported by the University of Michigan and Ohio State leadership researchers. The **Leadership Grid**® profiles leader behavior on two dimensions: **concern for people** and **concern for production**.[23,24] The word *concern* reflects how a leader's underlying assumptions about people at work and the importance of the bottom line affect leadership style. In that sense, then, the Leadership Grid deals with more than just behavior. Nonetheless, it is included in this chapter because it is such a direct descendant of earlier behavioral studies.

As Figure 7.2 shows, leaders can get scores ranging from 1 to 9 on both concern for people and concern for production depending on their responses to a leadership questionnaire. These two scores are then plotted on the Leadership Grid, and the two score combinations represent different leadership orientations. Each orientation reflects a unique set of assumptions for using power and authority to link people to production.[23] Amid the different leadership styles, the most effective leaders are claimed to have both high concern for people and high concern for production, and Leadership Grid training programs are designed to move leaders to a 9,9 leadership style. Whereas this objective seems intuitively appealing, where do you think the Supreme Leader of North Korea, Kim Jong-Il, or the Secretary-General of the United Nations, Ban Ki-Moon, score on these two dimensions? Do both of them show a high concern for production and people? Are there differences between the two leaders, or are both 9,9 leaders?

Although the Leadership Grid can be useful for describing or categorizing different leaders, we should note that the evidence to support the assertion that 9,9 leaders are the most effective comes primarily from Blake, Mouton, and their associates. However, other more recent research might shed some light on whether 9,9 leaders are really the most effective. Robie, Kanter, Nilsen, and Hazucha studied 1,400 managers in the United States, Germany, Denmark, the United Kingdom, Italy, Spain, France, and Belgium to determine whether the same leadership behaviors were related to effectiveness across countries. They reported that leadership behaviors associated with problem solving and driving for results (initiating structure or 9,1 leadership) were consistently related to successfully building teams, influencing a group to accomplish its goals, and getting results,

FIGURE 7.2
The Leadership Grid

Source: Robert R. Blake and Anne Adams McCanse, *Leadership Dilemmas—Grid Solutions* (Houston: Gulf Publishing, 1991), p. 29. Copyright 1991. Reprinted with permission of Grid International

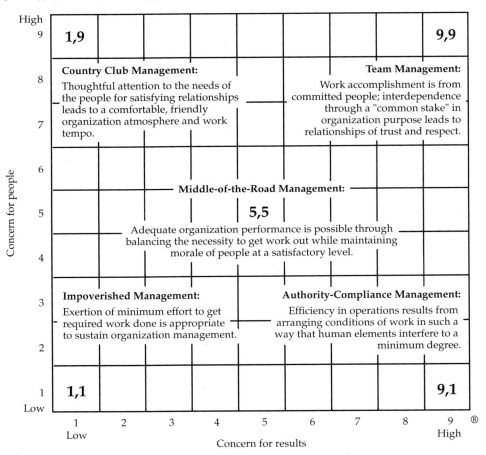

regardless of country.[25] Similar results about initiating structure and job performance were reported by Judge, Piccolo, and Ilies.[21] Using 800 managers in a U.S. high-tech firm, Goff reported that managers who spent more time building relationships (consideration or 1,9 leadership) also had more satisfied followers who were less likely to leave the organization.[26] Likewise, other researchers reported strong support for the notion that higher consideration behavior can reduce employee turnover.[21,22] These results seem to indicate that the most effective leadership style might depend on the criteria used to judge effectiveness. The context and style of leaders' behavior are also factors that affect their ability to build teams and get results through others (see Highlights 7.1 and 7.2).

Critical Leadership Behaviors in Wartime

HIGHLIGHT 7.2

It is likely that the behaviors needed to build teams and get results during peacetime and wartime operations may be different for officers in the U.S. military. A study sponsored by the Commanding General, U.S. Army Training and Doctrine Command, asked researchers to determine the critical behaviors leaders need to exhibit to build teams and get results while conducting Operation Iraqi Freedom (OIF). The researchers conducted extensive interviews with and administered surveys to 77 officers who had recently returned from OIF and asked them to identify the most important behaviors leaders need to exhibit when operating in a battlefield environment. Some of the most important behaviors leaders need to exhibit during wartime include these:

- Adapts quickly to new situations and requirements.
- Keeps cool under pressure.
- Clearly explains missions, standards, and priorities.
- Sees the big picture; provides context and perspective.
- Sets high standards with a "zero defects" mentality.

- Can handle "bad news."
- Gets out of headquarters and visits the troops.
- Sets a high ethical tone; demands honest reporting.
- Knows how to delegate and not "micromanage."
- Can make tough, sound decisions on time.
- Builds and supports teamwork within staff and among units.
- Is positive, encouraging, and reasonably optimistic.

Having identified these critical leadership behaviors, the U.S. Army is now conducting training to develop these behaviors *before* sending leaders over to Iraq. Although the U.S. Army should be commended for training its officers to exhibit these behaviors, are they all that different from the behaviors associated with effective leadership in peacetime?

Source: W. J. Ulmer Jr., M. D. Shaler, R. C. Bullis, D. F. DiClemente, and T. O. Jacobs, *Leadership Lessons at Division Command Level—2004*, report prepared under the direction of the U.S. Army War College, November 2004.

I don't do quagmires ... I don't do diplomacy ... I don't do foreign policy ... I don't do predictions ... I don't do numbers ...

Donald Rumsfeld, former U.S. Secretary of Defense

Competency Models

So far in this section we have described several ways to categorize leaders or leadership behaviors, but what are the implications of this research for leadership practitioners? Believe it or not, you can see the practical application of this leadership behavior research in just about every Global 1,000 company. **Competency models** describe the behaviors and skills managers need to exhibit if an organization is to be successful.[2,27-34] Just as leaders in different countries may need to exhibit behaviors uniquely appropriate to each setting to be successful, different businesses and industries within any country often emphasize different leadership behaviors. Therefore, it is not unusual to see different organizations having distinct competency models depending on the nature and size of each business, its business model, its level of globalization, and the role of technology or teams in the business.[6,27,28,30,35,36] An example of a typical competency model for middle managers can be found in Figure 7.3.

FIGURE 7.3
An Example of a Leadership Competency Model

Source: G. J. Curphy, K. Louiselle, and S. Bridges, *Talent Assessment Overview: 360-Degree Feedback Report* (Eagan, MN: Advantis Research & Consulting, 2003).

Rank	Competency
	Analyzing problems and making decisions: Effectively analyzes issues and makes sound, logical business decisions in a timely manner.
	Thinking strategically: Brings a broad perspective to bear on issues and problems (e.g., considers information from different industries, markets, competitors); deliberately evaluates strategic "fit" of possible decisions and actions.
	Financial and technical savvy: Demonstrates strong technical and financial knowledge when resolving customer, operational, and/or financial problems. Makes sound customer, operational, and financial trade-offs.
	Planning and organizing: Establishes clear goals and action plans, and organizes resources to achieve business outcomes.
	Managing execution: Directs and monitors performance, and intervenes as appropriate to ensure successful achievement of business objectives.
	Inspiring aligned purpose: Successfully engages people in the mission, vision, values, and direction of the organization; fosters a high level of motivation.
	Driving change: Challenges the status quo and looks for ways to improve team or organizational performance. Champions new initiatives and stimulates others to make changes.
	Building the talent base: Understands the talent needed to support business objectives (e.g., qualifications, capabilities); identifies, deploys, and develops highly talented team members.
	Fostering teamwork: Creates an environment where employees work together effectively to achieve goals.
	Creating open communications: Communicates clearly and creates an environment in which important issues are shared.
	Building relationships: Develops and sustains effective working relationships with direct reports, peers, managers, and others; demonstrates that maintaining effective working relationships is a priority.
	Customer focus: Maintains a clear focus on customer needs; demonstrates a strong desire to provide exemplary customer service; actively seeks ways to increase customer satisfaction.
	Credibility: Earns others' trust and confidence; builds credibility with others through consistency between words and actions and follow-through on commitments.
	Personal drive: Demonstrates urgency in meeting objectives and achieving results; pursues aggressive goals and persists to achieve them.
	Adaptability: Confidently adapts and adjusts to changes and challenges; maintains a positive outlook and works constructively under pressure.
	Learning approach: Proactively identifies opportunities and resources for improvement.

Many of the best organizations now have competency models for different levels of management. For example, the behaviors and skills needed by department supervisors, store managers, district managers, regional vice presidents, and division presidents at The Home Depot vary considerably, and these differences are reflected in the competency models for each management group. These models help to clarify expectations of performance for people in different leadership positions and describe the skills necessary for promotion. They also help human resource professionals design selection, development, performance management, and succession planning programs so organizations have a steady supply of leadership talent.[2,4,5,7,28,30,37-42]

According to Hogan and Warrenfelz, the skills and behaviors found in virtually every organizational competency model fall into one of four major categories. **Intrapersonal skills** are leadership competencies and behaviors having to do with adapting to stress, goal orientation, and adhering to rules. These skills and behaviors do not involve interacting with others, and they are among the most difficult to change. **Interpersonal skills** are those that involve direct interaction, such as communicating and building relationships with others. These skills are somewhat easier to develop. **Leadership skills** are skills and behaviors concerned with building teams and getting results through others, and these are more easily developed than the skills and behaviors associated with the first two categories. Finally, competencies concerned with analyzing issues, making decisions, financial savvy, and strategic thinking fall into the **business skills** category. These skills and competencies are often the focus of MBA programs and are among the easiest to learn of the four categories. The Hogan and Warrenfelz domain model of leadership competencies is important because it allows people to see connections between seemingly different organizational competency models and makes predictions about how easy or difficult it will be to change various leadership behaviors and skills.[41]

The Hogan and Warrenfelz model is also important because it points out what behaviors leaders need to exhibit to build teams and get results through others. Because organizational competency models are more alike than different, the behaviors needed to build teams and get results are fairly universal across organizations. Leaders wanting to build high-performing teams need to hire the right people, effectively cope with stress, set high goals, play by the rules, and hold people accountable. They also need to communicate and build relationships with others. Effective leaders also get followers involved in decisions, fairly distribute workloads, develop talent, keep abreast of events that could affect the team, and make sound financial and operational decisions. Thus competency models provide a sort of recipe for leaders wanting to build teams and get results in different organizations. Many of these leadership behaviors may be fairly universal across industries, but there may also be some important differences by company and leadership level. Ancona, Malone,

Does Humor Matter?

HIGHLIGHT 7.3

Leaders exhibit many kinds of behavior. Some are focused on task accomplishment, whereas others are more related to supporting followers. Some leaders are naturally funny, and others seem stern and humorless. Does a leader's sense of humor affect his or her ability to build teams, influence others, or get results? Researchers have examined this question and discovered the answer is not a simple yes or no. The effectiveness of humor seems to depend on the context, the outcomes leaders are trying to achieve, and the leadership style used. Laissez-faire leaders (1,1) who used humor reported having more satisfied followers but did not have higher-performing work groups. Task-focused leaders (9,1) who used humor actually had less satisfied and lower-performing work units. Apparently their use of humor seemed out of sync with their constant focus on goal setting, productivity, and cost-cutting initiatives.

Transformational leaders (9,9) and leaders with high levels of emotional intelligence who used humor seemed to have higher-performing work groups. The key lesson from this research appears to be that the impact of a leader's humor depends on the leader's style and the context in which it is delivered. Task-focused leaders should be keenly attuned to followers' needs when the company is facing an economic downturn or a difficult organizational dilemma, and should also be aware that the use of humor in these situations will probably have the opposite effect as intended.

Sources: B. J. Avolio, J. M. Howell, and J. J. Sosik, "A Funny Thing Happened on the Way to the Bottom Line: Humor as a Moderator of Leadership Style Effects," *Academy of Management Journal* 42, no. 2 (1999), pp. 219–27; F. Sala, "Laughing All the Way to the Bank," *Harvard Business Review,* September 2003, pp. 16–17; E. J. Romero and K. W. Cruthirds, "The Use of Humor in the Workplace." *Academy of Management Perspectives* 20, no. 2 (2006), pp. 58–69.

Orlikowski, and Senge aptly point out that most leaders don't possess all the skills listed in many competency models, but effective leaders are those who understand their strengths and have learned how to staff around the areas in which they are less skilled.[43] And longitudinal research has shown that the relative importance of certain competencies has changed over time. For example, building relationships, administrative/organizational skills, and time management skills have grown considerably more important over the past 15–20 years.[44] These results are not surprising when one considers the impact on managerial work of technology, globalization, and organizational restructuring and delayering.

The Leadership Pipeline

We started this chapter by exploring the notion that there was a universal set of behaviors associated with leadership effectiveness. Yet research shows that initiating structure, interactional facilitation, and 9,9 leadership can be important in some situations and relatively unimportant in others. Situational and follower factors play important roles in determining the relative effectiveness of different leadership behaviors, and researchers and human resource professionals have created competency models to describe the behaviors needed by leaders in particular jobs and companies. Leaders heading up virtual teams of people located around the globe or working in sales versus manufacturing organizations may need to exhibit different types of behaviors to be effective, and competency models are useful in capturing these differences. Although globalization, the industry, and the functional area affect the type of leadership behaviors needed, another factor that impacts leadership behavior is **organizational level.** For example, the behaviors first-line supervisors need to manifest to keep a group of call center employees motivated and on task differ from those a chief executive officer needs to exhibit when meeting a group of investors or running company business strategy sessions. Although both types of leaders need to build teams and get results through others, the types of teams they lead and the results they need to obtain are so dramatically different that they exhibit very different types of behaviors.

The **Leadership Pipeline** is a useful model for explaining where leaders need to spend their time, what they should be focusing on and what they should be letting go, and the types of behaviors they need to exhibit as they move from first-line supervisor to functional manager to chief executive officer.[45] The pipeline also describes the lessons people should learn as they occupy a particular organizational level and the challenges they will likely face as they transition to the next level. As such, this model provides a type of road map for people wanting to occupy the top leadership positions in any organization. And because people at different organizational levels need to exhibit different behaviors, many companies have created competency models to describe the behaviors needed to be successful at different organizational levels. According to the Leadership Pipeline model, the most effective leaders are those who can accurately diagnose the organizational level of their job and then exhibit behaviors commensurate with this level. The pipeline also provides potential explanations for why some people fail to advance: these individuals may not be focusing on the right things or may be exhibiting leadership behaviors associated with lower organizational levels.

A depiction of the seven organizational levels and their competency requirements, time application, and work values can be found in Table 7.2. The items listed in Table 7.2 correspond to a large for-profit organization; smaller for-profit or nonprofit organizations may not have all these levels. Nonetheless, the Leadership Pipeline provides a useful framework for thinking about how leadership competencies change as people are promoted through organizations.

According to the model, many people who fail to demonstrate the competencies, work values, and time applications commensurate with their positions will struggle with building teams and getting results through others. For example, functional leaders who have not given up acting like first-line supervisors and spend a lot of time coaching and monitoring the performance of the individual contributors not only have no time to build a vision

TABLE 7.2 The Leadership Pipeline

Source: R. Charan, S. Drotter, and J. Noel, *The Leadership Pipeline: How to Build the Leadership-Powered Company* (San Francisco: Jossey-Bass, 2001).

Organizational Level	Competency Requirements	Time Applications	Work Values
Individual contributor	Technical proficiency. Using company tools. Build relationships with team members.	Meet personal due dates. Arrive/depart on time.	Get results through personal proficiency. High-quality work. Accept company values.
First-line supervisor	Planning projects. Delegating work. Coaching and feedback. Performance monitoring.	Annual budget planning. Make time available for followers. Set priorities for team.	Get results through others. Success of followers. Success of the team.
Midlevel manager	Select, train, and manage first-line supervisors. Manage boundaries and deploy resources to teams.	Monitor performance of each team. Make time to coach first-line supervisors.	Appreciate managerial versus technical work. Developing first-line supervisors.
Functional leader	Manage the whole function. Communicate with and listen to everyone in the function. Make subfunction trade-offs. Interact with other functions.	Determine three-year vision for the function. Interact with business unit leader's team.	Clarify how the function supports the business. Value all subfunctions.
Business unit leader	Build cross-functional leadership team. Financial acumen. Balance future goals with short-term business needs.	Develop three-year vision for the business unit. Monitor financial results. Effectively manage time.	Value all staff functions. Value organizational culture and employee engagement.
Group manager	Manage business portfolio. Allocate capital to maximize business success. Develop business unit leaders.	Develop strategies for multiple business units. Monitor financial results for multiple businesses. Interact with CEO's team.	Value the success of all the business units. Interact with internal and external stakeholders.
CEO or enterprise leader	Analyze and critique strategy. Manage the entire company and multiple constituencies. Deliver predictable business results. Set company direction. Create company culture. Manage the board of directors.	Manage external stakeholders. Spend significant time reviewing financial results. Spend significant time doing strategic planning.	Value a limited set of key long-term objectives. Value advice from board of directors. Value inputs from a wide variety of stakeholders.

and manage the function; they also disempower the first-line supervisors and midlevel managers in their function. So one key to having a successful career is exhibiting competencies appropriate for your current organizational level and then letting go of these competencies and learning new ones when moving up the organizational ladder. Charan, Drotter, and Noel maintain that transitioning from individual contributor to first-line supervisor and from functional to business unit leader are the two hardest transitions for people.[45] It is difficult for people who have spent all their time

Indra Nooyi

PROFILES IN LEADERSHIP 7.3

PepsiCo is commonly acknowledged as having one of the best leadership talent management systems in the world. Pepsi's talent management systems make extensive use of competency models, 360-degree feedback tools, personality and intelligence assessments, in-basket simulations, and unit performance indexes. One of the people who has benefited from this in-depth assessment and development is Indra Nooyi. Nooyi is currently the chief executive officer of PepsiCo and is ranked by *Forbes* as the fourth most powerful woman in the world and the most powerful businesswoman in the world. Nooyi grew up in India and received an undergraduate degree from Madras Christian College and a postgraduate diploma in management from the Indian Institute in Management. She also has a degree from the Yale School of Management. While in college Nooyi fronted an all-female rock band, and she is refreshingly funny and candid when speaking in public. In May 2005 Nooyi started a controversy when she spoke to Columbia Business School graduates and said the United States "must be careful that when we extend our arm in either a business or a political sense, we take pains to ensure we are giving a hand … not the finger."

Before emigrating to the United States in 1978, Nooyi was a product manager for Johnson and Johnson and the textile firm Mettur Beardsell in India. Her first job after graduating from Yale was to work as a consultant with The Boston Consulting Group. She then took senior leadership positions at Motorola and Asea Brown Boveri before moving to PepsiCo in 1994. While at Pepsi Nooyi played a vital role in the spinoff of Tricon, which is now known as Yum! Brands Inc. (Taco Bell and Kentucky Fried Chicken are some of the franchises in Yum! Brands Inc.) She also took the lead in Pepsi's acquisition of Tropicana and Quaker Oats in the late 1990s. Nooyi was promoted to chief financial officer in 2001 and to the CEO position in 2006. As the head of PepsiCo, Nooyi heads up a company of 157,000 employees that generate $35 billion in annual revenues through the worldwide sales of products such as Pepsi, Mountain Dew, Tropicana, Gatorade, Aquafina, Dole, Lipton, Doritos, Ruffles, Lays, Quaker Oats, Life cereal, and Rice-A-Roni. Under Nooyi, Pepsi has developed new products and marketing programs through the liberal use of cross-cultural advisory teams.

Given Pepsi's global reach and emphasis on brand management, Nooyi's background seems well-suited for a recent leadership challenge. In 2006 a group of individuals in India claimed that both Coke and Pepsi products were tainted with pesticides. Later investigations disproved these allegations, but the surrounding publicity damaged Pepsi's brand in a large, developing market. Nooyi is now working hard to restore the Indian public's confidence in the safety of PepsiCo's products.

How do you think Indra Nooyi's career matches up to the Leadership Pipeline? What lessons do you think she learned as she traveled through the Leadership Pipeline that help her be a more effective CEO for Pepsico?

Sources: http://www.forbes.com/lists/2006/11/06/women_ Indra-Nooyi; http://www.Pepsico.com/PEP; http://www.businessweek.com/investor/content/aug2006/pi20060814; http://www.hoovers.com/pepsico.

selling to customers or writing code to transition to managing the people who do this work and for people whose entire career has been in sales or IT to manage, value, and leverage the work done by other functions.

Another career implication of this model is worth mentioning: people who skip organizational levels often turn out to be ineffective leaders. For example, it is not unusual for organizations to offer jobs to consultants. A consultant may have been called in to fix a particularly difficult problem, such as implementing a new sales initiative or IT program, and because the solution was so successful he or she is asked to join the company. The problem is that many of these job offers are for functional or business unit leader types of roles, and to a large extent consultants have spent their entire careers doing nothing but individual contributor–level work. Because consultants may have never formally led a team or managed multiple teams or functions, they continue to exhibit those behaviors they got rewarded for in the first place, which is individual contributor–level work. No matter how good these former consultants are at doing individual contributor work, these jobs they are put in are much too big for them to do all the sales calls, write all the computer code, or the like. If they do not adjust their leadership behaviors to fit the demands of the position, they quickly burn out and will be asked to pursue other options. So if your career aspirations include leading a function, business unit, or company, you need to think through the sequence of positions that will give you the right experiences and teach you the right competencies needed to prepare you for your ultimate career goal.

> *Never doubt that a group of thoughtful, committed citizens can change the world. Indeed, it is the only thing that ever has.*
> **Margaret Mead, anthropologist**

Community Leadership

Although organizational competency models have played a pervasive role in selecting, developing, and promoting government and business leaders, they have not been used much in community leadership. **Community leadership** is the process of building a team of volunteers to accomplish some important community outcome and represents an alternative conceptualization of leadership behavior.[46-48] Examples of community leadership might include forming a group to raise funds for a new library, gathering volunteers for a blood drive, or organizing a campaign to stop the construction of a Walmart. Thus community leadership takes place whenever a group of volunteers gets together to make something happen (or not happen) in their local community.

But leading a group of volunteers is very different from being a leader in a publicly traded company, the military, or a nongovernment agency. For one thing, community leaders do not have any position power; they cannot discipline followers who do not adhere to organizational norms, get tasks accomplished, or show up to meetings. They also tend to have fewer resources and rewards than most other leaders. And because there is no

FIGURE 7.4
The Components of Community Leadership

Source: J. Krile, G. Curphy, and D. Lund, *The Community Leadership Handbook: Framing Ideas, Building Relationships, and Mobilizing Resources* (St. Paul, MN: Fieldstone Alliance, 2006).

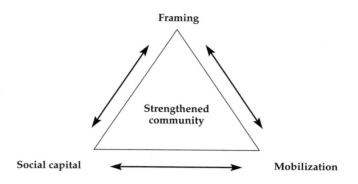

formal selection or promotion process, anyone can be a community leader. But whether such leaders succeed in their community change efforts depends on three highly interrelated competencies (see Figure 7.4). Just as you need the three ingredients of oxygen, fuel, and an igniter to start a fire, so do you need the three competencies of framing, building social capital, and mobilization to successfully drive community change efforts.

Framing is the leadership competency of helping a group or community recognize and define its opportunities and issues in ways that result in effective action. Framing helps the group or community decide *what* needs to be done, *why* it is important that it be done, and *how* it is to be done, and communicate that in clear and compelling ways. Any community could take on myriad potential projects, but many of these projects never get off the ground because the person "in charge" never framed the project in such a way that others could understand the outcome, how they would benefit by the outcome, and what they must do to achieve the outcome.

Building social capital is the leadership competency of developing and maintaining relationships that allow people to work together in the community across their differences. Just as financial capital allows individuals to make choices about what they can purchase, such as buying a new television, car, or house, social capital allows a community leader to make choices about which community change initiatives or projects are likely to be successful. If you have little money, your options are severely limited. Likewise, leaders lacking social capital will have a difficult time getting anything done in their communities because they will not be able to mobilize the resources necessary to turn their vision into reality. Social capital is the power of relationships shared between individuals, between an individual and a group, or between groups.

Engaging a critical mass to take action to achieve a specific outcome or set of outcomes is the leadership competency of **mobilization.** Community leaders will have achieved a critical mass when they have enough human and other resources to get what they want done. People, money, equipment, and facilities are often needed to pass bond issues or attract new businesses to a community. Mobilization is strategic, planned purposeful activity to achieve clearly defined outcomes. Almost anyone can get resources moving, but it takes leadership to get enough of the right resources moving toward the same target.

How would the community leadership model come into play if you wanted to have a new student union built on your campus? First, you would need to frame the issue in such a way that other students understood what was in it for them and what they would need to do to make a new student union become reality. Second, you would need to reach out and build relationships with all of the current and potential users of the new student union. You would need to identify the formal and informal leaders of the different user groups and meet with them to gain and maintain their trust. Third, you would need these different user groups to take action to get the new student union built. Some of these actions might

Father Greg Boyle

PROFILES IN LEADERSHIP 7.4

Father Greg Boyle grew up in a family of eight children in the Los Angeles area. Working on his father's dairy farm while growing up, Father Greg opted to become a Jesuit after graduating from high school and was ordained as a minister in 1984. After graduating with degrees from Gonzaga University, Loyola Marymount University, and Wheaton College, he spent several years teaching high school, running a mission in Los Angeles, and serving as a chaplain for Folsom Prison and Islas Marias Penal Colony in Mexico. It was while Father Greg was a pastor at the Dolores Mission in Los Angeles that he started Jobs for the Future (JFF), a program designed to keep gang-involved youths out of trouble. JFF involved developing positive alternatives, establishing an elementary school and day care centers, and providing jobs for disadvantaged youth.

Partly as a result of the civil unrest in Los Angeles in 1992, Father Greg started the first of several Homeboy businesses. Homeboy Bakery was created to teach gang-involved youths life and work skills and how to work side-by-side with rival gang members. Other businesses started by Father Greg include Homeboy Silkscreen, Homeboy Maintenance, Homeboy/Homegirl Merchandise, and Homegirl Café. All of these businesses provide needed business, conflict resolution, and teamwork skills to gang members who are eager to leave the streets.

Homeboy Industries has run as a nonprofit organization since 2001 and has expanded several times to keep up with the increasing demand for its services. The organization currently serves over 1,200 people as either employees or participants in its many outreach programs. Although Homeboy Industries generates revenues, it does not generate enough cash to fund all of its programs. In the past any shortfalls between revenues and costs were covered by donations and speaking fees. The economic recession has severely reduced these funding sources, and Homeboy Industries may have to close its doors unless some alternative funds can be found. The organization appealed to the City of Los Angeles for $15,000,000 in funding but was turned down because of the city's own financial crisis. Nonetheless, the City of Los Angeles managed to find $65,000,000 to give to its new Museum of Modern Art.

Where do the concepts of framing, social capital, and mobilization come into play with the startup or turnaround of Homeboy Industries? What skills does Father Greg possess that help him build teams and achieve results? Where do you think public money is better spent—keeping 1,200 gang members off the street or funding a new museum?

Source: http://www.homeboy-industries.org; T. Gross, "Interview with Greg Boyle," *Fresh Air*, May 21, 2010.

include raising funds, making phone calls, canvassing students to sign petitions, mounting a publicity campaign, and meeting with university and state officials who are the key decision makers about the issue.

It is worth noting that you need to do all three of the community leadership components well if you are to build teams of volunteers and successfully accomplish community outcomes. You might be able to succinctly frame the issue, but if you lacked social capital or could not get a critical mass mobilized, you would probably not get far in building the new student union. The same would be true if you had a broad and well-established network of students but did not frame the issue in such a way that followers could take action. It is likely that as many community change efforts fail as succeed, and the reasons for failure often have to do with inadequate framing, social capital, or mobilization. These three components are critical when it comes to building teams of volunteers and achieving community goals.

Assessing Leadership Behaviors: Multirater Feedback Instruments

One way to improve leader effectiveness is to give leaders feedback regarding the frequency and skill with which they perform various types of leadership behaviors. A $200 million industry has developed over the past three decades to meet this need. This is the **360-degree,** or **multirater, feedback** instrument industry, and it is difficult to overestimate its importance in management development both in the United States and overseas. Jack Welch, the former CEO of General Electric, has stated that these tools have been critical to GE's success.[49] Practically all of the Global 1,000 companies are using some type of multirater feedback instrument for managers and key individual contributors.[2,6,7,8,50-58] Multirater feedback instruments have been translated into 16 different languages, and well over 5 million managers have now received feedback on their leadership skills and behaviors from these instruments.[50] Because of the pervasiveness of multirater feedback in both the public and private sectors, it will be useful to examine some issues surrounding these instruments.

Many managers and human resource professionals have erroneously assumed that a manager's self-appraisal is the most accurate source of information regarding leadership strengths and weaknesses. This view has changed, however, with the introduction of multirater feedback instruments. These tools show that direct reports, peers, and superiors can have very different perceptions of a leader's behavior, and these perspectives can paint a more accurate picture of the leader's strengths and development needs than self-appraisals alone (see Figures 7.5 and 7.6). A manager may think he or she gets along well with others, but if 360-degree feedback ratings from peers and direct reports indicate that the manager is difficult to work with, the manager should gain new insights on what to do to

FIGURE 7.5
Sources for 360-Degree Feedback

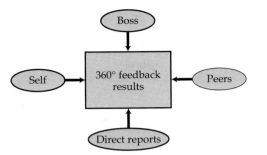

improve his or her leadership effectiveness. Prior to the introduction of 360-degree instruments, it was difficult for managers to get accurate information about how others perceived their on-the-job behaviors because the feedback they received from others in face-to-face meetings tended to be adulterated or watered down.[2,5,6,50-60] Moreover, the higher one goes in an organization, the less likely one is to ask for feedback, which results in bigger discrepancies between self and other perceptions.[2,60-62] And as described in Chapter 6, many of the most frequent behaviors exhibited by leaders are rooted in personality traits and occur almost automatically; as a result many leaders do not understand or appreciate their impact on others. It was difficult for managers to accurately determine their leadership strengths and development needs until the advent of 360-degree feedback instruments. Today most organizations use 360-degree tools as an integral part of the training, coaching, succession planning, and performance management components of a comprehensive leadership talent management system.[2,50,52,53,56,58]

Given the pervasive role 360-degree feedback plays in many organizations today, it is not surprising that there has been an extensive amount of research on the construction, use, and impact of these tools. Much of this research has explored how to use competency models to build effective 360-degree questionnaires, whether 360-degree feedback matters, whether self–observer perceptual gaps matter, whether leaders' ratings can improve over time, and whether there are meaningful culture/gender/race issues with 360-degree feedback ratings. With respect to the first issue, researchers have reported that the construction of 360-degree feedback questionnaires is very important. Poorly conceived competency models and ill-designed questionnaire items can lead to spurious feedback results, thus depriving managers of the information they need to perform at a higher level.[2,34,53,54,63] In terms of whether 360-degree feedback matters, a number of researchers have held that leaders who received 360-degree feedback had higher-performing work units than leaders who did not receive this type of feedback. These results indicate that 360-degree feedback ratings do matter.[2,64-73] But a study of 750 firms by Watson-Wyatt, a human resource consulting firm, reported that companies that used

FIGURE 7.6
Example of 360-Degree Feedback.

Source: K. Louiselle, G. J. Curphy, and S. Bridges, *C3 360-Degree Feedback Report* (Eagan, MN: Advantis Research and Consulting, 2003). Reprinted with permission of Advantis Research and Consulting.

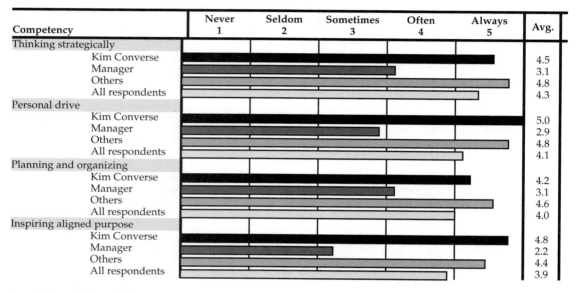

Competency	Never 1	Seldom 2	Sometimes 3	Often 4	Always 5	Avg.
Thinking strategically						
Kim Converse						4.5
Manager						3.1
Others						4.8
All respondents						4.3
Personal drive						
Kim Converse						5.0
Manager						2.9
Others						4.8
All respondents						4.1
Planning and organizing						
Kim Converse						4.2
Manager						3.1
Others						4.6
All respondents						4.0
Inspiring aligned purpose						
Kim Converse						4.8
Manager						2.2
Others						4.4
All respondents						3.9

Inspiring Aligned Purpose

Successfully engages people in the mission, vision, values, and direction of the organization; fosters a high level of motivation.

Average Ratings for Each Item and Respondent Type

Items	Self	Manager	Others	All Respondents
1. Communicates a compelling vision of the future.	5.0	1.0	4.5	3.8
2. Provides a clear sense of purpose and direction for the team.	5.0	3.0	4.3	4.0
3. Sets challenging goals and expectations.	5.0	4.0	4.5	4.4
4. Fosters enthusiasm and buy-in for the direction of the team/organization.	5.0	1.0	4.8	4.0
5. Supports initiatives of upper management through words and actions.	4.0	2.0	4.0	3.2

360-degree feedback systems had a 10.6 percent decrease in shareholder value.[74] Although this research provides strong evidence that 360-degree feedback may not "work," it is important to note how these systems were being used in these firms. For the most part, Pfau and Kay examined firms using 360-degree feedback for performance appraisal, not development purposes. This distinction is important because most 360-degree feedback systems are not designed to make comparisons *between* people. Instead these systems are designed to tell leaders about their own relative strengths and development needs. But because 360-degree feedback tools are data based and provide good development feedback, many organizations have decided to modify the process for performance appraisal purposes. This can be a mistake: many 360-degree feedback tools used in performance appraisals are poorly constructed and often result in such inflated ratings that the resulting feedback no longer differentiates between high, average, and low-level performers. The end result is a costly, time-intensive performance appraisal system that has little if any benefit to the individual or the boss and yields organizational results similar to those reported by Watson-Wyatt. The bottom line is that 360-degree feedback systems can add tremendous value, but only if they are well-conceived and constructed.[2,50,53,54,56-58,64,73,75]

As stated earlier, one advantage of 360-degree feedback is that it provides insight into self-perceptions and others' perceptions of leadership skills. But do self–observer gaps matter? Are leaders more effective if they have a high level of insight—that is, if they rate their strengths and weaknesses as a leader the same as others do? As depicted in Figure 7.6, some level of disagreement is to be expected because bosses, peers, and direct

Facebook, MySpace, and Online Personas

HIGHLIGHT 7.4

Social networking sites such as Facebook and MySpace have made it much easier for people to connect with others. In an effort to attract attention, many entries on these sites contain highly personal information about sexual practices, drug and alcohol use, philosophies toward life and work, and so on. Some of this information may be true and some just hyperbole, but all of it is in the public domain. The bad news is that companies are now searching these same sites and eliminating applicants based on their online personae. An interesting exercise is to identify a critical leadership position and define the organizational level, key competencies, time application, and work values needed to do this position. Then pick out four or five random online personae from MySpace and determine whether you would hire any of these individuals if they had applied for the position. Now look at your own online persona (if you have one). Would you get hired if an organization were looking for a competent manager to fill this position? What should carry more weight in determining a person's leadership potential—work experiences and education or online persona?

Source: Adapted from Alan Finder, "For Some, Online Persona Undermines Résumé," *The New York Times,* June 11, 2006.

In many cases the only person who is surprised by his or her 360-degree feedback results is the feedback recipient.

**Dianne Nilsen,
PDI-Ninth House**

reports may have different expectations for a leader. Nevertheless, insight does not seem to matter for leadership effectiveness. Even leaders with large self–observer gaps were effective as long as they had high observer ratings. On the other hand, the least effective leaders were those with high self and low others' ratings. The important lesson here is that leadership is in the eyes of others. And the key to high observer ratings is to develop a broad set of leadership skills that will help groups to accomplish their goals.[1,76-80]

Another line of research has looked at whether 360-degree feedback ratings improve over time. In other words, is it possible to change others' perceptions of a leader's skills? One would hope that this would be the case, given the relationship between others' ratings and leadership effectiveness. Walker and Smither reported that managers who shared their 360-degree feedback results with their followers and worked on an action plan to improve their ratings had a dramatic improvement in others' ratings over a five-year period.[81] Johnson and Johnson looked at 360-degree ratings over a two-year period and reported leadership productivity improvements of 9.5 percent for 515 managers in a manufacturing company.[82] A more recent article reviewed the findings from 24 different studies and concluded that 360-degree feedback ratings do change over time, but the amount of change tends to be small.[55] Other researchers aptly point out that 360-degree feedback alone is not a panacea to improve leadership skills. In addition to gaining insight from 360-degree feedback, leaders must also create a set of development goals and commit to a development plan if they want to see improvement in others' ratings (and, in turn, leadership effectiveness) over time.[2,50,81-85]

The last line of research has explored whether there are important cultural, racial, or gender issues with 360-degree feedback. In terms of cultural issues, some countries, such as Japan, do not believe peers or followers should give leaders feedback.[85,86] Other countries, such as Saudi Arabia, tend more to avoid conflict and provide only positive feedback to leaders. The latter phenomenon also appears in the United States, where researchers working in small organizations or in rural communities often report similar findings. People seem more hesitant to give leaders constructive feedback if they have to deal with the consequences of this feedback both at and away from work. These findings further support the notion that 360-degree feedback is not a management panacea; societal or organizational culture plays a key role in the accuracy and utility of the 360-degree feedback process.[2,4,32,33,50,52,60,74,86]

With respect to racial differences, a comprehensive study by Mount, Sytsma, Hazucha, and Holt looked at the pattern of responses from bosses, peers, and subordinates for over 20,000 managers from a variety of U.S. companies. In general, these researchers reported that blacks tended to give higher ratings to other blacks, irrespective of whether they were asked to provide peer, subordinate, or boss ratings. However, the overall size of this effect was small. White peers and subordinates generally gave about the same level of ratings to both black and white peers and bosses. This was not the case for white bosses, however, who tended to give significantly higher ratings to whites who reported directly to them. These findings imply that black leaders are likely to advance at a slower pace than their white counterparts because 80–90 percent of salary, bonus, and promotion decisions are made solely by bosses.[87,88]

With respect to gender issues, research indicates that there are some slight gender differences. Female managers tend to get higher ratings on the majority of skills, yet their male counterparts are generally perceived as having higher advancement potential. There does not appear to be any same-sex bias in 360-degree feedback ratings, and female managers tend to be lower self-raters. Male managers tend to have less accurate self-insight and more blind spots when compared to their female counterparts. In summary, male and female 360-degree feedback ratings are similar, and any differences are of little practical significance.

What should a leadership practitioner take away from this 360-degree feedback research? First, given the popularity of the technique, it is likely that you will receive 360-degree feedback sometime in your career. Second, 360-degree feedback should be built around a competency model, which will describe the leadership behaviors needed to achieve organizational goals. Third, the organization may have different competency models to reflect the different leadership behaviors needed to succeed at different organizational levels. Fourth, 360-degree feedback may be one of the best sources of "how" feedback for leadership practitioners. Leaders tend to get plenty of "what" feedback—what progress they are making toward group goals, what level of customer service is being achieved, win–loss records, and so on; but they get little feedback on how they should act to get better results. Multirater instruments provide feedback on the kinds of things leaders need to do to build cohesive, goal-oriented teams and get better results through others. Fifth, effective leaders seem to have a broad set of well-developed leadership skills—they do not do just one or two things well and do everything else poorly. Instead they seem to possess a broad array of leadership strengths. Sixth, leaders need to create specific goals and development plans in order to improve leadership skills—360-degree feedback results give leaders ideas on what to improve but may not be enough in and of themselves to affect behavioral change. Seventh, leadership behavior can change over time, but it may take a year or two to acquire new skills and for the changes to be reflected in 360-degree feedback ratings. Finally, some cultural, racial, and gender issues are associated with 360-degree feedback, and practitioners should be aware of these issues before implementing any 360-degree feedback process.[56,73,88,89]

Summary

People in leadership positions exhibit a wide variety of behaviors, and researchers have explored whether there is a universal set of behaviors that differentiates effective from ineffective leaders or if there are situational or follower factors that impact the types of behavior needed to build teams or get results through others. To answer the first question, there does not appear to be a universal set of leadership behaviors that guarantees success across many or all situations. Although some types of task and relationship-oriented leadership behaviors will likely improve the odds of success, the nature of the work to be performed, the situation, and the number and types of followers affect the specific kinds of task and relationship behaviors leaders need to demonstrate to be effective. Chapter 12 describes a much more comprehensive list of the situational factors affecting leadership behavior, but some of the key situational factors reviewed in this chapter include the setting (community or organization) and organizational level. Competency models and 360-degree feedback can be used to describe how well someone is performing the behaviors needed to succeed in a particular position.

Leadership practitioners need to realize that they will ultimately be judged by the results they obtain and the behaviors they exhibit. Yet prior experience, values, and attributes play critical roles in how leaders go about building teams and achieving results through others. For example, leaders who move into roles that involve solving complex business problems but lack relevant experience, analytic intelligence, and strong commercial values will struggle to be successful, and those with the opposite characteristics are much more likely to succeed. Having the right attributes, values, and experience does not guarantee that leaders will exhibit the right behaviors, but this improves the odds considerably.

This chapter offers some vital yet subtle suggestions on how to be effective as a leader. First, people moving into leadership roles need to understand the performance expectations for their positions. These expectations not only include the results to be achieved; they also include the behaviors that need to be exhibited. Organizational levels and competency models can help leaders determine the specific types of behaviors required to build teams and get results through others for the position in question. These frameworks also describe the behavioral changes leaders will need to make as they transition into new roles.

Second, understanding the behavioral requirements of various leadership positions and exhibiting needed behaviors can be two quite different things. That being the case, 360-degree feedback can give leaders insight into whether they need to do anything differently to build stronger teams or get better results through others. Although getting feedback from others can be an uncomfortable experience, this information is vital if people want to succeed as leaders. 360-degree feedback makes the process of getting feedback from others more systematic and actionable, and as such it is an important tool in the development of leaders.

Third, getting feedback from others in and of itself may not result in behavioral change. For example, many people know they need to lose weight, yet they may not do anything about it. But if they build a plan that includes a modified diet and regular exercise and get regular feedback and encouragement from others, they are much more likely to lose weight. The same holds true for changing leadership behaviors. Building development plans and getting coaching from others will improve the odds of changing targeted behaviors or acquiring needed skills, so leaders who want to be more effective should have written development plans.

Key Terms

Leader Behavior Description Questionnaire (LBDQ), 247
consideration, 247
initiating structure, 247
job-centered dimensions, 247
leadership behavior, 248
leadership skill, 248
goal emphasis, 248
work facilitation, 248
employee-centered dimensions, 248

leader support, 248
interaction facilitation, 248
Leadership Grid, 250
concern for people, 250
concern for production, 250
competency models, 252
intrapersonal skills, 254
interpersonal skills, 254
leadership skills, 254

business skills, 254
organizational levels, 256
Leadership Pipeline, 256
community leadership, 259
framing, 260
building social capital, 260
mobilization, 260
360-degree or multirater feedback, 262

Questions

1. Could you create a competency model for college professors? For college students? If you used these competency models to create 360-degree feedback tools, who would be in the best position to give professors and students feedback?

2. What competencies would be needed by a U.S.-born leader being assigned to build power plants in China? What competencies would be needed by a Chinese-born leader being assigned to run a copper mine in Kenya?

3. What are the competencies needed to be an effective U.S. senator? A famous musician or actor? How are these competencies similar or different?

4. Is the U.S.-based Tea Party movement an example of community leadership? Why or why not?

Activities

1. Identify two leadership positions and then determine the relative importance of the 16 competencies shown in Figure 7.3. You can do this by ranking each competency in order of importance, with the most important competency being assigned a 1, the second most important a 2, and so on. If you do this exercise with several partners ranking the same positions, does everyone give the 16 competencies about the same ranking? Why or why not?

2. Collect competency models from two organizations and assign them to the intrapersonal, interpersonal, leadership, and business categories described by Hogan and Warrenfelz. Do the competencies fit easily into the four categories? Which categories seem to be underrepresented or overrepresented by the competency models?

3. Identify two leadership positions at your school and determine their organizational levels using the Leadership Pipeline.

4. Given the model of community leadership described earlier in this chapter, analyze an ongoing community change initiative. Has the leader framed the issue in a way that makes it easy for others to take action? Do the group members have strong bonds with other groups? Have they created a plan and mobilized a critical mass of people and resources to make the change become reality?

Minicase

Paying Attention Pays Off for Andra Rush

Paying attention has been a key for Andra Rush. As a nursing school graduate she was paying attention when other nurses complained about unfair treatment and decided she wanted to do something about it—so she enrolled in the University of Michigan's MBA program so she could do something about how employees were treated. As she completed her business courses and continued to work as a nurse, she was paying attention when a patient described his experience in the transport business. The business sounded intriguing, and so, with minimal experience and minimal resources, Rush took a risk and started her own trucking business. She scraped together the funds to buy three trucks by borrowing money from family and using her credit cards. She specialized in emergency shipping and accepted every job that came her way, even if it meant driving the trucks herself. She answered phones, balanced her books, and even repaired the trucks. She paid attention to her customers and made a point of exceeding their expectations regardless of the circumstances. When the terrorist attacks of September 11, 2001, shut down local bridges, Rush rented a barge to make sure a crucial shipment for DaimlerChrysler made it to its destination on time.

Rush continues to pay attention and credits her listening skills as a major reason for her success. Rush is distinct in the traditionally white male–dominated trucking industry—a woman and a minority (Rush is Native American) who credits her heritage and the "enormous strength" of her Mohawk grandmother for helping her prevail:

> It is entirely possible that my Native spirit, communicated to me by my grandmother and my immediate family, have enabled me to overcome the isolation, historical prejudice, and business environment viewed as a barrier to Native- and woman-owned businesses. The willingness to listen, to understand first, and act directly and honestly with integrity is a lesson and code of conduct my elders have bequeathed to me. Being an entrepreneur has reinforced those lessons again and again.

Her Mohawk heritage is pervasive. Rush's company logo is a war staff with six feathers representing the Six Nations of the Iroquois: Mohawk, Onondaga, Oneida, Cayuga, Tuscarora, and Seneca. She believes in the power of a diverse workforce; as a result more than half of the 390 employees at Rush Trucking are women, and half are minorities.

Rush keeps close tabs on her company and its employees. Though the company has grown from its humble three-truck beginning to a fleet of 1,700 trucks, Rush still takes time to ride along with drivers. She has provided educational programs like "The Readers' Edge," a literacy program, to improve the skills and lives of her employees. Rush is actively involved in several organizations that work to improve the position of minorities—she's on the boards of directors of the Michigan Minority Business Development Council, the Minority Enterprise Development/Minority Business Development Agency, and the Minority Business Roundtable, and she has served as president of the Native American Business Alliance.

1. As we have discussed, competency models describe the behaviors and skills managers need to exhibit if an organization is to be successful. Consider the general competencies found in Figure 7.3 and apply these to Andra Rush, providing examples of how these competencies apply.
2. How does the Leadership Pipeline apply to Andra Rush?
3. Andra Rush belongs to several volunteer organizations. Would her leadership style need to change as the president of the Native American Business Alliance versus the CEO of Rush Trucking? How would the Community Leadership Model apply to Andra Rush?

Sources: http://www.inc.com/magazine/20040401/25rush.html; http://www.crains detroit.com/cgi-bin/page.pl?pageId=400; http://www.readfaster.com/pr20030912.pdf; http://www.turtle-tracks.org/issue41/i41_3.html; http://www.indiancountry. com/?2224.

End Notes

1. G. J. Curphy, "In-Depth Assessments, 360-Degree Feedback, and Development: Key Research Results and Recommended Next Steps," presentation at the Annual Conference for HR Managers at US West Communications, Denver, CO, January 1998.

2. G. J. Curphy, "What Role Should I/O Psychologists Play in Executive Education?" in *Models of Executive Education*, R. T. Hogan (chair). Presentation given at the 17th Annual Society for Industrial and Organizational Psychology, Toronto, Canada, April 2002.

3. G. J. Curphy, "Leadership Transitions and Teams," presentation given at the Hogan Assessment Systems International Users Conference, Istanbul, September 2003.

4. G. J. Curphy, "The Consequences of Managerial Incompetence," presentation given at the 3rd Hogan Assessment Systems International Users Conference, Prague, Czech Republic, September 2004.

5. G. J. Curphy, "Comments on the State of Leadership Prediction," in *Predicting Leadership: The Good, The Bad, the Indifferent, and the Unnecessary*, J. P. Campbell and M. J. Benson (chairs). Symposium conducted at the 22nd Annual Conference for the Society of Industrial and Organizational Psychology, New York, April 2007.

6. G. J. Curphy and M. E. Roellig, *Followership*, unpublished manuscript (North Oaks, MN: Author, 2010).

7. G. J. Curphy and R. T. Hogan, "What We Really Know about Leadership (But Seem Unwilling to Implement)," working paper, 2004.

8. R. T. Hogan and G. J. Curphy, *Leadership Effectiveness and Managerial Incompetence*, unpublished manuscript, 2007.

9. R. Charan and G. Colvin, "Why CEOs Fail," *Fortune*, June 21, 1999, pp. 69–82.

10. M. Goldsmith and M. Reiter, *What Got You Here Won't Get You There* (New York: Hyperion, 2007).

11. J. K. Hemphill, "The Leader and His Group," *Journal of Educational Research* 28 (1949), pp. 225–29, 245–46.

12. J. K. Hemphill and A. E. Coons, "Development of the Leader Behavior Description Questionnaire," in *Leader Behavior: Its Description and Measurement*, ed. R. M. Stogdill and A. E. Coons (Columbus: Ohio State University, Bureau of Business Research, 1957).

13. E. A. Fleishman, "Twenty Years of Consideration and Structure," In *Current Developments in the Study of Leadership*, ed. E. A. Fleishman and J. G. Hunt (Carbondale: Southern Illinois University Press, 1973).

14. A. W. Halpin and B. J. Winer, "A Factorial Study of the Leader Behavior Descriptions," in *Leader Behavior: Its Descriptions and Measurement*, ed. R. M. Stogdill and A. E. Coons (Columbus: Ohio State University, Bureau of Business Research, 1957).

15. E. A. Fleishman, *Examiner's Manual for the Supervisory Behavior Description Questionnaire* (Washington, DC: Management Research Institute, 1972).

16. E. A. Fleishman, *Examiner's Manual for the Leadership Opinion Questionnaire*, rev. ed. (Chicago: Science Research Associates, 1989).

17. R. M. Stogdill, *Individual Behavior and Group Achievement* (New York: Oxford University Press, 1959).

18. R. Likert, *New Patterns of Management* (New York: McGraw-Hill, 1961).

19. D. G. Bowers and S. E. Seashore, "Predicting Organizational Effectiveness with a Four Factor Theory of Leadership," *Administrative Science Quarterly* 11 (1966), pp. 238–63.

20. B. M. Bass, *Bass and Stogdill's Handbook of Leadership*, 3rd ed. (New York: Free Press, 1990).

21. T. A. Judge, R. F. Piccolo, and R. Ilies, "The Forgotten Ones? The Validity of Consideration and Initiating Structure in Leadership Research," *Journal of Applied Psychology* 89, no. 1 (2004), pp. 36–51.

22. R. Eisenberger, F. Stinglhamber, C. Vandenberghe, I. L. Sucharski, and L. Rhoades, "Perceived Supervisor Support: Contributions to Perceived Organizational Support and Employee Retention," *Journal of Applied Psychology* 87, no. 3 (2002), pp. 565–73.

23. R. R. Blake and A. A. McCanse, *Leadership Dilemmas—Grid Solutions* (Houston, TX: Gulf, 1991).

24. R. R. Blake and J. S. Mouton, *The Managerial Grid* (Houston, TX: Gulf, 1964).

25. C. Robie, K. Kanter, D. L. Nilsen, and J. Hazucha, *The Right Stuff: Understanding Cultural Differences in Leadership Performance* (Minneapolis, MN: Personnel Decisions International, 2001).

26. M. Goff, *Critical Leadership Skills Valued by Every Organization* (Minneapolis, MN: Personnel Decisions International, 2001).

27. S. Davis, J. Volker, R. C. Barnett, P. H. Batz, and P. Germann, *Leadership Matters: 13 Roles of High Performing Leaders* (Minneapolis, MN: MDA Leadership Consulting, 2006).

28. G. P. Hollenbeck, M. W. McCall, and R. F. Silzer, "Leadership Competency Models," *The Leadership Quarterly* 17 (2006), pp. 398–413.

29. L. Tischler, "IBM's Management Makeover," *Fast Company*, November 2004, pp. 112–16.

30. P. Lievens, J. I. Sanchez, and W. DeCorte, "Easing the Inferential Leap in Competency Modeling: The Effects of Task-Related Information and Subject Matter Expertise," *Personnel Psychology* 57 (2004), pp. 881–904.

31. A. W. King, S. W. Fowler, and C. P. Zeithaml, "Managing Organizational Competencies for Competitive Advantage: The Middle-Management Edge," *Academy of Management Executive* 15, no. 2 (2001), pp. 95–106.

32. G. J. Curphy, *The Blandin Education Leadership Program* (Grand Rapids, MN: The Blandin Foundation, 2004).

33. Ibid.

34. G. J. Curphy and R. T. Hogan, "Managerial Incompetence: Is There a Dead Skunk on the Table?" Working paper, 2004.

35. D. Ulrich, J. Zenger, and N. Smallwood, *Results-Based Leadership* (Boston: Harvard Business School Press, 1999).

36. D. B. Peterson, "Making the Break from Middle Manager to a Seat at the Top," *The Wall Street Journal*, July 7, 1998.

37. R. B. Kaiser and S. B. Craig, *Testing the Leadership Pipeline: Do the Behaviors Related to Managerial Effectiveness Change with Organizational Level?* Presentation given at the 1st Annual Leading Edge Consortium, St Louis, MO, 2008.

38. K. Louiselle, S. Bridges, and G. J. Curphy, "Talent Assessment Overview." Working paper, 2003.

39. S. H. Gebelein, "360-Degree Feedback Goes Strategic," *PDI Portfolio,* Summer 1996, pp. 1–3.

40. J. S. Shippmann, R. A. Ash, M. Battista, L. Carr, L. D. Eyde, B. Hesketh, J. Kehoe, K. Pearlman, E. P. Prien, and J. I. Sanchez, "The Practice of Competency Modeling," *Personnel Psychology* 53, no. 3 (2000), pp. 703–40.

41. R. T. Hogan and R. Warrenfelz, "Educating the Modern Manager," *Academy of Management Learning and Education* 2, no. 1 (2003), pp. 74–84.

42. A. H. Church, "Talent Management," *The Industrial-Organizational Psychologist* 44, no. 1 (2006), pp. 33–36.

43. D. Ancona, T. W. Malone, W. J. Orlikowski, and P. M. Senge, "In Praise of the Incomplete Leader," *Harvard Business Review,* February 2007, pp. 92–103.

44. W.A. Gentry, L.S. Harris, B.A. Becker, and J.B. Leslie, "Managerial Skills: What Has Changed since the Late 1980s," *Leadership & Organizational Development Journal* 29, no. 2 (2008), pp. 167–81.

45. R. Charan, S. Drotter, and J. Noel, *The Leadership Pipeline: How to Build the Leadership-Powered Company* (San Francisco: Jossey-Bass, 2001).

46. J. Krile, G. J. Curphy, and D. Lund, *The Community Leadership Handbook: Framing Ideas, Building Relationships and Mobilizing Resources* (St Paul, MN: Fieldstone Alliance, 2005).

47. B. C. Crosby and J. M. Bryson, "Integrative Leadership and the Creation and Maintenance of Cross-Sector Collaborations," *The Leadership Quarterly* 21 (2010), pp. 211–30.

48. J. E. Bono, W. Shen, and M. Snyder, "Fostering Integrative Community Leadership," *The Leadership Quarterly* 21 (2010), pp. 324–35.

49. N. M. Tichy and E. Cohen, *The Leadership Engine: How Winning Companies Build Leaders at Every Level* (New York: HarperCollins, 1997).

50. D. P. Campbell, G. J. Curphy, and T. Tuggle, *360-Degree Feedback Instruments: Beyond Theory.* Workshop presented at the 10th Annual Conference of the Society for Industrial and Organizational Psychology, Orlando, FL, May 1995.

51. G. J. Curphy, "Executive Integrity and 360-Degree Feedback," in *Assessing Executive Failure: The Underside of Performance,* R. T. Hogan (chair). Symposium presented at the 18th Annual Conference of the Society of Industrial and Organizational Psychology, Orlando, FL, 2003.

52. G. Toegel and J. A. Conger, "360-Degree Assessment: Time for Reinvention," *Academy of Management Learning and Education* 2, no. 3, pp. 297–311.

53. R. B. Kaiser and S. B. Craig, "Building a Better Mousetrap: Item Characteristics Associated with Rating Discrepancies in 360-Degree Feedback," *Consulting Psychology Journal* 57, no. 4 (2005), pp. 235–45.

54. F. Morgeson, T. V. Mumsford, and M. A. Campion, "Coming Full Circle: Research and Practice to Address 27 Questions about 360-Degree Feedback Programs," *Consulting Psychology Journal* 57, no. 3 (2005), pp. 196–209.

55. J. W. Smither, M. London, and R. R. Reilly, "Does Performance Improve Following Multisource Feedback? A Theoretical Model, Meta-analysis, and Review of Empirical Findings," *Personnel Psychology* 58 (2005), pp. 33–66.

56. K. M. Nowack, "Leveraging Multirater Feedback to Facilitate Successful Behavioral Change," *Consulting Psychology Journal: Practice and Research* 61, no. 4 (2009), pp. 280–97.

57. J. E. Bono and A. E. Colbert, "Understanding Responses to Multi-Source Feedback: The Core of Self-Evaluations," *Personnel Psychology* 58 (2005), pp. 171–203.

58. D. W. Bracken, C. W. Timmreck, and A. H. Church, *The Handbook of Multisource Feedback* (San Francisco: Jossey-Bass, 2000).

59. P. W. B. Atkins and R. E. Wood, "Self-Versus Others' Ratings as Predictors of Assessment Center Ratings: Validation Evidence for 360-Degree Feedback Programs," *Personnel Psychology* 55 (2002), pp. 871–84.

60. G. J. Curphy, "Some Closing Remarks about the Use of Self- and Other-Ratings of Personality and Behaviors," in *Multirater Assessment Systems: What We've Learned*, M. D. Dunnette (chair). Symposium conducted at the 99th American Psychological Association Convention, San Francisco, August 1991.

61. J. M. Jackman and M. H. Strober, "Fear of Feedback," *Harvard Business Review*, April 2003, pp. 101–8.

62. M. A. Peiperl, "Getting 360-Degree Feedback Right," *Harvard Business Review*, January 2001, pp. 142–48.

63. F. Sala, "Executive Blind Spots: Discrepancies between Self- and Other-Ratings," *Consulting Psychology Journal* 55, no. 4 (2003), pp. 222–29.

64. S. B. Craig and K. Hannum, "Research Update: 360-Degree Performance Assessment," *Consulting Psychology Journal* 58, no. 2 (2006), pp. 117–24.

65. D. Antonioni, "360-Degree Feedback for a Competitive Edge," *Industrial Management* 42 (2000), pp. 6–10.

66. F. Sala and S. A. Dwight, "Predicting Executive Performance with Multirater Surveys: Whom You Ask Makes a Difference," *Consulting Psychology Journal* 55, no. 3 (2003), pp. 166–72.

67. G. J. Curphy, "An Empirical Investigation of Bass' (1985) Theory of Transformational and Transactional Leadership," PhD dissertation, University of Minnesota, 1991.

68. G. J. Curphy, "The Effects of Transformational and Transactional Leadership on Organizational Climate, Attrition, and Performance," in *Impact of Leadership*, ed. K. E. Clark, M. B. Clark, and D. P. Campbell (Greensboro, NC: Center for Creative Leadership, 1992).

69. A. H. Church, "Managerial Self-Awareness in High-Performing Individuals in Organizations," *Journal of Applied Psychology* 82, no. 2 (1997), pp. 281–92.

70. A. H. Church, "Do Higher Performing Managers Actually Receive Better Ratings?" *Consulting Psychology Journal* 52, no. 2 (2000), pp. 99–116.

71. J. Ghorpade, "Managing Six Paradoxes of 360-Degree Feedback," *Academy of Management Executive* 14, no. 1 (2000), pp. 140–50.

72. G. J. Greguras, C. Robie, D. J. Schleicher, and M. Goff III, "A Field Study of the Effects of Rating Purpose on the Quality of Multisource Ratings," *Personnel Psychology* 56, no. 1 (2003), pp. 1–22.

73. A. H. Church and J. Waclawski, "A Five-Phase Framework for Designing a Successful Multisource Feedback System," *Consulting Psychology Journal* 53, no. 2 (2001), pp. 82–95.

74. K. Pfau, "Does 360-Degree Feedback Negatively Affect Company Performance?" *HR Magazine,* June 2002, pp. 55–59.

75. G. J. Curphy, *Afterburner 360 Training Manual* (North Oaks, MN: Curphy Consulting Corporation, 2003).

76. G. J. Greguras and C. Robie, "A New Look at Within-Source Interrater Reliability of 360-Degree Feedback Ratings," *Journal of Applied Psychology* 83, no. 6 (1998), pp. 960–68.

77. M. K. Mount, T. A. Judge, S. E. Scullen, M. R. Sytsma, and S. A. Hezlett, "Trait, Rater, and Level Effects in 360-Degree Performance Ratings," *Personnel Psychology* 51, no. 3 (1998), pp. 557–77.

78. C. Ostroff, L. E. Atwater, and B. J. Feinberg, "Understanding Self-Other Agreement: A Look at Rater and Ratee Characteristics, Context, and Outcomes," *Personnel Psychology* 57, no. 2 (2004), pp. 333–76.

79. L. E. Atwater, C. Ostroff, F. J. Yammarino, and J. W. Fleenor, "Self–Other Agreement: Does It Really Matter?" *Personnel Psychology* 51, no. 3 (1998), pp. 577–98.

80. J. W. Fleenor, C. D. McCauley, and S. Brutus, "Self-Other Rating Agreement and Leader Effectiveness," *Leadership Quarterly* 7, no. 4 (1996), pp. 487–506.

81. A. Walker and J. W. Smither, "A Five-Year Study of Upward Feedback: What Managers Do with Their Results Matters," *Personnel Psychology* 52, no. 2 (1999), pp. 395–423.

82. K. Johnson and J. Johnson, *Economic Value of Performance Change after 360-Degree Feedback* (Minneapolis, MN: Personnel Decisions International, 2001).

83. G. J. Curphy, *Role of the Supervisor Training Manual* (North Oaks, MN: Curphy Consulting Corporation, 2007).

84. J. W. Smither, M. London, R. Flautt, Y. Vargas, and I. Kucine, "Can Working with an Executive Coach Improve Multisource Feedback Ratings over Time? A Quasi-Experimental Field Study," *Personnel Psychology* 56, no. 1 (2003), pp. 23–44.

85. W. W. Tornow and M. London, *Maximizing the Value of 360-Degree Feedback* (San Francisco: Jossey-Bass, 1998).

86. J. S. Chhokar, F. C. Brodbeck, and R. J. House, *Culture and Leadership across the World: The Globe Book of In-Depth Studies of 25 Societies* (Mahwah, NJ: Lawrence Erlbaum Associates, 2007).

87. M. K. Mount, M. R. Sytsma, J. F. Hazucha, and K. E. Holt, "Rater–Ratee Effects in Development Performance Ratings of Managers," *Personnel Psychology* 50, no. 1 (1997), pp. 51–70.

88. H. J. Bernardin and R. W. Beatty, *Performance Appraisal: Assessing Human Behavior at Work* (Boston: Kent, 1984).

89. Personnel Decisions International, *PROFILOR® Certification Workshop Manual* (Minneapolis, MN: Author, 2007).

Chapter  8

Skills for Building Personal Credibility and Influencing Others

In this second chapter dealing with leadership skills, our focus is on some of the most "basic" skills with which almost every leader should be equipped:

- Building credibility.
- Communication.
- Listening.
- Assertiveness.
- Conducting meetings.
- Effective stress management.
- Problem solving.
- Improving creativity.

Building Credibility

Interviews with thousands of followers as well as the results of over half a million 360-degree feedback reports indicate that credibility may be one of the most important components of leadership success and effectiveness.[1,2] Employees working for leaders they thought were credible were willing to work longer hours, felt more sense of ownership in the company, felt more personally involved in work, and were less likely to leave the company over the next two years.[3] Given the difficulties companies are having finding and retaining talented leaders and workers and the role intellectual capital and bench strength play in organizational success, it would appear that credibility could have a strong bottom-line impact on many organizations. Credibility is a little like leadership in that many people have ideas about what credibility is, but there is little consensus on one "true" definition of credibility. This section will define what we believe credibility is, present the two components of credibility, and explore what leadership practitioners can do (and avoid doing) if they want to build their credibility.

The Two Components of Credibility

Credibility can be defined as the ability to engender trust in others. Leaders with high levels of credibility are seen as trustworthy; they have a strong sense of right and wrong, stand up and speak up for what they believe in, protect confidential information, encourage ethical discussions of business or work issues, and follow through with commitments. Sometimes dishonest leaders, personalized charismatic leaders, or power wielders can initially be seen by followers as credible, but their selfish and self-serving interests usually come to light over time. Credibility is made up of two components: expertise and trust. Followers will not trust leaders if they feel they do not know what they are talking about. Similarly, followers will not trust leaders if they feel confidential information will be leaked, if their leaders are unwilling to take stands on moral issues, or if their leaders do not follow through on their promises. Much about these two components of credibility has already been discussed in the Chapter 3 sections "Building Technical Competence," "Building Effective Relationships with Superiors," and "Building Effective Relationships with Peers." What follows is a brief overview of these three skills as well as some additional considerations that can help leaders build their credibility.

Building Expertise

Expertise consists of technical competence as well as organizational and industry knowledge, so building expertise means increasing your knowledge and skills in these three areas. Building technical competence, described earlier in this section, concerns increasing the knowledge and repertoire of behaviors you can bring to bear to successfully complete a task. To build technical competence, leadership practitioners must determine how their jobs contribute to the overall mission of the company or organization, become an expert in those jobs through formal training or teaching others, and seek opportunities to broaden their technical expertise.

Nonetheless, building expertise takes more than just technical competence. Leaders also need to understand the company and the industry they are in. Many followers not only want leaders to coach them on their skills—they also look to their leaders to provide some context for organizational, industry, and market events. Building one's organizational or industry knowledge may be just as important as building technical competence. However, the ways in which leadership practitioners build these two knowledge bases is somewhat different from building technical competence. Building technical competence often takes more of a hands-on approach to development, but it is hard to do this when building organizational or industry knowledge. One way to build your organizational or industry knowledge is by regularly reading industry-related journals, annual reports, *The Wall Street Journal, Fortune, Inc.,* or various Web sites. Many leaders spend 5–10 hours a week building their industry and organizational knowledge using this approach. Getting a mentor or being coached by your boss is another way to build such knowledge. Other leadership practitioners have taken stretch assignments where they work on special projects with senior executives. Often these assignments allow them to work closely with executives, and through this contact they better understand the competitive landscape, the organization's history and business strategies, and organizational politics. The bottom line is that your learning is not over once you have obtained your degree. In many ways, it will have just started.

Finally, remember that expertise is more than experience. As noted previously, some leaders get one year's worth of experience out of five years' work, whereas others get five years' worth of experience from one year's work. Leaders who get the most from their experience regularly discuss what they have been learning with a partner, and they frequently update their development plans as a result of these discussions.

Building Trust

The second component of credibility is building trust, which can be broken down into clarifying and communicating your values, and building relationships with others. In many ways leadership is a moral exercise. For example, one key difference between charismatic and transformational leaders is that the latter base their vision on their own and their followers' values, whereas the former base their vision on their own possibly selfish needs. Having a strong values system is an important component both in the building blocks model of skills and in leadership success. Because of the importance of values and relationships in building trust, the remainder of this section explores these two topics in more depth.

Chapter 5 defined *values* as constructs representing generalized behaviors or states of affairs that are considered by the individual to be important. Provided that leaders make ethical decisions and abide by organizational rules, however, differences in values among leaders and followers may be difficult to discern. People do not come to work with their values marked on their foreheads, so others typically make inferences about leaders' values based on their day-to-day behaviors. Unfortunately, in many cases leaders' day-to-day behaviors are misaligned with their personal values; they are not living their work lives in a manner consistent with their values.

An example of a leader not living according to his values might be illustrative. An executive with an oil and gas firm was responsible for all drilling operations in western Canada. Because he felt the discovery of new oil and gas fields was the key to the company's long-term success, he worked up to 18 hours a day, pushed his followers to work similar hours, had little patience for and would publicly disparage any oil rig operators who were behind schedule, and almost fired a manager who gave one of his followers a week off to see the birth of his son back in the United States. As these behaviors continued over time, more and more of his followers either requested transfers or quit to join other companies. Because of these problems with turnover and morale, he was asked to participate in a formal coaching program. Not surprisingly, his 360-degree feedback showed that his boss, peers, and followers found him difficult to work with. These results indicated that he put a premium on getting ahead and economic rewards; yet when he was asked to name the things he felt were most important to him as a leader, his priorities were his family, his religion, getting along with others, and developing his followers (altruism). Obviously there was a huge gap between what he truly believed in and how he behaved. He felt the company expected him to hold people's feet to the fire and get results no matter what the cost, yet neither his boss nor his peers felt that this was the case. The executive had misconstrued the situation and was exhibiting behaviors that were misaligned with his values.

Although this case is somewhat extreme, it is not unusual to find leaders acting in ways that are misaligned with their personal values. One way to assess the degree to which leaders are living according to their personal values is by asking what they truly believe in and what they spend their time and money on. For example, you could write down the five things you believe most strongly in (your top five values) and then review your calendar, daytimer, checkbook, and credit card statements to determine where you spend your time and money. If the two lists are aligned, you are likely living according to your values. If not, you may be living according to how others think you should act. And if there is some discrepancy between the two lists, what should you do? Of course some discrepancy is likely to occur because situational demands and constraints can influence how we behave. On the other hand, large discrepancies between the lists may indicate that you are not living consistently with your values, and those you interact with may infer that you have a different set of values than those you believe in. A good first step in clarifying such a discrepancy is to craft a personal mission statement or a leadership credo that describes what you truly believe in as a leader.

Examples of different leadership credos for managers across corporate America can be found in Highlight 8.1. Several aspects of leadership credos are worth additional comment. First, leadership credos are personal and are closely linked with a leader's values—a credo should describe what the leader believes in and will or will not stand for. Second, it should also describe an ideal state. A leader's behavior may never be perfectly aligned with his or her personal mission statement, but it should be a set of day-to-day behaviors that he or she will strive to achieve. Third, leadership

Sample Leadership Credos

HIGHLIGHT 8.1

As a leader, I . . .

. . . believe in the concept of whole persons and will seek to use the full range of talents and abilities of colleagues whenever possible.

. . . will seek to keep people fully informed.

. . . will more consistently express appreciation to others for a job well done.

. . . will take risks in challenging policies or protocol when they do not permit us to effectively serve our customers.

. . . will selectively choose battles to fight—rather than trying to fight all of the possible battles.

. . . will actively support those providing the most effective direction for our company.

. . . will seek to change the things I can in a positive direction and accept those things I have no chance or opportunity to change.

Source: *Impact Leadership* (Minneapolis: Personnel Decisions International, 1995).

credos should be motivating; leaders should be passionate and enthusiastic about the kind of leader they aspire to be. If the leader does not find his or her personal mission statement to be particularly inspiring, then it is hard to see how followers will be motivated by it. Much of the inspiration of a leadership credo stems from its being personal and values-based. Fourth, personal mission statements should be made public. Leaders need to communicate their values to others, and a good way to do this is to display their leadership credos prominently in their offices. This not only lets others know what you as a leader think is important; it also is a form of public commitment to your leadership credo.

Another key way to build trust is to form strong relationships with others. There is apt to be a high level of mutual trust if leaders and followers share strong relationships; if these relationships are weak, the level of mutual trust is apt to be low. Techniques for building relationships with peers and superiors have already been described in this section of the text. Perhaps the best way to build relationships with followers is to spend time listening to what they have to say. Because many leaders tend to be action-oriented and are paid to solve (rather than listen to) problems, some leaders overlook the importance of spending time with followers. Yet leaders who take the time to build relationships with followers are much more likely to understand their followers' perspectives on organizational issues, intrinsic motivators, values, levels of competence for different tasks, and career aspirations. Leaders armed with this knowledge may be better able to influence and get work done through others. More about building relationships with followers can be found in Chapter 11 under "Coaching."

Expertise × Trust

Leaders vary tremendously in their levels of both expertise and trust, and these differences have distinct implications for leaders wanting to improve

FIGURE 8.1
The Credibility Matrix

Source: G. J. Curphy, *Credibility: Building Your Reputation throughout the Organization* (Minneapolis: Personnel Decisions International, 1997).

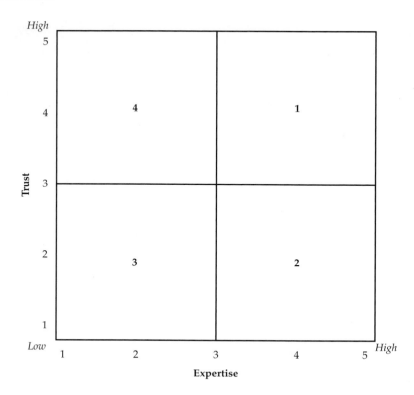

their credibility. Consider leaders who are in the first quadrant of Figure 8.1. These individuals have a high level of trust and a high level of expertise; they would likely be seen by others as highly credible. Individuals in the second quadrant might include leaders who have spent little time with followers, who do not follow through with commitments, or who are new to the organization and have had little time to build relationships with co-workers. In all three cases, leaders wanting to improve their credibility should include building relationships with co-workers as key development objectives. Leaders in the third quadrant may be new college hires or people joining the company from an entirely different industry. It is unlikely that either type of leader would have the technical competence, organizational or industry knowledge, or time to build relationships with co-workers. These leaders may be in touch with their values and have a personal mission statement, but they will need to share their statement with others and act in a manner consistent with this statement to build their credibility. Other development objectives could include building expertise and strong relationships with others. Leaders in the fourth quadrant might include those promoted from among peers or transferring from another department within the company. Both sets of leaders may be in touch with their values, have a leadership credo, share strong relationships with co-workers, and have organizational and industry knowledge, but the former may need to develop leadership knowledge or skills and the latter technical competence if they wish to increase their credibility. Finally, note that leaders who do not strive to live up to their ideals or fail to follow through with their developmental commitments are likely to be seen as less trustworthy than those who do.

Communication

Bass[4] has defined *communication effectiveness* as the degree to which someone tells others something and ensures that they understand what was said. In a more general sense, effective communication involves the ability to transmit and receive information with a high probability that the intended message is passed from sender to receiver. Few skills are more vital to leadership. Studies show that good leaders communicate feelings and ideas, actively solicit new ideas from others, and effectively articulate arguments, advocate positions, and persuade others.[5-7] It seems likely the same can be said of good followers, though far less study has gone into that question. Moreover, the quality of a leader's communication is positively correlated with subordinate satisfaction[8] as well as with productivity and quality of services rendered.[9] Effective communication skills are also important because they give leaders and followers greater access to information relevant to important organizational decisions.[10]

A systems view of communication is depicted in Figure 8.2. Communication is best understood as a process beginning with an intention to exchange certain information with others. That intention eventually takes form in some particular expression, which may or may not adequately convey what was intended. The next stage is reception. Just as with a weak or garbled radio signal or malfunctioning antenna, what is received is not always what was sent. Reception is followed by interpretation. If a driver asks, "Do I turn here?" and a passenger answers, "Right," did the passenger mean *yes* or *turn right*? Finally, it is not enough merely to receive and interpret information; others' interpretations may or may not be consistent with what was intended at the outset. Therefore, it always helps to have a feedback loop to assess any communication's overall effectiveness.

We also can use the scheme in Figure 8.2 to think about the knowledge, behaviors, and criteria used to evaluate communication skills. According to this model, the knowledge component of communication skills concerns the intentions of the leader, knowing what medium is most effective, and knowing whether the message was heard and understood. The behavioral component of communication skills concerns the behaviors associated with communicating verbally and nonverbally. Feedback concerning whether the message was understood by the receiver constitutes

FIGURE 8.2
A Systems View of Communication

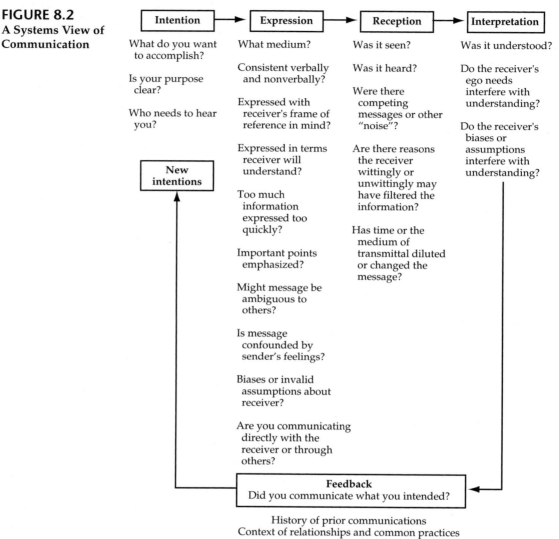

Intention	Expression	Reception	Interpretation

Intention

What do you want to accomplish?

Is your purpose clear?

Who needs to hear you?

Expression

What medium?

Consistent verbally and nonverbally?

Expressed with receiver's frame of reference in mind?

Expressed in terms receiver will understand?

Too much information expressed too quickly?

Important points emphasized?

Might message be ambiguous to others?

Is message confounded by sender's feelings?

Biases or invalid assumptions about receiver?

Are you communicating directly with the receiver or through others?

Reception

Was it seen?

Was it heard?

Were there competing messages or other "noise"?

Are there reasons the receiver wittingly or unwittingly may have filtered the information?

Has time or the medium of transmittal diluted or changed the message?

Interpretation

Was it understood?

Do the receiver's ego needs interfere with understanding?

Do the receiver's biases or assumptions interfere with understanding?

New intentions

Feedback
Did you communicate what you intended?

History of prior communications
Context of relationships and common practices
Concurrent events

the evaluative component of communication skills. An important aspect of feedback is that it is an outcome of the previous steps in the communication process. In reality, the effectiveness of the communication process depends on the successful integration of all the steps in the communication process. Effectiveness in just one step (such as speaking ability) is not enough. Successful communication needs to be judged in terms of the effective operation of the whole system.

The model also suggests a number of reasons why communication breakdowns might occur. For example, communication can break down because the purpose of the message was unclear, the leader's or follower's verbal and nonverbal behaviors were inconsistent, the message was not heard by the receiver, or someone may have misinterpreted the message. Most people see themselves as effective communicators, and senders and receivers of messages often seem disposed to believe communication breakdowns are the other person's fault. Communication breakdowns often lead to blaming someone else for the problem, or "finger pointing" (see Figure 8.3). One way to avoid the finger pointing associated with communication breakdowns is to think of communication as a process, not as a set of discrete individual acts (such as giving instructions to someone). By using the communication model, leadership practitioners can minimize the conflict typically associated with communication breakdowns.

The model in Figure 8.2 can give leadership practitioners many ideas about how to improve communication skills. They can do so by determining the purpose of their communication before speaking, choosing an appropriate context and medium for the message, sending clear signals, and actively ensuring that others understand the message. The following is a more detailed discussion of some different ways in which leaders can improve their communication skills.

Know What Your Purpose Is

You will communicate more effectively with others if you are clear about what you intend to communicate. By knowing purpose, a leader or follower can better decide whether to communicate publicly or privately, orally or in writing, and so on. These decisions may seem trivial, but often the specific content of a message will be enhanced or diminished by how and where it is communicated.

Choose an Appropriate Context and Medium

There is a rule of thumb that says leaders should praise followers in public and punish them in private. It points out the importance of selecting physical and social settings that will enhance the effectiveness of any communication. If the leader has an office, for example, how much communication with subordinates should occur in her office and how much in the followers' workplace?

FIGURE 8.3
Breakdowns in Communication Sometimes Lead to Finger Pointing

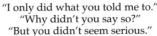

Person A   Person B

"You weren't listening!"
"That isn't what I said."
"You didn't follow directions."
"That isn't what you were supposed to do."

"I only did what you told me to."
"Why didn't you say so?"
"But you didn't seem serious."

Sometimes, of course, an office is the best place to talk. Even that decision, however, is not all a leader needs to consider. The arrangement of office furniture can enhance or interfere with effective communication. Informal, personal communications are enhanced when two people sit at a 90-degree angle and are relatively close to each other; more formal communication is enhanced when the follower remains standing when the leader is sitting or if the leader communicates across his desk to followers.

Additionally, a leader's communications often take place in a whole organizational context involving broader existing practices, policies, and procedures. Leaders need to take care that their words and deeds do not inadvertently undercut or contradict such broader organizational communications, including their own bosses'. Organizational factors also help determine whether any particular communication is most appropriately expressed orally or in writing. Oral communication is the most immediate, the most personal, the most dynamic, and often the most effective; it is ideal when communication needs to be two-way or when the personalized aspect is especially important. At the other extreme, a more permanent modality is probably most appropriate when the leader needs a record of the communication or when something needs to be expressed in a particular way to different people, at different times, in different settings.

Send Clear Signals

Leaders and followers can enhance the clarity of their communications in several ways. First, it is helpful to be mindful of others' level of expertise, values, experiences, and expectations and how these characteristics affect their *frames of reference.* For example, the leader may brief followers on a new organizational policy, and they may come up with different interpretations of this policy based on their values and expectations. By being sensitive to followers' frames of reference and modifying messages accordingly, leaders can minimize communication breakdowns. Another way to clarify messages is to create a common frame of reference for followers before communicating a message. For example, consider the following passage:

> With hocked gems financing him, our hero bravely defied all scornful laughter that tried to prevent his scheme. "Your eyes deceive," he had said. "An egg, not a table, correctly typifies this unexplored planet." Now, three sisters sought sturdy proof.
>
> Forging along, sometimes through calm vastness, yet more often over turbulent peaks and valleys, days became weeks as many doubters spread fearful rumors about the edge. At last, welcome winged creatures appeared signifying momentous success.[11]

Many are slow to recognize that this passage is about Christopher Columbus. Once the correct frame of reference is known, however, the previously confusing elements become sensible. Followers more readily understand new or ambiguous material when leaders paint a common frame of reference prior to introducing new material.

Another way to send clear signals is to use familiar terms, jargon, and concepts. This can clarify and abbreviate messages when receivers are familiar with the terms. However, messages containing jargon can also confuse receivers unfamiliar with those terms. For example, a freshman cadet at the U.S. Air Force Academy might say to another, "I hope we get an ONP this weekend, because after three GRs, a PCE, and a SAMI, I'll need it." Because the second cadet understands this organizational jargon, he or she would have no difficulty understanding what was said. However, a person unfamiliar with the Air Force Academy would not have the slightest idea what this conversation meant. Leaders should make sure followers understand any jargon they use—especially if the followers are relatively inexperienced. (In case you were wondering, the cadet said, "I hope we get a pass to go downtown this weekend, because after three academic tests, a military test, and a room inspection, I'll need it.")

Two other ways to improve the clarity of messages are to use unambiguous, concrete terms and to send congruent verbal and nonverbal signals. For example, a leader who tells a follower "Your monthly sales were down 22 percent last month" will more effectively communicate her concerns and cause less follower defensiveness than a leader who states, "Your performance has been poor." Thus the more specific the message, the less likely receivers will be confused about what it means. In addition, leaders will be more effective communicators if their nonverbal signals match the content of the message. Followers, like everyone, can get confused, and tend to believe nonverbal signals when leaders send mixed verbal and nonverbal messages.[12] Similarly, followers may send mixed messages to leaders; communication goes both ways.

One particularly destructive form of incongruent verbal and nonverbal signals is sarcasm. It is not the anger of the message per se but rather the implicit message conveyed by dishonest words that drives a wedge in the trust between leaders and followers. It is unwise for leaders to always share their transitory feelings with subordinates; but if a leader is going to share his or her feelings, it is important to do so in a congruent manner. Similarly, it can be just as unwise for followers to share transitory feelings with leaders; but if it's done, it's important for verbal and nonverbal behaviors to be congruent.

Actively Ensure That Others Understand the Message

Leaders and followers can ensure that others understand their messages by practicing two-way communication and by paying attention to others' emotional responses. Effective leaders and followers tend to actively engage in two-way communication (though this usually is more under the control of the leader than the follower). They can do so in many ways: by seeking feedback, by mingling in each other's work areas, and, in the case of leaders, by being sincere about having an open-door policy.[13]

Although such steps appear to be straightforward, leaders typically believe they utilize two-way communication more frequently than their followers perceive them to be using it.[14] Leaders can get clues about the clarity of their messages by paying attention to the nonverbal signals sent by their followers. When followers' verbal and nonverbal messages seem to be incongruent, it may be because the message sent to them was unclear. For example, followers may look confused when they verbally acknowledge that they understand a particular task. In this case, leaders may find it useful to address the mixed signals directly to clear up such confusion.

Listening

Our systems view of communication emphasized that effectiveness depends on both *transmitting* and *receiving* information. It may seem inconsistent, therefore, to distinguish the topic of listening from the more general topic of communication. Isn't listening part of communication? Of course; our separate treatment of listening is simply for emphasis. It seems to us that most discussions of communication emphasize the transmission side and neglect the receiving side. Good leaders and followers recognize the value of two-way communication. Listening to others is just as important as expressing oneself clearly to them. People in leadership roles are only as good as the information they have, and much of their information comes from watching and listening to what goes on around them.

At first it may seem strange to describe listening as a skill. Listening may seem like an automatic response to things being said, not something one practices to improve, like free throws. However, the best listeners are *active listeners*, not passive listeners.[15] In passive listening, someone may be speaking but the receiver is not focused on understanding the speaker. Instead the receiver may be thinking about the next thing he will say or how bored he is in listening to the speaker. In either case, the receiver is not paying attention to what the sender is saying. To get the fullest meaning out of what someone else says, we need to practice active listening. Individuals who are listening actively exhibit a certain pattern of nonverbal behaviors, do not disrupt the sender's message, try to put the sender's message into their own words, and scan the sender for various nonverbal signals. Knowing what nonverbal signals to send and correctly interpreting the sender's nonverbal signals are the knowledge component of listening skills. Nonverbal signals are the behavioral component, and how well we can paraphrase a sender's message makes up the evaluative component of listening skills.

In addition to helping us understand others better, active listening is a way to visibly demonstrate that we respect others. People, particularly those with high self-monitoring scores, can often sense when others are not truly paying attention to what they are saying. Followers will quickly decide it is not worth their time to give their leader information if they perceive they are not being listened to. Leaders may do the same. To avoid turning off others, leaders and followers can improve their active listening skills in a number of ways. Some of these tips include learning to model nonverbal signals associated with active listening, actively interpret the sender's message, be aware of the sender's nonverbal behaviors, and avoid becoming defensive. The following is a more detailed discussion of these four ways to improve active listening skills.

Demonstrate Nonverbally That You Are Listening

Make sure your nonverbal behaviors show that you have turned your attention entirely to the speaker. Many people mistakenly assume that listening is a one-way process. Although it seems plausible to think of information flowing only from the sender to the receiver, the essence of active listening is to see all communication, even listening, as a two-way process. Listeners show they are paying attention to the speaker with their own body movements. They put aside, both mentally and physically, other work they may have been engaged in. Individuals who are actively listening establish eye contact with the speaker, and they do not doodle, shoot rubber bands, or look away at other things. They show they are genuinely interested in what the speaker has to say.

Actively Interpret the Sender's Message

The essence of active listening is trying to understand what the sender means. It is not enough merely to be (even if you could) a perfect human tape recorder. We must look for the meaning behind someone else's words. In the first place, this means we need to keep our minds open to the sender's ideas. This, in turn, implies not interrupting the speaker and not planning what to say while the speaker is delivering the message. In addition, good listeners withhold judgment about the sender's ideas until they have heard the entire message. This way, they avoid sending the message that their minds are made up and avoid jumping to conclusions about what the sender is going to say. Another reason to avoid sending a closed-minded message is that it may lead others to *not* bring up things one needs to hear.

Another valuable way to actively interpret what the sender is saying is to *paraphrase* the sender's message. By putting the speaker's thoughts into their own words, leaders can better ensure that they fully understand what their followers are saying, and vice versa. The value of paraphrasing even a simple idea is apparent in the following dialogue:

Sarah: "Jim should never have become a teacher."

Fred: "You mean he doesn't like working with kids? Do you think he's too impatient?"

Sarah: "No, neither of those things. I just think his tastes are so expensive he's frustrated with a teacher's salary."

In this example, Fred indicated what he thought Sarah meant, which prompted her to clarify her meaning. If he had merely said, "I know what you mean," Fred and Sarah mistakenly would have concluded they agreed when their ideas were far apart. Paraphrasing also actively communicates your interest in what the other person is saying. Highlight 8.2 offers various "communication leads" that may help in paraphrasing others' messages to improve your listening skills.

Attend to the Sender's Nonverbal Behavior

People should use all the tools at their disposal to understand what someone else is saying. This includes paraphrasing senders' messages and being astute at picking up on senders' nonverbal signals. Much of the social meaning in messages is conveyed nonverbally, and when verbal and nonverbal signals conflict, people often tend to trust the nonverbal signals. Thus no one can be an effective listener without paying attention to nonverbal signals. This requires listening to more than just the speaker's words themselves; it requires listening for feelings expressed via the speaker's loudness, tone of voice, and pace of speech as well as watching the speaker's facial expressions, posture, gestures, and so on. These behaviors convey a wealth of information that is immensely richer in meaning than the purely verbal content of a message, just as it is richer to watch actors in a stage play rather than merely read their script.[16] Although there may not be any simple codebook of nonverbal cues with which we can decipher what a sender feels, listeners should explore what a sender is trying to say whenever they sense mixed signals between the sender's verbal and nonverbal behaviors.

Avoid Becoming Defensive

Defensive behavior is most likely to occur when someone feels threatened.[17] Although it may seem natural to become defensive when criticized, defensiveness lessens a person's ability to constructively use

---

Communication Leads for Paraphrasing and Ensuring Mutual Understanding

HIGHLIGHT 8.2

From your point of view . . .

It seems you . . .

As you see it . . .

You think . . .

What I hear you saying is . . .

Do you mean . . . ?

I'm not sure I understand what you mean; is it . . . ?

I get the impression . . .

You appear to be feeling . . .

Correct me if I'm wrong, but . . .

information. Acting defensively may also decrease followers' subsequent willingness to pass additional unpleasant information on to the leader or other followers, or even the leader's willingness to give feedback to followers. Defensiveness on the part of the leader can also hurt the entire team or organization because it includes a tendency to place blame, categorize others as morally good or bad, and generally question others' motives. Such behaviors on a leader's part do not build a positive work or team climate.

Leaders can reduce their defensiveness when listening to complaints by trying to put themselves in the other person's shoes. Leaders have an advantage if they can empathize with how they and their policies are seen by others; they can better change their behaviors and policies if they know how others perceive them. Leaders need to avoid the temptation to explain how the other person is wrong and should instead just try to understand how he or she perceives things. A useful warning sign that a leader may be behaving defensively (or perhaps closed-mindedly) is if he enters a conversation by saying, "Yes, but. . . ."

Assertiveness

What is *assertive behavior,* and what are assertiveness skills? Individuals exhibiting assertive behavior are able to stand up for their own rights (or their group's rights) in a way that also recognizes the concurrent right of others to do the same (see Highlight 8.3). Like the skills already discussed, assertiveness skills also have knowledge, behavioral, and evaluative components. The behavioral component of assertiveness skills was just described. The knowledge component of assertiveness skills concerns knowing where and when not to behave assertively. People who are overly assertive may be

---

Assertiveness Questionnaire

HIGHLIGHT 8.3

Do you let someone know when you think he or she is being unfair to you?

Can you criticize someone else's ideas openly?

Are you able to speak up in a meeting?

Can you ask others for small favors or help?

Is it easy for you to compliment others?

Can you tell someone else you don't like what he or she is doing?

When you are complimented, do you really accept the compliment without inwardly discounting it in your own mind?

Can you look others in the eye when you talk to them?

If you could answer most of these questions affirmatively for most situations, then you probably behave assertively.

Source: Adapted from R. E. Alberti and M. L. Emmons, *Your Perfect Right* (San Luis Obispo, CA: Impact, 1974).

perceived as aggressive and often may "win the battle but lose the war." Finally, the evaluative component comes into play when individuals are successful (or unsuccessful) in standing up for their own or their group's rights and continually working in an effective manner with others.

Perhaps the best way to understand assertiveness is to distinguish it from two other styles people have for dealing with conflict: acquiescence (nonassertiveness) and aggression.[18] *Acquiescence* is avoiding interpersonal conflict entirely either by giving up and giving in or by expressing our needs in an apologetic, self-effacing way. Acquiescence is *not* synonymous with politeness or helpfulness, though it is sometimes rationalized as such. People who are acquiescent, or nonassertive, back down easily when challenged. By not speaking up for themselves, they abdicate power to others and, in the process, get trampled on. Besides the practical outcome of not attaining our goals, an acquiescent style typically leads to many negative feelings such as guilt, resentment, and self-blame, as well as a low self-image.

Aggression, on the other hand, is an effort to attain objectives by attacking or hurting others. Aggressive people trample on others, and their aggressiveness can take such direct forms as threats, verbal attacks, physical intimidation, emotional outbursts, explosiveness, bullying, and hostility—and such indirect forms as nagging, passive–aggressive uncooperativeness, guilt arousal, and other behaviors that undermine an adversary's autonomy. It is important to understand that aggressiveness is not just an emotionally strong form of assertiveness. Aggressiveness tends to be reactive, and it tends to spring from feelings of vulnerability and a lack of self-confidence. Aggressive people inwardly doubt their ability to resolve issues constructively through the give-and-take of direct confrontation between mutually respecting equals. Aggressiveness is a form of interpersonal manipulation in which we try to put ourselves in a "top dog" role and others in a "bottom dog" role.[19] Additionally, aggressive people have difficulty expressing positive feelings.

Assertiveness is different from both acquiescence and aggression; it is not merely a compromise between them or a midpoint on a continuum. Assertiveness involves direct and frank statements of our own goals and feelings, and a willingness to address the interests of others in the spirit of mutual problem solving and a belief that openness is preferable to secretiveness and hidden agendas. Assertiveness is the behavioral opposite of both acquiescence and aggression, as depicted in Figure 8.4. The qualitative differences between these three styles are like the differences between fleeing (acquiescence), fighting (aggression), and problem solving (assertiveness).

It may seem axiomatic that leaders need to behave assertively with subordinates. Sometimes, however, leaders also need to be assertive with their own bosses. Followers often need to be assertive with other followers and with their leaders. For example, midlevel supervisors need to communicate

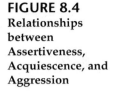

FIGURE 8.4
Relationships
between
Assertiveness,
Acquiescence, and
Aggression

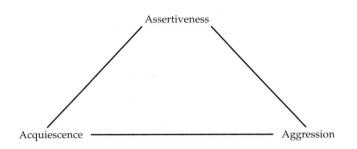

performance expectations clearly and directly to subordinates, and they need to be strong advocates for their subordinates' interests with senior supervisors. Likewise, leaders sometimes need to give their own superiors bad news, and it is best to do so directly rather than hesitantly and guardedly. Followers may sometimes need to be assertive with a peer whose poor work habits are adversely affecting the work group. In addition, leaders sometimes need to be assertive with representatives of other power-holding or special interest groups. For example, the leader of a community group seeking a new elementary school in a residential area may need to take an assertive stand with local school board officials.

Sometimes the hardest people to be assertive with are friends, family, and peers. Leaders who fail to be assertive with friends and peers run the risk of becoming victims of the Abilene paradox (see Highlight 8.4). The *Abilene paradox*[20] occurs when someone suggests that the group engage in a particular activity or course of action, and no one in the group really wants to do the activity (including the person who made the suggestion). However, because of the false belief that everyone else in the group wants to do the activity, no one behaves assertively and voices an honest opinion about it. Only after the activity is over does anyone voice an opinion (and it is usually negative). For example, someone in your group of friends may suggest that the group go to a particular movie on a Friday night. No one in the group really wants to go, yet because of the false belief that everyone else is interested, no one points out that the movie is not supposed to be good and the group should do something else instead. If group members' true opinions surface only *after* the movie, then the group has fallen victim to the Abilene paradox. We can avoid the Abilene paradox by being assertive when suggestions about group decisions and activities are first made.

Everyone can do several things to help themselves behave more assertively. These techniques include using "I" statements, speaking up for what we need, learning to say no, monitoring our inner dialogue, and being persistent. Next we discuss these assertiveness tips in more detail.

Use "I" Statements

Assertive people take responsibility for what they say. They are clear in their own minds and with others about what they believe and what they

The Abilene Paradox

HIGHLIGHT 8.4

That July afternoon in Coleman, Texas (population 5,607), was particularly hot—104 degrees according to the thermometer. In addition, the wind was blowing fine-grained west Texas topsoil through the house. But the afternoon was still tolerable—even potentially enjoyable. A fan was stirring the air on the back porch; there was cold lemonade; and finally, there was entertainment: dominoes—perfect for the conditions. The game requires little more physical exertion than an occasional mumbled comment, "Shuffle 'em," and an unhurried movement of the arm to place the tiles in their appropriate positions on the table. All in all, it had the makings of an agreeable Sunday afternoon in Coleman. That is, until my father-in-law suddenly said, "Let's get in the car and go to Abilene and have dinner at the cafeteria."

I thought, "What, go to Abilene? Fifty-three miles? In this dust storm and heat? And in an unair-conditioned 1958 Buick?"

But my wife chimed in with, "Sounds like a great idea. I'd like to go. How about you, Jerry?" Since my own preferences were obviously out of step with the rest, I replied, "Sounds good to me," and added, "I just hope your mother wants to go."

"Of course I want to go," said my mother-in-law. "I haven't been to Abilene in a long time."

So into the car and off to Abilene we went. My predictions were fulfilled. The heat was brutal. Perspiration had cemented a fine layer of dust to our skin by the time we arrived. The cafeteria's food could serve as a first-rate prop in an antacid commercial.

Some four hours and 106 miles later, we returned to Coleman, hot and exhausted. We silently sat in front of the fan for a long time. Then, to be sociable and to break the silence, I dishonestly said, "It was a great trip, wasn't it?"

No one spoke.

Finally, my mother-in-law said, with some irritation, "Well, to tell the truth, I really didn't enjoy it much and would rather have stayed here. I just went along because the three of you were so enthusiastic about going. I wouldn't have gone if you all hadn't pressured me into it."

I couldn't believe it. "What do you mean 'you all'?" I said. "Don't put me in the 'you all' group. I was delighted to be doing what we were doing. I didn't want to go. I only went to satisfy the rest of you. You're the culprits."

My wife looked shocked. "Don't call me a culprit. You and Daddy and Mama were the ones who wanted to go. I just went along to keep you happy. I would have had to be crazy to want to go out in heat like that."

Her father entered the conversation with one word. "Shee-it." He then expanded on what was already absolutely clear: "Listen, I never wanted to go to Abilene. I just thought you might be bored. You visit so seldom I wanted to be sure you enjoyed it. I would have preferred to play another game of dominoes and eat the leftovers in the icebox."

After the outburst of recrimination, we all sat back in silence. Here we were, four reasonably sensible people who—of our own volition—had just taken a 106-mile trip across a godforsaken desert in furnacelike heat and a dust storm to eat unpalatable food at a hole-in-the-wall cafeteria in Abilene, when none of us had really wanted to go. To be concise, we'd done just the opposite of what we wanted to do. The whole situation simply didn't make sense.

At least it didn't make sense at the time. But since that day in Coleman, I have observed, consulted with, and been a part of more than one organization that has been caught in the same situation. As a result, the organizations have taken journeys to Abilene when Dallas or Houston or Tokyo was where they really wanted to go. And for most of those organizations, the negative consequences of such trips, measured in terms of both human misery and economic loss, have been much greater than for our little Abilene group.

I now call the tendency for groups to embark on excursions that no group member wants "the Abilene paradox." Stated simply, when organizations blunder into the Abilene paradox, they take actions that contradict what they really want to do and therefore defeat the purpose they are trying to achieve. Business theorists typically believe that

continued

continued

managing conflict is one of the greatest challenges faced by an organization, but a corollary of the Abilene paradox states that the inability to manage agreement may be a major source of organization dysfunction.

Source: Jerry B. Harvey, "The Abilene Paradox: The Management of Agreement," *Organizational Dynamics,* Summer 1974. Copyright 1974. Reprinted with permission from Elsevier.

want. One of the easiest ways to do this is to use first-person pronouns when you speak. Highlight 8.5 provides examples of how to be more assertive by using first-person pronouns.

Speak Up for What You Need

No one has all of the skills, knowledge, time, or resources needed to do all the tasks assigned to their work group. Virtually everyone will need to ask superiors, peers, or subordinates for help at some time. Both effective leaders and effective followers ask for help from others when they need it. Highlight 8.5 also provides guidelines for making requests for help.

Learn to Say No

No one can be all things to all people, but it takes assertiveness to say no to others. Leaders, for example, may need to say no to their own superiors at times to stand up for their subordinates' or organization's rights and to keep from spreading themselves too thin and detracting from other priorities. Additionally, people who cannot (that is, who *do not*) say no often build up a reservoir of negative emotions, such as those associated with the feeling of being taken advantage of. Tips for assertively refusing to do something also can be found in Highlight 8.5.

Monitor Your Inner Dialogue

Most of us talk to ourselves, though not out loud. Such self-talk is natural and common, though not everyone is aware of how much it occurs or how powerful an influence on behavior it can be. Assertive people have self-talk that is positive and affirming. Nonassertive people have self-talk that is negative, doubtful, and questioning. Learning to say no is a good example of the role self-talk plays in assertiveness. Suppose someone is asked to serve on a volunteer committee he simply does not have time for and that he wants to say no. To behave assertively, the person would need to talk to himself positively. He would need to ensure that he is not defeated by his own self-talk. It would hardly help the person's resolve, for example, to have an inner dialogue that says, "They'll think I'm selfish if I don't say yes," or "If they can make time for this committee, I should be able to make time for it, too." In learning to behave more assertively, therefore, it is necessary for leaders to become more aware of their own counterproductive self-talk, confront it, and change it.

Tips for Being Assertive

HIGHLIGHT 8.5

EXAMPLES OF GOOD AND BAD "I" STATEMENTS

Bad: Some people may not like having to maintain those new forms.

Good: I don't think these new forms are any good. I don't think they're worth the effort.

Bad: Maybe that candidate doesn't have all the qualifications we're looking for.

Good: I think his academic record looks fine, but we agreed to consider only candidates with at least five years' experience. I think we should keep looking.

TIPS FOR SPEAKING UP FOR WHAT YOU NEED

Do not apologize too much or justify yourself for needing help or assistance (e.g., "I just hate to ask you, and I normally wouldn't need to, but . . . ").

At the same time, giving a brief reason for your request often helps.

Be direct. Do not beat around the bush, hinting at what you need and hoping others get the message.

Do not play on someone's friendship.

Do not take a refusal personally.

TIPS FOR SAYING NO

Keep your reply short and polite. Avoid a long, rambling justification.

Do not invent excuses.

Do not go overboard in apologizing because you cannot do it.

Be up-front about your limitations and about options you could support.

Ask for time to consider it if you need to.

Source: Adapted from K. Back and K. Back, *Assertiveness at Work* (New York: McGraw-Hill, 1982).

Be Persistent

Assertive individuals stick to their guns without becoming irritated, angry, or loud. They persistently seek their objectives, even while facing another person's excuses or objections. Exchanging merchandise can provide a good occasion for assertive persistence. Suppose someone purchased a shirt at a department store, wore it once, and then noticed a seam was poorly sewn. A person acting assertively might have an exchange much like that found in Highlight 8.6. An assertive person is similarly persistent in standing up for her own or her group's rights.

Conducting Meetings

Meetings are a fact of organizational life. It is difficult to imagine a leader who could (or should) avoid them, particularly when groups, committees, or teams have high levels of task or lateral interdependence. Well-planned and well-led meetings are a valuable mechanism for accomplishing diverse goals and are an important way of exchanging information and

Example Exchange between a Buyer and a Clerk

HIGHLIGHT 8.6

Buyer: "I bought this shirt last week, and it's poorly made."

Clerk: "It looks like you've worn it. We don't exchange garments that already have been worn."

Buyer: "I understand that is your policy, but it's not that I don't like the shirt. It is obviously defective. I didn't know it had these defects when I wore it."

Clerk: "Maybe this seam came loose because of the way you wore it."

Buyer: "I didn't do anything unusual. It is defective. I want it exchanged."

Clerk: "I'm sorry, but you should have returned it earlier. We can't take it back now."

Buyer: "I understand your point, but I didn't get what I paid for. You need to return my money or give me a new shirt."

Clerk: "It's beyond my authority to do that. I don't make the policies. I just have to follow them."

Buyer: "I understand you don't think you have the authority to change the policy. But your boss does. Please tell her I'd like to see her right now."

keeping open lines of communication within and between work groups or volunteer organizations.[21,22] Although meetings have many advantages, they also cost time and money. The annual cost of meetings in the corporate sector alone may well be in the billions of dollars. Furthermore, unnecessary or inefficient meetings can be frustrating and are often a source of dissatisfaction for participants. Given the investment of time and energy meetings require, leaders have a responsibility to make them as productive as possible. Guth and Shaw[23] have provided seven helpful tips for running meetings, which are discussed in the following paragraphs.

Determine Whether It Is Necessary

Perhaps the most important step in conducting a meeting is to take the time to *determine whether a meeting is really necessary.* If you are evaluating whether to have a meeting, assess what it can accomplish. Call a meeting only if the potential benefits outweigh the costs. As part of this process, get the opinions of the other participants beforehand if that is possible. Moreover, if meetings are regularly scheduled, you should have significant business to conduct in each meeting. If not, these meetings should probably be scheduled less frequently.

List the Objectives

Once you have decided that a meeting is necessary, you should *list your objectives for the meeting and develop a plan for attaining them* in an orderly manner. Prioritize what you hope to accomplish at the meeting. It is often helpful to indicate approximately how much time will be spent on each agenda item. Finally, get the agenda and issues to be covered to the participants well in advance; also let them know who else will be attending.

Stick to the Agenda

Once the meeting gets started, it is important for leaders to *stick to the agenda*. It is easy for groups to get sidetracked by tangential issues or good-natured storytelling. Although you should try to keep a cooperative and comfortable climate in the meeting, it is better to err on the side of being organized and businesslike than being lax. If items were important enough to put on the agenda, they are important enough to attend to in the time allotted for the meeting.

Provide Pertinent Materials in Advance

Besides having an agenda, a meeting is often more effective if leaders also give the other participants *pertinent reports or support materials well in advance.* Passing out materials and waiting for people to read them at the meeting itself wastes valuable time. Most people will come prepared, having read relevant material beforehand, if you have given it to them, and almost everyone will resent making a meeting longer than necessary doing work that could and should have been done earlier. In a similar vein, prepare for any presentations you will make. If you did not provide reports before the meeting, it is often helpful to provide an outline of your presentation for others to take notes on. Finally, of course, be sure the information you distribute is accurate.

Make It Convenient

Another way to maximize the benefits of meetings is to *pick a time and place as convenient as possible for all participants.* Besides maximizing attendance, this will help keep key participants from being distracted with thoughts of other pressing issues. Similarly, choose a place that is convenient for the participants and suitable for the nature of the meeting. Be sure to consider whether you need such things as a table for the meeting (with seating around it for all participants); a blackboard, an overhead projector, or similar audiovisual aids; coffee or other refreshments; and directions on how to find the meeting place. And start on time; waiting for stragglers is unfair to those who were punctual, and it sends the wrong signal about the seriousness of the meeting. Also plan and announce a time limit on the meeting beforehand, and stick to it.

Encourage Participation

Leaders have a responsibility to *encourage participation;* everyone at the meeting should have an opportunity to be heard and should feel some ownership in the meeting's outcome. In some cases you may need to solicit participation from quieter people at the meeting; these members often make valuable contributions to the group when given the chance. Furthermore, ensuring that the quieter members participate will also help you to avoid mistaking someone's quietness for implied consent or agreement. By the same token, you sometimes may need to curtail the participation of more outspoken participants. You can do this respectfully by merely indicating that the group has a good idea of their position and that it would be useful to hear from some others. You can also help encourage relevant participation by providing interim summaries of the group's discussion.

Keep a Record

During a meeting, the points of discussion and various decisions or actions taken may seem clear to you. However, do not trust your memory to preserve them all. *Take minutes for the record* so you and others can reconstruct what the participants were thinking and why you did or did not take some action. Record decisions and actions to be taken, including *who* will be responsible for doing it and *when* it is supposed to be accomplished. Such records are also useful for preparing future meeting agendas.

By following the preceding simple steps, both leaders and followers are likely to get much more out of their meetings, as well as appear organized and effective.

Effective Stress Management

People use the term *stress* in different ways. Sometimes people use the term to describe particular sorts of events or environmental conditions. For example, fans might speculate that a football coach's heart attack was caused by the pressures of his profession. Other examples might include receiving a failing grade on a physics exam, or arriving noticeably late to an important meeting, or playing a sudden-death overtime in hockey. But people also use the term in a quite different way. Sometimes it refers to the *effects* of environments. The phrase "I'm feeling a lot of stress" might refer to various symptoms a person is experiencing, such as muscular tension or difficulty concentrating. Before we proceed further, therefore, it will be useful to agree on some conventions of terminology.

We will define *stress* as the process by which we perceive and respond to situations that challenge or threaten us. These responses usually include increased levels of emotional arousal and changes in physiological symptoms, such as increases in perspiration and heart rate, cholesterol level, or blood pressure. Stress often occurs in situations that are complex, demanding, or unclear. Stressors are specific characteristics in individuals, tasks, organizations, or the environment that pose some degree of threat or challenge to people (see Highlight 8.7). Although all the factors in Highlight 8.7 probably have an adverse impact on people, the degree of stress associated with each of them depends on one's overall level of stress tolerance and previous experience with the stressor in question.[24] Similarly,

Stress Symptoms

HIGHLIGHT 8.7

Are you behaving unlike yourself?

Has your mood become negative, hostile, or depressed?

Do you have difficulty sleeping?

Are you defensive or touchy?

Are your relationships suffering?

Have you made more mistakes or bad decisions lately?

Have you lost interest in normally enjoyable activities?

Are you using alcohol or other drugs?

Do you seem to have little energy?

Do you worry a lot?

Are you nervous much of the time?

Have you been undereating or overeating?

Have you had an increase in headaches or back pains?

it is important to realize that stress is in the eye of the beholder—what one person may see as challenging and potentially rewarding, another may see as threatening and distressful.[25,26]

Who do you think typically experiences greater stress—leaders or followers? In one sense, the answer is the same as that for much psychological research: it depends. The role of leader certainly can be quite stressful. Leaders face a major stressful event at least once a month.[27] Followers' stress levels, on the other hand, often depend on their leaders. Leaders can help followers cope with stress or, alternatively, can actually increase their followers' stress levels. Many leaders recognize when followers are under a lot of stress and will give them time off, try to reduce their workload, or take other actions to help followers cope. On the other hand, about two out of three workers say their bosses play a bigger part in creating their stress than any other personal, organizational, or environmental factor.[28,29] Others have reported that working for a tyrannical boss was the most frequently cited source of stress among workers. It is clear that leaders play a substantial role in how stressful their followers' work experience is, for good or ill.[30]

Stress can either facilitate or inhibit performance, depending on the situation. Too much stress can take a toll on individuals and organizations that includes decreased health and emotional well-being, reduced job performance, and decreased organizational effectiveness (see Highlight 8.8 for an example of how too much stress impaired one person's performance).

To understand the effects of stress, an analogy might be helpful. Kites need an optimal amount of wind to fly; they will not fly on windless days, and the string may break on a day that is too windy. You can think of stress as being like the wind on a kite: a certain level is optimal, neither too little nor too much. Another analogy is your car. Just as an automobile engine operates optimally within a certain range of revolutions per minute (RPM), most people function best at certain levels of stress. Some

Stress on a TV Game Show

HIGHLIGHT 8.8

The television game show *Wheel of Fortune* pits contestants against each other in trying to identify common sayings. By spinning a wheel, contestants determine varying dollar amounts to be added to their potential winnings.

This is similar to the game of "Hangman" you may have played as a child. It begins with spaces indicating the number of words in a saying and the number of letters in each word. One player spins the wheel, which determines prize money, and then guesses a letter. If the letter appears somewhere in the saying, the player spins the wheel again, guesses another letter, and so on. The letters are "filled in" as they are correctly identified. A player may try to guess the saying after naming a correct letter.

If a player names a letter that does not appear in the saying, that prize money is not added to the

contestant's potential winnings, and play moves on to another contestant.

One day a contestant was playing for over $50,000 to solve the following puzzle. Perhaps because of the stress of being on television and playing for so much money, the contestant could not accurately name a letter for one of the four remaining spaces. Most people, not experiencing such stress, easily solve the problem. Can you? For the answer, see the end of this box.

```
THETHRI__
OF_I_TORY
ANDTHE
AGONYOF
DEFEAT
```

Answer: The Thrill of Victory and the Agony of Defeat.

stress or arousal is helpful in increasing motivation and performance, but too much stress can be counterproductive. For example, it is common and probably helpful to feel a little anxiety before giving a speech, but being too nervous can destroy one's effectiveness.

The optimal level of stress depends on a number of factors. One is the level of physical activity actually demanded by the task. Another is the perceived difficulty of the task. Performance often suffers when difficult tasks are performed under stressful situations. For example, think how one's performance might differ when first learning to drive a car with an instructor who is quiet and reserved rather than one who yells a lot. Chances are performance will be much better with the first instructor than with the second.

Note that task difficulty is generally a function of experience; the more experience one has with a task, the less difficult it becomes. Thus the more driving experience one has, the easier the task becomes. Moreover, people not only cope with stress more readily when performing easier tasks—but often need higher levels of stress to perform them optimally. One underlying purpose behind any type of practice (such as football, marching band, soccer, or drama) is to reduce task difficulty and help members or players perform at an even higher level under the stress of key performances and games.

Although stress can have positive effects, research has focused on the negative implications of too much stress on health and work. Stress has been linked to heart disease,[31] immune system deficiencies[32] and the growth rates of tumors.[33]And various studies have reported that work-related stress has caused a dramatic increase in drug and alcohol use in the workplace[34,35] and that stress is positively related to absenteeism, in-tentions to quit, and turnover.[36] Estimates in the 1980s were that the eco-nomic impact of stress to companies in the United States ranged between $70 billion and $150 billion annually.[37,38] Stress can also affect the decision-making process. Although leaders need to act decisively in crises, they may not make good decisions under stress.[39,40,41] Some have suggested that people make poor decisions under stress because they revert to their intuition rather than thinking rationally about problems.[42,43]

As we have noted, too much stress can take a toll on individuals and their organizations. Individuals can see their health, mental and emotional well-being, job performance, or interpersonal relationships suffer. For organiza-tions, the toll includes decreased productivity and increased employee absenteeism, turnover, and medical costs. It stands to reason, then, that lead-ers in any activity should know something about stress. Leaders should un-derstand the nature of stress because the leadership role itself can be stressful and because leaders' stress can impair the performance and well-being of followers. To prevent stress from becoming so excessive that it takes a toll in some important dimension of your own or your followers' lives, the follow-ing guidelines for effective stress management are provided.

Monitor Your Own and Your Followers' Stress Levels

One of the most important steps in managing stress is to *monitor your own and your followers' stress levels.* Although this seems straightforward, a par-adoxical fact about stress is that it often takes a toll without one's con-scious awareness. A person experiencing excessive stress might manifest various symptoms apparent to everyone but him or her. For that reason, it is useful to develop the habit of regularly attending to some of the warn-ing signs that your stress level may be getting too high. Some warning signs of stress are listed in Highlight 8.7. If you answer yes to these ques-tions, then your own or your followers' stress levels may be getting too high, and it would probably be a good idea to put some of the following stress management strategies into practice right away. On the other hand, answering some of the questions affirmatively does not necessarily mean your stress level is too high. There could, for example, be some other ex-planation.

Identify What Is Causing the Stress

Monitoring your stress will reduce the chances that it will build to an un-healthy level before you take action, but monitoring is not enough. Leaders also need to *identify what is causing the stress.* It may seem at first that the causes of stress always will be obvious, but that is not true. Sometimes the problems are clear enough even if the solutions are not (such as family finances or working in a job with a big workload and lots of deadlines). At other times, however, it may be difficult to identify the root problem. For example, a coach may attribute his anger to the losing record of his team, not recognizing that a bigger cause of his emotional distress may be the problems he is having at home with his teenage son. A worker may feel frustrated because her boss overloads her with work, not realizing that her own unassertiveness keeps her from expressing her feelings to her boss. Problem solving can be applied constructively to managing stress, but only if the problem is identified properly. Once the problem is identified, a plan for minimizing stress or the effects of the stressor can be developed.

Practice a Healthy Lifestyle

Practicing a healthy lifestyle is one of the best ways to minimize stress. There are no substitutes for balanced nutrition, regular exercise, adequate sleep, abstention from tobacco products, and drinking only moderate amounts of (if any) alcohol as keys to a healthy life. A long-term study of the lifestyles of nearly 7,000 adults confirmed these as independent factors contributing to wellness and the absence of stress symptoms.[44] Insufficient sleep saps energy, interferes with alertness and judgment, increases irritability, and lowers resistance to illness. Exercise, besides being a valuable part of any long-term health strategy, is also an excellent way to reduce tension.

Learn How to Relax

Believe it or not, some people just do not know how to relax. Although physical exercise is a good relaxation technique, sometimes you will need to relax but not have an opportunity to get a workout. *Practicing other relaxation techniques* will come in handy when a situation prevents strenuous exercise. Also, of course, some people simply prefer alternative relaxation techniques to exercise. Deep-breathing techniques, progressive muscle relaxation, and thinking of calming words and images can be powerful on-the-spot calming techniques. They are applicable in stressful situations ranging from job interviews to sports. The effectiveness of these techniques is a matter of personal preference, and no single one is best for all purposes or all people.

Develop Supportive Relationships

Another powerful antidote to stress is *having a network of close and supportive relationships* with others.[45] People who have close ties to others through marriage, church membership, or other groups tend to be healthier than those with weaker social ties. Also, social supports of various kinds (such as the supportiveness of one's spouse, co-workers, or boss) can buffer the impact of job stress,[46,47] and unit cohesion is believed to be a critical element of soldiers' ability to withstand even the extreme physical and psychological stresses of combat.[48] Leaders can play a constructive role in developing mutual supportiveness and cohesiveness among subordinates, and their own open and frank communication with subordinates is especially important when a situation is ambiguous as well as stressful.

Keep Things in Perspective

As we noted earlier, the stressfulness of any event depends partly on how we interpret it, not just on the event itself. For example, a poor grade on an examination may be more stressful for one student than for another, just as a rebuke from a boss may be more stressful for one worker than for another. This is partly due, of course, to the fact that individuals invest themselves in activities to different degrees because they value different things. A problem in an area of heavy personal investment is more stressful than one in an area of little personal investment. It goes deeper than that, however. Managing stress effectively depends on *keeping things in perspective*. This is difficult for some people because they have a style of interpreting events that aggravates their felt stress.

Individuals who have relatively complex self-concepts, as measured by the number of different ways they describe or see themselves, are less susceptible to common stress-related complaints than are people with lesser degrees of self-complexity.[49] Take, for example, someone who has suffered a setback at work, such as having lost out to a colleague for a desired promotion. Someone low in self-complexity (such as a person whose self-concept is defined solely in terms of professional success) could be devastated by the event. Low self-complexity implies a lack of resilience to threats to one's ego. Consider, on the other hand, someone with high self-complexity facing the same setback. The person could understandably feel disappointed and perhaps dejected about work, but if she were high in self-complexity, then the event's impact would be buffered by the existence of relatively uncontaminated areas of positive self-image. For example, she might base her feelings of professional success on more criteria than just getting (or not getting) a promotion. Other criteria, such as being highly respected by peers, may be even more important bases for her feelings of professional success. Furthermore, other dimensions of her life (like her leadership in the local Democratic Party or support to her family) may provide more areas of positive self-image.

The A-B-C Model

Unfortunately, because there are no shortcuts to developing self-complexity, it is not really a viable stress management strategy. There are other cognitive approaches to stress management, however, that can produce more immediate results. These approaches have the common goal of changing a person's self-talk about stressful events. One of the simplest of these to apply is called the *A-B-C model*.[50,51]

To appreciate the usefulness of the A-B-C model, it is helpful to consider the chain of events that precedes feelings of stress. Sometimes people think of this as a two-step sequence. Something external happens (a stressful event), and then something internal follows (symptoms of stress). We can depict the sequence like this:

A. Triggering event (such as knocking your boss's coffee onto his lap).

B. Feelings and behaviors (anxiety, fear, embarrassment, perspiration).

In other words, many people think their feelings and behaviors result directly from external events. Such a view, however, leaves out the critical role played by our thoughts, or self-talk. The actual sequence looks like this:

A. Triggering event (knocking your boss's coffee onto his lap).

B. Your thinking ("He must think I'm a real jerk.").

C. Feelings and behaviors (anxiety, fear, embarrassment, perspiration).

From this perspective you can see the causal role played by inner dialogue, or self-talk, in contributing to feelings of stress. Such inner dialogue can be rational or irrational, constructive or destructive—and which it will be is under the individual's control. People gain considerable freedom from stress when they realize that by changing their own self-talk they can control their emotional responses to events around them. Consider a different sequence for our scenario:

A. Triggering event (knocking your boss's coffee onto his lap).

B. Your thinking ("Darn it! But it was just an accident.").

C. Feelings and behavior (apologizing and helping clean up).

Thus a particular incident can be interpreted in several different ways, some likely to increase feelings of stress and distress, and others likely to maintain self-esteem and positive coping. You will become better at coping with stress as you practice listening to your inner dialogue and changing destructive self-talk to constructive self-talk. Even this is not a simple change to make, however. Changing self-talk is more difficult than you might think, especially in emotionalized situations. Because self-talk is covert, spontaneous, fleeting, and reflexive,[52] like any bad habit it can be difficult to change. Nevertheless, precisely because self-talk is just a habit, you can change it.

Finally, leaders need to recognize their role in their followers' stress levels. A leader in a stressful situation who is visibly manifesting some of the symptoms described in Highlight 8.7 is not going to set much of an example for followers. On the contrary, because followers look to leaders for guidance and support, these behaviors and symptoms could become contagious and increase followers' stress levels. Leaders need to recognize the importance of role modeling in reducing (or increasing) followers' stress levels. Leaders also need to make sure their style of interacting with subordinates does not make the leaders "stress carriers."

Problem Solving

Identifying Problems or Opportunities for Improvement

The first step in solving a problem is to state it so everyone involved in developing a solution has an informed and common appreciation and understanding of the task. This is a critical stage in problem solving and will take time and probably group discussion. It is dangerous to assume that everyone (or anyone) knows at the outset what the problem is. A hurried or premature definition of the problem (perhaps as a result of groupthink) may lead to considerable frustration and wasted effort. In counseling and advising, for example, a significant portion of the work with a client is devoted to clarifying the problem. A student may seek help at the school counseling center to improve his study skills because he is spending what seems to be plenty of time studying yet is still doing poorly on examinations. A little discussion, however, may reveal that he is having difficulty concentrating on schoolwork because of problems at home. If the counselor had moved immediately to develop the client's study skills, the real cause of his difficulties would have gone untreated, and the client might have become even more pessimistic about his abilities and the possibility that others could help him. Or consider a police chief who is concerned about the few volunteers willing to serve on a citizen's advisory committee to her department. There are many problems she might identify here, such as citizen apathy or poor publicity concerning the need and importance of the committee. The real problem, however, might be her own reputation for rarely listening to or heeding recommendations made by similar advisory committees in the past. If the chief were to take the time to explore and clarify the problem at the outset, she could discover this important fact and take steps to solve the real problem (her own behavior). If, on the other hand, she pressed ahead aggressively, trusting her own appraisal of the problem, nothing likely would change.

The reason it helps to take time to define a problem carefully is that sometimes people mistake symptoms for causes. In the case of the student, his poor studying was a symptom of another cause (family difficulties), not the cause of his poor grades. In the case of the police chief, lack of citizen participation on the advisory committee was a symptom of a problem, not the problem itself. If a plan addresses a symptom rather than the causes of a problem, the desired results will not be attained. It also is important during this stage to avoid scapegoating or blaming individuals or groups for the problem, which may trigger defensiveness and reduce creative thinking. This is a stage where conflict resolution techniques and negotiating skills can be important. Finally, the statement of a problem should not imply that any particular solution is the correct one.

As an application of these considerations, let us consider two pairs of problem statements that a teacher might present to his class as a first step in addressing what he considers to be an unsatisfactory situation. These samples of dialogue touch on many aspects of communication, listening, and feedback skills addressed earlier in this book. Here, however, our focus is on differences in defining problems. In each case, the second statement is the one more likely to lead to constructive problem solving.

A: I don't think you care enough about this course. No one is ever prepared. What do I have to do to get you to put in more time on your homework?

B: What things are interfering with your doing well in this course?

A: Your test grades are too low. I'm going to cancel the field trip unless they improve. Do you have any questions?

B: I'm concerned about your test scores. They're lower than I expected them to be, and I'm not sure what's going on. What do you think the problem is?

Another aspect of this first stage of problem solving involves identifying those factors that, when corrected, are likely to have the greatest impact on improving an unsatisfactory situation. Because there are almost always more problems or opportunities for improvement than time or energy to devote to them all, it is crucial to identify those whose solutions offer the greatest potential payoff. A useful concept here is the *Pareto principle,* which states that about 80 percent of the problems in any system are the result of about 20 percent of the causes. In school, for example, most discipline problems are caused by a minority of the students. Of all the errors people make on income tax returns, just a few kinds of errors (like forgetting to sign) account for a disproportionately high percentage of returned forms. We would expect about 20 percent of the total mechanical problems in a city bus fleet to account for about 80 percent of the fleet's downtime. The Pareto principle can be used to focus problem-solving efforts on those causes that have the greatest overall impact.

Analyzing the Causes

Once a problem is identified, the next step is to analyze its causes. Analysis of a problem's causes should precede a search for its solutions. Two helpful tools for identifying the key elements affecting a problem situation are a cause-and-effect diagram (also called a "fishbone" diagram because of its shape or an Ishikawa diagram after the person who developed it) and force field analysis. Cause-and-effect diagrams use a graphic approach to depict systematically the root causes of a problem, the relationships between different causes, and potentially a prioritization of which causes are most important (see Figure 8.5).

Force field analysis (see Figure 8.6) also uses a graphic approach; it depicts the opposing forces that tend to perpetuate a present state of affairs. It is a way of depicting any stable situation in terms of dynamic balance,

FIGURE 8.5
A Cause-and-Effect Diagram

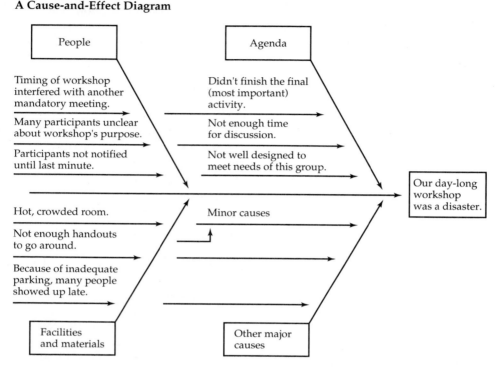

or equilibrium, between the forces that tend to press toward movement in one direction and other forces that tend to restrain movement in that direction. So long as the net sum of all the forces is zero, no movement occurs. When a change is desirable, force field analysis can be used to identify the best way to upset the balance between positive and negative forces so a different equilibrium can be reached.

Developing Alternative Solutions

A procedure called *nominal group technique* (NGT) is a good way to generate ideas pertinent to a problem.[53] This procedure is similar to brainstorming (see Highlight 8.9) in that it is an idea-generating activity conducted in a group setting. With NGT, however, group members write down ideas on individual slips of paper, which are later transferred to a blackboard or flipchart for the entire group to work with.

Selecting and Implementing the Best Solution

The first solution one thinks of is not necessarily the best solution, even if everyone involved finds it acceptable. It is better to select a solution on the basis of established criteria. These include questions such as the following:

FIGURE 8.6
Force Field Analysis Example: Starting a Personal Exercise Program

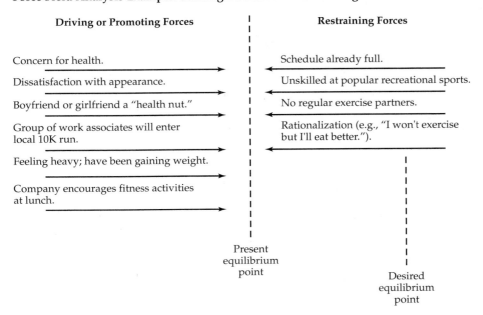

Driving or Promoting Forces

Restraining Forces

Concern for health.

Dissatisfaction with appearance.

Boyfriend or girlfriend a "health nut."

Group of work associates will enter local 10K run.

Feeling heavy; have been gaining weight.

Company encourages fitness activities at lunch.

Schedule already full.

Unskilled at popular recreational sports.

No regular exercise partners.

Rationalization (e.g., "I won't exercise but I'll eat better.").

Present equilibrium point

Desired equilibrium point

Have the advantages and disadvantages of all possible solutions been considered? Have all the possible solutions been evaluated in terms of their respective impacts on the whole organization, not just a particular team or department? Is the necessary information available to make a good decision among the alternatives?

Assessing the Impact of the Solution

We should not assume that the preceding steps will guarantee that the actions implemented will solve the problem. The solution's continuing impact must be assessed, preferably by measurable criteria of success that all parties involved can agree on.

Improving Creativity

Seeing Things in New Ways

Leaders can do several things to increase their own and their followers' creativity. Some of these facilitating factors have already been discussed and include assuring adequate levels of technical expertise, delaying and minimizing the evaluation or judgment of solutions, focusing on the intrinsic motivation of the task, removing unnecessary constraints on followers, and giving followers more latitude in making decisions. One

Steps for Enhancing Creativity through Brainstorming

HIGHLIGHT 8.9

Brainstorming is a technique designed to enhance the creative potential of any group trying to solve a problem. Leaders should use the following rules when conducting a brainstorming session:

1. Groups should consist of five to seven people; fewer than five can limit the number of ideas generated, but more than seven often can make the session unwieldy. It may be more important to carefully decide who should attend a session than how many people should attend.

2. Everybody should be given the chance to contribute. The first phase of brainstorming is idea generation, and members should be encouraged to spontaneously contribute ideas as soon as they get them. The objective in the first phase is quantity, not quality.

3. No criticism is allowed during the idea generation phase. This helps to clearly separate the activities of imaginative thinking and idea production from idea evaluation.

4. Freewheeling and outlandish ideas should be encouraged. With some modification, these ideas may be eventually adopted.

5. "Piggybacking" off others' ideas should be encouraged. Combining ideas or extending others' ideas often results in better solutions.

6. The greater the quantity and variety of ideas, the better. The more ideas generated, the greater the probability a good solution will be found.

7. Ideas should be recorded—ideally on a blackboard or large sheet of paper so members can review all the ideas generated.

8. After all the ideas have been generated, each idea should be evaluated in terms of pros and cons, costs and benefits, feasibility, and so on. Choosing the final solution often depends on the results of these analyses.

Source: A. F. Osborn, *Applied Imagination* (New York: Scribner's, 1963).

popular technique for stimulating creative thinking in groups is called *brainstorming* (which is discussed in Highlight 8.9).

An additional thing leaders can do to enhance creativity is to *see things in new ways,* or to look at problems from as many perspectives as possible. This is easier said than done. It can be difficult to see novel uses for things we are very familiar with. Psychologists call this kind of mental block *functional fixedness.*[54] Creative thinking depends on overcoming the functional fixedness associated with the rigid and stereotyped perceptions we have of the things around us.

One way to see things differently is to think in terms of analogies. This is a practical extension of Cronbach's definition of creativity—making fresh observations, or seeing one thing as something else.[55] In this case, the active search for analogies is the essence of the problem-solving method. In fact, finding analogies is the foundation of a commercial creative problem-solving approach called Synectics.[56] An actual example of use of analogies in a Synectics problem-solving group concerned designing a new roofing material that would adjust its color to the season, turning white in the summer to reflect heat and black in the winter to absorb heat. The group's first task was to find an analogy in nature, and it thought of fishes whose colors change to match their surroundings. The mechanism for such changes in fish is the movement of tiny compartments of pigments closer to or farther away from the skin's surface, thus changing its color. After some discussion, the group designed a black roof impregnated with tiny white plastic balls that would expand when it was hot, making the roof lighter, and contract when it was cold, making the roof darker.[57]

Another way to see things differently is to try putting an idea or problem into a picture rather than into words. Feelings or relationships that have eluded verbal description may come out in a drawing, bringing fresh insights to an issue.

Using Power Constructively

In addition to getting followers to see problems from as many perspectives as possible, a leader can also *use her power constructively to enhance creativity.* As noted earlier, groups may suppress creative thinking by being overly critical or by passing judgment during the solution generation stage. This effect may be even more pronounced when strong authority relationships and status differences are present. Group members may be reluctant to take the risk of raising a "crazy" idea when superiors are present, especially if the leader is generally perceived as unreceptive to new ideas; or they may be reluctant to offer an idea if they believe others in the group will take potshots at it in front of the leader. Leaders who wish to create a favorable climate for creativity need to use their power to encourage the open expression of ideas and to suppress uncooperative or aggressive reactions (overt or covert) between group members. Further, leaders can encourage creativity by rewarding successes and by not punishing mistakes. Leaders can also delegate authority and responsibility, relax followers' constraints, and empower followers to take risks. By taking these steps, leaders can help followers build idiosyncratic credits, which will encourage them to take risks and to be more creative. Along these same lines, the entire climate of an organization can be either more or less conducive to creative thinking—differences that may be due to the use of power within the organization. In an insightful turn of the familiar adage "Power corrupts," Kanter has noted how powerlessness also corrupts.[58] She pointed out how managers who feel powerless in an organization may spend more energy guarding their territory than collaborating with others in productive action. The need to actively support followers' creativity may be especially important for leaders in bureaucratic organizations because such organizations tend to be so inflexible, formalized, and centralized as to make many people in them feel relatively powerless.

Forming Diverse Problem-Solving Groups

Leaders can enhance creativity by *forming diverse problem-solving groups.* Group members with similar experiences, values, and preferences will be

Managing Creativity

HIGHLIGHT 8.10

R. T. Hogan and J. Morrison (1993) have maintained that people who are seen as more creative tend to have several distinguishing personality characteristics. In general, creative people are open to information and experience, have high energy, can be personally assertive and even domineering, react emotionally to events, are impulsive, are more interested in music and art than in hunting and sports, and finally are very motivated to prove themselves (that is, they are concerned with personal adequacy). Thus creative people tend to be independent, willful, impractical, unconcerned with money, idealistic, and nonconforming. Given that these tendencies may not make them ideal followers, the interesting question raised by Hogan and Morrison is this: How does one lead or manage creative individuals? This question becomes even more interesting when considering the qualities of successful leaders or managers. As discussed earlier, successful leaders tend to be intelligent, dominant, conscientious, stable, calm, goal-oriented, outgoing, and somewhat conventional. Thus we might think that the personalities of creative followers and successful leaders might be the source of considerable conflict and make them natural enemies in organizational settings. Because many organizations depend on creativity to grow and prosper, being able to successfully lead creative individuals may be a crucial aspect of success for these organizations. Given that creative people already possess technical expertise, imaginative thinking skills, and intrinsic motivation, Hogan and Morrison suggested that leaders take the following steps to successfully lead creative followers:

1. *Set goals:* Because creative people value freedom and independence, this step will be best accomplished if leaders set a high level of participation in the goal-setting process. Leaders should ask followers what they can accomplish in a particular time frame.

2. *Provide adequate resources:* Followers will be much more creative if they have the proper equipment to work with because they can devote their time to resolving problems rather than spending time finding the equipment to get the job done.

3. *Reduce time pressures, but keep followers on track:* Try to set realistic milestones and goals, and make organizational rewards contingent on reaching these milestones. Moreover, leaders need to be well organized to acquire necessary resources and to keep the project on track.

4. *Consider nonmonetary as well as monetary rewards:* Creative people often gain satisfaction from resolving the problem at hand, not from monetary rewards. Thus feedback should be aimed at enhancing their feelings of personal adequacy. Monetary rewards perceived as controlling may decrease rather than increase motivation toward the task.

5. *Recognize that creativity is evolutionary, not revolutionary:* Although followers can create truly novel products (such as the Xerox machine), often the key to creativity is continuous product improvement. Making next year's product faster, lighter, cheaper, or more efficient requires minor modifications that can, over time, culminate in major revolutions. Thus it may be helpful if leaders think of creativity more in terms of small innovations than major breakthroughs.

Source: R. T. Hogan and J. Morrison, "Managing Creativity," in *Create & Be Free: Essays in Honor of Frank Barron,* ed. A. Montouri (Amsterdam: J. C. Gieben, 1993).

less likely to create a wide variety of solutions and more apt to agree on a solution prematurely than more diverse groups. Thus selecting people for a group or committee with a variety of experiences, values, and preferences should increase the creativity of the group, although these differences may also increase the level of conflict within the group and make it more difficult for the leader to get consensus on a final solution. One technique for increasing diversity and creativity in problem-solving groups involves the use of the four preference dimensions of the Myers-Briggs Type Indicator (MBTI). Evidence to support this specific approach appears scanty,[59] but perhaps preferences assume significance only after certain other conditions for group creativity have been met. For example, diversity cannot make up for an absence of technical expertise. Although the MBTI dimensions may be useful in selecting diverse groups, this instrument should be used only after ensuring that all potential members have high levels of technical expertise. Choosing members based solely on MBTI preferences ignores the crucial role that technical expertise and intrinsic motivation play in creativity. Another aspect of the relationship between creativity and leadership is described in Highlight 8.10.

End Notes

1. Personnel Decisions International, *PROFILOR® Certification Workshop Manual* (Minneapolis, MN: Author, 1992).

2. J. M. Kouzes and B. Z. Posner, *The Credibility Factor* (San Francisco: Jossey-Bass, 1996).

3. J. M. Kouzes and B. Z. Posner, *The Credibility Factor* (San Francisco: Jossey-Bass, 1996).

4. B. M. Bass, *Bass and Stogdill's Handbook of Leadership*, 3rd ed. (New York: Free Press, 1990).

5. W. G. Bennis and B. Nanus, *Leaders: The Strategies for Taking Charge* (New York: Harper & Row, 1985).

6. R. M. Kanter, *The Change Masters* (New York: Simon & Schuster, 1983).

7. M. R. Parks, "Interpersonal Communication and the Quest for Personal Competence," in *Handbook of Interpersonal Communication*, ed. M. L. Knapp and G. R. Miller (Beverly Hills, CA: Sage, 1985).

8. R. J. Klimoski and N. J. Hayes, "Leader Behavior and Subordinate Motivation," *Personnel Psychology* 33 (1980), pp. 543–55.

9. R. A. Snyder and J. H. Morris, "Organizational Communication and Performance," *Journal of Applied Psychology* 69 (1984), pp. 461–65.

10. B. Fiechtner and J. J. Krayer, "Variations in Dogmatism and Leader-Supplied Information: Determinants of Perceived Behavior in Task-Oriented Groups," *Group and Organizational Studies* 11 (1986), pp. 403–18.

11. A. Sanford and S. Garrod, *Understanding Written Language* (New York: John Wiley, 1981).

12. M. S. Remland, "Developing Leadership Skills in Nonverbal Communication: A Situation Perspective," *Journal of Business Communication* 18, no. 3 (1981), pp. 17–29.

13. F. Luthans and J. K. Larsen, "How Managers Really Communicate," *Human Relations* 39 (1986), pp. 161–78.

14. P. J. Sadler and G. H. Hofstede, "Leadership Styles: Preferences and Perceptions of Employees of an International Company in Different Countries," *Mens en Onderneming* 26 (1972), pp. 43–63.

15. B. L. Davis, L. W. Hellervik, and J. L. Sheard, *The Successful Manager's Handbook*, 3rd ed. (Minneapolis, MN: Personnel Decisions International, 1989).

16. S. P. Robbins, *Organizational Behavior: Concepts, Controversies, and Applications* (Englewood Cliffs, NJ: Prentice Hall, 1986).

17. J. R. Gibb, "Defensive Communication," *Journal of Communication* 13, no. 3 (1961), pp. 141–48.

18. R. E. Alberti and M. L. Emmons, *Your Perfect Right* (San Luis Obispo, CA: Impact, 1974).

19. E. L. Shostrom, *Man, the Manipulator* (New York: Bantam, 1967).

20. J. B. Harvey, "The Abilene Paradox: The Management of Agreement," *Organizational Dynamics* 3 (1974), pp. 63–80.

21. B. M. Bass, *Bass and Stogdill's Handbook of Leadership*, 3rd ed. (New York: Free Press, 1990).

22. C. A. O'Reilly, "Supervisors and Peers as Informative Sources, Group Supportiveness, and Individual Decision-Making Performance," *Journal of Applied Psychology* 62 (1977), pp. 632–35.

23. C. K. Guth and S. S. Shaw, *How to Put on Dynamic Meetings* (Reston, VA: Reston, 1980).

24. P. E. Benner, *Stress and Satisfaction on the Job* (New York: Praeger, 1984).

25. C. D. McCauley, "Stress and the Eye of the Beholder," *Issues & Observations* 7, no. 3 (1987), pp. 1–16.

26. B. M. Staw, "Organizational Behavior: A Review and Reformulation of the Field's Outcome Variables," *Annual Review of Psychology* 35 (1984), pp. 627–66.

27. J. M. Ivancevich, D. M. Schweiger, and J. W. Ragan, "Employee Stress, Health, and Attitudes: A Comparison of American, Indian, and Japanese Managers," paper presented at the Academy of Management Convention, Chicago, 1986.

28. R. T. Hogan and A. M. Morrison, "The Psychology of Managerial Incompetence," paper presented at a joint conference of the American Psychological Association–National Institute of Occupational Safety and Health, Washington, DC, October 1991.

29. F. Shipper and C. L. Wilson, "The Impact of Managerial Behaviors on Group Performance, Stress, and Commitment," in *Impact of Leadership*, ed. K. E. Clark, M. B. Clark, and D. P. Campbell (Greensboro, NC: Center for Creative Leadership, 1992).

30. J. McCormick and B. Powell, "Management for the 1990s," *Newsweek*, April 1988, pp. 47–48.

31. M. Friedman and D. Ulmer, *Treating Type A Behavior-and Your Heart* (New York: Knopf, 1984); M. H. Frisch, "The Emerging Role of the Internal Coach," *Consulting Psychology Journal* 53, no. 4 (2001), pp. 240–50.

32. O. F. Pomerleau and J. Rodin, "Behavioral Medicine and Health Psychology," in *Handbook of Psychotherapy and Behavior Change,* 3rd ed., ed. S. L. Garfield and A. E. Bergin (New York: John Wiley, 1986).

33. A. Justice, "Review of the Effects of Stress on Cancer in Laboratory Animals: Importance of Time of Stress Application and Type of Tumor," *Psychological Bulletin* 98 (1985), pp. 108–38.

34. J. C. Latack, "Coping with Job Stress: Measures and Future Decisions for Scale Development," *Journal of Applied Psychology* 71 (1986), pp. 377–85.

35. D. Quayle, "American Productivity: The Devastating Effect of Alcoholism and Drug Use," *American Psychologist* 38 (1983), pp. 454–58.

36. M. Jamal, "Job Stress and Job Performance Controversy: An Empirical Assessment," *Organizational Behavior and Human Performance* 33 (1984), pp. 1–21.

37. D. Quayle, "American Productivity: The Devastating Effect of Alcoholism and Drug Use," *American Psychologist* 38 (1983), pp. 454–58.

38. K. Albrecht, *Stress and the Manager* (Englewood Cliffs, NJ: Prentice Hall, 1979).

39. F. E. Fiedler, "The Effect and Meaning of Leadership Experience: A Review of Research and a Preliminary Model," in *Impact of Leadership*, ed. K. E. Clark, M. B. Clark, and D. P. Campbell (Greensboro, NC: Center for Creative Leadership, 1992).

40. F. W. Gibson, "A Taxonomy of Leader Abilities and Their Influence on Group Performance as a Function of Interpersonal Stress," in *Impact of Leadership*, ed. K. E. Clark, M. B. Clark, and D. P. Campbell (Greensboro, NC: Center for Creative Leadership, 1992).

41. M. Mulder, R. D. de Jong, L. Koppelar, and J. Verhage, "Power, Situation, and Leaders' Effectiveness: An Organizational Study," *Journal of Applied Psychology* 71 (1986), pp. 566–70.

42. D. Weschler, *Weschler Adult Intelligence Scale: Manual* (New York: Psychological Corporation, 1955).

43. D. Tjosvold, "Stress Dosage for Problem Solvers," *Working Smart*, August 1995, p. 5.

44. J. Wiley, and T. Comacho, "Life-Style and Future Health: Evidence from the Alameda County Study," *Preventive Medicine* 9 (1980), pp. 1–21.

45. L. Berkman and S. L. Syme, "Social Networks, Host Resistance, and Mortality: A Nine-Year Follow-up Study of Alameda County Residents," *American Journal of Epidemiology* 109 (1979), pp. 186–204.

46. R. C. Cummings, "Job Stress and the Buffering Effect of Supervisory Support," *Group and Organizational Studies* 15, no. 1 (1990), pp. 92–104.

47. S. Jayaratne, D. Himle, and W. A. Chess, "Dealing with Work Stress and Strain: Is the Perception of Support More Important Than Its Use?" *Journal of Applied Behavioral Science* 24, no. 2 (1988), pp. 34–45.

48. West Point Associates, the Department of Behavior Sciences and Leadership, United States Military Academy, *Leadership in Organizations* (Garden City Park, NY: Avery, 1988).

49. P. W. Linville, "Self-Complexity as a Cognitive Buffer against Stress-Related Illness and Depression," *Journal of Personality and Social Psychology* 52, no. 4 (1987), pp. 663–76.

50. A. Ellis and R. Harper, *A New Guide to Rational Living* (Englewood Cliffs, NJ: Prentice Hall, 1975).

51. J. Steinmetz, J. Blankenship, L. Brown, D. Hall, and G. Miller, *Managing Stress before It Manages You* (Palo Alto, CA: Bull, 1980).

52. M. McKay, M. Davis, and P. Fanning, *Thoughts and Feelings: The Art of Cognitive Stress Intervention* (Richmond, CA: New Harbinger, 1981).

53. A. L. Delbecq, A. H. Van de Ven, and D. H. Gustafson, *Group Techniques for Program Planning: A Guide to Nominal and Delphi Processes* (Glenview, IL: Scott Foresman, 1975).

54. K. Duncker, "On Problem Solving," *Psychological Monographs* 58, no. 5 (1945).

55. L. J. Cronbach, *Essentials of Psychological Testing,* 4th ed. (San Francisco: Harper & Row, 1984).

56. W. J. J. Gordon, *Synectics* (New York: Harper & Row, 1961).

57. Ibid.

58. R. M. Kanter, *The Change Masters* (New York: Simon & Schuster, 1983).

59. P. W. Thayer, "The Myers-Briggs Type Indicator and Enhancing Human Performance," report prepared for the Committee on Techniques for the Enhancement of Human Performance of the National Academy of Sciences, 1988.

Refund Policy:

You may return any unused item for a refund provided that you deliver it to us in its original condition.

* 60 day rentals must be returned within 15 days of the original order date.
* 90 and 130 day rentals must be returned within 20 days of the original order date.

To return your rental, please log onto your CollegeBookRenter.com account. We supply a prepaid UPS return label for each order.
Returns will be shipped to:

College Book Renter
201 W Martin Luther King Dr
West Helena, AR 72390

Reason for return:_____

College Book Renter
201 W Martin Luther King Dr
West Helena, AR 72390

VIA: UPLS

SHIPPER NO.   NV873090

PKG. ID#

1Z8730901385162373

1321196

ANTON SAADEH
3903 TOPAZ LANE
LA VERNE CA 91750

Return Label

ORDER #   2475584

ANTON SAADEH
3903 TOPAZ LANE
LA VERNE CA 91750

College Book Renter
201 W Martin Luther King Dr
West Helena, AR 72390

REE1321196

SHIP ANTON SAADEH
TO: 3903 TOPAZ LANE
LA VERNE CA 91750

SHIPMENT NO.
1321196

Item Number	SHIP	Line	Item Description	Ord	Purchase Order No.
			SHIP VIA		
			UPS 1DAY AIR SAVER R		
9780078112652	1	001	LEADERSHIP ENHANCING THE LESSONS OF EXPE	1	
	1	...	TOTAL QUANTITY FOR ORDER ...	1	
			END OF ORDER 6/13/11 10:23:16		

ORDER NO.	PAGE NO.
2475584	1

DATE
6/13/11

723135138 - 000

College
BOOKRenter

Focus on the Followers

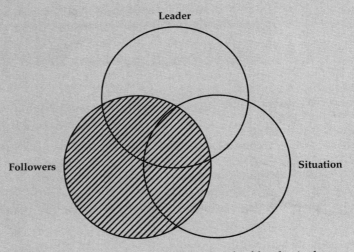

We began Part 2 with the notion that the individual leader is the most critical element of leadership. We begin Part 3 by qualifying that sentiment. Although the importance of a good leader cannot be denied, followers play an equally important, if often overlooked, role in the success of any group or organization. There can be no leaders without followers, but most research to date has focused on leadership. Researchers have only recently given serious consideration to the topics of followers and followership.

This research has revealed several interesting questions and findings. First, virtually everyone is a follower at some point in his or her life. And perhaps more importantly, anyone occupying a position of authority plays a followership role at times: first-line supervisors report to midlevel managers, midlevel managers report to vice presidents, vice presidents report to CEOs, and CEOs report to boards of directors. Because the same people play both leadership and followership roles, it is hardly surprising that the values, bases of power, personality traits, mental abilities, and behaviors used to describe effective leaders can also be used to describe effective followers. Followers vary in all the same ways that leaders vary.

Second, there are times when situational demands require that individuals in formal followership roles step into leadership roles. For example, a sergeant may take over a platoon when her lieutenant is wounded in battle, a volunteer may take over a community group when the leader moves away, a software engineer may be asked to lead a project because of unique programming skills, or team members can be asked to make decisions about team goals, work priorities, meeting schedules, and the like. That being the case, followers who are perceived to be the most effective are most likely to be asked to take the lead when opportunities arise. So understanding what constitutes effective followership and exhibiting those behaviors can help improve a person's promotion opportunities. Effective followership plays such an important role in the development of future leadership skills that freshman at all the U.S. service academies (the Air Force, Army, Navy, Coast Guard, and Merchant Marine Academies) spend their first year in formal follower roles. Following the path set by the service academies, perhaps the most effective people in any organization are those who are equally adept at playing *both* leadership and followership roles. Many people make great leaders but ultimately fail because of their inability to follow orders or get along with peers. And other people are great at following orders but cause teams to fail because of their reluctance to step into leadership roles.

> *Better followership often begets better leadership.*
> **Barbara Kellerman, Harvard University**

Third, it is important to remember the vital role followers play in societal change and organizational performance. The Civil Rights and more recent Tea Party movements are good examples of what happens when angry followers decide to do something to change the status quo. And this is precisely why totalitarian societies, such as North Korea, Myanmar, or Iran, tightly control the amount and type of information flowing through their countries. Organizational leaders should treat followers as important assets because they are the people creating the products, taking orders, serving customers, and collecting payments. Research has consistently shown that more engaged employees are happier, more productive, and more likely to stay with organizations than those who are disengaged.[1] Moreover, ethical followers can help leaders avoid making questionable decisions, and high-performing followers often motivate leaders to raise their own levels of performance.[2,3] Wars are usually won by armies with the best soldiers, teams with the best athletes usually win the most games, and companies with the best employees usually outperform their competitors—so it is to a leader's benefit to choose the best followers.

Fourth, although asking why anyone would want to be a leader is an interesting question, perhaps a more interesting question is asking why anyone would want to be a follower. Being a leader clearly has some advantages, but why would anyone freely choose to be a subordinate to someone else? Why would you be a follower? Evolutionary psychology hypothesizes that people follow because the benefits of doing so outweigh the costs of going it alone or fighting to become the leader of a group.[4] Thousands of years ago most people lived in small, nomadic groups, and these groups offered individuals more protection, resources for securing food, and mating opportunities than they would have had on their own. The groups with the best leaders and followers were more likely to survive, and those poorly led or consisting of bad followers were more likely to starve. Followers who were happy with the costs and benefits of membership stayed with the group; those who were not either left to join other groups or battled for the top spots. Evolutionary psychology also rightly points out that leaders and followers can often have different goals and agendas. In the workplace, leaders may be making decisions to maximize financial performance, whereas followers may be acting to improve job security. Therefore, leaders adopting an evolutionary psychology approach to followership must do all they can to align followers' goals with those of the organization and ensure that the benefits people accrue outweigh the costs of working for the leader; followers will either mutiny or leave if goals are misaligned or inequities are perceived.

However, social psychology tells us that something other than cost–benefit analyses may be happening when people choose to play followership roles. In some situations people seem too willing to abdicate responsibility and follow orders, even when it is morally offensive to do so. The famous Milgram experiments of the 1950s demonstrated that people would follow orders, even to the point of hurting others, if told to do so by someone they perceived to be in a position of authority. You would think the infamy of the Milgram research would subsequently inoculate people from following morally offensive or unethical orders, but a recent replication of the Milgram experiments showed that approximately 75 percent of both men and women will follow the orders of complete strangers who they believe occupy some position of authority.[5] Sadly, the genocides of Bosnia, Rwanda, and Darfur may be real examples of the Milgram effect. For leadership practitioners, this research shows that merely occupying positions of authority grants leaders a certain amount of influence over the actions of their followers. Leaders need to use this influence wisely.

Social psychology also tells us that identification with leaders and trust are two other reasons why people choose to follow. Much of the research in Chapter 14 concerning charismatic and transformational leadership shows that a leader's personal magnetism can draw in followers and convince them to take action. This effect can be so strong as to cause followers to give their lives for a cause. The 9/11/2001 terrorist attacks; the Mumbai, Bali, and London Tube bombings; the attempted bombing of a Delta airlines flight in December 2009; and suicide bomber attacks in Iraq and Afghanistan are examples of the personal magnetism of Osama bin Laden and the Al-Qaeda cause. Although most people do not have the personal magnetism of an Osama bin Laden or a Martin Luther King, those who do need to decide whether they will use their personal magnetism for good or evil.

Trust is a common factor in these hypotheses of cost–benefit analysis, compliance with authority, or willing identification with leaders. It is unlikely that people will follow leaders they do not trust.[3] It can be hard to rebuild trust once it has been broken, and followers' reactions to lost trust typically include disengagement, leaving, or seeking revenge on their leaders. Many acts of poor customer service, organizational delinquency, and workplace violence can be directly attributed to disgruntled followers,[6] and the recent economic downturn has put considerable strain on trust between leaders and followers. Many leaders, particularly in the financial services industry, seemed happy to wreck the global economy and lay off thousands of employees while collecting multimillion-dollar compensation packages. Given the lack of trust between leaders and followers in many organizations these days, we have to wonder what will happen to the best and brightest followers once the economy picks up and jobs become more readily available. Because of the importance of trust in team and organizational performance, leaders need to do all they can to maintain strong, trusting relationships with followers.

The final question or finding of the followership research concerns follower frameworks. Over the past 40 years or so researchers such as Zaleznik,[7] Kelley,[8] Chaleff,[9] Hollander,[3] Kellerman,[10] Potter and Rosenbach,[11] and Curphy[12] have developed various models for describing different types of followers. These models are intended to provide leaders with additional insight into what motivates followers and how to improve individual and team performance. The frameworks developed by these researchers have more similarities than differences, and for illustration a more detailed description of two of these models follows.

The Potter and Rosenbach Followership Model

Potter and Rosenbach[11] believe follower inputs are vital to team performance because followers are closest to the action and often have the best solutions to problems. Their model is based on two independent dimensions, which include follower performance levels and the strength of leader–follower relationships. The **performance initiative** dimension is concerned with the extent to which an individual follower can do his or her job, works effectively with other members of the team, embraces change, and views himself or herself as an important asset in team performance. Followers receiving higher scores on this dimension are competent, get along well with others, support leaders' change initiatives, and take care of themselves; those with lower scores do not have the skills needed to perform their jobs, do not get along with others, and actively resist change. The **relationship initiative** dimension is concerned with the degree to which followers act to improve their working relationships with their leaders. Followers receiving higher scores on this dimension are loyal and identify with their leaders' vision of the future but will raise objections and negotiate differences when need be; those with lower scores are disloyal, will not raise objectives even when it would be beneficial to do so, and pursue their own agendas even when they are misaligned with those of their boss.

Because the performance and relationship initiatives are independent dimensions, they can be placed on vertical and horizontal axes and used to describe four different types of followers. As shown in the diagram, the different types of followers include subordinates, contributors, politicians, and partners. Subordinates are followers in the more traditional sense; they do what they are told, follow the rules, are low to medium performers, and do not have particularly good relationships with their leaders. These individuals often rise in more bureaucratic, hierarchical organizations because they tend to remain with organizations for long periods, stay out of trouble, and do not make waves.

Potter and Rosenbach Followership Model

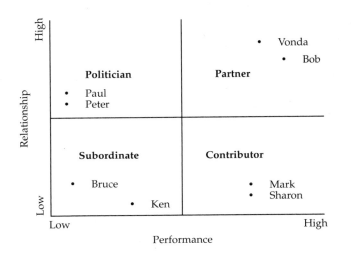

Contributors are different in that they are hard workers and often are motivated to be subject matter experts in their organizations. Although these individuals can be great researchers, programmers, or accountants, they have no interest in interpersonal dynamics or building stronger relationships with their leaders. They rarely seek out their leaders' perspectives, generally wait for direction, and work best in jobs where they can be left alone to do their thing.

Politicians are an interesting group: these individuals put much more emphasis on getting along well with their boss than getting things done. They are loyal and sensitive to interpersonal dynamics, and as such can give leaders good insights into other team members. There appear to be two types of politicians—some delight in playing the game and are good in positions that require lots of interaction with others. They often confuse activity with productivity, can be administratively challenged, and can often be found in sales or public relations because they are good at talking to people and closing deals. The other type of politician tends to be manipulative, selfish, and have unhealthy needs to be the center of attention. These people play games, start rumors, get little done but take credit for others' work, and jockey to been seen as indispensable to their leaders. Leaders who fall under this type of politician's spell often have teams with poor morale and performance.

Partners are individuals who are committed to high performance and building good relationships with their leaders. Partners take the time to understand their leaders' perspectives and buy into their vision for the team. Because they are strongly motivated to make an impact, partners work closely with their leaders to identify issues and work out solutions. Unlike politicians, partners are much more likely to raise uncomfortable issues and hold leaders accountable for decisions.

Several aspects of the Potter and Rosenbach followership model are worthy of additional comment. First, the situation plays an important role in determining followership types. Some individuals may be partners in one software firm but subordinates in another firm or may move from contributor to subordinate when working for a new boss. Organizational culture, the demands of the position, available resources, other team members, and the leader all affect followership types. Second, although it is natural for leaders to think partners make the best followers, Potter and Rosenbach maintain that all four types of followers can play valuable roles in organizations. Nonetheless, if leaders want to surround themselves with partners, they need to create team climates that encourage effective followership. To do this, leaders must clearly spell out their performance and relationship expectations for followers. Leaders also need to role model partner behavior for their followers when given opportunities to do so, seek followers' input on issues and decisions, and do debriefings on projects to demonstrate effective followership and build trust. If leaders take all these actions and team members choose to remain subordinates, contributors, or politicians, then leaders may want to consider replacing these individuals with those who have the potential to become partners.

Third, the Potter and Rosenbach followership model is useful in that it helps leaders understand their own followership type, the different kinds of followers, what kind of followers they currently have, and what they can do to create effective followership. As depicted in the figure, leaders often find followership scatter plots helpful in determining how to best motivate and lead members of their teams.

However, this model has two potential drawbacks. First, the model puts much of the onus of effective followership on followers. It is up to followers to identify with their leaders, buy into their leaders' vision, raise objections, and perform at a high level. But it is difficult for followers to take these actions if their leaders have not articulated a compelling vision of the future, encouraged constructive feedback, or provided the resources needed for followers to perform at high levels. Here we see that leaders and followers play equally important roles in effective followership.

This leads us to the second drawback of the model. As we will discuss in more detail in Chapter 15, it may be that over half the people occupying positions of authority are unable to build teams or get results through others. That being the case, what happens to followership when the leader is incompetent, unethical, or evil? The Potter and Rosenbach model states that the situation plays an important role in effective followership, but it may not take into account the role that ineffective leadership plays in followership. The next followership model, however, considers incompetent leadership.

The Curphy Followership Model

The Curphy followership model[12] builds on some of the earlier followership research of Kelley,[8] Hollander,[3] and Kellerman[10] and is similar to the Potter and Rosenbach model in that it also consists of two independent dimensions and four followership types. The two dimensions of the Curphy model are critical thinking and engagement. **Critical thinking** is concerned with a follower's ability to challenge the status quo, ask good questions, detect problems, and develop solutions. High scorers on critical thinking are constantly identifying ways to improve productivity or

Curphy Followership Model

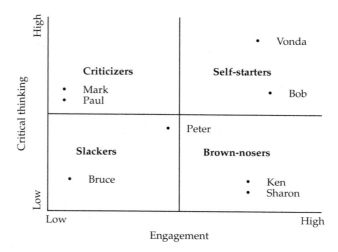

efficiency, drive sales, reduce costs, and so forth; those with lower scores believe it is the role of management to identify and solve problems.

Engagement is concerned with the level of effort people put forth at work. High scorers are optimistic and hardworking, put in long hours when needed, are enthusiastic about being part of the team, and are driven to achieve results; low scorers are lazy and disengaged and would rather be doing anything but the task at hand.

Like the Potter and Rosenbach followership model, the Curphy model can be used to assess current followership types. **Self-starters,** such as Bob and Vonda, are individuals who are passionate about the team and will exert considerable effort to make it successful. They are also constantly thinking of ways to improve team performance as they raise issues, develop solutions, and enthusiastically carry out change initiatives. When encountering problems, self-starters are apt to resolve issues and then tell their leaders what they did rather than waiting to be told what to do. This followership type also helps to improve their leaders' performance because they will voice opinions prior to and provide constructive feedback after bad decisions.

Self-starters are a significant component of high-performing teams and are by far the most effective followership type. Leaders who want to have these followers should keep in mind the underlying psychological driver of this type and the behaviors they need to exhibit if they want to encourage self-starters. In terms of the underlying psychological driver, leaders need to understand that self-starters fundamentally lack patience. They do not suffer fools gladly and expect their leaders to promptly clear obstacles and acquire the resources needed to succeed. Leaders who consistently make bad decisions, dither, or fail to quickly secure needed resources or follow through on commitments are not apt to have self-starters on their teams. It is important for leaders wanting to encourage self-starters to articulate a clear vision and goals for their teams because this type operates by seeking forgiveness rather than permission. If self-starters do not know where the team is going, they may make decisions and take actions that are counterproductive. And self-starters whose decisions get overruled too many times are likely to disengage and become criticizers or slackers. In addition to making sure they understand the team's vision and goals, leaders also need to provide self-starters with needed resources, interesting and challenging work, plenty of latitude and regular performance feedback, recognition for strong performance, and promotion opportunities. The bottom line is that self-starters can be highly rewarding but challenging team members, and leaders need to bring their best game to work if they want to successfully manage these followers.

Brown-nosers, such as Ken and Sharon, share the strong work ethic but lack the critical thinking skills of self-starters. Brown-nosers are earnest, dutiful, conscientious, and loyal employees who will do whatever their leaders ask them to do. They never point out problems, raise objections, or make any waves, and they do whatever they can to please their bosses. Brown-nosers constantly check in with their leaders and operate by seeking permission rather than forgiveness. It is not surprising that many leaders surround themselves with brown-nosers—these individuals are sources of constant flattery and tell everyone how lucky they are to be working for such great bosses. It may also not be surprising that brown-nosers often go quite far in organizations, particularly those not having good performance metrics. Organizations lacking clear goals and measures of performance often make personnel decisions on the basis of politics, and brown-nosers work hard to have no enemies (they can never tell who their next boss will be) and as such play politics well.

Because brown-nosers will not bring up bad news, put everything in a positive light, never raise objections to bad decisions, and are reluctant to make decisions, teams and organizations consisting of high percentages of brown-nosers are highly dependent on their leaders to be successful. Leaders can do several things to convert brown-nosers into self-starters, however, and perhaps the first step is to understand that fear of failure is the underlying psychological issue driving brown-noser behavior. Often brown-nosers have all the experience and technical expertise needed to resolve issues, but they do not want to get caught making "dumb mistakes" and lack the self-confidence needed to raise objections or make decisions. Therefore, leaders wanting to convert brown-nosers need to focus their coaching efforts on boosting self-confidence rather than the technical expertise of these individuals. Whenever brown-nosers come forward with problems, leaders need to ask them how they think these problems should be resolved; putting the onus of problem resolution back on this type boosts both their critical thinking skills and their self-confidence. Whenever practical, leaders need to support the solutions offered, provide reassurance, resist stepping in when solutions are not working out as planned, and periodically ask these individuals what they are learning by implementing their own solutions. Brown-nosers will have made the transition to self-starters when they openly point out both the advantages and disadvantages of various solutions to problems leaders are facing.

Bruce and Peter are **slackers**—they do not exert much effort toward work and believe they are entitled to a paycheck for just showing up and it is management's job to solve problems. Slackers are clever at avoiding work and are stealth employees: they often disappear for hours on end, make it a practice to look busy but get little done, have many excuses for not getting projects accomplished, and spend more time devising ways to avoid completing tasks then they would just getting them done. Slackers are content to spend entire days surfing the Internet, shopping online, chatting with co-workers, or taking breaks rather than being productive at work. Nonetheless, slackers want to stay off their boss's radar screens, so they often do just enough to stay out of trouble but never more than their peers.

Transforming slackers into self-starters can be challenging because leaders need to improve both the engagement and critical thinking skills of these individuals. Many leaders mistakenly believe slackers have no motivation; but it turns out that slackers have plenty of motivation that is directed toward activity unrelated to work. This type of follower can spend countless hours on videogames, riding motorcycles, fishing, side businesses, or other hobbies, and if you ask them about their hobbies, their passion shows. Slackers work to live rather than live to work and tend to see work as a means of paying for their other pursuits. Thus the underlying psychological driver for slackers is motivation for work; leaders need to find ways to get these individuals focused on and exerting considerably more effort toward job activities. One way to improve work motivation is to assign tasks that are more in line with these followers' hobbies. For example, assigning research projects to followers who enjoy surfing the Internet might be a way to improve work motivation. Improving job fit is another way to improve motivation for work. Many times followers lack motivation because they are in the wrong jobs, and assigning them to other positions within teams or organizations that are a better fit with the things they are interested in can improve both the engagement and critical thinking skills of these individuals.

At the end of the day the work still has to get done, and many times the leader does not have the flexibility to assign preferred tasks or new jobs to these individuals (or would not want to reward them for substandard efforts). In this case leaders need to set unambiguous objectives and provide constant feedback on work performance, and then gradually increase performance standards and ask for more input on solutions to problems. Because slackers dislike attention, telling these individuals they have a choice of either performing at higher levels or becoming the focus of their leaders' undivided attention can help improve their work motivation and productivity. Leaders should have no doubt, however, that converting slackers to self-starters is difficult and time-consuming. It may be easier to replace slackers with individuals who have the potential to become self-starters then spend time on these conversion efforts.

The last of the four types, **criticizers,** are followers who are disengaged from work yet possess strong critical thinking skills. But rather than directing their problem identification and resolution skills toward work-related issues, criticizers are instead motivated to find fault in anything their leaders or organizations do. Criticizers make it a point of telling co-workers what their leaders are doing wrong, how any change efforts are doomed to failure, how bad their organizations are compared to competitors, and how management shoots down any suggestions for improvement. Criticizers are the most dangerous of the four types because they believe it is their personal mission to create converts. They are often the first to greet new employees and "tell them how things really work around here." And because misery loves company, they tend to hang out with other criticizers. Effectively managing teams and organizations with criticizers can be among the most difficult challenges leaders face.

Because they are motivated to create converts, criticizers are like an organizational cancer. And like many cancers, criticizers respond best to aggressive treatments. Leaders need to understand that the need for recognition is the key psychological driver underlying criticizer behavior. At one time criticizers were self-starters who got their recognition needs satisfied through their work accomplishments. But for some reason they were not awarded a promotion they felt they deserved, an organizational restructuring took away some of their prestige and authority, or they worked for a boss who felt threatened by their problem-solving

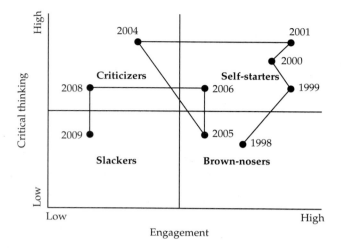

Curphy Followership Journey Line

skills. Criticizers act out because they crave recognition, and leaders can begin the reconversion to self-starters by finding opportunities to publicly recognize these individuals. As stated earlier, criticizers are good at pointing out how decisions or change initiatives are doomed to failure. When criticizers openly raise objections, leaders need to thank them for their inputs and then ask how they think these issues should be resolved. Most criticizers may initially resist offering solutions because they have drawers full of solutions that were ignored in the past and may be reluctant to share their problem-solving expertise in public. Leaders need to break through this resistance and may need to press criticizers for help. And once criticizers offer solutions that leaders can live with, leaders need to adopt these solutions and publicly thank criticizers for their efforts. Repeating this pattern of soliciting solutions, adopting suggestions, and publicly recognizing criticizers for their efforts will go a long way toward converting this group into self-starters. If leaders make repeated attempts to engage criticizers but they fail to respond, termination is a viable option for this type. Because of their need to create similar-minded co-workers, leaders who do not aggressively deal with these individuals may eventually find themselves leading teams made up of nothing but criticizers. In these situations it may be the leaders who are asked to look for another job rather than the one or two criticizers they failed to deal with properly.

Like the Potter and Rosenbach followership model, the Curphy followership model has several aspects that are worth additional comment. First, the model can help leaders assess follower types and determine the best ways to motivate direct reports. Second, leaders need to understand that followership types are not static; they change depending on the situation. The diagram here depicts how a person's followership type changed as she switched jobs, inherited different bosses, was given different responsibilities, and so on. This particularly individual started her professional career as a brown-noser, moved up to become a self-starter, spent some time as a criticizer, and is now a slacker. When asked why their followership type changed over time, most people say their immediate boss was the biggest factor in these changes. Thus leaders have a direct impact on effective followership—either by selecting direct reports with self-starter potential or developing direct reports into self-starters.

Third, it is not unusual for followers to start careers or new jobs as brown-nosers. New employees need time to learn the job before they feel comfortable making suggestions for improvement. The question for leaders is whether to take action to systematically convert brown-nosers into self-starters. Fourth, organizations having decent selection processes are more likely to hire brown-nosers and self-starters than criticizers and slackers. Additional research has shown the longer people stay in organizations, the more likely they will be criticizers. Over time people learn how to develop critical thinking skills about their functional expertise. It is usually only a matter of time before these finely honed critical thinking skills are trained on leaders, teams, and organizations.[13] That being said, teams and organizations populated with criticizers and slackers need to take a hard look at their leadership. The criticizer and slacker followership types may be ways that direct reports cope with clueless bosses.

Fifth, because people in positions of authority also play followership roles, they need to realize how their own followership type affects how they lead others. For example, leaders who are self-starters are likely to set high expectations, reward others for taking initiative, and give top performers plenty of latitude and needed resources. Leaders who are brown-nosers will squelch objections and demand that direct reports constantly check in. They will also expect their employees to do what they are told and not make waves. Leaders who are slackers are laissez-faire leaders who are disengaged from work, are unresponsive to followers' requests, and lead teams that get little accomplished. Leaders who are criticizers will complain not only about their organizations but also about their employees. As such, these leaders tend to manage by exception and find fault in everything their followers do.

We started Part 3 by stating that followers play an important role in team and organizational performance. We hope that some of the main research findings and questions about followership described in this section will prompt readers to give more thought to effective followership. The next two chapters will explore the topic of followers in considerably more detail. Individual followers differ in all the ways that individual leaders differ, but different things happen when groups of followers have to work together to get things done. Leaders wanting to build high-performing teams need to be aware of the role of group dynamics in team morale and performance.

9

Motivation, Satisfaction, and Performance

Introduction

Why do followers join some teams but not others? How do you get followers to exhibit enough of the critical behaviors needed for the team to succeed? And why are some leaders capable of getting followers to go above and beyond the call of duty? The ability to motivate others is a fundamental leadership skill and has strong connections to building cohesive, goal-oriented teams and getting results through others. The importance of follower motivation is suggested in findings that most people believe they could give as much as 15 percent or 20 percent more effort at work than they now do with no one, including their own bosses, recognizing any difference. Perhaps even more startling, these workers also believed they could give 15 percent or 20 percent *less* effort with no one noticing any difference. Moreover, variation in work output varies significantly across leaders and followers. The top 15 percent of workers in any particular job may produce 20 to 50 percent more output than the average worker, depending on the complexity of the job. Put another way, the best computer programmers or salesclerks might write up to 50 percent more programs or process 50 percent more customer orders.[1,2] Might better methods of motivating workers lead to higher productivity from *all* workers? Is motivating an individual follower different than motivating a group of followers? Are more motivated workers happier or more satisfied workers? Does money increase productivity and satisfaction, or can leaders do other things to increase the motivation and satisfaction levels of their followers? For example, the U.S. Army paid $85 million in retention bonuses in 2003 and over $1 billion in bonuses in 2007.[3] Is this money well spent?

Creating highly motivated and satisfied followers depends mostly on understanding others. Therefore, whereas motivation is an essential part

331

of leadership, it is appropriate to include it in this part of the book, which focuses on followers. As an overview, this chapter will address three key areas. First, we will examine the links among leadership, motivation, satisfaction, and performance—four closely related concepts. Second, we will review some major theories and research about motivation and satisfaction. Last, and perhaps most important, we will discuss what leaders can do to enhance the motivation and satisfaction of their followers if they implement these different theories.

Defining Motivation, Satisfaction, and Performance

Motivation, satisfaction, and performance seem clearly related. For example, Colin Powell was the former U.S. Army Chief of Staff during the first Gulf War and Secretary of State during the second Gulf War. Powell probably could have pursued a number of different vocations but was *motivated* to complete ROTC and join the U.S. Army. He was also motivated to put in extra time, energy, and effort in his various positions while in the U.S. Army and was judged or rated by his superiors as being an exceptional performer. His outstanding *performance* as an officer was crucial to his promotion as the head of the Joint Chiefs of Staff during the Reagan and George H. W. Bush administrations and his later appointment as Secretary of State. We could also infer that he was happy or *satisfied* with military life because he was a career officer in the U.S. Army. Figure 9.1 provides an overview of the general relationships among leadership, motivation, satisfaction, and performance. As we can see, some leadership behaviors, such as building relationships or consideration (Chapter 7), result in more satisfied followers. More satisfied followers are more likely to remain with the company and engage in activities that help others at work (organizational citizenship behaviors). Other leadership behaviors, such as setting goals, planning, providing feedback, and rewarding good performance (initiating structure from Chapter 7), appear to more directly influence followers to exert higher levels of effort toward the accomplishment of group goals. Research has shown that these follower behaviors result in higher levels of customer satisfaction and loyalty, which in turn lead to better team performance in retail, sales, or restaurant settings.[4-18] And individuals and teams with higher performance levels often achieve more rewards, which further increase follower satisfaction and performance.[19,20] Thus the leader's ability to motivate followers is vitally important to both the morale and performance of the work group. However, the leader's use of motivational techniques is not the only factor affecting group performance. Selecting the right people for the team, correctly using power and influence tactics, being seen as ethical and credible, possessing the right personality traits and high levels of intelligence, acquiring the necessary resources, and developing follower

FIGURE 9.1
Relationships among Leadership, Job Satisfaction, and Performance

Sources: M. A. Huselid, "The Impact of Human Resource Management Practices on Turnover, Productivity, and Corporate Financial Performance," *Academy of Management Journal* 38, no. 4 (1995), pp. 635–72; T. Butorac, *Recruitment and Retention: The Keys to Profitability at Carlson Companies*, presentation given at Personnel Decisions International, Minneapolis, MN, June 11, 2001; D. J. Koys, "The Effects of Employee Satisfaction, Organizational Citizenship Behavior, and Turnover on Organizational Effectiveness: A Unit-Level, Longitudinal Study," *Personnel Psychology* 54, no. 1 (2001), pp. 101–14; J. Husserl, "Allied's Organizational Life Cycle," *Management Education & Development* 24, no. 3 (1998), p. 8; Sirota Consulting, *Establishing the Linkages between Employee Attitudes, Customer Attitudes, and Bottom-Line Results* (Chicago, IL: Author, 1998); D. S. Pugh, J. Dietz, J. W. Wiley, and S. M. Brooks, "Driving Service Effectiveness through Employee–Customer Linkages," *Academy of Management Executive* 16, no. 4 (2002), pp. 73–84; B. Schneider, P. J. Hanges, D. B. Smith, and A. N. Salvaggio, "Which Comes First: Employee Attitudes or Organizational, Financial and Market Performance?" *Journal of Applied Psychology* 88, no. 5 (2003), pp. 836–51.

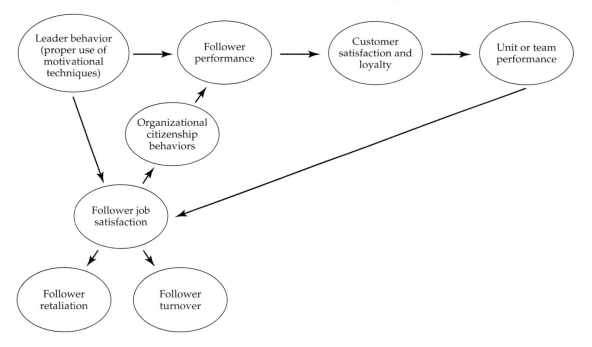

skills are other leadership factors affecting a group's ability to accomplish its goals.

Most people probably think of motivation as dealing with choices about what we do and how much effort we put into doing it. Most researchers define **motivation** as anything that provides *direction, intensity,* and *persistence* to behavior.[21,22,23] Thus motivation comes into play whenever someone chooses an activity or task to engage in, puts forth a certain level of effort toward this activity, and persists with this effort for some time. Like personality traits and types, motivation is not directly observable; it must be inferred from behavior. We would infer that one person is highly motivated to do well in school if she spent a lot of time studying for exams. She could choose to spend her time and energy on socializing, intramurals, or volunteer work, but because she is spending time outlining readings and

You have brains in your head. You have feet in your shoes. You can steer yourself in any direction you choose.

Dr. Seuss

reviewing class notes, we say she is motivated to do well in school. At work, if one person regularly assembles twice as many iPads as any other person in his work group—assuming all have the same abilities, skills, and resources—then we likely would say this first person is more motivated than the others. We use the concept of motivation to explain differences we see among people in the energy and direction of their behavior. Thus the energy and effort James Cameron expended creating *Avatar* or the government of Iran spends developing the country's nuclear capabilities would be examples of the direction, intensity, and persistence components of motivation.

Performance, on the other hand, concerns behaviors directed toward the organization's mission or goals or the products and services resulting from those behaviors. At work or school we can choose to perform a wide variety of behaviors, but performance would include only those behaviors related to the production of goods or services or obtaining good grades. Performance differs from **effectiveness,** which generally involves making judgments about the adequacy of behavior with respect to certain criteria such as work group or organizational goals. James Cameron spent several years creating the movie *Avatar*. The behaviors he exhibited in getting the film made constitute performance; the revenues generated and Academy Awards won by the movie indicate his effectiveness as a movie director. However, performance is affected by a variety of factors. Intelligence, skill, and the availability of key resources can affect a follower's behavior in accomplishing organizational goals (that is, performance) independently of that person's level of motivation. *Thus an adequate level of motivation may be a necessary but insufficient condition of effective performance.*

Job satisfaction is not how *hard* one works or how *well* one works, but rather how much one *likes* a specific kind of job or work activity. Job satisfaction deals with one's attitudes or feelings about the job itself, pay, promotion or educational opportunities, supervision, co-workers, workload, and so on.[11,24,25] Various polls over the past half-century have consistently shown that a majority of men and women report liking their jobs.[26-30] Research has also shown that people who are more satisfied with their jobs are more likely to engage in **organizational citizenship behaviors**—behaviors not directly related to one's job but helpful to others at work. Organizational citizenship behaviors create a more supportive workplace. Examples might include volunteering to help another employee with a task or project or filling in for another employee when asked. Happier workers tend to be more helpful workers.[31-36]

Although people generally like the work they do, several events have caused a downturn in job satisfaction levels among employees in the United States over the past decade. From roughly 2002 to 2007 the United States enjoyed strong economic growth, and companies rapidly expanded the products and services they provided. Because it took time to hire and train employees to meet increased demand, those already employed

A company is always perfectly designed to produce what it is producing. If it has quality problems, cost problems, or productivity problems, then the behaviors associated with these outcomes are being reinforced. This is not conjecture. This is the cold, hard reality of human behavior.

Anonymous

There is one virtue to the 35-hour workweek. It is one of the few French ideals that we don't need to worry about copyrighting. Nobody else wants it.

Nicolas Sarkozy, prime minister of France

had to cope with larger workloads. This period also saw a tremendous amount of consolidation (companies buying one another) and reorganization (restructuring functions, processes, and personnel) to better meet increased demand. Change was an overarching theme from 2002 to 2007, and leaders and followers were constantly devising new ways to deliver products and services to customers. This continuing cycle of consolidation, reorganization, and change made it difficult for employees to develop any loyalty for their organizations—they never knew if their work unit was going to be sold or merged with another work unit. This period, perhaps more than most, broke the implicit contract between employers and employees. Before 2002 many employees felt if they worked hard they could spend their entire careers at a single company. But after all the acquisitions, downsizings, and restructurings many employees developed more of a mercenary attitude toward employers. If they worked for a company that did not treat them well, had a bad boss, or did not get the pay or promotions they felt they deserved, they would find a position with another employer. And with the economy enjoying strong growth, there were plenty of opportunities for people to find other employment.

Although people were working longer hours and coping with more change than ever before, most people found 2002–2007 to be a cakewalk compared to what they experienced during the economic recession of 2008–2010. The global recession caused companies to freeze hiring and training programs and lay off record numbers of employees. The unemployment rate in the United States increased from 5 to over 10 percent, and many people went months or even years without finding meaningful work. Those lucky enough to remain employed wound up doing more than they did before with fewer resources and lower pay. Employees generally felt lucky to have a job and were not apt to complain (for fear of losing their jobs), but many were frustrated with their employers. This increased workload and sense of frustration cut job satisfaction to record lows, and a big question was whether the best and brightest employees would leave for other opportunities once the economy picked up.[37] Companies can ill afford to lose their best people just when their fortunes are improving, so many have implemented programs to retain their high-potential talent.[38]

Today many leaders face the dual challenges of having to achieve increasingly difficult team goals while having fewer followers available to do the work. The best leaders and organizations understand that one way to meet these challenges is to recruit, develop, and retain top leadership and technical talent. Savvy companies that spend considerably more time and effort attracting, developing, and retaining the best people often report superior financial results.[9,11,39-46] For example, many of the organizations appearing in *Fortune* magazine's "The 100 Best Companies to Work For" also do well when compared to the S&P 500 Index. *The best leaders may be those who can motivate workers to perform at a high level while maintaining an equally high level of job satisfaction.*

People don't leave companies, they leave bad bosses.
**Beverly Kaye,
CEO**

Productivity and Satisfaction across the Globe

HIGHLIGHT 9.1

The global recession has caused American businesses to downsize considerably, but many have been able to maintain customer satisfaction and revenue levels with fewer employees. In terms of the number of hours worked, the average U.S. employee works 137 hours per year more than the typical Japanese employee, 260 hours more per year compared to the average British employee, and 499 hours more than the average French employee. In other words, over a 40-year work career, U.S. employees will work the equivalent of 10 more years than the average French employee. Although American companies are noted for having some of the highest productivity in the world, might there also be a downside to these high productivity levels? Research has shown that some of the risks associated with longer workweeks include job dissatisfaction,

poorer physical and mental health, and distressed family and social relationships. As long as the U.S. economy is not adding jobs, many employees seem to prefer the consequences associated with longer work hours to those of being unemployed. But when the economy heats up and jobs become more readily available, leaders should not be surprised that many of these employees leave for greener pastures.

Why do you think U.S. employees put in longer hours than their European or Asian counterparts? Is working these longer hours a good or bad thing?

Sources: J. M. Brett and L. K. Stroh, "Working 61 Plus Hours a Week: Why Do Managers Do It?" *Journal of Applied Psychology* 88, no. 1 (2003), pp. 67–78; "Schumpeter: Overstretched" *The Economist*, May 22, 2010, p. 72; http://news.yahoo.com/s/ap/20100105/ap_on_bi_ge/us_unhappy_workers.

Having now defined motivation, performance, and job satisfaction, we can explore their relationships a bit further. We have already noted how motivation does not always ensure good performance. If followers lack the necessary skills or resources to accomplish a group task, then trying to motivate them more could be unproductive and even frustrating.[47,48] For example, no high school basketball team is likely to defeat the Los Angeles Lakers, however motivated the players may be. The players on the high school team simply lack the abilities and skills of the Lakers players. Higher motivation will usually affect performance only if followers already have the abilities, skills, and resources to get the job done. Motivating others is an important part of leadership, but not all of it; pep talks and rewards are not always enough.

The relationships between motivation and job satisfaction are more straightforward; in fact many theories of motivation are also theories of

Source: FUNKY WINKERBEAN © Baton, Inc. North American Syndicate.

Michelle Bachelet

PROFILES IN LEADERSHIP 9.1

Michelle Bachelet was inaugurated as president of Chile in March 2006 and is ranked by *Forbes* as the 17th most powerful female in the world. Bachelet is a surgeon, pediatrician, and epidemiologist with a master's degree in military studies from the Chilean Army War Academy and previous experience as the country's Health and Defense Minister. A moderate socialist who believes in free markets, Bachelet and her government have negotiated a number of bilateral trade agreements with other countries. Her government has also worked to reduce corruption, improve public transportation, resolve border disputes with Peru and Argentina, manage the aftermath of an 8.8 magnitude earthquake, and reduce the gap between rich and poor (Chile has one of the largest wealth gaps in the world).

Bachelet's father was a Chilean Air Force Brigadier General, and she moved a lot while growing up. While she was in high school her father got a two-year assignment to the Chilean embassy in Washington, D.C. Her family then moved back to Chile, where she graduated near the top of her high school class and applied to medical school. She had one of the highest scores ever recorded on the medical school entrance examination, but while she was in medical school Augusto Pinochet came to power and began to purge anyone associated with the previous administration. During this time Bachelet's father was working for the Salvadore Allende government as the head of the Food Distribution Office. He was arrested by Pinochet's forces and interrogated and tortured. He had a

heart attack and died while in prison. Shortly thereafter Michelle Bachelet and her mother were also arrested, interrogated, and tortured, but due to family connections they were granted exile in Australia. Bachelet then moved to East Germany to continue her medical studies. She remained in East Germany for three years before she was allowed to move back to Chile. Upon her return the country's medical establishment refused to honor the coursework and medical training Bachelet received in East Germany, so she had to repeat many of the courses she had taken earlier. She graduated near the top of her medical school class and then worked as a doctor helping the children of parents who were tortured or missing during the Pinochet administration's reign.

A fluent speaker of five languages, Bachelet is the first woman to be democratically elected as a head of state in Latin America who was not married to a previous head of state. Because the Chilean constitution prohibited her from running for two consecutive terms, Bachelet resigned from the presidency in March 2010. Had these constitutional prohibitions not been in place, it was likely that she would have been reelected because she had an 80 percent approval rating when she resigned.

What do you think motivates Bachelet? How would you measure her performance and effectiveness?

Sources: *The Economist,* March 31, 2007, p. 44; http://www.cwwl.org/bio-bachelet-michelle.html; http://www.notablebiographies.com/newsmakers2/2007-A-Co/Bachelet-Michelle.html; http://www.biography.com/articles/Michelle-Bachelet-37782?print.

job satisfaction. The implicit link between satisfaction and motivation is that satisfaction increases when people accomplish a task, particularly when the task requires a lot of effort. It might also seem logical that *performance* must be higher among more satisfied workers, but this is not always so.[12,17,24,49,50] Although satisfaction and performance are correlated, happy workers are not always the most productive ones; nor are unhappy or dissatisfied workers always the poorest performers. It is possible, for example, for poorly performing workers to be fairly satisfied with their jobs (maybe because they are paid well but do not have to work hard). It is also possible for dissatisfied workers to be relatively high performers (they may have a strong work ethic, have no other employment options, or be trying to improve the chances of getting out of their current job). Despite the intuitive appeal of believing that satisfied workers usually perform better, satisfaction has only an indirect effect on performance. Nevertheless, having both satisfied *and* high-performing followers is a goal leaders should usually strive to achieve.

Understanding and Influencing Follower Motivation

What do leaders do to motivate followers to accomplish group goals? Are all leaders and followers motivated the same way? Is there a universal theory of motivation? In other words, do Osama bin Laden and General David Petraeus, commander of U.S. forces in Afghanistan, use the same or different techniques to motivate their followers? As described in Highlight 9.2, organizations spend billions on motivating employees; but do these interventions actually improve job satisfaction, retention, and performance? Research can answer these questions, and few topics of human behavior have been the subject of so much attention as that of motivation. So much has been written about motivation that a comprehensive review of the subject is beyond the scope of this book. We will, however, survey several major approaches to understanding follower motivation, as well as address the implications of these approaches for follower satisfaction and performance. These motivational theories and approaches give leaders a number of suggestions to get followers to engage in and persist with different behaviors. However, some motivational theories are particularly useful in certain situations but not as applicable in others. Just as a carpenter can build better wooden structures or furniture by having a larger set of tools, so can leaders solve a greater number of motivational problems among followers by becoming familiar with different motivational theories and approaches. People who have only hammers in their toolkits are likely to see every problem as a nail needing hammering, and it is not unusual for less effective leaders to call on a limited number of approaches to any motivational problem. *Leaders who know about different motivational theories are more likely to choose the right theory for a particular follower and situation, and often have higher-performing and more satisfied employees as a result.*

Most performance problems can be attributed to unclear expectations, skill deficits, resource/equipment shortages, or a lack of motivation. Of these underlying causes, leaders seem to have the most difficulty in

Organizations Spend Billions on Motivational Programs for Employees, and All They Get Are Burned Feet

HIGHLIGHT 9.2

Organizations are constantly looking for quick fixes for their performance and effectiveness problems. The barriers to team or organizational performance often include a lack of resources and skills, unclear goals, poor performance or accountability standards, or incompetent leadership. But rather than adopting methods to directly address these issues, many organizations instead have employees listen to motivational speakers or engage in whitewater rafting, bungee jumping, or firewalking events. The motivational speaking circuit includes former professional athletes, astronauts, fighter pilots, and military generals, successful and failed business leaders, politicians, psychologists, and consultants. Motivational speaking engagements can be lucrative—one of the authors worked with a speaker who gave one speech in Las Vegas at lunch and the same speech that evening in Minneapolis and made $150,000 for the day. The author also has worked with a group of ex-fighter pilots who do half-day "Business Is Combat" seminars for $30,000–$75,000.

Companies think nothing of spending like this to motivate employees. For example, the software consulting firm EMC has spent $625,000 to have 5,000 employees walk over burning coals. But do expensive speakers and extreme activities actually improve organizational performance? Unfortunately exhaustive research has shown virtually no link between motivational spending and company revenues, profitability, or market share. Perhaps the biggest problem is that employees may find it difficult to see the link between walking over a bed of hot coals or participating in a Business Is Combat mission planning event and making another 20 sales calls every week. The problem is that these events do not address the root cause of many organizational woes but instead covertly shift the burden to "underperforming" employees. Other than bankrolling the motivation industry, these programs have another effect: nine U.S. Air Force recruiters had to go to the emergency room after they received second- and third-degree burns on their feet after one of these motivational programs.

Sources: D. Jones, "Firms Spend Billions to Fire Up Workers—With Little Luck," *USA Today,* May 10, 2001, pp. 1–2A; P. G. Chronis, "9 Burn Feet in National Guard Recruiters' Fire Walk," *Denver Post,* December 28, 1998, pp. 1A, 17A; G. J. Curphy and R. T. Hogan, "Managerial Incompetence: Is There a Dead Skunk on the Table?" working paper, 2004; G. J. Curphy, M. J. Benson, A. Baldrica, and R. T. Hogan, *Managerial Incompetence,* unpublished manuscript, 2007.

The truth of the matter is that you always know the right thing to do. The hard part is doing it.

Norman Schwarzkopf, United States Army

---

recognizing and rectifying motivation problems. An example might help to illustrate this point. A major airline was having serious problems with the customer service of its flight attendants. Passenger complaints were on the rise, and airplane loading (the average number of people per flight) was decreasing. The perceived lack of customer service was beginning to cost the airline market share and revenues; to fix the problem it decided to have all 10,000 flight attendants go through a two-day customer service training program. Unfortunately passenger complaints only got worse after the training. A thorough investigation of the underlying cause of the problem revealed that flight attendants knew what they were supposed to do, had all the skills necessary to perform the behaviors, and usually had the resources and equipment necessary to serve customers. The root cause was a lack of motivation to go the extra mile for customers. When asked what they found to be the most motivating aspect of being a flight attendant, most stated "time off." In other words, the flight attendants were most motivated when they were *not* at work. (Because of work schedules, flight attendants typically get two weeks off per month.) Given that a strong union represented the flight attendants, how would you go about solving this dilemma? The next section will give you some ideas on how to resolve this and other motivation problems that you may face as a leader.

As stated earlier, leaders can use many different theories and approaches to motivate followers. In this section we will discuss the key aspects of five popular and useful approaches to understanding motivation in work or leadership contexts. Some may wonder why these motivational approaches were included and others excluded from this section, and sound arguments could be made for changing the motivational approaches described. Our intention is to provide a broad view of different motivational approaches and not be so comprehensive as to overwhelm readers. The five theories and approaches are listed in Table 9.1. For illustrative purposes we will also discuss how leadership practitioners could apply these approaches to motivate two fictitious followers, Julie and Ling Ling. Julie is a 21-year-old ski lift operator in Banff, Alberta, Canada. Her primary job is to ensure that people get on and off her ski lift safely. She also does periodic equipment safety checks and maintains the lift lines and associated areas. Julie works from 8:30 a.m. to 5:00 p.m. five days a week, is paid a salary, and has a pass that allows her to ski for free whenever she is off work. Ling Ling is a 35-year-old real estate agent in Hong Kong. She works for an agency that locates and rents apartments for people on one- to three-year business assignments for various multinational companies. She works many evenings and weekends showing apartments, and she is paid a salary plus a commission for every apartment she rents. How the five approaches could be used to motivate Julie and Ling Ling will be discussed periodically throughout this section.

Maslow's Hierarchy of Needs: How Does Context Affect Motivation?

First rule of survival: Pack your own parachute.
T. L. Hakala

One way to get followers to engage in and persist with the behaviors needed to accomplish group goals is to appeal to their needs. **Needs** refer to internal states of tension or arousal, or uncomfortable states of deficiency people are motivated to change. Hunger would be a good example of a need: people are motivated to eat when they get hungry. Other needs might include the need to live in a safe and secure place, to belong to a group with common interests or social ties, or to do interesting and challenging work. If these needs were not being met, people would choose to engage in and persist with certain behaviors until they were satisfied. According to this motivational approach, leadership practitioners can get

TABLE 9.1
Five Motivational Approaches

Theory or Approach	Major Themes of Characteristics
Maslow's hierarchy of needs	Satisfy needs to change behavior.
Achievement orientation	Personality trait.
Goal setting	Set goals to change behavior.
Operant approach	Change rewards and punishments to change behavior.
Empowerment	Give people autonomy and latitude to increase their motivation for work.

followers to engage in and persist with certain behaviors by correctly identifying and appeasing their needs.

According to Maslow, people are motivated by five basic types of needs.[51] These include the need to survive physiologically, the need for security, the need for affiliation with other people (that is, belongingness), the need for self-esteem, and the need for self-actualization. Maslow's conceptualization of needs is usually represented by a triangle with the five levels of needs arranged in a **hierarchy of needs** (see Figure 9.2). According to Maslow, any person's behavior can be understood primarily as the effort directed to satisfy a particular level of need in the hierarchy. Which level happens to be motivating a person's behavior at any time depends on whether lower needs in the hierarchy have been satisfied. According to Maslow, lower-level needs must be satisfied before the next-higher level becomes salient in motivating behavior.

Maslow believed higher-level needs like those for self-esteem or self-actualization would not become salient (even when unfulfilled) until

FIGURE 9.2
Maslow's Hierarchy of Needs

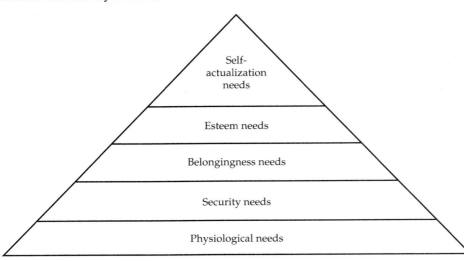

lower needs were satisfied. Thus a practical implication of his theory is that leaders can motivate follower behavior only by taking account of a follower's or team's position on the needs hierarchy. Applying Maslow's hierarchy to Julie, it might be inefficient to try to motivate our ski lift operator by appealing to how much pride she could take in a job well done (that is, to her self-esteem) if she was underdressed for weather conditions. If her boss wanted Julie to do more, she should first make sure that Julie's physiological needs were met, that she worked and lived in a secure place, and that she had ample opportunities to socialize with other employees. Only after these lower needs had been met should the boss try to increase Julie's self-esteem. Thus if leadership practitioners want to use Maslow's hierarchy of needs to motivate employees to work harder, they need to determine where their followers are on the needs hierarchy and ensure that all lower-order needs are satisfied before appealing to their followers' self-esteem or self-actualization needs. Leadership practitioners should watch for mismatches between their motivational efforts and followers' *lowest* (on the hierarchy) unsatisfied needs.

How could you determine the needs of flight attendants, and what kind of program would you implement to improve customer service? Although Maslow's theory provides some useful ideas on how to improve customer service, it has several limitations. For one thing, the theory does not make specific predictions about what an individual will do to satisfy a particular need. [21,52] For example, if Ling Ling was trying to get her belongingness needs met, she might exert considerable effort to establish new friendships at work, try to make friends outside work, or join several professional or business associations. This lack of specificity and predictive power limits the practical applicability of Maslow's theory in real-life settings. On the other hand, awareness of the general nature of the various sorts of basic human needs described in this theory seems fundamentally useful to leaders. Leaders will have a difficult time getting followers to maintain various work behaviors by emphasizing good relationships with co-workers or appealing to their sense of pride if the job pays only minimum wage and followers are having a difficult time making ends meet. A person may be reluctant to volunteer for a self-actualizing opportunity in support of a political campaign if such participation may risk that person's financial security. Perhaps the greatest insight provided by this theory is that leadership practitioners may need to address some basic, fundamental areas before their attempts to get followers and teams to expend more effort on work-related behaviors will be successful.

Along these lines, it may be interesting to look at how Maslow's hierarchy of needs could be applied to workers from 2002 to 2009. One could argue that during the economic growth years many workers were putting in long hours but operating at the esteem and self-actualization levels. However, with the recession of 2008–2010 those who remained employed switched their focus to meeting their security needs. These

Cadet Motivation

HIGHLIGHT 9.3

One of the toughest things for freshmen at a military academy to do is come back to school after winter break. For most freshmen it is the first time they have been home since June, and the contrast between civilian and military life is so great that many are tempted to leave military school. The freshmen at the U.S. Air Force Academy were asked to write a paper about why they returned to the institution after winter break. Read the following paper and determine what work values drive this individual:

Winter Break

So after our sunburns have faded and memories of our winter break have been reduced to pictures we've pinned on our desk boards, and once again we've exchanged T-shirts and swimsuits for flight suits and camouflage, there still remains the question that every cadet in Colorado Springs has asked themselves at some point: Why did we come back? Why, after spending two weeks with our family, could we return to one of the most demanding lifestyles in the country? After listening to our "friends" who are home from state or Ivy League schools chock full of wisdom about how the war in Iraq is unjust and unworldly, why would we return? And after watching the news and reading the papers, which only seem to condemn the military's every mistake and shadow every victory, why would we continue to think it is worth the sacrifice of a normal college life?

Is it because the institution to which we belong is tuition-free? Anyone who claims this has forgotten that we will, by the time we graduate, repay the U.S. taxpayer many times over in blood, sweat, and

tears. Is it because the schooling we are receiving is one of the best undergraduate educations in the country? While the quality of the education is second to none, anyone who provides this as a main reason has lost sight of the awesome responsibility that awaits those who are tough enough to graduate and become commissioned officers in the U.S. Air Force.

I come back to the Academy because I want to have the training necessary so that one day I'll have the incredible responsibility of leading the sons and daughters of America in combat. These men and women will never ask about my Academy grade point average; their only concern will be that I have the ability to lead them expertly—I will be humbled to earn their respect.

I come back to the Academy because I want to be the commander who saves lives negotiating with Arab leaders . . . in their own language. I come back to the Academy because, if called upon, I want to be the pilot who flies halfway around the world with three mid-air refuelings to send a bomb from 30,000 feet into a basement housing the enemy . . . through a ventilation shaft two feet wide. For becoming an officer in today's modern Air Force is so much more than just a command; it is being a diplomat, a strategist, a communicator, a moral compass, but always a warrior first . . .

Joseph R. Tomczak
Cadet Fourth Class
United States Air Force Academy

Given this letter, what level is Cadet Tomczak operating at according to Maslow's hierarchy of needs?

Some players you pat their butts, other players you kick their butts, and some players you leave alone.
Pete Rose

individuals were working longer hours than ever before, but this was to ensure they had a job versus making a meaningful contribution or being fulfilled. And many of those who were not gainfully employed may have spent much of their time just trying to get food on the table (physiological needs). As the economy recovers, it will be interesting to see if leaders will be able to convince followers that their lower-level needs will be met and get them to shift their focus to self-esteem and self-actualization needs.

Achievement Orientation: How Does Personality Affect Motivation?

Is it possible that some people are naturally more motivated or have "more fire in the belly" than others? Do some people automatically put forth a higher level of effort toward group goals simply because they are hardwired this way? Unlike Maslow's theory, which claims all people share some fundamental needs, this approach to motivation is simple. To improve group performance, leaders should select only followers who both possess the right skills and have a higher level of a personality trait called achievement orientation.

Atkinson has proposed that an individual's tendency to exert effort toward task accomplishment depends partly on the strength of his or her motivation to achieve success, or as Atkinson called it, **achievement orientation**.[21,53] McClelland further developed Atkinson's ideas and said that individuals with a strong achievement orientation (or in McClelland's terms, a strong *need for achievement*) strive to accomplish socially acceptable endeavors and activities. These individuals also prefer tasks that provide immediate and ample feedback and are moderately difficult (that is, tasks that require a considerable amount of effort but are accomplishable). Additionally, individuals with a strong need to achieve feel satisfied when they successfully solve work problems or accomplish job tasks. Individuals with a relatively low need to achieve generally prefer easier tasks and do not feel satisfied by solving problems or accomplishing assigned tasks. McClelland maintained that differences in achievement orientation are a primary reason why people differ in the levels of effort they exert to accomplish assignments, objectives, or goals. Thus achievement orientation is a bit like "fire in the belly"; people with more achievement orientation are likely to set higher personal and work goals and are more likely to expend the effort needed to accomplish them. People with low levels of achievement motivation tend to set lower personal and work goals and are less likely to accomplish them.[54]

Achievement orientation is also a component of the Five Factor Model or OCEAN model of personality dimension of conscientiousness (see Chapter 6). Conscientiousness has been found to be positively related to performance across virtually all jobs as well as predict success in school, in the military, in blue-collar and retail workers, and in management positions. All things being equal, people with higher levels of achievement orientation are likely to do better in school, pursue postgraduate degrees, get promoted more quickly, and get paid higher salaries and bonuses than their lower-scoring counterparts.[46,55-64]

Given that individuals with higher achievement orientation scores set high personal goals and put in the time and effort necessary to achieve them, it is hardly surprising that achievement orientation is often a key success factor for people who advance to the highest levels of the organization.

What Really Motivates Workers?

HIGHLIGHT 9.4

Which of the following items do you think best motivates workers?

A. Recognition

B. Incentives

C. Interpersonal support

D. Support for making progress

E. Clear goals

If you are like 600 managers who were asked this question in 2010, you would choose A. Recognition for good work. However, if we look over daily diaries of hundreds of employees over a multiyear period, the answer seems to be D. Support for making progress. Employees reported striving to do their best and having the strongest positive emotions on days when they felt they were making headway in their work assignments or got support to overcome obstacles. Emotions and drive were lowest on those days when they felt they were spinning their wheels

or encountered roadblocks. These research results indicate that leaders can best motivate followers and teams by providing meaningful goals, resources, and encouragement; being decisive; and minimizing irrelevant demands. Leaders can also help motivate followers by rolling up their sleeves and pitching in and not exerting time pressure so intense that even minor glitches are perceived as major crises.

The good news is that many of the things leaders can to do motivate followers are under their direct control. It is also worth noting that this research reported that recognition helps to improve motivation, but only if people feel they are making progress toward individual or team goals. How does making progress toward goals relate to Maslow's hierarchy of needs or to people with low or high levels of achievement orientation?

Source: T. M. Amabile and S. J. Kramer, "What Really Motivates Workers?" *Harvard Business Review*, January–February 2010, pp. 44–45.

For example, achievement orientation appears to be a common success factor underlying the careers of Michelle Bachelet, Mark Roellig, Wu Yi, and Richard Branson (Profiles in Leadership 9.1–9.4). Although achievement orientation is often associated with higher performance, high achievers can get demoralized when facing unclear or impossible tasks. Working with elite Army Ranger units, Britt found that these units almost always performed at high levels and were often successful. But when given unclear missions with few resources and impossible timelines, these same units could self-destruct quickly. In these situations the units felt they were being set up to fail, and fail they did. This phenomenon is clearly depicted in the movie *Black Hawk Down,* where Army Ranger units were sent to Mogadishu, Somalia, to capture a Somalian warlord. The important lesson here is that leaders need to give high achievers clear goals and the resources they need to succeed.[65]

How could a leader apply this knowledge of achievement orientation to improve the performance of Julie, Ling Ling, and the flight attendants? Perhaps the first step would be to ensure that the hiring process selected individuals with higher levels of achievement orientation. Assuming they had higher scores, we would expect Ling Ling to work with her boss to set aggressive goals for renting apartments and then work as many nights and weekends as were needed to achieve them. We might also expect Ling Ling to obtain her MBA from Hong Kong University over the next few years. Julie could also be expected to set high personal and work goals, but she may find that her job limits her ability to pursue these goals. Unlike Ling Ling, who can control the number of nights and weekends she works, Julie has no control over the number of people who ride on her lift. The job itself may limit Julie's ability to fulfill her high level of achievement orientation. As a result, she may pursue other activities, such as becoming an expert skier, joining the ski patrol, doing ski racing, looking for additional responsibilities or opportunities for advancement, or finding another job where she has the opportunity to achieve and get rewarded for her efforts. Because Julie would set and work toward high personal goals, a good boss would work closely with Julie to find work-related ways to capitalize on her achievement orientation. Thus achievement orientation may be a dual-edged sword. Leadership practitioners may be able to hire a group of highly motivated followers, but they also need to set clear expectations, provide opportunities for followers to set and achieve work-related goals, and provide feedback on progress toward goals. Otherwise followers may find different ways to fulfill their high levels of achievement orientation.

> *Capacity is its own motivation.*
> **David Campbell, Center for Creative Leadership**

Applying the achievement orientation approach to the flight attendant situation or to U.S. workers from 2002 to 2009 leads to some interesting thoughts. Perhaps the airline did not screen for conscientiousness when hiring flight attendants and does not have enough people with high scores to deliver good customer service. Or the company could have hired only people with high conscientiousness scores but not set any measurable goals, repeatedly ignored requests for better equipment, failed to back up staff when they were challenged by "bad" travelers, or not given any recognition for jobs well done. In this case the flight attendants could feel that they have been set up for failure. With respect to people working in the United States from 2002 to 2009, those with the highest levels of achievement orientation were most likely to get promoted during the economic boom and stay with their companies during the recession. However, because many companies went under or eliminated entire work units or functions, some achievement-oriented types found themselves out of jobs. Because work is so important to people with high levels of achievement orientation, some of these individuals probably found work elsewhere. Others may be devastated by their job loss and are bitter about being set up for failure.

> *A good goal is like strenuous exercise—it makes you stretch.*
> **Mary Kay Ashe, CEO**

Goal Setting: How Do Clear Performance Targets Affect Motivation?

One of the most familiar and easiest formal systems of motivation to use with followers is **goal setting.** From the leader's perspective, this involves setting clear performance targets and then helping followers create

Mark Roellig

PROFILES IN LEADERSHIP 9.2

Mark Roellig is currently the executive vice president and general counsel of MassMutual Financial Group. Growing up in Michigan, Mark attended the University of Michigan to obtain an undergraduate degree in mathematics in three years. He went on to earn his law degree at George Washington University and an MBA degree from the University of Washington. Mark started his professional career as an attorney practicing civil litigation at two law firms in Seattle before joining Pacific Northwestern Bell Telephone Company in 1983. He spent the next 17 years working in the law division of the company as it transformed from Pacific Northwestern Bell to US West to Qwest Communications. During this time Mark rapidly moved through the ranks and eventually became the executive vice president of public policy, human resources, and law for US West. In this role Mark managed a group of over 1,000 employees and an annual budget of $250,000,000.

After US West was acquired by Qwest, Mark spent some time as the general counsel for Storage Technology Corporation and Fisher Scientific International before moving into his current role in 2005. MassMutual Financial Group is a financial services company that has over $420,000,000,000 in assets under management and is ranked as a *Fortune* 100 firm. Mark is currently responsible for both the law and corporate services divisions and manages a team of 500 employees and a $160,000,000 annual budget. Having been the top lawyer and board secretary for four *Fortune* 500 companies, Mark has learned a number of valuable lessons about leadership and management over the years. Some of these key lessons include developing strategic plans that support

and advance the business objectives, surrounding oneself with top talent, setting clear goals to support plans, using metrics to track progress, rewarding top performers, building teams, and creating performance-based cultures. Some of Mark's accomplishments since joining MassMutual include these:

- A 57 percent reduction in outside counsel costs.
- A 27 percent reduction in total legal costs.
- An 18 percent reduction in dispute resolution costs.
- A 15 percent increase in customer satisfaction ratings.
- Consistently receiving some of the best employee satisfaction scores across the company.

Mark obsesses over talent and spends a considerable amount of time hiring top lawyers and then putting them in various training programs and rotational assignments to help them develop needed legal and leadership skills. Over the years a number of his direct reports have gone on to be general counsels or top lawyers in a number of other firms, and because of his unique combination of skills Mark is constantly asked to lead areas outside the legal area, as well as provide advice on complex business, public policy, board of director, and personnel issues.

How would you use Maslow's hierarchy of needs, achievement orientation, goal setting, and the operant approach to describe Mark Roellig's career? Which motivational approaches best describe his leadership philosophy?

Sources: http://boston.citybizlist.com/lstg/lstgDetail.aspx?id-4030; M. Roellig, *Summary of 2009 Law Division Activities*, presentation given to the MassMutual Audit Committee on April 13, 2010, in Springfield, MA.

systematic plans to achieve them. According to Locke and Latham, goals are the most powerful determinants of task behaviors. Goals direct attention, mobilize effort, help people develop strategies for achievement, and help people continue exerting effort until the goals are reached. This leads, in turn, to even higher goals.[66-69]

Locke and Latham reported that nearly 400 studies involving hundreds of tasks across 40,000 individuals, groups, and organizations in eight different countries have provided consistent support for several aspects of goal setting. First, this research showed goals that were both *specific* and *difficult* resulted in consistently higher effort and performance when contrasted to "do your best" goals. Second, *goal commitment* is critical. Merely having goals is not enough. Although follower participation in setting goals is one way to increase commitment, goals set either by leaders unilaterally or through participation with followers can lead to necessary levels of commitment. Commitment to assigned goals was often as high as commitment to goals followers helped to set, provided the leader was perceived to have legitimate authority, expressed confidence in followers, and provided clear standards for performance. Third, followers exerted the greatest effort when goals were accompanied by *feedback*; followers getting goals or feedback alone generally exerted less effort. (See Highlight 9.5 for a practical application of goal-setting theory.)

Several other aspects of goal setting are also worth noting. First, goals can be set for any aspect of performance, be it reducing costs, improving the quality of services and products, increasing voter registration, or winning a league championship. Nevertheless, leaders need to ensure that they do not set conflicting goals because followers can exert only so much effort over a given time.[70] Second, determining just how challenging to make goals creates a bit of a dilemma for leaders. Successfully completed goals give followers a sense of job satisfaction, and easy goals are more likely to be completed than difficult goals. However, easily attainable goals result in lower levels of effort (and performance) than do more difficult goals. Research suggests that leaders might motivate followers most effectively by setting moderately difficult goals, recognizing partial goal accomplishment, and making use of a continuous improvement philosophy by making goals incrementally more difficult.[71-76]

A leader's implicit and explicit expectations about goal accomplishment can also affect the performance of followers and teams. Research by Dov Eden and his associates in Israel has provided consistent support for the Pygmalion and Golem effects.[77,78] The **Pygmalion effect** occurs when leaders articulate high expectations for followers; in many cases these expectations alone will lead to higher-performing followers and teams. Unfortunately the **Golem effect** is also true—leaders who have little faith in their followers' ability to accomplish a goal are rarely disappointed. Thus a leader's expectations for a follower or team have a good chance of becoming a self-fulfilling prophecy (Chapter 2). These results indicate that leaders wanting to improve individual or team performance should set high but achievable goals and express confidence and support that the followers can get the job done.[79,80]

How could leadership practitioners apply goal setting to Julie and Ling Ling to increase their motivation levels? Given the research findings just

The Balanced Scorecard

HIGHLIGHT 9.5

A practical method for implementing goal setting in organizations involves the creation of balanced scorecards. Kaplan and Norton argue that most of the measures typically used to assess organizational performance are too limited in scope. For example, many organizations set goals and periodically review their financial performance, but these indicators suffer from time lags (it may take a month or longer before the financial results of specific organizational activities are available) and say little about other key organizational performance indicators, such as customer satisfaction, employee turnover, and key internal operational performance. To get around these problems, Kaplan and Norton advocate creating a set of goals and metrics for customers, employees, internal operations, and finance. Customer and employee goals and metrics make up leading indicators because problems with customer satisfaction and employee turnover often result in subpar operational and financial performance.

Curphy has developed balanced scorecards for rural Minnesota hospitals and school districts. For example, hospitals begin this process with a comprehensive review of their market demographics, customer trends, financial performance, internal operations (pharmacy, surgical use, infection rates, radiology and lab use, and so on), and staffing and facility data. Key community and health care leaders then create a new five-year vision for the hospital and set strategic priorities in the customer, financial, internal operations, and workforce and facilities categories. These priorities are refined further to create clear, measurable goals with readily available metrics to track monthly progress. These balanced scorecard goals are used to drive specific department goals and track hospital performance and have been very effective in helping all hospital employees understand how their efforts contribute to the hospital's overall performance. In several cases hospital performance has dramatically improved as

a result of these balanced scorecard efforts. A partial example of a typical balanced scorecard for one of these rural hospitals is as follows:

- **Customer:** Improve patient satisfaction ratings from 74 to 86 percent by 1 January 2012.
- **Customer:** Increase the number of live births from 12 to 20 per month by 1 January 2012.
- **Financial:** Reduce average accounts payable from 84 to 53 days by 1 January 2012.
- **Financial:** Increase operating margins from 2 to 6 percent by 1 January 2012.
- **Internal operations:** Increase orthopedic surgeries from 4 to 8 per day by 1 March 2012.
- **Internal operations:** Reduce patient infection rates from 1 to .5 percent by 1 March 2012.
- **Workforce:** Reduce days needed to hire nurses from 62 to 22 days by 1 March 2012.
- **Workforce:** Reduce employee turnover rates from 27 to 12 percent by 1 March 2012.

A monthly balanced scorecard report is included in all employee pay statements and is a key topic of discussion in hospital and department staff meetings. Staff members review goal progress and regularly devise strategies for achieving department and hospital goals. A nice thing about the balanced scorecard is that it helps employees be proactive and gives them permission to win. In too many organizations employees work hard but never see how their results contribute to team or organizational performance. Adopting balanced scorecards is a way to get around these problems.

Sources: G. J. Curphy, *The Blandin Education Leadership Program* (Grand Rapids, MN: The Blandin Foundation, 2004); R. S. Kaplan and D. P. Norton, "The Balanced Scorecard: Measures That Drive Performance," *Harvard Business Review,* January–February 1992, pp. 71–79; R. S. Kaplan and D. P. Norton, *The Balanced Scorecard* (Boston, MA: Harvard Business School Press, 1996); R. S. Kaplan and D. P. Norton, *The Strategy Focused Organization* (Boston, MA: Harvard Business School Press, 2001).

described, Julie and Ling Ling's bosses should work with these two followers to set specific and moderately difficult goals, express confidence that they can achieve their goals, and provide regular feedback on goal progress. Julie and her boss could look at Julie's past performance or other lift operators' performance as a baseline, and then set specific and measurable goals for the number of hours worked, the number of people who fall off the lift during a shift, customer satisfaction survey ratings from skiers, the length of lift lines, or the number of complaints from customers. Similarly, Ling Ling and her boss could look at some real estate baseline measures and set goals for the number of apartments rented for the year, the total monetary value of these rentals, the time it takes to close a lease and complete the necessary paperwork, customer complaints, and sales expenses. Note that both Ling Ling and Julie's bosses would need to take care that they do not set conflicting goals. For example, if Julie had a goal only for the number of people who fell off the lift, she might be likely to run the lift slowly, resulting in long lift lines and numerous customer complaints. In a similar vein, bosses need to ensure that individual goals do not conflict with team or organizational goals. Ling Ling's boss would need to make sure that Ling Ling's goals did not interfere with those of the other real estate agents in the firm. If Ling Ling's goals did not specify territorial limits, she might rent properties in other agents' territories, which might cause a high level of interoffice conflict. Both bosses should also take care to set measurable goals; that way they could give Julie and Ling Ling the feedback they need to stay on track.

Goal setting could also help the airline company motivate flight attendants to provide better service to customers. Airline executives may believe customer satisfaction is critically important for keeping planes full, but they may not have set a specific goal for or devised a good way to measure customer satisfaction on individual flights. Customer service may improve only when the airline sets a clear customer satisfaction goal, makes feedback against the goal readily available, and holds flight attendants accountable for improved customer satisfaction results. Likewise, goal setting was also very prevalent for U.S. workers from 2002 to 2009. The first five years of this period saw a steady increase in market share, revenues, new product, profitability, and similar goals set each year, but the economic recession resulted in most if not all corporate goals being scaled back to where they were five years earlier. For example, a company with a $500,000,000 revenue goal in 2003 and steady growth may have had a $700,000,000 revenue goal by 2007. With the recession this revenue goal may have been scaled back to $500,000,000 in 2008. Although many key organizational goals were scaled back during the 2008–2010 recession, most leaders had significantly fewer people to get the goals accomplished. In many cases those who remained found that they needed to get much more work done with many fewer people. Those who were laid off often set goals for finding new jobs and the activities they would engage in to make this happen. Because goal setting is such a widely used and powerful motivational technique, more about this topic can be found in Chapter 11.

The Operant Approach: How Do Rewards and Punishment Affect Motivation?

One popular way to change the direction, intensity, or persistence of behavior is through rewards and punishments. It will help at the outset of this discussion of the **operant approach** to define several terms. A **reward** is any consequence that *increases* the likelihood that a particular behavior will be repeated. For example, if Julie gets a cash award for a suggestion to improve customer service at the ski resort, she will be more likely to forward additional suggestions. **Punishment** is the administration of an aversive stimulus or the withdrawal of something desirable, each of which *decreases* the likelihood that a particular behavior will be repeated.[81] Thus if Ling Ling loses her bonus for not getting her paperwork in on time, she will be less likely to do so again in the future. Both rewards and punishments can be administered in a contingent or noncontingent manner. **Contingent** rewards or punishments are administered as *consequences of a particular behavior.* Examples might include giving Julie a medal immediately after she wins a skiing race or giving Ling Ling a bonus check for exceeding her sales quota. **Noncontingent** rewards and

Wu Yi

PROFILES IN LEADERSHIP 9.3

In 2008 Wu Yi retired as the Vice Premier and Minister of Health for the People's Republic of China. One of four premiers in charge of running the country, Wu Yi was ranked second on *Fortune's* list of the most powerful women in the world for three years. Wu Yi started her career by graduating from the Beijing Petroleum Institute with a degree in petroleum engineering. After school she started as a petroleum technician and eventually achieved the rank of deputy manager at the Beijing Dongfang Hong refinery. A Communist party member, Wu Yi was the party secretary at the Beijing Yanshan Petrochemical Corporation before being elected to be the deputy mayor of Beijing in 1988. She held this position during the Tiananmen Square protests and from 1991 to 1998 moved into positions of ever-increasing responsibility within the Communist party. A protégé of Zhu Rongji, she helped negotiate the country's entry into the World Trade Orga-

nization and reorganized the customs service after complaints about intellectual property theft. She also took charge of China's response to the SARS crisis when the previous minister had been fired for covering up the event and is heading up China's delegation in the six-country talks to persuade North Korea to give up its nuclear weapons. Firm and direct in her leadership style, she has been called by some the "Iron Lady of China." An able diplomat, she has negotiated and signed a number of trade agreements with other Asian countries and makes frequent inspection visits across the country.

Where do you think Maslow's hierarchy of needs, achievement orientation, goal setting, and the operant approach have come into play during Wu Yi's career?

Source: http://www.forbes.com/lists/2006/11/06women_Wu-Yi_GGD7.html; http://chineseculture.about.com/od/thechinesegovernment/p/WuYi.htm.

Professional Athlete and Executive Salary Demands

HIGHLIGHT 9.6

General managers are responsible for the overall performance of their professional sports teams. They help select players and coaches; negotiate media, player, coach, and stadium contracts; keep team morale at a high level; and take action to ensure the team wins the championship and makes money. One of the most difficult issues general managers deal with is negotiating contracts with players. Players look at their own pay and performance and compare them to those of other athletes in the league. If they feel their compensation is not consistent with that of other players, they usually ask to be traded or for a new contract to be negotiated. These comparisons have led to the $100 million–plus salaries now commanded by star players in basketball, football, and baseball. But what happens to team morale, the win–loss record, and financial performance when one or two players make substantially more money than the rest of the team? Research on professional baseball teams over an eight-year period indicated that teams with high pay dispersion levels (large gaps between the highest-and lowest-paid starting players) did less well financially and were less likely to win division championships. Researchers surmised that this drop in team performance was due to the high levels of pay dispersion, which eroded team performance and increased inequity for other players on the team. The trick for general managers seems to be to find enough financial rewards to induce higher levels of performance but not create inequity situations for the rest of the team.

The effects of pay inequity that are readily apparent with professional athletes' pay also hold true for top executives. Many boards of directors worry that if they do not pay their CEOs and top executives at least on par with those in other companies, they run the risk of executive turnover. But executives who negotiate large signing bonuses and big annual pay packages don't necessarily achieve better results than their lower-paid counterparts. Far too many executives tout the benefits of pay for performance but appear much more concerned with their own pay than their company's performance. For example, the compensation for the average United States worker rose at a 0.3 percent annual rate from 1980 to 2004, yet the average CEO's compensation grew at a rate of 8.5 percent annually. CEOs promised an average of 11.5 percent annual earnings growth over this period but actually only achieved 6 percent growth, which was slightly less than the annual percentage growth rate for the overall economy from 1980 to 2004. Despite the fact that the average CEO performed no better than the overall economy, in 1980 the average CEO made 42 times as much as the average worker, and by 2004 this had increased to 280 times the average worker's salary. The top executives in Japanese companies currently make 20–30 times more than the average employee, and one has to wonder if companies with high pay dispersions achieve the same suboptimal results as do professional athletic teams with high pay dispersions. With workers putting in longer hours for less pay and the people on top getting fat paychecks and bonuses irrespective of results, is it any wonder that workers are less satisfied and engaged?

Sources: M. Bloom, "The Performance Effects of Pay Dispersions on Individuals and Organizations," *Academy of Management Journal* 42, no. 1 (1999), pp. 25–40; J. Lublin, "Boards Tie CEO Pay More Tightly to Performance," *The Wall Street Journal,* February 21, 2006, pp. A1 and A14; L. A. Bebchuk and J. M. Fried, "Pay without Performance: Overview of the Issues," *The Academy of Management Perspectives* 20, no. 1 (2006), pp. 5–24; J. Bogle, "Reflections on CEO Compensation," *The Academy of Management Perspectives* 22, no. 2 (2008), pp. 21–25.

and do not violate organizational norms or policies. Julie might find driving the snow cat to be enjoyable, and her boss could use this reward to maintain or increase Julie's motivation levels for operating the ski lift. Finally, because the administration of noncontingent consequences has relatively little impact, *leadership practitioners should administer rewards and punishments in a contingent manner whenever possible.* Highlight 9.7 provides examples of the unintended consequences of implementing an operant approach to boost organizational performance.

The operant approach can also be used to improve customer service for flight attendants. Using the tenets described earlier, the airline would need to specify which customer satisfaction behaviors were important, determine if those behaviors were being reinforced or punished, determine what attendants found to be rewarding, and administered valued rewards whenever attendants demonstrated good customer service behaviors.

The operant approach to motivation was alive and well in the United States from 2002 to 2009 and continues to be a popular motivational technique in many companies today. Most organizations tout a "pay for performance" culture and pay bonuses or commissions for results obtained. This can most clearly be seen in sales positions, where salespeople are paid a percentage of the total dollars they sell. Needless to say, salespeople experienced a large drop in compensation when customers stopped buying products and services during the 2008–2010 recession, despite exhibiting all the behaviors needed to retain customers or get new business in the door. This example points out a shortcoming of the operant technique, which is that situational factors can overwhelm the effectiveness of a reward program. Sometimes people can get big bonuses or commissions without working hard because they are selling a hot product or the economy is experiencing a boom. Other times they may do all the right things but nobody wants to buy their products because of factors beyond their control (such as selling Hummers when gasoline is $4.00/gallon or selling Toyotas during that company's safety crisis).

Empowerment: How Does Decision-Making Latitude Affect Motivation?

Empowerment is the final approach to motivation that will be discussed in this chapter. In general, people seem to fall into one of two camps with respect to empowerment. Some people believe empowerment is about delegation and accountability; it is a top-down process in which senior leaders articulate a vision and specific goals and hold followers responsible for achieving them. Others believe empowerment is more of a bottom-up approach that focuses on intelligent risk taking, growth, change, trust, and ownership; followers act as entrepreneurs and owners who question rules and make intelligent decisions. Leaders tolerate mistakes and encourage cooperative behavior in this approach to empowerment.[95-99]

The Culture of Praise

HIGHLIGHT 9.8

There is no doubt that the generation of people entering the workforce these days has had more positive reinforcement while growing up than any previous generation. As children these individuals got positive strokes in the form of rewards, ribbons, plaques, and certificates for just showing up to athletic events or school activities. For example, one of this book's authors went to a school assembly for one of his children and watched teachers pass out awards to all 300 students in the elementary school. Some of the awards were for student achievement or citizenship, but many were for "completing your homework for three days in a row" and "having a nice smile." Thirty years ago it was difficult to earn an athletic letter in one or two sports, but some of today's athletic jackets have 10–15 awards and letters. This culture of praise was intended to boost self-esteem and better prepare students for life after high school, but as described in Highlight 9.7, the use of unconditional praise has had some unintended implications that organizations must deal with.

One implication is that people now entering the workforce are much more likely to be self-centered, "narcissistic praise junkies" than the people they are working for. Because of the constant positive reinforcement they received when growing up, a much higher percentage of people in this generation think they are special and should get rewarded for anything and everything they do. Organizations, recognizing this need in their youngest employees, are taking some extraordinary steps to boost the self-esteem of (and retain) these individuals. For example, Lands' End and Bank of America teach managers how to compliment employees using e-mail, prize packages, and public displays of appreciation. The Scooter Store has a "celebration assistant" whose job is to throw 25 pounds of confetti and pass out 100–500 helium balloons to employees each week. The Container Store estimates that one of its 4,000 employees is rewarded every 20 seconds.

But what is the impact of these praise and recognition programs? Company officials argue they would see high levels of turnover without these programs. But if this younger generation gets constant recognition just for meeting minimum standards, what happens when they get promoted into supervisory positions? The short-term consequence may be improved retention of young employees, but the long-term consequence may be leaders who are unable to deal with difficult business or personnel issues.

Source: J. Zaslow, "The Most Praised Generation Goes to Work," *The Wall Street Journal,* April 20, 2007, pp. W1 and W7.

Needless to say, these two conceptualizations of empowerment have very different implications for leaders and followers. And it is precisely this conceptual confusion that has caused empowerment programs to fail in many organizations.[95] Because of the conceptual confusion surrounding empowerment, companies such as Motorola will not use this term to describe programs that push decision making to lower organizational levels. These companies would rather coin their own terms to describe these programs, thus avoiding the confusion surrounding empowerment.

We define empowerment as having two key components. For leaders to truly empower employees, they must delegate leadership and decision making down to the lowest level possible. Employees are often the closest to the problem and have the most information, and as such can often make the best decisions. A classic example was the UPS employee who

Hemmed in by rules and treated as unimportant, people get even.
Rosabeth Moss Kanter, Harvard University

ordered an extra 737 aircraft to haul parcels that had been forgotten in the last-minute Christmas rush. This decision was clearly beyond the employee's level of authority, but UPS praised his initiative for seeing the problem and making the right decision. The second component of empowerment, and the one most often overlooked, is equipping followers with the resources, knowledge, and skills necessary to make good decisions. Often companies adopt an empowerment program and push decision making down to the employee level, but employees have no experience in creating business plans, submitting budgets, dealing with other departments within the company, or directly dealing with customers or vendors. Not surprisingly, ill-equipped employees can make poor, uninformed decisions, and managers in turn are likely to believe that empowerment was not all it was cracked up to be. The same happens with downsizing as employees are asked to take on additional responsibilities but are given little training or support. Such "forced" empowerment may lead to some short-term stock gains but tends to be disastrous in the long run. Thus empowerment has both delegation and developmental components; delegation without development is often perceived as abandonment, and development without delegation can often be perceived as micromanagement. Leaders wishing to empower followers must determine what followers are capable of doing, enhance and broaden these capabilities, and give followers commensurate increases in authority and accountability.

The psychological components of empowerment can be examined at both macro and micro levels. Three macro psychological components underlie empowerment: motivation, learning, and stress. As a concept, empowerment has been around since at least the 1920s, and the vast majority of companies that have implemented empowerment programs have done so to increase employee motivation and, in turn, productivity. As a motivational technique empowerment has a mixed record; often empowered workers are more productive than unempowered workers, but at times this may not be the case. When empowerment does not increase productivity, senior leaders may tend to see empowerment through rose-colored glasses. They hear about the benefits an empowerment program is having in another company but do not consider the time, effort, and changes needed to create a truly empowered workforce. Relatedly, many empowerment programs are poorly implemented—the program is announced with great fanfare, but little real guidance, training, or support is provided, and managers are quick to pull the plug on the program as soon as followers start making poor decisions. Adopting an effective empowerment program takes training, trust, and time; but companies most likely to implement an empowerment program (as a panacea for their poor financial situation) often lack these three attributes.[100,101] In addition, worker productivity and job dissatisfaction in the United States are at an all-time high. Many companies are dealing with high levels of employee burnout, and adding responsibilities to overfilled plates is likely to be counterproductive. As reported by Xie and Johns, some empowerment programs create positions that are just too big for a person to handle effectively, and job burnout is usually the result.[102]

Although the motivational benefits of empowerment are sometimes not realized, the learning and stress reduction benefits of empowerment are more clear-cut. Given that properly designed and implemented empowerment programs include a strong developmental component, a key benefit to these programs is that they help employees learn more about their jobs, company, and industry. These knowledge and skill gains increase the intellectual capital of the company and can be a competitive advantage in moving ahead. In addition to the learning benefits, well-designed empowerment programs can help reduce burnout. People can tolerate high levels of stress when they have a high level of control. Given that many employees are putting in longer hours than ever before and

Power and Empowerment

HIGHLIGHT 9.9

A famous Lord Acton quote is "Power corrupts," which essentially means that the more power one has the more likely one is to break laws, rules, and societal norms. Leadership researcher Rosabeth Moss Kanter has an interesting variation of this quote that relates to the concept of empowerment. According to Kanter, powerlessness also corrupts. In other words, if workers are only given a small amount of power, they will jealously guard whatever power they have. Employees with little power do not show their unhappiness by voicing their opinions but instead flex their muscles by demanding tribute before responding to requests. They rigidly adhere to the policies governing their position and ensure there are no exceptions to anyone following their rules. Customers are told to submit all required forms, get signed permissions from other entities, and follow bureaucratic procedures to the letter if they want anything done, and it will take requesters months to see tangible results. Because speed is an essential component of execution, powerlessness can paralyze companies needing to quickly build products, process orders, submit invoices, receive payments, or hire and train new

employees. One hallmark of organizations suffering from powerlessness is the hoarding of information. Information is power, so managers limit the amount of information given to followers and are constantly battling for information access and control and scarce resources.

About a year ago one of the textbook authors experienced all the frustrations associated with powerlessness. Being a graduate and former professor of the U.S. Air Force Academy, the author was asked to do two days of leadership training for the institution at a highly discounted rate. Wanting to help his alma mater, the author agreed and delivered a highly successful program. But because no good deed goes unpunished, it took the author another two days to complete all the paperwork and almost a full year before he was paid for this work. Until this episode the author had invoiced hundreds of other private and public sector clients and had never needed more than 30 minutes to process the paperwork needed to get paid. What motivational approaches would best describe the people responsible for processing this payment paperwork?

Source: R. Moss Kanter, "Powerlessness Corrupts," *Harvard Business Review,* July–August 2010, p. 36.

work demands are at an all-time high, empowerment can help followers gain some control over their lives and better cope with stress. Although an empowered worker may have the same high work demands as an unempowered worker, the empowered worker will have more choices in how and when to accomplish these demands and as such will suffer from less stress. And because stress is a key component of dysfunctional turnover, giving workers more control over their work demands can reduce turnover and in turn improve the company's bottom line.

There are also four micro components of empowerment. These components can be used to determine whether employees are empowered or unempowered, and include self-determination, meaning, competence, and influence.[95,96,102] Empowered employees have a sense of self-determination; they can make choices about what they do, how they do it, and when they need to get it done. Empowered employees also have a strong sense of meaning; they believe what they do is important to them and to the company's success. Empowered employees have a high level of competence: they know what they are doing and are confident they can get the job done. Finally, empowered employees have an impact on others and believe that they can influence their teams or work units and that co-workers and leaders will listen to their ideas. In summary, empowered employees have latitude to make decisions, are comfortable making these decisions, believe what they do is important, and are seen as influential members of their team. Unempowered employees may have little latitude to make decisions, may feel ill equipped and may not want to make decisions, and may have little impact on their work unit, even if they have good ideas. Most employees probably fall somewhere between the two extremes of the empowerment continuum, depicted in Figure 9.3.

Empowerment and the operant approach make an important point that is often overlooked by other theories of motivation: by changing the situation, leaders can enhance followers' motivation, performance, and satisfaction. Unfortunately many leaders naively assume it is easier to change an *individual* than it is to change the *situation,* but this is often not the case. The situation is not always fixed, and followers are not the only variable in the performance equation. Leaders can often see positive changes in followers' motivation levels by restructuring work processes and procedures, which in turn can increase their latitude to make decisions and add

FIGURE 9.3
The Empowerment Continuum

Empowered Employees ⟷ **Unempowered Employees**

- Self-determined.
- Sense of meaning.
- High competence.
- High influence.

- Other-determined.
- Not sure if what they do is important.
- Low competence.
- Low influence.

more meaning to work. Tying these changes to a well-designed and well-implemented reward system can further increase motivation. However, leaders are likely to encounter some resistance whenever they change the processes, procedures, and rewards for work, even if these changes are for the better. Doing things the old way is relatively easy—followers know the expectations for performance and usually have developed the skills needed to achieve results. Followers often find that doing things a new way can be frustrating because expectations may be unclear and they may not have the requisite skills. Leaders can help followers work through this initial resistance to new processes and procedures by showing support, providing training and coaching on new skills, and capitalizing on opportunities to reward progress. If the processes, procedures, and rewards are properly designed and administered, then in many cases followers will successfully work through their resistance and, over time, wonder how they ever got work done using the old systems. The successful transition to new work processes and procedures will rest squarely on the shoulders of leaders. How could you use empowerment to improve the performance of Julie or Ling-Ling or the customer service levels of flight attendants? What information would you need to gather, how would you implement the program, and what would be the potential pitfalls of your program? And what do you think happened to empowerment as companies went through the economic recession of 2008–2010?

Motivation Summary

Some people believe it is virtually impossible to motivate anyone, and leaders can do little to influence people's decisions regarding the direction, intensity, and persistence of their behavior. Clearly there is a lot followers bring to the motivational equation, but we feel that a leader's actions can and do affect followers' motivation levels. If leaders did not affect followers' motivation levels, it would not matter whom one worked for—any results obtained would be solely due to followers' efforts. But as you will read in Chapter 15, whom one works for matters a lot. We hope that after reading this chapter you will have a better understanding of how follower characteristics (needs and achievement orientation), leader actions (goal setting), and situational factors (contingent rewards and empowerment) affect how you and your followers are motivated (and demotivated). Moreover, you should be able to start recognizing situations where some theories provide better insights about problems in motivation levels than others. For example, if we go back to the survival situation described in Chapter 1, we can see that Maslow's hierarchy of needs provides better explanations for the behavior of the survivors than empowerment or the operant approach. On the other hand, if we think about the reasons we might not be doing well in a particular class, we may see that we have not set specific goals for our grades or that the rewards for doing well are not clear. Or if we are working in a bureaucratic organization, we may see few consequences for either substandard or superior performance; thus there is little reason to exert extra effort. Perhaps the best strategy for leaders is to be flexible in the types of interventions they consider to affect follower motivation. That will require, of course, familiarity with the strengths and weaknesses of the different theories and approaches presented here.

Similarly, we need to consider how the five motivational approaches can be used with both individuals and teams. Much of this section focused on applying the five approaches to individuals, but the techniques can also be used to motivate teams of followers. For example, leaders can set team goals and provide team rewards for achieving them. Leaders can also hire team members who have high levels of achievement orientation and then provide everyone on the team with the decision-making latitude and skills needed to adequately perform their jobs. Leaders can also assess where their teams are currently at on the hierarchy of needs and take actions to ensure that lower-order needs are satisfied. Again, having a good understanding of the five motivational approaches will help leaders determine which ones will be most effective in getting teams to change behavior and exert extra energy and effort.

One of the most important tools for motivating followers has not been fully addressed in this chapter. As described in Chapter 14, charismatic or transformational leadership is often associated with extraordinarily high levels of follower motivation, yet none of the theories described in this chapter can adequately explain how these leaders get their followers to do more than they thought possible. Perhaps this is due to the fact that the theories in this chapter take a rational or logical approach to motivation, yet transformational leadership uses emotion as the fuel to drive followers' heightened motivational levels. Just as our needs, thoughts, personality traits, and rewards can motivate us to do something different, so can our emotions drive us to engage in and persist with particular activities. A good example here may be political campaigns. Do people volunteer to work for these campaigns because of some underlying need or personal goals, or because they feel they will be rewarded by helping out? Although these are potential reasons for some followers, the emotions generated by political campaigns, particularly where the two leading candidates represent different value systems, often seem to provide a better explanation for the large amount of time and effort people contribute. Leadership practitioners should not overlook the interplay between emotions and motivation, and the better able they are to address and capitalize on emotions when introducing change, the more successful they are likely to be.

A final point concerns the relationship between motivation and performance. Many leadership practitioners equate the two, but as we pointed out earlier in this chapter, they are not the same concepts. Getting followers to put in more time, energy, and effort on certain behaviors will not help the team to be more successful if they are the wrong behaviors to begin with. Similarly, followers may not know how and when to exhibit behaviors associated with performance. Leadership practitioners must clearly identify the behaviors related to performance, coach and train their followers in how and when to exhibit these behaviors, and then use one or more of the theories described in this chapter to get followers to exhibit and persist with the behaviors associated with higher performance levels.

Understanding and Influencing Follower Satisfaction

As stated earlier, job satisfaction concerns one's attitudes about work, and there are several practical reasons why job satisfaction is an important concept for leaders to think about. Research has shown that satisfied workers are more likely to continue working for an organization.[22,104-109] Satisfied workers are also more likely to engage in organizational citizenship behaviors that go beyond job descriptions and role requirements and help reduce the workload or stress of others in the organization. Dissatisfied workers are more likely to be adversarial in their relations with leadership (filing grievances, for example) and engage in diverse counterproductive behaviors.[110-118] Dissatisfaction is a key reason why people leave organizations, and many of the reasons people are satisfied or dissatisfied with work are within the leader's control (see Table 9.2).[105-107,118]

Although the total costs of dissatisfaction are difficult to measure, the direct costs of replacing a first-line supervisor or an executive can range from $5,000 to $400,000 per hire, depending on recruiting, relocation, and training fees, and these costs do not include those associated with the productivity lost as a result of unfilled positions.[119] Other indirect costs include the loss of customers. A survey of major corporations showed that 49 percent switched to another vendor because of poor customer service.[120] Employees are probably not going to provide world-class service if they are unhappy with their job, boss, or company. The inability to retain customers directly affects revenues and makes investors think twice about buying stock in a company. Relatedly, Schellenbarger reported that 35 percent of investor decisions are driven by nonfinancial factors. Number 5 on a list of 39 factors investors weighed before buying stock was the company's ability to attract and retain talent. These findings imply that a company's stock price is driven not only by market share and profitability, but also by service and bench strength considerations. Thus employee satisfaction (or dissatisfaction) can have a major impact on the organization's bottom line.[121]

Seventy to ninety percent of the decisions not to repeat purchases of anything are not about product or price. They are about dimensions of service.

**Barry Gibbons,
Burger King**

Of these outcomes, perhaps employee turnover has the most immediate impact on leadership practitioners. It would be hard for Julie's or Ling Ling's bosses to achieve results if, respectively, ski resort or real estate personnel were constantly having to be replaced and the leader was spending

Improving Safety on Offshore Oil Platforms

HIGHLIGHT 9.10

One of the most dangerous jobs in the world is that of an offshore oil rig employee. These employees often work 12- to 16-hour days for two- to four-week shifts operating heavy equipment in confined spaces. Not only is the work long and hard, but many employees face additional dangers from high seas, cold weather, icebergs, hurricanes, and well blowouts. Because of these conditions and the nature of work, many energy companies are concerned with safety. But what can well managers do to create safe oil platforms? It turns out that using a combination of several motivational techniques may be the best way to reduce oil platform accidents.

To reduce accidents, well managers must first set clear goals and performance expectations for safety. If employees believe only production is important to well managers, they will do what they think is right to boost productivity and will pay little attention to safety issues. So managers must set the tone for safety by setting safety goals and constantly reminding employees of safety issues. Second, they must hire employees who are motivated to perform safe work behaviors. Well managers should use personality inventories to hire employees with higher conscientiousness scores because they tend to be risk averse and much more rule abiding than those with lower conscientiousness scores. Third, well managers must ensure that their compensation systems recognize and reward safe behaviors. If the compensation system rewards only productivity, employees will do what they need to in order to maximize their rewards. The same is true if the compensation system rewards both productivity *and* safety. Using this three-pronged approach will not eliminate all oil rig accidents, but it will go a long way toward reducing accident rates.

It appears that BP did not use these proven techniques to improve safety at the Deepwater Horizon oil rig in the Gulf of Mexico. Much of the evidence to date shows that instead BP emphasized productivity and cost cutting. BP used a cheaper (and less safe) well head design, and there were questions whether the equipment used would operate safely at a depth of 5,000 feet. There were ample warnings that the cementing process used to prevent blowouts was not working, and the company did not have good backup plans to deal with blowouts and spills occurring at these depths. The end result was an explosion on the Deepwater Horizon oil rig that killed 11 people and the biggest oil spill in U.S. history. It will take years for the Gulf of Mexico to recover from this environmental disaster, and BP has set aside $20,000,000,000 to cover cleanup and compensation costs.

Unfortunately BP has had a long history of poor safety and environmental performance. In 2005, 15 people were killed and 170 injured in a massive explosion at its Texas City refinery; since then BP refineries have accounted for 760 "egregious, willful" safety violations. These violations are administered when companies demonstrate an intentional disregard of the law or show indifference to employee safety and health. For comparison, other U.S. energy firms had a total of 19 such violations over the same period. What would you do to create an environmentally aware and safety-friendly culture at BP?

Source: R. Gregory, R. T. Hogan, and G. J. Curphy, "Risk-Taking in the Energy Industry," *Well Connected* 5, no. 6 (June 2003), pp. 5–7; http://online.wsj.com/article/SB12599149005978193.html; http://abcnews.go.com/WN/bps-dismal-safety-record/story?id=10763042; http://www.guardian.co.uk/environment/2010/jul/01/bp-deepwater-horizon-oil-spill.

an inordinate amount of time recruiting, hiring, and training replacements. Although some level of **functional turnover** is healthy for an organization (some followers are retiring, did not fit into the organization, or were substandard performers), dysfunctional turnover is not. **Dysfunctional turnover** occurs when the "best and brightest" in an organization become

TABLE 9.2 Why People Leave or Stay with Organizations

Sources: Pace Communication Inc., *Hemispheres Magazine*, November 1994, p. 155; "Keeping Workers Happy," *USA Today*, February 10, 1998, p. 1B.

Why Do People Leave Organizations?		Why Do People Stay with Organizations?	
Limited recognition and praise:	34%	Promises long-term employment:	82%
Compensation:	29%	Supports training and education:	78%
Limited authority:	13%	Hires/keeps hard-working, smart people:	76%
Personality conflicts:	8%	Encourages fun, collegial relationships:	74%
Other:	16%	Bases job evaluation on innovation:	72%

To reduce job satisfaction from 9 to 8 on the 10 point scale . . . would, for a family with a $65,000 income, have to be matched by an income increase of more than $30,000 a year to leave life satisfaction unchanged. . . . Moving from the 50th to the 75th percentile [in job satisfaction] would have a personal income equivalence, for someone of median income, of $17,000 per annum.

Charles Cook, Cook Computing

Would life on a slave ship be much better if the galley master first asked the rowers to help write a mission statement? What employers need to come to terms with is the economic, cultural, and societal benefits of being loyal to their employees. If they don't, eventually their abuses will bite them on the ass.

Daniel Levine, author

dissatisfied and leave. Dysfunctional turnover is most likely to occur when downsizing is the response to organizational decline (increased costs or decreased revenues, market share, or profitability). In these situations, dysfunctional turnover may have several devastating effects. First, those individuals in the best position to turn the company around are no longer there. Second, those who remain are even less capable of successfully dealing with the additional workload associated with the downsizings. Compounding this problem is that training budgets also tend to be slashed during downsizings. Third, organizations that downsize have a difficult time recruiting people with the skills needed to turn the company around. Competent candidates avoid applying for jobs within the organization because of uncertain job security, and the less competent managers remaining with the company may decide not to hire anyone who could potentially replace them. Because leaders can play an important role in followers' satisfaction levels, and because followers' satisfaction levels can have a substantial impact on various organizational outcomes, it is worth going into this topic in greater detail (see Highlight 9.11).[104,105,108,122,123,124]

Global, Facet, and Life Satisfaction

There are different ways to look at a person's attitudes about work, but researchers usually collect these data using some type of job satisfaction survey.[39,40,45,107,122,123,125,126] Such surveys typically include items such as those found in Table 9.2 and are usually sent to a representative sample of employees in the organization. Their responses are collected and tabulated, and the results are disseminated throughout the organization. Table 9.3 presents examples of three different types of items typically found on a job satisfaction survey. Item 1 is a **global satisfaction** item, which assesses the overall degree to which employees are satisfied with their organization and their job. Items 2 through 7 are **facet satisfaction** items, which assess the degree to which employees are satisfied with different aspects of work, such as pay, benefits, promotion policies, working hours and conditions, and the like. People may be relatively satisfied overall but still dissatisfied with certain aspects of work. For example, a study of junior officers in the

A Recipe for Success: The Gallup 12

HIGHLIGHT 9.11

More and more organizations are beginning to realize that their overall success depends on how they treat their employees. Hiring good people, setting high goals and performance expectations, providing needed resources, developing new skills, and holding people accountable for results seem to be important ingredients in organizational success. Leaders who use these techniques are likely to have more engaged employees, less turnover, and higher team and organizational level performance. The Gallup Organization has surveyed thousands of companies and has identified 12 key questions that assess employee engagement:

1. I know what is expected from me at work.
2. I have the materials and equipment I need to do my job right.
3. At work, I have the opportunity to do what I do best every day.
4. In the last seven days, I have received recognition and praise for doing good work.
5. My supervisor, or someone at work, seems to care about me as a person.
6. There is someone at work who encourages my development.
7. At work, my opinions seem to count.
8. The mission/purpose of my company makes me feel my job is important.
9. My associates (fellow employees) are committed to doing quality work.
10. I have a best friend at work.
11. In the last six months, someone at work has talked to me about my progress.
12. This past year, I have had the opportunities at work to learn and grow.

Leaders with higher scores on these 12 items consistently have more satisfied employees, lower dysfunctional turnover, and higher team performance. Leaders with lower scores generally have the opposite results. What is interesting about the Gallup 12 is that many of the items are related to the motivational techniques described earlier in this chapter and are under immediate supervisors' direct control. Often poor leaders blame followers, the organization, or the situation for poor results or high turnover, when the truth is that they would more likely pinpoint the source of the problem by looking in the mirror.

Sources: M. Buckingham and C. Coffman, *First, Break All The Rules* (New York: Simon & Schuster, 1999); G. J. Curphy and R. T. Hogan, "Managerial Incompetence: Is There a Dead Skunk on the Table?" working paper, 2004; G. J. Curphy and R. T. Hogan, "What We Really Know about Leadership (But Seem Unwilling to Implement)," working paper, 2004.

U.S. Army revealed that overall satisfaction among them has been in decline and is beginning to hurt reenlistment rates. A higher percentage of junior officers are choosing to leave the army than ever before; the two primary reasons for this high level of dysfunctional turnover seem to be dissatisfaction with immediate supervisors and top leadership. Many junior officers reported that they were tired of working for career-obsessed supervisors who had a strong tendency to micromanage and would just as soon throw them under a bus if it would advance their career.[127,128] And given the multiple tours and tour extensions supporting the conflict in Iraq and Afghanistan, employee dissatisfaction among National Guard and reserve units is probably high, which has driven up turnover and made

TABLE 9.3
Typical Items on a Satisfaction Questionnaire

1. Overall, I am satisfied with my job.
2. I feel the workload is about equal for everyone in the organization.
3. My supervisor handles conflict well.
4. My pay and benefits are comparable to those in other organizations.
5. There is a real future for people in this organization if they apply themselves.
6. Exceptional performance is rewarded in this organization.
7. We have a good health care plan in this organization.
8. In general, I am satisfied with my life and where it is going.
These items are often rated on a scale ranging from *strongly disagree* (1) to *strongly agree* (5).

recruitment more difficult. For example, retention bonuses for the U.S. military went from $80 million to $660 million between 2002 and 2008.[129,130] This decline in global satisfaction is not limited to the U.S. Army: the same phenomenon is happening in many companies today. Much of this decline can be attributed to higher follower expectations, greater follower access to information through technology, economic downturns, organizational downsizings, and incompetent bosses.[40,41]

Leadership practitioners should be aware of several other important findings regarding global and facet satisfaction. The first finding is that people generally tend to be happy with their vocation or occupation. They may not like the pay, benefits, or their boss, but they seem to be satisfied with what they do for a living. The second finding pertains to the **hierarchy effect:** in general, people with longer tenure or in higher positions tend to have higher global and facet satisfaction ratings than those newer to or lower in the organization.[131] Because people higher in the organization are happier at work, they may not understand or appreciate why people at lower levels are less satisfied. From below, leaders at the top can appear naive and out of touch. From above, the complaints about morale, pay, or resources are often perceived as whining. One of this book's authors once worked with a utilities company that had downsized and was suffering from all the ill effects associated with high levels of dysfunctional turnover. Unfortunately the executive vice president responsible for attracting and retaining talent and making the company "an employer of choice" stated that he had no idea why employees were complaining and that things would be a lot better if they just quit whining. Because the executive did not understand or appreciate the sources of employee complaints, the programs to improve employee morale completely missed the mark, and the high levels of dysfunctional turnover continued. The hierarchy effect also implies that it will take a considerable amount of top leaders' focus and energy to increase the satisfaction levels of nonmanagement employees—lip service alone is never enough. See Highlight 9.12 for an example of a well-intended but poorly considered attempt at improving employee morale.

The Hierarchy Effect and Stupid Corporate Tricks

HIGHLIGHT 9.12

The hierarchy effect can make people at the top oblivious to the frustrations and feelings of those at the bottom of organizations. One example of where the hierarchy effect is alive and well is the airline industry. The major airlines in the United States suffered tremendously after 9/11/2001. Many major carriers, such as United, Delta, and US Airways, had to declare bankruptcy as a result of reduced passenger loads and higher fuel prices. These carriers had to make massive personnel cuts and renegotiate contracts with the pilot, flight attendant, ground crew, and mechanics unions to regain financial solvency. Many union employee pensions were tied to airline stock and disappeared when their airline declared bankruptcy. In addition to their pension loss, employees were asked to put in 20 percent more hours while taking 20–30 percent pay cuts. Relationships between labor and management had always been problematic in the airline industry, but employee morale sank to new lows when these changes were implemented.

But executives were not blind to the plight of their employees. One major airline went so far as to create a booklet full of tips on how to help employees cope with reduced pay. This booklet was sent to 30,000 employees and contained such helpful ideas as these:

• Shop for jewelry at pawn shops.
• Take dates for a free walk in the woods.
• Do not be shy about pulling something you like out of the trash.

With sensitivity like this, can anyone wonder why this airline's customer service, lost baggage, and on-time arrival and departure statistics are poor? This airline is only now recognizing that employees are critical to its long-term success, but its efforts to engage employees have been limited to cheerleading events like those identified in Highlight 9.2. Rather than boosting morale, these mandatory activities have made employees even angrier. It is hard to get fired up to serve customers when top management's actions (loss of pension, increased workloads, and pay cuts) speak louder than the "concern for employee" messages coming out of these motivational events.

Source: "Tip No. 102: Avoid Our Overpriced Inflight Snacks," *Minnesota Monthly Magazine,* December 2006, p. 81.

Compensation is another facet of job satisfaction that can have important implications for leadership practitioners. As you might expect, the hierarchy effect can be seen in pay: a survey of 3 million employees reported that 71 percent of senior management, 58 percent of middle management, and only 46 percent of nonmanagers rate their pay as "very good." Of nonmanagers, 33 percent rate their pay as "so-so" and 20 percent rate their pay as "very poor."[132] Given the wage gap between males and females, a disproportionate number of females can probably be found in these less satisfied groups. Many of these females may be the highest performers in their positions; therefore, this wage discrepancy, in combination with relatively small annual pay increases over the past few years, may contribute to disproportionately high levels of dysfunctional turnover among females.

People who are happier with their jobs also tend to have higher life satisfaction ratings. **Life satisfaction** concerns one's attitudes about life in

Leaders are often the only people surprised by employee satisfaction results. In reality, employees have been talking about the issues identified in these surveys for quite some time.

Dianne Nilsen, PDI-Ninth House

general, and Item 8 in Table 9.3 is an example of a typical life satisfaction question. Because leaders are often some of the most influential people in their followers' lives, they should never underestimate the impact they have on their followers' overall well-being.

Job satisfaction surveys are used extensively in both public and private institutions. Organizations using these instruments typically administer them every one or two years to assess workers' attitudes about different aspects of work, changes in policies or work procedures, or other initiatives. Such survey results are most useful when they can be compared with those from some **reference group.** The organization's past results can be used as one kind of reference group—are people's ratings of pay, promotion, or overall satisfaction rising or falling over time? Job satisfaction ratings from similar organizations can be another reference group— are satisfaction ratings of leadership and working conditions higher or lower than those in similar organizations?

Figure 9.4 shows the facet and global satisfaction results for approximately 80 employees working at a medium-sized airport in the western United States. Employees completing the survey included the director of aviation and his supervisory staff ($n = 11$), the operations department ($n = 6$), the airfield maintenance department ($n = 15$), the communications department ($n = 6$), the airport facilities staff ($n = 12$), the administration department ($n = 10$), and the custodial staff ($n = 20$). The airport is owned by the city and has seen tremendous growth since the opening of its new terminal; in fact, less than two years later aircraft loads exceeded the capacity of the new terminal. Unfortunately staffing had remained the same

FIGURE 9.4
Results of a Facet Satisfaction Survey

Source: D. P. Campbell and S. Hyne, *Manual for the Revised Campbell Organizational Survey* (Minneapolis, MN: National Computing Systems, 1995).

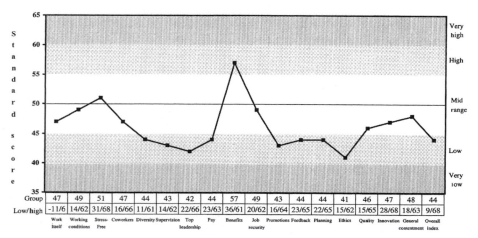

since the opening, and the resulting workload and stress were thought to be adversely affecting morale and job satisfaction. Because of these concerns, the director of aviation decided to use a job satisfaction survey to pinpoint problem areas and develop action plans to resolve them.

Scores above 50 on Figure 9.4 are areas of satisfaction; scores below 50 are areas of dissatisfaction when compared to national norms. Here we see that airport employees are very satisfied with their benefits, are fairly satisfied with the work itself, but are dissatisfied with top leadership, ethics, supervision, feedback, promotion opportunities, and the like. All airport employees got to review these results, and each department discussed the factors underlying the survey results and developed and implemented action plans to address problem areas. Top leadership, in this case the director of aviation, was seen as the biggest source of dissatisfaction by all departments. The director was a genuinely nice person and meant well, but he never articulated his vision for the airport, never explained how employees' actions were related to this mission, failed to set goals for each department, did not provide feedback, never clarified roles or areas of responsibilities for his staff, delegated action items to whomever he happened to see in the hall, often changed his mind about key decisions, and failed to keep his staff informed of airline tenant or city council decisions. When confronted with this information, the director placed the blame on the rapid growth of the airport and the lack of staffing support from the city (the fundamental attribution error from Chapter 2). The city manager then gave the director six months to substantially improve employee satisfaction levels. The director did not take the problem seriously; so, not surprisingly, the survey results six months later were no different for top leadership. The director was subsequently removed from his position because of his failure to improve the morale at the airport.

It is rarely enough to merely administer surveys. Leaders must also be willing to take action on the basis of survey results or risk losing credibility and actually increasing job dissatisfaction. Upon receiving the results of these surveys, leaders with bad results may feel tempted to not share any results with their followers, but this is almost always a mistake. Although the results may not be flattering, the rumors are likely to be much worse than the results themselves. Also, followers will be less willing to fill out subsequent satisfaction surveys if they see denial of the results and little change to the workplace. Furthermore, leaders feeling defensive about such results and tempted to hide them should remember that the bad results may surprise no one but themselves; therefore, what's to hide? On a practical level, leaders should never assess employees' attitudes about work unless they are willing to share the results and take action.

Three Theories of Job Satisfaction

As shown in Table 9.4, all five of the theories of motivation described earlier in this chapter provide insight into followers' levels of job satisfaction

The question: If you had to describe your office environment as a type of television show, what would it be? The responses: "Survivor," 38 percent; soap opera, 27 percent; medical emergency, 18 percent; courtroom drama, 10 percent; science fiction, 7 percent.
Andrea Nierenberg, New York University

TABLE 9.4
Eight Theories of Satisfaction

Theory or Approach	How Leaders Can Improve Job Satisfaction
Maslow's hierarchy of needs	Helping people get their needs satisfied.
Achievement orientation	Securing needed resources, clearing obstacles, and allowing people to work on activities that matter to them.
Goal setting	Setting high goals and helping people to accomplish them.
Operant approach	Administering rewards.
Empowerment	Giving people needed training and more decision-making authority.
Affectivity	Hiring happier people.
Herzberg's two-factor theory	Giving people more meaningful work.
Organizational justice	Treating people fairly.

too. For example, it would be difficult for Julie to be satisfied with her job if she was consistently underdressed for weather conditions or for Ling Ling to be satisfied if her goals were unclear, she was not given feedback, or she failed to be rewarded for good performance. Nonetheless, several other theories offer even better explanations for job satisfaction, including affectivity, Herzberg's two-factor theory, and organizational justice.

Affectivity: Is the Cup Half Empty or Half Full?

Affectivity refers to one's tendency to react to stimuli in a consistent emotional manner. People with a disposition for **negative affectivity** consistently react to changes, events, or situations in a negative manner. They tend to be unhappy with themselves and their lives, and are more likely to focus on the downside or disadvantages of a situation. People with a disposition for **positive affectivity** consistently react to changes, events, or situations in a positive manner. They are happy with their lives and tend to take an upbeat, optimistic approach when faced with new situations. People with a positive affective disposition tend to see a cup as half full; people with a negative affective disposition are more likely to describe a glass as half empty. These two groups of individuals are thought to attend to, process, and recall information differently, and these differences affect both job satisfaction and satisfaction with life itself. Researchers have found that negative affectivity is related to job dissatisfaction, and positive affectivity to job satisfaction. Of course such results are not surprising—we all know individuals who never seem happy whatever their circumstances, and others who seem to maintain a positive outlook even in the most adverse circumstances.[133-136]

These findings suggest that leadership initiatives may have little impact on a person's job satisfaction if her affective disposition is either extremely positive or negative. For example, if Ling Ling has a negative affective disposition, she may remain dissatisfied with her pay, working

Some people are next to impossible to please.
Anonymous

The Happiest Occupations, States, and Countries

HIGHLIGHT 9.13

Polls show that job and life satisfaction vary considerably by occupation, state, and even the country in which one lives. And although the United States is the richest nation in the world, it ranked only 16th in life satisfaction. Life satisfaction surveys of 130,000+ people reveal the following (listed in order):

Happiest occupations: business owners, professionals, managers/executives, and farming/forestry

Least happy occupations: transportation, services, installation, and construction

Happiest states: Utah, Hawaii, Wyoming, Colorado, and Minnesota

Least happy states: West Virginia, Kentucky, Mississippi, Ohio, and Arkansas

Happiest countries: Denmark, Finland, the Netherlands, and New Zealand

Least happy countries: Zimbabwe, Ukraine, Armenia, and Russia

Sources: http:// new.yahoo.com/s/livescience/20100701/sc_livescience/isrichestnationbutnothappiest; http://livescience.com/culture/091110-fifty-happy-states.html; http://finance.yahoo.com/news/Happy-business-owners-changes-apf-1598303505.html?x=0$.v=1; http://abcnews.go.com/Business/Economy/story?id=7585729&page=1; http://thehappinessshow.com/HappiestCountries.htm.

conditions, and so forth *no matter what her leader does.* This is consistent with the findings of a study of identical twins reared apart and together, which discovered that affectivity has a strong genetic component.[134,136,137] Given that leaders can do little to change followers' genetic makeup, these findings highlight the importance of using good selection procedures when hiring employees. Trying to increase followers' job satisfaction is a reasonable goal, but some followers may be hard to please.

From a leader's perspective, affectivity can have several implications in the workplace. First, a leader's own affectivity can strongly influence followers' morale or satisfaction levels. Say you worked for a leader with negative affectivity. Chances are he or she would always find fault in your work and constantly complain about organizational policies, resources, and so on. The opposite might be true if you worked for someone with positive affectivity. Second, leading a high percentage of followers having either positive or negative affectivity would likely result in very different leadership experiences. The positive group may be much more tolerant and willing to put up with organizational changes; the negative group would likely find fault in any change the leader made. Increasing job satisfaction through affectivity means hiring those with positive affectivity. However, few, if any, selection systems address this important workplace variable. Because negative affectivity may not be assessed or even apparent until a follower has been on the job for a while, perhaps the best advice for leadership practitioners is that some followers may have a permanent chip on their shoulders, and there may be little you can do to change it.

Role Ambiguity, Role Conflict, and Job Satisfaction

HIGHLIGHT 9.14

The eight theories of job satisfaction provide useful frameworks for understanding why people may or may not be happy at work. But two other key causes of job dissatisfaction do not fit neatly into one of these frameworks. The first has to do with **role ambiguity,** which occurs whenever leaders or followers are unclear about what they need to do and how they should do it. Many people come to work to succeed, but too many leaders set followers up for failure by not providing them with the direction, training, or resources they need to be successful. In these situations followers may exert a high level of effort, but they often are not working on the right things and as a result get little accomplished. This sense of frustration quickly turns to dissatisfaction and eventually causes people to look for someplace else to work. An example here is an executive vice president of human resources who left a position early in his career after he had been on the job for only two weeks. During those first two weeks he had never seen his boss, did not have a desk, and did not even have a phone. The irony was that he was working for a major Canadian phone company.

Role conflict occurs when leaders and followers are given incompatible goals to accomplish. For example, leaders may be told that their goals are to boost output while reducing headcount. It will be difficult to achieve both goals unless the leader is given some new process, technology, or product that significantly increases worker productivity. When given seemingly incompatible goals, leaders often focus their efforts on accomplishing some goals to the exclusion of others. This may have been the case with BP's Deepwater Horizon oil rig disaster, where managers were told to drill for oil safely and in an environmentally friendly manner while reducing costs and boosting production. The managers on the rig seemed to focus on production and cost reduction goals, and the end result was the death of 11 workers and an unprecedented environmental disaster.

Although role conflict is a source of dissatisfaction, people need to realize that a key challenge for leaders is to successfully achieve seemingly incompatible goals. If the team has only a productivity goal, many leaders are likely to be successful in helping their team to accomplish this goal. If the team has productivity and profitability goals, fewer leaders are likely to be successful. And if the team has productivity, profitability, safety, quality, and customer satisfaction goals, an even smaller subset of leaders will be successful in all of these areas. The fact is that most teams and organizations have more than one goal, and effective leaders are able to get their teams to successfully accomplish all assigned goals. Hiring achievement-oriented team members, setting clear goals, regularly measuring and reporting on goal progress, clearing obstacles, obtaining needed resources, and providing contingent rewards will go a long way toward the successful accomplishment of multiple goals and improved employee satisfaction.

Sources: G. J. Curphy, "What We Really Know about Leadership (But Seem Unwilling to Implement)," presentation given at the Minnesota Professionals for Psychology Applied to Work, Minneapolis, MN, January 2004; G. J. Curphy and R. T. Hogan, "Managerial Incompetence: Is There a Dead Skunk on the Table?" working paper, 2004; R. T. Hogan and G. J. Curphy, "Leadership Matters: Values and Dysfunctional Dispositions," working paper, 2004; G. J. Curphy, A. Baldrica, M. Benson, and R. T. Hogan, *Managerial Incompetence,* unpublished manuscript, 2007; G.J. Curphy and M. Roellig, *Followership,* unpublished manuscript, 2010.

Herzberg's Two-Factor Theory: Does Meaningful Work Make People Happy?

Herzberg developed the **two-factor theory** from a series of interviews he conducted with accountants and engineers. Specifically, he asked what satisfied them about their work and found that their answers usually could be sorted into five consistent categories. Furthermore, rather than assuming that what dissatisfied people was always just the opposite of what satisfied them, he also specifically asked what *dissatisfied* people about their jobs. Surprisingly, the list of satisfiers and dissatisfiers represented entirely different aspects of work.

Herzberg labeled the factors that led to *satisfaction* at work **motivators,** and he labeled the factors that led to *dissatisfaction* at work **hygiene factors.** The most common motivators and hygiene factors are listed in Table 9.5. According to the two-factor theory, efforts directed toward improving hygiene factors will not increase followers' motivation or satisfaction. No matter how much leaders improve working conditions, pay, or sick leave policies, for example, followers will not exert additional effort or persist longer at a task. For example, followers will probably be no more satisfied to do a dull and boring job if they are merely given pleasant office furniture. On the other hand, followers may be asked to work in conditions so poor as to create dissatisfaction, which can distract them from constructive work.[138,139,140]

Given limited resources on the leader's part, the key to increasing followers' satisfaction levels according to this two-factor theory is to just adequately satisfy the hygiene factors while maximizing the motivators for a particular job. It is important for working conditions to be adequate, but it is even more important (for enhancing motivation and satisfaction) to provide plenty of recognition, responsibility, and possibilities for advancement (see Figure 9.5). Although giving followers meaningful work and then recognizing them for their achievement seem straightforward enough, these techniques are underutilized by leaders.[40,45,140] In other words, Herzberg argues that leaders would be better off restructuring work to make it more meaningful and significant than giving out shirts with company logos or decreasing medical copays.

The two-factor theory offers leaders ideas about how to bolster followers' satisfaction, but it has received little empirical support beyond Herzberg's own results. Perhaps it is not an accurate explanation for job satisfaction despite its apparent grounding in data. We present it here partly because it has become such a well-known approach to work motivation and job satisfaction that this chapter would appear incomplete if

TABLE 9.5
Motivators and Hygiene Factors of the Two-Factor Theory

Source: Adapted from F. Herzberg, *Work and the Nature of Men* (Cleveland, OH: World Publishing, 1966).

Hygiene Factors	Motivators
Supervision	Achievement
Working conditions	Recognition
Co-workers	The work itself
Pay	Responsibility
Policies/procedures	Advancement and growth
Job security	

FIGURE 9.5
Herzberg's Two-
Factor Theory

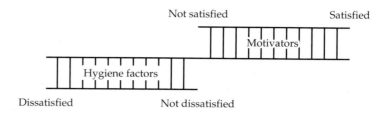

we ignored it. One problem with two-factor theory, however, seems to lie in the original data on which it was based. Herzberg developed his theory after interviewing only accountants and engineers—two groups who are hardly representative of workers in other lines of work or activity. Furthermore, his subjects typically attributed job satisfaction to *their* skill or effort, yet blamed their dissatisfaction on circumstances beyond their control. This sounds suspiciously like the fundamental attribution error described earlier in this book. Despite such limitations, the two-factor theory has provided useful insight into what followers find satisfying and dissatisfying about work.

Organizational Justice: Does Fairness Matter?

Organizational justice is a cognitive approach based on the premise that people who are treated unfairly are less productive, satisfied, and committed to their organizations. Moreover, these individuals are also likely to initiate collective action and engage in various counterproductive work behaviors.[141] According to Trevino, organizational justice is made up of three related components. **Interactional justice** reflects the degree to which people are given information about different reward procedures and are treated with dignity and respect. **Distributive justice** concerns followers' perceptions of whether the level of reward or punishment is commensurate with an individual's performance or infraction. Dissatisfaction occurs when followers believe someone has received too little or too much reward or punishment. Perceptions of **procedural justice** involve the process by which rewards or punishments are administered. If someone is to be punished, followers will be more satisfied if the person being punished has been given adequate warnings and has had the opportunity to explain his or her actions, and if the punishment has been administered in a timely and consistent manner.[142] Research has shown that these different components of organizational justice are related to satisfaction with the leader, pay, promotion, the job itself, organizational citizenship behaviors, and counterproductive work behaviors (in instances where perceived injustice was taking place).[143-150]

So what should leaders do to improve follower satisfaction and reduce turnover using organizational justice theory? The underlying principle for organizational justice is fairness; going back to our earlier characters, do

True patriotism hates injustice in its own land more than anywhere else.
**Clarence Darrow,
attorney**

Ling Ling or Julie feel that the process in which rewards or punishments are administered is fair? Are the potential rewards commensurate with performance? Do Julie and Ling Ling believe the reward system is unbiased? What would the flight attendants say about whether they were treated with dignity and respect, whether rewards were commensurate with performance, or whether rewards were administered fairly? How about the survivors and those who were laid off during the economic recession of 2008–2010? Leaders who want to improve job satisfaction using this approach need to ensure that followers answer yes to these three questions; if not, leaders need to change the reward and punishment system if they want to improve job satisfaction using organizational justice theory. Brockner notes that fairness in the workplace makes intuitive sense but is woefully lacking in many organizations. Too many managers play favorites, avoid rather than directly deal with uncomfortable situations, or for legal reasons cannot reveal how certain issues were handled.[36] These instances of perceived unfairness are often the underlying causes of job dissatisfaction in many organizations.

Richard Branson

PROFILES IN LEADERSHIP 9.4

Richard Branson is the chairman of Virgin Industries, which owns such companies as Virgin Airlines, Virgin Records, Virgin Galactic, Virgin Fuels, Virgin Media, Virgin Comics, and Virgin Health Care. An entrepreneur since the age of 16, Branson had his first business success publishing *Student* magazine in 1966. From there he started Virgin Records, which at the time was an audio record mail order business. In 1972 he owned a chain of record stores, Virgin Records, and installed a recording studio. At the time the studio was used by a number of top bands, including Mike Oldfield, the Sex Pistols, and Culture Club.

In the 1980s Branson ventured into the airline industry with the launch of Virgin Atlantic Airways. He expanded his airline holdings to include Virgin Express, a low-cost European carrier, and Virgin Blue, an Asia-Pacific carrier. In 2004 he partnered with Paul Allen and Burt Rutan to launch Virgin Galactic, a space tourism company. His Virgin Fuels business was launched to find more environmentally friendly fuels for automobiles and airplanes.

Having a long history of creating successful companies, selling them, and then using the proceeds to fund other business ventures, Branson sold Virgin Records to EMI for approximately $750,000,000 and sold Virgin Mobile for $1,500,000,000. Virgin Industries currently employs 50,000 people in 30 countries and generates $23,000,000,000 in annual revenues. With a personal net worth of over $4,000,000,000, Branson has turned his attention to more humanitarian causes. Working with the likes of Nelson Mandela, Jimmy Carter, and Desmond Tutu, Branson is looking to develop peaceful resolutions to long-standing conflicts. He is an active promoter of using entrepreneurship to solve environmental problems. What motivational approach would best describe Richard Branson?

Sources: http://www.solarnavigator.net/sponsorship/richard_branson.htm; http://renewableenergyaccess.com/rea/news/story?id=46071; http://groovygecko.net/anon.groovy/clients/akqa/projectamber/press/The_Elders-Press_Release.pdf; http://www.ft.com/cms/s/0/7f5dd8f32-bfa0-11dc-8052-0000779fd2ac.html; http://virgin.com/richard-branson/autobiography/; http://www.hoovers.com/company/Virgin_Group_Ltd/crjkji-1.html.

Summary

This chapter has reviewed research concerning motivation, satisfaction, and performance. Motivation was defined as anything that provides direction, intensity, and persistence to behavior. Although motivation is an important aspect of performance, performance and motivation are not the same thing. Performance is a broader concept than motivation; abilities, skills, group norms, and the availability of resources can all affect followers' levels of performance. Job satisfaction is a set of attitudes that people have about work. Although many people are generally satisfied with their jobs, they often have varying levels of satisfaction with different aspects of their jobs, such as pay, working conditions, supervisors, or co-workers.

Many of the approaches to understanding motivation have distinct implications for increasing performance and satisfaction. Therefore, several different theories of motivation were reviewed in this chapter. Maslow's hierarchy of needs assumes that people are motivated to satisfy a universal set of needs. Achievement orientation views motivation as a personality trait and assumes some people are hardwired to be more motivated than others. Goal setting examines motivation from a cognitive perspective. This approach assumes that people make rational, conscious choices about the direction, intensity, and persistence of their behaviors, and generally engage in behaviors that maximize payoffs and minimize costs. The last two theories, empowerment and operant approach, examine motivation from a situational perspective. Leadership practitioners likely will be more effective if they learn to recognize situations where various approaches, or the insights particular to them, may be differentially useful.

Several other theories seem to be more useful for explaining followers' attitudes about work. Some research suggests that individuals vary in the characteristic tenor of their affectivity; some people generally have positive attitudes about work and life whereas others are generally unhappy about work and life. Such differences have a genetic component and may limit the extent to which initiatives by leaders will change follower satisfaction. Leaders may be able to increase satisfaction levels by giving followers more meaningful work and by treating them fairly. Followers (and leaders) are more likely to have positive attitudes about work if they believe that what they do is important and that the reward and disciplinary systems are fair and just.

Key Terms

motivation, *333*
performance, *334*
effectiveness, *334*
job satisfaction, *334*

organizational
citizenship
behaviors, *334*
needs, *340*

hierarchy of
needs, *341*
achievement
orientation, *344*

goal setting, *346*
Pygmalion effect, *348*
Golem effect, *348*
operant approach, *351*
reward, *351*
punishment, *351*
contingent, *351*
noncontingent, *351*
extinction, *353*
empowerment, *355*
functional
turnover, *363*

dysfunctional
turnover, *363*
global satisfaction, *364*
facet satisfaction, *364*
hierarchy effect, *366*
life satisfaction, *367*
reference group, *368*
negative
affectivity, *370*
positive
affectivity, *370*
role ambiguity, *372*

role conflict, *372*
two-factor theory, *372*
motivators, *373*
hygiene factors, *373*
organizational
justice, *374*
interactional
justice, *374*
distributive justice, *374*
procedural justice, *374*

Questions

1. Why do you think there are so many different theories or approaches to understanding motivation? Shouldn't it be possible to determine which one is best and just use it? Why or why not?

2. Many good leaders are thought of as good motivators. How would you rate Barack Obama, Rachel Maddow, Sarah Palin, or Rush Limbaugh in terms of their ability to motivate others?

3. What is your own view of what motivates people to work hard and perform well?

4. Do you know of any examples where reward systems are inconsistent with desired behavior? How are personal values related to rewards?

5. What do you find personally satisfying or dissatisfying at work or school? For those things you find dissatisfying, how could you make them more satisfying? What theory of job satisfaction best explains your actions?

Activities

1. Earlier in this chapter you were asked how five motivation approaches could be used to improve the customer service levels of flight attendants. Break into five groups, and have each group discuss how they would design and implement a motivation program using one of these approaches. Each group should then give a 15-minute presentation on their findings. The presentation should include the approach they used, how they would collect any needed additional data, the program design, program implementation, potential barriers to the program, and their evaluation of the effectiveness of their program.

2. Interview someone in a leadership position about employee satisfaction and retention. Does the organization conduct regular satisfaction surveys? What do the survey results reveal about the organization? Is the organization having any turnover problems? Why or why not?

3. Interview someone in a leadership position who has been through a merger or a downsizing and determine their level of satisfaction before and after these events.

4. People often leave bosses, not organizations. Interview people with 10–20 years of work experience and ask them to list the reasons why they have left jobs. How many people left because of bad bosses? How did the reasons for leaving relate to the motivation and satisfaction approaches described in this chapter?

5. How would motivating a group of volunteers for a community project differ from motivating a group of employees in a for-profit business or a platoon of soldiers?

Minicase

Initech versus the Coffee Bean

Consider Peter Gibbons, an employee of the fictional Initech Corporation from the movie *Office Space*. Peter has been asked to meet with efficiency experts (Bob and Bob) to discuss his work environment. One of the Bobs is curious about Peter's tendency toward underperformance and confronts him about his lack of attention to office policies and procedures. It seems Peter has been turning in his TPS reports late and without the company-mandated cover sheet:

Peter: You see, Bob, it's not that I'm lazy, it's that I just don't care.

Bob: Don't? Don't care?

Peter: It's a problem of motivation, all right? Now if I work my butt off and Initech ships a few extra units, I don't see another dime, so where's the motivation? And here's another thing, I have eight different bosses right now.

Bob: Eight?

Peter: Eight, Bob. So that means when I make a mistake, I have eight different people coming by to tell me about it. That's my only real motivation, not to be hassled, that and the fear of losing my job. But you know, Bob, that will only make someone work just hard enough not to get fired.

The environment at Initech is an all too familiar one to many office workers. It is an environment in which success is directly proportional to how busy you look, where questioning authority is taboo, and where meticulous attention to paperwork is the only way to get promoted.

Contrast Initech to The Coffee Bean—a chain of gourmet coffee shops. In an effort to boost employee morale and increase productivity, the management team at The Coffee Bean decided to pursue the FISH philosophy.

FISH is a management training program that stresses fun in the work-place. It espouses four principles:

Play—"Work that is made fun gets done."

Make Their Day—"When you make someone's day through a small act of kindness or unforgettable engagement, you can turn even routine encounters into special memories."

Be There—"Being there is a great way to practice wholeheartedness and fight burnout."

Choose Your Attitude—"When you learn you have the power to choose your response to what life brings, you can look for the best and find opportunities you never imagined possible."

Stores in The Coffee Bean chain were encouraged to use these principles to make the stores a fun place for employees and customers. The stores have created theme days where employees dress up for themes (NFL day, basketball day, pajama day)—and then give discounts to customers who dress the same. There are also trivia games in which customers who can answer trivia questions get discounts on their coffee purchases. Nancy Feilen, a Coffee Bean store manager, explains, "We tried to come up with something that would help strike up a conversation with guests and engage fun in the stores for team members and guests." In other stores, customers play Coffee Craps. If a customer rolls a 7 or an 11, he gets a free drink. Some stores have used Fear Factor Fridays: if the store sells a certain number of drinks, one of the baristas will agree to some act—in one case a barista ate a cricket.

The results? One store increased the average check by 12 percent in six months; turnover has decreased significantly—general managers typically left after 22 months with the chain but now stay an average of 31 months; and the turnover rate for hourly employees dropped to 69 percent from more than 200 percent over a three-year period.

So where would you rather work?

1. How would you gauge Peter's achievement orientation? What are some of the needs not being met for Peter Gibbons at Initech? What changes might improve Peter's motivation?

2. Would you judge the leaders at Initech as more likely to invoke the Pygmalion or the Golem effect? What about the environment at The Coffee Bean—Pygmalion or Golem effect?

3. Why has The Coffee Bean seen such a significant reduction in its turnover?

Sources: http://www.findarticles.com/p/articles/mi_m3190/is_2_38/ai_112248126; http://www.imdb.com/title/tt0151804/quotes;
http://www.charthouse.com/home.asp;
http://www.gazettenet.com/business/02242003/3706.htm.

Part End Notes

1. G. Anders, "Management Leaders Turn Attention to Followers," *The Wall Street Journal*, January 24, 2007, p. B3.

2. S. Jones, "The Lost Art of Following," *The Minneapolis Star Tribune*, October 7, 2007, p. AA1–AA5.

3. E. Hollander, *Inclusive Leadership* (New York: Routledge/Taylor and Francis, 2008).

4. M. Van Vugt, R. Hogan, and R. B. Kaiser, "Leadership, Followership, and Evolution: Some Lessons from the Past," *American Psychologist* 63, no. 3, pp. 182–96.

5. J. M. Burger, "Replicating Milgram: Would People Still Obey Today?" *American Psychologist* 64, no. 1, pp. 1–11.

6. P. Bordia, S. L. D. Restubog, and R. L. Tang, "When Employees Strike Back: Investigating Mediating Mechanisms between Psychological Contract Breach and Workplace Deviance," *Journal of Applied Psychology* 93, no. 5, pp. 1104–17.

7. A. Zaleznik, "The Dynamics of Subordinacy," *Harvard Business Review*, May–June 1965.

8. R. E. Kelley, *The Power of Followership: How to Create Leaders People Want to Follow, and Followers who Led Themselves* (New York: Doubleday, 1982).

9. I. Chaleff, *The Courageous Follower* (San Francisco: Berrett-Koehler, 1995).

10. B. Kellerman, "What Every Leader Needs to Know about Followers," *Harvard Business Review*, December 2007, pp. 84–91.

11. E. H. Potter III and W. E. Rosenbach, "Followers as Partners: Ready When the Time Comes," in *Military Leadership*, 6th ed. (Boulder, CO: Westview Press, 2009).

12. G. J. Curphy and M. E. Roellig, *Followership*, unpublished manuscript (North Oaks, MN:, Author, 2010).

13. A. L. Blanchard, J. Welbourne, D. Gilmore, and A. Bullock, "Followership Styles and Employee Attachment to the Organization," *The Psychologist-Manager Journal* 12, no. 2, pp. 111–31.

Chapter End Notes

1. J. E. Hunter, F. L. Schmidt, and M. K. Judiesch, "Individual Differences in Output Variability as a Function of Job Complexity," *Journal of Applied Psychology* 74 (1990), pp. 28–42.

2. E. Matson and L. Prusak, "The Performance Variability Dilemma," *MIT Sloan Management Review* 45, no. 1 (2003), pp. 38–44.

3. Associated Press, "Democrats Hit Troop Extensions," April 12, 2007, http://www.military.com/NewsContent.

4. M. A. Huselid, "The Impact of Human Resource Practices on Turnover, Productivity, and Corporate Financial Performance," *Academy of Management Journal* 38, no. 4 (1995), pp. 635–72.

5. Sirota Consulting, *Establishing the Linkages between Employee Attitudes, Customer Attitudes, and Bottom-Line Results* (Chicago: Author, 1998).

6. D. J. Koys, "The Effects of Employee Satisfaction, Organizational Citizenship Behavior, and Turnover on Organizational Effectiveness: A Unit-Level, Longitudinal Study," *Personnel Psychology* 54, no. 1 (2001), pp. 101–14.

7. S. D. Pugh, J. Dietz, J. W. Wiley, and S. M. Brooks, "Driving Service Effectiveness through Employee–Customer Linkages," *Academy of Management Executive* 16, no. 4 (2002), pp. 73–81.

8. B. A. S. Koene, A. L. W. Vogelaar, and J. L. Soeters, "Leadership Effects on Organizational Climate and Financial Performance: Local Leadership Effect in Chain Organizations," *The Leadership Quarterly* 13, no. 3 (2002), pp. 193–216.

9. G. A. Gelade and M. Ivery, "The Impact of Human Resource Management and Work Climate on Organizational Performance," *Personnel Psychology* 56, no. 2 (2003), pp. 383–404.

10. J. Z. Carr, A. M. Schmidt, J. K. Ford, and R. P. DeShon, "Climate Perceptions Matter: A Meta-analytic Path Analysis Relating Molar Climate, Cognitive and Affective States, and Individual Level Work Outcomes," *Journal of Applied Psychology* 89, no. 4 (2004), pp. 605–19.

11. I. Smithey-Fulmer, B. Gerhart, and K. S. Scott, "Are the 100 Best Better? An Empirical Investigation of the Relationship between Being a 'Great Place to Work' and Firm Performance," *Personnel Psychology* 56, no. 4 (2003), pp. 965–93.

12. D. B. McFarlin, "Hard Day's Work: A Boon for Performance but a Bane for Satisfaction?" *Academy of Management Perspectives* 20, no. 4 (2006), pp. 115–16.

13. S. A. Hewlett and C. Buck Luce, "Extreme Jobs: The Dangerous Allure of the 70-Hour Work Week," *Harvard Business Review,* December 2006, pp. 48–49.

14. J. C. Rode, M. L. Arthaud-Day, C. H. Mooney, J. P. Near, T. T. Baldwin, W. H. Bommer, and R. S. Rubin, "Life Satisfaction and Student Performance," *Academy of Management Learning & Education* 4 no. 4 (2005), pp. 421–33.

15. J. D. Shaw, N. Gupta, and J. E. Delery, "Alternative Conceptualizations of the Relationship between Voluntary Turnover and Organizational Performance," *Academy of Management Journal* 48, no. 5 (2005), pp. 50–68.

16. K. Birdi, C. Clegg, M. Patterson, A. Robinson, C. B. Stride, T. D. Wall, and S. J. Wood, "The Impact of Human Resources and Operations Management Practices on Company Productivity," *Personnel Psychology* 61, no. 3 (2008), pp. 467–502.

17. A. G. Walker, J. W. Smither, and D. A. Waldman, "A Longitudinal Examination of Concomitant Changes in Team Leadership and Customer Satisfaction," *Personnel Psychology* 61, no. 3 (2008), pp. 547–78.

18. R. B. Kaiser, R. T. Hogan, and S. B. Craig, "Leadership and the Fate of Organizations," *American Psychologist* 63, no. 2 (2008), pp. 96–110.

19. C. Kiewitz, "Happy Employees and Firm Performance: Have We Been Putting the Cart before the Horse?" *Academy of Management Executive* 18, no. 2 (2004), pp. 127–29.

20. B. Schneider, P. J. Hanges, D. B. Smith, and A. N. Salvaggio, " Which Comes First: Employee Attitudes or Organizational Financial and Market Performance?" *Journal of Applied Psychology* 88, no. 5 (2003), pp. 836–51; J. Schneider, "The Cultural Situation as a Condition for the Condition of Fame," *American Sociology Review* 2 (1937), pp. 480–91.

21. R. Kanfer, "Motivation Theory in Industrial and Organizational Psychology," in *Handbook of Industrial and Organizational Psychology*, vol. 1, ed. M. D. Dunnette and L. M. Hough (Palo Alto, CA: Consulting Psychologists Press, 1990), pp. 75–170.

22. E. A. Locke and G. P. Latham, "What Should We Do about Motivation Theory? Six Recommendations for the Twenty-First Century," *Academy of Management Review* 29, no. 3 (2004), pp. 388–403.

23. R. M. Steers, R. T. Mowday, and D. L. Shapiro, "The Future of Work Motivation Theory," *Academy of Management Review* 29, no. 3 (2004), pp. 379–87.

24. F. E. Saal and P. A. Knight, *Industrial Organizational Psychology: Science and Practice* (Belmont, CA: Brooks/Cole, 1988).

25. T. A. Judge, C. J. Thoresen, J. E. Bono, and G. K. Patton, "The Job Satisfaction–Job Performance Relationship: A Qualitative and Quantitative Review," *Psychological Bulletin* 127 (2001), pp. 376–407.

26. D. P. Campbell and S. Hyne, *Manual for the Revised Campbell Organizational Survey* (Minneapolis, MN: National Computer Systems, 1995).

27. Health, Education, and Welfare Task Force, *Work in America* (Cambridge, MA: MIT Press, 1973).

28. R. Hoppock, *Job Satisfaction* (New York: Harper, 1935).

29. F. J. Smith, K. D. Scott, and C. L. Hulin, "Trends in Job-Related Attitudes in Managerial and Professional Employees," *Academy of Management Journal* 20 (1977), pp. 454–60.

30. G. L. Staines and R. P. Quinn, "American Workers Evaluate the Quality of Their Jobs," *Monthly Labor Review* 102, no. 1 (1979), pp. 3–12.

31. B. J. Tepper, M. K. Duffy, J. Hoobler, and M. D. Ensley, "Moderators of the Relationships between Coworkers' Organizational Citizenship Behaviors and Fellow Employees' Attitudes," *Journal of Applied Psychology* 89, no. 3 (2004), pp. 455–65.

32. R. Cropanzano, D. E. Rupp, and Z. S. Byrne, "The Relationship of Emotional Exhaustion to Work Attitudes, Job Performance, and Organizational Citizenship Behaviors," *Journal of Applied Psychology* 88, no. 1 (2003), pp. 160–69.

33. R. Ilies, B. A. Scott, and T. A. Judge, "The Interactive Effects of Personality Traits and Experienced States on the Intraindividual Patterns of Citizenship Behavior," *Academy of Management Journal* 49, no. 3 (2006), pp. 561–75.

34. B. R. Dineen, R. J. Lewicki, and E. C. Tomlinson, "Supervisory Guidance and Behavioral Integrity: Relationships with Employee Citizenship and Deviant Behavior," *Journal of Applied Psychology* 91, no. 3 (2006), pp. 622–35.

35. L. Y. Sun, S. Aryee, and K. S. Law, "High Performance Human Resource Practices, Citizenship Behavior, and Organizational Performance: A Relational Perspective," *Academy of Management Journal* 50, no. 3 (2007), pp. 558–77.

36. J. Brockner, "Why It's So Hard to Be Fair," *Harvard Business Review,* March 2006, p. 122–30.

37. D. S. Whitman, D. L. Van Rooy, and C. Viswesvaran, "Satisfaction, Citizenship Behaviors, and Performance in Work Units: A Meta-Analysis of Collective Construct Relations," *Personnel Psychology* 63, no. 1 (2010), pp. 41–81.

38. http://news.yahoo.com/s/ap/20100105/ap/_on_bi_ge/us_unhappy_workers.

39. "Schumpeter: Overstretched," *The Economist,* May 22, 2010, p. 72.

40. G. J. Curphy, M. J. Benson, A. Baldrica, and R. T. Hogan, *Managerial Incompetence,* unpublished manuscript, 2007.

41. G. J. Curphy, and R. T. Hogan, "Managerial Incompetence: Is There a Dead Skunk on the Table?" working paper, 2004.

42. R. Charan, S. Drotter, and J. Noel, *The Leadership Pipeline: How to Build the Leadership-Powered Company* (San Francisco: Jossey-Bass, 2001).

43. B. N. Pfau, and S. A. Cohen, "Aligning Human Capital Practices and Employee Behavior with Shareholder Value," *Consulting Psychology Journal* 55, no. 3 (2003), pp. 169–78.

44. M. A. Huselid, R. W. Beatty, and B. E. Becker, "'A Players' or 'A Positions'? The Strategic Logic of Workforce Management," *Harvard Business Review,* December 2005, pp. 110–21.

45. G. J..Curphy and R. T. Hogan, "What We Really Know about Leadership (But Seem Unwilling to Implement)," working paper, 2004.

46. R. T. Hogan, *Personality and the Fate of Organizations* (Mahwah, NJ: Lawrence Erlbaum Associates, 2007).

47. J. P. Campbell, "The Cutting Edge of Leadership: An Overview," in *Leadership: The Cutting Edge,* ed. J. G. Hunt and L. L. Larson (Carbondale: Southern Illinois University Press, 1977).

48. J. P. Campbell, "Training Design for Performance Improvement," in *Productivity in Organizations: New Perspectives from Industrial and Organizational Psychology,* ed. J. P. Campbell, R. J. Campbell, and Associates (San Francisco: Jossey-Bass, 1988), pp. 177–216.

49. M. T. Iaffaldano and P. M. Muchinsky, "Job Satisfaction and Job Performance: A Meta-analysis," *Psychological Bulletin* 97 (1985), pp. 251–73.

50. E. A. Locke and G. P. Latham, "Work Motivation and Satisfaction: Light at the End of the Tunnel," *Psychological Science* 1 (1990), pp. 240–46.

51. A. H. Maslow, *Motivation and Personality* (New York: Harper & Row, 1954).

52. E. L. Betz, "Two Tests of Maslow's Theory of Need Fulfillment," *Journal of Vocational Behavior* 24 (1984), pp. 204–20.

53. J. W. Atkinson, "Motivational Determinants of Risk Taking Behavior," *Psychological Review* 64 (1957), pp. 359–72.

54. D. C. McClelland, *Power: The Inner Experience* (New York: Irvington, 1975).

55. M. R. Barrick and M. K. Mount, "The Big Five Personality Dimensions and Job Performance: A Meta-analysis," *Personal Psychology* 44 (1991), pp. 1–26.

56. T. A. Judge and R. Ilies, "Relationship of Personality to Performance Motivation: A Meta-analytic Review," *Journal of Applied Psychology* 87, no. 4 (2002), pp. 797–807.

57. R. T. Hogan and G. J. Curphy, *Personality and Managerial Incompetence,* unpublished manuscript, 2007.

58. G. J. Curphy and K. D. Osten, *Technical Manual for the Leadership Development Survey,* Technical Report No. 93-14 (Colorado Springs, CO: U.S. Air Force Academy, 1993).

59. G. J. Curphy, *Users Guide and Interpretive Report for the Leadership Personality Survey* (Minneapolis, MN: Personnel Decisions International, 1998b).

60. R. T. Hogan and J. Hogan, *Manual for the Hogan Personality Inventory* (Tulsa, OK: Hogan Assessment Systems, 1992).

61. D. L. Nilsen, *Using Self and Observers' Rating of Personality to Predict Leadership Performance,* unpublished doctoral dissertation, University of Minnesota, 1995.

62. S. A. Hewlett, "Executive Women and the Myth of Having It All," *Harvard Business Review,* April 2002, pp. 66–67.

63. G. J. Curphy, *Hogan Assessment Systems Certification Workshop Training Manuals* (Tulsa, OK: Hogan Assessment Systems, 2003).

64. R. Gregory, R. T. Hogan, and G. J. Curphy, "Risk-Taking in the Energy Industry," *Well Connected* 5, no. 6 (June 2003), pp. 5–7.

65. T. W. Britt, "Black Hawk Down at Work," *Harvard Business Review*, January 2003, pp. 16–17.

66. E. A. Locke and G. P. Latham, "Building a Practically Useful Theory of Goal Setting and Task Motivation: A 35-Year Odyssey," *American Psychologist* 57, no. 9 (2002), pp. 705–18.

67. E. A. Locke, "Goal Setting Theory and Its Applications to the World of Business," *Academy of Management Executive* 18, no. 4 (2004), pp. 124–25.

68. G. P. Latham, "The Motivational Benefits of Goal Setting," *Academy of Management Executive* 18, no. 4 (2004), pp. 126–29.

69. E. A. Locke and G. P. Latham, "Has Goal Setting Gone Wild, or Have Its Attackers Abandoned Good Scholarship?" *Academy of Management Perspectives* 23, no. 1 (2009), pp. 17–23.

70. L. D. Ordonez, M. E. Schweitzer, A. D. Galinsky, and M. H. Bazerman, "Goals Gone Wild: The Systematic Side Effects of Overprescribing Goal Setting," *Academy of Management Perspectives* 23, no. 1 (2009), pp. 6–16.

71. S. Kerr and S. Landauer, "Using Stretch Goals to Promote Organizational Effectiveness and Personal Growth: General Electric and Goldman Sachs," *Academy of Management Executive* 18, no. 4 (2004), pp. 139–43.

72. Y. Fried and L. Haynes Slowik, "Enriching Goal-Setting Theory with Time: An Integrated Approach," *Academy of Management Review* 29, no. 3 (2004), pp. 404–22.

73. E. A. Locke, "Linking Goals to Monetary Incentives," *Academy of Management Executive* 18, no. 4 (2004), pp. 130–33.

74. K. A. Eddleston, D. L. Kidder, and B. E. Litzky, "Who's the Boss? Contending with Competing Expectations from Customers and Management," *Academy of Management Executive* 16, no. 4 (2002), pp. 85–94.

75. M. Imai, *Kaizen: The Key to Japan's Competitive Success* (New York: Random House, 1986).

76. D. D. Van Fleet, T. O. Peterson, and E. W. Van Fleet, "Closing the Performance Feedback Gap with Expert Systems," *Academy of Management Executive* 19, no. 3 (2005), pp. 35–42.

77. O. B. Davidson and D. Eden, "Remedial Self-Fulfilling Prophecy: Two Field Experiments to Prevent Golem Effects among Disadvantaged Women," *Journal of Applied Psychology* 83, no. 3 (2000), pp. 386–98.

78. D. Eden, D. Geller, A. Gewirtz, R. Gordon-Terner, I. Inbar, M. Liberman, Y. Pass, I. Salomon-Segev, and M. Shalit, "Implanting Pygmalion Leadership Style through Workshop Training: Seven Field Experiments," *Leadership Quarterly* 11, no. 2 (2000), pp. 171–210.

79. S. S. White and E. A. Locke, "Problems with the Pygmalion Effect and Some Proposed Solutions," *Leadership Quarterly* 11, no. 3 (2000), pp. 389–416.

80. D. B. McNatt, "Ancient Pygmalion Joins Contemporary Management: A Meta-analysis of the Result," *Journal of Applied Psychology* 83, no. 2 (2000), pp. 314–21.

81. R. D. Arvey and J. M. Ivancevich, "Punishment in Organizations: A Review, Propositions, and Research Suggestions," *Academy of Management Review* 5 (1980), pp. 123–32.

82. G. J. Curphy, "What We Really Know about Leadership (But Seem Unwilling to Implement)," presentation given at the Minnesota Professionals for Psychology Applied to Work, Minneapolis, MN, January 2004.

83. L. S. Anderson, *The Cream of the Corp* (Hastings, MN: Anderson Performance Improvement Company, 2003).

84. S. E. Markham, K. D. Scott, and G. H. McKee, "Recognizing Good Attendance: A Longitudinal Quasi-Experimental Field Study," *Personnel Psychology* 55, no. 3 (2002), pp. 639–60.

85. A. D. Stajkovic and F. Luthans, "Differential Effects of Incentive Motivators on Performance," *Academy of Management Journal* 44, no. 3 (2001), pp. 580–90.

86. F. Luthans and A. D. Stajkovic, "Reinforce for Performance: The Need to Go beyond Pay and Even Rewards," *Academy of Management Executive* 13, no. 2 (1999), pp. 49–57.

87. M. Bloom and G. T. Milkovich, "Relationships among Risk, Incentive Pay, and Organizational Performance," *Academy of Management Journal* 41, no. 3 (1998), pp. 283–97.

88. G. D. Jenkins, A. Mitra, N. Gupta, and J. D. Shaw, "Are Financial Incentives Related to Performance? A Meta-analytic Review of Empirical Research," *Journal of Applied Psychology* 83, no. 5 (1998), pp. 777–87.

89. J. L. Komacki, S. Zlotnick, and M. Jensen, "Development of an Operant-Based Taxonomy and Observational Index on Supervisory Behavior," *Journal of Applied Psychology* 71 (1986), pp. 260–69.

90. R. D. Pritchard, J. Hollenback, and P. J. DeLeo, "The Effects of Continuous and Partial Schedules of Reinforcement of Effort, Performance, and Satisfaction," *Organizational Behavior and Human Performance* 16 (1976), pp. 205–30.

91. F. Luthans and R. Kreitner, *Organizational Behavior Modification and Beyond: An Operant and Social Learning Approach* (Glenview, IL: Scott Foresman, 1985).

92. P. M. Podsakoff and W. D. Todor, "Relationships between Leader Reward and Punishment Behavior and Group Process and Productivity," *Journal of Management* 11 (1985), pp. 55–73.

93. P. M. Podsakoff, W. D. Todor, and R. Skov, "Effects of Leader Contingent and Noncontingent Reward and Punishment Behaviors on Subordinate Performance and Satisfaction," *Academy of Management Journal* 25 (1982), pp. 810–25.

94. R. D. Arvey, G. A. Davis, and S. M. Nelson, "Use of Discipline in an Organization: A Field Study," *Journal of Applied Psychology* 69 (1984), pp. 448–60.

95. R. E. Quinn and G. M. Spreitzer, "The Road to Empowerment: Seven Questions Every Leader Should Consider," *Organizational Dynamics*, Autumn 1997, pp. 37–49.

96. S. H. Wagner, C. P. Parker, and N. D. Christiansen, "Employees That Think and Act Like Owners: Effects of Ownership Beliefs and Behaviors on Organizational Effectiveness," *Personnel Psychology* 56, no. 4 (2003), pp. 847–71.

97. A. Srivastava, K. M. Bartol, and E. A. Locke, "Empowering Leadership in Management Teams: Effects on Knowledge Sharing, Efficacy, and Performance," *Academy of Management Journal* 49, no. 6 (2006), pp. 1239–51.

98. S. E. Seibert, S. R. Silver, and W. A. Randolph, "Taking Empowerment to the Next Level: A Multiple-Level Model of Empowerment, Performance, and Satisfaction," *Academy of Management Journal* 47, no. 3 (2004), pp. 332–49.

99. M. Ahearne, J. Mathis, and A. Rapp, "To Empower or Not Empower Your Sales Force? An Empirical Examination of the Influence of Leadership Empowerment Behavior on Customer Satisfaction and Performance," *Journal of Applied Psychology* 90, no. 5 (2005), pp. 945–55.

100. J. Combs, Y. Liu, A. Hall, and D. Ketchen, "How Much Do High Performance Work Practices Matter? A Meta-analysis of Their Effects on Organizational Performance," *Personnel Psychology* 59 (2006), pp. 502–28.

101. L. R. Offermann, "Leading and Empowering Diverse Followers," in *The Balance of Leadership and Followership,* ed. E. P. Hollander and L. R. Offerman, Kellogg Leadership Studies Project (College Park: University of Maryland Press, 1997), pp. 31–46.

102. J. L. Xie and G. Johns, "Job Scope and Stress: Can Job Scope Be Too High?" *Academy of Management Journal* 38, no. 5 (1995), pp. 1288–1309.

103. G. M. Spreitzer, "Psychological Empowerment in the Workplace: Dimensions, Measurement, and Validation," *Academy of Management Journal* 38, no. 5 (1995), pp. 1442–65.

104. J. C. McElroy, P. C. Morrow, and S. N. Rude, "Turnover and Organizational Performance: A Comparative Analysis of the Effects of Voluntary, Involuntary, and Reduction-in-Force Turnover," *Journal of Applied Psychology* 86, no. 6 (2001), pp. 1294–99.

105. J. A. Krug, "Why Do They Keep Leaving?" *Harvard Business Review,* February 2003, pp. 14–15.

106. S. Armour, "Bosses Held Liable for Keeping Workers," *USA Today,* April 12, 2000, p. 1B.

107. E. Sutherland, *Bosses Encouraged to Play Nice* (Minneapolis, MN: Personnel Decisions International, 2000).

108. D. Rigby, "Look before You Lay Off," *Harvard Business Review,* April 2002, pp. 20–21.

109. D. S. Levine, *Disgruntled: The Darker Side of the World of Work* (New York: Berkley Boulevard Books, 1998).

110. B. E. Litzky, K. E. Eddleston, and D. L. Kidder, "The Good, The Bad, and the Misguided: How Managers Inadvertently Encourage Deviant Behaviors," *Academy of Management Perspectives* 20, no. 1 (2006), pp. 91–103.

111. D. W. Organ and K. Ryan, "A Meta-analytic Review of Attitudinal and Dispositional Predictors of Organizational Citizenship Behavior," *Personnel Psychology* 48 (1995), pp. 775–802.

112. L. A. Bettencourt, K. P. Gwinner, and M. L. Meuter, "A Comparison of Attitude, Personality, and Knowledge Predictors of Service-Oriented Organizational Citizenship Behaviors," *Journal of Applied Psychology* 86, no. 1 (2001), pp. 29–41.

113. R. C. Mayer and M. B. Gavin, "Trust in Management and Performance: Who Minds the Shop While Employees Watch the Boss?" *Academy of Management Journal* 48, no. 5 (2005), pp. 874–88.

114. B. J. Tepper, M. K. Duffy, C. A. Henle, L. Schurer Lambert, "Procedural Injustice, Victim Precipitation, and Abusive Supervision," *Personnel Psychology* 59 (2006), pp. 101–23.

115. G. Strauss, "Workers Hone the Fine Art of Revenge: Acts of Violence, Harassment toward Boss on Rise in Corporate World," *Denver Post*, August 24, 1998, p. 6E.

116. A. E. Colbert, M. K. Mount, J. K. Harter, L. A. Witt, and M. R. Barrick, "Interactive Effects of Personality and Perceptions of the Work Situation on Workplace Deviance," *Journal of Applied Psychology* 89, no. 4 (2004), pp. 599–609.

117. B. Marcus and H. Schuler, "Antecedents of Counterproductive Behavior at Work: A General Perspective," *Journal of Applied Psychology* 89, no. 1 (2004), pp. 647–60.

118. R. P. Tett and J. P. Meyer, "Job Satisfaction, Organizational Commitment, Turnover Intention, and Turnover: Path Analyses Based on Meta-analytic Findings," *Personnel Psychology* 46 (1993), pp. 259–93.

119. G. J. Curphy, "In-Depth Assessments, 360-Degree Feedback, and Development: Key Research Results and Recommended Next Steps," presentation at the Annual Conference for HR Managers at US West Communications, Denver, CO, January 1998.

120. T. Peters, *The Circle of Innovation: You Can't Shrink Your Way to Greatness* (New York: Random House, 1997).

121. S. Schellenbarger, "Investors Seem Attracted to Firms with Happy Employees," *The Wall Street Journal*, March 19, 1997, p. I2.

122. A. G. Bedeian and A. A. Armenakis, "The Cesspool Syndrome: How Dreck Floats to the Top of Declining Organizations," *Academy of Management Executive* 12, no. 1 (1998), pp. 58–63.

123. P. W. Hom and A. J. Kinicki, "Towards a Greater Understanding of How Dissatisfaction Drives Employee Turnover," *Academy of Management Journal* 44, no. 5 (2001), pp. 975–87.

124. P. W. Hom, L. Roberson, and A. D. Ellis, "Challenging Conventional Wisdom About Who Quits: Revelations from Corporate America," *Journal of Applied Psychology* 93, no. 1 (2008), pp. 1–34.

125. D. P. Campbell, G. J. Curphy, and T. Tuggle, *360 Degree Feedback Instruments: Beyond Theory*, workshop presented at the 10th Annual Conference of the Society for Industrial and Organizational Psychology, Orlando, FL, May 1995.

126. P. Morrel-Samuels, "Getting the Truth into Workplace Surveys," *Harvard Business Review*, February 2002, pp. 111–20.

127. A. Stone, "Army Sees Leaders of the Future Leaving Today," *USA Today*, April 18, 2000, p. 10A.

128. http://www.strategicstudiesinstitute.army.mil/pubs/summary.cfm?q=912.

129. Associated Press, "Military Pay Soars," April 11, 2007, http://military.com/NewsContent.

130. http://www.armytimes.com/news/2007/09/army_bonuses_070910w/.

131. D. P. Campbell and S. Hyne, *Manual for the Revised Campbell Organizational Survey* (Minneapolis, MN: National Computer Systems, 1995).

132. C. Kleiman, "Survey: Job Satisfaction Can Be Costly to Employers," *Denver Post*, June 22, 1997, p. J–4.

133. T. A. Judge and R. Ilies, "Relationship of Personality to Performance Motivation: A Meta-analytic Review," *Journal of Applied Psychology* 87, no. 4 (2002), pp. 797–807.

134. R. Ilies and T. A. Judge, "On the Heritability of Job Satisfaction: The Mediating Role of Personality," *Journal of Applied Psychology* 88, no. 4 (2003), pp. 750–59.

135. T. A. Judge, J. E. Bono, and E. A. Locke, "Personality and Job Satisfaction: The Mediating Role of Job Characteristics," *Journal of Applied Psychology* 85, no. 2 (2000), pp. 237–49.

136. T. A. Judge and R. Ilies, "Is Positiveness in Organizations Always Desirable?" *Academy of Management Executive* 18, no. 4 (2004), pp. 151–55.

137. R. D. Arvey, T. J. Bouchard, Jr., N. L. Segal, and L. M. Abraham, "Job Satisfaction: Environmental and Genetic Components," *Journal of Applied Psychology* 74 (1989), pp. 187–92.

138. F. Herzberg, "The Motivation-Hygiene Concept and Problems of Manpower," *Personnel Administrator* 27 (1964), pp. 3–7.

139. F. Herzberg, *Work and the Nature of Man* (Cleveland, OH: World Publishing, 1966).

140. F. Herzberg, "One More Time: How Do You Motivate Employees?" *Harvard Business Review*, January 2003, pp. 87–96.

141. B. H. Sheppard, R. J. Lewicki, and J. W. Minton, *Organizational Justice: The Search for Fairness in the Workplace* (New York: Lexington Books, 1972).

142. L. K. Trevino, "The Social Effects of Punishment in Organizations: A Justice Perspective," *Academy of Management Review* 17 (1992), pp. 647–76.

143. P. A. Siegel, C. Post, J. Brockner, A. Y. Fishman, and C. Garden, "The Moderating Influence of Procedural Fairness on the Relationship between Work–Life Conflict and Organizational Commitment," *Journal of Applied Psychology* 90, no. 1 (2005), pp. 13–24.

144. J. A. Colquitt, "On the Dimensionality of Organizational Justice: A Construct Validation of a Measure," *Journal of Applied Psychology* 86, no. 2 (2001), pp. 386–400.

145. J. A. Colquitt, D. E. Conlon, M. J. Wesson, C. O. L. H. Porter, and K. Y. Ng, "Justice at the Millennium: A Meta-analytic Review of 25 Years of Organizational Justice Research," *Journal of Applied Psychology* 86, no. 2 (2001), pp. 425–45.

146. M. L. Ambrose and R. Cropanzano, "A Longitudinal Analysis of Organizational Fairness: An Examination of Reactions to Tenure and Promotion Decisions," *Journal of Applied Psychology* 88, no. 2 (2003), pp. 266–75.

147. B. J. Tepper and E. C. Taylor, "Relationships among Supervisors' and Subordinates' Procedural Justice Perceptions and Organizational Citizenship Behaviors," *Academy of Management Journal* 46, no. 1 (2003), pp. 97–105.

148. T. Simons and Q. Roberson "Why Managers Should Care about Fairness: The Effects of Aggregate Justice Perceptions on Organizational Outcomes," *Journal of Applied Psychology* 88, no. 3 (2003), pp. 432–43.

149. E. C. Hollensbe, S. Khazanchi, and S. S. Masterson, "How Do I Assess If My Supervisor and Organization Are Fair: Identifying the Rules Underlying Entity-Based Justice Perceptions," *Academy of Management Journal* 51, no. 6 (2008), pp. 1099–116.

150. B. C. Holtz and C. M. Harold, "Fair Today, Fair Tomorrow? A Longitudinal Investigation of Overall Justice Perceptions," *Journal of Applied Psychology* 94, no. 5 (2009), pp. 1185–99.

10

Groups, Teams, and Their Leadership

Introduction

As we have already discussed, leaders need to understand some things about themselves. Their skills, abilities, values, motives, and desires are important considerations in determining their leadership style and preferences. Leaders also need to understand, as much as possible, the same characteristics of their followers. But if you could know characteristics of both yourself and each of your followers, that would still not be enough. This is because groups and teams are different than solely the skills, abilities, values, and motives of those who compose them. Groups and teams have their own special characteristics.

Although much of the leadership literature today is about the individual who fills the leadership role, a survey of 35 texts about organizational behavior found that, in each one, the chapter about leadership is in the section about group behavior.[1] This should not be terribly surprising because groups (even as small as two people) are essential if leaders are to affect anything beyond their own behavior. What may be surprising is that the concept of groups is sometimes omitted entirely from books about leadership. The **group perspective** looks at how different group characteristics can affect relationships both with the leader and among the followers.

With *teams* and *teamwork* being current buzzwords, it is worth clarifying the difference between groups and teams, although this difference is mostly one of degree. We will begin the chapter with that clarification. The larger distinction, as just noted, is between the characteristics of groups and the characteristics of individuals. We will spend the first half of the chapter discussing some factors that are unique to groups. Given the high interest in organizational teamwork, the latter portion of this chapter will present a model developed to

We are born for cooperation, as are the feet, the hands, the eyelids, and the upper and lower jaws.

Marcus Aurelius

help leaders design, diagnose, and leverage high-impact factors to create the conditions that foster team effectiveness. This chapter will conclude with a section about virtual teams, which are becoming ever more present, if not popular.

Individuals versus Groups versus Teams

As noted previously, there is a significant difference between individual work and group work. But what is the difference between group work and teamwork?

You will learn, in the next section of this chapter, that two identifying characteristics of groups are mutual interaction and reciprocal influence. Members of teams also have mutual interaction and reciprocal influence, but we generally distinguish teams from groups in four other ways. First, team members usually have a stronger sense of identification among themselves than group members do. Often both team members and outsiders can readily identify who is and who is not on the team (athletic uniforms are one obvious example); identifying members of a group may be more difficult. Second, teams have common goals or tasks; these may range from developing a new product to winning an athletic league championship. Group members, on the other hand, may not have the same degree of consensus about goals that team members do. Group members may belong to the group for a variety of personal reasons, and these may clash with the group's stated objectives. (This phenomenon probably happens with teams, too, although perhaps not to the same extent.)

Third, task interdependence typically is greater with teams than with groups. For example, basketball players usually are unable to take a shot unless other team members set picks or pass the ball to them (see Profiles in Leadership 10.1 about Phil Jackson). On the other hand, group members often can contribute to goal accomplishment by working independently; the successful completion of their assigned tasks may not be contingent on other group members. Of course task interdependence can vary greatly even across teams. Among athletic teams, for example, softball, football, soccer, and hockey teams have a high level of task interdependence, whereas swimming, cross-country, and track teams have substantially lower levels of task interdependence.

Fourth, team members often have more differentiated and specialized roles than do group members. Group members often play a variety of roles within the group; however, team members often play a single, or primary, role on a team. Finally, it is important to bear in mind that the distinctions we have been highlighting probably reflect only matters of degree. We might consider teams to be highly specialized groups.

Phil Jackson

PROFILES IN LEADERSHIP 10.1

In Part 2 of this book, which discussed individual leadership characteristics, it was fairly easy to come up with a leader who typified the particular aspect of leadership we were illustrating. This is not quite so easy for teams. If you consider Ginnett's definition of leadership ("The leader's job is to create the conditions for the team to be successful"), the real team leader might be behind the scenes or, in this case, not even on the court.

Phil Jackson is a basketball coach, but not just any coach. Jackson was the coach of champion Michael Jordan and ultimately of the championship Chicago Bulls. Certainly basketball is a team sport; and as Michael Jordan and other Bulls found out, having arguably the best player in the sport does not necessarily translate to the best team in the game. In many of the years when Jordan won the individual scoring championship, the Bulls didn't win the championship. Jackson's job as head coach was to transform spectacular individual players into a spectacular team.

Perhaps the best way to get a sense of this challenge and the teamwork Jackson built to win the championship is to extract a few lines from his book *Sacred Hoops*:

> The most important part of the (coach's) job takes place on the practice floor, not during the game. After a certain point you have to trust the players to translate into action what they've learned in practice. Using a comprehensive system of basketball makes it easier for me to detach myself in that way. Once the players have mastered the system, a powerful group intelligence emerges that is greater than the coach's ideas or those of any individual on the team. When a team reaches that state, the coach can step back and let the game itself "motivate" the players. You don't have to give them any "win one for the Gipper" pep talks, you just have to turn them loose and let them immerse themselves in the action. . . .

> The sign of a great player was not how much *he* scored, but how much he lifted his teammate's performance. . . .

> You can't beat a good defensive team with one man. It's got to be a team effort. . . .

> It took a long time for Michael to realize he couldn't do it all by himself. Slowly, however, as the team began to master the nuances of the system, he learned that he could trust his teammates to come through in the clutch. It was the beginning of his transformation from a gifted solo artist into a selfless team player. . . .

> What appealed to me about the system was that it empowered everybody on the team by making them more involved in the offense, and demanded that they put their individual needs second to those of the group. This is the struggle every leader faces: how to get members of the team who are driven by the quest for individual glory to give themselves over wholeheartedly to the group effort.

Source: P. Jackson and H. Delehanty, *Sacred Hoops: Spiritual Lessons of a Hardwood Warrior* (New York: Hyperion, 1995).

The Nature of Groups

Perhaps we should begin by defining what a **group** is. A group can be thought of as "two or more persons who are interacting with one another in such a manner that each person influences and is influenced by each other person."[2] Three aspects of this definition are particularly important to the study of leadership. First, this definition incorporates the concept of reciprocal influence between leaders and followers—an idea considerably different from the one-way influence implicit in the dictionary's definition of followers. Second, group members interact and influence each other. Thus people waiting at a bus stop would not constitute a group because there generally is neither interaction nor influence between the various individuals. On the other hand, eight people meeting to plan a school bond election would constitute a group because there probably would be a high level of mutual interaction among the attendees. Third, the definition does not constrain individuals to only one group. Everyone belongs to a number of different groups; an individual could be a member of various service, production, sports, religious, parent, and volunteer groups simultaneously.

Although people belong to many groups, just as they do to many organizations, groups and organizations are not the same thing (groups, of course, can exist within organizations). Organizations can be so large that most members do not know most of the other people in the organization. In such cases there is relatively little intermember interaction and reciprocal influence. Similarly, organizations typically are just too large and impersonal to have much effect on anyone's feelings, whereas groups are small and immediate enough to affect both feelings and self-image. People often tend to identify more with the groups they belong to than with the organizations they belong to; they are more psychologically invested in their groups. Also, certain important psychological needs (like social contact) are better satisfied by groups than by organizations.

Perhaps an example will clarify the distinction between groups and organizations. Consider a church so large that it may fairly be described as an organization—so large that multiple services must be offered on Sunday mornings, dozens of different study classes are offered each week, and there are numerous different choirs and musical ensembles. In such a large church, the members could hardly be said to interact with or influence each other except on an occasional basis. Such size often presents both advantages and disadvantages to the membership. On one hand, it makes possible a rich diversity of activities; on the other hand, its size can make the church itself (the overall organization) seem relatively impersonal. It may be difficult to identify with a large organization other than in name only ("I belong to First Presbyterian Church"). In such cases many people identify more with particular groups within the church than with the church itself; it may be easier to *feel* a part of some smaller group such as the high school choir or a weekly study group.

Although groups play a pervasive role in society, in general people spend little time thinking about the factors that affect group processes and intragroup relationships. Therefore, the rest of this section will describe some group characteristics that can affect both leaders and followers. Much of the research on groups goes well beyond the scope of this chapter (see Gibbard, Hartman, & Mann, 1974; Shaw, 1981; Hackman, 1990), but six concepts are so basic to the group perspective that they deserve our attention.[2,3,42] These six concepts are group size, stages of group development, roles, norms, communication, and cohesion. Five of them will be addressed in the following sections. The sixth, communication, permeates them all.

Group Size

The size of any group has implications for both leaders and followers. First, leader emergence is partly a function of group size. The greater number of people in a large versus a small group will affect the probability that any individual is likely to emerge as leader. Second, as groups become larger, **cliques** are more likely to develop.[4] Cliques are subgroups of individuals who often share the same goals, values, and expectations. Because cliques generally wield more influence than individual members, they are likely to exert considerable influence—positively or negatively—on the larger group. Leaders need to identify and deal with cliques within their groups; many intragroup conflicts are the results of cliques having different values, goals, and expectations.

Third, group size also can affect a leader's behavioral style. Leaders with a large **span of control** tend to be more directive, spend less time with individual subordinates, and use more impersonal approaches when influencing followers. Leaders with a small span of control tend to display more consideration and use more personal approaches when influencing followers.[5–8] Fourth, group size also affects group effectiveness. Although some researchers have suggested the optimal number of workers for any task is between five and seven,[9,10] it probably is wise to avoid such a simple generalization. The answer to the question of appropriate group size seems to be "just big enough to get the job done." Obviously the larger the group, the more likely it is that it will involve differentiated skills, values, perceptions, and abilities among its members. Also, more "people power" will certainly be available to do the work as group size increases.

There are, however, limits to the benefits of size. Consider the question, "If it takes 1 person two minutes to dig a one-cubic-foot hole, how long will it take 20 people to dig the same size hole?" Actually, it probably will take the larger group considerably *longer,* especially if they all participate at the same time. Beyond the purely physical limitations of certain tasks,

A committee is an animal with four back legs.
Jean le Carre

there may be decreasing returns (on a per capita basis) as group size increases. This is true even when the efforts of all group members are combined on what is called an **additive task.** An additive task is one where the group's output simply involves the combination of individual outputs.[11] Such a case may be illustrated by the number of individuals needed to push a stalled truck from an intersection. One individual probably would not be enough—maybe not even two or three. At some point, though, as group size increases in this additive task, there will be enough combined force to move the truck. However, as the group size increases beyond that needed to move the truck, the individual contribution of each member will appear to decrease. Steiner[12] suggested this may be due to **process loss** resulting from factors such as some members not pushing in the right direction. Process losses can be thought of as the inefficiencies created by more and more people working together.

Group size can affect group effectiveness in a number of other ways. As group size increases, the diminishing returns of larger work groups may be due to **social loafing,**[13] which is the phenomenon of reduced effort by people when they are not individually accountable for their work. Experiments across different sorts of tasks have tended to demonstrate greater effort when every individual's work is monitored than when many individuals' outputs are anonymously pooled into a collective product. Recent evidence, however, suggests the process may be considerably more complicated than initially thought.[14] The performance decrement may be affected more by the level of task complexity or the reward structure (cooperative versus competitive) than by outcome attribution.

Sometimes working in the presence of others may actually increase effort or productivity through a phenomenon called **social facilitation.** Social facilitation was first documented in classic experiments at the Hawthorne plant of the Western Electric Company (see Highlight 10.1). However, social

Social Facilitation and the Hawthorne Effect

HIGHLIGHT 10.1

Social facilitation was first documented in experiments conducted at the Hawthorne plant of the Western Electric Company during the late 1920s and early 1930s. These classic studies were originally designed to evaluate the impact of different work environments.[18,19] Among other things, researchers varied the levels of illumination in areas where workers were assembling electrical components and found that production increased when lighting was increased. When lighting was subse-

quently decreased, however, production again increased. Faced with these confusing data, the researchers turned their attention from physical aspects of the work environment to its social aspects. As it turns out, one reason workers' production increased was simply because someone else (in this case the researchers) had paid attention to them. The term *Hawthorne effect* is still used today to describe an artificial change in behavior due merely to the fact that a person or group is being studied.

facilitation is not limited to research situations. It refers to any time people increase their level of work due to the presence of others. Typically this occurs when the presence of others increases individual accountability for work, in contrast to other occasions when being in a group reinforces individual anonymity and social loafing.[15]

Developmental Stages of Groups

Just as children go through different stages of development, so do groups. Tuckman's[16] review of over 60 studies involving leaderless training, experimental, or therapeutic groups revealed that groups generally went through four distinct stages of development. The first stage, **forming,** was characterized by polite conversation, the gathering of superficial information about fellow members, and low trust. The group's rejection of emerging potential leaders with negative characteristics also took place during the forming stage. The second stage, **storming,** usually was marked by intragroup conflict, heightened emotional levels, and status differentiation as remaining contenders struggled to build alliances and fulfill the group's leadership role. The clear emergence of a leader and the development of group norms and cohesiveness were the key indicators of the **norming** stage of group development. Finally, groups reached the **performing** stage when group members played functional, interdependent roles that were focused on the performance of group tasks.

The four stages of group development identified by Tuckman[17] are important for several reasons. First, people are in many more leaderless groups than they may realize. For example, many sports teams, committees, work groups, and clubs start out as leaderless teams. Team or club captains or committee spokespersons are likely to be the emergent leaders from their respective groups. On a larger scale, perhaps even many elected officials initially began their political careers as the emergent leaders of their cliques or groups, and were then able to convince the majority of the remaining members in their constituencies of their viability as candidates.

Another reason it is important to understand stages of group development is the potential relationships between leadership behaviors and group cohesiveness and productivity. Some experts have maintained that leaders need to focus on consideration or group maintenance behaviors during the norming stage to improve group cohesiveness, and on task behaviors during the performing stage to improve group productivity.[20,21] They also have suggested that leaders who reverse these behaviors during the norming and performing stages tend to have less cohesive and less productive groups. Thus being able to recognize stages of group development may enhance the likelihood that one will emerge as a leader as well as increase the cohesiveness and productivity of the group being led.

Tuckman's model is widely known if for no other reason than the fact that its components rhyme with each other; but it is not without criticism. Recall that the subjects for Tuckman's research were training,

If you start yelling and becoming obtrusive and beboppin' around, you give the impression of insecurity, and that becomes infectious. It bleeds down into the actors, and they become nervous; then it bleeds down into the crew, and they become nervous, and you don't get much accomplished that way. You have to set a tone and just demand a certain amount of tranquility.

Clint Eastwood on being a film director

Dysfunctional Roles

HIGHLIGHT 10.3

Dominating: Monopolizing group time, forcing views on others.

Blocking: Stubbornly obstructing and impeding group work, persistent negativism.

Attacking: Belittling others, creating a hostile or intimidating environment.

Distracting: Engaging in irrelevant behaviors, distracting others' attention.

Source: Adapted from K. D. Benne and P. Sheats, "Functional Roles of Group Members," *Journal of Social Issues* 4 (1948), pp. 41–49.

The Stanford Prison Experiment

HIGHLIGHT 10.4

A fascinating demonstration of the power of roles occurred when social psychologist Philip Zimbardo and his colleagues[25] created a simulated prison environment at Stanford University. From a larger group of volunteers, two dozen male college students were randomly assigned to be either "prisoners" or "guards." The simulation was quite realistic, with actual cells constructed in the basement of one of the university buildings. The guards wore uniforms and carried nightsticks and whistles; their eyes were covered by sunglasses. The prisoners were "arrested" at their homes by police cars replete with blazing sirens. They were handcuffed, frisked, blindfolded, and brought to the "jail." They were fingerprinted, given prisoner outfits, and assigned numbers by which they would henceforth be addressed.

It did not take long for the students' normal behavior to be overcome by the roles they were playing. The guards became more and more abusive with their power. They held prisoners accountable for strict adherence to arbitrary rules of prison life (which the guards themselves created) and seemed to enjoy punishing them for even minor infractions. They increasingly seemed to think of the prisoners— truly just other college students—as bad people. The

emotional stress on the prisoners became profound, and just six days into the two-week schedule the experiment was halted. This unexpected outcome occurred because participants' roles had become their reality. They were not just students role-playing guards and prisoners; to a disconcerting degree they became guards and prisoners.

What should people conclude from the Stanford prison study? At an abstract level, the study dramatically points out how behavior is partly determined by social role. Additionally, it is clear how just being in the role of leader, especially to the extent that it is attended by tangible and symbolic manifestations of power, can affect how leaders think and act toward followers. Still another lesson people might draw involves remembering that the volunteers all had many different roles in life than those assigned to them in the study, though being a guard or a prisoner was certainly the salient one for this period. Whereas everyone has many roles, the salience of one or another often depends on the situation, and a person's behavior changes as his or her role changes in a group.

Source: P. Zimbardo, C. Haney, W. Banks, and D. Jaffe, "The Mind Is a Formidable Jailer: A Pirandellian Prison," *New York Times Magazine,* April 8, 1973, pp. 38–60.

had better be perfect"). **Intersender role conflict** occurs when someone receives inconsistent signals from several others about expected behavior. Still another kind of role conflict is based on inconsistencies between different roles a person may have. Professional and family demands, for example, often create role conflicts. **Interrole conflict** occurs when someone is unable to perform all of his roles as well as he would like. A final type occurs when role expectations violate a person's values. This is known as **person–role conflict.** An example of person–role conflict might occur if a store manager encourages a salesperson to mislead customers about the quality of the store's products when this behavior is inconsistent with the salesperson's values and beliefs.

A different sort of role problem is called **role ambiguity.** In role conflict, one receives clear messages about expectations, but the messages are not all congruent. With role ambiguity, the problem is lack of clarity about exactly what the expectations are.[26,27] There may have been no role expectations established at all, or they may not have been clearly communicated. A person is experiencing role ambiguity if she wonders, "What am I supposed to be doing?" It is important for leaders to be able to minimize the degree to which dysfunctional roles, role conflict, and role ambiguity occur in their groups because these problems have been found to have a negative impact on organizational commitment, job involvement, absenteeism, and satisfaction with co-workers and supervisors.[28]

Group Norms

Norms are the informal rules groups adopt to regulate and regularize group members' behaviors. Although norms are only infrequently written down (see Highlight 10.5) or openly discussed, they nonetheless often have a powerful and consistent influence on behavior.[29] That is because most people are good at reading the social cues that inform them about existing norms. For example, most people easily discern the dress code in any work environment without needing written guidance. People also are apt to notice when a norm is violated, even though they may have been unable to articulate the norm before its violation was apparent. For example, most students have expectations (norms) about creating extra work for other students. Imagine the reaction if a student in some class complained that not enough reading was being assigned for each lesson or that the minimum length requirements for the term paper needed to be substantially raised.

Norms do not govern all behaviors—just those a group feels are important. Norms are more likely to be seen as important and are more apt to be enforced if they (1) facilitate group survival; (2) simplify, or make more predictable, what behavior is expected of group members; (3) help the group avoid embarrassing interpersonal problems; or (4) express the central values of the group and clarify what is distinctive about the group's identity.[31]

Putting It In Writing[30]

Rick Reilly

HIGHLIGHT 10.5

Why are sports' unwritten rules unwritten? Get a Xerox machine under these puppies and have a copy on everybody's desk in the morning.

After we gave up a touchdown in our first Touch Football/Pulled Groinathon of the year, the guys on the other team sneered and said, "Suckers walk."

"Says who?" asked our left tackle, Cementhead.

"It's an unwritten rule," explained the other side's captain. "Oh, yeah?" said Cementhead. "Show me where." Which is exactly my point. Why are sports' unwritten rules unwritten? Get a Xerox machine under these puppies and have a copy on everybody's desk in the morning.

The coach always sits in the first row on the team bus. If he is out sick or dead, the seat remains empty.

Apologize for a point won on a net cord.

Take two or three pitches if your pitcher just made the second out of the inning.

Never, ever put your finger in someone else's bowling ball.

The starting goalie is always the first player on the ice.

If a line judge makes a bad call in your favor, purposely double-fault the next point.

A manager never drinks at the same bar as his players.

Never knock in the tying run in the ninth inning of an exhibition game. Far better to lose than go extra innings in spring training.

No NBA player attempting a layup in the fourth quarter of a tight game should go unfouled.

In a losing clubhouse you must act as if there has been a death in the family.

Hand the manager the ball when he comes to the mound to take you out.

Never shoot the puck into the net after a whistle blows.

Do not talk to or sit near a pitcher with a no-hitter going. And never bunt to break one up.

A first base coach never stands in the first base coaching box.

Never blow your nose before a fight. (It makes the eyes swell easier later on.)

Stand as far away as possible from a skeet shooter with a perfect score going.

Never walk on a player's putting line, including the two feet on the other side of the cup.

Always clear the inside lane for faster runners.

Never stand behind the pool table pocket your opponent is shooting for.

Never let the interviewee hold the mike.

A catcher may complain to the ump all he wants about balls and strikes, as long as he doesn't turn around and do it face-to-face.

Never hit the quarterback during practice.

Never start the 100 meters in a decathlon into a wind. Trade false starts until the breeze is favorable.

When a soccer player is hurt, the opponents must kick the ball out of play.

Except for Rocky Marciano, the challenger always enters the ring first—and always will.

Throw a handful of salt into the air before your sumo wrestling match begins.

It's true: Suckers walk.

The bus may be delayed by superstars only.

When the coach finally wraps up a long meeting with "Any questions?" nobody better ask one.

Rookies shag balls, whether they are millionaires or not.

Never shoot high on the goalie during warm-ups.

The back nine is always pressed.

You must admit it when you hit a forehand on the second bounce.

continued

continued

On the playground, offense calls the fouls.

Never write down the score of a bowler who is on a run of strikes.

Never admit you trapped the ball while trying to make a catch.

No overhead smashes at women in mixed doubles.

The caddie of the last player to putt plants the flag.

NBA refs will take some trash from head coaches but not a word from an assistant.

Never steal with a five-run lead after the seventh inning.

You must alter your course to help a boat in distress.

Boxers never blink during a ref's prefight instructions.

When a receiver drops a pass, go back to him on the next play.

Card games are played in the back of the plane.

Scrubs stand during NBA timeouts.

Winners buy.

Got it, Cementhead?

The norms that group members value, such as those just listed, are essentially inward looking. They help the team take care of itself and avoid embarrassing situations caused by inappropriate member behaviors. Hackman[32] recommends that the leader has a responsibility to focus the team outwardly to enhance performance. Specifically, he suggests two core norms be created to enhance performance:

1. Group members should actively scan the environment for opportunities that would require a change in operating strategy to capitalize upon them.
2. The team should identify the few behaviors that team members must always do and those they should never do to conform to the organization's objectives.

By actively implementing these two norms, the team is forced to examine not only its organizational context but the much larger industry and environmental shells in which it operates. One irony about norms is that an outsider to a group often is able to learn more about norms than an insider. An outsider, not necessarily subject to the norms herself, is more apt to notice them. In fact, the more "foreign" an observer is, the more likely it is the norms will be perceived. If a man is accustomed to wearing a tie to work, he is less likely to notice that men in another organization also wear ties to work, but is *more* likely to note that the men in a third organization typically wear sweaters or sweatshirts around the office.

Group Cohesion

Group cohesion is the glue that keeps a group together. It is the sum of the forces that attract members to a group, provide resistance to leaving it, and motivate them to be active in it. Highly cohesive groups interact with and influence each other more than less cohesive groups do. Furthermore, a highly cohesive group may have lower absenteeism and lower turnover than a less cohesive group, and low absenteeism and turnover often contribute to higher group performance; higher performance can, in turn, contribute to even higher cohesion, thus resulting in an increasingly positive spiral.

However, greater cohesiveness does not always lead to higher performance. A highly cohesive but unskilled team is still an unskilled team, and such teams will often lose to a less cohesive but more skilled one. Additionally, a highly cohesive group may sometimes develop goals that are contrary to the larger organization's goals. For example, members of a highly cohesive research team at a particular college committed themselves to working on a problem that seemed inherently interesting to them. Their nearly zealous commitment to the project, however, effectively kept them from asking, or even allowing others to ask, if the research aligned itself well with the college's stated objectives. Their narrow and basic research effort deviated significantly from the college's expressed commitment to emphasize applied research. As a result, the college lost some substantial outside financial support.

Other problems also can occur in highly cohesive groups. Researchers[33,34] have found that some groups can become so cohesive they erect what amount to fences or boundaries between themselves and others. Such **overbounding** can block the use of outside resources that could make them more effective. Competitive product development teams can become so overbounded (often rationalized by security concerns or inordinate fears of "idea thieves") that they will not ask for help from willing and able staff within their own organizations.

One example of this problem was the failed mission to rescue U.S. embassy personnel held hostage in Iran during the Carter presidency. The rescue itself was a complicated mission involving many different U.S. military forces. Some of these forces included sea-based helicopters. The helicopters and their crews were carried on regular naval vessels, though most sailors on the vessels knew nothing of the secret mission. Senior personnel were so concerned that some sailor might leak information, and thus compromise the mission's secrecy, that maintenance crews aboard the ships were not directed to perform increased levels of maintenance on the helicopters immediately before the critical mission. Even if a helicopter was scheduled for significant maintenance within the next 50 hours of flight time (which would be exceeded in the rescue mission), crews were not told to perform the maintenance. According to knowledgeable sources, this practice affected the performance of at least one of the failed helicopters, and thus the overall mission.

Janis[35] discovered still another disadvantage of highly cohesive groups. He found that people in a highly cohesive group often become more concerned with striving for unanimity than objectively appraising different courses of action. Janis labeled this phenomenon **groupthink** and believed it accounted for a number of historic fiascoes, including Pearl Harbor and the Bay of Pigs invasion. It may have played a role in the *Challenger* disaster, and it also occurs in other cohesive groups ranging from business meetings to air crews, and from therapy groups to school boards.

What is groupthink? Cohesive groups tend to evolve strong informal norms to preserve friendly internal relations. Preserving a comfortable, harmonious group environment becomes a hidden agenda that tends to suppress dissent, conflict, and critical thinking. Unwise decisions may result when concurrence seeking among members overrides their willingness to express or tolerate deviant points of view and think critically. Janis[36] identified a number of symptoms of groupthink, which can be found in Highlight 10.6.

A policy-making or decision-making group displaying most of the symptoms in Highlight 10.6 runs a big risk of being ineffective. It may do a poor job of clarifying objectives, searching for relevant information, evaluating alternatives, assessing risks, and anticipating the need for contingency plans. Janis[37] offered the following suggestions as ways of reducing groupthink and thus of improving the quality of a group's input to policies or decisions. First, leaders should encourage all group members to take on the role of critical evaluator. Everyone in the group needs to appreciate the importance of airing doubts and objections. This includes the leader's willingness to listen to criticisms of his or her own ideas. Second, leaders should create a climate of open inquiry through their own impartiality and objectivity. At the outset, leaders should refrain from stating

Symptoms of Groupthink

HIGHLIGHT 10.6

An illusion of invulnerability, which leads to unwarranted optimism and excessive risk taking by the group.

Unquestioned assumption of the group's morality and therefore an absence of reflection on the ethical consequences of group action.

Collective rationalization to discount negative information or warnings.

Stereotypes of the opposition as evil, weak, or stupid.

Self-censorship by group members from expressing ideas that deviate from the group

consensus due to doubts about their validity or importance.

An illusion of unanimity such that greater consensus is perceived than really exists.

Direct pressure on dissenting members, which reinforces the norm that disagreement represents disloyalty to the group.

Mindguards who protect the group from adverse information.

Source: Adapted from I. L. Janis, *Groupthink,* 2nd ed. (Boston: Houghton Mifflin, 1982).

personal preferences or expectations that may bias group discussion. Third, the risk of groupthink can be reduced if independent groups are established to make recommendations on the same issue. Fourth, at least one member of the group should be assigned the role of devil's advocate—an assignment that should rotate from meeting to meeting.

One final problem with highly cohesive groups may be what Shephard[38] has called **ollieism.** Ollieism, a variation of groupthink, occurs when illegal actions are taken by overly zealous and loyal subordinates who believe that what they are doing will please their leaders. It derives its name from the actions of Lieutenant Colonel Oliver North, who among other things admitted he lied to the U.S. Congress about his actions while working on the White House staff during the Iran–Contra affair. Shephard cited the slaying of Thomas à Becket by four of Henry II's knights and the Watergate break-in as other prime examples of ollieism. We will probably see similar examples as the details of the Wall Street financial crisis and the BP Gulf oil spills are uncovered by investigators. Ollieism differs from groupthink in that the subordinates' illegal actions usually occur without the explicit knowledge or consent of the leader. Nevertheless, Shephard pointed out that, although the examples cited of ollieism were not officially sanctioned, the responsibility for them still falls squarely on the leader. It is the leader's responsibility to create an ethical climate within the group, and leaders who create highly cohesive yet unethical groups must bear the responsibility for the group's actions.

After reading about the uncertain relationships between group cohesion and performance, and the problems with overbounding, groupthink, and ollieism, you might think cohesiveness should be avoided. Nothing, however, could be further from the truth. First, problems with overly cohesive groups occur relatively infrequently, and in general leaders will be better off thinking of ways to create and maintain highly cohesive teams than not developing these teams out of concern for potential groupthink or overbounding situations. Second, perhaps the biggest argument for developing cohesive groups is to consider the alternative—groups with little or no cohesiveness. In the latter groups, followers would generally be dissatisfied with each other and the leader, commitment to accomplishing group and organizational goals may be reduced, intragroup communication may occur less frequently, and interdependent task performance may suffer.[39] Because of the problems associated with groups having low cohesiveness, leadership practitioners need to realize that developing functionally cohesive work groups is a goal they all should strive for.

In summary, the group perspective provides a complementary level of analysis to the individual perspective presented earlier in this chapter. A follower's behavior may be due to his or her values, traits, or experience (the individual perspective), or this behavior may be due to the followers' roles, the group norms, the group's stage of development, or the group's level of cohesiveness (the group perspective). Thus the group perspective can also provide both leaders and followers with a number of explanations for why individuals in groups behave in certain ways. Moreover, the six group characteristics just described can give leaders and followers ideas about factors that may be affecting their ability to influence other group members and how to improve their level of influence in the group.

Teams

With so much attention devoted to teams and teamwork in today's organizations, it is appropriate to spend a fair amount of time examining teams and the factors that impact their effectiveness. After considering some differential measures of team effectiveness, we will look at a comprehensive model of team leadership.

Effective Team Characteristics and Team Building

Teams definitely vary in their effectiveness. Virtually identical teams can be dramatically different in terms of success or failure (see Highlight 10.7). We must ask, therefore, what makes one team successful and another unsuccessful. Although this is an area only recently studied, exploratory work at the Center for Creative Leadership has tentatively identified several key characteristics for effective team performance (see Highlight 10.8 for an astronaut's perspective on teamwork).

The Center for Creative Leadership's research with teams indicated that successful and unsuccessful teams could be differentiated on the

---

Examples of Effective and Ineffective Teams

HIGHLIGHT 10.7

Most people can readily think of a number of examples of ineffective and effective teamwork. Consider the relative effectiveness of the teams depicted in the following two true stories:

Ineffective teamwork: After an airline flight crew failed to get a "nose gear down and locked" indicator light to come on while making a landing approach into Miami, all three crew members became involved in trying to change the burned-out indicator bulb in the cockpit. Nobody was flying the airplane, and none of them were monitoring the flight of the L-1011 as it descended into the Everglades and crashed.

Effective teamwork: The crew of a DC-10, having lost all capability to control the airplane through flight controls as a result of an engine explosion, realized they needed all the help they could get. Captain Al Haynes discovered that another experienced captain was traveling in the passenger cabin and invited him to come up to the cabin to help the regular crew out. Miraculously, their combined abilities enabled the crew—using techniques developed on the spot—to control the plane to within a few feet of the ground. Even though there were fatalities, over 180 people survived a nearly hopeless situation.

Women in Leadership: Teamwork from an Astronaut's Perspective

HIGHLIGHT 10.8

Dr. Bonnie J. Dunbar is an American astronaut. She has flown on four space shuttle missions. We asked her to share a few personal reflections about the meaning of teamwork and followership to her as she was growing up, as well as presently in her role in the space program. She wrote this during preparation for her flight in June 1992. She was payload commander for that space shuttle mission.

Above all, the success of a space flight depends upon teamwork: within the crew and between the ground controllers and the crew. Teamwork is a valued attribute among currently selected astronauts.

I was very fortunate as a young girl to have been exposed to that concept by my family. With four children and a multitude of chores to be performed, my mother and father impressed upon us our responsibilities within the family unit. Success of the farm (and our future) depended upon our contribution. As the oldest, I was expected to participate in all chores, including driving the tractor and "round-up" by horseback. There were no distinctions in these responsibilities between my brothers and me. Group experiences within the 4-H organization (showing steers, etc.) and playing on baseball, volleyball, and basketball teams reinforced the pride of sharing success together and consoling each other in defeat.

When I attended college, some of that team experience was missed. By virtue of my gender, I was considered an unwelcome minority by many in the engineering college. Therefore, I was never invited to the study groups or participated in group solution of the homework problems. Still, I found an outlet in group activities by belonging to Angel Flight (co-ed auxiliary to Air Force ROTC—I was elected Commander of 50 my junior year) and by continuing to play co-ed baseball. Ironically, my engineering classmates needed my athletic ability as first baseman on the playing field.

I was also supported by three very important individuals during this time: my father, my mother, and the chairman of the Ceramic Engineering Department, Dr. James I. Mueller. My parents always

encouraged me to pursue my "dreams" and to be the best person I could be. The fact that I was the first in the family to attend college was a source of pride for them. That I subscribed to their principles of hard work, human compassion, and honesty was probably a source of greater pride. They were proud of my selection as an astronaut, but my father was more concerned that I not forget how to get manure on my boots.

In my professional life, the closest I have come to real group esprit de corps has come through my association with the Astronaut Office. Perhaps it was due to the concept of "class training," or the similarity of individuals involved, but I consider those I work with as also my closest friends. Our successes are really those of a family team that extends out to the engineers, managers, and administrative support in the Space Shuttle program.

I am now on my third NASA Space Shuttle crew. As Payload Commander I have tried to convey to the noncareer payload specialists on my next flight the importance of being part of the crew . . . that we will share both the successes and the failures of the flight. It has been an interesting experience to assess others' ability to become "part of the team." I have seen what not being part of the team can do, and in a flight environment that can be highly risky. Not being a team member does more than cause internal friction within the crew; it can be hazardous.

So, what does being "part of the team" mean? It doesn't always mean being the smartest or the fastest. It does mean recognizing the big picture goal and the contribution that each individual brings to the whole. It may not mean being the life of the party, but it does mean being able to get along with people and to tread a fine line . . . knowing when to compromise and knowing when to stand firm. And, in an organization such as ours with competitive individuals used to being on top of the hill, it means knowing when to be a Chief and when to be an Indian. In the Astronaut Office, mission specialists rotate through technical jobs and different responsibilities during flights. Sometimes they are Indians instead of Chiefs. Those that perform best and appear to be well-regarded can do each equally well.

basis of eight key characteristics, the first six of which are primarily concerned with task accomplishment.[40] First, effective teams had a *clear mission* and *high performance standards.* Everyone on the team knew what the team was trying to achieve and how well he or she had to perform in order to achieve the team's mission. Second, leaders of successful teams often *took stock* of their equipment, training facilities and opportunities, and outside resources available to help the team. Leaders of effective teams spent a considerable amount of time *assessing the technical skills* of the team members. After taking stock of available resources and skills, good leaders would work to *secure resources and equipment* necessary for team effectiveness. Moreover, leaders of effective teams would spend a considerable amount of time *planning* and *organizing* to make optimal use of available resources, to select new members with needed technical skills, or to improve needed technical skills of existing members.

The last two characteristics of effective teams were concerned with the group maintenance or interpersonal aspects of teams. Hallam and Campbell's[41] research indicated that *high levels of communication* were often associated with effective teams. These authors believed this level of communication helped team members to stay focused on the mission and to take better advantage of the skills, knowledge, and resources available to the team. High levels of communication also helped to *minimize interpersonal conflicts* on the team, which often drained energy needed for team success and effectiveness. The characteristics of effective teams identified in this research provide leadership practitioners with a number of ideas about how they may be able to increase the effectiveness of their work units or teams.

A different avenue to group and team effectiveness has been to use a normative approach. One example of this technique is described in *Groups That Work (and Those That Don't).*[42] Ginnett[43,44] has developed an expanded model focusing specifically on team leadership, which we will examine in more detail later in this chapter. For now, our concern is with one of the three major leadership functions in Ginnett's model that focuses on team design. The model suggests four components of design of the team itself that help the team get off to a good start, whatever its task. This is important because it is not uncommon to find that a team's failure can be traced to its being set up inappropriately from the beginning. If a team is to work effectively, the following four variables need to be in place:

1. *Task:* Does the team know what its task is? Is the task reasonably unambiguous and consistent with the mission of the team? Does the team have a meaningful piece of work, sufficient autonomy to perform it, and access to knowledge of its results?

2. *Boundaries:* Is the collective membership of the team appropriate for the task to be performed? Are there too few or too many members? Do the members collectively have sufficient knowledge and skills to perform

the work? In addition to task skills, does the team have sufficient maturity and interpersonal skills to be able to work together and resolve conflicts? Is there an appropriate amount of diversity on the team? That is, are members different enough that they have varied perspectives and experiences, and yet similar enough to be able to communicate and relate to one another?

3. *Norms:* Does the team share an appropriate set of norms for working as a team? Norms can be acquired by the team in three ways: (a) they can be imported from the organization existing outside the team, (b) they can be instituted and reinforced by the leader or leaders of the team, or (c) they can be developed by the team itself as the situation demands. If the team is to have a strategy that works over time, it must ensure that conflicting norms do not confuse team members. It also needs to regularly scan and review prevailing norms to ensure that they support overall objectives.

4. *Authority:* Has the leader established a climate where her authority can be used in a flexible rather than a rigid manner? Has she, at one end of the authority continuum, established sufficient competence to allow the group to comply when conditions demand (such as in emergencies)? Has she also established a climate such that any member of the team feels empowered to provide expert assistance when appropriate? Do team members feel comfortable in questioning the leader on decisions where there are no clear right answers? In short, have conditions been created where authority can shift to appropriately match the demands of the situation?

Many of these team design components may be imported from preexisting conditions in the organization within which the team is forming, from the industry in which the organization operates, or even from the environment in which the industry exists. To help team leaders consider these various levels, Hackman and Ginnett[45,46] developed the concept of **organizational shells** (see Figure 10.1). Notice that the four critical factors for team design (task, boundary, norms, and authority) are necessary for the group to work effectively. In some cases, all the information about one of these critical factors may be input from the industry or organizational shell level. Here the leader need do little else but affirm that condition. In other cases, there may be too little (or even inappropriate) input from the organizational level to allow the team to work effectively. Here the leader needs to modify the factors for team design. Ideally this is done during the formation process—the final shell before the team actually begins work.

These ideas may require a new way of thinking about the relationship between a leader and followers. In many organizational settings, leaders are assigned. Sometimes, however, the people who create conditions for improved group effectiveness are not the designated leaders at all; they

FIGURE 10.1
Organizational Shells

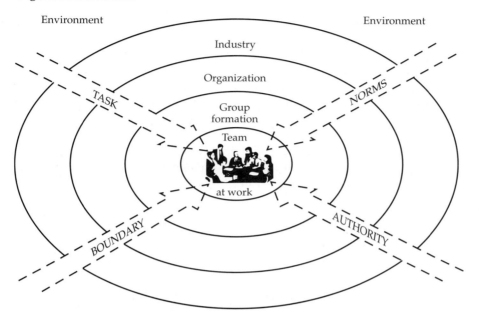

may emerge from the ranks of followers. This model has been used to differentiate between effective and ineffective "self-managing work groups"—teams where the followers and leaders were the same people. Moreover, because the model is prescriptive, it suggests what ineffective work groups can do to be successful. That same purpose underlies the following model as well.

Ginnett's Team Leadership Model

Because we have emphasized that leadership is a group or team function and have suggested that one measure of leadership effectiveness may be whether the team achieves its objectives, it is reasonable to examine a model specifically designed to help teams perform more effectively: the **Team Leadership Model,** or **TLM**[47,48,49] (shortened from earlier versions that called it the Team Effectiveness Leadership Model). Another way to think of this model is as a mechanism to first identify what a team needs to be effective, and then to point the leader either toward the roadblocks that are hindering the team or toward ways to make the team even more effective than it already is. This approach is similar to McGrath's[50] description of leadership, which suggested that the leader's main job is to determine the team's needs and then take care of them. This approach also will require us to think about leadership not as a function of the leader and his or her characteristics but as a function of the team. As the title of the model suggests, team effectiveness is the underlying driver.

We have mentioned this model of group or team effectiveness briefly before, but now we will explore it in greater detail. The original model for examining the "engine of a group" was developed by Richard Hackman and has been the basis for much research on groups and teams over the last 30 years.[51] The model presented here includes major modifications by Ginnett and is an example of a leadership model that has been developed primarily using field research. While there have been controlled experimental studies validating portions of the model,[52] the principal development and validation have been completed using actual high-performance teams operating in their own situational context. Examples of the teams studied in this process include commercial and military air crews in actual line flying operations, surgical teams in operating suites, executive teams, product development and manufacturing teams, and teams preparing the space shuttle for launch. A complete illustration of the model will be shown later. Because of its complexity, it is easier to understand by starting with a few simpler illustrations.

At the most basic level, this model (see Figure 10.2) resembles a systems theory approach with inputs at the base (individual, team, and organizational factors), processes or throughputs in the center (what the team actually does to convert inputs to outputs and what we can tell about the

FIGURE 10.2
An Iceberg Metaphor for Systems Theory Applied to Teams

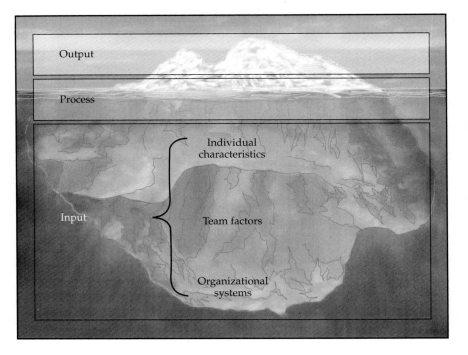

team by actually observing team members at work), and outputs at the top (how well the team did in accomplishing its objectives, ideally a high-performance team). It is often helpful to think of these components as parts of a metaphorical iceberg. While almost everyone can see the outputs of the team (the portion of the iceberg above the waterline), and some can see the processes, most of the inputs are in the organizational background (or underwater in the iceberg metaphor). But anyone who has seen an iceberg recognizes that most of its mass is the part that is underwater—and this part supports the part that is visible. So it is with the leadership work in teams. Much of the leadership work is done in the background, and many of the components may be developed before the team is constituted. As we will see, the leader's job is to create the conditions for the team to be effective, and much of that work is done at the input level.

As helpful as the iceberg is as a metaphor, an iceberg is unwieldy and a little messy in a classroom. Therefore, the TLM will be presented from here on as a four-sided pyramid. We will examine each of these major systems theory stages as they apply to the TLM. However, we will proceed through the model in reverse order—looking at outputs first, then the process stage, and then inputs.

Outputs

What do we mean by outputs? Quite simply, **outputs** (see Figure 10.3) are the results of the team's work. For example, a football team scores 24 points. A production team produces 24 valves in a day. A tank crew hits 24 targets on an artillery range. Such raw data, however, are insufficient for assessing team effectiveness.

How do we know if a team's output is good? How do we know if a team is effective? Even though it was possible for the three teams just mentioned to measure some aspect of their work, these measurements are not helpful in determining their effectiveness, either in an absolute sense or in a relative sense. For comparison and research purposes, it is desirable to have some measures of team effectiveness that can be applied across teams and tasks. Hackman[53] argued that a group is effective if (1) the team's productive output (goods, services, decisions) meets the standards of quantity, quality, and timeliness of the people who use it; (2) the group process that occurs while the group is performing its task enhances the ability of the members to work as members of a team (either the one they were on or any new teams they may be assigned to) in the future; and (3) the group experience enhances the growth and personal well-being of the individuals who compose the team.

Process

It should be obvious why leaders should be concerned with the outputs listed in the preceding section. After all, if a team does not "produce"

FIGURE 10.3
**Basic TLM Outputs:
Outcomes of High-
Performance Teams**

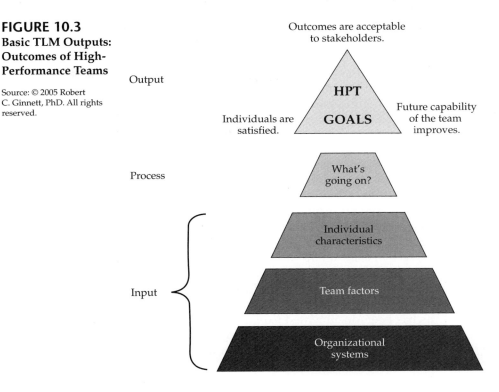

(output), it cannot be considered effective. But what is process? And why should a leader care about it? Actually, there are several reasons why a leader might want to pay attention to the team's process—how the team goes about its work. Some teams may have such a limited number of products that the leader can ill afford to wait until the product is delivered to assess its acceptability to the client. For example, a team whose task is to build one (and only one) satellite to be launched into orbit will have no second chances. There may be no opportunity to correct any problem once the satellite is launched (or, as was the case with the flawed Hubble Space Telescope, correction can be made only at great expense). Therefore, it may be desirable for the leader of such a team to assess the team's work while it is working rather than after the satellite is launched. Other kinds of teams have such high standards for routine work that there simply are not enough critical indicators in the end product to determine effectiveness from outcome measures. As an example of this situation, a team operating a nuclear power plant is surrounded by so many technical backup systems that it may be difficult to determine team effectiveness by looking at "safe operation" as a measurement criterion. But we have evidence that not all teams in nuclear power plants operate equally well (Chernobyl and Three Mile Island are two examples). There is emerging suspicion that poor teamwork was a contributing cause in the 2010 BP Deepwater Horizon accident in the Gulf of Mexico. It would seem helpful to be able to assess real teams "in process" rather than learn about team problems only after disastrous outcomes. Even leaders of noncritical teams might like to be able to routinely monitor their teams for evidence of effective or ineffective processes. So how teams work can provide useful information to the leader.

Because process assessment is so important, let us focus for a moment on the block containing the four process measures of effectiveness in Figure 10.4. These four **process measures** of effectiveness provide criteria by which we can examine how teams work. If a team is to perform effectively, it must (1) work hard enough, (2) have sufficient knowledge and skills within the team to perform the task, (3) have an appropriate strategy to accomplish its work (or ways to approach the task at hand), and (4) have constructive and positive group dynamics among its members. The phrase *group dynamics* refers to interactions among team members, including such aspects as how they communicate with others, express feelings toward each other, and deal with conflict with each other, to name but a few characteristics. Assessing and improving group process is no trivial matter, as has been documented extensively in a comprehensive view of group process and its assessment by Wheelan.[54]

What should the leader do if she discovers a problem with one of these four process measures? Paradoxically, the answer is not to focus her attention on that process per se. While the four process measures are fairly good diagnostic measures for a team's ultimate effectiveness, they are unfortunately not particularly good leverage points for fixing the problem.

FIGURE 10.4
TLM Process Variables: Diagnose the Team Using the Process Variables

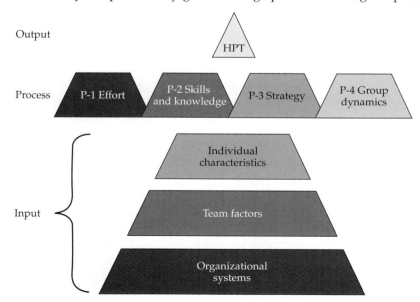

An analogy from medicine would be a doctor who diagnoses the symptoms of an infection (a fever) but who then treats the symptoms rather than attacking the true underlying cause (a nail in the patient's foot). Similarly at the team level, rather than trying to correct a lack of effort being applied to the task at hand (perhaps a motivation problem), the team leader would be better advised to discover the underlying problem and fix that than to assume that a motivational speech to the team will do the job. This is not to imply that teams cannot benefit from process help. It merely suggests that the leader should ensure that there are no design problems (at the input level) that should be fixed first.

Inputs

When a team outgrows individual performance and learns team confidence, excellence becomes a reality.

Joe Paterno, Penn State football coach

In a manufacturing plant, **inputs** are the raw materials that are processed into products for sale. Similarly in team situations, inputs are what is available for teams as they go about their work. However, an important difference between an industrial plant and a team is that for a plant, the inputs are physical resources. Often for team design, we are considering psychological factors. Levels of inputs range from the individual level to the environmental level. Some of these inputs provide little opportunity for the leader to have an influence—they are merely givens. Leaders are often put in charge of teams with little or no control over the environment, the industry, or even the organizational conditions. However, the leader can directly influence other inputs to create the conditions for effective teamwork.

Figure 10.2 shows the multiple levels in the input stage of the model. Note that there are input factors at the individual and organizational levels and that these levels both surround and affect the team design level.

Leadership Prescriptions of the Model

Creation

Following McGrath's[55] view of the leader's role (the leader's main job is to identify and help satisfy team needs), and Ginnett's definition that the leader's job is to create the conditions for the team to be successful, it is possible to use the TLM to identify constructive approaches for the leader to pursue. As described earlier in this chapter, what leaders do depends on where a team is in its development. Ideally we should build a team as we build a house or an automobile. We should start with a concept, create a design, engineer it to do what we want it to do, and then manufacture it to meet those specifications. The TLM provides the same linear flow for design of a team. The somewhat more complex version of the TLM model is shown in Figure 10.5, and the leader should, as just noted, begin at the base with the dream, proceed through all the design variables, and then pay attention to the development needs of the team. In this way she can implement the three critical functions for team leadership: **dream, design,** and **development.**

FIGURE 10.5
Three Functions of TLM Leadership

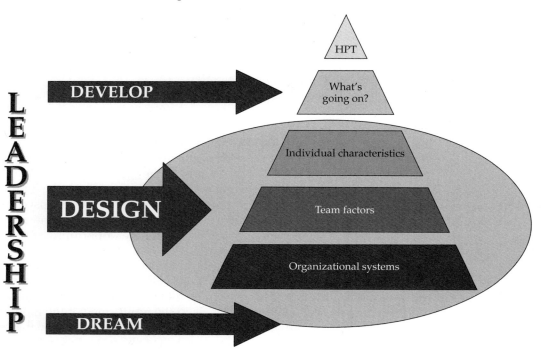

Dream

Obviously the team needs to have a clear vision. In their book *The Wisdom of Teams*[56] Katzenbach and Smith suggested that this may be the most important single step in teamwork. If the team has a challenging and demanding goal, teamwork may be necessary to accomplish the task. In highly effective work teams, the leader ensures that the team has a clear vision of where they are going. The communication of a vision frequently involves metaphorical language so that team members actually "paint their own pictures" of where the team is headed.

Design

If you've ever watched a great coach, you might have marveled at his or her calm demeanor while the game is being played. Perhaps one of the biggest reasons for this composure is that coaches realize most of their work is done by the time the game starts. They have recruited the right players, they have trained and equipped them, they have designed a strategy for their opponents, and they have instilled in the team the appropriate attitudes and values. In short, they have already done the design work.

The importance of the design function of leadership cannot be overstated. Whether in the start-up of a team or in the midstream assignment of leaders, designing the team is critical. Unfortunately this is also often the most frequently omitted step in the culture of many traditional organizations.

Managers have long been trained to detect deviations and correct them. But what if the deviations are not detectable until the output stage? At their best, managers often detect deviations at the process stage and attempt to fix them "right where they are seen." Far too often, little time or attention is focused at the organizational, team, and individual input levels. Senior-level leaders may resist changing the organizational systems for a number of reasons, including having a vested interest in maintaining the status quo (whatever it is, it has at least let them rise to their current position). And while individual team leaders may have little control over the organizational context and systems, they can always make an impact in their own team's design at both the individual and team levels.

Development

If the leader finds that the team has a clear sense of direction and vision, and the input variables at the individual, organizational, and team levels are contributing positively to team effectiveness (that is, the design portion of the leader's job has been taken care of), then she can turn her attention to the development level. Development is the ongoing work done with the team at the process level to continue to find ways to improve an already well-designed team. Given our individualistic culture, we have identified many teams in organizations that are apparently well designed and supported at the input level, but that have had no training or experience in the concept of teamwork. There are times when effective teamwork is based on very different concepts than effective individual work. For example, for a team to do well, the individuals composing the team must sometimes not maximize their individual effort. Referred to as *subsystem nonoptimization,* this concept is at first not intuitively obvious to many newly assigned team members. Nevertheless, consider the example of a high school football team that has an extremely fast running back and some good (but considerably slower) blocking linemen as members of the offense. Often team members are told they all need to do their absolute best if the team is going to do well. If our running back does his absolute best on a sweep around the end, he will run as fast as he can. By doing so, he will leave his blocking linemen behind. The team is not likely to gain much yardage on such a play, and the linemen and the running back, who have done their individual best, are apt to learn an important experiential lesson about teamwork. Most important, after several such disastrous plays, all the team members may be inclined to demonstrate poor team process (lower effort, poor strategy, poor use of knowledge, and poor group dynamics represented by intrateam strife). If we assume that all the input stage variables are satisfactorily in place, ongoing coaching may now be appropriate. The coach would get better results if he worked out a better coordination plan between the running back and the linemen. In this case, the fast running back needs to slow down (not perform maximally) to give the slower but excellent blockers a chance to do their work. After they have been given a chance to contribute to the play, the running back will have a much better chance to excel individually, and so will the team as a whole.

As straightforward as this seems, few leaders get the opportunity to build a team from the ground up. More often a leader is placed into a team that already exists, has most, if not all, of its members assigned, and is in a preexisting organizational context that might not be team friendly. Although this situation is more difficult, all is not lost. The TLM also provides a method for diagnosis and identification of key **leverage points** for on-the-fly change.

Diagnosis and Leverage Points

Let us assume that you, as a new leader, have been placed in charge of a poorly performing existing team. After a few days of observation, you have discovered that its members are just not working hard. They seem to be uninterested in the task, frequently wandering off or not even showing up for scheduled teamwork. By focusing on the process level of the TLM, we would diagnose this at the process level as a problem of effort. (The core or "engine" of the TLM is shown in Figure 10.6, which can be thought of as a four-sided pyramid.) Note that preceding the term *effort* at the process level is the label "P-1" and that all variables on this side of the pyramid have a "1" designation as well. Rather than just encouraging the team members to work harder (or threatening them), we should first look at the input level to see if there is some underlying problem. But you do not need to examine all 12 input variables. Because we have already diagnosed a P-1 level process problem, the TLM is designed to focus your attention on the key leverage points to target change for the specific problem identified in diagnosis. Each face of the pyramid shows the input variables at the individual, team, and organizational levels that most impact the process variable that we might diagnose. The factors on the "1" side of the pyramid are referred to as the leverage points for impacting P-1 effort. (See the "1" face of the pyramid in Figure 10.6.) The individual level (I-1) suggests that we look at the interests and motivations of the individual team members. These are referred to as **individual factors** in the model. If we have built a team to perform a mechanical assembly task, but the individuals assigned have little or no interest in mechanical work and instead prefer the performing arts, they may have little interest in contributing much effort to the team task. Here, using instruments such as the Campbell Interest and Skills Survey to select personnel may help our team's effort level from an individual perspective.[57]

FIGURE 10.6
Team Leadership Model

Source: R. C. Ginnett, *The Four Faces of the Pyramid of the Team Leadership Model.* © 2005 Robert C. Ginnett, PhD. All rights reserved.

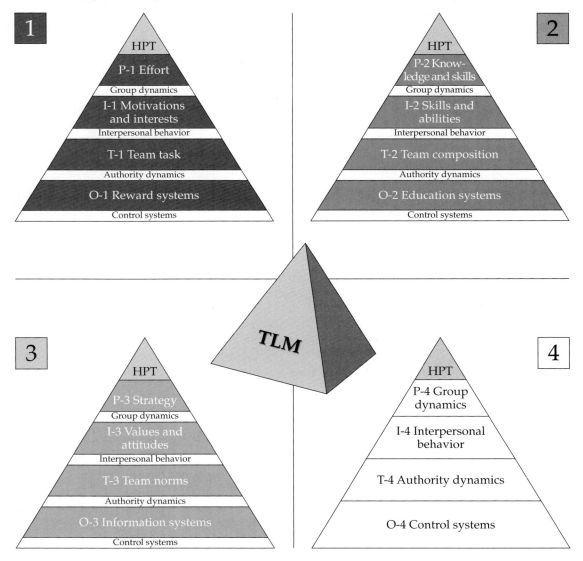

While it may seem tempting to move to the team-level inputs next, remember that this model emphasizes how teams are influenced by both individual and organizational-level inputs. Therefore, we will look at the **organizational level** next. At the organizational level (O-1), the model suggests that we should examine the reward system that may be impacting the team. If the individuals have no incentive provided by the organization for putting forth effort, they might not be inclined to work hard. Similarly, the reward system may be structured to reward only individual performance. Such a reward structure would be inconsistent with designs for a team task, where interdependence and cooperation among members are often underlying premises. If a professional basketball organization rewards players based only on individual points scored, with no bonuses for team performance (games won or making the playoffs), you can expect little passing, setting picks for teammates, and so on.

Both the individual and organizational-level variables contribute to the team's ability to perform the task. But there can also be problems at the **team design** level. Here (T-1) a poorly designed task is hypothesized to be unmotivating. If a job is meaningless, lacks sufficient autonomy, or provides no knowledge of results, we would not expect to see followers putting forth much effort.

Using the model, we found key leverage points at various levels of the input stage that affect how the team works (team process). In the example cited, we diagnosed a process-level problem with effort (P-1), so we examined the 1-level variables at the individual, organizational, and team levels as the most likely location for finding input-stage problems. By the way, the concept of leverage point does not imply that only factors at the corresponding "numbers" should be considered. For example, a team's effort might be affected by an oppressive and authoritarian leader. As we will discuss next, this foundation-level variable can have a tremendous impact on the other variables. Indeed, so powerful is this component that we should examine the process measure of group dynamics (P-4) and its corresponding leverage points in more detail. Consider the following two examples:

Surgical team: A surgical team composed of highly experienced members is involved in a surgical procedure that each member has participated in numerous times before. During one portion of the procedure, the surgeon asks for a particular instrument. The scrub nurse looks across the table at the assistant with a questioning gaze and then hands the surgeon the instrument he requested. Recognizing that the instrument he has been handed (and asked for) is not correct for the current procedure, he throws it down on the table and curses at the scrub nurse. All members of the surgical team take a half-step back from the table and all casual conversation stops. No one offers any further voluntary assistance to the surgeon.

Commercial airline crew: A commercial airline crew is making a routine approach into an uncrowded airport on a clear day. The captain is flying and has declared a visual approach. His final approach to the runway is not good, which greatly complicates the plane's landing, and the landing is poor. After taxiing to the gate, the captain and his entire crew debrief (discuss) the poor approach, and the team members talk about what they could do individually and collectively to help the captain avoid or improve a poor approach in the future. The captain thanks the members for their help and encourages them to consider how they could implement their suggestions in other situations.

Obviously the group dynamics are very different in these two cases. In the first example, the surgeon's behavior, coupled with his status, created a condition inappropriate for effective teamwork. The airline captain in the second example, even though not performing the task well, created a team environment where the team was much more likely to perform well in the future. In both of these cases, we would have observed unusual (one negative and one positive) group dynamics while the team was at work. These are examples of the group dynamics at the P-4 level.

Again returning to the model for determining points of leverage, we would check the I-4 variable at the individual level to determine if the team members involved had adequate interpersonal skills to interact appropriately. At the organizational level, the O-4 variable would suggest we check organizational components to determine if any organizational control systems inhibit or overly structure the way in which the team can make decisions or control its own fate. Such factors may include organizational design or organizational structure limitations (such as functional hierarchies or "silos"), or it may be a rigid computerized control system that specifies every minute detail of the tasks not only for the team as a whole but for all the individuals composing the team. These excessive controls at the organizational level can inhibit effective teamwork. Finally, at the team design level, the T-4 variable would have us examine authority dynamics created between the leader and the followers. Authority dynamics describe the various ways the team members, including the leader, relate and respond to authority. It is at the team level that the followers have opportunities to relate directly with the team's authority figure, the team leader. The intricacies of how these various authority dynamics can play themselves out in a team's life are more complex than is warranted for this chapter; suffice it to say that authority relationships range from autocratic to laissez-faire. (For a more detailed explanation of this concept, see Ginnett.[58]) But even without further description, it should be no surprise that the varied group dynamics observed in the previous two examples were leveraged by the leaders' different use of authority.

It would be simple if leaders could identify and specify in advance the ideal type of authority for themselves and their teams, and then work toward that objective. However, teams seldom can operate effectively under one fixed type of authority over time. The leader might prefer to use his or her favorite style, and the followers might also have an inherent preference for one type of authority or another; but if the team is to be effective, the authority dynamics they are operating with should complement the demands of the situation. Situations change over time, and so should the authority dynamics of the team. This idea is similar to a point made earlier in this book—that effective leaders tend to use all five sources of leader power.

In research on the behavior of leaders in forming their teams, Ginnett[59] found that highly effective leaders used a variety of authority dynamics in the first few minutes of a team's life. At one point in the first meeting of the team, the leader would behave directively, which enabled him to establish his competence and hence his legitimate authority. At another time, the same leader would actively seek participation from each member of the team. By modeling a range of authority behaviors in the early stages of team life, effective leaders laid the groundwork for continuing expectations of shifting authority as the situational demands changed.

Concluding Thoughts about Ginnett's Team Leadership Model

Not all components of the TLM have been discussed here because of its complexity. For example, we have not discussed **material resources.** Even if a team is well designed, has superior organizational systems supporting its work, and has access to superior-quality ongoing development, without adequate physical resources it is not likely to do well on the output level. Also note that background shells (discussed earlier in this chapter) representing the industry and the environment have not been included in this simplified depiction of the TLM. Although the team leader may have little opportunity to influence these shells, they will certainly have an impact on the team.

Finally, several feedback loops (not shown in the pyramid depictions of the TLM) provide information to various levels of the organization. Usually information is available to the organization as a whole (either formally or informally) about which teams are doing well and which are struggling. Whether leaders have access to this information is largely a function of whether they have created or stifled a safe climate. Feedback at the individual level can influence the perceived efficacy of the individual members of the team,[60,61] while the overall potency of the team is impacted even for tasks that the team has yet to attempt.[62]

Finally, let us reinforce a limitation noted earlier. For ease of use and guidance, this model has been presented as if it were a machine (for example, if P-2 breaks, check I-2, O-2, and T-2). As with other models of leadership or other human systems, however, nothing is that simple. Obviously other variables affect teams and team effectiveness. There are also complex interactions between the variables described in this model.

"Well, I guess I did it again, guys? Missed a field goal in the final seconds. But hey, we're a team, right? Right, guys? Guys?"

But we have considerable evidence that the model can be useful for understanding teams,[63] and, in light of the relationship between teams and leadership, we are now using it as an underlying framework in courses to help leaders more effectively lead their teams.

It has been shown that leaders can influence team effectiveness by (1) ensuring that the team has a clear sense of purpose and performance expectations; (2) designing or redesigning input-stage variables at the individual, organizational, and team design levels; and (3) improving team performance through ongoing coaching at various stages, but particularly while the team is actually performing its task. These midcourse corrections should not only improve the team outcomes but also help to avoid many of the team-generated problems that can cause suboptimal team performance.[64] Whether the leader gets the luxury of creation or is thrust into the leadership of an existing team, the TLM has been shown to be a useful tool in guiding leader behavior. It also is handy if you believe that a leader's job is to create the conditions for a team to be effective.

Let us integrate the variables from this model into our leader–follower–situation framework (see Figure 10.7). Clearly there are variables of importance in each of the three arenas. However, in this model leader characteristics play a lesser role because the leader's job is to work on what is not being provided for the team so it can perform its task. The focus thus has shifted from the leader to the followers and to the situation.

FIGURE 10.7
Factors from the Team Leadership Model and the Interactional Framework

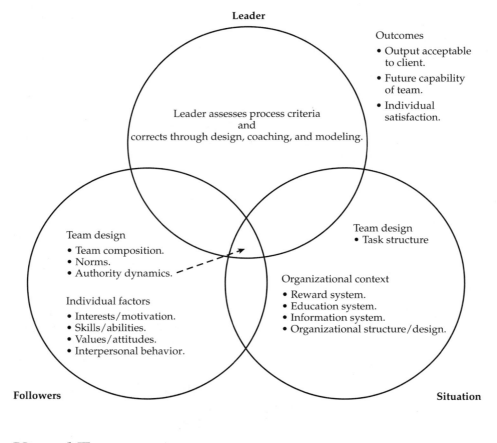

Virtual Teams

Just as teams and teamwork have become essential to the accomplishment of work in organizations, so will be an understanding of teams that are not in a single location. With the movement toward the global marketplace and the resultant globalization of organizations, it is appropriate to briefly consider the difficulties and recommended solutions for leading **geographically dispersed teams (GDTs).** There is considerable discussion about the labeling of such teams,[65] but for simplicity we will call them **virtual teams** here.

The marketplace for many firms is now the globe (see Highlight 10.9). Western corporations are recognizing that growth and development opportunities are often much greater in Russia and other nations of the former Soviet Union, China, Latin America, and Africa than they are in

What Is the "Global Population" of Your Classroom?

HIGHLIGHT 10.9

The authors of this book attended a training session conducted by a major corporation intended for its newly appointed executives. One session was devoted to demonstrating the need for a global perspective in today's environment. To illustrate the key point, the instructor divided the room into unequal groups representing the geographical distribution of the world's population and had each group stand up in turn. As each group stood, she told them the proportion of the global population they represented. The proportions she used are provided here.

You might try this in your classroom—it makes the point dramatically.

Australia and New Zealand	2%
North America	5%
Former Soviet Union	5%
Latin America	7%
Western/Eastern Europe	10%
Africa	12%
Asia	56%

the markets of North America and Europe. But this realization brings new challenges for leading teams that are not only dispersed geographically but are often culturally different as well. Fortunately, information and communication technology offers some new opportunities, if not solutions, for these problems. Personal computer sales should top 366 million in 2010; more than 2.5 billion people will use cellular phones with over 500 million of these users in China; and the Internet and World Wide Web will be used by nearly 2 billion users worldwide.[66] But is the mere opportunity to communicate electronically sufficient to ensure teamwork? Apparently not.

Researchers at the Conference Board[67] have reported that five major areas must change for global teams to work. The five listed were senior management leadership, innovative use of communication technology, adoption of an organization design that enhances global operations, the prevalence of trust among team members, and the ability to capture the strengths of diverse cultures, languages, and people.

Armstrong and Cole[68] did in-depth studies of virtual teams and have reported three conclusions that should be considered by leaders of these teams. First, the distance between members of a virtual team is multidimensional. "Distance" includes not just geographical distance but also organizational distance (different group or department cultures), temporal distance (different time zones), and differences in national culture. Second, the impact of such distances on the performance of a distributed work group is not directly proportional to objective measures of distance. In fact, Armstrong and Cole suggested that a new measure of distance between group members that reflects the degree of group cohesion and identity—a measure of psychological distance between members—would predict group performance better than geographical distance. Finally,

Leading Virtual Teams: 10 Principles

HIGHLIGHT 10.10

Terence Brake is the president of TMA-Americas and specializes in globalization. He suggests the following guidance for leaders of virtual teams:

Virtual when used in relation to teamwork is an unfortunate term. It implies there is almost teamwork, but not quite. *Virtual* has associations with *nearly, close to,* and *bordering on.* As one wit said, "If you want virtual results, create a virtual team." Alternatively, it is a fortunate term if taken to imply that greater efforts are needed to achieve real teamwork in virtual teams. What principles can help you do this?

1. *Be proactive.* We often talk of "virtual" teams (VTs) as if they were all of a kind, but each one has its unique challenges. Some have a high level of cultural diversity. Others are more homogeneous. Some use one primary technology for collaboration, while others use a diverse mix. Some are short-lived, targeted on solving an immediate problem. Others are longer-term and strategic. Some cross time zones, and others none. By understanding the most likely challenges to occur, you can take proactive measures and increase team confidence. Confidence is a building block of virtual team performance.

2. *Focus on relationships before tasks.* Early on, team communications should have a significant "getting to know you" component. They should also demonstrate enthusiasm and optimism. Members need to feel valued for who they are, not just what they do. They need to feel engaged and connected. Trust is usually built early on virtual teams, or not at all. Some observers talk of the "virtual paradox"—virtual teams being highly dependent on trust, but not operating under conditions supportive of trust building. Trust is often built on perceived similarities, but distance makes this process difficult. Chances for misunderstanding are also increased. Goodwill and engagement will solve most problems. Isolation and alienation create problems. Connect, and then collaborate.

3. *Seek clarity and focus early on.* Invest up-front time in clarifying the team's purpose and roles and responsibilities. There is enough uncertainty when working at a distance; it doesn't need to be added to by ambiguity and confusion. Clear purpose and accountabilities support cohesion. Translate purpose and overall accountabilities into specific objectives and tasks so that everyone knows what is expected, by whom, and by when. Virtual teams are highly susceptible to "focus drift" and fragmentation, so keep reminding the team of purpose, objectives, and so on.

4. *Create a sense of order and predictability.* In a world wanting us to embrace chaos, "order" and "predictability" might appear unfashionable. But they are critical to the success of virtual teams. Uncertainty creates anxiety, fear, and withdrawal. The result is a demotivated and unproductive team. Use common team tools, templates, and processes; have predetermined times for communicating together; check in with team members regularly without trying to micromanage; be accessible and an anchor point for the team. Shared expectations are psychological threads connecting separate minds.

5. *Be a cool-headed, objective problem solver.* Problems on virtual teams can appear larger than they actually are; people feeling isolated can lose perspective. Small issues, quickly resolved when working face-to-face, often fester and spread paranoia and distrust. You should establish yourself as someone who is totally fair; you don't play favorites, and you don't overburden some at the expense of others. You also need to be pragmatic. When there is a problem, you keep calm, you engage the team in finding practical solutions, and you communicate often. Panic is a virus that breeds exceptionally well in silent, isolated spaces.

6. *Develop shared operating agreements.* To reduce threats of uncertainty and ambiguity,

continued

continued

common methods and processes—operating agreements—need to be established quickly. These agreements provide the team with shared mental models for working together. Typically, operating agreements need to be created in areas such as planning, decision making, communicating, and coordination. A team charter acts as a common reference point and can help orient new team members. Take time during team "meetings" to review how well the operating agreements are working.

7. *Give team members personal attention.* Just as you would on a face-to-face team, allocate time to "meet" with individuals. Find out how he or she is feeling about things. Give each person an opportunity to share personal successes, challenges, needs, and wants. It can be difficult to do this in team "meetings" where the emphasis is on shared tasks and problem solving. Empathize with that person who is on the road, working at home, or in a remote office. Listening, caring, sympathizing, recognizing—they cost little, but benefit everyone.

8. *Respect the challenges of the virtual environment.* I once lived on a boat, and I soon learned to respect the power of nature—the winds, tides, swells, rain, ice, and drought. I had to pay very close attention to these elements or they could sink me, swamp me, or ground me. There is always the temptation to carry over habits from one environment (land, face-to-face teamwork) into another (river, working at a distance). We must recognize the differences and adapt. Listening, empathizing, communi-

cating, coordinating, engaging, energizing, and enabling all need to be enhanced.

9. *Recognize the limits of available technologies.* Unless you really have to, don't try and do everything via a virtual team. Sometimes teams are working on projects so complex that no matter how much video- or teleconferencing time they have, it will not be enough. Sometimes it pays dividends to bring people together for a few days. Never assume that because you have been designated a "virtual" team, you must always work in that mode. Focus on cost/benefit over the life of the project. Technology is a tool, and all tools are good for some tasks and not others.

10. *Stay people-focused.* Distance can make faceless abstractions of us all. Never lose sight of the fact that your virtual team members are people, with all that that entails—needs for belonging, meaning, accomplishment, and recognition; feelings of frustration, anger, excitement, boredom, and alienation; political pressures and personal pressures. Think about those features of your physical workplace that enable teams to work well together, such as formal meeting rooms, informal spaces, and the coffee area, and see what you can do to humanize your virtual workplace—team pictures and bios, bulletin boards, chat areas.

Applying these virtual team leadership principles will help you avoid *almost* and *close to* teamwork. Virtual teamwork is only going to increase, so many of us need to re-skill ourselves for leading at a distance.

---

differences in the effects of distance on work groups are due at least partially to two intervening variables: (1) integrating practices *within* a virtual team, and (2) integrating practices *between* a virtual team and its larger host organization.

With increasing numbers of virtual teams, we are beginning to see evidence that these teams, when designed and constructed properly, might be even more effective than in-place teams. In a study of successful "far-flung teams,"[69] three rules emerged that enhanced the teams' performance. First, the leaders needed to not only select for diversity but then exploit that diversity for the team's benefit. Second, technology needed to simulate reality. For example, e-mail was a poor way for a team to communicate because it either focused on one-on-one communications (as opposed to team-level) or drowned people in paperwork if everyone was copied. Surprisingly, the researchers didn't think much of videoconferencing. What seemed to work best was a specifically designed "virtual work space." This included not only a team Web space with a home page prominently displaying the team's mission but also pages for people, purpose, and a meeting center, among other features. Other teams have found wikis essential to keep global teams up to date.[70] Third, leaders must be particularly diligent to hold virtual teams together. Face-to-face teams can confront forces that splinter the groups, but such forces can be accentuated in virtual teams. Leaders of successful virtual teams overcommunicated, pushed for the adoption of a common language, and merged work practices. One particularly successful tactic was to have team members work in ad hoc pairs for a week or two so they would get to know each other better. This also seemed to discourage the formation of cliques. And, as described for the TLM earlier, the leaders spent a great deal of time working in the organizational background to ensure that team members were allotted sufficient time to work on the virtual project.

Finally, a number of frameworks under development can help leaders work with virtual teams, and these frameworks may provide specific useful factors. However, in our admittedly limited exposure to virtual teams in a pure research sense, a number of our clients have reported that the TLM has been quite useful in considering process problems and in suggesting appropriate leverage points for intervention. One thing is clear: virtual teams require more leadership, not less.

Summary

The group perspective showed that followers' behaviors can be the result of factors somewhat independent of the individual characteristics of followers. Group factors that can affect followers' behaviors include group size, stages of group development, roles, norms, and cohesion. Leadership practitioners should use these concepts to better understand followers' behaviors. Leaders should also use a team perspective for understanding follower behavior and group performance. Leadership practitioners need to bear in mind how a team's sense of identity, common goals or tasks, level of task interdependence, and differentiated roles affect functional and dysfunctional follower behavior. Additionally, because effective teams have several readily identifiable characteristics, leadership practitioners may want to use the suggestions provided by Hackman,[71] Ginnett,[72] or Hallam and Campbell[73] to develop more effective teams.

The Team Leadership Model posited that team effectiveness can best be understood in terms of inputs, processes, and outcomes. The input level consists of the individual characteristics of the followers; the design of the team itself; and various organizational systems that create the context in which the teams will operate. The process level concerns how teams behave while going about their tasks, and the output level concerns whether customers and clients are satisfied with the team's product, whether the team improves and develops as a performing unit, and whether followers are satisfied to be members of the team. By identifying certain process problems in teams, leaders can use the model to diagnose appropriate leverage points for action at the individual, team design, or organizational levels, or for ongoing development at the process level. Leaders concerned with teamwork in organizational settings have found this framework useful in helping them conceptualize factors affecting team effectiveness and identifying targets for change.

Key Terms

group perspective, *390*
group, *393*
cliques, *394*
span of control, *394*
additive task, *395*
process loss, *395*
social loafing, *395*
social facilitation, *395*
forming, *396*
storming, *396*
norming, *396*
performing, *396*
project teams, *397*
punctuated
equilibrium, *397*
group roles, *397*
task role, *397*
relationship role, *397*

dysfunctional
roles, *398*
role conflict, *398*
intrasender role
conflict, *398*
intersender role
conflict, *400*
interrole conflict, *400*
person–role
conflict, *400*
role ambiguity, *400*
norms, *400*
group cohesion, *402*
overbounding, *403*
groupthink, *404*
ollieism, *405*
organizational
shells, *409*

Team Leadership
Model (TLM), *410*
outputs, *412*
process measures, *414*
inputs, *415*
dream, *415*
design, *415*
development, *415*
leverage point, *418*
individual factors, *418*
organizational
level, *420*
team design, *420*
material resources, *422*
geographically
dispersed teams
(GDTs), *424*
virtual teams, *424*

Questions

1. How do the tenets of Ginnett's Team Leadership Model compare with the components of team performance described earlier?

2. Not all group norms are positive or constructive from the leader's perspective. If a group holds counterproductive norms, what should the leader do?

3. On the basis of what you know about global cultures, would people from the United States, Japan, or Chile be more comfortable with a group or team-based approach to work?

Activity:

NASA Exercise—Lost on the Moon

Your spaceship has crash-landed on the dark side of the moon and you are scheduled to rendezvous with the mother ship, which is 200 miles away on the lighted side of the moon. The crash has ruined the ship and destroyed all the equipment except for the 15 items listed here. Your crew's survival depends on reaching the mother ship, so you must choose the most critical items available to take on the 200-mile trip. Your task is to rank-order the 15 items in the order of their importance for your survival. Place a "1" beside the most important item, a "2" beside the second most important item, and so on until you have ranked all 15 items.

_____ Box of matches
_____ Food concentrate
_____ 50 feet of nylon rope
_____ Parachute silk
_____ Solar-powered portable heating unit
_____ Two .45 caliber pistols
_____ One case of dehydrated milk
_____ Two 100-pound tanks of oxygen
_____ Stellar map
_____ Self-inflating life raft
_____ Magnetic compass
_____ Five gallons of water
_____ Signal flares
_____ First-aid kit with hypodermic syringes
_____ Solar-powered FM transmitter/receiver

Your instructor has the "NASA Expert" answers and the instructions for completing the exercise.

Minicase

Integrating Teams at Hernandez & Associates

Marco Hernandez is president of Hernandez & Associates Inc., a full-service advertising agency with clients across North America. The company provides a variety of marketing services to support its diverse group of clients. Whether called on to generate a strategic plan, create interactive Web sites, or put together a full-blown media campaign, the team at Hernandez & Associates prides itself on creative solutions to its clients' marketing challenges.

The firm was founded in 1990 with an emphasis in the real estate industry. It quickly expanded its client base to include health care, as well as food and consumer products. Like many small firms, the company grew quickly in the "high-flying" 1990s, but its administrative costs to obtain and serve businesses also skyrocketed. And, as with many businesses, the agency's business was greatly affected by the terrorist attacks of September 11, 2001, and the economic downturn that followed. Clients' shrinking budgets forced them to scale back their business with Hernandez & Associates, and staff cutbacks meant that clients needed more marketing support services as opposed to full-scale campaigns.

Hernandez & Associates now faced a challenge—to adapt its business to focus on what the clients were asking for. Specifically, clients, with their reduced staffs, were looking for help responding to their customers' requests and looking for ways to make the most of their limited marketing budgets. Its small, cohesive staff of 20 employees needed to make some fast changes.

As president of Hernandez & Associates, Marco Hernandez knew his team was up for the challenge. He had worked hard to create an environment to support a successful team—he recruited people who had solid agency experience, and he consistently communicated the firm's mission to his team. He made sure the team had all the resources it needed to succeed and constantly took stock of these resources. He had built his team as he built his business and knew the group would respond to his leadership. But where to start? Getting the team to understand that growth depended on a shift in how it served its clients was not difficult—each of the employees of the small firm had enough contact with the clients that they knew client needs were changing. But making significant changes to the status quo at Hernandez & Associates would be difficult. Group roles had to change—creative folks had to think about how to increase a client's phone inquiries and Web site visits; account people needed a better understanding of the client's desire for more agency leadership. And everyone needed a better sense of the costs involved. The company as a whole required a more integrated approach to serving clients if they hoped to survive. Marco needed a plan.

1. Like many leaders, Marco has a team in place and does not have the luxury of building a new team to adapt to the changing business environment his firm now faces. Use the TLM to help Marco diagnose the problems faced by the firm and identify leverage points for change.
   a. Consider the major functions of the TLM—input, process, and output. Where do most of the firm's challenges fall?
   b. What are the team's goals for outputs?
2. Identify potential resources for Marco and his team in implementing a strategy to change the way they do business at Hernandez & Associates.

End Notes

1. R. C. Ginnett, "Effectiveness Begins Early: The Leadership Role in the Formation of Intra-Organizational Task Groups," unpublished manuscript, 1992.

2. G. S. Gibbard, J. J. Hartman, and D. Mann, *Analysis of Groups: Contribution to the Theory, Research, and Practice* (San Francisco: Jossey-Bass, 1974).

3. M. Shaw, *Group Dynamics: The Psychology of Small Group Dynamics,* 3rd ed. (New York: McGraw-Hill, 1981).

4. G. A. Yukl, *Leadership in Organizations,* 1st ed. (Englewood Cliffs, NJ: Prentice Hall, 1981).

5. I. J. Badin, "Some Moderator Influences on Relationships between Consideration, Initiating Structure, and Organizational Criteria," *Journal of Applied Psychology* 59 (1974), pp. 380–82.

6. B. E. Goodstadt and D. Kipnis, "Situational Influences on the Use of Power," *Journal of Applied Psychology* 54 (1970), pp. 201–07.

7. D. Kipnis, S. M. Schmidt, and I. Wilkinson, "Intraorganizational Influence Tactics: Explorations in Getting One's Way," *Journal of Applied Psychology* 65 (1980), pp. 440–52.

8. J. G. Udell, "An Empirical Test of Hypotheses Relating to Span of Control," *Administrative Science Quarterly* 12 (1967), pp. 420–39.

9. B. M. Bass, *Leadership, Psychology, and Organizational Behavior* (New York: Harper, 1960).

10. B. P. Indik, "Organizational Size and Member Participation: Some Empirical Tests of Alternative Explanations," *Human Relations* 18 (1965), pp. 339–50.

11. I. D. Steiner, *Group Process and Productivity* (New York: Academic Press, 1972).

12. Ibid.

13. B. Latane, K. Williams, and S. Harkins, "Social Loafing," *Psychology Today* (1979), p. 104.

14. D. B. Porter, M. Bird, and A. Wunder, "Competition, Cooperation, Satisfaction, and the Performance of Complex Tasks among Air Force Cadets," *Current Psychology Research and Reviews* 9, no. 4 (1991), pp. 347–54.

15. R. Zajonc, "Social Facilitation," *Science* 149 (1965), pp. 269–74.

16. B. W. Tuckman, "Developmental Sequence in Small Groups," *Psychological Bulletin* 63 (1965), pp. 384–99.

17. Ibid.

18. E. Mayo, *The Human Problems of an Industrial Civilization* (New York: Macmillan, 1933).

19. R. M. Stogdill, "Group Productivity, Drive, and Cohesiveness," *Organizational Behavior and Human Performance* 8 (1972), pp. 26–43.

20. Ibid.

21. J. R. Terborg, C. H. Castore, and J. A. DeNinno, "A Longitudinal Field Investigation of the Impact of Group Composition on Group Performance and Cohesion," paper presented at the annual meeting of the Midwestern Psychological Association, Chicago, 1975.

22. C. J. G. Gersick, "Time and Transition in Work Teams: Toward a New Model of Group Development," *Academy of Management Journal* 31 (1988), pp. 9–41.

23. R. C. Ginnett, "Airline Cockpit Crew," in *Groups That Work (and Those That Don't)*, ed. J. Richard Hackman (San Francisco: Jossey-Bass, 1990).

24. M. Jamal, "Job Stress and Job Performance Controversy: An Empirical Assessment," *Organizational Behavior and Human Performance* 33 (1984), pp. 1–21.

25. P. Zimbardo, C. Haney, W. Banks, and D. Jaffe, "The Mind Is a Formidable Jailer: A Pirandellian Prison," *New York Times Magazine*, April 8, 1973, pp. 38–60.

26. R. J. House, R. S. Schuler, and E. Levanoni, "Role Conflict and Ambiguity Scales: Reality or Artifact?" *Journal of Applied Psychology* 68 (1983), pp. 334–37.

27. J. R. Rizzo, R. J. House, and S. I. Lirtzman, "Role Conflict and Ambiguity in Complex Organizations," *Administrative Science Quarterly* 15 (1970), pp. 150–63.

28. C. D. Fisher, and R. Gitleson, "A Meta-analysis of the Correlates of Role Conflict and Ambiguity," *Journal of Applied Psychology* 68 (1983), pp. 320–33.

29. J. R. Hackman, "Group Influences on Individuals," in *Handbook of Industrial and Organizational Psychology*, ed. M. D. Dunnette (Chicago: Rand McNally, 1976).

30. R. Reilly, *Sports Illustrated* 104, no. 15 (2006), p. 76.

31. D. C. Feldman, "The Development and Enforcement of Group Norms," *Academy of Management Review*, January 1984, pp. 47–53.

32. J. R. Hackman, *Leading Teams—Setting the Stage for Great Performances* (Boston, MA: Harvard Business School Press, 2002).

33. C. P. Alderfer, "Group and Intergroup Relations," in *Improving Life at Work*, ed. J. R. Hackman and J. L. Suttle (Santa Monica, CA: Goodyear, 1977).

34. R. C. Ginnett, "The Formation Process of Airline Flight Crews," *Proceedings of the Fourth International Symposium on Aviation Psychology* (Columbus, OH, 1987).

35. I. L. Janis, *Groupthink*, 2nd ed. (Boston: Houghton Mifflin, 1982).

36. Ibid.

37. Ibid.

38. J. E. Shephard, "Thomas Becket, Ollie North, and You," *Military Review* 71, no. 5 (1991), pp. 20–33.

39. S. P. Robbins, *Organizational Behavior: Concepts, Controversies, and Applications* (Englewood Cliffs, NJ: Prentice Hall, 1986).

40. G. L. Hallam and D. P. Campbell, "Selecting Team Members? Start with a Theory of Team Effectiveness," paper presented at the Seventh Annual Meeting of the Society of Industrial/Organizational Psychologists, Montreal, Canada, May 1992.

41. Ibid.

42. J. R. Hackman, *Groups That Work (and Those That Don't)* (San Francisco: Jossey-Bass, 1990).

43. R. C. Ginnett, "Crews as Groups: Their Formation and Their Leadership," in *Crew Resource Management*, ed. B. Kanki, R. Helmreich, and J. Anca (San Diego, CA: Academic Press, 2010).

44. R. C. Ginnett, "Team Effectiveness Leadership Model: Identifying Leverage Points for Change," *Proceedings of the 1996 National Leadership Institute Conference* (College Park, MD: National Leadership Institute, 1996).

45. J. R. Hackman, "Group Level Issues in the Design and Training of Cockpit Crews," in *Proceedings of the NASA/MAC Workshop on Cockpit Resource Management*, ed.

H. H. Orlady and H. C. Foushee (Moffett Field, CA: NASA Ames Research Center, 1986).

46. R. C. Ginnett, "Crews as Groups: Their Formation and Their Leadership," in *Crew Resource Management,* ed. B. Kanki, R. Helmreich, and J. Anca (San Diego, CA: Academic Press, 2010).

47. Ibid.

48. R. C. Ginnett, "Team Effectiveness Leadership Model: Identifying Leverage Points for Change," *Proceedings of the 1996 National Leadership Institute Conference* (College Park, MD: National Leadership Institute, 1996).

49. R. C. Ginnett, "Team Effectiveness Leadership Model: Design & Diagnosis," *12th Annual International Conference on Work Teams* (Dallas, TX: 2001).

50. J. E. McGrath, *Leadership Behavior: Some Requirements for Leadership Training* (Washington, DC: Office of Career Development, U.S. Civil Service Commission, 1964).

51. J. R. Hackman, *Groups That Work (and Those That Don't)* (San Francisco: Jossey-Bass, 1990).

52. K. W. Smith, E. Salas, and M. T. Brannick, "Leadership Style as a Predictor of Teamwork Behavior: Setting the Stage by Managing Team Climate," paper presented at the Ninth Annual Conference of the Society for Industrial and Organizational Psychology, Nashville, TN, 1994.

53. J. R. Hackman, *Groups That Work (and Those That Don't)* (San Francisco: Jossey-Bass, 1990).

54. S. A. Wheelan, *Group Processes* (Needham Heights, MA: Allyn & Bacon, 1994).

55. J. E. McGrath, *Leadership Behavior: Some Requirements for Leadership Training* (Washington, DC: Office of Career Development, U.S. Civil Service Commission, 1964).

56. J. R. Katzenbach and B. K. Smith *The Wisdom of Teams* (Boston: HarperBusiness, 1994).

57. D. P. Campbell, S. Hyne, and D. L. Nilsen, *Campbell Interests and Skill Survey Manual* (Minneapolis, MN: National Computer Systems, 1992).

58. R. C. Ginnett, "Crews as Groups: Their Formation and Their Leadership," in *Crew Resource Management,* ed. B. Kanki, R. Helmreich, and J. Anca (San Diego, CA: Academic Press, 2010).

59. Ibid.

60. A. Bandura, "Self-Efficacy: Toward a Unifying Theory of Behavioral Change," *Psychological Review* 84 (1977), pp. 191–215.

61. D. H. Lindsley, D. J. Brass., and J. B. Thomas, " Efficacy-Performance Spirals: A Multilevel Perspective," *Academy of Management Review* 20 (1995), pp. 645–78.

62. R. A. Guzzo, P. R. Yost, R. J. Campbell, and G. P. Shea, "Potency in Teams: Articulating a Construct," *British Journal of Social Psychology* 32 (1993), pp. 87–106.

63. J. R. Hackman, *Groups That Work (and Those That Don't)* (San Francisco: Jossey-Bass, 1990).

64. I. D. Steiner, *Group Process and Productivity* (New York: Academic Press, 1972).

65. M. Kossler, and S. Prestridge, "Geographically Dispersed Teams," *Issues and Observations* 16 (1996), pp. 2–3.

66. J. Lipnack and J. Stamps, *Virtual Teams: Reaching across Space, Time and Organizations with Technology* (New York: John Wiley, 1997).

67. Conference Board, "Global Management Teams: A Perspective," *HR Executive Review* 4 (1996).

68. D. J. Armstrong and P. Cole, "Managing Distances and Differences in Geographically Distributed Work Groups," in *Distributed Work*, ed. P. Hinds and S. Kiesler (Cambridge, MA: MIT Press, 2002), pp. 167–89.

69. A. Majchrzak, A Malhotra, J. Stamps, and J. Lipnack, "Can Absence Make a Team Grow Stronger?" *Harvard Business Review*, May 2004, pp.131–37.

70. P. Dvorak, "How Teams Can Work Well Together from Far Apart," *The Wall Street Journal*, September 17, 2007, p. B-4.

71. J. R. Hackman, *Groups That Work (and Those That Don't)* (San Francisco: Jossey-Bass, 1990).

72. R. C. Ginnett, "Effectiveness Begins Early: The Leadership Role in the Formation of Intra-Organizational Task Groups," unpublished manuscript, 1992.

73. G. L. Hallam and D. P. Campbell, "Selecting Team Members? Start with a Theory of Team Effectiveness," paper presented at the Seventh Annual Meeting of the Society of Industrial/Organizational Psychologists, Montreal, Canada, May 1992.

Chapter

11

Skills for Developing Others

The skills chapter in Part 2 addressed what might be considered relatively basic leadership skills such as listening and communication. In this chapter we will cover a number of additional leadership skills that are somewhat more advanced and that pertain particularly to the leader's relationship with followers. The skills addressed in this section include

- Setting goals.
- Providing constructive feedback.
- Team building for work teams.
- Building high-performance teams—the Rocket Model.
- Delegating.
- Coaching.

Setting Goals

The Roman philosopher Seneca wrote, "When a man does not know what harbor he is making for, no wind is the right wind." Setting goals and developing plans of action to attain them are important for individuals and for groups. For example, the purpose or goal is often the predominant norm in any group. Once group goals are agreed on, they induce member compliance, act as a criterion for evaluating the leadership potential of group members, and become the criteria for evaluating group performance.[1]

Perhaps the most important step in accomplishing a personal or group goal is stating it right in the first place. The reason many people become frustrated with the outcomes of their New Year's resolutions is that their resolutions are so vague or unrealistic that they are unlikely to lead to demonstrable results. It is possible to keep New Year's resolutions, but we must set them intelligently. In a more general sense, some ways of writing goal statements increase the likelihood that we will successfully achieve the desired goals. Goals should be specific and observable, attainable and challenging, based on top-to-bottom commitment, and designed to provide feedback to personnel about their progress toward them. The following is a more detailed discussion of each of these points.

Goals Should Be Specific and Observable

As described in Chapter 9, research provides strong support for the idea that specific goals lead to higher levels of effort and performance than general goals. General goals do not work as well because they often do not provide enough information regarding which particular behaviors are to be changed or when a clear end state has been attained. This may be easiest to see with a personal example.

Assume that a student is not satisfied with her academic performance and wants to do something about it. She might set a general goal such as "I will do my best next year" or "I will do better in school next year." At first such a goal may seem fine; after all, as long as she is motivated to do well, what more would be needed? However, on further thought you can see that "do my best" or "do better" are so ambiguous as to be unhelpful in directing her behavior and ultimately assessing her success. General goals have relatively little impact on energizing and directing immediate behavior, and they make it difficult to assess, in the end, whether someone has attained them. A better goal statement for this student would be to attain a B average or to get no deficient grades this semester. Specific goals like these make it easier to chart progress. A more business-oriented example might be improving productivity at work. Specific goal statements in this case might include a 20 percent increase in the number of products produced by the work unit over the next three months or a 40 percent decrease in the number of products returned by quality control next year.

The idea of having specific goals is closely related to that of having observable goals. It should be clear to everyone when a goal has or has not been reached. It is easy to say your goal is to go on a diet, but a much better goal is "to lose 10 pounds by March." Similarly, it is easy to say a team should do better next season, but a better goal is to say the team will win more than half of next season's games. Note that specific, observable goals are also time limited. Without time limits for accomplishing goals, there would be little urgency associated with them. Neither would there be a finite point at which it is clear whether a person or group has accomplished the goals. For example, it is better to set a goal of improving the next quarter's sales figures than just improving sales.

Goals Should Be Attainable but Challenging

Some people seem to treat goals as a sort of loyalty oath they must pass, as if it would be a break with their ideals or reflect insufficient motivation if any but the loftiest goals were set. Yet to be useful, goals must be realistic. The struggling high school student who sets a goal of getting into Harvard may be unrealistic, but it may be realistic to set a goal of getting into the local state university. A civil rights activist may wish to eliminate prejudice completely, but a more attainable goal might be to eliminate racial discrimination in the local housing project over the next five years. A track team is not likely to win every race, but it may be realistic to aim to win the league championship.

The corollary to the preceding point is that goals should also be challenging. If goals merely needed to be attainable, then there would be nothing wrong with setting goals so easy that accomplishing them would be virtually guaranteed. As we have seen previously, setting easy goals does not result in high levels of performance; higher levels of performance come about when goals stretch and inspire people toward doing more than they thought they could. Goals need to be challenging but attainable to get the best out of ourselves.

Goals Require Commitment

There is nothing magical about having goals; having goals per se does not guarantee success. Unless supported by real human commitment, goal statements are mere words. Organizational goals are most likely to be achieved if there is commitment to them at both the top and the bottom of the organization. Top leadership needs to make clear that it is willing to put its money where its mouth is. When top leadership sets goals, it should provide the resources workers need to achieve the goals and then should reward those who do. Subordinates often become committed to goals simply by seeing the sincere and enthusiastic commitment of top leadership to them. Another way to build subordinate acceptance and commitment to goals is to have subordinates participate in setting the goals. Research on the effects of goal setting demonstrates that worker acceptance and satisfaction tend to increase when workers are allowed to participate in setting goals.[2,3]

On the other hand, research is less conclusive about whether participation in goal setting actually increases performance or productivity. These mixed findings about participation and performance may be due to various qualities of the group and the leader. In terms of the group, groupthink may cause highly cohesive groups to commit to goals that are unrealistic and unachievable. Group members may not have realistically considered equipment or resource constraints or have the technical skills needed to successfully accomplish the goal. In addition, group members may not have any special enthusiasm for accomplishing a goal if the leader is perceived to have little expert power or is unsupportive, curt, or inept.[4,5,6] However, if leaders are perceived to be competent and supportive, followers may have as much goal commitment as they would if they had participated in setting the goal. Thus participation in goal setting often leads to higher levels of commitment and performance if the leader is perceived to be incompetent, but it will not necessarily lead to greater commitment and performance than are achieved when a competent leader assigns a goal. Again, these findings lend credence to the importance of technical competence in leadership effectiveness.

Goals Require Feedback

One of the most effective ways to improve any kind of performance is to provide feedback about how closely a person's behavior matches some criterion, and research shows that performance is much higher when goals are accompanied by feedback than when either goals or feedback are used alone. Goals that are specific, observable, and time limited are conducive to ongoing assessment and performance-based feedback, and leaders and followers should strive to provide and seek regular feedback. Moreover, people should seek feedback from a variety of sources or provide feedback using a variety of criteria. Often, different sources and criteria can paint diverse pictures of goal progress, and people can get a better idea of the true level of their progress by examining the information provided and integrating it across the various sources and criteria.

Providing Constructive Feedback

Giving constructive feedback involves sharing information or perceptions with another about the nature, quality, or impact of that person's behavior. It can range from giving feedback pertaining specifically to a person's work (performance feedback) to impressions of how aspects of that person's interpersonal behavior may be pervasively affecting relationships with others. Our use of the term *feedback* here is somewhat different from its use in the systems view of communication (Figure 8.2 in Chapter 8). In the communication model, the feedback loop begins with actively checking the receiver's interpretation of your own message and then initiating or modifying subsequent communications as necessary. A simple example of that meaning of feedback might be noting another person's quizzical expression when you try to explain a complicated point and realizing you'd better say it differently. The skill of giving constructive feedback, however, inherently involves actively giving feedback to someone else.

Getting helpful feedback is essential to a subordinate's performance and development. Without feedback, a subordinate will not be able to tell whether she's doing a good job or whether her abrasiveness is turning people off and hurting her chances for promotion. And it's not just subordinates who need constructive feedback to learn and grow. Peers may seek feedback from peers, and leaders may seek feedback from subordinates. Besides fostering growth, effective supervisory feedback also plays a major role in building morale.

In many ways, the development of good feedback skills is an outgrowth of developing good communication, listening, and assertiveness skills. Giving good feedback depends on being clear about the purpose of the feedback and on choosing an appropriate context and medium for giving it. Giving good feedback also depends on sending the proper nonverbal signals and trying to detect emotional signals from whoever may be receiving the feedback. In addition, giving good feedback depends on being somewhat assertive in providing it, even when it may be critical of a person's performance or behavior. Although feedback skills are related to communication, listening, and assertiveness skills, they are not the same thing. Someone may have good communication, listening, and assertiveness skills but poor feedback skills. Perhaps this distinction can be made clearer by examining the knowledge, behavior, and evaluative components of feedback skills.

The knowledge component of feedback concerns knowing when, where, and what feedback is to be given. For example, knowing when, where, and how to give positive feedback may be very different from knowing when, where, and how to give negative feedback. The behavioral component of feedback concerns how feedback actually is delivered (as contrasted with knowing how it should be delivered). Good feedback is specific, descriptive, direct, and helpful; poor feedback is often too watered down to be useful to the recipient. Finally, one way to evaluate feedback is to examine whether recipients actually modify their behavior accordingly after receiving it. Of course this should not be the only way to evaluate feedback skills. Even when feedback is accurate in content and delivered skillfully, a recipient may fail to acknowledge it or do anything about it.

Although most leaders probably believe that feedback is an important skill, research has shown that leaders also believe they give more feedback than their subordinates think they do.[7] There are many reasons why leaders may be reluctant to give feedback. Leaders may be reluctant to give positive feedback because of time pressures, doubts about the efficacy of feedback, or lack of feedback skills.[8] Sometimes supervisors hesitate to use positive feedback because they believe subordinates may see it as politically manipulative, ingratiating, or insincere.[9] Leaders also may give positive feedback infrequently if they rarely leave their desks, if their personal standards are too high, or if they believe good performance is expected and should not be recognized at all.[10] Other reasons may explain the failure to give negative feedback,[11] such as fear of disrupting leader–follower relations[12] or fear of employee retaliation.[13]

Although there are a number of reasons why leaders are hesitant to provide both positive and negative feedback, leaders need to keep in mind that followers, committee members, or team members will perform at a higher level if they are given accurate and frequent feedback. It is difficult to imagine how work group or team performance could improve without feedback. Positive feedback is necessary to tell followers they should keep doing what they are doing well, and negative feedback is needed to give followers or team members ideas for how to change their behavior to improve their performance. Although accurate and frequent feedback is necessary, there are several other aspects of feedback that everyone can work on to improve their feedback skills, including making sure it's helpful, being direct, being specific, being descriptive, being timely, being flexible, giving both positive and negative feedback, and avoiding blame and embarrassment when giving feedback. Highlight 11.1 gives examples of each of these different aspects of feedback, and the following is a more complete description of ways leaders can improve their feedback skills.

Make It Helpful

The purpose of feedback is to provide others with information they can use to change their behavior. Being clear about the intent and purpose is important because giving feedback sometimes can become emotional for both the person giving it and the person receiving it. If the person giving feedback is in an emotional state (such as angry), she may say things that make her temporarily feel better but that only alienate the receiver. To be helpful, individuals need to be clear and unemotional when giving feedback, and they should give feedback only about behaviors actually under the other person's control.

Tips for Improving Feedback Skills

HIGHLIGHT 11.1

BEING HELPFUL

Do not: "I got better scores when I was going through this program than you just did."

Do: "This seems to be a difficult area for you. What can I do to help you master it better?"

BEING DIRECT

Do not: "It's important that we all speak loud enough to be heard in meetings."

Do: "I had a difficult time hearing you in the meeting because you were speaking in such a soft voice."

BEING SPECIFIC

Do not: "Since you came to work for us, your work has been good."

Do: "I really like the initiative and resourcefulness you showed in solving our scheduling problem."

BEING DESCRIPTIVE

Do not: "I'm getting tired of your rudeness and disinterest when others are talking."

Do: "You weren't looking at anyone else when they were talking, which gave the impression you were bored. Is that how you were feeling?"

BEING TIMELY

Do not: "Joe, I think I need to tell you about an impression you made on me in the staff meeting last month."

Do: "Joe, do you have a minute? I was confused by something you said in the meeting this morning."

BEING FLEXIBLE

Do not (while a person is crying, or while they are turning red with clenched teeth in apparent anger): "There's another thing I want to tell you about your presentation yesterday . . . "

Do: When a person's rising defenses or emotionality gets in the way of really listening, deal with those feelings first, or wait until later to finish your feedback. Do not continue giving information.

People can improve the impact of the feedback they give when it is addressed to a specific individual. A common mistake in giving feedback is addressing it to "people at large" rather than to a specific individual. In this case, the individuals for whom the feedback was intended may not believe the feedback pertains to them. To maximize the impact of the feedback, people should try to provide it to specific individuals, not large groups.

Be Specific

Feedback is most helpful when it identifies particular behaviors that are positive or negative. One of the best illustrations of the value of specific feedback is in compositions or term papers written for school. If someone turned in a draft of a paper to the instructor for constructive comments and the instructor's comments about the paper were "Good start, but needs work in several areas," the writer would not know what to change or correct. More helpful feedback from the instructor would be specific comments like "This paragraph does not logically follow the preceding one" or "Cite an example here." The same is true of feedback in work situations. The more specifically leaders can point out which behaviors to change, the more clearly they let the other person know what to do.

Be Descriptive

In giving feedback, it is good to stick to the facts as much as possible, being sure to distinguish them from inferences or attributions. A behavior description reports actions that others can see, about which there can be little question or disagreement. Such descriptions must be distinguished from inferences about someone else's feelings, attitudes, character, motives, or traits. It is a behavior description, for example, to say that Sally stood up and walked out of a meeting while someone else was talking. It is an inference, though, to say she walked out because she was angry. However, sometimes it is helpful to describe both the behavior itself and the corresponding impressions when giving feedback. This is particularly true if the feedback giver believes that the other person does not realize how the behavior negatively affects others' impressions.

Another reason to make feedback descriptive is to distinguish it from evaluation. When a person gives feedback based mostly on inferences, he often conveys evaluations of the behavior as well. For example, saying "You were too shy" has a more negative connotation than saying "You had little to say." In the former case, the person's behavior was evaluated unfavorably and by apparently subjective criteria. Yet evaluation is often an intrinsic part of a supervisor's responsibilities, and good performance feedback may necessitate conveying evaluative information to a subordinate. In such cases, leaders are better off providing evaluative feedback when clear criteria for performance have been established. Filley and Pace have described criteria that can be used to provide evaluative feedback; some are listed in Highlight 11.2.[14]

Types of Criteria to Use for Evaluative Feedback

HIGHLIGHT 11.2

1. Compare behavior with others' measured performance. With this method, the subordinate's behavior is compared with that of her peers or co-workers; this is also called norm-referenced appraisal. For example, a subordinate may be told her counseling load is the lightest of all 10 counselors working at the center.

2. Compare behavior with an accepted standard. An example of this method would be a counselor being told her workload was substantially below the standard of acceptable performance set at 30 cases per week. This is known as criterion-referenced appraisal.

3. Compare behavior with a previously set goal. With this method, the subordinate must participate in setting and agree with a goal. This is a form of criterion-referenced appraisal, with the subordinate's "ownership" and acceptance of the goal before the fact critical to the feedback procedure.

4. Compare behavior with past performance.

Source: Adapted from A. C. Filley and L. A. Pace, "Making Judgments Descriptive," in *The 1976 Annual Handbook for Group Facilitators,* ed. J. E. Jones and J. W. Pfeiffer (La Jolla, CA: University Associates Press, 1976), pp. 128–31.

An issue related to impressions and evaluative feedback concerns the distinction between job-related (that is, performance) feedback and more personal or discretionary feedback. Although leaders have a right to expect followers to listen to their performance feedback, that is not necessarily true concerning feedback about other behaviors. Sharing perceptions of a person's behavior could be helpful to that person even when the behavior doesn't pertain specifically to his formal responsibilities; in such cases, however, it is the follower's choice whether to hear it or, if he hears it, whether to act on it.

Be Timely

Feedback usually is most effective when it is given soon after the behavior occurs. The context and relevant details of recent events or behaviors are more readily available to everyone involved, thus facilitating more descriptive and helpful feedback.

Be Flexible

Although feedback is best when it is timely, sometimes waiting is preferable to giving feedback at the earliest opportunity. In general, everyone should remember that the primary purpose of feedback is to be helpful. Feedback sessions should be scheduled with that in mind. For example, a subordinate's schedule may preclude conveniently giving him feedback right away, and it may not be appropriate to give him feedback when it will distract him from a more immediate and pressing task. Furthermore, it may not be constructive to give someone else feedback when the person receiving it is in an emotional state (whether about the behavior in question or other matters entirely). Moreover, it is important to be attentive to the other person's emotional responses while giving feedback and to be ready to adjust your own behavior accordingly.

A final important part of being flexible is to give feedback in manageable amounts. In giving feedback, you do not need to cover every single point at one time; doing so would only overload the other person with information. Instead, anyone who needs to give a lot of feedback to someone else may want to spread out the feedback sessions and focus on covering only one or two points in each session.

Give Positive as Well as Negative Feedback

Giving both positive and negative feedback is more helpful than giving only positive or negative feedback alone. Positive feedback tells the other person or the group only what they are doing right, and negative feedback tells the other person or group only what they are doing wrong. Providing both kinds of feedback is best.

Avoid Blame or Embarrassment

Because the purpose of feedback is to give useful information to other people to help them develop, talking to them in a way merely intended (or likely) to demean or make them feel bad is not helpful. Followers tend to be more likely to believe feedback if it comes from leaders who have had the opportunity to observe their behavior and are perceived to be credible, competent, and trustworthy.[15,16,17] Bass has pointed out that followers will continue to seek feedback even if their leaders are not competent or trustworthy—though they will not seek it from their leaders.[18] They will seek it from others they trust, such as peers or other superiors.

Team Building for Work Teams

Few activities have become more commonplace in organizations these days than "team-building workshops." One reason for this level of activity is the powerful shift that has occurred in the workplace from a focus primarily on individual work to team-centered work. Unfortunately, however, these activities do not always achieve their objectives. As noted earlier in this text, it doesn't make sense to hold teams responsible for work if nothing else in the organizational environment changes. Team-building interventions, at the team level, may help team members understand why they are having so much difficulty in achieving team objectives, and even suggest coping strategies for an intolerable situation. They are not, however, likely to remove root causes of problems. To better understand the importance of looking at teams this way, let's use an example of this kind of erroneous thinking from a different context.

Team-Building Interventions

Suppose you have decided that the next car you drive must have outstanding ride and handling characteristics. Some cars you test, such as some huge American-made automobiles, have outstanding ride characteristics, but you are not happy with their handling. They sway and "float" in tight slalom courses. Other cars you test have just the opposite characteristics. They are as tight and as stable as you could hope for in turns and stops, but their ride is so hard that your dental work is in jeopardy. But you do find one car that seems to meet your requirements: a Mercedes-Benz provides both a comfortable ride and tremendous road handling characteristics in high-performance situations. There is, however, one small problem. The Mercedes costs a lot of money up front—more than you are willing to put into this project. So you arrive at an alternative solution. You find a used Yugo, a small car built in Yugoslavia and no longer imported into the United States, largely because of inferior quality. But it is cheap, and after purchasing it, you know you will have lots of money left over to beef up the suspension, steering, and braking systems to provide you with the Mercedes-Benz ride you really want.

Ludicrous! Obviously you are never going to get a Mercedes-Benz ride unless you are willing to put in considerable money and effort *up front* rather than doing little up front and putting all your money into repair work. But that is precisely what many organizations attempt to do with teams. They do not seem willing to create the conditions necessary for teamwork to occur naturally (a point we will discuss in the section "Team Building at the Top" in Chapter 16), but when the teams struggle in a hostile environment, as they invariably will, the leaders seem willing to pour tremendous amounts of money into team-building interventions to fix the problem. These types of team-building problems are those we would categorize as "top-down."

An equally vexing problem occurs when organizations are committed to teamwork and are willing to change structures and systems to support it, but are not committed to the "bottom-up" work that is required. This is best illustrated in the rationale for team training shown in Figure 11.1. In our work with organizations, we are frequently asked to help teams that are struggling. In Figure 11.1 we would place these requests at the "TEAM" level, which is the third platform up from the bottom. We believe this type of intervention will work only if the team members have achieved a stable platform from which to work. In this case, that would include the two previous platforms in Figure 11.1. If the foundation is not well established, the solely team-based intervention often leads to intrateam competition or apathy and withdrawal.

As a basis for any work at the team level, individual team members must first be comfortable with themselves. They must be able to answer the questions "What do I bring to the team?" and "What do I need from the team?" Not answering these questions breeds inherent fear and mistrust.

FIGURE 11.1
A Rationale for Individual, Interpersonal, Team, and Organizational Training

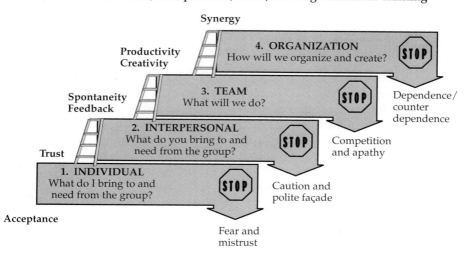

When these questions have been answered, team members are in a position to begin dealing at the interpersonal level, where they may now comfortably ask, "What do *you* bring to the team and what do *you* need from the team?" Not resolving these issues results in caution in dealing with other members, and interactions at the "polite façade" level rather than at the level of truth and understanding. If the first- and second-level platforms are in place, a true team-building intervention can be useful. (Incidentally, just because team members have not stabilized themselves at levels 1 and 2 does not mean an intervention cannot be conducted. Rather, it means a more extensive intervention will be required than a solely team-based effort.)

What Does a Team-Building Workshop Involve?

Hundreds, if not thousands, of team-building interventions are being conducted today. Many good sources, such as the *Team and Organization Development Sourcebook,* contain team-based activities such as conflict resolution, problem solving, development of norms, trust building, or goal setting, to name a few.[19] Rather than trying to describe all these suggestions, however, we will describe a few recommendations that we have found useful and then share a few examples of interventions we have used.

At the Center for Creative Leadership, staff are frequently asked to design custom team interventions for mid- to upper-level teams. While we enter these design meetings with no agenda of activities, neither do we enter with a completely blank slate. We believe an intervention at the team level must meet three general requirements to be successful, and at least one activity must be included in the intervention pertaining to each of those three requirements.

The first requirement involves awareness raising. As we noted in our previous chapters, not all cultures are equally prepared or nurtured in the concepts of teamwork. In fact, many of the lessons we think we have learned about teams are incorrect. So we need to dispel such myths and include a healthy dose of team-based research findings about how teams *really* work as a critical element of a workshop. Second, we need some diagnostic, instrument-based feedback so team members can have a reasonably valid map of where they and their teammates now are located. Finally, each intervention must include a practice field, to use Senge's term.[20] Practice is necessary for athletic success, and it is necessary in organizations too. It would be foolish to design a whole new series of plays for a hockey team to implement, talk about them in the locker room, but never actually practice any of them before expecting the team to implement them in a game. Similarly, if you are asking people to change their behaviors in the way they interact to improve teamwork, it is only fair to give them a practice field upon which they can test their new behaviors in a reasonably risk-free, protected environment.

This is where experiential exercises can be useful, and here the quality of the team-building facilitator is important. Conducting a pencil-and-paper exercise in the classroom does not require the same facilitator skill set as that required to conduct, say, a team-rappelling exercise off the face of a cliff—few facilitators get those requirements wrong, and we have seldom discovered problems here. Where we have seen a significant breakdown in facilitator skills is in being able to link the exercise to the real world in which the team will be asked to perform. Facilitators must have not only a good sense of real-time team dynamics but also a sense of the business in which the team operates. They must help the participants make the links back to team dynamics that occur on the manufacturing floor or in the boardroom, and this seems to be the skill that distinguishes highly effective facilitators.

Examples of Interventions

Now let us provide a few examples of the range of interventions that can be included in team building. Ginnett conducted an intervention with three interdependent teams from a state youth psychiatric hospital. The teams included members of the administrative services, the professional staff, and the direct care providers. The members of each team were dedicated to their roles in providing high-quality service to the youths under their care, but the three groups experienced difficulty in working with each other. Extensive diagnosis of the groups revealed two underlying problems. First, each group had a different vision of what the hospital was or should be. Second, each group defined themselves as "care givers," thus making it difficult for them to ask others for help because, in their minds, asking for help tended to put them in the role of their patients. We conducted a series of workshops to arrive at a common vision for the hospital, but the second problem required considerably more work. Because the staff members needed to experientially understand that asking for help did not place them in an inherently inferior position, a "wilderness experience" was designed where the entire staff was asked to spend four days together in a primitive wilderness environment with difficult hiking, climbing, and mountaineering requirements. By the end of the experience, everyone had found an occasion to ask someone else for help. Even more important, everyone found that actually asking others for help—something they had previously resisted—moved the overall team much higher in its ability to perform. Considerable time was spent each evening linking the lessons of the day with the work in the hospital.[21]

In one of the more interesting programs we've conducted, a team of senior executives spent a week together at a ranch in Colorado. Each morning the team met for a series of awareness sessions and data feedback sessions. Afternoons were reserved by the chief operating officer for fun and relaxation, with the only requirement being that attendees participate as a team or subteams. As facilitators, we actively participated with the teams and related their team experiences each day to the lessons of the next morning, as well as to challenges facing the team in its normal work. In interventions like this we have learned that team building can be fun, and that the venues for it are almost limitless. Second, we have learned that being able to observe and process team activity in a real-time mode is essential for team-building facilitators. There is no substitute for firsthand observation as a basis for discerning group dynamics and noting the variety of revealing behaviors that emerge in unstructured team activities.

Building High-Performance Teams: The Rocket Model

As stated throughout this text, leadership is not an individual process. Rather, it involves influencing a group to pursue some type of overarching goal. From Chapter 10 we know that teams vary in a number of important factors, such as group size, norms, development stages, and cohesion. We also know leaders need to take these factors into consideration when creating and leading teams. The Team Leadership Model in Chapter 10 provides a comprehensive description of team dynamics and what leaders must do if they want to create high-performing teams. What follows is a simpler and more pragmatic model of team effectiveness. The **Rocket Model of Team Effectiveness** is both a prescriptive and a diagnostic model of team building.[22,23,24,25] The model is prescriptive in that it tells leaders what steps to take and when to take them when building new teams. The model can also be used as a diagnostic tool for understanding where existing teams are falling short and what leaders need to do to get them back on track.

The Rocket Model is based on extensive research on and experience with teams in the health care, education, retail, manufacturing, service, software, telecommunications, energy, and financial service industries. The model has been used with executive teams at Home Depot, Waste Management, and the Strategic Health Authority in the United Kingdom; midmanagement teams at Waste Management, Pfizer, and a number of rural hospitals and school districts; and project teams at Qwest Communications and Hewlett-Packard. The model seems to work equally well with different types of teams at different organizational levels in different industries. Leaders particularly like the Rocket Model because of its straightforward and practical approach to team building.

A diagram of the Rocket Model can be found in Figure 11.2. As shown, building a team can be analogous to building a rocket. Just as the booster stage is critical for getting a rocket off the ground, so are the mission and talent stages critical for starting a team. Once the mission and talent issues have been addressed, leaders need to work with team members to sort out team norms and buy-in, and so on. Research shows that the teams with the best results are usually those who report a high level of team functioning

FIGURE 11.2
The Rocket Model

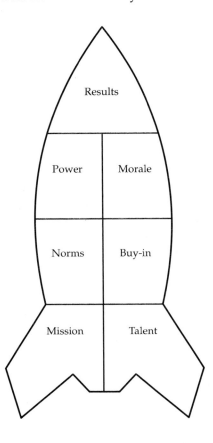

on all the components of the Rocket Model. Teams reporting a high level of functioning in only some of these components usually report mediocre results, and those with low functioning on all the components usually achieve few if any results. The following is a more in-depth description of the seven components of the Rocket Model.

Mission

When building a new team, the first thing a leader must do is clarify the team's purpose and goals, set team performance standards, and ensure that individual team member goals are aligned with the team's goals. Thus the mission component of the Rocket Model is concerned with setting a common direction for the team. In some cases the leader works closely with team members to sort out these issues; in other cases the leader makes these determinations; and in other cases the organization may make these decisions. For this component of the model, who makes these decisions is not as important as ensuring that all the team members understand what the team is trying to accomplish and how they personally contribute to team success. Teams with this common understanding often experience much lower levels of role ambiguity and conflict.

Of all the components in the Rocket Model, mission may be the most important one because it drives all the other components of the model. The mission of the team will play a big role in determining the number and skills of people needed to achieve results (talent), the rules by which the team operates (norms), and the equipment and budget needed (power). Because mission plays such a vital role in team building, leaders of underperforming teams often find it worthwhile to first review the team's purpose, goals, and performance standards when striving to improve team performance.

If we were to apply the Rocket Model to a learning team in a college leadership course, then the first thing the team should do is clarify what the team wants to accomplish. This might include such things as everyone on the team getting an A on the midterm, final exam, and overall course. Once the overall mission and team goals are determined, the learning team would need to decide who would do what and what the performance standards would be for each team member.

Talent

Teams with too many or too few people or with team members lacking the skills needed to achieve team goals often will report lower talent scores than teams having the right number of people with the right skills. Selecting the right kind of people and continuously developing those skills needed to achieve team goals are two key leadership activities in this component of the Rocket Model. And the selection and development of talent are precisely where many teams fall short. Professional athletic and elite military combat teams obsess over hiring decisions and spend countless hours practicing; they actually spend little time performing. Most other teams seem to do just the opposite: they throw a group of available people together and expect them to produce. These latter teams do not think through who needs to be on the team, spend little if any time developing needed skills, and never practice.

In the learning team example, talent would come into play if team leaders selected their teammates on the basis of GPA and how well potential team members got along with others. Once the teams were assembled, team leaders would determine what skills they still needed to develop and work to ensure the team improved in these areas. Team skills could be developed through coaching, training programs, practice test sessions, and so on. Of course this scenario assumes the leader gets to pick team members. Many times leaders do not have this luxury. If leaders do not get to pick team members, it is imperative that they assess and develop those skills needed to accomplish team goals.

Norms

Once team members are selected and clearly understand the team's purpose and goals, leaders need to address the norms component of the Rocket Model. Norms are the rules that govern how teams make decisions, conduct meetings, get work done, hold team members accountable for results, and share information. Several important aspects of norms are worth noting. First, the decisions the team makes, the way in which it makes decisions, how often and how long the team meets, and so forth should all be driven by the team's purpose and goals. Second, norms happen. If the team or team leader is not explicit about setting the rules that govern team behavior, they will simply evolve over time. And when they are not explicitly set, these rules may run counter to the team's purpose and goals. For example, one of the authors was working with a software development team that was responsible for delivering several new products in a six-month period. The time frame was aggressive, but one of the team norms that had evolved was that it was okay for team members to show up late to team meetings, if they even bothered to show up. However, the team meetings were important to the success of the team because they were the only time the team could discuss problems and coordinate its software development efforts. Team member behavior did not change until an explicit norm was set for team meeting participation.

Third, there are many team norms. These norms might include where people sit in meetings, what time team members come in to work, what team members wear, the acronyms and terms they use, and so on. But of the domain of possible norms, those involving decision making, communication, meetings, and accountability seem to be the most important to team functioning. High-performance teams are explicit about what decisions the team makes and how it makes those decisions. These teams have also set rules about the confidentiality of team meetings, when team members speak for themselves or speak for the team, and how difficult or controversial topics are raised in team meetings. High-performance teams also have explicit rules about team meetings and team member account-ability. In our learning team example, the team would need to decide how it would prepare for the midterm exam, what the format and quality of the prep material would be, how often and where they would meet to prepare for the exam, what they would do both in and outside of the prep-aration meetings, and how they would use the results of the midterm ex-ams to adjust their preparations for the final exam. Corporate teams often fail because they do not explicitly set decision making, communication, meeting, and accountability norms or ask themselves if the rules they have adopted are still working or need to be improved.

Buy-In

Just because team members understand the team's purpose and goals and the rules by which the team operates does not necessarily mean they will automatically be committed to them. Many times team members will nod their agreement on the team's goals, rules, and action steps in team meet-ings, but then turn around and do something entirely different after the meetings. This is an example of a team that lacks buy-in. Teams with high levels of buy-in have team members who believe in what the team is try-ing to accomplish and will enthusiastically put forth the effort needed to make the team successful.

There are three basic ways team leaders can build buy-in. One way to build buy-in is to develop a compelling team vision or purpose. Many times team members want to be part of something bigger than themselves, and a team can be one venue for fulfilling this need. Whether or not team members will perceive the team to have a compelling vision will depend to a large extent on the degree to which the team's purpose and goals match up to their personal values. Charismatic or transformational leaders (Chap-ter 14) are particularly adept at creating visions aligned with followers' personal values. A second way to create buy-in is for the team leader to have a high level of credibility. Leaders with high levels of relevant exper-tise who share trusting relationships with team members often enjoy high levels of buy-in. Team members often question the judgment of team lead-ers who lack relevant expertise, and they question the agendas of team leaders they do not trust. And because people prefer to make choices as opposed to being told what to do, a third way to enhance team buy-in is to involve team members in the goal, standard, and rule-setting process.

In our learning team example, team buy-in would likely be enhanced if the team got together and jointly determined its purpose, goals, roles, and rules. Alternatively, the team leader could assemble a group of students who wanted to achieve the same means and believed being part of a team would be the best way to make an A in the class. Team buy-in might be somewhat lower if the instructor determined the learning team's mission and norms. Many teams in the public and private sector world fail because team members do not trust the team leader, believe the team leader to be incompetent, do not see how they personally benefit from being on the team, or were not involved with setting the team's goals.

Power

The power component of the Rocket Model concerns the decision-making latitude and resources the team has to accomplish its goals. Teams reporting high levels of power have considerable decision-making authority and all the equipment, time, facilities, and funds needed to accomplish team goals. Teams with low power often lack the necessary decision-making authority or resources needed to get things done. One of the authors was working with a group of public school administrators who felt they had little power to make decisions affecting the school district. The district had had three superintendents over the past four years, and as a result the school board had stepped in to take over the day-to-day operation of the school district.

To improve the power component of the Rocket Model, team leaders will first need to determine if they have all the decision-making latitude and resources they need to accomplish group goals. If they do not have enough power, they will need to lobby higher-ups to get what they need, devise ways to get team goals accomplished with limited resources, or revise team goals in light of the resource shortfalls. Most teams do not believe they have all the time, resources, or decision-making latitude they need to succeed, but more often than not they have enough of these things to successfully accomplish their goals. Good teams figure out ways to make do with what they have or devise ways to get what they need; dysfunctional teams spend their time and energy complaining about a perceived lack of resources rather than figuring out ways to achieve team goals. Along these lines, many poorly performing teams often make false assumptions or erect barriers that do not really exist. Team leaders need to challenge these assumptions and break barriers if they are to help the team succeed.

Team power will play a role in our learning team. In this case, the team leader may need to secure a room or facility to conduct the study sessions, obtain computer resources for team members, or even work with the instructor to see if the members could take group rather than individual exams. The team also must determine how much time will be needed to adequately prepare for the examinations and whether all the team members can devote the time needed for the team to succeed. If the team does not have all the necessary resources or time, the team will either have to find ways to make do with what it has or revise the team's goals downward.

Morale

Just because individual team members understand what the team is trying to accomplish, are committed to achieving team objectives, and understand the rules by which the team gets work done does not necessarily mean team members will all get along with each other. Teams that report high levels of morale tend to effectively deal with interpersonal conflict and have high levels of cohesion. This does not mean that highly cohesive teams do not experience interpersonal conflict. Instead, teams with high morale scores have learned how to get conflict out in the open and deal with it in an effective manner. One way leaders can improve morale is to work with team members to determine the rules for addressing team conflict. On the other hand, some of the best techniques for destroying team morale are for leaders to either ignore interpersonal conflict or to tell team members to "quit fighting and just get along."

Because of values differences, workload inequities, miscommunication, and differing levels of commitment, it is likely that our learning team will experience some level of interpersonal conflict. If the learning team wanted to improve cohesiveness, it would need to discuss how members were going to address conflict in the group. These discussions should happen relatively early in the group's formation, and team conflict should be a regular topic in team meetings. Interestingly enough, many public and private sector teams report low morale scores and often take some kind of action to improve team cohesiveness. Usually these actions include sending the team to some sort of team-building program, such as an outdoor learning or high ropes course. In almost all these cases, these interventions have little if any long-term effect on team cohesiveness because the morale component of the Rocket Model is often a symptom of a deeper team problem. More often than not, team members do not get along because of unclear goals and roles, ill-defined performance standards or accountability norms, a lack of commitment or resources, and so forth. In other words, the reason why team members fight has to do with a problem in one or more of the other components of the Rocket Model. Successfully addressing these problem components will not only improve results but will also help develop team morale.

Results

The mission through morale components of the Rocket Model describe the "how" of team building. In other words, these components tell team leaders what they specifically need to do to improve team mission, norms, and so forth. The results component of the Rocket model describes the "what" of team building—what did the team actually accomplish? Like morale, results are a symptom or an outcome of the other components of the Rocket Model. High-performing teams get superior results because they have attended to the other six components of the Rocket Model. Those teams achieving suboptimal results can improve their performance by focusing on problematic components of the Rocket Model. In our learning team example, if the team received a B on the midterm exam, the team could reexamine its purpose and goals, determine if it had some talent gaps, review its rules to see if they were spending enough time practicing the right things, find another venue or time to study, and so on.

One thing we know about high-performing teams is that they often build executable action plans with clear timelines and accountable parties to achieve results. These plans include key milestones and metrics, and good teams regularly review team progress and revise their plans accordingly. Many times these plans include specific action steps to improve team functioning as well as the actions specific team members need to take for the team to achieve results.

Implications of the Rocket Model

As stated at the beginning of this section, the Rocket Model is both prescriptive and diagnostic, and the model works equally well with student-through executive-level teams. When building a new team or determining where an existing team is falling short, leaders should always start with the mission and talent components before moving to other parts of the model. Just as a rocket needs a large booster to get off the ground, so do teams need a clear purpose and the right players to succeed. Along these lines, the Team Assessment Survey was designed to give teams feedback on where they stand with respect to the seven components of the Rocket Model. Figures 11.3 and 11.4 show the assessment results for two executive-level

FIGURE 11.3
Team Assessment Results for a Dysfunctional Health Care Team

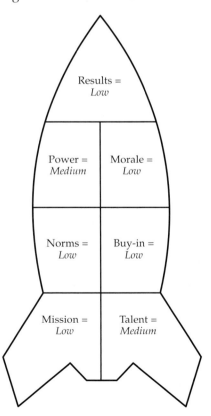

Results = *Low*

Power = *Medium*

Morale = *Low*

Norms = *Low*

Buy-in = *Low*

Mission = *Low*

Talent = *Medium*

FIGURE 11.4
Team Assessment
Results for a High-
Performing Retail
Team

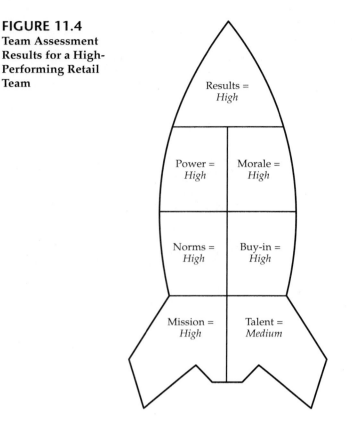

Results =
High

Power =
High

Morale =
High

Norms =
High

Buy-in =
High

Mission =
High

Talent =
Medium

teams. Figure 11.3 is a highly dysfunctional group of executives who led a billion-dollar health care organization. Because these executives never learned how to work together as a team, many were let go less than six months after their Team Assessment Survey was completed. Figure 11.4 shows the results for a top executive team running a $6 billion retail organization. This team was more or less hitting on all cylinders; its only real issue was grooming a successor for the soon-to-retire division president.

Second, the components of the Rocket Model roughly correspond to Tuckman's four development stages of groups.[26] According to Tuckman, forming is the first stage teams go through. Team leaders can help teams to successfully work through this stage by focusing on the mission and talent components of the Rocket Model. Tuckman maintained that teams then go into the storming stage, during which team leaders should concentrate on the norms and buy-in components of the model. Team leaders should focus on power and morale in Tuckman's norming phase and the results component of the Rocket Model in Tuckman's performing stage.

Delegating

Delegation is a relatively simple way for leaders to free themselves of time-consuming chores; give followers developmental opportunities; and increase the number of tasks accomplished by the work group, team, or committee. However, delegation is often an overlooked and underused management option.[27,28] Delegation implies that someone has been empowered by a leader, boss, or coach to take responsibility for completing certain tasks or engaging in certain activities. Delegation gives the responsibility for decisions to those individuals most likely to be affected by or to implement the decision, and delegation is more concerned with autonomy, responsibility, and follower development than with participation. Research has shown that leaders who delegate authority more frequently often have higher-performing businesses,[29] but followers are not necessarily happier when their leaders frequently delegate tasks.[30] Bass maintained that the latter findings were due to subordinates who felt they were not delegated the authority needed to accomplish delegated tasks, monitored too closely, or delegated only tasks leaders did not want to do.[31] Nevertheless, Wilcox showed that leaders who delegated skillfully had more satisfied followers than leaders who did not delegate well.[32] Because leaders who delegate skillfully often have more satisfied and higher-performing work groups, teams, or committees, the following suggestions from Taylor are provided to help leadership practitioners delegate more effectively and successfully. Taylor provided useful ideas about why delegating is important, common reasons for avoiding delegation, and principles of effective delegation.[33]

Why Delegating Is Important

Delegation Frees Time for Other Activities

The essence of leadership is achieving goals through others, not trying to accomplish them by oneself. Learning to think like a leader partly involves developing a frame of mind wherein you think in terms of the whole group's or organization's capabilities and not just your own. This requires a new frame of reference for many individuals, especially those whose past successes resulted primarily from personal achievement in interpersonally competitive situations. Still, leaders typically have so many different responsibilities that they invariably must delegate some of them to others.

It is not just the mere quantity of work that makes delegation necessary. There is a qualitative aspect, too. Because leaders determine what responsibilities will be delegated, the process is one by which leaders can ensure that their time is allocated most judiciously to meet group needs. The leader's time is a precious commodity that should be invested wisely in those activities that the leader is uniquely suited or situated to accomplish and that will provide the greatest long-term benefits to the group. What the leader *can* delegate, the leader *should* delegate.

Delegation Develops Followers

Developing subordinates is one of the most important responsibilities any leader has, and delegating significant tasks to them is one of the best ways to support their growth. It does so by providing opportunities for initiative, problem solving, innovation, administration, and decision making. By providing practical experience in a controlled fashion, delegation allows subordinates the best training experience of all: learning by doing.

Delegation Strengthens the Organization

Delegation is an important way to develop individual subordinates, but doing so also strengthens the entire organization. For one thing, an organization that uses delegation skillfully will be a motivating one to work in. Delegation sends an organizational signal that subordinates are trusted and their development is important. Moreover, skillful delegation inherently tends to increase the significance and satisfaction levels of most jobs, thus making subordinates' jobs better. Delegation also can be seen as a way of developing the entire organization, not just the individuals within it. To the extent that a whole organization systematically develops its personnel using delegation, its overall experience level, capability, and vitality increase. Finally, delegation stimulates innovation and generates fresh ideas and new approaches throughout the whole organization.

Common Reasons for Avoiding Delegation

Delegation Takes Too Much Time

Delegation saves time for the leader in the long run, but it costs the leader time in the short run. It takes time to train a subordinate to perform any new task, so it often really does take less time for a leader to do the task herself than to put in the effort to train someone else to do it. When a task is a recurring or repetitive one, however, the long-term savings will make the additional effort in initial training worth it—both for the leader and for the subordinate.

Delegation Is Risky

It can feel threatening to delegate a significant responsibility to another person because doing so reduces our direct personal control over the work we will be judged by.[34] Delegation may be perceived as a career risk by staking our own reputation on the motivation, skill, and performance of others. It is the essence of leadership, though, that the leader will be evaluated in part by the success of the entire team. Furthermore, delegation need not and should not involve a complete loss of control by the leader over work delegated to others. The leader has a responsibility to set performance expectations, ensure that the task is understood and accepted, provide training, and regularly monitor the status of all delegated tasks and responsibilities.[35]

The Job Will Not Be Done as Well

Often the leader can do many specific tasks or jobs better than anyone else. That is not surprising—the leader is often the most experienced person in the group. This fact, however, can become an obstacle to delegation. The leader may rationalize not delegating a task to someone else because the follower lacks technical competence and the job would subsequently suffer.[36] However, this may be true only in the short term, and letting subordinates make a few mistakes is a necessary part of their development, just as it was for the leader at an earlier stage in her own development. Few things are likely to be so stifling to an organization as a leader's perfectionist fear of mistakes. When thinking about delegating tasks to others, leaders should remember what their own skill levels used to be, not what they are now. Leaders should assess subordinates' readiness to handle new responsibilities in terms of the former, not the latter.

The Task Is a Desirable One

A leader may resist delegating tasks that are a source of power or prestige. He may be willing to delegate relatively unimportant responsibilities but may balk at the prospect of delegating a significant one having high visibility.[37,38] The greater the importance and visibility of the delegated task, though, the greater will be the potential developmental gains for the subordinate. Furthermore, actions always speak louder than words, and nothing conveys trust more genuinely than a leader's willingness to delegate major responsibilities to subordinates.

Others Are Already Too Busy

A leader may feel guilty about increasing a subordinate's already full workload. It is the leader's responsibility, though, to continually review the relative priority of all the tasks performed across the organization. Such a review might identify existing activities that could be eliminated, modified, or reassigned. A discussion with the subordinate about her workload and career goals would be a better basis for a decision than an arbitrary and unilateral determination by the leader that the subordinate cannot handle more work. The new responsibility could be something the subordinate wants and needs, and she might also have some helpful ideas about alternative ways to manage her present duties.

Principles of Effective Delegation

Decide What to Delegate

The first step leaders should take when deciding what to delegate is to identify all their present activities. This should include those functions regularly performed and decisions regularly made. Next leaders should estimate the actual time spent on these activities. This can be done fairly easily by developing and maintaining a temporary log. After collecting this information, leaders need to assess whether each activity justifies the time they are spending on it. In all likelihood, at least some of the most time-consuming recurring activities should be delegated to others. This process will probably also identify some activities that could be done more efficiently (either by the leader or someone else) and other activities that provide so little benefit they could be eliminated completely.

Decide Whom to Delegate To

There might be one individual whose talent and experience make her the logical best choice for any assignment. However, leaders must be careful not to overburden someone merely because that individual always happens to be the best worker. Additionally, leaders have a responsibility to balance developmental opportunities among all their followers. Leaders should look for ways to optimize, over a series of assignments, the growth of all subordinates by matching particular opportunities to their respective individual needs, skills, and goals.

Make the Assignment Clear and Specific

As with setting goals, leaders delegating an assignment must be sure the subordinate understands what the task involves and what is expected of him. Nevertheless, at times leaders provide too brief an explanation of the task to be delegated. A common communication error is overestimating our own clarity, and in the case of delegation this can happen when the leader already knows the ins and outs of the particular task. Some of the essential steps or potential pitfalls in an assignment that seem self-evident to the leader may not be as obvious to someone who has never done the assignment before. Leaders should welcome questions and provide a complete explanation of the task. The time leaders invest during this initial training will pay dividends later. When giving an assignment, leaders should ensure that they cover all the points listed in Highlight 11.3.

Assign an Objective, Not a Procedure

Indicate what is to be accomplished, not *how* the task is to be accomplished. End results are usually more important than the methods. It is helpful to demonstrate procedures that have worked before, but not to specify rigid methods to follow in the future. Leaders should not assume their ways always were and always will be best. Leaders need to be clear about the criteria by which success will be measured, but allowing subordinates to achieve it in their own ways will increase their satisfaction and encourage fresh ideas.

Points to Cover When Delegating a Task

HIGHLIGHT 11.3

How does the task relate to organizational goals?

When does the subordinate's responsibility for the task begin?

How has the task been accomplished in the past?

What problems were encountered with the task in the past?

What sources of help are available?

What unusual situations might arise in the future?

What are the limits of the subordinate's authority?

How will the leader monitor the task (such as by providing feedback)?

Finally, in covering these points, be sure to convey high confidence and expectations.

Allow Autonomy, but Monitor Performance

Effective delegation is neither micromanagement of everything the subordinate does nor laissez-faire indifference toward the subordinate's performance. Leaders need to give subordinates a degree of autonomy (as well as time, resources, and authority) in carrying out their new responsibilities, and this includes the freedom to make certain kinds of mistakes. An organizational climate where mistakes are punished suppresses initiative and innovation. Furthermore, mistakes are important sources of development. Knowing this, one wise executive reassured a subordinate who expected to be fired for a gigantic mistake by saying, "Why should I fire you when I've just invested $100,000 in your development?"[39]

Once a task has been delegated, even though the subordinate's training and development are continuing, the leader should be cautious about providing too much unsolicited advice or engaging in "rescue" activities. An exception would be when a subordinate's mistake would put significant organizational assets at risk. On the other hand, the leader needs to establish specific procedures for periodically reviewing the subordinate's performance of the delegated task. Leaders need to maintain good records of all the assignments they have delegated, including appropriate milestones and completion dates for each one.

Give Credit, Not Blame

Whenever leaders delegate, they must give subordinates *authority* along with responsibility. In the final analysis, however, leaders always remain fully responsible and accountable for any delegated task. If things should go wrong, the leaders should accept responsibility for failure fully and completely and never try to pass blame on to subordinates. On the other hand, if things go well, as they usually will, leaders should give all the public credit to the subordinates. Also, when providing performance feedback privately to a subordinate, emphasize what went right rather than what went wrong. Leaders should not ignore errors in judgment or implementation, but they need not dwell on them, either. One helpful approach to performance feedback is called the "sandwich technique." With this technique, negative feedback is placed between two pieces of positive feedback. It affirms the subordinate's good work, puts the subordinate at least somewhat at ease, and keeps the ratio of positive and negative comments in balance. The idea of a sandwich, however, should not be taken too literally. There is nothing magical about two pieces of positive feedback for one piece of negative feedback. In fact, from the receiver's point of view the balance between positive and negative feedback may seem "about right" when the ratio is considerably higher than 2:1.

Coaching

People who are coaches will be the norm. Other people won't get promoted.

**Jack Welch,
former General
Electric CEO**

A key success factor in most organizations today is having leaders and followers with the right knowledge and skills. More and more, companies are looking at "bench strength" as a competitive advantage. There are essentially two ways to acquire bench strength: employers can either buy (that is, hire) the talent they need, or they can build their existing talent through development and coaching programs. Given that many employers face a labor shortage in certain critical positions, many are looking to build their own internal talent.[40] Much of this talent is being developed through informal coaching. As we noted in Chapter 2, most leaders engage in some form of informal coaching. But how good are they at coaching? The authors' conversations with a multitude of leaders indicate that almost every single one was unsure what to do as a coach. Some thought coaching involved directing their employees in how to do tasks. Others thought it involved counseling employees on personal problems. One stated that his only example of coaching came from his high school football coach, and he wouldn't wish that on anyone.

Two thought leaders in this area are Peterson and Hicks,[41] who have described coaching as the "process of equipping people with the tools, knowledge, and opportunities they need to develop themselves and become more successful." According to Peterson and Hicks, good coaches orchestrate rather than dictate development. Good coaches help followers clarify career goals, identify and prioritize development needs, create and stick to development plans, and create environments that support learning and coaching. Coaching is really a blend of several different leadership skills. Being a good coach means having well-developed skills, determining where a follower is in the coaching process, and intervening as appropriate. The five steps of coaching give leaders both a good road map and a diagnostic model for improving the bench strength of their followers.

Peterson and Hicks pointed out that this model works particularly well for high performers—individuals who tend to benefit the most from, but are often overlooked by, leaders when coaching. We noted in Chapter 9 that high performers produce 20–50 percent more than average employees,[42] so coaching can have a considerable impact on the bottom line if it is targeted at high performers. Further support for the idea that top performers may benefit the most from coaching comes from athletics. If you watch the Olympics, you have probably seen that many of the world's top athletes have at least one and sometimes two or three coaches. If these world-class athletes feel that coaching can enhance their performance, it is likely that good coaches can also enhance the performance of any organization's top employees. Although the five-step model described here also works with poorly performing employees, more appropriate interventions might also include diagnosing performance problems, goal setting, providing rewards and constructive feedback, and punishing these individuals, particularly if informal coaching is not achieving desired results.

Forging a Partnership

The first step in informal coaching involves establishing a relationship built on mutual trust and respect with a follower. If a follower does not trust or respect her leader, it is unlikely that she will pay much attention to his ideas for her development. There are several things leaders can do to forge a partnership with coachees. First, it will be much easier for leaders with high credibility to build strong partnerships with followers than this will be for leaders with low credibility. Therefore, leaders need to assess their credibility (see Chapter 8), and they may need to take appropriate developmental steps to improve their credibility before their coaching suggestions will have much impact. These developmental steps may include building technical and organizational knowledge as well as building strong relationships with the individuals they want to coach. Understanding the context in which the employee operates can be as important as the relationship the leader shares with the employee.

In Chapter 8 we noted that leaders also need to spend time listening to their coachees; they need to understand coachees' career aspirations, values, intrinsic motivators, view of the organization, and current work situation. Good coaches can put themselves in their coachees' shoes and can understand how coachees may view issues or opportunities differently than themselves. While forging a partnership, leaders can also provide coachees with realistic career advice—sometimes coachees have unrealistic estimations of their skills and opportunities. For example, a new graduate from a top MBA program might want to be a partner at a consulting firm after two years with the company, but company policy may dictate that this decision will not be made until she has been with the firm for at least eight years. Her coach should inform her of this policy and then work with her to map out a series of shorter-term career objectives that will help her become a partner in eight years. If coaches do not know what drives their coachees' behaviors, then another step to forging a partnership is to start asking questions. This is an excellent opportunity for leaders to practice their listening skills so as to better understand their coachees' career aspirations and intrinsic motivators.

Inspiring Commitment: Conducting a GAPS Analysis

This step in the coaching process is similar to the GAPS analysis and the gaps-of-the-GAPS analysis that were discussed in the "Development Planning" section in Chapter 3. The only difference is that these two analyses are now done from the coachee's perspective. Figure 11.5 might help to clarify this difference in perspective. In the goals quadrant of the GAPS

FIGURE 11.5
A GAPS Analysis for an Employee

Source: D. B. Peterson, and M. D. Hicks, *Leader as Coach* (Minneapolis, MN: Personnel Decisions International, 1996); G. J. Curphy, *The Leadership Development Process Manual* (Minneapolis, MN: Personnel Decisions International, 1998).

Goals: Where do you want to go?	**Abilities:** What can you do now?
Step 1: Career objectives: Career strategies:	*Step 2:* What strengths do you have for your career objectives? *Step 3:* What development needs will you have to overcome?
Standards: What does your boss or the organization expect?	**Perceptions:** How do others see you?
Step 5: Expectations:	*Step 4:* 360-degree and performance review results, and feedback from others: • *Boss* • *Peers* • *Direct reports*

analysis the leader should write the coachee's career objectives, and in the perceptions quadrant the leader would write how the coachee's behavior affects others. It is possible that the leader may not be able to complete all of the quadrants of the GAPS for a coachee. If so, the leader will need to gather more information before going any further. This information gathering may include discussing career goals and abilities with the coachee, reviewing the coachee's 360-degree feedback results, asking peers about how the coachee comes across or impacts others, or asking human resources about the educational or experience standards relevant to the coachee's career goals. One way to gather additional information is to have both the leader and the coachee complete a GAPS analysis independently, and then get together and discuss areas of agreement and disagreement. This can help ensure that the best information is available for the GAPS analysis and also help to build the partnership between the leader and coachee. During this discussion the leader and coachee should also do a gaps-of-the-GAPS analysis to identify and prioritize development needs. Usually leaders will get more commitment to development needs if coachees feel they had an important role in determining these needs, and a gaps-of-the-GAPS discussion is a way to build buy-in. This discussion can also help ensure that development needs are aligned with career goals.

Growing Skills: Creating Development and Coaching Plans

Once the coachee's development needs are identified and prioritized, coachees will need to build development plans to overcome targeted needs. These plans are identical to those described in the "Development Planning" section in Chapter 3. Leaders generally do not build development plans for their coachees. Instead they may want to go over a sample (or their own) development plan and coach their coachees on the seven steps in building a plan. They can then either jointly build a plan or have the coachee individually build a plan for the leader to review. Giving coachees an important role in development planning should increase their level of commitment to the plan. Once a draft development plan is created, the leader and coach can use the development planning checklist in Table 11.1 to review the plan.

In addition to the development plan, leaders must build a coaching plan that outlines the actions they will take to support their coachees' development. Some of these actions might include meeting with the coachees regularly to provide developmental feedback, identifying developmental resources or opportunities, or helping coachees reflect on what they have learned. As with development plans, leaders should share their coaching plans so coachees know what kind of support they will be getting. This will also publicly commit the leaders to the coachees' development, which will make it more likely that they will follow through with the coaching plan.

TABLE 11.1 **Development Plan Checklist**

Source: G. J. Curphy, *The Leadership Development Process Manual* (Minneapolis, MN: Personnel Decisions International, 1998).

Objectives:
- One-year career objective identified?
- No more than a total of two or three development goals?
- Areas in which the employee is motivated and committed to change and develop?

Criteria for Success
- Is the new behavior clearly described?
- Can the behavior be measured or observed?

Action Steps
- Specific, attainable, and measurable steps?
- Mostly on-the-job activities?
- Includes a variety of types of activities?
- Are activities divided into small, doable steps?

Seek Feedback and Support
- Involvement of a variety of others?
- Includes requests for management support?
- Are reassessment dates realistic?

Stretch Assignments
- Do the stretch assignments relate to the employee's career objectives?

Resources
- Uses a variety of books, seminars, and other resources?

Reflect with a Partner
- Includes periodic reviews of learning?

Promoting Persistence: Helping Followers Stick to Their Plans

Having development and coaching plans in place is no guarantee that development will occur. Sometimes coachees build development plans with great enthusiasm, but then take no further action. This step in the coaching process is designed to help coachees "manage the mundane." An example of managing the mundane might be illustrative. One of the authors successfully completed a triathlon. The most difficult part of this accomplishment was not the event itself, but rather doing all the training needed to successfully complete the event. Similarly, the inability to stick to a diet or keep a New Year's resolution is primarily due to an inability to manage the mundane; people are initially committed to these goals but have a difficult time sticking to them. The same is true with development planning. Conducting a GAPS analysis and creating a development plan are relatively easy; sticking to the plan is more difficult. From the leader's perspective, a large part of coaching is helping followers stick to their development plans.

Several development planning steps are specifically designed to promote persistence. For example, ensuring alignment between career and development objectives, getting feedback from multiple sources on a regular basis, and reflecting with a partner can help keep coachees focused on their development. If the leader is a coachee's developmental partner, then reflection sessions can help followers persist with their development. If leaders are not designated as partners in the development plan, they should commit to meeting regularly with the coachees to discuss progress, what the leaders can do to support development, developmental opportunities, developmental feedback, and so forth.

Leaders can also help to promote persistence by capitalizing on coachable moments. Say a coachee was working on listening skills, and the leader and coach were in a staff meeting together. If the leader provides feedback to the coachee about her listening skills immediately after the staff meeting, the leader has capitalized on a coachable moment. To capitalize on a coachable moment, leaders must know the followers' developmental objectives, be in situations where they can observe followers practicing their objectives, and then provide immediate feedback on their observations. Few coaches capitalize on coachable moments, but they can go a long way toward promoting persistence in coachees. Note that capitalizing on coachable moments should take little time, often less than two minutes. In the example here, the leader could provide feedback to the coachee during their walk back to the office after the staff meeting.

Transferring Skills: Creating a Learning Environment

To build bench strength, leaders need to create a learning environment so that personal development becomes an ongoing process rather than a one-time event. As Tichy and Cohen[43] aptly point out, the most successful organizations are those that emphasize the learning and teaching process—they focus on constantly creating leaders throughout the company. In reality, leaders have quite a bit of control over the learning environments they want to create for their followers, and they can use several interventions to ensure that development becomes an ongoing process. Perhaps the most important intervention is for leaders to role-model development. In that regard, if leaders are not getting regular feedback from followers, they are probably not doing a good job of role-modeling development. By regularly soliciting feedback from followers, leaders are also likely to create a feedback-rich work environment. Once feedback becomes a group norm, people will be much more willing to help build team member skills, which in turn can have a catalytic effect on group performance. The leader will play a large role in this group norm because if the leader is feedback averse, feedback will be difficult to encourage among followers.

Leaders can also create learning environments by regularly reviewing their followers' development. Perhaps the easiest way to do this is by making leaders and followers development partners; then both parties can provide regular feedback and ongoing support. During these discussions leaders and followers should review and update their development plans to capitalize on new development opportunities or acquire new skills. Leaders and followers can also review coaching plans to see what is and is not working and make the necessary adjustments.

Concluding Comments

Perhaps one of the greatest misperceptions of coaching, and the primary reason why leaders state that they do not coach others, is that it takes a lot of time. In reality, nothing could be further from the truth. Leaders are working to build credibility, build relationships with followers, and understand followers' career aspirations and views of the world. Although these take time, they are also activities leaders should be engaged in even if they are not coaching followers. Doing GAPS analyses, identifying and prioritizing development needs, helping followers create development plans, and creating coaching plans often take less than four hours. Although leaders will need to take these steps with all their followers, this time can be spread out over a four- to six-week period. As stated earlier, meeting with followers regularly to review development (perhaps monthly) and capitalizing on coachable moments also take little time. Finally, many of the actions outlined in "Transferring Skills: Create a Learning Environment" in Chapter 3 either take little time or are extensions of actions outlined earlier. The bottom line is that coaching really takes little additional time; it is more a function of changing how you spend time with followers so you can maximize their development.

Do what you can, where you are at, with what you have.
Theodore Roosevelt

Another note about the coaching model is that good coaches are equally versatile at all five steps of coaching. Some leaders are good at forging a partnership but then fail to carry development to the next level by conducting GAPS analyses or helping followers build development plans. Other leaders may help followers build development plans but do nothing

FIGURE 11.6
The Empowerment Continuum

Empowered Employee ◄──────► **Unempowered Employees**

- Self-determined.
- Sense of meaning.
- High competence.
- High influence.

- Other-determined.
- Not sure if what they do is important.
- Low competence.
- Low influence.

to promote persistence or create a learning environment. Just as leaders need to develop their technical skills, so might they need to assess and develop coaching skills. It is important to remember that coaching is a dynamic process—good coaches assess where followers are in the coaching process and intervene appropriately. By regularly assessing where they are with followers, they may determine that the relationship with a particular follower is not as strong as they thought, and this lack of relationship is why followers are not sticking to their development plans. In this case a good coach would go back to forging a partnership with the follower and, once a trusting relationship had been created, go through another GAPS analysis, and so forth.

Finally, it is important to note that people can and do develop skills on their own. Nevertheless, leaders who commit to the five steps of informal coaching outlined here will both create learning organizations and help to raise development to a new level. Given the competitive advantage of companies that have a well-developed and capable workforce, in the future it will be hard to imagine leadership excellence without coaching. Good leaders are those who create successors, and coaching may be the best way to make this happen.

End Notes

1. B. M. Bass, *Bass and Stogdill's Handbook of Leadership*, 3rd ed. (New York: Free Press, 1990).
2. M. Erez, P. C. Earley, and C. L. Hulin, "The Impact of Participation on Goal Acceptance and Performance: A Two-Step Model," *Academy of Management Journal*, 1985, pp. 359–72.
3. E. A. Locke, G. P. Latham, and M. Erez, "Three-Way Interactive Presentation and Discussion," "A Unique Approach to Resolving Scientific Disputes," and "Designing Crucial Experiments," papers presented at the Society of Industrial and Organizational Psychology Convention, Atlanta, GA, 1987.
4. R. J. House, "Power in Organizations: A Social Psychological Perspective," unpublished manuscript, University of Toronto, 1984.
5. G. P. Latham and T. W. Lee, "Goal Setting," in *Generalizing from Laboratory to Field Settings*, ed. E. A. Locke (Lexington, MA: Lexington Books, 1986).
6. E. A. Locke, G. P. Latham, and M. Erez, "Three-Way Interactive Presentation and Discussion," "A Unique Approach to Resolving Scientific Disputes," and "Designing Crucial Experiments," papers presented at the Society of Industrial and Organizational Psychology Convention, Atlanta, GA, 1987.
7. M. M. Greller, "Evaluation of Feedback Sources as a Function of Role and Organizational Development," *Journal of Applied Psychology* 65 (1980), pp. 24–27.
8. J. L. Komacki, "Why We Don't Reinforce: The Issues," *Journal of Organizational Behavior Management* 4, nos. 3–4 (1982), pp. 97–100.
9. B. M. Bass, *Bass and Stogdill's Handbook of Leadership*, 3rd ed. (New York: Free Press, 1990).

10. S. Deep and L. Sussman, *Smart Moves* (Reading MA: Addison-Wesley, 1990).

11. J. R. Larson Jr. "Supervisors' Performance Feedback to Subordinates: The Impact of Subordinate Performance Valence and Outcome Dependence," *Organizational Behavior and Human Decision Processes* 37 (1986), pp. 391–408.

12. E. L. Harrison, "Training Supervisors to Discipline Effectively," *Training and Development Journal* 36, no. 11 (1982), pp. 111–13.

13. C. K. Parsons, D. M. Herold, and M. L. Leatherwood, "Turnover during Initial Employment: A Longitudinal Study of the Role of Causal Attributions," *Journal of Applied Psychology* 70 (1985), pp. 337–41.

14. A. C. Filley and L. A. Pace, "Making Judgments Descriptive," in *The 1976 Annual Handbook for Group Facilitators*, eds. J. E. Jones and J. W. Pfeiffer (La Jolla, CA: University Associates Press, 1976).

15. R. W. Coye, "Subordinate Responses to Ineffective Leadership," *Dissertation Abstracts International* 43, no. 6A (1982), p. 2070.

16. P. L. Quaglieri and J. P. Carnazza, "Critical Inferences and the Multidimensionality of Feedback," *Canadian Journal of Behavioral Science* 17 (1985), pp. 284–93.

17. D. L. Stone, H. G. Gueutal, and B. MacIntosh, "The Effects of Feedback Sequence and Expertise of Rater of Perceived Feedback Accuracy," *Personal Psychology* 37 (1984), pp. 487–506.

18. B. M. Bass, *Bass and Stogdill's Handbook of Leadership,* 3rd ed. (New York: Free Press, 1990).

19. M. Silberman and P. Philips (Eds). *2005 ASTD Team & Organization Development Sourcebook* (Alexandria VA: ASTD Press, 2005).

20. P. M. Senge, *The Fifth Discipline: The Art and Practice of the Learning Organization* (New York: Doubleday/Currency, 1994).

21. R. C. Ginnett, "To the Wilderness and Beyond: The Application of a Model for Transformal Change," *Proceedings of the Ninth Psychology in the Department of Defense Symposium* (Colorado Springs, CO, 1984).

22. G. J. Curphy and R. T. Hogan, "Managerial Incompetence: Is There a Dead Skunk on the Table?" working paper, 2004.

23. G. J. Curphy, "A Roadmap for Creating High Performing Teams," presentation given at the Strategic Staff Meeting of the Mid-Atlantic Division of The Home Depot, Atlantic City, NJ, September 2000.

24. J. E. Krile, G. J. Curphy, and D. R. Lund, *The Community Leadership Handbook* (St. Paul, MN: The Fieldstone Alliance, 2006).

25. G. J. Curphy, "Leadership Transitions and Succession Planning," in *Developing and Implementing Succession Planning Programs*, J. Lock (chair). Symposium conducted at the 19th Annual Conference for the Society of Industrial and Organizational Psychology, Chicago April 2004.

26. B. W. Tuckman, "Developmental Sequence in Small Groups," *Psychological Bulletin* 63 (1965), pp. 384–99.

27. B. M. Bass, *Bass and Stogdill's Handbook of Leadership,* 3rd ed. (New York: Free Press, 1990).

28. C. R. Leana, "Power Relinquishment vs. Power Sharing: Theoretical Clarification and Empirical Comparison of Delegation and Participation," *Journal of Applied Psychology* 72 (1987), pp. 228–33.

29. D. Miller and J. M. Toulouse, "Strategy, Structure, CEO Personality and Performance in Small Firms," *American Journal of Small Business,* Winter 1986, pp. 47–62.

30. R. M. Stogdill and C. L. Shartle, *Methods in the Study of Administrative Performance* (Columbus, OH: Ohio State University, Bureau of Business Research, 1955).

31. B. M. Bass, *Bass and Stogdill's Handbook of Leadership,* 3rd ed. (New York: Free Press, 1990).

32. W. H. Wilcox, "Assistant Superintendents' Perceptions of the Effectiveness of the Superintendent, Job Satisfaction, and Satisfaction with the Superintendent's Supervisory Skills," PhD dissertation, University of Missouri, Columbia, 1982.

33. H. L. Taylor, *Delegate: The Key to Successful Management* (New York: Warner Books, 1989).

34. H. D. Dewhirst, V. Metts, and R. T. Ladd, "Exploring the Delegation Decision: Managerial Responses to Multiple Contingencies," paper presented at the Academy of Management Convention, New Orleans, LA, 1987.

35. B. M. Bass, *Bass and Stogdill's Handbook of Leadership,* 3rd ed. (New York: Free Press, 1990).

36. H. D. Dewhirst, V. Metts, and R. T. Ladd, "Exploring the Delegation Decision: Managerial Responses to Multiple Contingencies," paper presented at the Academy of Management Convention, New Orleans, LA, 1987.

37. B. M. Bass, *Bass and Stogdill's Handbook of Leadership,* 3rd ed. (New York: Free Press, 1990).

38. H. D. Dewhirst, V. Metts, and R. T. Ladd, "Exploring the Delegation Decision: Managerial Responses to Multiple Contingencies," paper presented at the Academy of Management Convention, New Orleans, LA, 1987.

39. M. W. McCall Jr., M. M. Lombardo, and A. M. Morrison, *The Lessons of Experience: How Successful Executives Develop on the Job* (Lexington, MA: Lexington Books, 1988).

40. N. M. Tichy and E. Cohen, *The Leadership Engine: How Winning Companies Build Leaders at Every Level* (New York: HarperCollins, 1997).

41. D. B. Peterson and M. D. Hicks, *Leader as Coach: Strategies for Coaching and Developing Others* (Minneapolis, MN: Personnel Decisions International, 1996), p. 14.

42. J. E. Hunter, F. L. Schmidt, and M. K. Judiesch, "Individual Differences in Output Variability as a Function of Job Complexity," *Journal of Applied Psychology* 74 (1990), pp. 28–42.

43. N. M. Tichy and E. Cohen, *The Leadership Engine: How Winning Companies Build Leaders at Every Level* (New York: HarperCollins, 1997).

Part 4

Focus on the Situation

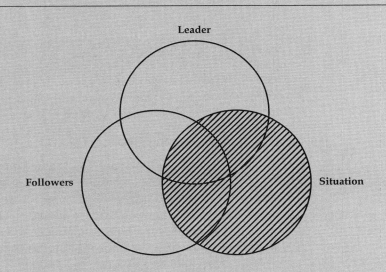

In previous chapters we noted that understanding leaders and followers is much more complicated than many people think. For example, we examined how leaders' personality characteristics, behaviors, and attitudes affect the leadership process. Similarly, followers' attitudes, experience, personality characteristics, and behaviors, as well as group norms and cohesiveness, also affect the leadership process. Despite the complexities of leaders and followers, however, perhaps no factor in the interactional framework is as complex as the situation. Not only do a variety of task, organizational, and environmental factors affect behavior, but the relative salience or strength of these factors varies dramatically across people. What one person perceives to be the key situational factor affecting his or her behavior may be relatively unimportant to another person.

Moreover, the relative importance of the situational factors also varies over time. Even during a single soccer game, for example, the situation changes constantly: the lead changes, the time remaining in the game changes, weather conditions change, injuries occur, and so on. Given the dynamic nature of situations, it may be a misnomer to speak of "the" situation in reference to leadership.

Because of the complex and dynamic nature of situations and the substantial role that perceptions play in the interpretation of situations, no one has been able to develop a comprehensive taxonomy describing all the situational variables affecting a person's behavior. In all likelihood, no one ever will. Nevertheless, considerable research about situational influences on leadership has been accomplished. Leadership researchers have examined how different task, organizational, and environmental factors affect both leaders' and followers' behavior, though most have examined only the effects of one or two situational variables on leaders' and followers' behavior. For example, a study might have examined the effects of task difficulty on subordinates' performance yet ignored how broader issues, such as organizational policy or structure, might also affect their performance. This is primarily due to the difficulty of studying the effects of organizational and environmental factors on behavior. As you might imagine, many of these factors, such as societal culture or technological change, do not easily lend themselves to realistic laboratory experiments where conditions can be controlled and interactions analyzed. Nonetheless, it is virtually impossible to understand leadership without taking the situation into consideration. We examine various factors and theories pertaining especially to the situation in Part 4.

Chapter 12

The Situation

Introduction

April 16, 2007, was a dark day at Virginia Tech. On that day Cho Seung Hui went on a shooting rampage that killed 32 students and faculty and injured a host of others. There is no doubt that Cho was a villain, if not a deranged one, as he created a situation of terror in Norris Hall. But in that same awful situation, heroes were created. One was Zach Petkewicz.

Zach and his fellow classmates were in a classroom near the one where Cho initiated his massacre. They heard the initial gunshots through the walls and could hear them getting closer. At first everyone experienced fear and hid behind whatever they could find for protection. But it occurred to Zach that "there's nothing stopping him from coming in here. We were just sitting ducks." And that's when Zach and others took action.

Zach grabbed a table and shoved it against the door. Seeing his plan, other students joined him, pinning the table against the cinderblock walls around the door frame. They were just in time. Cho tried to get into their classroom next. Having tried the door handle and then brute force, Cho emptied a clip of ammunition through the door before giving up and moving on to another room.

Days after the assault, Zach Petkewicz was interviewed by Matt Lauer on NBC's *Today Show*. Lauer asked Zach if he could have predicted, before the shooting, how he would react. The young hero, whose first reaction had been fear, said that's not possible for anyone. "There's no way of telling what I would have done until you're put in that situation."

Zach was right about two things. First, as he said, it is difficult to predict anyone's behavior unless you take the situation into account. Second, we are coming to understand that the situation is one of the most powerful variables in the leadership equation. And that is the topic of this chapter. It is important to understand how the situation influences leaders and followers and, furthermore, that the situation is not just a "given" that leaders and followers must adapt to; sometimes, at least, leaders and followers can change the situation and thereby enhance the likelihood of desired outcomes. That's what Zach did: he changed the situation. Of course Zach reacted to a situation he was tragically confronted with, but leaders do not always need to be reactive. Leaders also can use their knowledge of how the situation affects leadership to proactively *change* the situation in order to enhance the likelihood of success. All too often, leaders and followers overlook how changing the situation can help them to change their behavior. This is called **situational engineering.**

Suppose, for example, that a leader received developmental feedback that she needed to spend more time interacting with subordinates. Even with the best intentions, such a goal can prove difficult to achieve, just as numerous New Year's resolutions fail. In both cases an important barrier to success is that the person does not adequately address challenges posed by the situation in which they find themselves. After the holidays, many well-intentioned dieters don't lose weight because they fail to reduce the number of food cues around them. And a leader who may genuinely desire greater interaction with subordinates may nonetheless unwittingly subvert her own goal by continuing to define her tasks in the same way she always had. A better strategy could be to review her own tasks and then delegate some of them to subordinates. This would free up some of the leader's time and also create opportunities to interact with subordinates in ways like mutually setting performance goals and meeting regularly to review their progress.[1]

Highlight 12.1 presents ways in which various versions of a familiar situation may significantly affect your own likelihood of being a "good follower." Highlight 12.2 examines how leaders in dangerous situations might have to adopt different strategies to be successful than they would in more normal situations.

In a book designed to introduce students to the subject of leadership, a chapter about "the situation" poses some challenging obstacles and dilemmas. The breadth of the topic is daunting: it could include almost everything else in the world that has not been covered in the previous chapters! To the typical student who has not yet begun a professional career, pondering the magnitude of variables making up the situation is a formidable request. For one thing, the situation you find yourself in is often seen as completely beyond your control. How many times have you heard someone say, "Hey, I don't make the rules around here—I just follow them"? The subject is made more difficult by the fact that most students have limited organizational experience as a frame of reference. So why bother to introduce the material in this chapter? Because the situation we are in often explains far more about what is going on and what kinds of leadership behaviors will be best than any other single variable we have discussed so far!

In this chapter we will try to sort out some of the complexity and magnitude of this admittedly large topic. First, we will review some of the research that has led us to consider these issues. Then, after considering a

> *When you've exhausted all possibilities, remember this: You haven't!*
> **Robert H. Schuller**

> *Trying to change individual and/or corporate behavior without addressing the larger organizational context is bound to disappoint. Sooner or later bureaucratic structures will consume even the most determined of collaborative processes. As Woody Allen once said, "The lion and the lamb may lie down together, but the lamb won't get much sleep." What to do? Work on the lion as well as the lamb designing teamwork into the organization. . . . Although the Boston Celtics have won 16 championships, they have never had the league's leading scorer and never paid a player based on his individual statistics. The Celtics understand that virtually every aspect of basketball requires collaboration.*
> **Robert W. Keidel**

The College Classroom as Situation

HIGHLIGHT 12.1

One way to appreciate the variety of ways in which the situation affects leadership is to look at one of the most familiar situations to you: the college classroom and its associated work. Let's define the leadership challenge in every case as "getting the best out of you" in terms of your study, your work on assignments, and enhancing the experience of the course for everyone. With those criteria of effective leadership (or followership, if you prefer), reflect on how the challenges you face as a follower are affected by the variations in the series of classroom situations described here:

Situation 1	Situation 2	Situation 3 (in some Cases)
You're in a seminar with 15 other students.	You're in a 200-student lecture hall.	You're taking the course virtually over the Internet.
This is an elective course in your major.	This is a required general education course at your school.	
There's much student autonomy in the course in determining course paper topics.	Highly specific writing assignments are prescribed for you.	
A group project is an important part of your grade, and you're working on it with three good friends who are all good students.	A group project is an important part of your grade, and you're working on it with three strangers who are doing poorly in the course.	
Your class meets at 8 a.m.	Your class meets at 2 p.m.	Your class meets at 7 p.m.
You're a full-time student living in a dorm at your college.	You're a part-time student taking the class at a "commuter college" after you finish your regular day job.	

huge situational change that is now occurring, we will present a model to help us consider key situational variables. Finally, we will take a look forward through an interesting lens. Throughout the chapter, though, our objective will be primarily to increase awareness rather than to prescribe specific courses of leader action.

The appropriateness of a leader's behavior with a group of followers often makes sense only when you look at the situational context in which the behavior occurs. For example, severely disciplining a follower might seem a poor way to lead; but if the follower in question had just committed a safety violation endangering the lives of hundreds of people, the leader's actions might be exactly right. In a similar fashion, the situation may be the primary reason personality traits, experience, or cognitive abilities are related less consistently to leadership effectiveness

Leading in Extremis

HIGHLIGHT 12.2

Colonel Tom Kolditz is head of the Department of Behavioral Sciences and Leadership at the U.S. Military Academy at West Point. He's the author of a book called *In Extremis Leadership*, which looks at leadership in dangerous contexts. In doing research for the book, Kolditz and his colleagues interviewed leaders of SWAT teams, parachuting teams, special operations soldiers, mountain climbing guides, and others who led in dangerous situations. Kolditz identified several characteristics of effective in extremis leaders:

- They embrace continuous learning because dangerous situations demand it.
- They share risks with their followers.
- They share a common lifestyle with their followers.
- They are highly competent themselves in ways specific to the dangerous situation.
- They inspire high competence and mutual trust and loyalty with others.

Source: T. Kolditz, *In Extremis Leadership: Leading as If Your Life Depended on It* (San Francisco: Jossey-Bass, 2007).

The way of the superior is threefold, but I am not equal to it. Virtuous, he is free from anxieties; wise, he is free from perplexities; bold, he is free from fear.

Confucius

---

than to leadership emergence.[2,3] Most leadership emergence studies have involved leaderless discussion groups, and for the most part the situation is quite similar across such studies. In studies of leadership effectiveness, however, the situation can and does vary dramatically. The personal attributes needed by an effective leader of a combat unit, chemical research and development division, community service organization, or fast-food restaurant may change considerably. Because the situations facing leaders of such groups may be so variable, it is hardly surprising that studies of leader characteristics have yielded inconsistent results when looking at leadership effectiveness across jobs or situations. Thus the importance of the situation in the leadership process should not be overlooked.

Historically, some leadership researchers emphasized the importance of the situation in the leadership process in response to the Great Man theory of leadership. These researchers maintained that the situation, not someone's traits or abilities, plays the most important role in determining who emerges as a leader.[4,5,6] As support for the situational viewpoint, these researchers noted that great leaders typically emerged during economic crises, social upheavals, or revolutions; great leaders were generally not associated with periods of relative calm or quiet. For example, Schneider[7] noted that the number of individuals identified as great military leaders in the British armed forces during any period depended on how many conflicts the country was engaged in—the higher the number of conflicts, the higher the number of great military leaders. Moreover, researchers advocating the situational viewpoint believed leaders were made, not born, and that prior leadership experience helped forge effective leaders.[8] These early situational theories of leadership tended to be popular in the United States because they fit more closely with American ideals of equality and meritocracy and ran counter to the genetic views of leadership that were popular among European researchers at the time.[9] (The fact that many of these European researchers had aristocratic backgrounds probably had something to do with the popularity of the Great Man theory in Europe.)

More recent leadership theories have explored how situational factors affect leaders' behaviors. In **role theory,** for example, a leader's behavior was said to depend on a leader's perceptions of several critical aspects of the situation: rules and regulations governing the job; role expectations of subordinates, peers, and superiors; the nature of the task; and feedback about subordinates' performance.[10] Role theory clarified how these situational demands and constraints could cause role conflict and role ambiguity.[11] Leaders may experience role conflict when subordinates and superiors have conflicting expectations about a leader's behavior or when company policies contradict how superiors expect tasks to be performed. A leader's ability to successfully resolve such conflicts may well determine leadership effectiveness.[12]

Another effort to incorporate situational variables into leadership theory was Hunt and Osborn's[13] **multiple-influence model.** Hunt and Osborn distinguished between microvariables (such as task characteristics) and macrovariables (such as the external environment) in the situation. Although most researchers looked at the effects tasks had on leader behaviors, Hunt and Osborn believed macrovariables have a pervasive influence on the ways leaders act. Both role theory and the multiple-influence model highlight a major problem in addressing situational factors, which was noted previously: that situations can vary in countless ways. Because situations can vary in so many ways, it is helpful for leaders to have an abstract scheme for conceptualizing situations. This would be a step in knowing how to identify what may be most salient or critical to pay attention to in any particular instance.

One of the most basic abstractions is **situational levels.** The idea behind situational levels may best be conveyed with an example. Suppose someone asked you, "How are things going at work?" You might respond by commenting on the specific tasks you perform ("It is still pretty tough. I am under the gun for getting next year's budget prepared, and I have never done that before"). Or you might respond by commenting on aspects of the overall organization ("It is really different. There are so many rules you have to follow. My old company was not like that at all"). Or you might comment on factors affecting the organization itself ("I've been really worried about keeping my job—you know how many cutbacks there have been in our whole industry recently"). Each response deals with the situation, but each refers to a different level of abstraction: the task level, the organizational level, and the environmental level. Each of these three levels provides a different perspective with which to examine the leadership process (see Figure 12.1).

FIGURE 12.1
**An Expanded
Leader–Follower–
Situation Model**

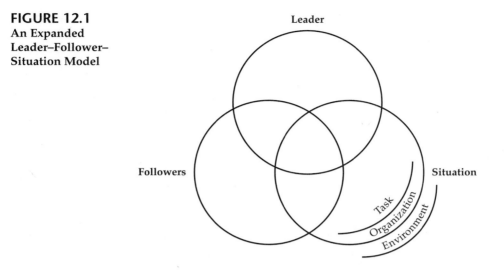

These three levels certainly do not exhaust all the ways in which situations vary. Situations also differ in terms of physical variables like noise and temperature levels, workload demands, and the extent to which work groups interact with other groups. Organizations also have unique "corporate cultures," which define a context for leadership. And there are always even broader economic, social, legal, and technological aspects of situations within which the leadership process occurs. What, amid all this situational complexity, should leaders pay attention to?

The Task

How Tasks Vary, and What That Means for Leadership

The most fundamental level of the situation involves the tasks to be performed by individuals or teams within the organization. Several ways in which tasks vary are particularly relevant to leadership. Industrial and organizational psychologists spent much of the last half-century classifying and categorizing tasks to better understand how to enhance worker satisfaction and productivity. Some of this research has great relevance to leadership, particularly the concepts of task autonomy, feedback, structure, and interdependence.

Task autonomy is the degree to which a job provides an individual with some control over what he does and how he does it. Someone with considerable autonomy would have discretion in scheduling work and deciding the procedures used in accomplishing it. Autonomy often covaries with technical expertise: workers with considerable expertise will be given more latitude, and those with few skills will be given more instruction

The brain is a wonderful organ; it begins working the moment you get up in the morning and does not stop until you get to the office.

Robert Frost

If you want to give a man credit, put it in writing. If you want to give him hell, do it on the phone.

Charles Beacham

and coaching when accomplishing tasks.[14,15] Moreover, responsibility and job satisfaction often increase when autonomy increases.[16]

Another important way in which tasks vary is in terms of **task feedback,** which refers to the degree to which a person accomplishing a task receives information about performance *from performing the task itself.* In this context feedback is received not from supervisors but rather from what is intrinsic to the work activity itself. Driving a car is one example of feedback intrinsic to a task. If you are a skilled driver on a road with a number of twists and turns, you get all the feedback you need about how well you are accomplishing the task merely by observing how the car responds to your inputs. This is feedback from the job itself as opposed to feedback from another person (who in this example would be a classic backseat driver). Extending this example to work or team settings, leaders sometimes may want to redesign tasks so that they (the tasks) provide more intrinsic feedback. Although this does not absolve the leader from giving periodic performance feedback, it can free up some of the leader's time for other work-related activities. Additionally, leaders should understand that followers may eventually become dissatisfied if leaders provide high levels of feedback for tasks that already provide intrinsic feedback.[17,18,19]

Perhaps the easiest way to explain **task structure** is by using an example demonstrating the difference between a structured task and an unstructured task. Assume the task to be accomplished is solving for x given the formula $3x + 2x = 15$. If that problem were given to a group of people who knew the fundamental rules of algebra, everyone would arrive at the same answer. In this example there is a known procedure for accomplishing the task; there are rules governing how one goes about it; and if people follow those rules, there is one result. These features characterize a *structured task.*

On the other hand, if the task is to resolve a morale problem on a team, committee, or work group, there may be no clear-cut method for solving it. There are many different ways, perhaps none of which is obvious or necessarily best for approaching a solution. Different observers may not see the problem in the same way; they may even have different ideas of what morale is. Solving a morale problem, therefore, exemplifies an *unstructured task.*

People vary in their preferences for, or ability to handle, structured versus unstructured tasks. With the Myers-Briggs Type Indicator (MBTI), for example, perceivers are believed to prefer unstructured situations, whereas judgers prefer activities that are planned and organized.[20] Individuals with high tolerance for stress may handle ambiguous and unstructured tasks more easily than people with low tolerance for stress.[21] Aside from these differences, however, we might ask whether there are any general rules for how leaders should interact with followers as a function of task structure. One consideration here is that while it is *easier* for a leader or coach to give instruction in structured tasks, it is not necessarily the most helpful thing to do.

We can see this by returning to the algebra problem described earlier. If a student had never seen such an algebra problem before, it would be relatively easy to teach the student the rules needed to solve the problem. Once any student has learned the procedure, however, she can solve similar problems on her own. Extending this to other situations, once a subordinate knows or understands a task, a supervisor's continuing instruction (that is, initiating structure or directive behavior) may provide superfluous information and eventually become irritating.[22,23] Subordinates *need* help when a task is unstructured, when they do not know what the desired outcome looks like, and when they do not know how to achieve it. Anything a supervisor or leader can do to increase subordinates' ability to perform unstructured tasks is likely to increase their performance and job satisfaction.[24] Paradoxically, though, unstructured tasks are by nature somewhat ill defined. Thus they often are more difficult for leaders themselves to analyze and provide direction in accomplishing. Nonetheless, reducing the degree of ambiguity inherent in an unstructured situation is a leadership behavior usually appreciated by followers.

Finally, **task interdependence** concerns the degree to which tasks require coordination and synchronization for work groups or teams to accomplish desired goals. Task interdependence differs from autonomy in that workers or team members may be able to accomplish their tasks in an autonomous fashion, but the products of their efforts must be coordinated for the group or team to succeed. Tasks with high levels of interdependence place a premium on leaders' organizing and planning, directing, and communication skills.[25] In one study, for example, coaches exhibiting high levels of initiating-structure behaviors had better-performing teams for sports requiring relatively interdependent effort, such as football, hockey, lacrosse, rugby, basketball, and volleyball; the same leader behaviors were unrelated to team performance for sports requiring relatively independent effort, such as swimming, track, cross-country, golf, and baseball.[26] Thus the degree of task interdependence can dictate which leader behaviors will be effective in a particular situation.

Problems and Challenges

Astronaut Jim Lovell's words during the *Apollo 13* lunar mission, "Houston, we have a problem," launched a remarkable tale of effective teamwork and creative problem solving by NASA engineers working to save the lives of the imperiled crew when two oxygen tanks exploded en route to the moon. The problem they faced was urgent, critical, and novel: no one had ever confronted a problem like this before, no one had even anticipated it, and there were no established checklists, emergency procedures, or backup equipment that could be counted on to reach a viable solution. We might say, of course, that the engineers' task was to devise a solution, but we want to stress a distinction here between the connotation of *task* as it was examined in the preceding section and that of completely novel problems or challenges for which routine solutions do not exist. As we noted earlier, up to this point our treatment of tasks has derived largely from the perspective of industrial and organizational psychology wherein the task dimensions just described (and many others) represent ways to systematically and objectively describe relatively enduring aspects of routine work or jobs. Obviously the situation that the NASA engineers and astronauts faced was anything but routine.

Ronald Heifetz has been studying the leadership implications of problems and challenges like that for many years. He says that often we face problems or challenges for which the problem-solving resources already exist. In general, you can think of these resources as having two aspects: specialized methods and specialized expertise. There are many technical problems that we can solve by applying widely known though specialized methods for solution. A simple example might be determining the gas mileage your car gets on a cross-country trip. The rules are simple to follow, and they always work if you follow them correctly. At other times we may not know the answers, but it may be relatively easy to find the people who do. Maybe we can't fix the rattle coming from the car engine, but we believe the mechanic can do so. We may not know how to fix our ailment, but we believe the physician will know what to do. We may not know how to use a new software system, but we believe we can master it with assistance from an expert. Problems like these are what Heifetz calls **technical problems.** Even though they may be complex, there are expert solutions to them, and experts know how to solve them even if we don't.[27]

Rough waters are truer tests of leadership. In calm water every ship has a good captain.
Swedish proverb

But not all problems are like that. Some problems, by their nature, defy even expert solution. Some problems cannot be solved using currently existing resources and ways of thinking. In fact, it's the nature of such problems that *it can be quite difficult even reaching a common definition of what the problem really is.* Solving such problems requires that the systems facing them make fundamental changes of some kind. Heifetz calls these **adaptive problems.** Whereas technical problems can be solved without changing the nature of the social system itself within which they occur, *adaptive problems can only be solved by changing the system itself.*

At work, the most important issue in addressing technical problems is making sure they get to someone with the authority to manage the solution. According to Heifetz, however, most social problems turn out to be adaptive in nature. Almost by definition, then, significant organizational change is at least in part an adaptive challenge. Even a seemingly simpler leadership challenge at work, like getting someone else to take more seriously some constructive feedback, is actually an adaptive challenge rather than a technical one. But here is where the distinction between technical problems and adaptive problems can become blurred. Go back to our earlier example of seeing a physician for a medical problem—but let's assume

TABLE 12.1
Adaptive and Technical Challenges

	What's the Work?	Who Does the Work?
Technical	Applying current know-how.	Authorities.
Adaptive	Discovering new ways.	The people facing the challenge.

it's your elderly parent rather than yourself who is the patient. Let's further assume that the physician correctly solves the technical problem and provides the correct technical solution—a particular medication that has a noticeable but tolerable side effect. Getting your parent to take the medicine if he doesn't want to turns this seemingly simple technical problem into a challenging adaptive one.

How do you know when a challenge is mostly a technical challenge or mostly an adaptive challenge? It's an adaptive challenge either wholly or mostly

- When people's hearts and minds need to change, and not just their standard or habitual behaviors.
- By a process of elimination—if every technical solution you can think of has failed to improve the situation, it is more likely to be an adaptive challenge.
- If there is continuing conflict among people struggling with the challenge.
- In a crisis, which may reflect an underlying or unrecognized adaptive problem.

Some problems are so complex that you have to be highly intelligent and well informed just to be undecided about them.

Laurence J. Peter,
management
consultant

Different leadership approaches are required to solve adaptive problems than are required to solve technical problems. That's because adaptive problems involve people's *values*, and finding solutions to problems that involve others' values requires the active engagement of *their* hearts and minds—not just the leader's. This is what Heifetz calls **adaptive leadership.** The importance of the difference between adaptive and technical problems will become clearer as we look later in the chapter at the organizational and environmental levels of the situation.

To summarize, Table 12.1 shows the relationship between whether a problem or a challenge is mostly technical or adaptive in nature, the kind of work required to effectively address the challenge, and whom should be thought of as the "problem solver."[28]

The Organization

From the Industrial Age to the Information Age

All of us have grown up in the age of industry, but perhaps in its waning years. Starting just before the American Civil War and continuing through the last quarter of the 20th century, the industrial age supplanted the age of agriculture. During the industrial age, companies succeeded according to how well they could capture the benefits from "economies of scale and scope."[29] Technology mattered, but mostly to the extent that companies could increase the efficiencies of mass production. Now a new age is emerging, and in this information age many of the fundamental assumptions of the industrial age are becoming obsolete.

Kaplan and Norton[30] have described a new set of operating assumptions underlying the information age and contrasted them with their predecessors in the industrial age. They described changes in the following ways companies operate.

Cross Functions   Industrial age organizations gained competitive advantage through specialization of functional skills in areas like manufacturing, distribution, marketing, and technology. This specialization yielded substantial benefits, but over time also led to enormous inefficiencies and slow response processes. The information age organization operates with integrated business processes that cut across traditional business functions.

Links to Customers and Suppliers   Industrial age companies worked with customers and suppliers via arm's-length transactions. Information technology enables today's organizations to integrate supply, production, and delivery processes and to realize enormous improvements in cost, quality, and response time.

Customer Segmentation   Industrial age companies prospered by offering low-cost but standardized products and services (remember Henry Ford's comment that his customers "can have whatever color they want as long as it is black"). Information age companies must learn to offer customized products and services to diverse customer segments.

Global Scale   Information age companies compete against the best companies throughout the entire world. In fact, the large investments required for new products and services may require customers worldwide to provide adequate returns on those costs.

Innovation   Product life cycles continue to shrink. Competitive advantage in one generation of a product's life is no guarantee of success for future generations of that product. Companies operating in an environment of rapid technological innovation must be masters at anticipating customers' future needs, innovating new products and services, and rapidly deploying new technologies into efficient delivery processes.

Knowledge Workers   Industrial companies created sharp distinctions between an intellectual elite on the one hand (especially managers and engineers) and a direct labor workforce on the other. The latter group performed tasks and processes under direct supervision of white-collar engineers and managers. This typically involved physical rather than mental capabilities. Now all employees must contribute value by what they know and by the information they can provide.

Growing Up with The Gap

HIGHLIGHT 12.3

The Gap, Inc., is growing up in the information age. The retail company got its start in 1969 when Don and Doris Fisher opened the first Gap store in San Francisco. The Fishers' goal was to appeal to young consumers and bridge "the generation gap" they saw in most retail stores. Their first store sold only jeans and targeted customers mainly in their 20s. As Gap customers have grown up, so has the brand. In 1983 The Gap acquired Banana Republic mainly for its thriving catalog business and evolved the company from its original travel theme to an upscale alternative to the more casual Gap stores. In 1990 Baby Gap was born, appealing to young parents looking for stylish alternatives for their children. In 1994 Old Navy stores were introduced as the Gap looked for ways to appeal to value-oriented shoppers. The Piperline brand was created in 2006, retailing footwear online, and Athleta, a women's athletic wear line was added in 2009. From young adult, to career professional, to parent, to cost-conscious family, to aging baby boomer, The Gap has stuck close to its customers and evolved to offer products that would appeal to their changing needs.

Sources: http://www.sfgate.com/cgi-bin/article.cgi?file=/c/a/2004/08/20/BUG8288V9244.DTL&type=printable; http://www.gapinc.com/financmedia/press_releases.htm; http://www.gapinc.com/about/ataglance/milestones.htm.

One needs only to reflect upon Kaplan and Norton's list of changing operating assumptions to recognize that the situation leaders find themselves in today is different from the situation of 20 years ago. What's more, it is probably changing at an ever-increasing rate. In a real sense, the pace of change today is like trying to navigate whitewater rapids; things are changing so rapidly it can be difficult to get one's bearings. You can see how one well-known company has been trying to navigate these changing waters in Highlight 12.3. To understand how organizations cope with change, it will be helpful to look at two different facets of organizations: the formal organization and the informal organization, or organizational culture.

The Formal Organization

The study of the **formal organization** is most associated with the disciplines of management, organizational behavior, and organizational theory. Nonetheless, many aspects of the formal organization have a profound impact on leadership, and so we will briefly review some of the most important of them.

A man may speak very well in the House of Commons, and fail very completely in the House of Lords. There are two distinct styles requisite.
Benjamin Disraeli

Level of authority concerns our hierarchical level in an organization. The types of behaviors most critical to leadership effectiveness can change substantially as we move up an organizational ladder. First-line supervisors, lower-level leaders, and coaches spend a considerable amount of time training followers, resolving work unit or team performance problems, scheduling practices or arranging work schedules, and implementing policies. Leaders at higher organizational levels have more autonomy and spend relatively more time setting policies, coordinating activities,

Despite the dramatic changes in the way people work, the organizations in which they carry out that work have changed much less than might be expected.

The Economist, January 21, 2006

and making staffing decisions.[31,32] Moreover, leaders at higher organizational levels often perform a greater variety of activities and are more apt to use participation and delegation.[33,34] A quite different aspect of how level of authority affects leadership is presented in Highlight 12.4.

Organizational structure refers to the way an organization's activities are coordinated and controlled, and represents another level of the situation in which leaders and followers must operate. Organizational structure is a conceptual or procedural reality, however, not a physical or tangible one. Typically it is depicted in the form of a chart that clarifies formal authority relationships and patterns of communication within the organization. Most people take organizational structure for granted and fail to realize that structure is really just a tool for getting things done in organizations. Structure is not an end in itself, and different structures might exist for organizations performing similar work, each having unique advantages and disadvantages. There is nothing sacrosanct or permanent about any structure, and leaders may find that having a basic

The Glass Ceiling and the Wall

HIGHLIGHT 12.4

While the past 25 years have been marked by increasing movement of women into leadership positions, women still occupy only a small percentage of the highest leadership positions. Researchers at the Center for Creative Leadership embarked on the Executive Woman Project to understand why.[35]

They studied 76 women executives in 25 companies who had reached the general management level or the one just below it. The average woman executive in the sample was 41 and married. More than half had at least one child, and the vast majority were white.

The researchers expected to find evidence of a "glass ceiling," an invisible barrier that keeps women from progressing higher than a certain level in their organizations *because they are women.* One reason the women in this particular sample were interesting was precisely because they had apparently "broken" the glass ceiling, thus entering the top 1 percent of the workforce. These women had successfully confronted three different sorts of pressure throughout their careers, a greater challenge than their male counterparts faced. One pressure was that from the job itself, and this was no different for women than for men. A second level of pressure, however, involved being a female executive, with attendant stresses such as being particularly visible, excessively scrutinized, and a role model for other women. A third level of pressure involved the demands of coordinating personal and professional life. It is still most people's expectation that women will take the greater responsibility in a family for managing the household and raising children. And beyond the sheer size of such demands, the roles of women in these two spheres of life are often at odds (such as being businesslike and efficient, maybe even tough, at work yet intimate and nurturing at home).

Resear Researchers identified the "lessons for success" of this group of women who had broken through the glass ceiling, and they also reported a somewhat unexpected finding. Breaking through the glass ceiling presented women executives with an even tougher obstacle. They "hit a wall" that kept them out of the very top positions. The researchers estimated that only a handful of the women executives in their sample would enter the topmost echelon, called senior management, and that none would become president of their corporation.

understanding of organizational structure is not only useful but impera-tive. Leaders may wish to design a structure to enhance the likelihood of attaining a desired outcome, or they may wish to change a structure to meet future demands.

One important way in which organizational structures vary is in terms of their complexity. Concerning an organizational chart, **horizontal com-plexity** refers to the number of "boxes" at any particular organizational level. The greater the number of boxes at a given level, the greater the horizontal complexity. Typically greater horizontal complexity is associ-ated with more specialization within subunits and an increased likelihood for communication breakdowns between subunits. **Vertical complexity** refers to the number of hierarchical levels appearing on an organizational chart. A vertically simple organization may have only two or three levels from the highest person to the lowest. A vertically complex organization, on the other hand, may have 10 or more. Vertical complexity can affect leadership by impacting other factors such as authority dynamics and communication networks. **Spatial complexity** describes geographical dis-persion. An organization that has all its people in one location is typically less spatially complex than an organization that is dispersed around the country or around the world. Obviously spatial complexity makes it more difficult for leaders to have face-to-face communication with subordinates in geographically separated locations, and to personally administer re-wards or provide support and encouragement. Generally all three of these elements are partly a function of organizational size. Bigger organizations are more likely to have more specialized subunits (horizontal complexity) and a greater number of hierarchical levels (vertical complexity), and to have subunits that are geographically dispersed (spatial complexity).

Organizations also vary in their degree of **formalization,** or degree of standardization. Organizations having written job descriptions and stan-dardized operating procedures for each position have a high degree of formalization. The degree of formalization in an organization tends to vary with its size, just as complexity generally increases with size.[36] For-malization also varies with the nature of work performed. Manufacturing organizations, for example, tend to have fairly formalized structures, whereas research and development organizations tend to be less formal-ized. After all, how could there be a detailed job description for develop-ing a nonexistent product or making a scientific discovery?

The degree of formalization in an organization poses both advantages and disadvantages for leaders and followers. Whereas formalizing proce-dures clarifies methods of operating and interacting, it also may constitute demands and constraints on leaders and followers. Leaders may be con-strained in the ways they communicate requests, order supplies, or re-ward or discipline subordinates.[37] If followers belong to a union, then union rules may dictate work hours, the amount of work accomplished per day, or who will be the first to be laid off.[38] Other aspects of the impact

Is There Any Substitute for Leadership?

HIGHLIGHT 12.5

Are leaders always necessary? Or are certain kinds of leader behaviors, at least, sometimes unnecessary? Kerr and Jermier proposed that certain situational or follower characteristics may effectively neutralize or substitute for leaders' task or relationship behaviors. *Neutralizers* are characteristics that reduce or limit the effectiveness of a leader's behaviors. *Substitutes* are characteristics that make a leader's behaviors redundant or unnecessary.

Kerr and Jermier developed the idea of **substitutes for leadership** after comparing the correlations between leadership behaviors and follower performance and satisfaction with correlations between various situational factors and follower performance and satisfaction. Those subordinate, task, and organizational characteristics having higher correlations with follower performance and satisfaction than the two leadership behaviors were subsequently identified as substitutes or neutralizers. The following are a few examples of the situational factors Kerr and Jermier found to substitute for or neutralize leaders' task or relationship behaviors:

- A subordinate's ability and experience may substitute for task-oriented leader behavior. A subordinate's indifference toward rewards overall may neutralize a leader's task and relationship behavior.

- Tasks that are routine or structured may substitute for task-oriented leader behavior, as can tasks that provide intrinsic feedback or are intrinsically satisfying.

- High levels of formalization in organizations may substitute for task-oriented leader behavior, and unbending rules and procedures may even neutralize the leader's task behavior. A cohesive work group may provide a substitute for the leader's task and relationship behavior.

Source: S. Kerr and J. M. Jermier, "Substitutes for Leadership: Their Meaning and Measurement," *Organizational Behavior and Human Performance* 22 (1978), pp. 375–403.

of formalization and other situational variables on leadership are presented in Highlight 12.5

The centralization refers to the diffusion of decision making throughout an organization. An organization that allows decisions to be made by only one person is highly centralized. When decision making is dispersed to the lowest levels in the organization, the organization is very decentralized. Advantages of decentralized organizations include increased participation in the decision process and, consequently, greater acceptance and ownership of decision outcomes. These are both desirable outcomes. There are also, however, advantages to centralization, such as uniform policies and procedures (which can increase feelings of equity) and clearer coordination procedures.[39] The task of balancing the degree of centralization necessary to achieve coordination and control, on one hand, and gaining desirable participation and acceptance, on the other, is an ongoing challenge for the leader.

The Informal Organization: Organizational Culture

The word that sums up the **informal organization** better than any other is its *culture*. Although most people probably think of culture in terms of very large social groups, the concept also applies to organizations. **Organizational culture** has been defined as a system of shared backgrounds, norms, values, or beliefs among members of a group,[40] and **organizational climate** concerns members' subjective reactions to the organization.[41,42] These two concepts are distinct in that organizational climate is partly a function of, or reaction to, organizational culture; our feelings or emotional reactions about an organization are probably affected by the degree to which we share the prevailing values, beliefs, and backgrounds of organizational members.[43] If a person does not share the values or beliefs of the majority of members, then in all likelihood this person would have a fairly negative reaction about the organization overall. Thus organizational climate (and indirectly organizational culture) is related to how well organizational members get along with each other.[44,45] Also note that organizational climate is narrower in scope but highly related to job satisfaction. Generally, organizational climate has more to do with nontask perceptions of work, such as feelings about co-workers or company policies, whereas job satisfaction usually also includes perceptions of workload and the nature of the tasks performed.

Just as there are many cultures across the world, there are a great number of different cultures across organizations. Members of military organizations typically have different norms, background experiences, values, and beliefs, for example, from those of the faculty at most colleges or universities. Similarly, the culture of an investment firm is different from the culture of a research and development firm, a freight hauling company, or a college rugby team. Cultural differences can even exist between different organizations within any of these sectors. The culture of the U.S. Air Force is different from the culture of the U.S. Marine Corps, and Yale University has a different culture than the University of Colorado even though they are both fine institutions of higher learning. Questions that suggest further ways in which organizational cultures may differ are listed in Table 12.2.

One of the more fascinating aspects of organizational culture is that it often takes an outsider to recognize it; organizational culture becomes so second nature to many organizational members that they are unaware of how it affects their behaviors and perceptions.[46] Despite this transparency to organizational members, a fairly consistent set of dimensions can be used to differentiate between organizational cultures. For example, Kilmann and Saxton[47] stated that organizational cultures can be differentiated based on

TABLE 12.2   Some Questions That Define Organizational Culture

Source: Adapted from R. H. Kilmann and M. J. Saxton, *Organizational Cultures: Their Assessment and Change* (San Francisco: Jossey-Bass, 1983).

- What can be talked about or not talked about?
- How do people wield power?
- How does a person get ahead or stay out of trouble?
- What are the unwritten rules of the game?
- What are the organization's morality and ethics?
- What stories are told about the organization?

members' responses to questions like those found in Table 12.2. Another way to understand an organization's culture is in terms of myths and stories, symbols, rituals, and language.[48] A more detailed description of the four key factors identified by Schein can be found in Highlight 12.6.

Here is an example of how stories contribute to organizational culture. A consultant was asked to help a plant that had been having morale and

Schein's Four Key Organizational Culture Factors

HIGHLIGHT 12.6

Myths and stories are the tales about the organization that are passed down over time and communicate a story of the organization's underlying values. Virtually any employee of Walmart can tell you stories about Sam Walton and his behavior—how he rode around in his pickup truck, how he greeted people in the stores, and how he tended to "just show up" at different times. The Center for Creative Leadership has stories about its founder, H. Smith Richardson, who as a young man creatively used the mail to sell products. Sometimes stories and myths are transferred between organizations even though the truth may not lie wholly in either one. A story is told in AT&T about one of its founders and how he trudged miles and miles through a blizzard to repair a faulty component so that a woman living by herself in a rural community could get phone service. Interestingly enough, this same story is also told in MCI (now Verizon).

Symbols and artifacts are objects that can be seen and noticed and that describe various aspects of the culture. In almost any building, for example, symbols and artifacts provide information about the organization's culture. For example, an organization may believe in egalitarian principles, and that might be reflected in virtually everyone having the same size office. Or there can be indications of opulence, which convey a very different message. Even signs might act as symbols or artifacts of underlying cultural values. At one university that believed students should have first priority for facilities, an interesting sign showed up occasionally to reinforce this value. It was not a road sign, but a sign appearing on computer monitors. When the university's main computer was being overused, the computer was programmed to identify nonstudent users, note the overload, and issue a warning to nonstudent users to sign off. This was a clear artifact, or symbol, underlying the priority placed on students at that school.

Rituals are recurring events or activities that reflect important aspects of the underlying culture. An organization may have spectacular sales meetings for its top performers and spouses every two years. This ritual would be an indication of the value placed on high sales and meeting high quotas. Another kind of ritual is the retirement ceremony. Elaborate or modest retirement ceremonies may signal the importance an organization places on its people.

Language concerns the jargon, or idiosyncratic terms, of an organization and can serve several different purposes relevant to culture. First, the mere fact that some know the language and some do not indicates who is in the culture and who is not. Second, language can also provide information about how people within a culture view others. Third, language can be used to help create a culture. A good example of the power of language in creating culture is in the words employees at Disneyland or Walt Disney World use in referring to themselves and park visitors. Employees—all employees, from the costumed Disney characters to popcorn vendors—are told to think of themselves as members of a cast, and never to be out of character. Everything happening at the park is part of the "show," and those who paid admission to enter the park are not mere tourists, but rather "the audience." Virtually everyone who visits the Disney parks is impressed with the consistently friendly behavior of its staff, a reflection of the power of words in creating culture. (Of course a strict and strongly enforced policy concerning courtesy toward park guests also helps.)

production problems for years. After talking with several individuals at the plant, the consultant believed he had located the problem. It seems everyone he talked to told him about Sam, the plant manager. He was a giant of a man with a terrible temper. He had demolished unacceptable products with a sledgehammer, stood on the plant roof screaming at workers, and done countless other things sure to intimidate everyone around. The consultant decided he needed to talk to this plant manager. When he did so, however, he met an agreeable person named Paul. Sam, it seems, had been dead for nearly a decade, but his legacy lived on.[49]

Leaders must realize that they can play an active role in changing an organization's culture, not just be influenced by it.[50,51,52,53] Leaders can change culture by attending to or ignoring particular issues, problems, or projects. They can modify culture through their reactions to crises, by rewarding new or different kinds of behavior, or by eliminating previous punishments or negative consequences for certain behaviors. Their general personnel policies send messages about the value of employees to the organization (such as cutting wages to avoid layoffs). They can use role modeling and self-sacrifice as a way to inspire or motivate others to work more vigorously or interact with each other differently. Finally, leaders can also change culture by the criteria they use to select or dismiss followers.

Changing an organization's culture, of course, takes time and effort, and sometimes it may be extremely difficult. This is especially true in very large organizations or those with strong cultures. New organizations, on the other hand, do not have the traditions, stories or myths, or established rites to the same extent that older companies do, and it may be easier for leaders to change culture in these organizations. Still another way to think about organizational culture change is described in Highlights 12.7 and 12.8.

Why would a leader *want* to change an organization's culture? It all should depend on whether the culture is having a positive or a negative impact on various desirable outcomes. We remember one organization with a very polite culture, an aspect that seemed positive at first. There were never any potentially destructive emotional outbursts in the organization, and there was an apparent concern for other individuals' feelings in all interactions. However, a darker side of that culture gradually became apparent. When it was appropriate to give feedback for performance appraisals or employee development, supervisors were hesitant to raise negative aspects of behavior; they interpreted doing so as not being polite. And so the organization continued to be puzzled by employee behavior that tended not to improve; the organization was a victim of its own culture.

At other times, organizational culture itself can be a victim of changes initially considered to be merely technical. A classic example of this pertains to the coal mining industry in England. For hundreds of years coal was mined by teams of three people each. In England coal is layered in narrow seams, most only a few feet high. In the past the only practical means to get the coal out was to send the three-person teams of miners

Stages of Leadership Culture Development

HIGHLIGHT 12.7

Researchers at the Center for Creative Leadership have been studying different kinds of leadership cultures, which they define as the values, beliefs, and often taken-for-granted assumptions about how people work together in an organization, reflecting its collective approach to achieving direction, alignment, and commitment. While virtually all large organizations include aspects of all three types, often one of these cultures will be most dominant. Furthermore, these types of leadership culture are thought to represent successive stages of culture development, each one better adapted to deal with increasingly complex challenges. An important practical purpose of this work is to help organizations transform their cultures in ways better suited to the organization's current and future challenges.

Dependent leadership cultures are characterized by widespread beliefs and practices that it's primarily people in positions of authority who are responsible for leadership. This assumption may lead to organizations that emphasize top-down control and deference to authority. In general, you can think of dependent cultures as "conforming" cultures. Other characteristics often associated with dependent cultures include these:

- There may be a command and control mind-set.
- Seniority and position levels are important bases of respect.
- There's great emphasis on keeping things running smoothly.
- Most people operate with the philosophy that it's usually safest to check things out with one's boss before taking a new direction.

Independent leadership cultures are characterized by widespread beliefs and practices that leadership emerges as needed from a variety of individuals, based on knowledge and expertise. There's great emphasis on individual responsibility; decentralized decision making; and the promotion of experts, professionals, and individual contributors into positions of authority. In general, you can think of independent cultures as "achievement-oriented" cultures. Other characteristics associated with independent cultures include these:

- The results that leaders achieve, whatever it takes, are an important basis of respect.
- Even during times of stress, there is great pressure not to let performance numbers go down.
- Bold and independent action that gets results is highly prized.
- The organization is successful because of its large number of highly competent and ambitious individuals.

Interdependent leadership cultures are characterized by widespread beliefs and practices that leadership is a collective activity requiring mutual inquiry and learning. There's widespread use of dialogue, collaboration, horizontal networks, valuing of differences, and a focus on learning. In general, you can think of interdependent cultures as "collaborative" cultures. Other characteristics associated with interdependent cultures include these:

- Many people wear several hats at once, and roles change frequently as the organization continually adapts to changing circumstances.
- People believe it's important to let everyone learn from your experience, even your mistakes.
- There's a widely shared commitment to doing what it takes to make the entire organization be successful, not just one's own group.
- Openness, candor, and building trust across departments are valued.

Metaphors of Leadership Culture

HIGHLIGHT 12.8

Highlight 12.7 described a theory of organizational culture based on the idea that different cultures represent different stages of development. In that theory, interdependent cultures represent a higher stage of development than independent cultures, and independent cultures represent a higher stage of development than dependent cultures. In line with the old saying that a picture is worth a thousand words, here are some pictures that represent different metaphors of leadership culture. Try your hand at aligning each picture (thinking of it as a metaphor) with the type of culture it most represents: dependent, independent, or interdependent.

Answers: evangelistic preachers = dependent culture; player coaches = interdependent culture; pool of sharks = independent culture; motivational coaches = independent culture; network of peers = interdependent culture; nurturing parents = dependent culture.

Source: Reprinted with permission of the Center for Creative Leadership, 2010. www.CCLExplorer.org.

down into the mines to dig coal from the seam and then haul it to the surface on a tram. These mining teams had extremely high levels of group cohesiveness. A technological development called the long-wall method of coal extraction upset these close relationships, however. In the long-wall method, workers were arrayed all along an entire seam of coal rather than in distinct teams, and the method should have resulted in higher productivity among the miners. However, the breakdown of the work teams led to unexpected decreases in productivity, much higher levels of worker dissatisfaction, and even disruption of social life among the miners' families. Although the long-wall method was technically superior to the three-person mining team, the leaders of the coal-mining companies failed to consider the cultural consequences of this technological advancement.[54]

These examples help make the point that while organizational culture is a powerful aspect of the situation, it can also seem fairly elusive and unresponsive to simple executive orders to change. For those reasons and others changing an organization's culture is usually both difficult and time-consuming, usually taking years in large organizations. To put it differently, it is much easier to change formal aspects of the organization like its structure or policies than it is to change its culture. In our view, however, it is precisely those organizational change efforts that focus solely or primarily on the formal organization that tend to fail. Truly significant organizational change or transformation is unlikely to be successful without addressing organizational culture as well as the formal organization.

Furthermore, a change effort is more likely to be successful if it is based on an established theory of organizational culture, and not merely subjective preferences about what needs to change. Absent a guiding theory, misguided and superficial targets of change may be selected that miss the point and usually create problems rather than produce desired results. For example, efforts to create a more collaborative culture that only target surface behaviors such as "we'll dress and talk less formally" and "we'll spend more time in meetings together" invariably miss the point, waste energy, and breed cynicism.

You may not be surprised to learn that there are a number of theories of organizational culture, and we will not try to summarize or even list them all here. It will be sufficient for our purposes to examine just one to illustrate how culture theories systematically use abstract dimensions to depict the variety of ways in which living and working in one organization can feel so different from another. The theory we will focus on is Cameron and Quinn's **Competing Values Framework**.[55]

A Theory of Organizational Culture

The Competing Values Framework is depicted in Figure 12.2. It derives its name from the fact that the values depicted on opposite ends of each axis are inherently in tension with each other. They represent competing assumptions about the desired state of affairs in the organization. The core

FIGURE 12.2
The Competing Values Framework

Source: K. S. Cameron and R. E. Quinn, *Diagnosing and Changing Organizational Culture* (Reading, MA: Addison-Wesley, 1999), p. 32.

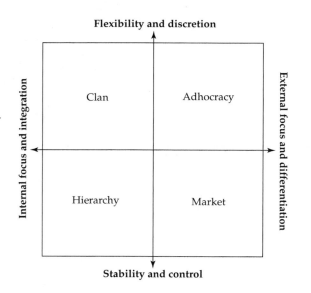

values at one end of each axis or continuum are opposed to the core values at the opposite end. Thus it's impossible that an organization could be both extremely flexible and extremely stable all the time. An organization's culture represents a balance or trade-off between these competing values that tends to work for that organization in its particular competitive environment.

Organizational cultures are not usually designed intentionally. That's one reason we noted earlier in this section that people tend not to be consciously aware of their own organization's culture. In fact, it's usually only when an organization's culture is impeding organizational performance (typically in a changing competitive environment) that people become aware of any need for culture change. It's at just such times that it can be useful for people within an organization to consider something different. The Competing Values Framework was designed to help organizations be more deliberate in identifying a culture more likely to be successful given their respective situations, and in transitioning to it.

As you can see in Figure 12.2, the intersection of the competing values axes creates four quadrants describing four different combinations of values. The distinctive sets of values in these quadrants define four unique organizational cultures.

Organizations that emphasize stability and control, and also focus their attention inward (on how people within the organization interact with each other, on whether internal operating procedures are followed, and so forth), have a **hierarchy culture.** Organizations with a hierarchy culture tend to have formalized rules and procedures; they tend to be highly structured places to work. Following standard operating procedures, or

SOPs, is the rule of the day. The emphasis is on ensuring continuing efficiency, smooth functioning, and dependable operations. Examples of hierarchy cultures are government agencies, fast-food chains, and traditional large manufacturing companies.[56]

Organizations that, like hierarchy cultures, emphasize stability and control but focus their attention primarily on the external environment (outside the organization itself) are called **market cultures.** Their interest is more on interactions with external constituencies like customers and suppliers. Market cultures are competitive and results-oriented, and the results that count most are typically financial measures of success such as profit. To ensure discipline in achieving these ends, there is great emphasis on achieving measurable goals and targets. Fundamentally, what characterizes market cultures is a pervasive emphasis on winning, often defined simply as beating the competition.[57]

Organizations that emphasize having a high degree of flexibility and discretion, and that also focus primarily inward rather than outward, are known as **clan cultures** because in many ways they can be thought of as an extended family. A strong sense of cohesiveness characterizes clan cultures along with shared values and a high degree of participativeness and consensus building. Clan cultures believe their path to success is rooted in teamwork, loyalty, and taking care of people within the organization, including their continuing development. In a real sense clan cultures can be thought of as *relationship* cultures.[58]

Finally, organizations that emphasize having a high degree of flexibility and discretion, and that focus primarily on the environment outside the organization, are called **adhocracy cultures.** In many ways adhocracy cultures represent an adaptation to the transition from the industrial age to the information age described earlier in that this form of organizational culture is most responsive to the turbulent and rapidly changing conditions of the present age. The name *adhocracy* has roots in the phrase *ad hoc,* which means temporary or specialized. Adhocracy cultures are by nature dynamic and changing so as to best foster creativity, entrepreneurship, and staying on the cutting edge. This requires a culture that emphasizes individual initiative and freedom.[59]

In actuality, these four cultures represent idealized forms; no real organization probably exists whose culture can be completely described by just one quadrant. The complexities and necessities of organizational life and survival inevitably require that all cultures include elements from all four of the cultures (that is, all cultures put some value on all the competing values). What differentiates one culture from another, then, is the relative predominance of one culture type over the others. Nonetheless, it should be apparent that quite different approaches to leadership are called for based on which of these four distinctive cultures dominates any organization.

Leadership in hierarchy cultures, for example, emphasizes careful management of information, monitoring detailed aspects of operations, and assuring operational dependability and reliability. In contrast, leadership in market cultures places a premium on aggressiveness, decisiveness, productivity (which is not the same thing as stability or continuity), and outperforming external competitors. Leadership in a clan culture focuses on process more than output, especially as it pertains to minimizing conflict and maximizing consensus. A premium is placed on leadership that is empathetic and caring and that builds trust. And leadership in adhocracy cultures requires vision, creativity, and future-oriented thinking.

An Afterthought on Organizational Issues for Students and Young Leaders

Let us conclude this section by adding an afterthought about what relevance organizational issues may have for students or others at the early stages of their careers, or at lower levels of leadership within their organizations. It is unlikely that such individuals will be asked soon to redesign their organization's structure or change its culture. As noted earlier, this chapter is not intended as a how-to manual for changing culture. On the other hand, it has been our experience that younger colleagues sometimes develop biased impressions of leaders or have unrealistic expectations about decision making in organizations, based on their lack of familiarity with, and appreciation of, the sorts of organizational dynamics discussed in this section. In other words, a primary reason for being familiar with such organizational variables is the context they provide for understanding the leadership process at your own level in the organization. Finally, we have worked with some senior leaders of huge organizations who have been with their companies for their entire careers. They have often been unable to identify *any* of the dimensions of their culture because they have never seen anything else. In these cases we were amazed by how junior managers were far better at describing the culture of the large organization. While these junior people may have had only five to eight years of total work experience, if that experience was obtained in several different organizations, they were much better prepared to describe the characteristics of their new large organization's culture than were the senior executives.

The Environment

The environmental level of the situation refers to factors outside the task or organization that still affect the leadership process. We will focus on two interrelated aspects of these extra-organizational aspects of the situation: (1) the ways in which leaders increasingly confront situations that are unexpected, unfamiliar, complex, and rapidly changing; and (2) the growing importance of leadership across different societal cultures.

Are Things Changing More Than They Used To?

One general aspect of the situation that affects leadership is the degree of change that's occurring. Leading in a relatively stable situation presents different challenges—generally simpler ones—than does leading in a dynamic situation. Many people think things *are* changing more than they used to, and at an increasing pace, but that's not so simple a question as it first might appear. For example, it may seem as though no age could possibly rival ours in terms of the transformative effect technology has had on our lives. On the other hand, a good case can be made that technologies introduced to most Americans during the early to mid-20th century like indoor electric lighting, refrigerators, electric and natural gas ovens, and indoor plumbing, changed life to a much greater degree than new technologies of the past decade.[60]

Nonetheless, while there's no argument that the generations growing up in the early part of the 20th century experienced profound transformations in life (television, the automobile, air travel, and atomic energy, to name a few), we believe that the nature of challenges facing leaders is changing as never before. Ronald Heifetz argues that leaders not only are facing more crises than ever before but that a new mode of leadership is needed because we're in a *permanent* state of crisis.[61] Thomas Friedman provocatively titled his book *The World Is Flat* to convey how globalization and technology are radically changing how we live and work.[62] And Army General David Petraeus used an oddly anachronistic painting in speaking with the troops he was soon to take command of in what was widely known as "the surge" in Iraq. The painting was *The Stampede* (see Figure 12.3), painted by western artist Frederic Remington in 1908. It depicts a cowboy in the 1800s riding desperately to survive a stampeding herd of cattle panicked by a thunderstorm. As Thomas Ricks tells the story in his account of the surge *The Gamble*, Petraeus used the painting to convey to his subordinates his notion of command. "I don't need to be hierarchical," he explained. "I want to flatten organizations. I'm comfortable with a slightly chaotic environment. I know that it's okay if some of you get out ahead of us.

FIGURE 12.3
The Stampede, by Frederic Remington

Reprinted with permission.

Some of the cattle will get out ahead and we will catch up with them. And some will fall behind and we will circle back and we won't leave them behind. . . . We're just trying to get the cattle to Cheyenne."[63]

To appreciate the significance of what Petraeus was saying, contrast the language and images used here ("don't need to be hierarchical," "some of the cattle will get out") with the stereotypical notions of command and control in the military. Situational changes are being met with new approaches to leadership even within what is often regarded as the epitome of traditional top-down leadership.

We think Heifetz, Friedman, and Petraeus illuminate important ways in which the challenge of leadership is changing. It might be useful, therefore, to introduce a variation of Figure 12.1, which depicted the task, organizational, and environmental levels of the situation. In Figure 12.4 we've added two vectors to the original diagram to highlight how two contrasting and multidimensional kinds of environments affect leadership. We don't intend the two vectors to imply there's a simple categorization of environments or that there are just two basic kinds of environment. In reality each dimension in the vectors is better conceptualized as a continuum (such as simple to complex), but we prefer the simpler representation for illustrative purposes.

Another purpose of the vectors is to underscore how different levels of the situation interact. Thus relatively narrow and specific descriptions of job tasks tend to be most common and most appropriate in more formal and highly structured organizations having more hierarchical cultures. This set of situational levels is reasonably aligned to deal with what Heifetz called technical problems. Adaptive or wicked problems, on the other hand, are more likely to be effectively addressed when tasks for individuals and teams are more fluid, in organizations that are less formal, less structured, and more agile and that have adhocracy-like cultures.

FIGURE 12.4
**Contrasting
Environments in the
Situational Level**

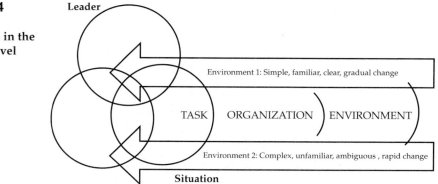

Leader

Environment 1: Simple, familiar, clear, gradual change

TASK ORGANIZATION ENVIRONMENT

Environment 2: Complex, unfamiliar, ambiguous , rapid change

Situation

Of course we are not saying that once situational variables have been identified as corresponding more closely to the bottom vector, it's a simple matter for a leader to just "turn on" adaptive leadership. The whole point is that such leadership is inherently more than an individual leader or his behavior or skills. Certain kinds of established relationships with followers are vital, and distinctive skill sets on their parts are needed, as is a certain kind of organizational culture.

In addition, Heifetz has described a thorny leadership challenge that can raise its head even after a challenge is recognized as an adaptive one. Followers generally want their leaders to be experts having all the answers (recall that by definition, adaptive problems don't have expert solutions). He said, "When you attain a position of significant authority, people inevitably expect you to treat adaptive challenges as if they were technical—to provide for them a remedy that will restore equilibrium with the least amount of pain and in the shortest amount of time."[64] Furthermore, leaders themselves easily fall prey to the same expectation. People in positions of authority often take personal pride in being able to solve problems that others can't solve. When facing an adaptive challenge, it can be difficult for them to admit they've come to the limit of their expertise.[65] To put it differently, leadership has never been easy and appears to be growing more difficult. A number of trends driving the changing nature of leadership are listed in Highlight 12.9.

> *I claim not to have controlled events, but confess plainly that events have controlled me.*
>
> **Abraham Lincoln**

Workplace Trends

HIGHLIGHT 12.9

In response to increasing competitiveness, uncertainty, globalization, and the pace of change, a number of leadership trends have been identified in how organizations can best face the future:

- Recognize that complex challenges are on the rise, and therefore that new approaches to leadership and leadership development will be required.
- Embrace innovation as a driver of future organizational success.
- Prepare for ever-greater levels of and need for virtual leadership, and that the skills it requires are different than those needed for face-to-face leadership.
- Collaboration across organizational boundaries (across teams, departments, units, regions, and so on) will be essential to organizational success.

- Because trust and respect will be vital, leaders will need to be more authentic in their roles than ever before.
- The next generation of leaders will place new kinds of leadership demands on their organizations.
- A crisis of talent in organizations is coming, and so organizations that have credible and established programs of talent development and succession planning will be at an advantage.
- Ensuring the health and fitness of all employees, leaders included, must become an organizational priority.

Source: A. Martin, *What's Next: The 2007 Changing Nature of Leadership Survey*, CCL Research White Paper (Greensboro, NC: Center for Creative Leadership,).

". . . Then it's agreed. As a crowd, we'll be subdued in innings one through seven, then suddenly become a factor in innings eight and nine . . ."

Source: © Tribune Media Services. All rights reserved. Reprinted with permission.

Leading across Societal Cultures

A telling illustration of the role societal culture can play in leadership is provided by Malcolm Gladwell in his book *Outliers*. It concerns the role that culture played in a series of airline crashes, including that of Korean Air Flight 801 in 1997, which killed 228 of the 254 people on board. In fact, the loss rate (deaths per number of departing passengers) for Korean Air in the period from 1988 to 1998 was 17 times what it was for a representative American carrier. It may seem initially that the likely cause of such a difference would be deficiencies in the Korean pilots' technical flying expertise or knowledge, but that was not the case—nor is it usually the case. The kinds of errors that cause crashes are almost always errors of teamwork and communication rather than errors of flying skill. Careful analysis of those crashes reveals that a root cause was the Korean pilots' customary cultural deep respect for authority. The same factor also played a role in crashes of airliners piloted by crews of other nationalities sharing a similar respect for authority. Respect for authority in itself is neither a good nor a bad thing, but it can be a problem when it interferes with clear and direct communication about an emergency situation. That's just what was happening in these crashes. Strange as it may sound, the crews did not make the criticality of their situations crystal clear to air traffic controllers. Conversing with the controllers as equals, such as by correcting the

Taking Charge

HIGHLIGHT 12.10

A critical period for any leader often involves those first few moments and days of assuming command. This is a time when first impressions are formed and expectations are set. It is a crucial time for any leader in any situation, but it can be a matter of life or death for a young leader in a combat situation. Here are one young officer's first reactions upon arriving in Southeast Asia to command a platoon:

> I was alone. That was my first sensation as a leader. The men were going about the morning's business—breaking out C rations, relieving themselves, shaving, brushing their teeth. They moved among each other comfortably, a word here, a smile there. I could hear snatches of conversation: "A good night's sleep . . . " "Only 90 days left." Occasionally a man would nod in my direction, or glance at me for a fleeting moment.

I gathered up my belongings—weapon, web gear, and rucksack—and moved toward the command post. I needed a few minutes to gather my thoughts before I made my debut as a platoon leader. I knew it was going to be a tricky business.

I had assumed that I would have a company commander nearby to give me my orders. But I had not even met him yet; I would not meet him for weeks. The fact was I was totally on my own. What should I do? Whose advice could I ask? The platoon sergeant's? The squad leaders'? In time I would listen to their ideas and incorporate them

with my own, but I could hardly begin my tour with "Well what do you think we ought to do, men?" No, I knew that the basic decisions were mine to make.

The first few moments would be crucial. Obviously, I was the object of interest that morning. Everyone was wondering what the new lieutenant would be like, and I would be telling them with my first words, my gestures, my demeanor, my eyes. I would have no grace period in which to learn my way around. This was a life and death environment. If I began with a blunder, my credibility as a leader would be shot, and so might some of the men.

I decided to begin by giving my attention to tactics. In a military environment, everything is determined by tactical considerations. Where you sleep, when you sleep, where you go, what you do, and in whose company you do it—all are dictated by underlying tactical necessities. I would communicate my style of leadership through my tactical instructions.

As I surveyed the soldiers, the nearby village, the distant rice paddies, the heavy undergrowth, the varied terrain, my mind raced back over the years of tactical training I had received. Conscious of the stares of the men, I hoped to appear composed as I fought back the panic of having to decide, both quickly and correctly.

Source: J. M. McDonough, *Platoon Leader* (San Francisco: Presidio Press, 1985), pp. 30–31. Reprinted with permission.

---

controllers' understanding of the actual situations, would have seemed disrespectful from the crew's cultural perspective. (As a footnote, Korean Air has corrected its procedures and now has an exemplary safety record.)[66]

This is admittedly a dramatic illustration, and airline crashes are fortunately rare events. The point the story makes, however, applies to leaders of all sorts and in all places: cultural differences—especially when they are not recognized and addressed—can create significant challenges to communication and teamwork. It's no surprise, then, that in recent years an increasing number of empirical studies have examined the challenges of leading across societal cultures. One value of such studies is that their findings can point out myths, mistaken assumptions, or invalid generalizations people have or make about leadership.

Global Leadership

HIGHLIGHT 12.11

There is no doubt about it: the world is getting smaller. Globalization has allowed goods and services to be manufactured, traded, and delivered in places no one thought possible just 10 or 20 years ago. World business leaders, such as Jeffery Immelt of General Electric, Carlos Ghosn of Renault and Nissan Motors, and Steve Ballmer of Microsoft all believe these global trends are irreversible and gaining momentum. But what are the implications of globalization for leadership? It is clear that the ways in which leaders get results through others and build cohesive, goal-oriented teams will vary somewhat from one country to the next. For example, Malaysian leadership culture inhibits assertive, confrontational behavior and puts a premium on maintaining harmony. Effective leaders are expected to show compassion while demonstrating more of an autocratic than participatory leadership style. German leadership culture does not value compassion, and interpersonal relationships are straightforward and stern. Effective leaders in Germany generally value autonomy and participation but have a low team orientation.

So how does one lead in a global economy? Certainly appreciating what different cultures value and how things get done in different countries is an important first step. But do leaders need to do fundamentally different things to build teams or get results through others in India, Zimbabwe, or Estonia? Will leaders of the future need to speak multiple languages or actually live in other countries to be effective? The answers to these questions will depend to some extent on the global orientation of the organization. Some organizations, such as Waste Management or ServiceMaster, operate primarily in Canada and the United States and probably will not need to have leaders who have lived in other countries or speak multiple languages. Other organizations, such as 3M, Hewlett-Packard, Pfizer, BP, Levono, Nike, Toyota, or the British military have significant manufacturing, marketing, sales, or other operations in multiple countries. These organizations often use a global competency model to outline the expectations for leaders in all countries, and these models tend to vary more by company than by country (see Figure 7.3 for an example of a competency model).

It seems likely that leaders who have spent time in other countries, have applied the action–observation–reflection model to maximize the lessons learned from their expatriot experiences, and can speak multiple languages would be better able to lead international organizations. But currently this is conjecture; more research is needed before we can definitively say whether international experience matters, how much and what kinds of experience are needed, what the key lessons to be learned from these experiences are, and how we should select and develop leaders to successfully lead international organizations. The good news here is that a group of 150 social scientists working on the GLOBE (Global Leadership and Organizational Behavior Effectiveness) project are actively seeking the answers to these questions and will soon be publishing their findings.

Sources: S. Green, F. Hassan, J. Immelt, M. Marks, and D. Meiland, "In Search of Global Leaders," *Harvard Business Review,* August 2003, pp. 38–45; J. C. Kennedy, "Leadership in Malaysia: Traditional Values, International Outlook," *The Academy of Management Executive,* 16, no. 3 (2002), pp. 15–24; F. Brodbeck, M. Frese, M. Javidan, and F. G. Kroll, "Leadership Made in Germany: Low on Compassion, High in Performance," *The Academy of Management Executive* 16, no. 1 (2002), pp. 16–30; GLOBE program: http://mgmt3.ucalgary.ca/web/globe.nsf/index.

For example, a person regarded as an effective leader in one society may not be perceived as effective in another. That's what one study found in comparing evaluations by supervisors of the leadership effectiveness of female managers in Malaysia with those by supervisors of female managers in Australia. These findings appeared to be based not on an objective appraisal of the female managers' capability but rather on strongly held cultural beliefs about appropriate roles for women in society. There was a clear culturally based readiness by both male and female supervisors in Australia to value equality between the roles of men and women generally and in organizational roles specifically; this was not the case in Malaysia, where more gender-specific stereotypes were held. While these findings were not unexpected, they point out how research findings in Western cultures may not be transferable to developing cultures.[67]

Such findings have a practical importance beyond mere academic or scholarly interest. A survey of executives in the 500 largest corporations in the world showed that having competent global leaders was the most important contributor to business success. What's more, 85 percent of those executives did not think their companies had sufficient numbers of competent global leaders.[68]

Without competent global leaders, misunderstandings and slights can occur when people from different cultures are working together. Here are two specific examples. First consider the historic U.S. emphasis on individualism (the focus on *self*-confidence, *self*-control, *self*-concept, *self*-expression, or the way rugged individualists are heroically portrayed in film, television, and literature) and how it might impact work. Given an individualist perspective, certain management practices and expectations seem self-evident, such as the idea of individual accountability for work. When individual accountability is valued, for example, decision-making authority tends to be delegated to individual managers. What's more, those same managers may be inclined to take personal credit when the job is well done. A different norm, however, applies in industrialized Japan. Decision making is often time-consuming to ensure that everyone who will be affected by a decision has input on it beforehand. Another self-evident principle to the U.S. mind is that individual career progress is desirable and good. In some other cultures, however, managers resist competing with peers for rewards or promotions so as not to disturb the harmony of the group or appear self-interested.

Another example of potential conflict or misunderstanding can be seen in the case of orientation to authority—how people should handle power and authority relationships with others. The United States is a relatively young and mobile country, populated mostly by immigrants. Relative to other countries, there is little concern with family origin or class background. There is a belief that success should come through an individual's hard work and talent, not by birthright or class standing. This all leads to relative informality at work, even among individuals of strikingly different position within a company. Subordinates expect their bosses to be accessible, even responsive in some ways to their subordinates. In some other cultures, however, higher status in a company confers nearly unchallengeable authority, and an expectation as well that most decisions will be referred *up* to them (as distinguished from delegated down to others).

What Is Societal Culture?

Before we look at more specific findings about leading across societal cultures, it will be useful first to clarify what the term *societal culture* means. **Societal culture** refers to those learned behaviors characterizing the total way of life of members within any given society. Cultures differ from one another just as individuals differ from one another. To outsiders, the most salient aspect of any culture typically involves behavior—the distinctive actions, mannerisms, and gestures characteristic of that culture. Americans visiting Thailand, for example, may find it curious and even bothersome to see male Thais hold hands with each other in public. They may react negatively to such behavior because it is atypical to them and laden with North American meaning ("It's okay for women to hold hands in public, but men shouldn't do that"). Salient as such behaviors are, however, they are just the tip of the iceberg. The mass of culture is not so readily visible, just as most of an iceberg lies beneath the water. Hidden from view are the beliefs, values, and myths that provide context to manifest behaviors.[69] A clear implication for business leaders in the global context, therefore, is the need to become aware and respectful of cultural differences and cultural perspectives. Barnum pointed out the importance of being able to look at one's own culture through the eyes of another:

> Consciously or unconsciously they will be using their own beliefs as the yardsticks for judging you, so know how to compare those yardsticks by ferreting out their values and noting where they differ the least and most from yours. For example, if their belief in fatalism outweighs your belief in accountability, there will be conflicts down the road. This is a severe problem in the Middle East, for instance, and affects management styles in companies and even the ability to market life insurance, which is frowned upon in communities where Muslim observances are strong.[70]

The GLOBE Study

I do believe in the spiritual nature of human beings. To some it's a strange or outdated idea, but I believe there is such a thing as a human spirit. There is a spiritual dimension to man which should be nurtured.

Aung San Suu Kyi

GLOBE is an acronym for a research program called the Global Leadership and Organizational Behavior Effectiveness Research Program. It is the most comprehensive study of leadership and culture ever attempted, involving data collected from over 17,000 managers representing 950 companies in 62 countries.[71,72]

Hofstede was one of the pioneers in the study of beliefs and culture, and his seminal work provided some of the early roots of the GLOBE study.[73] He identified five fundamental dimensions of cultural values and beliefs, and these, as well as dimensions drawn from the work of other researchers, became the nine dimensions of societal culture used in the GLOBE study. Because of the number of scales and complexity of findings, we'll look at representative findings from just two of those scales to convey the flavor of some of these cross-cultural findings. We'll look at the dimensions of future orientation and collectivism–individualism. Here's a brief definition of each of them:[74]

Future orientation: The degree to which individuals in organizations or societies engage in future-oriented behaviors like planning and investing in the future.

Collectivism: The degree to which individuals express pride, loyalty, and cohesiveness in their organizations, families, or similar small groups.

Table 12.3 presents some of the representative findings that differentiate cultures high or low on each of these dimensions. Cross-cultural differences on these and the other seven dimensions of culture used in GLOBE constitute a foundation for the GLOBE findings on differences in leadership across cultures.

The heart of the conceptual model in the GLOBE research is what's called **implicit leadership theory.** This theory holds that individuals have implicit beliefs and assumptions about attributes and behaviors that distinguish leaders from followers, effective leaders from ineffective leaders, and moral from immoral leaders. The GLOBE model further posits that relatively distinctive implicit theories of leadership characterize different societal cultures from each other as well as organizational cultures within those societal cultures. GLOBE calls these **culturally endorsed implicit theories of leadership** (CLT).

After detailed analysis of findings, GLOBE researchers identified six dimensions that were determined to be applicable across all global

TABLE 12.3   **Representative Societal Differences on Two GLOBE Dimensions**

Societies Higher on Collectivism Tend to	Societies Higher on Individualism Tend to
• Have a slower pace of life. • Have lower heart attack rates. • Assign less weight to love in marriage decisions. • Have fewer interactions, but interactions tend to be longer and more intimate.	• Have a faster pace of life. • Have higher heart attack rates. • Assign greater weight to love in marriage decisions. • Have more social interactions, but interactions tend to be shorter and less intimate.
Societies Higher on Future Orientation Tend to	**Societies Lower on Future Orientation Tend to**
• Achieve economic success. • Have flexible and adaptive organizations and managers. • Emphasize visionary leadership that is capable of seeing patterns in the face of chaos and uncertainty.	• Have lower rates of economic success. • Have inflexible and maladaptive organizations and managers. • Emphasize leadership that focuses on repetition of reproducible and routine sequences.

cultures for assessing CLT. Here are those six dimensions and a brief description of each:[75]

- **Charismatic/value-based leadership** reflects the ability to inspire, motivate, and expect high performance from others on the basis of firmly held core values.
- **Team-oriented leadership** emphasizes effective team building and implementation of a common purpose or goal among team members.
- **Participative leadership** reflects the degree to which managers involve others in making and implementing decisions.
- **Humane-oriented leadership** reflects supportive and considerate leadership as well as compassion and generosity.
- **Autonomous leadership** refers to independent and individualistic leadership.
- **Self-protective leadership** focuses on ensuring the safety and security of the individual or group member.

After analyzing the data from all the societies in the study, GLOBE researchers categorized them into 10 different societal clusters (such as Eastern Europe, Nordic Europe, Latin America, Southern Asia, and Anglo). Societies were included in a cluster based on criteria of relative similarity of values and beliefs *within* each cluster, and *differentiation* from other societal clusters. Again, it is beyond our purposes here to present a comprehensive description of all these societal clusters. It will suffice to look at just three of them so you will have a general sense of the nature of the GLOBE findings. Table 12.4 presents the relative rankings (high, medium, or low) for three different societal clusters on each of the six global CLT dimensions.[76]

The considerable variation in views of what constitutes good leadership across different societal clusters evident in Table 12.4 makes it clear that behaving effectively as a leader (and being perceived as effective) requires awareness of the cultural values and practices in the society within which one is working.

A final set of interesting findings coming out of GLOBE concerns the **universality of leadership attributes.** These findings both refine and temper the distinctiveness of societal CLTs exemplified in Table 12.4. They temper the impression we may get that different societies have completely

TABLE 12.4   Relative Rankings of Selected Societal Clusters on CLT Leadership Dimensions

Societal Cluster	Charismatic/ Value-Based	Team-Oriented	Participative	Humane-Oriented	Self-Protective
Eastern Europe	Medium	Medium	Low	Medium	High
Anglo	High	Medium	High	High	Low
Middle East	Low	Low	Low	Medium	High

Nelson Mandela and Francois Pienaar

PROFILES IN LEADERSHIP 12.1

The idea of "leading across cultures" sometimes involves leading across cultures within the same country. That was the challenge facing Nelson Mandela during the early stage of his presidency of South Africa—a dramatic time portrayed in the film *Invictus*. The film focuses on the year just after Mandela was elected president of South Africa. What made his election such an unbelievable and inspiring event is that for 27 years before he had been held prisoner in a South African jail cell for fighting apartheid in his own country.

The film focuses on Mandela's efforts to help the South African rugby team win the World Cup, which would be played in South Africa in 1995. Mandela was a rugby fan, but his motivation went far deeper: he wanted to use the South African team's path to the World Cup as an opportunity to unite a bitterly divided country.

This would be no small feat: the team was detested by the South African black majority precisely because it had for so long been loved by South African whites; the team was an insulting and painful reminder to blacks of apartheid. But Mandela saw the team in a way no one else in South Africa did— as a possible vehicle for national reconciliation. This was no mere gracious gesture on Mandela's part. In fact, while Mandela and South African blacks had won a political victory, economic power was still controlled by the white majority. Mandela knew he needed to bring the country together, and he saw the team and the World Cup as an opportunity to do so. His unlikely ally in the cause was the team's captain, Francois Pienaar. When it appeared to most that the team's success in the World Cup seemed hopeless, Mandela gave Pienaar a poem that had sustained his own spirit during his long years of captivity.

The poem that Mandela shared with Pienaar was the basis of the film's title: *Invictus*. It was written by the English poet William Henley in the 19th century. Henley, too, overcame major hardships in life. His leg was amputated when he was 24 due to tuberculosis of the bone, and he wrote this poem from his hospital bed. This is the poem that sustained and strengthened Mandela during his 27 years in prison and that he gave to Pienaar to help inspire the heavily disadvantaged South African Springbok rugby team:

> *Out of the night that covers me,*
> *Black as the pit from pole to pole,*
> *I thank whatever gods may be*
> *For my unconquerable soul.*
>
> *In the fell clutch of circumstance*
> *I have not winced nor cried aloud.*
> *Under the bludgeonings of chance*
> *My head is bloody, but unbowed.*
>
> *Beyond this place of wrath and tears*
> *Looms but the Horror of the shade,*
> *And yet the menace of the years*
> *Finds and shall find me unafraid.*
>
> *It matters not how strait the gate,*
> *How charged with punishments the scroll,*
> *I am the master of my fate:*
> *I am the captain of my soul.*

Mandela knew that his own hopes and vision for South Africa required a transformation in the hearts and minds of both blacks and whites, and his ability to touch the heart of one particular man. That man, Pienaar, in turn touched the hearts of his team, and that team's success changed a nation.

Source: A. Getz, "Sports, Politics, and Mandela," December 10, 2009, http://www.newsweek.com/2009/12/09/sports-politics-and-mandela.html.

Autocrats, Democrats, and Meritocrats

HIGHLIGHT 12.12

Many people take for granted that similar attitudes about leadership are shared among businesspeople, at least in Western nations. However, a recent poll of senior executives in the United Kingdom, Germany, and France revealed some striking differences in national attitudes concerning different aspects of leadership. These differences led the researchers to label French business leaders as "autocrats," German business leaders as "democrats," and British business leaders as "meritocrats."

Here are some of the findings that led to those designations:

- Although you may assume that no bosses like being challenged about decisions they make, fewer than 3 in 10 French bosses said they were happy about such challenges compared to half of German bosses and more than 9 out of 10 business leaders in the United Kingdom.

- Nearly two-thirds of French bosses said that one of the three best things about being a leader was "the freedom to make decisions with minimum interference."

- 50 percent of German bosses and 70 percent of British bosses said that the best thing about the job is developing talent in the company. Only 14 percent of French bosses rated this among the top three benefits of leadership.

- French leaders are three times more likely than British leaders and eight times more likely than German leaders to consider "being in a position of power" one of the best things about the job.

Source: Adapted from Alison Maitland, "Le Patron, der Chef, and the Boss," *The Financial Times Limited,* January 9, 2006, *Business Life,* p. 1. Copyright © 2006 The Financial Times Limited. Reprinted with permission.

different notions of what constitutes good and bad leadership by demonstrating that actually there is consensus across cultures on a number of desirable leadership attributes as well as consensus on what are considered to be universally negative leadership traits. But these findings also provide further insight into which attributes see much of the variability across cultures. GLOBE researchers identified 22 specific attributes and behaviors that are viewed universally across cultures as contributing to leadership effectiveness.[77] They are listed in Table 12.5. In addition, the

TABLE 12.5
Leader Attributes and Behaviors Universally Viewed as Positive

Source: Adapted from House et al., *Cultural Influences on Leadership and Organizations: Project Globe. Advances in Global Leadership,* vol. 1 (JAI Press, 1999), pp. 171–233.

Trustworthy	Positive	Intelligent
Just	Dynamic	Decisive
Honest	Motive arouser	Effective bargainer
Foresighted	Confidence builder	Win–win problem solver
Plans ahead	Motivational	Administratively skilled
Encouraging	Dependable	Communicative
Informed	Coordinator	Team builder
Excellence oriented		

TABLE 12.6   **Leader Attributes and Behaviors Universally Viewed as Negative**

Source: Adapted from House et al., *Cultural Influences on Leadership and Organizations: Project Globe. Advances in Global Leadership*, vol. 1 (JAI Press, 1999), pp. 171–233.

Loner	Nonexplicit
Asocial	Egocentric
Noncooperative	Ruthless
Irritable	Dictatorial

TABLE 12.7   **Examples of Leader Behaviors and Attributes That Are Culturally Contingent**

Source: Adapted from House et al., *Cultural Influences on Leadership and Organizations: Project Globe. Advances in Global Leadership*, vol. 1 (JAI Press, 1999), pp. 171–233.

Ambitious	Logical
Cautious	Orderly
Compassionate	Sincere
Domineering	Worldly
Independent	Formal
Individualistic	Sensitive

project identified eight characteristics that are universally viewed as impediments to leader effectiveness (see Table 12.6). And GLOBE researchers identified 35 leader characteristics that are viewed as positive in some cultures but negative in others (some of these are listed in Table 12.7). This large set of culturally contingent characteristics apparently accounts for most of the variance across societal cultures.

Implications for Leadership Practitioners

The perspectives and findings presented in this chapter have significant implications for leadership practitioners. Perhaps most important, leadership practitioners should expect to face a variety of challenges to their own systems of ethics, values, or attitudes during their careers. Additionally, values often are a source of interpersonal conflict. Although we sometimes say two people don't get along because of a personality conflict, often these conflicts are due to differences in value systems, not personality traits. Often people on either side of an issue see only themselves and their own side as morally justifiable. Nonetheless, people holding seemingly antithetical values may need to work together, and dealing with diverse values will be an increasingly common challenge for leaders. As noted earlier, interacting with individuals and groups holding divergent and conflicting values will be an inevitable fact of life for future leaders. This does not mean, however, that increased levels of interpersonal conflict are inevitable. Both leaders and followers might be well advised to minimize the conflict and tension often associated with value differences. Leaders in particular have a responsibility not to let their own personal values interfere with professional leader–subordinate relationships unless the conflicts pertain to issues clearly relevant to the work and the organization.

Summary

The situation may be the most complex factor in the leader–follower–situation framework. Moreover, situations vary not only in complexity but also in strength. Situational factors can play such a pervasive role that they can effectively minimize the effects of personality traits, intelligence, values, and preferences on leaders' and followers' behaviors, attitudes, and relationships. Given the dynamic nature of leadership situations, finding fairly consistent results is a highly encouraging accomplishment for leadership researchers.

As an organizing framework, this chapter introduced the concept of situational levels as a way to consider many situational factors. At the lowest level, leaders need to be aware of how various aspects of tasks can affect both their own and their followers' behaviors, and how they might change these factors to improve followers' satisfaction and performance. The organizational level includes both the formal organization and informal organization. The formal organization involves the ways authority is distributed across various organizational levels and how organizational structure impacts the way activities in the organization are coordinated and controlled. The informal organization or the organizational culture can have a profound impact on the way both leaders and followers behave—and may be the least recognizable because it is the water in the bowl where all the fish are swimming. An increasingly important variable at the environmental level is societal culture, which involves learned behaviors that guide the distinctive mannerisms, ways of thinking, and values within particular societies.

Key Terms

situational engineering, *476*
role theory, *479*
multiple-influence model, *479*
situational levels, *479*
task autonomy, *480*
task feedback, *481*
task structure, *481*
task interdependence, *482*
technical problems, *483*
adaptive problems, *483*
adaptive leadership, *484*
formal organization, *486*
level of authority, *486*
organizational structure, *487*
horizontal complexity, *488*
vertical complexity, *488*
spatial complexity, *488*
formalization, *488*

centralization, *489*
substitutes for
leadership, *489*
informal
organization, *489*
organizational
culture, *489*
organizational
climate, *490*
myths and
stories, *491*
symbols and
artifacts, *491*
rituals, *491*
language, *491*
dependent leadership
culture, *493*
independent
leadership culture, *493*
interdependent
leadership
culture, *493*
Competing Values
Framework, *495*
hierarchy
culture, *496*
market culture, *497*
clan culture, *497*
adhocracy culture, *497*
societal culture, *506*
GLOBE, *506*
future orientation, *507*
collectivism, *507*
implicit leadership
theory, *507*
culturally endorsed
implicit theories of
leadership, *507*
charismatic/values-
based leadership, *508*
team-oriented
leadership, *508*
participative
leadership, *508*
humane-oriented
leadership, *508*
autonomous
leadership, *508*
self-protective
leadership, *508*
universality of
leadership
attributes, *508*

Questions

1. The term *bureaucratic* has a pejorative connotation to most people. Can you think of any positive aspects of a bureaucracy?
2. Think of a crisis situation you are familiar with involving a group, team, organization, or country, and analyze it in terms of the leader–follower–situation framework. For example, were the followers looking for a certain kind of behavior from the leader? Did the situation demand it? Did the situation, in fact, contribute to a particular leader's emergence?
3. Can you identify reward systems that affect the level of effort students are likely to put forth in team or group projects? Should these reward systems be different than those for individual effort projects?

Activity

Your instructor has several exercises available that demonstrate the impact of situational factors on behavior. They are not described here because identifying the situational factors being manipulated in an exercise undercuts the purpose of that exercise.

Minicase

Innovation at IKEA

Redecorating and renovating have become a popular international pastime. In a world facing persistent terrorist alerts and lagging economies, more and more people are opting to stay home and make their homes safe havens. This phenomenon has contributed tremendously to the success of IKEA, the Swedish home furniture giant. In the past 10 years sales for IKEA have tripled, growing from over $4 billion in 1993 to over $12 billion in 2003.

Much of IKEA's success can be attributed to its founder, Ingvar Kamprad. Kamprad used graduation money to start IKEA in the small Swedish village where he was born. He started off selling belt buckles, pens, and watches—whatever residents in the small local village of Agunnaryd needed. Eventually Kamprad moved on to selling furniture. One day in 1952, while struggling to fit a large table in a small car, one of Kamprad's employees came up with the idea that changed the furniture industry forever—he decided to remove the legs. IKEA's flat-pack and self-assembly methodology was born, and it rocketed the company past the competition. "After that [table] followed a whole series of other self-assembled furniture, and by 1956 the concept was more or less systematized," writes Kamprad.

Kamprad is dedicated to maintaining the corporate culture he has helped define over the past 50 years. He is a simple man—his idea of a luxury vacation is riding his bike. He is fiercely cost-conscious and, even though his personal wealth has been estimated in the billions, he refuses to fly first class. He values human interaction above all, and, even though retired, he still visits IKEA stores regularly to keep tabs on what is going on where the business really happens.

The culture at IKEA is a culture closely connected with Kamprad's simple Swedish farm roots. It is a culture that strives "to create a better everyday for the many people." IKEA supports this culture by

- Hiring co-workers (IKEA prefers the word *co-workers* to *employees*) who are supportive and work well in teams.
- Expecting co-workers to look for innovative, better ways of doing things in every aspect of their work.
- Respecting co-workers and their views.
- Establishing mutual objectives and working tirelessly to realize them.
- Making cost consciousness part of everything they do from improving processes for production to purchasing wisely to traveling cost-effectively.
- Avoiding complicated solutions—simplicity is a strong part of the IKEA culture.
- Leading by example, so IKEA leaders are expected to pitch in when needed and create a good working environment.
- Believing that a diverse workforce strengthens the company overall.

The IKEA culture is one that resonates for many. The buildings are easy to identify—the giant blue and gold warehouses that resemble oversized Swedish flags are hard to miss. Millions of customers browse through the

Klippan sofas and Palbo footstools (Nordic names are given to all IKEA products) in the stark, dimly lit warehouses. The surroundings may not be lavish and the service may be minimal, but customers keep going back not just for the bargains but to experience the IKEA culture as well.

1. Discuss the three input components of the Congruence Model as they apply to the success of IKEA.

2. Consider Schein's four key organizational culture factors as described in Highlight 12.6. What examples can you identify within the IKEA organization that contribute to the company's strong corporate culture?

3. Based on the level of technological complexity and the degree of environmental uncertainty present at IKEA, what type of organizational structure would you expect?

Sources: http://archive.cinweekly.com/content/2004/03/24/0324travelikea.asp; http://www.azcentral. com/home/design/articles/0812ikea12.html; http://strategis.ic.gc.ca/epic/internet/inimr-ri.nsf/en/gr-76894e.html; http://www.geocities.com/TimesSquare/1848/ikea.html; http://www.sustainability.com/news/press-room/JE-teflon-shield-Mar01. asp?popup=1; http://www.benefitnews.com/retire/detail.cfm?id=345.

End Notes

1. T. J. Peters and R. H. Waterman, *In Search of Excellence* (New York: Harper & Row, 1982).

2. R. T. Hogan and J. Hogan, *Manual for the Hogan Personality Inventory* (Tulsa, OK: Hogan Assessment Systems, 1992).

3. G. Yukl, *Leadership in Organizations,* 2nd ed. (Englewood Cliffs, NJ: Prentice Hall, 1989).

4. A. J. Murphy, "A Study of the Leadership Process," *American Sociological Review* 6 (1941), pp. 674–87.

5. H. S. Person, "Leadership as a Response to Environment," *Educational Record Supplement*, no. 6 (1928), pp. 9–21.

6. G. Spiller, "The Dynamics of Greatness," *Sociological Review* 21 (1929), pp. 218-32.

7. J. Schneider, "The Cultural Situation as a Condition for the Condition of Fame," *American Sociology Review* 2 (1937), pp. 480–91.

8. H. S. Person, "Leadership as a Response to Environment," *Educational Record Supplement* no. 6 (1928), pp. 9–21.

9. B. M. Bass, *Bass and Stogdill's Handbook of Leadership,* 3rd ed. (New York: Free Press, 1990).

10. R. K. Merton, *Social Theory and Social Structure* (New York: Free Press, 1957).

11. J. Pfeffer and G. R. Salancik, "Determinants of Supervisory Behavior: A Role Set Analysis," *Human Relations* 28 (1975), pp. 139–54.

12. A. Tsui, "A Role Set Analysis of Managerial Reputation," *Organizational Behavior and Human Performance* 34 (1984), pp. 64–96.

13. J. G. Hunt and R. N. Osborn, "Toward a Macro-Oriented Model of Leadership: An Odyssey," in *Leadership: Beyond Establishment Views,* ed. J. G. Hunt, U. Sekaran, and C. A. Schriesheim (Carbondale: Southern Illinois University Press, 1982), pp. 196–221.

14. P. Hersey and K. H. Blanchard, *Management of Organizational Behavior: Utilizing Human Resources,* 3rd ed. (Englewood Cliffs, NJ: Prentice Hall, 1977).

15. P. Hersey and K. H. Blanchard, *Management of Organizational Behavior: Utilizing Human Resources,* 4th ed. (Englewood Cliffs, NJ: Prentice Hall, 1984).

16. J. R. Hackman and G. R. Oldham, *Work Redesign* (Reading, MA: Addison-Wesley, 1980).

17. R. J. House and G. Dressler, "The Path-Goal Theory of Leadership: Some Post Hoc and A Priori Tests," in *Contingency Approaches to Leadership,* ed. J. G. Hunt and L. L. Larson (Carbondale: Southern Illinois University Press, 1974).

18. J. P. Howell and P. W. Dorfman, "Substitute for Leadership: Test of a Construct," *Academy of Management Journal* 24 (1981), pp. 714–28.

19. S. Kerr and J. M. Jermier, "Substitutes for Leadership: Their Meaning and Measurement," *Organizational Behavior and Human Performance* 22 (1978), pp. 375–403.

20. I. B. Myers and B. H. McCaulley, *Manual: A Guide to the Development and Use of the Myers-Briggs Type Indicator* (Palo Alto, CA: Consulting Psychologists Press, 1985).

21. B. M. Bass, *Bass and Stogdill's Handbook of Leadership,* 3rd ed. (New York: Free Press, 1990).

22. J. D. Ford, "Department Context and Formal Structure as Constraints on Leader Behavior," *Academy of Management Journal* 24 (1981), pp. 274–88.

23. G. Yukl, *Leadership in Organizations,* 2nd ed. (Englewood Cliffs, NJ: Prentice Hall, 1989).

24. M. Siegall and L. L. Cummings, "Task Role Ambiguity, Satisfaction, and the Moderating Effect of Task Instruction Source," *Human Relations* 39 (1986), pp. 1017–32.

25. J. Galbraith, *Designing Complex Organizations* (Menlo Park, CA: Addison-Wesley, 1973).

26. L. Fry, W. Kerr, and C. Lee, "Effects of Different Leader Behaviors under Different Levels of Task Interdependence," *Human Relations* 39 (1986), pp. 1067–82.

27. R. A. Heifetz, *Leadership without Easy Answer* (Cambridge, MA: Belknap, 1998).

28. R. A. Heifetz and M. Linsky, *Leadership on the Line: Staying Alive through the Dangers of Leading* (Boston: Harvard Business School Press, 2002).

29. A. D. Chandler, *Scale and Scope: The Dynamics of Industrial Capitalism* (Cambridge: Harvard University Press, 1990).

30. R. S. Kaplan and D. P. Norton, *The Balanced Scorecard: Translating Strategy into Action* (Boston: Harvard Business School Press, 1996).

31. F. Luthans, S. A. Rosenkrantz, and H. W. Hennessey, "What Do Successful Managers Really Do? An Observational Study of Managerial Activities," *Journal of Applied Behavioral Science* 21 (1985), pp. 255–70.

32. R. C. Page and W. W. Tornow, "Managerial Job Analysis: Are We Any Further Along?" paper presented at a meeting of the Society of Industrial Organizational Psychology, Atlanta, GA, 1987.

33. G. Chitayat and I. Venezia, "Determinates of Management Styles in Business and Nonbusiness Organizations," *Journal of Applied Psychology* 69 (1984), pp. 437–47.

34. L. B. Kurke and H. E. Aldrich, "Mintzberg Was Right! A Replication and Extension of the Nature of Managerial Work," *Management Science* 29 (1983), pp. 975–84.

35. A. M. Morrison, R. P. White, and E. Van Velsor, *Breaking the Glass Ceiling* (Reading, MA: Addison-Wesley, 1987); Morse, G. "Why We Misread Motives," *Harvard Business Review,* January 2003, p. 18.

36. S. P. Robbins, *Organizational Behavior: Concepts, Controversies, and Applications* (Englewood Cliffs, NJ: Prentice Hall, 1986).

37. P. M. Podsakoff, "Determinants of a Supervisor's Use of Rewards and Punishments: A Literature Review and Suggestions for Future Research," *Organizational Behavior and Human Performance* 29 (1982), pp. 58–83.

38. T. H. Hammer and J. Turk, "Organizational Determinants of Leader Behavior and Authority," *Journal of Applied Psychology* 71 (1987), pp. 674–82.

39. B. M. Bass, *Bass and Stogdill's Handbook of Leadership,* 3rd ed. (New York: Free Press, 1990).

40. E. H. Schein, *Organizational Culture and Leadership: A Dynamic View* (San Francisco: Jossey-Bass, 1985).

41. B. M. Bass, *Bass and Stogdill's Handbook of Leadership,* 3rd ed. (New York: Free Press, 1990).

42. S. W. J. Kozlowski and M. L. Doherty, "Integration of Climate and Leadership: Examination of a Neglected Issue," *Journal of Applied Psychology* 74 (1989), pp. 546–53.

43. B. Schneider, P. J. Hanges, D. B. Smith, and A. N. Salvaggio, " Which Comes First: Employee Attitudes or Organizational Financial and Market Performance?" *Journal of Applied Psychology* 88, no. 5 (2003), pp. 836–51; J. Schneider, "The Cultural Situation as a Condition for the Condition of Fame," *American Sociology Review* 2 (1937), pp. 480–91.

44. B. M. Bass, *Bass and Stogdill's Handbook of Leadership,* 3rd ed. (New York: Free Press, 1990).

45. S. W. J. Kozlowski and M. L. Doherty, "Integration of Climate and Leadership: Examination of a Neglected Issue," *Journal of Applied Psychology* 74 (1989), pp. 546–53.

46. B. M. Bass, *Bass and Stogdill's Handbook of Leadership,* 3rd ed. (New York: Free Press, 1990).

47. R. H. Kilmann and M. J. Saxton, *Organizational Cultures: Their Assessment and Change* (San Francisco: Jossey-Bass, 1983).

48. E. H. Schein, *Organizational Culture and Leadership: A Dynamic View* (San Francisco: Jossey-Bass, 1985).

49. B. Dumaine, "Creating a New Company Culture," *Fortune,* 1990, pp. 127–131.

50. B. M. Bass, *Leadership and Performance beyond Expectations* (New York: Free Press, 1985).

51. J. M. Kouzes and B. Z. Posner, *The Leadership Challenge: How to Get Extraordinary Things Done in Organizations* (San Francisco: Jossey-Bass, 1987).

52. E. H. Schein, *Organizational Culture and Leadership: A Dynamic View* (San Francisco: Jossey-Bass, 1985).

53. N. M. Tichy and M. A. Devanna, *The Transformational Leader* (New York: John Wiley, 1986).

54. F. E. Emery and E. L. Trist, "The Causal Texture of Organizational Environments," *Human Relations* 18 (1965), pp. 21–32.

55. C. S. Cameron and R. E. Quinn, *Diagnosing and Changing Organizational Culture* (Reading, MA: Addison-Wesley, 1999).

56. Ibid.

57. Ibid.

58. Ibid.

59. Ibid.

60. M. Lind, "The Boring Age," *Time,* March 22, 2010, pp. 58–59.

61. R. Heifetz, A. Grashow, and M. Linsky, "Leadership in a (Permanent) Crisis," *Harvard Business Review,* July–August 2009, pp. 62–69.

62. Friedman, T. *The World Is Flat: A Brief History of the Twenty-First Century* (New York: Farrar, Straus and Giroux, 2005).

63. T. Ricks, *The Gamble* (New York: The Penguin Press, 2009).

64. R. Heifetz, "An Interview with Ronald A. Heifetz: Interview by James Nelson," http://www.managementfirst.com/management_styles/interviews/heifetz.htm, accessed June 5, 2006.

65. Ibid.

66. M. Gladwell, *Outliers* (New York: Little, Brown and Company, 2005).

67. U. D. Jogulu and G. J. Wood, "A Cross-Cultural Study into Peer Evaluations of Women's Leadership Effectiveness," *Leadership & Organization Development Journal* 29, no. 7 (2008), pp. 606–16.

68. M. Javidan and R. J. House, "Cultural Acumen for the Global Manager: Lessons from Project GLOBE," *Organizational Dynamics* 29 (2001), pp. 289–305.

69. L. R. Kohls, *Survival Kit for Overseas Living* (Boston: Intercultural Press, 2001).

70. D. F. Barnum, "Effective Membership in the Global Business Community," in *New Traditions in Business,* ed. J. Renesch (San Francisco: Berrett-Koehler, 1992), p. 153.

71. R. House, P. Hanges, M. Javidan, P. Dorfman, and V. Gupta (ed.), *Culture, Leadership and Organizations: The GLOBE Study of 62 Societies* (Thousand Oaks, CA: Sage, 2004).

72. J. S. Chhokar, F. C. Brodbeck, and R. J. House (ed.), *Culture and Leadership around the World: The GLOBE Book of In-Depth Studies of 25 Societies* (Mahwah, NJ: Lawrence Erlbaum, 2007).

73. G. Hofstede, *Cultural Consequences: Comparing Values, Behaviors, Institutions and Organizations across Nations,* 2nd ed. (Thousand Oaks, CA: Sage Publications, 2001).

assumed to have a positive effect on group or organizational outcomes. Thus these theories maintain that leadership effectiveness is maximized when leaders correctly make their behaviors *contingent* on certain situational and follower characteristics. Because of these similarities,[2] Chemers argued that these contingency theories are more similar than they were different. He said they differ primarily in terms of the types of situational and follower characteristics upon which various leader behaviors should be contingent.

Leader–Member Exchange (LMX) Theory

In Chapter 1 we first noted a contingency when we mentioned the "in-group" and "out-group" interactions between leaders and followers. These relationships were originally described as vertical dyad linkages[3] but have developed over time into what is most often referred to today as **leader–member exchanges** (LMX). The main premise of these theories has remained unchanged, however. Fundamentally, LMX argues that leaders do not treat all followers as if they were a uniform group of equals. Rather, the leader forms specific and unique linkages with each subordinate, thus creating a series of dyadic relationships. In general, as just noted, the linkages tend to be differentiated into two major groups.

In the out-group, or low-quality exchange relationships, interpersonal interaction is largely restricted to fulfilling contractual obligations.[4] With other subordinates (the in-group), leaders form high-quality exchange relationships that go well beyond "just what the job requires." These high-quality relationships are indeed "exchanges" because both parties benefit. In exchange for higher levels of task performance[5] from subordinates, leaders may contribute empowerment,[6] sponsorship of subordinates in social networks,[7] and mentoring.[8]

There has been considerable evolution in leader–member exchange research and thinking in the last 20 years. Early on, the focus was on stages of development as the process of the relationship developed over time. These stages typically were described as follows:

1. **Role-taking** happens early in a follower's work experience. Here the leader offers opportunities and evaluates the follower's performance and potential.
2. **Role-making** is the next phase where a role is created based on a process of trust building. This is a fragile stage, and any perceived betrayals can lead to the follower being dropped from the developing in-group and assigned to the out-group.
3. **Routinization** occurs as the relationship becomes well established. It is in this phase that similarities (for the in-group) and differences (often accentuated for the out-group) become cemented.

TABLE 13.1
The Cycle of
Leadership Making

Source: Adapted from G. B.
Graen and M. Uhl-Bien,
"Relationship-Based
Approach to Leadership:
Development of Leader–
Member Exchange (LMX)
Theory over 25 Years: Apply-
ing a Multi-Level Multi-
Domain Perspective,"
Leadership Quarterly 6 (1995),
pp. 219–47.

	TIME →		
Characteristic	**Stranger**	**Acquaintance**	**Maturity**
Relationship building phase	Role-taking	Role-making	Role routinization
Reciprocity	Cash and carry	Mixed	In-kind
Time span of reciprocity	Immediate	Some delay	Indefinite
Leader–member exchange	Low	Medium	High
Incremental influence	None	Limited	Almost unlimited

Perhaps the biggest leap forward in LMX came 25 years after its introduction in an article by Graen and Uhl-Bien.[9] In this publication, the authors expanded the descriptive portion of the model, which continued to
focus on the dyadic processes between the leader and followers. However,
the model also changed from merely describing the process to proposing
a prescriptive process that would enhance organizational effectiveness.
Most of us can identify with the descriptive components of LMX portion
by thinking back to coaches or teachers from our past that had in-groups
and out-groups. Now the model suggests behaviors that the leader should
engage in to actively develop relationships (hence the prescriptive label)
and build more in-group relations across the follower pool. This process
of leadership is outlined in Table 13.1.

The LMX leadership making process moves from left to right in the table as indicated by the time arrow. Perhaps most important in the prescriptive notion of the model is the focus on the leader's responsibility to
enhance overall organizational effectiveness by developing more in-
groups and reducing the number of out-groups. In summary, the leadership making process prescribes that the leader should work to develop
special relationships with *all* followers, should offer each follower an opportunity for new roles, responsibilities, and challenges, should nurture
high-quality exchanges with all followers, and should focus on ways to
build trust and respect with all subordinates—resulting in the entire work
group becoming an in-group rather than accentuating the differences between in-groups and out-groups.

Concluding Thoughts about the LMX Model

In its earlier form (the vertical dyad linkage model), LMX was one of the
simplest of the contingency models. Looking at our leader–follower–
situation model, it is easy to see that LMX, even today, is largely about the

process of relationship building between the leader and the follower. The situation has barely crept in, and only if we consider the desire to increase organizational effectiveness by maximizing the number of in-groups the leader might develop. From an application perspective, perhaps the biggest limitation of LMX is that it does not describe the specific behaviors that lead to high-quality relationship exchanges between the leader and the follower. Nonetheless, LMX, as opposed to some of the subsequent contingency models, continues to generate research into the present decade.[10,11]

The Normative Decision Model

Obviously in some situations leaders can delegate decisions to subordinates or should ask subordinates for relevant information before making a decision. In other situations, such as emergencies or crises, leaders may need to make a decision with little, if any, input from subordinates. The level of input that subordinates have in the decision-making process varies substantially depending on the issue at hand, followers' level of technical expertise, or the presence or absence of a crisis. Although the level of participation changes due to various leader, follower, and situational factors,[12] Vroom and Yetton maintained that leaders can often improve group performance by using an optimal amount of participation in the decision-making process. Thus the normative decision model is directed solely at determining how much input subordinates should have in the decision-making process. Precisely because the normative decision model is limited only to decision making and is not a grand, all-encompassing theory, it is a good model to examine next.

Levels of Participation

Like the other theories in this chapter, the **normative decision model**[13] was designed to improve some aspects of leadership effectiveness. In this case Vroom and Yetton explored how various leader, follower, and situational factors affect the degree of subordinates' participation in the decision-making process and, in turn, group performance. To determine which situational and follower factors affect the level of participation and group performance, Vroom and Yetton first investigated the decision-making processes leaders use in group settings. They discovered a continuum of decision-making processes ranging from completely autocratic (labeled "AI") to completely democratic, where all members of the group have equal participation (labeled "GII"). These processes are listed in Highlight 13.1.

Decision Quality and Acceptance

After establishing a continuum of decision processes, Vroom and Yetton[14] established criteria to evaluate the adequacy of the decisions made—criteria they believed would be credible to leaders and equally applicable

Levels of Participation in the Normative Decision Model

HIGHLIGHT 13.1

Autocratic Processes

AI: The leader solves the problem or makes the decision by himself or herself using the information available at the time.

AII: The leader obtains any necessary information from followers, then decides on a solution to the problem herself. She may or may not tell followers the purpose of her questions or give information about the problem or decision she is working on. The input provided by them is clearly in response to her request for specific information. They do not play a role in the definition of the problem or in generating or evaluating alternative solutions.

Consultative Processes

CI: The leader shares the problem with the relevant followers individually, getting their ideas and suggestions without bringing them together as a group. Then he makes a decision. This decision may or may not reflect the followers' influence.

CII: The leader shares the problem with her followers in a group meeting. In this meeting, she obtains their ideas and suggestions. Then she makes the decision, which may or may not reflect the followers' influence.

Group Process

GII: The leader shares the problem with his followers as a group. Together they generate and evaluate alternatives and attempt to reach agreement (consensus) on a solution. The leader's role is much like that of a chairman, coordinating the discussion, keeping it focused on the problem, and making sure the critical issues are discussed. He can provide the group with information or ideas that he has, but he does not try to press them to adopt "his" solution. Moreover, leaders adopting this level of participation are willing to accept and implement any solution that has the support of the entire group.

Source: Adapted from V. H. Vroom and P. W. Yetton, *Leadership and Decision Making* (Pittsburgh, PA: University of Pittsburgh Press, 1973).

across the five levels of participation. Although a wide variety of criteria could be used, Vroom and Yetton believed decision quality and decision acceptance were the two most important criteria for judging the adequacy of a decision.

Decision quality means simply that if the decision has a rational or objectively determinable "better or worse" alternative, the leader should select the better alternative. Vroom and Yetton[15] intended quality in their model to apply when the decision could result in an objectively or measurably better outcome for the group or organization. In the for-profit sector, this criterion can be assessed in several ways, but perhaps the easiest to understand is, "Would the decision show up on the balance sheet?" In this case, a high-quality (or, conversely, low-quality) decision would have a direct and measurable impact on the organization's bottom line. In the public sector, we might determine if there was a quality component to a decision by asking, "Will one alternative have a greater cost saving than the other?" or "Does this decision improve services to the client?" Although it may seem that leaders should always choose the alternative with the highest decision quality, this is not always the case. Often leaders have equally good (or bad) alternatives. At other times, the issue in question is trivial, rendering the quality of the decision relatively unimportant.

Decision acceptance implies that followers accept the decision as if it were their own and do not merely comply with the decision. Acceptance of the decision outcome by the followers may be critical, particularly if the followers will bear principal responsibility for implementing the decision. With such acceptance, there will be no need for superiors to monitor compliance, which can be a continuing and time-consuming activity (and virtually impossible in some circumstances, such as with a geographically dispersed sales staff).

As with quality, acceptance of a decision is not always critical for implementation. For example, most organizations have an accounting form that employees use to obtain reimbursement for travel expenses. Suppose a company's chief financial officer (CFO) has decided to change the format of the form for reimbursing travel expenses and has had the new forms printed and distributed throughout the company. Further, she has sent out a notice that, effective June 1, the old forms will no longer be accepted for reimbursement—only claims made using the new forms will be processed and paid. Assuming the new form has no gross errors, problems, or omissions, our CFO really has no concern with acceptance as defined here. If people want to be reimbursed for their travel expenses, they will use the new form. This decision, in essence, implements itself.

On the other hand, leaders sometimes assume that they do not need to worry about acceptance because they have so much power over their followers that overt rejection of a decision is not likely to occur. A corporate CEO is not apt to see a junior accountant stand up and openly challenge the CEO's decision to implement a new policy, even though the young accountant may not buy into the new policy at all. Because followers generally do not openly object to the decisions made by leaders with this much power, these leaders often mistakenly assume that their decisions have been accepted and will be fully implemented. This is a naive view of what really goes on in organizations. Just because the junior subordinate does not publicly voice his opposition does not mean he will rush to wholeheartedly implement the decision. In fact, the junior accountant has a lot more time to destructively undermine the policy than the CEO does to ensure that it is being carried out to the letter.

The Decision Tree

Having settled on quality and acceptance as the two principal criteria for effective decisions, Vroom and Yetton then developed a normative decision model. (A normative model is based on what ought to happen rather than describing what does happen.) They also developed a set of questions to protect quality and acceptance by eliminating decision processes

FIGURE 13.1
Vroom and Yetton's Leadership Decision Tree

Source: Reprinted from V. H. Vroom and P. W. Yetton, *Leadership and Decision Making*, by permission of the University of Pittsburgh Press, © 1973 University of Pittsburgh Press.

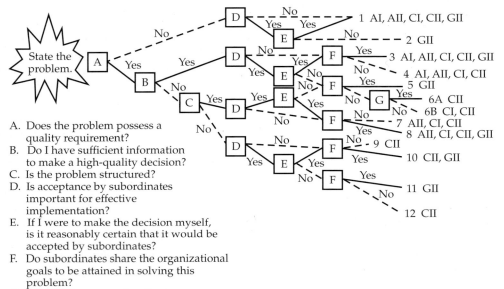

A. Does the problem possess a quality requirement?
B. Do I have sufficient information to make a high-quality decision?
C. Is the problem structured?
D. Is acceptance by subordinates important for effective implementation?
E. If I were to make the decision myself, is it reasonably certain that it would be accepted by subordinates?
F. Do subordinates share the organizational goals to be attained in solving this problem?
G. Is conflict among subordinates over preferred solutions likely?

that would be wrong or inappropriate. Generally, these questions concern the problem itself, the amount of pertinent information possessed by the leader and followers, and various situational factors.

To make it easier for leaders to determine how much participation subordinates should have to optimize decision quality and acceptance, Vroom and Yetton[16] incorporated these questions into a decision tree (see Figure 13.1). To use the decision tree, we start at the left by stating the problem and then proceed through the model from left to right. Every time a box is encountered, the question associated with that box must be answered with either a yes or a no response. Eventually all paths lead to a set of decision processes that, if used, will lead to a decision that protects both quality and acceptance.

Having reached a set of feasible alternatives that meet the desirable criteria for quality and acceptance among followers, the leader may then wish to consider additional criteria. One practical consideration is the amount of time available (see Highlight 13.2). If time is critical, the leader should select the alternative in the feasible set that is farthest to the *left*, again noting that the feasible set is arranged from AI through GII. It generally takes less time to make and implement autocratic decisions than it does to make consultative or group decisions. Nevertheless, the first step

How Much Time Do I Have?

HIGHLIGHT 13.2

In a world of instant messages that require lightning-fast responses, Steven B. Sample, president of the University of Southern California, is touting the benefits of "artful procrastination." In his course on leadership and his book *The Contrarian's Guide to Leadership,* a key lesson is never make a decision today that can reasonably be put off to tomorrow:

> With respect to timing, almost all great leaders have understood that making quick decisions is typically counterproductive. I'm not talking about what to have for breakfast or what tie to wear today. President Harry Truman almost personified this concept. When anyone told him they needed a decision, the first thing he would ask is "How much time do I have—a week, 10 seconds, six months?" What he understood was that the nature of the

decision that a leader makes depends to a large extent on how much time he has in which to make it. He also understood that delaying a decision as long as reasonably possible generally leads to the best decisions being made.

Other lessons from Sample include these:

- Think gray. Don't form opinions if you don't have to.
- Think free. Move several steps beyond traditional brainstorming.
- Listen first, talk later. And when you listen, do so artfully.
- You can't copy your way to the top.

Sources: http://www.usc.edu/president/book/; http://www.refresher.com/!enescontrarian.html; http://bottomlinesecrets.com/blpnet/article.html?article_id=33302.

is to protect quality and acceptance (by using the model). Only *after* arriving at an appropriate set of outcomes should leaders consider time in the decision-making process. This tenet is sometimes neglected in the workplace by leaders who overemphasize time as a criterion. Obviously there are some situations where time is absolutely critical, as in life-or-death emergencies. Certainly no one would have expected U.S. Airways Captain Chesley "Sully" Sullenberger to pull out his Vroom-Yetton decision model after his Airbus A320 struck a flock of geese and he found himself plummeting toward the Hudson River in what had become a very large glider. But too often leaders ask for a decision to be made as if the situation were an emergency when, in reality, they (the leaders, not the situation) are creating the time pressure. Despite such behavior, it is difficult to imagine a leader who would knowingly prefer a fast decision that lacks both quality and acceptance among the implementers to one that is of high quality and acceptable to followers but that takes more time.

Another important consideration is follower development. Again, after quality and acceptance have been considered using the decision tree, and if the leader has determined that time is not a critical element, she may wish to follow a decision process more apt to allow followers to develop their own decision-making skills. This can be achieved by using the decision tree and then selecting the alternative within the feasible set that is farthest to the *right.* The arrangement of processes from AI to GII provides an increasing amount of follower development by moving from autocratic to group decisions.

Finally, if neither time nor follower development is a concern and multiple options are available in the feasible set of alternatives, the leader may select a style that best meets his or her needs. This may be the process with which the leader is most comfortable ("I'm a CII kind of guy"), or it may be a process in which he or she would like to develop more skill.

Concluding Thoughts about the Normative Decision Model

Having looked at this model in some detail, we will now look at it from the perspective of the leader–follower–situation (L-F-S) framework. To do this, we have used the different decision processes and the questions from the decision tree to illustrate different components in the L-F-S framework (see Figure 13.2). Several issues become apparent in this depiction. First,

FIGURE 13.2
Factors from the Normative Decision Model and the Interactional Framework

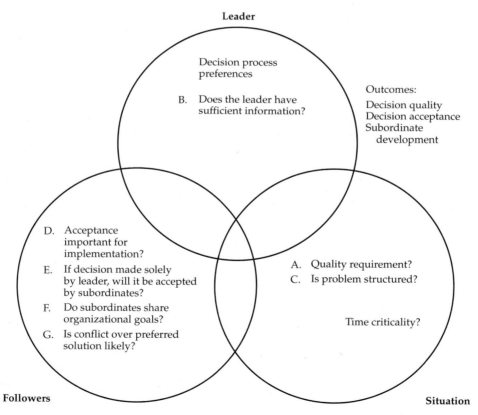

*Irrationally held truths
may be more harmful
than reasoned errors.*
Thomas Huxley

for ease of presentation we have placed each question or factor solely within one circle or another. Nevertheless, we could argue that some of the questions could or should be placed in another part of the model. For example, the question "Do I have sufficient information to make a high-quality decision?" is placed in the leader block. It might be argued, however, that no leader could answer this question without some knowledge of the situation. Strictly speaking, therefore, perhaps this question should be placed in the intersection between the leader and the situation. Nonetheless, in keeping with our theme that leadership involves interactions among all three elements, it seems sufficient at this point to illustrate them in their simplest state.

A second issue also becomes apparent when the normative decision model is viewed through the L-F-S framework. Notice how the Vroom and Yetton[17] model shifts focus away from the leader toward both the situation and, to an even greater degree, the followers. There are no questions about the leader's personality, motivations, values, or attitudes. In fact, the leader's preference is considered only after higher-priority factors have been considered. The only underlying assumption is that the leader is interested in implementing a high-quality decision (when quality is an issue) that is acceptable to followers (when acceptance is critical to implementation). Given that assumption and a willingness to consider aspects of the situation and aspects of the followers, the leader's behavior can be channeled into more effective decision-making processes.

A third issue is that the L-F-S framework organizes concepts in a familiar conceptual structure. This is an advantage even for a theory with as limited a focus as the normative decision model (that is, decision making); it will be even more helpful later as we consider more complex theories.

Finally, because the normative decision model is a *leadership theory* rather than Vroom and Yetton's personal opinions, a number of empirical studies have investigated the model's efficacy. Research conducted by Field[18] and Vroom and Jago[19,20] provided strong support for the model; these studies showed that leaders were much more likely to make effective or successful decisions when they followed its tenets than when they ignored them. Nevertheless, although leaders may be more apt to make effective decisions when using the model, there is no evidence to show that these leaders are more effective overall than leaders not using the model.[21] The latter findings again point out that both the leadership process and leadership effectiveness are complex phenomena; being a good decision maker is not enough to be a good leader (although it certainly helps). Other problems with the model are that it views decision making as taking place at a single point in time,[22] assumes that leaders are equally skilled at using all five decision procedures,[23] and assumes that some of the prescriptions of the model may not be the best for a given situation. For example, the normative decision model prescribes that leaders use a GII decision process if conflict may occur over a decision, but leaders may be more effective if they instead make an AI decision and avoid intra-group conflict.[24] Despite these problems, the normative model is one of the best supported of the five major contingency theories of leadership, and leaders would be wise to consider using the model when making decisions.

The Situational Leadership® Model

It seems fairly obvious that leaders do not interact with all followers in the same manner. For example, a leader may give general guidelines or goals to her highly competent and motivated followers but spend considerable time coaching, directing, and training her unskilled and unmotivated followers. Or leaders may provide relatively little praise and assurances to followers with high self-confidence but high amounts of support to followers with low self-confidence. Although leaders often have different interactional styles when dealing with individual followers, is there an optimum way for leaders to adjust their behavior with different followers and thereby increase their likelihood of success? And if there is, what factors should the leader base his behavior on—the follower's intelligence? Personality traits? Values? Preferences? Technical competence? A model called **Situational Leadership**® offers answers to these two important leadership questions.

Leader Behaviors

The Situational Leadership® model has evolved over time. Its essential elements first appeared in 1969,[25] with roots in the Ohio State studies, in which the two broad categories of leader behaviors, initiating structure and consideration, were initially identified (see Chapter 7). As Situational Leadership® evolved, so did the labels (but not the content) for the two leadership behavior categories. Initiating structure changed to **task behaviors,** which were defined as the extent to which a leader spells out the responsibilities of an individual or group. Task behaviors include telling people what to do, how to do it, when to do it, and who is to do it. Similarly, consideration changed to **relationship behaviors,** or how much the leader engages in two-way communication. Relationship behaviors include listening, encouraging, facilitating, clarifying, explaining why a task is important, and giving support.

When the behavior of actual leaders was studied, there was little evidence to show these two categories of leader behavior were consistently related to leadership success; the relative effectiveness of these two behavior dimensions often depended on the situation. Hersey's Situational Leadership® model explains why leadership effectiveness varies across these two behavior dimensions and situations. It arrays the two orthogonal dimensions as in the Ohio State studies and then divides each of them

FIGURE 13.3
Situational
Leadership®

Source: P. Hersey, K.
Blanchard, and D. Johnson,
*Management of Organizational
Behavior: Utilizing Human
Resources,* 7th ed.
(Englewood Cliffs, NJ:
Prentice Hall, 1996), p. 200.
Copyright © 2006. Reprinted
with permission of the
Center for Leadership
Studies, Inc., Escondido, CA
92025. All rights reserved.

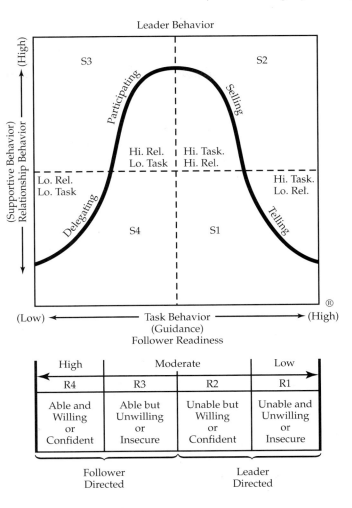

into high and low segments (see Figure 13.3). According to the model, depicting the two leadership dimensions this way is useful because certain combinations of task and relationship behaviors may be more effective in some situations than in others.

For example, in some situations high levels of task but low levels of relationship behaviors are effective; in other situations, just the opposite is true. So far, however, we have not considered the key follower or situational characteristics with which these combinations of task and relationship behaviors are most effective. Hersey says these four combinations of task and relationship behaviors would increase leadership effectiveness if they were made contingent on the readiness level of the individual follower to perform a given task.

Follower Readiness

In Situational Leadership®, **follower readiness** refers to a follower's ability and willingness to accomplish a particular task. Readiness is not an assessment of an individual's personality, traits, values, age, and so on. It's not a personal characteristic, but rather how ready an individual is to perform a particular task. Any given follower could be low on readiness to perform one task but high on readiness to perform a different task. An experienced emergency room physician would be high in readiness on tasks like assessing a patient's medical status, but could be relatively low on readiness for facilitating an interdepartmental team meeting to solve an ambiguous and complex problem like developing hospital practices to encourage collaboration across departments.

Prescriptions of the Model

Now that the key contingency factor, follower readiness, has been identified, let us move on to another aspect of the figure—combining follower readiness levels with the four combinations of leader behaviors described earlier. The horizontal bar in Figure 13.3 depicts follower readiness as increasing from right to left (not in the direction we are used to seeing). There are four segments along this continuum, ranging from R1 (the lowest) to R4 (the highest). Along this continuum, however, the assessment of follower readiness can be fairly subjective. A follower who possesses high levels of readiness would clearly fall in the R4 category, just as a follower unable and unwilling (or too insecure) to perform a task would fall in R1.

To complete the model, a curved line is added that represents the leadership behavior that will most likely be effective given a particular level of follower readiness. To apply the model, leaders should first assess the readiness level (R1–R4) of the follower relative to the task to be accomplished. Next a vertical line should be drawn from the center of the readiness level up to the point where it intersects with the curved line in Figure 13.3. The quadrant in which this intersection occurs represents the level of task and relationship behavior that has the best chance of producing successful outcomes. For example, imagine you are a fire chief and have under your command a search-and-rescue team. One of the team members is needed to rescue a backpacker who has fallen in the mountains, and you have selected a particular follower to accomplish the task. What leadership behavior should you exhibit? If this follower has both substantial training and experience in this type of rescue, you would assess his readiness level as R4. A vertical line from R4 would intersect the curved line in the quadrant where both low task and low relationship behaviors by the leader are most apt to be successful. As the leader, you should exhibit a low level of task and relationship behaviors and delegate this task to the follower. On the other hand, you may have a brand-new member of the fire department who still has to learn the ins and outs of firefighting.

A Developmental Intervention Using SLT

HIGHLIGHT 13.3

Dianne is a resident assistant in charge of a number of students in a university dorm. One particular sophomore, Michael, has volunteered to work on projects in the past but never seems to take the initiative to get started on his own. Michael seems to wait until Dianne gives him explicit direction, approval, and encouragement before he will get started. Michael can do a good job, but he seems to be unwilling to start without some convincing that it is all right, and unless Dianne makes explicit what steps are to be taken. Dianne has assessed Michael's readiness level as R2, but she would like to see him develop, both in task readiness and in psychological maturity. The behavior most likely to fit Michael's current readiness level is selling, or high task, high relationship. But Dianne has decided to implement a developmental intervention to help Michael raise his readiness level. Dianne can be most helpful in this intervention by moving up one level to participating, or low task, high relationship. By reducing the amount of task instructions and direction while encouraging Michael to lay out a plan on his own and supporting his steps in the right direction, Dianne is most apt to help Michael become an R3 follower. This does not mean the work will get done most efficiently, however. As we saw in the Vroom and Yetton model earlier, if part of the leader's job is development of followers, then time may be a reasonable and necessary trade-off for short-term efficiency.

Because this particular follower has low task readiness (R1), the model maintains that the leader should use a high level of task and a low level of relationship behaviors when initially dealing with this follower.

Hersey suggests one further step leaders may wish to consider. The model just described helps the leader select the most appropriate behavior given the current level of follower readiness. However, there may be cases when the leader would like to see followers increase their level of readiness for particular tasks by implementing a series of **developmental interventions** to help boost follower readiness levels. The process would begin by first assessing a follower's current level of readiness and then determining the leader behavior that best suits that follower in that task. Instead of using the behavior prescribed by the model, however, the leader would select the next higher leadership behavior. Another way of thinking about this would be for the leader to select the behavior pattern that would fit the follower if that follower were one level higher in readiness. This intervention is designed to help followers in their development, hence its name (see Highlight 13.3).

Concluding Thoughts about the Situational Leadership® Model

In Figure 13.4 we can see how the factors in Situational Leadership® fit within the L-F-S framework. In comparison to the Vroom and Yetton model, there are fewer factors to consider in each of the three elements. The only situational consideration is knowledge of the task, and the only

FIGURE 13.4
Factors from the Situational Leadership® Model and the Interactional Framework

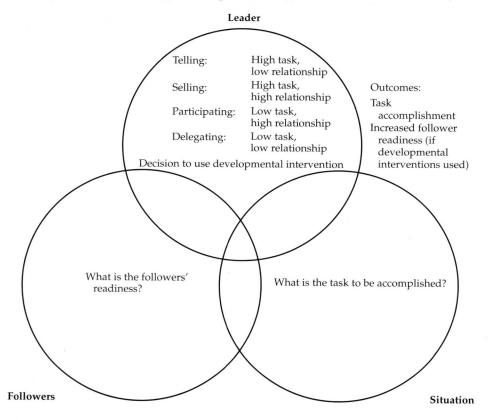

Leader

Telling: High task,
                low relationship
Selling: High task,
                high relationship
Participating: Low task,
                high relationship
Delegating: Low task,
                low relationship
Decision to use developmental intervention

Outcomes:
Task
  accomplishment
Increased follower
  readiness (if
  developmental
  interventions used)

What is the followers' readiness?

What is the task to be accomplished?

Followers

Situation

follower factor is readiness. On the other hand, the theory goes well beyond decision making, which was the sole domain of the normative decision model.

Situational Leadership® is usually appealing to students and practitioners because of its commonsense approach as well as the ease of understanding it. Unfortunately there is little published research to support the predictions of Situational Leadership® in the workplace.[26,27] A great deal of research has been done within organizations that have implemented Situational Leadership®, but most of those findings are not available for public dissemination.

In 2007 Blanchard modified the Situational Leadership® prescriptions to specify more clearly the four definitions of follower developmental level and their four corresponding optimal styles of leadership.[28] Although this revision of the model, perhaps as a result of much criticism concerning the lack of prescriptive specificity, does create a more discrete typology of follower styles, recent research suggests that the original model is a better predictor of subordinate performance and attitudes than the revised version.[29]

Nevertheless, even with these shortcomings, Situational Leadership® is a useful way to get leaders to think about how leadership effectiveness may depend somewhat on being flexible with different subordinates, not on acting the same way toward them all.

The Contingency Model

Although leaders may be able to change their behaviors toward individual subordinates, leaders also have dominant behavioral tendencies. Some leaders may be generally more supportive and relationship-oriented, whereas others may be more concerned with task or goal accomplishment. The contingency model[30] recognizes that leaders have these general behavioral tendencies and specifies situations where certain leaders (or behavioral dispositions) may be more effective than others.

Fiedler's[31] **contingency model** of leadership is probably the earliest and most well-known contingency theory, and is often perceived by students to be almost the opposite of SLT. Compared to the contingency model, SLT emphasizes flexibility in leader behaviors, whereas the contingency model maintains that leaders are much more consistent (and consequently less flexible) in their behavior. Situational Leadership theory maintains that leaders who *correctly base their behaviors* on follower maturity will be more effective, whereas the contingency model suggests that leader effectiveness is primarily determined by *selecting the right kind of leader for a certain situation or changing the situation* to fit the particular leader's style. Another way to say this is that leadership effectiveness depends on both the leader's style and the favorableness of the leadership situation. Some leaders are better than others in some situations but less effective in other situations. To understand contingency theory, therefore, we need to look first at the critical characteristics of the leader and then at the critical aspects of the situation.

The Least Preferred Co-worker Scale

To determine a leader's general style or tendency, Fiedler developed an instrument called the **least preferred co-worker (LPC) scale.** The scale instructs a leader to think of the single individual with whom he has had the greatest difficulty working (that is, the least preferred co-worker) and then to describe that individual in terms of a series of bipolar adjectives (such as friendly–unfriendly, boring–interesting, and sincere–insincere). Those ratings are then converted into a numerical score.

In thinking about such a procedure, many people assume that the score is determined primarily by the characteristics of whatever particular individual the leader happened to identify as his least preferred co-worker. In the context of contingency theory, however, the score is thought to *represent something about the leader, not the specific individual the leader evaluated.*

The current interpretation of these scores is that they identify a leader's *motivation hierarchy.*[32] Based on their LPC scores, leaders are categorized into two groups: **low-LPC leaders** and **high-LPC leaders.** In terms of their motivation hierarchy, low-LPC leaders are motivated primarily by the task, which means these leaders gain satisfaction primarily from task accomplishment. Thus their dominant behavioral tendencies are similar to the initiating structure behavior described in the Ohio State research or the task behavior of SLT. However, if tasks are being accomplished in an acceptable manner, low-LPC leaders will move to their secondary level of motivation, which is forming and maintaining relationships with followers. Thus low-LPC leaders will focus on improving their relationships with followers *after* they are assured that assigned tasks are being satisfactorily accomplished. If tasks are no longer being accomplished in an acceptable manner, however, low-LPC leaders will refocus their efforts on task accomplishment and persist with these efforts until task accomplishment is back on track.

In terms of motivation hierarchy, high-LPC leaders are motivated primarily by relationships, which means these leaders are satisfied primarily by establishing and maintaining close interpersonal relationships. Thus their dominant behavioral tendencies are similar to the consideration behaviors described in the Ohio State research or the relationship behaviors in SLT. If high-LPC leaders have established good relationships with their followers, they will move to their secondary level of motivation, which is task accomplishment. As soon as leader–follower relations are jeopardized, however, high-LPC leaders will cease working on tasks and refocus their efforts on improving relationships with followers.

You can think of the LPC scale as identifying two different sorts of leaders, with their respective motivational hierarchies depicted in Figure 13.5. Lower-level needs must be satisfied first. Low-LPC leaders will move "up" to satisfying relationship needs when they are assured the task is being satisfactorily accomplished. High-LPC leaders will move "up" to emphasizing task accomplishment when they have established good relationships with their followers.

Because all tests have some level of imprecision, Fiedler[33] suggested that the LPC scale cannot accurately identify the motivation hierarchy for individuals with intermediate scores. Research by Kennedy[34] suggested an alternative view. Kennedy has shown that individuals within the intermediate range of LPC scale scores may more easily or readily switch between being task- or relationship-oriented leaders than those individuals with more extreme scale scores. They may be equally satisfied by working on the task or establishing relationships with followers.

FIGURE 13.5
Motivational
Hierarchies for
Low- and High-LPC
Leaders

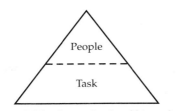

Low-LPC leader motivational hierarchy

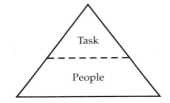

High-LPC leader motivational hierarchy

Situational Favorability

The other important variable in the contingency model is **situational favorability,** which is the amount of control the leader has over the followers. Presumably the more control a leader has over followers, the more favorable the situation is, at least from the leader's perspective. Fiedler included three subelements in situation favorability. These were leader–member relations, task structure, and position power.

Leader–member relations are the most powerful of the three subelements in determining overall situation favorability. They involve the extent to which relationships between the leader and followers are generally cooperative and friendly or antagonistic and difficult. Leaders who rate leader–member relations as high feel they have the support of their followers and can rely on their loyalty.

Task structure is second in potency in determining overall situation favorability. Here the leader objectively determines task structure by assessing whether there are detailed descriptions of work products, standard operating procedures, or objective indicators of how well the task is being accomplished. The more one can answer these questions affirmatively, the higher the structure of the task.

Position power is the weakest of the three elements of situational favorability. Leaders who have titles of authority or rank, the authority to administer rewards and punishments, and the legitimacy to conduct follower performance appraisals have greater position power than leaders who lack them.

The relative weights of these three components, taken together, can be used to create a continuum of situational favorability. When using the

FIGURE 13.6
Contingency Model Octant Structure for Determining Situational Favorability

	High ← Overall situation favorability						Low
Leader–member relations	Good				Poor		
Task structure	Structured		Unstructured		Structured		Unstructured
Position power	High	Low	High	Low	High	Low	High	Low
Octant	1	2	3	4	5	6	7	8

contingency model, leaders are first asked to rate items that measure the strength of leader–member relations, the degree of task structure, and their level of position power. These ratings are then weighted and combined to determine an overall level of situational favorability facing the leader.[35] Any particular situation's favorability can be plotted on a continuum Fiedler divided into octants representing distinctly different levels of situational favorability. The relative weighting scheme for the subelements and how they make up each of the eight octants are shown in Figure 13.6.

You can see that the octants of situational favorability range from 1 (highly favorable) to 8 (very unfavorable). The highest levels of situational favorability occur when leader–member relations are good, the task is structured, and position power is high. The lowest levels of situational favorability occur when there are high levels of leader–member conflict, the task is unstructured or unclear, and the leader does not have the power to reward or punish subordinates. Moreover, the relative weighting of the three subelements can easily be seen by their order of precedence in Figure 13.6, with leader–member relations appearing first, followed by task structure, and then position power. For example, because leader–member relations carry so much weight, it is impossible for leaders with good leader–member relations to have anything worse than moderate situational favorability, regardless of their task structure or position power. In other words, leaders with good leader–member relations will enjoy situational favorability no worse than octant 4; leaders with poor leader–member relations will face situational favorability no better than octant 5.

Prescriptions of the Model

Fiedler and his associates have conducted numerous studies to determine how different leaders (as described by their LPC scores) have performed in different situations (as described in terms of situational favorability). Figure 13.7 describes which type of leader (high or low LPC) Fiedler found to be most effective, given different levels of situation favorability. The solid dark line represents the relative effectiveness of a low-LPC

FIGURE 13.7

Leader Effectiveness Based on the Contingency between Leader LPC Score and Situation Favorability

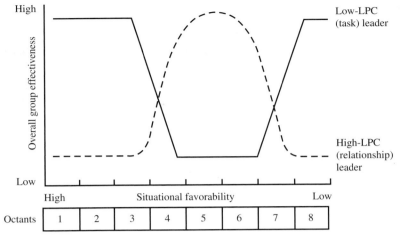

leader, and the dashed line represents the relative effectiveness of a high-LPC leader. It is obvious from the way the two lines cross and recross that there is some interaction between the leader's style and the overall situation favorability. If the situational favorability is moderate (octants 4, 5, 6, or 7), then those groups led by leaders concerned with establishing and maintaining relationships (high-LPC leaders) seem to do best. However, if the situation is either very unfavorable (octant 8) or highly favorable (octants 1, 2, or 3), then those groups led by the task-motivated (low-LPC) leaders seem to do best.

Fiedler suggested that leaders will try to satisfy their primary motivation when faced with unfavorable or moderately favorable situations. This means that low-LPC leaders will concentrate on the task and high-LPC leaders will concentrate on relationships when faced with these two levels of situational favorability. Nevertheless, leaders facing highly favorable situations know that their primary motivations will be satisfied and thus will move to their secondary motivational state. This means that *leaders will behave according to their secondary motivational state only when faced with highly favorable situations* (see Highlight 13.4).

Several interesting implications of Fiedler's[36] model are worthy of additional comment. Because leaders develop their distinctive motivation hierarchies and dominant behavior tendencies through a lifetime of experiences, Fiedler believed these hierarchies and tendencies would be difficult to change through training. Fiedler maintained it was naive to believe that sending someone to a relatively brief leadership training program could substantially alter any leader's personality or typical way of acting in leadership situations; after all, such tendencies had been developed over many years of experience. Instead of trying to change the leader,

High- and Low-LPC Leaders and the Contingency Model

HIGHLIGHT 13.4

Suppose we have two leaders, Tom Low (a low-LPC or task-motivated leader) and Brenda High (a high-LPC or relationship-motivated leader). In unfavorable situations, Tom will be motivated by his primary level and will thus exhibit task behaviors. In similar situations, Brenda will also be motivated by her primary level and as a result will exhibit relationship behaviors. Fiedler found that in unfavorable situations, task behavior will help the group to be more effective, so Tom's behavior would better match the requirements of the situation. Group effectiveness would not be aided by Brenda's relationship behavior in this situation.

In situations with moderate favorability, both Tom and Brenda are still motivated by their primary motivations, so their behaviors will remain the same. Because the situation has changed, however, group effectiveness no longer requires task behavior. Instead the combination of situational variables leads to a condition where a leader's relationship behaviors will make the greatest contribution to group effectiveness. Hence Brenda will be the most effective leader in situations of moderate favorability.

In highly favorable situations, Fiedler's explanation gets more complex. When leaders find themselves in highly favorable situations, they no longer have to be concerned about satisfying their primary motivations. In highly favorable situations, leaders switch to satisfying their secondary motivations. Because Tom's secondary motivation is to establish and maintain relationships, in highly favorable situations he will exhibit relationship behaviors. Similarly, Brenda will also be motivated by her secondary motivation, so she would manifest task behaviors in highly favorable situations. Fiedler believed that leaders who manifested relationship behaviors in highly favorable situations helped groups to be more effective. In this case, Tom is giving the group what it needs to be more effective.

Fiedler concluded, training would be more effective if it showed leaders how to recognize and change key situational characteristics to better fit their personal motivational hierarchies and behavioral tendencies. Thus, according to Fiedler, the content of leadership training should emphasize situational engineering rather than behavioral flexibility in leaders. Relatedly, organizations could become more effective if they matched the characteristics of the leader (in this case LPC scores) with the demands of the situation (situational favorability) than if they tried to change the leader's behavior to fit the situation. These suggestions imply that high- or low-LPC leaders in mismatched situations should either change the situation or move to jobs that better match their motivational hierarchies and behavioral patterns.

Concluding Thoughts about the Contingency Model

Before reviewing the empirical evidence, perhaps we can attain a clearer understanding of the contingency model by examining it through the L-F-S framework. As shown in Figure 13.8, task structure is a function of the situation, and LPC scores are a function of the leader. Because position power is not a characteristic of the leader but of the situation the leader finds himself

FIGURE 13.8
Factors from Fiedler's Contingency Theory and the Interactional Framework

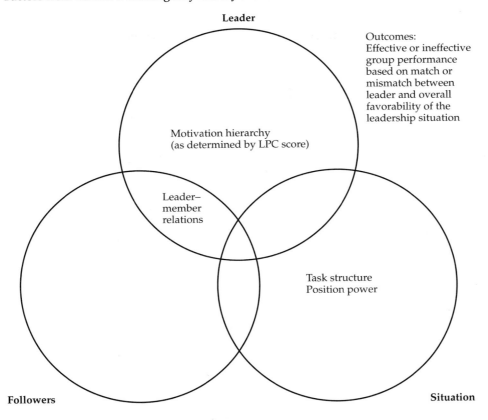

Leader

Outcomes:
Effective or ineffective
group performance
based on match or
mismatch between
leader and overall
favorability of the
leadership situation

Motivation hierarchy
(as determined by LPC score)

Leader–
member
relations

Task structure
Position power

Followers

Situation

or herself in, it is included in the situational circle. Leader–member relations are a joint function of the leader and the followers; thus they belong in the overlapping intersection of the leader and follower circles.

As opposed to the dearth of evidence for Hersey and Blanchard's[37,38] situational theory, Fiedler and his fellow researchers have provided considerable evidence that the predictions of the model are empirically valid, particularly in laboratory settings.[39–43] However, a review of the studies conducted in field settings yielded only mixed support for the model.[44] Moreover, researchers have criticized the model for the uncertainties surrounding the meaning of LPC scores,[45–47] the interpretation of situational favorability,[48,49] and the relationships between LPC scores and situational favorability.[50–52] Despite such questions, however, the contingency model has stimulated considerable research and is the most validated of all leadership theories.

The Path–Goal Theory

Perhaps the most sophisticated (and comprehensive) of the five contingency models is path–goal theory. The underlying mechanism of **path–goal theory** deals with expectancy—a cognitive approach to understanding motivation where people calculate effort-to-performance probabilities (If I study for 12 hours, what is the probability I will get an A on the final exam?), performance-to-outcome probabilities (If I get an A on the final, what is the probability of getting an A in the course?), and assigned valences or values of outcomes (How much do I value a higher GPA?). Theoretically at least, people are assumed to make these calculations on a rational basis, and the theory can be used to predict what tasks people will put their energies into, given some finite number of options.

Path–goal theory uses the same basic assumptions as expectancy theory. At the most fundamental level, the effective leader will provide or ensure the availability of valued rewards for followers (the goal) and then help them find the best way of getting there (the path). Along the way, the effective leader will help the followers identify and remove roadblocks and avoid dead ends; the leader will also provide emotional support as needed. These task and relationship leadership actions essentially involve increasing followers' probability estimates for effort-to-performance and performance-to-reward expectancies. In other words, the leader's actions should strengthen followers' beliefs that if they exert a certain level of effort, they will be more likely to accomplish a task, and if they accomplish the task, they will be more likely to achieve some valued outcome.

Although uncomplicated in its basic concept, the model has added more variables and interactions over time. Evans[53] is credited with the first version of path–goal theory, but we will focus on a later version developed by House and Dressler.[54] Their conceptual scheme is ideally suited to the L-F-S framework because they described three classes of variables that include leader behaviors, followers, and the situation. We will examine each of these in turn.

Leader Behaviors

The four types of leader behavior in path–goal theory can be seen in Table 13.2. Like SLT, path–goal theory assumes that leaders not only may use varying styles with different subordinates but might also use differing styles with the same subordinates in different situations. Path–goal theory suggests that, depending on the followers and the situation, these different leader behaviors can increase followers' acceptance of the leader, enhance their level of satisfaction, and raise their expectations that effort will result in effective performance, which in turn will lead to valued rewards (see Highlight 13.5).

**TABLE 13.2
The Four Leader
Behaviors of
Path–Goal Theory**

Directive leadership. These leader behaviors are similar to the task behaviors from SLT. They include telling the followers what they are expected to do, how to do it, when it is to be done, and how their work fits in with the work of others. This behavior would also include setting schedules, establishing norms, and providing expectations that followers will adhere to established procedure and regulations.

Supportive leadership. Supportive leadership behaviors include having courteous and friendly interactions, expressing genuine concern for the followers' well-being and individual needs, and remaining open and approachable to followers. These behaviors, which are similar to the relationship behaviors in SLT, also are marked by attention to the competing demands of treating followers equally while recognizing status differentials between the leader and the followers.

Participative leadership. Participative leaders engage in the behaviors that mark the consultative and group behaviors described by Vroom and Yetton.[56] As such, they tend to share work problems with followers; solicit their suggestions, concerns, and recommendations; and weigh these inputs in the decision-making process.

Achievement-oriented leadership. Leaders exhibiting these behaviors would be seen as both demanding and supporting in interactions with their followers. First they would set challenging goals for group and follower behavior, continually seek ways to improve performance en route, and expect the followers to always perform at their highest levels. But they would support these behaviors by exhibiting a high degree of ongoing confidence that subordinates can put forth the necessary effort; will achieve the desired results; and, even further, will assume even more responsibility in the future.

The Followers

Path–goal theory contains two groups of follower variables. The first relates to the *satisfaction of followers,* and the second relates to the *followers' perception of their own abilities* relative to the task to be accomplished. In terms of followers' satisfaction, path–goal theory suggests that leader behaviors will be acceptable to followers to the degree that followers see the leader's behavior either as an immediate source of satisfaction or as directly instrumental in achieving future satisfaction. In other words, followers will actively support a leader as long as they view the leader's actions as a means for increasing their own levels of satisfaction. However, there is only so much a leader can do to increase followers' satisfaction levels because satisfaction also depends on characteristics of the followers themselves.

A frequently cited example of how followers' characteristics influence the impact of leader behaviors on followers' levels of satisfaction involves the trait of locus of control. People who believe they are "masters of their own ship" are said to have an internal locus of control; people who believe

Shifting Behaviors at Caterpillar

HIGHLIGHT 13.5

James Despain was a leader with a very directive leadership style. He began his career at Caterpillar Inc. as a young man, sweeping the factory floor. He followed the lead of others of his generation—the 1950s were a time when leaders were the ultimate authority and words like *participative* and *consultative* were unheard of. Despain worked his way into supervisory positions and finally was named vice president of the track-type tractor division. Despain claims he "spent much of [his] career as a manager focusing on what employees were doing wrong." He focused on the tasks at hand and little else. But in the early 1990s Despain had to face some hard facts: his $1.2 billion division was losing millions of dollars per year, his management team was getting hundreds of grievances from their employees, and morale at the Caterpillar plant was extremely low.

Despain and his leadership group identified the need for a strategic plan to transform the working culture. Key to the plan was determining a strategy for dealing with employee attitudes and behavior. Despain and his transformation team identified nine behaviors or "common values" that they wanted every employee to emulate every day—trust, mutual respect, customer satisfaction, a sense of urgency, teamwork, empowerment, risk taking, continuous improvement, and commitment.

Employee evaluations were based on the manifestation of these behaviors. Above and beyond those behaviors, top executives and management were expected to lead by example and commit themselves to practice 100 positive leadership traits. Statements such as "I will know every one of my employees by name . . . will recognize their accomplishments with praise . . . will trust my employees to do their work" became the new mantras for those in charge.

Through this process, Despain came to understand that "the most important thing for employees in the workplace is to achieve self-worth." The principal change he was striving to achieve was to make employees accountable for how their jobs got done; for workers that meant stretching a little more every day to achieve their full potential. For managers it meant shifting away from achieving traditional metrics and toward drawing desired behavior from workers. "And we found that the more we focused on behavior, the better the metrics got." The result: Despain's division cut its break-even point in half within five years of launching the transformation.

Sources: http://www.tribuneindia.com/2004/20040509/spectrum/book2.htm; http://www.sodexho-usa.com/printer_friendly.htm; http://www.stchas.edu/press/despain.shtml

they are (relatively speaking) "pawns of fate" are said to have an external locus of control. Mitchell, Smyser, and Weed[55] found that follower satisfaction was not directly related to the degree of participative behaviors manifested by the leader; that is, followers with highly participative leaders were no more satisfied than followers with more autocratic leaders. However, when followers' locus-of-control scores were taken into account, a contingency relationship was discovered. As shown in Figure 13.9, internal-locus-of-control followers, who believed outcomes were a result of their own decisions, were much more satisfied with leaders who exhibited participative behaviors than they were with leaders who were directive. Conversely, external-locus-of-control followers were more satisfied with directive leader behaviors than they were with participative leader behaviors.

FIGURE 13.9
Interaction between Followers' Locus of Control Scores and Leader Behavior in Decision Making

Source: Adapted from T. R. Mitchell, C. M. Smyser, and S. E. Weed, "Locus of Control: Supervision and Work Satisfaction," *Academy of Management Journal* 18 (1975), pp. 623–30.

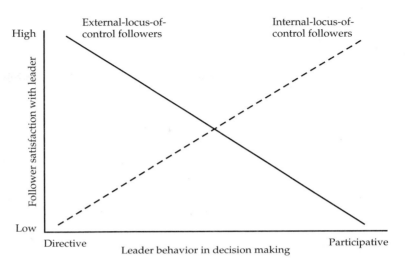

Followers' perceptions of their own skills and abilities to perform particular tasks can also affect the impact of certain leader behaviors. Followers who believe they are perfectly capable of performing a task are not as apt to be motivated by, or as willing to accept, a directive leader as they would a leader who exhibits participative behaviors. Using the same rationale as for locus of control, we can predict the opposite relationship for followers who do not perceive that they have sufficient abilities to perform a task. Once again, the acceptability of the leader and the motivation to perform are in part determined by followers' characteristics. Thus path–goal theory suggests that both leader behaviors and follower characteristics are important in determining outcomes.

The Situation

Path–goal theory considers three situational factors that impact or moderate the effects of leader behavior on follower attitudes and behaviors. These include *the task, the formal authority system,* and *the primary work group.* Each of these three factors can influence the leadership situation in one of three ways. These three factors can serve as an independent motivational factor, as a constraint on the behavior of followers (which may be either positive or negative in outcome), or as a reward.

However, these variables can often affect the impact of various leader behaviors. For example, if the task is structured and routine, the formal authority system has constrained followers' behaviors, and the work group has established clear norms for performance, then leaders would be serving a redundant purpose by manifesting directive or achievement-oriented behaviors. These prescriptions are similar to some of those noted in substitutes for leadership theory[57] because everything the follower needs to understand the effort-to-performance and performance-to-reward links is provided by the situation. Thus redundant leader behaviors might be interpreted by followers as either a complete lack of understanding or empathy by the leader, or an attempt by the leader to exert excessive control. Neither of these interpretations is likely to enhance the leader's acceptance by followers or increase their motivation.

Although we have already described how follower characteristics and situational characteristics can impact leader behaviors, path–goal theory also maintains that follower and situational variables can impact each other. In other words, situational variables, such as the task performed, can also impact the influence of followers' skills, abilities, or personality traits on followers' satisfaction. Although this seems to make perfect sense, we hope you are beginning to see how complicated path–goal theory can be when we start considering how situational variables, follower characteristics, and leader behaviors interact in the leadership process.

Prescriptions of the Theory

In general, path–goal theory maintains that leaders should first assess the situation and select a leadership behavior appropriate to situational demands. By manifesting the appropriate behaviors, leaders can increase followers' effort-to-performance expectancies, performance-to-reward expectancies, or valences of the outcomes. These increased expectancies and valences will improve subordinates' effort levels and the rewards attained, which in turn will increase subordinates' satisfaction and performance levels and the acceptance of their leaders. Perhaps the easiest way to explain this complicated process is through an example. Suppose we have a set of followers who are in a newly created work unit and do not understand the requirements of their positions. In other words, the followers have a high level of role ambiguity. According to path–goal theory, leaders should exhibit a high degree of directive behaviors to reduce the role ambiguity of their followers. The effort-to-performance link will become clearer when leaders tell followers what to do and how to do it in ambiguous situations, which in turn will cause followers to exert higher effort levels. Because role ambiguity is assumed to be unpleasant, these directive leader behaviors and higher effort levels should eventually result in higher satisfaction levels among followers. Figure 13.10 illustrates this process. Similarly, leaders may look at the leadership situation and note that followers' performance levels are not acceptable. The leader may also conclude that the current situation offers few, if any, incentives for increased performance. In this case the leader may use directive behaviors to increase the value of the rewards (or valence), which in turn will increase followers' effort levels and performance.

FIGURE 13.10
Examples of Applying Path–Goal Theory

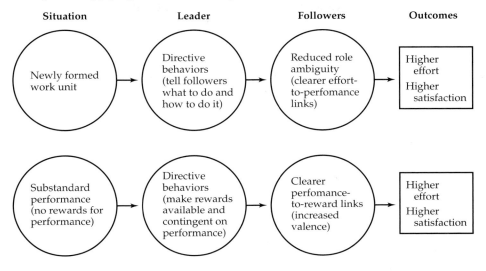

Concluding Thoughts about the Path–Goal Theory

Before getting into the research surrounding path–goal theory, you may wish to examine the theory using the L-F-S framework. As shown in Figure 13.11, the components of path–goal theory fit nicely into the L-F-S model. The four leader behaviors fit into the leader circle, the characteristics of the followers fit into the follower circle, and the task and the formal authority system fit into the situation circle. Of all the components of path–goal theory, the only "mismatch" with the L-F-S model deals with the primary work group. The norms, cohesiveness, size, and stage of development of groups are considered to be part of the follower function in the L-F-S model but are part of the situation function in path–goal theory. In that regard, we hasten to note we use the L-F-S framework primarily for heuristic purposes. Ultimately the concepts described in these five theories are sufficiently complex and ambiguous that there probably is no right answer in any single depiction.

In terms of research, the path–goal theory has received only mixed support to date.[58–61] Although many of these mixed findings may be due to the fact that the path–goal theory excludes many of the variables found to impact the leadership process, that may also be due to problems with the theory. Yukl[62] maintained that most of these criticisms deal with the methodology used to study path–goal theory and the limitations of expectancy theory. Moreover, the path–goal theory assumes that the only way to increase performance is to increase followers'

FIGURE 13.11
Factors from Path–Goal Theory and the Interactional Framework

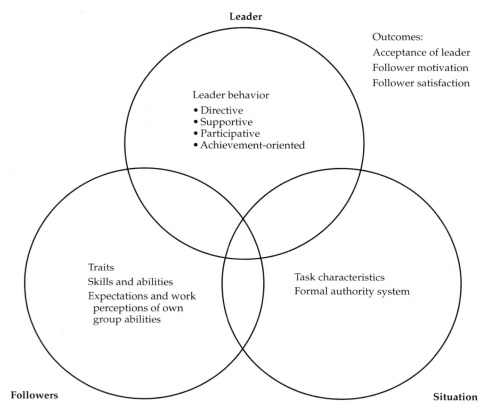

Leader

Leader behavior
• Directive
• Supportive
• Participative
• Achievement-oriented

Outcomes:
Acceptance of leader
Follower motivation
Follower satisfaction

Traits
Skills and abilities
Expectations and work
  perceptions of own
  group abilities

Task characteristics
Formal authority system

Followers

Situation

To act is easy; to think is hard.

Goethe

motivation levels. The theory ignores the roles leaders play in selecting talented followers, building their skill levels through training, and redesigning their work.[63]

Nonetheless, path–goal theory is useful for illustrating two points. First, as noted by Yukl,[64] "path–goal theory has already made a contribution to the study of leadership by providing a conceptual framework to guide researchers in identifying potentially relevant situational moderator variables." Path–goal theory also illustrates that, as models become more complicated, they may be more useful to researchers and less appealing to practitioners. Our experience is that pragmatically oriented students and in-place leaders want to take something from a model that is understandable and can be applied in their work situation right away. This does not mean they prefer simplicity to validity—they generally appreciate the complexity of the leadership process. But neither do they want a model that is so complex as to be indecipherable.

Summary

This chapter has provided an overview of five well-known contingency theories of leadership, which include leader–member exchange theory, the normative decision model,[65] the Situational Leadership® model, the contingency model[66] and the path–goal theory.[67] All five models are similar in that they specify that leaders should make their behaviors contingent on certain aspects of the followers or the situation to improve leadership effectiveness. In addition, all five theories implicitly assume that leaders can accurately assess key follower and situational factors. However, as the material regarding perception in Chapter 2 shows, it is entirely possible that two leaders in the same situation may reach different conclusions about followers' levels of knowledge, the strength of leader–follower relationships, the degree of task structure, or the level of role ambiguity being experienced by followers. These differences in perception could lead these two leaders to reach different conclusions about the situation, which may in turn cause them to take different actions in response to the situation. Furthermore, these actions may be in accordance or in conflict with the prescriptions of any of these five theories. Also, the fact that leaders' perceptions may have caused them to act in a manner not prescribed by a particular model may be an underlying reason why these five theories have reported conflicting findings, particularly in field settings.

Another reason these theories have generally found mixed support in field settings is that they are all limited in scope. Many factors that affect leader and follower behaviors in work group, team, or volunteer committee settings are not present in laboratory studies but often play a substantial role in field studies. For example, none of the models take into account how levels of stress, organizational culture and climate, working conditions, technology, economic conditions, or types of organizational design affect the leadership process. Nevertheless, the five contingency theories have been the subject of considerable research; and even if only mixed support for the models has been found, this research has added to our knowledge about leadership and has given us a more sophisticated understanding of the leadership process.

Key Terms

leader–member exchange, *521*
role-taking, *521*
role-making, *521*
routinization, *521*
normative decision model, *523*
decision quality, *524*

autocratic processes, *524*
consultative processes, *524*
group process, *524*
decision acceptance, *525*

Situational Leadership®, *530*
task behaviors, *530*
relationship behaviors, *530*
follower readiness, *532*

developmental
interventions, *533*
contingency
model, *535*
least preferred
co-worker (LPC)
scale, *535*
low-LPC leaders, *536*

high-LPC
leaders, *536*
situational
favorability, *537*
path–goal theory, *542*
directive
leadership, *543*

supportive
leadership, *543*
participative
leadership, *543*
achievement-oriented
leadership, *543*

Questions

1. Given the description of the leadership situation facing the airplane crash survivors described in Chapter 1, how would leader–member exchange, the normative decision model, the situational leadership theory, the contingency model, and the path–goal theory prescribe that a leader should act?

2. Can leaders be flexible in how they interact with others? Do you believe leaders can change their behavior? Their personalities?

3. Think of a leadership situation with which you are familiar. Apply each of the theories in this chapter to the situation. Which theory best fits the interaction of the leader, followers, and situation in your example? Does any theory allow you to predict a likely or preferred outcome for a current challenge?

Minicase

Big Changes for a Small Hospital

As F. Nicholas Jacobs toured the Windber Medical Center facility, he was dismayed by the industrial pink-painted walls, the circa-1970 furniture, and the snow leaking through the windows of the conference room. Employees earned 30 percent less than their counterparts in the area, and turnover was steep. As Windber's newest president, Jacobs knew he was the facility's last hope—if he couldn't successfully turn around the aging facility, it would mean closing the doors forever.

Coming to Windber Medical Center in 1997, Jacobs was keenly aware that the hospital could be the next in a series of small hospitals that had fallen victim to a struggling economy. Determined to see that not happen, he began by making connections with the employees of the hospital and the community at large. Jacobs's first step was to interview the employees to find out firsthand what they wanted for the Windber community and the medical center. He also looked to members of local community groups like the local library, the Agency on Aging, and local politicians and asked these groups what they wanted from their local medical facility. When Jacobs realized that octogenarians made up a larger percentage of the population in Windber, Pennsylvania, than in all of Dade County, Florida, he made it a priority to provide more options to seniors for improving their health and quality of life. He set forth a vision of a medical center that was more of a community center—a center that would allow members of the community to exercise in a state-of-the-art facility while having access to professionals to answer health-related questions. Jacobs realized that keeping people in the community both physically and mentally healthy also meant keeping the hospital financially healthy. He made the center's new preventative care philosophy clear to the public: "Work out at our hospital so you can stay out of our hospital."

Jacobs's efforts have paid off—in an era when small hospitals are closing left and right, Windber Medical Center is thriving. Under Jacobs's leadership Windber has established an affiliation with the Planetree treatment system, which integrates meditation, massage, music, and other holistic methods into traditional health care. Windber's wellness center, which offers fitness training, yoga, and acupuncture, among other treatments, opened in January 2000 and now generates over $500,000 annually. Gone are the pink walls and dated furniture—replaced with fountains, plants, and modern artwork. Jacobs recruited a former hotel manager to oversee food service. And despite the dismissal of about 32 employees (those used to a more traditional hospital setting had a tough time in the new environment), the staff has nearly doubled to 450 employees, and pay has improved. Windber has raised more than $50 million in public and private funding and has forged research partnerships with the Walter Reed Army Health System and the University of Pittsburgh, among others. The Windber Research Institute, Windber's heart disease reversal program, has treated about 250 patients.

1. Consider the factors from the situational leadership theory outlined in Figure 13.4. Apply these factors to Jacobs and Windber.

2. How do you think Jacobs would score on the least preferred co-worker (LPC) scale? Why?

3. Based on the success of Windber, in what range would you guess the overall situational favorability might fall for Jacobs on the continuum illustrated in Figure 13.6?

Sources: http://www.careerjournaleurope.com/columnists/inthelead/20030827 inthelead.html; http://www.haponline.org/ihc/hospitalshealthsystems/models2.asp; http://www.post-gazette.com/pg/04013/260747.stm.

End Notes

1. F. E. Fiedler, "Reflections by an Accidental Theorist," *Leadership Quarterly* 6, no. 4 (1995), pp. 453–61; F. E. Fiedler, *A Theory of Leadership Effectiveness* (New York: McGraw-Hill, 1967).

2. M. M. Chemers, "The Social, Organizational, and Cultural Contest of Effective Leadership," in *Leadership: Multidisciplinary Perspectives*, ed. B. Kellerman (Englewood Cliffs, NJ: Prentice Hall, 1984).

3. G. Graen and J. F. Cashman, "A Role-Making Model of Leadership in Formal Organization: A Developmental Approach," in *Leadership Frontiers,* ed. J. G. Hunt and L. L. Larson (Kent, OH: Kent State University Press), pp. 143–65, 1976.

4. R. C. Linden and G. Graen, "Generalizability of the Vertical Dyad Linkage Model of Leadership," *Academy of Management Journal* 23 (1980), pp. 451–65.

5. S. J. Wayne, L. M. Shore, and R. C. Linden, "Perceived Organizational Support and Leader-Member Exchange: A Social Exchange Perspective," *Academy of Management Journal* 40 (1997), pp. 82–111.

6. G. Chen, B. L. Kirkman, R. Kanfer, D. Allen, and B. Rosen, "A Multilevel Study of Leadership Empowerment and Performance in Teams," *Journal of Applied Psychology* 92 (2007), pp. 331–46.

7. R. T. Sparrowe and R. C. Linden, "Two Routes to Influence: Integrating Leader-Member Exchange and Social Network Perspectives," *Administrative Science Quarterly* 50 (2005), pp. 505–35.

8. T. A. Scandura and C. A. Schriesheim, "Leader-Member Exchange and Supervisor Career Mentoring as Complementary Constructs in Leadership Research," *Academy of Management Journal* 37 (1994), pp. 1588–1602.

9. G. B. Graen and M. Uhl-Bien, "Relationship-Based Approach to Leadership: Development of Leader-Member Exchange (LMX) Theory over 25 Years: Applying a Multi-Level Multi-Domain Perspective," *Leadership Quarterly* 6 (1995), pp. 219–47.

10. D. J. Henderson, R. C. Liden, B. C. Glibkowski, and A. Chaudhry, "LMX Differentiation: A Multilevel Review and Examination of Its Antecedents and Outcomes," *Leadership Quarterly* 20 (2009), pp. 517–34.

11. L. Atwater and A. Carmeli, "Leader-Member Exchange, Feelings of Energy, and Involvement in Creative Work," *Leadership Quarterly* 20 (2010), pp. 264–75.

12. V. H. Vroom and P. W. Yetton, *Leadership and Decision Making* (Pittsburgh, PA: University of Pittsburgh Press, 1973).

13. Ibid.

14. Ibid.

15. Ibid.

16. Ibid.

17. Ibid.

18. R. H. G. Field, "A Test of the Vroom-Yetton Normative Model of Leadership," *Journal of Applied Psychology* 67 (1982), pp. 523–32.

19. V. H. Vroom and A. G. Jago, "Leadership and Decision Making: A Revised Normative Model," paper presented at the Academy of Management Convention, Boston, MA, 1974.

20. V. H. Vroom and A. G. Jago, *The New Theory of Leadership: Managing Participation in Organizations* (Englewood Cliffs, NJ: Prentice Hall, 1988).

21. J. B. Miner, "The Uncertain Future of the Leadership Concept: An Overview," in *Leadership Frontiers,* ed. J. G. Hunt and L. L. Larson (Kent, OH: Kent State University, 1975).

22. G. Yukl, *Leadership in Organizations*, 2nd ed. (Englewood Cliffs, NJ: Prentice Hall, 1989).

23. G. A. Yukl and D. D. Van Fleet, "Theory and Research on Leadership in Organizations," in *Handbook of Industrial & Organizational Psychology*, vol. 3, ed. M. D. Dunnette and L. M. Hough (Palo Alto, CA: Consulting Psychologists Press, 1992), pp. 1–51.

24. A. Couch and P. W. Yetton, "Manager Behavior, Leadership Style, and Subordinate Performance: An Empirical Extension of the Vroom-Yetton Conflict Rule," *Organizational Behavior and Human Decision Processes* 39 (1987), pp. 384–96.

25. P. Hersey and K. H. Blanchard, "Life Cycle Theory of Leadership," *Training and Development Journal* 23 (1969), pp. 26–34.

26. R. P. Vecchio, "Situational Leadership Theory: An Examination of a Prescriptive Theory," *Journal of Applied Psychology* 72 (1987), pp. 444–51.

27. G. A. Yukl and D. D. Van Fleet, "Theory and Research on Leadership in Organizations," in *Handbook of Industrial & Organizational Psychology*, vol. 3, ed. M. D. Dunnette and L. M. Hough (Palo Alto, CA: Consulting Psychologists Press, 1992), pp. 1–51.

28. K. H. Blanchard, *Leading at a Higher Level* (Upper Saddle River, New Jersey: Prentice-Hall, 2007).

29. G. Thompson and R. P. Vecchio, "Situational Leadership Theory: A Test of Three Versions," *Leadership Quarterly* 20 (2009), pp. 837–48.

30. F. E. Fiedler, "Reflections by an Accidental Theorist," *Leadership Quarterly* 6, no. 4 (1995), pp. 453-61; F. E. Fiedler, *A Theory of Leadership Effectiveness* (New York: McGraw-Hill, 1967).

31. Ibid.

32. F. E. Fiedler, "The Contingency Model and the Dynamics of the Leadership Process," in *Advances in Experimental Social Psychology*, ed. L. Berkowitz (New York: Academic Press, 1978).

33. Ibid.

34. J. K. Kennedy, "Middle LPC Leaders and the Contingency Model of Leader Effectiveness," *Organizational Behavior and Human Performance* 30 (1982), pp. 1–14.

35. F. E. Fiedler and M. M. Chemers, *Improving Leadership Effectiveness: The Leader Match Concept*, 2nd ed. (New York: John Wiley, 1982).

36. F. E. Fiedler, "Reflections by an Accidental Theorist," *Leadership Quarterly* 6, no. 4 (1995), pp. 453–61; F. E. Fiedler, *A Theory of Leadership Effectiveness* (New York: McGraw-Hill, 1967).

37. P. Hersey and K. H. Blanchard, "Life Cycle Theory of Leadership," *Training and Development Journal* 23 (1969), pp. 26–34.

38. P. Hersey and K. H. Blanchard, *Management of Organizational Behavior: Utilizing Human Resources*, 4th ed. (Englewood Cliffs, NJ: Prentice Hall, 1982).

39. F. E. Fiedler, "The Contingency Model and the Dynamics of the Leadership Process," in *Advances in Experimental Social Psychology*, ed. L. Berkowitz (New York: Academic Press, 1978).

40. F. E. Fiedler, "Cognitive Resources and Leadership Performance," *Applied Psychology: An International Review* 44, no. 1 (1995), pp. 5–28.

41. F. E. Fiedler and M. M. Chemers, *Improving Leadership Effectiveness: The Leader Match Concept,* 2nd ed. (New York: John Wiley, 1982).

42. L. H. Peters, D. D. Hartke, and J. T. Pohlmann, "Fiedler's Contingency Theory of Leadership: An Application of the Meta-analytic Procedures of Schmidt and Hunter," *Psychological Bulletin* 97 (1985), pp. 274–85.

43. M. J. Strube and J. E. Garcia, "A Meta-analytic Investigation of Fiedler's Contingency Model of Leadership Effectiveness," *Psychological Bulletin* 90 (1981), pp. 307–21.

44. L. H. Peters, D. D. Hartke, and J. T. Pohlmann, "Fiedler's Contingency Theory of Leadership: An Application of the Meta-analytic Procedures of Schmidt and Hunter," *Psychological Bulletin* 97 (1985), pp. 274–85.

45. J. K. Kennedy, "Middle LPC Leaders and the Contingency Model of Leader Effectiveness," *Organizational Behavior and Human Performance* 30 (1982), pp. 1–14.

46. R. W. Rice, "Construct Validity of the Least Preferred Co-Worker Score," *Psychological Bulletin* 85 (1978), pp. 1199–1237.

47. C. A. Schriesheim and S. Kerr, "Theories and Measures of Leadership: A Critical Appraisal of Current and Future Directions," in *Leadership: The Cutting Edge,* ed. J. G. Hunt and L. L. Larson (Carbondale, IL: Southern Illinois University Press, 1977).

48. A. G. Jago and J. W. Ragan, "The Trouble with Leader Match Is That It Doesn't Match Fiedler's Contingency Model," *Journal of Applied Psychology* 71 (1986), pp. 555–59.

49. A. G. Jago and J. W. Ragan, "Some Assumptions Are More Troubling Than Others: Rejoinder to Chemers and Fiedler," *Journal of Applied Psychology* 71 (1986), pp. 564–65.

50. A. G. Jago and J. W. Ragan, "The Trouble with Leader Match Is That It Doesn't Match Fiedler's Contingency Model," *Journal of Applied Psychology* 71 (1986), pp. 555–59.

51. A. G. Jago and J. W. Ragan, "Some Assumptions Are More Troubling Than Others: Rejoinder to Chemers and Fiedler," *Journal of Applied Psychology* 71 (1986), pp. 564–65.

52. R. P. Vecchio, "Assessing the Validity of Fiedler's Contingency Model of Leadership Effectiveness: A Closer Look at Strube and Garcia," *Psychological Bulletin* 93 (1983), pp. 404–8.

53. M. G. Evans, "The Effects of Supervisory Behavior on the Path-Goal Relationship," *Organizational Behavior and Human Performance* 5 (1970), pp. 277–98.

54. R. J. House and G. Dressler, "The Path–Goal Theory of Leadership: Some Post Hoc and A Priori Tests," in *Contingency Approaches to Leadership,* ed. J. G. Hunt and L. L. Larson (Carbondale, IL: Southern Illinois University Press, 1974).

55. T. R. Mitchell, C. M. Smyser, and S. E. Weed, "Locus of Control: Supervision and Work Satisfaction," *Academy of Management Journal* 18 (1975), pp. 623–30.

56. V. H. Vroom and P. W. Yetton, *Leadership and Decision Making* (Pittsburgh, PA: University of Pittsburgh Press, 1973).

57. S. Kerr and J. M. Jermier, "Substitutes for Leadership: Their Meaning and Measurement," *Organizational Behavior and Human Performance* 22 (1978), pp. 375–403.

58. C. A. Schriesheim and A. S. DeNisi, "Task Dimensions as Moderators of the Effects of Instrumental Leadership: A Two Sample Replicated Test of Path–Goal Leadership Theory," *Journal of Applied Psychology* 66 (1981), pp. 589–97.

59. C. A. Schriesheim and S. Kerr, "Theories and Measures of Leadership: A Critical Appraisal of Current and Future Directions," in *Leadership: The Cutting Edge*, ed. J. G. Hunt and L. L. Larson (Carbondale, IL: Southern Illinois University Press, 1977).

60. G. Yukl, *Leadership in Organizations*, 2nd ed. (Englewood Cliffs, NJ: Prentice Hall, 1989).

61. C. A. Schriesheim, S. L. Castro, X. Zhou, and L. A. DeChurch, "An Investigation of Path–Goal and Transformational Leadership Theory Predictions at the Individual Level of Analysis," *Leadership Quarterly* 17 (2006), pp. 21–38.

62. G. Yukl, *Leadership in Organizations*, 2nd ed. (Englewood Cliffs, NJ: Prentice Hall, 1989).

63. G. A. Yukl and D. D. Van Fleet, "Theory and Research on Leadership in Organizations," in *Handbook of Industrial & Organizational Psychology*, vol. 3, ed. M. D. Dunnette and L. M. Hough (Palo Alto, CA: Consulting Psychologists Press, 1992), pp. 1–51.

64. G. Yukl, *Leadership in Organizations*, 2nd ed. (Englewood Cliffs, NJ: Prentice Hall, 1989), p. 104.

65. V. H. Vroom and P. W. Yetton, *Leadership and Decision Making* (Pittsburgh, PA: University of Pittsburgh Press, 1973).

66. F. E. Fiedler, "Reflections by an Accidental Theorist," *Leadership Quarterly* 6, no. 4 (1995), pp. 453–61.

67. R. J. House and G. Dressler, "The Path–Goal Theory of Leadership: Some Post Hoc and A Priori Tests," in *Contingency Approaches to Leadership*, ed. J. G. Hunt and L. L. Larson (Carbondale, IL: Southern Illinois University Press, 1974).

Chapter 14

Leadership and Change

Introduction

Organizations today face myriad potential challenges. To be successful they must cope effectively with the implications of new technology, globalization, changing social and political climates, new competitive threats, shifting economic conditions, industry consolidation, swings in consumer preferences, and new performance and legal standards. Think how technology affected James Cameron's ability to make *Avatar* or the changes the U.S. military had to make as it shifted from stemming the tide of communism to fighting more regionalized conflicts. And consider how the events of 9/11/2001, the wars in Iraq and Afghanistan, the threats of global terrorism, the emergence of the European Union, the growth of the Chinese and Indian economies, the economic recession of 2008–2010, and global warming have affected leaders in both the private and public sectors around the world. Leading change is perhaps the most difficult challenge facing any leader, yet this skill may be the best differentiator of managers from leaders and of mediocre from exceptional leaders. The best leaders are those who recognize the situational and follower factors inhibiting or facilitating change, paint a compelling vision of the future, and formulate and execute a plan that moves their vision from a dream to reality.

The scope of any change initiative varies dramatically. Leaders can use goal setting, coaching, mentoring, delegation, or empowerment skills to effectively change the behaviors and skills of individual direct reports. But what would you need to do if you led a pharmaceutical company of 5,000 employees and you had just received FDA approval to introduce a revolutionary new drug into the marketplace? How would you get the research and development, marketing, sales, manufacturing, quality, shipping, customer service, accounting, and information technology departments to work together to ensure a profitable product launch? Or what would you do if you had to reduce company expenses by 40 percent for the next two years or deal with a recent acquisition of a competitor?

It is not necessary to change. Survival is not mandatory.

W. Edwards Deming, quality expert

Obviously change on this scale involves more than individual coaching and mentoring. Because this chapter builds on much of the content of the previous chapters, it is fitting that it appears toward the end of the text. To successfully lead larger-scale change initiatives, leaders need to attend to the situational and follower factors affecting their group or organization (Chapters 9, 10, and 12). They must also use their intelligence, problem-solving skills, creativity, and values to sort out what is important and formulate solutions to the challenges facing their group (Chapters 5–7). But solutions in and of themselves are no guarantee for change; leaders must use their power and influence, personality traits, coaching and planning skills, and knowledge of motivational techniques and group dynamics in order to drive change (Chapters 2, 3, 4, 8, 9, 11, and 16). An example of what it takes to drive large-scale organizational change can be found in Highlight 14.1.

As an overview, this chapter begins by revisiting the leadership versus management discussion from Chapter 1. We then describe a rational approach to organizational change and spell out what leaders can do if they want to be successful with their change efforts. This model also provides a good diagnostic framework for understanding why many change efforts fail. We conclude the chapter with a discussion of an alternative approach to change—charismatic and transformational leadership. The personal magnetism, heroic qualities, and spellbinding powers of these leaders can have unusually strong effects on followers, which often lead to dramatic organizational, political, or societal change. Unlike the rational approach to change, the charismatic and transformational leadership framework places considerable weight on followers' heightened emotional levels to drive organizational change. Much of the leadership research over the past 30 years has helped us better understand the situational, follower, and leader characteristics needed for charismatic or transformational leadership to occur. The chapter concludes with an overview of these factors and a review of the predominant theory in the field, Bass's theory of transformational and transactional leadership.[1]

The Rational Approach to Organizational Change

A number of authors have written about organizational change, including O'Toole,[2] Pritchett,[3] McNulty,[4] Heifetz and Linsky,[5] Moss Kanter,[6,7] Krile, Curphy, and Lund,[8] Ostroff,[9] Rock and Schwartz,[10] Kotter,[11] Curphy,[12,13] Burns,[14] Marcus and Weiler,[15] Bennis and Nanus,[16] Tichy and Devanna,[17] Bridges,[18] Collins and Porras,[19] Treacy and Wiersma,[20] Beer,[21,22] Heifetz and Laurie,[23] and Collins.[24,25] All these authors have unique perspectives on leadership and change, but they also share a number of common characteristics. Beer[21,22] has offered a rational and straightforward approach to

Change in the Waste Industry

HIGHLIGHT 14.1

Even something as mundane as trash disposal can present some significant leadership challenges. One company, Waste Management, acquired over 1,600 smaller waste disposal companies from 1995 to 2004. All of the acquired companies had their own financial systems, pay scales and benefits, trucks and equipment, and operating procedures. None of the IT or financial systems could "talk" to each other, drivers followed different operating procedures and had different performance standards and compensation packages, many of the companies were former competitors that now had to collaborate in order to achieve overall company goals, and few if any supervisors had been through any type of leadership training. The board of directors brought in an outsider, Maury Myers from Yellow Freight, to integrate all these acquisitions into a single company. As CEO, Maury's first task was to create a common financial system so that all the company's revenues and expenses could be consolidated into a single financial statement. And given the large number of acquired companies, this in itself was no small task. He also created a system that allowed supervisors and drivers to set goals and measure daily productivity and customer satisfaction rates and introduced other major organizational change initiatives to improve safety and vehicle maintenance, optimize vehicle use, and reduce operating expenses.

The results of these change initiatives have been nothing short of spectacular. Waste Management is now the industry leader in the waste industry, consisting of approximately 50,000 employees who create $1.5 billion in profits on a $12 billion annual revenue stream. Driver productivity, customer satisfaction, and driver safety have improved over 50 percent, and operating expenses have been dramatically reduced. Maury Myers retired from the CEO role in November 2004 and was replaced by David Steiner, the former CFO.

Since taking the reins at Waste Management David Steiner has focused on three critical initiatives, which include operational excellence, growth, and rebranding. In terms of operational excellence, the company has implemented a number of companywide initiatives to improve the safety and productivity of employees. Some of these include the Mission for Success Safety program, the Business Process Improvement initiative, and Waste Route, a route optimization program. These programs have helped Waste Management to become the best in the industry in terms of safety and worker productivity. The company is vigorously pursuing a number of organic growth opportunities to generate additional profits, such as capturing landfill gases to fuel garbage trucks, taking the lead in electronic recycling and disposal, placing power generating windmills at landfills, and developing new waste-to-energy power plants. In terms of rebranding, Waste Management has been repositioning itself with its "Think Green" television, radio, and magazine ads; the use of natural gas–powered trucks; and an aggressive landfill remediation program. It is looking at how it can play a lead role in sustainability because many companies, such as Walmart, have corporate goals of reducing store waste by 95 percent in the next five years. If these customers dramatically reduce their waste streams, what will Waste Management have to do to remain a good investment for shareholders? Although Waste Management has seen some dramatic changes over the past 10 years, waste stream reduction, alternative energy sources, and global warming may force Waste Management to undergo even more dramatic changes. What would you do if you were running a waste disposal company that made most of its money from landfills and the country adopted a strong sustainability mind-set?

Change in a Rural Community

HIGHLIGHT 14.2

There is no limit to what an organized group can do if it wants to.

George McLean, newspaper editor

Change does not just happen in organizations; it also occurs in communities. Whereas many suburbs are experiencing dramatic growth, most urban and rural communities are experiencing declines in population and business. Some rural communities are working hard to attract new businesses, such as ethanol plants, and build new schools or new community centers; others are organizing to prevent Walmart or other large retailers from building stores in their communities. One of the real success stories of how a community transformed itself is Tupelo, Mississippi. Tupelo is famous for being the birthplace of Elvis Presley; in 1940 it also had the distinction of being the county seat of the poorest county in the poorest state in the country. But Lee County now has a medical center with over 6,000 employees, boasts 18 *Fortune* 500 manufacturing plants, and has added 1,000 new manufacturing jobs in each of the past 13 years. Tupelo now has a symphony, an art museum, a theater group, an 8,000-seat coliseum, and an outstanding recreational program. Its public schools have won national academic honors, and its athletic programs have won several state championships.

So how was Tupelo able to transform itself from a poor to a vibrant rural community? The town had no natural advantages, such as a harbor or natural resources, which would give it a competitive advantage. It also had no interstate highways, and the closest metropolitan centers were over 100 miles away. The key to Tupelo's success was the ability of the town's citizens to work together. More specifically, the citizens of Tupelo were able to (1) collaborate effectively in identifying the problems and needs of the community; (2) achieve a working consensus on goals and priorities; (3) agree on ways and means to implement goals and priorities; and (4) collaborate effectively in the agreed actions.

Tupelo's success started when local community members pooled resources to acquire a siring bull. The bull's offspring were used to start local ranches. Farmers shifted from planting cotton to growing crops needed to support the ranchers and local populace, and farming and ranching equipment distributors started up local operations. George McLean, the local newspaper publisher, kept the community focused on economic development and helped local entrepreneurs by subsidizing office and warehouse space. With various tax breaks and incentives from local bankers, furniture manufacturers started moving to town. A number of other businesses then sprang up to support the manufacturers, and community leaders made a concerted effort to expand and improve local health care and educational facilities to support the new workforce. Despite the successes to date, Tupelo is now facing even bigger challenges, as many of the local furniture manufacturers are being threatened by low-cost manufacturers in China. But if any community were to succeed in the face of challenge, it would likely be Tupelo. The community seems to have the leaders needed to help citizens fully understand these new challenges and what to do to meet them. What would you do to preserve jobs and attract new businesses if you were the mayor of Tupelo?

Source: V. L. Grisham Jr., *Tupelo: The Evolution of a Community* (Dayton, OH: Kettering Foundation Press, 1999).

organizational change that addresses many of the issues raised by the other authors. Beer's model also provides a road map for leadership practitioners wanting to implement an organizational change initiative, as well as a diagnostic tool for understanding why change initiatives fail. According to Beer,

$$C = D \times M \times P > R$$

The *D* in this formula represents followers' **dissatisfaction** with the current status quo. *M* symbolizes the **model** for change and includes the leader's vision of the future as well as the goals and systems that need to change to support the new vision. *P* represents **process,** which concerns developing and implementing a plan that articulates the who, what, when, where, and how of the change initiative. *R* stands for **resistance;** people resist change because they fear a loss of identity or social contacts, and good change plans address these sources of resistance. Finally the *C* corresponds to the **amount of change.** Notice that leaders can increase the amount of change by increasing the level of dissatisfaction, increasing the clarity of vision, developing a well-thought-out change plan, or decreasing the amount of resistance in followers. You should also note that the $D \times M \times P$ is a multiplicative function—increasing dissatisfaction but having no plan will result in little change. Likewise, if followers are content with the status quo, it may be difficult for leaders to get followers to change, no matter how compelling their vision or change plan may be. This model maintains that organizational change is a systematic process, and large-scale changes can take months if not years to implement.[15,21,22] Leadership practitioners who understand the model should be able to do a better job developing change initiatives and diagnosing where their initiatives may be getting stuck. Because change is an important component of leadership, we will go into more detail about each of the components of Beer's model.

Dissatisfaction

Followers' level of satisfaction is an important ingredient in a leader's ability to drive change. Followers who are relatively content are not apt to change; malcontents are much more likely to do something to change the situation. Although employee satisfaction is an important outcome of leadership, leaders who want to change the status quo may need to take action to *decrease* employee satisfaction levels. Follower's emotions are the fuel for organizational change, and change often requires a considerable amount of fuel. The key for leadership practitioners is to increase dissatisfaction (*D*) to the point where followers are inclined to take action, but not so much that they decide to leave the organization. So what can leaders do to increase follower dissatisfaction levels? Probably the first step is to determine how satisfied followers are with the current situation. This information can be gleaned from employee satisfaction surveys, grievance records, customer complaints, or conversations with followers. To increase dissatisfaction, leaders can talk about potential competitive, technology, or legal threats or employee concerns about the status quo. They can also capitalize on or even create some type of financial or political crisis, compare benchmarks against other organizations, or substantially increase performance standards. All of these actions can potentially heighten followers' emotional levels; however, leaders must ensure that

Constructive Dissatisfaction and Employee Engagement

HIGHLIGHT 14.3

As stated earlier, it may be difficult to drive organizational change if employees are happy with the status quo. And as described in Chapter 9, employees can have high levels of job satisfaction and low levels of job performance. The key ingredients in organizational change may be constructive dissatisfaction and employee engagement. **Constructive dissatisfaction** defines a state where followers are unhappy with their current situation and are willing to do something to change it. They are not so happy to be content with the status quo or so demoralized to think the situation is hopeless. Leaders implementing the rational approach to change want to create a state of constructive dissatisfaction in followers, where followers willingly suggest ideas and exert energy to change the status quo.

Another factor leaders need to be aware of when driving organizational change is **employee engagement.** Engaged employees are those who

- Exert high levels of effort that go beyond expectations.
- Persist with difficult tasks.
- Help others.
- Voice recommendations for improvement.
- Readily adapt to change.

A leader's ability to drive change will depend to a large extent on the degree to which he or she manages a highly engaged workforce. Those who create teams of engaged employees are more likely to make organizational change happen; those who do not are likely to see their organizational change efforts fail. So what should leaders do to create engaged employees? Some of the key things leaders can do to engage followers is to have them do meaningful work, create work cultures where followers feel safe raising difficult issues with leaders, treat people fairly, and give them the training and resources needed to get work completed. Employee engagement is a huge buzzword in corporate America these days, but there is some uncertainty whether employee engagement (and the actions needed to create engaged employees) is really anything new. How do employee engagement and the key leadership behaviors relate to the material described in Chapters 7 and 9?

Sources: B. Schneider, W. H. Macey, K. M. Barbera, S. A. Young, and W. Lee, *Employee Engagement: Everything You Wanted to Know about Engagement but Were Afraid to Ask* (Rolling Meadows, IL: Valtera Corporation, 2006); W. H. Macey and B. Schneider, "The Meaning of Employee Engagement," *Industrial and Organizational Psychology: Perspectives on Science and Practice* 1, no. 1 (2008), pp. 3–30; J. K. Harter and F. L. Schmidt, "Conceptual versus Empirical Distinctions among Constructs: Implications for Discriminant Validity," *Industrial and Organizational Psychology: Perspectives on Science and Practice* 1, no. 1 (2008), pp. 36–39.

these emotions are channeled toward the leader's vision for the organization (see Highlight 14.3).

Model

Without a compelling vision, there is no way for people who lose the most to reconcile their losses.

Bill Mease, Mease & Trudeau

There are four key components to the model (*M*) variable in the change formula, and these include environmental scanning, a vision, the setting of new goals to support the vision, and needed system changes. As discussed earlier, organizations are constantly bombarded with economic, technological, competitive, legal, and social challenges. Good leaders constantly scan the external environment to assess the seriousness of these threats. They are also adept at internal scanning; they understand where the organization is doing well and falling short. Thus keeping up to date on current events, spending time reviewing organizational reports, and taking time to listen to followers' concerns are some techniques leaders use to conduct external and internal scans.[2,8,11,12,15,22,26] This information in turn is used to formulate a vision for the change initiative. What would a new organization look like if it were to successfully counter the gravest external threats, take advantage of new market opportunities, and overcome organizational shortcomings? What would be the purpose of the new organization, and why would people want to work in it? A good vision statement should answer these questions. Fortunately a vision statement does not have to be a solo effort on the part of the leader. Often leaders will either solicit followers for ideas or work with a team of followers to craft a vision statement.[8,15-17,27,28] Both of these actions can help to increase followers' commitment to the new vision.

It is important to understand the difference between an organization's vision and goals. Just as ancient mariners used the stars to navigate, so should a vision provide guidance for an organization's actions. A vision helps an organization make choices about what it should and should not do, the kind of people it should hire and retain, the rules by which it should operate, and so on.[10,20,27-29] But just as the stars were not the final destination for the mariners, a vision is not the final destination for an organization. An organization's goals are the equivalent of the mariners' final destination, and they should spell out specifically what the organization is trying to accomplish and when they will get done.[2,8,19,26-29] Depending on the organization, these goals might concern market share, profitability, revenue or customer growth, quality, the implementation of new customer service or information technology systems, the number of patents awarded, school test scores, fund-raising targets, or the reduction of crime rates. Thus an organization's goals can be externally or internally focused or both, depending on the results of the environmental scan and the vision of the organization. Highlight 14.4 provides an example of a vision statement and organizational goals for a waste-to-energy power company. (This company burns trash to create electricity.)

After determining the organization's goals, the leader will need to determine which systems need to change for the organization to fulfill its vision and accomplish its goals. In other words, how do the marketing, sales, manufacturing, quality, human resource, shipping, accounting, or customer service systems need to change if the organization is to succeed? And does the current organizational structure or culture support or interfere with the new vision? Leaders wanting their organizational change initiatives to succeed will need to take a systems thinking approach after setting organizational goals.[15,26,27,30] A **systems thinking approach** asks leaders to think about the organization as a set of interlocking systems, and explains how changes in one system can have intended and unintended consequences for other parts of the organization. For example, if a company wanted to grow market share and revenue, it might change the

Without a clear vision and an explicit set of goals, all decisions are based on politics.
Pete Ramstad, Toro

An Example of a Vision Statement and Organizational Goals

HIGHLIGHT 14.4

Vision Statement

To be the industry leader in waste-to-energy operating companies.

Selected Organizational Goals

- Increase profitability growth from 5 to 8.5 percent.
- Hold maintenance and repair spending to 2011 levels.
- Maintain 92 percent boiler availability rate across all plants.
- Reduce unscheduled boiler downtime by 29 percent.

- Reduce accounting costs by 12 percent by centralizing the accounting function.
- Achieve zero recordables and zero lost time safety incidents across all plants.
- Implement a metals recovery system across all plants in order to boost recycle revenues by 26 percent.
- Win five new waste-to energy plant operating contracts in 2011.

Source: G. J. Curphy, *The Competitive Advantage Program for Wheelabrator Technologies Incorporated* (North Oaks, MN: Author, 2010).

compensation system to motivate salespeople to go after new customers. However, this approach could also cause a number of problems in the manufacturing, quality, shipping, accounting, and customer service departments. Leaders who anticipate these problems make all of the necessary systems changes to increase the odds of organizational success. Leaders may need to set goals and put action plans in place for each of these system changes. These actions can be contrasted to **siloed thinking,** where leaders act to optimize their part of the organization at the expense of suboptimizing the organization's overall effectiveness.[15,26,27,30] For example, the vice president of sales could change the sales compensation plan if she believed her sole concern was annual revenues. This belief could be reinforced if her compensation was based primarily on hitting certain revenue targets. If she were a siloed thinker, she would also believe that profitability, quality, or customer service were not her concerns. However, this mode of thinking could ultimately lead to her downfall: quality and order fulfillment problems might cause customers to leave faster than new customers buy products.

Figure 14.1 is a graphic depiction of a systems model for leadership practitioners. All the components of this model interact with and affect all the other components of the model. Therefore, leaders changing organizational vision or goals will need to think through the commensurate changes in the organization's structure, culture, systems, and leader and follower capabilities. Similarly, changes in the information or hiring systems can affect the organization's capabilities, culture, structure, or ability to meet its goals. One of the keys to successful organizational

FIGURE 14.1
The Components of Organizational Alignment

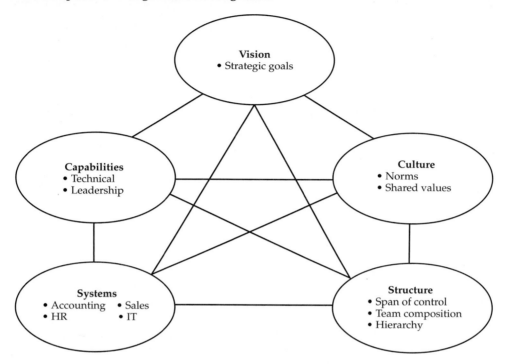

change is ensuring that all components in Figure 14.1 are in alignment. A common mistake for many leaders is to change the organization's vision, structure, and systems and overlook the organization's culture and leader and follower capabilities. This makes sense in that it is relatively easy to create a new vision statement, organizational chart, or compensation plan. Leaders either discount the importance of organizational culture and capabilities, falsely believe they are easy to change, or believe they are a given because they are so difficult to change. It is possible to change the culture and capabilities of an organization, but it takes considerable time and focused effort. Unfortunately about 70 percent of change initiatives fail, and the underlying cause for many of these failures is the leader's inability or unwillingness to address these culture and capabilities issues.[5-8,11,22,23,27,31-35]

Process

At this point in the change process, the leader may have taken certain steps to increase follower dissatisfaction. She may also have worked with followers to craft a new vision statement, set new team or organizational goals, and determined what organizational systems, capabilities, or structures need to change. In many ways, the *D* and *M* components of the change model are the easiest for leadership practitioners to alter. The process (*P*) component of the change model is where the change initiative becomes tangible and actionable because it consists of the development and execution of the **change plan**.[8,12,27,33,36] Good change plans outline the sequence of events, key deliverables, timelines, responsible parties, metrics, and feedback mechanisms needed to achieve the new organizational goals. They may also include the steps needed to increase dissatisfaction and deal with anticipated resistance, an outline of training and resource needs, and a comprehensive communication plan to keep all relevant parties informed.

Depending on the depth and breadth of change, change plans can be detailed and complicated. For example, the waste-to-energy company described earlier could no longer do what it had always done if it were to reach its goals outlined in Highlight 14.3. The company needed new behaviors, metrics, and feedback systems to achieve these goals. The company's change plan was quite extensive and consisted of an overall plan for the company as well as plant-specific goals and change plans. Each of these plans outlined the action steps, responsible parties, metrics, and due dates; progress against the plans was regularly reviewed in monthly plant business and operational reviews. The goals and change plans were constantly adjusted in these meetings to take into account unforeseen barriers, sooner-than-expected progress, and so on.

Of course the plan itself is only a road map for change. Change will occur only when the action steps outlined in the plan are actually carried out. This is another area where leadership practitioners can run into trouble. One of the reasons why CEOs fail is an inability to execute, and this is also one of the reasons why first-line supervisors through executives derail.[36–39] Perhaps the best way to get followers committed to a change plan is to have them create it. This way followers become early adopters and know what, why, when, where, who, and how things are to be done. Nevertheless, many times it is impossible for all the followers affected by the change to be involved with plan creation. In these cases follower commitment can be increased if the new expectations for behavior and performance are explicit, the personal benefits of the change initiative are made clear, and followers already have a strong and trusting relationship with their leader.[8,15,28] Even after taking all of these steps, leadership practitioners will still need to spend considerable time regularly reviewing progress and holding people accountable for their roles and responsibilities in the change plan. Followers face competing demands for time and effort, and a lack of follow-through will cause many followers to drop the change initiative off of their radar screens. Leaders should also anticipate shifts in followership types once the change plan is implemented. Self-starters may shift to become criticizers, brown-nosers to slackers, or slackers to criticizers. Leaders who address these shifts in types and inappropriate

Joel Klein

PROFILES IN LEADERSHIP 14.1

The comment that best summarized the situation as I moved into the chancellor's role was when somebody told me that the Department of Education was there not to serve the kids, but to serve the employees.

Joel Klein, Chancellor, New York City Department of Education

Prior to becoming the chancellor of the Department of Education in New York City, Joel Klein was the head of the Antitrust Division in the Department of Justice during the Clinton administration and played the role of lead prosecutor during the Microsoft antitrust case. Klein received his BA from Columbia University and his law degree from Harvard. After graduating from Harvard, Klein worked as a clerk for U.S. Supreme Court Justice Lewis Powell and then went into private practice and specialized in appellate cases. Immediately prior to the chancellor position, he was the general counsel for Bertelsmann.

Upon getting elected as the mayor of New York City, Michael Bloomberg determined that upgrading the public education system was his number one priority. The department was spending approximately $15 billion a year to educate over 1.1 million students, yet only 48 percent were graduating from high school. Because the department was spending nearly twice as much per pupil than other school districts but achieving much lower graduation rates, Bloomberg determined that giving the department more money would not improve results. Bloomberg needed someone who could change the way education was delivered by the department and asked Joel Klein to be the lead change agent for the department.

Upon assuming the chancellor position, Klein noted that the Department of Education was subdivided into different school districts, with each district having its own school board, administration, teachers, and students. The school districts were run autonomously and had dramatically different educational goals and curriculums. However, internal politics, favoritism, poor district–community relationships, and a lack of results and accountability seemed to permeate all the districts. One of the first things Klein did was to eliminate the school districts and their boards and create one consolidated board for the Department of Education. The next thing Klein did was to create common reading, writing, and math educational standards and curriculum across all 1,400 schools in the department. Needless to say, these changes caused a considerable amount of conflict within the department and became grist for the New York City media. But as dramatic and unpopular as these changes were, they were nothing compared to what Klein did next.

The next major change Klein introduced was to create charter schools. These schools were often located within an existing school, but students had to achieve set educational goals and adhere to strict behavioral standards. Teachers and administrators were freed from many of the rules and regulations governing education but had to achieve specific educational goals. Students, teachers, and administrators were held accountable to these goals and standards and would be dismissed from the charter school if they failed to achieve results. Due to the popularity of the program the department now has over 400 charter schools. This program was even more unpopular than those earlier changes, with much of the resistance coming from the 80,000 members of the United Federation of Teachers. The department had 3,000 teachers whom no one wanted, but because of seniority rules many young and motivated teachers were bumped to make room for older and unmotivated teachers. The charter school system eliminated the seniority system, and the United Federation of Teachers generated a lot of negative publicity to kill the charter school concept. Despite this negative publicity from the teachers' union, the charter schools have continued to deliver superior results and the public remains firmly behind this approach to education.

What would you do to improve the quality of primary and secondary education in your area? What steps would you need to take? Who would be the key stakeholders? How would you overcome resistance to change?

Sources: J. Alter, "Stop Pandering on Education," *Newsweek*, February 12, 2007; G. J. Curphy, *Team 100 Leadership Program for the New York City Department of Education* (North Oaks, MN: Author, 2005); http://en.wikipedia.org/wki/Joel_Klein.

follower behaviors in a swift and consistent manner are more likely to succeed with their change initiatives.

Resistance

In terms of barriers to change, there is not a single rural community that wouldn't benefit from a few timely deaths.

**Jim Krile,
community
researcher**

Why would followership styles shift as a result of a change initiative? One reason is that it may take some time before the benefits of change are realized. Leaders, followers, and other stakeholders often assume that performance, productivity, or customer service will immediately improve upon the acquisition of new equipment, systems, behaviors, and so on. However, there is often a temporary drop in performance or productivity as followers learn new systems and skills. This difference between initial expectations and reality is called the **expectation–performance gap** and can be the source of considerable frustration (see Figure 14.2). If not managed properly, it can spark resistance (*R*), causing followers to revert back to old behaviors and systems to get things done. Leaders can help followers deal with their frustration by setting realistic expectations, demonstrating a high degree of patience, and ensuring that followers gain proficiency with the new systems and skills as quickly as possible. Good change plans address the expectation–performance gap by building in training and coaching programs to improve follower skill levels.[27,28,39]

Everybody resists change, particularly those who have to change the most.

**James O'Toole,
Aspen Institute**

Another reason why followers might resist change is a fear of loss.[3-5,8-10, 21,23,27,33,34,40] Because of the change, followers are afraid of losing power, close relationships with others, valued rewards, and their sense of identity or, on the other hand, being seen as incompetent. According to Beer,[21] the fear of

**FIGURE 14.2
The Expectation–
Performance Gap**

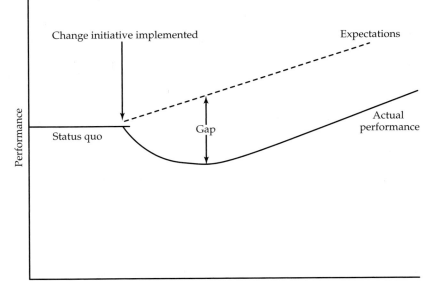

Change initiative implemented · Expectations · Status quo · Gap · Actual performance · Performance · Time

TABLE 14.1
Common Losses with Change

Loss of	Possible Leader Actions
Power	Demonstrate empathy, good listening skills, and new ways to build power.
Competence	Coaching, mentoring, training, peer coaching, job aids, and so forth.
Relationships	Help employees build new relationships before change occurs or soon thereafter.
Rewards	Design and implement new reward system to support change initiative.
Identity	Demonstrate empathy; emphasize value of new roles.

loss is a predictable and legitimate response to any change initiative, and some of a leader's responses to these fears can be found in Table 14.1. Change initiatives are more likely to be successfully adopted if their change plans identify and address potential areas of resistance. People also seem to go through some predictable reactions when confronted with change. An example might help to clarify the typical stages people go through when coping with change. Suppose you were working for a large company that needed to lay off 30 percent of the workforce due to a slowdown in the economy and declining profits. If you were one of the people asked to leave, your first reaction might be shock or surprise. You might not have been aware that market conditions were so poor or that you would be among those affected by the layoff. Next you would go through an anger stage. You might be angry that you had dedicated many long evenings and weekends to the company and now the company no longer wanted your services. After anger would come the rejection stage. In this stage you would start to question whether the company really knew what it was doing by letting you go and perhaps rationalize that they would probably be calling you back. In the final stage, acceptance, you would realize that the company might not ask you back, and you would start to explore other career options. These four reactions to change—shock, anger, rejection, and acceptance—make up what is known as the **SARA model.**[41] Most people go through these four stages whenever they get passed over for a promotion, receive negative feedback on a 360-degree report, get criticized by their boss, or the like.

But what should a leadership practitioner do with the SARA model? Perhaps the first step is to simply recognize the four reactions to change. Second, leaders need to understand that individual followers can take more or less time to work through the four stages. Leaders can, however, accelerate the pace in which followers work though the four stages by maintaining an open door policy, demonstrating empathy, and listening to concerns. Third, it is important to note that people are not likely to take any positive action toward a change initiative until they reach the acceptance stage. This does not mean they are happy with the change—only

FIGURE 14.3
Reactions to Change

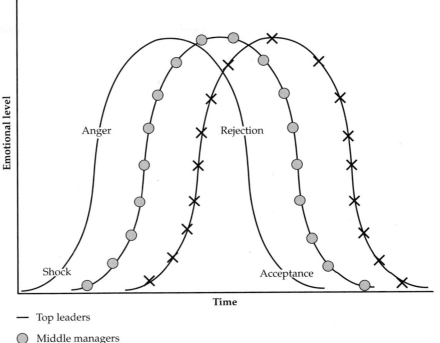

Top leaders

○ Middle managers

✕ Individual contributors

that they accept the inevitability of the change. Fourth, leaders also need to understand that where people are in the SARA model often varies according to organization level. Usually the first people to realize that a change initiative needs to be implemented are the organization's top leaders. Like everyone else, they go through the four stages, but they are the first to do so. The next people to hear the news are middle managers, followed by first-line supervisors and individual contributors. These three groups also go through the emotional stages of the SARA model but do so at different times. These differences in emotional reactions by organizational level are depicted in Figure 14.3. What is interesting in Figure 14.3 is that just when top executives have reached the acceptance stage, first-line supervisors and individual contributors are in the anger or rejection stages. By this time top leaders are ready to get on with the implementation of the change initiative and may not understand why the rest of the organization is still struggling. Because they are already at the acceptance stage, top leaders may fail to demonstrate empathy and listening skills, and this may be another reason for the depressed performance depicted in Figure 14.2.

Concluding Comments about the Rational Approach to Organizational Change

The situational, follower, and leader components of the rational approach to organizational change are shown in Figure 14.4. Although organizational vision, goals, and change plans are often a collaborative effort between the leader and followers, they are the primary responsibility of the leader. Leaders also need to think about the importance of critical mass for driving change.[8,15,27,29,35] They may be more successful by initially focusing their change efforts on early adopters and those on the fence rather than on those followers who are the most adamant about maintaining the status quo. Once a critical mass is reached, the adopters can exert peer pressure on followers who are reluctant to change.[8,22,27,29] This approach also maintains that the leader needs both good leadership and good management skills if a change initiative is to succeed over the long term. Leadership skills are important for determining a new vision for the organization, increasing dissatisfaction, coaching followers on how to do things differently, and overcoming resistance. Management skills are important when setting new goals and creating, implementing, and reviewing progress on change plans. Both sets of skills not only are important components in organizational change but also may play a key role in determining

FIGURE 14.4
The Rational Approach to Organization Change and the Interactional Framework

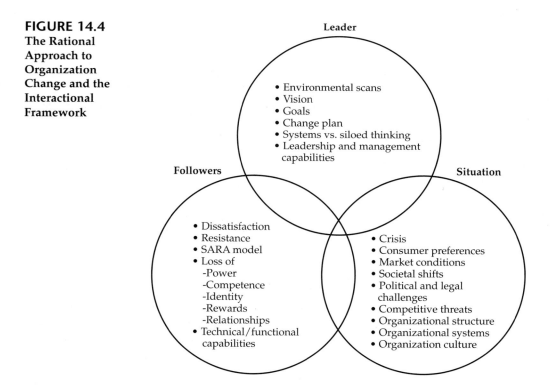

whether a new company will succeed or fail. Because of their strong leadership skills, entrepreneurs are often good at starting up new organizations. Many of these individuals can get people excited about their vision for the new company. However, if entrepreneurs fail to possess or appreciate the importance of management skills, they may not create the systems, policies, and procedures necessary to keep track of shifting consumer preferences, revenues, customer satisfaction, quality, and costs. As a result, these individuals may not have the information they need to make good operational and financial decisions, and their companies eventually file for bankruptcy. On the other hand, it is hard to see how planning and execution skills alone will result in the formation of a new company or drive organizational change. It is almost impossible to start up a new company—or for an organization to successfully change—if the person in charge does not have a compelling vision or fails to motivate others to do something different. Many of the other reasons why organizational change initiatives fail have their roots in underdeveloped leadership or management skills.[11,37]

Although both sets of skills are important, leadership practitioners should recognize that there is a natural tension between leadership and management skills. In many ways management skills help to maintain the status quo; they help to ensure consistency in behaviors and results. Leadership skills are often used to change the status quo; they help to change the purpose and processes by which an organization gets things done. Leaders who overuse or overemphasize either set of skills are likely to suboptimize team or organizational performance. Nonetheless, two leadership and management skills seem vitally important to driving change and are worth discussing in more detail. **Adaptive leadership** involves behaviors associated with being able to successfully flex and adjust to changing situations. Change, challenge, and adversity seem to be part of most organizations today, and the most effective leaders are those who readily adapt their leadership styles to changing situational demands.[42,43] And because of the constant bombardment of change, learning agility also seems to play a vital role in leadership effectiveness. **Learning agility** is the capability and willingness to learn from experience and apply these lessons to new situations.[44] The most effective leaders are those with high levels of learning agility and adaptability—not only do they know how to build teams and get results through others in changing situations, but also they can flex and adjust their behavior as needed to adapt to situational demands. The first part of this chapter was designed to help leadership practitioners better understand when to use leadership and management skills in the change process, and education and experience can help leadership practitioners improve both sets of skills.

Finally, it is worth noting that the rational approach gives leaders a systematic process for driving change and increasing understanding of why change initiatives succeed or fail in their respective organizations. Leadership practitioners can use the $C = D \times M \times P > R$ model as a road map for

A Tool for Understanding Rational Change: Force Field Analysis

HIGHLIGHT 14.5

If you really want to understand something, then try to change it.

Kurt Lewin, researcher

Force field analysis (FFA) is a tool that can be used to gain a better understanding of organiza-tional change. FFA uses vectors to graphically de-pict the driving forces and the barriers to an organizational change. Stronger forces and barri-ers are represented by larger vectors; weaker forces and barriers are represented by smaller vec-tors. Here is an example of an FFA for a rural school district trying to improve third grade stu-dent achievement test scores in math:

Drivers		**Barriers**
Compelling Vision ⟶	⟵	Budget Reductions
SMART Goals ⟶	⟵	Poor Math Curriculum
Board Support ⟶	⟵	Lack of Parental Involvement
Teacher Buy-In ⟶	⟵	Reduced Number of Teachers
Open Enrollment ⟶	⟵	Increased Class Size
Published Test Results ⟶	⟵	No Mentor Program
		Current State

The first step in an FFA is to graphically depict the current state as shown here. In many cases the driv-ers and barriers to change in the current state should more or less balance out because they rep-resent the current status quo. The second step in an FFA is to formulate strategies to increase the drivers or reduce the barriers to organizational change. (Leaders will often get better results if they focus on reducing barriers rather than increasing the num-ber or size of the drivers for change.) The third and final step in an FFA is to create and implement change plans that outline the steps, accountable parties, and timelines for increasing drivers and re-ducing the barriers to change.

Use an FFA to depict a change initiative going on at your school or in the local community. What would you recommend doing to drive change based on your FFA?

Source: K. Lewin, "Field Theory and Experiment in Social Psychology: Concepts and Methods," *American Journal of Sociology* 44 (1939) pp. 868–96.

creating a new vision and goals, changing the products and services their organizations provide, or changing the IT, financial, operations, mainte-nance, or compensation systems used to support organizational goals. Likewise, leadership practitioners can also use this model to diagnose where their change initiatives have fallen short—perhaps followers were reasonably satisfied with the status quo or did not buy into the new vision and goals, critical systems changes were not adequately identified, or change plans were incomplete or improperly implemented. Given the ex-planatory power of the model, the rational approach to change gives lead-ers a useful heuristic for driving organizational and community change.

The Emotional Approach to Organizational Change: Charismatic and Transformational Leadership

The world of the 1990s and beyond will not belong to "managers" or those who can make numbers dance. The world will belong to passionate, driven leaders—people who not only have enormous amounts of energy but can energize those they lead.

Jack Welch, former CEO of General Electric

Although the rational approach provides a straightforward model for organizational change, it seems that many large-scale political, societal, or organizational changes were not this formulaic. For example, it is doubtful that Jesus Christ, Muhammad, Joan of Arc, Vladimir Lenin, Adolf Hitler, Mahatma Gandhi, Mao Zedong, Martin Luther King Jr., the Ayatollah Khomeini, Nelson Mandela, Fidel Castro, Hugo Chávez, or Osama bin Laden followed some change formula or plan, yet these individuals were able to fundamentally change their respective societies. Although these leaders differ in a number of important ways, one distinct characteristic they all share is charisma. Charismatic leaders are passionate, driven individuals who can paint a compelling vision of the future. Through this vision they can generate high levels of excitement among followers and build particularly strong emotional attachments with them. The combination of a compelling vision, heightened emotional levels, and strong personal attachments often compels followers to put forth greater effort to meet organizational or societal challenges. The enthusiasm and passion generated by charismatic leaders seems to be a dual-edged sword, however. Some charismatic movements can result in positive and relatively peaceful organizational or societal changes; some examples might include the Falun Gong movement in China, Al Gore and the global warming awareness movement, and Louis Farrakhan's Million Man March. On the downside, when this passion is used for selfish or personal gains, history mournfully suggests it can have an equally devastating effect on society. Examples here might include David Koresh of Waco, Texas, Adolf Hitler, the Serbian leader Slobodan Milosevic, or Zimbabwe President Robert Mugabe.

What is it about charismatic leadership that causes followers to get so excited about future possibilities that they may willingly give up their lives for a cause? Even though many people conjure up images of charismatic individuals when thinking about leadership, the systematic investigation of charismatic leadership is relatively recent. The remainder of this chapter begins with a historical review of the research on charismatic leadership and the leader–follower–situation components of charismatic leadership. We will then review the most popular conceptualization of charisma: Bass's theory of transformational and transactional leadership. We conclude this chapter by comparing and contrasting the rational and emotional approaches to organizational change.

Charismatic Leadership: A Historical Review

Prior to the mid-1970s charismatic leadership was studied primarily by historians, political scientists, and sociologists. Of this early research,

Nelson Mandela

PROFILES IN LEADERSHIP 14.2

South Africa was ruled by a white minority government for much of the past 200 years. Although blacks made up over 75 percent of the populace, whites owned most of the property, ran most of the businesses, and controlled virtually all the country's resources. Moreover, blacks did not have the right to vote and often worked under horrible conditions for little or no wages. Seeing the frustration of his people, Nelson Mandela spent 50 years working to overturn white minority rule. He started by organizing the African National Congress, a nonviolent organization that protested white rule through work stoppages, strikes, and riots. Several whites were killed in the early riots, and in 1960 the police killed or injured over 250 blacks in Sharpeville. Unrest over the Sharpeville incident caused 95 percent of the black workforce to go on strike for two weeks, and the country declared a state of emergency. Mandela then orchestrated acts of sabotage to further pressure the South African government to change. The organization targeted installations and took special care to ensure that no lives were lost in the bombing campaign. Mandela was arrested in 1962 and spent the next 27 years in prison. While in prison he continued to promote civil unrest and majority rule, and his cause eventually gained international recognition. He was offered but turned down a conditional release from prison in 1985. After enormous international and internal pressure, South African President F. W. de Klerk "unbanned" the ANC and unconditionally released Nelson Mandela from prison. Nonetheless South Africa remained in turmoil, and in 1992 4 million workers went on strike to protest white rule. Because of this pressure, Mandela forced de Klerk to sign a document outlining multiparty elections. Mandela won the 1994 national election and was the first democratically elected leader of the country.

Do you think Nelson Mandela is a charismatic leader? Why or why not?

Sources: M. Fatima, *Higher Than Hope: The Authorized Biography of Nelson Mandela* (New York: Harper & Row, 1990); S. Clark, *Nelson Mandela Speaks: Forming a Democratic, Nonracist South Africa* (New York: Pathfinder Press, 1993).

> *An institution is the lengthened shadow of one man.*
>
> **Ralph Waldo Emerson, writer**

Max Weber arguably wrote the single most important work. Weber was a sociologist interested primarily in how authority and religious and economic forces affected societies over time. Weber maintained that societies could be categorized into one of three types of authority systems: traditional, legal–rational, and charismatic.[45]

In the **traditional authority system,** the traditions or unwritten laws of the society dictate who has authority and how this authority can be used. The transfer of authority in such systems is based on traditions such as passing power to the first-born son of a king after the king dies. Historical examples would include the monarchies of England from the 1400s to 1600s or the dynasties of China from 3000 BC to the 1700s. Some modern examples of the traditional authority system include Saudi Arabia, Kuwait, Syria, North Korea, Brunei, and Libya. But these examples should not be limited to countries—many of the CEOs in privately held companies or publicly traded companies that are controlled by a majority shareholder are often the children or relatives of the previous CEO. Examples include Ford, Marriott, Anheuser-Busch, Cargill, Marriott Hotels, Amway, and Carlson Companies (owners of T.G.I. Friday's restaurants and Radisson Hotels).

In the **legal–rational authority system** a person possesses authority not because of tradition or birthright but because of the laws that govern the position occupied. For example, elected officials and most leaders in nonprofit or publicly traded companies are authorized to take certain actions because of the positions they occupy. The power is in the position itself rather than in the person who occupies the position. Thus Hillary Clinton can take certain actions not because of whom she is or is related to but because of her role as U.S. Secretary of State.

These two authority systems can be contrasted to the **charismatic authority system,** in which people derive authority because of their exemplary characteristics. Charismatic leaders are thought to possess superhuman qualities or powers of divine origin that set them apart from ordinary mortals. The locus of authority in this system rests with the individual possessing these unusual qualities; it is not derived from birthright or laws. According to Weber, charismatic leaders come from the margins of society and emerge as leaders in times of great social crisis. These leaders focus society both on the problems it faces and on the revolutionary solutions proposed by the leader. Thus charismatic authority systems are usually the result of a revolution against the traditional and legal–rational authority systems. Examples of these revolutions might be the overthrow of the Shah of Iran by the Ayatollah Khomeini, the ousting of the British in India by Mahatma Gandhi, the success of Martin Luther King Jr. in changing the civil rights laws in the United States, or the economic and social change movements led by Hugo Chavez in Venezuela. Unlike traditional or legal–rational authority systems, charismatic authority systems tend to be short-lived. Charismatic leaders must project an image of success in order for followers to believe they possess superhuman qualities; any failures will cause followers to question the divine qualities of the leader and in turn erode the leader's authority.

A number of historians, political scientists, and sociologists have commented on various aspects of Weber's conceptualization of charismatic authority systems. Of all these comments, however, probably the biggest controversy surrounding Weber's theory concerns the locus of charismatic leadership. Is charisma primarily the result of the situation or social context facing the leader, the leader's extraordinary qualities, or the strong relationships between charismatic leaders and followers? A number of authors have argued that charismatic movements could not take place unless the society was in a crisis.[46-48] Along these lines, Friedland, Gerth and Mills, and Kanter have argued that before a leader with extraordinary qualities would be perceived as charismatic, the social situation must be such that followers recognize the relevance of the leader's qualities.[49-51] Others have argued that charismatic leadership is primarily a function of the leader's extraordinary qualities, not the situation. These qualities include having extraordinary powers of vision, the rhetorical skills to communicate this vision, a sense of mission, high self-confidence and intelligence, and setting high expectations for followers.[52,53] Finally,

Kleptocracies and Authority Systems

HIGHLIGHT 14.6

The difference between a kleptocrat and a wise states-man, between a robber baron and a benefactor, is merely one of degree.

Jared Diamond, researcher

In the book *Guns, Germs, and Steel* author Jared Diamond describes the historic, geographic, climatic, technologic, demographic, and economic factors that have caused human societies to emerge, thrive, or disappear. One phenomenon that appears across many groups as they grow to 100 or so people is the emergence of some form of government. Sometimes this government is based on the power of a family (traditional authority); other times it is more fomalized (legal–rational authority); and at times it is based on a single leader (charismatic authority). Governments emerge because groups this size begin to recognize that they can solve common problems, such as finding food and shelter and defending against enemies by pooling resources rather than working as individuals. Thus members of the group give up certain liberties and resources but gain services they could ill afford on their own. Some people perceive this exchange to be relatively fair; the services they receive seem to offset their costs in terms of taxes, food, and so on. But at other times these governments appear to be nothing more than kleptocracies—people pay large tributes to a small group of people at the top but get little in return. Kleptoc-

racies can be found in traditional authority systems; what do British citizens get in return for paying taxes to support having a queen? Kleptocracies can also be found in legal–rational systems; the collapse of the financial services and automobile industries in 2008–2009 are examples of executives ripping off customers, employees, and shareholders. Charismatic leaders can also head up kleptocracies. At one time Robert Mugabe was seen as a charismatic leader by many of his citizens, but with his $2 million birthday party, poverty rates at an all-time high, and inflation hovering at 8,000 percent per year, it seems that most citizens of Zimbabwe are not enjoying the same fruits of success.

Because charismatic leaders are more likely to emerge in a crisis, they may be more likely to appear when citizens believe their fees, taxes, goods, cattle, or people payments are misaligned with the benefits they are getting by keeping their government in place. This is precisely what happened when Mao, Lenin, and Castro led their communist revolutions in China, Russia, and Cuba. More recently this same phenomenon has allowed charismatic leaders to be elected into the presidential suites in Venezuela and Ecuador. And the (un)fairness of the tax versus service exchange is often used by politicians in the United States to gain votes and get elected into office.

Is your current government a kleptocracy? Why or why not? What information would you use to justify your answer?

Source: J. Diamond, *Guns, Germs, and Steel: The Fates of Human Societies* (New York: W.W. Norton, 1999).

---

several authors have argued that the litmus test for charismatic leadership does not depend on the leader's qualities or the presence of a crisis, but rather on followers' reactions to their leader. According to this argument, charisma is attributed only to those leaders who can develop particularly strong emotional attachments with followers.[54-58]

The debate surrounding charismatic leadership shifted dramatically with the publication of James MacGregor Burns's *Leadership*. Burns was a prominent political scientist who had spent a career studying leadership in the national political arena. He believed that leadership could take one of two forms. **Transactional leadership** occurred when leaders and followers were in some type of exchange relationship to get needs met. The exchange could be economic, political, or psychological, and examples might include exchanging money for work, votes for political favors, loyalty for consideration, and so forth. Transactional leadership is common but tends to be transitory in that there may be no enduring purpose to hold parties together once a transaction is made. Burns also noted that while this type of leadership could be quite effective, it did not result in organizational or societal change and instead tended to perpetuate and legitimize the status quo.[14]

The second form of leadership is **transformational leadership,** which changes the status quo by appealing to followers' values and their sense of higher purpose. Transformational leaders articulate the problems in the current system and have a compelling vision of what a new society or organization could be. This new vision of society is intimately linked to the values of both the leader and the followers; it represents an ideal that is congruent with their value systems. According to Burns, transformational leadership is ultimately a moral exercise in that it raises the standard of human conduct. This implies that the acid test for transformational leadership might be the answer to the question "Do the changes advocated by the leader advance or hinder the development of the organization or society?" Transformational leaders are also adept at **reframing** issues; they point out how the problems or issues facing followers can be resolved if they fulfill the leader's vision of the future. These leaders also teach followers how to become leaders in their own right and incite them to play active roles in the change movement (see Profiles in Leadership 14.1–14.5).

All transformational leaders are charismatic, but not all charismatic leaders are transformational. Transformational leaders are charismatic because they can articulate a compelling vision of the future and form strong emotional attachments with followers. However, this vision and these relationships are aligned with followers' value systems and help them get their needs met. Charismatic leaders who are *not* transformational can convey a vision and form strong emotional bonds with followers, but they do so to get their own (that is, the leader's) needs met. Both charismatic and transformational leaders strive for organizational or societal change; the difference is whether the changes are for the benefit of the leader or the followers. Finally, transformational leaders are always controversial. Charismatic leadership almost inherently raises conflicts over values or definitions of the social good. Controversy also arises because the people with the most to lose in any existing system will put up the most resistance to a transformational change initiative. The emotional levels of those resisting the transformational leadership movement are often just as great as those who embrace it, and this may be the underlying cause for the violent ends to Martin Luther King Jr., John F. Kennedy, Mahatma Gandhi, Joan of Arc, and Jesus Christ. Burns stated that transformational leadership always involves conflict and change, and transformational leaders must be willing to embrace conflict, make enemies, exhibit a high level of self-sacrifice, and be thick-skinned and focused to perpetuate their cause (see Profiles in Leadership 14.3).[59-65]

Leadership researchers Gary Yukl, Jerry Hunt, and Jay Conger have all maintained that the publication of *Leadership* played a key role in renewing interest in the topic of leadership.[66-68] As a result, research over the past 35 years has explored cross-cultural, gender, succession, leader, follower, situational, and performance issues in charismatic or transformational leadership. From these efforts we now know that charismatic or transformational leadership is both common and rare. It is common because it can occur in almost every social stratum across every culture. For example, a high school student leader in France, a military cadet leader at the U.S. Naval Academy, a Kenyan community leader, an Indonesian hospital leader, or a Russian business executive could all be perceived as charismatic or transformational leaders. But it is also rare because most people in positions of authority are not perceived to be charismatic or transformational leaders. We also know that females such as Sarah Palin, Carly Fiorina, or Oprah Winfrey tend to be perceived as more charismatic than their male counterparts and that transformational leadership results in higher group performance than transactional leadership.[69-88] Although charismatic or transformational leadership often results in large-scale organizational change and higher organizational performance, there is little evidence that these changes remain permanent in organizational settings after the leader moves on.[89,90] In addition, some researchers have found that charismatic or transformational leaders did not result in higher organizational performance, but they did earn higher paychecks for themselves.[89,91-93] In other words, these leaders were good at garnering attention, hogging credit, and changing their respective organizations, but many of these changes did not result in higher organizational performance.

As a result of this research, we also have three newer theories of charismatic or transformational leadership. Conger and Kanungo used a stage model to differentiate charismatic from noncharismatic leaders. Charismatic leaders begin by thoroughly assessing the current situation and pinpointing problems with the status quo. They then articulate a vision that represents a change from the status quo. This vision represents a challenge and is a motivating force for change for followers. The vision must be articulated in a way that increases dissatisfaction with the status quo and compels followers to take action. In the final stage, leaders build trust in their vision and goals by personal example, risk taking, and their total commitment to the vision.[94] The theory developed by House and his colleagues describes how charismatic leaders achieve higher performance by changing followers' self-concepts. Charismatic leaders are believed to motivate followers by changing their perceptions of work itself, offering an appealing vision of the future, developing a collective identity among followers, and increasing their confidence in getting the job done.[95-97] Avolio and Bass's theory of transformational and transactional leadership is essentially an extension of Burns's theory. Unlike Burns, who viewed transactional and

Osama bin Laden

PROFILES IN LEADERSHIP 14.3

Osama bin Laden is a member of the prestigious bin Laden family in Saudi Arabia and is the founder of al-Qaeda. Bin Laden was born in Riyadh, Saudi Arabia, and was brought up as a devout Sunni Muslim. He attended the Al-Thager Model School in Jeddah, "the school of the elite," and was exposed to many teachings of the Muslim Brotherhood while growing up. He attended university after his secondary schooling, but it is uncertain what he majored in or whether he obtained a degree. At the age of 17 he married his first wife and reportedly has had up to four wives and fathered anywhere between 12 and 24 children. In person he is said to be soft-spoken, charming, respectful, and polite. He appears to live a life of discipline, simplicity, and self-sacrifice, preferring that his wealth be used to benefit al-Qaeda rather than improve his personal lifestyle.

Bin Laden first engaged in militant activities in the late 1970s, when he moved to Pakistan to help the mujahedeen fight a guerilla war to oust the Soviet Union from Afghanistan. His family connections and wealth helped to fund many of the mujahedeen's efforts over the next 10 years. Some of his money and arms may have come from the Central Intelligence Agency: the United States also wanted to get the Soviet Union out of Afghanistan.

After Iraq invaded Kuwait in 1990, bin Laden offered to protect Saudi Arabia with 12,000 armed men, but his offer was rebuffed by the Saudi royal family. Shortly thereafter bin Laden publicly denounced the presence of coalition troops ("infidels") on Saudi soil and wanted all U.S. bases on the Arab peninsula to be closed. He eventually left Saudi Arabia to take up residence in Sudan, where he established a new base for mujahedeen operations. The purpose of his African organization was to propagate Islamist philosophy and recruit new members to the cause. In 1996 bin Laden left Sudan and went to Afghanistan to set up a new base of operations, where he forged a close relationship with the leaders of the new Taliban government.

Bin Laden issued fatwas in 1996 and 1998 that stated that Muslims should kill civilians and military personnel from the United States and allied countries until they withdraw support for Israel and withdraw military forces from Islamic countries. It is believed he was either directly involved with or funded the 1992 bombing of the Gold Mihor Hotel in Aden, Yemen; the massacre of German tourists in Luxor, Egypt, in 1997; the 1998 bombings of two United States embassies in Africa; and the World Trade Center and Pentagon bombings on 9/11/2001. He, al-Qaeda, and its splinter movements have been involved with the London subway bombing, the wars in Afghanistan and Iraq, and unrest in the Philippines, Thailand, Indonesia, and Somalia. Given his ability to evade capture and track record, it is likely the world will see more violence from these groups.

It is clear that bin Laden has a following, and that following has grown into the tens of thousands over the past 20 years. These followers are very devoted; some are so committed that they volunteer to be suicide bombers. A much larger group may not play active roles in al-Qaeda but are clearly sympathetic to its cause. But as strong as these followers' feelings are about bin Laden, others are just as intent to see him dead or behind bars.

Is Osama bin Laden a charismatic leader or a transformational leader? Would your answer to this question change if you were sympathetic to the al-Qaeda cause?

Sources: http://topics.nytimes.com/reference/timestopics/people/b/osama_bin_laden/index.html; http://www.infoplease.com/spot/osamabinladen.html.

transformational leadership as the extremes of a single continuum, Avolio and Bass viewed these two concepts as independent leadership dimensions. Thus leaders can be transformational and transactional, transactional but not transformational, and so on. Transformational leaders are believed to achieve stronger results because they heighten followers' awareness of goals and the means to achieve them, they convince followers to take action for the collective good of the group, and their vision of the future helps followers satisfy higher-order needs. Because Avolio and Bass created a questionnaire to assess a leader's standing on transactional and transformational leadership, this theory is by far the most thoroughly researched and will be discussed in more detail later in this chapter.[98]

What Are the Common Characteristics of Charismatic and Transformational Leadership?

Although there are some important differences in the theories offered by Conger and Kanungo, House, and Avolio and Bass, in reality they are far more similar than different. These researchers either do not differentiate charismatic from transformational leadership, or see charisma as a component of transformational leadership. Therefore, we will use these terms somewhat interchangeably in the next section, although we acknowledge the fundamental difference between these two types of leadership. A review of the common leader, follower, and situational factors from Burns and the three

The ultimate measure of a man is not where he stands in moments of comfort and convenience, but where he stands in moments of challenge and controversy.

Martin Luther King Jr., civil rights leader

FIGURE 14.5
Factors Pertaining to Charismatic Leadership and the Interactional Framework

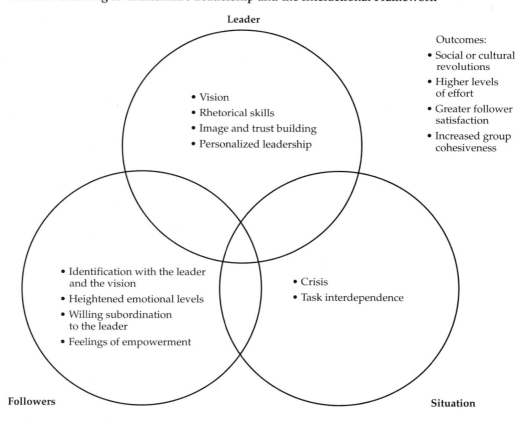

Leader

- Vision
- Rhetorical skills
- Image and trust building
- Personalized leadership

Outcomes:
- Social or cultural revolutions
- Higher levels of effort
- Greater follower satisfaction
- Increased group cohesiveness

- Identification with the leader and the vision
- Heightened emotional levels
- Willing subordination to the leader
- Feelings of empowerment

- Crisis
- Task interdependence

Followers

Situation

more recent theories can be found in Figure 14.5. Like the past debates surrounding charismatic leadership, modern researchers are divided on whether charismatic leadership is due to the leader's superhuman qualities, a special relationship between leaders and followers, the situation, or some combination of these factors. Irrespective of the locus of charismatic leadership, the research provides overwhelming support for the notion that transformational leaders are effective at large-scale societal or organizational change.

Leader Characteristics

Charismatic leaders are meaning makers. They pick and choose from the rough materials of reality and construct pictures of great possibilities. Their persuasion then is of the subtlest kind, for they interpret reality to offer us images of the future that are irresistible.

**Jay Conger,
University of
Southern California**

Leadership researchers have spent considerably more time and effort trying to identify the unique characteristics of charismatic leaders than they have exploring follower or situational factors. This is partly because some researchers believe that it is possible to drive higher levels of organizational change or performance through the selection or training of charismatic leaders.[64,70,76,77,82,83,99,100] Although some scholars have argued that the leader's personal qualities are the key to charismatic or transformational leadership, we do not believe the leader's qualities alone result in charismatic leadership. [101,102] We do, however, acknowledge several common threads in the behavior and style of both charismatic and transformational leaders, and these include their vision and values, rhetorical skills, ability to build a particular kind of image in the hearts and minds of their followers, and personalized style of leadership.

Vision

Both transformational and charismatic leaders are inherently future-oriented. They involve helping a group move "from here to there." Charismatic leaders perceive fundamental discrepancies between the way things are and the way things can (or should) be. They recognize the shortcomings of the present order and offer an imaginative **vision** to overcome them. A charismatic leader's vision is not limited to grand social movements; leaders can develop a compelling vision for any organization and organizational level. This vision can have both a stimulating and a unifying effect on the efforts of followers, which can help drive greater organizational alignment and change and higher performance levels by followers (see Figure 14.6).[103-105] Paradoxically, the magic of a leader's vision is often that the more complicated the problem, the more people may be drawn to simplistic solutions.

Never underestimate the power of purpose.
**Price Pritchett,
consultant**

Rhetorical Skills

In addition to *having* vision, charismatic leaders are gifted in *sharing* their vision. As discussed earlier, charismatic and transformational leaders have superb **rhetorical skills** that heighten followers' emotional levels and inspire them to embrace the vision. As it turns out, both the content of

FIGURE 14.6
A Leader's Vision of the Future Can Align Efforts and Help Groups Accomplish More

Source: Adapted from P. M. Senge, *The Fifth Discipline* (New York: Doubleday, 1990).

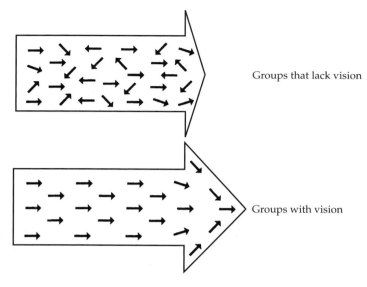

Groups that lack vision

Groups with vision

Facts tell, but stories sell.

Bob Whelan,
NCS Pearson

a transformational leader's speeches and the way they are delivered are vitally important.[104-114] Charismatic leaders make extensive use of metaphors, analogies, and stories rather than abstract and colorless rational discourse to reframe issues and make their points. Often the delivery of the speech is even more important than the content itself—poor delivery can detract from compelling content. Adolf Hitler mastered his delivery techniques so well that his speeches can have hypnotic power even to people who do not understand German. Similarly, many people consider Martin Luther King Jr.'s "I Have a Dream" speech one of the most moving speeches they have ever heard. Note his use of different speech techniques and his masterful evocation of patriotic and cultural themes in the speech found at www.mlkonline.net/video-i-have-a-dream-speech.html.

Image and Trust Building

Setting an example is not the main means of influencing another; it is the only means.

Albert Einstein,
physicist

As demonstrated in Profiles in Leadership 14.2 and 14.3, transformational leaders build trust in their leadership and the attainability of their goals through an **image** of seemingly unshakable self-confidence, strength of moral conviction, personal example and self-sacrifice, and unconventional tactics or behavior.[63,95,115-120] They are perceived to have unusual insight and ability and act in a manner consistent with their vision and values. Whereas transformational leaders **build trust** by showing commitment to followers' needs over self-interest, some charismatic leaders are so concerned with their image that they are not beyond taking credit for others' accomplishments or exaggerating their expertise.[115]

Political Campaigns and the Attribution of Charisma

HIGHLIGHT 14.7

Political campaigns are a big business in the United States. It is estimated that the 2008 presidential election alone cost candidates over $1 billion in campaign funds. Most of this money was used for various types of advertisements with the lion's share going to television commercials. These commercials tend to be of two extremes. At one extreme, if the commercial is sponsored by the candidate (or a group that supports the candidate), it contains only information that paints the candidate in a favorable light. This positive spin is intended to leave a favorable impression on the audience so they will vote for the candidate in the upcoming election. At the other extreme, negative attack ads usually consist of half-truths, unflattering photographs, or comments and video clips that are taken out of context and/or modified so the audience questions the integrity, competence, judgment, and personality of candidates. For example, negative attack ads questioned the integrity, bravery, and legitimacy of 2004 U.S. presidential candidate John Kerry, a decorated Vietnam War veteran. Curiously enough, the Democratic party did not run negative ads about George W. Bush's Vietnam record, who avoided fighting in the Vietnam War by "protecting Texas from Oklahoma" as part of the Texas Air National Guard. People tend to remember negative attack ads more than those with positive spin,

so candidates have been using them with more and more frequency.

Given the unflattering nature of negative attack ads, we must wonder if it is possible to perceive political candidates as charismatic leaders. Followers' perceptions are critical in the attribution of charisma, and in the day and age of negative attack ads, unverified blogs, and unflattering video clips and cell phone photos, it may be impossible for anyone wanting to hold an elected office to be seen as charismatic. With technology it is far too easy to catch candidates saying or doing something that destroys their image and trust-building capabilities. On the other hand, positive spin campaigns may help to create the perception of charisma when candidates are anything but charismatic. What does seem true is that technology will give voters more information about candidates than they ever had in the past and that candidates need to be mindful of how anything they say or do can show up on the Internet and national television in just a few hours.

How have technology and the media affected the attribution of charisma to Sarah Palin? Barack Obama? Evo Morales? Kim Jong-Il?

Source: R. E. Riggio, "It's the Leadership, Stupid—An I/O Psychology Perspective on the 2004 U.S. Presidential Election," *The Industrial-Organizational Psychologist* 42, no. 3 (2005), pp. 21–25.

Personalized Leadership

Never tell people how to do things. Tell them what to do, and they will surprise you with their ingenuity.

George S. Patton, U.S. Army general

One of the most important aspects of charismatic and transformational leadership is the personal nature of the leader's power. These leaders share strong, personal bonds with followers, even when the leader occupies a formal organizational role. It is this **personalized leadership** style that seems to be responsible for the feelings of empowerment notable among followers of charismatic or transformational leaders. Charismatic leaders seem more adept at picking up social cues and tend to be emotionally expressive, especially through such nonverbal channels as their eye contact, posture, movement, gestures, tone of voice, and facial expressions. Transformational leaders also empower followers by giving them tasks that lead to heightened self-confidence and creating environments of heightened expectations and positive emotions.[1,61,62,64, 77,89,116,119,121-124]

Follower Characteristics

If charismatic leadership were defined solely by a leader's characteristics, it would be relatively easy to identify individuals with good vision, rhetorical, and impression management skills and place them in leadership positions. Over time we would expect that a high percentage of followers would embrace and act on these leaders' visions. However, a number of leaders appear to possess these attributes yet are not seen as charismatic. They may be good, competent leaders, but they seem unable to evoke strong feelings in followers or to get followers to do more than they thought possible. In reality, charisma is probably more a function of the followers' reactions to a leader than of the leader's personal characteristics. If followers do not accept the leader's vision or become emotionally attached to the leader, then the leader simply will not be perceived to be either charismatic or transformational. Thus **charisma** is in the eyes and heart of the beholder; it is a particularly strong emotional reaction to, identification with, and belief in some leaders by some followers. Note that this definition is value-free—leaders seen as charismatic may or may not share the same values as their followers or meet Burns's criteria for transformational leadership. A recent example of followers' divergent reactions can be seen with U.S. President Barack Obama. Some followers, particularly those in the Democratic party, perceive President Obama to be a very charismatic leader. Most Republicans think he does not share the same values as the American people and is out to destroy the United States, yet he is clearly the same person. Many of the more popular conceptualizations of charisma and charismatic leadership today also define charisma in terms of followers' reactions to the leader.[1,77,94,111,125-127] Defining charisma as a reaction that followers have toward leaders makes it reasonable to turn our attention to the four unique characteristics of these reactions.

Identification with the Leader and the Vision

Two of the effects associated with charismatic leadership include a strong affection for the leader and a similarity of follower beliefs with those of the leader. These effects describe a sort of bonding or **identification with the leader** personally and a parallel psychological investment to a goal or activity (a "cause") bigger than oneself. Followers bond with a leader because they may be intensely dissatisfied with the status quo and see the implementation of the vision as a solution to their problems. Being like the leader, or approved by the leader, also becomes an important part of followers' self-worth.[128-134]

Heightened Emotional Levels

Charismatic leaders are able to stir followers' feelings, and this **heightened emotional level** results in increased levels of effort and performance.[61,62,64,122,132,135-138] Emotions are often the fuel driving large-scale initiatives for change, and charismatic leaders will often do all they can to maintain them, including getting followers to think about their dissatisfaction with the status quo or making impassioned appeals directly to followers. But charismatic leaders need to keep in mind that some people will become alienated with the vision and movement and can have emotions just as intense as those of the followers of the vision. This polarizing effect of charismatic leaders may be one reason why they tend to have violent deaths: those alienated by a charismatic leader are almost as likely to act on their emotions as followers within the movement.[139]

Willing Subordination to the Leader

We're not worthy; we're not worthy!
Wayne and Garth, "Wayne's World"

Whereas the preceding factor dealt with followers' emotional and psychological closeness to the leader, **willing subordination to the leader** involves their deference to his or her authority.[130] Charismatic leaders often seem imbued with superhuman qualities. As a result, followers often naturally and willingly submit to the leader's apparent authority and superiority. Followers seem to suspend their critical thinking skills; they have few doubts about the intentions or skills of the leader, the correctness of the vision or change initiative, or the actions they need to take in order to achieve the vision.

Feelings of Empowerment

Followers of charismatic leaders are moved to expect more of themselves, and they work harder to achieve these higher goals. Charismatic leaders set high expectations while expressing confidence in their abilities and providing ongoing encouragement and support. Somewhat paradoxically, followers feel stronger and more powerful at the same time they willingly subordinate themselves to the charismatic leader. These **feelings of empowerment,** when combined with heightened emotional levels and a leader's vision of the future, often result in increases in organizational, group, or team performance or significant social change.[81,116,122,140] (See Table 14.2 for typical reactions to change requests.)

TABLE 14.2
Followers'
**Responses to
Change**

Source: B. Yager (Boise, ID: The Bryan Yager Group, 2003).

Malicious compliance: This occurs when followers either ignore or actively sabotage change requests.
Compliance: This takes place when followers do no more than abide by the policies and procedures surrounding change requests.
Cooperation: Followers willingly engage in those activities needed to make the change request become reality.
Commitment: Followers embrace change requests as their own and often go the extra mile to make sure work gets done. Charismatic and transformational leaders are adept at getting followers committed to their vision of the future.

Barack Obama

PROFILES IN LEADERSHIP 14.4

Barack Obama is the president of the United States and rode into office on a promise of change. Born of a Kenyan father and a white mother from Kansas, Obama spent most of his formative years in Hawaii and Indonesia. Upon graduation from high school, Obama attended Columbia University, where he graduated with a BA in political science. He then moved to Chicago and spent three years working for a nonprofit organization that helped local churches provide job training programs. He next attended Harvard Law School, where he was the first black man to be elected class president in the school's 104-year history. He graduated magna cum laude with a JD and moved back to Chicago to work in a law firm.

While in Chicago Obama organized voter registration drives, lectured on constitutional law at the University of Chicago, and was elected to represent the Hyde Park district in the Illinois State Senate. He spent eight years as a state senator before running for United States senator in 2004. While in the Senate Obama sponsored or supported legislation on immigration and election reform, tightening the rules for lobbying and the use of corporate jets for legislator travel, the reduction of greenhouse gases, the creation of a universal health care program, continuing sanctions against Iran's nuclear enrichment program, and ending the war in Iraq. He gained national prominence with an electrifying keynote address at the 2004 Democratic National Convention.

A smart, articulate, engaging, and charismatic public speaker, Obama has been able to leverage these assets to become the president of the United States.

Since taking office in early 2009 Obama has faced a number of major crises. The U.S. economy continued in a major recession, the financial services and automobile industries had failed, the country was fighting wars in both Iraq and Afghanistan, Iran continued pursuing a nuclear agenda, North Korea threatened the United States and South Korea, there was a major environmental disaster in the Gulf of Mexico, health care costs continued to escalate, and immigration became a major political issue. To address some of these issues, the Obama administration spearheaded major economic recovery and stimulus packages, passed landmark financial services and health care reform legislation, drew down troops in Iraq while adding another 30,000 to the Afghanistan campaign, and ran up the largest national debt in U.S. history. President Obama's approval ratings have dropped over 30 percent since he took office, and there is some doubt whether he will be elected for a second term.

How do these situational factors and the media play into Barack Obama being perceived as a charismatic leader? Is he an effective leader? What would you use to evaluate his performance as a leader?

Sources: http://www.reuters.com/people/barack-obama; http://www.ontheissues.org/barack_obama.htm; http://www.biography.com/articles/Barack-Obama-12782369.

Situational Characteristics

Many researchers believe that situational factors also play an important role in determining whether a leader will be perceived as charismatic. Perhaps individuals possessing the qualities of charismatic leaders are perceived as charismatic *only when confronting certain types of situations.* Because the situation may play an important role in the attribution of charisma, it will be useful to review some of the situational factors believed to affect charismatic leadership.

Crises

Perhaps the most important situational factor associated with charismatic leadership is the presence or absence of a **crisis.** Followers who are content with the status quo are relatively unlikely to perceive a need for a charismatic leader or be willing to devote great effort to fundamentally change an organization or society. On the other hand, a crisis often creates "charisma hungry" followers who are looking for a leader to alleviate or resolve their crisis. Leaders are given considerably more latitude and autonomy and may temporarily (or sometimes permanently) suspend accepted rules, policies, and procedures to pull the organization out of the crisis. Some leaders may even create or manufacture crises to increase followers' acceptance of their vision, the range of actions they can take, and followers' level of effort. Although a crisis situation does not necessarily make every leader look charismatic, such a situation may set the stage for particular kinds of leader behaviors to be effective.[80,82,92,101,102,121,142-144]

Social Networks

Communication is the currency of leadership.
David Lee, Personal Decisions International

Social networks can also affect the attribution of charisma. Attributions of charisma will spread more quickly in organizations having well-established social networks, where everybody tends to know everyone else. And more often than not charismatic leaders have bigger social networks and play a more central role in their networks than leaders seen as less charismatic.[145,146]

Other Situational Characteristics

Two other situational characteristics may help or hinder the emergence of a charismatic leader. One of these is outsourcing and organizational downsizing. Many people believe that downsizing destroys the implicit contract between employer and employee and leaves many employees disillusioned with corporate life. Because charismatic or transformational leadership is intensely relational in nature, destroying the implicit contract between leaders and followers greatly diminishes the odds of charismatic leadership emergence. But of all the situational variables affecting charismatic leadership, perhaps the most important and overlooked variable is **time.** Charismatic or transformational leadership does not happen overnight. It takes time for leaders to develop and articulate their vision, heighten followers' emotional levels, build trusting relationships with followers, and direct and empower followers to fulfill the vision. A crisis may compress the amount of time needed for charismatic leadership to emerge, whereas relatively stable situations lengthen this period.

Rules are good servants, but not always good masters.
Russell Page, master landscaper

Concluding Thoughts about the Characteristics of Charismatic and Transformational Leadership

Several final points about the characteristics of charismatic leadership need to be made. First, although we defined charisma as a quality attributed to certain leaders based on the relationships they share with followers, charismatic leadership is most fully understood when we also consider how leader and situational factors affect this attribution process. The special relationships charismatic leaders share with followers do not happen by accident; rather, they are often the result of interaction between the leader's qualities, the degree to which a leader's vision fulfills followers' needs, and the presence of certain situational factors. Second, it seems unlikely that all the characteristics of charismatic leadership need to be present before charisma is attributed to a leader. The bottom line for charisma seems to be the relationships certain leaders share with followers, and there may be a variety of ways in which these relationships can develop. This also implies that charisma may be more of a continuum than an all-or-nothing phenomenon. Some leaders may be able to form particularly strong bonds with a majority, others with a few—and still others may not get along well with any followers. Third, it seems that charismatic leadership can happen anywhere—schools, churches, communities, businesses, government organizations, and nations—and does not happen only on the world stage.

Fourth, given that there are a number of ways to develop strong emotional attachments with followers, one important question is whether it is possible to attribute charisma to an individual based solely on his or her position or celebrity status. Some individuals in positions of high public visibility and esteem (film stars, musicians, athletes, television evangelists, or politicians) can develop (even cultivate) charismatic images among their fans and admirers. In these cases it is helpful to recognize that charismatic leadership is a two-way street. Not only do followers develop strong emotional bonds with leaders, but leaders also develop strong emotional bonds with followers and are concerned with follower development.[14,81,140] It is difficult to see how the one-way communication channels of radio and television can foster these two-way relationships or enhance follower growth. Thus, although we sometimes view certain individuals as charismatic based on media manipulation and hype, this is not transformational leadership.

So what can leadership practitioners take from this research if they want to use an emotional approach to drive organizational change? They will probably be more successful at driving organizational change if they capitalize on or create a crisis. They also need to be close enough to their followers to determine their sources of discontent and ensure that their vision provides a solution to followers' problems and paints a compelling picture of the future. Leaders must passionately articulate their vision of the future; it is difficult to imagine followers being motivated toward a vision that is unclear or presented by a leader who does not seem to really care about it. Leadership practitioners also need to understand that they alone cannot make the vision a reality; they need their followers' help and support to create organizational or societal changes. Along these lines, they will need to be a role model and coach followers on what they should (and should not) be doing, provide feedback and encouragement, and

Good to Great: An Alternative Framework to the Rational and Emotional Approaches to Organizational Change

HIGHLIGHT 14.8

An alternative conceptualization of organizational change comes from the book *Good to Great.* Collins and his research team reviewed the financial performance of 1,435 companies that appeared on the *Fortune* 500 list from 1965 to 1995. From this list, 11 companies made the leap from being a good to a truly great company—a company that yielded financial returns much higher than those for the overall stock market or industry competitors for at least 15 consecutive years. For example, a dollar invested in these 11 companies in 1965 would have yielded $471 in January 2000, whereas the same dollar invested in the stock market would have returned $56. Collins's research indicates that these 11 companies all followed the same six rules:

1. *Level 5 leadership:* The *Good to Great* companies were led not by high-profile celebrity leaders but rather by humble, self-effacing, and reserved individuals who also possessed an incredibly strong drive to succeed.

2. *First who, then what:* Before developing a future vision or goals, these leaders first made sure they had the right people with the right skills in the right jobs. Leadership talent management was a key focus of these top companies.

3. *Confront the brutal facts (yet never lose faith):* These leaders met reality head-on—they did not sugarcoat organizational challenges or difficulties. But they also had an unshakable faith in their organizations' ability to meet these challenges.

4. *The hedgehog concept:* These companies all focused on being the best in the world at what

they did, were deeply passionate about their business, and identified one or two key financial or operational metrics to guide their decision making and day-to-day activities.

5. *A culture of discipline:* Companies that had disciplined people did not need hierarchies, bureaucracies, or excessive controls because the people in the field knew what they needed to do and made sure it happened.

6. *Technology accelerators:* All these companies selectively used technology as a means for enhancing business operations, but they were not necessarily leaders in technical innovation.

There were several other surprising findings in Collins's research. First, none of these top-performing companies was led by transformational or charismatic leaders. Second, because these top companies were constantly undergoing small but noticeable changes, they did not need to launch major change initiatives or organizational restructuring programs. Third, companies need to abide by all six of these rules to go from good to great; three or four of the six rules were not enough for companies to make the leap to becoming top performers.

How do you think a *Good to Great* leader would perform in a crisis? What would he or she do differently than a charismatic leader? What role does talent play in *Good to Great* companies versus those led by charismatic leaders?

Source: J. Collins, *Good to Great* (New York: Harper-Collins, 2001); J. Collins, "Level 5 Leadership: The Triumph of Humility and Fierce Resolve," *HBR on Point* (Boston, MA: Harvard Business School Press, 2004).

persuade followers to take on more responsibilities as their skills and self-confidence grow. Finally, leadership practitioners using this approach to organizational change also need to be thick-skinned, resilient, and patient (see Highlight 14.8). They will need to cope with the polarization effects of charismatic leadership and understand that it takes time for the effects of this type of leadership to yield results. However, the rewards appear to be well worth the efforts. There appears to be overwhelming evidence that charismatic or transformational leaders are more effective than their non-charismatic counterparts, whether they be presidents of the United States,[147] CEOs,[80,84,148] military cadets and officers,[78,79,149,150] college professors,[151] or first-line supervisors and middle-level managers in a variety of public and private sector companies.[77,82,85,86-88,122,152,153]

Bass's Theory of Transformational and Transactional Leadership

Much of what we know about the leader, follower, and situational characteristics associated with charismatic or transformational leaders comes from research on Bass's **theory of transformational and transactional leadership.**[1,117,121] Bass believed that transformational leaders possessed those leader characteristics described earlier and used subordinates' perceptions or reactions to determine whether a leader was transformational. Thus transformational leaders possess good vision, rhetorical, and impression management skills and use them to develop strong emotional bonds with followers. Transformational leaders are believed to be more successful at driving organizational change because of followers' heightened emotional levels and their willingness to work toward the accomplishment of the leader's vision. In contrast, transactional leaders do not possess these leader characteristics, nor are they able to develop strong emotional bonds with followers or inspire followers to do more than followers thought they could. Instead transactional leaders were believed to motivate followers by setting goals and promising rewards for desired performance.[1,98,116,117,119,124] Avolio and Bass maintained that transactional leadership could have positive effects on follower satisfaction and performance levels, but they also stated that these behaviors were often underutilized because of time constraints, a lack of leader skills, and a disbelief among leaders that rewards could boost performance.[77,98] Bass also maintained that transactional leadership only perpetuates the status quo; a leader's use of rewards does not result in the long-term changes associated with transformational leadership.[117]

Like the initiating structure and consideration behaviors described in Chapter 7, Bass hypothesized that transformational and transactional leadership comprised two independent leadership dimensions. Thus individuals could be high transformational but low transactional leaders, low transformational and low transactional leaders, and so on. Bass developed a questionnaire, known as the **Multifactor Leadership Questionnaire (MLQ),** to assess the extent to which leaders exhibited transformational or transactional leadership and the extent to which followers were satisfied with their leader and believed their leader was effective. The MLQ is a 360-degree feedback instrument that assesses five transformational and three transactional factors and a nonleadership

Bill Roberts

PROFILES IN LEADERSHIP 14.5

Although transformational leaders come from all walks of life, one common characteristic they share is their ability to drive change and get things done. One of the best examples of a transformational leader is Bill Roberts, the vice president of operations for Wheelabrator Technologies, Inc. (WTI). Wheelabrator Technologies runs a fleet of 22 waste-to-energy facilities—power plants that burn trash to create electricity and steam for residential and commercial customers. These plants are environmentally friendly in that only 10 percent of the trash they burn is returned to landfills; they have much lower air pollution emissions than coal-fired plants; and all the metals in the trash are recovered and recycled. As the vice president of operations, Roberts is responsible for the financial, operational, safety, and environmental performance of the fleet. When he took over operations three years ago, Roberts recognized that the fleet was not performing nearly as well as it could. Boiler availability (a measure of operating capacity) was down, safety performance was eroding, and the fleet's financial performance had substantial room for improvement. At about the same time WTI embraced an aggressive growth strategy and was looking to expand both domestically and internationally. The fleet needed to perform at a much higher level to fund these business development efforts as well as provide the operating, safety, and environmental statistics needed to give WTI a competitive advantage when bidding for new business.

Since taking over Roberts has driven a number of major changes across the fleet. An engaging and dynamic speaker, Roberts painted a compelling picture of the future of WTI and set clear expectations of performance for all his plant managers. He empowered his plant managers to find ways to improve boiler availability, safety, and financial performance and provided training to help them think more like business owners. By constantly reviewing results with the plant managers, Roberts kept challenging and encouraging his staff to find ways to continuously improve performance. He rewarded plant managers who improved plant performance and coached or removed those who could not meet his expectations. By getting plant managers to work together to solve mutual problems, Roberts also broke down the walls that had previously existed between his staff and got them to work together as a high-performing team.

From an operational perspective, the 22 plants are running about 10 percent better than they were when he took over. The fleet now has an impeccable environmental and safety record, and the plant managers have a much stronger understanding of plant financials. Because of these efforts, WTI has achieved world-class operational, safety, and environmental performance and has been able to use these results to expand the business in the United States, the United Kingdom, and China.

Given this description of Bill Roberts, do you think he is more of a charismatic or Level 5 leader? What other information would you need to make this assessment?

factor.[117,154-158] The transformational leadership factors assess the degree to which the leader instills pride in others, displays power and confidence, makes personal sacrifices or champions new possibilities, considers the ethical or moral consequences of decisions, articulates a compelling vision of the future, sets challenging standards, treats followers as individuals, and helps followers understand the problems they face. The three transactional leadership factors assess the extent to which leaders set goals, make rewards contingent on performance, obtain necessary resources, provide rewards when performance goals have been met, monitor followers' performance levels, and intervene when problems occur. The MLQ also assesses another factor called laissez-faire leadership, which assesses the extent to which leaders avoid responsibilities, fail to make decisions, are absent when needed, or fail to follow up on requests.

Research Results of Transformational and Transactional Leadership

To date, over 350 studies have used the MLQ to investigate transformational and transactional leadership across a wide variety of situations. These results indicated that transformational leadership can be observed in all countries, institutions, and organizational levels, but it was more prevalent in public institutions and at lower organizational levels.[70,77,78,82,119] In other words, there seemed to be more transformational leaders in the lower levels of the military or other public sector organizations than anywhere else. Second, there is overwhelming evidence that transformational leadership is a significantly better predictor of organizational effectiveness than transactional or laissez-faire leadership. Transformational leaders, whether they are U.S. presidents, CEOs, school administrators, or plant managers, seem to be more effective than transactional leaders at driving organizational change and getting results. Avolio and Bass also believed that transformational leadership augments performance above and beyond what is associated with transactional leadership.[77] Third, as expected, laissez-faire leadership was negatively correlated with effectiveness.

Given that the MLQ can reliably identify transformational leaders and that these leaders can drive higher levels of organizational change and effectiveness than their transactional counterparts, it seems reasonable to ask whether it is possible to train or select charismatic leaders. Fortunately researchers have looked at the effects of transformational leadership training on the performance of military, public sector, and private industry leaders in the United States, Canada, and Israel. Usually these training programs consisted of several one- to five-day training sessions in which participants learned about the theory of transformational and transactional leadership; received MLQ feedback on the extent to which they exhibit transformational, transactional, and laissez-faire leadership; and then went through a series of skill-building exercises and activities to improve their leadership effectiveness. This research provided strong evidence that it is possible for leaders to systematically develop their transformational and transactional leadership skills.[70,77,82,83,99,156,159,160]

An alternative to training leaders to be more transformational is to select leaders with the propensity to be transformational or charismatic in the first place. Several researchers have looked at the importance of childhood experiences, leadership traits, and even genetics in transformational

TABLE 14.3 **Correlations between Five Factor Model Dimensions and Charismatic Leadership Characteristics for 125 Corporate CEOs and Presidents**

Source: D. Nilsen, "Using Self and Observers' Ratings for Personality to Predict Leadership Performance," unpublished doctoral dissertation, University of Minnesota, Minneapolis, 1995.

Personality Dimension	Transformational Leadership Characteristics			
	Visionary Thinking	Empowering Others	Inspiring Trust	High-Impact Delivery
Extraversion	.32	.33	.16	.47
Conscientiousness	−.08	−.01	.06	−.04
Agreeableness	.02	.52	.48	.35
Neuroticism	−.03	.29	.38	.22
Openness to experience	.47	.30	.14	.40

leadership. Zacharatos, Barling, and Kelloway reported that adolescents who were rated by coaches and peers to be more transformational were also more likely to have parents who were transformational leaders.[161] There is also evidence that certain Five Factor Model (FFM) leadership traits (Chapter 6) can be reliably used to identify transformational leaders.[76,124,139,162-166] Some of the most compelling evidence comes from Nilsen, who looked at the relationships between FFM personality traits and 125 CEOs. As shown in Table 14.3, not only are the FFM personality dimensions strongly correlated with certain components of transformational leadership, but the pattern of high and low correlations seems to make sense.[165] Given that certain leadership traits are related to transformational leadership, and that leadership traits have a genetic component, it is not surprising that some researchers also believe that some aspect of transformational leadership is heritable.[100]

Despite this evidence that it may be possible to select and train transformational leaders, the fact remains that charisma ultimately exists in the eye of the beholder. Thus there can be no guarantee that leaders who have the right stuff and are schooled in the appropriate techniques will be seen as charismatic by followers. As discussed earlier, follower and situational variables play a key role in determining whether leaders are perceived as transformational and drive organizational change. Certain leaders may get higher transformational leadership scores as a result of a training program; but do they actually heighten followers' emotional levels, get followers to exert extra effort, and as a result achieve greater organizational change or performance after the program? Given what we know about individual differences and leadership skills training, it seems likely that a leader's personality will also play a major role in determining whether he or she will benefit from such training.

Finally, several other important comments about the theory of transformational and transactional leadership are worth noting. First, and perhaps most important, this theory has generated a considerable amount of interest among leadership researchers. This research has helped leadership practitioners better understand the leader, follower, and situational components of charismatic or transformational leadership, whether transformational leaders are born or made, and so forth. Nevertheless, this approach to leadership may be more a reflection of socially desirable leadership behaviors than the full range of skills needed by leaders. For example, it seems likely that business leaders wanting to drive organizational change or performance need to have a good understanding of the industry, business operations, market trends, finance, strategy, and technical or functional knowledge; they also need to effectively cope with stress, negotiate contracts with vendors, demonstrate good planning skills, and develop and monitor key metrics. Yet none of these attributes and skills is directly measured by the MLQ. This leads us to another point, which is that a primary problem with this theory is that there is only one way to be an effective leader, and that is by demonstrating transformational leadership skills. The contingency theories of leadership no longer matter, and situational or follower factors have little impact on leadership effectiveness. In all likelihood leaders probably need to do more than just exhibit transformational leadership skills if they wish to achieve greater organizational change and performance.

Summary

This chapter has reviewed two major approaches to organizational change. Although independent lines of research were used to develop the rational and emotional approaches to change, in reality these approaches have several important similarities. With the rational approach, leaders increase follower dissatisfaction by pointing out problems with the status quo, systematically identifying areas of needed change, developing a vision of the future, and developing and implementing a change plan. In the emotional approach, leaders develop and articulate a vision of the future, heighten the emotions of followers, and empower followers to act on their vision. Charismatic leaders are also more likely to emerge during times of uncertainty or crisis, and may actually manufacture a crisis to improve the odds that followers will become committed to their vision of the future. The rational approach puts more emphasis on analytic, planning, and management skills, whereas the emotional approach puts more emphasis on leadership skills, leader–follower relationships, and the presence of a crisis to drive organizational change. This chapter also described the steps leadership practitioners must take if they wish to drive organizational change. There is ample evidence to suggest that either the rational or the emotional approach can result in organizational change, but the effectiveness of the change may depend on which approach leadership practitioners are most comfortable with and the skill with which they can carry it out.

Key Terms

$C = D \times M \times P > R$, *559*
dissatisfaction, *560*
model, *560*
process, *560*
resistance, *560*
amount of change, *560*
constructive
dissatisfaction, *561*
employee
engagement, *561*
systems thinking
approach, *562*
siloed thinking, *562*
change plan, *565*
expectation–
performance gap, *567*
SARA model, *568*
adaptive
leadership, *571*

learning agility, *571*
force field analysis
(FFA), *572*
traditional authority
system, *574*
legal–rational
authority system, *575*
charismatic authority
system, *575*
transactional
leadership, *576*
transformational
leadership, *577*
reframing, *577*
vision, *581*
rhetorical skills, *581*
image, *582*
build trust, *582*
personalized
leadership, *583*

charisma, *584*
identification with
the leader, *584*
heightened emotional
level, *585*
willing subordination
to the leader, *585*
feelings of
empowerment, *585*
crisis, *586*
social networks, *587*
time, *587*
theory of
transformational
and transactional
leadership, *590*
Multifactor
Leadership
Questionnaire
(MLQ), *590*

Questions

1. Are Sarah Palin, Barack Obama, and Andrea Merkel transformational or charismatic leaders? What data would you need to gather to answer this question?

2. Are Vladimir Putin and Hamid Karzai charismatic or transformational leaders? Would your answers differ if you were a Russian or Afghanistan citizen?

3. Research shows that females are seen as more transformational leaders, yet they hold relatively few top leadership positions compared to men. Why do you think this is the case? What, if anything, could you do to change this situation?

4. How does the model of community leadership (Chapter 7) compare to the rational and emotional approaches to organizational change?

5. Can leaders lack intelligence (as described in Chapter 6) and still be seen as charismatic?

6. How do charismatic and transformational leadership relate to the four followership types described in the "Focus on the Followers" section of this book?

7. Suppose you wanted to build a new student union at your school. What would you need to do to make this happen if you used a rational versus an emotional approach to organizational change?

Activities

1. Break into teams and identify something that needs to change at your school or at work. Use the rational approach to change $(C = D \times M \times P > R)$ to develop a plan for your change initiative.

2. Interview a midlevel leader or executive and ask about the biggest change initiative she or he was ever a part of. Did this leader use more of a rational or emotional approach to organizational change, and was the change initiative successful? Why or why not?

3. Create a force field analysis diagram for a change you would like to see happen at your work or school.

Minicase

Keeping Up with Bill Gates

Bill Gates inherited intelligence, ambition, and a competitive spirit from his father, a successful Seattle attorney. After graduating from a private prep school in Seattle, he enrolled in Harvard but dropped out to pursue his passion—computer programming. Paul Allen, a friend from prep school, presented Gates with the idea of writing a version of the BASIC computer language for the Altair 8800, one of the first personal computers on the market. Driven by his competitive nature, Gates decided he wanted to be the first to develop a language to make the personal computer accessible for the general public. He and Allen established the Microsoft Corporation in 1975. Gates's passion and skill were programming—he would work night and day to meet the extremely aggressive deadlines he set for himself and his company. Eventually Gates had to bring in other programmers; he focused on recent college graduates. "We decided that we wanted them to come with clear minds, not polluted by some other approach, to learn the way that we liked to develop software, and to put the kind of energy into it that we thought was key."

In the early days of Microsoft, Gates was in charge of product planning and programming while Allen was in charge of the business side. He motivated his programmers with the claim that whatever deadline was looming, no matter how tight, he could beat it personally if he had to. What eventually developed at Microsoft was a culture in which Gates was king. Everyone working under Gates was made to feel they were lesser programmers who couldn't compete with his skill or drive, so they competed with each other. They worked long hours and tried their best to mirror Gates—his drive, his ambition, his skill. This internal competition motivated the programmers and made Microsoft one of the most successful companies in the computer industry, and one of the most profitable. The corporation has created a tremendous amount of wealth—many of its employees have become millionaires while working at Microsoft, including, of course, Bill Gates, currently one of the richest men in the world. During the 1990s Bill Gates's net worth grew at an average rate of $34 million per day; that's $200 million per week!

Gates needed a castle for his kingdom, so he built a much-talked-about house on Lake Washington. The house lies mainly underground and looks like a set of separate buildings when viewed from above. The house was conceived as a showcase for Microsoft technology—it took $60 million, seven years of planning and construction, and three generations of computer hardware before it was finally finished. A feature of the house that reveals a lot about its owner is the house's system of electronic badges. These badges let the house computers know where each resident and visitor is in the house. The purpose of the badges is to allow the computer to adjust the climate and music to match the preferences of people in the house as they move from room to room. What happens when more than one person is in a room? The computer defaults to Gates's personal preferences.

1. Would you classify Bill Gates as a charismatic or transformational leader? Why?
2. Consider the followers and employees of Gates. What are some unique characteristics of Gates's followers that might identify him as charismatic or transformational?

Sources: http://www.microsoft.com;
http://news.bbc.co.uk/1/hi/programmes/worlds_most_powerful/3284811.stm;
http://ei.cs.vt.edu/~history/Gates.Mirick.html;
http://www.time.com/time/time100/builder/profile/gates3.html;
http://www.pbs.org/cringely/pulpit/pulpit20001123.html.

End Notes

1. B. M. Bass, *Leadership and Performance beyond Expectations* (New York: Free Press, 1985).
2. J. O'Toole, *Leading Change* (San Francisco: Jossey-Bass, 1995).
3. P. Pritchett, *Firing Up Commitment during Organizational Change* (Dallas, TX: Pritchett and Associates, 2001).
4. E. McNulty, "Welcome Aboard (But Don't Change a Thing)," *Harvard Business Review,* October 2002, pp. 32–41.
5. R. A. Heifetz and M. Linsky, "A Survival Guide for Leaders," *Harvard Business Review,* June 2002, pp. 65–75.
6. R. Moss Kanter, "Leadership and the Psychology of Turnarounds," *Harvard Business Review,* June 2003, pp. 58–64.
7. R. M. Kanter, *The Change Masters* (New York: Simon & Schuster, 1983).
8. J. Krile, G. J. Curphy, and D. Lund, *The Community Leadership Handbook: Framing Ideas, Building Relationships and Mobilizing Resources* (St. Paul, MN: Fieldstone Alliance, 2005).
9. F. Ostroff, "Change Management in Government," *Harvard Business Review,* May 2006, pp. 141–53.
10. D. Rock and J. Schwartz, "The Neuroscience of Leadership: Why Organizational Change Hurts," *Strategy + Business* 43 (2006) pp. 71–79.

11. J. Kotter, "Leading Change: Why Transformation Change Efforts Fail," *Harvard Business Review,* January 2007, pp. 96–103.

12. G. J. Curphy, *The Competitive Advantage Program for Wheelabrator Technologies Incorporated* (North Oaks, MN: Author, 2006).

13. G. J. Curphy, *Leadership, Teams, and Change Program for the New York City Leadership Academy* (North Oaks, MN: Author, 2005).

14. J. M. Burns, *Leadership* (New York: Harper & Row, 1978).

15. R. Marcus and R. Weiler, *Aligning Organizations: The Foundation of Performance* (Camden, ME: Brimstone Consulting Group, 2010).

16. W. G. Bennis and B. Nanus, *Leaders: The Strategies for Taking Charge* (New York: Harper & Row, 1985).

17. N. M. Tichy and M. A. Devanna, *The Transformational Leader* (New York: John Wiley, 1986).

18. W. Bridges, *Managing Transitions: Making the Most of Change* (Reading, MA: Addison-Wesley, 1991).

19. J. C. Collins and J. I. Porras, *Built to Last: Successful Habits of Visionary Companies* (Reading, MA: Perseus Books, 1997).

20. M. Treacy and F. Wiersma, *The Discipline of Market Leaders* (Reading, MA: Perseus Books, 1997).

21. M. Beer, *Leading Change,* Reprint No. 9-488-037 (Boston: Harvard Business School Publishing Division, 1988).

22. M. Beer, "Developing Organizational Fitness: Towards a Theory and Practice of Organizational Alignment," paper presented at the 14th Annual Conference of the Society of Industrial and Organizational Psychology, Atlanta, GA, 1999.

23. R. A. Heifetz and D. L. Laurie, "The Work of Leadership," *Harvard Business Review,* December 2001, pp. 131–40.

24. J. Collins, *Good to Great* (New York: HarperCollins, 2001).

25. J. Collins, *How the Mighty Fall* (New York: HarperCollins, 2009).

26. N. M. Tichy and N. Cardwell, *The Cycle of Leadership: How Great Companies Teach Their Leaders to Win* (New York: HarperBusiness, 2002).

27. G. J. Curphy, *The Blandin Education Leadership Program* (Grand Rapids, MN: The Blandin Foundation, 2003).

28. G. J. Curphy and R. T. Hogan, *A Guide to High Performing Teams* (North Oaks, MN: Author, 2010).

29. M. Roellig and G. J. Curphy, *How to Hit the Ground Running: A Guide to Successful Executive On-Boarding* (North Oaks, MN: Author, 2010).

30. P. M. Senge, *The Fifth Discipline: The Art and Practice of the Learning Organization* (New York: Doubleday/Currency, 1994).

31. M. W. Dickson, D. B. Smith, M. W. Grojean, and M. G. Ehrhart, "An Organizational Climate Regarding Ethics: The Outcome of Leader Values and the Practices That Reflect Them," *Leadership Quarterly* 12, no. 2 (2001), pp. 197–218.

32. M. L. Marks and P. H. Mirvis, "Making Mergers and Acquisitions Work," *Academy of Management Executive* 15, no. 2 (2001), pp. 80–94.

33. P. Pritchett and R. Pound, *Smart Moves: A Crash Course on Merger Integration Management* (Pritchett and Associates, 2001).

34. C. M. Ruvolo and R. C. Bullis, "Essentials of Cultural Change: Lessons Learned the Hard Way," *Consulting Psychology Journal* 55, no. 3 (2003), pp. 155–68.

35. Q. N. Huy, "In Praise of Middle Managers," *Harvard Business Review,* September 2001, pp. 72–81.

36. L. Bossidy and R. Charan, *Execution: The Discipline of Getting Things Done* (New York: Crown Business Publishing, 2002).

37. G. J. Curphy, A. Baldrica, and R. T. Hogan, *Managerial Incompetence,* unpublished manuscript, 2009.

38. R. Charan and G. Colvin, "Why CEOs Fail," *Fortune,* June 21, 1999, pp. 69–82.

39. L. Hirschhorn, "Campaigning for Change," *Harvard Business Review,* July 2002, pp. 98–106.

40. J. D. Ford, L. W. Ford, and A. D'Amelio, "Resistance to Change: The Rest of the Story," *Academy of Management Review* 33, no. 2 (2008), pp. 362–90.

41. E. Kübler-Ross, *Living with Death and Dying* (New York: Macmillan, 1981).

42. R. B. Kaiser, "Introduction to the Special Issue on Developing Flexible and Adaptable Leaders for an Age of Uncertainty," *Consulting Psychology Journal: Practice and Research* 62, no. 2 (2010), pp. 77–80.

43. G. A. Yukl and R. Mahsud, "Why Flexible and Adaptable Leadership Is Essential," *Consulting Psychology Journal: Practice and Research* 62, no. 2 (2010), pp. 81–93.

44. K. De Muese, G. Dai, and G. S. Hallenbeck, "Learning Agility: A Construct Whose Time Has Come," *Consulting Psychology Journal: Practice and Research* 62, no. 2 (2010), pp. 119–30.

45. M. Weber, *The Theory of Social and Economic Organization,* ed. Talcott Parsons, trans. A. M. Henderson and T. Parsons (New York: Free Press, 1964).

46. P. M. Blau, "Critical Remarks on Weber's Theory of Authority," *American Political Science Review* 57, no. 2 (1963), pp. 305–15.

47. E. Chinoy, *Society* (New York: Random House, 1961).

48. H. Wolpe, "A Critical Analysis of Some Aspects of Charisma," *Sociological Review* 16 (1968), pp. 305–18.

49. W. H. Friedland, "For a Sociological Concept of Charisma," *Social Forces,* no. 1 (1964), pp. 18–26.

50. H. H. Gerth and C. W. Mills, *Max Weber: Essays in Sociology* (New York: Oxford University Press, 1946).

51. R. M. Kanter, *Commitment and Community* (Cambridge: Harvard University Press, 1972).

52. R. C. Tucker, "The Theory of Charismatic Leadership," *Daedalus* 97 (1968), pp. 731–56.

53. T. E. Dow, "The Theory of Charisma," *Sociological Quarterly* 10 (1969), pp. 306–18.

54. B. R. Clark, "The Organizational Saga in Higher Education," *Administrative Science Quarterly* 17 (1972), pp. 178–84.

55. G. Deveraux, "Charismatic Leadership and Crisis," in *Psychoanalysis and the Social Sciences,* ed. W. Muensterberger and S. Axelrod (New York: International University Press, 1955).

56. J. V. Downton, *Rebel Leadership: Commitment and Charisma in the Revolutionary Process* (New York: Free Press, 1973).

57. J. T. Marcus, "Transcendence and Charisma," *Western Political Quarterly* 16 (1961), pp. 236–41.

58. E. Shils, "Charisma, Order, and Status," *American Sociological Review* 30 (1965), pp. 199–213.

59. N. Turner, J. Barling, O. Eptiropaki, V. Butcher, and C. Milner, "Transformational Leadership and Moral Reasoning," *Journal of Applied Psychology* 87, no. 2 (2002), pp. 304–11.

60. T. L. Price, "The Ethics of Authentic Transformational Leadership," *Leadership Quarterly* 14, no. 1 (2003), pp. 67–82.

61. R. S. Rubin, D. C. Munz, and W. H. Bommer, "Leading from Within: The Effects of Emotion Recognition and Personality on Transformational Leadership Behavior," *Academy of Management Journal* 48, no. 5 (2005), pp. 845–58.

62. J. E. Bono and R. Ilies, "Charisma, Positive Emotions, and Mood Contagion," *Leadership Quarterly* 17 (2006), pp. 317–34.

63. S. Parameshwar, "Inventing Higher Purpose through Suffering: The Transformation of the Transformational Leader," *Leadership Quarterly* 17 (2006), pp. 454–74.

64. M. Greer, "The Science of Savoir Faire," *Monitor on Psychology,* January 2005, pp. 28–30.

65. J. M. Strange and M. D. Mumford, "The Origins of Vision: Effects of Reflection, Models, and Analysis," *Leadership Quarterly* 16 (2005) pp. 121–48.

66. G. Yukl, "An Evaluation of Conceptual Weaknesses in Transformational and Charismatic Leadership Theories," *Leadership Quarterly* 10, no. 2 (1999), pp. 285–306.

67. J. G. Hunt, "Transformational/Charismatic Leadership's Transformation of the Field: An Historical Essay," *Leadership Quarterly* 10, no. 2 (1999), pp. 129–44.

68. J. A. Conger and J. G. Hunt, "Charismatic and Transformational Leadership: Taking Stock of the Present and Future," *Leadership Quarterly* 10, no. 2 (1999), pp. 121–28.

69. E. E. Duehr and J. E. Bono, "Personality and Transformational Leadership: Differential Prediction for Male and Female Leaders," in *Predicting Leadership: The Good, The Bad, the Different, and the Unnecessary,* J. P. Campbell and M. J. Benson (chairs), annual meeting of Society of Industrial and Organizational Psychology, New York, April 2007.

70. B. M. Bass, "Two Decades of Research and Development in Transformational Leadership," *European Journal of Work and Organizational Psychology* 8, no. 1 (1999), pp. 9–32.

71. D. N. Den Hartog, R. J. House, P. J. Hanges, S. A. Ruiz-Quintanilla, P. W. Dorfman, and associates, "Culture Specific and Cross-Culturally Generalizable Implicit Leadership Theories: Are Attributes of Charismatic/Transformational Leadership Universally Endorsed?" *Leadership Quarterly* 10, no. 2 (1999), pp. 219–56.

72. A. H. Eagly and L. L. Carli, "The Female Leadership Advantage: An Evaluation of the Evidence," *Leadership Quarterly* 14 (2003), pp. 807–34.

73. J. B. Rosener, "Ways Women Lead," *Harvard Business Review* 68 (1990), pp. 119–25.

74. V. U. Druskat, "Gender and Leadership Style: Transformational and Transactional Leadership in the Roman Catholic Church," *Leadership Quarterly* 5, no. 1 (1994), pp. 99–120.

75. B. M. Bass and F. J. Yammarino, *Long-term Forecasting of Transformational Leadership and Its Effects among Naval Officers: Some Preliminary Findings,* Technical Report No. ONR-TR-2 (Arlington, VA: Office of Naval Research, 1988).

76. S. M. Ross and L. R. Offermann, "Transformational Leaders: Measurement of Personality Attributes and Work Group Performance," paper presented at the Sixth Annual Society of Industrial and Organizational Psychologists Convention, St. Louis, MO, April 1991.

77. B. J. Avolio and B. M. Bass, *Developing a Full Range of Leadership Potential: Cases on Transactional and Transformational Leadership* (Binghamton: State University of New York at Binghamton, 2000).

78. B. M. Bass, "Thoughts and Plans," in *Cutting Edge: Leadership 2000,* ed. B. Kellerman and L. R. Matusak (Carbondale, IL: Southern Illinois University Press, 2000), pp. 5–9.

79. G. J. Curphy, "An Empirical Investigation of Bass' (1985) Theory of Transformational and Transactional Leadership," PhD dissertation, University of Minnesota, 1991.

80. D. A. Waldman, G. G. Ramirez, R. J. House, and P. Puranam, "Does Leadership Matter? CEO Leadership Attributes and Profitability under Conditions of Perceived Environmental Uncertainty," *Academy of Management Journal* 44, no. 1 (2001), pp. 134–43.

81. T. Dvir, D. Eden, B. J. Avolio, and B. Shamir, "Impact of Transformational Leadership on Follower Development and Performance: A Field Experiment," *Academy of Management Journal* 45, no. 4 (2002), pp. 735–44.

82. J. E. Bono, "Transformational Leadership: What We Know and Why You Should Care!" Presentation delivered to the Minnesota Professionals for Psychology Applied to Work, Minneapolis, MN, September 2002.

83. B. M. Bass, B. J. Avolio, D. I. Jung, and Y. Berson, "Predicting Unit Performance by Assessing Transformational and Transactional Leadership," *Journal of Applied Psychology* 88, no. 2 (2003), pp. 207–18.

84. D. A. Waldman, M. Javidan, and P. Varella, "Charismatic Leadership at the Strategic Level: A New Application of Upper Echelons Theory," *Leadership Quarterly* 15, no. 3 (2004), pp. 355–80.

85. T. A. Judge and R. F. Piccolo, "Transformational and Transactional Leadership: A Meta-analytic Test of Their Relative Validity," *Journal of Applied Psychology* 89, no. 5 (2004), pp. 755–68.

86. R. T. Keller, "Transformational Leadership, Initiating Structure, and Substitutes for Leadership: A Longitudinal Study of Research and Development Project Team Performance," *Journal of Applied Psychology* 91, no. 1 (2006), pp. 202–10.

87. J. L. Whittington, V. L. Goodwin, and B. Murray, "Transformational Leadership, Goal Difficulty, and Job Design: Independent and Interactive Effects on Employee Outcomes," *Leadership Quarterly* 15, no. 5 (2004), pp. 593–606.

88. L. A. Nemanich and R. T. Keller, "Transformational Leadership in an Acquisition: A Field Study of Employees," *Leadership Quarterly* 18, no. 1 (2007), pp. 49–68.

89. J. A. Conger, "Charismatic and Transformational Leadership in Organizations: An Insider's Perspective on These Developing Streams of Research," *Leadership Quarterly* 10, no. 2 (1999), pp. 145–80.

90. B. Tranter, "Leadership and Change in the Tasmanian Environmental Movement," *The Leadership Quarterly* 20, no. 5 (2009), pp. 708–24.

91. R. Khurana, "The Curse of the Superstar CEO," *Harvard Business Review*, September 2002, pp. 60–67.

92. H. L. Tosi, V. F. Misangyi, A. Fanelli, D. A. Waldman, and F. J. Yammarino, "CEO Charisma, Compensation, and Firm Performance," *Leadership Quarterly* 15, no. 3 (2004), pp. 405–20.

93. B. R. Agle, N. J. Nagarajan, J. A. Sonnenfeld, and D. Srinivasan, "Does CEO Charisma Matter? An Empirical Analysis of the Relationships among Organizational Performance, Environmental Uncertainty, and Top Management Team Perceptions of Charisma," *Academy of Management Journal* 49, no. 1 (2006), pp. 161–74.

94. J. A. Conger and R. N. Kanungo, *Charismatic Leadership in Organizations* (Thousand Oaks, CA: Sage, 1998).

95. R. J. House, "A 1976 Theory of Charismatic Leadership," in *Leadership: The Cutting Edge,* ed. J. G. Hunt and L. L. Larson (Carbondale, IL: Southern Illinois University Press, 1977).

96. R. J. House and B. Shamir, "Toward an Integration of Transformational, Charismatic, and Visionary Theories," in *Leadership Theory and Research Perspective and Directions,* ed. M. Chemers and R. Ayman (Orlando, FL: Academic Press, 1993), pp. 577–94.

97. B. Shamir, R. J. House, and M. B. Arthur, "The Motivation Effects of Charismatic Leadership: A Self-Concept Based Theory," *Organizational Science* 4 (1993), pp. 577–94.

98. B. J. Avolio and B. M. Bass, "Transformational Leadership, Charisma, and Beyond," in *Emerging Leadership Vistas,* ed. J. G. Hunt, B. R. Baliga, and C. A. Schriesheim (Lexington, MA: D. C. Heath, 1988).

99. A. J. Towler, "Effects of Charismatic Influence Training on Attitudes, Behavior, and Performance," *Personnel Psychology* 56, no. 2, pp. 363–82.

100. R. Hooijberg and J. Choi, "From Selling Peanuts and Beer in Yankee Stadium to Creating a Theory of Transformational Leadership: An Interview with Bernie Bass," *Leadership Quarterly* 11, no. 2 (2000), pp. 291–300.

101. K. M. Boal and J. M. Bryson, "Charismatic Leadership: A Phenomenal and Structural Approach," in *Emerging Leadership Vistas,* ed. J. G. Hunt, B. R. Baliga, H. P. Dachler, and C. A. Schriesheim (Lexington, MA: Heath Company, 1988).

102. M. Kets de Vries, *The Leadership Mystique: A User's Guide for the Human Enterprise* (London: Financial Times/Prentice Hall, 2001).

103. J. M. Strange and M. D. Mumford, "The Origins of Vision: Charismatic versus Ideological Leadership," *Leadership Quarterly* 13, no. 4 (2002), pp. 343–78.

104. J. S. Mio, R. E. Riggio, S. Levin, and R. Reese, "Presidential Leadership and Charisma: The Effects of Metaphor," *Leadership Quarterly* 16 (2005), pp. 287–94.

105. L. J. Naidoo and R. G. Lord, "Speech Imagery and Perceptions of Charisma: The Mediating Role of Positive Affect," *The Leadership Quarterly* 19, no. 3 (2008), pp. 283–96.

106. R. McKee, "Storytelling That Moves People: A Conversation with Screenwriting Coach Robert McKee," *Harvard Business Review,* June 2003, pp. 51–57.

107. C. J. Palus, D. M. Horth, A. M. Selvin, and M. L. Pulley, "Exploration for Development: Developing Leaders by Making Shared Sense of Complex Challenges," *Consulting Psychology Journal* 55, no. 1 (2003), pp. 26–40.

108. Y. Berson, B. Shamir, B. J. Avolio, and M. Popper, "The Relationship between Vision Strength, Leadership Style, and Context," *Leadership Quarterly* 12, no. 1 (2001), pp. 53–74.

109. B. Shamir, M. B. Arthur, and R. J. House, "The Rhetoric of Charismatic Leadership: A Theoretical Extension, a Case Study, and Implications for Research," *Leadership Quarterly* 5 (1994), pp. 25–42.

110. Y. Berson, B. Shamir, B. J. Avolio, and M. Popper, "The Relationship between Vision Strength, Leadership Style, and Context," *Leadership Quarterly* 12, no. 1 (2001), pp. 53–74.

111. A. R. Willner, *The Spellbinders: Charismatic Political Leadership* (New Haven: Yale University Press, 1984).

112. V. Seyranian and M. C. Bligh, "Presidential Charismatic Leadership: Exploring the Rhetoric of Social Change," *The Leadership Quarterly* 19, no. 1 (2008), pp. 54–76.

113. K. B. Boal and P. L. Schultz, "Storytelling, Time, and Evolution: The Role of Strategic Leadership in Complex Adaptive Systems," *The Leadership Quarterly* 18, no. 3 (2007), pp. 411–28.

114. W. Liu, R. Zhu, and Y. Yang, "I Warn You Because I Like You: Voice Behavior, Employee Identifications, and Transformational Leadership," *The Leadership Quarterly* 21, no. 1 (2010), pp. 189–202.

115. J. A. Conger, *The Charismatic Leader* (San Francisco: Jossey-Bass, 1989).

116. B. M. Bass and B. J. Avolio, eds., *Increasing Organizational Effectiveness through Transformational Leadership* (Thousand Oaks, CA: Sage, 1994).

117. B. M. Bass, "Does the Transactional–Transformational Leadership Paradigm Transcend Organizational and National Boundaries?" *American Psychologist* 52, no. 3 (1997), pp. 130–39.

118. B. M. Bass and P. Steidlmeier, "Ethics, Character, and Authentic Transformational Leadership Behavior," *Leadership Quarterly* 10, no. 2 (1999), pp. 181–218.

119. J. J. Sosik, B. J. Avolio, and D. I. Jun, "Beneath the Mask: Examining the Relationship of Self-Presentation and Impression Management to Charismatic Leadership," *Leadership Quarterly* 13, no. 3 (2002), pp. 217–42.

120. R. Pillai, E. A. Williams, K. B. Lowe, and D. I. Jung, "Personality, Transformational Leadership, Trust, and the 2000 Presidential Vote," *Leadership Quarterly* 14, no. 2 (2003), pp. 161–92.

121. B. M. Bass, *Bass and Stogdill's Handbook of Leadership*, 3rd ed. (New York: Free Press, 1990).

122. J. E. Bono and T. A. Judge, "Self-Concordance at Work: Toward Understanding the Motivational Effects of Transformational Leaders," *Academy of Management Journal* 46, no. 5 (2003), pp. 554–71.

123. G. J. Curphy, *Hogan Assessment Systems Certification Workshop Training Manuals* (Tulsa, OK: Hogan Assessment Systems, 2003).

124. J. Antonakis and R. J. House, "On Instrumental Leadership: Beyond Transactions and Transformations," presentation delivered at the UNL Gallup Leadership Summit, June 2004, Lincoln, Nebraska.

125. J. M. Howell and P. Frost, "A Laboratory Study of Charismatic Leadership," *Organizational Behavior and Human Decision Processes* 43 (1988), pp. 243–69.

126. J. M. Howell and B. Shamir, "The Role of Followers in the Charismatic Leadership Process: Relationships and Their Consequences," *Academy of Management Review* 30, no. 1 (2005), pp. 96–112.

127. M. E. Brown and L. K. Trevino, "Leader–Follower Values Congruence: Are Socialized Charismatic Leaders Better Able to Achieve It?" *Journal of Applied Psychology* 94, no. 2 (2009), pp. 478–90.

128. M. G. Ehrhart and K. J. Klein, "Predicting Followers' Preferences for Charismatic Leadership: The Influence of Follower Values and Personality," *Leadership Quarterly* 12, no. 2 (2001), pp. 153–80.

129. R. G. Lord and D. J. Brown, "Leadership, Values, and Subordinate Self-Concepts," *Leadership Quarterly* 12, no. 2 (2001), pp. 133–52.

130. R. Kark, B. Shamir, and G. Chen, "The Two Faces of Transformational Leadership: Empowerment and Dependency," *Journal of Applied Psychology* 88, no. 2 (2003), pp. 246–55.

131. O. Epitopaki and R. Martin, "The Moderating Role of Individual Differences in the Relation between Transformational/Transactional Leadership Perceptions and Organizational Identification," *Leadership Quarterly* 16 (2005), pp. 569–89.

132. S. M. Campbell, A. J. Ward, J. A. Sonnenfeld, and B. R. Agle, "Relational Ties That Bind: Leader–Follower Relationship Dimensions and Charismatic Attribution," *Leadership Quarterly* 19, no. 5 (2008), pp. 556–68.

133. B. M. Galvin, P. Balkundi, and D. D. Waldman, "Spreading the Word: The Role of Surrogates in Charismatic Leadership Processes," *Academy of Management Review* 35, no. 3 (2010), pp. 477–94.

134. F. O. Walumbwa, B. J. Avolio, and W. Zhu, "How Transformational Leadership Weaves Its Influence on Individual Job Performance: The Role of Identification and Efficacy Beliefs," *Personnel Psychology* 61, no. 4 (2008), pp. 793–826.

135. S. Fox and Y. Amichai-Hamburger, "The Power of Emotional Appeals in Promoting Organizational Change Programs," *The Academy of Management Executive* 15, no. 4 (2001), pp. 84–94.

136. J. E. Bono, H. Foldes, G. Vinson, and J. P. Muros, "Workplace Emotions: The Role of Supervision and Leadership," *Journal of Applied Psychology* 92, no. 5 (2007), pp. 1357–67.

137. A. Erez, V. F. Misangyi, D. E. Johnson, M. A. LePine, and K. C. Halverson, "Stirring the Hearts of Followers: Charismatic as the Transferral of Affect," *Journal of Applied Psychology* 93, no. 3 (2008), pp. 602–16.

138. S. K. Johnson, "I Second That Emotion: Effects of Emotional Contagion and Affect at Work on Leader and Follower Outcomes," *Leadership Quarterly* 19, no. 1 (2008), pp. 1–19.

139. R. J. House, J. Woycke, and E. M. Fodor, "Charismatic and Noncharismatic Leaders: Differences in Behavior and Effectiveness," in *Charismatic Leadership: The Elusive Factor in Organizational Effectiveness,* ed. J. A. Conger and R. N. Kanungo (San Francisco: Jossey-Bass, 1988), pp. 98–121.

140. M. Popper and O. Mayseless, "Back to Basics: Applying a Parenting Perspective to Transformational Leadership," *Leadership Quarterly* 14, no. 1 (2003), pp. 41–66.

141. J. M. Beyer, "Training and Promoting Charisma to Change Organizations," *Leadership Quarterly* 10, no. 2 (1999), pp. 307–30.

142. J. G. Hunt, K. B. Boal, and G. E. Dodge, "The Effects of Visionary and Crisis-Responsive Charisma on Followers: An Experimental Examination of Two Kinds of Charismatic Leadership," *Leadership Quarterly* 10, no. 3 (1999), pp. 423–48.

143. B. S. Pawar and K. K. Eastman, "The Nature and Implications of Contextual Influences on Transformational Leadership: A Conceptual Examination," *Academy of Management Review* 22, no. 1 (1997), pp. 80–109.

144. I. Boga and N. Ensari, "The Role of Transformational Leadership and Organizational Change on Perceived Organizational Success," *The Psychologist-Manager Journal* 12, no. 4 (2009), pp. 235–51.

145. J. C. Pastor, J. R. Meindl, and M. C. Mayo, "A Network Effects Model of Charismatic Attributions," *The Academy of Management Journal* 45, no. 2 (2002), pp. 410–20.

146. J. E. Bono and M. H. Anderson, "The Advice and Influence Networks of Transformational Leaders," *Journal of Applied Psychology* 90, no. 6, pp. 1301–14.

147. R. J. Deluga, "American Presidential Proactivity, Charismatic Leadership and Rated Performance," *Leadership Quarterly* 9, no. 2 (1998), pp. 265–92.

148. A. Fanelli and V. F. Misangyi, "Bringing Out Charisma: CEO Charisma and External Stakeholders," *Academy of Management Review* 31, no. 4 (2006), pp. 1049–61.

149. G. J. Curphy, "The Effects of Transformational and Transactional Leadership on Organizational Climate, Attrition, and Performance," in *Impact of Leadership,* ed. K. E. Clark, M. B. Clark, and D. P. Campbell (Greensboro, NC: Center for Creative Leadership, 1992).

150. J. Adams, H. T. Prince, D. Instone, and R. W. Rice, "West Point: Critical Incidents of Leadership," *Armed Forces and Society* 10 (1984), pp. 597–611.

151. A. S. Labak, "The Study of Charismatic College Teachers," *Dissertation Abstracts International* 34 (1973), p. 1258B.

152. S. J. Shin and J. Zhou, "Transformational Leadership, Conservation, and Creativity: Evidence from Korea," *Academy of Management Journal* 46, no. 6, pp. 703–14.

153. A. H. B. De Hoogh, D. N. Den Hartog, P. L. Koopman, H. Thierry, P. T. Van den Berg, J. G. Van der Weide, and C. P. M. Wilderom, "Leader Motives, Charismatic Leadership, and Subordinates' Work Attitude in the Profit and Voluntary Sector," *Leadership Quarterly* 16 (2005), pp. 17–38.

154. A. E. Rafferty and M. A. Griffen, "Dimensions of Transformational Leadership: Conceptual and Empirical Extensions," *Leadership Quarterly* 15, no. 3 (2004), pp. 329–54.

155. J. Antonakis, B. J. Avolio, and N. Sivasubramainiam, "Context and Leadership: An Examination of the Nine Factor Full Range Leadership Theory Using the Multifactor Leadership Questionnaire," *Leadership Quarterly* 15, no. 2 (2003), pp. 261–95.

156. B. M. Bass and B. J. Avolio, *The Multifactor Leadership Questionnaire Report* (Palo Alto, CA: Mind Garden, 1996).

157. J. Rowold and K. Heinitz, "Transformational and Charismatic Leadership: Assessing the Convergent, Divergent, and Criterion Validity of the MLQ and CKS," *Leadership Quarterly* 18, no. 1 (2007), pp. 121–33.

158. R. F. Piccolo, J. E. Bono, T. A. Judge, E. E. Duehr, and J. P. Muros, "Which Leader Behaviors Matter Most: Comparing Dimensions of the LBDQ and MLQ," paper presented in J. P. Campbell and M. J. Benson (chairs), *Predicting Leadership: The Good, The Bad, the Different, and the Unnecessary,* Annual Meeting of Society of Industrial and Organizational Psychology, New York, April, 2007.

159. M. Frese, S. Beimel, and S. Schoenborn, "Action Training for Charismatic Leadership: Two Evaluations of Studies of a Commercial Training Module on Inspirational Communication of a Vision," *Personnel Psychology* 56, no. 3 (2003), pp. 671–97.

160. J. Barling, C. Loughlin, and E. K. Kelloway, "Development and Test of a Model Linking Safety–Specific Transformational Leadership and Occupational Safety," *Journal of Applied Psychology* 87, no. 3 (2002), pp. 488–96.

161. A. Zacharatos, J. Barling, and E. K. Kelloway, "Development and Effects of Transformational Leadership in Adolescents," *Leadership Quarterly* 11, no. 2 (2000), pp. 211–26.

162. T. A. Judge and J. E. Bono, "Five-Factor Model of Personality and Transformational Leadership," *Journal of Applied Psychology* 85, no. 5 (2000), pp. 751–65.

163. R. T. Hogan, G. J. Curphy, and J. Hogan, "What Do We Know about Personality: Leadership and Effectiveness?" *American Psychologist* 49 (1994), pp. 493–504.

164. G. J. Curphy, "New Directions in Personality," in *Personality and Organizational Behavior,* R. T. Hogan (chair). Symposium presented at the 104th Annual Meeting of the American Psychological Association, Toronto, Canada, 1996.

165. D. L. Nilsen, *Using Self and Observers' Rating of Personality to Predict Leadership Performance,* unpublished doctoral dissertation, University of Minnesota, Minneapolis, 1995.

166. R. J. House, W. D. Spangler, and J. Woycke, "Personality and Charisma in the U.S. Presidency: A Psychological Theory of Leadership Effectiveness," *Administrative Science Quarterly* 36 (1991), pp. 364–96.

15

The Dark Side of Leadership

Introduction

Back in May 2005 one of the authors of this book was on a flight from Columbus, Ohio, to Minneapolis, Minnesota. Northwest Airlines Flight 1495 had a heavy passenger load and a crew of two pilots and three flight attendants. The two-hour flight seemed routine, but upon landing the author noticed the runway was lined with ambulances and fire trucks. The plane taxied off the runway and stopped some distance short of the gate. After waiting five minutes, one of the pilots got on the intercom and announced, "The plane has experienced a systems malfunction." The pilots and flight attendants did not say anything more, and about five minutes later the DC-9 began moving again.

The DC-9 had been traveling about 10 seconds when suddenly a loud boom filled the cabin and the plane came to an abrupt stop. Passengers were thrown violently forward in their seats, but luckily everyone was still wearing their seatbelts. The author and other passengers had assumed the plane was taxiing to its gate, but a look out the window showed that the DC-9 had collided with another aircraft. Apparently the pilots of the DC-9 had left the engines running and the plane had experienced a hydraulics failure, which caused it to lose all steering and braking capabilities. The DC-9 collided with a Northwest Airlines A-319 that was being pushed back from its gate, and the wing of the A-319 peeled back the first 10 feet of the roof of the DC-9 during the collision.

After the plane had stopped, the lead flight attendant unbuckled her seat belt and started running up and down the aisle yelling, "Assume the crash position! Assume the crash position!" The passengers were wondering how putting our heads between our knees was going to help when the plane had already come to a stop, but we dutifully complied with the flight attendant's request. After two to three minutes of running up and down the aisle and barking orders, the lead flight attendant hyperventilated and collapsed in a heap behind the first-class bulkhead. The two remaining flight attendants then got out of their seats to check on the lead flight attendant.

Most of the passengers started easing out of the crash position and began looking to the other flight attendants for guidance on what to do, but none was forthcoming. The author then got up and went to the cockpit door because he could tell that the wing of the A-319 had come in through the cockpit, and he was concerned about the pilots. He asked the pilots whether they needed any help, and one of them meekly replied that they needed medical attention. The author tried to open the door, but the door reinforcements added after 9/11/2001 made it impossible to get in.

As the author was tugging on the cockpit door handle, he could overhear the two flight attendants discussing whether they should deplane the aircraft. One attendant asked, "Should we keep them on or get them off?" The other attendant replied, "I don't know, what do you think?" This conversation continued for three to four minutes, with the lead flight attendant still whispering in the background, "Assume the crash position. Assume the crash position." During this time one of the flight attendants came up to the cockpit door and asked the pilots what to do, but there was no response. She then went back to attend to the lead flight attendant.

At this time the author noticed that jet fuel from the wing of the A-319 had leaked into the cockpit of the DC-9 and had seeped into the first-class cabin. He realized that his shoes and pants were covered in jet fuel and an errant spark would light up two planes full of people. He then turned and yelled at the flight attendants, "I am standing in jet fuel. Get everyone off the plane. NOW!" The two coherent flight attendants got up and proceeded to hustle everyone off the plane using the DC-9's rear exit. Being in the front of the cabin at the cockpit door, the author was the last in line to get off the plane. You can imagine how happy he was to see passengers at the rear of the aircraft taking the time to open the overhead bins and retrieve their luggage while he was standing in jet fuel. The flight attendants did not intervene more than giving some mild reminders to passengers to just exit the aircraft and leave the luggage behind.

All the passengers from both aircraft escaped with only a few minor injuries. The flight attendants were okay; the two DC-9 pilots needed some medical attention but were released the next day. But this incident provides several vivid examples of failures in leadership. The pilots failed to warn the passengers of the impending collision and did not use the thrust reversers to stop the plane. The lead flight attendant's instructions to assume the crash position after the plane was at a complete stop and then collapsing two to three minutes later did not instill confidence.

The other two flight attendants needed to step into a leadership role and take over the situation but were unable to make a decision or tell passengers what to do. Northwest Airlines failed by having standard operating procedures (SOPs) that instructed pilots to leave the engines running in the event of an aircraft hydraulics failure. Instead the SOP should have instructed pilots to shut down the engines and have the plane towed to a gate. The airline also failed when the author called in several times offering to describe the incident in order to improve training and was ignored. Later he learned that the airline formally rewarded the two pilots and three flight attendants for their outstanding actions during the emergency.

Although this may appear a bit self-serving, in our minds leadership is the most important topic in the world today. Leadership determines whether countries are democracies or dictatorships or are at peace or war, whether businesses are good investments or kleptocracies, whether teams win or lose, whether health care and education reforms fail or succeed, and whether rural communities thrive or merely survive. Leadership plays a role in determining where you live, what schools you get into, what laws and rules you must obey, what occupations you enter, whether you have a successful career, and how your children are raised. It plays such a pervasive part in our lives that it is easy to overlook its impact on our day-to-day behaviors. Because of the profound ways in which leadership affects us all, it would be nice if the people in positions of authority were actually good at it. But research shows that most people are woefully inadequate when it comes to influencing an organized group toward accomplishing its goals. The purpose of this chapter is to describe the most common reasons why people fail in leadership positions and the steps we can take to improve our odds of success.

It is fitting that this chapter appears at the end of the book because it draws on much of the leader, follower, and situation material described in earlier chapters. As an overview, we will review the research pertaining to and some practical steps for avoiding bad leadership, managerial incompetence, and managerial derailment. **Bad leadership** is associated with individuals who are effective at building teams and getting results through others, but who obtain results that are morally or ethically challenged. An example here might be Adolf Hitler. Hitler was clearly able to rally an entire country around a common cause and conquered a number of countries, yet the end result was a continent in ruins and the death of over 20,000,000 people. Unlike bad leadership, **managerial incompetence** concerns a person's *inability* to build teams or get results through others. A majority of people in positions of authority can (1) build teams but not get results; (2) get results but destroy team morale and cohesiveness; or (3) neither build teams nor get results. **Managerial derailment** describes the common reasons why people in

If you put on a blindfold and threw a dart at a map of the world, then there is a 70 percent chance that whatever country the dart lands on is run by some form of dictatorship.

RT Hogan, Hogan Assessment Systems

positions of authority have difficulties building teams or getting results through others. Knowing the six root causes of managerial derailment and what to do to avoid these pitfalls can help you be more effective as a leader.

Bad Leadership

One way to evaluate leadership effectiveness is to look at a person's ability to build teams and get results through others. Effective leaders are those who can meet both criteria, where ineffective leaders have trouble building teams or getting results. As described in Chapter 14, James MacGregor Burns has maintained that truly effective leaders need to meet an additional criterion, which is to raise the standard of human conduct and improve the lives of everyone they touch.[1] In other words, effective leaders must make the organizations or societies they belong to better places to work or live. Given these three criteria, we can see that there is a subset of leaders who are good at painting a compelling picture of the future and getting followers to drive the organizational or societal changes needed to make their vision become reality, yet the end result may be morally or ethically reprehensible. Some of these leaders are among the most infamous in history and include Alexander the Great, Genghis Kahn, Attila the Hun, Ivan the Terrible, Vlad the Impaler, Napoleon Bonaparte, Adolf Hitler, Joseph Stalin, Mao Zedong, Pol Pot, Idi Amin, Saddam Hussein, Kim Jong-Il, Robert Mugabe, Fidel Castro, and Osama bin Laden. No one could argue about whether these individuals had a major impact on their countries and societies, but their collective influence killed hundreds of millions of innocent people. And such leaders who are still alive lead incredibly repressed societies or followers who are bent on delivering death and destruction (see Profiles in Leadership 15.1.)

To crush your enemies, see them driven before you, and listen to the lamentation of the women.

Conan the Barbarian

Bad leadership is not limited to government or political leaders—it occurs in virtually all other settings. The recession of 2008–2010 can be partially attributed to a number of bad leaders in the financial services industry. Many greedy bank and insurance executives did a good job of building teams and generating profits, but the profits were gained by cooking the books, selling financial products that were doomed to fail, or funding subprime mortgages that owners could ill afford. The problem was so widespread in the financial services industry that it almost caused the collapse of the entire global economy (see Profiles in Leadership 15.2). Similarly, the massacres at My Lai, Serbia, Bosnia, Croatia, Rwanda, and Darfur show that bad leadership also occurs in military settings. In the

Robert Mugabe

PROFILES IN LEADERSHIP 15.1

Robert Mugabe was elected president of Zimbabwe at the end of 1987 and has remained in this role for the past 20+ years. Mugabe's administration has moved Zimbabwe from impressive success to one of the biggest collapses in the last 100 years. He has attracted international criticism for corruption, economic and land reform mismanagement, deteriorating human rights, antigay crusades, and stifling all political opposition to his rule. He is generally blamed for driving Zimbabwe's annual inflation rate so high that the money needed to buy a brick house with a tennis court and pool in 1990 could not buy a single brick today. Widely despised by his own citizens and the international community, Mugabe is also seen by many as charismatic, well-educated,

and clever. A near vegetarian and a nondrinking workaholic, Mugabe starts each day with a heavy regimen of yoga and exercise before putting in 14 hours of work. Educated as a teacher and currently possessing seven academic degrees, Mugabe also has a self-proclaimed "degree in violence." Rival leaders, members of the opposition, and journalists are beaten regularly or killed. Many predicted his demise 10 years ago, yet Mugabe's iron rule and ability to constantly reinvent himself makes his position as president seem as safe as ever.

Sources: *The Economist,* "Robert Mugabe; The Man Behind the Fist," March 31, 2007, pp. 27–23; C. Shepherd, "News of the Weird," *Minneapolis Star Tribune,* March 15, 2007, p. E3; http://news.bbc.co.uk/2/hi/africa/643737.stm.

spirit of seeking revenge or ethnic cleansing, military commanders will rally the troops to kill everyone in particular villages and towns—even those who are not military combatants. Religious leaders can also exhibit bad leadership. Jim Jones and David Koresh are two examples of highly charismatic religious leaders who developed cultlike followings and lead their adherents to commit suicide (see Profiles in Leadership 15.3). And bad leadership can occur at a variety of levels in organizations. Sometimes first-line supervisors, midlevel managers, and executives who disagree with company policies and strategies will motivate their followers to pursue courses of action that are not aligned with organizational interests. These actions and their subsequent results often lead to poor customer service, duplicative efforts, high levels of team conflict, and ultimately suboptimal financial performance. Although these leaders and followers may believe they are doing the right thing, their actions harm their organizations.[2-4]

Barbara Kellerman correctly points out that the United States has an overly optimistic outlook on leadership. Most of the leadership books written for U.S. consumption have an overly positive tone and generally maintain that leadership is relatively easy to learn.[5] Similarly, many leadership training programs delivered in the United States are built on the erroneous assumption that leaders are inherently good and

Richard Fuld

PROFILES IN LEADERSHIP 15.2

Richard Fuld was the CEO of Lehman Brothers, a 150-year-old investment bank with 25,000 employees, when the company declared bankruptcy in September 2008. After receiving an MBA from New York University in 1973, Fuld joined Lehman Brothers as a commercial paper trader and worked his way through the ranks to become CEO in 1993. As the leader of the fourth largest investment bank in the world, he was known as the "scariest man on Wall Street" and his nickname was "the Gorilla." Fuld loved beating up on the competition and was highly focused on achieving strong results for his bank and its shareholders. Although some were intimidated by his leadership style, Fuld was able to build a loyal following of employees who believed in his strategy and vision for Lehman Brothers. This strategy involved making a number of risky investments and then (unknown to many people) engaging in accounting tricks to make the company's financial performance look much better than warranted. From 2003 to 2008 Fuld was paid over $300,000,000 for his efforts, yet when the financial crisis hit Wall Street, Lehman Brothers fell like a house of cards. The Lehman Brothers bankruptcy cost 25,000 employees their jobs and shareholders many billions of dollars in equity. The collapse of Lehman Brothers also brought the global financial system to the brink of failure and is seen as the starting point of the global recession. Yet before the crisis many employees and shareholders believed in Lehman Brothers and completely bought into Fuld's vision for the company.

Sources: R.T. Hogan, *Personality and Financial Management* (Tulsa, OK: Hogan Assessment Systems, 2009); http://topics.nytimes.com/top/reference/timestopics/people/f/richard_s_fuld_jr/index.html.

---

effective; bad or incompetent leadership is the exception rather than the rule. Yet Jared Diamond's book, *Guns, Germs, and Steel: The Fates of Human Societies,* shows that most societies from the earliest times to today have been kleptocracies.[6] Some are legitimized kleptocracies, where kings, queens, and elected officials dictate laws or write rules to increase their power or personal wealth. Dictators who emerge after violent overthrows of previous governments seem to benefit greatly from their change in status but rarely if ever improve the lot of commoners (see Profiles in Leadership 15.1). Thus bad leadership occurs when people in positions of authority use their team-building skills to achieve greedy and selfish results. And as history mournfully suggests, evil, corrupt, greedy, and selfish leaders will likely be around for a long time.

A final note about bad leadership is worth discussing further: what may be considered bad versus good leadership may be in the eye of the beholder. Although most people believe Kim Jong-Il and Charles Taylor are egomaniacal despots, those loyal to these two individuals may see them as great leaders. And in reality those who are loyal to bad leaders generally are rewarded for their efforts. Sometimes this reward comes in the form of a bullet (Joseph Stalin, Mao Zedong, and Idi Amin did not hesitate to kill loyal followers whom they perceived as rivals), but more

Iraq is clearly hubris carried to the point of insanity—it's damn hard to convince people that you are killing them for their own good.
Molly Ivins, writer

David Koresh

PROFILES IN LEADERSHIP 15.3

In April 1993 approximately 85 people died at a religious compound outside of Waco, Texas. Many of them died in the fire that consumed the compound, but a single bullet to the head had killed others. Twenty-five of the deceased were children. How did this happen? The story of David Koresh is a classic example of what can go wrong when bad leaders take charge.

By all accounts David Koresh (born as Vernon Wayne Howell) had a miserable childhood. His mother was only 14 when David was born and went through two divorces before she was 20. David was abused by his uncle while growing up and his mother decided to attend the local Seventh Day Adventist church when he turned nine. Apparently David loved church and religion and was spellbound during sermons. He memorized large portions of scripture and could effortlessly recite endless passages. However, in his later teen years Koresh began to question why the church believed in modern-day prophets yet claimed that none had walked the earth for a long time. He also began to question the biblical interpretations of elders and eventually left the Seventh Day Adventists to join the Branch Davidians. The Branch Davidians believed not only in modern-day prophets but also in Armageddon. At the age of 24 Koresh took over

the Branch Davidians by having intimate relations with their 67-year-old leader. He also secretly married a 14-year-old member of the sect and was subsequently kicked out of the church. He and many of the Branch Davidians left to start their own chapter outside Waco, Texas.

While starting his own church Koresh became increasingly temperamental and violent. He made fellow members watch violent war movies and listen to his rock sessions, and he put them through long fasts and strange diets. At first Koresh abided by his own rules, but eventually he claimed that God had told him it was all right for him, and only him, to violate these rules. Koresh took a number of wives, all of whom were under 15. He eventually told the males that all the females in the church were to become his wives and their marriages were no longer valid. This bizarre behavior continued until agents from the Alcohol, Tobacco, and Firearms Bureau came to the compound to investigate allegations of firearms violations and child abuse in early 1993. Rather than allowing the agents to investigate, Koresh burned down the compound, killed many of his followers, and commited suicide.

Source: K. R. Samples, E. M. deCastro, R. Abanes, and R. J. Lyle, *Prophets of the Apocalypse: David Koresh and the Other American Messiahs* (Grand Rapids, MI: Baker Books, 1994).

For every person who's a manager and wants to know how to manage people, there are 10 people who are being managed and would like to figure out how to make it stop.

Scott Adams,
creator of "Dilbert"

often than not loyal followers are richly rewarded with titles, wealth, and power. The same perspective could be applied to Osama bin Laden. Most people from Western cultures see Osama bin Laden as a threat, but his followers see his vision as a path to heaven. This concept of good versus bad leadership could also be applied to President Barack Obama. Many Democrats see Barack Obama as a great U.S. president, but members of the Tea Party think the United States is heading in the wrong direction and is destined to fail under his leadership. Sometimes political, religious, or business leaders advocate what many believe are the wrong things, but these turn out to be the right things over time. Lee Iacocca's push for a government bailout of Chrysler, Martin Luther King Jr.'s vision for civil rights, and Bill Clinton's intervention in the Yugoslavian civil war are all examples of leaders accused of doing bad things at the time but who in retrospect improved the organizations and societies they led. Thus bad leadership might not be quite so clear-cut as we might think.

Managerial Incompetence

Whereas bad leadership is associated with individuals who build teams to achieve corrupt or evil ends, incompetent management is associated with individuals who either cannot build teams or cannot get results through others. In other words, incompetent managers have difficulties building loyal followings or getting anything done. Research shows that there may be more incompetent than competent managers; the **base rate of managerial incompetence** may be 50–75 percent.[7,8] You might think the base rate of managerial incompetence could not be this high—too many countries, businesses, government and other nonprofit organizations, or volunteer organizations would simply fail if riddled with such a high percentage of incompetent leaders. But consider the following facts:

- Most countries are run by some form of dictatorship. Most ordinary citizens in Saudi Arabia, Egypt, Libya, Jordan, Chad, Zimbabwe, Iran, Turkmenistan, China, and Russia do not have much say over who is in charge, what laws are made, and so on. Although the leaders of these countries have a following among a minority of people, the majority has little input into who leads them.

- Many leaders of democratic countries are perceived as being unable to build teams or get results. U.S. President George W. Bush saw his approval ratings drop from 85 to 30 percent over his eight-year term. Barack Obama experienced a 25-point approval rating drop during his first 18 months in office, and in the summer of 2010 the U.S. Congress had only an 11 percent approval rating from likely voters.[9-11]

- There were 1,132 CEO departures in the first nine months of 2008, up from 700 per year from 2002 to 2004. Fifty percent of *Fortune* 500 CEOs will be dismissed for poor performance over the next three years. Worldwide confidence in business leaders is the lowest it has ever been for the past 10 years.[12-15]

- Employee satisfaction surveys show that more than 75 percent of all respondents indicate that the most stressful part of their job is their immediate boss.[8] This finding holds true across countries and industries.

- A study published in *Harvard Business Review* reported that only 30 percent of businesses had "healthy and respectful" work climates. A majority of organizations had dysfunctional and unhealthy work climates.[16]

- At any one time the 800,000 employees of the U.S. Postal Service have filed 150,000 grievances against their supervisors.[8]

- Research shows that 50–90 percent of all new businesses fail within five years. This finding seems consistent across all business types and countries. Most of the failures can be attributed to managerial incompetence.[17-20]

- BP, the energy company responsible for the Gulf of Mexico environmental disaster in 2010, has been cited 760 times and paid fines of $373,000,000 for safety and environmental violations since 2005. The root causes of most major industrial accidents and incidents, such as the Bhopal, India, chemical spill, the Exxon Valdez disaster, or the Texas City refinery explosion can be traced back to poor management oversight or management cost-cutting initiatives.[21,22]

- Research also shows that 67 percent of all IT projects fail to deliver promised functionality, are not delivered on time, or do not stay within budgeted costs. This IT project failure rate has not improved much over the past 10 years, and U.S. businesses are now spending over $55 billion annually on poorly scoped or executed IT projects.[23]

- Over 70 percent of all mergers and acquisitions fail to yield projected improvements in profitability and synergies. Examples might include ATT's acquisition of NCR or Daimler's ill-fated acquisition of Chrysler.[24]

- A majority of large-scale organizational change initiatives fail to achieve their intended results.[25]

As unflattering as these statistics are, these examples may seem out of the realm of most readers. So let's make the concept of managerial incompetence a little more personal. One easy way to determine the level of incompetence among people in positions of authority is to do the **Dr. Gordy test.**[7] To use this test, begin by counting the total number of people you have been led by or worked for in the past. This total should include past bosses, athletic coaches, team captains, choir directors, camp directors, and so on. In other words, it should include anyone with whom you played a formal followership role. Once you have arrived at a total, count the number of people in this group for whom you would willingly play, sing, or work again. In other words, how many of these people would you play a followership role for again if given a choice? Now calculate the percentage of competent leaders in the total group of leaders. When health care, education, business, military, and community leaders are asked the same question, most need only the digits on a single hand to count the number of leaders for whom they would willingly work again. The percentage of competent leaders people would willingly work for again varies dramatically across individuals, but the percentage seems to hover between 25 and 40 percent.[7] This means that most people would not work for a majority of leaders they have been exposed to.

FIGURE 15.1
The Two
Dimensions
of Managerial
Incompetence

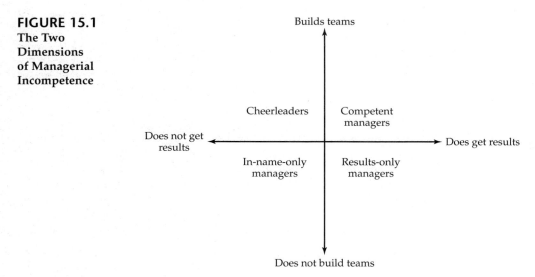

We believe that those occupying positions of authority are paid to get results, and they get results by building teams.[7,8] As shown in Figure 15.1, **competent managers** are good at building teams and getting results through others. Although they are the types of leaders most people aspire to be, most people in positions of authority fall into one of the other three categories. **Results-only managers** are often good at achieving results, such as financial targets or win–loss records, but tend to treat followers so poorly that these results tend to be short-lived. Nonetheless, some results-only managers are effective at turning around failing businesses. Because these managers do not care for people, they can make the tough decisions needed to right a sinking ship, and some are so good at turnarounds that they spend their entire careers moving from one floundering company to another. Other results-only managers are good at projecting an image of success by launching **programs for promotions initiatives** that garner a lot of attention but have no real chance of success. Superiors get caught up in the hyperbole and often promote these results-only managers before the consequences of their poorly conceived initiatives and lack of team-building skills become evident (see Highlight 15.1). And because results-only managers have impressive track records, they are often hired away to wreak havoc on other organizations.

Cheerleaders are people in positions of authority who are people-centered and make a point of getting along with everyone. Thanks to their focus on making the workplace warm and fun, most people like working for cheerleaders. However, cheerleaders spend so much time making the workplace enjoyable that they forget why they are paid to be

An Example of a Results-Only Manager

HIGHLIGHT 15.1

The following is a story about a sales manager who is a results-only manager. What advice would you give to the writer to fix the problem?

I've been working in a medium-sized manufacturing company for the past 20 years. I'm not in sales, but interact with salespeople on a daily basis. Over the past year or so, I have noticed the sales force has been frustrated. After numerous conversations not only with the sales force, but also with other people in all aspects of the company, I have realized that the poison is coming from one person: Mike, the sales manager. Mike has been with the company for over 10 years and has successfully maneuvered his way to the position of sales manager. All of his promotions were given to him because of his own self-promotion. He has an enormous ego. His tactics of bulldog management, double standards, and outright lying are driving his sales force out and are frustrating people all over the company. He is disliked, even hated, by almost everyone in the company.

Amazingly, Mike doesn't realize what people think of him. I believe the owners tolerate Mike's behavior because he has produced decent sales over the years. This year sales are substantially down. I believe the company is going to start to lose good salespeople because of Mike. Here's why: Nobody will confront him because if they do, he threatens them or makes them do some ridiculous assignment. All conversations with Mike are one-sided. If you bring up a concern that involves him, he will change the subject and dismiss you. It's like he is afraid of the truth. He is dishonest and essentially a loose cannon. I believe the owners know the truth about Mike but they continue to let him act this way. I believe Mike will never leave because he knows he could never get away with the things he does here anywhere else. My concern is that if the owners don't fix the "Mike problem" they will start to lose good salespeople. Any advice?

Source: J. Lloyd, "Good Firms Work to Find Out Truth about Bad Managers," *Milwaukee Journal Sentinel,* August 20, 2000, p. 20.

in leadership positions, which is to get results. Cheerleaders also tend to be involved with a number of different activities and stay very busy. But cheerleaders tend to confuse activity with productivity and thus work hard but get little accomplished. They also tend to have a difficult time doing anything that could potentially erode their relationships with followers, which includes dealing with conflict or confronting performance problems. Nevertheless, because they are loyal and dutiful, avoid making enemies, engage in strategic ingratiation, and are well liked by followers, cheerleaders often are promoted into senior positions in organizations (see Highlight 15.2).

In-name-only managers do not play to win; they play to not lose. They may not be complete failures at building teams and getting results, but they could be a lot better at both of these endeavors. Many times in-name-only managers do just enough to stay out of trouble and avoid the spotlight. The last thing in-name-only managers want is attention because this might raise superiors' expectations for their performance. So if their team is starting to exceed expectations, they may hold back or even sabotage

An Example of a Cheerleader

HIGHLIGHT 15.2

Every business depends on its account receivables department. This department collects payments from customers, and problems in collections will hurt company performance. An office supply company was having serious cash flow problems and had been using its credit line to pay its bills, primarily because accounts receivable time had increased from 36 to 52 days. To try to turn around this problem, Helen was made manager of accounts receivable because of her performance during a major sales software conversion. Helen approached her new role with great enthusiasm, and motivational posters started appearing everywhere. The poster titled "The Power of One" was particularly amusing because she was the one person who did everything but her job.

Helen was easy to get along with and well liked by her staff. She knew everyone's personal problems, regularly organized potluck lunches, and brought in weekly treats. When peers inquired about the status of invoices, Helen always told them she would "get right on it," but it usually took another three to four calls before they could determine what was really happening. After three months the only gains in the department were on the waistlines of the staff, who had made no progress in reducing the time it was taking customers to pay the company. A few months later Helen brought in outside consultants to help fix the accounts receivable problem. Helen constantly extolled the virtues of her hardworking staff and consultants and provided pleasant but somewhat ridiculous excuses for her department's lack of progress. After a year of posters, potlucks, and ever-worsening accounts receivables results, Helen was promoted into another position. The keys to her success were flattering her boss and making everyone on her team happy—team results were not important.

If you were Helen's boss, what would you do to achieve better accounts receivable results?

Source: G. J. Curphy, A. Baldrica, and R. T. Hogan, *Managerial Incompetence,* unpublished manuscript, 2009.

There are three kinds of people in the world: those who can count, and those who can't.

Anonymous

---

team performance to avoid having to meet higher expectations in the future. Thus followers who are self-starters can get frustrated and leave organizations when they find out they are working for in-name-only managers (see Highlight 15.3).

There are variations of in-name-only managers. Some have a hard time building teams and getting results because they are so intellectually and interpersonally challenged. It is hard to build a team and get results if you are completely clueless about people and repeatedly demonstrate poor business judgment. Other in-name-only managers want to succeed but demonstrate irritating, counterproductive behaviors that interfere with their ability to build teams or get results through others. Some lack the motivation needed to build teams or get results. Put another way, these individuals simply do not care if they lead cohesive teams or obtain better-than-average results. Situational factors may also affect the prevalence of in–name-only managers in organizations—some managers may find themselves in situations where they lack the equipment,

An Example of an In-Name-Only Manager

HIGHLIGHT 15.3

Steve Jones was a salesman who learned the car business and then convinced a local bank to lend him the money to open his own Ford dealership. Over the years Steve added Dodge, Suzuki, BMW, Nissan, Rover, and Volkswagen automobile and Yamaha motorcycle dealerships to his company; annual revenues grew from less than $1,000,000 to over $200,000,000. As Steve grew older he became concerned with succession and wanted his oldest son Scott to take over the business. Growing up in a privileged environment, Scott was a poor student in high school and flunked out of college, but Steve brought him into the business and put him in charge of purchasing. One of his responsibilities was to purchase life and health insurance for employees.

Scott asked a local insurance representative to make an insurance sales presentation for him and 15 other executives from the dealerships. During the presentation Scott asked several irrelevant questions and criticized the other executives and the representative for not following his line of questioning. He had strong opinions about, but no grasp of, life and health insurance. Unfortunately Scott acted no differently at the sales presentation than he did in his day-to-day interactions with customers, vendors, managers, and employees—he treated everyone with equal distain. Scott did not care about the people on his purchasing team, and the dealership began making bad purchasing decisions. The other managers and employees tried to keep Scott from making mistakes, but Scott ignored any advice on how to obtain better results. After several major purchasing blunders, Steve removed Scott from his position and told him never to return to work. Although Steve saved his business, Scott continues to treat others as "little people" who are unworthy of his presence.

Source: G. J. Curphy, A. Baldrica, and R. T. Hogan, *Managerial Incompetence,* unpublished manuscript, 2009.

systems, budget, or talent needed to succeed. For example, a fire chief may find it nearly impossible to build a cohesive, effective team of firefighters if the department lacks fire trucks or a fire station or has no budget to train staff.

If the base rate of managerial incompetence is 50–75 percent, we might wonder how organizations can succeed with such a high percentage of ineffective people in positions of authority. Although managerial incompetence can be found in any organization, many businesses still make money, the U.S. military is capable of waging wars, children continue to get educated, and most people receive high-quality health care when they need it. The good news is that organizations may not actually need every person in a position of authority to be a competent manager. The keys to success may be for organizations to ensure that they have a higher percentage of competent managers than their competitors and that these individuals are in pivotal leadership roles. Research shows that organizations with higher percentages of competent managers occupying critical positions are more successful than those with fewer

When the dog is dead, the fleas are gone.
Puerto Rico folk saying

The Moronization of Management

HIGHLIGHT 15.4

Carl Icahn is a multibillionaire who made his fortune buying up companies that were poorly managed, straightening out their operations and finances, and then reselling them for a profit. Senior managers dislike Icahn because they often lose their jobs when he buys their companies; but many would argue that if they were doing their jobs, the company performance would be so good that Icahn would not see an opportunity to buy the company and flip it to make a profit. Icahn has a theory about U.S. businesses: many senior executives are the "guys you knew in college, the fraternity president—not too bright, back slapping, but a survivor, politically astute, a nice guy." According

to Icahn, to be a chief executive people need to know how not to tread on anyone's toes on the way up. Eventually a person becomes the number two in the company and needs to be just a little worse than number one in order to survive. When the number two gets promoted to be the CEO, he in turn promotes someone a little less capable than him as the second-in-command. "It is survival of the unfittest—eventually we are all going to be run by morons." Icahn calls this phenomenon of promoting people slightly less capable than the incumbent leader the **moronization of management.**

Source: Adapted from *The Economist,* February 11, 2006, p. 42.

competent managers who are not well placed.[26-28] The purpose of this chapter and book is to increase the odds of you becoming a competent manager and securing positions where you can have an impact on the success of your organization.

Managerial Derailment

So far we have described five different leadership and management types. Bad leadership is associated with individuals who have good team-building skills but achieve results that are morally or ethically reprehensible. Results-only managers tend to get good results but run over people and erode team cohesiveness while doing so. Cheerleaders are very busy and care about followers but fail to get anything done. In-name-only managers have difficulties building teams and getting results because they are clueless, do not care, or are in situations that make it impossible to succeed. Competent managers make up a minority of people in positions of authority and are those who can build teams and achieve results that improve organizations, societies, or countries. Of course, if it were easy to be a competent manager, many more people would be in this category. Given that most people in positions of authority are either bad or incompetent leaders, there must be many ways in which people can fail as leaders. The purpose of this section is to describe the most common reasons why people fail in leading others.

Over the past 30 years a considerable amount of research has been done on managerial derailment, and it is worthwhile to describe the lessons of these efforts because they apply to virtually anyone in a position of authority. Initial research on managerial derailment—whereby individuals who at one time were on the fast track only to have their careers derailed—was conducted in the early 1980s by researchers at the Center for Creative Leadership. The researchers went to the human resources departments in a number of *Fortune* 100 companies seeking lists of their **high-potential managers.** McCall and Lombardo defined *high potentials* as individuals who had been identified as eventually becoming either the CEO/president or one of his or her direct reports sometime in the future. They waited for three years and then returned to these organizations to ask what had happened to the people on the lists. They discovered that roughly a quarter of the high potentials had been promoted to one of the top two levels in the organization, and an equal percentage had not yet been promoted but would be as soon as a position became available. Another 25 percent had left the companies; some had quit to form their own companies, and others were given better offers somewhere else. Finally, about a quarter of the people on the list were no longer being considered for promotion. Most of these individuals were let go or demoted to less influential and visible positions. This last group of individuals represented cases of managerial derailment.[29]

Several other researchers have investigated the managerial derailment phenomenon.[30–41] This additional research used much larger samples (one researcher examined over 600 derailed managers), European samples, and more sophisticated assessment tools (such as 360-degree feedback instruments). Moreover, a substantially higher percentage of women and minorities were represented in this later research; the initial high-potential list was dominated by white males. As Van Veslor and Leslie point out, this research focused on identifying factors that helped derailment candidates initially get identified as high potentials as well as factors contributing to their ultimate professional demise.[34] Although these studies varied in many ways, there are many consistent findings across them. Both successful and derailed candidates were smart, ambitious, and willing to do whatever it took to get the job done, and they had considerable technical expertise. In other words, all of the high-potential candidates had impressive track records in their organizations.

On the other hand, the derailed candidates exhibited one or more behavioral patterns not evident in the high potentials who succeeded. Five key derailment themes run through the research results listed in Table 15.1 and are described in more detail here. Note that the derailment themes included in Table 15.1 have been consistently reported by researchers in both the United States and Europe. One derailment pattern identified in Table 15.1 is a **failure to meet business objectives.** Although both successful and derailed managers experienced business downturns, the two

TABLE 15.1 Common Themes in Derailment Research

Source: J. Hogan, R. T. Hogan, and R. Kaiser, "Managerial Derailment," in *APA Handbook of Industrial and Organizational Psychology*, Vol. 3, ed. S. Zedeck (Washington, DC: American Psychological Association, 2011), pp. 555–76.

Skill Domain / *Definition*		Research Study					
	Benz (1985a)	McCall and Lombardo (1983)	Morrison, White, and Van Velsor (1987)	McCauley and Lombardo (1990)	Lombardo and Eichinger (2006)	Rasch, Shen, Davies, and Bono (2008)
Business						
Ability to plan, organize, monitor, and use resources.	Lacked business skill.	Specific business problems.	Performance problems.	Difficulty in molding a staff.	Poor administrative skills.	Poor task performance.
	Unable to deal with complexity.	Unable to think strategically.	Not Strategic.	Difficulty in making strategic transition.	Lack of strategic thinking.	Poor planning, organization, and/or communication.
	Reactive and tactical.	Unable to staff effectively.	Restricted business experience.	Strategic differences with management.	Difficulty making tough choices.	
Leadership						
Ability to influence, build, and maintain a team; role modeling.	Unable to delegate.	Overmanaging— failing to delegate.	Can't manage subordinates.		Failure to build a team.	Failure to nurture and manage talent.
	Unable to build a team.					Avoiding conflict and people problems.
						Overcontrolling.

TABLE 15.1 (*Continued*)

Interpersonal

Social skill, empathy, and maintaining relationships.	Unable to maintain relationships with a network.	Insensitivity (abrasive, intimidating, bully). Cold, aloof, arrogant.	Poor relationships.	Problems with interpersonal relationships.	Poor political skills. No interpersonal savy. Unable to deal with conflict.	Failure to consider human needs.

Intrapersonal

Self-awareness and self-control, emotional maturity, integrity.	Lets emotions cloud judgment. Slow to learn. An "overriding personality defect."	Unable to adapt to a boss with a different style. Too dependent on an advocate. Too ambitious. Betrayal of trust.	Unable to adapt to boss. Too ambitious.	Too dependent on an advocate. Lack of follow-through.	Questionable integrity. Low self-awareness.	Procrastination and time delays. Poor emotional control. Rumor-mongering and inappropriate use of information.

groups handled setbacks quite differently. Successful managers took personal responsibility for their mistakes and sought ways to solve the problem. Derailed managers tended to engage in finger-pointing and blamed others for the downturn. *But as long as things were going well,* it was difficult to differentiate these two groups on this factor. Some of these managers were also untrustworthy. They blatantly lied about business results, cooked the books, or failed to keep promises, commitments, or deadlines. Others failed because they were not particularly smart or did not have an in-depth understanding of the business and as a result exercised poor judgment.

Although the research cited in Table 15.1 focused on failed high-potential candidates, the inability to achieve business results is not limited to this audience. Many people in positions of authority may not be high-potential candidates but are nonetheless unable to achieve business or organizational results. These individuals tend to be either cheerleaders or in-name-only managers and simply cannot get anything accomplished. As described earlier, some are popular but confuse activity with productivity; others want their teams to get just enough done to stay off their boss's radar screens. Some may be motivated to achieve results but consistently make bad decisions or alienate team members by exhibiting behaviors that interfere with team cohesiveness, such as an inability to make decisions, micromanaging team members, or taking credit for others' work. One hallmark of effective leadership is the ability to get results across a variety of situations; those who cannot get anything noteworthy accomplished are destined to fail the Dr. Gordy test.

The second derailment pattern identified by Hogan, Hogan, and Kaiser was an **inability to build and lead a team.**[33] Some high-potential candidates derailed because they simply did not know how to build teams. Others failed by hiring staff members that were just like themselves, which only magnified their own strengths and weaknesses. Some wanted to stay in the limelight and hired staff less capable than they were. Still others micromanaged their staffs and wanted their followers to "check their brains at the door" before coming to work, even when they lacked relevant subject matter expertise. People in positions of authority who spend too much time doing activities that should be done by direct reports can also have difficulty building teams because they disempower all the managers who work for them. Because these leaders are making the decisions that their followers would normally make, followers become disengaged with work and team performance suffers.[7,42]

Like the failure to meet business objectives, the inability to build or lead teams is a common reason why many people in positions of authority are seen as incompetent managers. Two underlying reasons for the inability to build teams are a lack of team-building know-how and dark-side personality traits. Many people can easily describe the best and worst teams they have ever been on, but when asked what process they would use to build high-performing teams, they are surprisingly inarticulate. In other words, most people in positions of authority understand the importance of teamwork but have no clue how to make it happen. This lack of team-building knowhow is one reason why some people are seen as in-name-only or results-only managers, but another key reason is the presence of dark-side personality traits. These attributes will be described in more detail later in this chapter.

A third derailment pattern has to do with an **inability to build relationships** with co-workers. The derailed managers exhibiting this pattern of behavior were insensitive to the needs and plights of their followers and co-workers, and they were often overly competitive, demanding, and domineering. They embraced the "my way or the highway" school of management, and many would be categorized as results-only managers. Many were extremely arrogant and truly believed no one in their organizations was as good as they were, and they let their co-workers know this every time they could. Some of these derailed managers also did whatever they felt necessary to get the job done, even if it meant stepping on a few toes. Unfortunately this is not a recommended technique for winning friends and influencing people. It is wise to remember the old adage that you should be careful whom you step on going up a ladder because you may meet them again on your way down. Many of these managers left a trail of bruised people who were waiting for the right opportunity to bring these leaders down.

The inability to get along with others is a fairly common derailment pattern among high potentials and anyone else in positions of authority. An example is a female vice president of marketing and sales for a cellular phone company who was fired from her $200,000-a-year job for exhibiting many of the behaviors just listed. She was very bright, had an excellent technical background (she was an engineer), had already been the CEO of several smaller organizations, and worked long hours. Although she also had a strong leaderlike personality, she would quickly identify and capitalize on others' faults, constantly comment on their incompetence, talk down to people, run over her peers when she needed resources or support, promote infighting among her peers and subordinates, and expect to be pampered. Interestingly, she had no idea she was having such a debilitating effect on those she worked with until she received some 360-degree feedback. Had she received this feedback sooner, she might have been able to stop her career from derailing.

The inability to build relationships is not limited to results-only managers; in-name-only managers also have difficulties getting along with others. But rather than exhibiting a "my way or the highway" attitude, in-name-only managers fail to build relationships with followers because they regularly exhibit emotional outbursts and temper tantrums, falsely believe that followers are out to get them, fail to provide followers with needed resources or support, or burn out team members with constantly shifting priorities. These irritating, counterproductive behavioral tendencies are manifestations of dark-side personality traits, which will be described in more detail later in this chapter.

Charan and Colvin, Dotlich and Cairo, Hogan, and Curphy have all stated that people problems are also one of the primary reasons why CEOs fail. However, unlike derailed first-line supervisors or midlevel managers, most CEOs get along with others in the company. The problem with some CEOs is that they get along with some of their direct reports too well and do not take timely action to address problem performers. More specifically, some CEOs fail because they place loyal subordinates into jobs they are incapable of handling, falsely believe they can help poorly performing subordinates to change ineffective behavior, do not want to offend Wall Street or the board by letting popular (but ineffective) executives go, or do not feel comfortable hiring outsiders to fill key executive positions.[7,8,30,33,41]

Another derailment profile has to do with a leader's **inability to adapt** to new bosses, businesses, cultures, or structures. As pointed out earlier in this chapter, business situations require different leadership behaviors and skills, and some derailed managers could not adapt or adjust their styles to changing bosses, followers, and situations. They persisted in acting the same way when it was no longer appropriate to new circumstances. For example, a first-line supervisor for an electronics firm that built video poker machines was having a difficult time transitioning from his old job as a missile guidance repairman in the U.S. Air Force. He thought he should lead his subordinates the way he led others in the military: his staff should be willing to work long hours and over the weekends without being told to do so and to travel for extended periods with short notice. Their thoughts or opinions about ways to improve work processes did not matter to him, and he expected everyone to maintain cool and professional attitudes at work. After half of his staff quit as a direct result of his supervision, he was demoted and replaced by one of his subordinates.

In the past, organizations could afford to take their time in identifying and developing leadership talent. And as described earlier in this book, many of the best organizations today have strong programs for systematically developing leadership bench strength. However, organizations today are under increasing pressure to find good leaders quickly, and they are increasingly asking their own high-potential but inexperienced leadership talent to fill these key roles. Although these new leaders are bright and motivated, they often have narrow technical backgrounds and lack the leadership breadth and depth necessary for the new positions. The unfortunate result is that many of these leaders leave their organizations because of **inadequate preparation for promotion.** For example, a relatively young woman attorney was promoted to be the vice president of human resources in a large telecommunications firm. Although she was

The Sea Witch

PROFILES IN LEADERSHIP 15.4

Holly Graf was the first female in the U.S. Navy to command a cruiser, the second largest surface vessel in the fleet. Graf's father was a commander in the U.S. Navy, and as a child she dreamed of someday commanding a ship. Pursuing her dreams, Graf graduated from the U.S. Naval Academy and rapidly advanced through a series of leadership roles in destroyer tenders, frigates, destroyers, and finally a guided missile cruiser. Intelligent and ambitious, she also obtained three masters degrees and did a stint at the Pentagon during her shore assignments. Graf's troubles in leading and managing others were noted relatively early in her career. When a destroyer she was commanding stopped suddenly while leaving port, she began screaming and swearing at the navigator, thinking he had run the ship aground, which would have been a career-ending episode for Graf. It turned out that one of the screws on the destroyer had failed; but when the crew heard about the ship running aground, they all broke out in song: "Ding, dong, the witch is dead!" She allegedly ran over a whale during ship maneuvers; choked one of her subordinates during a "training session"; regularly pushed, screamed, swore at, and questioned the manhood of her staff; routinely tossed coffee cups at those bearing bad news; and thought it was acceptable for junior officers to play piano at her personal Christmas parties and walk her dogs.

When a chaplain visiting one of her ships tried to give her feedback about her leadership style and its debilitating effect on the crew, she quickly dismissed the chaplain and did not speak to him for the rest of the cruise. The ship's crew let out a loud cheer when she was formally relieved of command and promoted into another command position.

For a number of years the complaints about Graf fell on deaf ears, but eventually they became so pervasive as to warrant a formal investigation. Based on the results of this investigation, Graf was relieved of command; shortly thereafter a popular Navy blog had 190 posts about Graf. Nearly all the posts were negative; the four supportive posts came from individuals who had never served under Graf. It was evident that Graf had a toxic effect on almost everyone she worked with, yet she continued to get promoted despite strong evidence showing that she was unable to build teams. A key question that remains unanswered is why the navy not only tolerated but actually rewarded these behaviors in a leader. Perhaps the navy's lack of leadership accountability played as much of a role in Graf's promotions and ultimate demise as Graf herself.

What would you have done if you were Graf's commanding officer? Or one of her direct reports?

Sources: http://www.time.com/time/nation/article/0,8599,1969602-2,00.html; http://www.susankatzkeating.com/2010/01/captain-holly-graf-plows-down-whale.html.

---

bright and ambitious, her previous management experience involved leading a team of six attorneys, whereas her promotion put her in charge of 300 human resources professionals. It soon became apparent that she lacked the skills and knowledge needed to manage a large, geographically dispersed human resources organization. Although she tried hard to succeed, she kept acting as a front-line supervisor instead of a functional leader and failed to earn the respect of her staff. After six months she was given a generous separation package and asked to leave the company.

Most derailed managers manifest several of these themes; the presence of only one of these behavioral patterns is usually not enough for derailment. The only exception to this rule is a failure to meet business objectives. Managers who do not follow through with commitments, break promises, lie, are unethical, and do not get results do not stay on the high-potential list for long. Although this research focused on derailment patterns for high-potential candidates, it seems likely that these five reasons for failure are universal. It would be difficult to perceive someone as a competent manager if he or she could not obtain business results or had difficulties adapting to new situations, building teams, or getting along with others. A bigger concern is why these managerial derailment patterns appear to be fairly obvious, yet so many people fail as leaders. In other words, if you asked a group of people why people in positions of authority fail, it is likely that you would hear the five reasons described in this section. Because these derailment factors are more or less public knowledge, it seems that simply being aware of the reasons why people fail in leadership positions does not seem to be enough to prevent it from happening. If we assume that most people move into managerial positions with positive intent and generally know the pitfalls to avoid in order to be successful, yet they are likely to be perceived as incompetent managers, then there must be something else going on. We believe that managerial incompetence and derailment have some underlying root causes, and knowing what they are and what to do to minimize their impact will improve the odds of being perceived as a competent manager. Many of these root causes are variations of concepts presented earlier in this book.

The Six Root Causes of Managerial Incompetence and Derailment

The research on managerial derailment provides a good starting point for investigating the underlying reasons why a majority of people in positions of authority are seen as results-only managers, cheerleaders, or in-name-only managers. Clearly a failure to achieve business objectives, an inability to build a team, or an inability to adapt to changing conditions will make leaders fail. But what causes people to fail to achieve business results or get along with others? Are these management failures due to character flaws on the part of the leader, pervasive situational factors, problematic followers, or some combination of all three factors? As shown in Figure 15.2, leader, follower, and situational factors all play roles in managerial derailment. Sometimes leaders are put in situations where it is virtually impossible to build teams or achieve results; at other times a leader's own shortcomings cause managerial incompetence and derailment. Looking over Figure 15.2, we might think it is next to impossible to be a competent manager because there are so many ways in which people in positions of authority can fail. For example, the global economy could take a significant downturn, hurricanes or terrorist events could disrupt supply chains, key followers could retire or be hired away by competitors, organizations could downsize or be acquired by other companies, new

FIGURE 15.2
The Root Causes of Managerial Derailment and the Leader–Follower–Situation Model

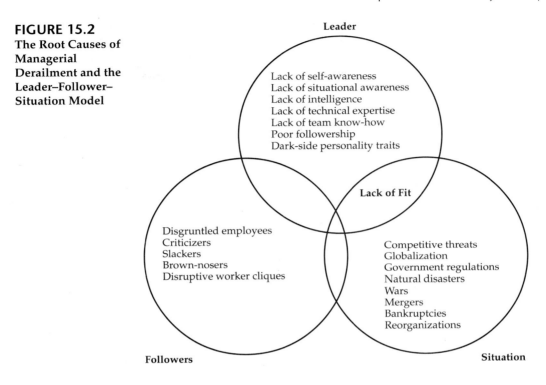

Leader

Lack of self-awareness
Lack of situational awareness
Lack of intelligence
Lack of technical expertise
Lack of team know-how
Poor followership
Dark-side personality traits

Lack of Fit

Disgruntled employees
Criticizers
Slackers
Brown-nosers
Disruptive worker cliques

Competitive threats
Globalization
Government regulations
Natural disasters
Wars
Mergers
Bankruptcies
Reorganizations

Followers   **Situation**

competitors could develop disruptive technologies and dominate the market, workers could go on strike, or the new CEO could be a results-only manager. The good news is that we can mitigate managerial derailment by understanding the six root causes, assessing the extent to which they are affecting our ability to build teams and get results through others, and then adopting some of the suggestions found in this section to minimize their effects.

As shown in Figure 15.2 and Table 15.2, there are six root causes of managerial derailment. Table 15.2 is not meant to be a comprehensive list of root causes—there are other reasons why results-only managers, in-name-only managers, and cheerleaders occur so frequently. However, these six are likely to describe why many people are unable to build teams or get results. As an overview, certain situational and follower factors can make it difficult to build teams and get results. An example might include a commercial airline crew trying to deliver a planeload of international passengers to an airport that suddenly closes down due to a terrorist threat. The captain may have done a good job of getting the crew to work as a cohesive team to provide great passenger service but will not be able to achieve her on-time arrival goal because of the airport closure. Although situational and follower factors can sometimes play key roles, leader factors are much more likely to cause managerial incompetence

TABLE 15.2
Bad Leadership,
Managerial
Incompetence,
Managerial
Derailment, and
Root Causes

Leadership Type	Managerial Derailment Factors	Root Causes of Derailment
Bad leadership.	Failure to meet business objectives.	Situational and follower factors.
Competent managers.	Inability to build and lead teams.	Lack of organizational fit.
Results-only managers.	Inability to build relationships.	Lack of situational or self-awareness.
Cheerleaders.	Inability to adapt.	Lack of intelligence, technical expertise, or team-building know-how.
In-name-only managers.	Inadequate preparation for promotion.	Poor followership; dark-side personality traits.

Savvy managers figure out how to get things done, no matter what obstacles they face.

**Mark Roellig,
MassMutual**

and derailment. Some leaders cannot see how they impact others, some consistently exercise poor judgment, others do not value building teams or getting results, and others are such poor followers that they are fired from their leadership positions.

Stuff Happens: Situational and Follower Factors in Managerial Derailment

The story in Highlight 15.5 concerns a relatively short-lived scenario in which a situational factor interfered with a person's ability to build teams and get results through others. Similar events, many of which are more dramatic and longer-lived, occur frequently. Think about a person's ability

---

The Role of Situational Factors in Managerial Incompetence

HIGHLIGHT 15.5

In the late summer of 2001 one of this textbook's authors was the manager of a relatively large office of consultants based in the United States. One of his responsibilities was to manage a large succession planning project for Saudi Aramco, the national oil company in Saudi Arabia. Succession planning is simple in Saudi Arabia: if someone is related to the royal family, he is automatically promoted into a key leadership position in the company regardless of his talent for management. Because the House of Saud is relatively small, the consultant's job was to identify nonfamily employees who could best fill the remaining leadership positions. The author was ending a three-week consulting engagement in Saudi Arabia when he watched the airplanes hit the World Trade Center and Pentagon on CNN. Because all flights to the United States were canceled and international phone circuits became overloaded, the author was unable to communicate with his family or his staff until he returned to the United States six days later. His inability to communicate with his team limited his effectiveness as a leader during this time.

Source: G. J. Curphy, A. Baldrica, and R. T. Hogan, *Managerial Incompetence,* unpublished manuscript, 2009.

to be a competent manager if he was a civic leader in Haiti immediately after the Port au Prince earthquake, a midlevel automobile parts manufacturing manager right after she was told her plant would be closing in the next six months, or a U.S. Army Reserve captain who was preparing his unit to be deployed to Afghanistan for the fifth time in seven years. It seems somewhat obvious, but situational and follower factors significantly affect a person's ability to build teams and get results.[7] Here are some of the factors that can interfere with a person's ability to be seen as a competent manager:

- New competitive threats, globalization, technology, changing customer preferences, unreliable suppliers, new government regulations, unfavorable media coverage, natural disasters, and wars.
- Mergers, acquisitions, divestitures, bankruptcies, new strategies, reorganizations, and incidents of workplace violence or environmental disasters.
- New bosses, peers, direct reports; disengaged or disgruntled employees; disruptive worker cliques; and strikes or dysfunctional turnover.
- New jobs, responsibilities, or projects.

Figuring out how to build teams and get things done despite potentially disruptive situational and follower factors is part of any leadership role, but at times these external factors can be so overwhelming that there may be little a person can do to build teams or get results. What is interesting is how the four managerial types react when facing hopeless challenges. Competent managers take time to reflect on the situation, determine what they need to do differently, and then ensure that their decisions are executed. Competent managers often succeed where others fail because they investigate all the alternatives and then make the changes needed to maintain team cohesiveness and performance. Interestingly, one of these alternatives may include changing jobs or leaving the organization if the leader feels that others are better able to help the team cope with these challenges. Leaders may also believe that switching teams is a better option than remaining in the role and risk becoming cheerleaders, results-only managers, or in-name-only managers.

Incompetent managers facing hopeless situations tend to act quite differently: they are likely to keep doing what they have always done but expect to achieve different results. For example, when faced with challenging followers or situations, results-only managers tend to focus more closely on goals, metrics, and bottom-line results and spend even less time with the people on their teams. Cheerleaders increase their team-building and relationship-building behaviors and try to keep teammates happy rather than making them more productive. And in-name-only managers are even less likely to make decisions, take stands, lay out courses of action, or push team members to perform. All three types of incompetent managers try to leverage their strengths rather than change, which erodes their ability to build teams and get results.

Two additional points about these overwhelming situational and follower factors are worth noting. Although many situational and follower factors are beyond a manager's control, the manager can control his or her reactions to these events. A manager can step back, reflect upon the new situation, and determine what he or she needs to do differently; or the manager can continue to leverage his or her strengths and expect a different outcome. Reflection may be the key success factor when facing difficult situations, but too often people in positions of authority overreact, withhold information, and rush to judgment rather than explaining difficult facts and soliciting team members for ideas.

A second point concerns the concepts of episodic versus chronic incompetence. **Episodic managerial incompetence** occurs when people in positions of authority face extremely tough situational or follower events that temporarily interfere with their ability to build teams and get results. However, once they have reflected upon and taken action to cope with the event, they quickly regain their ability to successfully build teams and get results. **Chronic managerial incompetence** occurs when taxing situational or follower events permanently disrupt a person's ability to build teams or get results. All competent managers experience occasional episodic managerial incompetence; the trick is to limit the frequency and duration of these occurrences. But given their preferred ways of dealing with challenging events, cheerleaders, results-only managers, and in-name-only managers seem to exemplify chronic managerial incompetence.

The Lack of Organizational Fit: Stranger in a Strange Land

The previous section described the role that situational and follower factors play in managerial competence and incompetence. Organizational culture also plays an important role in this matter. Chapter 12 defined organizational culture as a system of shared backgrounds, norms, values, or beliefs among members of a group. All organizations have cultures, but the content and strength of the beliefs underlying these cultures can vary dramatically. For example, the shared beliefs, norms, and values of the U.S. Marine Corps are quite different from those of PETA or Greenpeace.

Organizational culture is not one of those pervasive situational factors that doom managers to fail, but a person's fit with an organization's culture can cause him or her to be seen as incompetent. **Organizational fit** can be defined as the degree of agreement between personal and organizational values and beliefs.[42,43] If a person does not share the values or beliefs of the majority of members, then in all likelihood this person will be a poor fit with the organization. Many times people who do not fit with an organization's culture wield diminishing levels of influence, which interferes with their ability to build teams and get results. Highlight 15.6

Organizational Fit and Managerial Derailment

HIGHLIGHT 15.6

Ann had spent the past 30 years as a sales executive in the insurance industry. Savvy, sophisticated, and successful, over the years Ann had developed deep expertise in marketing, sales, contracting, invoicing, budgeting, and compensation. She also had over 20 years of sales leadership experience and had consistently built cohesive teams that exceeded their sales quotas. After a successful career of selling insurance, Ann was looking for a new challenge, and one of the local nonprofit organizations needed an executive to head up its fund-raising function. The nonprofit had been around for over 50 years, employed over 300 people, and specialized in helping developmentally disabled adults live more independent lives. To achieve this mission the nonprofit provided lodging, skills training, transportation, and other services to its constituents. Ann was hired because the organization was running out of money—revenues were shrinking, expenses were rapidly rising, and donors were scaling back on their contributions. The main donor base was also growing old, and many major contributors were literally dying off.

Attracted to the mission and by the challenge of doing something new, Ann joined the organization and was told by the president to do whatever was needed to secure the existing funding base and find new sources of revenue. Ann started this effort by reviewing the donor database and soon discovered that the organization had done nothing more than send form thank-you letters to the major donors over the past five years. The organization had not visited or invited the donors to any functions or solicited funding from any new donors. She developed a strategic marketing plan that called for the senior staff to engage in a number of outreach activities with new and existing donors.

Ann was surprised by the organization's reaction to her strategic marketing plan. The president felt it was beneath her to engage in fund-raising activities and did not want the organization to be seen as having anything to do with fund solicitation. The president emphatically stated that the mission of the organization was to serve the developmentally disabled, not raise money. The rest of the senior staff wholeheartedly agreed with the president. Ann responded that the organization's costs were exceeding its revenues, and if the senior staff did not want to help generate more funding, then the alternative was to cut expenses. She reminded the staff that she had been told to do whatever was needed to raise cash, and now that her plan was put forward, it appeared that this was not really the case. The president said that money was not their concern and it was up to Ann, and Ann alone, to make things happen. Because of the organization's lack of urgency and genuine distaste for fund-raising, Ann felt like a fish out of water. The things she cared about were of no interest to the senior leadership team, even though her plan would allow the organization to continue its mission. Because of this lack of fit, Ann left the organization less than a year later, and the organization laid off staff members to reduce expenses.

Source: G. J. Curphy, A. Baldrica, and R. T. Hogan, *Managerial Incompetence,* unpublished manuscript, 2009.

describes a classic example of how the lack of organizational fit can cause someone to be perceived as an incompetent manager. In many ways Ann was precisely what the organization needed to turn things around. She had all the knowledge and skills necessary to succeed, but the senior staff felt their other responsibilities were more important than fund-raising. Thus Ann recognized that she was in a no-win situation and left the organization.

Organizations often realize that continuing to do things the same way will eventually result in failure, and one approach to fostering new ways of thinking is to hire people from the outside with different work experiences. New hires may have good ideas to remedy a situation, but whether they and their ideas are accepted will depend to a large extent on an organization's culture. The farther these ideas stray from the organization's prevailing values and beliefs, the more likely they are to be dismissed. Managers hired from the outside suffer the same fate as transplanted organs—those who are seen as a good fit are accepted, and those who are not are rejected. What is interesting about this phenomenon is that outsiders often possess exactly the knowledge and skills an organization needs to succeed, but because the solutions proposed are so antithetical to its culture, the ideas are attacked or discounted. The organizational fit phenomenon occurs not only when outsiders are brought in; it also happens when companies hire new CEOs or acquire other organizations. New CEOs often take steps to mold the organization's culture around their own personal values and beliefs, and some managers may no longer fit into the new culture. Likewise, managers from an acquired company can have considerable difficulty fitting into the other organization's culture. Because of this lack of fit, leaders from "old" culture or acquired companies can be perceived as incompetent even though they may have all the skills needed to build teams and get results through others. Acquiring organizations often act on these perceptions and limit the influences and resources provided to these managers, essentially setting them up for failure. As described earlier in this book, many mergers and organizational changes fail, and this is often due to cultural fit issues.[24,25]

What can leaders do to avoid being seen as organizational culture misfits? Perhaps the best thing to do is to minimize the risk of it happening at all. The first step in this process is to understand their own values, beliefs, and attitudes toward work. Some people go to work to make money, others are motivated by job security, and still others are driven to help others or make a difference. There are no right or wrong answers here, but it is important that people understand what they want out of a job. Once people clearly see what they want from work, the second step in the process is to determine the extent to which the cultures of potential employers are aligned with these beliefs. Determining an organization's culture may not be straightforward, however, because the underlying beliefs, norms, stories, and values are often unwritten. One way to determine an organization's culture is through informational interviews, in which employees are asked how things really get done, how employees treat each other, what is valued or punished, what the unwritten rules are, and so on. This information should help leaders determine the extent to which their personal values and beliefs are aligned with those of various employers. We realize there are times when people need to take jobs for the money and benefits, but they also need to realize that their level of satisfaction and ability to build teams and get results will be affected by the degree of fit between their personal values and the organization's culture. Those who do not fit run the risk of being seen as incompetent and may find that working elsewhere can help them be seen as competent managers.

More Clues for the Clueless: Lack of Situational and Self-Awareness

Most aircraft accidents are the result of pilot errors, and a lack of situational awareness is the leading cause of pilot errors.[44] **Situational awareness** refers to a pilot's ability to be cognizant of and accurately assess risks before, during, and after a flight.[45] In other words, pilots with good situational awareness know what their aircraft is doing, the weather, the positions of other aircraft in the area, the relationship of their aircraft to the ground, and the like. Like pilots, people in positions of authority must also have a high degree of situational awareness if they want to be seen as competent managers. This means competent managers must accurately read the situational and follower factors affecting their teams and remain vigilant for changes. Competent managers not only have high levels of situational awareness—they also have high levels of **self-awareness.** As described in Chapter 2, individuals who are keenly aware of their own strengths and shortcomings often find ways to either manage or staff around their personal knowledge and skill gaps. In contrast, cheerleaders, in-name-only managers, and results-only managers tend to have major situational and self-awareness blind spots (see Highlight 15.7). They either are unaware of or discount the impact of key situational or follower events and overestimate their ability to build teams and get results.

Research shows that in many cases incompetence is bliss, at least for the person demonstrating incompetence. Researchers Dunning and Kruger conducted a series of experiments that asked people to rate the funniness of 65 jokes. They then asked eight professional comedians to do the same and compared the differences between the experts' and test subjects' ratings. They found that some participants could not predict what others would find funny, yet they described themselves as excellent judges of humor. Similarly, Nilsen and Campbell reported that managers who consistently overrated their performance on 360-degree feedback instruments tended to overrate their performance on everything they did. Not only did these individuals believe they were good leaders, they also believed they were excellent drivers, mothers and fathers, athletes, dancers, judges of character, and so on, and they tended to overlook evidence that pointed to the contrary.[46,47]

There appear to be two reasons why some cheerleaders, results-only managers, and in-name-only managers lack situational and self-awareness. One reason is that some incompetent managers are self-deluding, and the most incompetent managers may be those who are the most self-deluding.[48] Another reason why some incompetent managers lack situational

Situational and Self-Awareness and Managerial Incompetence

HIGHLIGHT 15.7

Dick was the chief of police in a medium-sized midwestern town. Because of a series of easily avoidable but high-profile blunders, the local newspaper and television stations were regularly running stories about department foul-ups. The city council began pressuring Dick to clean up the department's image, and he felt the best way to rectify the situation was to send a memo to the entire department. In the past Dick had relied on his executive assistant to write all his correspondence, but she was on vacation and he felt the memo could not wait until her return. He wrote the following memo and posted it at the department's main entrance:

Date: August 20th, 2004

From: Dick Thompson, Chief of Police

Subject: Profesionalism

To: All Police Department Personal

It has come to my atention that the deparment lack profesionalism. I have seen several officers with dirty uniforms and untucked shirts and some of you need haircuts. We need to do a better job with our police reports—some have typological errors are not profesional. We need better in court too. Officers who can not meet these standards will be unpromotionable. if you have any questions see you Captain.

Less than a day later the posted memo looked like this:

Date: August 20th, 2004

From: Dick Thompson, Chief of Police

Subject: Profesionalism *[Spelling]*

To: All Police Department Personal *[Spelling]*

It has come to my atention *[Spelling]* that the deparment lack *[Spelling]* profesionalism. *[Spelling]* I have seen several officers with dirty uniforms and untucked shirts; and some of you also need haircuts. We need to do a better job with our police reports—some have typological *[typographical]* errors are not profesional. *[Spelling]* We need to be better in court too.

Officers who can not meet these standards will be unpromotionable. *[Is this a word?]* if you have any questions see you Captain.

Unfortunately for Dick, this memo was just the tip of the iceberg—he had a long history of misjudging events and making bad policy decisions, and as a result department morale was in the dumps. The city council finally came to its senses and asked the chief to leave. However, Dick was hired as the chief of police in another midwestern town, thus perpetuating incompetent management.

Source: G. J. Curphy, A. Baldrica, and R. T. Hogan, *Managerial Incompetence,* unpublished manuscript, 2009.

and self-awareness is that they fail to heed direct report feedback. Cheerleaders and other incompetent leaders may spend considerably more time paying attention to and developing relationships with those who control their fate (that is, superiors) than with team members. They are also in a position where they can and often do ignore any feedback from their staff, even when this information would help them build teams and get results through others. And by regularly shooting the messenger, results-only and in-name-only managers effectively dampen any additional feedback that would make them more effective and push self-starters over to the dark side of followership.

So what can people in positions of authority do to eliminate a lack of situational and self-awareness as an underlying cause of managerial derailment and incompetence? Given the research findings, it is imperative that people wanting to be competent managers get regular feedback on their performance, ideally in the form of 360-degree feedback. It is also imperative that people in positions of authority regularly ask team members for ideas on improving team performance and find ways to stay abreast of important situational and follower events. By building teams of self-starters, competent managers encourage team members to share ideas and solutions for improving team morale and performance, even if this means telling leaders what they personally need do differently in order to be more effective.

Lack of Intelligence, Subject Matter Expertise, and Team-Building Know-How: Real Men of Genius

People are put into positions of authority to make decisions. Each of these decisions is essentially a problem-solving exercise, and the history and success of any organization are the cumulative sum of these problem-solving exercises. Organizations that do a better job of identifying the right problems to solve and developing effective solutions to these problems are often more successful than those that solve the wrong problems or develop ineffective solutions. The famous management consultant Peter Drucker has said that most businesses get into trouble because senior managers exercise bad judgment.[49] Business leaders are supposed to direct resources toward activities that increase profitability, but they often decide to spend time and money completing projects that do not matter.

As described in Chapter 6, intelligence can be defined as the ability to think clearly. Some significant components of thinking clearly involve learning new information quickly, making good assumptions and inferences, seeing connections between seemingly unrelated issues, accurately prioritizing issues, generating potential solutions, understanding the implications of various decision options, and being quick on one's feet. Although research has shown that people in positions of authority are generally brighter than others, the intelligence of managers varies greatly.[50]

Because a manager's intelligence is directly related to his or her ability to make decisions, intelligence also affects managers' ability to build cohesive teams and get results.[51,52] Smart managers tend to do a better job of recognizing problems, prioritizing issues, assigning team member roles, developing work processes, allocating workloads, hiring staff, and resolving problems, whereas less intelligent managers do more poorly on these issues. In other words, being smart improves the odds of being a competent manager; being less intelligent improves the odds of being a cheerleader or an in-name-only manager.

But intelligence alone does not equal good judgment. A shortfall in critical knowledge also decreases a person's ability to solve problems and make decisions and increases the odds of managerial incompetence. **Subject matter expertise** can be defined as the relevant knowledge or experience a person can leverage to solve a problem. People with high expertise have a lot of relevant knowledge and experience, whereas those with low expertise are unfamiliar with the task or problem at hand. For example, a marketing executive with 10 years of experience living overseas will have a lot more knowledge of how to effectively drive sales in Europe than will someone new to marketing who has never lived in another country. People with a lot of relevant expertise know *what* is to be done, *how* to get things done, and the *interconnections* between different processes and activities. They know which levers to pull to obtain a particular outcome and understand how decisions can affect activities three or four steps later in a procedure. Managers with relevant expertise have "street smarts"; they can use their knowledge of the what, how, and interconnections to help their teams set the right goals, adopt efficient work processes, and get superior results.

All positions of authority require some level of technical expertise. For example, manufacturing managers need to understand the ins and outs of the manufacturing process, suppliers, maintenance and operations procedures, safety, process control methods, budgets, and their interconnections. People run the risk of being seen as incompetent managers any time they move into jobs that are unrelated to their technical or functional expertise (see Highlight 15.8). Like intelligence, however, technical expertise is no guarantee that a person will be a competent manager. Too many people are promoted into positions of authority because of their technical expertise but fail as managers. Often the best programmers or accountants do a great job writing programs or reconciling the books but have difficulty getting teams of people to write great software or conduct effective audits. Put another way, having relevant expertise increases the odds of being a competent manager, and lacking this expertise increases the likelihood of being perceived as a cheerleader, an in-name-only manager, or a results-only manager.

Whereas subject matter expertise pertains to the knowledge and skills associated with a particular functional area or process, such as accounting or contracting, **team-building know-how** can be defined as the degree to which a leader knows the steps and processes needed to build high-performing teams.[7,8,52] As described earlier in this textbook, most people spend their careers working in groups but lack a fundamental understanding of what it takes to build cohesive, goal-oriented teams. Chances are good that most of these teams were led by cheerleaders, in-name-only managers, or results-only managers and were more dysfunctional than effective. These experiences lead to a lack of team-building know-how, which contributes to the high base rate of managerial incompetence.

Relevant Expertise and Managerial Derailment

HIGHLIGHT 15.8

Debbie was a general manager at a management consulting firm. Debbie's job was to ensure her office met its revenue, profitability, and productivity numbers each year. Her track record against these three criteria was less than stellar, however: she had consistently missed her targets since taking over as the office leader. But she managed to convince the firm's senior leaders that the office's financial woes were primarily a function of the local economy and everyone in her office was working really hard. In reality, Debbie ran the office like a social club and was constantly buying lunch for the office staff, setting up Friday night socials, and praising office staff for their performance (even though the office was not hitting its financial goals). Eventually everyone in the office came to believe that they were special and corporate would never understand the unique challenges they faced. Debbie often bragged that she had little financial savvy and even less interest in the performance of the office and truly believed her job was to improve staff morale.

One of Debbie's multibillion-dollar clients asked for help in hiring a new executive vice president of human resources. The previous head of human resources had been let go because he had been unable to resolve some major staffing, compensation, and HRIS issues that were hurting the company's bottom line. Debbie's firm specialized in the assessment of executive talent, and she led the effort to evaluate the top three candidates for the executive vice president position. Debbie determined that all three candidates had significant shortcomings and suggested that the client consider her as a candidate. Desperate to fill the position, the client decided to hire Debbie on the spot. Had the client followed the process used to evaluate the other candidates, it would have discovered that Debbie lacked any corporate, senior executive, board of director, compensation, or HRIS experience, was likely to run human resources like a social club, and would foster a we–they mentality between her department and the rest of the company.

Although she was offered executive coaching from a former head of human resources to help her transition into her new role, Debbie felt she already knew what she needed to know and did not capitalize on this resource. Less than a month after starting she made the first of what would be a series of fatal errors. Debbie looked somewhat frumpy and disheveled at her first board of directors meeting, and her presentation painted the CEO and several business unit leaders in an unflattering light. When the board raised questions about the costs and benefits of the strategic initiatives in her presentation, she stated that the company needed to do these things and costs were irrelevant. Board members were left scratching their heads and hoped that Debbie's performance would improve at subsequent meetings. The CEO then asked Debbie to provide more detailed cost and ROI estimates for her strategic initiatives at the next senior staff meeting. When pressed for details, it became apparent that Debbie had no idea how much these initiatives would cost and whether any benefits would drop to the bottom line. Over the next few months several major HRIS problems occurred, and the new compensation system devised by Debbie caused unprecedented levels of turnover among sales staff. To counter these problems Debbie added about 20 percent more staff and quickly began overspending her budget. The CFO kept reminding Debbie about the company's financial woes, but she countered that her people were the hardest working in the company and it would be some time before all their efforts paid off. As she had before, Debbie instituted regular lunches and happy hours and started pitting her staff against the rest of the organization. This went on for another six months before she was called into the CEO's office and let go. She got a nice six-figure severance package for her efforts, but it was clear that Debbie's lack of relevant expertise was one reason why she was eventually dismissed.

Source: G. J. Curphy, A. Baldrica, and R. T. Hogan, *Managerial Incompetence,* unpublished manuscript, 2009.

Although most people readily acknowledge the importance of teamwork, most managers have no idea how to make teamwork happen.

What can leaders do to make up for a lack of intelligence, relevant subject matter expertise, or team-building know-how? Technology and staffing can make up for shortfalls in intelligence and subject matter expertise. Some companies, such as McDonald's, Target, UPS, and Best Buy, have sophisticated systems that give managers real-time information about revenues, costs, inventory turns, and the like to help them make better store staffing and stocking decisions. Generally speaking, the better the systems, the lower the intelligence needed to operate the systems. What is fascinating is that people with managerial aspirations and lower intelligence often gravitate to organizations with good systems. In other words, it is not unusual to find less intelligent but competent managers in organizations having good systems. These managers have learned how to leverage technology to make good judgments, which in turn helps them build teams and get results. Another way people with less intelligence and subject matter expertise can improve the odds of becoming competent managers is to surround themselves with smart, experienced people. People in positions of authority can leverage the intelligence and experience of their staffs to identify and prioritize problems and develop solutions that help their teams succeed. A third way to improve the odds of becoming a competent manager is through hard work. There are many ways to succeed in any particular job, and people can sometimes compensate for their lower intelligence and expertise by putting in extra effort and working longer hours. Modeling a strong work ethic can also have a contagious effect on team members, which in turn can build team cohesiveness and drive team success. Attending training programs can also help leaders build relevant expertise and understand how to build high-performing teams. Along these lines, the Rocket Model© described earlier in this textbook gives managers a practical framework for understanding the critical components of and actions needed to improve team functioning and performance.

Adherent: Noun. A follower who has not yet obtained all that he expects to get.

Ambrose Bierce, journalist

Poor Followership: Fire Me, Please

Chapter 1 introduced the concept of followership and how anyone in a position of authority has to play both leader and follower roles. Part 3 of this textbook provided a more detailed explanation of followership and introduced the Curphy Followership Model. As a reminder, this model states that followers vary on two dimensions, which are critical thinking and engagement. Self-starters are followers who seek forgiveness rather than permission, voice opinions, offer alternative solutions, go the extra mile, make things happen, and follow orders even when they disagree with them. Brown-nosers work hard but are loyal sycophants who never challenge their bosses; slackers do all they can to get out of work; and criticizers believe their purpose in life is to point out all the things their bosses and organizations are doing wrong. As

An Example of Poor Followership

HIGHLIGHT 15.9

Stanley McChrystal had been the commander of all United States and Allied forces in Afghanistan for about a year before he was fired in the summer of 2010 for making disparaging remarks about the Obama administration. McChrystal graduated from the U.S. Military Academy at West Point in 1976 and over the next 25 years rose through the ranks by doing stints in the infantry, intelligence, joint operations, air assault, training, and special forces. During this time he was also a senior fellow at the Kennedy School of Government and deployed to Saudi Arabia for Operations Shield and Desert Storm. He was promoted to Brigadier General in 2001, and in 2003 McChrystal was selected to deliver all nationally televised briefings of U.S. military operations on Iraq. In 2005 he took over the Joint Special Forces Operations Command, where he led what *Newsweek* called the most secretive force in the U.S. military. Under McChrystal's leadership the command captured Saddam Hussein and a number of other key Iraqi leaders and killed a number of Al-Qaeda leaders, including Abu Musab al-Zarqawi, the head of al-Qaeda in Iraq. But McChrystal and his staff also made some major mistakes, some of which included the commission of torture at Camp Nama in Iraq and the cover-up of the fratricide of former NFL player Pat Tillman.

Shortly after he was appointed to take over the command of all U.S. forces in Afghanistan, McChrystal's staff leaked a report that stated the war would be lost without an immediate influx of an additional 30,000-40,000 troops. The public release of the report was unprecedented: any recommendations on military strategy by military officers are supposed to be vetted by the secretary of defense and the president before going public. McChrystal's decision to leak the report was heavily criticized, and many in Congress thought the general should have been fired for insubordination. President Barack Obama acquiesced to McChrystal's request and sent an additional 30,000 troops to support an Afghanistan surge campaign. But apparently the additional soldiers were not enough to satisfy McChrystal and his staff; they spent the next year repeatedly disparaging a number of military, civilian, allied, and Afghani officials. When these unflattering comments became public in a *Rolling Stones* article, McChrystal was summoned to Washington and dismissed.

Sources: M. Hastings, "The Runaway General," *Rolling Stone* 1108–1109, July 8–22, 2010; http://wwwrollingstone.com/politics/news/17390/119236; http://www.ny-dailynews.com/news/politics/2-1-/06/22/2010-06-22_gen_s...ystal_ordered_back_to_dc_white_house_on_possible_firing_all_opt.html; http://www.nytimes.com/2010/07/24/us/24mcchrystal.html?hp.

described in Highlight 15.9, Stanley McChrystal appeared to be someone who spent much of his career as a self-starter but became a criticizer shortly after taking command in Afghanistan. Although he was able to build a loyal staff, his ability to get results was severely limited once his criticisms became public. Angering one's boss through **poor followership** is not a particularly effective career advancement strategy, and McChrystal paid the price for his subordination.

Highlight 15.9 illustrates how people in positions of authority who are criticizers often become incompetent managers. People in positions of authority who are brown-nosers and slackers are also likely to be seen as incompetent managers. With their eagerness to do whatever their superiors tell them to do and inability to make independent decisions, brown-nosers are likely to be seen as cheerleaders or in-name-only managers.

Slackers are so disconnected with the workplace that they are unlikely to build teams or get results, and they will be perceived as in-name-only managers. Thus followership not only affects how one leads; it also determines whether one is seen as a competent or incompetent manager.[53]

So what can leaders do to avoid being seen as incompetent managers due to their followership types? The first thing they need to do is to realize that everything done at work (or even outside of work) counts. Day-to-day actions, work activities, Facebook entries, tweets, blogs, and e-mail all affect their perceived followership types. It may not be enough to just build cohesive teams and get results—competent managers also need to build good relationships with peers and superiors if they want to get resources and decision-making latitude. Second, leaders need to honestly assess their follower type. If they are criticizers, brown-nosers, or slackers, they need to figure out why they are these less effective follower types and what they need to do to become self-starters. As described in Part 3, a person's immediate boss is the leading cause of dysfunctional follower types. A leader may be working for a boss who is a cheerleader, an

---

The Negative Consequences of Dark-Side Personality Traits

HIGHLIGHT 15.10

From 1999 to 2004 the U.S. Navy relieved of duty at least 80 commanding officers for various performance problems. Roughly a third of these dismissals were due to mishaps such as ship collisions or the deaths of crew members. But many of the other dismissals were due to inappropriate behavior, such as adultery, inappropriate relationships with subordinates, or alcohol abuse. The good news is that only a small percentage of the people occupying one of the 1,300 commanding officer positions in the U.S. Navy were dismissed. At first this sounds like the prevalence of dark-side traits among U.S. Navy officers (or at least the manifestation of these traits) is quite low. But remember that many of the officers exhibiting dark-side tendencies either failed to get promoted, voluntarily resigned, or were dismissed or discharged before they got a chance to assume a command position. In these cases the U.S. Navy's succession planning system worked: many of these people were weeded out before assuming a command position. It is also likely that some of the officers occupying command positions are exhibiting dark-side behaviors, but these tendencies may not be problematic enough for dismissal (but will make life unpleasant for subordinates as described in Profiles in Leadership 15.4.)

The bad news is that the prevalence of dark-side traits among people in significant positions of authority may be even higher in the business world than it is in the U.S. military. From 1978 to 2002 federal regulators initiated 585 investigations of financial misrepresentation by publicly traded companies. These investigations involved 2,310 individuals in 657 firms and resulted in $16.5 billion in fines and civil penalties to individuals and $8.4 billion in fines and damages to the companies they worked for. And these monetary damages were assessed only on the individuals and firms that got caught. The costs associated with lost productivity, poor morale, and high turnover are truly staggering if all the unchecked dark-side traits exhibited by people in positions of authority across all private and public sector organizations are factored in.

Sources: Associated Press, "Navy Assesses Troubling Performance Problems among Commanding Officers," *Minneapolis Star Tribune*, December 23, 2004, p. A3; K. Cools, "Ebbers Rex," *The Wall Street Journal*, March 22, 2005, p. B2.

in-name-only manager, or a results-only manager, in which case finding another boss may be a viable option.

Dark-Side Personality Traits: Personality as a Method of Birth Control

Dark-side personality traits are irritating, counterproductive behavioral tendencies that interfere with a leader's ability to build cohesive teams and cause followers to exert less effort toward goal accomplishment.[7,8,30,33,36,54,55,56,57] A listing of 11 common dark-side traits can be found in Table 15.3. Any of these 11 tendencies, if exhibited regularly, will decrease the leader's ability to get results through others. And if you consider some of the worst bosses you have worked for, chances are these individuals possessed some of these 11 dark-side personality traits.

TABLE 15.3   Dark-Side Personality Traits

Source: Hogan Assessment Systems, *The Hogan Development Survey* (Tulsa, OK: 2002).

Excitable	Leaders with these tendencies have difficulties building teams because of their dramatic mood swings, emotional outbursts, and inability to persist on projects.
Skeptical	Leaders with this dark-side trait have an unhealthy mistrust of others, are constantly questioning the motives and challenging the integrity of their followers, and are vigilant for signs of disloyalty.
Cautious	Because these leaders are so fearful of making "dumb" mistakes, they alienate their staffs by not making decisions or taking action on issues.
Reserved	During times of stress these leaders become extremely withdrawn and are uncommunicative, difficult to find, and unconcerned about the welfare of their staffs.
Leisurely	These passive–aggressive leaders will exert effort only in the pursuit of their own agendas and will procrastinate on or not follow through with requests that are not in line with their agendas.
Bold	Because of their narcissistic tendencies, these leaders often get quite a bit done. But their feelings of entitlement, inability to share credit for success, tendency to blame their mistakes on others, and inability to learn from experience often result in trails of bruised followers.
Mischievous	These leaders tend to be quite charming but take pleasure in seeing if they can get away with breaking commitments, rules, policies, and laws. When caught, they also believe they can talk their way out of any problem.
Colorful	Leaders with this tendency believe they are "hot" and have an unhealthy need to be the center of attention. They are so preoccupied with being noticed that they are unable to share credit, maintain focus, or get much done.
Imaginative	Followers question the judgment of leaders with this tendency because these leaders think in eccentric ways, often change their minds, and make strange or odd decisions.
Diligent	Because of their perfectionist tendencies, these leaders frustrate and disempower their staffs through micromanagement, poor prioritization, and an inability to delegate.
Dutiful	These leaders deal with stress by showing ingratiating behavior to superiors. They lack spines, are unwilling to refuse unrealistic requests, won't stand up for their staffs, and burn them out as a result.

FIGURE 15.3
Leadership Challenge Profile

Source: Adapted with permission of Hogan Assessment Systems.

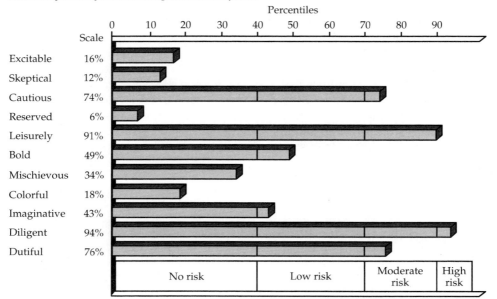

Several aspects of dark-side personality traits are worth noting. First, everyone has at least one dark-side personality trait. Figure 15.3 shows a graphic output from a typical dark-side personality measure, which shows that this individual has strong leisurely and diligent tendencies and moderate cautious and dutiful tendencies (scores above the 90th percentile indicate a high risk and within the 70–89th percentiles indicate a moderate risk of dark-side tendencies). The results in Figure 15.3 indicate that when in a crisis this leader will slow down the decision-making process, not follow though on commitments, tend to micromanage others, and not stand up for his or her followers and get them the resources they need. Second, dark-side traits usually emerge during crises or periods of high stress and are coping mechanisms for dealing with stress. People act differently when under stress, and the behaviors associated with dark-side traits help leaders deal with stress more effectively. The problem is that although these coping behaviors *positively affect leaders'* ability to deal with stress, these same behaviors *negatively affect followers'* motivation and performance. Although yelling and temper tantrums might help leaders blow off steam (excitable), such behavior makes followers feel like they are walking on eggshells and wonder if they are going to be the next target of their leader's tirades.

Third, dark-side traits have a bigger influence on performance for people in leadership versus followership roles. Individual contributors might have leisurely or cautious tendencies, but because they do not have to get work done through others these tendencies have less impact on their work units than if these same individuals were first-line supervisors or business unit leaders. These individual contributors may not be fun to work with, but their counterproductive tendencies will not be as debilitating as they would be if these people were leading teams. Fourth, dark-side traits are usually apparent only when leaders are not attending to their public image. In other words, people will not see the behaviors associated with dark-side traits when leaders are concerned with how they are coming across to others. These tendencies are much more likely to appear under times of stress, when leaders are multitasking or focusing on task accomplishment, during crises, or when leaders feel comfortable enough around others to "let their guard down."[7,8,30,33,36,57] And given the high levels of stress, challenge, and complexity associated with most leadership positions, the conditions are ripe for the appearance of dark-side traits.

Fifth, many dark-side traits covary with social skills and are difficult to detect in interviews or assessment centers or with bright-side personality inventories.[7,8,30,33,36,55,57] In other words, people who possess bold, mischievous, colorful, and imaginative dark-side traits often do well in interviews and get hired as a result. Only after these individuals have been on the job for some time do their dark-side tendencies begin to emerge. Sixth, the 11 dark-side personality traits are related to extreme FFM or OCEAN scores. For example, being diligent is often associated with extremely high conscientious scores, and being excitable is associated with extremely low neuroticism scores. However, just because a person has an extremely high or low OCEAN dimension score does not necessarily mean that he or she also possesses the corresponding dark-side personality trait. Seventh, the behaviors associated with dark-side personality traits can occur at any leadership level, and many times organizations tolerate these behaviors because a leader is smart or experienced or possesses unique skills (see Profiles in Leadership 15.1–15.5). Along these lines, people with bold tendencies are particularly adept at moving up in organizations. Nothing ever got launched without a healthy dose of narcissism, and leaders with bold tendencies are quick to volunteer for new assignments, take on seemingly impossible challenges, and consistently underestimate the amount of time, money, and effort it will take to get a job accomplished. In some cases these leaders pull off the seemingly impossible and get promoted because of their accomplishments. But when things go badly (which they often do), these same leaders are quick to blame the situation or others for their failures and as a result never learn from their mistakes.[7,8,30,33,36,57]

The final point to be made about dark-side tendencies is that they are probably the leading cause of managerial incompetence. Dark-side traits are prevalent (everybody has at least one), they are virtually impossible to detect using the most common selection techniques (interviews and résumés), and they tend to emerge during periods of stress (workloads, workplace stress, and burnout are at all-time highs these days). Competent managers are those who have gained insight into their dark-side traits and have found ways to negate their debilitating effects on followers. Results-only managers are likely to exhibit excitable, reserved, bold, and diligent tendencies, and cheerleaders usually suffer from unchecked leisurely, mischievous, colorful, and dutiful tendencies. In-name-only managers often exhibit the behaviors associated with skeptical, cautious, and imaginative dark-side traits.

Ted Haggard

PROFILES IN LEADERSHIP 15.5

Ted Haggard was the founder and former pastor at the New Life Church in Colorado Springs, Colorado. He was also the founder of the Association of Life-Giving Churches and the leader of the 30,000,000-member National Association of Evangelicals from 2003 to 2006. Known as Pastor Ted to his parishioners, Haggard grew up in Indiana; his father was a veterinarian who founded an international charismatic ministry. "Born again" in 1972, Ted Haggard received an undergraduate degree from Oral Roberts University and got married in 1978. While working in various ministries and raising his five children, Haggard had a vision to build a church in Colorado Springs. Starting in his basement in 1984, Ted Haggard recruited new members and eventually had to rent space in various strip malls to accommodate his ever-expanding flock. His membership grew so large that he eventually built the New Life Church in the northern suburbs of Colorado Springs. By late 2006 the New Life Church had 14,000 active members. Based on his success as a minister, *Time* named Ted Haggard one of the top 25 influential evangelicals in the nation. A firm supporter of G. W. Bush, Haggard was credited with rallying evangelicals around the country to vote for President Bush in the 2004 election. As depicted in the movie *Jesus Camp*, Haggard is a believer in biblical literalism and has spoken out prominently against homosexuality and same-sex marriage. In the fall of 2006 the citizens of Colorado were to vote on a state amendment that defined marriage as being between a man and a woman, and Ted Haggard was an active spokesperson for the amendment's passage. Unfortunately for Haggard, a former male prostitute named Mike Jones publicly stated that he had been having sex and doing drugs with Haggard from 2003 to 2006. Haggard initially denied these charges but stated in a later press release, "I am guilty of sexual immorality, and take responsibility for the entire problem. I am a deceiver and a liar. There is a part of my life that is so dark that I've been warring against it all of my adult life. . . . The accusations that have been leveled against me are not all true, but enough of them are true that I have been appropriately and lovingly removed from ministry."

Haggard was stripped of his ministry in November 2006 because of these alleged incidents with Mike Jones, but prior to his downfall he was clearly a competent manager—he was able to build cohesive teams, and these teams were able to consistently achieve results. He was one of the most influential religious leaders in America, and his leadership helped elect President Bush to his second term and create a 14,000-member church. His values and bright-side traits helped him to achieve greatness, but his dark-side traits eventually led to his downfall.

What bright-side personality traits do you think contributed to Haggard's success? What dark-side traits do you think led to his downfall?

Sources: http://www.washingtonpost.com/wp-dyn/content/ article/2006/11/02/AR2006.

If virtually everyone has dark-side personality tendencies, what can individuals and organizations do about them? First and foremost, leaders and leaders-to-be need to identify their dark-side personality traits. This can be done by asking trusted others about how they act under pressure or what behaviors interfere with their ability to build teams, or by completing a dark-side personality assessment. Once these counterproductive

How the Mighty Fall

HIGHLIGHT 15.11

Chapter 14 included a highlight about Jim Collins's book *Good to Great*, which describes an alternative approach to organizational change. Collins and his research team investigated the performance of 1,400 publicly traded companies and determined that the top performers shared some common attributes. Several years later Collins and his team reexamined this database to determine if there were any common themes among once highly successful companies that subsequently failed. Some of these formerly high-flying companies included Zenith, Rubbermaid, Bear Sterns, Lehmann Brothers, Circuit City, Ames Department Stores, and AIG. Collins believed companies that stumble go through the following five-stage process:

- *Stage 1—hubris born of success:* Great businesses become insulated by success, and leaders with strong business results often become arrogant, adopt an entitlement mentality, and lose sight of what made their companies successful. They often get away with poor business and staffing decisions because their companies have such strong balance sheets.

- *Stage 2—undisciplined pursuit of more:* Because of the arrogance in stage 1, top leaders focus on growth, acclaim, and whatever those in charge deem as "success" and pursue ideas that are unrelated to the core business. Organizations that cannot fill all their key positions with internal talent because of their growth initiatives are probably in stage 2 decline.

- *Stage 3—denial of risk and peril:* As the warning signs from stage 2 begin to emerge, companies place the blame for their lack of success on external factors rather than on their own risky decisions to expand. In this stage vigorous, fact-based discussions disappear, and top leaders explain away or discount negative information.

- *Stage 4—grasping for salvation:* As the warning signs translate to actual business results and companies begin to drown in red ink, they often grasp at anything that will save them. This salvation sometimes comes from outside charismatic leaders, bold but untested strategies, hoped-for blockbuster products, or game-changing acquisitions. The initial results from these activities may appear positive but are often short-lived.

- *Stage 5—capitulation to irrelevance or death:* Accumulated setbacks and the continuous erosion of financial performance causes top leaders to lose hope and sell out; and the longer companies remain in stage 4, the more likely they will be declared bankrupt or be acquired by their competitors.

Collins believes most companies go through some of these stages, but the successful ones recognize when they are in stages 1 or 2 and then take steps to avoid moving into stages 3 or 4. The farther companies slide down the five-stage process, the harder it is for them to turn things around.

Although Collins does not write about managerial incompetence or derailment in this book, what role do you think these concepts play in his five-stage process? Where do the root causes of managerial incompetence and derailment come into play in this five-stage process?

Source: J. Collins, *How the Mighty Fall* (New York: HarperCollins, 2009).

tendencies are identified, leaders need to understand the situations or conditions in which these tendencies are likely to appear. Again, dark-side traits are most likely to appear under stress and heavy workloads, so finding ways to better manage stress and workloads will help reduce the impact of these dark-side tendencies. Just being aware of our dark-side tendencies and understanding the circumstances in which they appear will go a long way toward controlling the manifestation of counterproductive leadership behaviors. Exercise and other stress reduction techniques, and having trusted followers who can tell leaders when they are exhibiting dark-side traits, can also help control these tendencies. Finally, having lower scores on the OCEAN dimension of neuroticism also helps with some of these dimensions because these leaders seem to be better able to cope with stress than those with high scores.

Summary

As stated at the beginning of this chapter, leadership is arguably the most important concept in the world today. Who is in charge determines whom you can marry, where you work, how your kids will be educated, and whether you can travel freely or express your opinions. Although many in Western societies take these freedoms (and to some extent leadership) for granted, it is important to recognize that most people in the world today do not enjoy these privileges. Most people live under some form of dictatorship and have little say in what they do, whom they interact with, or who is in charge. Although the people in charge of dictatorships may find leadership to be relatively easy, those in positions of authority in more democratically oriented countries often find leadership to be a tremendously complex task. To succeed in these roles, leaders need to build teams and get results through others, but accomplishing these two ends is challenging. There are many ways for people in positions of authority to fail, and unfortunately most people are not particularly effective leaders.

This chapter began with a discussion of bad leadership. Bad leaders are those who can build teams but achieve results that are morally or ethically reprehensible. The current heads of North Korea, Belarus, Myanmar, and Turkmenistan could be considered bad leaders in that they have built loyal teams of followers but have done little to improve the lives of the vast majority of their citizens. Bad leadership is not restricted to the world stage: many community and nonprofit leaders, first-line supervisors, mid-level managers, and executives who can build teams also get results that are misaligned with the needs of a majority of their constituents or their parent organizations. And exactly what constitutes good or bad leadership may not be straightforward—initiatives initially deemed bad might prove to be good in the long run.

Managerial incompetence describes people in positions of authority who have difficulties either in building teams or in getting results through others. There appear to be four managerial types: competent managers, cheerleaders, in-name-only managers, and results-only managers. Research shows that the majority of people in positions of authority fall into one of these latter three types and are perceived as incompetent by many of their followers.

Managerial derailment is closely related to managerial incompetence and pertains to the reasons why competent managers can become cheerleaders, in-name-only managers, or results-only managers. Some of the reasons why high-potential leaders become ineffective managers are because of their unpreparedness for promotion or inability to build teams, achieve business objectives, get along with others, or adapt to new situations. Although the managerial derailment research has been conducted on people who were once seen as high-potential candidates, it seems likely that these reasons for failure can apply to anyone in a position of authority.

The fact that most people know why leaders fail shows that simply knowing the common reasons for derailment is not enough to prevent it from happening. Something else must be occurring to cause a majority of persons in positions of authority to be seen as cheerleaders, in-name-only managers, or results-only managers. Some not-so-obvious root causes for managerial incompetence and derailment include overwhelming situational and follower factors; a lack of organizational fit; a lack situational and self-awareness; a lack of intelligence, relevant subject matter expertise, and team-building know-how; poor followership; and dark-side personality traits. Unfortunately any one of these factors can cause people in positions of authority to fail, and many times a combination of these underlying causes may be at fault. The good news is that leaders and leaders-to-be can take steps to mitigate the impact of these factors on their ability to build teams and get results.

Key Terms

bad leadership, *610*
managerial incompetence, *610*
managerial derailment, *610*
base rate of managerial incompetence, *614*
Dr. Gordy test, *615*
competent managers, *616*
results-only managers, *616*
programs for promotions initiatives, *616*
cheerleaders, *616*

in-name-only managers, *617*
moronization of management, *620*
high-potential managers, *621*
failure to meet business objectives, *621*
inability to build and lead a team, *625*
inability to build relationships, *625*
inability to adapt, *626*
inadequate preparation for promotion, *626*

episodic managerial incompetence, *632*
chronic managerial incompetence, *632*
organizational fit, *632*
situational awareness, *635*
self-awareness, *635*
subject matter expertise, *638*
team building know-how, *638*
poor followership, *641*
dark-side personality traits, *643*

Questions

1. The base rate of managerial incompetence is estimated to be 50–75 percent. This means that a majority of people in positions of authority have difficulties getting a group of people to work effectively together or get results. What do you think about this percentage of incompetent managers? For example, is it too high or low, and why?

2. Think about the ineffective leaders you have worked or played for. What dark-side traits did these leaders possess that caused them to be ineffective?

3. Do you know anyone who has derailed from a leadership position? What did the person do? Use the leader–follower–situation model and the six underlying causes of derailment to explain what happened.

4. What role would downsizing play in an organization's overall level of subject matter expertise?

5. Is Hugo Chavez, the president of Venezuela, a bad leader? What data could you use to make this evaluation? Would your evaluation of Chavez change if you lived in a slum in Caracas or owned a large business in Venezuela?

Activities

1. Count how many leaders you have worked, played, or performed for in the past. This number should include anyone for which you were in a followership role. Once you have a total, count how many of these leaders you would willingly work, play, or perform for again. Then calculate the ratio of effective managers to total managers. Who were the worst and best leaders you have worked for, and what did they do that made them effective or ineffective leaders?

2. Get into small groups and discuss whether the following people were good or bad leaders. Provide the rationale and facts to support your positions.

   - Hugo Chavez
   - Evo Morales
   - Nancy Pelosi
   - Rush Limbaugh
   - David Cameron
   - Vladimir Putin
   - Goodluck Jonathan
   - Hosni Mubarak
   - Benjamin Netanyahu
   - Wen Jiabao

3. Investigate and prepare short presentations about the underlying causes of derailment or incompetence for the following people:

   - Robert Nardelli
   - Stanley O'Neal
   - Rick Waggoner
   - Conrad Black
   - Rodney Blagojevich
   - Gordon Brown
   - Silvio Berlusconi
   - Hamid Karzai
   - Asif Ali Zardari
   - Thabo Mbeki

Minicase

You Can't Make Stuff Like This Up

Steve once worked as a regional sales director for a large health insurance company called Blue Star Health. Blue Star Health was once quite successful but had become complacent over the past five years. Competitors gained market share using aggressive marketing and sales tactics, and Blue Star was selling antiquated products and using inefficient processes for settling claims. With falling revenues and margins, Blue Star became an acquisition target and was bought by Anthum, a *Fortune* 100 company. At the conclusion of the deal Anthum brought in an injection of cash, a reputation for operational excellence, and a new vice president of sales, Jim Blaylock. The CEO of Anthum described Jim as bright, experienced, successful, and "more energetic than the Energizer Bunny." Jim had joined the corporation immediately after college; because of his "potential" the company sent him to law school and rapidly promoted him into increasingly responsible positions. Senior management had tremendous confidence in Jim's leadership abilities and appointed him as the vice president of sales in Blue Star Health, even though he had no previous sales experience.

Steve was initially impressed with Jim's freshness and energy; he was constantly touting "Midwestern values" and the "work ethic of the Midwest." However, the sales management team soon became disenchanted with his views: Steve and his sales team were working 70 to 80 hours a week and becoming exhausted and frazzled. Moreover, Jim's interactions with internal and external clients were lessons in poor human relations. He seemed to seek confrontations, and as time passed, his behavior became steadily more extreme. Jim harangued people, ignored appointments and made no excuses for missing them, made promises he never kept, called sales directors at 6:00 a.m. with insignificant questions, and abused brokers. Those who questioned Jim's leadership were summarily dismissed.

One day Jim asked Steve to arrange a meeting with a broker at 9:00 p.m. The broker was from a large benefit house and was older, and the meeting time was late. However, he was a longtime personal friend of Steve's and as a courtesy agreed to the meeting. Jim did not show up for the appointment and would not answer Steve's calls to his cell phone. After an hour, Steve and the broker went home. When Steve asked Jim why he missed the appointment, he said he was drinking with a friend and did not think the meeting with the broker was important. Jim refused to apologize to the broker and was surprised when business with the broker's organization came to an end.

Jim loved working on high-visibility projects and landed an opportunity to convert the membership of another acquired company to Anthum. This was an important project for Anthum, and shortly thereafter

Jim set up an elaborate "war room" in which all sales planning and action would take place. He asked Steve to lead the conversion project, repeatedly announcing that the acquisition was to garner new contracts and to bring quality employees into the organization. At this point Steve had over 70 direct reports in five different locations across the state and some aggressive sales targets. It would be impossible for Steve to hit his revenue numbers and run the conversion project. But Jim cut Steve no slack, and the computer system intended to convert the contracts did not work. Jim spent no time with any of the newly acquired sales team members, and as a result they showed no interest in working for Anthum. Yet Jim made grandiose statements about the quality of the sales force at the acquired company, which implied the current sales employees were unsatisfactory and fostered a sense of mistrust in both sales organizations.

Because of Jim's shoddy treatment, the long hours, and poor sales and invoicing processes, the morale of the sales team began to plummet. Tantrums and tears occurred frequently, and Steve spent a lot of time smoothing feathers and telling team members that things would get better over time. But there was only so much Steve could do, and as team members began to quit, Jim blamed Steve for the decline in department morale. As the situation continued to deteriorate, Steve requested that Jim meet with the remaining staff to talk about their frustrations with Anthum. Jim opted to set up an all-employee breakfast at a local restaurant to address their concerns.

The night before the meeting a major snowstorm hit the city, and the streets were covered with a foot of snow. Some employees had to drive 40 miles to attend the meeting, but everyone made it to the restaurant. The only person missing was Jim, and Steve started calling him 10 minutes before the meeting start time to check on his status. Jim did not answer, so Steve began to call and leave messages every five minutes. Jim finally answered his phone 30 minutes after the meeting start time and told Steve that the reason he was not at the meeting was that he decided to go skiing and people would have to meet with him another day. He also asked Steve to quit bugging him by leaving messages every five minutes. Steve could do little to put a positive spin on this message, and the employees left the restaurant bitter and hurt. Of the 60 people who showed up for the meeting, only one was still with Anthum six months later. Jim never acknowledged his behavior and was "shocked" at the turnover in the sales group. Despite the turnover and declining sales revenues, Jim was still considered the company's darling, and it was commonly believed that the CEO tacitly condoned his behavior.

1. Was Jim Blaylock a bad leader, a competent manager, an in-name-only manager, a results-only manager, or a cheerleader? What data would you use to make this determination?

2. If Jim was an incompetent manager, what do you think were the underlying root causes of his incompetence?

3. Why do you think Jim was seen as a high-potential candidate? Why did the CEO still think he was a high performer?

4. What would you do if you were Jim's boss and heard about the information described here?

5. What would you do if you were Steve?

Source: G. J. Curphy, A. Baldrica, and R. T. Hogan, *Managerial Incompetence,* unpublished manuscript, 2009.

End Notes

1. J. M. Burns, *Leadership* (New York: Harper & Row, 1978).

2. S. Einarsen, M. Schanke Aasland, and A. Skogstad, "Destructive Leadership Behavior: A Definition and Conceptual Model," *The Leadership Quarterly* 18 (2007), pp. 207–16.

3. A. Padilla, R. T. Hogan, and R. B. Kaiser, "The Toxic Triangle: Destructive Leaders, Susceptible Followers, and Conducive Environments," *The Leadership Quarterly* 18 (2007), pp. 176–94.

4. J. Schaubroeck, F. O. Walumbwa, D. C. Ganster, and S. Kepes, "Destructive Leadership Traits and the Neutralizing Influence of an 'Enriched' Job," *The Leadership Quarterly* 18 (2007), pp. 235–51.

5. B. Kellerman, *Bad Leadership: What It Is, How It Happens, Why It Matters (Leadership for the Common Good)* (Boston, MA: Harvard Business School Press, 2004).

6. J. Diamond, *Guns, Germs, and Steel: The Fates of Human Societies* (New York: W.W. Norton, 1999).

7. G. J. Curphy, A. Baldrica, and R. T. Hogan, *Managerial Incompetence,* unpublished manuscript, 2009.

8. R. T. Hogan, *Personality and the Fate of Organizations* (Mahwah, NJ: Lawrence Erlbaum, 2007).

9. http://www.pollingreport.com/Congjpb/htm.

10. http://www.rasmussenreports.com/public_content/politics/mood_of_america/congressional_performance.

11. http://wwwpolitisite.com/2010/07/22/congress-approval-rating-at-lowest-since-the-70s-at-11/.

12. D. A. Nadler, "The CEO's Second Act," *Harvard Business Review,* January 2007, pp. 66–75.

13. C. Lucier, P. Kocourek, and R. Habbel, "CEO Succession 2005: The Crest of the Wave," *Strategy + Business* 43 (2006), pp. 40–50.

14. L. Bossidy and R. Charan, *Execution: The Discipline of Getting Things Done* (New York: Crown Business, 2002).

15. D. Jones, "Leadership Crisis Blamed for Some of the Nation's Problems," *USA Today,* November 5, 2008, p. 6B.

16. G. L. Neilson, B. A. Pasternack, and K. E. Van Nuys, " The Passive-Aggressive Organization," *Harvard Business Review,* October 2005, pp. 82–95.

17. K. E. Klein, "What's Behind High Small-Biz Failure Rates," *Frontier Advice and Columns*, September 30, 1999, http://www.businessweek.com/smallbiz/news/ coladvice/ask/sa990930.htm.

18. C. Denbow, "Small Business Failure," http://www.elib.org/articles/292/small-business.

19. C. Tushabomwe-Kazooba, "Causes of Small Business Failure in Uganda: A Case Study from Bushenyi and Mbarara," *African Studies Quarterly* 8, no. 4 (2006), pp. 1–12.

20. S. Ward, "Part 4: Avoiding Business Failure," *Small Business: Canada,* 1997. http://sbinfrocanada.about.com/cs/startup/a/startownbiz.

21. http://www.thescienceofpersonality.com/2010/08/bps-deepwater-sunset-disaster-waiting.html.

22. C. Johnson, *Visualizing the Relationship between Human Error and Organizational Failure*, 1998, http://www.dcs.gla.ac.uk/~johnson/papers/fault_trees/organizational_error.

23. The Standish Group, *Latest Standish Group CHAOS Report Shows Project Success Rates Have Improved 50%,* March 25, 2003, www.standishgroup.com/press/article.

24. J. A. Warden and L. A. Russell, *Winning in Fast Time* (Montgomery, AL: Venturist Publishing, 2002).

25. J. P. Kotter, *Leading Change* (Boston: Harvard Business School Press, 1996).

26. M. A. Huselid, R. W. Beatty, and B. E. Becker, "'A Players' or 'A Positions'? The Strategic Logic of Workforce Management," *Harvard Business Review*, December 2005, pp. 110–21.

27. J. W. Boudreau and P. M. Ramstad, "Talentship and the New Paradigm for Human Resource Management: From Professional Practices to Strategic Talent Decision Science," *Human Resource Planning* 28, no. 2 (2005), pp. 17–26.

28. J. Dowdy, S. Dorgan, T. Rippen, J. Van Reenen, and N. Bloom, *Management Matters* (London: McKinsey & Company, 2005).

29. M. W. McCall Jr. and M. M. Lombardo, "Off the Track: Why and How Successful Executives Get Derailed," Technical Report No. 21 (Greensboro, NC: Center for Creative Leadership, 1983).

30. D. L. Dotlich and P. E. Cairo, *Why CEOs Fail: The 11 Behaviors That Can Derail Your Climb to the Top and How to Manage Them* (New York: Wiley, 2001).

31. J. F. Hazucha, *PDI Indicator: Competence, Potential, and Jeopardy. What Gets Managers Ahead May Not Keep Them out of Trouble* (Minneapolis, MN: Personnel Decisions, September 1992).

32. M. M. Lombardo, M. N. Ruderman, and C. D. McCauley, "Explorations of Success and Derailment in Upper-Level Management Positions," paper presented at meeting of the Academy of Management, New York, 1987.

33. J. C. Hogan, R. T. Hogan, and R. B. Kaiser, "Managerial Derailment," in *APA Handbook of Industrial and Organizational Psychology*, Vol. 3, ed. S. Zedeck (Washington, DC: American Psychological Association, 2011), pp. 555–76.

34. E. Van Velsor and J. B. Leslie, "Why Executives Derail: Perspectives across Time and Cultures," *Academy of Management Executive* 9, no. 4 (1995), pp. 62–71.

35. H. J. Foldes and D. S. Ones, "Wrongdoing among Senior Managers: Critical Incidents and their Co-Occurrence," in *Predicting Leadership: The Good, The Bad, the Indifferent, and the Unnecessary,* J. P. Campbell and M. J. Benson (chairs). Symposium conducted at the 22nd Annual Conference for the Society of Industrial and Organizational Psychology, New York, April 2007.

36. M. J. Benson and J. P. Campbell, "Derailing and Dark Side Personality: Incremental Prediction of Leadership (In)Effectiveness," in *Predicting Leadership: The Good, The Bad, the Indifferent, and the Unnecessary,* J. P. Campbell and M. J. Benson (chairs). Symposium conducted at the 22nd Annual Conference for the Society of Industrial and Organizational Psychology, New York, April 2007.

37. V. J. Bentz, "Research Findings from Personality Assessment of Executives," in *Personality Assessment in Organizations,* ed. J. H. Bernadin and D. A. Bownas (New York: Praeger, 1985), pp. 82–144.

38. A. M. Morrison, R. P. White, and E. Van Velsor, *Breaking the Glass Ceiling* (Reading, MA: Addison-Wesley, 1987).

39. R. Rasch, W. Shen, S. E. Davies, and J. Bono, *The Development of a Taxonomy of Ineffective Leadership Behaviors,* paper presented at the 23rd Annual Conference of the Society for Industrial and Organizational Psychology, San Francisco, CA, 2008.

40. R. Charan, S. Drotter, and J. Noel, *The Leadership Pipeline: How to Build the Leadership-Powered Company* (San Francisco: Jossey-Bass, 2001).

41. R. Charan and G. Colvin, "Why CEOs Fail," *Fortune,* June 21, 1999, pp. 69–82.

42. G. J. Curphy, *The Role of a Supervisor* (North Oaks, MN: Curphy Consulting Corporation, 2004).

43. J. Hogan and R. T. Hogan, *Motives, Values and Preferences Inventory Manual* (Tulsa, OK: Hogan Assessment Systems, 1996).

44. http://www.dynamicflight.com/avcfibook/glossary/.

45. P. A. Craig, *Controlling Pilot Error: Situational Awareness* (New York: McGraw-Hill, 2001).

46. J. Kruger and D. Dunning, "Unskilled and Unaware of It: How Difficulties in Recognizing One's Own Incompetence Lead to Inflated Self-Assessments," *Journal of Personality and Social Psychology* 77, no. 6 (1999), pp. 1121–34.

47. D. L. Nilsen, *Using Self and Observers' Ratings of Personality to Predict Leadership Performance,* unpublished doctoral dissertation, University of Minnesota, 1995.

48. http://blogs.hbr.org/cs/2010/06/some_bosses_live_in_a_fools_pa.html?cm_mmc=npv.

49. P. F. Drucker, "The Theory of the Business," *Harvard Business Review,* September–October 1994.

50. R. T. Hogan and J. Hogan, *The Hogan Business Reasoning Inventory* (Tulsa, OK: Hogan Assessment Systems, 2007).

51. R. T. Hogan, *Intelligence and Good Judgment* (Tulsa, OK: Hogan Assessment Systems, 2008).

52. G. J. Curphy and R. T. Hogan, *A Guide to Building High Performing Teams* (North Oaks, MN: Curphy Consulting Corporation, 2010).

53. G. J. Curphy and R. M. Roellig, *Followership* (North Oaks, MN: Curphy Consulting Corporation, 2010).

54. M. J. Benson and J. P. Campbell "To Be, or Not to Be, Linear: An Expanded Representation of Personality and Its Relationship to Leadership Performance," *International Journal of Selection and Assessment* 15 (2007), pp. 232–49.

55. G. J. Curphy and R. T. Hogan, *Managerial Incompetence: Is There a Dead Skunk on the Table?* working paper, 2004.

56. G. J. Curphy and R. T. Hogan, *What We Really Know about Leadership (but Seem Unwilling to Implement)*, working paper, 2004.

57. R. T. Hogan and J. C. Hogan, "Assessing Leadership from the Dark Side," *International Journal of Selection and Assessment* 9, no. 1–2 (2001), pp. 40–51.

16

Skills for Optimizing Leadership as Situations Change

In this final chapter we offer some ideas about skills appropriate to the last element of the interactional framework. These skills include relatively advanced leadership skills useful in various specific situational challenges:

- Creating a compelling vision.
- Managing conflict.
- Negotiation.
- Diagnosing performance problems in individuals, groups, and organizations.
- Team building at the top.
- Punishment.

Creating a Compelling Vision

Suppose you are running the computer department at an electronics store. Overall the store has been having a good year: sales of cell phones, HDTVs and in-home theater equipment, and digital cameras have all been strong. But computer sales are lagging, and the store manager is exerting considerable pressure on you to increase sales. Your 11 sales associates are all relatively new to sales, and many do not have strong computer backgrounds. Your assistant department manager recently moved to the in-home theater department, and you have been screening candidates for this opening on your team. After failing to be impressed with the first four candidates interviewed, you notice that the next candidate, Colleen, has just moved to town and has a strong background in electronics sales. During the interview you become even more convinced that Colleen would be an ideal assistant department manager. Toward the end of the interview you ask Colleen if she has any questions about the position, and she states that she is considering several job offers and is asking all her prospective employers the same question, which is "Why should I work for you?"

What would you say if someone asked you this question? Would you be able to close the sale and make a strong case for getting someone to join your team? Believe it or not, many leaders cannot provide a compelling description of how they add value; as a result they have difficulty getting anyone excited to become part of their groups. And these struggles are not limited to new leaders—many seasoned leaders either do not have or cannot effectively articulate a clear and dynamic leadership vision. Yet many followers want to know where their team or group is going, how it intends to get there, and what they need to do to win. A leader's vision can answer these questions, explain why change is necessary, and keep team members motivated and focused. Because a leader's vision can have a pervasive effect on followers and teams, it is worth describing a process for building a compelling leadership vision.[1,2]

Before discussing the four components of leadership vision, it is worth noting that most people don't get particularly excited about a leader's vision by sitting though lengthy PowerPoint presentations or formal speeches. People tend to get more involved when leaders use stories, analogies, and personal experiences to paint compelling pictures of the future. As such, a leader's vision should be a personal statement that should help listeners answer the following questions:

- Where is the team going, and how will it get there?
- How does the team win, and how does it contribute to the broader organization's success?
- How does the speaker define leadership?
- What gets the speaker excited about being a leader?
- What are the speaker's key values? In other words, what are the leader's expectations for team members, and what will she or he not tolerate as a leader?

If you are currently in a leadership position, ask yourself how your direct reports would answer these questions. Would their answers to all five questions be the same, or would their answers differ? Alternatively, how would you answer these questions for your boss? If followers do not provide the same answers for these questions, leaders may need to create or better articulate their leadership vision. As shown in Figure 16.1, a leadership vision consists of four related components.

Ideas: The Future Picture

The idea component of a leader's vision begins with an honest assessment of the current situation facing the team.[3] Leaders need to clearly identify

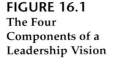

FIGURE 16.1
The Four Components of a Leadership Vision

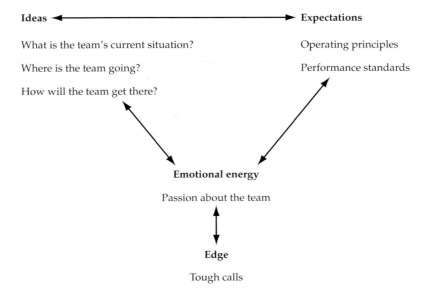

Ideas ⟷ Expectations

What is the team's current situation?

Where is the team going?

How will the team get there?

Operating principles

Performance standards

Emotional energy

Passion about the team

Edge

Tough calls

Stories, analogies, and metaphors

what the team is doing well, what it is not doing well, how it is performing compared to the competition, and what challenges it faces. Leaders should not pull any punches when assessing team performance because downplaying or overlooking team shortcomings will likely result in mediocrity. Once a leader has accurately assessed a team's strengths, weaknesses, and potential, he or she needs to clearly define where the team needs to be over the next 12–36 months. This future picture needs to describe the team's upcoming goals; the reputation it needs to have within the organization, among competitors, and with customers; and what strategies the team will pursue to achieve these outcomes. Ideas should also describe what changes the team must make to accomplish its major goals, explain why these changes are necessary, and give listeners hope for the future.[4]

Although leaders can complete the ideas component by themselves, they will often get considerably more commitment by working with their teams to assess the situation, set future team goals, and identify the changes needed for success. Whether the idea component is a solo or team effort, leaders will have successfully articulated their future pictures when everyone on their teams shares the same understanding of the situation and what they need to do to win.

Expectations: Values and Performance Standards

A leader's vision also needs to clearly describe her or his expectations for team member behavior. More specifically, what behaviors do leaders want team members to exhibit, and just as importantly, what behaviors will they not tolerate from team members? A leader's expectations for team members are highly related to his or her values. For example, if a leader believes winning is an important value, then he or she needs to say something about the levels of performance and commitment needed by team members. Or if leaders believe collaboration is an important value, they need to define how team members are supposed to work together. Because values and operating principles play such an important role in defining team member expectations, leaders should spend time identifying the team's core values and the positive and negative behaviors associated with these values. To improve understanding and buy-in, leaders can work with team members to jointly define a team's core values.

One important leadership role is to ensure that a team's core values are aligned with its future picture. For example, if the team has some aggressive performance goals, then its core values should include something about the performance and commitment expectations for individual team members. Team goals represent *what* a team must do to succeed; core values and operating principles represent *how* team members should behave if the team is to win. In addition, leaders should strive to implement a fairly limited (five to eight) set of core values. Team members often have difficulty recalling more than a half dozen core values, so the operating principles should be limited to only those values that are most directly related to team goals.

Leaders not only need to be a role model for these core values—they also need to hold team members accountable for behaving in accordance with these operating principles. Nothing will erode a leader's credibility or team morale more quickly then leaders or team members not being held accountable for exhibiting behaviors that are misaligned with a team's operating principles. Leaders will have successfully conveyed their operating principles when everyone on the team understands and is behaving in accordance with the team's core values.

Emotional Energy: The Power and the Passion

The last two components of leadership vision, emotional energy and edge, are concerned more with delivery than content. Emotional energy is the level of enthusiasm leaders use to convey the future vision and the team's operating principles. Nothing kills follower enthusiasm and motivation for a leader's vision more quickly than a dull, monotone delivery. If leaders are not excited about where the team is going and how it will get there, it will be difficult to get others to join the effort. However, leaders who are excited about where their teams are going still need to make sure this enthusiasm is clear in the delivery of their vision. Emotional appeals make for compelling messages, and leaders should use a range of emotions when describing the future picture and operating principles. Leaders will have effectively mastered the emotional energy component when team members see that they are excited about where the team is going and being in a leadership role.

Edge: Stories, Analogies, and Metaphors

Perhaps the most difficult component to master when it comes to creating a leadership vision is edge. Edge pertains to lessons of leadership learned through personal experience that are related to the team's future picture and core values. Edge includes personal stories and examples that can help color a team's future picture. For example, edge might include stories about teams leaders have been on or have led in the past through similar situations. Edge would also include stories that illustrate why some of the team's core values are so important—examples of how team members did or did not act in accordance with a particular value and what happened as a result. Edge can also include slogans, analogies, and metaphors to help clarify and simplify where the team is going or what it stands for. In general, the more personal the examples and the simpler the stories, the more likely leaders will leave an impression on team members.

Leaders should not spend too much time worrying about edge until the team's future picture and core values are clearly defined. However, once these issues are clearly understood, leaders need to reflect on how their personal experiences can help team members understand where the team is going and why certain behaviors are important. They should also spend time brainstorming analogies, metaphors, and slogans that can distill team goals and behaviors into simple but memorable messages. As was described for the future picture and core values, these analogies and slogans do not have to be solo efforts; leaders can solicit team members' help in creating slogans that convey simple but compelling messages about the future direction for their teams.

Although ideas, expectations, emotional energy, and edge make up the four components of a leader's vision, several other leadership vision issues are worth noting. First, the delivery of a leader's vision improves with practice. The four components can help leaders define what they need to say and how they need to say it, but leaders should practice the delivery of their vision a number of times before going live with team members. Ideally they should use video recordings of some of these practice deliveries to ensure that key messages are being conveyed, the personal stories being used make sense and are easy to follow, and excitement and emotion are evident. Second, leaders need to remember that the most compelling leadership visions are relatively short and make sparing use of PowerPoint slides. Many of the best leadership visions are less than 10 minutes long and consist of no more than three to four slides. Third, leaders need to constantly tie team events back to their vision and core values. Reminding team members how delegated tasks relate to the team's vision, tying team member feedback to core values, and explaining how staff and strategy changes relate to team goals and operating principles are all effective ways to keep team members focused and motivated toward a leader's vision. And fourth, having a clear and compelling leadership vision should go a long way in answering the question posed at the beginning of this section, which was "Why should I work for you?"

Managing Conflict

We read or hear in the daily news about various types of negotiations. Nations often negotiate with each other over land or fishing rights, trade agreements, or diplomatic relations. Land developers often negotiate with city councils for variances of local zoning laws for their projects. Businesses often spend considerable time negotiating employee salaries and fringe benefits with labor unions. In a similar fashion, negotiations every day cover matters ranging from high school athletic schedules to where a new office copying machine will be located. In one sense, all these negotiations, big or small, are similar. In every case, representatives from different groups meet to resolve some sort of conflict. Conflict is an inevitable fact of life and an inevitable fact of leadership. Researchers have found that first-line supervisors and midlevel managers can spend more than 25 percent of their time dealing with conflict,[5] and resolving conflict has been found to be an important factor in leadership effectiveness.[6] In fact, successfully resolving conflicts is so important that it is a central theme in some of the literature about organizations.[7-9] Moreover, successfully resolving conflicts will become an increasingly important skill as leadership and management practice moves away from authoritarian directives and toward cooperative approaches emphasizing rational persuasion, collaboration, compromise, and solutions of mutual gain.

What Is Conflict?

Conflict occurs when opposing parties have interests or goals that appear to be incompatible.[10] There are a variety of sources of conflict in team, committee, work group, and organizational settings. For example, conflict can occur when group or team members (1) have strong differences in values, beliefs, or goals; (2) have high levels of task or lateral interdependence; (3) are competing for scarce resources or rewards; (4) are under high levels of stress; or (5) face uncertain or incompatible demands—that is, role ambiguity and role conflict.[11] Conflict can also occur when leaders act in a manner inconsistent with the vision and goals they have articulated for the organization.[12] Of these factors contributing to the level of conflict within or between groups, teams, or committees, probably the most important source of conflict is the lack of communication between parties.[13] Because many conflicts are the result of misunderstandings and communication breakdowns, leaders can minimize the level of conflict within and between groups by improving their communication and listening skills, as well as spending time networking with others.[14]

Before we review specific negotiation tips and conflict resolution strategies, it is necessary to describe several aspects of conflict that can have an impact on the resolution process. First, the size of an issue (bigger issues are more difficult to resolve), the extent to which parties define the problem egocentrically (how much they have personally invested in the problem), and the existence of hidden agendas (unstated but important concerns or objectives) can all affect the conflict resolution process. Second, seeing a conflict situation in win–lose or either–or terms restricts the perceived possible outcomes to either total satisfaction or total frustration. A similar but less extreme variant is to see a situation in zero-sum terms. A zero-sum situation is one in which intermediate degrees of satisfaction are possible, but increases in one party's satisfaction inherently decrease the other party's satisfaction, and vice versa. Still another variant can occur when parties perceive a conflict as unresolvable. In such cases neither party gains at the expense of the other, but each continues to perceive the other as an obstacle to satisfaction.[15]

Is Conflict Always Bad?

So far we have described conflict as an inherently negative aspect of any group, team, committee, or organization. This certainly was the prevailing view of conflict among researchers during the 1930s and 1940s, and it probably also represents the way many people are raised today (that is, most people have a strong value of minimizing or avoiding conflict). However, researchers studying group effectiveness today have come to a different conclusion. Some level of conflict may help bolster innovation and performance. Conflict that enhances group productivity is viewed as useful, and conflict that hinders group performance is viewed as counterproductive.[16] Various possible positive and negative effects of conflict are listed in Highlight 16.1.

Along these lines, researchers have found that conflict can cause a radical change in political power,[17,18] as well as dramatic changes in organizational structure and design, group cohesiveness, and group or organizational effectiveness.[19,20] Nevertheless, it is important to realize that this current conceptualization of conflict is still somewhat limited in scope. For example, increasing the level of conflict within a group or team may enhance immediate performance but may also have a disastrous effect on organizational climate and turnover. Leaders may be evaluated in terms of many criteria, however, only one of which is group performance. Thus leaders should probably use criteria such as turnover and absenteeism rates and followers' satisfaction or organizational climate ratings in addition to measures of group performance when trying to determine whether conflict is good or bad. Leaders are cautioned against using group performance alone because this may not reveal the overall effects of conflict on the group or team.

Possible Effects of Conflict

HIGHLIGHT 16.1

Possible Positive Effects of Conflict	Possible Negative Effects of Conflict
Increased effort.	Reduced productivity.
Feelings get aired.	Decreased communication.
Better understanding of others.	Negative feelings.
Impetus for change.	Stress.
Better decision making.	Poorer decision making.
Key issues surface.	Decreased cooperation.
Critical thinking stimulated.	Political backstabbing.

Conflict Resolution Strategies

In addition to spending time understanding and clarifying positions, separating people from the problem, and focusing on interests, leaders can use five strategies or approaches to resolve conflicts. Perhaps the best way to differentiate between these five strategies is to think of conflict resolution in terms of two independent dimensions: cooperativeness versus uncooperativeness and assertiveness versus unassertiveness (see Figure 16.2). Parties in conflict vary in their commitment to satisfy the other's concerns, but they also vary in the extent to which they assertively stand up for their own concerns.[21] Thus conflict resolution can be understood in terms of how cooperative or uncooperative the parties are and how assertive or unassertive they are.

Using this two-dimension scheme, Thomas[22] described five general approaches to managing conflict:

1. *Competition* reflects a desire to achieve one's own ends at the expense of someone else. This is domination, also known as a win–lose orientation.
2. *Accommodation* reflects a mirror image of competition—entirely giving in to someone else's concerns without making any effort to achieve one's own ends. This is a tactic of appeasement.
3. *Sharing* is an approach that represents a compromise between domination and appeasement. Both parties give up something, yet both parties get something. Both parties are moderately, but incompletely, satisfied.
4. *Collaboration* reflects an effort to fully satisfy both parties. This is a problem-solving approach that requires the integration of each party's concerns.
5. *Avoidance* involves indifference to the concerns of both parties. It reflects a withdrawal from or neglect of any party's interests.

FIGURE 16.2
Five Conflict-Handling Orientations, Plotted According to the Parties' Desire to Satisfy Own and Other's Concerns

Source: K. W. Thomas, "Conflict and Conflict Management," in *Handbook of Industrial and Organizational Psychology,* ed. M. D. Dunnette (Chicago: Rand McNally, 1976). Reprinted with permission of Marvin D. Dunnette.

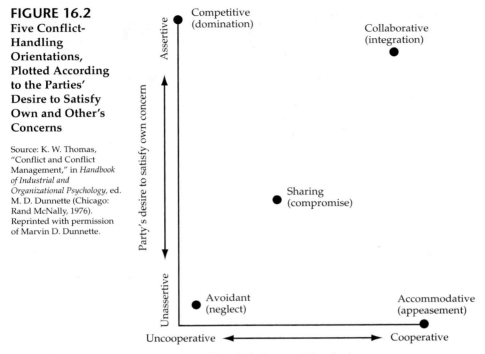

Does one of these approaches seem clearly better than the others to you? Each of them does, at least, reflect certain culturally valued modes of behavior.[23] For example, the esteem many people hold for athletic, business, and military heroes reflects our cultural valuation of competition. Valuation of a pragmatic approach to settling problems is reflected in the compromising approach. Cultural values of unselfishness, kindness, and generosity are reflected in accommodation, and even avoidance has roots in philosophies that emphasize caution, diplomacy, and turning away from worldly concerns. These cultural roots to each of the approaches to managing conflict suggest that no single one is likely to be right all the time. There probably are circumstances when each of the modes of conflict resolution can be appropriate. Rather than seeking a single best approach to managing conflict, it may be wisest to appreciate the relative advantages and disadvantages of all the approaches, as well as the circumstances when each may be most appropriate. A summary of experienced leaders' recommendations for when to use each strategy is presented in Highlight 16.2.

Finally, winning a negotiation at your counterpart's expense is likely to be only a short-term gain. Leaders should attempt to work out a resolution

Situations in Which to Use the Five Approaches to Conflict Management

HIGHLIGHT 16.2

COMPETING

1. When quick, decisive action is vital—such as emergencies.
2. On important issues where unpopular actions need implementing—cost cutting, enforcing unpopular rules, discipline.
3. On issues vital to company welfare when you know you're right.
4. Against people who take advantage of noncompetitive behavior.

COLLABORATING

1. To find an integrative solution when both sets of concerns are too important to be compromised.
2. When your objective is to learn.
3. To merge insights from people with different perspectives.
4. To gain commitment by incorporating concerns into a consensus.
5. To work through feelings that have interfered with a relationship.

COMPROMISING

1. When goals are important, but not worth the effort or potential disruption of more assertive modes.
2. When opponents with equal power are committed to mutually exclusive goals.
3. To achieve temporary settlements of complex issues.
4. To arrive at expedient solutions under time pressure.
5. As a backup when collaboration or competition is unsuccessful.

AVOIDING

1. When an issue is trivial or more important issues are pressing.
2. When you perceive no chance of satisfying your concerns.
3. When potential disruption outweighs the benefits of resolution.
4. To let people cool down and regain perspective.
5. When gathering information supersedes immediate decisions.
6. When others can resolve the conflict more effectively.
7. When issues seem tangential to or symptomatic of other issues.

ACCOMMODATING

1. When you find you are wrong—to allow a better position to be heard, to learn, and to show your reasonableness.
2. When issues are more important to others than yourself—to satisfy others and maintain cooperation.
3. To build social credits for later issues.
4. To minimize loss when you are outmatched and losing.
5. When harmony and stability are especially important.
6. To allow subordinates to develop by learning from mistakes.

Source: K. W. Thomas, "Toward Multidimensional Values in Teaching: The Example of Conflict Management," *Academy of Management Review* 2, no. 3 (1977), pp. 484–90. Copyright © 1977 Academy of Management, via Copyright Clearance Center.

How to Swim with Sharks

HIGHLIGHT 16.3

It is dangerous to swim with sharks, but not all sharks are found in the water. Some people may behave like sharks, and a best-selling book for executives written a few years ago took its title from that theme. However, an article appeared in the journal *Perspectives in Biology and Medicine* over three decades ago claiming to be a translated version of an essay written in France more than a century earlier for sponge divers. The essay notes that while no one wants to swim with sharks, it is an occupational hazard for certain people. For those who must swim with sharks, it can be essential to follow certain rules. See if you think the following rules for interacting with the sharks of the sea serve as useful analogies for interacting with the sharks of everyday life:

Rule 1: Assume any unidentified fish is a shark. Just because a fish may be acting in a docile manner does not mean it is not a shark. The real test is how it will act when blood is in the water.

Rule 2: Don't bleed. Bleeding will prompt even more aggressive behavior and the involvement of even more sharks. Of course, it is not easy to keep from bleeding when injured. Those who cannot do so are advised not to swim with sharks at all.

Rule 3: Confront aggression quickly. Sharks usually give warning before attacking a swimmer. Swimmers should watch for indications an attack is imminent and take prompt counterac-

tion. A blow to the nose is often appropriate because it shows you understand the shark's intentions and will respond in kind. It is particularly dangerous to behave in an ingratiating manner toward sharks. People who once held this erroneous view often can be identified by a missing limb.

Rule 4: Get out of the water if anyone starts bleeding. Previously docile sharks may begin attacking if blood is in the water. Their behavior can become so irrational, even including attacking themselves, that it is safest to remove yourself entirely from the situation.

Rule 5: Create dissension among the attackers. Sharks are self-centered and rarely act in an organized fashion with other sharks. This significantly reduces the risk of swimming with sharks. Every now and then, however, sharks may launch a coordinated attack. The best strategy then is to create internal dissension among them because they already are quite prone to it; often sharks will fight among themselves over trivial or minor things. By the time their internal conflict is settled, sharks often have forgotten about their organized attack.

Rule 6: Never divert a shark attack toward another swimmer. Please observe this final item of swimming etiquette.

Source: V. Cousteau, "How to Swim with Sharks: A Primer," *Perspectives in Biology and Medicine,* Summer 1973, pp. 525–28.

by looking at long-term rather than short-term goals, and they should try to build a working relationship that will endure and be mutually trusting and beneficial beyond the present negotiation. Along these lines, leaders should always seek win–win outcomes that try to satisfy both sides' needs and continuing interests. It often takes creative problem solving to find new options that provide gains for both sides. Realistically, however, not all situations may be conducive to seeking win–win outcomes (see Highlight 16.3).

Negotiation

Negotiation is an approach that may help resolve some conflicts. The following negotiating tips, from Fisher and Ury,[24] include taking the time to prepare for a negotiating session; keeping the people and problems separate; and focusing on interests rather than on positions.

Prepare for the Negotiation

To successfully resolve conflicts, leaders may need to spend considerable time preparing for a negotiating session. Leaders should anticipate each side's key concerns and issues, attitudes, possible negotiating strategies, and goals.

Separate the People from the Problem

Fisher and Ury also advised negotiators to separate the people from the problem.[25] Because all negotiations involve substantive issues and relationships between negotiators, it is easy for these parts to become entangled. When that happens, parties may inadvertently treat the people and the problem as though they were the same. For example, a group of teachers angry that their salaries have not been raised for the fourth year in a row may direct their personal bitterness toward the school board president. However, reactions such as these are usually a mistake because the decision may be out of the other party's hands, and personally attacking the other party often makes the conflict even more difficult to resolve.

Leaders can do several things to separate the people from the problem. First, leaders should not let their fears color their perceptions of each side's intentions. It is easy to attribute negative qualities to others when we feel threatened. Similarly, it does no good to blame the other side for our own problems.[26] Even if this is justified, it is still usually counterproductive. Another thing leaders can do to separate the people from the problem is to communicate clearly. Earlier in this text we suggested techniques for active listening. Those guidelines are especially helpful in negotiating and resolving conflicts.

Focus on Interests, Not Positions

Another of Fisher and Ury's main points is to focus on interests, not positions. Focusing on interests depends on understanding the difference between interests and positions. Here is one example. Say Raoul has had the same reserved seats to the local symphony every season for several years, but he was just notified that he will no longer get his usual tickets. Feeling irate, he goes to the ticket office to complain. One approach he could take would be to demand the same seats he has always had; this would be his *position*. A different approach would be to find alternative seats that are just as satisfactory as his old seats were; this would be his *interest*. In negotiating,

Opportunities

Performance can also be limited when followers lack the resources needed to get the job done. At other times followers may lack the opportunity to demonstrate acquired skills. Such is the case when passengers are hungry but flight attendants have no meals to pass out during the flight. In this situation the flight attendants could have high levels of customer service goals, capabilities, and motivation but will still not be able to satisfy customer needs. Leaders must ensure that followers and teams have the needed equipment, financial resources, and opportunities to exhibit their skills if they want to eliminate this constraint on performance.

Motivation

Many performance problems can be attributed to a lack of motivation. The critical issue here is whether followers or groups choose to perform or exhibit the level of effort necessary to accomplish a task. If this does not occur, the leader should first try to learn why people are unmotivated. Sometimes the task may involve risks the leader is not aware of. At other times individuals or groups may run out of steam to perform the task, or there may be few consequences for superior or unsatisfactory performance. Leaders have several options to resolve motivation problems in followers and teams. First, they can select followers who have higher levels of achievement or intrinsic motivation for the task. Second, they can set clear goals or do a better job of providing performance feedback. Third, they can reallocate work across the team or redesign the tasks to improve skill variety, task significance, and task identity. Fourth, they can restructure rewards and punishments so they are more closely linked to performance levels. See the "Motivation, Satisfaction, and Performance" chapter (Chapter 9) for more information about motivating followers.

Concluding Comments on the Diagnostic Model

In summary, this model provides an integrative framework for many of the topics affecting performance previously reviewed in this text. It reviews some of the factors that affect performance and suggests ideas for rectifying performance problems. However, this model addresses only follower, group, and organizational performance. Leaders need to remember that there are other desirable outcomes, too, such as organizational climate and job satisfaction, and that actions to increase performance (especially just in the short term) may adversely impact these other desirable outcomes.

Team Building at the Top

In certain ways, executive teams are similar to any other teams. For example, just about any group of senior executives that has faced a dire crisis and survived will note that teamwork was essential for its survival.

In a nutshell, then, *when teamwork is critical,* all the lessons of the Chapter 11 section "Building High-Performance Teams" apply. More specifically, to really benefit from a team-building intervention, individual members must be comfortable with their own strengths and weaknesses and the strengths and weaknesses of their peers. But this raises a question: If all this is true, why do we include a separate section about team building for top teams? Because two important differences between most teams and "teams at the top" should be addressed.

Executive Teams Are Different

As opposed to other kinds of work teams, not all the work at the executive level requires all (or even any) of the team to be present. An example might help. In our research on teams we studied the air crews that fly the B-1 bomber. These are four-person teams comprising an aircraft commander, a copilot, an offensive systems officer, and a defensive systems officer. While each has individual responsibilities, in every bombing run we observed, it was essential that the team work together to accomplish the mission. They had all the components of a true team (complex and common goal, differentiated skills, interdependence), and no individual acting alone could have achieved success. But this is not always the case for executive teams.

As Katzenbach has observed,[30] many top leadership challenges do not require teamwork at all. Furthermore, many top leadership challenges that do constitute real team opportunities do not require or warrant full involvement by everyone who is officially on the team. In fact, an official "team at the top" rarely functions as a collective whole involving all the formal members. Thus the real trick for executive teams is to be able to apply both the technical individual skills that probably got the individuals to the team and the skills required for high-performance teamwork when a team situation presents itself.

Applying Individual Skills and Team Skills

There are two critical requirements if this is to work. First, leaders must have the diagnostic skills to discern whether a challenge involves an individual situation or a team situation. Then leaders must "stay the course" when a team situation is present. This means, for example, when pressure for results intensifies, not slipping back into the traditional modes of assigning work to an individual (such as one member of that top team), but rather allowing the team to complete the work *as a team.* Again, Katzenbach stated this clearly:

> Some leadership groups, of course, err in the opposite way, by attempting to forge a team around performance opportunities that do not call for a team approach. In fact, the increasing emphasis that team proponents place on "team-based organizations" creates real frustrations as top leadership groups try to rationalize good executive leadership instincts into

time-consuming team building that has no performance purpose. Catalyzing real team performances at the top does not mean replacing executive leadership with executive teams; it means being rigorous about the distinction between opportunities that require single-leader efforts and those that require team efforts—and applying the discipline that fits.[31]

To summarize this point, executives do not always need to perform as a team to be effective. But when they do need to perform as a team, the same lessons of team building discussed earlier can help enhance their team performance.

The second difference with executive teams is that they have an opportunity to enhance teamwork throughout their organization that few others have. It is our experience that *only the executive team can change organizational systems.* Recall that in Chapter 10 we described the Team Leadership Model and mentioned four systems issues critical to team performance. These systems were all located at the organizational level and consisted of reward systems, education systems, information systems, and control systems. The impact of these systems can be so pervasive across the entire organization that a small change in a system can have monumental impact in the organization. In a sense, then, the executive team has the power to do widespread team building in a manner different than we have discussed to this point. For example, consider the impact of changing a compensation system from an individual-based bonus plan to a team-based bonus plan.

Tripwire Lessons

Finally, our experience in working with executives has taught us that leaders at this level have important lessons to learn about team building at the top. Richard Hackman, in preparing the huge editorial task of having many people produce one coherent book (by his own admission, not necessarily the best of team tasks), assembled the various authors at a conference center. As one of the contributors, one of this text's authors (RCG) recalls the frustrating task of attempting to put together a simple checklist of steps to ensure that a team developed properly. As this arduous process dragged on and tempers flared, it became obvious that "Teamwork for Dummies" was never going to emerge. But something else did emerge. It became clear that *some behaviors leaders engaged in could virtually guarantee failure for their teams.* While not the intent, this experience yielded a worthwhile set of lessons. A condensed version of those lessons, labeled "trip wires" by Hackman, concludes our discussion of team building at the top.[32]

Trip Wire 1: Call the Performing Unit a Team But Really Manage Members as Individuals   One way to set up work is to assign specific responsibilities to specific individuals and then choreograph individuals' activities so their products coalesce into a team product. A contrasting strategy is to assign a team responsibility and accountability for an entire piece of work and let members decide among themselves how they will proceed to accomplish the work. Although either of these strategies can be effective, a choice must be made between them. A mixed model, in which people are told they are a team but are treated as individual performers with their own specific jobs to do, sends mixed signals to members, is likely to confuse everyone, and in the long run is probably untenable.

To reap the benefits of teamwork, a leader must actually build a team. Calling a set of people a team or exhorting them to work together is insufficient. Instead explicit action must be taken to establish the team's boundaries, to define the task as one for which members are collectively responsible and accountable, and to give members the authority to manage both their internal processes and the team's relations with external entities such as clients and co-workers. Once this is done, management behavior and organizational systems gradually can be changed as necessary to support teamwork.

Trip Wire 2: Create an Inappropriate Authority Balance   The exercise of authority creates anxiety, especially when a leader must balance between assigning a team authority for some parts of the work and withholding it for other parts. Because both managers and team members tend to be uncomfortable in such situations, they may collude to clarify them. Sometimes the result is the assignment of virtually all authority to the team—which can result in anarchy or a team that heads off in an inappropriate direction. At other times managers retain virtually all authority, dictating work procedures in detail to team members and, in the process, losing many of the advantages that can accrue from teamwork. In both cases the anxieties that accompany a mixed model are reduced, but at significant cost to team effectiveness.

Achieving a good balance of managerial and team authority is difficult. Moreover, merely deciding how much authority will be assigned to the group and how much will be retained by management is insufficient. Equally important are the domains of authority that are assigned and retained. Our findings suggest that managers should be unapologetic and insistent about exercising their authority over *direction*—the end states the team is to pursue—and over *outer-limit constraints on team behavior*—the things the team must always do or never do. At the same time managers should assign to the team full authority for the means by which it accomplishes its work—and then do whatever they can to ensure that team members understand and accept their responsibility and accountability for deciding how they will execute the work.

Few managerial behaviors are more consequential for the long-term existence of teams than those that address the partitioning of authority between managers and teams. It takes skill to accomplish this well, and this skill has emotional and behavioral as well as cognitive components. Just knowing the rules for partitioning authority is insufficient; leaders also need practice in applying those rules in situations where anxieties, including their own, are likely to be high. Especially challenging for managers are the early stages in the life of a team (when managers often are tempted to give away too much authority) and times when the going gets rough (when the temptation is to take authority back too soon). The management of authority relations with task-performing teams is much like walking on a balance beam, and our evidence suggests that it takes a good measure of knowledge, skill, and perseverance to keep from falling off.

Trip Wire 3: Assemble a Large Group of People, Tell Them in General Terms What Needs to Be Accomplished, and Let Them "Work Out the Details" Traditionally, individually focused designs for work are plagued by constraining structures that have built up over the years to monitor and control employee behavior. When groups perform work, such structures tend to be viewed as unnecessary bureaucratic impediments to team functioning. Thus, just as managers sometimes (and mistakenly) attempt to empower teams by relinquishing all authority to them, so do some attempt to get rid of the dysfunctional features of existing organizational structures simply by taking down all the structures they can. Apparently the hope is that removing structures will release teams and enable members to work together creatively and effectively.

Managers who hold this view often wind up providing teams with less structure than they actually need. Tasks are defined only in vague, general terms. Group composition is unclear or fluid. The limits of the team's authority are kept deliberately fuzzy. The unstated assumption is that there is some magic in the group interaction process and that, by working together, members will evolve any structures the team needs.

This is a false hope; there is no such magic. Indeed, our findings suggest the opposite: groups that have appropriate structures tend to develop healthy internal processes, whereas groups with insufficient or inappropriate structures tend to have process problems. Worse, coaching and process consultation are unlikely to resolve these problems precisely because they are rooted in the team structure. For members to learn how to interact well within a flawed or underspecified structure is to swim upstream against a strong current.

Trip Wire 4: Specify Challenging Team Objectives, but Skimp on Organizational Supports Even if a work team has clear, engaging direction and an enabling structure, its performance can go sour—or at least can fall below the group's potential—if the team is not well supported. Teams in high-commitment organizations fall victim to this trip wire when given "stretch" objectives but not the wherewithal to accomplish them; high initial enthusiasm soon changes into disillusionment.

It is no small undertaking to provide these supports to teams, especially in organizations designed to support work by individuals. Corporate compensation policy, for example, may make no provision for team bonuses and indeed may explicitly prohibit them. Human resource departments may be primed to identify individuals' training needs and provide first-rate courses to fill those needs, but training in team skills may be unavailable. Existing performance appraisal systems, which may be state-of-the-art for measuring individual contributions, are likely to be inappropriate for assessing and rewarding work done by teams. Information systems and control systems may give managers the data they need to monitor and control work processes, but they may be neither available nor appropriate for use by work teams. Finally, the material resources required for the work may have been prespecified by those who originally designed it, and there may be no procedure in place for a team to secure the special configuration of resources it needs to execute the particular performance strategy it has developed.

Aligning existing organizational systems with the needs of teams often requires managers to exercise power and influence upward and laterally in the organization. An organization set up to provide teams with full support for their work is noticeably different from one whose systems and policies are intended to support and control individual work, and many managers may find the prospect of changing to a group-oriented organization both unsettling and perhaps even vaguely revolutionary.

It is hard to provide good organizational support for task-performing teams, but generally it is worth the trouble. The potential of a well-directed, well-structured, well-supported team is tremendous. Moreover, stumbling over the organizational support trip wire is perhaps the saddest of all team failures. When a group is both excited about its work and all set up to execute it superbly, it is especially shattering to fail merely because the organizational supports required cannot be obtained. This is like being all dressed up and ready to go to the wedding only to have the car break down en route.

Trip Wire 5: Assume That Members Already Have All the Competence They Need to Work Well as a Team   Once a team is launched and operating under its own steam, managers sometimes assume their work is done. As we have seen, there are indeed some good reasons for giving a team ample room to go about its business in its own way; inappropriate or poorly timed managerial interventions have impaired the work of more than one group in our research. However, a strictly hands-off managerial stance also can limit a team's effectiveness, particularly when members are not already skilled and experienced in teamwork.

Punishment

In an ideal world, perhaps everyone would be dependable, achievement oriented, and committed to their organization's goals. However, leaders sometimes must deal with followers who are openly hostile or insubordinate, create conflicts among co-workers, do not work up to standards, or openly violate important rules or policies. In such cases leaders may need to administer punishment to change the followers' behavior.

Of all the different aspects of leadership, few are as controversial as punishment. Some of the primary reasons for this controversy stem from myths surrounding the use of punishment, as well as lack of knowledge of the effects of punishment on followers' motivation, satisfaction, and performance. This section is designed to shed light on the punishment controversy by (1) addressing several myths about the use of punishment, (2) reviewing research findings concerning the relationships between punishment and various organizational variables, and (3) giving leadership practitioners advice on how to properly administer punishment.

Myths Surrounding the Use of Punishment

We should begin by repeating the definition of punishment stated earlier in the book. Punishment is the administration of an aversive event or the withdrawal of a positive event or stimulus, which in turn decreases the likelihood that a particular behavior will be repeated.[33] Examples of punishment might include verbal reprimands, being moved to a less prestigious office, having pay docked, being fired, being made to run several laps around an athletic field, or losing eligibility for a sport entirely. We should note that, according to this definition, only those aversive events administered on a contingent basis are considered to be forms of punishment; aversive events administered on a noncontingent basis may constitute harsh and abusive treatment but are not punishment. Additionally, punishment appears to be in the eye of the beholder; aversive events that effectively change the direction, intensity, or persistence of one follower's behavior may have no effect on another's.[34] It is even possible that some followers may find the administration of a noxious event or the removal of a positive event to be reinforcing. For example, it is not uncommon for some children to misbehave if that increases the attention they receive from parents, even if the latter's behavior outwardly may seem punishing. (To the children, some parental attention of any kind may be preferable to no attention.) Similarly, some followers may see the verbal reprimands and notoriety they receive by being insubordinate or violating company policies as forms of attention. Because these followers enjoy being the center of attention, they may find this notoriety rewarding, and they may be even more likely to be insubordinate in the future.

We will examine some myths surrounding the use of punishment. Three of these myths were reviewed by Arvey and Ivancevich and include beliefs that the use of punishment results in undesirable emotional side effects on the part of the recipient, is unethical and inhumane, and rarely works anyway (that is, it seldom eliminates the undesirable behavior).[35]

B. F. Skinner's work in behavioral psychology lent support to the idea that punishment is ineffective and causes undesirable side effects. He based his conclusions on the unnatural behaviors manifested by rats and pigeons punished in various conditioning experiments.[36] Despite the dangers of generalizing from the behavior of rats to humans, many people accepted Skinner's contention that punishment is a futile and typically counterproductive tool for controlling human behavior. This was so despite the fact that considerable research regarding the emotional effects of punishment on humans did not support Skinner's claim.[37-39] Parke, for example, suggested that undesirable emotional side effects of punishment might occur only when punishment was administered indiscriminately or was particularly harsh.[40]

With respect to the myth that punishment is unethical or inhumane, it's been suggested that there is an ethical distinction between "future-oriented" and "past-oriented" punishment. Future-oriented punishment, intended to help improve behavior, may be effective in diminishing or eliminating undesirable behavior. Past-oriented punishment, or what we commonly think of as retribution, on the other hand, is simply a payback for past misdeeds. This sort of punishment may be more questionable ethically, especially when it is intended *only* as payback and not, say, as deterrent to others. Moreover, when considering the ethics of administering punishment, we must also consider the ethics of failing to administer punishment. The costs of failing to punish a potentially harmful behavior, such as unsafe workplace practices, may far outweigh those associated with the punishment itself.[41]

A third myth concerns the efficacy of punishment. Skinner[42] and others claimed that punishment did not result in permanent behavior change but instead only temporarily suppressed behavior.[43] Evidence to support this claim was found in one study in which incarcerated prisoners had a recidivism rate of 85 percent.[44] However, this high recidivism rate may be due to the fact that criminals may have received punishment primarily for retribution rather than for corrective purposes. Judicious administration of sanctions, combined with advice about how to avoid punishment in the future, may successfully eliminate undesirable behaviors on a more permanent basis.[45] Furthermore, it may be a moot point to argue (as Skinner did) that punishment only temporarily suppresses behavior; so long as sanctions for misdeeds remain in place, their impact on behavior should continue. In that regard, the "temporary" effects of punishment on behavior are no different from the "temporary" effects of reinforcement on behavior.

Punishment, Satisfaction, and Performance

It appears that properly administered punishment does not cause undesirable emotional side effects, is not unethical, and may effectively suppress undesirable behavior. However, we also should ask what effect punishment has on followers' satisfaction and performance. Most people probably would predict that leaders who use punishment frequently will have less satisfied and lower-performing followers. Interestingly, this does not appear to be the case—at least when punishment is used appropriately. Let us look more closely at this issue.

Several researchers have looked at whether leaders who administer punishment on a contingent basis also administered rewards on a contingent basis. Generally, researchers have found that there is a moderate positive relationship between leaders' contingent reward behaviors and contingent punishment behaviors.[46-48] There also are consistently strong negative correlations between leaders' contingent reward and noncontingent punishment behaviors. Thus leaders meting out rewards on a contingent basis are also more likely to administer punishment only when followers behave inappropriately or are not performing up to standards.

Keller and Szilagyi maintained that punishment can serve several constructive organizational purposes.[49,50] They said it can help clarify roles and expectations, as well as reduce role ambiguity. Several other authors have found that contingent punishment either is unrelated to followers' satisfaction with their supervisor or has a low positive relationship with it.[51,52] In other words, leaders who follow certain rules in administering punishment need not have dissatisfied subordinates. In fact, judicious and appropriate use of punishment by leaders may result in somewhat higher overall satisfaction of followers. These findings make sense when the entire work unit is considered; failing to use punishment when it seems called for in most followers' eyes may lead to perceptions of inequity, which may in turn reduce group cohesiveness and satisfaction.[53,54]

With respect to followers' work behaviors, Arvey and Jones reported that punishment has generally been found to reduce absenteeism and tardiness rates.[55] Nevertheless, the evidence about punishment's impact on performance appears mixed. Some authors report a strong positive relationship between punishment and performance,[56-59] whereas others found either no relationship between punishment and performance or a negative one.[60,61]

Despite such mixed findings, several points about the relationship between punishment and performance findings are worth noting. First, the levels of punishment as well as the manner in which it was administered across studies could have differed dramatically, and these factors could have affected the results. Second, of the studies reporting positive results, Schnake's experiment studying the vicarious effects of punishment is by far the most provocative. Schnake hired college students for a temporary job and, after several hours at work, publicly reduced the pay or threatened to reduce the pay of a confederate in the work group. As predicted, the more severe the punishment witnessed (either the threat of reduced pay or the reduction of pay), the higher the subsequent performance of other work group members.[62]

Although these findings demonstrated that merely witnessing rather than receiving punishment could increase performance, these results should be interpreted with caution. Because most of the individuals in the experiment did not know each other and had been working together only for several hours, there was probably not enough time for group cohesiveness or norms to develop. It is unclear whether members of cohesive groups or groups with strong norms would react in the same way if they observed another group member being punished. Third, one of the studies reporting less favorable punishment–performance results made an important point about the opportunities to punish. It examined the relationships between Little League coaches' behaviors and their teams' win–loss records. They found that coaches who punished more often had less successful teams. These coaches also, however, had less talented players and therefore had many more opportunities to use punishment. Coaches of successful teams had little if any reason to use punishment. Fourth, many behaviors that are punished may not have a direct link to job performance. For example, being insubordinate, violating company dress codes, and arriving late to meetings are all punishable behaviors that may not be directly linked to solving work-related problems or producing goods or services.[63]

Finally, almost all these studies implicitly assumed that punishment enhanced performance (by correcting problem behaviors), but Curphy and his associates were the only researchers who actually tested this assumption. They collected over 4,500 incidents of documented punishment and performance data from 40 identical organizations over a three-month period. (The punishment and performance data were collected monthly.) They found that low performance led to higher levels of punishment. Moreover, they found that inexperienced leaders administered almost twice as much punishment as experienced leaders. The authors hypothesized that inexperienced leaders used punishment (that is, relied on their coercive power) more frequently because, by being the newest arrivals to the organization, they lacked knowledge of the organizational norms, rules, and policies (expert power); had not yet established relationships with followers (referent power); and were severely limited in the rewards they could provide to followers (reward power).[64]

In summary, the research evidence shows that punishment can lead to positive organizational outcomes if administered properly. When administered on a contingent basis, it may help increase job satisfaction, may decrease role ambiguity and absenteeism rates, and, depending on the behaviors being punished, may improve performance. However, administering intense levels of punishment in a noncontingent or capricious manner can have a devastating effect on the work unit. Group cohesiveness may suffer, followers are likely to become more dissatisfied and less apt to come to work, and they may perform at a lower level in the long term. Thus learning how to properly administer punishment may be the key to maximizing the benefits associated with its use.

Administering Punishment

Usually leaders administer punishment to rectify some type of behavioral or performance problem at work. However, not every behavior or performance problem is punished, and leaders probably weigh several different factors before deciding whether to administer punishment. Green and Mitchell maintained that leaders' decisions concerning punishment depended on whether leaders made internal or external attributions about a subordinate's substandard performance. Leaders making internal attributions were more likely to administer punishment; leaders making external attributions were more likely to blame the substandard performance on situational factors beyond the follower's control.[65]

Attribution theory maintains that leaders weigh three factors when making internal or external attributions about a follower's substandard performance. Specifically, leaders would be more likely to make an internal attribution about a follower's substandard performance (and administer punishment) if the follower had previously completed the task before, if other followers had successfully completed the task, and if the follower had successfully completed other tasks in the past. Moreover, it was found that leaders were biased toward making internal attributions about followers' poor performance (the fundamental attribution error) and thus more likely to use punishment to modify a follower's behavior.[66,67]

Because leaders are biased toward making internal attributions about followers' substandard performance, leaders can administer punishment more effectively by being aware of this bias and getting as many facts as possible before deciding whether to administer punishment. Leaders also can improve the manner or skill with which they administer punishment by using certain tips, such as that punishment is administered most effectively when it focuses on the act, not the person.[68] Followers probably cannot change their personalities, values, or preferences, but they can change their behaviors. By focusing on specific behaviors, leaders minimize the threat to followers' self-concepts. Also, punishment needs to be consistent across both behaviors and leaders; the same actions need to have the same consequences across work groups, or feelings of inequity and favoritism will pervade the organization. One way to increase consistency of punishment is through the establishment of clearly specified organizational policies and procedures.

Administering punishment properly depends on effective two-way communication between the leader and follower. Leaders need to provide a clear rationale for punishment and indicate the consequences for unacceptable behavior in the future. Finally, leaders need to provide followers with guidance about how to improve. This guidance may entail role-modeling proper behaviors for followers, suggesting that followers take training courses, or giving followers accurate feedback about their behavior at work.[69]

Overall, it may be the manner in which punishment is administered, rather than the level of punishment, that has the greatest effect on followers' satisfaction and performance. Leaders need to realize that they may be biased toward administering punishment to rectify followers' substandard performance, and the best way to get around this bias is to collect as much information as possible before deciding whether to punish. By collecting the facts, leaders will be better able to focus on the act, not the person; be able to administer a punishment consistent with company policy; provide the rationale for the punishment; and give guidance to followers on how to improve.

A final caution that leaders need to be aware of concerns the reinforcing or rewarding nature of punishment. Behaviors that are rewarded are likely to be repeated. When leaders administer punishment and subsequently see improvement in a follower's behavior, the leaders will be rewarded and be more apt to use punishment in the future. Over time this may lead to an overreliance on punishment and an underemphasis on the other motivational strategies as means of correcting performance problems. Again, by collecting as much information as possible and by carefully considering the applicability of goal setting, job characteristics theory, and so on, to the problem, leaders may be able to successfully avoid having only one tool in their motivational toolkit.

End Notes

1. N. N. Tichy and N. Cardwell, *The Cycle of Leadership: How Great Companies Teach Their Leaders to Win* (New York: HarperBusiness, 2002).

2. G. J. Curphy, *The Role of the Supervisor Program for Andersen Corporation* (North Oaks, MN: Author, 2005).

3. J. Collins, *Good to Great* (New York: HarperCollins, 2001).

4. J. Krile, G. J. Curphy, and D. Lund. *The Community Leadership Handbook: Framing Ideas, Building Relationships, and Mobilizing Resources* (St. Paul, MN: Fieldstone Alliance, 2005).

5. K. W. Thomas and W. H. Schmidt, "A Survey of Managerial Interests with Respect to Conflict," *Academy of Management Journal* 19 (1976), pp. 315–18.

6. J. J. Morse and F. R. Wagner, "Measuring the Process of Managerial Effectiveness," *Academy of Management Journal* 21 (1978), pp. 23–35.

7. L. D. Brown, *Managing Conflict at Organizational Interfaces* (Reading, MA: Addison-Wesley, 1983).

8. W. G. Ouchi, *How American Business Can Meet the Japanese Challenge* (Reading, MA: Addison-Wesley, 1981).

9. T. J. Peters and R. H. Waterman, *In Search of Excellence* (New York: Harper & Row, 1982).

10. S. P. Robbins, *Organizational Behavior: Concepts, Controversies, and Applications* (Englewood Cliffs, NJ: Prentice Hall, 1986).

11. G. Yukl, *Leadership in Organizations*, 2nd ed. (Englewood Cliffs, NJ: Prentice Hall, 1989).

12. M. F. R. Kets de Vries and D. Miller, "Managers Can Drive Their Subordinates Mad," In *The Irrational Executive: Psychoanalytic Explorations in Management,* ed. M. F. R. Kets de Vries (New York: International Universities Press, 1984).

13. K. W. Thomas and W. H. Schmidt, "A Survey of Managerial Interests with Respect to Conflict," *Academy of Management Journal* 19 (1976), pp. 315–18.

14. G. Yukl, *Leadership in Organizations,* 2nd ed. (Englewood Cliffs, NJ: Prentice Hall, 1989).

15. K. W. Thomas, "Conflict and Conflict Management," in *Handbook of Industrial and Organizational Psychology,* ed. M. D. Dunnette (Chicago: Rand McNally, 1976).

16. S. P. Robbins, *Organizational Behavior: Concepts, Controversies, and Applications* (Englewood Cliffs, NJ: Prentice Hall, 1986).

17. B. M. Bass, *Leadership and Performance beyond Expectations* (New York: Free Press, 1985).

18. A. R. Willner, *The Spellbinders: Charismatic Political Leadership* (New Haven: Yale University Press, 1984).

19. N. C. Roberts and R. T. Bradley, "Limits of Charisma," in *Charismatic Leadership: The Elusive Factor in Organizational Effectiveness,* ed. J. A. Conger and R. N. Kanungo (San Francisco: Jossey-Bass, 1988), pp. 253–75.

20. R. M. Kanter, *The Change Masters* (New York: Simon & Schuster, 1983).

21. K. W. Thomas, "Conflict and Conflict Management," in *Handbook of Industrial and Organizational Psychology,* ed. M. D. Dunnette (Chicago: Rand McNally, 1976).

22. Ibid.

23. K. W. Thomas, "Toward Multidimensional Values in Teaching: The Example of Conflict Management," *Academy of Management Review* 2, no. 3 (1977), pp. 484–90.

24. R. Fisher and W. Ury, *Getting to Yes* (Boston: Houghton Mifflin, 1981).

25. Ibid.

26. R. R. Blake, H. A. Shepard, and J. S. Mouton, *Managing Intergroup Conflict in Industry* (Houston, TX: Gulf, 1964).

27. J. P. Campbell, "The Cutting Edge of Leadership: An Overview," in *Leadership: The Cutting Edge,* ed. J. G. Hunt and L. L. Larson (Carbondale, IL: Southern Illinois University Press, 1977).

28. J. P. Campbell, R. A. McCloy, S. H. Oppler, and C. E. Sager, "A Theory of Performance," in *Frontiers in Industrial/Organizational Psychology and Personnel Selection,* ed. N. Schmitt and W. C. Borman (San Francisco: Jossey-Bass, 1993), pp. 35–70.

29. J. W. Boudreau and P. Ramstad, *Beyond HR: The New Science of Human Capital* (Boston, MA: Harvard Business School Press, 2007).

30. J. R. Katzenbach, *Teams at the Top* (Boston: Harvard Business School Press, 1998).

31. Ibid.

32. J. R. Hackman, *Groups That Work (and Those That Don't)* (San Francisco: Jossey-Bass, 1990).

33. R. D. Arvey and J. M. Ivancevich, "Punishment in Organizations: A Review, Propositions, and Research Suggestions," *Academy of Management Review* 5 (1980), pp. 123–32.

34. G. J. Curphy, F. W. Gibson, B. W. Asiu, C. P. McCown, and C. Brown, "A Field Study of the Causal Relationships between Organizational Performance, Punishment, and Justice," working paper, 1992.

35. R. D. Arvey and J. M. Ivancevich, "Punishment in Organizations: A Review, Propositions, and Research Suggestions," *Academy of Management Review* 5 (1980), pp. 123–32.

36. B. F. Skinner, *The Behavior of Organisms* (New York: Appleton-Century-Crofts, 1938).

37. A. E. Kazdin, *Behavior Modification in Applied Settings* (Homewood, IL: Dorsey, 1975).

38. J. M. Johnston, "Punishment of Human Behavior," *American Psychologist* 27 (1972), pp. 1033–54.

39. R. L. Solomon, "Punishment," *American Psychologist* 19 (1964), pp. 239–53.

40. R. D. Parke, "Some Effects of Punishment on Children's Behavior," in *The Young Child: Reviews of Research*, Vol. 2, ed. W. W. Hartup (Washington, DC: National Association for the Education of Young Children, 1972).

41. R. D. Arvey and J. M. Ivancevich, "Punishment in Organizations: A Review, Propositions, and Research Suggestions," *Academy of Management Review* 5 (1980), pp. 123–32.

42. B. F. Skinner, *The Behavior of Organisms* (New York: Appleton-Century-Crofts, 1938).

43. F. Luthans, *Organizational Behavior*, 5th ed. (New York: McGraw-Hill, 1992).

44. J. Huberman, "Discipline without Punishment," *Harvard Business Review*, July–August 1964, p. 62.

45. R. D. Arvey and J. M. Ivancevich, "Punishment in Organizations: A Review, Propositions, and Research Suggestions," *Academy of Management Review* 5 (1980), pp. 123–32.

46. R. D. Arvey, G. A. Davis, and S. M. Nelson, "Use of Discipline in an Organization: A Field Study," *Journal of Applied Psychology* 69 (1984), pp. 448–60.

47. P. M. Podsakoff and W. D. Todor, "Relationships between Leader Reward and Punishment Behavior and Group Process and Productivity," *Journal of Management* 11 (1985), pp. 55–73.

48. S. Strasser, R. C. Dailey, and T. S. Bateman, "Attitudinal Moderators and Effects of Leaders' Punitive Behavior," *Psychological Reports* 49 (1981), pp. 695–98.

49. R. T. Keller and A. D. Szilagyi, "Employee Reactions for Leader Reward Behavior," *Academy of Management Journal* 19 (1976), pp. 619–27.

50. R. T. Keller and A. D. Szilagyi, "A Longitudinal Study of Leader Reward Behavior, Subordinate Expectancies, and Satisfaction," *Personnel Psychology* 11 (1978), pp. 119–29.

51. R. D. Arvey, G. A. Davis, and S. M. Nelson, "Use of Discipline in an Organization: A Field Study," *Journal of Applied Psychology* 69 (1984), pp. 448–60.

52. P. M. Podsakoff, W. D. Todor, R. A. Grover, and V. L. Huber, "Situational Moderators of Leader Reward and Punishment Behaviors: Fact or Fiction?" *Organizational Behavior and Human Performance* 34 (1984), pp. 21–63.

53. G. J. Curphy, F. W. Gibson, B. W. Asiu, C. P. McCown, and C. Brown, "A Field Study of the Causal Relationships between Organizational Performance, Punishment, and Justice," working paper, 1992.

54. G. H. Dobbins and J. M. Russell, "The Biasing Effects of Subordinate Likeableness on Leaders' Responses to Poor Performance," *Personnel Psychology* 39 (1986), pp. 759–77.

55. R. D. Arvey and A. P. Jones, "The Use of Discipline in Organizational Settings: A Framework for Future Research," in *Research in Organizational Behavior,* Vol. 7, ed. L. L. Cummings and B. M. Staw (Greenwich, CT: JAI, 1985), pp. 367–408.

56. J. M. Beyer and H. M. Trice, "A Field Study in the Use and Perceived Effects of Discipline in Controlling Work Performance," *Academy of Management Journal* 27 (1984), pp. 743–64.

57. D. Katz, N. Maccoby, G. Gurin, and L. G. Floor, *Productivity, Supervision, and Morale among Railroad Workers* (Ann Arbor, MI: University of Michigan, Survey Research Center, Institute of Social Research, 1951).

58. P. M. Podsakoff and W. D. Todor, "Relationships between Leader Reward and Punishment Behavior and Group Process and Productivity," *Journal of Management* 11 (1985), pp. 55–73.

59. M. E. Schnake, "Vicarious Punishment in a Work Setting," *Journal of Applied Psychology* 71 (1986), pp. 343–45.

60. G. J. Curphy, F. W. Gibson, B. W. Asiu, C. P. McCown, and C. Brown, "A Field Study of the Causal Relationships between Organizational Performance, Punishment, and Justice," working paper, 1992.

61. B. Curtis, R. E. Smith, and F. L. Smoll, "Scrutinizing the Skipper: A Study of Behaviors in the Dugout," *Journal of Applied Psychology* 64 (1979), pp. 391–400; M. A. Dalton, "Using 360-Degree Feedback Successfully," *Leadership in Action* 18, no. 1 (1998), pp. 2–11.

62. M. E. Schnake, "Vicarious Punishment in a Work Setting," *Journal of Applied Psychology* 71 (1986), pp. 343–45.

63. G. J. Curphy, F. W. Gibson, B. W. Asiu, C. P. McCown, and C. Brown, "A Field Study of the Causal Relationships between Organizational Performance, Punishment, and Justice," working paper, 1992.

64. Ibid.

65. S. G. Green and T. R. Mitchell, "Attributional Processes of Leaders in Leader–Member Interactions," *Organizational Behavior and Human Performances* 23 (1979), pp. 429–58.

66. T. R. Mitchell, S. G. Green, and R. E. Wood, "An Attributional Model of Leadership and the Poor Performing Subordinate: Development and Validation," in *Research in Organizational Behavior,* ed. B. M. Staw and L. L. Cummings (Greenwich, CN: JAI, 1981), pp. 197–234.

67. T. R. Mitchell and R. E. Wood, "Supervisors' Responses to Subordinate Poor Performance: A Test of an Attributional Model," *Organizational Behavior and Human Performance* 25 (1980), pp. 123–38.

68. R. D. Arvey and J. M. Ivancevich, "Punishment in Organizations: A Review, Propositions, and Research Suggestions," *Academy of Management Review* 5 (1980), pp. 123–32.

69. Ibid.

Name Index

Note: Page numbers followed by *n* indicate source notes and endnotes.

Abanes, R., 613*n*
Aberman, R., 222, 225, 226, 240*n*108–109
Abraham, L. M., 388*n*137
Abrahams, M., 86*n*70
Acton, Lord, 118, 137, 358
Adams, J., 605*n*150
Adams, S., 613
Agle, B. R., 187*n*62, 602*n*93, 604*n*132
Aguero, S., 244, 245
Ahearne, M. J., 386*n*99
Alberti, R. E., 291*n*, 314*n*18
Albrecht, K., 315*n*38
Alderfer, C. P., 433*n*33
Aldrich, H. E., 517*n*34
Alexander the Great, 610
Allen, D., 552*n*6
Allen, P., 375, 596–597
Allen, T. D., 86*n*67–68, 86*n*72–73
Allen, W., 6
Allende, S., 337
Allinger, G. M., 40*n*28, 234*n*4
Allport, G. W., 235*n*19
Alter, J., 566*n*
Amabile, T. M., 216, 217*n*, 239*n*83–84, 239*n*95–97, 345*n*
Ambrose, M. L., 388*n*146
Amichai-Hamburger, Y., 604*n*135
Amin, I., 610, 612
Ancona, D., 254–255, 274*n*43
Anders, G., 380*n*1
Andersen, J. A., 187*n*56
Anderson, L. S., 385*n*83
Anderson, M. H., 605*n*146
Anderson, N. 237*n*58
Antonakis, J., 240*n*114, 604*n*124, 606*n*155
Antonioni, D., 275*n*65
Argyris, C., 54–56, 83*n*18, 212*n*
Aristotle, 190
Armenakis, A. A., 387*n*122
Armour, S., 386*n*106
Armstrong, D. J., 425–427, 435*n*68
Arthaud-Day, M. L., 381*n*14
Arthur, M. B., 602*n*97, 603*n*109
Arthur, W. Jr., 85*n*44

Arvey, R. D., 237*n*46, 385*n*81, 385*n*94, 388*n*137, 677, 679, 683*n*33, 684*n*35, 684*n*41, 684*n*45–46, 684*n*51, 685*n*55, 685*n*68
Arvidson, D., 84*n*41
Aryee, S., 382*n*35
Ash, R. A., 274*n*40
Ashkanasy, N. M., 241*n*124
Asiu, B. W., 684*n*34, 684*n*53, 685*n*60, 685*n*63
Astin, A. W., 41*n*59
Atkins, P. W. B., 275*n*59
Atkinson, J. W., 344, 383*n*53
Atwater, L. E., 276*n*78–79, 552*n*11
Avolio, B. J., 74, 114*n*23, 169, 185*n*8, 186*n*44, 186*n*47, 186*n*49, 186*n*51, 187*n*52, 255*n*, 578–580, 590, 601*n*77, 601*n*81, 601*n*83, 602*n*98, 603*n*108, 603*n*110, 603*n*116, 603*n*119, 604*n*134, 606*n*155–156
Axelrod, S., 599*n*55
Ayman, R., 602*n*96
Azar, B., 238*n*66

Bachelet, M., 337, 345
Back, K. and K., 296*n*
Bacon, F., 60
Badin, I. J., 432*n*5
Baer, J., 238*n*74
Baird, C. A., 185*n*11
Baker, S. D., 40*n*32
Baldrica, A., 7*n*, 114*n*37, 339*n*, 372*n*, 382*n*40, 599*n*37, 618*n*, 630*n*, 633*n*, 636*n*, 639*n*, 653*n*, 653*n*7
Baldwin, B., 157*n*
Baldwin, S., 4
Baldwin, T. T., 381*n*14
Baliga, B. R., 114*n*23, 602*n*98, 602*n*101
Balkundui, P., 604*n*133
Ballmer, S., 504
Baltzell, E. D., 40*n*30
Banaji, M. R., 185*n*24
Bandura, A., 166, 167, 186*n*36–37, 186*n*39, 434*n*60
Banki, B., 433*n*43, 434*n*58
Banks, W., 399*n*, 433*n*25

Barbera, K. M., 561*n*
Barling, J., 593, 600*n*59–61
Barlow, C. B., 41*n*45
Barnes, C., 186*n*33
Barnes, F., 147*n*29
Barnett, R. C., 273*n*27
Barnum, D. F., 506, 518*n*70
Bar-On, R., 222, 223*n*, 224, 225, 227, 240*n*107, 241*n*117–118
Barrett, A., 46*n*
Barrick, M. R., 235*n*22, 235*n*24, 383*n*55, 387*n*116
Bartol, K. M., 239*n*94, 386*n*97
Basadur, M., 239*n*89
Bass, B. M., 5, 39*n*12, 40*n*35, 113*n*21, 114*n*23, 146*n*7, 273*n*20, 283, 313*n*4, 314*n*21, 432*n*9, 444, 457, 469*n*1, 469*n*9, 470*n*18, 470*n*27, 471*n*31, 471*n*35, 471*n*37, 515*n*9, 516*n*21, 517*n*39, 517*n*41, 517*n*44, 517*n*46, 518*n*50, 557, 578–580, 590, 597*n*1, 600*n*70, 601*n*75, 601*n*77–78, 601*n*83, 602*n*98, 603*n*116–118, 604*n*121, 606*n*156, 683*n*17
Bateman, T. S., 684*n*48
Battista, M., 274*n*40
Batz, P. H., 273*n*27
Bazerman, M. H., 185*n*24, 384*n*70
Beacham, C., 481
Beatty, R. W., 276*n*88, 383*n*44, 654*n*26
Bebchuck, L. A., 352*n*, 354*n*
Becker, B. A., 274*n*44
Becker, B. E., 383*n*44, 654*n*26
Becket, T. à, 405
Bedeian, A. G., 387*n*122
Beer, M., 557, 559, 567–568, 568*n*, 569, 598*n*21–22
Beeson, J., 46*n*
Behar, K., 84*n*41
Behling, O., 39*n*7
Beimel, S., 606*n*159
Bell, S. T., 85*n*44
Benne, K. D., 398*n*, 399*n*
Benner, P. E., 314*n*24
Bennett, W. Jr., 85*n*44
Bennis, W. G., 39*n*4, 39*n*14, 39*n*16, 151, 184*n*4, 313*n*5, 557, 598*n*16

Benson, M. J., 7*n*, 114*n*37, 199*n*, 236*n*36, 272*n*5, 339*n*, 372*n*, 382*n*40, 600*n*69, 606*n*158, 655*n*35–36, 656*n*54

Bentz, V. J., 622, 655*n*37

Bergin, A. E., 315*n*32

Berglas, S., 75*n*

Berkman, L., 315*n*45

Berkowitz, L., 83*n*9, 553*n*32, 553*n*39

Berle, A. A., Jr., 141

Bernardin, H. J., 276*n*88

Bernthal, P., 82*n*2

Berson, Y. B., 601*n*83, 603*n*108, 603*n*110

Bertua, C., 237*n*58

Bettencourt, L. A., 386*n*112

Betz, E. L., 383*n*52

Beyer, J. M., 605*n*141, 685*n*56

Bickman, L., 147*n*18

Bierce, A., 640

bin Laden, O., 320, 338, 573, 579, 610, 613

Bird, M., 432*n*14

Birdi, K., 381*n*16

Bisqueret, C., 236*n*33

Blake, R. R., 250, 251*n*, 273*n*23–24, 683*n*26

Blanchard, A. L., 380*n*13

Blanchard, K. H., 516*n*14–15, 531*n*, 534, 541, 553*n*25, 553*n*28, 553*n*37–38

Blankenship, J., 316*n*51

Blau, P. M., 99, 113*n*15, 599*n*46

Blaylock, J., 651–653

Bliese, P. D., 235*n*25

Bligh, M. C., 603*n*112

Block, P., 41*n*44

Bloom, M., 352*n*, 385*n*87

Bloom, N., 654*n*28

Bloomberg, M., 566

Boal, K. B., 603*n*113, 605*n*142

Boal, K. M., 602*n*101

Boga, I., 605*n*144

Bogle, J., 352*n*

Bommer, W. H., 381*n*14, 600*n*61

Bono, J. E., 234*n*8, 235*n*26, 274*n*48, 275*n*57, 382*n*25, 388*n*135, 600*n*62, 600*n*69, 601*n*82, 604*n*122, 604*n*136, 605*n*146, 606*n*158, 606*n*162, 622, 655*n*39

Boone, M. F., 28*n*

Bordia, P., 380*n*6

Borman, W. C., 113*n*6, 683*n*28

Bossidy, L., 599*n*36, 653*n*14

Botes, C., 6, 6*n*, 217

Bouchard, T. J., Jr., 40*n*21, 388*n*137

Boudreau, J. W., 654*n*27, 683*n*29

Bowers, D. G., 273*n*19

Bowles, S. V., 85*n*57

Boyatzis, R. E., 135–137, 148*n*39, 148*n*42, 148*n*47, 185*n*9, 224–225, 227, 240*n*112–113, 241*n*126

Boyle, G., 261

Bracken, D. W., 275*n*58

Bradberry, T., 241*n*123

Bradford, D. L., 106, 114*n*36, 114*n*38

Bradley, J. C., 235*n*25

Bradley, R. T., 683*n*19

Brake, T., 426–427

Brandes, G., 18

Brannick, M. T., 434*n*52

Branson, R., 37–39, 345, 375

Brass, D. J., 434*n*61

Bray, D. W., 113*n*17

Breland, J. W., 148*n*50

Bremer, P., 245

Brenner, O. C., 41*n*55

Brett, J. M., 336*n*

Bridges, S., 253*n*, 264*n*, 274*n*38

Bridges, W., 557, 598*n*18

Brin, S., 216

Britt, T. W., 345, 384*n*65

Brockner, J., 382*n*36, 388*n*143

Brodbeck, F. C., 276*n*86, 504*n*, 518*n*72, 519*n*74–75

Brooks, S. M., 333*n*, 380*n*7

Brouwers, A., 85*n*55

Brown, C., 684*n*34, 684*n*53, 685*n*60, 685*n*63

Brown, D. J., 604*n*129

Brown, L., 316*n*51

Brown, L. D., 682*n*7

Brown, M. E., 184*n*1, 186*n*45, 604*n*127

Brown, R. P., 163, 186*n*33

Brutus, S., 276*n*80

Bryson, J. M., 274*n*47, 602*n*101

Buck, J. H., 147*n*27

Buckingham, M., 365*n*

Buck Luce, C., 381*n*13

Buddha, 160

Bugental, D. E., 113*n*8

Bullis, R. C., 252*n*, 599*n*34

Bullock, A., 380*n*13

Bunker, K. A., 57–58, 83*n*19

Burger, J. M., 380*n*5

Burger, W. E., 129

Burke, A., 195

Burnett, D. D., 235*n*18

Burns, J. M., 18, 40*n*34, 146*n*5, 151, 184*n*3, 557, 576–581, 598*n*14, 610, 653*n*1

Bush, G. H. W., 332

Bush, G. W., 204, 583, 614, 646

Butcher, V., 600*n*59

Butorac, T., 333*n*

Butts, M., 86*n*69

Byrne, Z. S., 382*n*32

Byron, Lord, 121

Cairo, P. E., 626, 654*n*30

Cameron, C. S., 518*n*55

Cameron, J., 244, 334, 556

Cameron, K. S., 495, 496*n*

Campbell, D. P., 39*n*8, 126, 148*n*52, 153, 238*n*80, 239*n*82, 274*n*50, 275*n*68, 314*n*29, 315*n*39–40, 346, 368*n*, 382*n*26, 387*n*125, 388*n*131, 408, 428, 433*n*40, 434*n*57, 435*n*73, 605*n*149, 626

Campbell, J. P., 199*n*, 236*n*36, 272*n*5, 383*n*47, 383*n*48, 600*n*69, 606*n*158, 635, 655*n*35–36, 656*n*54, 683*n*27–28

Campbell, K., 29

Campbell, R. J., 383*n*48, 434*n*62

Campbell, S. M., 604*n*132

Campion, M. A., 274*n*54

Cardwell, N., 598*n*26, 682*n*1

Carli, L. L., 41*n*58, 601*n*72

Carmeli, A., 552*n*11

Carnazza, J. P., 470*n*16

Carr, J. Z., 381*n*10

Carr, L., 274*n*40

Carranza, J., 81–82

Carre, J. le, 394

Carsten, M., 187*n*63

Carter, J., 375, 403

Cartwright, D., 147*n*20

Caruso, D. R., 222–223, 223*n*, 225, 227, 240*n*106, 240*n*111, 241*n*117

Casciaro, J., 214*n*

Case, T., 148*n*54–55, 149*n*60

Cashman, J. F., 40*n*24, 552*n*3

Castore, C. H., 432*n*21

Castro, F., 573, 576, 610

Castro, S. L., 555*n*61

Cha, S. E., 187*n*69

Chaleff, I., 20*n*, 187*n*52, 320, 380*n*9

Chandler, A. D., 516*n*29

Charan, R., 257*n*, 258, 272*n*9, 274*n*45, 382*n*42, 599*n*36, 599*n*38, 626, 653*n*14, 655*n*40–41

Chaudhry, A., 552*n*10
Chávez, H., 573, 575
Chemers, M. M., 521, 551*n*2, 553*n*35, 554*n*41, 602*n*96
Chen, G., 552*n*6, 604*n*130
Chess, W. A., 315*n*47
Chhokar, J. S., 276*n*86, 518*n*72, 519*n*74
Chien, I., 209
Ching, H., 144–146
Chinoy, E., 599*n*47
Chitayat, G., 517*n*33
Cho, J., 148*n*50
Choi, J., 602*n*100
Christiansen, N. D., 385*n*96
Chronis, P. G., 339*n*
Chugh, D., 185*n*24
Church, A. H., 227, 229*n*, 274*n*42, 275*n*58, 275*n*69–70, 275*n*73
Cialdini, R. B., 147*n*17
Cicero, 163
Ciulla, J. B., 59, 84*n*28
Clark, B. R., 599*n*54
Clark, K. E., 113*n*17, 148*n*52, 238*n*80, 239*n*82, 275*n*68, 314*n*29, 315*n*39–40, 605*n*149
Clark, M. B., 113*n*17, 148*n*52, 238*n*80, 239*n*82, 275*n*68, 314*n*29, 315*n*39–40, 605*n*149
Clark, S., 574*n*
Clegg, C., 381*n*16
Clinton, B., 566, 613
Clinton, H., 575
Coffman, C., 365*n*
Cohen, A. R., 106, 114*n*36, 114*n*38
Cohen, E., 274*n*49, 467, 471*n*40, 471*n*43
Cohen, S. A., 383*n*43
Colbert, A. E., 234*n*7, 275*n*57, 387*n*116
Cole, P., 425–427, 435*n*68
Collins, J., 197, 197*n*, 557, 589, 589*n*, 598*n*24–25, 647, 647*n*, 682*n*3
Collins, J. C., 598*n*19
Collins, M. A., 239*n*83
Colquitt, J. A., 388*n*144–45
Columbus, C., 286
Colvin, G., 272*n*9, 599*n*38, 626, 655*n*41
Comacho, T., 315*n*44
Combs, J., 386*n*100
Conan Doyle, A., 521
Conan the Barbarian, 610
Confucius, 478

Congdon, D., 160*n*
Conger, J. A., 63, 84*n*31, 84*n*34, 274*n*52, 578, 580, 581, 600*n*68, 602*n*89, 602*n*94, 603*n*115, 605*n*139, 683*n*19
Conlin, M., 41*n*49
Conlon, D. E., 388*n*145
Connaughton, S. L., 161*n*
Conway, F., 147*n*30
Cook, C., 364
Coolidge, C., 194
Cools, K., 642*n*
Coons, A. E., 272*n*12, 272*n*14
Cornell, A., 531
Corrigall, E., 42*n*62
Costa, P. T., Jr., 235*n*23
Cote, S., 241*n*121
Cotton, J. L., 85*n*60, 86*n*71
Couch, A., 553*n*24
Coughlin, T. M., 114*n*22
Cousteau, V., 667*n*
Covey, S. R., 152, 179, 187*n*70
Cowell, S., 195, 196
Coy, R., 186*n*24
Coye, R. W., 470*n*15
Craig, J. R., 113*n*13
Craig, P. A., 655*n*45
Craig, S. B., 273*n*37, 274*n*53, 275*n*64, 381*n*18
Cronbach, L. J., 237*n*55, 310, 316*n*55
Cropanzano, R., 382*n*32, 388*n*146
Crosby, B. C., 274*n*47
Cruthirds, K. W., 255*n*
Csikszentmihalyi, M., 83*n*25, 112*n*2
Cummings, L. L., 83*n*13, 516*n*24, 685*n*55, 685*n*66
Cummings, R. C., 315*n*46
Cummings, W. H., 236*n*43
Curphy, G. J., 7, 7*n*, 39*n*10, 40*n*27, 68*n*, 75*n*, 84*n*43, 85*n*50, 88, 110*n*, 112*n*1, 112*n*4, 114*n*24, 114*n*37, 187*n*58, 199*n*, 200, 234*n*5, 235*n*12, 235*n*14–16, 236*n*31, 236*n*36, 236*n*44, 237*n*61–62, 238*n*63–64, 241*n*, 243*n*, 253*n*, 260*n*, 264*n*, 272*n*1–8, 273*n*32, 273*n*34, 274*n*38, 274*n*46, 274*n*50–51, 275*n*60, 275*n*67–68, 276*n*75, 276*n*83, 282*n*, 320, 323, 324, 339*n*, 349, 349*n*, 363*n*, 365*n*, 372*n*, 380*n*12, 382*n*40–41, 383*n*45, 383*n*57–59, 384*n*63–64, 385*n*82, 387*n*119, 387*n*125, 466*n*, 470*n*22–25, 557,

566*n*, 597*n*8, 598*n*12–13, 598*n*27–29, 599*n*37, 601*n*79, 604*n*123, 605*n*149, 606*n*163–164, 618*n*, 619*n*, 626, 630*n*, 633*n*, 636*n*, 639*n*, 640, 653*n*, 653*n*7, 655*n*42, 655*n*52, 656*n*53, 656*n*55, 656*n*56, 680, 682*n*2, 682*n*4, 684*n*34, 684*n*53, 685*n*60, 685*n*63
Curran, K. E., 148*n*54
Curtis, B., 685*n*61
Cushing, R., 239*n*91

Dai, G., 599*n*44
Dailey, R. C., 684*n*48
Dalgarno, G., 243
Dalton, M. A., 685*n*61
D'Amelio, A., 599*n*40
Dansereau, F., 187*n*71
Darley, J., 167–168, 186*n*40
Darrow, C., 374
Davidson, O. B., 384*n*77
Davies, S. E., 622, 655*n*39
Davis, B. L., 115*n*47, 314*n*15
Davis, G. A., 385*n*94, 684*n*46, 684*n*51
Davis, M., 316*n*52
Davis, S., 273*n*27
Dawes, W., 22
Dawson, A., 211
Day, D. V., 82*n*1
Deal, J. J., 185*n*17
Deary, J. J., 235*n*20
deCastro, E. M., 613*n*
DeChurch, L. A., 555*n*61
Deci, E. L., 147*n*25
DeCorte, W., 273*n*30
Deep, S., 470*n*10
De Fruyt, F., 237*n*58
DeGeneres, E., 195, 196
De Hoogh, A. H. B., 606*n*153
De Janasz, S. C., 86*n*65
De Jong, R. D., 147*n*19, 315*n*41
Delbecq, A. L., 316*n*53
Delehanty, H., 392*n*
DeLeo, P. J., 385*n*90
Delery, J. E., 381*n*15
Dell, M., 127
Deluga, R. J., 605*n*147
Deming, W. E., 557
De Muese, K., 599*n*44
Denbow, C., 654*n*18
Den Hartog, D. N., 600*n*71, 606*n*153
DeNinno, J. A., 432*n*21
DeNisi, A. S., 555*n*58

DeShon, R. P., 381*n*10
Despain, J., 544
DeVader, C. L., 40*n*28, 234*n*4
Devanna, M. A., 518*n*53, 557, 598*n*17
Deveraux, G., 599*n*55
Dewhirst, H. D., 113*n*11, 471*n*34, 471*n*36, 471*n*38
Diamond, J., 576, 576*n*, 612, 653*n*6
Dickens, C., 59
Dickson, M. W., 598*n*31
Dickson, P., 22
DiClemente, D. F., 252*n*
Dietz, J., 333*n*, 380*n*7
Dilchert, S., 235*n*28
Dimotakis, N., 237*n*53
Dineen, B. R., 382*n*34
Dingfelder, S. F., 217*n*, 239*n*88
DioGuardi, K., 195
Dionne, S. D., 187*n*71
Disraeli, B., 17, 34, 486
Dobbins, G. H., 685*n*54
Dodge, G. E., 605*n*142
Doherty, M. L., 517*n*42, 517*n*45
Donnell, S. M., 152, 185*n*6
Donno, D., 146*n*2
Dorfman, P. W., 516*n*18, 518*n*71, 519*n*75, 600*n*71
Dorgan, S., 654*n*28
Dosier, L., 148*n*55, 149*n*60
Dotlich, D. L., 626, 654*n*30
Doughty, R., 65*n*
Dow, T. E., 599*n*53
Dowdy, J., 654*n*28
Downton, J. V., 600*n*56
Dressler, G., 516*n*17, 542, 554*n*54, 555*n*67
Drotter, S., 257*n*, 258, 274*n*45, 382*n*42, 655*n*40
Drucker, P. F., 350, 637, 655*n*49
Druett, J., 243, 243*n*
Druskat, V. U., 241*n*120, 601*n*74
Dubner, S. J., 354*n*
Dubois, P. H., 236*n*45
Duchler, H. P., 602*n*101
Duchon, D. S., 113*n*10, 114*n*25
Duehr, E. E., 600*n*69, 606*n*158
Duffy, M. K., 382*n*31, 387*n*114
Duke, A. B., 148*n*50
Dukerich, J. M., 11*n*
Dumaine, B., 517*n*49
Dunbar, B. J., 407
Duncker, K., 316*n*54
Dungy, A. K., 69, 71

Dunnette, M. D., 234*n*6, 275*n*60, 381*n*21, 433*n*29, 553*n*23, 553*n*27, 555*n*63, 665*n*
Dunning, D., 635, 655*n*46
Dvir, T., 601*n*81
Dvorak, P., 354*n*, 435*n*70
Dwight, S. A., 275*n*66
Dylan, B., 317

Eagly, A. H., 41*n*58, 601*n*72
Earley, P. C., 469*n*2
Eastman, K. K., 605*n*143
Eastwood, C., 396
Eby, L. T., 86*n*67–69, 86*n*72–73
Eckert, R., 233
Eddleston, K. A., 384*n*74, 386*n*110
Eden, D., 53, 83*n*16, 348, 384*n*77–78, 601*n*81
Edens, P. S., 85*n*44
Edmondson, A. C., 187*n*69
Ehrhart, M. G., 598*n*31, 604*n*128
Ehrlich, S. B., 11*n*, 39*n*2
Ehrlichman, J., 122, 146*n*15
Eichinger, R. W., 115*n*48, 622
Einarsen, S., 653*n*2
Einstein, A., 51, 160, 582
Eisenberger, R., 273*n*22
Eisenhower, D. D., 119, 128, 130
Eliot, T. S., 48
Ellis, A. D., 316*n*50, 387*n*124
Ellsworth, B., 84*n*41
Elman, N. S., 85*n*59
Emerson, R. W., 190, 574
Emery, F. E., 518*n*54
Emmons, M. L., 291*n*, 314*n*18
England, L., 131
Ensari, N., 605*n*144
Ensley, M. D., 382*n*31
Epitopaki, O., 604*n*131
Eptiropaki, O., 600*n*59
Erez, A., 236*n*35, 605*n*137
Erez, M., 469*n*2, 469*n*6
Erickson, G., 183–184
Evans, M. G., 542, 554*n*53
Evers, W. J. G., 85*n*55
Eyde, L. D., 274*n*40

Fairhurst, G. T., 149*n*58
Fanelli, A., 602*n*92, 605*n*148
Fanning, P., 316*n*52
Farrakhan, L., 573
Farris, G. F., 113*n*9
Fatima, M., 574*n*
Feinberg, B. J., 276*n*78

Feist, G. J., 238*n*76
Feldman, D. C., 433*n*31
Fiechtner, B., 313*n*10
Fiedler, A., 40*n*22
Fiedler, F. E., 15, 39*n*5, 218–220, 238*n*80, 239*n*81, 240*n*100, 240*n*101, 315*n*39, 520, 535–541, 551*n*1, 553*n*30, 553*n*32, 553*n*35, 553*n*36, 553*n*39–41, 555*n*66
Field, R. H. G., 529, 552*n*18
Filipczak, B., 185*n*16
Filley, A. C., 442, 443*n*, 470*n*14
Finder, A., 265*n*
Fiorini, C., 197, 578
Fischoff, B., 40*n*18
Fisher, C. D., 433*n*28
Fisher, D. and D., 486
Fisher, R., 668, 683*n*24
Fishman, A. Y., 388*n*143
Flaubert, G., 637
Flautt, R., 276*n*84
Fleenor, J. W., 276*n*79–80
Fleishman, E. A., 39*n*11, 272*n*13, 272*n*15–16
Floor, L. G., 685*n*57
Florida, R., 239*n*90–91
Fodor, E. M., 135, 148*n*41, 605*n*139
Foldes, H. J., 604*n*136, 655*n*35
Foley, D. M., 86*n*63
Foley, E., 185*n*19
Ford, H., 58
Ford, J. D., 516*n*22, 599*n*40
Ford, J. K., 381*n*10
Ford, L. W., 599*n*40
Foushee, H. C., 8, 39*n*13
Fowler, S. W., 273*n*31
Fox, S., 604*n*135
Frank, B., 141
Franken, A., 173
Franklin, B., 54, 61, 154
French, J., 125–134, 147*n*20
Frese, M., 504*n*, 606*n*159
Freud, S., 190, 234*n*11
Freytag-Loringhoven, H. von, 19
Fried, J. M., 352*n*, 354*n*
Fried, Y., 384*n*72
Friedland, W. H., 575, 599*n*49
Friedman, M., 315*n*31
Friedman, T., 499, 500
Friman, H., 65*n*
Frisch, M. H., 315*n*31
Frost, P., 604*n*125
Frost, R., 480
Fry, L., 516*n*26

Fudge, A., 232–234
Fuld, R., 197, 612

Gabarro, J. J., 114n30
Gaddis, B., 239n92
Gailor-Loflin, H., 185n17
Galbraith, J., 516n25
Galinsky, A. D., 137, 148n49, 384n70
Galvin, B. M., 604n133
Gandhi, M., 160, 573, 575, 577
Ganster, D. C., 653n4
Garcia, J. E., 218–220, 240n100, 554n43
Garden, C., 388n143
Gardner, H., 238n67
Gardner, J. W., 78, 86n75, 119, 146n3, 151, 184n2, 262
Gardner, W. L., 185n8, 186n44, 186n47, 186n51
Garfield, S. L., 315n32
Garfunkel, A., 200
Garrod, A., 185n23
Garrod, S., 313n11
Gates, G., 239n91
Gates, W., 26, 213, 596–597
Gavin, M. B., 387n113
Gebelein, S. H., 274n39
Geher, G., 241n118
Gelade, G. A., 381n9
Geller, D., 384n78
Genghis Khan, 610
Gentry, W. A., 186n34, 274n44
Gerhardt, M. W., 234n8
Gerhart, B., 381n11
Germann, P., 273n27
Gersick, C. J. G., 397, 432n22
Gerth, H. H., 575, 599n50
Getz, A., 509n
Gewirtz, R., 384n78
Ghiselli, E. E., 238n79
Ghorpade, J., 275n71
Ghosn, C., 504
Giancola, F., 185n21
Gibb, J. R., 314n17
Gibbard, G. S., 394, 432n2
Gibbons, B., 362
Gibson, F. W., 220, 236n44, 239n82, 315n40, 684n34, 684n53, 685n60, 685n63
Gilmore, D. C., 380n13
Gilson, L. L., 239n87
Ginnett, R. C., 39n9, 392, 397, 408, 409, 410–415, 411n, 413n, 414n, 415, 416n, 419n, 421, 422, 428,

432n1, 433n23, 433n34, 433n43–44, 434n46, 434n48–49, 434n58, 435n72, 447, 470n21
Gitleson, R., 433n28
Gladwell, M., 22, 22n, 26, 26n, 502
Glibkowski, C. B., 552n10
Goethe, J. W. von, 548
Goff, M., III, 251, 273n26, 275n72
Goldsmith, J., 151, 184n4
Goldsmith, M., 272n10
Goldwyn, S., 169
Goleman, D., 222, 223n, 224–225, 227, 228, 240n104, 240n110, 240n112–113
Goodnight, J., 239n90
Goodstadt, B. E., 432n6
Goodwin, V. L., 602n87
Gordon, G. G., 83n21
Gordon, L. V., 185n7
Gordon, W. J. J., 316n56
Gordon-Terner, R., 384n78
Gore, A., 573
Graen, G. B., 40n24, 40n39, 522, 522n, 552n3, 552n4, 552n9
Graf, H., 627
Grashow, A., 518n61
Graves, S. B., 187n75
Greaves, J., 241n123
Green, S., 504n
Green, S. G., 83n12–13, 113n10, 114n25, 149n58, 681, 685n65, 685n66
Greenleaf, R. K., 170, 187n54
Greenwald, A. G., 185n25
Greer, M., 600n64
Gregory, R., 384n64
Gregory, R. A., 363n
Greguras, G. J., 275n72, 276n76
Greller, M. M., 469n7
Grey, R. J., 83n21
Griffen, M. A., 606n154
Grigorenko, E. L., 238n73–76
Grimson, S., 211
Grisham, V. L., Jr., 559n
Grojean, M. W., 598n31
Gronsky, B., 85n46, 85n54
Grover, R. A., 684n52
Gueutal, H. G., 470n17
Guigard, J. H., 238n75
Guilford, J. P., 238n77
Gupta, N., 381n15, 385n88
Gupta, V., 518n71, 519n75
Gurin, G., 685n57
Gustafson, D. H., 316n53

Guth, C. K., 297, 314n23
Guzzo, R. A., 434n62
Gwinner, K. P., 386n112

Habbel, R., 653n13
Hackman, J. R., 394, 409, 411, 412, 428, 433n23, 433n29, 433n32–33, 433n42, 433–434n45, 434n51, 434n53, 434n63, 435n71, 516n16, 673, 683n32
Haggard, T., 646
Haidt, J., 186n32
Hakala, T. L., 340
Halberstam, D., 168, 186n43
Hall, A., 386n100
Hall, D., 316n51
Hall, J., 152, 185n6
Hallam, G. L., 408, 428, 433n40, 435n73
Hallenbeck, G. S., 599n44
Halpin, A. W., 272n14
Halverson, K. C., 605n137
Hambrick, D. C., 83n22
Hammer, T. H., 517n38
Haney, C., 399n, 433n25
Hanges, P. J., 333n, 381n20, 517n43, 518n71, 519n75, 600n71
Hannum, K., 275n64
Harding, F. D., 39n11
Harkins, S., 432n13
Harold, C. M., 389n150
Harper, R., 316n50
Harris, L. S., 274n44
Harris, M. H., 236n33
Harrison, E. L., 470n12
Hartel, C. E. J., 241n124
Harter, J. K., 387n116, 561n
Hartke, D. D., 554n42, 554n44
Hartman, J. J., 394, 432n2
Harvey, J. B., 314n20
Haslam, S. A., 42n63
Hass, J. W., 85n46, 85n54
Hassan, F., 504n
Hastings, M., 641n
Hayes, N. J., 313n8
Haynes, A., 406
Haynes Slowik, L., 384n72
Hazucha, J. F., 84n38, 115n44, 250, 266–267, 273n25, 276n87, 654n31
Heifetz, R. A., 483–484, 499–501, 516n27–28, 518n61, 518n64, 557, 597n5, 598n23
Heinitz, K., 606n157

Heinlein, R., 348
Hellervik, L. W., 115*n*47, 314*n*15
Helmreich, R., 433*n*43, 434*n*58
Hemphill, J. K., 272*n*11–12
Henderson, D. J., 552*n*10
Henle, C. A., 387*n*114
Henley, W., 509
Hennessey, H. W., 516*n*31
Henry, P., 152
Henry II, 405
Herman, C. P., 84*n*36
Hernandez, M., 430–431
Hernez-Broome, G., 84*n*33
Herold, D. M., 470*n*13
Herrnstein, R. J., 237*n*60
Hersey, P., 516*n*14–15, 531, 531*n*, 533,
    541, 553*n*25, 553*n*37–38
Herz, J. A., 114*n*22
Herzberg, F., 373*n*, 373–374,
    388*n*138–140
Hesketh, B., 274*n*40
Heskett, J. L., 181, 187*n*76
Hesse, H., 170
Hewlett, S. A., 381*n*13, 383*n*62
Hezlett, S. A., 84*n*38, 115*n*44, 115*n*46,
    276*n*77
Hicks, M. D., 66, 69, 70*n*, 72*n*, 84*n*37,
    84*n*40, 85*n*47, 85*n*51, 85*n*53,
    106, 108*n*, 110*n*, 114*n*41–42,
    462–463, 464*n*, 471*n*41
Hill, N., 146*n*1, 344
Himle, D., 315*n*47
Hinds, P., 435*n*68
Hinkin, T. R., 134, 146*n*4, 146*n*13,
    147*n*34
Hirschhorn, L., 599*n*39
Hitler, A., 8, 573, 582, 610
Hofstede, G. H., 314*n*14, 518*n*73
Hogan, J. C., 39*n*10, 40*n*27, 113*n*7,
    187*n*57, 200, 234*n*5, 234*n*10,
    235*n*17, 236*n*34, 236*n*37,
    238*n*65, 383*n*60, 515*n*2, 606*n*63,
    622*n*, 624, 642, 654*n*33, 655*n*43,
    655*n*50, 656*n*57
Hogan, R. T., 7, 7*n*, 39*n*10, 40*n*27,
    75*n*, 84*n*26, 113*n*7, 114*n*37,
    187*n*57–60, 200, 221, 221*n*,
    234*n*5–6, 234*n*10, 235*n*13,
    235*n*15–16, 236*n*30, 236*n*32,
    236*n*34, 236*n*37, 238*n*63, 238*n*65,
    243*n*, 254, 272*n*2, 272*n*7–8,
    273*n*34, 274*n*41, 274*n*51, 312,
    312*n*, 314*n*28, 339*n*, 363*n*,
    365*n*, 372*n*, 381*n*18, 382*n*40–41,

383*n*45–46, 383*n*57, 383*n*60,
    384*n*64, 470*n*22, 515*n*2, 598*n*28,
    599*n*37, 606*n*64, 606*n*163, 610,
    612*n*, 618*n*, 622*n*, 624, 626, 630*n*,
    633*n*, 636*n*, 639*n*, 642, 653*n*,
    653*n*3, 653*n*7–8, 654*n*33, 655*n*43,
    655*n*50–51, 656*n*55–57
Holding, R., 243
Holland, B., 235*n*17
Hollander, E. P., 15, 15*n*, 40*n*23,
    40*n*31, 147*n*36, 320, 323, 380*n*3,
    386*n*101
Hollenback, J., 385*n*90
Hollenbeck, G. P., 273*n*28
Hollensbe, E. C., 389*n*149
Holt, K. E., 266–267, 276*n*87
Holtz, B. C., 389*n*150
Hom, P. W., 387*n*123–124
Hoobler, J., 382*n*31
Hooijberg, R., 602*n*100
Hoover, J. E., 122
Hoppock, R., 382*n*28
Horth, D. M., 603*n*107
Hosking, D. M., 39*n*7
Hough, L. E., 235*n*27
Hough, L. M., 199*n*, 234*n*6, 381*n*21,
    553*n*23, 553*n*27, 555*n*63
House, R. J., 146*n*6, 276*n*86, 433*n*26–27,
    469*n*4, 510*n*, 511*n*, 516*n*17,
    518*n*68, 518*n*71–72, 519*n*74–75,
    519*n*77, 542, 554*n*54, 555*n*67,
    578, 580, 600*n*71, 601*n*80,
    602*n*95–97, 603*n*109, 604*n*124,
    605*n*139, 606*n*166
Howard, A. 113*n*16–17
Howard, R., 218
Howell, J. M., 255*n*, 604*n*125–26
Howell, J. P., 516*n*18
Huber, V. L., 684*n*52
Huberman, J., 684*n*44
Hughes, M. W., 57*n*
Hughes, R. L., 65*n*, 84*n*33
Hui, C. S., 475
Hulin, C. L., 382*n*29, 469*n*2
Hunt, J. G., 39*n*7, 40*n*24, 114*n*23,
    272*n*13, 479, 516*n*13, 516*n*17,
    552*n*3, 552*n*21, 554*n*54, 555*n*59,
    555*n*67, 578, 600*n*67–68,
    602*n*98, 602*n*101, 605*n*142
Hunt, J. T., 554*n*47
Hunter, J. E., 85*n*49, 112*n*5, 237*n*48,
    380*n*1, 471*n*42
Huselid, M. A., 333*n*, 380*n*4, 383*n*44,
    654*n*26

Hussein, S., 221, 610
Husserl, J., 333*n*
Huxley, T., 529
Huy, Q. N., 599*n*35
Hyne, S., 368*n*, 382*n*26, 388*n*131,
    434*n*57

Iacocca, L., 613
Iaffaldano, M. T., 383*n*49
Icahn, C., 620
Ilies, R., 234*n*7–8, 237*n*53, 239*n*85,
    251, 273*n*21, 382*n*33, 383*n*56,
    388*n*133–134, 388*n*136, 600*n*62
Imai, M., 384*n*75
Immelt, J., 504, 504*n*
Inbar, M., 384*n*78
Indik, B. P., 432*n*10
Ingrassia, P., 221*n*
Instone, D., 605*n*150
Ivancevich, J. M., 314*n*27, 385*n*81,
    677, 683*n*33, 684*n*35, 684*n*41,
    684*n*45, 685*n*68
Ivan the Terrible, 610
Ivery, M., 381*n*9
Ivins, M., 584, 612

Jackman, J. M., 275*n*61
Jackson, J., 151
Jackson, Peter, 6, 152
Jackson, Phil, 392, 392*n*
Jackson, R., 195
Jacobs, F. N., 550–551
Jacobs, T. O., 39*n*11, 252*n*
Jaffe, D., 399*n*, 433*n*25
Jago, A. G., 41*n*47, 529, 552*n*19–20,
    554*n*48–51
Jamal, M., 315*n*36, 433*n*24
Janis, I. L., 83*n*20, 403–404, 404*n*,
    433*n*35
Javidan, M., 504*n*, 518*n*68, 518*n*71,
    519*n*75, 601*n*84
Jayaratne, S., 315*n*47
Jellison, J., 565
Jenkins, G. D., 385*n*88
Jennings, G., 83*n*23
Jensen, M., 385*n*89
Jerdee, T. H., 113*n*14
Jermier, J. M., 489, 489*n*, 516*n*19,
    555*n*57
Jesus Christ, 160, 170–171, 573, 577
Joan of Arc, 573, 577
Jobs, S., 60
Jogulu, U. D., 518*n*67
Johns, G., 358, 386*n*102

Johnson, C., 654*n*22
Johnson, C. E., 181, 187*n*66, 187*n*67
Johnson, D., 531*n*
Johnson, D. E., 605*n*137
Johnson, J., 266, 276*n*82
Johnson, K., 266, 276*n*82
Johnson, L. B., 132–133
Johnson, S. K., 605*n*138
Johnston, J. M., 684*n*38
Jones, A. P., 679, 685*n*55
Jones, C., 148*n*54
Jones, D., 339*n*, 653*n*15
Jones, E. E., 53*n*, 83*n*11, 83*n*15
Jones, J., 8, 133, 611
Jones, J. E., 443*n*, 470*n*14
Jones, M., 646
Jones, S., 380*n*2, 619
Jong-Il, K., 221, 250, 583, 610, 612
Jonson, B., 74
Jordan, M., 392
Jordan, P. J., 241*n*124
Joseph, D. L., 240*n*116
Judge, T. A., 234*n*7–8, 235*n*26, 235*n*28, 236*n*35, 237*n*53–54, 273*n*21, 276*n*77, 382*n*25, 382*n*33, 383*n*56, 388*n*133–136, 601*n*85, 604*n*122, 606*n*158, 606*n*162
Judiesch, M. K., 85*n*49, 380*n*1, 471*n*42
Jung, C. G., 202, 236*n*38
Jung, D. I., 601*n*83, 603*n*119–120
Justice, A., 315*n*33

Kaiser, R. B., 273*n*37, 274*n*53, 380*n*4, 381*n*18, 599*n*42, 622*n*, 624, 653*n*3, 654*n*33
Kamprad, I., 513–515
Kanfer, R., 381*n*21, 552*n*6
Kanouse, D. E., 83*n*11
Kant, I., 151, 165
Kanter, K., 250, 273*n*25
Kanter, R. M., 40*n*29, 311, 313*n*6, 316*n*58, 357, 358, 358*n*, 557, 575, 597*n*6–7, 599*n*51, 683*n*20
Kanungo, R. N., 578, 580, 602*n*94, 605*n*139, 683*n*19
Kaplan, R. S., 349, 349*n*, 485–486, 516*n*30
Karamanlis, C., 194
Kark, R., 604*n*130
Karp, D. A., 121*n*
Katz, D., 685*n*57

Katzenbach, J. R., 416, 434*n*56, 672–673, 683*n*30
Kaufman, J. C., 238*n*74
Kay, M., 346
Kaye, B., 335
Kazdin, A. E., 684*n*37
Kehoe, J., 274*n*40
Keidel, R. W., 476
Keller, R. T., 601*n*86, 602*n*88, 679, 684*n*49–50
Kellerman, B., 318, 320, 323, 380*n*10, 551*n*2, 611, 653*n*5
Kelley, H. H., 83*n*11
Kelley, R. E., 21, 21*n*, 103, 114*n*31, 320, 323, 380*n*8
Kelloway, E. K., 593, 606*n*160–161
Kelly, E. M., 4
Kelly, K., 224*n*
Kennedy, J. C., 504*n*
Kennedy, J. F., 45, 577
Kennedy, J. K., 536, 553*n*34, 554*n*45
Kepes, S., 653*n*4
Kerr, S., 354, 354*n*, 384*n*71, 489, 489*n*, 516*n*19, 554*n*47, 555*n*57, 555*n*59
Kerr, W., 516*n*26
Kerry, J., 583
Kersting, L. M., 238*n*71
Ketchen, D., 386*n*100
Kets de Vries, M. F. R., 602*n*102, 683*n*12
Kettering, C. F., 58
Keys, B., 148*n*54–55, 149*n*60
Khaire, M., 217*n*, 239*n*95
Khazanchi, S., 389*n*149
Khomeini, Ayatollah, 573, 575
Khurana, R., 197*n*, 602*n*91
Kidder, D. L., 384*n*74, 386*n*110
Kidder, R., 164–165, 186*n*35
Kiesler, S., 435*n*68
Kiewitz, C., 381*n*19
Kilmann, R. H., 490*n*, 490–491, 517*n*47
Ki-Moon, B., 250
King, A. W., 273*n*31
King, M. L., Jr., 7, 9, 320, 573, 575, 577, 580, 582, 613
King, S. N., 56*n*
Kipnis, D. S., 137–138, 148*n*51, 148*n*53, 148*n*57, 149*n*59, 432*n*6, 432*n*7
Kirkman, B. L., 552*n*6
Kleiman, C., 388*n*132
Klein, J., 566

Klein, K. E., 654*n*17
Klein, K. J., 604*n*128
Klein, S. B., 147*n*28
Kleiner, K., 20, 20*n*
Klerk, F. W. de, 574
Klimoski, R. J., 313*n*8
Klinger, R. L., 237*n*54
Knapp, M. L., 313*n*7
Knight, P. A., 382*n*24
Kocourek, P., 653*n*13
Koene, B. A. S., 381*n*8
Koestner, R., 147*n*26
Kohl, H., 191
Kohlberg, L., 158, 159*n*, 185*n*22
Kohls, L. R., 518*n*69
Kolb, D. A., 82*n*5, 185*n*9
Kolditz, T., 478, 478*n*
Komacki, J. L., 385*n*89, 469*n*8
Konrad, A. M., 42*n*62
Koonce, B. A., 115*n*46
Koopman, P. L., 606*n*153
Koppelar, L., 147*n*19, 315*n*41
Korb, L. J., 147*n*27
Korda, M., 13
Koresh, D., 573, 611, 613
Korn, W. S., 41*n*59
Kossler, M., 434*n*65
Kotter, J. P., 114*n*30, 181, 187*n*76, 557, 598*n*11, 654*n*25
Kottler, P., 187*n*74
Kouzes, J. M., 41*n*42, 114*n*35, 278, 313*n*2–3, 518*n*51
Koys, D. J., 333*n*, 380*n*6
Kozlowski, S. W. J., 517*n*42, 517*n*45
Kramer, S. J., 239*n*84, 345*n*
Krayer, J. J., 313*n*10
Kreitner, R., 385*n*91
Krile, J. E., 260*n*, 274*n*46, 470*n*24, 557, 567, 597*n*8, 682*n*4
Kroll, F. G., 504*n*
Krug, J. A., 386*n*105
Kruger, J., 635, 655*n*46
Kübler-Ross, E., 599*n*41
Kucine, I., 276*n*84
Kummerow, J. M., 236*n*41
Kuncel, N. R., 215*n*
Kurke, L. B., 517*n*34

Labak, A. S., 605*n*151
Ladd, E. C., 185*n*20
Ladd, R. T., 113*n*11, 471*n*34, 471*n*36, 471*n*38
Ladkin, D. 65*n*

Lall, R., 86*n*64
Landauer, S., 384*n*71
Larsen, J. K., 314*n*13
Larson, J. R., Jr., 470*n*11
Larson, L. L., 40*n*24, 516*n*17, 552*n*3, 552*n*21, 554*n*47, 554*n*54, 555*n*59, 555*n*67
Latack, J. C., 315*n*34
Latane, B., 432*n*13
Latham, G. P., 113*n*18, 347–348, 381*n*22, 383*n*50, 384*n*66, 384*n*68–69, 469*n*3, 469*n*5–6
Lauer, M., 475
Laurie, D. L., 557, 598*n*23
Lauterbach, K. E., 140*n*
Law, K. S., 241*n*125, 382*n*35
Lay, K., 180
Layden, F., 211
Lazarsfeld, P. E., 40*n*20
Le, H., 237*n*52
Leana, C. R., 113*n*12, 470*n*28
Leatherwood, M. L., 470*n*13
Lee, C., 516*n*26
Lee, D., 587
Lee, N., 187*n*74
Lee, T. W., 469*n*5
Lee, W., 561*n*
LeFevre, A., 185*n*19
Lenin, V. I., 119, 573, 576
Lentz, E., 86*n*67–68, 86*n*72–73
LePine, M. A., 605*n*137
Lepsinger, R., 148*n*52
Leslie, J. B., 274*n*44, 621, 654*n*34
Levanoni, E., 41*n*40, 433*n*26
Levin, S., 603*n*104
Levina, N., 146*n*8
Levine, D. S., 364, 386*n*109
Levitt, S. D., 354*n*
Lewicki, R. J., 382*n*34, 388*n*141
Lewin, K., 572, 572*n*
Lewis, K., 197
Liberman, Y., 384*n*78
Liden, R. C., 552*n*10
Lieb, P., 42*n*62
Lievens, F., 236*n*33
Lievens, P., 273*n*30
Light, G., 83*n*17
Likert, R., 273*n*18
Lima, L., 86*n*67
Lincoln, A., 175, 192, 197, 338, 501
Lind, M., 518*n*60
Linden, R. C., 552*n*4–5, 552*n*7
Lindsley, D. H., 434*n*61
Linn, R. L., 237*n*49

Linsky, M., 516*n*28, 518*n*61, 557, 597*n*5
Linville, P. W., 316*n*49
Lipman-Blumen, J., 20*n*, 187*n*52
Lipnack, J., 435*n*66, 435*n*69
Lippitt, R., 41*n*43
Lirtzman, S. I., 433*n*27
Litzky, B. E., 384*n*74, 386*n*110
Liu, W., 603*n*114
Liu, Y., 386*n*100
Lloyd, J., 617*n*
Lobo, M. S., 214*n*
Locke, E. A., 347–348, 381*n*22, 383*n*50, 384*n*66–67, 384*n*69, 384*n*73, 384*n*79, 386*n*97, 388*n*135, 469*n*5–6
Locke, J., 112*n*4
Lockwood, A., 86*n*69
Lombardo, M. M., 82*n*4, 86*n*76, 114*n*34, 115*n*48, 147*n*37, 471*n*39, 622, 654*n*29, 654*n*32
London, M., 274*n*55, 276*n*84, 276*n*85
Long, H., 8
Longfellow, H. W., 3
Loong, L. H., 144–146
Lopez, S., 186*n*49
Lord, R. G., 40*n*28, 234*n*4, 603*n*105, 604*n*129
Loughlin, C., 606*n*160
Louiselle, K., 253*n*, 264*n*, 274*n*38
Lovell, J., 482–483
Lowe, K. B., 603*n*120
Lowin, A., 113*n*13
Lubart, T. I., 238*n*72, 238*n*75
Lublin, J. S., 352*n*, 354*n*
Lucia, T., 148*n*52
Lucier, C., 653*n*13
Lund, D. R., 260*n*, 274*n*46, 470*n*24, 557, 597*n*8, 682*n*4
Luthans, F., 185*n*8, 314*n*13, 350, 353, 385*n*85–86, 385*n*91, 516*n*31, 684*n*43
Lykken, D. T., 40*n*21
Lyle, R. J., 613*n*

Maccoby, M., 185*n*14
Maccoby, N., 685*n*57
Macey, W. H., 561*n*
Machiavelli, N., 118, 210, 556
MacIntosh, B., 470*n*17
MacKinnon, D. W., 186*n*34
MacLeish, A., 67
Macrorie, K., 41*n*41
Madonna, 213

Magee, J. C., 137, 148*n*49
Mahsud, R., 599*n*43
Maitland, A., 510*n*
Majchrzak, A., 435*n*69
Malhotra, A., 435*n*69
Malone, D. M., 114*n*22
Malone, T. W., 65*n*, 254–255, 274*n*43
Mandela, N., 25, 375, 509, 573, 574
Mann, D. D., 394, 432*n*2
Mann, R. D., 234*n*3
Mao Zedong, 573, 576, 610, 612
Marcus, B., 387*n*117, 624
Marcus, J. T., 600*n*57
Marcus, R., 557, 598*n*15
Marcus Aurelius,, 390
Marcy, R. T., 186*n*34
Markham, S., E., 385*n*84
Marks, M., 504*n*
Marks, M. L., 598*n*32
Marr, M., 224*n*
Martin, A., 501*n*
Martin, R., 604*n*131
Martorana, P. V., 197*n*
Maslow, A. H., 169, 341–342, 344, 360, 383*n*51
Massey, M., 185*n*15
Masterson, S. S., 389*n*149
Mathis, J., 386*n*99
Matson, E., 380*n*2
Maxwell, J., 195
May, D., 185*n*8
Mayer, J. D., 222–223, 223*n*, 225, 227, 240*n*105–106, 240*n*111, 241*n*117
Mayer, R. C., 387*n*113
Mayo, E., 432*n*18
Mayo, M. C., 605*n*145
Mayseless, O., 605*n*140
McCall, M. W., Jr., 45, 82*n*3–4, 86*n*76, 114*n*34, 147*n*37, 273*n*28, 471*n*39, 622, 654*n*29
McCanse, A. A., 251*n*, 273*n*23
McCauley, C. D., 84*n*39, 276*n*80, 314*n*25, 622, 654*n*32
McCaulley, B. H., 236*n*42, 516*n*20
McChrystal, S., 641
McClelland, D. C., 135–137, 142, 147*n*38, 148*n*39, 148*n*42–43, 148*n*47, 344, 383*n*54
McCloy, R. A., 683*n*28
McCormick, J., 314*n*30
McCown, C. P., 684*n*34, 684*n*53, 685*n*60, 685*n*63
McCrae, R. R., 235*n*23
McDonough, J. M., 503*n*

McElroy, J. C., 386n104
McFarlin, D. B., 381n12
McGhee, D. E., 185n25
McGrath, J. E., 410–411, 415, 434n50, 434n55
McGregor, D., 151, 184n5
McKay, M., 316n52
McKee, A., 224–225, 240n112–113
McKee, G. H., 385n84
McKee, R., 603n106
McLean, G., 559
McNamara, R., 168
McNatt, D. B., 384n80
McNulty, E., 557, 597n4
Mead, M., 259
Mease, B., 348, 561
Meindl, J. R., 11n, 39n2, 605n145
Melland, D., 504n
Menkes, J., 237n59
Merkel, A., 191
Merton, R. K., 39n6, 515n10
Metcalf, S., 211
Metts, V., 113n11, 471n34, 471n36, 471n38
Meuter, M. L., 386n112
Meyer, J. P., 387n118
Milgram, S., 124, 124n, 131, 319
Milkovich, G. T., 385n87
Miller, D. T., 83n10, 471n29, 683n12
Miller, G., 316n51
Miller, G. R., 313n7
Miller, J. S., 85n60, 86n71
Miller, T., 148n54
Miller, W. R., 84n35
Millier, J., 85n56
Mills, C. W., 575, 599n50
Milner, C., 600n59
Milosevic, S., 573
Mims, V., 147n26
Miner, J. B., 136–137, 148n44–45, 552n21
Minton, J. W., 388n141
Mintzberg, H., 45
Mio, J. S., 603n104
Mirvis, P. H., 598n32
Misangyi, V. F., 602n92, 605n137, 605n148
Mitchell, T. R., 52, 83n12–14, 544, 545n, 554n55, 681, 685n65–67
Mitra, A., 385n88
Moneta, G. B., 239n84
Mooney, C. H., 381n14
Moore, L. I., 40n38

Morales, E., 583
Morgeson, F. P., 274n54
Morrel-Samuels, P., 387n126
Morris, J. H., 313n9
Morrison, A. M., 41n56, 82n4, 86n76, 314n28, 471n39, 517n35, 622, 655n38
Morrison, J., 312, 312n
Morrow, B., 84n41
Morrow, J. E., 84n39
Morrow, P. C., 386n104
Morse, G., 517n35
Morse, J. J., 682n6
Moscoso, S., 237n58
Mount, M. K., 235n22, 266–267, 276n77, 276n87, 383n55, 387n116
Mountbatten, L., 160
Mouton, J. S., 250, 273n24, 683n26
Mowday, R. T., 382n23
Muchinsky, P. M., 383n49
Mueller, J. I., 407
Mueller, R., 41n54
Muensterberger, W., 599n55
Mugabe, R., 573, 576, 610, 611
Muhammad, 573
Mulcahy, A., 208
Mulder, M., 147n19, 315n41
Mumford, M. D., 39n11, 239n92, 600n65, 603n103
Mumsford, T. V., 274n54
Munz, D. C., 600n61
Murkison, G., 148n55
Muros, J. P., 604n136, 606n158
Murphy, A. J., 515n4
Murphy, S. E., 84n28, 223n, 237n47, 239n81, 240n111
Murray, B., 602n87
Murray, C., 237n60
Musab, A., 641
Musgrave, T., 243
Muskie, E., 141
Mycielska, K., 83n8
Myers, I. B., 236n42, 516n20
Myers, K. D., 203, 236n40
Myers, M., 558
Myers, P. B., 203, 236n40

Nadler, D. A., 653n12
Nagarajan, N. J., 602n93
Naidoo, L. J., 603n105
Nanus, B., 39n14, 313n5, 557, 598n16
Napoleon Bonaparte, 117, 610

Neal, D., 65n
Near, J. P., 381n14
Neilson, G. L., 653n16
Nelson, J., 146n9
Nelson, S. M., 385n94, 684n46, 684n51
Nemanich, L. A., 602n88
Nevins, M., 84n32
Nevitt, C., 211
Newman, D. A., 240n116
Ng, K. Y., 388n145
Nierenberg, A., 369
Nilsen, D. L., 214, 250, 266, 273n25, 368, 383n61, 434n57, 593n, 606n165, 635, 655n47
Nisbett, R. E., 83n11
Noel, J., 257n, 258, 274n45, 382n42, 655n40
Nooyi, I., 258
North, O., 405
Norton, D. P., 349, 349n, 485–486, 516n30
Novak, M. A., 40n39
Nowack, K. M., 275n56

Obama, B., 190, 244, 583, 584, 586, 613, 614, 641
O'Brien, B., 174, 187n61
Odbert, H. S., 235n19
O'Driscoll, T., 65n
Offermann, L. R., 40n31, 147n36, 386n101, 601n76
Oh, I., 237n52
Ohlott, P. J., 55n, 56n, 84n39
Oldfield, M., 38, 375
Oldham, G. R., 516n16
Omilusik, W., 84n41
Ones, D. S., 235n28, 655n35
Oppler, S. A., 113n6
Oppler, S. H., 683n28
Ordonez, L. D., 384n70
O'Reilly, B., 173
O'Reilly, C. A., 314n22
O'Reilly, J. B., 58
Organ, D. W., 386n111
Orlikowski, W. J., 146n8, 254–255, 274n43
Osborn, A. F., 310n
Osborn, R. N., 479, 516n13
Osland, J., 185n9
Osten, K. D., 236n31, 383n58
Ostroff, C., 276n78–79
Ostroff, F., 557, 597n9
Oswald, F. L., 199n, 235n27

O'Toole, J., 557, 567, 597*n*2
Ouchi, W. G., 682*n*8
Owens, P. D., 197*n*

Pace, L. A., 442, 443*n*, 470*n*14
Padilla, A., 653*n*3
Page, R. C., 517*n*32, 587
Palin, S., 578, 583
Palus, C. J., 603*n*107
Panzer, K., 56*n*
Parameshwar, S., 600*n*63
Parke, R. D., 678, 684*n*40
Parker, C. P., 385*n*96
Parker, D. A., 241*n*117
Parks, M. R., 313*n*7
Parrott, S. A., 41*n*59
Parsons, C. K., 470*n*13
Pass, I., 384*n*78
Pasternak, B. A., 653*n*16
Pastor, J. C., 605*n*145
Paterno, J., 415
Patterson, M., 381*n*16
Patton, G. K., 382*n*25
Patton, G. S., 209, 583
Pauling, L., 213
Pawar, B. S., 605*n*143
Pearlman, K., 274*n*40
Peiperl, M. A., 275*n*62
Penner, D. D., 114*n*22
Person, H. S., 515*n*5, 515*n*8
Peter, L. J., 181, 484
Peters, L. H., 554*n*42, 554*n*44
Peters, T. J., 147*n*23, 387*n*120, 515*n*1,
        632, 682*n*9
Peterson, D. B., 67, 68, 69, 70*n*, 72, 74*n*,
        84*n*40, 84*n*42, 85*n*47, 85*n*51,
        85*n*53, 85*n*56, 85*n*58, 106,
        108*n*, 110*n*, 114*n*41–43, 115*n*45,
        273*n*36, 462–463, 464*n*, 471*n*41
Peterson, K., 185*n*18
Peterson, M. D., 84*n*37
Peterson, R. S., 197*n*
Peterson, S., 186*n*44, 186*n*47
Peterson, T. O., 384*n*76
Petkewicz, Z., 475–476
Petraeus, D., 338, 499–500
Pfau, B. N., 383*n*43
Pfau, K., 265, 276*n*74
Pfeffer, J., 147*n*37, 515*n*11
Pfeiffer, J. W., 443*n*, 470*n*14
Philips, P., 470*n*19
Picano, J. J., 85*n*57
Piccolo, R. F., 251, 273*n*21, 601*n*85,
        606*n*158

Pienaar, F., 509
Pillai, R., 603*n*120
Pilliod, C., 139
Pink, D., 262
Pinochet, A., 337
Piraro, D., 16, 16*n*
Pirozzolo, F. J., 223*n*, 237*n*47, 239*n*81,
        240*n*111
Pirsico, J., 83*n*6
Podsakoff, P. M., 113*n*19, 134,
        147*n*33, 385*n*92–93,
        517*n*37, 684*n*47, 684*n*52,
        685*n*58
Pohlmann, J. T., 554*n*42, 554*n*44
Polivy, J., 84*n*36
Polk, T., 211
Pol Pot, 610
Pomerleau, O. F., 315*n*32
Popper, M., 603*n*108, 603*n*110,
        605*n*140
Porras, J. I., 557, 598*n*19
Porter, C. O. L. H., 388*n*145
Porter, D. A., 114*n*26
Porter, D. B., 432*n*14
Posner, B. Z., 41*n*42, 114*n*35, 278,
        313*n*2–3, 518*n*51
Post, C., 388*n*143
Post, J. M., 644
Poteet, M. L., 86*n*67
Potter, F. H., III, 320–324, 328–329,
        380*n*11
Pound, R., 598*n*33
Powell, B., 314*n*30
Powell, C., 48–49, 83*n*6, 220, 332
Powell, L., 566
Presley, E., 559
Prestridge, S., 434*n*65
Price, T. L., 600*n*60
Prien, E. P., 274*n*40
Prince, G. M., 240*n*99
Prince, H. T., 161, 161*n*, 605*n*150
Pritchard, R. D., 385*n*90
Pritchett, P., 557, 581, 597*n*3,
        598*n*33
Prusak, L., 380*n*2
Pugh, D. S., 333*n*
Pugh, S. D., 380*n*7
Pulakos, E. D., 113*n*6, 114*n*28
Pulley, M. L., 603*n*107
Puranam, P., 601*n*80

Quaglieri, P. L., 470*n*16
Quayle, D., 315*n*35, 315*n*37
Quenk, N. L., 236*n*39, 236*n*41

Quinn, R. E., 385*n*95, 495, 496*n*,
        518*n*55
Quinn, R. P., 382*n*30

Raddatz, M., 245*n*
Rafferty, A. E., 606*n*154
Ragan, J. W., 314*n*27, 554*n*48–51
Ragins, B. R., 85*n*60, 86*n*71, 146*n*10
Raines, C., 185*n*16
Ramirez, G. G., 601*n*80
Ramstad, P. M., 562, 624, 654*n*27,
        683*n*29
Randolph, W. A., 386*n*98
Rapp, A., 386*n*99
Rasch, R., 622, 655*n*39
Raven, B. H., 125–134, 147*n*20
Read, P. P., 2–3, 39*n*1
Reagan, R., 332
Reason, J., 83*n*8
Reese, R., 603*n*104
Reeves, B., 65*n*
Regan, D. T., 27
Reich, W., 186*n*37
Reichard, R., 187*n*52
Reilly, R. R., 274*n*55, 401–402, 433*n*30
Reiter, M., 272*n*10
Reiter-Palmon, R., 239*n*85
Remington, F., 499
Remland, M. S., 314*n*12
Rest, J., 185*n*23
Restubog, S. L. D., 380*n*6
Revere, P., 22
Rhoades, L., 273*n*22
Rice, R. W., 554*n*46, 605*n*150
Rich, S., 40*n*21
Richards, H. S., 491
Ricks, T., 499
Rigby, D., 386*n*108
Riggio, R. E., 20*n*, 58, 59, 84*n*27,
        84*n*28, 187*n*52, 223*n*, 237*n*47,
        239*n*81, 240*n*111, 583*n*,
        603*n*104
Rippen, T., 654*n*28
Ritchie, J. E., Jr., 42*n*62
Rizzo, J. R., 433*n*27
Roach, C. F., 39*n*7
Robbins, S. P., 314*n*16, 433*n*39,
        517*n*36, 682*n*10, 683*n*16
Roberson, L., 387*n*123–124
Roberson, Q., 389*n*148
Roberts, B., 591
Roberts, B. W., 187*n*57, 234*n*10,
        235*n*13
Roberts, N. C., 683*n*19

Robie, C., 250, 273*n*25, 275*n*72, 276*n*76
Robinson, C. B., 381*n*16
Rock, D., 557, 597*n*10
Rode, J. C., 381*n*14
Rodin, J., 315*n*32
Roellig, M. E., 88, 112*n*1, 272*n*6, 345, 347, 347*n*, 372*n*, 380*n*12, 598*n*29, 630
Roellig, R. M., 656*n*53
Rogers, C., 169, 186*n*48
Rogers, G., 211
Rogers, W., 50, 210
Roglio, K. D., 83*n*17
Rokeach, M., 153*n*, 185*n*10
Rolland, J. P., 237*n*58
Rollnick, S., 84*n*35
Romero, E. J., 255*n*
Roosevelt, T., 69, 468
Rose, P., 343
Rosen, B., 113*n*14, 552*n*6
Rosenbach, W. E., 320–324, 328–329, 380*n*11
Rosener, J. B., 31–33, 41*n*57, 601*n*73
Rosenkranz, S. A., 516*n*31
Ross, L., 83*n*9
Ross, M., 83*n*10
Ross, S. M., 601*n*76
Rowold, J., 606*n*157
Rubin, I. M., 185*n*9
Rubin, R. S., 381*n*14, 600*n*61
Rude, S. N., 386*n*104
Ruderman, M. N., 56*n*, 84*n*39, 654*n*32
Rudin, S., 224
Ruiz-Quintanilla, S. A., 600*n*71
Rumsfeld, D., 212, 252
Rupp, D. E., 382*n*32
Rush, A., 270–271
Russell, J. M., 685*n*54
Russell, L. A., 654*n*24
Rutan, B., 375
Ruvolo, C. M., 599*n*34
Ryan, B. 126
Ryan, E. M., 147*n*26
Ryan, K., 386*n*111
Ryan, M. K., 42*n*63

Saal, F. E., 382*n*24
Saavedra, R., 241*n*121
Sadler, P. J., 314*n*14
Sager, C. E., 683*n*28
Sala, F., 255*n*, 275*n*63, 275*n*66
Salancik, G. R., 515*n*11
Salas, E., 434*n*52

Saleh, D. H., 41*n*40
Sales, C. A., 41*n*40
Salgado, J. F., 200, 236*n*29, 237*n*58
Salomon-Segev, I., 384*n*78
Salovey, P., 222–223, 223*n*, 225, 227, 240*n*105–106, 240*n*111, 241*n*117
Salvaggio, A. N., 333*n*, 381*n*20, 517*n*43
Sample, S. B., 527
Samples, K. R., 613*n*
Sanchez, J. I., 273*n*30, 274*n*40
Sandberg, J., 214*n*
Sanford, A., 313*n*11
Sarkozy, N., 334
Sax, L. J., 41*n*59
Saxton, M. J., 490*n*, 490–491, 517*n*47
Scandura, T. A., 40*n*39, 552*n*8
Scarr, S., 207, 237*n*49
Schaffer, J., 237*n*52
Schanke Aasland, M., 653*n*2
Schatzel, E. A., 239*n*84
Schaubroeck, J., 653*n*4
Schein, E. H., 83*n*24, 491, 517*n*40, 517*n*48, 518*n*52
Schein, V. E., 29, 41*n*52–55
Schellenbarger, S., 362, 387*n*121
Schleicher, D. J., 275*n*72
Schlesinger, A. Jr., 132
Schmidt, A. M., 381*n*10
Schmidt, E., 244
Schmidt, F. L., 85*n*49, 112*n*4, 237*n*48, 237*n*52, 380*n*1, 471*n*42, 561*n*
Schmidt, S. M., 148*n*51, 148*n*53, 148*n*57, 432*n*7
Schmidt, W. H., 682*n*5, 683*n*13
Schmitt, N., 683*n*28
Schnake, M. E., 679, 685*n*59, 685*n*62
Schneider, B., 115*n*44, 333*n*, 381*n*20, 517*n*43, 561*n*
Schneider, J., 515*n*7
Schneider, R. J., 84*n*38
Schoenborn, S., 606*n*159
Schonpflug, W., 220, 240*n*102
Schriesheim, C. A., 39*n*7, 114*n*23, 134, 146*n*4, 146*n*13, 147*n*33–34, 187*n*71, 516*n*13, 552*n*8, 554*n*47, 555*n*58–59, 555*n*61, 602*n*98, 602*n*101
Schuler, H., 387*n*117
Schuler, R. S., 113*n*19, 433*n*26
Schuller, R. H., 476
Schultz, H., 14
Schultz, P. L., 603*n*113
Schurer Lambert, L., 387*n*114
Schwartz, J., 557, 597*n*10

Schwartz, J. L. K., 185*n*25
Schwartz, T., 241*n*119
Schwarzkopf, N., 243, 339
Schweiger, D. M., 314*n*27
Schweitzer, M. E., 384*n*70
Scott, B. A., 382*n*33
Scott, G. M., 239*n*92
Scott, K. D., 382*n*29, 385*n*84
Scott, K. S., 381*n*11
Scott, W. W., 5
Scullen, S. E., 276*n*77
Seashore, S. E., 273*n*19
Segal, N. L., 40*n*21, 388*n*137
Seibert, S. E., 386*n*98
Sekaran, U., 516*n*13
Selvin, A. M., 603*n*107
Seneca, 60, 123, 436
Senge, P. M., 41*n*46, 187*n*61, 254–255, 274*n*43, 470*n*20, 582*n*, 598*n*30
Seuss, Dr., 333
Seyranian, V., 603*n*112
Shackelford, C., 211
Shakespeare, W., 19, 19*n*, 118
Shaler, M. D., 252*n*
Shalit, M., 384*n*78
Shalley, C. E., 239*n*87
Shamir, B., 601*n*81, 602*n*96–97, 603*n*108–110, 604*n*126, 604*n*130
Shani, A. B., 53, 83*n*16
Shapiro, D. L., 382*n*23
Shartle, C. L., 471*n*30
Shaw, B. M., 314*n*26
Shaw, J. D., 381*n*15, 385*n*88
Shaw, M., 394, 432*n*3
Shaw, S. S., 297, 314*n*23
Shea, G. P., 434*n*62
Sheard, J. L., 115*n*47, 314*n*15
Sheats, P., 398*n*, 399*n*
Shelley, G., 168
Shen, W., 274*n*48, 622, 655*n*39
Shepard, H. A., 683*n*26
Shephard, J. E., 405, 433*n*38
Shepherd, C., 611*n*
Sheppard, B. H., 388*n*141
Shils, E., 600*n*58
Shin, S. J., 605*n*152
Shipper, F., 314*n*29
Shippmann, J. S., 274*n*40
Shirer, W. L., 160, 160*n*
Shore, L. M., 552*n*5
Shostrom, E. L., 314*n*19
Siegall, M., 516*n*24
Siegel, P. A., 388*n*143
Siegelman, J., 147*n*30

Silberman, M., 470*n*19
Silver, S. R., 386*n*98
Silzer, R. F., 227, 229*n*, 273*n*28
Simon, P., 200
Simon, S., 237*n*54
Simon, S. A., 86*n*69
Simons, T., 389*n*148
Singer, I. B., 246
Singer, J. L., 238*n*73–76
Sivasubramainian, N., 606*n*155
Skelly, F. R., 185*n*9
Skilling, J., 180
Skinner, B. F., 546, 677–678, 684*n*36, 684*n*42
Skogstad, A., 653*n*2
Skov, R., 385*n*93
Slovic, P., 40*n*18
Smallwood, N., 273*n*35
Smith, B. K., 434*n*56
Smith, D. B., 197*n*, 333*n*, 381*n*20, 517*n*43, 598*n*31
Smith, F. J., 382*n*29
Smith, H., 141, 141*n*
Smith, K. W., 416, 434*n*52
Smith, R. E., 685*n*61
Smither, J. W., 266, 274*n*55, 276*n*81, 276*n*84, 381*n*17
Smithey-Fulmer, L. B., 381*n*11
Smoll, F. L., 685*n*61
Smyser, C. M., 544, 545*n*, 554*n*55
Snavely, B. K., 149*n*58
Snowden, D. F., 28*n*
Snyder, M., 274*n*48
Snyder, R. A., 313*n*9
Soeters, J. L., 381*n*8
Sohenshein, S., 186*n*30
Solomon, R. L., 684*n*39
Sonnenfeld, J. A., 197*n*, 602*n*93, 604*n*132
Sorenson, G. J., 59, 84*n*28
Sorrell, M., 232–233
Sosik, J. J., 255*n*, 603*n*119
Spangler, W. D., 606*n*166
Sparrowe, R. T., 552*n*7
Spears, L., 187*n*53
Spielberg, S., 218
Spiller, G., 515*n*6
Spreitzer, G. M., 385*n*95, 386*n*103
Sprewell, L., 353
Springsteen, B., 196
Srinivasan, D., 602*n*93
Srivastava, K. M., 386*n*97
Stahl, M. J., 135, 148*n*40
Staines, G. L., 382*n*30

Stajkovic, A. D., 353, 385*n*85–86
Stalin, J., 610, 612
Stamps, J., 435*n*66, 435*n*69
Staw, B. M., 83*n*13, 685*n*55, 685*n*66
Steers, R. M., 382*n*23
Steidlmeier, P., 603*n*118
Steinberg, A. G., 86*n*63
Steiner, D., 558
Steiner, I. D., 395, 432*n*11, 434*n*64
Steinmetz, J., 316*n*51
Sternberg, R. J., 210, 213, 237*n*50–51, 237*n*56–57, 238*n*68–70, 238*n*72–76, 238*n*78, 239*n*83, 239*n*93
Stevenson, R. L., 23
Stewar, R., 39*n*7
Stewart, M., 174
Stinglhamber, F., 273*n*22
Stock, G., 164*n*
Stogdill, R. M., 5, 40*n*25–26, 131, 188, 234*n*1–2, 272*n*12, 272*n*14, 272*n*17, 432*n*19, 471*n*30
Stone, A., 387*n*127
Stone, D. L., 470*n*17
Strange, J. M., 239*n*92, 600*n*65, 603*n*103
Strasser, S., 684*n*48
Strauss, G., 387*n*115
Stricker, A., 65*n*
Stride, C. B., 381*n*16
Strober, M. H., 275*n*61
Stroh, L. K., 336*n*
Strube, M. J., 554*n*43
Stubbs, E. C., 227, 241*n*126
Stumpf, S., 84*n*32
Sucharski, I. L., 273*n*22
Sullenberger, Chesley (Sully), 527
Sullivan, S. E., 86*n*65
Sun, L. Y., 382*n*35
Sun Tzu, 173
Sussman, L., 470*n*10
Sutherland, E., 386*n*107
Suttle, J. L., 433*n*33
Sutton, C. D., 40*n*37
Sutton, W., 139–140, 203
Suu Kyi, A. S., 25, 140, 181, 506
Swope, J., 244, 245
Sy, T. S., 241*n*121
Syme, S. L., 315*n*45
Sytsma, M. R., 266–267, 276*n*77, 276*n*87
Szilagyi, A. D., 679, 684*n*49–50

Taber, T. D., 113*n*10, 114*n*25
Taft. W. H., 10

Tang, R. L., 380*n*6
Tanoff, G. F., 41*n*45
Taylor, C., 612
Taylor, E. C., 227, 388*n*147
Taylor, F. W., 331
Taylor, H. L., 457, 471*n*33
Taylor, S. N., 241*n*126
Taylor, S. S., 65*n*
Tellegen, A., 40*n*21
Tepper, B. J., 382*n*31, 387*n*114, 388*n*147
Terborg, J. R., 432*n*21
Tett, R. P., 235*n*18, 387*n*118
Thaues, B., 156
Thayer, P. W., 316*n*59
Theisman, J., 211
Thierry, H., 606*n*153
Thomas, D. A., 76–78, 85*n*61, 86*n*74
Thomas, J. B., 434*n*61
Thomas, K. W., 664, 665*n*, 666*n*, 682*n*5, 683*n*13, 683*n*15, 683*n*21, 683*n*23
Thompson, G., 553*n*29
Thoresen, C. J., 235*n*25, 382*n*25
Thoresen, J. D., 235*n*25
Thornburgh, R., 172
Thurstone, L. L., 235*n*21
Tichy, N. M., 274*n*49, 467, 471*n*40, 471*n*43, 518*n*53, 557, 598*n*17, 598*n*26
Tichy, N. N., 682*n*1
Tillman, P., 641
Timmreck, C. W., 275*n*58
Ting Fong, C., 241*n*122
Tischler, L., 273*n*29
Tjosvold, D., 315*n*43
Todor, W. D., 113*n*19, 385*n*92–93, 684*n*47, 684*n*52, 685*n*58
Toegel, G., 84*n*34, 274*n*52
Toffler, A., 469
Tomczak, J. R., 343
Tomic, W., 85*n*55
Tomkiewicz, J., 41*n*55
Tomlinson, E. C., 382*n*34
Tornow, W. W., 276*n*85, 517*n*32
Tosi, H. L., 602*n*92
Toulouse, J. M., 471*n*29
Tourish, D., 180*n*
Towler, A. J., 602*n*99
Tranter, B., 602*n*90
Trautman, N., 166*n*
Treacy, M., 557, 598*n*20
Treadway, D. C., 137, 148*n*50
Trevino, L. K., 184*n*1, 186*n*45, 187*n*62, 388*n*142, 604*n*127

Tribus, M., 560
Trice, H. M., 685n56
Trist, E. L., 518n54
Trovas, S., 157n
Truman, H., 527
Tsui, A., 515n12
Tucker, R. C., 599n52
Tuckman, B. W., 396–397, 432n16, 456, 470n26
Tuggle, T., 274n50, 387n125
Tumlin, G. R., 161n
Turk, J., 517n38
Turner, N., 600n59
Tushabomwe-Kazooba, C., 654n19
Tutu, Desmond, 375
Twenge, J. M., 42n60–61

Udell, J. G., 432n8
Uhl-Bien, M., 187n63, 522, 522n, 552n9
Ulmer, D., 315n31
Ulmer, W. J., Jr., 252n
Ulrich, D., 273n35
Ury, W., 668, 683n24

Valins, S., 83n11
Van den Berg, J. G., 606n153
Vandenberghe, C., 273n22
Van der Weide, J. G., 606n153
Van de Ven, A. H., 316n53
Van Fleet, D. D., 384n76, 553n23, 553n27, 555n63
Van Fleet, E. W., 384n76
Van Keer, E., 236n33
Van Nuys, K. E., 653n16
Van Reenen, J., 654n28
Van Rooy, D. L., 240n115, 382n37
Van Velsor, E., 41n56, 57n, 517n35, 621, 622, 654n34, 655n38
Van Vugt, R. H., 380n4
Varella, P., 601n84
Vargas, Y., 276n84
Vatcha, N., 180n
Vecchio, R. P., 553n26, 553n29, 554n52
Venezia, I., 517n33
Venter, C., 244
Verhage, J., 147n19, 315n41
Vinson, G., 604n136
Viswesvaran, C., 235n28, 240n115, 382n37
Vlad the Impaler, 610
Vogelaar, A. L. W., 381n8
Volker, J., 273n27

Vroom, V. H., 41n47, 523–530, 524n, 526n, 533–534, 552n12, 552n19–20, 554n56, 555n65

Waclawski, J., 275n73
Waddock, S. A., 187n75
Wagner, F. R., 682n6
Wagner, S. H., 385n96
Wakin, M. M., 147n27
Waldman, D. A., 85n59, 381n17, 601n80, 601n84, 602n92
Waldman, D. D., 604n133
Waldrop, M., 176
Walker, A., 266, 276n81
Walker, A. G., 381n17
Walker, T. G., 113n20
Wall, T. D., 381n16
Walumbwa, F., 185n8, 186n44, 186n47, 604n134
Walumbwa, F. O., 653n4
Ward, A. J., 604n132
Ward, S., 654n20
Warden, J. A., 654n24
Warhol, A., 193
Warner, N., 19n
Warrenfelz, R., 84n26, 236n34, 254, 274n41
Washington, G., 25
Wasylyshyn, K. M., 85n46, 85n54
Waterman, R. H., 147n23, 515n1, 682n9
Watson, T. Sr., 213
Wayne, S. J., 552n5
Weaver, G., 187n62
Webb, A., 57–58, 83n19
Weber, M., 574, 575, 599n45
Weed, S. E., 544, 545n, 554n55
Weiler, R., 557, 598n15
Weiner, B. J., 83n11, 140n
Weiss, H. M., 114n29
Welbourne, J., 380n13
Welch, J., 106, 262, 462, 560, 573
Wellins, R., 82n2
Wells, L., 65n
Wenzel, L. H., 72, 85n45, 85n52
Wernsing, T., 186n44, 186n47, 186n49
Weschler, D., 315n42
Wesson, M. J., 388n145
Wexley, K. N., 113n18, 114n28
Wheatley, M. A., 126
Whelan, B., 582
White, L. A., 113n6

White, R. P., 41n56, 517n35, 622, 655n38
White, S. S., 384n79
Whiting, V., 86n65
Whitman, D. S., 382n37
Whittington, J. L., 602n87
Wiener, E., 433n43, 434n58
Wiersma, F., 557, 598n20
Wilcox, F. B., 13
Wilcox, K. J., 40n21
Wilcox, W. H., 457, 471n32
Wilderom, C. P. M., 606n153
Wiley, J. W., 315n44, 380n7
Wiley, W., 333n
Wilkinson, I., 432n7
Williams, E. A., 603n120
Williams, K., 432n13
Willner, A. R., 603n111, 683n18
Wilson, C. L., 314n29
Wilson, J. A., 85n59
Wilson, P. R., 146n16
Winchester, S., 10n
Winer, B. J., 272n14
Winfrey, O., 59, 578
Winkel, D. E., 146n10
Wiseman, R., 50, 50n
Witt, L. A., 387n116
Wolff, S. B., 241n120
Wolpe, H., 599n48
Wong, C. S., 241n125
Wood, G., 40n19
Wood, G. J., 518n67
Wood, R. E., 83n13–14, 275n59, 685n66–67
Wood, S. J., 381n16
Woodman, R. W., 40n37
Woods, T., 126
Woycke, J., 605n139, 606n166
Wozniak, S., 60
Wriston, W. B., 12
Wunder, A., 432n14
Wu Yi, 345, 351

Xie, J. L., 358, 386n102

Yager, B., 585n
Yammarino, F. J., 187n71, 276n79, 601n75, 602n92
Yang, J., 148n50
Yang, Y., 603n114
Yetton, P. W., 523–530, 524n, 526n, 533–534, 552n12, 553n24, 554n56, 555n65
Yew, L. K., 144

Yoels, W. C., 121*n*
York, A., 166
Yost, P. R., 434*n*62
Young, S. A., 561*n*
Yukl, G. A., 112*n*3, 114*n*27, 134,
     147*n*24, 147*n*31, 147*n*35,
     148*n*52, 432*n*4, 515*n*3, 516*n*23,
     547–548, 553*n*22–23, 553*n*27,
     555*n*60, 555*n*62–64, 578,
     599*n*43, 600*n*66, 682*n*11,
     683*n*14

Zaccaro, S. J., 39*n*11, 220, 234*n*9,
     240*n*103
Zacharatos, A., 593, 606*n*161
Zajonc, R., 432*n*15
Zaleznik, A., 9, 39*n*15, 320, 380*n*7
Zaslow, J., 356*n*
Zedeck, S., 654*n*33
Zeithaml, C. P., 273*n*31
Zemke, R., 154–155, 185*n*16
Zenger, J. H., 273*n*35
Zhang, X., 239*n*94

Zhou, J., 216, 217*n*, 239*n*86, 240*n*98,
     605*n*152
Zhou, X., 555*n*61
Zhu, R., 603*n*114
Zhu, W., 604*n*134
Zhu Rongji, 351
Zimbardo, P., 131, 399, 399*n*,
     433*n*25
Zlotnick, S., 385*n*89
Zuckerberg, M., 244

Subject Index

A-B-C model, 304–305
Abilene paradox, 293, 294–295
Abilities, in GAPS analysis, 108, 464
Ability model, of emotional
   intelligence, 222–224
Academic tradition in leadership
   research, 7
Acceptance, in SARA model, 568–569
Accommodation, in conflict
   resolution, 664, 665, 666
Accountability
   empowerment and, 468
   social loafing and, 395
Achievement orientation, 344–346, 493
Achievement-oriented cultures, 493
Achievement-oriented leadership, 543
Acquiescence, 291–292, 293
Action
   in leadership development, 47, 48
   perception and, 52–54
   in spiral of experience, 47–48,
      52–54
Action learning, 64–66
Action-Observation-Reflection
   (A-O-R) model, 46–78, 106–107
   action and, 47, 48
   leadership development in,
      106–107, 112
   observation and, 47, 48
   perception and, 49–54
   reflection and, 47, 48, 51–52, 54–56
   spiral of experience and, 47–48,
      49–54
Action steps, in development
   plans, 111
Active followers, 21
Active listening, 288–291
Actor/observer difference, 51–52
Adaptation, inability to adapt, 626
Adaptive leadership, 484, 501, 571
Adaptive problems, 483–484
Additive task, 395
Adhocracy cultures, 497–498
Advantageous comparison, 167
Affectivity, 370–371
Afghanistan, 133, 579, 641
Agendas
   hidden, 404
   meeting, 298

Aggression, 291–292, 293, 667
Agreeableness, 193, 195
Aguero, Shane (profile), 245
AIG, 647
Airline crews, 81–82, 339–340, 346,
   350, 355, 367, 397, 421,
   502–503, 527, 607–609, 629
Alienated followers, 21
Alive (Read), 2–3
Al-Qaeda, 221, 320, 579, 641
American Express Financial
   Advisors (AEFA), 225–226
American Idol (TV program), 195, 196
Ames Department Stores, 647
Amount of change, 560
Amway, 574
Analytic intelligence, 210–212, 213,
   215, 218–219
Anger
   in coercive power, 133
   in SARA model, 568–569
Anheuser Busch, 574
Animal research, on power and
   dominance, 121
Apollo 13 lunar mission, 482–483
Apple Computer, 60, 229
Apprentice, The (TV program), 195
Artifacts and symbols, 491
   of power, 122–123
Art of War, The (Sun Tzu), 173
Asea Brown Boveri, 258
Asian Tigers, 145
Assertive behavior, 291–296
   Abilene paradox and, 293, 294–295
   acquiescence versus, 291–292, 293
   aggression versus, 291–292,
      293, 667
   inner dialogue and, 295
   "I" statements in, 293–295, 296
   nature of, 292–293
   persistence, 296, 466–467
   sample exchange, 297
   saying "no," 295, 296
   stating needs, 295, 296
   tips for, 296
Assessment
   leadership. *See* Leadership
      assessment personality, 135,
      199, 200, 202–207, 313, 481

Association of Life-Giving
   Churches, 646
Athleta, 486
Athletes. *See* Sports
AT&T, 99, 135, 136, 615
Attitudes. *See also* Job satisfaction;
   Values of leader toward
   self, 304
Attribution, 51–52
   attribution theory, 681
   of blame, 167
Authentic leadership, 169–170, 179
Authoritarian leaders, 140–141
Authority
   charismatic authority system,
      575–576
   in effective teams, 406–410
   in executive team building,
      674–675
   influence without, 104
   kleptocracies and, 576, 612
   legal-rational authority system,
      575, 576
   level of, 486–487
   power and, 122–125
   traditional authority system,
      574, 576
Autocratic leadership style, 510
Autocratic processes, 524
Autonomous leadership, 508
Autonomy
   in delegation, 461
   task, 480–481
Avatar (film), 244, 334, 556
Avoidance
   in conflict resolution, 664–666
   of delegation, 458–459
Awareness, in servant leadership, 171

Baby Boomers, values of, 155
Baby Gap, 486
Bachelet, Michelle (profile), 337
Bad leadership, 610–614
   defined, 609
   derailment factors, 630
   examples of, 609, 610–613
Balanced Scorecard, 349
Banana Republic, 486
Band of Brothers (film), 19

Bank of America, 356

Bar-On Emotional Quotient, 225

Base rate of managerial incompetence, 614

Bass's Theory of Transformational and Transactional Leadership, 590–594

Bass & Stogdill's Handbook of Leadership (Bass), 5

Bear Stearns, 647

Behavior change
coaching in, 73–74
leadership behavior, 243–244

Behaviorism, 189
operant approach to motivation, 351–355

Beijing Yanshan Petrochemical Corporation, 351

Best Buy, 229, 640

Bhagavad Gita, 173

bin Laden, Osama (profile), 579

Black Hawk Down (film), 345

Blame
attribution of, 167
avoiding, 285, 306–307, 444, 461–462

Bonuses, 129–130, 352, 355

Boston Consulting Group, 258

Boyle, Greg (profile), 261

BP, 197, 363, 372, 405, 413–414, 504, 615

Brainstorming, 309–310

Branson, Richard (profile), 375

Breaking the Glass Ceiling (Morrison et al.), 29–30

BRIC economies (Brazil, Russia, India, and China), 218

British Petroleum (BP), 197, 363, 372, 405, 413–414, 504, 615

Brown-nosers, in Curphy Followership Model, 325–326, 329, 641–642

Building community, in servant leadership, 171

Building social capital, 260

Build trust, 279–283, 582. *See also* Trust

Bureaucratic power, 128

Burger King, 232

Burma, 25

Business skills, 46, 254

BusinessWeek magazine, 162

Buy-in, and Rocket Model for Team Effectiveness, 452–453

$C = D \times M \times P > R$, 559–560, 571–572

California Psychological Inventory, 30

Campbell Interest and Skills Survey, 418

Campbell Leadership Index (CLI), 153

Capabilities, diagnosing problems with, 670

Care-based thinking, 165

Career objectives, in development plans, 111

Cargill, 574

Carlson Companies, 574

Case studies, 61

Catalyst, 28

Caterpillar, Inc., 544

Cause-and-effect diagrams (fishbone diagrams), 307, 308

Center for Creative Leadership
Executive Woman Project, 487
high-potential managers, 621
organizational culture factors, 491
self-rating of ethical behavior, 153
stages of leadership culture development, 493
team building and, 406–408, 446
women as leaders and, 55, 487
Women's Leadership Program, 55

Centralization, 489

Challenger space shuttle disaster, 404

Change. *See also* Behavior change; Organizational change
new leaders and, 93–94
process of, 560, 564–567
in rural communities, 559

Change plan, 565

Charisma
attribution of, 583
defined, 584

Charismatic authority system, 575–576

Charismatic leadership, 197, 319–329, 573–590
comparison with transformational leadership, 580–587
in cults, 180
described, 508
emotions and, 221–222, 573–581, 585
examples of, 8, 9, 133, 180, 578, 582
Five Factor Model (FFM) of Personality and, 593

follower characteristics in, 584–585
historical review of, 573–580
leader characteristics in, 581–584, 587–590
political campaigns and attribution of charisma, 583, 587–588
situational characteristics and, 586–587
trust and, 279, 582, 583

Cheerleaders
dark-side personality traits of, 624, 638, 641–642
derailment factors, 630
example of, 618
nature of, 616–617

Chernobyl nuclear power plant accident, 413

Chicago Bears, 71

Chicago Blackhawks, 211

Chicago Bulls, 392

Chicago Cubs, 211

Chief executive officers (CEOs)
bad leadership and, 610–614
compensation demands, 352, 354
decision acceptance and, 525
disillusionment of employees with, 177–179
executive team building, 671–676
Level 5 Leadership and, 197, 589
managerial derailment and, 620–648
managerial incompetence, 614–615
moronization of management and, 620
transformational leadership characteristics, 593
women as, 144–146, 208, 232–234, 258, 270–271

Children, beliefs about leadership, 62

Chile, 337

China, 218, 351

Chronic managerial incompetence, 632

Circuit City, 647

Civil Rights movement, 318, 575

Clan cultures, 497–498

Clarity
of communication, 286–287
of delegated assignment, 460

Clif Bar Inc., 183–184

Cliques, 106, 122, 394, 428

Clothing, power and, 123
Coaching, 69–74, 462–469
    coaching plans in, 70–73, 465–466
    commitment in, 464–465
    development plans in, 465–466
    executive, 75
    forging partnership in, 463–464
    formal, 73–74
    GAPS analysis and, 464–469
    informal, 69–73, 462–469
    learning environment in, 467–468
    persistence in, 296, 466–467
    remote, 72
    sports and, 71, 99, 680
    steps in, 70–72
Coaching plans, 70–73, 465–466
Coalition tactics, 138, 139
Coca-Cola, 197
Coercive power, 130–133
Cognitive resources theory (CRT),
    218–220
Cognitive theories of motivation,
    expectancy theory, 348–350
Collaboration, in conflict resolution,
    664–666
Collaborative cultures, 493
Collectivism, 507
College. *See also* Education and
    training; U.S. service
    academies
    classroom as situation, 477
    leader development in, 59–62
Color Purple, The (film), 59
Command and control, 175–176
Commitment
    in coaching, 464–465
    of followers, 585
    to goals, 438–439
    in servant leadership, 171
Common sense, 11–12
Communication, 283–288. *See also*
    Listening
    breakdowns in, 284–285, 287
    checking for understanding,
        287–288
    clarity of, 286–287
    context for, 285–286
    effective, 283–288
    in effective teams, 497
    medium of, 285–286
    purpose in, 285
    rhetorical skills of charismatic
        and transformational leaders,
        581–582

sending clear signals, 286–287
    systems view of, 283–285
    two-way, 287–288
Community
    building in servant leadership, 171
    individualism versus, 164
Community leadership, 259–262
Compaq, 217
Compensation
    job satisfaction and, 352, 354,
        363, 367
    professional athlete salary
        demands, 352
Competence, loss of, 568
Competency models, 252–255
Competent managers
    dark-side personality traits
        and, 214
    derailment factors, 630
    nature of, 616
Competing Values Framework,
    495–498
    adhocracy cultures, 497–498
    clan cultures, 497–498
    hierarchy cultures, 496–498
    market cultures, 497–498
Competition, in conflict resolution,
    664–666
Complexity
    organizational, 488
    self-, 304
Compliance, of followers, 585
Compromise, in conflict
    resolution, 666
Computer Center Corporation, 26
Conceptualization, in servant
    leadership, 171
Concern for people, 250–251
Concern for production, 250–251
Conference Board, 46, 425
Confidential information, 278
Conflict management, 662–667
    avoidance in, 664–666
    competition in conflict resolution,
        664–666
    conflict, defined, 662–663
    conflict resolution strategies,
        664–667
    effects of conflict, 663–664
    interpersonal conflict, 172–173, 408
    intragroup conflict, 394, 396
    intrapersonal conflict, 172–173
    managing creativity, 312
    role conflict and, 372, 398–400, 479

strategies for, 664–667
    swimming with sharks, 667
    values in, 173, 177
Conflicts of interest, 162–163
Conforming cultures, 493
Conformist followers, 21
Connector, 22
Conscientiousness, 193, 194, 344
Consideration, 247
Consistency, as component of
    leadership, 151
Constructive dissatisfaction, 561
Constructive feedback, 439–444
    avoiding blame and
        embarrassment in, 444
    criteria for, 443
    importance of, 439–440
    positive and negative, 440–441, 444
    360-degree, 66–67, 69, 70, 262–267,
        280, 635
    tips for improving, 441
Consultants, Leadership Pipeline
    and, 259
Consultation, 138, 524
Container Store, Inc., 356
Context, for communication, 285–286
Contingency Model, 535–541
    Leader-Follower-Situation (L-F-S)
        framework and, 520
    least preferred coworker scale,
        535–536
    prescriptions of, 538–540
    situational favorability, 537–538
Contingency theories of leadership,
    520–549
    Contingency Model, 535–541
    followers in, 535–545, 547–548
    leader-follower-situation (L-F-S)
        framework, 528–530
    Leader-Member Exchange (LMX)
        theory, 520, 521–523
    leaders in, 547–548
    normative decision model,
        523–530
    path-goal theory, 542–548
    Situational Leadership® Model,
        530–535
    situation in, 537–538, 547–548
Contingent rewards, 351
Contrarian's Guide to Leadership, The
    (Sample), 527
Contributors, in Potter and
    Rosenbach followership
    model, 322

Conventional level, of moral reasoning, 158, 159
Convergent thinking, 213
Conversion, in cults, 180
Cooperation, of followers, 585
Corporate culture, 180, 479–480
Corruption
    of "numbers games," 168, 363
    power and, 118, 137
Council of Women World Leaders, 29
Creation, as function for team leadership, 415
Creative intelligence, 213, 215–218
    components of, 215–218
    creativity killers, 217
Creativity, 309–313
    brainstorming and, 309–310
    divergent thinking and, 213
    managing, 312
    personality and, 213, 313
    power and, 311
    problem-solving groups and, 311–313
    seeing things in new ways, 309–311
Credibility, 277–283
    components of, 278
    defined, 278
    expertise in, 278–279, 281–283
    leadership credos, 280–281, 282–283
    trust in, 278, 279–283, 320
Credos, leadership, 280–281, 282–283
Creeping elegance, 217
Crises
    in charismatic and transformational leadership, 586–587
    dark side of leadership and, 607–609
    leadership response to, 10
    power and, 123–125
Critical thinking, 21, 323–324, 327–328, 329
Criticizers, in Curphy Followership Model, 327–328, 329, 641–642
Cross functions, 485
Cults, 133, 611, 613
    qualities of, 180
Culturally endorsed implicit theories of leadership (CLT), 507–508
Culture. See also Organizational culture
    coaching and, 72
    leadership style and, 502–505, 506–511

leading across cultures, 502–505
    in multirater feedback instruments, 266
    stages of leadership, 493
    universality of leadership attributes, 508–511
Curphy Followership Model, 323–330, 640–643
Customer segmentation, 485

DaimlerChrysler, 615
Dalgarno, George (profile), 243
Dark side of leadership, 607–649
    bad leadership, 610–614, 630
    crisis situations and, 607–609
    in-name-only managers versus, 624, 625–626, 638, 641–642
    managerial derailment, 609–610, 620–648
    managerial incompetence, 609, 614–620, 628–648
    root causes, 628–648
Dark-side personality traits, 643–648
    anonymous feedback and, 177
    leadership challenge profile, 644
    list of, 643
    managerial incompetence and, 645–646
    negative consequences of, 214, 642
    stress and, 220, 299–303
DBS Bank, 145
Decision acceptance, 525
Decision making
    importance of, 221
    leader role in, 28
Decision quality, 524–525
Decision tree, 525–528
Defensiveness, avoiding, 290–291
Dehumanization, 167
Delegation, 457–467
    avoidance of, 458–459
    as empowerment, 356–357
    importance of, 457–458
    nature of, 457
    points to cover in, 461
    principles of effective, 459–462
    reasons for avoiding, 458–459
Dell, Inc., 127, 229
Dell, Michael (profile), 127
Delta Airlines, 367
Democratic leaders, 140–141, 151, 510
Dependability, 104

Dependent, uncritical thinking, 21
Dependent leadership cultures, 493, 494
Descriptiveness, of feedback, 441, 442–443
Design, as function for team leadership, 415, 416–417, 420
Development, as function for team leadership, 415, 417–418
Developmental interventions, 533
Development objectives, in development plans, 111
DevelopMentor, 111
Development planning, 66–69, 106–112
    building plans, 110–112
    in coaching, 465–466
    GAPS analysis in, 106–112
    importance of, 97–98
    modifying plans, 112
    transfer learning to new environment, 112
Development plans, 67–69
Diagnostic Model
    expectations and, 670
    opportunities and, 671
Diagnostic model, 669–671
    capabilities and, 670
    motivation and, 671
Diffusion of responsibility, 167
Dilbert comic strip, 244–245
Directive leadership, in path-goal theory, 543
Directness, of feedback, 441
Disasters. See Crises
Disneyland, 491
Disney World, 491
Displacement of responsibility, 167
Disregard of consequences, 167
Dissatisfaction, 560–561
    costs of, 362
Distortion of consequences, 167
Distributive justice, 374–375
Divergent thinking, 213. See also Creativity
Diversity. See Culture
Domain model of leadership, 254
Dominance, gestures of, 121, 122
Double-loop learning, 56, 212
Dream, as function for team leadership, 415, 416
Dr. Gordy test, 615
Dungy, Tony (profile), 71

Dysfunctional roles, 398, 399
Dysfunctional turnover, 363–366

Edge, in vision of leader, 661–662
Education and training. *See also*
  Leadership development
  in emotional intelligence,
    225–226, 227
  leader development in college,
    59–62
  leadership training programs, 61,
    63–66, 252, 611–612
  motivation programs, 339–340
  U.S. service academies and, 44,
    287, 318, 343, 358, 478,
    578, 627
Effective communication, 283–288
Effectiveness
  defined, 334
  leader, 610
  leadership, 34–35, 136–137,
    169–170
  managing upward, 140
  porcupine leadership style
    and, 141
  team, 406–410, 497
Ego, 190
Embarrassment, avoiding, 444
EMC, 339
Emergencies. *See* Crises
EMI, 375
Emotional Competence Inventory
  (ECi), 225
Emotional intelligence, 220–229
  ability model of, 222–224
  defined, 222
  Five Factor Model (FFM) of
    Personality and, 224–225,
    227, 228
  humor and, 255
  implications of, 226–228
  measuring and developing,
    225–226
  mixed model of, 223,
    224–225
  nature of, 220–225
Emotional Intelligence (Goleman),
  222, 225
Emotional quotient (EQ), 220–229
Emotions
  charismatic leadership and,
    221–222, 573–581, 585
  leadership as emotional, 6–8
  in vision of leader, 660

Empathy
  as component of leadership, 151
  in servant leadership, 171
Employee-centered dimensions,
  248–249
Employee engagement, 561
Empowerment, 135, 311, 355–360
  best practices of, 468–469
  continuum of, 468
  defined, 355
  delegation in, 356–357
  developing others, 467–468
  of followers of charismatic and
    transformational leaders, 585
  motivational benefits of, 358–359
  nature of, 355–356
  operant approach and, 359–360
  power and, 358
  psychological components of,
    357–358
  as term, 134
Ends-based thinking, 165
Engagement, in Curphy
  Followership Model, 324
Enron, 29, 174, 180
Environment, 498–511
  changes in, 499–501
  creativity and, 213
  as situational factor, 498–511
Environmental factors, 213
Episodic managerial
  incompetence, 632
Ethical climates
  creating and sustaining,
    176–181, 405
  nature of, 175–176
Ethical dilemmas, 164–165
Ethics, 150–182. *See also* Values
  creating ethical climate,
    176–181, 405
  critical elements of ethical
    leadership, 161
  defined, 151
  doing the right things, 150–168
  morals versus, 154, 155
  in organizational leadership,
    172–181
  self-rating of, 153
  trust and, 279
Euphemistic labeling, 166–167
Evaluative feedback, 442–443
Evolutionary psychology, 319
Exchange, 138, 139
Executive coaching, 75

Executive team building, 671–676
Exemplary followers, 21
Exercise, in stress reduction, 303
Expectation-performance gap,
  567–569, 669–671
Expectations
  clarifying, 103–104, 292–293
  in diagnostic model, 670
  in leading by example, 175
  performance and, 348–350
  in social interaction, 53
  in vision of leader, 659–660
Experience
  cognitive resources theory (CRT)
    and, 218–220
  leadership development through,
    49–54, 94–98
  learning from others and, 96
  learning to learn from, 57–78,
    94–98
  in spiral of experience, 47–48,
    49–54
  women in leadership and, 56
Expertise. *See also* Technical
    competence
  components of, 278–279
  in credibility, 278–279, 281–283
  improving, 278–279
  managerial derailment and,
    637–640
  subject matter, 638, 639
Expert power, 125–126, 135–137
Extinction, in operant approach, 353
Extraversion
  extraversion-introversion, 203
  in Five Factor Model (FFM), 193,
    194–195
Extremis Leadership (Kolditz), 478
Extrinsic rewards, 130

Facebook, 89, 229, 244, 265
Facet satisfaction, 364–367, 368–369
Failure to meet business objectives,
  621–624, 627–628
Fairness, in leading by example,
  174–175
FBI, 122
Feedback. *See also* Constructive
    feedback; Observation
  anonymous, 177
  in coaching, 467–468
  constructive, 439–444
  creating opportunities to get, 95
  in delegation process, 461–462

descriptiveness of, 441, 442–443
in development plans, 111
evaluation versus, 442
goal setting and, 439–444
individualized, 61
multirater, 75, 262–267,
280, 635
in organizational settings, 63–64
positive, 440–441, 444
task, 481
Team Assessment Survey,
455–456
360 degree, 66–67, 69, 70, 262–267,
280, 635
Feelings of empowerment, 585
First impressions, 89–90
Five Factor Model (FFM) of
Personality, 192–200, 201, 344
advantages of, 198–200
charismatic leadership and, 593
described, 192–197
dimensions of, 193–197
emotional intelligence and,
224–225, 227, 228
implications of, 196–200
Flexibility, of feedback, 441, 443–444
Follower(s). *See also* Delegation;
Motivation
adapting to superior's style,
103–104
of charismatic and
transformational leaders,
584–585
in contingency theories of
leadership, 535–545, 547–548
in Curphy Followership Model,
323–330, 640–643
followership styles, 21
influence of, 104–106
in interactional framework, 15,
18–25, 34–35, 317–320,
547–548
Leader-Member Exchange (LMX)
theory, 520
leaders in follower role, 329
leaders versus, 188–189
in managerial incompetence,
630–632
managing upward, 140
monitoring stress levels of,
302, 305
motivation of, 338–362
obedience to power, 124, 319
in path-goal theory, 543–545

performance of. *See* Performance;
Performance problems
poor followership, 640–643
in Potter and Rosenbach
followership model, 320–323,
328–329
in rational approach to
organizational change,
570–572
relationships with peers, 104–106,
281, 625–626
relationships with superiors,
101–104, 281
satisfaction of. *See* Job satisfaction
styles of, 21
technical competence of, 98–101
toxic, 214
types of, 321–330
Follower readiness, 532
Followership. *See also* Follower(s)
defined, 19
leadership and, 18–25
Force field analysis (FFA), 307–308,
309, 572
Ford Motor Company, 168, 574
Foresight, in servant leadership, 171
Formal coaching, 73–74
Formalization, 488–489
Formal mentoring, 76–77
Formal organization, 486–489
level of authority, 486–487
organizational structure, 487–488
Forming stage of group, 396, 456
For Your Improvement (Lombardo &
Eichinger), 111
Frames of reference, 286–287
Framing, 260
Free agency, 155
Friendship
assertive behavior in, 293
personal appeals and, 138
referent power and, 126–128
Fuld, Richard (profile), 612
Functional fixedness, 310
Functional turnover, 363–364
Fundamental attribution error, 51
Furniture arrangement
communication and, 286
power and, 122
Future orientation, 507

Gallup Organization, 331, 365
Gamble, The (Ricks), 499
Games, 61

Gandhi, Mahatma (profile), 160
Gap, Inc., The, 486
GAPS analysis, 106–112
bridging gaps in, 110–112
coaching and, 464–469
conducting, 107–109
development needs in, 109–110
development planning and,
106–112
gaps of GAPS in, 109–110
sample, 108
Gates, Bill (profile), 26
Gender differences. *See also* Women
in leadership
in leadership style, 31–33, 140
in learning from experience, 57
in multirater feedback
instruments, 267
General Electric (GE), 197, 229, 262, 504
General Motors, 221
Gen Xers
generational archetypes and, 156
main events in lives of, 157
values of, 155–156
Geographically dispersed teams
(GDT), 424–428
Germany, 191
Gestures, of power and dominance,
121, 122
Glass ceiling effect, 29–30, 487
Glass cliff, 33–34
Globalization
geographically dispersed teams
(GDT) in, 424–428
global scale and, 485
leadership style and, 510
leading across cultures, 502–505
leading in a global economy, 504
organizational culture, 501
virtual teams and, 424–428
workplace trends and, 501
Global recession of 2008–2010,
334–336, 350, 610
Global satisfaction, 364–367, 368–369
GLOBE (Global Leadership and
Organizational Behavior
Effectiveness) project, 504,
506–511
Goal emphasis, 248
Goal setting, 346–351, 436–439
attainable goals, 437–438
challenging goals, 437–438
commitment to goals, 438–439
common interests and, 104–105

Goal setting—*Cont.*
empowerment and, 468
feedback and, 439–444
in GAPS analysis, 107, 464
observable goals in, 437
specific goals in, 437
for teams, 216–217
Goal specificity, 437
Golden Rule, 165
Golem Effect, 348–350
Good Samaritan, 163
Good to Great (Collins), 589, 647
Google, 229, 244
Great Depression, 155
Great Man theory, 130, 188–189,
478–479
Group(s), 390–429
cohesion of, 402–406
defined, 393
developmental stages of,
396–397, 456
individuals versus, 391
nature of, 393–406
norms of, 400–402, 409
organizations versus, 393
size of, 393–396
teams versus, 390–391
Group boundaries, 408–409
Group cohesion, 402–406
Group dynamics, influence on
behavior, 8
Group perspective, 390–406
defined, 390
development stages in,
396–397, 456
group, defined, 393
group cohesion in, 402–406
group norms in, 400–402, 409
group roles in, 397–400
group size in, 393–396
individuals versus groups versus
teams, 391
nature of groups, 391, 393–406
teams versus groups, 390–391
Group process, 524
Group roles, 397–400
*Groups That Work (and Those That
Don't)* (Hackman), 408
Groupthink, 306, 403–405
Guns, Germs, and Steel (Diamond),
576, 612

Haggard, Ted (profile), 646
Hawthorne effect, 395

Hawthorne experiments, 395
Healing, in servant leadership, 171
Healthy lifestyle, stress and, 303
Hedgehog leadership style, 589
Heightened emotional levels, 585
Helpfulness, of feedback, 441–442
Hernandez & Associates Inc.,
430–431
Heroic theory, 27
Herzberg's two-factor theory of
motivation, 372–374
Hewlett-Packard, 449, 504
Hidden agendas, 404
Hierarchical power, 175
Hierarchy cultures, 496–498
Hierarchy effect, 366–367
Hierarchy of needs (Maslow),
340–343, 360–361
High-LPC leaders, 536, 537–540
High-potential managers,
defined, 621
Hogan, Robert "RT" (profile), 200
Hogan Assessment Systems, 200
Homeboy Industries, 261
Home Depot, 254, 449
Honesty, 104–106, 154
Horizontal complexity, 488
Humane-oriented leadership, 508
Humor, 255
Hurricane Katrina (2005), 10
Hygiene factors, 372–374

IBM, 197, 229
Id, 190
Ideas, in vision of leader, 658–659
Identification with the leader, 584
Identity, loss of, 568
Ideology, of ethical climate, 176–177
IKEA, 513–515
Image building, of charismatic and
transformational leaders,
582, 583
Implicit leadership theory, 507
Implicit prejudice, 161–163
Inability
to adapt, 626
to build and lead a team, 624–625
to build relationships, 625–626
Inadequate preparation for
promotion, 626–628
Inauthentic leadership, 170
In-basket exercises, 63
Incompetence, managerial. *See*
Managerial incompetence

Independent, critical thinking, 21
Independent leadership cultures,
493, 494
India, 145, 160, 218, 258
Indianapolis Colts, 71
Individual development plans, 68
Individual differences
in achievement orientation,
344–346
leadership behavior and, 242–244
Individual factors, 418
Individualism, 505, 507
Individualized feedback, 61
Individual versus community, 164
Indoctrination, in cults, 180
Industrial age, 484–486
Influence
without authority, 104
defined, 119
of followers, 104–106
generalizations about, 134
leader motives for, 134–137
in managing upward, 140
power versus, 119–120
Influence Behavior Questionnaire
(IBQ), 138–139
Influence tactics, 137–142
defined, 119
nonverbal, 120, 121
power and, 139–142
types of, 138–139
Influence without authority, 104
Informal coaching, 69–73,
462–469
Informal mentoring, 76–77
Informal organization, 489–498
Information age, 484–486
Ingratiation, 138, 139
In-group, 16, 521
In-group favoritism, 162
Initiating structure, 247
In-name-only managers
dark-side personality traits of,
624, 625–626, 638, 641–642
derailment factors, 630
example of, 619
nature of, 617–618
Inner dialogue (self-talk), 295
Innovation, 485
in emerging economies, 218
in leadership development, 65
Inputs, team, 415
Inspirational appeals, 138
Instrumental values, 153–154

Integrity, 104
   as component of leadership,
      151, 154
   in ethical climate, 177
Intel, 229
Intelligence, 208–220
   analytic, 210–212, 213, 215, 218–219
   athleticism versus, 211
   creative, 213, 215–218
   defined, 209–210
   as domain specific, 211–212
   emotional (EQ), 220–229
   judgment and, 221
   managerial derailment and, 637
   nature of, 208–210
   practical, 210–212, 213, 215, 218–219
   single- versus double-loop
      learning, 54–56, 212
   stress and, 218–220
   triarchic theory of, 210–218,
      224–225
Interaction, 34–35
Interactional framework, 15–27
   followers in, 15, 18–25, 34–35,
      317–320, 547–548
   Leader-Follower-Situation
      interactions, 34–35, 520,
      523–530, 534, 547, 548
   leader in, 15, 16–17, 34–35, 117,
      547–548
   overview of, 15–27
   situation in, 15, 26–27, 34–35,
      473–480, 545–548
   Team Leadership Model (TLM)
      and, 424
   women in leadership roles, 25,
      27–34
Interactional justice, 374–375
Interaction facilitation, 248
Interactions, 15
Interactive leadership, 31–33
Interdependence, 391, 482
Interdependent leadership cultures,
   493, 494
International business. *See*
   Globalization
Internet, online personas and,
   89, 265
Interpersonal behaviors, in leading
   by example, 174
Interpersonal conflict, 172–173, 408
Interpersonal level of leadership, 179
Interpersonal skills, 254
Interrole conflict, 400

Interrupting, 121, 289
Intersender role conflict, 400
Interventions
   developmental, 533
   in Situational Leadership®
      Model, 533
   in team building, 444–448
Intragroup conflict, 394, 396
Intrapersonal conflict, 172–173
Intrapersonal skills, 254
Intrasender role conflict, 398–400
Intrinsic rewards, 130
Invictus (film), 509
Iran-Contra affair, 405
Iran hostage crisis, 403
Iraq
   Abu Ghraib prison, 131, 133
   coercive power in, 131, 133
   war in, 131, 133, 221, 245, 252,
      499–500
Island of the Lost (Druett), 243
"I" statements, 293–295, 296

Jackson, Peter (profile), 6
Jackson, Phil (profile), 392
Japanese management style, 173
Jargon, 287
Jesuits, 261
Jesus Camp (film), 646
Job-centered dimensions, 247, 249
Job descriptions, 103
Jobs, Steve (profile), 60
Job satisfaction, 362–375
   affectivity and, 370–371
   compensation and, 352, 354,
      363, 367
   costs of dissatisfaction, 362
   defined, 334, 362
   facet satisfaction, 364–367, 368–369
   global satisfaction, 364–367,
      368–369
   life satisfaction and, 367–368
   motivation and, 333–338, 362–375
   organizational justice and, 374–375
   productivity and, 336
   punishment and, 678–680
   relationship with leadership and
      performance, 334–335
   role ambiguity and, 372, 400, 479
   surveys of, 368–369
   theories of, 369–375
Jobs for the Future (JFF), 261
Johnson & Johnson, 258
Jonestown massacre, 133

Journals, 96–97
Journey to the East (Hesse), 170
Judging-perceiving, 204–205
Justice
   versus mercy, 165
   organizational, 374–375
   procedural, 374–375
   types of, 374

Kansas City Chiefs, 71
Kentucky Fried Chicken, 129,
   232, 258
Keppel Corp., 145
Klein, Joe (profile), 566
Kleptocracy, 576, 612
Knowledge workers, 485
Korean Air, 502–503
Koresh, David (profile), 613
Kraft Foods, 232–233
Kravis Leadership Institute, 58–59

Laissez-faire leadership, 255
Lands' End, 356
Language
   nonverbal. *See* Nonverbal
      language
   in organizational culture, 491
Leader(s). *See also* New leaders;
      Profiles in leadership;
      Superior(s)
   attitude toward self, 304
   charismatic. *See* Charismatic
      leadership
   in contingency theories of
      leadership, 547–548
   in follower role, 329
   followers versus, 188–189
   identification with, 584
   in interactional framework, 15,
      16–17, 34–35, 117, 547–548
   in leadership equation, 34–35
   mission and, 100
   power of. *See* Power
   in rational approach to
      organizational change,
      570–572
   sources of power, 122–125
   technical competence of, 98–101
   transactional. *See* Transactional
      leadership
   transformational. *See*
      Transformational leadership
Leader Behavior Description
      Questionnaire (LBDQ), 246–247

Leader development, 43–79
  Action-Observation-Reflection
    model, 46–78, 106–107
  arts-based approaches to, 65
  in college, 59–62
  development planning in, 66–69
  dilemmas for women, 55
  through experience, 49–54, 94–98
  key points for, 45
  leadership development versus, 43
  in organizational settings, 61, 63–64
  perception in spiral of experience,
    49–54
  self-image and, 78
  spiral of experience in, 47–48,
    49–54
  technology-based approaches
    to, 65
Leader-Follower-Situation (L-F-S)
    framework
  causes of managerial
    incompetence, 629, 630–632
  contingency model and, 520
  described, 34–35
  normative decision model and,
    523–530
  path-goal theory and, 548
Leader-Member Exchange (LMX)
    theory, 520, 521–523
Leader-member relations, 537
Leadership. *See also* Charismatic
    leadership; Profiles in
    leadership; Transactional
    leadership; Transformational
    leadership
  as art, 5–6
  characteristics of effective, 34–35,
    136–137, 169–170
  community, 259–262
  components of, 151
  defined, 3–5, 188
  as emotional, 6–8
  followership and, 18–25
  functions of, 415–422
  interactional framework for. *See*
    Interactional framework
  leader responses to crises, 10
  Level 5 Leadership, 197, 589
  management and, 8–9
  nature of, 3–14
  negative forms of, 510–511
  positive forms of, 168–172, 510–511
  power and. *See* Power
  as rational, 6–8, 557–572

relationship with job satisfaction
    and performance, 334–335
  romance of, 11
  as science, 5–6
  servant, 170–172
  stages of culture development, 493
  substitutes for, 489
  task variance, 480–482
  universality of positive attributes,
    508–511
Leadership (Burns), 576–578
Leadership assessment
  emotional intelligence in, 225–226
  importance of, 229
  leader motives in, 134–137
  multirater feedback instruments,
    262–267
  personality tests, 135, 199, 200, 213
Leadership attributes, 188–230
  emotional intelligence, 220–229
  Great Man theory, 130, 188–189,
    478–479
  intelligence, 208–220
  personality traits, 189–207
  personality types, 201–207
Leadership behavior, 242–269
  competency models and, 252–255
  group roles and, 397–400
  importance of studying, 244–246
  individual differences and,
    242–244
  Leader Behavior Description
    Questionnaire (LBDQ),
    246–247
  Leadership Grid® and, 250–251
  leader traits versus, 242–244
  in path-goal theory, 542–543
  research on, 244–259
  in Situational Leadership® Model,
    530–531
  skills versus, 248. *See also*
    Leadership skills
  360-degree feedback and, 280
  in wartime, 128, 131, 168, 245,
    252, 499–500, 503, 641
Leadership development. *See also*
    Education and training
  Action-Observation-Reflection
    (A-O-R) model in, 106–107, 112
  community leadership, 259–262
  through experience, 49–54, 94–98
  leader development versus, 43
  Leadership Pipeline and, 255–259
  myths that hinder, 11–14

for new leaders. *See* New leaders
  peers in, 104–106
Leadership Grid®, 250–251
Leadership Opinion Questionnaire
    (LOQ), 247
Leadership Pipeline, 255–259
Leadership research
  academic tradition in, 7
  on followers, 320–330
  on implicit prejudice, 161–163
  on leadership behavior, 244–255
  on managerial derailment, 620–628
  on power dynamics, 119, 121, 124,
    131, 140–141, 142, 319
  theories of job satisfaction, 369–375
  on transformational and
    transactional leadership,
    592–594
  troubadour tradition in, 7
  on values of Gen Xers, 156
Leadership skills, 94–112, 657–682
  assertiveness, 291–296
  behavior versus, 248
  coaching, 462–469
  communication, 283–288
  conducting meetings, 296–299
  conflict management, 662–667
  constructive feedback, 439–444
  creativity, 309–313
  credibility, 277–283
  delegating, 457–467
  development planning, 106–112
  diagnosing performance
    problems, 669–671
  empowerment, 311, 355–360
  goal setting, 436–439
  learning from experience, 94–98
  listening, 288–291
  nature of, 254
  needed in 2010, 46
  negotiation, 668–669
  problem solving, 306–309
  punishment, 676–682
  relationships with peers, 104–106,
    281, 625–626
  relationships with superiors,
    101–104, 281
  stress management, 299–305
  team building at the top, 624–625,
    671–676
  team building for work teams,
    444–448
  technical competence, 98–101
  vision of leader, 657–662

Leadership style, 151–152. *See also*
  Charismatic leadership;
  Transactional leadership;
  Transformational leadership
 achievement-oriented
  leadership, 543
 adapting to superior's, 103–104
 authentic leaders, 169–170, 179
 authoritarian leaders, 140–141
 autocratic leaders, 510
 autonomous leadership, 508
 culture and, 502–505, 506–511
 democratic leadership, 140–141,
  151, 510
 directive leadership, 543
 humane-oriented leadership, 508
 humor and, 255
 leading by example, 174–176
 Level 5 Leadership, 197, 589
 participative leadership, 508, 543
 self-protective leadership, 508
 servant leadership, 170–172
 supportive leadership, 345, 543
 team-oriented leadership, 508
 Theory X, 151–152
 Theory Y, 105–106, 151–152
 Theory Z, 173
 of women, 31–33, 140
Leadership theories. *See also*
  Contingency theories of
  leadership; Interactional
  framework
 Great Man theory, 130, 188–189,
  478–479
 multiple-influence model, 479
 role theory, 479
 situational levels, 479–480
Leader support, 248
Leading by example, 174–176
Learning agility, 571
Learning environment, 467–468
Learning from experience,
  94–98
 development plan in, 97–98
 gender and, 57
 getting feedback, 95
 journals, 96–97
 learning from others, 96
 learning to learn, 57–78, 94–98
 luck and, 50
 new leaders and, 94–98
 spiral of experience in, 47–48,
  49–54
 10 percent stretch and, 95–96

Least preferred coworker (LPC)
  scale, 535–536
Legal-rational authority system,
  575, 576
Legitimate power, 128
Legitimizing tactics, 138–139
Lehman Brothers, 612, 647
Level 5 Leadership, 197, 589
Level of authority, 486–487
Leverage points, 418–422
Levono, 504
Life satisfaction, 367–368
LinkedIn, 89
Links to customers and suppliers, 485
Listening, 288–291
 active, 288–291
 avoiding defensiveness, 290–291
 in coaching process, 463
 interpreting sender's message in,
  289–290
 nonverbal signals and, 289–290
 in servant leadership, 171
Lord of the Rings trilogy (films), 6, 152
Los Angeles Lakers, 336
Low-LPC leaders, 536, 537, 539, 540
Luck, learning from experience
  and, 50

Macho culture, 29, 180
Management
 defined, 8
 leadership and, 8–9
 managerial incompetence, 609,
  614–620, 628–648
Managerial derailment, 620–648
 common themes, 622–623
 defined, 609–610
 expertise and, 637–640
 failure to meet business
  objectives, 621–624, 627–628
 follower factors in, 630–632
 high-potential managers, 621
 inability to adapt, 626
 inability to build and lead a team,
  624–625
 inability to build relationships,
  625–626
 inadequate preparation for
  promotion, 626–628
 intelligence and, 637
 leader factors in, 628–630
 organizational fit and, 633
 relevant expertise and, 639
 root causes of, 628–648

 situational factors in, 630–632
 themes in, 620–628
Managerial incompetence, 614–620,
  628–648
 chronic, 632
 dark-side personality traits,
  645–646
 defined, 609
 episodic, 632
 examples of, 614–615
 rate of, 619–620
 root causes of, 628–648
 situational factors in, 630, 636
Managerial level of leadership, 179
Mandela, Nelson (profile), 509, 574
Market cultures, 497–498
Marriott Hotels, 574
Mars missions, 213
Maslow's hierarchy of needs,
  340–343, 360–361
MassMutual Financial Group, 347
Material resources, 422
Mattel, 233
Mayer, Salovey, and Caruso
  Emotional Intelligence Test
  (MSCEIT), 225, 227
McDonald's, 129, 640
MCI, 491
Meetings, 296–299
 agendas for, 298
 convenience of, 298
 determining need for, 297
 encouraging participation in,
  298–299
 minutes of, 299
 of new leaders with staff, 90–92,
  93–94
 objectives of, 297–298
 off-site, 93–94
 one-on-one, 90
 providing pertinent materials
  for, 298
Mentors and mentoring, 74–78
Menttium Corporation, 77
Mercy, justice versus, 165
Meritocratic leadership style, 510
Merkel, Angela (profile), 191
Mettur Beardsell, 258
Microsoft Corporation, 26, 229, 504,
  596–597
Milgram studies, 124, 131, 319
Millennials, values of, 156
Miner's Sentence Completion Scale
  (MSCS), 136

Minnesota Vikings, 71
Minority groups
  leader characteristics, 76–78
  mentors and, 76–78
Minutes of meetings, 299
Mission statements, 100
  nature of, 450
  in Rocket Model for Team
    Effectiveness, 450
Mixed model, of emotional
    intelligence, 223, 224–225
Mobilization, 260–261
Möbius strip, 22–23
Model, for change, 559–560, 561–564
Moral dimension of leadership, 151
Morale
  and Rocket Model for Team
    Effectiveness, 453–454
  task structure and, 481–482
Moral justification, 166–168
Moral managers, 168–169
Moral person, 168–169
Moral reasoning, 157–166
  acts versus words and, 163–164
  bias and, 161–163
  defined, 157–158
  ethical dilemmas, 164–165
  self-evaluation of, 163–164, 166
  stages of moral development,
    158–161
Morals, ethics versus, 154, 155
Moronization of management, 620
Motivation, 331–362
  achievement orientation and,
    344–346
  defined, 333–334
  in diagnostic model, 671
  empowerment and, 358–359
  goal setting and, 346–351
  job satisfaction and, 333–338,
    362–375
  leader motives and power, 134–137
  to manage, 136–137
  need theories of, 340–343,
    360–361, 372–374
  operant approach to, 351–355,
    359–360
  performance and, 334–338,
    361–362
  performance problems and, 671
  personality and, 344–346
  praise and, 356
  in reward power, 130
  understanding follower, 338–362

Motivators, 372–374
Motorola, 258, 356
Mugabe, Robert (profile), 611
Mulcahy, Anne (profile), 208
Multifactor Leadership
    Questionnaire (MLQ), 590–594
Multiple-influence model, 479
Multirrater feedback, 75, 262–267,
    280, 635
Musgrave, Thomas (profile), 243
Myers-Briggs Type Indicator (MBTI),
    202–207, 313, 481
MySpace, 265
Myths and stories, 11–14, 491, 677–678

National Association of
    Evangelicals, 646
National Institute of Ethics, 166
NCR, 615
Need for power, 135–136
Needs
  defined, 340–341
  stating, 295, 296
Need theories of motivation
  Herzberg's two-factor theory,
    372–374
  Maslow's hierarchy of needs,
    340–343, 360–361
Negative affectivity, 370–371
Negative feedback, 440–441, 444
Negative forms of leadership, 510–511
Negotiation, 668–669
  interests versus positions in,
    668–669
  people versus problem in, 668
  preparing for, 668
Neptune Orient Lines, 145
Neuroticism, 193, 195–196
Neutralizers, 489
New leaders, 87–112
  development planning and,
    66–69, 106–112
  driving change, 93–94
  first 90 days, 88–94
  first impressions and, 89–90
  homework of, 88–89
  influence of followers and, 120
  laying the foundation, 90–92
  learning from experience, 94–98
  onboarding roadmap, 88
  relationships with peers, 104–106
  relationships with superiors,
    101–104
  team performance and, 93

  team strategy and, 92–93
  team structure and, 93
  technical competence of,
    98–101
New Life Church, 646
New Orleans Saints, 211
New York Giants, 71
NeXT Computer, 60
Nexters
  generational archetypes and, 156
  values of, 156
Nike, 504
Nissan Motors, 504
"No," saying, 295
Nominal Group Technique
    (NGT), 308
Noncontingent rewards, 351–353
Nonverbal language
  congruent, 287
  influence tactics in, 120–121
  listening and, 289–290
  sending clear signals, 286–287
Nooyi, Indra (profile), 258
Norm(s)
  defined, 400
  group, 400–402, 409
  in Rocket Model for Team
    Effectiveness, 451–452
Normative decision model, 523–530
  decision acceptance in, 525
  decision quality in, 524–525
  decision tree in, 525–528
  follower development in, 527–528
  levels of participation in, 523, 524
Norming stage of group, 396, 456
Northwest Airlines, 607–609
"No," saying, 296
Nuclear power plant accidents, 413

Obama, Barack (profile), 586
Obedience, 124, 319
Objectives
  assigning, versus procedures, 460
  failure to meet, 621–624, 627–628
  of meetings, 297–298
  in team building, 675–676
Observable goals, 437
Observation, 49–51
  in Action-Observation-Reflection
    (A-O-R) model, 47, 48
  perception and, 49–51
  self-observer gaps, 265–266
  in spiral of experience, 47–48,
    49–51

OCEAN model of personality, 192–200, 201, 227, 228, 344
The Office (TV program), 244–245
Office Space (film), 378–379
Off-site meetings, 93–94
Ohio State University, 246–249, 250, 530–531, 536
Old Navy, 486
Ollieism, 405
Onboarding roadmap, 88
One-on-one meetings, 90
Open-door policy, 95
Openness to experience, 193–194
Operant approach, 351–355, 359–360
Operation Iraqi Freedom (OIF), 252
Opportunities
   to get feedback, 95
   performance problems and, 671
Oracle, 229
Organization, 484–498
   formal organization, 486–489
   informal organization, 489–498
Organizational alignment, 564
Organizational change, 556–594
   examples of, 558–559
   fall of the mighty and, 647
   inability to adapt to, 626
   rational approach to, 557–572
   role of executive teams in, 672–673
   Theory of Transformational and Transactional Leadership, 590–594
Organizational citizenship behaviors, 334
Organizational climate, defined, 489–490
Organizational complexity, 488
Organizational culture
   changing, 490–495
   corporate culture, 180, 479–480
   defined, 489–490
   globalization and, 501
   leadership cultures in, 493, 494
   organizational fit and, 632–635
   theory of, 495–498
Organizational fit, 632–635
Organizational goals, sample, 563
Organizational justice, 374–375
Organizational level of leadership, 179, 256–259, 420
Organizational shells, 409, 410
Organizational structure, 487–488
   centralization, 489
   complexity, 488

formal organization, 486–489
   team building and, 675–676
Orientation to authority, 505
Out-group, 16, 521
Outliers (Gladwell), 26, 502
Outputs, team, 412
Overbounding, 403
Overclaiming credit, 162

Pacific Northwestern Bell Telephone Company, 347
Paper-and-pencil measures, in team building, 447
Paraphrasing, 289–290
Pareto principle, 307
Participative leadership, 508, 543
Partnering, 463–464
Partners, in Potter and Rosenbach followership model, 322
Passion, in vision of leader, 660
Passive followers, 21
Path-goal theory, 542–548
   applying, 547
   followers in, 543–545
   leader behaviors and, 542–543
   Leader-Follower-Situation (L-F-S) framework and, 547–548
   prescriptions of, 546
   situation in, 545–546
PDI Development Pipeline®, 67
Pecking order, 121
Peers
   assertive behavior with, 293
   building effective relationships with, 104–106, 281, 625–626
   common interests and goals, 104–105
   in leadership development process, 104–106
PepsiCo, 229, 258
Perception
   action and, 52–54
   in GAPS analysis, 109, 464
   in leadership development, 49–54
   observation and, 49–51
   reflection and, 51–52
   in spiral of experience, 49–54
Perceptual set, 49–51
Performance
   defined, 334
   in expectation-performance gap, 567–569, 669–671
   expectations and, 348–350
   goal setting and, 346–351

model of, 669–671
   monitoring, in delegation process, 461
   motivation and, 334–338, 361–362
   punishment and, 678–680
   relationship with leadership and job satisfaction, 334–335
Performance initiative, 321
Performance measurement, 167–168, 177, 363
Performance problems, 669–671
   capabilities and, 670
   expectations and, 670
   motivation and, 671
   opportunities and, 671
Performing stage of group, 396, 456
Persistence, 296, 466–467
Personal appeals, 138
Personality, 189–207
   creativity and, 213, 313
   defined, 189
   Five Factor Model of, 192–200, 201, 224–225, 227, 228, 344, 593
   Great Man theory of leadership, 130, 188–189, 478–479
   leader motives and, 134–137
   motivation and, 344–346
   nature of, 189–192
   presidency and, 190, 192, 586
Personality tests, 135, 199, 200, 202–207, 313, 481
Personality traits, 189–207
   assessing, 135, 199, 200, 202, 207, 313, 481
   nature of, 189–192
   personality types versus, 201, 202
Personality typology, 201–207
   defined, 201
   implications of, 205–207
   psychological preferences as, 202–207
Personalized leadership, of charismatic and transformational leaders, 583–584
Personalized power, 135
Personal level of leadership, 179
Person-role conflict, 400
Perspective, stress and, 304
Persuasion
   in group decision making, 3
   rational, 138, 139
   in servant leadership, 171
Pfizer, 449, 504

Philadelphia Eagles, 126
Pittsburgh Steelers, 71
Pixar, 60
Platoon (film), 215
Plaxo, 89
Pointing, 121
Policies and procedures, ethics in, 176
Political campaigns
    attribution of charisma and, 583, 587–588
    negative attack ads, 583
Politicians, in Potter and Rosenbach followership model, 322
Poor followership, 640–643
Porcupine leadership style, 141
Position power, 537
Positive affectivity, 370–371
Positive feedback, 440–441, 444
Positive forms of leadership, 168–172, 510–511
Postconventional level, of moral reasoning, 158, 159
Potter and Rosenbach followership model, 320–323, 328–329
Power, 118–143
    aspects of, 118–119
    authority and, 122–125
    coercive, 130–133
    constructive use of, 311
    creativity and, 311
    defined, 118
    empowerment and, 358
    expert, 125–126, 135–137
    generalizations about, 134
    hierarchical, 175
    influence tactics and, 139–142
    influence versus, 119–120
    leader motives for, 134–137
    loss of, 568
    need for, 135–136
    referent, 105, 126–128, 139
    reward, 129–130
    and Rocket Model for Team Effectiveness, 453
    sources of leader, 122–125
    Stanford Prison experiment, 131, 399
    taxonomy of, 125–134
    in vision of leader, 660
Power Game, The (Smith), 141
Power-sharing activities, 134
Practical intelligence, 210–212, 213, 215, 218–219
Pragmatist followers, 21

Praise
    motivation and, 356
    in reward power, 130
Preconventional level, of moral reasoning, 158, 159
Presidency, personality and, 190, 192, 586
Pressure tactics, 138
Prince, The (Machiavelli), 118
Principle-centered leadership, 179
Prisons
    Abu Ghraib, 131, 133
    Stanford Prison experiments, 131, 399
Problem solving, 306–309
    alternative solutions in, 308–309
    analyzing causes, 307–308
    assessing impact of solution, 309
    identifying problems, 306–307
    importance of, 221
    problem-solving groups and, 311–313
    selecting and implementing solutions, 308–309
Procedural justice, 374–375
Procedures, assigning objectives versus, 460
Process
    of change, 560, 564–567
    team, 412–415
    Team Leadership Model (TLM), 412–415
Process loss, 395
Process measures, 414
Procrastination, 527
Procter & Gamble, 229
Productivity, job satisfaction and, 336
Product life cycle, 485
Profiles in leadership
    Shane Aguero, 245
    Michelle Bachelet, 337
    Osama bin Laden, 579
    Greg Boyle, 261
    Richard Branson, 375
    George Dalgarno, 243
    Michael Dell, 127
    Tony Dungy, 71
    Richard Fuld, 612
    Mahatma Gandhi, 160
    Bill Gates, 26
    Ted Haggard, 646
    Robert "RT" Hogan, 200
    Peter Jackson, 6
    Phil Jackson, 392

    Steve Jobs, 60
    Joel Klein, 566
    David Koresh, 613
    Nelson Mandela, 509, 574
    Angela Merkel, 191
    Robert Mugabe, 611
    Anne Mulcahy, 208
    Thomas Musgrave, 243
    Indra Nooyi, 258
    Barack Obama, 586
    Paul Revere, 22
    Bill Roberts, 591
    Mark Roellig, 347
    Scott Rudin, 224
    Howard Schultz, 14
    Aung San Suu Kyi, 25
    Jerry Swope, 245
    Oprah Winfrey, 59
    Wu Yi, 351
Programs for promotions initiatives, 616
Projective personality test, 135
Projective psychological tests, 65
Project teams, 397
Promotion, inadequate preparation for, 626–628
Punctuated equilibrium, 397
Punishment, 676–682. *See also* Reward(s)
    administering, 124, 319, 681–682
    defined, 351
    job satisfaction and, 678–680
    myths concerning, 677–678
    in operant approach, 351
    performance and, 678–680
    power and, 124, 319
Pygmalion Effect, 348–350

Questionnaires, 246–249. *See also specific questionnaires*
Questions, in becoming an expert, 100–101
Qwest Communications, 347, 449

Race, in multirater feedback instruments, 266–267
Rational approach to organizational change, 557–572
    alternative to, 589
    amount of change, 560
    dissatisfaction, 560–561
    force field analysis (FFA), 572
    leaders in, 570–572
    model, 559–560, 561–564

process, 560, 564–567
resistance, 560, 567–569
Rational persuasion, 138, 139
Reciprocal influence, 134
Reference group, 368
Referent power, 105, 126–128, 139
Reflection
  in Action-Observation-Reflection
    (A-O-R) model, 47, 48, 51–52,
    54–56
  in becoming an expert, 100
  in development planning, 112
  double-loop learning, 56, 212
  in leadership development, 54–56
  perception and, 51–52
  single-loop learning, 54–56, 212
  in spiral of experience, 47–48,
    51–52
Reframing, 577
Rejection, in SARA model, 568–569
Relationship(s)
  of followers with peers, 104–106,
    281, 625–626
  of leaders with peers, 104–106
  loss of, 568
  with superiors, 101–104, 281
  supportive, and stress, 303–304
Relationship behaviors, 530
Relationship initiative, 321
Relationship role, 397–398
Relaxation, 303
Remote coaching, 72
Renault, 504
Research Researchers, 487
Resistance, to change, 560, 567–569
Resources
  cognitive resources theory (CRT),
    218–220
  in development plans, 111
  material, 422
Respect, reinforcing, 105
Results, in Rocket Model for Team
    Effectiveness, 454–455
Results-only managers
  dark-side personality traits of,
    625, 638
  example of, 617
  nature of, 616
Revere, Paul (profile), 22
Reward(s), 682. *See also* Punishment
  defined, 351
  loss of, 568
  in operant approach, 351,
    352, 354

reward power and, 129–130
  understanding peers', 105
Reward power, 129–130
Rhetorical skills, of charismatic and
    transformational leaders,
    581–582
Risk-taking behaviors, delegation as,
    458–459
Rituals, 491
Roberts, Bill (profile), 591
Rocket Model for Team Effectiveness,
    448–456
  buy-in and, 452–453
  diagrams of, 449, 455, 456
  implications of, 455–456
  mission in, 450
  morale and, 453–454
  norms in, 451–452
  power and, 453
  results in, 454–455
  talent and, 450–451
  users of, 449
Roellig, Mark (profile), 347
Role ambiguity, 372, 400, 479
Role conflict, 372, 398–400, 479
Role-making, in Leader-Member
    Exchange (LMX) theory, 521
Role-play simulations, 61
Role-taking, in Leader-Member
    Exchange (LMX) theory, 521
Role theory, 479
Rorschach Inkblot test, 65
Routinization, in Leader-Member
    Exchange (LMX) theory, 521
Rubbermaid, 647
Rudin, Scott (profile), 224
Rule-based thinking, 165
Rural communities, change in, 559
Rush Trucking, 270–271

Sacred Hoops (Jackson and
    Delehanty), 392
Safety
  motivation programs and, 363
  team effectiveness and, 405,
    413–414
San Francisco 49ers, 71
San Francisco earthquake and fire
    (1906), 10
SARA model, 568–569
Sarcasm, 287
Satisfaction. *See* Job satisfaction
Scapegoating, avoiding, 306–307,
    444, 461–462

Schultz, Howard (profile), 14
Scooter Store, 356
Self-actualization, 169, 340–343
Self-awareness, 635–637
Self-complexity, 304
Self-concept, 304
Self-development. *See* New leaders
Self-esteem, 340–343
Self-expectations, in leading by
    example, 175
Self-fulfilling prophecy, 53, 207,
    348–350
Self-image, in leadership
    development, 78
Self-interest, in moral
    development, 158
Self-protective leadership, 508
Self-sacrifice, 135
Self-serving bias, 51
Self-starters, in Curphy Followership
    Model, 324–325, 329
Sensing-intuition, 203–204
Servant leadership, 170–172
Service learning, 60
ServiceMaster, 504
Sex roles, 28–29
Sharing, in conflict resolution,
    664, 665
Shock, in SARA model, 568–569
"Shock generator" experiments
    (Milgram), 124, 131, 319
Short-term versus long-term, 165
Siloed thinking, 563
Simpsons, The (TV program), 128, 194
Simulations, 61
Singapore Airlines, 145
Singapore Telecommunications, 145
Single-loop learning, 54–56, 212
Situation
  background of, 475–480
  and charismatic and
    transformational leadership,
    586–587
  in contingency theories of
    leadership, 537–538, 547–548
  environmental characteristics,
    498–511
  industrial age, 484–486
  information age, 484–486
  in interactional framework, 15,
    26–27, 34–35, 473–480, 545–548
  Leader-Follower-Situation (L-F-S)
    framework and, 34–35, 520,
    528–530, 534, 547–548

Situation—*Cont.*
  in managerial incompetence,
    630–632
  multiple-influence model, 479
  organization in, 484–498
  in path-goal theory of leadership,
    545–546
  in rational approach to
    organizational change, 570–572
  role theory and, 479
  situational awareness and,
    635–637
  situational engineering and,
    476–479
  situational levels, 479–480
  task in, 480–484
  understanding superiors', 102–103
Situational awareness, 635–637
Situational engineering, 476–479
Situational favorability, 537–538
Situational Leadership® Model,
    530–535
  developmental intervention
    using, 533
  follower readiness in, 532
  leader behaviors in, 530–531
  prescriptions of, 532–533
Situational levels, 479–480
Skepticism, of Gen Xers, 156
Skill(s). *See also* Leadership skills
  growing, in coaching, 467–468
  rhetorical, 581–582
Slackers, in Curphy Followership
    Model, 326–327, 329,
    641–642
Social capital, 260
Social facilitation, 395–396
Socialized power, 135
Social loafing, 395
Social networking sites, 89, 265
Social networks
  of charismatic and
    transformational leaders, 587
  nature of, 587
Social psychology, 319–320
Social reputation, 189–190
Societal culture, 506
South Africa, 509, 574
Space Shuttle program, 404, 407
Span of control, 394
Spatial complexity, 488
Specificity
  of communication, 287
  of delegated assignment, 460

of feedback, 441, 442
  goal, 437
Spiral of experience, 47–48, 49–54
Sports
  athleticism versus intelligence
    in, 211
  coaching and, 71, 99, 680
  free agency and, 155
  group roles in, 397
  praise and, 356
  professional athlete salary
    demands, 352
  task interdependency of
    teams, 391
  unwritten rules of, 401–402
Standards, in GAPS analysis, 109, 464
Stanford Prison experiment, 131, 399
Starbucks, 14, 176–177
Staring, 121
Stars, new leaders and, 90–91
Star Trek: The Next Generation (TV
    program), 124–125
Stewardship, in servant
    leadership, 171
Storage Technology Corporation, 347
Stories and myths, 11–14, 491,
    677–678
Storming stage of group, 396, 456
Strategic Health Authority (UK), 449
Stress, 299–305
  A-B-C model, 304–305
  cognitive resources theory and,
    218–220
  dark-side personality traits and,
    220, 299–303
  defined, 299–300
  effects of, 299–301
  healthy lifestyle and, 303
  identifying cause of, 302–303
  monitoring follower, 302, 305
  perspective and, 304
  relaxation and, 303
  supportive relationships and,
    303–304
  symptoms of, 299–300, 302, 305
Stretch
  stretch assignments in
    development planning, 111
  stretch assignments to build
    expertise, 279
  10 percent, 95–96
Strong situations, 191–192
Subject matter expertise, managerial
    derailment and, 638, 639

Subordinate(s). *See also* Follower(s)
  in Potter and Rosenbach
    followership model, 321
  as term, 5
Substitutes for leadership, 489
Success
  criteria for, 111
  skills for successful leaders, 46
  Successful Manager's Handbook, The
    (Davis et al.), 111
Superego, 190
Superior(s). *See also* Leader(s)
  adapting to style of, 103–104
  building effective relationships
    with, 101–104, 281
  defined, 101
  managing upward by
    followers, 140
  understanding world of, 102–103
Supervisory Descriptive Behavior
    Questionnaire (SDBQ), 247
Supportive leadership
  in path-goal theory, 543
  research on, 345
Supportive relationships, 303–304
Surgical teams, 420
Survey of Organizations, 248
Suu Kyi, Aung San (profile), 25
Swope, Jerry (profile), 245
Symbols and artifacts, 491
  of power, 122–123
Synectics, 310–311
Systems thinking approach, 283–285,
    562–564

Taco Bell, 258
Talent, in Rocket Model for Team
    Effectiveness, 450–451
Tampa Bay Buccaneers, 71
Target, 229, 640
Task(s), 480–484
  of effective teams, 408
  problems and challenges of,
    482–484
Task autonomy, 480–481
Task behaviors, 530
Task feedback, 481
Task-focused leadership, 255
Task interdependence, 482
Task role, 397–398
Task structure, 481–482, 537
Team(s), 406–428. *See also* Team
    building
  authority in effective, 406–410

groups versus, 390–391
individuals versus, 391
project, 397
virtual, 424–428
Team Assessment Survey, 455–456
Team building, 444–448
    effective teams, 406–410, 497
    examples of interventions, 447–448
    executive team, 624–625, 671–676
    inability to build and lead a team,
        624–625
    ineffective teams, 406
    interventions in, 444–448
    Rocket Model for Team
        Effectiveness, 448–456
    team-building know-how,
        618–620, 638
    team-building workshops, 446–447
    teams versus groups, 390–391
    tripwire lessons in, 673–676
    work team, 444–448
Team-building know-how,
    618–620, 638
Team design, 415, 416–417, 420
Team Effectiveness Leadership
    Model (TELM). See Team
    Leadership Model (TLM)
Team Leadership Model (TLM),
    410–422
    concluding thoughts about,
        422–424
    diagnosis and leverage points,
        418–422
    inputs, 415
    interactional framework and, 424
    leadership prescriptions of,
        415–422
    material resources in, 422
    outputs, 412
    prescriptions of, 415–422
    process, 412–415
    systems view of, 417–418
Team-oriented leadership, 508
Teamwork
    inability to build and lead a team,
        624–625
    women in leadership and, 407
Tea Party movement, 318, 613
Technical competence, 98–101
    becoming an expert, 100–101
    defined, 98
    expert power and, 125–126, 135–137
    of followers, 98–101
    job in overall mission, 100

of leaders, 98–101
    opportunities to broaden
        experience, 101
Technical problems, 483–484
Temasek Holdings, 144–146
10 percent stretch, 95–96
Terminal values, 153–154
Texas A&M, 211
Texas Instruments (TI), 216–217
Thematic Apperception Test
    (TAT), 135
Theory, leadership. See Leadership
    theories
Theory of Transformational and
    Transactional Leadership,
    590–594
Theory X, 151–152
Theory Y, 105–106, 151–152
Theory Z, 173
Thinking-feeling, 204
3M, 213, 504
360-degree feedback, 66–67, 69, 70,
    262–267, 280, 635
Three Mile Island nuclear power
    plant accident, 413
Time
    artful procrastination, 527
    in charismatic and
        transformational
        leadership, 587
    in delegation process, 457–460
Timeliness, of feedback, 441, 443
Titles, power and, 122–123
Touching, 121
Toxic followers, 214
Toyota, 504
Traditional authority system,
    574, 576
Training. See Education and training
Training programs, 64–66
Trait(s), 189–230
    behavior versus, 242–244
    defined, 190
    emotional intelligence, 220–229
    personality, 189–207
Trait approach, defined, 190
Transactional leadership
    Bass's theory of, 590–594
    described, 576–577
    Hollander's approach to, 15
    research results of, 592–594
Transformational leadership, 255,
    319–329
    Bass's theory of, 590–594

comparison with charismatic
    leadership, 580–587
described, 577–578
emotions and, 221–222, 585
follower characteristics in,
    584–585
leader characteristics in, 581–584,
    587–590
research results of, 592–594
situational characteristics and,
    586–587
trust and, 279, 582, 583
Triarchic theory of intelligence,
    210–218, 224–225
    components of, 210–213
    implications of, 213–218
Tripwire lessons, in executive team
    building, 673–676
Troubadour tradition in leadership
    research, 7
Trust
    building, 279–283, 582
    for charismatic and
        transformational leaders, 279,
        582, 583
    charismatic/transformational
        leaders and, 279
    in credibility, 278, 279–283, 320
    expertise and, 281–283
    sarcasm and, 287
    in true leadership, 151
Truth versus loyalty, 164
TRW, 26
Tupelo Model, 559
Two-factor theory of motivation,
    372–374
Two-way communication, 287–288
Tyco, 174

Unconscious, 190
Unethical climates, 175–176
Unions
    numbers games and, 168
    power of, 128
United Airlines, 232, 367
United Parcel Service (UPS), 81–82,
    356–357, 640
U.S. Air Force
    motivational programs of, 343
    organizational culture in, 489
    Recruiting Service, 225
    service academy, 44, 318,
        343, 358
U.S. Airways, 367, 527

U.S. Army
Abu Ghraib prison and, 131, 133
disasters and, 10
Iraq war and, 131, 133, 245
job satisfaction in, 332, 364–366
mentors in, 76
retention bonuses, 331
service academy, 478
Training and Doctrine
Command, 252
World War II and, 19, 128
U.S. Congress, leadership style
and, 141
U.S. Government Accountability
Office, 28
U.S. Marine Corps, organizational
culture in, 489
U.S. Navy
dark-side personality traits and,
627, 642
mentors in, 76
service academy, 578
U.S. Post Office, 10, 615
U.S. service academies, 44, 287, 318,
343, 358, 478, 578, 627
Universality of leadership attributes,
508–511
University of Colorado, 490
University of Houston, 211
University of Michigan, 246–249, 250
University of Pittsburgh, 211
UPS (United Parcel Service), 81–82,
356–357, 640
Upward ethical leadership, 175
US West, 347
Utah Jazz, 211

Values, 150–182
defined, 152, 279
development of, 154–157
doing the right things, 150–168
generational differences in,
154–157
good people doing bad things,
166–168
implications for leadership
practitioners, 511–512

nature of, 152–154
in organizational leadership,
172–181
positive forms of leadership,
168–172
terminal versus instrumental,
153–154
trust and, 279–281
in vision of leader, 659–660
Verizon, 491
Vertical complexity, 488
Veterans, values of, 155
Vietnam War, 168, 583
Virgin Industries, 37–39, 375
Virtual teams, 424–428
Vision
of charismatic and
transformational leaders, 581,
582, 584
compelling, 657–662
as component of leadership, 151
in cults, 180
empowerment and, 468
follower identification with, 584
sample vision statement, 563

Wall Street Journal, 11
Walmart, 197, 259
Walt Disney World, 491
Wartime
coercive power in, 131, 133
follower behaviors in, 641
intelligence and judgment
during, 221
leadership behaviors in, 128, 131,
168, 245, 252, 499–500, 503, 641
legitimate power in, 128
Waste Management, 449, 504, 558
Watergate break-in, 405
Watson-Wyatt, 263–265
Weak situations, 191–192
Western Electric Company, 395–396
Wheelabrator Technologies, 591
Wheel of Fortune (TV program), 301
Willing subordination to the
leader, 585
Winber Medical Center, 550–551

Winfrey, Oprah (profile), 59
Wisdom of Teams, The (Katzenbach
and Smith), 416
Witness to Power (Ehrlichman), 122
Women in leadership
astronaut teamwork, 407
CEOs, 144–146, 208, 232–234, 258,
270–271
charismatic leaders, 578
dark-side personality traits, 627
development of, 55, 56, 77,
81–82, 487
dilemmas for women, 55
finding good women leaders,
27–34
glass ceiling effect and, 29–30, 487
government leaders, 191,
337, 351
interactional framework for, 25,
27–34
leadership style and, 31–33, 140
learning from experience, 57
managing upward, 140
mentoring programs for, 77
military service, 627
profiles of, 25, 59, 191, 208,
258, 337
role of personal experience
in, 56
sex role stereotypes, 28–30
Work facilitation, 248
Working with Emotional Intelligence
(Goleman), 222
WorldCom, 174
World Is Flat, The (Friedman),
499–500
World War II, 19, 128, 155
WPP Group, 232
Wu Yi (profile), 351

Xerox, 208

Yale University, 124, 490
Young & Rubicam, 232–234

Zenith, 647
Zimbabwe, 611